VOLUME 1, SPRING 2001

THE ABOVE-THE-LINE RESOURCE GUIDE FOR AND ABOUT PRODUCERS

Publisher: Dan Bolton

Senior Editor: Debbie Hennessey
Assistant Editor: Kevin Oaks
Special Guest Appearance: Bryan Cuprill

Editorial Staff:
Paige Cline, Jonathan D. Ekedahl, Robert Gonzales, Renee Harris, Gerard Karsenty,
Jesse Mackey, Jessica Meyerson, Alfredo Ramirez, Samantha C. Wood

Contributing Editors: Rita Street, Ferdinand Lewis

Director of Editorial & Production: Dale E. Norley
Graphic Design: Donna Greiner
Layout Artist: Orlando Rios

Director of Sales/Associate Publisher: Brian McOwen
Advertising Sales/Art Coordinator: Marjorie V. Goldberg
Account Representatives: Heather Wimett, Clare Jacoby, Paulette Miechle, Sean Killebrew
Sales Assistant: Celestine Cronin

Marketing Manager: Beve Regas

Director of Information Technology: Aaton Cohen-Sitt
Information Systems Specialist: James Dennis
Web Developer: Micah Brown

Business Manager: Stefanie Mount
Fulfillment Manager: Kathie Rackham
Customer Service Representative: Clarice Abert
Accounting Assistant: Roxanne Morganstern
Production Assistant: Luana Norman

Thanks to everyone who worked so hard to create Producers 411. A special thanks to the editorial team, your efforts, talents and especially your sense of humor are greatly appreciated. Now, about that agent's book...

Marc Teren
CEO

Cahners
A Division of Reed Elsevier, Inc.

Mike Roggero
Group Publisher

Tad Smith
President of Media Division

Dan Hart
Vice President of Finance

The Publisher has taken all reasonable measures to ensure the accuracy of the information in this edition of Producers 411 but cannot accept responsibility for any errors or omissions or any liability resulting from the use or misuse of any such information. The entire contents of the Vol. 1 Spring edition of Producers 411 by LA 411 Publishing Company may not be reproduced or transmitted in any form or by any graphic, digital, electronic, mechanical or other means including photocopying, recording, taping or information storage and retrieval systems of any nature without the prior written permission of the Publisher. All rights reserved. Producers 411 reserves the right to remove and/or requalify listings at any time. Address all correspondence to: LA 411 Publishing Company, 7083 Hollywood Boulevard, Suite 501, Los Angeles, California 90028-8901 USA.

Telephone 323/460-6304 or 800/545-2411. Facsimile 323/460-6305.
http://www.la411publishing.com

TABLE OF CONTENTS

ARTICLES

The A-List—Roundtable interview with *Lili Fini Zanuck, Mark Johnson, Dan Jinks, Bruce Cohen and David Friendly* . . . . .page 4
In Defense of Aliens . . . . .page 10
Top Twenty Sci Fi . . . . .page 12
Eyeful of Reality . . . . .page 15
Rigging Reality . . . . .page 16
Spotty Future . . . . .page 19
Listening to Convergence . . . . .page 21
Historical Impact . . . . .page 24
Seeing the Present in Our Past . . . . .page 26
Music Video Vet . . . . .page 27
The Creative Producer . . . . .page 31
Wrangling the Web . . . . .page 32
Pitch a Caster . . . . .page 36
Ready to Produce for the Internet . . . . .page 37
Marketcast Report . . . . .page 38

PRODUCTION COMPANY CATEGORY KEY . . . . .page 41
A reference key of the categories found in Producers 411 with corresponding production companies.

PRODUCTION COMPANIES . . . . .page 53
Complete listings for production companies.
Feature Film, TV, Commercials, Video, Music Video, Interactive Multimedia

FREELANCE PRODUCER CATEGORY KEY . . . . .page 285
A reference key of categories with corresponding freelance producers.

FREELANCE PRODUCERS . . . . .page 287
Complete listings for freelance producers.
Feature Film, TV, Commercials, Video, Music Video, Interactive Multimedia

TV SHOWS . . . . .page 307
Listings of current TV shows including production companies and casting directors.

STUDIO & NETWORK QUICK REFERENCE . . . . .page 327
Contact information for film studios, television networks and their divisions.

TRADE ASSOCIATIONS/UNIONS/GUILDS . . . . .page 331
Contact information for organizations that support the entertainment industry.

AWARDS/EXPOS/FESTIVALS . . . . .page 335
Contact information and dates for many major film events throughout the world.

EXECUTIVES/PERSONNEL ALPHA KEY . . . . .page 337
An alphabetical reference of executives and personnel with corresponding companies and phone numbers.

PRODUCTION COMPANY & FREELANCE PRODUCER ALPHA INDEX . . . . .page 363
An alphabetical reference of production companies and freelance producers with corresponding page numbers.

ADVERTISER'S INDEX . . . . .page 375

How To Picture
Perfect Creative Harmony.

Talent and Technology.

Keep Me Posted is a full service postproduction design studio that offers
a unique array of computer-generated graphics, digital compositing and visual effects
for commercials, music videos, broadcast programming and promos,
feature films and interactive media.

Whether you're looking to hire our talent or a home for your talent,
we provide a perfect blend of creative professionals and creative space
readied with cutting-edge technology including
Discreet* Logic fire, Quantel* Magnum Editbox, Avid Symphony, Avid Media Composer 9000,
Digidesign Pro Tools Audio and a Component Linear Edit Bay.

10640 Riverside Drive Toluca Lake, CA 91602
Telephone 738-7000

(left to right)

Mark Johnson, Bruce Cohen, Lili Fini Zanuck, Dan Jinks, and David Friendly

Photos by Jilly Wendell

The A-List

Hollywood Producers Talk Shop

By Rita Street

Few things raise the eyebrows of the *Daily Variety* staff. When it comes to stars, for instance, they've seen it all. Producers, however, are another story. Entertainment journalists all understand that producers are the real backbone of the business, the folks who actually make Hollywood tick. So when Producers 411 tromped five of the industry's most respected into *Daily Variety*'s conference room for a lunchtime roundtable, more than a few reporters sat up and took notice.

Gathered to chat about their jobs and their challenges were Lili Fini Zanuck (*Cocoon; Driving Miss Daisy*), David Friendly (*Dr. Dolittle; Courage Under Fire*), Dan Jinks (*American Beauty; Nothing to Lose*), Bruce Cohen (*American Beauty; To Wong Foo, Thanks For Everything, Julie Newmar*) and Mark Johnson (*Rain Man; Good Morning Vietnam*).

What we were looking for was a basic job description for Hollywood Producer. What we got was a whole heckuva lot of passion – for the writers, directors, and artistry that goes into making a great motion picture.

Producers411: Bluntly put, what does a producer do?

Zanuck: We find the material. We find the director. We try to get our movies made. We are involved in all of the below-the-line decisions in terms of who we crew up with. A lot of us even have crews that we ask directors to quasi-inherit.

Friendly: In a perfect world, I like to stay with the movies I produce from cradle-to-grave. Some producers, fortunately for them, have a number of movies shooting at once. Obviously though, if you're producing three movies at once, you're doing a different job than if you're producing one.

Jinks: I think the most important thing a producer can do is support the writer and director. To me the hardest part about producing is finding really good material, which is like finding a needle in a haystack, and when you find really good material you want to fight for that vision. When you find a director who sees the movie the same way you do, you want to support that director throughout the entire journey.

Cohen: The actual day-to-day is one of the really exciting things about being the types of producers that we all are. It's such a different job from preproduction. Looking for material and trying to put things together is very different from shooting, which is very different from post. But I don't think we would ever want to be the type of producers who didn't get involved in all those phases.

Friendly: It's a dual existence. You're developing, sitting in rooms with writers trying to find ideas or fix scripts, and then when you're making a movie, you get to show up in the morning and trucks are rolling and people are there and it's very exciting. But it's two very different disciplines, each of equal importance.

Johnson: There are some producers that are very good at developing but not particularly good at – or don't even care to be around – the making-of. It doesn't make them any less of a producer, because developing good material is next to impossible. Some of us come from production backgrounds and our affinities are more in the making of the movie. But there aren't really that many producers who are successful from beginning to end.

Producers 411: Where does your passion come from?

Friendly: What I think the passion comes from is loving the process, and loving the product. But it takes a really proactive personality. There are a lot of days when nobody is calling you. You're generating every single phone call, so you have to be somebody who can start with a blank page and still get it done. I've never been handed a movie. I'd like it to happen, but it never will.

Zanuck: You have to have incredible enthusiasm. You're the one selling the project – to actors, to studios, to everybody. Even after you get your director, there's a lot of hard times. You're the one that's keeping everybody's spirits up. You're the one that's always selling it, only you're not selling anything really tangible. You're selling your belief in the project. Everybody wants to say no and that is occurring more and more often. The fear factor is so high; things are so expensive that I really think you have to have great agency skills.

Johnson: People talk about creative producers versus non-creative producers, but listen, to be a producer you have to be creative. You have to be as much of a filmmaker as the director, and once you've made a movie that you believed in – you formed it into a screenplay, got it made, went through all these battles and it resembles what you wanted it to be – the feeling is sublime. You've made something that has an effect, hopefully, on a lot of people. One of the movies I'm proudest of is *A Little Princess*. I look at that movie and I see myself all over it. It's completely the director's movie. The director did a spectacular job, but I can watch that movie today and I don't have to say a word. It's the most articulate way of me saying to myself, "That's why I'm a producer."

Producers 411: Let's talk more about development. Where do you find your projects?

Jinks: The most obvious place is the spec screenplay market, which really is very difficult. You read a lot, and a lot of scripts are badly written, or else not original or just not a story. But to ignore the spec market is crazy. *American Beauty*, which Bruce and I produced,

Above: The A-List laughs and kibitzes over victories and defeats.

Right: *American Beauty* co-producer Dan Jinks contemplates his passion for the biz and the desire to tell a good story while maintaining sanity in an ever-changing job.

was a spec screenplay. You can find great things there, but to sit around waiting for a great screenplay is suicide. You can't do that. We all meet with writers, try to generate our own ideas. We all look at books and plays. No matter what you're doing in your life, you never stop looking for a good movie idea or a writer with a wonderful voice that you want to support.

Producers 411: Can you tell if a script is good within the first few pages?

Zanuck: You can tell good writing quickly, but there may be a very good idea that the person hasn't executed in the first act.

Cohen: I think endings are hugely important and are underestimated as the key to brilliant movies. How often in your filmgoing experience is the ending a problem for you? The story doesn't tie up, or doesn't have the emotional depth you thought it was going to. Or you end up asking, "What was the movie about?"

Zanuck: Those movies also don't succeed because there were so many cooks in the kitchen. You read these scripts all the time, and you can see that the notes were contradictory, that Joe Blow said, "Make the mother this," and somebody else said, "Make her that." The desire to please all people was so strong that the script is now about nothing. With a director it's different. As a producer you have a kind of a pride of ownership, but as soon as you hire the director you have to be prepared to share that, because they're going to execute their vision. But you know that going in, that's the director's purpose.

Friendly: It's a great point, and it relates to a bigger point about producing. I think you're being paid for your instincts and as a producer you have to marry that instinct with the product, that's your goal. I want my instinct in the product, but without smothering anybody, the director, the writer. The problem is, there are all these other instincts knocking against your instincts, wanting to go some other way. *On Big Mama's House,* there were a number of times when my instincts were questioned and I learned to say, "You know what? Let me try it my way." Wrong or right, a producer has to trust his instincts. This is what I believe.

Lili Fini Zanuck speaks out against "too many cooks in the kitchen."

Producers 411: But how do you do that if you're a first-time producer?

Cohen: You have to be really passionate, really persistent, and you can be, because you don't have anything to lose.

Zanuck: You haven't been broken yet. You haven't gone through the situation where sticking to your instincts means you go into turnaround. You haven't gone through those things yet, so it's easy to fight.

Friendly: This is what frustrates me. I wish more studio executives trusted people. If you don't trust a producer, don't put him on the lot. If you trust Mark Johnson, who has made thirty movies in the last thirty years, let him make the movie. It's basic logic.

Cohen: Why do we have to ask everyone's opinion? Let us do what we believe.

Zanuck: None of our pictures were obvious sells. Mark had Tom Cruise, but *Rain Man* was still about an autistic man and his brother, it wasn't *Mission Impossible 2.*

Cohen: And yet *Rainman, American Beauty* and *Driving Miss Daisy* all succeeded because there wasn't a [studio] development process. When you have to pool a room, by the seventh or eighth opinion you lose sight of the path.

Producers 411: Let's talk about production. How do you create a team, how do find a director, how do you stay on budget?

Johnson: There's a list of directors, and we all have the same list. Our private list we don't share with anybody else, but believe me, within a name or two they're the same list. Everybody wants Peter Weir, everybody wants Steven Spielberg. But there are also probably a dozen certifiably great directors who, for just about any movie, you could say "Okay fine, we're there." You ask yourself, "Have there been other movies like the one I'm making, whose directors synchronize — thematically and stylistically—with this project?" Then you go after that list. And this has to be a producer's decision, not a committee decision.

Friendly: The irony of this too, is that you have a movie that is greenlit, subject to getting a director and you literally can't get a director to say yes to your project. So it's not just "Oh, I like Barry Levinson, he'd be great." In my case the studio has to approve that director, and the director has to be available, and all the other factors. You can't believe how many times you've got a movie just sitting there ready to go and you can't find a director. That's hard, and surprising, and it happens all the time.

Johnson: This speaks to another problem we all go through, which is the question of whether it's the producer's job to get the movie made, or to get the movie made well. There's a real distinction there. Sometimes, because of a deal you have with a studio, or because you haven't made a picture in a year, or maybe the pocketbook speaks, you might say, "I'm willing to do this thing and to put so-and-so on it," even though your instincts say no. Every mistake I've made has been based on not following my instincts.

Zanuck: You really are mad at yourself when you're sitting in the dailies or you're watching your rough cut or you're previewing and you knew. You knew that this director could not deliver the picture. You knew and you didn't listen to yourself.

Jinks: And that happens with other positions too. You know you don't have the right actor sometimes. You know you don't have the right first assistant director which is a very key position. You know you don't have the right director of photography. There are a million of those elements.

Johnson: I remember David Putnam said, "If the producer has done his or her job right, the job is really only pre-production and post." Obviously there are emergencies, but the truth of the matter is that if you've cast the right people and crewed the film correctly you should just be there to be supportive. I can't think of any director I've worked with who wanted to know what lens I thought he should use.

Friendly: There's one thing I disagree about: Yeah, in the perfect world once the movie starts your job should be easier, but today I find myself spending a lot of time, along with the director, dealing with talent. Because the talent is at the top of the pyramid, it's become complicated. You're paying an actor $20 million dollars, and you're paying the director $2 million. Well, guess who's kind of running the show, and it's not the director. Then I find myself pulled into that triangle. It's become a very important part of the producer's job.

Zanuck: I think you're right, that this is unfortunately becoming a bigger part of the job, the balance of power.

Jinks: When you're shooting a movie, the pressures are so enormous, it's a crazy, crazy job. A lot of what our job is during shooting is doing everything we can to allow the director to concentrate on making the day, and trying to relieve him of everything else that is going on.

Cohen: The director literally has no free time. There is not a minute available. When a studio executive wants to talk dailies or anything that isn't involved with the shot at hand, you've got to handle it, so the director can stay focused.

Producers 411: How involved are you in the post process?

Friendly: I think it depends on the director you're with. There have been movies where I have had very little to do with actual post, because I was working with someone who has his own crew and ideas and doesn't want me in the editing room, and will show me the first cut. But then again, the last director I worked with was completely collaborative and I saw the movie the day after we finished shooting. So for me, it depends on who you're working with.

Johnson: I agree, it all depends. When we did *A Perfect World* with Clint Eastwood, we got along great, but he

> **Every mistake I've made has been based on not following my instincts**
> **—Mark Johnson**

has his way of working and he'll show you the movie when he's ready to show it to you. I was involved later in the process than I normally like to be, but I understood, I got the joke. By the way, you crew a postproduction unit the same way you do production: I remember that Barry Levinson and I went straight from *Tin Men* to *Good Morning Vietnam*, and everybody who worked on *Tin Men*, the cameraman, the sound person, the assistant director, they weren't right for *Good Morning Vietnam*, just because of sensibilities and experiences, situations in terms of working in a foreign country and whatever else. Same thing happens in postproduction. I think a producer who is not involved in postproduction really isn't doing the job

Jinks: So often the normal sequence of postproduction, how it's supposed to work, just isn't the case. You have budgetary issues so that you need to see the movie or there's marketing problems so you have to preview before you're done, or the composer is not available, so a lot of times the reason why producers need to get very involved in post is because we've got a very complicated situation. We're going to directors and we're explaining to them the advantages of showing something way before it's done and if they don't want to do it, I'm 100% supportive but I still need to explain that there are going to be ramifications.

Johnson: You know there's a real downside to that. I know in the case of Dreamworks we showed *Galaxy Quest* way too soon. It was a Christmas release and they had to see it, but because the film needed a lot of visual effects, when they saw it they thought it was a mess and unfortunately that defined their views of the movie. By the time the movie was finished and somebody looked at it and said, "Wow, this is a really good movie," it was almost too late.

Jinks: And we had the opposite on *American Beauty*. We showed them a finished movie, and we felt like this was the finished film, which was unusual because usually you've got more work to do, usually you know stuff is coming out. In this case we really had to support our director. He said he wanted to present it to them and say, "'Here it is.'" Of course, the huge risk was that they think it's theirs and then you don't know, sometimes directors like to keep a scene in their pocket or they know there's a little fat and they want to work together. In this case, he thought it was done.

Johnson: You had the advantage that nobody knew what to expect. With other movies, sometimes the expectations are so high. In our case, we had a big Christmas movie, and you had this wonderful present for them that I know some people didn't know what to expect, some people probably didn't have high expectations and all of a sudden you show them this movie that you say is almost finished.

Jinks: I can think of an exception to that. We could see that *American Beauty* was going to be an incredibly difficult movie to cut a trailer for. I mean, we've all sat in movie theaters where there is a trailer that doesn't work and you can feel it in the audience. A bad trailer really hurts you. Well, an advertising guy that Bruce and I had separately worked with, and we both had a very good history with him,

American Beauty Co-Producer Bruce Cohen believes in sticking to your guns, especially when it comes to fighting for a trailer that best represents your movie.

we convinced Sam Mendes (director, *American Beauty*) that this marketing guy should see the film very early on so that he could start working on the trailer early, and the first couple of attempts were not successful. But had there not been that extra time to really find the trailer, it could have gone off in the wrong direction.

Zanuck: Also, in the old days, production would hand a movie to distribution and say, "Figure it out." When my husband ran Fox he didn't ask marketing in advance how to sell *M.A.S.H.* because they would have said there's no way to sell it, it wouldn't have gotten made. Now, distribution has input into production and marketing, and actually it should be like it was in the old days. You figure it out. It's amazing to me how often I watch a movie on video, one that I end up enjoying very much, and wonder if it was just a bad trailer that caused me to put off seeing the movie in the theater. Because I would have seen the movie, I wouldn't have waited. *Driving Miss Daisy* was billed as, "The Comedy That Won A Pulitzer," because they were so afraid that nobody would see it if it wasn't sold as funny, which was fine, but it wasn't really a comedy.

Cohen: I think David really nailed something with what he said about instinct, and it really applies here. It's probably the most important part of the job, those key instinct moments. We've all learned that the trailer is one of those moments, that if your instinct tells you it's good but its not great, that's what you've got to stay on the studio about day after day, week after week.

You have to tell them, "It's not good enough. You're not selling our film well enough," and then hopefully you get somewhere. Because that sitting in the theater and seeing a trailer that's not putting your movie forward is the worst.

Zanuck: And marketing thinks it's their movie because they cut the trailer, and they have so much pride in this trailer that they've cut with some vendor that they love and you're saying, "This doesn't work," and they're acting like they're the director.

Friendly: I think that's why a lot of what we do is politics, it's just the nature of the job. I became very friendly with the marketing department at Fox, and I would say to them, "Don't show it to me as a formality. I'm not one of these guys who you're going to show the trailer to and I'm just going to sign off and we're done. Let me have input. Don't show it as an afterthought," which is often what they do now. "Okay, come on in and we'll show you the trailer," and then you find out there's a green band on it and its done. I think you have to go in up front and say, "Okay, I don't know how it works with everybody else, but this is how I would like it to work," and the way you get that is by befriending these people and having them trust you, and you trust them. It's very hard.

Cohen: We should all be experts in television commercials because that's really where the movies are sold.

Zanuck: The one-sheet really is a thing of the past. In L.A. they happen to be on a lot of bus shelters, but they're not on bus shelters all over the country.

Johnson: On Sunset Boulevard, those billboards are all vanity. Dreamworks has theirs, Warners has theirs, and they put them up and it makes you feel good and you drive by them and all that, but it's money misspent.

Producers 411: What is your favorite part of the job?

Zanuck: When they say your name at the Oscars.

Jinks: That's a moment that's hard to beat.

Above right: Dave Friendly.
Above left: Mark Johnson (right) and Dan Jinks (left) talk about the importance of casting a crew.

Producers 411 wishes to thank Vivian Mayer of DreamWorks SKG and Ronni Chasen of Chasen & Company for their assistance in producing this roundtable. We would also like to thank Stephanie Haymes and Cicada Restaurant & Bar for catering this event.

tonedog
www.tonedog.com

Music & Sound Design for New Media

contact: andrea@tonedog.com
2017 s. westgate avenue
west los angeles, ca. 90025
vox: (310) 826-2550 fax: (310) 207-2587

Producers 411

In Defense of Aliens

The Staying Power of Science Fiction

By Rita Street

Preliminary artwork for Jean Giraud's upcoming computer animated feature *The Mobius Strip*.

Science fiction is both the bane and blessing of Hollywood. Films like last summer's expensive and less-than-successful *Battlefield Earth* put studio execs off the genre. At the same time, the triumphs of the *Star Wars* series and *The Matrix* make the same folks drool.

When science fiction works, it really works. When it fails, it fails with all the decisiveness of its oft-overburdened special effects. *Entertainment Tonight*'s Leonard Maltin believes this is true because Tinsel Town is sometimes blind to the real power of the genre – its inherent ability to change the way we think. "This is not a very good time for science fiction, mainly because everyone equates it with special effects," says Maltin, "That's not what science fiction is all about. It's about imagination, speculation, the future and mankind."

Legendary French illustrator/designer Moebius (a.k.a Jean Giraud) agrees. In Los Angeles to guide the design of his feature length, fully computer-animated science fiction project, *The Mobius Strip*, Mobius took a break from pre-production last Fall to ponder the question, "Why is science fiction such a strong genre?" Mobius posited, "Science fiction is the eternal frontier. It is the struggle against the unknown. Through science fiction we tease the monster, the monster in this case being our greatest fears. Through science fiction we even resolve problems of cultural development."

Considering the same question, executive producer Lucas Foster took time out from production on an as-yet-untitled science fiction feature in Berlin. Like Moebius, Lucas is one of the genre's champions, evidenced by his eight years tramping around Hollywood trying to sell *Stainless Steel Rat*, a property based on Harry Harrison's ten books of the same name. *Rat* never lost its appeal to Foster during that entire time, he insists. Finally, in June of 2000, Fox signed a deal with Foster and director Jon De Bont.

With science fiction, says Foster, "You can really reach people and make them take a look at things that might seem corny or overly familiar if they were to look at them more directly. Because a story is set in a fictional place, in another time or another reality, it's a good way to peek at the consequences of our current attitudes, political ideas, ethics and feelings."

Science fiction doesn't always get the kind of appreciation around Hollywood that its box office popularity ought to engender, however, mainly because motion pictures with out-of-this-world storylines often cost a digital arm-and-a-leg to make. "There have always been many sci-fi projects in development, but this hasn't necessarily been an indicator of Hollywood's appreciation for the reliability or the success of the genre," adds Foster. "I don't think most executives in the upper reaches of a studio really consider sci-fi a good bet. It's typically more expensive to make these effects-laden movies, requiring bigger stars to make them viable – in their eyes. That being said, no one who's paying attention can help but notice that the biggest movie franchise ever is a sci-fi property, *Star Wars*. I would say that the ridiculous success of the re-release and of *Episode I* woke a few people up to the enormous potential that science fiction movies — and really the broader adventure genre — has to offer."

Many science fiction producers, especially those involved with visual effects, are constantly battling to keep costs in line with shrinking below-the-line numbers. Jeff Olsen, visual effects producer for Industrial Light + Magic and *Star Wars Episode I: The Phantom Menace*, spends most of his time devising work-arounds that not only meet artistic demands but also fit the studios' ever-tightening pocketbooks. "Our job is to feed the story. For a movie to work, it can't be about the special effects. Still, for the story to be believable, we have to be able to establish the look of a world. You have to work closely with the producer and director to define the money shots and then continue to sell the reality through clues and illusions. For example with a movie like *Star Trek*, you have to spend a certain amount of money outside, say, the Enterprise hull as an establishing (often computer-generated) shot, but when you cut back you can continue to spin the illusion through less expensive in-camera shots – interior sets populated by actors with Star Fleet costumes." Olsen adds that contrary to common belief, the ILM team will often opt to build a miniature rather than create a more expensive digital model.

"You just get a lot of things for 'free' with models, like shadows and interactive lighting."

Both Olsen and Foster feel that although science fiction's upside is definitely its box office appeal, its downside is often its audacious difficulty. Says Foster, "If you asked me what challenges I face as a producer of science fiction, I would say the better question is 'What challenges don't I face?' Comedy producers and directors don't have to establish a world all that often. They deal with tone, and how far to go, but the basic reality is already understood by the audience. We, on the other hand are often building a creature one cell at a time."

Even when heavy-hitters are attached, science fiction features can be difficult to make, evidenced by the current stall on Mel Gibson's pet project, a remake of *Farenheit 451*. On the other hand, says Sheila Williams, Executive Editor of *Asimov's Science Fiction Magazine*, science fiction will always draw audiences because it's difficult – difficult to believe, that is. "Science Fiction makes us think about unexpected consequences," she says. "It dramatizes what might happen in a nuclear war, like *On The Beach*, or what might happen if artificial intelligence runs wild like *The Matrix*. It is powerful because it asks us to consider other things than our jobs or our paychecks."

But mostly, Williams says, "It asks us to stop and think."

Lucas Foster, Producer, *Stainless Steel Rat*

> "If you asked me what challenges I face as a producer of science fiction, I would say the better question is 'What challenges don't I face?'"
>
> —*Lucas Foster*

Top Twenty Science Fiction Box Office Hits
Source: Variety, compiled by Anthony D'Alessandro

1. *Star Wars: Episode IV - A New Hope* (Fox; 1977; dir., G. Lucas; prod., G. Kurtz) $460,998,007*
2. *Star Wars: Episode I - The Phantom Menace* (Fox; 1999; dir., G. Lucas; prod., G. Lucas/R. McCallum) $431,088,295
3. *E.T. - The Extra-Terrestrial* (Universal, 1982; dir., S. Spielberg; prod., S. Spielberg/K. Kennedy) $399,804,539
4. *Return of the Jedi* (Fox; 1983; dir., R. Marquand; prod., H. Kazanjian/G. Lucas) $309,205,079*
5. *Independence Day* (Fox; 1996; dir., R. Emmerich; prod., D. Devlin) $306,169,268
6. *The Empire Strikes Back* (Fox; 1980; dir., I. Kershner; prod., G. Lucas/G. Kurtz) $290,271,960*
7. *Men in Black* (Sony; 1997; dir., B. Sonnenfeld; prod., W. Parkes/L. MacDonald) $250,016,330
8. *Back to the Future* (Universal; 1985; dir., R. Zemeckis; prod., B. Gale/N. Canton/S. Spielberg/F. Marshall/K. Kennedy) $208,242,016
9. *Terminator 2* (TriStar; 1991; dir., J. Cameron; prod., J. Cameron/G.A. Hurd/M. Kassar) $204,843,345
10. *Armageddon* (Buena Vista; 1998; dir., M. Bay; prod., J. Bruckheimer) $201,578,182
11. *The Matrix* (Warner Bros.; 1999; dir., The Wachowski Brothers; prod., J. Silver/B.Berman/B. Osborne/A. Mason II/E. Stoff) $171,479,930
12. *Close Encounters of the Third Kind* (Columbia; 1977; dir., S. Spielberg; prod., J. & M. Phillips) $155,691,323
13. *Deep Impact* (Paramount; 1998; dir., M. Leder; prod., R. Zanuck/D. Brown) $140,464,664
14. *Total Recall* (TriStar; 1990; dir., P. Verhoeven; prod., B. Feitshans/R. Shusett/M. Kassar/A. Vajna) $119,394,839
15. *Back to the Future II* (Universal; 1989; dir., R. Zemeckis; prod., B. Gale/N. Canton/S. Spielberg/F. Marshall/K. Kennedy) $118,450,002
16. *Star Trek IV: The Voyage Home* (Paramount; 1986; dir., L. Nimoy; prod., H. Bennett) $109,713,132
17. *Contact* (Warner Bros.; 1997; dir., R. Zemeckis; prod., R. Zemeckis/S. Starkey) $100,803,906
18. *Star Trek: First Contact* (Paramount; 1996; dir., J. Frakes; prod., R. Berman) $92,027,888
19. *Space Cowboys* (Warner Bros., 2000; dir., C. Eastwood; prod., C. Eastwood, T. Rooker, A. Lazar) $89,699,441
20. *Waterworld* (Universal;1995; dir., K. Reynolds; prod., C. Gordon/J. Davis/K. Costner) $88,246,220

*includes grosses from recent re-releases

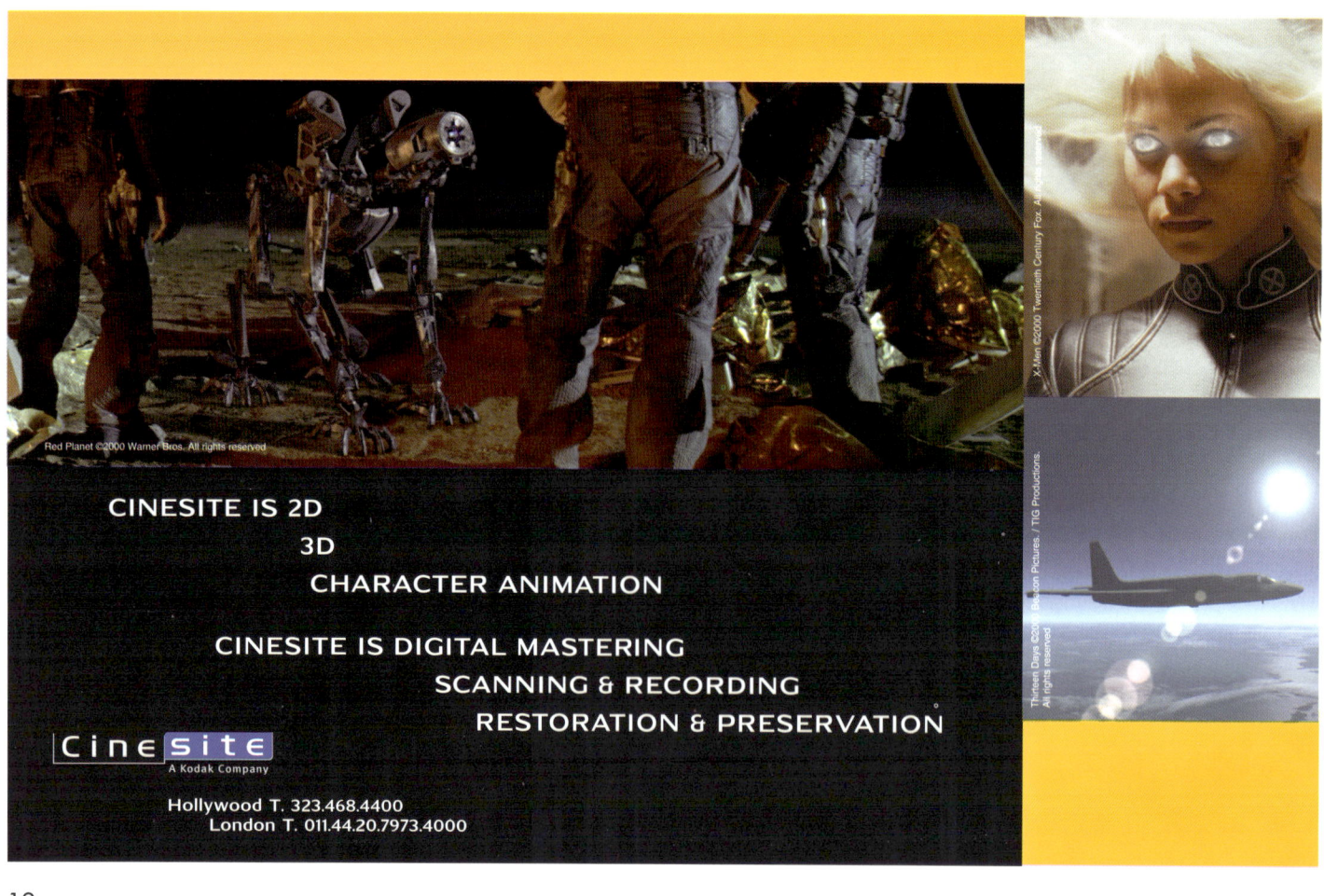

More of Everything.

Videotape, Film, Data Media, Storage, Cameras, Display, VTRs & much more.

We supply professional motion picture stock, datamedia, videotape and audio recording media to companies and individuals in the entertainment, corporate, educational, advertising and broadcast industries.

We are the West Coast's largest reseller of Fuji Film and represent many other major manufacturers such as Sony Data Media, Maxell, BASF, Quantegy and Quantum. Recently, we've expanded our operation to include equipment sales!

Call us and ask for our full line card!

Ask about our new line of drives!

SONY   FUJIFILM   maxell   QUANTEGY   Quantum   BASF by EMTEC

MEDIA DISTRIBUTORS
Products To Capture Imagination

10960 Ventura Blvd, Studio City, CA 91604 Toll Free: 888-889-3130 www.mediadistributors.com

featureFILMS

comMERCials

broadCAST

COMPUTERCAFE
3D animation - visual FX

santa **MONICA** california

310 395-9013   fax 310 395-9814

santa **MARIA** california

805 922-9479   fax 805 922-3225

www.computercafe.com

Eyeful of Reality
CBS's Burnett, Romer & Ross

By Ferdinand Lewis

After the ratings of summer 2000, everyone wanted to know what the Eye Net put in its water. With two major reality hits, *Survivor* and *Big Brother*, CBS had the lock on the genre. To find out their secrets, *Producers 411* visited the executive producers of both shows as they were winding up — *Survivor*'s Mark Burnett already on his way to Australia for *Survivor II*; *Big Brother*'s Paul Romer talking wistfully of seeing his kids back in Holland and Douglas Ross on his way to the wrap party.

"'Will it be inspiring?' is the question that I always ask myself," said Burnett, describing his personal acid test for Reality development. "If I sat down at dinner with someone not in the television business and told them this idea, would they be inspired?" Likewise, Ross put simplicity first. "I have this idea of the 'well thought out show,' which is easy to explain in a way that's solid, that doesn't have a lot of twists and turns. That helps when you're out in the field because you're not trying to make something work that isn't there." Romer, who was imported with the original show from Holland, also believes that

Big Brother's technolgy was strategized to the smallest detail. Inset: the Control Room

complex production must rely on one simple idea. "Ten million people watched *Big Brother* every night for the fun of being amateur psychologists. With these shows, the viewer feels he knows what the people on the show should do and so he is involved."

No matter how simple your message is, however, if you can't translate it to your American audience, you might as well be speaking Dutch. As Ross observed, "We found that not everything that worked in the Dutch version of *Big Brother* worked in the United States. European audiences are used to watching serialized soap operas six nights a week. Americans aren't. A lot of the show is made up of nuances. If you don't watch regularly you may not catch them. So it took time to work out our format and for the numbers to solidify."

Burnett also said that successful Reality shows in the coming year will be those that are shepherded by producers who have a personal commitment to the product. Affectionately monickered "The Method Producer" by his *Survivor* crew, Burnett insists on personally undergoing every trial that his contestants are asked to undertake. "Just because a show like [*Who Wants To Be A*] *Millionaire* works on one network doesn't mean it'll work everywhere else. You can't just pull producers in on projects and then expect those projects to be inspired. The producer has to be inspired too. And

The unassuming exterior of the Big Brother compound on the CBS lot.

that's especially true when the show has no script because at some point the producer is all there is to the show. That's when passion is the key."

All three producers agreed that the single most important element to successful Reality TV is its cast. "Take care of your contestants," says Burnett. "With this kind of show, you're building a world and in order for it to work you have to have the trust and loyalty of the cast. I told each member of the original *Survivor* cast, 'This isn't going to be *Jerry Springer*. I'm not here to make you look stupid. We won't manipulate you.'"

"This kind of show is more than just the shoot. It's this whole enormous marketing machine and if these ordinary people aren't part of the team they won't be team players. You have to care for your crew in the same way, so they're all part of the same team," said Burnett. Romer concurred, adding, "Your contestants are your best promotion for a second series. You want to show the world that you do your work in a responsible way because people will hear about it, and they'll know. These are the people who make your show. As a producer you have an obligation to take care of the people who make your success."

Ross added that contestants are unlikely to reveal their true natures – the meat on the Reality TV viewer's plate – unless they feel absolutely comfortable. "You have to get the authentic, natural quality out of the people you're featuring, so you have to earn their trust. On *Big Brother*, when one of our houseguests tried to organize a walk-out, we started to figure out how they were going to exit the show, contacting the alternates and contacting their families. If this is reality, then the houseguests control our destiny. As it turned out, when we told them that we would let them all go if they wanted to, they all decided to stay."

Contestants, these producers pointed out, must be carefully prepared for the long strange trip of a *Big Brother* houseguest. "We have no secrets from our contestants," said Romer. "We tell them about the consequences for their families at home. Psychologists do confidential evaluations with each candidate to tell us if a person is a good candidate or not. When a candidate is suitable, we prepare them for what will happen to their lives after the show. During production those same psychologists observe the show and tell us if a guest needs a consult or some extra help and these are private and not taped. When the show is over, houseguests have a debriefing with their psychologist who then tells us if the guest needs extra counciling, which the show provides. We also provide houseguests with publicists who support them with all the interviews and advise them if they want to pursue the entertainment business."

On the Reality set the only person without support is the producer. Of course, if Burnett is any sort of indicator, Reality producers thrive on life without a safety net. "When I was a child, hiking with my family in the Scottish mountains, then later with the military all over the world, I was inspired by nature in the raw. It makes me feel like a human being. My programs are all about that. It's what I love about them. But, it's really hard work doing unscripted material on such a big scale. There's just no control. You can't say 'cut,' so it's hard, incredibly hard work. Still I just love it."

In fact, he added, "You could say I've had a great time suffering."

Rigging Reality

By Ferdinand Lewis

"Reality TV requires you to think faster and better. You have no choice but to be innovative," says Chris Thompson. He oughta know. Thompson is President of Wexler Video Inc., the world's largest privately owned rental house and home

Chris Thompson

of the engineering brains that rig some of the most complex productions in television history. Wexler Video is not only responsible for shows like *Survivor*, but MTV's *Fear*, for which the company had only a week to outfit a prison with 45 cameras. Explains Thompson, "For Reality TV, you have to create an organic solution rather than just handing over a box."

Working on shows like MTV's *Real World*, MTV's *Road Rules* and ABC's *Making The Band* prepared Thompson and crew for the slings and arrows of last year's full-bore Reality boom. "No two productions are alike," adds Thompson. "We refined the microwave video link that made *Real World* possible, but for *Survivor*, we went with the most basic technology. That show was more a question of discipline, making sure that everything worked all the time. The bleeding edge of technology doesn't help our clients when they're shooting on a rowboat in the middle of the ocean."

Yet Thompson shrugs off the difficulty of his work. "The toughest job isn't ours, it's the producer's. They have to make incredible TV in impossible circumstances, with very little time, and very little money."

Alliance Post Productions, LLC

On-Site Rentals · AVID Bays · Service · Support

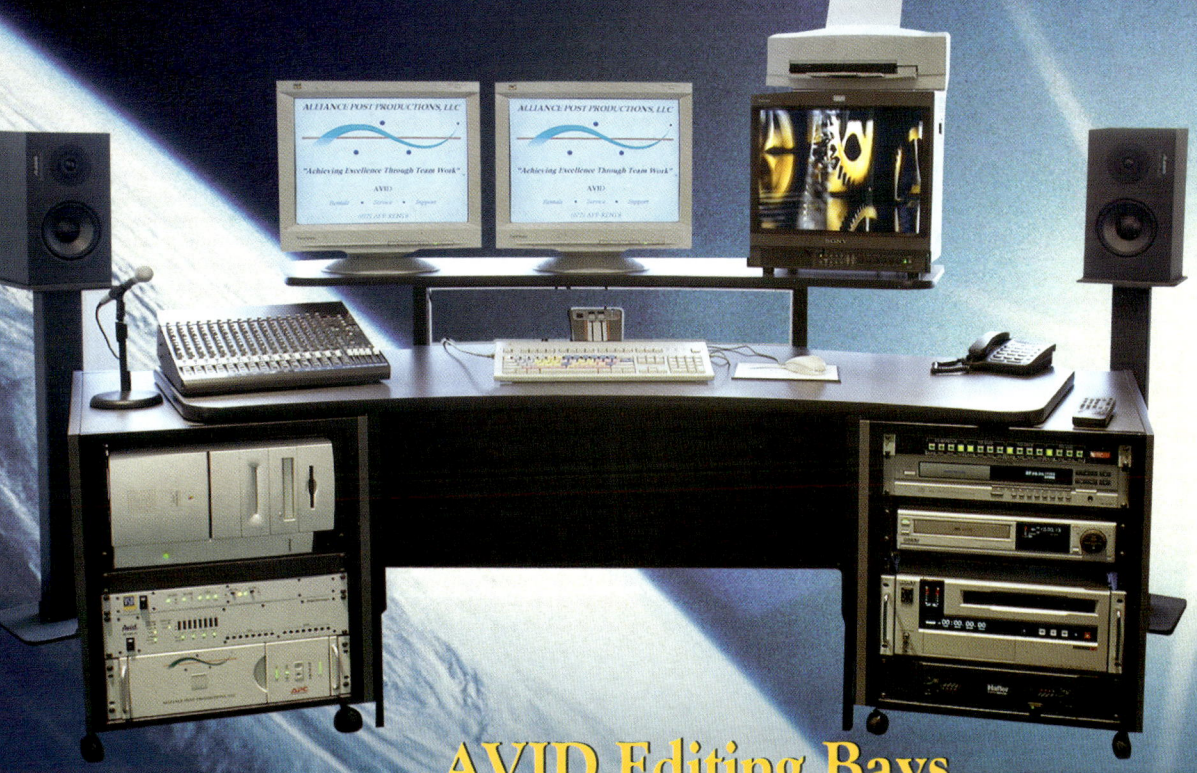

AVID Editing Bays

- Located in the City of Burbank at 210 North Glenoaks Blvd., Suite A, Burbank, CA 91502
- Bays are Fully Furnished
- Service and Support 24 Hours a Day, 7 Days a Week
- Fine Food Nearby For Dining In or Take Out
- Easy Freeway Access And Ample Parking

Relax in Our Dining Area

- Enjoy our 50's Style Dining Area
- We Have a Kitchen Area for your Convenience Including: Refrigerator, Microwave and More

We Have a Seat Waiting for You!

Phone: (818) 609-1600 · Fax: (818) 837-9101
Web Site: www.alliancepost.com

When you're on location, you gotta stay connected.

We keep you connected. Anywhere.

Internet Connections and Support.
Any Time, Any Place, Any Speed. Wired or Wireless.

Hollywood runs on connections . . .
—and those connections aren't just personal, they're electronic.
Whether you're shooting in a sound stage or up the Columbia River, you need to stay in touch.

No Wires? No Hassle.
Location Connect from TK Media Services delivers it all:

- High-speed Internet
- Access on location, any location
- Full-service computer, voice, wiring and network installation
- Consulting and 24-hour support.

Our people come on site, hook you to the Internet, keep your network secure, and move with you. Even if the nearest phone line is in the next county, you'll be:

- Viewing digital dailies
- Sending stills to the publicist, and
- e-mailing Mom

. . . in less than four hours. All with no wires, no prep, and no hassle.

And, back at home, we'll keep your office connections running great, too.

Call us to see how we do it.
Location Connect: *We Connect. You Create.*

Locationconnect.com **1·800·818·TECH**
(626) 792-0000
(626) 844-1001 FAX
info@locationconnect.com

Spotty Future?
Commercial Production At The Crossroads

By Ferdinand Lewis

Main Picture: Celluloid's spot "Bubble Boys" for Bud Light.

Inset: Visa spot produced by Headquarters.

In the middle of a recent meeting, one of Frank Scherma's clients put his head down on the conference table and cried, "I just want to go back to the way it was!" Scherma, CEO of the commercial production house @radical.media, explains that when working out the future of convergence and its affect on advertising, such client meltdowns are not atypical. Fortunately, Scherma handles it all with the aplomb of a experienced counselor.

"We're in the midst of a revolution," says Scherma. "But our business is not over. Remember when VCR's were going to destroy the movies, but in the end they created a whole new business? We have to embrace convergence and be excited about it, and in that excitement we'll find out what it can do for our clients, for our talent, and for everyone involved."

Commercial producers across the spectrum agree that production is at a crossroads. Should producers focus on

Producers 411

Visitor's Olivier Katz

Frank Scherma, @radical.media

With the advent of personal video recorders like Tivo and Replay, consumers can now trim commercials out of their nightly viewing schedules. This new threat to advertising presence initially kept spot producers and agency types up nights, however, the latest word from the frontlines is increasingly reassuring. Olivier Katz, chief of production house Celluloid, believes that production is quickly responding to digital media with its strongest suit — creativity.

"TV has been a passive sport," says Katz. "Now all that is changing and it's going to force advertisers and ad agencies to elevate the level of entertainment in advertising. That means that viewers aren't going to discriminate against advertising; it means they're going to discriminate against bad advertising and that's good news for everyone." Katz, along with many of his peers, believes that within two years new long-form commercials will "have the kind of impact that music videos and MTV had on the music industry fifteen years ago."

Additional good news for the commercial production arena comes in the form of a little thing called personalized viewer profiling. "The new technology," says Scherma, "is building a profile on everybody who uses it. Eventually, if you watch a lot of golf, for instance, they can then send a golf-specific spot. If you can target people with things they're interested in, they're more likely to watch." Michael Porte, founder of the B-to-B site for commercial production Wheresspot.com, adds, "In five years, we'll know exactly who's sitting in the living room."

It is already clear that the new viewer profiling increases a client's ability to target, but what remains unclear is whether or not personalized targeting will increase sales. Until that is figured out, a number of convergence strategists are experimenting with the best uses for online profiling. One tactic gaining considerable traction is yet another spin on advertising-as-entertainment: sponsored programming.

"In the old days," says Porte, "it was smart for one client to sponsor a whole show because they knew exactly who they were reaching. But media evolved and the idea of sponsorship went away. Now, we're reaching back in time because the technology is leaping forward. We're again able to target that specifically." Alex Blum, Partner and Executive Producer for Headquarters, interprets this as proof of commercial production's mercurial ability to adapt to any consumer environment. "A business that moves like ours always has to be thinking about how it's going to look in the years to come. The big question concerns the evolution of the entire business and in what ways producing commercials is going to change."

Tommy Means and Mekanism were recently presented with an opportunity to push that evolution, with the interactive campaign for Rock The Vote, co-produced by MTV, last Fall. "This was the first election where you could register to vote online, and our goal was to drive as many young voters to register as possible," Means explains. "It was a powerful message, and we had to enable the audience to speak back to that message, to create a dialogue with the spots, which is what's so powerful about taking commercials to the Internet."

Tommy Means of Mekanism

retraining existing talent for parallel production, i.e., the ability to create content for both broadcast and broadband? Or should producers simply continue to make their advertising content more entertainment-friendly? Either answer is an attempt to address the central phenomenon of convergence, which Mekanism's Executive Producer, Tommy Means, phrases this simply: "The audience is talking back."

"Viewers aren't going to discriminate against advertising... they're going to discriminate against bad advertising."

—Olivier Katz

Using the broadcast commercial's provocative imagery, Mekanism created supersticials with Flash animation, interactive rollovers, and a haunting, persistent score that emphasized the gravity of a voter's responsibility. At the end of the piece, users had the option to register online or write to the candidates. Other important placements were triggers built into Rock The Vote's broadcast commercial for Web TV, alerting viewers that the commercial is interactive, enabling them to register online via picture-in-picture, without interrupting regular programming. In addition, in-stream ads for Rock The Vote ran on the Real Broadcast Network and the Sony Music Video Network, with the ability to click through and register to vote.

Means proudly quoted the figures: as of the first week of October 2000, the supersticial ads garnered an 18% clickthrough, the most successful ad on Altavista to-date. The streaming video version of the broadcast ad had a click-through rate of 15.2 %, the Real Broadcast Network's most successful ad ever. Means said that Rock the Vote estimates that the online campaign will have been seen by 10 million, and that with a month of campaign to go, an estimated 130,000 voters had already registered online.

But what does that mean for the future of advertising? "The creatives from both sides have to collaborate now, online and broadcast," says Means. "Broadcast is king and will be for a long time, but you still have to think of the technology at the head-in, and craft the imagery and dialogue and audio for both venues." Blum believes that the Rock the Vote campaign was successful because its amalgam of message, audience and medium were apt to the moment. "(Rock The Vote) was a perfect use (of interactivity). It's a very specific thing, though, that they were trying to get people to do, so that was a good convergence of function." Yet Blum adds that the campaign was also relatively uncomplex, suggesting that a full-blown mating of Internet and broadcast would be far more unwieldy to produce.

Tony Hazard, CEO of Random Order, is well aware of that unwieldiness. "Right now there can be 20 different technologies employed in a project, and they all have constraints, so you have to have a full understanding of the spectrum," he says, adding that no one in commercial production can afford to stay out of the fray — not even for the time it takes to rest their heads on a desk and moan. "If a client needs an interactive commercial, and one company has experience with it and one doesn't, they're gonna go with the experienced one."

Listening To Convergence

By Ferdinand Lewis

In traditional commercial production, post is usually pretty far downstream in the process. "Editing houses are by nature reactive, not proactive," says consultant/strategist Valerie Petrusson. However, with the dawn of webcasting and interactive television, editorial is presented with a unique opportunity to fish a little further upstream. "Traditionally, editorial is hanging fire until everything else is decided," says Petrusson, "But the new technology is shaking all that up."

One post house swimming resolutely upstream is the audio editorial company Ear-To-Ear, a Petrusson client. Ear-To-Ear's new Interactive Division is working with a new plug-in for Internet sound that will stake a big claim at the headwaters of TV/Internet convergence. There's already a demand for it, explains Ear-To-Ear's Executive Director Christine Cash. "Web sites are looking more and more like television commercials, and so users are starting to expect the highest quality sound from the Internet. Right now, though, Internet audio is all MP3 and streaming audio, button clicks and rollover sounds. We're going to take it to the next level."

Christine Cash

If Ear-To-Ear's new audio platform can set the standard for the Internet, Cash is betting, it'll be only a short swim to interactive television. "We're already strategically partnered with the developers of interactive TV," Cash says. "This is absolutely going to be the platform for interactive audio in the years to come."

Woodland Hills
818.316.1000

Hollywood
323.464.3800

Orlando
407.363.0990

Chicago
773.267.1500

Wilmington
910.343.8796

Dallas
972.929.8585

New York
212.606.0700

Toronto
416.444.7000

Vancouver
604.291.7262

Melbourne
011.613.9646.3044

Sydney
011.612.9436.1844

Brisbane
011.617.5588.6543

Wellington
011.644.384.4191

Auckland
011.649.378.9492

London
011.44.181.839.7333

Manchester
011.44.161.872.4766

Shepperton
011.44.1932.572440

Glasgow
011.44.141.221.5175

Dublin
011.353.12.860811

Paris
011.331.4462.2020

Marseille
011.334.91.21.43.14

Gennevilliers
011.331.46.13.92.10

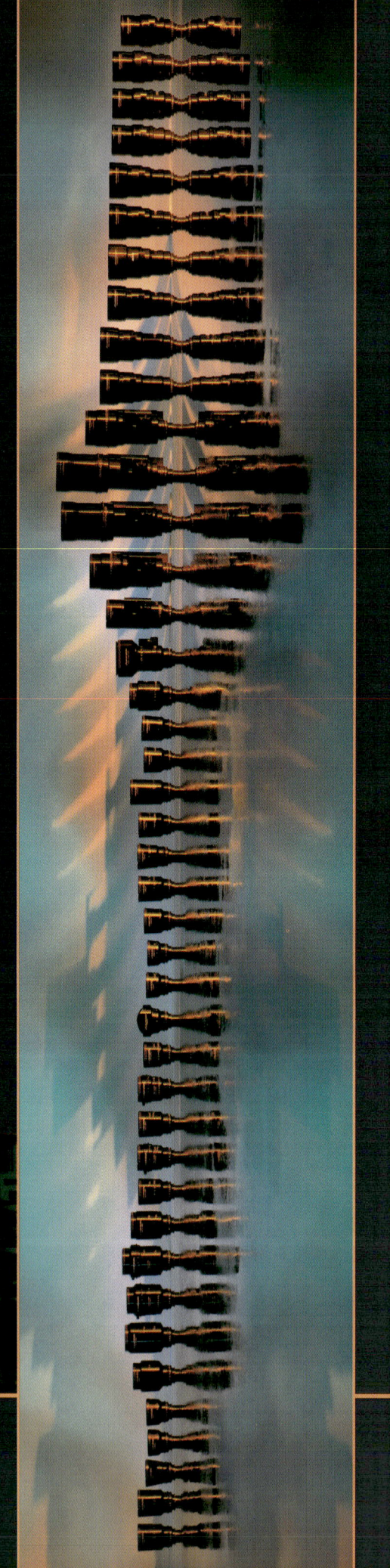

stages
locations
equipment
audio post
editorial facilities

UNIVERSAL STUDIOS

800.892.1979

the filmmakers destination

competitive rates to the
production community
· television
· commercials
· features
· music videos
· independent projects
· wrap parties/special events

UNIVERSAL

UNIVERSAL STUDIOS
OPERATIONS GROUP

800.892.1979
THE FILMMAKERS DESTINATION
WWW.UNIVERSALSTUDIOS.COM/STUDIO

Producers 411

Historical Impact
Charlie Maday Brings the Personal Touch to History Channel Docs

By Ferdinand Lewis

At first, it seems a little odd. When you ask the History Channel's Vice President of Programming, Charles Maday, how he accounts for the cabler's success he answers, "Television lives off of good stories about individuals, personal stories." But how can that be when the History Channel has built its market share on documentaries about the biggest, most sweeping events in human history, like the Civil War and the Industrial Revolution?

For *Producers 411*, Maday talks about the historical documentary form, how it has changed over the years, and what the History Channel looks for in historical documentary production.

Producers 411: How is your approach to historical docs different from most?

Maday: We're about the stories rather than the analysis of history. We don't look at a battle, for instance, we look at individuals who were in it. Our audience looks to us for a perspective on history, rather than scholarship. It's a perspective of individuals confronting challenges and overcoming odds. Through these personal stories you get a perspective on the issues. The human stories are what make the History Channel unique.

Producers 411: That sounds more like fiction. Aren't documentaries

Charles Maday, History Channel's Vice President of Programming

As Maday explains, finding the personal in the epic — the unique approach to historical documentaries that he and the History Channel have pioneered — is key. Proof of this success is found in the History Channel's loyal and steadily growing audience of 25-54 year-olds. For almost twenty-four months the cablers' monthly ratings have beaten those of the previous years'.

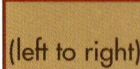

(left to right) History Channel's *History Center, A History of Britian, History IQ, This Week in History, A History of Britian,* and *History Alive.*

24

responsible for accuracy?

Maday: For us, storytelling doesn't mean just setting up a camera and having someone tell you a story and then you're done. We're dealing with history so these stories have to have first class scholarship behind them. They have to be supported by the best research. The difference between us and a more scholarly survey is that historians use quantitative information; we use human information. But the two work together.

Producers 411: Do you program more for story or for history?

Maday: We program according to what the major historical trends are. We watch the news but we're not about the news. Instead, we look for the small story within the big one, the detail within the great sweep of history. The premiere episode of *This Week in History* this past summer for instance, was about the Berlin Wall but instead of the broad point-of-view we looked at the guard who stamped the last passport before the wall was torn down.

Producers 411: The History Channel also tends to avoid nostalgia. Why is that? Nostalgia can be so powerful.

Maday: Nostalgia is the cheap route to emotion. The harder road is through detail. Accurate, rich detail is what makes a story universal rather than something that only a handful of people care about. I was watching a piece on the Kennedy-Nixon debates and thinking, "Why isn't everyone in the world watching this?" and then I recalled that half the world wasn't even alive when those debates took place. You have to bring these great events down to earth through a personal story. Detail is what makes a story universal. Of course, with ancient history there's no nostalgia but that's a different challenge.

Producers 411: How do you develop the human aspect of a history story?

Maday: It all begins with research. When you produce a history documentary you don't grab a camera and go shoot like you would for other types of documentary. With history, you have to spend months in research, or else find a book that has already done the research, but even then you've got to be a thinker before you're a shooter.

Just to illustrate the point about how good the research has to be, you ought to be able to literally put together the documentary and never touch a camera; just make it out of archive footage and voice-overs. The ideal show, of course, has great interviews, good visuals, and a terrific archive, but I'm trying to illustrate the level of research we expect.

Producers 411: History is finite. Is it possible to run out of subjects?

Maday: I've been in the business thirty years and I've seen everything that's been made. You have to either find something people don't already know about, or else find a new approach to some aspect of history that's very familiar. One program of ours that's taking a new approach to an old subject is *The Unfinished Civil War*, which is the story of Civil War re-enactors. We look at their lives and the details of their love for the Civil War and through that we learn about the war.

The Unfinished Civil War is the first thing I've done here that's shot in a more vérité style. The Civil War has been done so much there needed to be a new way of looking at it. So this is a new style for us but it comes out of that same need.

Producers 411: What's your take on the evolution of the documentary form as viable programming and what does the future hold for the genre?

Maday: Over the years the definition of documentary has broadened. That's because in the beginning, most documentaries had an underlying desire to change the human condition. They began with a social concern and that social aspect has evolved into many different forms. Today documentaries are used for education, entertainment, training — many things, not just documenting problems in society. The social aspect will always be there but now there are so many ways into it. A documentary can show us our world through the history of the automobile, for example, which we've done by literally taking a car apart and examining history through every part of the car.

Is the Internet in our future? It hasn't changed what we do in terms of documentaries, but it enhances what we do. We're now producing in parallel for the Internet and broadcast. You're going to see more and more of that parallel development, of course. The two worlds are different — Internet and broadcast — but anything that can enhance the broadcast, we're going to do, like streaming the dedication of the World War II Memorial in Washington, D.C., for instance.

The History IQ quiz show that launched last fall is fully interactive. You can play it in real time at home against the contestants on the air but it also has a game that can be accessed 24x7.

On a practical, day-to-day basis, the Internet hasn't changed what we do that much. It's a great source for research but dangerous too, because search engines don't discriminate between good research and bad.

Producers 411: Any advice for producers who want to move into this genre?

Maday: In documentary, nothing's casual. You have to plan. It might seem casual to the audience but if it's in there, somebody had to want it to be. With documentary it seems like there's so much you can't control, but the truth is you can. In topic selection, in editing, in the shots you choose, you have a lot of control. The most successful documentaries are planned, planned, planned.

In the end, though, television lives off of good stories about individuals, personal stories. That's always been the case and it will always be the case.

David Haugland On: Seeing The Present In Our Past

By Ferdinand Lewis

David Haugland believes that although history is long, memory is brief. The Oscar-nominated documentary producer observes, however, that when history is retold through an individual perspective, imagination can stand in for memory.

Says Haugland, "It can be so hard to understand the German Occupation, for instance, but when you think of Anne Frank and what she went through, you have a character to identify with. Through her perspective, you learn about what happened." The former President of the International Documentary Association adds, "What fiction works so hard to achieve -the audience identifying with the characters- can be automatic in documentaries."

The most important thing that historical documentaries help us recall isn't our past, Haugland concludes, but ourselves. "Documentaries help us to interpret our lives by giving us a context. That's very powerful. I give the History Channel a lot of credit for their approach. They're helping us all make sense of the past."

Producers 411

Sam Aslanian, Executive Producer D.N.A.

inset photo by Libby Simon

Music Video Vet
In The Trenches With Sam Aslanian

By Rita Street

Executive producer Sam Aslanian digs his work. Even after twelve years he's still hooked. As head of production for Hollywood-based David Naylor & Associates (D.N.A.), Aslanian is in charge of one of the busiest and most successful music video production stables on the planet. Week in, week out, artists like Ricky Martin, Lauryn Hill, Jennifer Lopez and Brian McKnight depend on him and the directors at D.N.A. to consistently pull off the impossible: a four-minute piece of art produced in an impossibly short amount of time. Though his company wrangles between two and four of these grueling miracles a week, he's still gonzo about making "mini-music-movies."

Oh sure, he does admit to having it a little tough sometimes, but it's all fun. "One job we booked recently came in on a Friday afternoon at 2:00 p.m. and we had to be shooting by Monday," he says with a shrug. "But, by 5:00 p.m. we had our equipment and camera on hold, a sound stage booked and an art director ready to start work. The set went up over the weekend and by 7:00 p.m. Monday we were ready to shoot until dawn."

To pull off something like that you have to have a great database on your Palm Pilot and a heck of a lot of moxy. Aslanian has both. Here's how he keeps his passion for the craft alive, and his wits about him, while producing the work of some of the world's greatest clip directors.

Producers 411: How did you get started in the business?

Aslanian: I was always into film. I got my BA and MFA from UCLA Film School, worked as a production manager and then went on to write, produce and direct my first low-budget feature. It actually had a theatrical release in the mid-'80s but I don't think I want to tell you the name. I would have kept doing that but I figured out that I really hate writing; it's exhausting. Then a friend pulled me on to a music video set and I never went back. Not long after I was brought on at D.N.A. to handle a fairly low-budget job. Within a year I was producing. I'm looking back over the master list of videos I've been involved with now, and its over 530.

Producers 411: Let's talk about the directors in your stable, and how you shape their careers.

Aslanian: We work with artists like Lili Fini Zanuck who directed Faith Hill's "Breathe," [winner of the Country Music Association's Music Video of the year for Artist and Director, 1999] and Jean Baptiste Mondino for Madonna, as well as Award-Winning directors Francis Lawrence, Liz Friedlander, Rocky

> "The most important part of my job is taking care of directors. I try to keep them out of political and creative struggles and pitfalls."
> —Sam Aslanian

Schenck and Mark Webb. Limp Bizkit's Fred Durst also directs his own videos with us.

The most important part of my job is taking care of directors. I try to keep them out of political and creative struggles and pitfalls. Creatively I always tell them how I feel. They can count on me to be honest. It also definitely helps that I have a filmmaking background because we speak the same language. That's especially important when it comes to sitting down with a director on a piece that's not working or when we need to take a blue pencil through a concept. I love working with young directors because they aren't jaded, not stuck in a formula. Francis and Liz started their careers here, and now they've grown into A-list directors. That's really the best part of the job, nurturing and watching directors grow.

Producers 411: How do you nurture them?

Aslanian: I just make sure they don't get complacent; recycle old ideas. I used to work with this director years ago who had a concept file that he would consult whenever he had to make a bid. He'd say, "Oh, I think this needs a concept 'H.'" And he'd go to the file and get it out, literally. He also had a file of whip pans that he kept. That was sort of his trademark and they would just appear in video after video. But videos aren't about tricks, they're about taking a piece of music and giving it visual life.

Producers 411: It's been a while since MTV made its move to original content. What's the fall-out from that?

Aslanian: We used to make a lot of videos at lower budgets, dozens of jobs under $100,000. Now those are rare. The lower end is more like $250,000 and we regularly produce with budgets of around $800,000 to $1.4 million. That's because there are fewer slots for air and each label wants to make sure their video makes an impression and actually gets shown. Because MTV shows directors' credits, bands know which directors they want, so it's harder now for young directors to break in. The Internet is also generating more work for us. Let's say we do a video that's going to be marketed on MTV, on DVD, home video and the Internet: once the marketplace expands, our budget expands because every band gets a certain amount out of a label's various marketing categories. The more categories of delivery there are, the more money a band sees to make their clip.

Producers 411: What does it take to be an executive producer in music videos?

Aslanian: You have to be very quick on your feet. The commercials division of D.N.A. sometimes gets a whole three weeks to prep. We're lucky if we get a few days. Our directors usually get about two days to shoot. It gets pretty scary; sometimes we wonder if we'll actually make it but we always do – even in situations where you're asked to shoot in some remote town in Texas in a day and a half and part of that limited time will be taken up by the director actually driving to the location because there are no airports close by. It helps being in Los Angeles because everything is available twenty-four hours a day.

Producers 411: What's the next big trend?

Aslanian: Definitely visual effects. They're getting more affordable now and I think there will be a time soon when almost everything we do will be in front of a green screen and art directors will be guys on computers. We came close to that with the Ricky Martin clip *Private Emotion* directed by Francis. That hotel room goes up in flames and then freezes and none of that was real.

Producers 411: What's the best thing about your job?

Aslanian: When a director walks into the office with the finished product. They've just left the editor and they come to our conference room and the whole staff joins in for a screening. When Francis comes in with something like McKnight's *Back At One* and people actually cry. Music videos are like pieces of art. I know some people will think I'm insane for saying that, but that's what I believe. If I didn't, I wouldn't be doing this…

Plus, what other job pays you to be up at four in the morning blasting really loud music?

Director Francis Lawrence

Are you ready for Rich Media?

ANNOUNCING

Web-n-Flow™

L.A.'s first interactive rich-media production facility for rent.

According to Forrester Research, 92% of online consumers will communicate via rich media in the next four years. The boom has started, and the time to re-purpose existing content and explore the hottest production methods is now. So how do you get your hands on the best technology?

At Web-n-Flow, we provide everything you need to produce innovative multimedia content. You can integrate video with Javascript, Flash and HTML on an editing timeline, then compress it to Quicktime, Windows Media or Real Video for website uploading or output to DVD. Our featured equipment list includes iMedia100 web design tools, a Compression/Motion-Graphics Workstation, and a DVD authoring station complete with a 24/7 technical support team. You can bring your own talent, or if you prefer, hire ours. You'll find us downtown, in the state-of-the-art Los Angeles Center Studios.

Call today to set up a demo, or visit us online at www.webnflow.tv.

Sales • Rentals • Solutions
1201 West 5th Street, Los Angeles, CA 90017
Telephone: 323-537-6060 Fax 323-537-6061
Toll Free: 877-Web-n-Flow

Break Down the Barriers of Blue Screen Technology

The HoloRing, attached to the camera lens, emits a blue (or green) light toward the set.

The magic of chroma keying has always been limited by the logistical hurdles of expensive and complex lighting systems, extensive set-up time, talent clothing color considerations, and fixed set locations. HoloSet overcomes all of these limitations with a simple hardware based keying system.

HOW IT WORKS

HoloSet consists of a blue or green LED ring that attaches to the camera lens, an LED Intensity Controller, and a roll of retro-reflective gray fabric with millions of small glass beads on its surface. Light from the LED ring is reflected by the glass beads on the fabric directly back into the camera lens. The camera reads this reflected light from the fabric as an even blue or green key source depending on the color of the LED ring you choose.

The blue light from the HoloRing is reflected back into the camera from HoloSet's proprietary synthetic fabric.

EXTREME PORTABILITY AND FLEXIBILITY

HoloSet can be carried on location in a camera bag and set up in just minutes. Because the optically advanced fabric can reflect light even from extreme angles, no cove or hard cyc is required. All of the corners, seams, edges and wrinkles that would ruin a traditional key become invisible to the camera. And since HoloSet is a hardware solution, it works with any chroma keyer from software rendered keyers to Ultimatte.®

Regardless of set lighting, the camera sees the reflected light as a blue glow, perfect for chroma keying.

AVAILABLE NOW

See for yourself how HoloSet will change the television production industry. Experience the power of HoloSet at your local Authorized Trinity Dealer. For more info, visit www.play.com.

HoloSet gives you the freedom to use standard weather map techniques or even place actors into three dimensional virtual sets.

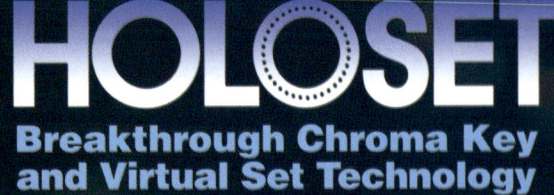

HOLOSET
Breakthrough Chroma Key and Virtual Set Technology

Play Incorporated • 2890 Kilgore Road • Rancho Cordova, CA 95670
Phone 916.851.0800 • www.play.com

PLAY

The Creative Producer
Oxymoron, Or Job Description?

When director Francis Lawrence writes a concept pitch for a music video he doesn't have to waste time second-guessing his own creativity. Instead he drops his work into the waiting arms of Executive Producer Sam Aslanian. As atypical as this might sound, Lawrence and the rest of the directors at the A-List Hollywood-based clip house D.N.A. rely on the right side of their exec's brain as much as the left. Says Lawrence, "If he doesn't like it, then I probably never really liked it in the first place."

It helps that Aslanian not only has a film degree but has also written, produced and directed movies. It means that Lawrence and his producer speak the same language. "Sam never tells me what to do with a concept, but he knows how I can get my ideas across more clearly. He's helped me with my aesthetic and my style and whether I should take a certain job because it would advance my career or just because it would be a cool thing to do creatively."

No sooner did Lawrence join D.N.A., some five years ago, than Aslanian began to steer the yet-to-be-established director toward a solid track record and the heights of clip-helming-stardom. "Sam took me under his wing and nurtured my career," Lawrence says, observing that thoughtful — and informed — creative input is what makes a great producer. "I don't really know how other producers work, but personally, I wouldn't have it any other way."

(left to right)

Stills from D.N.A. produced videos for Destiny's Child, Lil' Kim and Madonna.

Producers 411

Wrangling The Web

Rogue Producers Stake Internet Claims

By Rita Street

The first made-for-Internet Indie Feature *Quantum Project*.

Producing for the Internet is Hollywood's new Wild West. Out there on the Net, you can do anything you want. As Matt Diamond, head of development for webcentric production studio FDG-I points out, "With no FCC regulations you can create stuff that's more risky than broadcast."

Out there, you can make history. As Barnet Bain, co-producer of *What Dreams May Come* and the first Hollywood-style made-for-Internet movie *Quantum Project*, points out, you can still stake a claim. "We realized there was a window of opportunity that had never existed before, for an indie to produce a made-for-Internet motion picture. So with *Quantum*, we actually set out to produce an Internet version of *The Jazz Singer*; a property that would be the equivalent to the first talkie."

Out there, you can still break in. As young indie filmmaker Mitchell Rose says, the Internet can also be "a stepping stone to a Hollywood project." Rose, a former choreographer, has a webisode deal with Universal to produce Mitchell Rose's *Modern Daydreams*. Mitchell's oddball original short, *Deere John*, about an exec who imagines himself in a loving ballet with a backhoe, helped land him the digital mini-series.

Yup, out there, in virgin cyberspace you'll have your creative freedom, your X-minutes of fame, and even your chance to influence the majors.

What you won't have out there is money.

Yeah sure, some folks, like producer Joseph Levy have struck gold. Levy and his team hit

(left to right)

Stephen Simon and Barnet Bain co-producers of *What Dreams May Come* and *Quantum Project*.

32

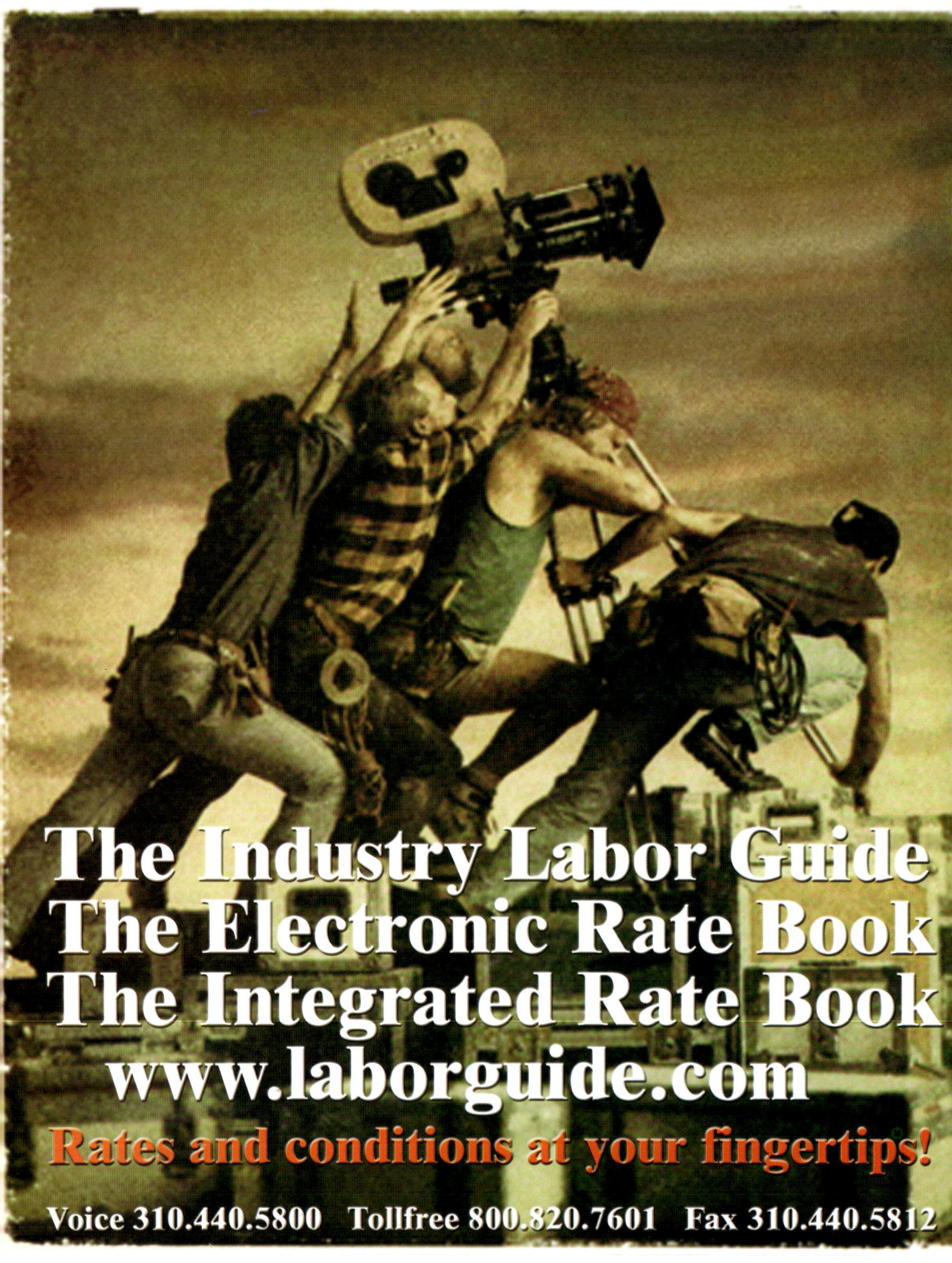

> "There is simply no business model in the arena."
> —Barnet Baine

the Internet motherload with *George Lucas In Love*, a nine-minute parody of the mega-filmmaker's college days, and his struggle to write a science fiction screenplay. According to MediaTrip, the on-line caster that debuted the short in '99, *Lucas* has received well over a million free downloads, each of which increases actual sales potential through outlets like Amazon.com and Tower Records. The collector mentality of webviewers, in turn, has earned some 50,000 VHS unit sales for the short. Amazon.com reports that the parody was its bestselling short subject in 2000 and the best all-time seller in its *Advantage Title*, offering a program which showcases indie product.

Likewise *Quantum Project*, which received $3 million in production financing from SightSound.com and will earn attractive stock options in the same for Bain's Metafilmics, garnered over a million attempted downloads in its first week — a healthy sum at $3.95 a pop. "But hits [in this case, blockbusters rather than clicks], are not a business," says Bain, who adds that he is definitely not into "playing the lottery" when it comes to opportunities for consistent production.

That is the problem with producing for the Internet. "There is," according to Bain and many of his peers, "simply no business model in the arena." Of the total number of Internet users in America today, only about 2 million are paying for home-based broadband access fast enough to comfortably view streaming media, and that's not a particularly attractive number for banner ad or sponsor-based advertisers.

Low ad dollars, of course, mean low production budgets. "There just aren't enough eyeballs out there yet to justify high-production costs," says Jim Rush, director of development for webcaster Neurotrash. Filmmakers picked up for deals with Rush, "get a bare bones budget, under $5,000, and a digital camera for production." The rest is up to them.

So if the chances of striking it rich are slim, and potential backing for production ventures are scarce, why head toward the new digital West? In part, because it is the nature of filmmakers to seek out the unknown; to try something different. As Bain puts it, there is nothing quite like, "setting sail into unknown country." Also, it is the nature of prospectors to get there first and stake large claims in hopes of retaining the biggest shares.

"By 2003," says Rush, "there will be between 13 and 19 million customers with high-speed connections. With numbers like that, we can talk about an actual business plan." In the meantime, innovative Inter-preneurs are patching together quilt-type business models that should keep them afloat, at least until convergence or broadband (or both) begin to grow the kind of gold veins this industry needs — solid advertising dollars.

"I think what a lot of producers intend to do is multi-platform," says Diamond. "That's one of those new terms everyone is throwing around, which basically means taking your projects to multiple mediums. A lot of producers intend to use their Internet products as the equivalent of TV pilots. And we always make sure our properties are character-driven so that we can build franchises out of them." Diamond even intends to move into toy sales.

Webcasters like AtomFilms think along the same lines. Atom, unlike the failed DEN and the aborted Pop, remains viable by relying on distribution monies from ancillary-to-net outlets like airlines and cablers. Monies brought in from sponsors on their free-to-view site are icing on the Atomfilm P&L cake. Others, like Internet agent Lisa Lindo of Acme

Matt Diamond
Head of Development, FDG-I.

Pitch A Caster, Any Caster

(For your next cyberspace pitching adventure, may we humbly suggest the following.)

www.01films.com

www.atom-bomb.com

www.atomfilms.com

www.bijoucafe.com

www.cinemanow.com

www.cinemapop.com

www.craptv.com

www.dfilm.com

www.dotcomix.com

www.dreamspan.com

www.entertaindom.com

www.icebox.com

www.mediatrip.com

www.mondominishows.com

www.neurotrash.com

www.shockwave.com

www.sightsound.com

www.sputnik7.com

www.television.com

www.tv.tv

www.undergroundfilm.com

www.z.com

FDG-I's Cornbread and Coyote Sound-off.

Management, are beginning to tap into pop culture's latest event mentality.

"Unless you're doing theater, entertainment is all about advertising. With that in mind, I'm trying to come up with a new kind of syndication model. The problem with selling a show to one content source is that it is limited to that site, so less eyeballs. To increase the eyeballs, you create an event that travels from site-to-site. So let's say you have a travel show: First you might take it to a food site, where you could sell food or recipes that relate to your show. Then you'd take your show to a clothing site and sell clothing for travel. As the show gets picked up by more and more sites you get more and more viewers."

Lindo and Internet guru peers like Austin Harrison, founder of Mediatrip, have learned to create their own opportunities. Says Harrison, "We put a lot of effort into underground marketing, viral e-mails – aggressive e-mails that aren't SPAMS, but get the word out – seeding news groups and

> "This is just a golden opportunity for young indies to go out and shoot stuff, put it up and make a name for themselves."
>
> —Matt Diamond

lots of press. For instance, when we were featured on NPR with *George Lucas In Love* we sold a couple thousand videos at $8 each."

MediaTrip's *'Lil Pimp* (a webisode about the adventures of an elementary school-age panderer), has not only been picked up for feature film production based on its popularity with over 350,000 monthly viewers, but offers a unique model for promotion. As an episode loads, a message gives viewers the heads-up. In the middle of the Flash cartoon they'll have a chance to click on the "bean poem juice," a zippy juice-box animation, for a chance to win a free T-shirt.

This gimmick definitely fits into the quirky look of *'Lil Pimp*, and the alternative-entertainment feel of the Net. It also offers up a possible profit center in the form of "sponsored-by" advertising.

For most Internet producers, however, production dollars based on advertisements aren't the real treasure. Producers of Internet product typically get to see their work distributed. Instead of getting turned down by television executives who are looking for mainstream properties, most Internet producers are actually in production. "This is just a golden opportunity for young indies to go out and shoot stuff, put it up and make a name for themselves," says Diamond. "That's mainly because, for the most part, pitching for the Internet is not the bureaucratic nightmare that television has become."

Diamond, who is producing two of his own pilots for www.craptv.com, gets to be a Wild West cowboy. Finally, he's making his own really "out there" properties — *Whore*, a spoof of cheesy game shows and *Cornbread and Coyote*, a dysfunctional puppet show featuring a raggedy foul-mouthed canine and a piece of cornbread. And that, for him, is paydirt.

Ready to Produce for the Internet?

Here are some tips from the experts

By Rita Street

When it comes to developing your script, think short and funny. According to producer Matt Diamond, "Comedy is selling best, because it's easily produced in short segments." Whenever possible, serialize. Webcasters prefer webisode buys.

Check out TheGroupHome.org for Internet casting, crewing and kibitzing. This sub-group of Wheresspot.com – a collective for resources in advertising – is an e-mail-based bulletin group designed especially for producers of online entertainment.

Plan on working with a digital camera and a desktop editing system. The preferred set-up for Internet post-production is a Apple G-3 or G-4 running Final Cut or Adobe's After Effects and Photoshop. If you include animation, Macromedia's Flash is the web standard for production software. Keep it simple. Really simple. Austin Harrison, president of webcaster MediaTrip explains, "Don't think in terms of what you would see in the movie theater or on television. Think functionally for the Internet, which is typically a small frame that lacks clarity. So, a shot of some guy standing on the horizon won't work." As often as possible, go for close-up and medium shots and locked-off cameras.

Think Calling Card. Forget about making it rich with your Internet production. That's playing the lottery. Do think about what interest your work will garner. "Young filmmakers and cinematographers wanting to break into directing use the Internet as a way to cut their teeth," says Jim Rush of Neurotrash. Attracting attention on the Web may get you your next non-digital deal, on broadcast air or on the silver screen.

Producers 411

The Summer of 2000:

Notable Trends in Major Releases

By Marketcast

As the movie industry looks toward this coming summer, last year's successes and failures are faint history. This report analyzes the box-office for Summer 2000, using data from MarketCast's Movie Tracking Study that, on a daily basis, measures the awareness and interest of moviegoers in seeing upcoming movies. To determine the audience for each movie, we use tracking data collected the night before each movie's opening day.

THE ILLUSION OF A WEAK SUMMER

For the first time since 1994, the summer of 2000 showed no increase in summer box-office. The 5% decline in 2000 compared to 1999 triggered extensive speculation about the prospects of continuing declines during the next summer as well.

So what happened? Let's look at the facts:

* Every summer since 1994 registered an increase in total gross over the preceding year (of at least 1%), except this past summer 2000. This summer was 5% lower than last year.

* This decrease was in stark contrast to the Summer of 1999 which registered the largest increase in recent years, up 12% from the summer of 1998. If we look closely at the Summer of 1999, we can see that this extraordinary increase was a consequence of *Star Wars: Episode 1 – The Phantom Menace*, which grossed $431 million. Without *Episode 1*, the increase in Summer 1999 would have been much closer to the normal 4%.

* The Summer of 2000, like the Summer of 1999, had ten movies grossing over $100 million. There was no decline in the number of high grossing movies, and-outside of *Episode 1* – the grosses for these blockbusters were as high or higher.

* If *Episode 1* had been a "normal blockbuster," then the Summer of 2000 would have easily surpassed Summer of 1999. For example, if *Episode 1* box-office had been $200 million instead of $431 million, then the Summer of 2000 would have ranked as the highest grossing ever. Or if *Mission Impossible 2* (the top grossing film of Summer 2000 at $213 million) had opened in the summer of 1999 and *Episode 1* had opened this summer, then Summer of 1999 would have shown a 3% increase over Summer of 1998 and Summer of 2000 would have shown a record 12% increase over the year before.

* Summer of 2000 was just fine. The decline was caused by the huge box office of *Star Wars: Episode 1*.

SEGMENTED ENTHUSIASM

A few movies, that are usually "blockbusters", have general appeal and attract moviegoers across the board: old and young, male and female, and upscale and downscale. However, most movies are targeted to specific demographic segments. In this section, we take a quick look at the movies that generated the greatest heat with each important audience segment-as measured by day-of-release enthusiasm.

Teen Turn on's:

* If a movie tracked well with teens this past summer it generally meant box-office success, even if other segments were not on board.

Teenage boys got excited about two broad movies (*Mission Impossible 2 and Gladiator*), and three movies that were teen targeted. True to their historic taste, all these Teen Turn On's featured action or comedy or both.

Teenage girls shared only *Scary Movie* with teenage boys; the rest of their top five were different. It included Bring It On a surprise hit based only on teen girls (no other segment got excited about it) and *The Klumps*, an appeal teen girls shared with Gen X women and non-whites. And instead of action, they chose horror-*What Lies Beneath*-a favorite with all female groups; and *The Hollow Man*.

Teen Males:

Movie	Total Interest in Movie	Box Office
Mission Impossible 2	46%	$215 Million
Scary Movie	41%	$156 Million
X Men	40%	$156 Million
Road Trip	40%	$ 69 Million
Gladiator	36%	$186 Million

Teen Females:

Movie	Total Interest in Movie	Box Office
Scary Movie	46%	$156 Million
Bring It On	43%	$ 63 Million
Nutty Professor 2, The Klumps	40%	$121 Million
The Hollow Man	38%	$ 73 Million
What Lies Beneath	31%	$152 Million

Generation X (Moviegoers in Their Twenties):

MarketCast's tracking research has shown that dividing audiences arbitrarily into two age groups, under and over 25, obscures the move taste difference of people in their twenties. Therefore, our research distinguished between teens, Gen X moviegoers, and those 30 and older.

Mission Impossible 2 was the number one choice for Generation X moviegoers. Considering that teen women did not even put this movie in their top five choices, it appears that teen girls don't warm up to Tom Cruise like their older sisters do. Generation X women also found *What Lies Beneath* (the female horror film of the season) appealing, as well as *The Klumps* (liked by teenage girls), and *The Patriot* (which they shared with moviegoers over 30).

The Gen X men went for action with a touch of horror, with *Gladiator* (like all men), *Gone in Sixty Seconds* (like older men), and *The Hollow Man* (which they shared with teenage girls).

Gen X. Males:

Movie	Total Interest in Movie	Box Office
Mission Impossible 2	41%	$215 Million
Gladiator	37%	$186 Million
Shaft	34%	$ 70 Million
Gone in 60 Seconds	34%	$101 Million
The Hollow Man	30%	$ 73 Million

Gen X. Females:

Movie	Total Interest in Movie	Box Office
Mission Impossible 2	41%	$215 Million
What Lies Beneath	34%	$152 Million
Nutty Professor 2, The Klumps	32%	$121 Million
The Patriot	28%	$113 Million
Shaft	27%	$ 70 Million

Boomers at the Box-Office:

The baby boomers (over 30) exhibited much less gender disagreement. Like almost everyone else, they placed *Mission Impossible 2* at the top, but they also agreed on *The Patriot* (like Gen X women) and *Shaft* (with all Gen Xers). After this they disagreed, with the men choosing *Gladiator* (the male movie of the year) and *Gone in Sixty Seconds* (with Gen X men); and the women going for *What Lies Beneath* and *The Perfect Storm* (all to themselves).

Females over 30:

Movie	Total Interest in Movie	Box Office
Mission Impossible 2	41%	$215 Million
What Lies Beneath	30%	$152 Million
The Perfect Storm	29%	$181 Million
Shaft	28%	$ 70 Million
The Patriot	28%	$113 Million

Males over 30:

Movie	Total Interest in Movie	Box Office
Mission Impossible 2	39%	$215 Million
The Patriot	33%	$113 Million
Gladiator	31%	$186 Million
Gone in 60 Seconds	30%	$101 Million
Shaft	28%	$ 70 Million

Ethnic Enthusiasm:

Four of the top five movies favored by non-whites featured African American stars, (even *Mission Impossible 2*, although in a secondary role). However, this is not a matter of segregated taste: two of the four were also hot with key segments in the general audience – *The Klumps* (with women under 30) and *Scary Movie* (with teens) – and *Big Momma's House* almost made the teen list as well. Only *Kings of Comedy*-one of the surprise hits of the Summer-appealed exclusively to non-whites. All in all, Summer of 2000 showed that whites are being "integrated" into non-white movie tastes; and that non-whites can support a strong opening without them.

Movie	Total Interest in Movie	Box Office
Kings of Comedy	45%	$ 37 Million
Mission Impossible 2	42%	$215 Million
Big Mommas House	39%	$117 Million
Nutty Professor 2, The Klumps	37%	$121 Million
Scary Movie	36%	156 Million

MOVIE BREAKDOWN

Every year there are a few movies that wreak havoc with common sense and accepted wisdom.

Box office successes usually have visible stars and high interest, even before the marketing campaign begins. But Shooting Stars achieve their visibility and popularity during the marketing campaign. They start meekly, but shoot up the charts during the last three weeks before opening, and hit opening weekend running.

For almost all major releases, a strong opening weekend is the key to a long and successful run. But a few, the Supernovas, burn brightly on opening weekend and burn out after that. They have a high opening and a low total. Alternatively, movies with Great Legs, do not open at the top of the market, but just keep rolling along until they achieve blockbuster status.

In this section we look at the Shooting Stars, Supernovas and Great Legs of the Summer of 2000.

Shooting Stars

Gladiator was a star maker and a record breaker. Before the marketing campaign, only few moviegoers (25%) had even heard of the movie and a tiny number (10%) were excited about seeing it. In fact, with three weeks to go before release, *Gladiator* was behind more than 90% of all the major releases in terms of audience enthusiasm. A superbly crafted marketing campaign changed all that. By opening day, enthusiasm had tripled and visibility had almost tripled, bringing *Gladiator* to the top 20% in awareness and interest and a $34 million opening weekend.

Shooting Star number two this summer was the biggest surprise of the summer – *Scary Movie*. When *Scary Movie* first came on the tracking, there were no indications that it was going to having anything more than a moderate opening-visibility and enthusiasm were well below the average for all movies. Three weeks later, visibility had almost tripled and enthusiasm had more than doubled, exceeding 80% of all major releases. With teens, the increases in enthusiasm were astonishing, registering 30-point gains and exceeding 99% of all movies on opening day.

Increase during time on tracking until opening in:

Movie	Awareness	Overall Definite Interest
Gladiator	37%	21%
Scary Movie	25%	9%

Supernovas

The only Supernova this summer was *Pokemon, The Movie 2000*. It opened well, reaching almost $20 million on opening weekend ($19.6M). But then it died, recording only $43.7 million total.

Movie	Weekend B.O.	Total B.O.	Opening Weekend As A Percent Of The Total
Pokemon, The Movie 2000	$19.6	$43.7	45%

Great Legs

After a respectable, but not spectacular $17 million opening, *Chicken Run* ran forever and grossed $106 million. That is, only 17% of its total gross was captured on the first weekend. In a world where the average movie makes about a third of its gross during the opening, this proves that chicken legs are Great Legs.

And then there was Disney's *The Kid*. After a moderate $13 million opening, it hung on to total $69 million. That's almost six times the opening weekend.

Movie	Weekend B.O.	Total B.O.	Opening Weekend As A Percent Of The Total
Chicken Run	$17.5	$106	17%
Disney's The Kid	$12.7	$69.1	18%
Gladiator	$34.8	$186.6	19%

Gladiator was not far behind. It started well ($35M), but it ended better, finally totaling $187 million. Less than one fifth (19%) of the final total came on opening weekend.

MarketCast, Inc. is a strategic research company for the movie and other entertainment industries. The company specializes in reseach on the development and marketing of entertainment products including research screenings, trailer, TV spot and print ad testing, movie and video tracking studies, and media and positioning research. For additional information, please call Joseph Helfgot (310) 312-5577.

CICADA
RESTAURANT & BAR

The Center of L.A's Downtown Dining.

Unique and Almost Indescribable Combination of Contemporary Californian-Italian Cuisine and Original Art Deco Architecture.

617 S. Olive Street (between 7th and 6th)
Downtown Los Angeles
Phone: 213.488.9488
Lunch • Dinner • Valet Parking • Shuttle to Music Center
Private Parties • Weddings • Corporate Events
www.cicadarestaruant.com

Production Company Category Key

Feature Film

3 Arts Entertainment
30 Second Films
40 Acres & A Mule Filmworks, Inc.
5th Gear Entertainment
A&E Television Networks
A Band Apart
Ab'-strakt Pictures
Abby Lou Entertainment
Acappella Pictures
Act III Productions
Adelson Entertainment
Orly Adelson Productions
Adobe Pictures
AEI
Aerial Focus Productions
Afra-Film Enterprises, Inc.
Alameda Filmworks, Inc.
Albrecht & Associates, Inc.
Alchemy Entertainment
All Girl Productions
Allen & Associates
Alliance Atlantis
Alphaville
AM Productions & Management
Amalgamated, Inc.
Amblin Entertainment
Amen Ra Films
American Entertainment Co.
American World Pictures
American Zoetrope
Craig Anderson Productions
Angel Ark Productions
Another Diversion
Apatow Productions
Apostle Pictures
Mark Archer Entertainment
The Arnet/Kerner Co.
Artisan Entertainment
The Artists' Colony
Ashley Productions
Asset Pictures
Atkinson Way Films
Atlantic Streamline
Atlas Entertainment
Automatic Pictures, Inc.
Avalanche! Entertainment
AVD Productions, Inc/AV Designs
Avenue Pictures
Axelrod Entertainment
Axelson-Weintraub Productions
Back Home Pictures
Backyard Productions
The Badham Company
The Baer Animation Company, Inc.
Baer Entertainment Group

BallPark Productions
Ballyhoo, Inc.
Baltimore/Spring Creek Pictures, LLC
Bandeira Entertainment
Banner Entertainment
Barnholtz Entertainment
Barnstorm Films
Barwood Films
Bassett Productions
Suzanne Bauman Productions
Barbara L. Baumann, Inc.
Baumgarten/Prophet Entertainment
Bay Films
Beacon Communications, LLC
June Beallor Productions
The Bedford Falls Company
Bel-Air Entertainment
Belisarius Productions
Bella Productions
Belladonna Productions
Bender-Spink
Benjamin Productions, Inc.
Rick Berman Productions
Jay Bernstein Productions
Bettina Productions, Ltd.
Black & Blu Entertainment
Black Entertainment Television (BET)
Black Sheep Entertainment
Bleecker Street Films
Christal Blue Productions
Blue Bay Productions
Blue Relief
Blue Tulip Productions
Blue Wolf Productions
Blumberg Productions & Management
Carol Bodie Entertainment
Bona Fide Productions
Bonfire Films of America
Boxing Cat Productions
Boyington Studios, Inc.
Boz Productions
Braga Productions
Brayton/Carlucci Productions
Paulette Breen Productions
The Bregman Entertainment Company
Brillstein-Grey Entertainment
Brooksfilms, Ltd.
Brookwell McNamara Entertainment
Jerry Bruckheimer Films
The Bubble Factory
The Buena Vista Motion Pictures Group
Bungalow 78 Productions
Bushwood Pictures
Butchers Run Films
C'est Tout Productions
Cairo/Simpson Entertainment, Inc.
Calar
Calico World Entertainment
Calm Down Productions, Inc.

Camera Marc
Cannell Studios
The Canton Company
Canvas House Films
Capella Films, Inc.
Capital Arts Entertainment
Capo Productions, Inc.
Cappa Productions
Mark Carliner Productions
Carlyle Productions & Management
Carrie Productions
Castle Rock Entertainment
Centropolis Entertainment
Chancellor Entertainment
Chapter 10 Productions
Chartoff Productions
Stanley Chase Productions, Inc.
The Chelmar Group
Cherry Alley Productions
Chesler/Perlmutter Productions
Chicagofilms
Chiodo Bros. Productions, Inc.
Cine Excel Entertainment
Cinergi Pictures
Cineville, Inc.
Circle Associates Ltd.
Cohen Pictures
Collaborative Artists
Colomby/Keaton Productions
Columbia Pictures/Columbia Tristar
    Motion Picture Group
Connection III Entertainment Corp.
Constantin Film
Conundrum Entertainment
Cornice Entertainment
The Cort/Madden Company
Cosgrove-Meurer Productions
Cindy Cowan Entertainment, Inc.
CPC Entertainment
Crane Wexelblatt Entertainment
Wes Craven Films
Creative Impulse Entertainment
Crusader Entertainment
Ctonic Flikz
Danamation Studios
Danjaq, Inc.
Dark Horse Entertainment
Davis Classics
Davis Entertainment Co.
Daybreak Productions
Dino De Laurentiis Company
Deja View Productions, Inc.
Denali Productions, Inc.
Desert Heart Productions
Destination Films
Di Novi Pictures
DIC Entertainment
Louis DiGiaimo & Associates
Dimension Films

Production Company Category Key

The Walt Disney Company
Walt Disney Pictures/Touchstone Pictures
Distant Horizon
Dockry Productions
The Donners' Company
Bruce Dorn Films
Jean Doumanian Productions
DreamWorks SKG
Dreyfuss/James Productions
Duck Soup Studios
E.M.E., Inc.
Echo Lake Productions
Edmonds Entertainment
Rona Edwards Productions
Ralph Edwards/Stu Billett Productions
Egg Pictures
El Norte Productions
Elephant Walk Entertainment
EMK Productions
Enchantment Films
Ensemble Entertainment
Enteraktion, Inc.
Epiphany Productions, Inc.
Erratic Entertainment, Inc.
Esparza-Katz Productions
The Robert Evans Company
Everyman Pictures
Face Productions
Fair Dinkum Productions
Fast Carrier Pictures
Fat Chance Films
Fate Junkie Films, Inc.
The Edward S. Feldman Co.
Fenady Associates, Inc.
FGM Entertainment
Adam Fields Productions
Film Roman, Inc.
FilmColony, Ltd.
FilmWorld, Inc.
Fine Line Features
Wendy Finerman Productions
Fireworks Pictures
First Avenue Films
Flip Your Lid, Inc.
Flower Films, Inc.
Flying Freehold Productions
Forest Hills Pictures
Fortis Films
Forward Pass, Inc.
David Foster Productions
Foundation Entertainment
Fountainbridge Films
Fountainhead Pictures
Four Square Productions, Inc.
Fox Searchlight Pictures
FR Productions
Franchise Pictures, Inc.
Joel Freeman Productions, Inc.

Fresh Produce Company
Daniel Fried Productions
Fried Films
Friendly Productions
Mark Frost Productions
Further Films
Genrebend Productions, Inc.
Roger Gimbel Productions, Inc.
Ginty Films
Gittes, Inc.
GMR Productions
Go Film
Goepp Circle Productions
Jeff Gold Productions, Inc.
Gold'N Hen Productions
Golden Eagle Pix
Goldenring Productions
The Goldstein Company
Samuel Goldwyn Films
Good Machine
Lawrence Gordon Productions
Gracie Films
Grade A Entertainment
Graham/Rosenzweig Films
Grammnet Productions (Film)
Grazka Taylor Productions
Green Communications
Green Grass Blue Sky Company, Inc.
Green Moon Productions
The Greif Company/A Day With, Inc.
The Alan Greisman Company
Merv Griffin Entertainment
Ken Gross Management
Gross Productions
Beth Grossbard Productions
Gullane Pictures
H-Gun Labs
Hallway Pictures
Halsted Pictures
Hammer Films
Handprint Entertainment
Harbor Lights Productions
Harpo Films
David Haugland Productions
Havoc Inc.
Hawk Entertainment
Headquarters
Heller Highwater
Hennessey Entertainment, Ltd.
The Jim Henson Company
Debra Hill Productions
Hofflund-Polone
Hogan Moorhouse Pictures
Hollane Corp./Martin Poll Films, Ltd.
Horseshoe Bay Productions
The House Production Company
Hunt-Tavel Productions
Hy-Tone Productions
Icon Productions, Inc.

Ideal Entertainment, Inc.
Image G
Image Movers
Imaginary Forces
Imagine Entertainment
IMAX Corporation
Impact PSA, Inc.
In Play Media Arts
Incognito Entertainment
IndieGal Productions, LLC
InFront Productions
Initial Entertainment Group
Instinct Pictures
Intermedia Films
International Television Group (ITG)
Irish DreamTime
Itasca Pictures, Inc.
ITB CineGroup/Television
The Jacobson Company
Jaffilms
Jaret Entertainment
Jeff Wald Entertainment
Jersey Films
Jersey Shore Films
The Jinks/Cohen Company
JKR Productions, Inc.
JLT Productions
Don Johnson Productions
Mark Johnson Productions
Quincy Jones Media Group, Inc.
Jumbo Pictures, Inc.
Junction Entertainment
Kahn Power Pictures
Kandoo Films, Inc.
Perry Katz Productions
Marty Katz Productions
The Kaufman Company
David E. Kelley Productions
The Kennedy/Marshall Company
Killer Films
Kandice King Productions, Inc.
Kingsgate Films
Kingsize Entertainment
Kinowelt USA, Inc.
David Kirschner Productions
Klasky Csupo, Inc.
The Koch Company
Konrad Pictures
Kontrast Films
Kopelson Entertainment
Kouf-Bigelow Productions
Krainin Productions, Inc.
The Jonathan Krane Group
Sid & Marty Krofft Pictures
Kurtz & Friends
Kushner-Locke Company
Kuzui Enterprises, Inc.
LA Productions
The Ladd Company

Production Company Category Key

Lakeshore Entertainment Corporation
Lakota Productions
Langley Productions
Lawton Entertainment
Le Monde Entertainment
Leading Pictures, Inc.
Stan Lee Media, Inc.
Malcolm Leo Productions
Let There Be Light Productions
Michael I. Levy Enterprises
Simon Lewis Productions, Inc.
Licht/Mueller Films
Lighthouse Productions
Lightmotive, Inc.
Lightstorm Entertainment
Lion Rock Productions
Lions Gate Entertainment
Si Litvinoff Productions
Warren Lockhart Productions, Inc.
Logo Entertainment
Longboard Productions, Inc.
Longfellow Pictures
Lotus Films
Love Spell Entertainment
LucasFilm Ltd.
Lucid Film
Lucid Media
Lumiere Films, Inc.
Luminosity Productions
Lux Pictures, Inc.
M.H.S. Productions
William J. MacDonald Productions
MacGillivray Freeman Films
Mad Chance
Make It Happen Productions, Inc.
Charles Malcolm Video Productions
Malpaso Productions
Mandalay Pictures
Mandolin Entertainment
The Manhattan Project
Manifest Film Company
Marca-Relli Productions, LLC
Mariposa
Laurence Mark Productions
Marvel Characters, Inc.
Niki Marvin Productions
Matador Pictures
Matovich Productions
Matrix Communications
The Matthau Company, Inc.
Maverick Films
MDP Worldwide
Megahertz Pictures
Barry Mendel Productions
Merchant-Ivory Productions
Metafilmics
Metro-Goldwyn-Mayer Studios, Inc.
Michael/Finney Productions, Inc.
The Miller Entertainment Group, Inc.

Miller/Boyett Productions
Mindfire Entertainment
MindStorm Productions, LLC
Minervision
Mirage Enterprises
Miramax Films
Miss Jones
MM2K
Mo Jo Productions, Inc.
Monarex Hollywood Corporation
Montage Entertainment
The Montecito Picture Company
Morgan Creek Productions
Morra, Brezner, Steinberg & Tenenbaum
Mostow/Lieberman
Moushel Productions
Moving Pictures
Moving Target
Mozark Productions
Mr. Mudd Productions
MT. Tabor Productions
MTV Films
Muse Productions
Music Room Pictures
Mutant Enemy, Inc.
Mutual Film Company
MWG Productions
National Geographic Feature Films
National Lampoon
Neild Street Prod., Inc.
Nelvana Entertainment
Nemiroff Productions
Neo Art & Logic
Mace Neufeld Productions
Neverland Films, Inc.
New Concorde
New Crime Productions
New Line Cinema, Inc.
New Millennium Studios
New Regency Productions
Newmark Films, Inc.
Nickelodeon Movies
Nitestar Productions
No Prisoners
Noble Productions, Inc.
Norah Films
North Hall Productions
Nova Pictures
Nuance Productions
NXT Entertainment
O Entertainment
Oak Island Films, Inc.
Lynda Obst Productions
Ocean Pictures
Lin Oliver Productions
Olmos Productions, Inc.
OMNIBUS
One Step Productions
Open Road Productions, Ltd.

Orbit Entertainment Group
Original Film, Inc.
Original Voices, Inc.
Our Productions, Inc.
Outerbanks Entertainment
Outlaw Productions
Overbrook Entertainment
P.A.T. Productions
George Paige Associates, Inc.
Paradox Productions, Inc.
Paramount Classics
Paramount Pictures - Motion Picture Group
Parkway Productions
Patchett Kaufman Entertainment
Patchwork Productions
Pavlic/Raimondi Pictures
Peak Productions
Pendragon Film Ltd.
James Pentecost Productions
Permut Presentations
Persistent Entertainment, Inc.
Lester Persky Productions, Inc.
Perspective Films
Peters Entertainment
Pfeffer Film
Phase I Productions
Philmco
Phoenix Pictures
Pico Creek Productions
Picture Mill
The Frederick S. Pierce Company, Inc.
Pixar Animation Studios
PlasterCITY Productions
Pleasant Productions
Polestar Entertainment Group, LLC
Pongo Productions
Pop/Art Film Factory
Popular Arts Entertainment, Inc.
Producers Group, Ltd.
Production Analysis Corporation
Proletariat Filmworks
Propaganda Films
Proud Mary Entertainment
Punch Productions
Quasar Studios
Quinn Productions
Radar Pictures
Radiant Productions
Raffaella Productions, Inc.
Rainmaker Productions
Raintree Productions
Randwell Productions
Martin Ransohoff Productions, Inc.
Rastar Productions
Patrick Raymond Entertainment, Inc.
Realitory Productions
Rearguard Productions, Inc.
Red Bird Productions

Production Company Category Key

Red Hots Entertainment
Red Hour Films
Red House Entertainment
Red Wagon
Red-Horse Productions
Dan Redler Entertainment
Regent Entertainment, Inc.
Rick Reinert Pictures
Renaissance Pictures
Reveal Entertainment
Revelations Entertainment
Revolution Studios
Revolver Films, LLC
RGH/Lions Share Pictures
Rhythm & Hues Studios
Rice & Beans Productions
Ridini Entertainment Corporation
RJ Lauren
RJN Productions, Inc.
RKO Pictures, Inc.
RoadKill Films
Roadside Attractions, LLC
Dolores Robinson Entertainment
Stan Rogow Productions
Rogue Entertainment
Phil Roman Entertainment
Alex Rose Productions
Howard Rosenman Productions
Roundtable Ink
Ruddy Morgan Organization
Scott Rudin Productions
Rumbalara Films
S.E.R. Filmworks
Saban Entertainment
Alan Sacks Productions, Inc.
Samuelson Productions
Sanford/Pillsbury Productions
Santa Monica Pictures
Sarabande Productions
Saturn Films
Schapiro Entertainment Group
Edgar J. Scherick & Associates, Inc.
Paul Schiff Productions
Scholastic Entertainment
Joel Schumacher Productions
Bernard Schwartz Productions
Kristine Schwarz Productions
Scott Free Productions
Scotti Productions
Screen Gems
Section Eight Pictures
Dylan Sellers Productions
Seven Arts Pictures
Shady Acres Entertainment
Shanghai'd Films
Shearman Entertainment, Inc.
Shoelace Productions, Inc.
Shonkyte Productions, Inc.
Shoreline Entertainment

Signature Entertainment
Signature Films
Silver Lining Productions, Inc.
Silver Lion Films
Silver Pictures Television
Silvereye Productions
Silverline Pictures
SimEx Digital Studios
Simian Films
The Gene Simmons Company
Randy Simon Productions
The Robert Simonds Company
Single Spark Pictures
Sitting Ducks Productions
Skylark Entertainment, Inc.
Skylark Films, Ltd.
Sladek Entertainment Corporation
Snapdragon Films, Inc.
Sneak Preview Entertainment, Inc.
SNL Studios
Snow Leopard Productions
Sonnenfeld/Josephson Worldwide Entertainment
Sony Pictures Classics
Sony Pictures Entertainment
South Fork Productions
Southern Skies, Inc.
The Spark Factory
Spin Pictures Intertainment, LLC
Spoke Film
Spyglass Entertainment
St. Clare Entertainment
J. Stack Productions
Stagescreen Productions
Stampede Entertainment
Star Entertainment Group, Inc.
Stargazer, Inc.
Jane Startz Productions, Inc.
State Street Pictures
Steamroller Productions
Stefanino Productions
The Howard Stern Production Company
Stone vs. Stone
Stonelock Pictures
Storm Entertainment
Straw Dogs
Strom Magallon Entertainment
Mel Stuart Productions, Inc.
Mike Sullivan Productions, Inc.
Summerland Entertainment
Summers Entertainment
Sundog Productions
Martin Tahse Productions
Talent Entertainment Group
Talisman Pacific
Talking Rings Entertainment
Tapestry Films, Inc.
Taurus Entertainment Company
Tavel Entertainment

Taylor-Bedell Entertainment
Team Todd
Telescene Film Group, Inc.
Telling Pictures, Inc.
Ten Thirteen Productions
Teocalli Entertainment, Inc.
Terra Bella Entertainment
Threshold Entertainment
Tidewater Entertainment
The Steve Tisch Company
TLC Entertainment
Tollin/Robbins Productions
Totem Productions
Tribe Pictures
Tribeca Productions
The Tribunal
Triology Entertainment Group
Triumph Pictures, Inc.
True Blue Productions
Simon Tse Productions, Inc.
The Turman-Morrissey Company
Jon Turtle Productions
Twentieth Century Fox Pictures
Twilight Time Films
Two Stepp Productions
UBU Productions
Ufland Productions
Unapix Films
Undergrace Productions
Unger Productions, Inc.
United Artists Films
Universal Pictures
Universal Studios, Inc.
Upstart Entertainment
USA Films
Val D'Oro Entertainment
Renée Valente Productions
Valhalla Motion Pictures
Vanguard Productions
The Vault, Inc.
VCA Productions
Ventana Films
Venture Entertainment Group
Verdon-Cedric Productions
Verhoeven/Marshall Films
Viacom Entertainment Group
View Askew Productions, Inc.
Village Roadshow Pictures
Visionbox
Raymond Wagner Productions, Inc.
Ken Walz Productions
Warner Bros.
Warner Bros. Animation
Warner Bros. Pictures Production
Watershed Films
Weed Road Pictures
Jerry Weintraub Productions
Weintraub/Kuhn Productions
Roni Weisberg Productions

Production Company Category Key

John Wells Productions
Bill White Productions
Whitewater Films
Wicked Monkey Productions
Wild Things Productions
Wildwood Enterprises, Inc./South Fork Pictures
WIN Ventures, LLC.
Winchester Films
Wind Dancer Production Group
Winkler Films
Ralph Winter Productions, Inc.
Witt/Thomas/Harris Productions
Wonderland Films
The Woofenill Works, Inc.
Working Title Films
World of Wonder Productions
Marvin Worth Productions
Norton Wright Productions
Wychwood Productions
Yak Yak Pictures
Mark Yellen Productions
Bud Yorkin Productions
Yorktown Productions, Inc.
Zaloom Film
The Zanuck Company
Zeal Pictures
Zide/Perry Entertainment
Zooma Zooma Corporation
Zucker Productions
Zucker/Netter Productions
Zuckerman Entertainment
Zystar Films, Inc.

TV

21st Century Man Productions
3 Arts Entertainment
30 Second Films
A&E Television Networks
A Band Apart
Ab'-strakt Pictures
Abby Lou Entertainment
ABC Entertainment Television Group
ABC, Inc./ABC Television Network
Acappella Pictures
Act III Productions
The Ad-Files
Adelson Entertainment
Orly Adelson Productions
AEI
Aerial Focus Productions
Afra-Film Enterprises, Inc.
Albrecht & Associates, Inc.
Alchemy Entertainment
All Girl Productions
Allen & Associates
Alliance Atlantis
Alta Vista Productions
AM Productions & Management

Amalgamated, Inc.
Ambitious Entertainment
Amen Ra Films
American Entertainment Co.
American Movie Classics/Romance Classics
American Sports Network, Inc.
American Video Group
American World Pictures
American Zoetrope
Craig Anderson Productions
Angel Ark Productions
Apatow Productions
Apostle Pictures
Mark Archer Entertainment
The Arnet/Kerner Co.
Artisan Entertainment
The Artists' Colony
Artists Television Group
Asset Pictures
The Association, Inc.
Atkinson Way Films
Avenue Pictures
Axelrod Entertainment
Axelson-Weintraub Productions
The Badham Company
BallPark Productions
Ballyhoo, Inc.
Bandeira Entertainment
Barnstorm Films
Barwood Films
Suzanne Bauman Productions
Barbara L. Baumann, Inc.
Baumgarten/Prophet Entertainment
Bay Films
BCProductions, Inc./BCTV Productions
June Beallor Productions
The Bedford Falls Company
Belisarius Productions
Bell-Phillip Television Productions, Inc.
Bella Productions
Bender-Spink
Robert Benedetti Productions, Inc.
Benjamin Productions, Inc.
Rick Berman Productions
Jay Bernstein Productions
Bettina Productions, Ltd.
Big Daddy Productions
Big Ticket Television
Black & Blu Entertainment
Black Entertainment Television (BET)
Black Sheep Entertainment
Bleecker Street Films
Blue Relief
Blue Tulip Productions
Blumberg Productions & Management
Bob Booker Productions
Steven Bochco Productions
Carol Bodie Entertainment

Bonfire Films of America
Boz Productions
Braga Productions
Brayton/Carlucci Productions
Paulette Breen Productions
The Bregman Entertainment Company
Bright-Kauffman-Crane Productions
Brillstein-Grey Entertainment
Broadway Video
Brookwell McNamara Entertainment
Jerry Bruckheimer Films
Buena Vista Television
Bungalow 78 Productions
Bunim-Murray Productions
Burrud Productions
Al Burton Productions
Bushwood Pictures
Cairo/Simpson Entertainment, Inc.
Calar
Calico World Entertainment
Calm Down Productions, Inc.
Cannell Studios
The Canton Company
Canvas House Films
Capital Arts Entertainment
Capo Productions, Inc.
Mark Carliner Productions
Carlyle Productions & Management
Carrie Productions
The Carsey-Werner, LLC.
Castle Rock Entertainment
Cates/Doty Productions
CBS Enterprises
CBS Entertainment
CBS Television
Celluloid
Chancellor Entertainment
Charles Bros. Productions
Stanley Chase Productions, Inc.
Cherry Alley Productions
Chesler/Perlmutter Productions
Chicagofilms
Chiodo Bros. Productions, Inc.
Chris/Rose Productions
Cinemagic Productions
Circle Associates Ltd.
Dick Clark Productions, Inc.
Clifden Productions
Coast Media Teleproductions, Inc.
Collaborative Artists
Colomby/Keaton Productions
Columbia TriStar Television
Comedy Central
Connection III Entertainment Corp.
Cornice Entertainment
The Cort/Madden Company
Cosgrove-Meurer Productions
Cossette Productions
Cindy Cowan Entertainment, Inc.

45

Production Company Category Key

- CPC Entertainment
- Crane Wexelblatt Entertainment
- Wes Craven Films
- Creative Impulse Entertainment
- Crusader Entertainment
- Crystal Pyramid Productions
- D.L.T. Entertainment Ltd.
- Dalrymple Productions
- dapTV associates
- Dark Horse Entertainment
- Davis Classics
- Davis Entertainment Co.
- Daybreak Productions
- Deja View Productions, Inc.
- Denali Productions, Inc.
- Desert Heart Productions
- Di Novi Pictures
- DIC Entertainment
- Louis DiGiaimo & Associates
- Discovery Networks/Discovery Communications, Inc.
- Walt Disney Television Animation
- The Disney Channel
- Disney Telefilms
- Distant Horizon
- The Donners' Company
- Double Whammy Productions
- Jean Doumanian Productions
- DreamWorks SKG
- Dreyfuss/James Productions
- E! Entertainment Television
- E.M.E., Inc.
- Edmonds Entertainment
- Rona Edwards Productions
- Ralph Edwards/Stu Billett Productions
- El Norte Productions
- Elephant Walk Entertainment
- Eleventh Day Entertainment
- EMK Productions
- Peter Engel Productions
- Ensemble Entertainment
- Enteraktion, Inc.
- Entertainment Television Services, Inc.
- Epiphany Productions, Inc.
- Erratic Entertainment, Inc.
- Esparza-Katz Productions
- Evolution Film
- Face Broadcast Productions
- Fair Dinkum Productions
- Fast Carrier Pictures
- Fat Chance Films
- The Edward S. Feldman Co.
- Fenady Associates, Inc.
- Adam Fields Productions
- Film Roman, Inc.
- The Film Syndicate
- Fireworks Television
- First Avenue Films
- Flip Your Lid, Inc.

- Flower Films, Inc.
- Forest Hills Pictures
- Forward Pass, Inc.
- David Foster Productions
- Foundation Entertainment
- Fountainhead Pictures
- Four Square Productions, Inc.
- Fox Broadcasting Company
- Fox Family Channel
- Fox Kids Network
- Fox Television Studios
- Woody Fraser Productions
- Fried Films
- Mark Frost Productions
- Furman Films, Inc.
- FX Networks, LLC
- Gallo & Gallo, Inc.
- Gears Communications
- Genrebend Productions, Inc.
- Roger Gimbel Productions, Inc.
- Ginty Films
- GMR Productions
- Goepp Circle Productions
- Jeff Gold Productions, Inc.
- Gold'N Hen Productions
- Golden Eagle Pix
- Goldenring Productions
- Goodman/Rosen Productions
- Gracie Films
- Grade A Entertainment
- Grammnet Productions (TV)
- Granada Entertainment USA
- Grazka Taylor Productions
- Green Communications
- Green Moon Productions
- The Greif Company/A Day With, Inc.
- Greystone Communication Group, Inc./Greystone Films
- Merv Griffin Entertainment
- Ken Gross Management
- Gross Productions
- Beth Grossbard Productions
- Grub Street Productions
- Gullane Pictures
- H-Gun Labs
- Hallmark Entertainment
- Hallmark Hall of Fame Productions, Inc.
- Halsted Pictures
- Handprint Entertainment
- Harbor Lights Productions
- Dean Hargrove Productions
- Harpo Films
- David Haugland Productions
- Hawk Entertainment
- HBO
- HBO Films
- HBO Independent Productions/HBO Downtown Productions
- HBO Original Programming

- Hearst Entertainment Productions
- Heller Highwater
- Hennessey Entertainment, Ltd.
- The Jim Henson Company
- Debra Hill Productions
- The History Channel
- Hodge Film & Video
- Hofflund-Polone
- Hollane Corp./Martin Poll Films, Ltd.
- Horseshoe Bay Productions
- Howard Rosenman Productions
- Hy-Tone Productions
- Icon Productions Inc.
- Image G
- Imagine Entertainment
- In-Finn-Ity Productions, Inc.
- IndieGal Productions, LLC
- InFront Productions
- Intelliscape Films, LLC
- International Television Group (ITG)
- Itasca Pictures, Inc.
- ITB CineGroup/Television
- Michael Jacobs Productions
- Jaret Entertainment
- Jersey Films
- JKR Productions, Inc.
- Don Johnson Productions
- Mark Johnson Productions
- Quincy Jones Media Group, Inc.
- Jumbo Pictures, Inc.
- Just Singer Entertainment
- Kahn Power Pictures
- Katie Face Productions
- The Kaufman Company
- Kedzie Productions
- David E. Kelley Productions
- Kelley Productions International
- The Kennedy/Marshall Company
- Diana Kerew Productions
- Kingsgate Films
- David Kirschner Productions
- Klasky Csupo, Inc.
- Kontrast Films
- Kopelson Entertainment
- Kouf-Bigelow Productions
- Krainin Productions, Inc.
- Sid & Marty Krofft Pictures
- Kurtz & Friends
- Kushner-Locke Company
- Kuzui Enterprises, Inc.
- LA Productions
- The Ladd Company
- Langley Productions
- Lawton Entertainment
- Le Monde Entertainment
- Malcolm Leo Productions
- Let There Be Light Productions
- The Levinson/Fontana Company
- Michael I. Levy Enterprises

Production Company Category Key

Simon Lewis Productions, Inc.
Licht/Mueller Films
Lifetime Television (East Coast)
Lifetime Television (West Coast)
Lightmotive, Inc.
Lightning Bolt PIX: Barnyard Productions
Lion Rock Productions
Lions Gate Entertainment
Si Litvinoff Productions
Warren Lockhart Productions, Inc.
Logo Entertainment
LucasFilm Ltd.
Lucid Film
Lucid Media
Lumination Inc.
M.H.S. Productions
William J. MacDonald Productions
Make It Happen Productions, Inc.
Mandalay Television
Mandolin Entertainment
The Manhattan Project
March Hare Entertainment at
   Jaffe-Braunstein
Jeff Margolis Productions
Laurence Mark Productions
Marvel Characters, Inc.
Niki Marvin Productions
John Masius Productions, Inc.
Matador Pictures
The Matthau Company, Inc.
Mesita
Metafilmics
Metro-Goldwyn-Mayer/Worldwide TV
Miller/Boyett Productions
Mindfire Entertainment
MindStorm Productions, LLC
Minervision
MM2K
Mo Jo Productions, Inc.
Monarex Hollywood Corporation
Morgan Creek Productions
Morra, Brezner, Steinberg
   & Tenenbaum
Moving Pictures
Moving Target
Mozark Productions
Mr. Mudd Productions
MTV Networks (East Coast)
MTV Networks (West Coast)
Muse Productions
Mutant Enemy, Inc.
Mutual Film Company
MWG Productions
National Geographic Feature Films
National Lampoon
NBC Entertainment, Inc.
NBC Entertainment (West Coast)
Neild Street Prod., Inc.
Nelvana Entertainment

Nemiroff Productions
Mace Neufeld Productions
New Concorde
New Millennium Studios
New Regency Productions
New Screen Concepts, Inc.
Nickelodeon/Nick at Nite
Noble Productions, Inc.
Norah Films
North Hall Productions
Nova Pictures
Nuance Productions
NXT Entertainment
Lynda Obst Productions
October Productions
Lin Oliver Productions
OMNIBUS
One Step Productions
Original Film, Inc.
Our Gang Productions
Our Productions, Inc.
Outerbanks Entertainment
Overbrook Entertainment
P.A.T. Productions
George Paige Associates, Inc.
Paradox Productions, Inc.
Paramount Domestic Television
Paramount International Television
Paramount Network Television
Paramount Television Group
Patchett Kaufman Entertainment
Patchwork Productions
PaxTV/Paxson Communications
PBS
Peak Productions
Pearson Television
Pendragon Film Ltd.
James Pentecost Productions
Permut Presentations
Persistent Entertainment, Inc.
Lester Persky Productions, Inc.
Perspective Films
Dorothea G. Petrie Productions, Inc.
Phase I Productions
Pico Creek Productions
Pie Town Productions
The Frederick S. Pierce Company, Inc.
Pirates' Cove Entertainment, Inc.
PlasterCITY Productions
Point of View Productions
Polestar Entertainment Group, LLC
Popular Arts Entertainment, Inc.
Producers Group, Ltd.
Production Analysis Corporation
Production Partners, Inc.
Proletariat Filmworks
Proud Mary Entertainment
Quasar Studios
Radiant Productions

Raffaella Productions, Inc.
Raimondi Films, Inc.
Rainmaker Productions
Randwell Productions
Ken Raskoff Productions
Raven Productions, Inc.
Patrick Raymond Entertainment, Inc.
Rearguard Productions, Inc.
Red Bird Productions
Red Hots Entertainment
Red Hour Films
Red House Entertainment
Red-Horse Productions
Dan Redler Entertainment
Reel Orange
Marian Rees Associates
Regent Entertainment, Inc.
Tim Reid Productions, Inc.
Rick Reinert Pictures
Revelations Entertainment
Revolver Films, LLC
Rice & Beans Productions
Ridini Entertainment Corporation
Roadside Attractions, LLC
Dolores Robinson Entertainment
Stan Rogow Productions
Phil Roman Entertainment
Freyda Rothstein Productions
Roundtable Ink
Ruddy Morgan Organization
RumRunner Cine Service
S.E.R. Filmworks
Saban Entertainment
Alan Sacks Productions, Inc.
Samuelson Productions
Sanford/Pillsbury Productions
Santa Monica Pictures
Sarabande Productions
Edgar J. Scherick & Associates, Inc.
George Schlatter Productions
Scholastic Entertainment
Bernard Schwartz Productions
Kristine Schwarz Productions
Scott Free Productions
Dylan Sellers Productions
Seven Arts Pictures
Shady Acres Entertainment
Shearman Entertainment, Inc.
Shoreline Entertainment
Showtime Networks, Inc.
Shukovsky English Entertainment
Sí TV
Signature Entertainment
Silver Lining Productions, Inc.
Silver Pictures Television
Silvereye Productions
Silverline Pictures
The Fred Silverman Company
The Gene Simmons Company

47

Production Company Category Key

Randy Simon Productions
The Robert Simonds Company
David A. Simons Productions
Single Spark Pictures
Sitting Ducks Productions
Skylark Entertainment, Inc.
Skylark Films, Ltd.
Sladek Entertainment Corporation
Snapdragon Films, Inc.
Sneak Preview Entertainment, Inc.
SNL Studios
Snow Leopard Productions
Sofronski Productions
Sonnenfeld/Josephson Worldwide Entertainment
Sony Pictures Entertainment
South Fork Productions
Southern Skies, Inc.
Spelling Television, Inc.
SplendidLight Media Productions
Spring Creek Productions
Spyglass Entertainment
St. Clare Entertainment
J. Stack Productions
Stagescreen Productions
StarToons International, LLC
Jane Startz Productions, Inc.
Starz Encore Entertainment Group
State Street Pictures
Stefanino Productions
The Howard Stern Production Company
Mel Stuart Productions, Inc.
Studios USA
Mike Sullivan Productions, Inc.
Summerland Entertainment
Summers Entertainment
Sundog Productions
Sweet Lorraine Productions, Inc.
Taffner Entertainment
Talent Entertainment Group
Taurus Entertainment Company
Tavel Entertainment
Taylor-Bedell Entertainment
TBS Superstation
Team Todd
Telescene Film Group, Inc.
Telling Pictures, Inc.
Ten Thirteen Productions
Teocalli Entertainment, Inc.
Terra Bella Entertainment
Threshold Entertainment
Tidewater Entertainment
TLC Entertainment
Tollin/Robbins Productions
Tribeca Productions
The Tribunal
Tribune Entertainment Company
Triology Entertainment Group
Triumph Pictures, Inc.

True Blue Productions
The Turman-Morrissey Company
Turner Entertainment Group
Turner Network Television (TNT)
Jon Turtle Productions
TVA Productions
TVP Studios
Twentieth Century Fox Television
Twilight Time Films
Two Oceans Entertainment
Two Stepp Productions
UBU Productions
Ufland Productions
Unapix Films
Undergrace Productions
Unger Productions, Inc.
Universal Studios, Inc.
Universal Television
UPN (United Paramount Network)
Upstart Entertainment
USA Network
Val D'Oro Entertainment
Renée Valente Productions
Valhalla Motion Pictures
Vanguard Productions
Venture Entertainment Group
Verité Productions
VH1
Viacom Entertainment Group
Viacom Productions
Video Hollywood Productions
Videowerks
Videox
View Askew Productions, Inc.
Vihlene & Associates, Inc.
Vin Di Bona Productions
Visionbox
Raymond Wagner Productions, Inc.
Jeff Wald Entertainment
Wallach Entertainment
Ken Walz Productions
Warner Bros. Animation
Warner Bros. International Television
Warner Bros. Telepictures Production
Warner Bros. Television
Watershed Films
WB Television Network
Ed Weinberger Productions
Weintraub/Kuhn Productions
Roni Weisberg Productions
Weller/Grossman Productions
John Wells Productions
Western Branch Productions, Inc.
Bill White Productions
Whitewater Films
Wicked Monkey Productions
Wild Things Productions
WildRice Productions
Wilshire Court Productions

WIN Ventures, LLC.
Wind Dancer Production Group
Ralph Winter Productions, Inc.
Wolf Films, Inc.
The Wolper Organization
Wonderland Films
The Woofenill Works, Inc.
World of Wonder Productions
World Wide Pants, Inc
Marvin Worth Productions
Linda Wright Productions
Norton Wright Productions
Wychwood Productions
Yak Yak Pictures
Bud Yorkin Productions
Yorktown Productions, Inc.
Zaloom Film
Zooma Zooma Corporation
Zucker/Netter Productions
Zuckerman Entertainment
Zystar Films, Inc.

Commercials
1171 Production Group
21st Century Man Productions
2EZ, LLC
30 Second Films
40 Acres & A Mule Filmworks, Inc.
A Band Apart Commercials
Abby Lou Entertainment
AbsoluteFilms.net
Access Film
Acme Filmworks, Inc.
The Ad-Files
Ad-Lib Marketing & Advertising
Alameda Filmworks, Inc.
Albrecht & Associates, Inc.
Allen & Associates
Alta Vista Productions
Ambitious Entertainment
American Video Group
Angel City Productions
Another Diversion
Another Large Production
Area 51 Films
Arsenal, Inc.
The Artists Company/The A&R Group
Ashley Productions
The Association, Inc.
Atlas Pictures
Avalanche! Entertainment
AVD Productions, Inc/AV Designs
Back Home Pictures
Backyard Productions
The Baer Animation Company, Inc.
Bandolero Films
Barking Weasel Productions, Inc.
Bassett Productions

Production Company Category Key

Barbara L. Baumann, Inc.
BCProductions, Inc./BCTV Productions
Beantown Productions, Inc.
Beard Boy Productions
Bella Productions
Bjoin Films
Brian Bleak Films
Christal Blue Productions
Blue Goose Productions
Bob Industries
Bonfire Films of America
Boyington Studios, Inc.
Brownstone Films
Bungalow 3
Burke/Triolo Productions
c.2K Entertainment
C'est Tout Productions
Calar
Calico World Entertainment
Canvas House Films
Canyon Pictures, Inc.
Carbo Films
Katie Carlson Kasting
Celluloid
The Chelmar Group
Chelsea Pictures
Chiari Cook Company, Inc.
Chicago Story
Chiodo Bros. Productions, Inc.
Cinemanix
Coast Media Teleproductions, Inc.
Cohn & Company
Commercials While-U-Wait, Inc.
Coppos Films
Michael Cowan, Inc.
CPProds
Creative Chaos
The Creative Department, LLC
Cronenweth Films
Crossroads Films
Cylo
Dalrymple Productions
dapTV associates
Dektor Film
Denali Productions, Inc.
DNA, Inc.
Doom, Inc.
Bruce Dorn Films
Bruce Dowad Associates
Drive Media
Duck Soup Studios
E.M.E., Inc.
Eleventh Day Entertainment
Evil Twin Productions
Fate Junkie Films, Inc.
FDG
Film Planet
The Film Syndicate
First Avenue Films

Flying Tiger Films
FM Rocks
Four Sisters Production
Four Square Productions, Inc.
Fuel
Fusion Films
Galanty & Company, Inc.
Gartner
Ginty Films
Glass Guns
Go Film
Jeff Gold Productions, Inc.
Gold'N Hen Productions
Golden Eagle Pix
Graying & Balding, Inc.
Green Communications
Green Dot Films, Inc.
GreenWater Pictures
Gross Productions
H-Gun Labs
Hallowes Productions
Headquarters
The Jim Henson Company
HKM Productions
Hodge Film & Video
Hokus Pokus Productions, Inc.
Horizon Shine, Inc.
Hot Spots Television
The House Production Company
HSI Productions, Inc.
Image G
Imaginary Forces
Impact PSA, Inc.
In Play Media Arts
In-Finn-Ity Productions, Inc.
Industrial Light + Magic Commercial Productions
Infomercial Solutions, Inc.
Instinct Pictures
Intelliscape Films, LLC
International Television Group (ITG)
IPS Productions
JGF
JKR Productions, Inc.
The Joneses
Carolyn Judd & Associates, Inc.
kaboom
Kandoo Films, Inc.
Kelley Productions International
Klasky Csupo, Inc.
Kontrast Films
Kurtz & Friends
LA Productions
Legacy Films
Let There Be Light Productions
Level 7 Productions
The Lieberman Company
Life of Riley, Inc.
Lightning Bolt PIX: Barnyard Productions

Little T Television
Long Coat Productions
Longboard Productions, Inc.
Lotus Films
Lucid Media
Lumination Inc.
Luminosity Productions
Lux Pictures, Inc.
Lyon Studios
M-80 Films
Mad Heart
Make It Happen Productions, Inc.
Charles Malcolm Video Productions
John Marias Productions
Mariposa
Mars Media, Inc.
Matrix Communications
Ross McCanse & Associates, Inc.
Megahertz Pictures
Mekanism
Carey Melcher Productions, Inc.
Mesita
Metro Pictures
The Miller Entertainment Group, Inc.
Mirella Film Co.
Miss Jones
MM2K
Mo Jo Productions, Inc.
Morton Jankel Zander, Inc.
Moving Image
Moving Target
Moxie Pictures
MPH Films
Music Room Pictures
Nemiroff Productions
New Millennium Studios
Nitestar Productions
No Prisoners
Nonfiction Spots
Nova Pictures
NXT Entertainment
Nydrle
October Productions
Omaha Pictures
OneSuch Films
Onyx Productions, Inc.
Orbit Entertainment Group
Our Gang Productions
Our Productions, Inc.
Ovation Entertainment
Pacific Star Productions
Edward Pacio & Associates
George Paige Associates, Inc.
Pearson Television
Perseverance Productions
Perspective Films
Philmco
Picture Park
Piper Productions

49

Production Company Category Key

Plum Productions
PMC Pictures
Point of View Productions
Polestar Film & Photographic Production
Pongo Productions
Pop/Art Film Factory
Porter Film Company
Post Modern Edit
Producers Group, Ltd.
Production Analysis Corporation
The Production Asylum
Proletariat Filmworks
Propaganda Films
Proud Mary Entertainment
Joseph Pytka Productions, Inc.
@radical.media
Raimondi Films, Inc.
Raintree Productions
Ranch Exit Films, Inc.
Rapport Films, Inc.
Raven Productions, Inc.
Patrick Raymond Entertainment, Inc.
Ken Rayzor Sound Design
Red Hots Entertainment
Dan Redler Entertainment
Reel Orange
Regent Films, Inc.
Renegade Animation, Inc.
Revolver Films, LLC
Kavich Reynolds Productions, Inc.
Rhythm & Hues Studios
RJ Lauren
Roaring Tiger Films
RumRunner Cine Service
Satellite Films
Kristine Schwarz Productions
Scotti Productions
Scream, LLC.
Sharpcut Productions
Signature Entertainment
Silver Lining Productions, Inc.
Silvereye Productions
Jay Silverman Productions
SimEx Digital Studios
Smillie Films
Sodas & Shoes
Sonic Films, Inc.
Sound Concepts Inc.
South Fork Productions
The Spark Factory
SplendidLight Media Productions
Sports' Cinematography Group
J. Stack Productions
StarBoard Productions
Stargazer, Inc.
Steam
Stefanino Productions
Kris Stevens Enterprises Inc.
Stiefel + Company

Straw Dogs
Strom Magallon Entertainment
Sun Spots
Tag Team
Tango Films
Tool of North America
Totem Productions
Trafficanda Studios, Inc.
Tropix Films
Tuesday Films
TVA Productions
TVP Studios
Vanguard Productions
VCA Productions
Ventana Films
Venture Entertainment Group
Venus Entertainment
Video Hollywood Productions
Videowerks
Vihlene & Associates, Inc.
Villains
Visitor, LLC
Roni Weisberg Productions
Western Branch Productions, Inc.
Bill White Productions
WildLife Management
Windmill Lane Productions
Wyld Spots
X-1 Films
X-Ray Productions
Yada/Levine Productions
Mark Yellen Productions
Zeal Pictures
Zooma Zooma Corporation
Zystar Films, Inc.

Video

21st Century Man Productions
30 Second Films
40 Acres & A Mule Filmworks, Inc.
A&E Television Networks
A Story Untold Productions
Abby Lou Entertainment
AbsoluteFilms.net
Ad-Lib Marketing & Advertising
Aerial Focus Productions
Alameda Filmworks, Inc.
Albrecht & Associates, Inc.
Ambitious Entertainment
American Sports Network, Inc.
American Video Group
Another Large Production
Joel Asher Studio
The Association, Inc.
AVD Productions, Inc/AV Designs
BCProductions, Inc./BCTV Productions
Beard Boy Productions
Pat Blessing Productions
Christal Blue Productions

Burrud Productions
Calar
CBIE, Inc.
The Chelmar Group
Coast Media Teleproductions, Inc.
The Creative Department, LLC
Crystal Pyramid Productions
Dalrymple Productions
dapTV associates
Denali Productions, Inc.
Digital Visionaries
Digivision Productions
Doom, Inc.
Eleventh Day Entertainment
Epiphany Productions, Inc.
Face Broadcast Productions
Fat Chance Films
Forest Hills Pictures
Four Square Productions, Inc.
Furman Films, Inc.
Galanty & Company, Inc.
Gears Communications
Geronimo Film Productions, Inc.
Jeff Gold Productions, Inc.
GreenWater Pictures
Greystone Communication Group, Inc./Greystone Films
Hallmark Entertainment
David Haugland Productions
The Jim Henson Company
Hodge Film & Video
Horizon Shine, Inc.
The House Production Company
Hy-Tone Productions
Impact PSA, Inc.
In Play Media Arts
Infomercial Solutions, Inc.
Intelliscape Films, LLC
International Television Group (ITG)
IPS Productions
JKR Productions, Inc.
Kavich Reynolds Productions, Inc.
Kelley Productions International
Let There Be Light Productions
Lightning Bolt PIX: Barnyard Productions
Lucid Media
Lyon Studios
Make It Happen Productions, Inc.
Charles Malcolm Video Productions
Niki Marvin Productions
Matrix Communications
Megahertz Pictures
MM2K
Monarex Hollywood Corporation
Music Room Pictures
Nemiroff Productions
New & Unique Videos
Nitestar Productions
NXT Entertainment

Production Company Category Key

October Productions
One Step Productions
Onyx Productions, Inc.
Our Productions, Inc.
Ovation Entertainment
P.A.T. Productions
Edward Pacio & Associates
George Paige Associates, Inc.
Perseverance Productions
Perspective Films
Picture Mill
Point of View Productions
Polestar Film & Photographic Production
Post Modern Edit
Producers Group, Ltd.
Production Analysis Corporation
The Production Asylum
Proletariat Filmworks
Quasar Studios
Patrick Raymond Entertainment, Inc.
Realitory Productions
Red Hots Entertainment
Red-Horse Productions
Reel Orange
Rick Reinert Pictures
Revolver Films, LLC
Ridini Entertainment Corporation
Rogue Entertainment
RumRunner Cine Service
Scotti Productions
Silver Lining Productions, Inc.
Snapdragon Films, Inc.
Sneak Preview Entertainment, Inc.
South Fork Productions
SplendidLight Media Productions
Stefanino Productions
Stereomedia 3D Video Productions
Strom Magallon Entertainment
Mel Stuart Productions, Inc.
Suzanne Bauman Productions
Telling Pictures, Inc.
Teocalli Entertainment, Inc.
Time-Life Video
Tribe Pictures
TVA Productions
TVP Studios
Vanguard Productions
Venture Entertainment Group
Verité Productions
Video Hollywood Productions
Videowerks
Vihlene & Associates, Inc.
Weintraub/Kuhn Productions
Weller/Grossman Productions
Western Branch Productions, Inc.
Bill White Productions
Yada/Levine Productions
Zeal Pictures
Zystar Films, Inc.

Music Video
1171 Production Group
21st Century Man Productions
40 Acres & A Mule Filmworks, Inc.
5th Gear Entertainment
A Band Apart Commercials
A Few Miles North
AbsoluteFilms.net
Ad-Lib Marketing & Advertising
Albrecht & Associates, Inc.
Alta Vista Productions
American Sports Network, Inc.
Arsenal, Inc.
The Artists Company/ The A&R Group
Ashley Productions
Backyard Productions
The Baer Animation Company, Inc.
Suzanne Bauman Productions
Bella Productions
Black Dog Films (RSA USA)
Blue Goose Productions
Bob Industries
Bonfire Films of America
Boyington Studios, Inc.
The Bregman Entertainment Company
Canvas House Films
The Chelmar Group
Coast Media Teleproductions, Inc.
CPProds
The Creative Department, LLC
Cylo
dapTV associates
Dayton/Faris, Inc.
DNA, Inc.
Doom, Inc.
Duck Soup Studios
E.M.E., Inc.
Fat Chance Films
Fate Junkie Films, Inc.
The Film Syndicate
FM Rocks
Fuel
Galanty & Company, Inc.
Gears Communications
Geronimo Film Productions, Inc.
Ginty Films
Glass Guns
Go Film
Jeff Gold Productions, Inc.
Graying & Balding, Inc.
GreenWater Pictures
H-Gun Labs
David Haugland Productions
The Jim Henson Company
Hodge Film & Video
Horizon Shine, Inc.
In-Finn-Ity Productions, Inc.
Industrial Light + Magic Commercial
   Productions

Instinct Pictures
LA Productions
Legacy Films
Let There Be Light Productions
Lightning Bolt PIX: Barnyard Productions
Make It Happen Productions, Inc.
Mars Media, Inc.
Matrix Communications
The Miller Entertainment Group, Inc.
MM2K
Mo Jo Productions, Inc.
Moxie Pictures
Music Room Pictures
Nemiroff Productions
New Millennium Studios
No Prisoners
Orange Soda
Our Gang Productions
Our Productions, Inc.
Ovation Entertainment
Overbrook Entertainment
George Paige Associates, Inc.
Perseverance Productions
Perspective Films
Planet, Inc.
Pop/Art Film Factory
Production Analysis Corporation
Proletariat Filmworks
Propaganda Films
Proud Mary Entertainment
Red Hots Entertainment
Satellite Films
Shady Acres Entertainment
Sharpcut Productions
Sneak Preview Entertainment, Inc.
Sodas & Shoes
South Fork Productions
Sports' Cinematography Group
J. Stack Productions
Stargazer, Inc.
Stefanino Productions
Stereomedia 3D Video Productions
Strom Magallon Entertainment
Summerland Entertainment
Tango Films
TVP Studios
Vanguard Productions
Ventana Films
Vide-U
Villains
Bill White Productions
Windmill Lane Productions
X-Ray Productions
Mark Yellen Productions
Zeal Pictures
Zooma Zooma Corporation
Zystar Films, Inc.

Production Company Category Key

Interactive Media

AbsoluteFilms.net
AntEye.com
Atom Films
Bender-Spink
Bunnygrenade
Cairo/Simpson Entertainment, Inc.
Calico World Entertainment
Canned Interactive
CinemaNow
CinemaPop
Cineville, Inc.
Coast Media Teleproductions, Inc.
Connection III Entertainment Corp.
CRAPtv
Ctonic Flikz
Cylo
D.Film
Digital Planet
Digital Visionaries
Doom, Inc.
dotcomix
Duck Soup Studios
E.M.E., Inc.
Enteraktion, Inc.
FDG Internet
Flip Your Lid, Inc.
Woody Fraser Productions
Gears Communications
Ginty Films
Glass Guns
Gracie Films
Grade A Entertainment
GreenWater Pictures
H-Gun Labs
Hawk Entertainment
Hennessey Entertainment, Ltd.
The Jim Henson Company
Hy-Tone Productions
Icebox
Industrial Light + Magic Commercial Productions
Jaret Entertainment
Killer Films
Langley Productions
Stan Lee Media, Inc.
Lineup Technologies, Inc.
Lucid Film
Mariposa
Matrix Communications
Mediatrip
Mekanism
Metafilmics
Mindfire Entertainment
National Lampoon
Nemiroff Productions
New Millennium Studios
NXT Entertainment
Orbit Entertainment Group
Our Gang Productions
George Paige Associates, Inc.
Perspective Films
Quasar Studios
Patrick Raymond Entertainment, Inc.
Realitory Productions
Dan Redler Entertainment
Renegade Animation, Inc.
Rice & Beans Productions
Phil Roman Entertainment
Santa Monica Pictures
Kristine Schwarz Productions
Sightsound.com
Silver Lining Productions, Inc.
Snapdragon Films, Inc.
The Spark Factory
Stereomedia 3D Video Productions
Streamedia.net
Tavel Entertainment
Threshold Entertainment
Undergroundfilm.com
Val D'Oro Entertainment
Videowerks
Z.com
ZeroOneFilms.com
Zooma Zooma Corporation

Production Companies - Feature Film

3 ARTS ENTERTAINMENT
9460 Wilshire Blvd., 7th Fl.
Beverly Hills, CA 90212
Phone: ....(310) 888-3200
....(212) 262-6565
Fax: ....(310) 888-3210
Key Executives/Personnel:
    Dave Becky, Manager
    Jeff Golenberg, Manager
    Howard Klein, Manager
    Molly Madden, Manager
    David Miner, Manager
    Daniel Rappaport, Manager
    Dave Rath, Manager
    Michael Rotenberg, Manager
    Mark Schulman, Manager
    Lainie Sorkin, Manager
    Erwin Stoff, Manager
    Kara Welker-Ryder, Manager
    Nick Frenkel, Manager
Specialties: Studio; Independent
Other Categories: TV
Credits: King of the Hill; The Chris Rock Show; The Hughleys
First Look/Development Deals: Twentieth Century Fox Television

30 SECOND FILMS
3019 Pico Blvd.
Santa Monica, CA 90405
Phone: ....(310) 315-1750
Fax: ....(310) 315-1757
www.30secondfilms.com
info@30secondfilms.com
Key Executives/Personnel:
    Alan Stamm, Executive Producer
    Bob Kronovet, Producer & Director
    Scott Baio, Director
    Debbie Allen, Director
    Tony Dow, Director
    Branscombe Richmond, Director
Specialties: Independent; Shorts; Documentaries; Trailers
Other Categories: TV; Commercials; Video
Credits: American Tigers; Ghostown; Broken Bars; L.A. Task Force

40 ACRES & A MULE FILMWORKS, INC.
124 Dekalb Ave.
Brooklyn, NY 11217
Phone: ....(718) 624-3703
Fax: ....(718) 624-2008
Key Executives/Personnel:
    Spike Lee, CEO
    Sam Kitt, President of Production
    Andre Hereford, Director of Development
    Heather Parish, Business Manager
Specialties: Studio; Independent; Documentaries; Trailers
Other Categories: Commercials; Video; Music Video
Credits: Bamboozled; Summer of Sam; He Got Game; Malcolm X
Additional Info: NY Development Office: 75 S. Elliot Pl., 3rd Fl.
    Brooklyn, NY 11217

5TH GEAR ENTERTAINMENT
5657 Wilshire Blvd., Ste. 230
Los Angeles, CA 90036
Phone: ....(323) 954-0555
Fax: ....(323) 936-9421
centralhq@aol.com
Key Executives/Personnel:
    Carl Craig, Executive Producer
Specialties: Independent
Other Categories: Music Video
Credits: Players Club; Hollywood Shuffle; Book of Love

A&E TELEVISION NETWORKS
235 E. 45th St.
New York, NY 10017
Phone: ....(212) 210-1400
Fax: ....(212) 210-1308
www.aande.com
Key Executives/Personnel:
    Nickolas Davatzes, President & CEO
    Gerard Gruosso, CFO & Sr. VP of Finance
    Whitney Goit, Executive VP of Sales & Marketing
    Dan Davids, Executive VP & General Manager
    Jim Greiner, Sr. VP of Operations & Business Development
    Delia Fine, VP of Drama & Film Programming
    Ed Hersh, VP of Documentary Programming
    Carol Anne Dolan, Director of Documentary Programming
Specialties: Direct-to-Video
Other Categories: TV; Video
Credits: Biography; American Justice; Investigative Reports

A BAND APART
7966 Beverly Blvd.
Los Angeles, CA 90048
Phone: ....(323) 951-4600
Fax: ....(323) 951-4601
Key Executives/Personnel:
    Lawrence Bender, Producer
    Quentin Tarantino, Writer & Director
    John Baldecchi, Producer
    Laura Bickford, Producer
    Julie Kirkham, Sr. VP of Production
    Kevin Brown, Executive Producer, TV
    Christian D'Andrea, VP of Production
    Nicole Pennington, VP of Development
    Janet Jeffries, Story Editor & Assistant to Ms. Kirkham
    Robin Reinhardt, Assistant to Mr. Brown
    David Zerr, Assistant to Mr. Baldecchi
Specialties: Studio; Independent
Other Categories: TV
Credits: Pulp Fiction; Anna And The King; Good Will Hunting; Jackie Brown
First Look/Development Deals: Miramax Films, Twentieth Century Fox

AB'-STRAKT PICTURES
100 N. Crescent Dr.
Beverly Hills, CA 90210
Phone: ....(310) 385-6611
....(310) 385-6608
Fax: ....(310) 385-4306
lupe_rilova@yahoo.com
Key Executives/Personnel:
    Gail Mutrux, Producer
    Valerie Dean, VP of Production
Specialties: Studio; Documentaries
Other Categories: TV
Credits: Nurse Betty; Donnie Brasco; Quiz Show
First Look/Development Deals: USA Films

ABBY LOU ENTERTAINMENT
1411 Edgehill Pl.
Pasadena, CA 91103
Phone: ....(626) 795-7334
Fax: ....(626) 795-4013
ale@full-moon.com
Key Executives/Personnel:
    George LeFave, Executive Producer
    Chryl Pestor, Executive VP of Development
Specialties: Independent

Production Companies – Feature Film

Other Categories: TV; Commercials; Video
Credits: Adventures in Whispering Gardens; A Christmas Whisper

ACAPPELLA PICTURES
Phone: ....(323) 782-8200
Fax: ....(323) 782-8210
charlie@acapellapictures.com
Key Executives/Personnel:
  Charles Evans Jr., President & Producer
  Benjamin Sztajnkrycer, VP of Development & Production
  Scott Stein, Story Editor
  Jason Amos, Assistant
Specialties: Independent
Other Categories: TV
Credits: The Brave

ACT III PRODUCTIONS
100 N. Crescent Dr., Ste. 250
Beverly Hills, CA 90210
Phone: ....(310) 385-4111
Fax: ....(310) 385-4148
Key Executives/Personnel:
  Norman Lear, Chairman & CEO
  John Baskin, President
  Rachel Davidson, VP of Feature & TV Development
Specialties: Studio; Independent
Other Categories: TV

ADELSON ENTERTAINMENT
2601 Ocean Park Blvd., Ste. 112
Santa Monica, CA 90405
Phone: ....(310) 314-9151
Fax: ....(310) 314-9669
Key Executives/Personnel:
  Andrew Adelson, Producer & Partner
  Tracey Alexander, Executive Producer & Partner
  Laurie Arent, Director of Development
Specialties: Independent
Other Categories: TV
Credits: Hiroshima; Her Own Rules; Critical Choices

ORLY ADELSON PRODUCTIONS
12304 Santa Monica Blvd., Ste. 115
Los Angeles, CA 90025
Phone: ....(310) 442-2012
Fax: ....(310) 442-2013
orly@orlyadelson.com
Key Executives/Personnel:
  Orly Adelson, President
  J. J. Jamieson, Executive Producer
  Jada Miranda, Story Editor
Specialties: Studio
Other Categories: TV
Credits: The Truth About Jane; On Hostile Ground; To Love, Honor & Betray; No Greater Love

ADOBE PICTURES
3727 W. Magnolia Blvd., Ste. 189
Burbank, CA 91510
Phone: ....(818) 955-8345
....(818) 955-8378
Fax: ....(818) 955-7650
www.adobepictures.com
jadair@adobepictures.com
Key Executives/Personnel:
  Joed W. Adair, Producer, Director & Writer
Specialties: Independent
Credits: Wanna Be In Pictures; Sweet Mama; Tourist Court

AEI
9601 Wilshire Blvd., Ste. 1202
Beverly Hills, CA 90210
Phone: ....(323) 932-0407
www.aeionline.com
webaei@aol.com
Key Executives/Personnel:
  Ken Atchity, President
  Chi-Li Wong, VP
  Brenna Lui, Director of Development
  Gordon H. Lui, Development Executive
  Jennifer Pope, Submissions Coordinator
Specialties: Studio; Animation
Other Categories: TV
Credits: Me; Henry's List of Wrongs; The Kill Martin Club

AERIAL FOCUS PRODUCTIONS
8 Camino Verde
Santa Barbara, CA 93103
Phone: ....(805) 962-9911
Fax: ....(805) 962-9536
www.aerialfocus.com
aerialfcs@aol.com
Key Executives/Personnel:
  Tom Sanders, Executive Producer
  David Stanfield, Segment Producer
Specialties: Shorts
Other Categories: TV; Video
Credits: Over The Edge; The Best Boogie Continues; Royal Sky Celebration
Trade Assoc./Guilds/Unions: AFTRA, SAG

AFRA-FILM ENTERPRISES, INC.
137 S. Robertson Blvd., Ste. 254
Beverly Hills, CA 90211
Phone: ....(323) 882-6193
Fax: ....(323) 882-6032

Celebrating Over 20 Years as
Your Payroll & Software Solution

Payroll

Service & Value
Personalized processing from industry experts
Low SUI & Workers' Comp rates
Handling fee applies only to
  gross payroll - not fringes

Feature /
Television
Payroll all types
  of production
No budget too small
No budget too large
Production accounting
  Onsite or at our offices
  Includes free hardware
  & Media software
Residual & music payroll processing

Commercial /
Video / Industrial
Significant pool savings
Caps on handling fees
  Payroll processing with full benefits
  ...al talent processing

Accounting
Windows Programs
MediaWin™ Feature/TV
MediaWin™ Commercial

DOS Programs
MPAS™ - Media Production
  Accounting System
MCAS™ - Media Commercial
  Accounting System

Production
Movie Magic Budgeting
  & Scheduling
RepTools
ShowBiz Forms
Automated Contracts for Film/TV
Automated Contracts for Music
Storyboard Artist & Storyboard Quick
Cinergy 2000 Production System

Bidding & Actualization

Software

 ...ay to discuss all we have to offer!
Angeles   New York
  9696   212.366.9390
Website: www.media-services.com

Production Companies – Feature Film

sidazfor@earthlink.net
Key Executives/Personnel:
    Anatoly A. Fradis, President
    Jeff Ratner, VP of Finance
    Felix Kleiman, VP of Development
    Olga Fradis, VP of Production
Specialties: Studio; Independent
Other Categories: TV
Credits: Arena; Iron Maiden; Red Shoe Diaries; Business For Pleasure

ALAMEDA FILMWORKS, INC.
Phone: ....(818) 846-4074
afwinc@att.net
Key Executives/Personnel:
    Wendy Yorkshire, Producer
Specialties: Trailers
Other Categories: Commercials; Video
Trade Assoc./Guilds/Unions: AICP, DGA

ALBRECHT & ASSOCIATES, INC.
3442 Dorothy Rd.
Topanga, CA 90290
Phone: ....(818) 222-4836
jaalbrecht@yahoo.com
Specialties: Independent; Direct-to-Video
Credits: Carol King One to One; Mickey's 60th Birthday
Trade Assoc./Guilds/Unions: DGA, SAG, WGA

ALCHEMY ENTERTAINMENT
73 Market St.
Venice, CA 90291
Phone: ....(310) 396-5937
Fax: ....(310) 450-4988
Key Executives/Personnel:
    Andy Tennant, Writer & Director
    Jon Jashni, Producer
    Wink Mordaunt, Producer
Specialties: Studio
Other Categories: TV
Credits: Anna and the King; Ever After

ALL GIRL PRODUCTIONS
4024 Radford Ave., Bungalow 20
Studio City, CA 91604
Phone: ....(818) 655-6000
Fax: ....(818) 655-8380
Key Executives/Personnel:
    Bette Midler, Actress & Producer
    Bonnie Bruckheimer, Producer
    Yvette Taylor, Executive VP
    Julia Eisenman, Sr. VP
    Laura Mueller, Development Assistant
    Robert Nguyen, Assistant to Ms. Bruckheimer
Specialties: Studio; Independent
Other Categories: TV
Credits: Bette; Beaches; Diva Las Vegas; Man of the House
First Look/Development Deals: Sony Pictures Entertainment

ALLEN & ASSOCIATES
5304 Ballone Ln.
Culver City, CA 90230
Phone: ....(310) 390-5522
sportstape@aol.com
Key Executives/Personnel:
    Donald V. Allen, Producer
Specialties: Independent; Direct-to-Video; Shorts; Documentaries; Trailers
Other Categories: TV; Commercials
Credits: The Home Show; Suburbia; Car Wash; Super Picnic
Trade Assoc./Guilds/Unions: AFTRA, NARAS, SAG

ALLIANCE ATLANTIS
808 Wilshire Blvd., 3rd Fl.
Santa Monica, CA 90401
Phone: ....(310) 899-8000
....(416) 967-1174
Fax: ....(310) 899-8100
www.allianceatlantis.com
Key Executives/Personnel:
    Peter Sussman, President
    John Morayniss, Executive VP of TV Production
    Ed Gernon, VP of TV Movies & Miniseries
    Noreen Halpern, VP of TV Series Production
    Janine Coughlin, VP of TV Series Production
Specialties: Studio; Independent; Direct-to-Video; Documentaries; Animation
Other Categories: TV
Credits: Joan of Arc; Beastmaster (TV series); Sunshine; The Sweet Hereafter

ALPHAVILLE
5555 Melrose Ave., DeMille Bldg., 2nd Fl.
Los Angeles, CA 90038
Phone: ....(323) 956-4803
Fax: ....(323) 862-1616
firstname@aville.com
Key Executives/Personnel:
    Sean Daniel, Producer & Partner
    Jim Jacks, Producer & Partner
    Caldecot Chubb, President of Production
    Jennifer Moyer, Director of Development
    Chris Palmer, Office Manager
    Ty Warren, Assistant to Mr. Daniel
    Laura Kotcharian, Assistant to Mr. Jacks
    Melissa Maxwell, Assistant to Mr. Chubb
Specialties: Studio
Credits: The Mummy; Tombstone; Dazed and Confused; Michael
First Look/Development Deals: Paramount Pictures - Motion Picture Group

AM PRODUCTIONS & MANAGEMENT
8899 Beverly Blvd., Ste. 713
Los Angeles, CA 90048
Phone: ....(310) 275-9081
Fax: ....(310) 275-9082
Key Executives/Personnel:
    Ann Margret, Executive Producer & Actor
    Burt Reynolds, Executive Producer, Director & Actor
    Alan Margulies, Executive Producer
    Roger Smith, Executive Producer & Writer
    Christina King, Administration
Specialties: Studio; Independent
Other Categories: TV
Credits: Mystery Alaska; Hard Time; Life of the Party

AMALGAMATED, INC.
6565 Sunset Blvd., Ste. 525
Los Angeles, CA 90028
Phone: ....(323) 466-5400
Fax: ....(323) 960-9283
Key Executives/Personnel:
    Erik Feig, Producer
    Dawn Ebert-Byrnes, Assistant
Specialties: Studio
Other Categories: TV
Credits: I Know What You Did Last Summer; I Still Know What You Did Last Summer; Slackers

AMBLIN ENTERTAINMENT
1000 Flower St.
Glendale, CA 91201

Production Companies – Feature Film

Phone: (818) 733-4600
Specialties: Studio
Additional Info: See DreamWorks SKG

AMEN RA FILMS
301 N. Cañon Dr., Ste. 228
Beverly Hills, CA 90210
Phone: (310) 246-6510
Fax: (310) 550-1932
firstname@amenrafilms.com
Key Executives/Personnel:
  Wesley Snipes, Producer & Actor
  Kimiko Fox, President & Producer
  Victor McGauley, Sr. VP & Producer
  Carmen Baker, Comptroller
  Julian Chang Zolkin, Creative Executive
  Clay Rivers, Director of Design & Marketing
  Glennis Bastien, Physical Production
  Trudy Snipes Baylock, Human Resources
  Rachelle L. Thomas, Special Projects
  Lori Davis, Executive Assistant to Mr. Snipes
  Jeanie Lee, Executive Assistant to Ms. Fox
  Waraire Boswell, Executive Assistant to Mr. McGauley
Specialties: Studio; Independent
Other Categories: TV
Credits: Blade; Disappearing Acts; Money Train; The Art of War

AMERICAN ENTERTAINMENT CO.
5225 Wilshire Blvd., Ste. 615
Los Angeles, CA 90036
Phone: (323) 939-6746
Fax: (323) 939-6747
Key Executives/Personnel:
  Bill Paxton, Producer & President
  Tom Huckabee, Producer & VP
  Xander Maksik, Creative Executive
  Mike Culbert, Creative Executive
Specialties: Studio; Independent; Documentaries
Other Categories: TV
Credits: Traveller; Mexicali; Frailty; Beer Ban

AMERICAN WORLD PICTURES
21700 Oxnard St., Ste. 660
Woodland Hills, CA 91367
Phone: (818) 715-1480
Fax: (818) 715-1081
awpics@earthlink.net
Key Executives/Personnel:
  Mark L. Lester, President & CEO
  Dana Dubovsky, President of Production
  Brian R. Etting, VP of Production
  Terese Linden Kohn, VP of Int'l. Sales & Acquisitions
  Jenny Dillon, Director Int'l.
  Anna Montgomery, Production Executive
Specialties: Independent; Direct-to-Video
Other Categories: TV
Credits: Blowback; Sacrifice; The Ex; Misbegotten

AMERICAN ZOETROPE
808 Wilshire Blvd., 3rd Fl.
Santa Monica, CA 90401
Phone: (310) 899-8000
(415) 788-7500
Fax: (310) 899-8100
www.zoetrope.com
Key Executives/Personnel:
  Francis Ford Coppola, no title
  Linda Reisman, President (NY)
  Jay Shoemaker, CEO (SF)
  Tara McCann, Sr. VP, Head of TV & Producer (LA)
  Bobby Rock, VP of Features Production & Acquisitions (LA)
  Aude Soichet, Creative Executive, TV (LA)
  Shannon Lail, Assistant to Mr. Coppola
Specialties: Studio; Independent
Other Categories: TV
Credits: The Virgin Suicides; The Godfather I, II, III; The Third Miracle; Sleepy Hollow
First Look/Development Deals: MGM, Inc., Alliance Atlantis

CRAIG ANDERSON PRODUCTIONS
9696 Culver Blvd., Meralta Plaza, Ste. 208
Culver City, CA 90232
Phone: (310) 841-2555
Fax: (310) 841-5934
Key Executives/Personnel:
  Craig Anderson, Owner & Executive Producer
  Phil Kruner, VP of Development
  Chris St. George, Creative Executive
  Noah Jones, Creative Development Executive
  Marty Schwartz, Production Supervisor
Specialties: Independent
Other Categories: TV
Credits: The Piano Lesson

ANGEL ARK PRODUCTIONS
12711 Ventura Blvd., Ste. 330
Studio City, CA 91604
Phone: (818) 508-3338
Fax: (818) 508-2009
Key Executives/Personnel:
  Jason Alexander, Partner
  Jenny Birchfield-Eick, Partner
  Michael A. Jackman, Partner
  Christopher May, VP of TV
  Colin Martin, Assistant
  Vera Wagman, Assistant
Specialties: Studio; Independent
Other Categories: TV
Credits: Just Looking; Rocky & Bullwinkle; On Edge

ANOTHER DIVERSION
Phone: (818) 763-0338
(818) 802-0758
Fax: (818) 763-0504
omokyra@aol.com
Key Executives/Personnel:
  Kyra Shelgren, Executive Producer
Specialties: Independent
Other Categories: Commercials
Credits: Motorola; Gatorade; Dodge; Jeep
Trade Assoc./Guilds/Unions: DGA

APATOW PRODUCTIONS
1438 N. Gower, Bldg. 38, Ste. 557
Hollywood, CA 90028
Phone: (323) 860-7825
Fax: (323) 860-7849
Key Executives/Personnel:
  Judd Apatow, Producer & Writer
  Maureen Jennings, Internet
  John Hayes, Assistant
Specialties: Studio
Other Categories: TV
Credits: The Cable Guy; Freaks & Geeks; The Larry Sanders Show
First Look/Development Deals: DreamWorks SKG

APOSTLE PICTURES
1697 Broadway, Ste. 906
New York, NY 10019

Integrated Post Production Services

Astound your audiences with the very best images possible

"David's passion for excellence, his steadfast and masterly dedication to this film, our company and the 70mm format continue to set the standard for our industry."
GREG MACGILLIVRAY Producer/Director, Everest

"DKP's vast experience in the 70mm format was invaluable throughout the making of Michael Jordan to the Max, their ability to channel this expertise into uncharted territory with digital effects was particularly critical for this film and really pushed the envelope for this medium."
STEVE KEMPF Producer, Michael Jordan to the Max

- 35mm ADDITIVE PRINTDOWN DAILIES
- 35mm REDUCTION NEGATIVES
- 35mm & 65mm PROJECTION
- 2D & 3D 15/70 PROJECTION
- IN THREE SCREENING ROOMS
- RELEASE PRINT & ELEMENT STORAGE
- TITLES & OPTICALS
- DIGITAL IMAGE RENDERING
- DIGITAL CRT & LASER FILM RECORDING
- DIGITAL 2D PROJECTION

- 65,000 SQUARE FEET
- PRESENTATION ROOMS WITH TELECONFERENCING CAPABILITIES
- A THEATRE FOR YOUR NEXT 70/35/DIGITAL SCREENING
- AVID & KEM EDITING SUITE
- SUPERVISION & QUALITY ASSURANCE OF 70mm DAILIES, ANSWER PRINTS, RELEASE PRINTS & DUPLICATE NEGATIVES
- NEGATIVE CUTTING
- 3M SCOTCHGARD™ FILM PROTECTOR
- VIDEO MASTERING & DUPLICATION

Contact David Keighley
DAVID KEIGHLEY PRODUCTIONS 70MM INC.
3003 Exposition Blvd.   Santa Monica, CA 90404
Tel (310) 255-5552   Fax (310) 315-7199
e-mail dkeighley@imax.com

THE WORLD OF VARIETY

DAILY VARIETY GOTHAM

Published every weekday

Global show business news with a focus on New York's entertainment, financial and media-related industries

VARIETY

Published weekly

Provides essential entertainment business news

News coverage and analysis to global industry leaders in 84 countries

eV

Published monthly

This unique monthly is focused on the business of entertainment and the digital economy, featuring in-depth coverage and analysis of technology's impact on the global entertainment industry

DAILY VARIETY

Published every weekday

This leading business publication delivers breaking entertainment news in Hollywood and around the world

VARIETY.COM

Launched January, 1998

Variety's two-tiered web site features daily news, reviews, columns, charts, awards coverage, international box office analysis and more

- *Variety.com* (free service) is geared towards the mainstream entertainment consumer

- *VarietyExtra* (subscription-based service) targets entertainment industry professionals

---

LOS ANGELES 323-857-6600 • **NEW YORK** 212-337-7002 • **LONDON** 44-20-7520-5222
MADRID/LATIN AMERICA 34-91-766-1356 • **SYDNEY** 61-2-9422-8630

Production Companies – Feature Film

Phone: .... (212) 541-4323
Fax: .... (212) 541-4330
Key Executives/Personnel:
  Dennis Leary, Producer & Director
  Jim Serpico, President
  Tom Sellitti, Creative Executive
  Barstow Church, Assistant to Producers
  Steve Hochmuth, Assistant to Mr. Leary
Specialties: Studio; Independent
Other Categories: TV
Credits: Blow
First Look/Development Deals: DreamWorks SKG

MARK ARCHER ENTERTAINMENT
1910 St. Joe Center Rd., Ste. 22
Fort Wayne, IN 46825
Phone: .... (219) 486-8831
Fax: .... (219) 486-8971
www.markarcherentertainment.com
development@markarcherentertainment.com
Key Executives/Personnel:
  Mark Archer, President & CEO
  Johnathan Brouwer, VP of Production & Operations
Specialties: Independent; Documentaries
Other Categories: TV
Credits: In the Company of Men; American Reel; The Life Between

THE ARNET/KERNER CO.
3815 Hughes Ave.
Culver City, CA 90232
Phone: .... (310) 838-2500
Key Executives/Personnel:
  Jon Avnet, Director & Producer
  Jordan Kerner, Producer
  Carol Chacamaty, Sr. VP of Finance
  Lisa Lindstrom, Sr. VP of Feature Development & Production
  Paul Neesan, Sr. VP of Development & Production
  Sandra Hodges, VP of Operations
  Marsha Oglesby, VP of Development & Production
  Jason Abril, Story Editor
Specialties: Studio; Independent
Other Categories: TV
Credits: Inspector Gadget; George of the Jungle; Fried Green Tomatoes; Red Corner
Trade Assoc./Guilds/Unions: DGA, SAG, WGAw

ARTISAN ENTERTAINMENT
2700 Colorado Ave., 2nd Fl
Santa Monica, CA 90404
Phone: .... (310) 449-9200
.... (212) 577-2400
Fax: .... (310) 255-3920
www.artisanent.com
Key Executives/Personnel:
  Amir Malin, CEO
  Bill Block, President
  John Shestack, President of Production & Development
  Steve Beeks, President of Home Entertainment
  Glenn Ross, President of Family Home Entertainment
  Ken Schapiro, COO of Artisan Pictures
  Jim Keegan, Executive VP & CFO
  Nick Van Dyk, Executive VP of Corporate Development & Strategic Planning
  Caitlin Scanlon, Executive VP of Production
  Meltem Demirer, VP of Production
  Andrew Golov, Executive VP of Production
  Patrick Gunn, Sr. VP
  Gary Rubin, Sr. VP of TV
  Nancy V. Coleman, Sr. VP of Human Resources
  Rachel Cohen, VP of Acquisitions & Production (NY)

  Leilani Forby, VP of Film Acquisitions
  Cybelle Greenman, VP of Development & Production
  Marc Danon, Manager of Production
Specialties: Studio; Independent; Direct-to-Video; Shorts; Documentaries; Animation; Trailers
Other Categories: TV
Credits: Blair Witch I & II; The Way of the Gun; The Limey; Reservoir Dogs

THE ARTISTS' COLONY
7421 Beverly Blvd., Ste. 13
Los Angeles, CA 90036
Phone: .... (323) 930-7900
Fax: .... (323) 930-7919
www.theartistscolony.com
las@theartistscolony.com
Key Executives/Personnel:
  Lloyd A. Silverman, President & Producer
  Ginnina d'Orazio, Development Executive
  Julian Bernard, Urban Markets
  Caelyn Smith, Assistant
Specialties: Studio; Independent
Other Categories: TV
Credits: Snow Falling On Cedars; Shattered Image; Solid Ones; Till The End of Time

ASHLEY PRODUCTIONS
5225 Canyon Crest Dr., Ste. 71-340
Riverside, CA 92507
Phone: .... (909) 781-6597
www.ashleyproductions.com
info@ashleyproductions.com
Key Executives/Personnel:
  Jacqueline Ashley, President & CEO
  William Ashley II, VP & CFO

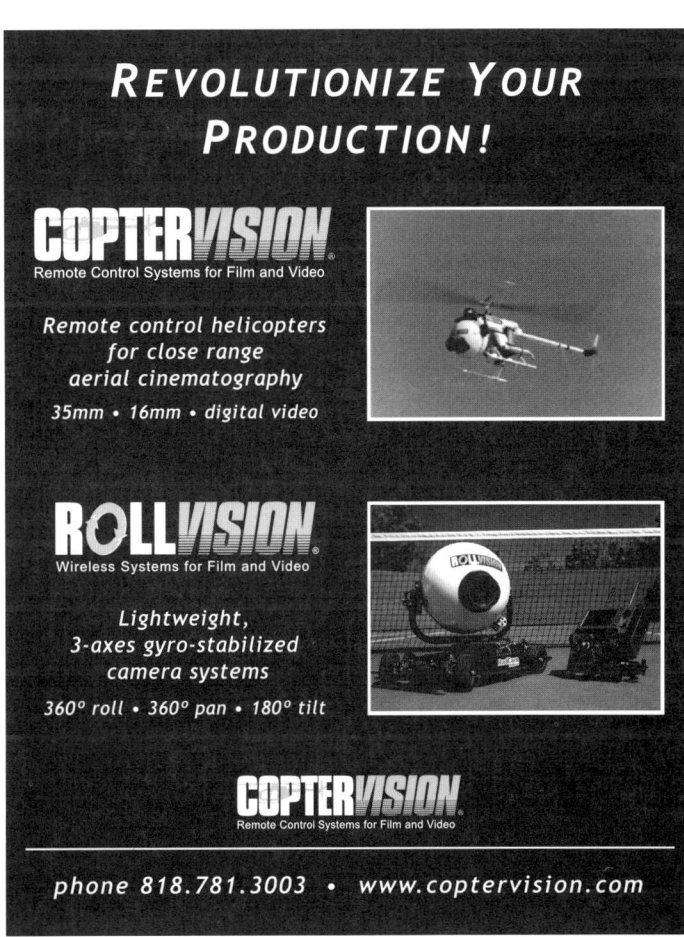

Production Companies – Feature Film

Specialties: Independent; Shorts; Documentaries
Other Categories: Commercials; Music Video
Credits: Between Friends; Stolen Moments; The Right Crowd

ASSET PICTURES
526 W. 26th St., Ste. 813
New York, NY 10001
Phone: ....(212) 255-6187
Fax: ....(212) 242-8345
www.fivewives.com
asetpix@aol.com
Key Executives/Personnel:
    Tessa Blake, President
    Jason Lyon, Producer
Specialties: Independent; Documentaries
Other Categories: TV
Credits: Five Wives; Three Secretaries & Me
Trade Assoc./Guilds/Unions: AIVF, IDA, IFP
Additional Info: LA Partner: Joe Messian, 1218 N. Bronson Ave.,
    Hollywood, CA 90038

ATKINSON WAY FILMS
6121 Santa Monica Blvd., Ste. 100
Los Angeles, CA 90038
Phone: ....(323) 465-3350
Fax: ....(323) 465-3344
Key Executives/Personnel:
    Sam Waterson, Owner
    Beth Colt, Owner
    Andew Myler, Director of Development
    Erika Coleman, Development
Specialties: Studio; Independent
Other Categories: TV
Credits: Chuck & Buck; A House Divided; Star Maps; Journey of August King
First Look/Development Deals: NBC Entertainment, Inc.

ATLANTIC STREAMLINE
1323 A Third St.
Santa Monica, CA 90401
Phone: ....(310) 319-9366
Fax: ....(310) 319-9235
www.atlanticstreamline.com
info@atlanticstreamline.com
Key Executives/Personnel:
    Marco Weber, President & CEO
    Fran Lucci, Sr. VP of Production & Finance
    Diana Lesmez, VP of Creative Affairs
    Dana Taprogge, Development Coordinator
    Jill Simpson, Executive Assistant to Mr. Weber
    Gaycia Bowen, Assistant
Specialties: Independent
Credits: You're Dead; The Thirteenth Floor; Don't Do It; Project Assassins
First Look/Development Deals: Baltimore/Spring Creek Pictures, LLC

ATLAS ENTERTAINMENT
9169 Sunset Blvd.
Los Angeles, CA 90069
Phone: ....(310) 724-7350
Fax: ....(310) 724-7345
Key Executives/Personnel:
    Allen Shapiro, President
    Charles Roven, Producer & Partner
    Todd Smith, Manager & Producer
    Dianne Gunn, VP of Finance
    Kelley Smith-Wait, Producer
    Douglas Segal, Producer
    Richard Suckle, Producer
    Alan Glazer, Associate Producer
    Tom Brennan, Feature Development
    Gloria Fan, Feature Development
    Cee Cee Capotosto, Assistant to Mr. Shapiro
    A. D. Harris, Assistant to Mr. Suckle
    Maia Winters, Assistant to Mr. Roven
    Dave Bithers, Assistant to Mr. Roven
    Heather Dennis, Assistant to Mr. Smith
Specialties: Studio
Credits: City of Angels; Three Kings; Rollerball; 12 Monkeys

AUTOMATIC PICTURES, INC.
5225 Wilshire Blvd., Ste. 525
Los Angeles, CA 90036
Phone: ....(323) 935-1800
Fax: ....(323) 395-8040
Key Executives/Personnel:
    Frank Beddor, Producer
    Liz Cavalier, Creative Executive
    Matthew Lloyd, Assistant
Specialties: Independent; Animation
Credits: There's Something About Mary; Wicked
First Look/Development Deals: Pathé Pictures, Bel-Air Entertainment, Summit Entertainment

AVALANCHE! ENTERTAINMENT
506 Santa Monica Blvd., Ste. 322
Santa Monica, CA 90401
Phone: ....(310) 395-3660
Fax: ....(310) 395-8322
info@avalanche-ent.com
Key Executives/Personnel:
    Richard Hull, President
    Anthony Ross, Director of Development
    Rodney Lee Conover, Co-President of New Media
    Jeff Hause, Co-President of New Media
    Ken Dupuis, Director
Specialties: Studio; Independent
Other Categories: Commercials
Credits: She's All That; Getting Over Allison; Jekyll Island; Within The Lines

AVD PRODUCTIONS, INC/AV DESIGNS
Phone: ....(310) 379-5818
dondavol@pacbell.net
Key Executives/Personnel:
    Genie Davis, Producer, Writer & Director
    Don Davis, Producer
Specialties: Independent
Other Categories: Commercials; Video
Credits: Relentless; IHOP; Taco Bell
First Look/Development Deals: Smith Hemion Productions
Trade Assoc./Guilds/Unions: WGAw

AVENUE PICTURES
11111 Santa Monica Blvd., Ste. 525
Los Angeles, CA 90025
Phone: ....(310) 996-6800
Fax: ....(310) 473-4376
www.avepix.com
Key Executives/Personnel:
    Cary Brokaw, President & CEO
    Sheri Halfon, Sr. VP & CFO
    Judy Geletko, Controller
    David Tellefsen, Assistant to Mr. Brokaw
    Geoff Goodman, Office Manager & Assistant
Specialties: Independent; Direct-to-Video; Documentaries
Other Categories: TV
Credits: Drugstore Cowboy; The Player; Short Cuts; Restoration
First Look/Development Deals: Pearson Television, Intermedia Films

Production Companies – Feature Film

AXELROD ENTERTAINMENT
5555 Melrose Ave., B Annex 1
Hollywood, CA 90038
Phone: ....(323) 956-3705
Fax: ....(323) 862-0079
Key Executives/Personnel:
  Jonathan Axelrod, Executive Producer
  Stacey Ackman, Assistant to Mr. Axelrod
Specialties: Studio
Other Categories: TV
Credits: Kiss Me Guido; Dave's World; Brother's Keeper; Movie Stars
First Look/Development Deals: Paramount Pictures
Additional Info: Formerly Axelrod/Widdoes Entertainment

AXELSON-WEINTRAUB PRODUCTIONS
4421 Riverside Dr., Ste. 208
Burbank, CA 91505
Phone: ....(818) 954-8661
Fax: ....(818) 954-0468
aw-prods@earthlink.net
Key Executives/Personnel:
  John Axelson, Executive Producer & Director
  Barbara Weintraub, Executive Producer
Specialties: Documentaries
Other Categories: TV
Credits: An Affectionate Look at Fatherhood; The Really Naked Truth; The New Adventures of Robin Hood; Strip Poker

BACK HOME PICTURES
6918 Santa Monica Blvd.
Los Angeles, CA 90038
Phone: ....(323) 962-8500
bhpictures@aol.com
Key Executives/Personnel:
  Charles Abehsera, Director
  Shelley O'Connor, Producer
  Diona Pavinsky, Producer
  Moshe Abehsera, Sales Representative
Specialties: Independent
Other Categories: Commercials
Credits: Viatel Communications; Econophone; Destia; AC Transit

BACKYARD PRODUCTIONS
248 Main St.
Venice, CA 90291
Phone: ....(310) 314-1122
Fax: ....(310) 314-1123
www.backyard.com
mail@backyard.com
Key Executives/Personnel:
  Blair Stribley, President & Executive Producer
  Roy Skillicorn, Head of Sales
  Sheila Stepanek, Executive Producer
  Peter Steinzeig, Head of Production
  Ann Edgar, VP of Development
  Kevin Smith, Director
  Rob Pritts, Director
  Don Rase, Director
  Shaun Conrad, Director
  Chace Strickland, Director
  Eddy Chu, Director
  Peter Keenan, Producer
  Kris Mathur, Producer
Specialties: Studio; Independent
Other Categories: Commercials; Music Video
Credits: American Express; Anheuser-Busch; AT&T; Delta Airlines

THE BADHAM COMPANY
3344 Clerendon Rd.
Beverly Hills, CA 90210
Phone: ....(818) 990-9495
Fax: ....(818) 981-9163
www.badhamcompany.com
Key Executives/Personnel:
  John Badham, Director & Producer
  Cammie Crier-Herbert, Co-Producer & Development
Specialties: Studio; Independent
Other Categories: TV
Credits: Saturday Night Fever; War Games; The Jack Bull
First Look/Development Deals: HBO, Paramount Pictures

THE BAER ANIMATION COMPANY, INC.
7743 Woodrow Wilson Dr.
Los Angeles, CA 90046
Phone: ....(323) 874-9122
....(818) 760-8666
Fax: ....(323) 874-7690
www.baeranimation.com
baer@baeranimation.com
Key Executives/Personnel:
  Jane Baer, President & Executive Producer
  Hope Parker, VP & Director of Administration & Marketing
  Milt Vallas, Producer
Specialties: Direct-to-Video; Animation
Other Categories: Commercials; Music Video
Credits: Annabelle's Wish (feature); Coca-Cola (commercial); Chevrolet (commercial); Disney World (commercial)
Trade Assoc./Guilds/Unions: AMPAS, ATAS, IATSE
Additional Info: Production of all styles of animation. Specializes in integrating with live action.

BAER ENTERTAINMENT GROUP
9229 Sunset Blvd., Ste. 401
Los Angeles, CA 90069
Phone: ....(310) 777-3680
Fax: ....(310) 777-3685
Key Executives/Personnel:
  Thomas Baer, Producer
  Michael Steinhardt, Partner
  Mario Acosta, Director of Development
Specialties: Studio; Independent
Credits: The Long Run

BALLPARK PRODUCTIONS
P.O. Box 508
Venice, CA 90294
Phone: ....(310) 827-1328
Fax: ....(310) 577-9626
Key Executives/Personnel:
  Michael Schiffer, Producer & Writer
  Sally Allen, VP of Development
Specialties: Studio; Independent
Credits: Very Bad Things; Lean on Me

BALLYHOO, INC.
6738 Wedgewood Place
Los Angeles, CA 90068
Phone: ....(323) 874-3396
Fax: ....(323) 883-0265
mbesman@wgn.net
Key Executives/Personnel:
  Michael Besman, President
  Brian Cosgrove, Story Editor
Specialties: Studio
Other Categories: TV
Credits: Seven Years In Tibet; The Opposite of Sex; Bounce; About Schmidt

BALTIMORE/SPRING CREEK PICTURES, LLC
4000 Warner Blvd., Bldg. 76, Rm. 8
Burbank, CA 91522
Phone: ....(818) 954-1210

Production Companies – Feature Film

Fax: ....(818) 954-2737
Key Executives/Personnel:
  Barry Levinson, Producer, Director & Writer
  Paula Weinstein, Producer
  Amy Solan, CFO & Business Affairs
  Len Amato, Executive VP
Specialties: Studio; Independent
Credits: Analyze This; The Perfect Storm; Liberty Heights
First Look/Development Deals: Warner Bros.

BANDEIRA ENTERTAINMENT
8447 Wilshire Blvd., Ste. 212
Beverly Hills, CA 90211
Phone: ....(323) 866-3535
Fax: ....(323) 866-3599
Key Executives/Personnel:
  Beau Flynn, Producer
  Christine Johnson, Director of Development
Specialties: Studio
Other Categories: TV
Credits: Fear (TV series); The Love Letter; Judas Kiss
First Look/Development Deals: DreamWorks SKG

BANNER ENTERTAINMENT
8265 Sunset Blvd., Ste. 200
Los Angeles, CA 90046
Phone: ....(323) 848-2880
Fax: ....(323) 848-2255
Key Executives/Personnel:
  Mickey Liddell, President & Producer
Specialties: Independent
Credits: The Broken Hearts Club; Go; Telling Lies In Amercia; Traveller

BARNHOLTZ ENTERTAINMENT
31770 Cottontail Lane
Malibu, CA 90265
Phone: ....(310) 457-7484
Fax: ....(310) 589-2681
bbarnholtz@aol.com
Key Executives/Personnel:
  Barry Barnholtz, President & CEO
  Murray Gilden, CFO
  Katherine L. Miller, Director of Acquisitions
  Irina Piyevsky, Legal Affairs
  Matthew Fladell, Sr. VP of Business Affairs
Specialties: Studio; Independent; Direct-to-Video; Trailers
Credits: Sir Arthur Conan Doyle's The Lost World; The Mangler; The First 9 1/2 Weeks; Backyard Dogs

BARNSTORM FILMS
73 Market St.
Venice, CA 90291
Phone: ....(310) 396-5937
Fax: ....(310) 450-4988
Key Executives/Personnel:
  Tony Bill, Producer & Director
  Helen Bartlett, Producer
Specialties: Studio; Independent
Other Categories: TV
Credits: Harlan County War; Taxi Driver; The Sting; Untamed Heart

BARWOOD FILMS
330 W. 58th St., Ste. 301
New York, NY 10019
Phone: ....(212) 765-7191
Fax: ....(212) 765-6988
Key Executives/Personnel:
  Barbra Streisand, Owner, Producer & Director
  Cis Corman, President
  Evan Cohen, VP of Development
  Jane Mendle, Story Editor

Specialties: Independent; Documentaries
Other Categories: TV
Credits: What Makes A Family; Prince of Tides; Serving in Silence

BASSETT PRODUCTIONS
125 Primose Rd.
Burlingame, CA 94010
Phone: ....(650) 579-1313
Fax: ....(650) 579-4414
www.bassettproductions.com
debra@bassettproductions.com
Key Executives/Personnel:
  Debra Bassett, Executive Producer
Specialties: Independent
Other Categories: Commercials
Credits: Wisdom of the Elders, The Last Owl (feature); Epinions.com (commercial); Wall St. Journal (commercial); HBO (commercial)

SUZANNE BAUMAN PRODUCTIONS
21901 Velicata St.
Woodland Hills, CA 91364
Phone: ....(818) 348-4342
Fax: ....(818) 348-6482
Key Executives/Personnel:
  Suzanne Bauman, Producer & Director
  Toni Pace, Producer
  John Marzilli, Director of Development
Specialties: Independent; Documentaries
Other Categories: TV; Video; Music Video
Credits: Jackie: Behind the Myth; Jack Hanna's Animal Adventures; La Belle Epoque; Women of Summer
Trade Assoc./Guilds/Unions: DGA, WGAw

BARBARA L. BAUMANN INC.
13428 Maxella Ave., Ste. 460
Marina Del Rey, CA 90292
Phone: ....(310) 821-2429
....(310) 569-7991
Fax: ....(310) 821-1429
skyenm@aol.com
Key Executives/Personnel:
  Barbara L. Bauman, Producer
Specialties: Documentaries
Other Categories: TV; Commercials
Credits: A Displaced Person (documentary); One River, Many Voices (documentary); Toyota (commercial); Visa (commercial)

BAUMGARTEN/PROPHET ENTERTAINMENT
1640 S. Sepulveda Blvd., Ste. 218
Los Angeles, CA 90025
Phone: ....(310) 996-1885
Fax: ....(310) 996-1892
Key Executives/Personnel:
  Craig Baumgarten, Producer
  Melissa Prophet, Manager
  Adam Merims, Producer
  Jessica Berlinski, Manager
  Ruth Vester, Assistant to Mr. Baumgarten
  Jackie Tallarido, Assistant to Ms. Prophet
  Shawn Minton, Second Assistant to Mr. Baumgarten & Ms. Prophet
  Eric Morris, Assistant to Mr. Merims
Specialties: Independent
Other Categories: TV
Credits: Universal Soldier: The Return; Love Stinks; Blank Check; Hook

BAY FILMS
2110 Broadway
Santa Monica, CA 90404
Phone: ....(310) 829-7799
Fax: ....(310) 829-7099
Key Executives/Personnel:

Michael Bay, Director & Partner
Jennifer Klein, VP
Matthew Cohan, Creative Executive
Scott Windhauser, Story Editor
Specialties: Studio
Other Categories: TV
Credits: Armageddon; Pearl Harbor; The Rock
First Look/Development Deals: The Walt Disney Company

BEACON COMMUNICATIONS, LLC
120 Broadway, Ste. 200
Santa Monica, CA 90401
Phone: ....(310) 260-7000
Fax: ....(310) 260-7050
www.beaconpictures.com
Key Executives/Personnel:
  Armyan Bernstein, Chairman
  Marc Abraham, President
  Thomas Bliss, COO
  Paul Green, Executive VP of Business & Legal Affairs
  Suzann Ellis, Sr. VP of Development & Production
  Eric Newman, Sr. VP of Development & Production
  Nancy Rae Stone, Sr. VP of Production
  Cynthia McWethy, Sr. VP of Finance
  Merry Rose, Director of Human Resources & Administration
Specialties: Independent
Credits: Air Force One; The Commitments; End Of Days; The Hurricane

JUNE BEALLOR PRODUCTIONS
100 Universal City Plaza, Bldg. 477
Universal City, CA 91608
Phone: ....(818) 777-9000
Fax: ....(818) 866-2161
Key Executives/Personnel:
  June Beallor, Producer
  Susan M. Baker, Associate Producer
  Dawn Spiwak, Development Associate
  Vanessa Lee, Assistant to Ms. Beallor
Specialties: Studio; Independent
Other Categories: TV
Credits: Survivors of the Holocaust; The Lost Children of Berlin; The Last Days
First Look/Development Deals: DreamWorks SKG

THE BEDFORD FALLS COMPANY
409 Santa Monica Blvd., PH
Santa Monica, CA 90401
Phone: ....(310) 394-5022
Fax: ....(310) 394-5825
Key Executives/Personnel:
  Marshall Herskovitz, Executive Producer, Writer & Director
  Edward Zwick, Executive Producer, Writer & Director
  Richard Solomon, President
  Lisa Moiselle, Sr. VP of Production
  Robin Budd, Director of Development
Specialties: Studio
Other Categories: TV
Credits: Shakespeare in Love; Once and Again; Dangerous Beauty; thirtysomething
First Look/Development Deals: ABC Entertainment Television Group

BEL-AIR ENTERTAINMENT
4000 Warner Blvd., Bldg. 66, Rm. 100
Burbank, CA 91522
Phone: ....(818) 954-4040
Fax: ....(818) 954-2838
Key Executives/Personnel:
  Steve Reuther, Chairman & CEO
  Philip Elway, COO
  Allyn Stewart, President of Production
  John Schimmel, Executive VP of Production
  Keri Selig, Sr. VP of Production
  Kirk Borcherding, VP of Production Administration
  Carol Dantuono, VP of Post Production
  Ann L. Duval, VP of Business & Legal Affairs
  Heather Courtney, Creative Executive
  Leslie Goott, Story Editor
Specialties: Studio
Credits: Pay It Forward; Proof of Life; Sweet November
First Look/Development Deals: Warner Bros.

BELISARIUS PRODUCTIONS
5555 Melrose Ave., Clara Bow Bldg., Ste. 204
Los Angeles, CA 90038
Phone: ....(323) 956-8660
Fax: ....(323) 862-0250
Key Executives/Personnel:
  Donald P. Bellisario, Executive Producer, Director & Writer
  Floyd Johnson, Co-Executive Producer
  Ed Zuckerman, Co-Executive Producer
  Steven Zito, Co-Executive Producer & Writer
  Mark Saraceni, Producer
  David Bellisario, Producer
  Dana Coen, Producer
  Avery Drewe, Producer
  Mark M. Horowitz, Producer
  Julie Watson, Producer
  Paul Levine, Executive Story Editor
Specialties: Independent
Other Categories: TV
Credits: JAG
First Look/Development Deals: Paramount Pictures

GIANT STUDIOS

Animation • Visual Effects
Digital Character Development
Motion Capture • Motion Control

"The films are demanding in that we are faced with the task of creating tens of thousands of digital extras and creatures which have to share the frame believably with live actors. Giant's state-of-the-art capture system and software allows us to apply performance capture with an ease and lifelike nuance that's never been seen before. Their collaboration with us in this effort has made it all possible."

Charlie McClellan, Visual Effects Producer
Weta Digital, Lord of the Rings

Santa Monica
1313 Stewart Street, Suite 2000
Santa Monica, CA 90404
Phone: 310.315.0085

Atlanta
2160 Hills Avenue, Suite A
Atlanta, GA 30318
Phone: 404.367.1999

e-mail: info@giantstudios.com
website: www.giantstudios.com

Production Companies – Feature Film

BELLA PRODUCTIONS
4250 Beethoven St.
Los Angeles, CA 90066
Phone: ....(310) 823-3115
Fax: ....(310) 823-8366
bella1@earthlnk.net
Key Executives/Personnel:
  Cami Taylor, Executive Producer
  Bill Hayden, Executive Producer
  Herb Ritts, Director
  Mark Story, Director
  Peter Abraham, Executive Producer
  Audrey Pask, Executive Producer
Specialties: Independent; Documentaries
Other Categories: TV; Commercials; Music Video
Credits: Nike (commercial); Little Caesar's (commercial); Pac Bell (commercial)
Trade Assoc./Guilds/Unions: DGA

BELLADONNA PRODUCTIONS
2704 11th St.
Santa Monica, CA 90405
Phone: ....(310) 452-0399
Key Executives/Personnel:
  Diane Campbell, Producer & Writer
Specialties: Independent
Credits: Never Leave Nevada
Additional Info: No unsolicited calls or submissions.

BENDER-SPINK
1149 North Poinsettia Place
West Hollywood, CA 90046
Phone: ....(323) 845-1640
Fax: ....(323) 512-5347
Key Executives/Personnel:
  Chris Bender, no title
  J. C. Spink, no title
  Charlie Gogolak, no title
  Roy Lee, no title
  Jim Valdes, no title
  Shane Thueson, no title
  Nicole Harb, no title
  Bryan O'Donnell, no title
  Brian Spink, no title
Specialties: Studio
Other Categories: TV; Interactive Multimedia
Credits: American Pie; Cheaters; Like Cats and Dogs
First Look/Development Deals: Twentieth Century Fox Television, New Line Cinema, Inc.

BENJAMIN PRODUCTIONS, INC.
10451 Valley Spring Ln.
North Hollywood, CA 91602
Phone: ....(818) 752-8500
Fax: ....(818) 752-4928
Key Executives/Personnel:
  Stuart Benjamin, Producer
  Alise Benjamin, Producer
Specialties: Studio; Independent; Animation
Other Categories: TV

RICK BERMAN PRODUCTIONS
5555 Melrose Ave., Cooper Bldg., Rm. 232
Los Angeles, CA 90038
Phone: ....(323) 956-5037
Fax: ....(323) 862-1076
Key Executives/Personnel:
  Rick Berman, Executive Producer
  Dave Rossi, Supervisor, Star Trek Projects
  Joanna Fuller, Assistant to Mr. Berman
Specialties: Studio
Other Categories: TV
Credits: Star Trek (features & TV series)
First Look/Development Deals: Paramount Pictures

JAY BERNSTEIN PRODUCTIONS
P.O. Box 1148
Beverly Hills, CA 90213
Phone: ....(310) 851-2126
Fax: ....(310) 858-1607
Specialties: Studio; Independent; Direct-to-Video
Other Categories: TV
Credits: Mickey Spillane's Mike Hammer; Double Jeopardy; Diamond Trap
Trade Assoc./Guilds/Unions: AFTRA, DGA, PGA, SAG, WGAw

BETTINA PRODUCTIONS, LTD.
624 S. June St.
Los Angeles, CA 90005
Phone: ....(323) 937-2101
Fax: ....(323) 937-2103
Key Executives/Personnel:
  Walter Doniger, President
Specialties: Large Format
Other Categories: TV
Credits: Rope of Sand; Kentucky Woman; Stone Cold

BLACK & BLU ENTERTAINMENT
10202 W. Washington Blvd., Lean Bldg., Rm. 333
Culver City, CA 90232
Phone: ....(310) 244-8833
Fax: ....(310) 244-2151
Key Executives/Personnel:
  Todd Black, Producer
  Jason Blumenthal, Producer
  Brian Morewitz, Sr. VP
  Chrissy Blumenthal, VP of Development
Specialties: Studio
Other Categories: TV
Credits: A Knight's Tale
First Look/Development Deals: Sony Pictures Entertainment

BLACK ENTERTAINMENT TELEVISION (BET)
811 S. San Fernando Rd.
Burbank, CA 91502
Phone: ....(818) 566-9948
....(202) 608-2000
Fax: ....(818) 566-1655
www.bet.com
Key Executives/Personnel:
  Robert Johnson, Chairman & CEO
  Debra Lee, President & COO
  Curtis Gadson, Sr. VP of Entertainment, Programming & Network Operations
  Andre Barnwell, VP of Development
  Stephen Hill, VP of Music
  Gina Holland, VP of Production & Technical Operations
  Philip Johnson, VP of Network Operations & Business Administration
  Veronica Hatchinson, VP of Programming
Specialties: Studio
Other Categories: TV
Additional Info: 1 B.E.T. Plaza, 1900 W. Place, NE Washington, DC 20018

BLACK SHEEP ENTERTAINMENT
4063 Radford Ave., Ste. 203-A
Studio City, CA 91604
Phone: ....(818) 769-2227
Fax: ....(818) 769-2228
blacksheepent@aol.com
Key Executives/Personnel:
  Steven Feder, Writer, Director, Producer & Owner

Jeff Mazzola, Producer
Mark Groubert, Producer
Tracey Morton, Development Executive
Specialties: Studio; Independent
Other Categories: TV
Credits: The Big Gig; The Cottonwood; It Had To Be You; With A Bullet
Trade Assoc./Guilds/Unions: WGAw

BLEECKER STREET FILMS
1438 N. Gower St., Ste. 22
Los Angeles, CA 90028
Phone: ...(323) 993-7386
Fax: ...(323) 993-7387
bleeckerfilms@aol.com
Key Executives/Personnel:
Lois Bonfiglio, President
Simone Study, Director of Development
Specialties: Studio
Other Categories: TV
Credits: Boss of Bosses; Broken Trust; A Bright Shining Lie; Old Gringo
First Look/Development Deals: Turner Network Television (TNT)

CHRISTAL BLUE PRODUCTIONS
5723 Melrose Ave.
Los Angeles, CA 90038
Phone: ...(323) 466-9083
Fax: ...(323) 466-9583
www.christalblue.com
christalblucast@aol.com
Key Executives/Personnel:
Christal Blue, Producer
Specialties: Shorts
Other Categories: Commercials; Video
Credits: Smart & Final (corp. video); Airwalk (commercial); Spanish Entertainment (educational video); English Education (educational video)

BLUE BAY PRODUCTIONS
1119 Colorado Ave., Ste. 100
Santa Monica, CA 90401
Phone: ...(310) 440-9904
bluebay99@aol.com
Key Executives/Personnel:
Rodney Liber, Owner & Producer
Jennifer Hughes, VP of Development
Wendy Means, Assistant to Mr. Liber
Specialties: Studio
Credits: Big Momma's House; Wild Things; Dunston Checks In

BLUE RELIEF
301 N. Cañon Dr., Ste. 205
Beverly Hills, CA 90210
Phone: ...(310) 275-7900
Fax: ...(310) 724-5820
Key Executives/Personnel:
Diane Keaton, Producer & Director
Bill Robinson, Producer
Jennifer Glianna, Assistant to Ms. Keaton
Erin Corzine, Assistant to Mr. Robinson
Specialties: Studio; Independent
Other Categories: TV
Credits: Hanging Up; Northern Lights; Plan B
First Look/Development Deals: USA Films, Brillstein-Grey Entertainment

BLUE TULIP PRODUCTIONS
1658 10th St.
Santa Monica, CA 90404
Phone: ...(310) 752-7900
Fax: ...(310) 752-7920

Key Executives/Personnel:
Jan De Bont, Producer & Director
Lucas Foster, Producer & Partner
Jessica Borsiceky, Head of Production & Development
Erin Davis, Creative Executive
Specialties: Studio; Independent
Other Categories: TV
Credits: Librium; Minority Report; Speed 2; SLC-Punk
First Look/Development Deals: Twentieth Century Fox Pictures

BLUE WOLF PRODUCTIONS
39 Mesa St., Ste. 201
San Francisco, CA 94129
Phone: ...(415) 561-6655
Fax: ...(415) 561-6650
Key Executives/Personnel:
Robin Williams, no title
Marsha Williams, no title
Daniel Spencer, no title
Cyndi Margolis, no title
Jennifer Garces Cerchiai, no title
Specialties: Studio
Credits: Patch Adams; Mrs. Doubtfire; Jakob the Liar

BLUMBERG PRODUCTIONS & MANAGEMENT
833 Moraga Dr., Ste. 12
Los Angeles, CA 90049
Phone: ...(310) 472-6410
Fax: ...(310) 472-5705
mgblumberg@earthlink.net
Key Executives/Personnel:
Barry Blumberg, Producer
Specialties: Independent
Other Categories: TV
Credits: Sensation; West Side Waltz; Plato's Run

CAROL BODIE ENTERTAINMENT
9465 Wilshire Blvd., Ste. 420
Beverly Hills, CA 90212
Phone: ...(310) 247-8181
Fax: ...(310) 247-8555
entcbe@aol.com
Key Executives/Personnel:
Carol Bodie, CEO & Producer
Steven Dubin, COO
Jennifer Choi, Executive Assistant
Specialties: Studio; Independent; Documentaries
Other Categories: TV
Credits: Girl, Interrupted

BONA FIDE PRODUCTIONS
8899 Beverly Blvd., Ste. 804
Los Angeles, CA 90048
Phone: ...(310) 273-6782
Fax: ...(310) 273-7821
Key Executives/Personnel:
Albert Berger, Producer
Ron Yerxa, Producer
Kristin Landholt, Story Editor
Specialties: Studio; Independent
Credits: Election; King of the Hill; Cold Mountain; The Wishbones
First Look/Development Deals: New Line Cinema, Inc.

BONFIRE FILMS OF AMERICA
4655 Kingswell Ave., Ste. 213
Los Angeles, CA 90027
Phone: ...(323) 953-6815
Fax: ...(323) 953-0623
Key Executives/Personnel:
Shirley Moyers, Executive Producer
A. J. Schnack, Executive Producer

Production Companies – Feature Film

John McGinnis, Director's Rep
Specialties: Shorts
Other Categories: TV; Commercials; Music Video

BOXING CAT PRODUCTIONS
11500 Hart St.
North Hollywood, CA 91605
Phone: ....(818) 765-4870
Fax: ....(818) 765-4975
Key Executives/Personnel:
 Tim Allen, Producer & Actor
 Brian Reilly, Producer
 Matt Carroll, Director of Development
Specialties: Studio
Credits: The Santa Clause; Jungle to Jungle
First Look/Development Deals: Touchstone Pictures

BOYINGTON STUDIOS, INC.
17 Galleon St.
Marina Del Rey, CA 90292
Phone: ....(310) 822-2360
Fax: ....(310) 822-0430
www.boyingtonfilms.com
pboy@gte.net
Key Executives/Personnel:
 Paul Boyington, Producer, Director & Effects Supervisor
 Tibor Takacs, Director
 Foster Corder, Director
 Anthony Mabin, Director & Effects Supervisor
 Robert Scopinich, Director & Effects Supervisor
Specialties: Independent
Other Categories: Commercials, Music Videos
Credits: Sweet Talk; Fox Sports (Promo); Megadeath - Hangar 18; Keith Richards - Take It So Hard

BOZ PRODUCTIONS
1632 N. Sierra Bonita Ave.
Los Angeles, CA 90046
Phone: ....(323) 876-3232
Fax: ....(323) 876-3231
boz51@aol.com
Key Executives/Personnel:
 Bo Zenga, Producer & Writer
 Jeff Monarch, Director of Development
Specialties: Studio; Independent
Other Categories: TV
Credits: Scary Movie; Everything's Jake

BRAGA PRODUCTIONS
5555 Melrose Ave, Hart Bldg., Ste. 205
Hollywood, CA 90038
Phone: ....(323) 956-5799
Fax: ....(323) 862-8503
Key Executives/Personnel:
 Brannon Braga, President
 Michael O'Halloran, VP of Production & Development
 Robert Gillan, Story & Script Reader
Specialties: Studio
Other Categories: TV
Credits: Star Trek (TV series); Star Trek: Voyager
First Look/Development Deals: Paramount Pictures

BRAYTON/CARLUCCI PRODUCTIONS
1640 S. Sepulveda Blvd., 4th Fl.
Los Angeles, CA 90025
Phone: ....(310) 478-1700
Fax: ....(310) 478-2202
Key Executives/Personnel:
 Anne Carlucci, Executive Producer
 Marian Brayton, Executive Producer
 Larry Grimaldi, Director of Development & Co-Producer
Specialties: Studio; Independent
Other Categories: TV
Credits: Out-of-Sync; Sex and Mrs. X; The Soul Collector; Dangerous Evidence
First Look/Development Deals: Hearst Entertainment Productions

PAULETTE BREEN PRODUCTIONS
6920 Texhoma Avenue, Ste. 101
Van Nuys, CA 91406
Phone: ....(818) 342-0228
Fax: ....(818) 342-0228
breenpg@aol.com
Key Executives/Personnel:
 Paulette Breen, President & Producer
 Diane Biederbeck, VP of Creative Affairs
 Kathy Page, Creative Assistant
Specialties: Independent
Other Categories: TV
Credits: Haven; Down Will Come Baby; Separated by Murder; Stranger Within

THE BREGMAN ENTERTAINMENT COMPANY
1950 Sawtelle Blvd., Ste. 360
Los Angeles, CA 90025
Phone: ....(213) 833-6207
Fax: ....(323) 876-1957
budboy@worldnet.att.net
Key Executives/Personnel:
 Buddy Bregman, President
 Marie DePuthod, Writer, Director & Producer
Specialties: Studio; Independent
Other Categories: TV; Music Video
Credits: Ain't Misbehavin'; The American Civil War; Olivia Newton John; Nancy Wilson Show
First Look/Development Deals: Gen X Entertainment, Int'l. Filmed Entertainment
Trade Assoc./Guilds/Unions: AFM, DGA, PGA, WGAw

BRILLSTEIN-GREY ENTERTAINMENT
9150 Wilshire Blvd., Ste. 350
Beverly Hills, CA 90212
Phone: ....(310) 275-6135
Fax: ....(310) 275-6180
Key Executives/Personnel:
 Bernie Brillstein, Consultant
 Brad Grey, Chairman & CEO
 Kevin Reilly, President of BGTV
 Steve Blume, CFO
 Matthew Baer, Head of Motion Picture Division
 Sandy Wernick, Sr. Executive VP
 Jonathan Liebman, Executive VP
 Marc Gurvitz, Executive VP of Management
 Peter Travgott, Executive VP of BGTV
 Susie Fitzgerald, Sr. VP of TV
 Tony Carey, VP of TV Production
 Laura Hopper, VP of Motion Pictures
 Denise Stewart, VP of Motion Pictures
Specialties: Studio; Independent
Other Categories: TV
Credits: The Sopranos; Scary Movie; Just Shoot Me
First Look/Development Deals: Miramax Films

BROOKSFILMS, LTD.
c/o Culver Studios, 9336 W. Washington Blvd.
Culver City, CA 90232
Phone: ....(310) 202-3292

Production Companies – Feature Film

Fax: ....(310) 202-3225
Key Executives/Personnel:
   Mel Brooks, President
   Leah Zappy, VP of Production Services
   Jennifer Yale, Development
Specialties: Studio
Credits: The Fly I & II; Frances; Elephant Man; My Favorite Year

BROOKWELL MCNAMARA ENTERTAINMENT
5433 Beethoven St.
Los Angeles, CA 90066
Phone: ....(310) 306-2151
Fax: ....(310) 823-7026
Key Executives/Personnel:
   David Brookwell, Executive Producer
   Sean McNamara, Executive Producer
Specialties: Studio; Independent
Other Categories: TV
Credits: Even Stevens; Race to Space; The Trial Of Old Drum; Wild Grizzly

JERRY BRUCKHEIMER FILMS
1631 10th St.
Santa Monica, CA 90404
Phone: ....(310) 664-6260
Key Executives/Personnel:
   Jerry Bruckheimer, Producer
   Mike Stenson, President
   Chad Oman, President of Production
   Jonathan Littman, Executive VP of TV
   Kristie Anne Groelinger, Director of Production
Specialties: Studio
Other Categories: TV
Credits: Gone in 60 Seconds; Remember the Titans; Armageddon; Coyote Ugly
First Look/Development Deals: Walt Disney Pictures/Touchstone Pictures

THE BUBBLE FACTORY
8840 Wilshire Blvd., 3rd Fl.
Beverly Hills, CA 90211
Phone: ....(310) 358-3000
Fax: ....(310) 358-3299
Key Executives/Personnel:
   Sid Sheinberg, Partner
   Bill Sheinberg, Partner
   Jon Sheinberg, Partner
   Gerald S. Barton, Consultant of Business Affairs
   Gerald Bocaccio, Sr. VP of Creative Affairs
   Tom Prince, Sr. VP of Production
   Kevin D. Forester, VP of Finance & Operations
   Gwen Osborne, Director of Development
   Cory M. Lidschin, Manager of Media & Consumer Products
   Kim Gross, Office Manager
Specialties: Studio; Independent; Direct-to-Video
Credits: A Simple Wish; McHale's Navy; That Old Feeling; Playing Mona Lisa

THE BUENA VISTA MOTION PICTURES GROUP
500 South Buena Vista St.
Burbank, CA 91521
Phone: ....(818) 560-1000
www.buenavista.com
Key Executives/Personnel:
   Richard Cook, Chairman
   Dean Hallett, President & CFO, Walt Disney Studios
   Nina Jacobson, President
   Oren Aviv, President of Marketing
   Bruce Hendricks, President of Physical Production
   Kathy Nelson, President of Theatrical Music
   Mark Zoradi, President of Buena Vista Int'l.
   Michael Mendenhall, President of Synergy
   Jason Reed, Sr. VP
   Phil Barlow, Executive VP
   Bernadine Brandis, Executive VP of Legal Affairs
   Steve Bardwil, Sr. VP of Legal Affairs
   Scott Holtzman, Sr. VP of Music Business & Legal Affairs
   Ron Lynch, Sr. VP of Features Production
   Stephanie Mangano, Sr. VP of Casting Administration
   Jeffrey Miller, Sr. VP of Character Voices & Dubbing
   Phillip Muhl, Sr. VP of Business Affairs
   Art Repola, Sr. VP of Visual Effects & Productions
   Marcia Ross, Sr. VP of Casting
   Fred Tio, Sr. VP of Creative Services & Animation
   Karen Glass, VP
   Jerry Ketcham, VP of Features Production
   Donna Morong, VP of Casting
   Jason Reed, VP of Production
   Jeff Clifford, VP of Production
   Gail Goldberg, Director of Features Casting
Specialties: Studio

BUNGALOW 78 PRODUCTIONS
5555 Melrose Ave., Lasky Bldg., Ste. 200
Los Angeles, CA 90038
Phone: ....(323) 956-4440
Fax: ....(323) 862-2090
Key Executives/Personnel:
   Barry Kemp, Executive Producer & Writer
   Devorah Moos-Hankin, President of Feature Production
   Bess Walkes, Director of Development
Specialties: Studio
Other Categories: TV
Credits: Catch Me If You Can; Patch Adams; Romy & Michelle's High Reunion
First Look/Development Deals: Paramount Pictures

BUSHWOOD PICTURES
320 S. Irving Blvd.
Los Angeles, CA 90020
Phone: ....(323) 936-1659
Fax: ....(323) 936-1977
Key Executives/Personnel:
   Sandy Isaac, Producer & Writer
   Margaret French Isaac, Producer
Specialties: Studio
Other Categories: TV
Credits: Jack and Jill; Never Been Kissed; Stepmom; To Die For

BUTCHERS RUN FILMS
8978 Norma Pl.
West Hollywood, CA 90069
Phone: ....(310) 246-4630
Fax: ....(310) 246-1033
Key Executives/Personnel:
   Robert Duvall, Producer & Director
   Rob Carliner, Producer & Manager
   Adam Prince, Director of Development
Specialties: Studio; Independent
Credits: The Apostle; A Shot at Glory; A Family Thing; The Man Who Captured Eichmann

C'EST TOUT PRODUCTIONS
10792 Rochester Ave.
Los Angeles, CA 90024
Phone: ....(310) 475-5615
zensat@aol.com
Key Executives/Personnel:

Production Companies – Feature Film

Nancy Kissock, Producer
Specialties: Independent; Shorts; Trailers
Other Categories: Commercials
Credits: Catillion 65 (feature); Shelter (feature); Mission Impossible (trailer); Frasier (promo)

CAIRO/SIMPSON ENTERTAINMENT, INC.
9255 Sunset Blvd., Ste. 507
West Hollywood, CA 90069
Phone: ....(310) 888-1262
Fax: ....(310) 887-1813
judycairo@aol.com
Key Executives/Personnel:
Judy Cairo, Executive Producer
Michael Simpson, Producer, Director & Writer
Specialties: Studio; Independent
Other Categories: TV; Interactive Multimedia
Credits: Her Deadly Rival; Twisted Desire; Perfect Body; What We Did That Night

CALAR
335 N. Maple Dr., Ste. 245
Beverly Hills, CA 90210
Phone: ....(310) 271-2202
Fax: ....(310) 271-8990
Key Executives/Personnel:
Caylyn E. Morris, Executive Producer
Alex Muñoz, Director
Specialties: Independent
Other Categories: TV; Commercials; Video

CALICO WORLD ENTERTAINMENT
10200 Riverside Dr., Ste. 203
North Hollywood, CA 91602
Phone: ....(818) 755-3800
Fax: ....(818) 755-4643
www.calicoworld.com
tom@calicoworld.com
Key Executives/Personnel:
Tom Burton, Executive Director & Producer
Claudia Zeitlin Burton, Managing Director
Ken Leonard, Art Director
Joel Fajnor, Producer & Director
Mary Cim, Producer & Director
Jim Livolsi, Executive Producer & Marketing
Pedram Shohadai, Digital Animator
Specialties: Animation
Other Categories: TV; Commercials; Interactive Multimedia
Credits: Denver, The Lost Dinosaur; Bad Baby; Kid's Songs of Woody Guthrie; Ghosts Legends of the Queen Mary

CALM DOWN PRODUCTIONS, INC.
1360 N. Crescent Heights Blvd., Ste. 3B
Los Angeles, CA 90046
Phone: ....(323) 650-4027
Fax: ....(323) 654-1104
Key Executives/Personnel:
Kevin Pollak, CEO
Lucy Webb, President & Producer
Lana Estrada, Executive Assistant
Amy Barnes, Creative Development
Specialties: Studio
Other Categories: TV
Credits: Work With Me; Grant & Lee; The Underworld; Stop With The Kicking

CAMERA MARC
4605 Lankershim Blvd., Ste. 201
North Hollywood, CA 91602
Phone: ....(818) 753-9901
Fax: ....(818) 753-9921
Key Executives/Personnel:
Marc Frydman, CEO & Producer
Marc Rocco, Producer & Director
Kent Walters, Assistant to Mr. Frydman
Specialties: Independent

CANNELL STUDIOS
7083 Hollywood Blvd., Ste. 600
Hollywood, CA 90028
Phone: ....(323) 465-5800
Fax: ....(323) 856-7390
www.cannell.com
Key Executives/Personnel:
Stephen J. Cannell, CEO
Wayne S. Williams, VP of Development
Specialties: Studio; Independent
Other Categories: TV
Credits: Dawg; Terror.net; Director's Cut

THE CANTON COMPANY
4000 Warner Blvd., Bldg. 81, Ste. 200
Burbank, CA 91522
Phone: ....(818) 954-2130
Fax: ....(818) 954-2967
Key Executives/Personnel:
Mark Canton, CEO & President
Chris Carter, no title
Anna DeRoy, no title
Nathan Kahane, no title
Barbara Kalish, no title
Ben Hurivtz, no title
Scott Coleman, no title
Nicole Fitzpatrick, no title
Michael Gordon, no title
Jim Miller, no title
Sabrina Steele, no title
Specialties: Independent
Other Categories: TV
Credits: Get Carter; Red Planet; Angel Eyes; Jack & Jill

CANVAS HOUSE FILMS
3671 Bear St., Ste. E
Santa Ana, CA 92704
Phone: ....(714) 850-1964
....(323) 459-0609
teteemley@aol.com
Key Executives/Personnel:
Mitch Teemley, Writer & Producer
Elizabeth Gray, Associate Producer
Specialties: Studio; Independent; Direct-to-Video; Shorts
Other Categories: TV; Commercials; Music Video
Credits: Out Of Time (TV series); Lennar Homes (commercial); The Limited (feature); Kragira (feature)

CAPELLA FILMS, INC.
9242 Beverly Blvd., Ste. 280
Beverly Hills, CA 90210
Phone: ....(310) 247-4700
Fax: ....(310) 247-4701
Key Executives/Personnel:
David Korda, President
Jean-Louis Rubin, President, Capella Int'l.
Craig Arrington, CFO
Alessandra McAliley, Executive VP
Specialties: Studio
Credits: Austin Powers; Shattered; Drop Dead Gorgeous

CAPITAL ARTS ENTERTAINMENT
Phone: ....(310) 581-3020
Fax: ....(310) 581-3023

Production Companies – Feature Film

www.capitalarts.com
capartsent@aol.com
Key Executives/Personnel:
   Mike Elliott, Co-President
   Rob Kerchner, Co-President
Specialties: Independent; Direct-to-Video
Other Categories: TV
Credits: Skipped Parts; After The Storm; Northface; Rocket's Red Glare
First Look/Development Deals: Fox Family Channel, Trimark Pictures, Saban Entertainment

CAPO PRODUCTIONS, INC.
Phone: ....(310) 477-4234
capoprod@aol.com
Key Executives/Personnel:
   Deborah Capogresso, President
Specialties: Independent
Other Categories: TV
Credits: Just a Little Harmless Sex; The Hot Spot; Other Voices

CAPPA PRODUCTIONS
445 Park Ave., 7th Fl.
New York, NY 10022
Phone: ....(212) 906-8800
Fax: ....(212) 906-8891
Key Executives/Personnel:
   Martin Scorsese, Director
Specialties: Studio; Independent; Documentaries
Credits: Kundun; Casino; Goodfellows

MARK CARLINER PRODUCTIONS
4121 1/2 Radford Ave
Studio City, CA 91604
Phone: ....(818) 763-4783
mcarliner@aol.com
Key Executives/Personnel:
   Mark Carliner, Producer
   B. J. Heath, Assistant to Mr. Carliner
Specialties: Independent
Other Categories: TV
Credits: Rose Red; Storm of the Century; The Shining (miniseries); Stalin

CARLYLE PRODUCTIONS & MANAGEMENT
2050 Laurel Canyon Rd.
Los Angeles, CA 90046
Phone: ....(323) 848-4960
Fax: ....(323) 650-8249
carlyle@earthlink.net
Key Executives/Personnel:
   Phyllis Carlyle, Producer & Manager
   Devin Klein, Manager
   Joseph O'Connor, Creative Executive
Specialties: Independent
Other Categories: TV
Credits: Seven; The Accidental Tourist; Mean Streak

CARRIE PRODUCTIONS
4444 Riverside Dr., Ste. 110
Burbank, CA 91505
Phone: ....(818) 567-3292
Fax: ....(818) 567-3296
Key Executives/Personnel:
   Danny Glover, Executive Producer
   Carolyn McDonald, Executive Producer
   Judith Alonso, Creative Executive
Specialties: Independent
Other Categories: TV
Credits: Freedom Song; America's Dream; Buffalo Soldiers

CASTLE ROCK ENTERTAINMENT
335 N. Maple Dr., Ste. 135
Beverly Hills, CA 90210
Phone: ....(310) 285-2300
Fax: ....(310) 285-2345
Key Executives/Personnel:
   Rob Reiner, Producer & Director
   Andrew Scheinman, Producer & Director
   Martin Shafer, President, Castle Rock Pictures
   Glenn Padnick, President, Castle Rock TV
   Greg Paul, COO
   Liz Glotzer, President of Production, Features
   Jeffrey Stott, Executive VP of Production Management
   Brady Thomas, Creative Executive
   Jess Wittenberg, Executive VP
Specialties: Studio
Other Categories: TV
Credits: The Green Mile; The Shawshank Redemption; A Few Good Men; Seinfeld
First Look/Development Deals: Warner Bros.

CENTROPOLIS ENTERTAINMENT
10202 W. Washington Blvd.
Culver City, CA 90232
Phone: ....(310) 244-4300
Fax: ....(310) 244-4360
www.centropolis.com
Key Executives/Personnel:
   Roland Emmerich, Partner
   Dean Devlin, Partner
   Ute Emmerich, Partner
   William Fay, President
   Peter Winther, Sr. VP
   Marc Roskin, VP of Development
   Philippe Maigret, Head of Business Development
Specialties: Studio
Credits: The Patriot; Thirteenth Floor; Godzilla; Independence Day
First Look/Development Deals: Sony Pictures Entertainment

CHANCELLOR ENTERTAINMENT
10600 Holman Ave., Ste. 1
Los Angeles, CA 90024
Phone: ....(310) 474-4521
Fax: ....(310) 470-9273
chaent@aol.com
Key Executives/Personnel:
   Bob Marcucci, President & CEO
Specialties: Independent
Other Categories: TV
Credits: The Razors Edge; Letter to Three Wives; Stitches
Trade Assoc./Guilds/Unions: AMPAS, ASCAP, BMI, NARAS, PGA, WGAw

CHAPTER 10 PRODUCTIONS
1746 N. Orange Dr., Ste. 504
Los Angeles, CA 90028
Phone: ....(323) 460-6665
Fax: ....(323) 460-6665
Key Executives/Personnel:
   Bryan Cuprill, Owner & Producer
   Paige Cline, Owner & Producer
Specialties: Independent
Credits: The Eleventh Hour; Bombastic; The Saga of Snappy Goldfarb

CHARTOFF PRODUCTIONS
1250 Sixth St., Ste. 101
Santa Monica, CA 90401
Phone: ....(310) 319-1960
Fax: ....(310) 319-3469
Key Executives/Personnel:

Production Companies – Feature Film

    Robert Chartoff, President & CEO
    Lynn Hendee, Executive VP
    Lori Imbler Vernon, Production Associate
Specialties: Studio; Independent
Credits: Rocky; The Right Stuff; Raging Bull

STANLEY CHASE PRODUCTIONS, INC.
1937 S. Beverly Glen Blvd.
Los Angeles, CA 90025
Phone: ....(310) 475-4236
Fax: ....(310) 474-5720
chaseprods@aol.com
Key Executives/Personnel:
    Stanley Chase, President
    Dorothy Rice, VP
Specialties: Studio; Independent
Credits: Mack The Knife; The Guardian; American Xmas Carol; Colossus: The Forbin Project
Trade Assoc./Guilds/Unions: AMPAS

THE CHELMAR GROUP
PMB# 345, 411 E. Huntington Dr., Bldg. 107
Arcadia, CA 91006
Phone: ....(626) 358-4001
chelmar@earthlink.net
Key Executives/Personnel:
    Richard James, Executive Producer
    Michelle Palmer, Producer
Specialties: Documentaries; Trailers
Other Categories: Commercials; Video; Music Video
Credits: Renewable Power (documentary); The View From Malabar (documentary); Salvation Army (commercial); Coca-Cola (commercial)

CHERRY ALLEY PRODUCTIONS
1250 Sixth St., Ste. 200
Santa Monica, CA 90401
Phone: ....(310) 458-8886
Key Executives/Personnel:
    Goldie Hawn, CEO
    Deloris Horn, Assistant
    Patty Davis, Assistant
Specialties: Studio; Independent
Other Categories: TV
Credits: The Out of Towners; Hope

CHESLER/PERLMUTTER PRODUCTIONS
1045 Gayley Ave., Ste. 200
Los Angeles, CA 90024
Phone: ....(310) 443-9650
Fax: ....(310) 443-9524
chesper1@aol.com
Key Executives/Personnel:
    Lewis B. Chesler, CEO
    David Perlmutter, CEO (Toronto)
    Kevin Commins, VP of Development
    Rob Vaughn, VP of Production
    Hank McCann, VP of Talent
    Michael Cote, Director of Finance (Toronto)
    Gaille LeDrew, Development Executive (Toronto)
    Roberta Harron, Administrative Executive (Toronto)
    Beth Blum, Office Coordinator
    Edie Monroe, Accounting (Toronto)
    Rob Carpio, Development Assistant
    Steve Stromberg, Assistant
Specialties: Independent; Direct-to-Video
Other Categories: TV
Credits: Hostile Intent; The Hidden Room; The Hitchhiker; Undertow
First Look/Development Deals: HBO, Canal +

Additional Info: 129 Yorkville Ave, Ste. 200, Toronto, ON M5R IC4 Canada, (416) 927-0016 phone, (416) 960-8447 fax

CHICAGOFILMS
250 W. 57th St., Ste. 2217
New York, NY 10107
Phone: ....(212) 307-0050
Fax: ....(212) 307-9066
Key Executives/Personnel:
    Bob Balaban, Producer & Director
    Allison Shigo, Director of Development
Specialties: Studio; Independent
Other Categories: TV

CHIODO BROS. PRODUCTIONS, INC.
110 W. Providencia Ave.
Burbank, CA 91502
Phone: ....(818) 842-5656
Fax: ....(818) 848-0891
www.chiodobros.com
klowns@chiodobros.com
Key Executives/Personnel:
    Edward Chiodo, Producer & Development
    Stephen Chiodo, Director & Development
    Charles Chiodo, Design & Development
    Paul Kemp, COO & Development
Specialties: Studio; Independent; Direct-to-Video; Shorts
Other Categories: TV; Commercials
Credits: Killer Klowns from Outer Space (feature); Amazing Live Sea Monkeys (TV series); The Crayon Box (TV series); Skwid Zone (TV pilot)

CINE EXCEL ENTERTAINMENT
Phone: ....(818) 848-4478
Fax: ....(818) 848-1590
www.cineexcel.com
david@cineexcel.com
Key Executives/Personnel:
    David Huey, Producer
Specialties: Independent; Direct-to-Video; Trailers

CINERGI PICTURES
2308 Broadway
Santa Monica, CA 90404
Phone: ....(310) 315-6000
Fax: ....(310) 828-0443
Key Executives/Personnel:
    Andrew Vajna, Chairman & CEO
    Samuel Falconello, Sr. VP of Finance
    Beverly Cusack, Controller
Specialties: Studio
Credits: Basic Instinct 2; Evita; Shadow Conspiracy; Die Hard: With a Vengeance

CINEVILLE, INC.
225 Santa Monica Blvd., 7th Fl.
Santa Monica, CA 90401
Phone: ....(310) 394-4699
Fax: ....(310) 394-3052
www.cineville.com
cineville@aol.com
Key Executives/Personnel:
    Bob Joyce, VP of Production
    Mavrizio Bizzarri, VP of Marketing & Sales, Cineville.com
    Annabelle Frankl, Director of Development
    Gina Carollo, Controller
    Carl-Jan Colpaert, Administration
    Christoph Henkel, Administration
Specialties: Independent
Other Categories: Interactive Multimedia
Credits: Swimming With Sharks; Hurlyburly; Gas Food Lodging; The Whole Wide World

Production Companies – Feature Film

CIRCLE ASSOCIATES LTD.
P.O. Box 5730
Santa Monica, CA 90409
Phone: ...(310) 823-4024
Fax: ...(310) 574-1950
Key Executives/Personnel:
 Mike Kaplan, President
Specialties: Independent; Documentaries
Other Categories: TV
Credits: Luck Trust & Ketchup; The Whales of August

COHEN PICTURES
7966 Beverly Blvd.
Los Angeles, CA 90048
Phone: ...(323) 951-4250
Fax: ...(323) 655-1594
bobby_cohen@yahoo.com
Key Executives/Personnel:
 Bobby Cohen, Executive Producer
 Wittney Horton, Development
Specialties: Studio
Credits: Bounce; The Cider House Rules; Down to You; Rounders
First Look/Development Deals: Miramax Films

COLLABORATIVE ARTISTS
445 S. Beverly Dr., Ste. 100
Beverly Hills, CA 90212
Phone: ...(310) 274-4800
Fax: ...(310) 274-4803
www.collaborativeartisits.com
labird@mindspring.com
Key Executives/Personnel:
 Steve Leon, no title
 Leslie A. Bird, no title
Specialties: Studio; Independent
Other Categories: TV

COLOMBY/KEATON PRODUCTIONS
2110 Main St., Ste. 302
Santa Monica, CA 90405
Phone: ...(310) 399-8881
Fax: ...(310) 392-1323
www.colombykeaton.com
Key Executives/Personnel:
 Harry Colomby, Partner
 Michael Keaton, Partner
 Jennifer Keohane, Producer
 Helen Baines, Story Editor
 Ford Delman, Creative Associate
Specialties: Studio; Independent; Documentaries; Animation
Other Categories: TV
Credits: Body Shots

COLUMBIA PICTURES/COLUMBIA TRISTAR MOTION PICTURE GROUP
10202 W. Washington Blvd.
Culver City, CA 90232
Phone: ...(310) 244-4000
Fax: ...(310) 244-2626
www.spe.sony.com
Key Executives/Personnel:
 Amy Pascal, Chairman
 Gareth Wigan, Vice Chairman, CTMPG
 Kenneth Lemberger, President, CTMPG
 Peter Schlessel, President of Production
 Robert Levin, President, SPE Worldwide Marketing
 Gary Martin, President of Columbia Production Administration
 Josh Goldstine, Sr. Executive VP of Marketing
 Amy Baer, Executive VP of Production
 Doug Belgrad, Executive VP of Production
 Michael Costigan, Executive VP of Production
 Matt Tolmach, Executive VP of Production
 Blaise Noto, Executive VP of Worldwide Publicity
 Robert Geary, Executive VP of Business Affairs & Operations
 Paul Smith, Executive VP, CTMPG
 James Honore, Executive VP of Post Production
 Lia Vollack, Executive VP of Music Creative Affairs
 Andrea Giannetti, Sr. VP of Production
 Lori Goldklang-Furie, Sr. VP of Production
 Carrie Richman, Sr. VP of Production
 Michelle Abbrecht, Sr. VP of Publicity
 Christine Birch, Sr. VP of North American Theatrical Marketing
 Andre Caraco, Sr. VP of Publicity
 Cherie Crane, Sr. VP of Media
 Neil Dick, Sr. VP of Creative Advertising
 Joseph Foley, Sr. VP of Worldwide Marketing Services
 Jamie Geller Hawtof, Sr. VP of Publicity
 Dennis P. Higgins, Sr. VP of Publicity
 George Leon, Sr. VP of Promotions
 Susan Levin, Sr. VP of Publicity
 Linda Middleton, Sr. VP of Market Research
 Dana Precious, Sr. VP of Creative Advertising
 Cynthia Swartz, Sr. VP of Publicity
 Susan Tick, Sr. VP of Media Relations
 Bill Ewing, Sr. VP of Production Administration
 Jon Gibson, Sr. VP of Business Affairs
 Alan Krieger, Sr. VP of Business Affairs
 John Levy, Sr. VP of Business Affairs
 Ray Zimmerman, Sr. VP of Production Administration
 Dwight Caines, VP of Internet Marketing Strategy, CPM
 Kim Carey, VP of Special Events
 Diana Hawkins, VP of Creative Affairs (London)
 Debbie Kreger, VP of Market Research
 Stephanie Napoli, VP of Media, CPM
 Peter Corral, VP of Production Administration
 Mark Horowitz, VP of Business Affairs Administration
 Donald Kennedy, VP of Music Licensing
 Larry Kohorn, VP of Music Business Affairs
 Pilar McCurry, VP of Music Creative Affairs
 Kathy McDermott, VP of Production Administration
 Karen Moy, VP of Story Department
 Russ Paris, VP of Post Production
 Raul Perez, VP of Music Administration
 Thomas Stack, VP of Business Affairs Contract Administration
 Mark Wyman, VP of Business Affairs
 Rita Zak, VP of Music Publishing
Specialties: Studio

CONNECTION III ENTERTAINMENT CORP.
8489 W. 3rd St.
Los Angeles, CA 90048
Phone: ...(323) 653-3400
www.connection3.com
Key Executives/Personnel:
 Cleveland O'Neal, Producer
Specialties: Independent
Other Categories: TV; Interactive Multimedia
Credits: What About Your Friends; The Garage Club; Phat Beach
Trade Assoc./Guilds/Unions: PGA

CONSTANTIN FILM
9200 Sunset Blvd., Ste. 730
Los Angeles, CA 90069
Phone: ...(310) 247-0300
Fax: ...(310) 247-0305
Key Executives/Personnel:
 Bernd Eichinger, no title
 Lisa Kregness, no title
 Cynthia Pruett, no title
 Mitch Horwits, no title
 Marsha Metz, no title

Production Companies – Feature Film

Robert Kulzer, no title
Elizabeth Wang Lee, no title
Specialties: Independent
Credits: The Calling; House of the Spirits; Smilla's Sense of Snow

CONUNDRUM ENTERTAINMENT
325 Wilshire Blvd., Ste. 201
Santa Monica, CA 90401
Phone: (310) 319-2800
Fax: (310) 319-2808
Key Executives/Personnel:
Bobby Farrelly, no title
Peter Farrelly, no title
Bradley Thomas, no title
Mark Charpentier, no title
Clemens Frenek, no title
Sarah Lopez, no title
Matt Smith, no title
Kris Meyer, no title
Specialties: Studio; Animation
Credits: Me, Myself & Irene; There's Something About Mary; Kingpin; Dumb & Dumber
First Look/Development Deals: Twentieth Century Fox Pictures

CORNICE ENTERTAINMENT
190 N. Cañon Dr., PH
Beverly Hills, CA 90210
Phone: (310) 777-0200
Fax: (310) 777-0357
Key Executives/Personnel:
Michael Marcus, no title
Carroll Kemp, no title
Marcie Hartley, no title
Specialties: Studio; Independent
Other Categories: TV
First Look/Development Deals: The Buena Vista Motion Pictures Group

THE CORT/MADDEN COMPANY
5555 Melrose Ave., Marx Bros. Bldg., Ste. 107
Hollywood, CA 90038
Phone: (323) 956-5884
Fax: (323) 862-1408
Key Executives/Personnel:
Robert Cort, Producer
Scarlett Lacey, VP
Eric Hertzel, Creative Executive
Specialties: Studio
Other Categories: TV
Credits: Save The Last Dance; Runaway Bride; Out of Towners; Harlen County War
First Look/Development Deals: Paramount Pictures

COSGROVE-MEURER PRODUCTIONS
4303 W. Verdugo Ave.
Burbank, CA 91505
Phone: (818) 843-5600
Fax: (818) 843-8585
Key Executives/Personnel:
Terry Meurer, Partner & President
John Cosgrove, Partner & CEO
Stuart Schwartz, VP of Reality Development
Rebecca Whittington, VP of Development
Joe Levi, Director of Feature Development
Specialties: Independent
Other Categories: TV
Credits: Yesterday's Children; Unsolved Mysteries; The Inheritance

CINDY COWAN ENTERTAINMENT, INC.
8265 Sunset Blvd., Ste. 205
Los Angeles, CA 90046
Phone: (323) 822-1082
Fax: (323) 822-1086
jjaggars@cowanent.com
Key Executives/Personnel:
Cindy Cowan, President & Producer
Carole McGorrian, Head of Production
Josh R. Jaggars, Director of Development
Specialties: Studio; Independent
Other Categories: TV
Credits: Very Bad Things; Savior; Little City; Dr. T and the Women

CPC ENTERTAINMENT
840 N. Larrabee St., Ste. 2322
West Hollywood, CA 90069
Phone: (310) 652-8194
Fax: (310) 652-4998
www.cpcentertainment.com
chane@compuserve.com
Key Executives/Personnel:
Peggy Chane, President, Producer & Director
Clayton Herzog, Development Associate
Louis Farber, Development Associate
Sylvia De La Riviere, Development Associate
Specialties: Independent
Other Categories: TV
Credits: Eyes of a Stranger; River to Greyrock; Under the Mummy's Spell; Zero Hour
Trade Assoc./Guilds/Unions: ATAS, IFP, PGA, WIF

CRANE WEXELBLATT ENTERTAINMENT
6061 Galahad Dr.
Malibu, CA 90265
Phone: (310) 457-4821
Fax: (310) 457-3888
twomoguls@aol.com
Key Executives/Personnel:
Peter Crane, Producer & Director
Linda Curran Wexelblatt, Producer
Specialties: Independent
Other Categories: TV
Credits: Lily Dale; The Passion of Ayn Rand
Trade Assoc./Guilds/Unions: DGA

WES CRAVEN FILMS
11846 Ventura Blvd., Ste. 208
Studio City, CA 91604
Phone: (818) 752-0197
Fax: (818) 752-1789
Key Executives/Personnel:
Wes Craven, Director & Producer
Marianne Maddalena, President & Producer
Rene Garcia, President of Production
Alix Taylor, VP of Development
Specialties: Studio
Other Categories: TV
Credits: Scream 1, 2 & 3; Music of the Heart
First Look/Development Deals: Miramax Films

CREATIVE IMPULSE ENTERTAINMENT
4524 Tujunga Ave., Ste. 15
Studio City, CA 91602
Phone: (818) 623-8260
Key Executives/Personnel:
Rockne S. O'Bannon, Executive Producer, Writer & Director
Robin Johanssen, VP of Development
Specialties: Studio
Other Categories: TV
Credits: Farscape; Seaquest

Production Companies – Feature Film

CRUSADER ENTERTAINMENT
132B Laskey Dr.
Beverly Hills, CA 90212
Phone: (310) 248-6360
Fax: (310) 248-6370
Key Executives/Personnel:
   Howard Baldwin, President
   Stewart Benjamin, Executive VP
   Karen Baldwin, Executive VP of Creative Affairs
   Jennifer Smith, VP of Television
Specialties: Studio
Other Categories: TV
Credits: Mystery Alaska; Gidion; La Bamba; Everybody's All American

CTONIC FLIKZ
5540 Hollywood Blvd., 2nd Fl.
Los Angeles, CA 90028
Phone: (323) 957-7824
Fax: (323) 957-8531
ctonic@aol.com
Key Executives/Personnel:
   Catalaine Knell, Executive Producer
Specialties: Studio; Independent; Animation
Other Categories: Interactive Multimedia

DANAMATION STUDIOS
1077 Montana Ave., Ste. 434
Santa Monica, CA 90403
Phone: (310) 433-4836
Fax: (310) 317-0718
danamation@netzero.net
Specialties: Studio; Independent; Animation
Trade Assoc./Guilds/Unions: ASIFA, SAG

DANJAQ, INC.
2401 Colorado Ave., Ste. 330
Santa Monica, CA 90404
Phone: (310) 449-3185
Fax: (310) 449-3189
Key Executives/Personnel:
   Dana Broccoli, Co-Chairman
   Michael Wilson, President & CEO
   David Pope, COO
   Barbara Broccoli, VP of Production & Development
Specialties: Studio
Credits: James Bond films
First Look/Development Deals: MGM, Inc.

DARK HORSE ENTERTAINMENT
100 Universal City Plaza, John Ford Bldg., Ste. 3G
Universal City, CA 91608
Phone: (818) 777-5830
Fax: (818) 866-5939
www.dhorse.com
Key Executives/Personnel:
   Mike Richardson, President & Producer
   Steven Gilder, VP of Production
   Kevin Hageman, Creative Executive
Specialties: Studio; Animation
Other Categories: TV
Credits: The Mask; Time Cop; Mystery Men; Big Guy & Rusty
First Look/Development Deals: Universal Pictures

DAVIS CLASSICS
c/o Davis Entertainment, 2121 Ave. of the Stars, Ste. 2900
Los Angeles, CA 90067
Phone: (310) 551-2266
Fax: (310) 556-3760
Key Executives/Personnel:
   J. Todd Harris, Producer
   Jourdan Krauss, VP of Development
   Craig Roth, VP of Production
   Corey Witte, Creative Executive
   Nichols Thurkettle, Story Editor
Specialties: Independent
Other Categories: TV
Credits: Urbania; Digging to China; Bad Manners; Denise Calls Up

DAVIS ENTERTAINMENT CO.
2121 Ave. of the Stars, Ste. 2900
Los Angeles, CA 90067
Phone: (310) 556-3550
Fax: (310) 556-3688
Key Executives/Personnel:
   John A. Davis, Chairman
   Paul Spadone, President of Series TV
   Teddy Zee, President of Features
   Brooke Brooks, Executive VP of Administration
   Wyck Godfrey, Executive VP of Production & Development
   Liz Phillips, Creative Executive
   Amy Palmer, Director of Development, TV
   Chris Aldrich, Assistant to Mr. Davis
Specialties: Studio
Other Categories: TV
Credits: Predator; Courage Under Fire; Grumpy Old Men; Breakers
First Look/Development Deals: Twentieth Century Fox Pictures

DAYBREAK PRODUCTIONS
100 Universal City Plaza, Bungalow 4172
Universal City, CA 91608
Phone: (818) 777-0277
Fax: (818) 866-0285
Key Executives/Personnel:
   Charles Gordon, Producer
   Marc Sternberg, President
   James Abraham, Assistant to Mr. Gordon
   Andrew Hong, Assistant to Mr. Sternberg
Specialties: Studio; Independent
Other Categories: TV
Credits: Die Hard 1 & 2; Waterworld; Field of Dreams; October Sky
First Look/Development Deals: Universal Pictures

DINO DE LAURENTIIS COMPANY
100 Universal City Plaza, Bungalow 5195
Universal City, CA 91608
Phone: (818) 777-2111
Fax: (818) 866-5566
Key Executives/Personnel:
   Dino De Laurentiis, Consultant
   Martha De Laurentiis, President & Producer
   Scott Browning, Business Affairs
Specialties: Studio; Independent
Credits: Hannibal; U-571; Breakdown

DEJA VIEW PRODUCTIONS, INC.
7603 Atron Ave.
West Hills, CA 91304
Phone: (818) 704-9185
Fax: (818) 704-6001
dejavprods@aol.com
Key Executives/Personnel:
   Robyn Evans-Jones, Producer & Partner
   Dennis E. Jones, Producer, UPM & Partner
Specialties: Studio; Independent
Other Categories: TV
Credits: The Flintstones in Viva Rock Vegas; Glory, Glory (TV pilot); OutBreak; Pacific Heights
Trade Assoc./Guilds/Unions: DGA

Production Companies – Feature Film

DENALI PRODUCTIONS, INC.
Studio One, 6743 Fernhill Dr.
Malibu, CA 90265
Phone: (310) 457-7566
Fax: (310) 457-5789
www.denaliproductions.com
bcarmic@earthlink.net
Key Executives/Personnel:
  Doug Millington, Executive Producer
  Bobby Carmichael, Director
Specialties: Documentaries; Large Format
Other Categories: TV; Commercials; Video
Credits: Merrill-Lynch (commercial); Sprite (commercial); Cadillac (commercial); Dayton 500 (documentary)

DESERT HEART PRODUCTIONS
685 Venice Blvd.
Venice, CA 90291
Phone: (310) 399-0013
Fax: (310) 396-4047
ddietchco@aol.com
Key Executives/Personnel:
  Donna Deitch, Director & Producer
  Scott Foundas, Assistant to Ms. Deitch
Specialties: Studio; Independent; Documentaries
Other Categories: TV
Credits: Desert Hearts; Angel on My Shoulder

DESTINATION FILMS
1299 Ocean Ave., 5th Fl.
Santa Monica, CA 90401
Phone: (310) 434-2700
Fax: (310) 434-2701
Key Executives/Personnel:
  Brent Baum, President
  Barry London, CEO
  John Bertolli, Executive VP & Co-Head of Production
  Brad Jenkel, Executive VP & Co-Head of Production
  Mark Jacobson, VP of Production
  J. J. Klein, VP of Production
  Mark Morgan, VP of Production
  Rick Joseph, Creative Executive
Specialties: Independent
Credits: Beautiful; Eye of the Beholder; Drowning Mona

DI NOVI PICTURES
3110 Main St., Ste. 220
Santa Monica, CA 90405
Phone: (310) 581-1355
Fax: (310) 399-0499
Key Executives/Personnel:
  Denise Di Novi, Producer
  Ed McDonnell, President
  Alison Greenspan, VP of Development
Specialties: Studio
Other Categories: TV
Credits: Little Women; Ed Wood; Edward Scissorhands

DIC ENTERTAINMENT
303 N. Glenoaks Blvd., 4th Fl.
Burbank, CA 91502
Phone: (818) 955-5400
Fax: (818) 955-5696
Key Executives/Personnel:
  Andy Heyward, President & CEO
  Jeff Wernick, Executive VP of Operations & COO
  Robby London, Executive VP of Creative Affairs
  Kaaren Brown, Executive Director of Creative Affairs
  Michael Maliani, Executive VP of Development
  Stacey Gallishaw, VP of Production
Specialties: Direct-to-Video; Animation
Other Categories: TV
Credits: Meet the Deedles; Carmen San Diego; Inspector Gadget; Madeline

LOUIS DIGIAIMO & ASSOCIATES
214 Sullivan St., Ste. 2C
New York, NY 10012
Phone: (212) 253-5510
Fax: (212) 253-5540
l.digiaimo@att.net
Key Executives/Personnel:
  Louis DiGiaimo, Producer
  Lou DiGiaimo Jr., Producer
  Stephanie Corsalini, Director of Development
Specialties: Studio; Independent
Other Categories: TV
Credits: Donnie Brasco; Falcone; Everlasting Piece; Dinner Rush
Additional Info: Also casting director

DIMENSION FILMS
375 Greenwich St.
New York, NY 10013
Phone: (212) 941-3800
         (323) 951-4200
Fax: (212) 941-3949
www.dimensionfilms.com
Key Executives/Personnel:
  Bob Weinstein, Co-Chairman
  Andrew Rona, Co-Head of Production
  Brad Weston, Co-Head of Production
  Michael Helfant, Sr. Executive VP of Business & Legal Affairs
  Peter Schwerin, Production Executive
  Andrew Gumpert, Sr. VP of Legal & Business Affairs
  Clark Henderson, Sr. VP of Post Production
  Kevin Hyman, Sr. VP of Physical Production
  Jane Evans, VP of Physical Production
  Jim Glander, VP of Physical Production
Specialties: Studio; Independent
Credits: Scream 1, 2 & 3; Scary Movie; Reindeer Games
Additional Info: 7966 Beverly Blvd., Los Angeles, CA 90048

THE WALT DISNEY COMPANY
500 S. Buena Vista St.
Burbank, CA 91521
Phone: (818) 560-1000
www.disney.com
Key Executives/Personnel:
  Michael D. Eisner, Chairman & CEO
  Roy E. Disney, Vice Chairman of the Board
  Bob Iger, President & CEO
  Peter E. Murphy, Sr. Executive VP & Chief Strategic Officer
  Thomas O. Staggs, Sr. Executive VP & CFO
  Louis M. Meisenger, Executive VP & Chief General Counsel
  John J. Garand, Sr. VP of Planning & Control
  Marsha L. Reed, VP & Corporate Secretary
Specialties: Studio

WALT DISNEY PICTURES/TOUCHSTONE PICTURES
500 S. Buena Vista St.
Burbank, CA 91521
Phone: (818) 560-1000
Fax: (818) 563-1598
www.disney.com
Key Executives/Personnel:
  Peter Schneider, Chairman of Walt Disney Studios
  Thomas Schumacher, President of Feature Animation & Theatrical Productions
  Michael Mendenhall, President of Synergy, Walt Disney Studios
  Phil Barlow, Executive VP of E-Cinema & Nech Technology, Walt Disney Motion Picture Group
  Bruce Hendricks, Executive VP of Motion Picture Production

Production Companies – Feature Film

Andrea Marozas, Sr. VP of Communications, Walt Disney Studios
Steve Bardwil, Sr. VP of Theatrical Animation
Kevin W. Breen, Sr. VP of Theatrical Animation
Tim Engel, Sr. VP of Production, Walt Disney Feature Animation
Scott Holtzman, Sr. VP of Music Business & Legal Affairs
Robert W. Johnson, Sr. VP of Labor Relations
Phil Lofarno, Sr. VP of Production, Walt Disney Feature Animation
David McCann, Sr. VP of Motion Picture & Television Post Production
Phillip Muhl, Sr. VP of Business & Legal Affairs
Doug Carter, VP of Business Affairs
William Clark, VP of Participation & Residuals
Chris Floyd, VP of Business Affairs
Steven W. Gerse, VP of Business & Legal Affairs
Stephanie J. Harris, VP of Credit & Title Administration
Bob Lambert, VP of New Technology & Development
Stuart Oken, VP of Creative Affairs, Walt Disney Feature Productions
Marjorie Randolph, VP of Human Resources, Walt Disney Feature Animation
Howard Safenowitz, VP of Business Affairs
Clark Spencer, VP of Financial & Planning Analysis
Paul Steinke, VP of Production Finance
Paul Yanover, VP of Technology, Walt Disney Feature Animation
Jeff Daitch, Director of Business
Sylvia J. Krask, Director of Music Business Affairs
Sherri Feldman, Sr. Attorney
Kal Walthers, Sr. Attorney

Specialties: Studio

DISTANT HORIZON
8282 Sunset Blvd., Ste. A
Los Angeles, CA 90046
Phone: ....(323) 848-4140
Fax: ....(323) 848-4144
www.distant-horizon.com
distanth@pacbell.net
Key Executives/Personnel:
Avant Singh, President
Brian Cox, Producer
Tyler Steele, Production Coordinator
Specialties: Studio; Independent; Documentaries; Animation
Other Categories: TV
Credits: The Theory of Flight; Twin Dragons; Cry The Beloved Country; Get Real

DOCKRY PRODUCTIONS
Phone: ....(310) 274-0761
Fax: ....(310) 274-0762
dockryproductions@mail.com
Key Executives/Personnel:
Nancy Dockry, President
Victor Williams, VP of Production
Sue Cazen, Sr. VP of Development
Walter Edwards, Executive VP
James Mark, Legal Affairs
Adolph Kaczynski, Treasurer
Specialties: Independent
Credits: Context; Yes, Yes, Yes; Ancient Ties; We Too

THE DONNERS' COMPANY
Phone: ....(818) 954-3611
    ....(818) 954-3961
Fax: ....(818) 954-3475
Key Executives/Personnel:
Lauren Shuler Donner, Producer
Richard Donner, Producer & Director
Julie Durk, Development Executive
Michael Aguilar, Development Executive
Specialties: Studio
Other Categories: TV
Credits: Leathal Weapon 1, 2 & 3; Free Willy 1, 2 & 3; X-Men; Dave
First Look/Development Deals: NBC Entertainment, Inc., Warner Bros.

BRUCE DORN FILMS
466-A Foothill Blvd., PMB 319
La Cañada, CA 91011
Phone: ....(818) 790-3080
Key Executives/Personnel:
Bruce Dorn, Owner
Specialties: Documentaries; Trailers
Other Categories: Commercials

JEAN DOUMANIAN PRODUCTIONS
595 Madison Ave., Ste. 2200
New York, NY 10022
Phone: ....(212) 486-2626
Fax: ....(212) 688-6236
Key Executives/Personnel:
Jean Doumanian, Producer & President
John Logigian, VP of Business Affairs
Adam Schlesinger, Director of Development
Kimberly Jose, Story Editor
Specialties: Independent
Other Categories: TV
Credits: Small Time Crooks; Sweet & Lowdown; The Spanish Prisoner; Everyone Says I Love You

DREAMWORKS SKG
100 Universal Plaza, Bldg. 10
Universal City, CA 91608
Phone: ....(818) 733-7000
Fax: ....(848) 733-7574
www.dreamworks.com
Key Executives/Personnel:
Steven Spielberg, Principal
Jeffrey Katzenberg, Principal
David Geffen, Principal
Helene Hahn, Legal
Ron Nelson, Finance
Ann Daly, Animation & Home Video
Laurie MacDonald, Production
Walter Parkers, Production
Adam Goodman, Theatrical Production
Marc Haimes, Theatrical Production
Leah Keith, Theatrical Production
Damien Stevenson, Theatrical Production
Mark Sourian, Theatrical Production
Paul Lister, Theatrical Production
Glenn Williamson, Theatrical Production
Michael Grillo, Production
Andrea McCall, Production
Leslee Feldman, Production
Steve Molen, Production
Terry Press, Marketing
Jim Tharp, Theatrical Distribution
Brian Edwards, Legal Affairs, Motion Pictures
Andy Spahn, Corporate Affairs
Dan McDermott, TV
Justin Falvey, TV
Darryl Frank, TV
Hal Richardson, TV Worldwide & Pay TV
Michael Ostin, Music
Mo Ostin, Music
Lenny Waronker, Music
Tony Hull, Finance
Laura Fox, Theatrical Business Affairs
Art Frazier, Theatrical Business Affairs
Alan Myerson, Animation Business Affairs
Barbara Zipperman, Animation Business Affairs
Pamela Baron, TV Business Affairs

Production Companies – Feature Film

Anne Globe, Consumer Products
Brad Globe, Consumer Products
Specialties: Studio; Animation
Other Categories: TV

DREYFUSS/JAMES PRODUCTIONS
1041 Formosa Ave., Pickford Bldg., Rm. 110
West Hollywood, CA 90046
Phone: (323) 850-3140
Fax: (323) 850-3141
Key Executives/Personnel:
Richard Dreyfuss, Partner & Executive Producer
Judith James, Partner & Executive Producer
Greg Szimonisz, Director of Development
Audrey Bamber, Assistant
Specialties: Studio; Independent
Other Categories: TV
Credits: Having Our Say; Mr. Holland's Opus; Quiz Show

DUCK SOUP STUDIOS
2205 Stoner Ave.
Los Angeles, CA 90064
Phone: (310) 478-0771
Fax: (310) 478-0773
www.ducksoupla.com
ducksoupla@aol.net
Key Executives/Personnel:
Mark Medernach, Executive Producer
Carolyn Bates, Producer
Specialties: Shorts; Animation
Other Categories: Commercials; Music Video; Interactive Multimedia
Credits: Starkist; Dean's Milk; Bell Atlantic; McDonald's

E.M.E., INC.
Phone: (310) 330-8841
emeinc@earthlink.net
Specialties: Studio; Animation; Trailers
Other Categories: TV; Commercials; Music Video; Interactive Multimedia

ECHO LAKE PRODUCTIONS
213 Rose Ave., 2nd Fl.
Venice, CA 90291
Phone: (310) 399-9164
Fax: (310) 399-9278
contact@echolakeproductions.com
Key Executives/Personnel:
Doug Mankoff, President
Robin Alper, VP of Production & Development
Peter Wetherell, Executive Producer
Mark Dempsey, Creative Executive
Kelly Rouse, Creative Executive
Specialties: Independent
Credits: The City (LA Ciudad)

EDMONDS ENTERTAINMENT
1635 N. Cahuenga Blvd., 5th Fl.
Los Angeles, CA 90028
Phone: (323) 860-1550
Fax: (323) 860-1554
Key Executives/Personnel:
Tracey Edmonds, President & CEO
Kenneth "Babyface" Edmonds, President & CEO
Bridget D. Davis, VP of Film
Patrick-Ian Polk, VP of E2 Filmworks
Shelia Ducksworth, Director of Development
Specialties: Studio; Independent
Other Categories: TV
Credits: Soul Food (feature); Hav Plenty; Light It Up; Soul Food (TV series)
First Look/Development Deals: Fox 2000 Productions

RONA EDWARDS PRODUCTIONS
264 S. La Cienega Blvd., Ste. 1052
Beverly Hills, CA 90211
Phone: (323) 466-3013
Fax: (323) 467-1258
Key Executives/Personnel:
Rona Edwards, Producer & Manager
Specialties: Studio; Independent
Other Categories: TV
Credits: Out of Sync; I Know What You Did; The Companion; One Special Victory

RALPH EDWARDS/STU BILLETT PRODUCTIONS
6922 Hollywood Blvd., Ste. 415
Hollywood, CA 90028
Phone: (323) 462-2212
Fax: (323) 461-1224
Key Executives/Personnel:
Ralph Edwards, Partner & Executive Producer
Stu Billett, Partner & Executive Producer
Gary Edwards, VP & Executive Producer
James B. Pollock, COO & General Counsel
Barbara Dunn-Leonard, Executive Producer
Specialties: Independent; Direct-to-Video
Other Categories: TV
Credits: The People's Court

EGG PICTURES
5555 Melrose Ave., Jerry Lewis Bldg. Annex
Los Angeles, CA 90038
Phone: (323) 956-8400
Fax: (323) 862-1414
Key Executives/Personnel:
Jodi Foster, no title
Meg LeFauve, President
Lisa Buono, VP
Erin O'Donnell, Executive Assistant
Lorielle Mallue, Development Assistant
Specialties: Studio; Independent
Credits: Nell; Home For the Holidays; Waking the Dead; The Dangerous Lives of Alter Boys
First Look/Development Deals: Paramount Pictures

EL NORTE PRODUCTIONS
8701 W. Olympic Blvd.
Los Angeles, CA 90035
Phone: (310) 360-1194
Fax: (310) 360-1199
Key Executives/Personnel:
Gregory Nava, Director & Producer
Barbara Martinez-Jitner, VP of TV
Darlene Caamano, Sr. VP of Development & Production
Laura Flores, Production & Development Assistant
Specialties: Studio; Documentaries
Other Categories: TV
Credits: El Norte; Selena; Mi Familia; Why Do Fools Fall in Love
First Look/Development Deals: New Line Cinema, Inc.

ELEPHANT WALK ENTERTAINMENT
Phone: (310) 887-3977
elephantwalk@earthlink.net
Key Executives/Personnel:
Doug McHenry, Producer & Director
Lana Campbell, Director of Development
Specialties: Studio; Independent
Other Categories: TV
Credits: The Brothaz; Mr. Murder; Malcolm & Eddie; Thin Line Between Love and Hate
Additional Info: Office address subject to change.

Production Companies – Feature Film

EMK PRODUCTIONS
1401 Ocean Ave., Ste. 300
Santa Monica, CA 90401
Phone: ....(310) 260-3362
Fax: ....(310) 260-3343
aweiss@regententertainment.com
Key Executives/Personnel:
    Ellen Krass, President
    Karen Frost, Director of Development
Specialties: Studio; Independent
Other Categories: TV
Credits: Lesson Before Dying; Other People's Money; Intimate Portrait: Jackie Onassis; The Kathy & Mo Show
First Look/Development Deals: Regent Entertainment, Inc.

ENCHANTMENT FILMS
11526 Burbank Blvd., Ste. 20
North Hollywood, CA 91601
Phone: ....(818) 506-5249
................................(505) 247-3880
Key Executives/Personnel:
    Steve Anderson, Director, Writer & Producer
    Scott Kimball, Producer
    Mark Anderson, Producer
Specialties: Studio; Independent; Shorts
Credits: Hearts of Stone; South Central; Columbia Pictures Discovery Program
First Look/Development Deals: Megellin Filmed Entertainment

ENSEMBLE ENTERTAINMENT
10474 Santa Monica Blvd., Ste. 380
Los Angeles, CA 90025
Phone: ....(310) 882-8900
Fax: ....(310) 882-8901
jbdead@aol.com
Key Executives/Personnel:
    Jon Brown, Producer & Manager
    Brian Jarvis, Assistant
Specialties: Studio; Independent
Other Categories: TV
Credits: The Tie That Binds
First Look/Development Deals: Showtime, Warner Bros. Television Productions

ENTERAKTION, INC.
2401 E. Atlantic Blvd., Ste. 410
Pompano Beach, FL 33062
Phone: ....(954) 785-5070
Fax: ....(954) 785-5042
www.enteraktion.com
enteraktion@enteraktion.com
Key Executives/Personnel:
    Tom Walsh, Producer, Co-Chairman & CEO
    Ronald Hilton, Producer & Co-Chairman
    Adriana Walsh, Producer & Sr. VP
    Claire Le Covac, Director of Marketing
    Michael Laughlin, Digital Director
    Lloyd Gross, Producer
Specialties: Independent
Other Categories: TV; Interactive Multimedia
Credits: Denial; We Dare You!; House to House; Mismatch

EPIPHANY PRODUCTIONS, INC.
10623 Esther Ave.
Los Angeles, CA 90064
Phone: ....(310) 815-1266
................................(310) 505-1133
Fax: ....(310) 815-1269
roadog@concentric.net
Key Executives/Personnel:
    Dan Halperin, Producer
    Mark Frazel, Director of Development
    Scott JT Frank, Producer
    Karen Anderson, Line Producer
Specialties: Independent
Other Categories: TV; Video
First Look/Development Deals: Liberty International Entertainment

ERRATIC ENTERTAINMENT, INC.
1131 Alta Loma Rd., Ste. 331
Los Angeles, CA 90069
Phone: ....(310) 657-0922
Fax: ....(310) 657-1360
erraticent@aol.com
Key Executives/Personnel:
    Graham Ludlow, Producer & Partner
    Sam Okun, Producer & Partner
    Matt Miller, Creative Executive
    Tom Damien, Director of Development
    Arlene Pachasa, Assistant to Producers
Specialties: Studio; Independent; Direct-to-Video; Documentaries
Other Categories: TV
Credits: The Call of the Wild; Anya's Bell

ESPARZA-KATZ PRODUCTIONS
8899 Beverly Blvd., Ste. 506
Los Angeles, CA 90048
Phone: ....(310) 281-3770
Fax: ....(310) 281-3770
esparzakatz@msn.com
Key Executives/Personnel:
    Moctesuma Esparza, Producer
    Robert Katz, Producer
Specialties: Studio; Independent; Direct-to-Video; Documentaries; Trailers
Other Categories: TV
Credits: Gettysburg; Selena; Introducing Dorothy Dandridge

THE ROBERT EVANS COMPANY
5555 Melrose Ave., Lubitsch Bldg., Ste. 117
Los Angeles, CA 90038
Phone: ....(323) 956-8800
Fax: ....(323) 862-0070
Key Executives/Personnel:
    Robert Evans, Chairman
    Christine Forsyth-Peters, President
    Robin Guthrie, Executive VP
    Cynthia Matzeger, Director of Development
    Samuel Dowe-Sanders, Story Editor
    James Smith, Development Assistant
Specialties: Studio
Credits: The Saint; Jade; Sliver; How to Lose a Guy in 10 Days
First Look/Development Deals: Paramount Pictures

EVERYMAN PICTURES
10202 W. Washington Blvd., Old Lab Bldg., Ste. 1043
Culver City, CA 90232
Phone: ....(310) 244-1686
Fax: ....(310) 244-1315
Key Executives/Personnel:
    Jay Roach, Producer & Director
    Gina Marcheschi, no title
Specialties: Studio
Credits: Meet the Parents; The Empty Mirror; Blown Away

FACE PRODUCTIONS
335 N. Maple Dr., Ste. 135
Beverly Hills, CA 90210
Phone: ....(310) 285-2300
Fax: ....(310) 285-2386
Key Executives/Personnel:
    Billy Crystal, Producer

Production Companies – Feature Film

Samantha Sprecher, VP of Development
Annette Mathews, Story Editor
Carol Sidlow, Assistant to Mr. Crystal
Specialties: Studio
Credits: 61*; Analyze This; My Giant; Forget Paris
First Look/Development Deals: Castle Rock Entertainment

FAIR DINKUM PRODUCTIONS
2500 Broadway St., Bldg. E-5018
Santa Monica, CA 90404
Phone: (310) 586-8471
Fax: (310) 586-8469
Key Executives/Personnel:
Henry Winkler, Executive Producer, Director & Actor
Michele McCole Moss, Executive Assistant to Mr. Winkler
Specialties: Studio
Other Categories: TV
Credits: MacGyver; Sightings; Dead Man's Gun; So Weird

FAST CARRIER PICTURES
c/o Showtime, 10880 Wilshire Blvd., Ste. 1500
Los Angeles, CA 90024
Phone: (310) 234-5376
Fax: (310) 234-5393
steve.rubin@showtime.net
Key Executives/Personnel:
Steven Jay Rubin, President
Rory J. Aylward, VP of Development
Specialties: Studio; Independent; Documentaries
Other Categories: TV
Credits: Combat!; The Errand Boy; The Battle of Hollywood

FAT CHANCE FILMS
3751 Motor Ave., Ste. 928
Los Angeles, CA 90034
Phone: (323) 882-4130
bobmardis2@aol.com
Key Executives/Personnel:
Bobby Mardis, Producer & Director
Specialties: Independent; Direct-to-Video; Documentaries
Other Categories: TV; Video; Music Video
Credits: Midnight Blue; Circle of Pain; Why Colors; One Last Time
Trade Assoc./Guilds/Unions: DGA, WGAw

FATE JUNKIE FILMS, INC.
4555 Matilija Ave.
Sherman Oaks, CA 91423
Phone: (818) 905-1333
(818) 929-7500
Fax: (818) 907-1333
stacey33@pacbell.net
Key Executives/Personnel:
Stacy Schachter, Owner & Producer
Specialties: Independent
Other Categories: Commercials; Music Video
Credits: Politically Incorrect (commercial); Frito Lay (commercial); Mattel (commercial); Tupac (music video)
Trade Assoc./Guilds/Unions: DGA

THE EDWARD S. FELDMAN CO.
500 S. Buena Vista St.
Burbank, CA 91521
Phone: (818) 972-3304
Fax: (818) 972-3309
esfeldman@aol.com
Key Executives/Personnel:
Winship Cook, Creative Associate
Specialties: Studio; Independent
Other Categories: TV
Credits: 102 Dalmations; The Truman Show; Witness; The Doctor

FENADY ASSOCIATES, INC.
249 N. Larchmont Blvd., Ste. 6
Los Angeles, CA 90004
Phone: (323) 466-6375
Fax: (323) 466-6376
Key Executives/Personnel:
Andrew J. Fenady, President
Duke Fenady, VP of Creative Affairs
Specialties: Studio; Independent
Other Categories: TV
Credits: The Man With Bogart's Face; The Love She Sought; Yes Virginia, There is a Santa Claus; The Sea Wolf

FGM ENTERTAINMENT
8670 Wilshire Blvd., Ste. 301
Beverly Hills, CA 90211
Phone: (310) 358-1370
Fax: (310) 358-1380
Key Executives/Personnel:
Frank Mancuso, Jr., President & Producer
Vikki Williams, Line Producer
Jenni Villegas, Executive Assistant to Mr. Mancuso
Specialties: Studio
Credits: Species; Internal Affairs; Ronin; Stigmata
Additional Info: Does not accept unsolicited submissions or query letters.

ADAM FIELDS PRODUCTIONS
10390 Santa Monica Blvd., Ste. 350
Los Angeles, CA 90025
Phone: (310) 552-8244
Fax: (310) 552-8247
Key Executives/Personnel:
Adam Fields, President
John Harman, VP of Creative Affairs
Specialties: Studio
Other Categories: TV
Credits: Ravenous; Money Train; Brokedown Palace; Great Balls of Fire
First Look/Development Deals: Twentieth Century Fox

FILM ROMAN, INC.
12020 Chandler Blvd., Ste. 300
North Hollywood, CA 91607
Phone: (818) 761-2544
Fax: (818) 985-2973
www.filmroman.com
Key Executives/Personnel:
John Hyde, CEO
Michael Winchester, CFO
Peter Schankowitz, President of TV Programming & Development
Mitch Solomon, President of Features
Uriel Sigala, CTO
Sidney Clifton, VP of TV
Kathee Schneider, VP of Commercial Division
Eric Radomski, Creative Director
Mike Wolf, Head of Animation Production
Specialties: Studio; Independent; Animation
Other Categories: TV
Credits: The Simpsons; King of the Hill; My First Mister (feature); Level13.net

FILMCOLONY, LTD.
7966 Beverly Blvd., 3rd Fl.
Los Angeles, CA 90048
Phone: (323) 951-4650
Fax: (323) 951-4660
Key Executives/Personnel:
Richard Gladstein, Producer & President
Gary Binkow, Sr. VP of Production & Co-Producer
Stacy Zand, Director of Development

Production Companies – Feature Film

Sharra Stende, Assistant to Mr. Binkow
Elinor Vizio, Assistant to Mr. Gladstein
David Iserson, Second Assistant to Mr. Gladstein
Specialties: Studio
Credits: The Cider House Rules; She's All That; Jackie Brown; Pulp Fiction
First Look/Development Deals: Miramax Films

FILMWORLD, INC.
304 N. Edinburgh Ave.
Los Angeles, CA 90048
Phone: ....(323) 655-7705
Fax: ....(323) 655-7706
Key Executives/Personnel:
  Menahem Golan, Chairman
  Mark Tolner, CEO
  John Daly, President
  Kendra Dousette, Production Coordinator
  Toni Obee, Sr. Executive Assistant
  Alexander Walker Jr., Office Manager
Specialties: Studio; Independent
Credits: Crime & Punishment (2000); Captain America; Night of the Living Dead; A Cry in the Dark

FINE LINE FEATURES
116 N. Robertson Blvd., Ste. 200
Los Angeles, CA 90048
Phone: ....(310) 854-5811
Fax: ....(310) 659-1453
www.flf.com
Key Executives/Personnel:
  Mark Ordesky, President
  Steve Friedlander, Executive VP of Distribution
  Marian Kolta, Executive VP of Marketing
  Rachel Horovitz, Sr. VP of Production & Acquisitions
  Ileen Maisel, Sr. VP of Productions & Acquisitions
  Marc Halperin, VP & General Sales Manager
  Beth R. Scheffres, VP & Sales Administration
  Nina Baron, Executive Director of East Coast Publicity
  Jennifer Stott, Executive Director of Publicity
  Anthony Bolinsky, Director of Co-op Advertising
  Anna Osso, Director of National Print Services
  Joseph A. Revitte, Creative Executive
Specialties: Studio; Independent; Direct-to-Video; Shorts; Documentaries
Credits: Dancer in the Dark; State and Main; Saving Grace; Tumbleweeds
Additional Info: 888 Seventh Ave, 20th Fl., New York, NY 10016
  212-649-4800 phone, 212-956-1942 fax

WENDY FINERMAN PRODUCTIONS
10201 W. Pico Blvd., Bldg. 52
Los Angeles, CA 90035
Phone: ....(310) 369-8800
....(212) 586-6000
Fax: ....(310) 369-8808
Key Executives/Personnel:
  Wendy Finerman, Producer
  Greg Mooradian, President of Production
  David Stephanov, VP of Production
  Jennifer Goldstein, Creative Executive
  Tiffany Ericksen, Creative Executive
  Timothy Record, Office Manager
  Lisa Zupan, Assistant to Ms. Finerman
  Debbie Lintz, Assistant to Ms. Finerman
Specialties: Studio
Credits: Forrest Gump; Stepmom; The Fan; Sugar & Spice
Additional Info: 140 W. 57th St., Ste. 10D
  New York, NY 10019

FIREWORKS PICTURES
1041 N. Formosa
Los Angeles, CA 90046
Phone: ....(310) 854-2429
Fax: ....(310) 854-2436
Key Executives/Personnel:
  Jay Firestone, Chairman & CEO
  Adam Haight, President & COO
  Daniel Diamond, President
  Bob Aaronson, VP of Acquisition & Co-Production
  Pamela Delaney, Director of Legal Affairs
  Maura T. Hoy, Director of Int'l. Sales
Specialties: Studio
Credits: There's No Fish Food In Heaven; 9 1/2 Weeks
Additional Info: A division of Fireworks Entertainment,
  111 George St., 3rd Fl., Toronto, ON M5A 2N4 Canada

FIRST AVENUE FILMS
567 MossHill Rd.
Orcas, WA 98280
Phone: ....(360) 376-3737
www.firstavenuefilms.com
info@firstavenuefilms.com
Key Executives/Personnel:
  John G. Ginnes, Executive Producer
  Leslie Kahan, Executive Producer
Specialties: Independent
Other Categories: TV; Commercials
Credits: Madonna - You Must Love Me; Out Of The Silence; Anheuser-Busch
Trade Assoc./Guilds/Unions: AICP, DGA

FLIP YOUR LID, INC.
23501 Park Sorrento, Ste. 207
Calabasas, CA 91302
Phone: ....(818) 222-0700
Fax: ....(818) 222-9166
www.flipyourlid.com
jay@flipyourlid.com
Key Executives/Personnel:
  Steve Soffer, Co-President & Executive Producer
  Jay Jacoby, Co-President & Creative Director
  Gay Murdock, Controller
  John Kokum, Producer
Specialties: Shorts; Animation
Other Categories: TV; Interactive Multimedia
Credits: Forty & Shorty; Undercover Brother; Shapes

FLOWER FILMS, INC.
9220 Sunset Blvd., Ste. 309
Los Angeles, CA 90069
Phone: ....(310) 285-0200
Fax: ....(310) 285-0827
Key Executives/Personnel:
  Drew Barrymore, Partner
  Nancy Juvonen, Partner
  Stephanie Savage, VP of Development
  Linda McDonough, Director of Development, TV & New Media
Specialties: Studio
Other Categories: TV
Credits: Charlie's Angels; Never Been Kissed; Donnie Darko; Olive, the Other Reindeer
First Look/Development Deals: Fox 2000 Productions

FLYING FREEHOLD PRODUCTIONS
5555 Melrose Ave., Clara Bow Bldg., Ste. 120
Los Angeles, CA 90038
Phone: ....(323) 956-8838
Fax: ....(323) 862-1031
judson-grubbs@paramount.com
Key Executives/Personnel:

Production Companies – Feature Film

Wendy Neuss, President
Patrick Stewart, CEO
Adam Robinson, VP of Development
Jud Grubbs, Creative Executive
Jackie Edwards, Executive Assistant to Mr. Stewart
Specialties: Studio; Independent
Credits: Christmas Carol; Rogue Element; Assassination Bureau
First Look/Development Deals: Paramount Pictures

FOREST HILLS PICTURES
P.O. Box 49694
Los Angeles, CA 90049
Phone: ....(310) 207-6462
www.foresthillspictures.com
howeis@aol.com
Key Executives/Personnel:
Howard Weisman, President & Executive Producer
Specialties: Studio; Independent
Other Categories: TV; Video
Credits: Lovestruck

FORTIS FILMS
8581 Santa Monica Blvd., Ste. 1
West Hollywood, CA 90069
Phone: ....(310) 659-4533
Fax: ....(310) 659-4373
Key Executives/Personnel:
Sandra Bullock, Owner
Gesine Bullock, Executive VP
Lillian Dean, Director of Development
Maggie Biggar, Production Executive
Bryan Moore, Office Manager
Specialties: Studio
Credits: Ms. Congeniality; Practical Magic; Hope Floats

FORWARD PASS, INC.
12233 W. Olympic Blvd., Ste. 340
Los Angeles, CA 90064
Phone: ....(310) 571-3443
Key Executives/Personnel:
Michael Mann, Writer, Producer & Director
Michael Schulman, VP of Development & Production
Nancy Peardon, VP of Business Affairs
Specialties: Studio
Other Categories: TV
Credits: Insider; Heat; Last of the Mohicans; Ali
First Look/Development Deals: Walt Disney Pictures/Touchstone Pictures

DAVID FOSTER PRODUCTIONS
4000 Warner Blvd., Producers Bldg. 1, Ste. 211
Burbank, CA 91522
Phone: ....(818) 954-4113
Fax: ....(818) 954-4449
Key Executives/Personnel:
David Foster, Producer
Pierre Weidemann, Director of Development
Specialties: Studio
Other Categories: TV
Credits: Hearts War; The Mask of Zorro; The River Wild; The Getaway 1 & 2

FOUNDATION ENTERTAINMENT
8800 Venice Blvd., Ste. 217
Los Angeles, CA 90034
Phone: ....(310) 204-4686
Fax: ....(310) 204-4603
www.foundent.com
Key Executives/Personnel:
John Manulis, President
Steve Przybylowski, Development
Specialties: Studio; Independent
Other Categories: TV
Credits: Daybreak; Swing Kids

FOUNTAINBRIDGE FILMS
10202 W. Washington Blvd., Crawford Bldg.
Culver City, CA 90232
Phone: ....(310) 244-8080
Fax: ....(310) 244-8484
Key Executives/Personnel:
Sean Connery, Owner & Producer
Rhonda Tollefson, President & Producer
Lynnette Ramirez, Creative Executive
Joanna Butan, Executive Assistant
Joyce Tollefson, Office Manager
Specialties: Studio
Credits: Entrapment; Just Cause; Finding Forester
First Look/Development Deals: Columbia Pictures/Columbia Tristar Motion Picture Group

FOUNTAINHEAD PICTURES
8670 Burton Way, Ste. 319
Los Angeles, CA 90048
Phone: ....(310) 276-5583
Fax: ....(310) 276-5583
fountpix@pacbell.net
Key Executives/Personnel:
Aaron J. Shuster, Director, Writer & Producer
Kimberly Norton, Producer & Manager
Jonathan King, Creative Affairs
Morgan Richards, Assistant
Specialties: Studio; Independent; Shorts
Other Categories: TV
Credits: Pictures At The Beach; Straight & Narrow; Sandor; Baraba

FOUR SQUARE PRODUCTIONS, INC.
5205 Kearny Villa Way
San Diego, CA 92123
Phone: ....(858) 874-1900
www.foursq.com
Key Executives/Personnel:
John DeBello, Director
Scott Sorensen, Sr. Producer
David Craven, Sr. Producer
Specialties: Direct-to-Video
Other Categories: TV; Commercials; Video
Credits: This Week in Sports; SPA War (video); SignOnSanDiego.com; The Guide

FOX SEARCHLIGHT PICTURES
10201 W. Pico Blvd., Bldg. 38
Los Angeles, CA 90035
Phone: ....(310) 369-4402
Fax: ....(310) 369-2359
www.foxsearchlight.com
Key Executives/Personnel:
Peter Rice, President
Joseph De Marco, Executive VP of Business Affairs
Claudia Lewis, Executive VP of Production
Joe Pichirallo, Sr. VP of Production
Tony Safford, Sr. VP of Acquisitions
Breena Camden, Sr. VP of Publicity & Promotions
Stephanie Allen, Sr. VP of Creative Advertising & Marketing
Jill Gwen, VP of Business Finance
Rosanne Korenberg, VP of Acquisitions
Liz Sayre, VP of Physical Production
Jamie Taylor, VP of Legal Affairs
Joshua Deighton, Creative Executive
Nancy Utley, President of Marketing
Specialties: Independent
Credits: Woman on Top; Bootmen; The Full Monty; Quills

Production Companies – Feature Film

FR PRODUCTIONS
2980 Beverly Glen Circle, Ste. 200
Los Angeles, CA 90077
Phone: (310) 470-9212
Fax: (310) 470-4905
Key Executives/Personnel:
   Fred Roos, President & Producer
   Thi Ngyuen, Development
Specialties: Studio; Independent

FRANCHISE PICTURES, INC.
8228 Sunset Blvd.
Los Angeles, CA 90046
Phone: (323) 822-0730
Fax: (323) 822-2165
Key Executives/Personnel:
   Elie Samaha, Chairman
   Andrew Stevens, President & CEO
   Mark McGarry, Sr. VP of Production
   Trancee Stanley, President of Development
   Andrew Kramer, Executive VP of Business & Legal Affairs
   Hans Turner, Sr. VP & CFO
   James Holt, VP of Finance
   Lori Drazen, Executive VP of Worldwide Marketing
   Lisa Wilson, President of Int'l. Sales
   Dawn Miller, VP of Development
   Emily Cummins, Development Executive
   Chay Gross, Story Editor
   Allison Semenza, Executive in Charge of Production
   Maureen Norton, Post Production Supervisor
   Liza-Maria el Khazen, Development Executive
   Kristen Figeroid & James Valdez, Assistants to Mr. Stevens
   Erik Anderson & Rodney Itier, Assistants to Ms. Samaha
Specialties: Studio; Independent
Credits: The Whole Nine Yards; Art of War; 3000 Miles to Graceland

JOEL FREEMAN PRODUCTIONS, INC.
15323 Weddington St., Ste. 102
Sherman Oaks, CA 91411
Phone: (818) 995-1189
(818) 995-1638
joelfree@earthlink.net
Key Executives/Personnel:
   Joel Freeman, President, CEO & Producer
   Betty Freeman, VP
Specialties: Independent
Credits: Heart is a Lonely Hunter; Octagon; Shaft; Love At First Bite
Trade Assoc./Guilds/Unions: AMPAS, DGA, PGA

FRESH PRODUCE COMPANY
5820 Wilshire Blvd., Ste. 403
Los Angeles, CA 90036
Phone: (323) 931-3700
Fax: (323) 931-8649
fpc@ix.nextcom.net
Key Executives/Personnel:
   Joyce Schweickert, Executive Producer
   Annette Vait, Producer
   Peter Torres, Director of Development
Specialties: Studio; Independent
Credits: Still Breathing; Twin Falls Idaho; Kill The Man; Cherry Falls

DANIEL FRIED PRODUCTIONS
Phone: (310) 452-7646
Fax: (310) 452-8022
kidfried@home.com
Key Executives/Personnel:
   Daniel Fried, Producer
Specialties: Studio; Independent
Credits: O; 29 Palms

FRIED FILMS
4503 Glencoe Ave.
Marina Del Rey, CA 90292
Phone: (310) 754-2676
Fax: (310) 778-9596
Key Executives/Personnel:
   Robert Fried, Producer
   Richard Zinman, Producer
   Marisa Forrest, Creative Executive
Specialties: Studio
Other Categories: TV
Credits: Rudy; Godzilla; Winchell; So I Married an Axe Murder
First Look/Development Deals: HBO

FRIENDLY PRODUCTIONS
10201 W. Pico Blvd., Bldg. 41
Los Angeles, CA 90035
Phone: (310) 369-3973
Fax: (310) 369-7436
Key Executives/Personnel:
   David T. Friendly, no title
   David W. Higgins, no title
   Noessa Higa, no title
   Michael McGahey, no title
   Kori Nelson, no title
   Will Rowbotham, no title
Specialties: Studio; Independent
Credits: Big Momma's House; Dr. Dolittle; Courage Under Fire
Additional Info: Company name will change beginning 2001.

MARK FROST PRODUCTIONS
5700 Wilshire Blvd.
Los Angeles, CA 90036
Phone: (323) 965-5785
Key Executives/Personnel:
   Mark Frost, Executive Producer
   Susie Putnam, Assistant
Specialties: Independent
Other Categories: TV
Credits: The Repair Shop; Buddy Faro; Twin Peaks: Fire Walk With Me

FURTHER FILMS
100 Universal City Plaza, Bldg. 1320, Ste. 4E
Universal City, CA 91608
Phone: (818) 777-6700
(212) 333-1421
Fax: (818) 866-1278
Key Executives/Personnel:
   Michael Douglas, Producer
   Allison Segan, Producer
   Angela Congelose, Controller
   Marcy Drogin, VP of Creative Affairs (NY)
   Jackie Levine, VP
Specialties: Studio
Credits: One Night At McCool's
First Look/Development Deals: Universal Pictures, USA Films
Additional Info: 825 Eighth St., 30th Fl., New York, NY 10019

GENREBEND PRODUCTIONS, INC.
1875 Century Park East, 2nd Fl.
Los Angeles, CA 90067
Phone: (310) 284-7312
Fax: (310) 284-7317
Key Executives/Personnel:
   David Nutter, President & Director
   Tom Lavagnino, Writer & VP of Creative Affairs
   Brian Vanderwilt, Director of Development

Production Companies – Feature Film

Specialties: Studio; Independent
Other Categories: TV
Credits: Dark Angel; Millennium; Roswell
First Look/Development Deals: Twentieth Century Fox

ROGER GIMBEL PRODUCTIONS, INC.
1675 Old Oak Rd.
Los Angeles, CA 90049
Phone: .... (310) 459-3838
gimpix1@ix.netcom.com
Key Executives/Personnel:
    Roger Gimbel, Producer
    Mark Trabulus, Producer
    Stephanie Young, Development
Specialties: Independent
Other Categories: TV
Credits: The Amazing Howard Hughes; Chernobyl, The Final Warning; A Perfect Mother; Murder Between Friends
First Look/Development Deals: Showtime
Trade Assoc./Guilds/Unions: PGA

GINTY FILMS
16255 Ventura Blvd., Ste. 625
Encino, CA 91436
Phone: .... (310) 274-9691
.... (310) 277-1408
Fax: .... (310) 274-9692
www.robertginty.com
rwginty@aol.com
Key Executives/Personnel:
    Robert Ginty, CEO
    Skip Heinecke, (Ireland)
    Shira Zeltzer, Executive Assistant
    Layla Bennett, Executive Assistant
    Lyndi Vanderhout, (Paris)
    Moira Proletti, (Rome)
    Jean Diamond, (London)
    John Gallagher, (New York)
    John Mein, (Vancouver)
Specialties: Studio; Independent; Large Format
Other Categories: TV; Commercials; Music Video; Interactive Multimedia
Credits: Bounty Hunter; Woman of Desire; Day of Reckoning
Trade Assoc./Guilds/Unions: BAFTA, DGA, SAG, WGAw

GITTES, INC.
10202 W. Washington Blvd., Poitier Bldg., Ste. 1200
Culver City, CA 90232
Phone: .... (310) 244-4333
Fax: .... (310) 244-1711
Key Executives/Personnel:
    Harry Gittes, Producer
    Edward C. Wang, Director of Development
Specialties: Studio
Credits: About Schmidt; Breaking In; Little Nikita; Goin' South
First Look/Development Deals: Columbia Pictures

GMR PRODUCTIONS
1333 Sixth Ave.
Venice, CA 90291
Phone: .... (310) 401-1400
Fax: .... (310) 401-1200
Key Executives/Personnel:
    Gina Resnick, Executive Producer
Specialties: Independent
Other Categories: TV
Credits: Female Perversions; Clockwatchers; 13 Conversations About One Thing

GO FILM
51 E. 12th St., 6th Fl.
New York, NY 10003
Phone: .... (212) 677-7500
Fax: .... (212) 677-7555
www.gofilm.net
Key Executives/Personnel:
    Jonathan Weinstein, Partner
    Robert Wherry, Partner
    Preston Lee, Executive Producer
    Caitlin Felton, Director
    Gary McKendry, Director
    Frank W. Ockenfels 3, Director
    Nick Rafter, Director
    Rad-ish, Director
Specialties: Independent
Other Categories: Commercials; Music Video
Additional Info: 1103 Abbot Kinney Blvd., Venice, CA 90291 (310) 581-1992 phone, (310) 581-4994 fax

GOEPP CIRCLE PRODUCTIONS
5555 Melrose Ave., Cooper Bldg., Ste. 116
Los Angeles, CA 90049
Phone: .... (323) 956-4620
Fax: .... (323) 862-1119
Key Executives/Personnel:
    Jonathan Frakes, Director & Producer
    Lisa J. Olin, Producer
    Daisy Gardner, Story Editor
Specialties: Studio
Other Categories: TV
Credits: Roswell; Dying to Live
First Look/Development Deals: Paramount Pictures

JEFF GOLD PRODUCTIONS, INC.
13900 Panay Way, Ste. 309
Marina Del Rey, CA 90292
Phone: .... (310) 827-9165
j47737@yahoo.com
Specialties: Independent
Other Categories: TV; Commercials; Video; Music Video
Credits: The Alpha Section; Talking Heads; Career Bed; Changing Times
Trade Assoc./Guilds/Unions: DGA

GOLD'N HEN PRODUCTIONS
12301 Wilshire Blvd., Ste. 402
Los Angeles, CA 90024
Phone: .... (310) 820-1308
Fax: .... (310) 820-1398
judy@groupmsi.com
Key Executives/Personnel:
    Joel Goldstein, Chairman
    Judy Henry, President
    Dale Eldridge Kaye, VP
    Jamie Goldstein, VP
Specialties: Studio
Other Categories: TV; Commercials
Credits: Replacing Dad; Nelson Diebel Story; Spy Girl

GOLDEN EAGLE PIX
475 Ravensbury St.
Thousand Oaks, CA 91361
Phone: .... (805) 381-9095
.... (805) 907-1860
Fax: .... (805) 381-9096
www.goldeneaglepix.com
goldeneaglepix@hotmail.com
Key Executives/Personnel:
    Peter B. Good, Producer
Specialties: Independent; Documentaries
Other Categories: TV; Commercials
Credits: Roller Coasters; Fireworks; Beyond Bizarre; Death Valley

Production Companies – Feature Film

GOLDENRING PRODUCTIONS
11271 Ventura Blvd., Rm. 506
Studio City, CA 91604
Phone: ....(323) 969-0354
Fax: ....(323) 969-8581
Key Executives/Personnel:
   Jane Goldenring, President
   Victoria R. Farwell, Associate
Specialties: Independent
Other Categories: TV
Credits: On The Second Day Of Christmas; Widows; My First Mister
First Look/Development Deals: Von Zerneck-Sertner Films

THE GOLDSTEIN COMPANY
1644 Courtney Ave.
Los Angeles, CA 90046
Phone: ....(310) 659-9511
Fax: ....(310) 659-8779
Key Executives/Personnel:
   Gary W. Goldstein, Executive Producer
   Sandra Tomita, Associate Producer
Specialties: Studio; Independent
Credits: Ringmaster; Under Siege 2: Dark Territory; The Hunted; Pretty Woman

SAMUEL GOLDWYN FILMS
9570 W. Pico Blvd., Ste. 400
Los Angeles, CA 90035
Phone: ....(310) 860-3100
Fax: ....(310) 860-3195
Key Executives/Personnel:
   Samuel Goldwyn Jr., Chairman of the Board
   Meyer Gottlieb, President
   Tom Quinn, Director of Acquisitions
   Chris Rowe, Production & Development
   Julie Huey, Production & Development
Specialties: Studio; Independent
Credits: Oneign; King of Masks; Big Blue; Solas
First Look/Development Deals: New Line Cinema, Inc.

GOOD MACHINE
417 Canal St., 4th Fl.
New York, NY 10013
Phone: ....(212) 343-9230
Fax: ....(212) 343-9645
www.goodmachine.com
Key Executives/Personnel:
   Ted Hope, Co-Chairman
   James Schamus, Co-Chairman
   David Linde, President of Good Machine Int'l.
   Anthony Bregman, VP of Production
   Noreen Ward, VP of Operations
   Glen Basner, VP of Sales
   Ross Katz, Director of Production
   Bobby Anderson, Sr. Accountant
Specialties: Independent
Credits: The Ice Storm; Walking and Talking; The Brothers McMullen; The Tao of Steve

LAWRENCE GORDON PRODUCTIONS
100 Universal City Plaza, Bungalow 4171
Universal City, CA 91608
Phone: ....(818) 777-7933
Fax: ....(818) 866-5068
Key Executives/Personnel:
   Lawrence Gordon, Owner
Specialties: Studio

GRACIE FILMS
10202 W. Washington Blvd., Sidney Poitier Bldg.
Culver City, CA 90232
Phone: ....(310) 244-4222
Fax: ....(310) 244-1530
Key Executives/Personnel:
   James L. Brooks, Producer, Director & Writer
   Richard Sakai, President
   Julie Ansell, President of Motion Pictures
   Denise Sirkot, Executive VP
Specialties: Studio
Other Categories: TV; Interactive Multimedia
Credits: As Good As It Gets; Jerry Maguire; Bottle Rocket; Riding in Cars with Boys
First Look/Development Deals: Columbia Pictures/Columbia Tristar Motion Picture Group
Additional Info: Simpson's production office: 10201 W. Pico Blvd., Los Angeles, CA 90035

GRADE A ENTERTAINMENT
368 N. La Cienega Blvd.
Los Angeles, CA 90048
Phone: ....(310) 358-8600
Fax: ....(310) 652-0718
gradeaprod@aol.com
Key Executives/Personnel:
   Andy Cohen, Producer
Specialties: Studio; Independent
Other Categories: TV; Interactive Multimedia
Credits: Captain Ron; It Takes Two; A Chance of Snow; Billboard Dad

GRAHAM/ROSENZWEIG FILMS
3000 Olympic Blvd., Ste. 2332
Santa Monica, CA 90404
Phone: ....(310) 264-3956
Fax: ....(310) 264-3958
grfilms@mindspring.com
Key Executives/Personnel:
   Tracie Graham, Producer
   Alison Rosenzweig, Producer
Specialties: Studio; Independent
Credits: Windtalkers; Phoenix; Dumb and Dumber; Threesome

GRAMMNET PRODUCTIONS (FILM)
5555 Melrose Ave., Bob Hope Bldg., Ste. 202
Los Angeles, CA 90038
Phone: ....(323) 956-5840
       ....(323) 956-5832
Fax: ....(323) 862-1433
Key Executives/Personnel:
   Kelsey Grammer, Producer & CEO
   Joanne Weiss, VP of Features Production
   Jessica Hochman, Story Editor
   Xochitl Olivas, Production Manager
Specialties: Studio
First Look/Development Deals: Paramount Pictures

GRAZKA TAYLOR PRODUCTIONS
9899 Santa Monica Blvd., Ste. 206
Beverly Hills, CA 90212
Phone: ....(310) 201-0806
Fax: ....(310) 201-0711
grazkat@aol.com
Key Executives/Personnel:
   Grazka Taylor, Producer
Specialties: Independent; Documentaries
Other Categories: TV
Credits: Tricks; Mahalia Jackson; Prophecies; The Operation

GREEN COMMUNICATIONS
303 N. Glen Oaks, Ste. 605
Burbank, CA 91502

Production Companies – Feature Film

Phone: (818) 557-0050
Fax: (818) 557-0056
www.greenfilms.com
tcaptan@greenfilms.com
Key Executives/Personnel:
  Talaat Captan, President
Specialties: Independent
Other Categories: TV; Commercials
Credits: Ground Control; Living in Peril; Apex; Space Marines

GREEN GRASS BLUE SKY COMPANY, INC.
4717 Laurel Canyon Blvd., Ste. 206
Valley Village, CA 91607
Phone: (818) 760-8243
ggbscompany@hotmail.com
Key Executives/Personnel:
  Frank Catalano, President
  Ronald J. Wong, Development
  Sandra Carlso, Development
  Anthony Catalano, Co-Production
  Gregory Snegoff, Rome
Specialties: Studio; Independent
Credits: Almost Classix; Bed Time Stories; Adventures of Dynamo Duck
Additional Info: 156 Viale Cortina D'Ampezzo,
  Rome, 00135 Italy, 011-396-331-4045

GREEN MOON PRODUCTIONS
3110 Main St., Ste. 205
Santa Monica, CA 90405
Phone: (310) 450-6111
Fax: (310) 450-1333
name@greenmoon.com
Key Executives/Personnel:
  Antonio Banderas, Producer & Actor
  Melanie Griffith, Producer & Actor
  Diane Sillan Isaacs, President
Specialties: Studio; Independent; Documentaries; Animation
Other Categories: TV
Credits: Crazy In Alabama; The Body; Loving Lulu; Tart
First Look/Development Deals: HBO

THE GREIF COMPANY/A DAY WITH, INC.
9233 W. Pico Blvd., Ste. 218
Los Angeles, CA 90035
Phone: (310) 385-1200
Fax: (310) 385-1207
leslie@greifco.cncdsl.com
Key Executives/Personnel:
  Leslie Greif, Executive Producer
  Tiffany Mclinn Lore, Producer
  Kristen Stabile, Executive in Charge of Production
Specialties: Independent
Other Categories: TV
Credits: Meet Wally Sparks; Keys to Tulsa; Lifetime, Intimate Portraits

THE ALAN GREISMAN COMPANY
335 N. Maple Dr., Ste. 135
Beverly Hills, CA 90210
Phone: (310) 205-2766
Fax: (310) 285-2345
Key Executives/Personnel:
  Alan Greisman, Producer
  Keith Lesser, Assistant
Specialties: Studio; Independent
Credits: Earthly Possessions; Soapdish; Fletch
First Look/Development Deals: Castle Rock Entertainment

MERV GRIFFIN ENTERTAINMENT
9860 Wilshire Blvd.
Beverly Hills, CA 90210
Phone: (310) 385-3160
Fax: (310) 385-3162
Key Executives/Personnel:
  Merv Griffin, Chairman
  Lawrence Cohen, CEO
  Ernest Chambers, Sr. VP of Production
  Robert Kosberg, Producer
  Scott Manville, Manager of Development
  Rick Upshaw, Director of Multimedia Development
  Jim Bradley, Executive Producer
  Kira Mason, Development Executive
  Diana Redman, Contract Administrator
Specialties: Studio; Independent
Other Categories: TV

KEN GROSS MANAGEMENT
7919 Sunset Blvd., 2nd Fl.
Los Angeles, CA 90046
Phone: (323) 512-2999
Fax: (323) 512-2699
kgrossm@msn.com
Key Executives/Personnel:
  Ken Gross, President
  Stephanie Gaines, VP
  Jenz Bergren, Coordinator
Specialties: Studio; Independent; Large Format
Other Categories: TV

GROSS PRODUCTIONS
1 Skyline Dr.
Burbank, CA 91501
Phone: (818) 557-7335
Fax: (818) 557-7336
www.grosspro.com
callgross@aol.com
Key Executives/Personnel:
  Chris Gross, Producer & Director
Specialties: Trailers
Other Categories: TV; Commercials
Credits: Gloria Estefan & Carribean Soul; La Femme Nikita; Duckman
Trade Assoc./Guilds/Unions: ASCAP

BETH GROSSBARD PRODUCTIONS
10202 W. Washington Blvd., Meralta Bldg., Ste. 308
Culver City, CA 90232
Phone: (310) 841-2555
Fax: (310) 841-5934
bethgcap@aol.com
Key Executives/Personnel:
  Beth Grossbard, Producer
  K. Jacobs, Development Associate
Specialties: Independent
Other Categories: TV
Credits: No One Could Protect Her; Range of Motion
First Look/Development Deals: Craig Anderson Productions

GULLANE PICTURES
1351 Third St., Ste. 200
Santa Monica, CA 90401
Phone: (310) 451-5111
Fax: (310) 451-5321
Key Executives/Personnel:
  Britt Allcroft, Co-Chairman
  Charles Falzon, Co-Chairman
  Meredith Metz, Head of Development & Packaging
  Jesse Stovin, Development Executive
Specialties: Studio; Independent; Direct-to-Video; Documentaries; Animation
Other Categories: TV
Credits: Thomas & The Magic Railroad; Thomas the Tank Engine & Friends; What Katy Did

Production Companies – Feature Film

H-GUN LABS
587 Shotwell St.
San Francisco, CA 94110
Phone: ....(415) 648-4386
....(773) 561-5354
Fax: ....(415) 920-3911
www.hgun.com
info@hgun.com
Key Executives/Personnel:
  James Deloye, Executive Producer
  Sara Kraft, Producer
  Nancy Williams, Lab Manager
Specialties: Trailers
Other Categories: TV; Commercials; Music Video; Interactive Multimedia

HALLWAY PICTURES
1041 N. Formosa, Formosa Bldg., Ste. 221
West Hollywood, CA 90046
Phone: ....(323) 850-2680
Fax: ....(323) 850-2681
hallwaypictures@earthlink.net
Key Executives/Personnel:
  Paul Hall, Producer
  Wendy Park, VP of Production
  Lloyd D'Souza, Executive Assistant
Specialties: Studio
Credits: Higher Learning; Why Do Fools Fall in Love; Shaft
First Look/Development Deals: Warner Bros.

HALSTED PICTURES
15 Brooks Ave., Unit B
Venice, CA 90291
Phone: ....(310) 450-7804
Fax: ....(310) 450-8174
Key Executives/Personnel:
  Dan Halsted, Executive Producer
  David Scheer, Creative Executive
  Ryan Lewis, Story Editor
Specialties: Independent; Studio
Other Categories: TV
Credits: Servicing Sarah; The Art of War; Any Given Sunday; The Virgin Suicides
First Look/Development Deals: Mandalay Pictures

HAMMER FILMS
6311 Romaine St., Ste. 7316
Los Angeles, CA 90038
Phone: ....(323) 463-9156
Fax: ....(323) 463-8130
www.hammerfilm.com
postmaster@hammerfilm.com
Specialties: Trailers
Credits: American Psycho; Get Real; Crash

HANDPRINT ENTERTAINMENT
1100 Glendon Ave., Ste. 1000
Los Angeles, CA 90024
Phone: ....(310) 481-4400
Fax: ....(310) 481-4419
Key Executives/Personnel:
  David Guillod, Partner
  Benny Medina, Partner
  Jeff Pollack, Partner
  Jay Polstein, Producer
Specialties: Studio; Independent
Other Categories: TV
Credits: Standoff; Eve's Bayou; Above the Rim; Fresh Prince of Bel Air
First Look/Development Deals: Miramax Films

HARBOR LIGHTS PRODUCTIONS
8634 Oak Park Ave.
Northridge, CA 91325
Phone: ....(818) 993-5255
Fax: ....(818) 993-5266
movierock@aol.com
Key Executives/Personnel:
  Rocky Lang, Producer & Director
Specialties: Studio; Independent
Other Categories: TV
Credits: White Squall; Titanic (miniseries)

HARPO FILMS
345 N. Maple Dr., Ste. 315
Beverly Hills, CA 90210
Phone: ....(310) 278-5559
....(312) 633-1000
Key Executives/Personnel:
  Oprah Winfrey, Chairman & CEO
  Kate Forte, President
  Lisa Halliday, Director of Media & Corporate Relations
  Susan Heyer, Director of Development, TV
  Valerie Scoon, Director of Development, Features
  Tim Tortora, Director of Production
Specialties: Studio
Other Categories: TV
Credits: Tuesday's With Morrie; Beloved; David & Lisa; Before Women Had Wings
First Look/Development Deals: ABC Entertainment Television Group, The Walt Disney Company
Additional Info: Oprah Winfrey Show office: 110 N. Carpenter, Chicago, IL 60607

DAVID HAUGLAND PRODUCTIONS
8961 Sunset Blvd., Ste. 2D
West Hollywood, CA 90069
Phone: ....(310) 550-1556
Fax: ....(310) 550-1584
dkhaugland@earthlink.net
Key Executives/Personnel:
  David Haugland, Producer & Director
  Christopher Miller, Assistant
Specialties: Independent; Documentaries
Other Categories: TV; Video; Music Video
Credits: Changing Our Minds; World and Time Enough; The Oscar Legacy; The Portrait
Trade Assoc./Guilds/Unions: DGA, WGAw

HAVOC INC.
16 W. 19th St., 12th Fl.
New York, NY 10011
Phone: ....(212) 924-1629
Fax: ....(212) 924-3105
Key Executives/Personnel:
  Tim Robbins, Producer, Writer & Director
  Nadia Benamara, Assistant to Mr. Robbins
Specialties: Independent
Credits: The Cradle Will Rock; The Typewriter, the Rifle, and the Movie Camera; Dead Man Walking

HAWK ENTERTAINMENT
8888 W. 3rd St., Ste. 306
Los Angeles, CA 90048
Phone: ....(310) 859-7779
Fax: ....(310) 859-7797
hawkentertain@aol.com

Production Companies – Feature Film

    Key Executives/Personnel:
        John Crededio, Partner
        Paul Pompian, Partner
        Ron DeRosa, Producer
    Specialties: Studio; Independent; Large Format
    Other Categories: TV; Interactive Multimedia
    Credits: The Watcher; Time Served; Vincent Verelli
    Additional Info: Chicago Studio City, 5660 W. Taylor St., Chicago, IL 60644

HEADQUARTERS
3015 Main St., 4th Fl.
Santa Monica, CA 90405
Phone: ....(310) 752-5200
Fax: ....(310) 752-5220
hesh@hqfilm.com
Key Executives/Personnel:
    Alex Blum, Partner
    Tom Mooney, Partner
    Andrew Denyer, Executive Producer
    Philip Fox-Mills, Head of Sales
    Hesh Rephun, West Coast Sales & Public Relations
    Jared Shapiro, Midwest Sales
    David Cornell, Director & Cinematographer
    John Moore, Director
    Sean Mullens, Director
    Joe Public, Director
    Lloyd Stein, Director
    Eric Steinman, Director
    Craig Champion, Director
    Neil Harris, Director
Specialties: Independent; Documentaries
Other Categories: Commercials
Credits: Capitol One; Southwest Bell; G.M.; Visa
Additional Info: 7 W. 18th St., 6th Fl., New York, NY 10011 (212) 255-9000 phone, (212) 255-9009 fax

HELLER HIGHWATER
5917 Foothill Dr.
Los Angeles, CA 90068
Phone: ....(323) 467-9490
Fax: ....(323) 468-8074
Key Executives/Personnel:
    Peter Heller, Producer
Specialties: Studio; Independent
Other Categories: TV
Credits: Bones; Caught Up; Hotel De Love; Barb Wire

HENNESSEY ENTERTAINMENT, LTD.
P.O. Box 481164
Los Angeles, CA 90048
Phone: ....(323) 876-2400
Fax: ....(323) 876-2444
www.hennesseyentertainment.com
a_sleuth@hotmail.com
Key Executives/Personnel:
    Ellis A. Cohen, Producer, Writer & CEO
    Leonard H. Cohen, Creative Executive
    Jerome Cohen, Creative Executive
Specialties: Independent
Other Categories: TV; Interactive Multimedia
Credits: Dangerous Evidence; Love, Mary; First Steps; Aunt Mary
Trade Assoc./Guilds/Unions: ATAS, PGA, WGAw

THE JIM HENSON COMPANY
1416 N. La Brea Ave.
Los Angeles, CA 90028
Phone: ....(323) 802-1500
Fax: ....(323) 802-1825
www.henson.com
Key Executives/Personnel:
    Brian Henson, Chairman
    Charles H. Rivkin, President & CEO
    Linda Govreau, Executive VP of Corporate Finance & CFO
    Lisa Henson, President, Jim Henson Pictures
    John Stephenson, Executive VP & Creative Supervisor, Jim Henson's Creature Shop
    Juliet Blake, Executive VP & Co-Head, Jim Henson Television Group Worldwide
    Angus Fletcher, Executive VP & Co-Head, Jim Henson Television Group Worldwide
    Peter Schube, General Counsel & Executive VP of Business & Legal Affairs
    Michael Bolingbroke, Sr. VP of Finance & Operations, Jim Henson's Creature Shop
    Craig Allen, Sr. VP & General Manager, Jim Henson Interactive
    Robert Norton, Sr. VP of Business & Legal Affairs
    Ritamarie Peruggi, Sr. VP of Production Worldwide
    Robert Wozniak, VP of Production Administration & Finance/Production Executive
    Kristine Belson, Production, Jim Henson Pictures
    Louis Philips, VP of Production Administration
    Halle Stanford Grossman, VP of Creative Affairs, Jim Henson Television
    Ruth Caruso, VP of Development, Jim Henson Television
    Michele Martell, VP of Business Affairs & Interactive Business Development
    Antonia Downey, VP of International Legal & Business Affairs
    Pete Coogan, VP of Physical Production
    David Barrington-Holt, Creative Supervisor, Jim Henson's Creature Shop
    Debbie McClellan, Sr. Director of Corporate Communications & Special Projects
    Omar Camacho, Director of Current Programming, Jim Henson Television
Specialties: Studio
Other Categories: TV; Commercials; Video; Music Video; Interactive Multimedia
Credits: Farscape; Story Telling with Tomie de Paola; Rat; Muppets From Space

DEBRA HILL PRODUCTIONS
1250 Sixth St., Ste. 205
Santa Monica, CA 90401
Phone: ....(310) 319-0052
Fax: ....(310) 260-8502
Key Executives/Personnel:
    Debra Hill, Producer, Writer & Director
    Barri Evins, President
    Patrick List, Director of Development
Specialties: Independent
Other Categories: TV
Credits: The Fisher King; Halloween; Crazy in Alabama; Escape From New York

HOFFLUND-POLONE
9465 Wilshire Blvd., Ste 820
Beverly Hills, CA 90212
Phone: ....(310) 859-1971
Fax: ....(310) 859-7250
Key Executives/Personnel:
    Judy Hofflund, Partner
    Gavin Polone, Partner
    Vivian Cannon, Production Executive
Specialties: Studio; Independent
Other Categories: TV
Credits: Stir of Echoes; Drop Dead Gorgeous; 8mm; The Gilmore Girls (TV series)

HOGAN MOORHOUSE PICTURES
1250 Sixth St., Ste. 305
Santa Monica, CA 90401
Phone: ....(310) 319-9299

Fax: . . . .(310) 319-1889
Key Executives/Personnel:
  P. J. Hogan, Writer & Director
  Jocelyn Moorhouse, Writer & Director
  Liza Moore, Sr. VP of Production
  Holly Brix, Executive Assistant
  Cori Carlson, Executive Assistant
Specialties: Studio
Credits: Muriel's Wedding; My Best Friends Wedding; How to Make an American Quilt; Unconditional Love
First Look/Development Deals: Sony Pictures Entertainment

HOLLANE CORP./MARTIN POLL FILMS, LTD.
P.O. Box 17137
Beverly Hills, CA 90209
Phone: . . . .(323) 876-8873
Fax: . . . .(323) 876-8892
Key Executives/Personnel:
  Martin Poll, President
  Shirley Mellner, VP
Specialties: Studio; Independent
Other Categories: TV
Credits: Nighthawks; The Lion In Winter; My Heroes Have Always Been Cowboys; Diana: Her True Story (miniseries)

HORSESHOE BAY PRODUCTIONS
500 S. Buena Vista St., Animation Bldg., Ste. 1G
Burbank, CA 91521
Phone: . . . .(818) 560-3229
Fax: . . . .(818) 848-6832
Key Executives/Personnel:
  Greg S. Foster, Producer
  Mark Steven Johnson, Producer, Writer & Director
  Julia Dray, President of Production
  Erik Baiers, Director of Development
Specialties: Studio
Other Categories: TV
Credits: The Score; Simon Birch; Sleepless in Seattle
First Look/Development Deals: Walt Disney Pictures/Touchstone Pictures

THE HOUSE PRODUCTION COMPANY
1429 N. Spaulding Ave.
Los Angeles, CA 90046
Phone: . . . .(323) 851-5151
. . . .(323) 697-3830
Fax: . . . .(323) 851-9598
Key Executives/Personnel:
  Bonnie Matchinga, Executive Producer
  Alleda Harrison, Marketing Director
  Bob Scwartz, Director
Specialties: Independent; Shorts
Other Categories: Commercials; Video
Credits: Poligrip; Total Telcom Media; Birds and the Bees
Trade Assoc./Guilds/Unions: DGA

HUNT-TAVEL PRODUCTIONS
10202 W. Washington Blvd., Astaire Bldg., Ste. 2410
Culver City, CA 90232
Phone: . . . .(310) 244-3144
Fax: . . . .(310) 244-0164
Key Executives/Personnel:
  Helen Hunt, Partner
  Connie Tavel, Partner
  Dana Jackson, Sr. VP
  Jason D. Scott, Creative Executive
  Ellen Huang, Story Editor
  Stacey Berns, Assistant to Ms. Hunt
Specialties: Studio; Independent
First Look/Development Deals: Columbia Pictures/Columbia Tristar Motion Picture Group

HY-TONE PRODUCTIONS
26349 Fairside Rd.
Malibu, CA 90265
Phone: . . . .(310) 456-3052
Fax: . . . .(310) 456-9659
www.notelvis.com
hytone@aol.com
Key Executives/Personnel:
  Robert Jaye, Producer, Director & Cinematographer
  Walter Hoylman, Producer, Director & Editor
Specialties: Documentaries
Other Categories: TV; Video; Interactive Multimedia
Credits: Some of the King's Men; Mustang America; Art and Sex; Fire Engine

ICON PRODUCTIONS INC.
5555 Melrose Ave., Wilder Bldg.
Los Angeles, CA 90038
Phone: . . . .(323) 956-2100
Fax: . . . .(323) 862-2121
Key Executives/Personnel:
  Bruce Davey, President
  Jim Lemley, President of TV
  Michael Lustig, President of Music
  Vicki Christianson, Sr. VP of Business
  Eveleen Bandy, VP of TV
  Karen J. Glasser, VP of Creative Affairs
Specialties: Studio; Independent
Other Categories: TV
Credits: Bless the Child; Payback; Three Stooges; Braveheart
First Look/Development Deals: Paramount Pictures

IDEAL ENTERTAINMENT, INC.
Phone: . . . .(323) 939-3399
shapiro@flash.net
Key Executives/Personnel:
  Jon Shapiro, Producer & President
  Pete Shapiro, Producer
  Kelly Knight, Producer
Specialties: Studio; Large Format
Credits: Richie Rich; All Access

IMAGE G
10900 Ventura Blvd.
Studio City, CA 91604
Phone: . . . .(818) 761-6644
Fax: . . . .(818) 761-8397
www.imageg.com
Key Executives/Personnel:
  Nick Paine, Producer
  Tom Barron, Producer
Specialties: Independent
Other Categories: TV; Commercials
Credits: Nestle; Del Monte; Spy Kids

IMAGE MOVERS
100 Universal City Plaza, Bldg. 484
Universal City, CA 91608
Phone: . . . .(818) 733-8313
Fax: . . . .(818) 733-8333
Key Executives/Personnel:
  Robert Zemeckis, Producer, Writer & Director
  Steve Starkey, Producer
  Jack Rapke, Producer
  Jennifer Perini, Head of Creative Affairs
  Steven Boyd, Associate Producer

Production Companies – Feature Film

    Bennett Schneir, Creative Executive
    Kelsey Clark, Assistant to Mr. Zemeckis
    Sharon Felder, Assistant to Mr. Zemeckis
    Heather Smith, Assistant to Mr. Starkey
Specialties: Studio; Independent
Credits: Forrest Gump; Contact; Romancing the Stone; Back to the Future 1, 2 & 3

IMAGINARY FORCES
6526 Sunset Blvd.
Los Angeles, CA 90028
Phone: ....(323) 957-6868
Fax: ....(323) 957-9577
www.imaginaryforces.com
information@imaginaryforces.com
Key Executives/Personnel:
    Kyle Cooper, Creative Director & Managing Partner
    Chip Houghton, Executive Producer & Managing Partner
    Peter Frankfurt, Creative Director & Managing Partner
    Saffron Kenny, Head of Production & Partner
    Mikon Van Gastel, Creative Director & Partner
    Karin Fong, Creative Director & Partner
    Kurt Mattila, Creative Director & Partner
    Michael Riley, Creative Director & Partner
    Linda Nakagawa, CFO & Partner
Specialties: Studio; Large Format; Trailers
Other Categories: Commercials
Credits: Blade; Blade 2; Coors Lite; Janus

IMAGINE ENTERTAINMENT
9465 Wilshire Blvd., 7th Fl.
Beverly Hills, CA 90212
Phone: ....(310) 858-2000
Fax: ....(310) 858-2020
www.imagine-entertainment.com
Key Executives/Personnel:
    Brian Grazer, Co-Chairman
    Ron Howard, Co-Chairman
    Tony Krantz, Co-Chairman & CEO
    Michael Rosenberg, President
    Karen Kehela, Co-Chair of Imagine Films
    Skip Chasey, Executive VP of Business Affairs, TV
    Robin Barris, Sr. VP of Administration & Operations
    Maureen Peyrot, Sr. VP of Motion Pictures
    Jim Whitaker, Sr. VP of Motion Pictures
    Jan Geniesse, VP of Motion Pictures
    Kim Roth, VP of Motion Pictures
    Suzy Barbier, VP of Motion Pictures
    Gayle Pillsbury, VP of Talent & Casting, TV
    Katie O'Connell, VP of Current TV Programming & Development
    Jennifer Robinson, VP of Current TV Programming & Development
    Mike Vorndian, Creative Executive
    Barry Jossen, Production Consultant
Specialties: Studio; Documentaries
Other Categories: TV
Credits: The Grinch; Bowfinger; Felicity; Sports Night

IMAX CORPORATION
3003 Exposition Blvd.
Santa Monica, CA 90404
Phone: ....(310) 255-5500
....(905) 403-6500
Fax: ....(310) 255-5551
www.imax.com
Key Executives/Personnel:
    Bradley J. Wechsler, Co-Chairman & Co-CEO
    Richard L. Gelfond, Co-Chairman & Co-CEO
    John Davidson, COO
    David Keighley, Executive VP of Post Production
    Udo von Karhan, Executive VP of Worldwide Sales & Marketing
    Andrew Gellis, Sr. VP & Distribution
    Patrick Murray, VP of Operations
    Wendi Mirabella, Director of Development
Specialties: Large Format
Credits: Cyberworld 3D; Destiny in Space; T-Rex: Back to the Cretaceous; Across the Sea of Time
Additional Info: 2525 Speakman Dr., Mississauga, ON L5K 1B1 Canada

IMPACT PSA, INC.
1429 N. Spaulding Ave.
Los Angeles, CA
Phone: ....(323) 851-5151
....(323) 697-3830
Fax: ....(323) 851-9598
Key Executives/Personnel:
    Bonnie Matchinga, Executive Producer
    Alleda Harrison, Director of Marketing
Specialties: Independent
Other Categories: Commercials; Video
Credits: Spilled Milk (PSA); A Place For Me (documentary)
Trade Assoc./Guilds/Unions: DGA

IN PLAY MEDIA ARTS
4174 Ince Blvd.
Culver City, CA 90232
Phone: ....(310) 839-7497
....(800) 260-6580
Fax: ....(310) 839-5365
www.inplaymediaarts.com
dutydukes@aol.com
Key Executives/Personnel:
    Gary Hoffman, no title
Specialties: Trailers
Other Categories: Commercials; Video

INCOGNITO ENTERTAINMENT
345 N. Maple Dr., Ste. 348
Beverly Hills, CA 90210
Phone: ....(310) 246-1500
Fax: ....(310) 246-0469
info@incognitoent.com
Key Executives/Personnel:
    Lawrence Abramson, CEO
    Larry Weinberg, Producer
    Andrew Howard, Manager
    Helena Bartuccio, Director of Development
    Kathy Carter, Manager
Specialties: Studio; Independent
Credits: Three to Tango; The Last Supper; Morning; Modern Vampires

INDIEGAL PRODUCTIONS, LLC
14350 Little Tujunga Canyon Rd.
San Fernando, CA 91342
Phone: ....(818) 890-6111
Fax: ....(818) 890-5851
indiegal_prods@hotmail.com
Key Executives/Personnel:
    Angela P. Shapiro, Partner
    Laura Keats, Partner
    Gail Harris, Partner
    Jan Marlyn Reesman, VP of Creative Affairs
    Deborah Zimmerly, VP of Development
    Susanna Midnight, Director of Creative Affairs
    Jeanne Yu, Director of Development
Specialties: Studio; Independent
Other Categories: TV
Credits: To Protect and Serve; The Iron Triangle; He's My Girl

Production Companies – Feature Film

INFRONT PRODUCTIONS
10201 W. Pico Blvd., Bldg. 3 North
Los Angeles, CA 90035
Phone: (310) 369-5890
Fax: (310) 369-8356
Key Executives/Personnel:
  Danny Jacobson, Writer & Producer
  Marjorie Weitzman, Producer
  Jennifer Hertrich, VP of Feature Development
Specialties: Independent
Other Categories: TV
Credits: Mad About You; Two Guys and a Girl; Roseanne
First Look/Development Deals: Twentieth Century Fox Pictures

INITIAL ENTERTAINMENT GROUP
3000 W. Olympic Blvd., Ste. 1550
Santa Monica, CA 90404
Phone: (310) 315-1722
Fax: (310) 315-1723
Key Executives/Personnel:
  Graham King, President & CEO
  Colin Cotter, COO
  David A. Jones, VP of Creative Affairs
Specialties: Independent
Credits: Dr. T and the Women; The Dangerous Lives of Alter Boys; Gangs of New York

INSTINCT PICTURES
520 Washington Blvd., Ste. 257
Marina Del Rey, CA 90292
Phone: (310) 578-9778
(213) 426-7211
zenueg@yahoo.com
Specialties: Independent
Other Categories: Commercials; Music Video
Credits: The Shelter (feature); Best Buddies (PSA); APLA (PSA)

INTERMEDIA FILMS
8490 W. Sunset Blvd., Ste. 700
Los Angeles, CA 90069
Phone: (310) 777-0007
Fax: (310) 777-0008
Key Executives/Personnel:
  Guy East, Co-Chairman
  Nigel Sinclair, Co-Chairman
  Kathy Goodman, President
  Julie Golden, Sr. VP of Production
  Karen Belanger, VP of Creative Affairs
  Rob McEntegart, VP of Business Affairs
  Tobin Armbrust, Manager of Production
Specialties: Studio; Independent
Credits: The Wedding Planner; Sliding Doors; Hilary and Jackie; Playing By Heart

INTERNATIONAL TELEVISION GROUP (ITG)
1322 Second St., Ste. 6
Santa Monica, CA 90401
Phone: (310) 656-9100
Fax: (310) 656-9104
intvg@aol.com
Key Executives/Personnel:
  Teresa Campbell, VP of Production & Development
  Lou La Monte, Producer
Specialties: Studio; Independent
Other Categories: TV; Commercials; Video
Credits: Cat on a Hot Tin Roof (1985); Uncle Wally's General Store

IRISH DREAMTIME
2450 Broadway, Ste. E-5021
Santa Monica, CA 90404
Phone: (310) 449-3411
Fax: (310) 586-8138
Key Executives/Personnel:
  Pierce Brosnan, Producer
  Beau St. Clair, Producer
  Angelique Higgins, VP of Development
  Cynthia Palormo, Creative Executive
  Amanda Scarano, Production Executive
Specialties: Studio; Independent
Credits: The Thomas Crown Affair; The Match; The Nephew
First Look/Development Deals: MGM, Inc.

ITASCA PICTURES, INC.
345 N. Maple Dr., Ste. 278
Beverly Hills, CA 90210
Phone: (310) 273-6505
Fax: (310) 273-1475
Key Executives/Personnel:
  Robert Snukal, Producer & Chairman
  Dan Grudnik, CEO & Producer
  Kandia Stroh, Associate Producer
Specialties: Studio; Independent
Other Categories: TV
Credits: Morton Orwell; Cletis Tout; Higher Love; Powder

ITB CINEGROUP/TELEVISION
3839 Brilliant Dr.
Los Angeles, CA 90065
Phone: (323) 258-5564
Fax: (323) 258-6634
quixotic@att.net
Key Executives/Personnel:
  Mark Byers, Writer & Producer
  Frank Antonelli, Writer & Producer
  Heather Ashley, Development
Specialties: Independent
Other Categories: TV
Credits: The Treatment; Criminal Act; Deception; Race, Religion, & Racism
First Look/Development Deals: Timeless Entertainment Corporation

THE JACOBSON COMPANY
500 S. Buena Vista, Animation Bldg., Ste. 2C-7
Burbank, CA 91521
Phone: (818) 560-1600
Fax: (818) 567-4010
Key Executives/Personnel:
  Tom Jacobson, Producer
  Jim Wedaa, Executive VP
  Tom Hoffman, VP of Production
  Leigh Rodwick, Assistant to Mr. Jacobson
  Brede Hovland, Assistant to Mr. Jacobson
  Rachel Kaiser, Assistant to Mr. Wedaa
  Mark Deetjen, Assistant to Mr. Hoffman
Specialties: Studio
Credits: Big Trouble; Mighty Joe Young; Mission To Mars
First Look/Development Deals: Walt Disney Pictures/Touchstone Pictures

JAFFILMS
12233 W. Olympic Blvd., Ste. 158
Los Angeles, CA 90064
Phone: (310) 820-2200
(212) 262-4700
Fax: (310) 820-1202
Key Executives/Personnel:
  Stanley Jaffe, Producer & Partner
  Bob Jaffe, Producer & Partner
Specialties: Independent
Credits: Madeline; I Dreamed of Africa
Additional Info: 152 W. 57th St., 52nd Fl., New York, NY 10019

Production Companies – Feature Film

JARET ENTERTAINMENT
2017 Pacific Ave., Ste. 2
Venice, CA 90291
Phone: .... (310) 883-8807
Fax: .... (310) 822-0916
www.jaretentertainment.com
sjaret@jaretentertainment.com
Key Executives/Personnel:
   Seth Jaret, CEO & Producer
   Susan Sullivan, Development Associate & Story Editor
   Amy O'Brien, Assistant
Specialties: Studio
Other Categories: TV; Interactive Multimedia
Credits: Rounders; 10 Things I Hate About You

JEFF WALD ENTERTAINMENT
3000 W. Olympic Blvd., Bldg. 2, Ste. 1400
Santa Monica, CA 90404
Phone: .... (310) 264-4156
Fax: .... (310) 264-4157
Key Executives/Personnel:
   Jeff Wald, President & CEO
   Steven Thomas, Sr. VP
   Dana Gonshor, Creative Associate
Specialties: Studio; Independent
Other Categories: TV
Credits: 2 Days in the Valley; Pensacola: Wings of Gold; The Roseanne Show

JERSEY FILMS
10351 Santa Monica Blvd., Ste. 200
Los Angeles, CA 90025
Phone: .... (310) 203-1000
Fax: .... (310) 203-1010
Key Executives/Personnel:
   Danny DeVito, Co-Chairman
   Michael Shamberg, Co-Chairman
   Stacey Sher, Co-Chairman
   John Landgraf, President of TV
   Richard Klubeck, COO
   Pamela Abdy, Sr. VP of Production
   Carla Santos Shamberg, VP of Special Projects
   Adrienne Biddle, Story Editor
   Sindy Lin, Story Editor
   David Kurs, Assistant Story Editor
   Monica Hall, Manager of Finance
   Amy Hurdelbrink, Office Manager
Specialties: Studio; Independent
Other Categories: TV
Credits: Man on the Moon; Erin Brockovich; Get Shorty; Out of Sight
First Look/Development Deals: Universal Pictures

JERSEY SHORE FILMS
130 W. 57th St., Ste. 11B
New York, NY 10019
Phone: .... (212) 333-3377
Fax: .... (212) 333-3346
www.jerseyfilms.com
Key Executives/Personnel:
   Dan Levine, Sr. VP
   Mandy Key, Assistant
   Lee Meyer, Assistant
Specialties: Studio; Independent
Credits: Drowning Mona; The Filth & The Fury; The Caveman's Valentine
First Look/Development Deals: Universal Pictures

THE JINKS/COHEN COMPANY
100 Universal City Plaza, Bldg. 5171
Universal City, CA 91608
Phone: .... (818) 733-9880
Fax: .... (818) 733-9893
Key Executives/Personnel:
   Dan Jinks, Producer
   Bruce Cohen, Producer
   Albert Page, Director of Development
Specialties: Studio
Credits: American Beauty; Mousehunt; Nothing to Lose; The Flintstones
First Look/Development Deals: DreamWorks SKG

JKR PRODUCTIONS, INC.
Phone: .... (310) 826-3666
jimruxin@aol.com
Key Executives/Personnel:
   Jim Ruxin, Producer
Specialties: Independent; Documentaries; Trailers
Other Categories: TV; Commercials; Video
Credits: Stoogemania; Defense Play; In God We Trust
Trade Assoc./Guilds/Unions: DGA; IALocal700

JLT PRODUCTIONS
1438 N. Gower St., Box 11
Hollywood, CA 90028
Phone: .... (323) 993-7093
Fax: .... (323) 993-7095
Key Executives/Personnel:
   Jenny Lew Tugend, Producer
Specialties: Studio; Independent
Credits: Return To Me; Free Willy 1, 2 & 3; Star Kid
Trade Assoc./Guilds/Unions: AMPAS, PGA, SAG

DON JOHNSON PRODUCTIONS
3400 Riverside Dr., Ste. 100
Burbank, CA 91505
Phone: .... (818) 238-2200
Key Executives/Personnel:
   Don Johnson, Executive Producer & CEO
   Marc Granirer, COO
   Nick Kelley, President
   David Buelow, Executive VP of Creative Affairs
Specialties: Studio; Independent
Other Categories: TV
Credits: Nash Bridges; The Marshall; In The Company of Darkness

MARK JOHNSON PRODUCTIONS
8490 Sunset Blvd., Ste. 700
West Hollywood, CA 90069
Phone: .... (310) 777-0007
Fax: .... (310) 777-0008
Key Executives/Personnel:
   Mark Johnson, Producer
   Tiffany Daniel, President
Specialties: Studio
Credits: Rain Man; Good Morning Vietnam; Galaxy Quest; The Little Princess

QUINCY JONES MEDIA GROUP, INC.
3800 Barham Blvd., 5th Fl.
Los Angeles, CA 90068
Phone: .... (323) 874-2009
Fax: .... (323) 874-3364
Key Executives/Personnel:
   Quincy Jones, CEO
   Joel Simon, President
   Jill Tanner, VP
   Debborah Foreman, Executive Assistant to Mr. Jones

Production Companies – Feature Film

Specialties: Studio
Other Categories: TV
Credits: Passing Glory
First Look/Development Deals: Warner Bros.

JUMBO PICTURES, INC.
161 Avenue of the Americas, 15th Fl.
New York, NY 10013
Phone: ...(212) 337-0077
Fax: ...(212) 337-0437
Key Executives/Personnel:
    Jim Jinkins, President
    David Campbell, Executive VP
    Jack Spillum, VP of Production
    Ellie Copland, VP of Finance
    Beldeen Fortunato, VP of Adminitration
Specialties: Animation
Other Categories: TV
Credits: Doug's First Movie; PB & J Otter; Doug (TV series)

JUNCTION ENTERTAINMENT
500 S. Buena Vista St.
Burbank, CA 91521
Phone: ...(818) 560-2800
Fax: ...(818) 841-3176
Key Executives/Personnel:
    Jon Turteltaub, Producer & Director
    Christina Steinberg, President & Producer
    Nikki Reed, Director of Development
    Victor Constantino, Creative Executive
    Karim Zreik, Creative Associate
    Dominique Fichera, Creative Associate
    Dan Shotz, Creative Associate
Specialties: Studio
Credits: The Kid; Instinct
First Look/Development Deals: Walt Disney Pictures/Touchstone Pictures

KAHN POWER PICTURES
818 N. Doheny Dr.
Los Angeles, CA 90049
Phone: ...(310) 550-0770
...(310) 967-6566
Fax: ...(310) 550-6292
Ilene.kahn@newline.com
Key Executives/Personnel:
    Ilene Kahn Power, President & Producer
    Derek Power, Partner
    Mark McCoy, Director of Development
    Jeremy Kahn, VP of New Media
Specialties: Independent
Other Categories: TV
Credits: Gia (1998); Stalin; Roswell; Fatherland
First Look/Development Deals: New Line Cinema, Inc.
Trade Assoc./Guilds/Unions: ATAS, BAFTA

KANDOO FILMS, INC.
4515 Van Nuys Blvd., Ste. 100
Sherman Oaks, CA 91403
Phone: ...(818) 789-6777
Fax: ...(818) 789-2299
www.kandoofilms.com
info@kandoofilms.com
Specialties: Trailers
Other Categories: Commercials
Credits: CBS (promo); Mad About You (promo); Friends (promo)

PERRY KATZ PRODUCTIONS
Phone: ...(818) 981-0232
Fax: ...(310) 260-6451

pkatz1@aol.com
Key Executives/Personnel:
    Perry Katz, President
Specialties: Studio
Credits: Flipper; McHale's Navy

MARTY KATZ PRODUCTIONS
1250 Sixth St., Ste. 205
Santa Monica, CA 90401
Phone: ...(310) 260-8501
Fax: ...(310) 260-8502
Key Executives/Personnel:
    Marty Katz, Producer
    Frederick Levy, VP of Development
    Andrew Friedman, Story Editor
    Campbell Katz, Development Associate
    Tiffany Tiesiera, Assistant to Mr. Katz
Specialties: Studio; Independent
Credits: Impostor; Reindeer Games; Mr. Wrong; Man of the House
First Look/Development Deals: Miramax Films, Dimension Films

THE KAUFMAN COMPANY
808 Wilshire Blvd., 3rd Fl.
Santa Monica, CA 90401
Phone: ...(310) 899-8080
Fax: ...(818) 899-8081
www.thekaufmancompany.com
info@thekaufmancompany.com
Key Executives/Personnel:
    Paul Kaufman, Executive Producer
    Helene Lynn-Nash, VP of Creative Affairs
    Gregg Tilson, Director of Development
    Erin Tierneu, Executive Assistant
Specialties: Independent
Other Categories: TV
Credits: Jewel; Run the Wild Fields; Emma's Wish; Thirst
First Look/Development Deals: Alliance Atlantis
Trade Assoc./Guilds/Unions: DGA, WGAw

DAVID E. KELLEY PRODUCTIONS
1600 Rosecrans Ave., Bldg. 4B
Manhattan Beach, CA 90266
Phone: ...(310) 727-2200
Fax: ...(310) 727-2423
Key Executives/Personnel:
    David E. Kelley, CEO, Writer & Executive Producer
    Pamela Wisne, Executive VP & Producer
    Rick Silverman, COO
    Veronica Wilson, VP of Legal Affairs
    Roseann M. Keris, Director of Marketing & Publicity
    Neely Swanson, Director of Business Affairs
    Bob Breech, Executive Producer
    Gary M. Strangis, Co-Executive Producer
    Bill D'Elia, Executive Producer
    Alice West, Co-Executive Producer
    Mike Listo, Supervising Producer
    Jonathan Pontell, Co-Executive Producer
    Shea Farrell, Manager of Creative Affairs
    Elisa Todd, Manager of Creative Affairs
Specialties: Studio
Other Categories: TV
Credits: The Practice; Ally McBeal; Boston Public; Mystery Alaska
First Look/Development Deals: Twentieth Century Fox

THE KENNEDY/MARSHALL COMPANY
1351 Fourth St., 4th Fl.
Santa Monica, CA 90401
Phone: ...(310) 656-8400
Fax: ...(310) 656-8430
Key Executives/Personnel:

Production Companies – Feature Film

    Zanne Devine, President
    Kathleen Kennedy, Producer
    Frank Marshall, Producer & Director
    Mark Ross, Development Executive
    Nancy Cavello, Story Editor
    Mary Radford, Assistant to Mr. Marshall
    Crissy Thomas-Taylor & Henrik Knudsen, Assistants to Ms. Kennedy
    John Tantillo, Assistant to Ms. Devine
Specialties: Studio; Large Format
Other Categories: TV
Credits: Milk Money; Congo; Snow Falling On Cedars; The Sixth Sense
First Look/Development Deals: Universal Pictures

KILLER FILMS
380 Lafayette St., Ste. 302
New York, NY 10003
Phone: ....(212) 473-3950
Fax: ....(212) 473-6152
www.killerfilms.com
dwagner@killerfilms.com
Key Executives/Personnel:
    Christine Vachon, Producer & President
    Pamela Koffler, Producer & President
    Katie Roumel, Head of Production
    Jon Marcus, Production Executive
    Brad Simpson, Head of Development
    Jocelyn Hayes, Development Executive
    Laird Adamson, Director of Creative Affairs
    Daniel Wagner, Office Manager
Specialties: Independent; Shorts
Other Categories: Interactive Multimedia
Credits: Boys Don't Cry; Velvet Goldmine; Officer Killer; Kiss Me Guido
First Look/Development Deals: John Wells Productions, Clear Blue Sky Productions

KANDICE KING PRODUCTIONS, INC.
12555 W. Jefferson Blvd., Ste. 321
Los Angeles, CA 90066
Phone: ....(310) 822-9502
Fax: ....(310) 822-9532
www.kandicekingprods.com
Key Executives/Personnel:
    Kandice King, President & Producer
    Tim Plant, VP of Production
    June Hatch, VP of Distribution
    Cori Gibson, Controller
Specialties: Independent; Direct-to-Video
Credits: Luck of the Draw; Bittersweet; Diary of a Serial Killer; Sunset Heat

KINGSGATE FILMS
8954 W. Pico Blvd., 2nd Fl.
Los Angeles, CA 90035
Phone: ....(310) 281-5880
Key Executives/Personnel:
    Nick Nolte, Producer
    Greg Shapiro, Producer
    Heather Edison, Executive Assistant
Specialties: Independent; Studio
Other Categories: TV
Credits: Affliction; Simpatico; Investigating Sex

KINGSIZE ENTERTAINMENT
639 N. Larchmont Blvd., Ste. 201
Los Angeles, CA 90004
Phone: ....(323) 467-7199
    ....(213) 400-3886
Fax: ....(323) 467-7201
www.kingsizeentertainment.com
mark@kingsizeentertainment.com
Key Executives/Personnel:

    Mark Roberts, Producer
    Lorena David, Director
Specialties: Independent
Credits: Plump Fiction; Single Action; Poor White Trash; Eastside

KINOWELT USA, INC.
9720 Wilshire Blvd., Ste. 500
Beverly Hills, CA 90212
Phone: ....(310) 205-9600
Fax: ....(310) 205-9610
www.kinowelt-usa.com
info@kinowelt-usa.com
Key Executives/Personnel:
    Chris Sievernich, CEO & Co-Chairman
    Matt Milich, Director of Development
Specialties: Independent
Credits: Lightning Over Water; The State Of Things; Paris, Texas; The Dead

DAVID KIRSCHNER PRODUCTIONS
400 S. June St.
Los Angeles, CA 90020
Phone: ....(323) 939-0230
Fax: ....(323) 930-0753
dkps@pacbell.net
Key Executives/Personnel:
    David Kirschner, Producer
    Corey Sienega, VP
    Karen Loop, Director of Development
Specialties: Studio; Animation
Other Categories: TV
Credits: The Flintstones; Hocus Pocus; Child's Play 1-4; An American Tail

KLASKY CSUPO, INC.
6353 Sunset Blvd.
Los Angeles, CA 90028
Phone: ....(323) 463-0145
www.klaskycsupo.com
Key Executives/Personnel:
    Gabor Csupo, Founder & Co-Chair
    Arlene Klasky, Founder & Co-Chair
    Terry Thoren, President & CEO
Specialties: Animation; Direct-to-Video
Other Categories: TV; Commercials
Credits: Rugrats; Duckman; The Simpsons; The Rugrats Movie

THE KOCH COMPANY
4000 Warner Blvd, Trailer 7
Burbank, CA 91522
Phone: ....(818) 954-7964
Key Executives/Personnel:
    Howard "Hawk" Koch Jr., Producer
    Tina Deocalis, Assistant to Mr. Koch
Specialties: Studio
Credits: Frequency; Keeping the Faith; Primal Fear; The Temp

KONRAD PICTURES
10202 W. Washington Blvd., Tristar Bldg., Ste. 222
Culver City, CA 90232
Phone: ....(310) 244-3555
Fax: ....(310) 244-0555
Key Executives/Personnel:
    Cathy Konrad, Producer
    Jeanne Allgood, Director of Development
    Carolyn Barber, Executive Assistant to Ms. Konrad
    Nicole Romero, Assistant to Ms. Konrad
    Andrew Storms, Development Assistant
Specialties: Studio
Credits: Girl, Interrupted; Scream 1, 2 & 3; Teaching Mrs. Tingle; Citizen Ruth

Production Companies – Feature Film

First Look/Development Deals: Columbia Pictures/Columbia Tristar Motion Picture Group

KONTRAST FILMS
315 W. Verdugo Ave.
Burbank, CA 91502
Phone: ....(818) 840-9333
Fax: ....(818) 840-9358
www.kontrastfilms.com
maureen@kontrastfilms.com
Key Executives/Personnel:
    Greg Gears, Producer
    Steven Kovner, VP of Production
    Valerio Ventura, Director
    Maureen English, VP of Sales
Specialties: Independent; Direct-to-Video; Shorts; Documentaries; Animation; Trailers
Other Categories: TV; Commercials
Credits: Cart Racing (commercial)

KOPELSON ENTERTAINMENT
2121 Avenue of the Stars, Ste. 1400
Los Angeles, CA 90067
Phone: ....(310) 369-7555
Fax: ....(310) 369-7501
Key Executives/Personnel:
    Arnold Kopelson, Producer & Co-Chairperson
    Anne Kopelson, Producer & Co-Chairperson
    Nana Greenwald, President of Creative Affairs
    Matthew Gross, Executive VP of Production
    David Goldman, Sr. VP
    Sherryl Clark, VP of Creative Affairs
    Mark Stein, Creative Executive
    Lara Wood, Creative Executive
    Claudia O'Hehir, Executive Assistant to Ms. Kopelson
    Elaine Mongeon, Executive Assistant to Mr. Kopelson
Specialties: Studio
Other Categories: TV
Credits: Platoon; The Fugitive (feature & TV series); Seven; A Perfect Murder

KOUF-BIGELOW PRODUCTIONS
10061 Riverside Dr., PMB 1024
Toluca Lake, CA 91602
Phone: ....(818) 508-1010
Fax: ....(818) 508-1079
Key Executives/Personnel:
    Jim Kouf, Producer, Writer & Director
    Lynn Bigelow-Kouf, Producer
Specialties: Independent
Other Categories: TV
Credits: Gang Related; Stakeout; Rush Hour
Additional Info: No unsolicited material accepted.

KRAININ PRODUCTIONS, INC.
8 Century Rd.
Palisades, NY 10964
Phone: ....(914) 359-0445
Fax: ....(914) 359-0446
krainin@rockland.net
Key Executives/Personnel:
    Julian Krainin, President, Producer & Director
    Michael Lawrence, Producer
    Todd Philips, Development
    Martye Wayne, VP
    Jason Hart, Special Projects
Specialties: Studio; Independent; Documentaries
Other Categories: TV
Credits: Quiz Show; George Wallace; Disaster At Silo Seven; To America

THE JONATHAN KRANE GROUP
8033 Wilshire Blvd., Ste. 6750
Los Angeles, CA 90046
Phone: ....(310) 278-0142
Fax: ....(310) 278-0925
Key Executives/Personnel:
    Jonathan Krane, Chairman & CEO
    Rino Vetrone, COO
    Maria Vallen, Assistant
Specialties: Independent; Studio
Credits: Lucky Numbers; Face/Off; Phenomenon

SID & MARTY KROFFT PICTURES
14144 Ventura Blvd., Ste. 110
Sherman Oaks, CA 91423
Phone: ....(818) 386-1918
Fax: ....(818) 386-9790
Key Executives/Personnel:
    Marty Krofft, President
    Sid Krofft, Executive VP
    Randy Pope, Sr. VP of Production
Specialties: Studio
Other Categories: TV
Credits: H.R. Pufnstuf; The Bugaloos; Land of the Lost

KURTZ & FRIENDS
2312 W. Olive Ave.
Burbank, CA 91506
Phone: ....(818) 841-8188
Fax: ....(818) 841-6263
www.kurtzandfriends.com
bobkurtz@aol.com
Key Executives/Personnel:
    Bob Kurtz, Director, Writer & Designer
    Boo Lopez, Producer
    Robert Peluce, Designer & Director
Specialties: Animation
Other Categories: TV; Commercials
Credits: Smokey the Bear (commercial)

KUSHNER-LOCKE COMPANY
11601 Wilshire Blvd., 21st Fl.
Los Angeles, CA 90025
Phone: ....(818) 841-8188
Fax: ....(818) 841-6263
www.kushner-locke.com
Key Executives/Personnel:
    Donald Kushner, Co-Chairman
    Peter Locke, Co-Chairman
    Bruce Lilliston, President & COO
    Rob Aft, President of Int'l. Distribution
    Richard Marks, Executive VP of Business Affairs
    Adam Moss, Executive VP of Production
    Steve Rosen, Executive VP of Operations & Finance
    Brett Robinson, Sr. VP & CFO
    Cynthia Griffith, VP of Int'l. Distribution
    Bob Wenokur, VP of Post Production
    Dana Scanlan, VP of Feature Films
Specialties: Independent; Direct-to-Video
Other Categories: TV
Credits: They Nest; Mambo Cafe; Beowolf

KUZUI ENTERPRISES, INC.
1041 N. Formosa Ave., Ste. B
Los Angeles, CA 90046
Phone: ....(323) 850-1195
Fax: ....(323) 850-5465
uskuzui@earthlink.net
Key Executives/Personnel:
    Kaz Kuzui, President
    Fran Kuzui, Co-President

Production Companies – Feature Film

Dawn Haber, Director of Creative Affairs
Specialties: Independent
Other Categories: TV
Credits: Tokyo Pop; Buffy The Vampire Slayer; Telling Lies in America; Orgazmo

LA PRODUCTIONS
Phone: (323) 874-9487
(323) 871-1982
Fax: (323) 874-9487
Key Executives/Personnel:
Herb Linsey, Executive Producer
John Arnow, Executive Producer
Stephen Paul, Executive Producer
Thomas Cost, Executive Producer
Specialties: Studio; Independent; Direct-to-Video
Other Categories: TV; Commercials; Music Video
Credits: Curad Bandages; Goodyear Tires; Johnson & Johnson; Wrangler Clothes

THE LADD COMPANY
9465 Wilshire Blvd., Ste. 910
Beverly Hills, CA 90212
Phone: (310) 777-2060
Fax: (310) 777-2061
Key Executives/Personnel:
Alan Ladd Jr., President
Keiliann Ladd, Producer
Natalia Chydzik, Creative Executive
Peter Bisanz, Assistant to Mr. Ladd
Lucy Rimalower, Assistant to Mr. Ladd
Specialties: Studio
Other Categories: TV
Credits: Chariots of Fire; Bladerunner; The Brady Bunch Movie; Braveheart

LAKESHORE ENTERTAINMENT CORPORATION
5555 Melrose Ave., Gloria Swanson Bldg.
Hollywood, CA 90038
Phone: (323) 956-4222
Fax: (323) 862-1190
Key Executives/Personnel:
Tom Rosenberg, Co-Chairman & CEO
Ted Tannebaum, Co-Chairman
Eric Reid, COO
Gary Lucchesi, President of Lakeshore Entertainment
Peter Rogers, President of Lakeshore Entertainment
Richard Wright, Executive VP & Head of Production
Robert Benun, Sr. VP of Business & Legal Affairs
Andre Lamal, VP of Physical Production
Renee Mancuso, VP of Finance
Bob McMinn, VP of Development
Christine Buckley, Executive Director of Business & Legal Affairs
Bic Tran, Director of Acquisitions
Kjose Elliot, Office Manager
Chris Brown, Story Editor
Beth Sekul, Development Assistant
Elisabeth Costa De Beauregard, Assistant to Mr. Rogers
Meg Dyer, Assistant to Mr. Lucchesi
Grant Grabowski, Assistant to Mr. Wright
Max Smerling, Assistant to Mr. Reid & Mr. Benum
Willow Reed, Executive Assistant to Mr. Rosenberg & Mr. Tannebaum
Anthony Striecher, Assistant to Mr. Lamal
Specialties: Studio; Independent
Credits: The Mothman Prophecies; The Apartment; Runaway Bride; Next Best Thing
First Look/Development Deals: Paramount Pictures

LAKOTA PRODUCTIONS
7080 Hollywood Blvd., Ste. 201B
Hollywood, CA 90028
Phone: (323) 464-8462
Fax: (323) 464-8305
Key Executives/Personnel:
Neil Canton, President & Producer
Specialties: Studio
Credits: Angel Eyes; Get Carter; Duets; Back to the Future 1, 2 & 3
First Look/Development Deals: Paramount Pictures

LANGLEY PRODUCTIONS
2225 Colorado Ave.
Santa Monica, CA 90404
Phone: (310) 449-5300
Key Executives/Personnel:
John Langley, President, Executive Producer, Director & Writer
Murray Jordan, Producer
Doug Waterman, Producer
Elie Cohn, Producer
Karen Hori, VP of TV Development
Specialties: Independent
Other Categories: TV; Interactive Multimedia
Credits: Cops; Anatomy of a Crime; Code 3; Wild Side
First Look/Development Deals: Twentieth Century Fox

LAWTON ENTERTAINMENT
419 N. Larchmont, PMB 27
Los Angeles, CA 90004
Phone: (323) 467-5677
Fax: (323) 467-5755
lawtonenter@earthlink.net
Key Executives/Personnel:
J. F. Lawton, President
Specialties: Studio
Other Categories: TV
Credits: V.I.P.; Under Seige

LE MONDE ENTERTAINMENT
808 Wilshire Blvd., 3rd Fl.
Santa Monica, CA 90404
Phone: (310) 899-8000
(416) 967-1174
Fax: (310) 899-8100
www.allianceatlantis.com
Key Executives/Personnel:
Marc Forby, Director of Creative Affairs
Specialties: Independent
Other Categories: TV
Credits: Second Skin; Cara Cara; Teacher's Pet; Falling Through

LEADING PICTURES, INC.
8981 Sunset Blvd., Ste. 311
West Hollywood, CA 90069
Phone: (310) 385-0951
Fax: (310) 385-9408
leadingpixae@aol.com
Key Executives/Personnel:
Anthony Esposito, Producer & President
Raymond Lee, VP of Finance
Danielle Probst, Director of Development
Nicole Cherill, Executive Assistant to Mr. Esposito
Specialties: Studio; Independent
Credits: Camouflage; Looking for an Echo; Lured Innocence; Special Delivery

STAN LEE MEDIA, INC.
15821 Ventura Blvd., Ste. 675
Encinco, CA 91436
Phone: (818) 461-1757
Fax: (818) 461-1760
www.stanleemedia.com
info@stanleemedia.com

Production Companies – Feature Film

Key Executives/Personnel:
    Stan Lee, Chairman & CCO
    Ken Williams, President & CEO
    Peter Paul, Co-Founder
    Stephen Brain, Executive VP of Production
    Stephen Gordon, Executive VP of Operations
    Jamie Wilkenson, Executive VP of Internet Strategy
    George Hamilton, President of Global Branded Entertainment
    Dana Moreshead, VP of Creative Services
Specialties: Independent
Other Categories: Interactive Multimedia
Credits: 7th Portal (feature); The Drifter (multimedia); The Backstreet Project (multimedia)
First Look/Development Deals: Shockwave.com, The Mark Canton Company

MALCOLM LEO PRODUCTIONS
6536 Sunset Blvd.
Los Angeles, CA 90028
Phone: ....(323) 464-4448
Fax: ....(323) 856-8755
Key Executives/Personnel:
    Malcolm Leo, Executive Producer & Director
    David Fairfield, Producer
    Nat Segaloff, Producer
    Edick Hossepian, Editorial
    Lionel Banes, Operations Manager
Specialties: Documentaries
Other Categories: TV
Credits: Rock 'n Roll Moments; Laverne & Shirley Reunion; This Is Elvis; Rolling Stone - 20 Years of Rock 'n Roll
Trade Assoc./Guilds/Unions: AFTRA, BMI, DGA, SAG, WGAw

LET THERE BE LIGHT PRODUCTIONS
4240 Lost Hills Rd., Ste. 2801
Agoura Hills, CA 91301
Phone: ....(818) 880-4717
Fax: ....(818) 880-4717
littnet@cs.com
Key Executives/Personnel:
    Robert Litt, Producer
Specialties: Independent; Direct-to-Video; Shorts; Trailers
Other Categories: TV; Commercials; Video; Music Video
Credits: Jenny Craig; WorldFreeNet.com; MPI/LA Tourism Bureau; Turbo - Take It To The Limit
First Look/Development Deals: Summer Storm Pictures

MICHAEL I. LEVY ENTERPRISES
6404 Wilshire Blvd., Ste. 520
Los Angeles, CA 90048
Phone: ....(323) 866-1802
Fax: ....(323) 866-1820
Key Executives/Personnel:
    Michael I. Levy, Producer
    Stephen Macias, VP of Creative Affairs
    Mark Saffian, Director of Development
    Georgette Waas, Executive Assistant
Specialties: Independent
Other Categories: TV
Credits: Prelude to a Kiss; Article 99; O

SIMON LEWIS PRODUCTIONS, INC.
16002 Meadowcrest Rd.
Sherman Oaks, CA 91403
Phone: ....(818) 906-7677
Fax: ....(818) 906-2836
Key Executives/Personnel:
    Simon R. Lewis, President
Specialties: Studio; Independent
Other Categories: TV
Credits: Look Who's Talking; The Chocolate War; Age Old Friends; Howie From Maui

LICHT/MUELLER FILMS
132A S. Lasky Dr., Ste. 200
Beverly Hills, CA 90212
Phone: ....(310) 205-5500
Fax: ....(310) 205-5590
Key Executives/Personnel:
    Andrew Licht, Partner & Producer
    Jeffery Mueller, Partner & Producer
    Ben Sitzer, Director of Development
    Doug Hammond, Creative Assistant
Specialties: Independent
Other Categories: TV
Credits: Idle Hands; License to Drive; The Cable Guy; Waterworld

LIGHTHOUSE PRODUCTIONS
120 El Camino Dr., Ste. 212
Beverly Hills, CA 90212
Phone: ....(310) 859-4923
Fax: ....(310) 859-7511
Key Executives/Personnel:
    Michael Phillips, Producer
    Juliana Maio, Producer
    John Frank Rosenblum, Producer
    Alia Tabet, Development Executive
Specialties: Studio
Credits: The Sting; Close Encounters; Taxi Driver; Mimic

LIGHTMOTIVE, INC.
10351 Santa Monica Blvd., Ste. 402
Los Angeles, CA 90025
Phone: ....(310) 282-0660
Fax: ....(310) 282-0990
Key Executives/Personnel:
    Roland Joffe, Chairman & CEO
    Ethan Markowitz, Creative Director
    Brian Lhee, Executive Assistant to Mr. Joffe
Specialties: Studio; Independent
Other Categories: TV
Credits: Fat Man and Little Boy; City of Joy; Undressed (TV series); Goodbye Lover

LIGHTSTORM ENTERTAINMENT
919 Santa Monica Blvd.
Santa Monica, CA 90401
Phone: ....(310) 656-6100
Fax: ....(310) 656-6102
Key Executives/Personnel:
    James Cameron, Chairman & CEO
    Carol Henry, CFO
    Rae Sanchini, President
    Jon Landau, Co-President
    Stacy Maes, VP of Development
    Jay Sanders, Director of Development
    Tom Cohen, Story Editor
Specialties: Studio
Credits: Titanic; Aliens; True Lies; Strange Days

LION ROCK PRODUCTIONS
2450 Broadway, Ste. 590
Santa Monica, CA 90404
Phone: ....(310) 449-3205
Fax: ....(310) 449-3512
Key Executives/Personnel:
    John Woo, Director & Producer
    Terence Chang, Producer
    Caroline Bruce, VP
    Suzanne Zizzi, VP
    Annie Hughes, Creative Executive

Production Companies – Feature Film

Specialties: Studio
Other Categories: TV
Credits: Windtalkers; The Big Hit; Broken Arrow; Face Off
First Look/Development Deals: MGM, Inc.

LIONS GATE ENTERTAINMENT
5750 Wilshire Blvd., Ste. 501
Los Angeles, CA 90036
Phone: (323) 692-7300
(310) 314-2000
Fax: (323) 692-7395
www.lionsgate.ent.com
www.lionsgate.ent.com
Key Executives/Personnel:
  Michael Paseornek, President of Production
  Mark Amin, Board of Directors
  Mark Urman, Co-President of Releasing
  Tom Ortenberg, Co-President of Releasing
  Cami Winikoff, Executive VP
  Peter Block, Executive VP of Distribution, Acquisitions & New Media
  Kevin Beggs, Executive VP of TV Series
  Doug Shwartz, Executive Producer
  Sergei Yershov, Sr. VP of Int'l. Sales
  Ellen Burditt, Sr. VP of TV Series
  Andy Reimer, Sr. VP of Worldwide Television
  Robin Schorr, Sr. VP of Production
  Ron Schwartz, Sr. VP of Home Video
  Richard Jordan, Sr. VP of Physical Operations
  Joella West, Sr. VP of Business Affairs
  James L. Zemelman, Sr. VP of Business Affairs
  Peter Marshall, VP of TV Production
  Guy Stodel, VP of Acquisitions
  Tracy Ames, VP of Worldwide Home Video Marketing
  Sarah Lash, Director of Acquisitions & Development
Specialties: Independent; Direct-to-Video; Documentaries
Other Categories: TV
Credits: American Psycho; Buffalo 66; Shadow of the Vampire; Jerry & Tom
Additional Info: Recently merged with Trimark Pictures. Personnel titles subject to change.

SI LITVINOFF PRODUCTIONS
2825 Woodstock Rd.
Los Angeles, CA 90046
Phone: (323) 848-6907
Fax: (323) 848-6908
slitvinoff@aol.com
Key Executives/Personnel:
  Si Litvinoff, President
  Paul Madden, VP of Development
  Ian Litvinoff, VP
Specialties: Studio; Independent
Other Categories: TV
Credits: A Clockwork Orange; The Man Who Fell To Earth; Walkabout; The Queen
Trade Assoc./Guilds/Unions: AMPAS

WARREN LOCKHART PRODUCTIONS, INC.
P.O. Box 11629
Marina Del Rey, CA 90295
Phone: (310) 821-1414
Fax: (310) 301-0536
warren@lockhartproductions.com
Key Executives/Personnel:
  Warren Lockhart, Producer & Writer
  Mackenzie Allen, VP of Development
Specialties: Studio; Independent; Documentaries; Animation
Other Categories: TV
Trade Assoc./Guilds/Unions: MPAA

LOGO ENTERTAINMENT
1888 Century Park East, Ste. 1900
Los Angeles, CA 90067
Phone: (310) 276-6700
Fax: (310) 284-3290
logoent@earthlink.net
Key Executives/Personnel:
  Louis Gossett Jr., President
  Dennis Considine, Executive Producer
  Laurie Ferneau, Development
Specialties: Direct-to-Video
Other Categories: TV
Credits: The Color of Love: Jacey's Story; For Love of Olivia; The Inspectors; The Inspectors 2: A Shred of Evidence
First Look/Development Deals: TeleVest, Inc.

LONGBOARD PRODUCTIONS, INC.
P.O. Box 2130
Elk Grove, CA 95759
Phone: (916) 684-5085
(916) 825-5390
Fax: (916) 684-5085
longboardproductions.com
fbernhardt@jps.net
Key Executives/Personnel:
  Ernie Cabral, President, Producer & Screenwriter
  Fred Bernhardt, VP, CFO & Producer
  Roland Ozzie Smith, VP, DP & Producer
  Michael Dryhurst, Producer
Specialties: Studio; Independent
Other Categories: Commercials
First Look/Development Deals: Digital Magic Company

LONGFELLOW PICTURES
145 Hudson St., 9th Fl.
New York, NY 10013
Phone: (212) 431-5550
Fax: (212) 435-5822
longfellow@mindspring.com
Key Executives/Personnel:
  Andrew Karsch, President & CEO
  Jane Garnett, Director of Development
  Amy Wood, Development Assistant
Specialties: Studio; Independent
Credits: Princess Caraboo; Curtain Call; Town and Country

LOTUS FILMS
6063 Sunset Blvd.
Los Angeles, CA 90028
Phone: (626) 292-1015
(626) 695-1112
Fax: (626) 292-1002
www.lotusfilms.com
lotusfilms@excite.com
Key Executives/Personnel:
  Dawn Fanning, Producer
  Mark Taylor, Director
  Gail Brooks, Director
  Paul McIlvaine, Director of Photography
Specialties: Shorts
Other Categories: Commercials
Credits: Room; Forever; McDonald's

LOVE SPELL ENTERTAINMENT
10202 W. Washington Blvd., Gable Bldg., Ste. 103
Culver City, CA 90232
Phone: (310) 244-6040
Fax: (310) 244-0740
jill-gilbert@spe.sony.com

Production Companies – Feature Film

Key Executives/Personnel:
   Jennifer Love Hewitt, Producer
   Jill Gilbert, Producer
Specialties: Studio; Independent
Credits: Girl in the Curl; Bunny; Park Jester; 13 Seconds
First Look/Development Deals: Columbia Pictures/Columbia Tristar Motion Picture Group

LUCASFILM LTD.
5858 Lucas Valley Rd.
Nicasio, CA 94946
Phone: (415) 662-1800
Specialties: Independent
Other Categories: TV
Additional Info: P.O. Box 2009, San Rafael, CA 94912

LUCID FILM
8490 Sunset Blvd., Ste. 700
West Hollywood, CA 90069
Phone: (310) 777-0007
Fax: (310) 360-8613
www.lucidfilm.com
Key Executives/Personnel:
   Ryan Phillippe, Producer
   David E. Siegel, Producer
Specialties: Studio; Independent; Shorts; Animation
Other Categories: TV; Interactive Multimedia
First Look/Development Deals: Intermedia Films

LUCID MEDIA
Phone: (818) 764-8580
www.loop.com/~macbravo
macbravo@loop.com
Key Executives/Personnel:
   Marino Colmano, Producer
Specialties: Independent; Shorts; Documentaries
Other Categories: TV; Commercials; Video
Credits: Reservoirs of Strength; End of the Rainbow

LUMIERE FILMS, INC.
8079 Selma Ave.
Los Angeles, CA 90046
Phone: (323) 650-6773
Fax: (323) 650-7339
lila@lumiere-films.com
Key Executives/Personnel:
   Lila Cazes, Head of Worldwide Production
   Steve Shedd, Head Administrator
Specialties: Independent
Credits: Leaving Las Vegas; Fresh; Touch; Somebody to Love

LUMINOSITY PRODUCTIONS
4220 Lankershim Blvd., 3rd Fl.
North Hollywood, CA 91602
Phone: (818) 752-3318
        (310) 620-0403
Fax: (818) 752-3311
www.luminosityprod.com
marla@luminosityprod.com
Key Executives/Personnel:
   Marla Friedler, Executive Producer
   Debbie Pinckes, Production Rep.
   Michael Kahn, Director
   Johnathan Kahn, Director
   Gregg Marquette, Director
   Pascal Franchot, Director
   Matthew Curry, Director
   David Kennedy, Director
Specialties: Independent

Other Categories: Commercials
Credits: Planned Parenthood; Apponline; Protest Clothing
Additional Info: 219 Broadway, Ste. 209, Laguna Beach CA 92651

LUX PICTURES, INC.
120 Mildred Ave.
Venice, CA 90291
Phone: (310) 301-0101
Fax: (310) 301-0153
www.luxpix.com
Key Executives/Personnel:
   James Magowan, President & Executive Producer
   Fiona Banister, Sr. Executive Producer & Partner
   Martin Kistler, Sr. Producer
   Mark Ching, Producer
Specialties: Independent; Documentaries
Other Categories: Commercials
Credits: Charles E. Merril: An American Tycoon

M.H.S. PRODUCTIONS
9336 W. Washington Blvd., Bldg. 0, Rm. 202
Culver City, CA 90232
Phone: (310) 202-3336
Fax: (310) 202-3320
Key Executives/Personnel:
   Joan Hyler, Producer
   Alfred Molina, Producer & Actor
   Larry Scissors, Business Affairs
   Adam Gascoine, Director of Development
   Joey Chang, Development Assistant
Specialties: Independent
Other Categories: TV
Credits: Ladies Man
First Look/Development Deals: Columbia Pictures/Columbia Tristar Motion Picture Group

WILLIAM J. MACDONALD PRODUCTIONS
3100 Donald Douglas Loop North, Box 17, Hangar 5
Santa Monica, CA 90405
Phone: (310) 581-4840
Fax: (310) 581-6111
wjmprods@aol.com
Key Executives/Personnel:
   Bill MacDonald, Producer
   Erik Mountain, Development
Specialties: Studio; Independent
Other Categories: TV
Credits: Sliver; The Saint; Jade; Molly

MACGILLIVRAY FREEMAN FILMS
P.O. Box 205
Laguna Beach, CA 92652
Phone: (949) 494-1055
Fax: (949) 494-2079
www.macfreefilms.com
Key Executives/Personnel:
   Greg MacGillivray, President, Director & Producer
   Alec Lorimore, VP Production/Development & Producer
   Stephen Judson, VP Post Production, Director, Writer & Producer
   Bill Bennett, President, MFF Distribution Co.
Specialties: Large Format
Credits: Adventures in Wild California; Dolphins; Everest; Magic of Flight

MAD CHANCE
4000 Warner Blvd., Bungalow 3
Burbank, CA 91522
Phone: (818) 954-3803

Production Companies – Feature Film

Fax: (818) 954-3447
Key Executives/Personnel:
    Andrew Lazar, Producer
    Jody Heiden, Co-Producer
    Doug Davison, VP of Production
    Far Shariat, Director of Creative Affairs
Specialties: Studio
Credits: Lucky Numbers; Space Cowboys; 10 Things I Hate About You
First Look/Development Deals: Warner Bros.

MAKE IT HAPPEN PRODUCTIONS, INC.
Phone: (323) 851-6444
Fax: (323) 851-6465
www.billyfrank.com
mihpi@aol.com
Key Executives/Personnel:
    Billy Frank, President & Producer
    Todd Denkin, Director & Producer
    Mark Eberle, Director of Photography
    Caroline Hileman, Assistant to President & Coordinator
Specialties: Independent; Direct-to-Video; Documentaries; Trailers
Other Categories: TV; Commercials; Video; Music Video
Credits: Wap!; Toughman (specials); Australian Experience
First Look/Development Deals: ABC Entertainment Television Group, FX Networks, LLC
Trade Assoc./Guilds/Unions: SAG, WGAw

CHARLES MALCOLM VIDEO PRODUCTIONS
P.O. Box 1772
Newport Beach, CA 92646
Phone: (714) 963-4222
charlesmalcolm@yahoo.com
Key Executives/Personnel:
    Charles Malcolm, Owner
Specialties: Independent
Other Categories: Commercials; Video

MALPASO PRODUCTIONS
4000 Warner Blvd., Bldg. 81
Burbank, CA 91522
Phone: (818) 954-3367
Fax: (818) 954-4803
Key Executives/Personnel:
    Clint Eastwood, Producer, Actor & Director
    Melissa Rooker, Director of Development
    Joel Cox, Editor
Specialties: Studio; Independent
Credits: Space Cowboys; The Bridges of Madison County; Unforgiven
First Look/Development Deals: Warner Bros.

MANDALAY PICTURES
5555 Melrose Ave., Lewis Bldg.
Hollywood, CA 90038
Phone: (323) 956-2400
Fax: (323) 862-2266
Key Executives/Personnel:
    Peter Guber, Chairman
    Paul Schaeffer, Vice Chairman
    Adam Platnick, President
    Darrell Walker, Executive VP of Business Affairs
    John Zabel, Executive VP & CFO
    Karen Teicher, Executive VP of Production
    David Zelon, Executive VP of Production Administration
Specialties: Studio
Credits: Seven Years in Tibet; Gloria; Sleepy Hollow; I Know What You Did Last Summer

MANDOLIN ENTERTAINMENT
1741 Ivar Ave.
Los Angeles, CA 90028
Phone: (323) 802-6950

Fax: (323) 802-6951
Key Executives/Personnel:
    Mimi Polk Gitlin, Producer
    Tanna Thompson, Director of Development
    Lisa Kelly, Story Editor & Assistant
Specialties: Studio; Independent
Other Categories: TV
Credits: Thelma & Louise; White Squall; Black Rain; The Browning Version
First Look/Development Deals: Propaganda Films
Trade Assoc./Guilds/Unions: AMPAS

THE MANHATTAN PROJECT
1775 Broadway, Ste. 410
New York, NY 10019
Phone: (212) 258-2541
Fax: (212) 258-2546
Key Executives/Personnel:
    David Brown, President & Producer
    Kit Golden, Sr. VP of Production
    Doris Wood, Executive Assistant
Specialties: Studio; Independent
Other Categories: TV
Credits: Enigma; Angela's Ashes; Deep Impact; A Few Good Men

MANIFEST FILM COMPANY
1247 Euclid St.
Santa Monica, CA 90404
Phone: (310) 899-5554
Fax: (310) 899-5553
manifilm@aol.com
Key Executives/Personnel:
    Janet Yang, Producer & Partner
    Lisa Henson, Producer & Partner
    Naomi Despres, Sr. VP
    Josh Cowing, Executive Assistant to Mr. Yang
    Kevin Kelly, Executive Assistant to Ms. Henson
Specialties: Studio; Independent
Credits: People vs. Larry Flynt; Joy Luck Club; Zero Effect; The Weight of Water

MARCA-RELLI PRODUCTIONS, LLC
6208 Ramirez Mesa Dr.
Malibu, CA 90265
Phone: (310) 457-8867
Fax: (310) 457-5656
marcaprods@aol.com
Key Executives/Personnel:
    Rob Marcarelli, Producer & Director
    Joe Marroquin, Associate Producer
    Steve Blinn, Associate Producer
Specialties: Independent
Credits: The Omega Code; The Emissary; Out of Jerusalem; I Don't Buy Kisses Anymore

MARIPOSA
Phone: (805) 527-9990
Fax: (805) 527-9990
www.surfbit.com
nadar@pacbell.net
Key Executives/Personnel:
    Bridget Gardner, Director & Producer
    Carole Gardner, Production Manager
Specialties: Independent
Other Categories: Commercials; Interactive Multimedia
Credits: American Cancer Society; NAMES Project; MADD; SurfBit.com

LAURENCE MARK PRODUCTIONS
10202 W. Washington Blvd., Poitier Bldg., Ste. 3111
Culver City, CA 90232
Phone: (310) 244-5239
Key Executives/Personnel:
    Laurence Mark, Producer

Production Companies – Feature Film

Jonathon King, President of Production
John McNamara, VP of Development & Film
Ilene Berg, VP of Development & TV
Specialties: Studio
Other Categories: TV
Credits: Finding Forrester; Center Stage; As Good As It Gets; Jerry Maguire
First Look/Development Deals: Columbia Pictures/Columbia Tristar Motion Picture Group

MARVEL CHARACTERS, INC.
10474 Santa Monica Blvd., Ste. 206
Los Angeles, CA 90025
Phone: ....(310) 234-8991
Fax: ....(310) 234-8481
www.marvel.com
Key Executives/Personnel:
    Stan Lee, Chairman Emeritus
    Avi Arad, President & CEO
    Rich Ungar, President of Marvel Characters Group
    Carlos Lopez, Executive Director of Creative Development
    Matt Sullivan, Director of Development
    Michael Kelly, Executive Assistant to Mr. Lee
    Amy Lewis, Executive Assistant to Mr. Ungar
    Victoria Tapscott, Executive Assistant to Mr. Arad
Specialties: Studio; Independent; Animation
Other Categories: TV
Credits: Spider-man; X-Men; Blade

NIKI MARVIN PRODUCTIONS
8919 Harratt St., Ste. 304
Los Angeles, CA 90069
Phone: ....(310) 274-6320
Key Executives/Personnel:
    Niki Marvin, President
Specialties: Studio; Independent; Direct-to-Video; Documentaries
Other Categories: TV; Video
Credits: Nightmare On Elm Street 3; Buried Alive 1 & 2; The Shawshank Redemption

MATADOR PICTURES
12424 Wilshire Blvd., Ste. 770
Los Angeles, CA 90025
Phone: ....(310) 820-5866
Fax: ....(310) 207-2275
www.matadorpictures.com
lauri@matadorpictures.com
Key Executives/Personnel:
    Lauri Apelian, Producer
    Nigel Thomas, Producer
    Peter Watson-Wood, Producer
Specialties: Independent
Other Categories: TV
Credits: Mad Dogs & Englishmen; The Fall; Dead Funny; Mortal Kombat
Trade Assoc./Guilds/Unions: IFPW, PGA

MATOVICH PRODUCTIONS
P.O. Box 5744
Beverly Hills, CA 90209
Phone: ....(661) 250-0644
Fax: ....(661) 250-0167
matpro@eatthlink.net
Key Executives/Personnel:
    Mitchel Matovich, President
    Elayne Herscovici, Finance
    Patte Dee, Executive Secretary
Specialties: Independent
Credits: Social Suicide - AKA Prima Donnas; I Don't Buy Kisses Anymore; Lightning In A Bottle; Deadly Delusions
Trade Assoc./Guilds/Unions: ASCAP, ATAS, DGA, PGA

MATRIX COMMUNICATIONS
2522 Torrance Blvd.
Torrance, CA 90503
Phone: ....(310) 782-8400
Key Executives/Personnel:
    Marta Houske, Executive Producer & Director
Specialties: Shorts
Other Categories: Commercials; Video; Music Video; Interactive Multimedia
Credits: Zimbabwe Legit (music video); A Stitch in Time (documentary); Times Mirror (commercial); In Search of ... (TV series)

THE MATTHAU COMPANY, INC.
11661 San Vicente Blvd., Ste. 609
Los Angeles, CA 90049
Phone: ....(310) 454-3300
Key Executives/Personnel:
    Charles Matthau, President
    Michael McDavitt, President of Management Division
    Lana Morgan, Director of Creative Affairs
    Kristina Jeffers, Director of Business Affairs
    Jessica Cooper, Office Manager
Specialties: Studio; Independent
Other Categories: TV
Credits: Hanging up; Mrs. Lambert Remembers Love; The Grass Harp; Grumpy Old Men

MAVERICK FILMS
9348 Civic Center Dr., Mezzanine Level
Beverly Hills, CA 90210
Phone: ....(310) 276-6177
Fax: ....(310) 276-9477
Key Executives/Personnel:
    Madonna, no title
    Guy Oseary, no title
    Caresse Henry, no title
    Gary Ventimiglia, no title
Specialties: Studio
Credits: Going Down

MDP WORLDWIDE
1925 Century Park East, Ste. 1700
Los Angeles, CA 90067
Phone: ....(310) 226-8300
Fax: ....(310) 226-8350
info@behaviourww.com
Key Executives/Personnel:
    Mark Damon, Chairman & CEO
    Dick Kiratsonlis, COO
    Matthew Carson, CFO
    Todd Olsson, VP of Int'l. Sales & Acquisitions
    David Gaynes, Sr. VP of Marketing & Publicity
    Tatyana Joffe, Director of Int'l. Operations
    Devin Cutler, Director of Corporate Finance
    Kristine Knudson, Director of Acquisitions & Development
Specialties: Independent
Credits: The Body; Eye of the Beholder; Dog of Flanders; Love and Sex

MEGAHERTZ PICTURES
1600 Rosecrans Ave., Bldg. 2B, 1st. Fl.
Manhattan Beach, CA 90266
Phone: ....(310) 727-2600
Fax: ....(310) 727-2601
www.directorsite.com
megahertz@directorsite.com
Key Executives/Personnel:
    John Harris, Executive Producer

Production Companies – Feature Film

Francis Mohajerin, Executive Producer
Suzanne O'Keefe, Producer & Writer
Masashi Nagadoi, Producer & Writer
Specialties: Independent
Other Categories: Commercials; Video
Credits: She Said I Love You

BARRY MENDEL PRODUCTIONS
100 Universal City Plaza, Bungalow 5163
Universal City, CA 91608
Phone: ....(818) 733-3076
Fax: ....(818) 733-4070
Key Executives/Personnel:
Barry Mendel, no title
Jennifer Simpson, no title
Beth Irizarry, no title
Heather Magee, no title
Jason Miller, no title
Specialties: Studio; Independent
Credits: The Sixth Sense; Rushmore; Unbreakable; Flora Plum
First Look/Development Deals: Universal Pictures

MERCHANT-IVORY PRODUCTIONS
250 W. 57th St., Ste. 1825
New York, NY 10107
Phone: ....(212) 582-8049
Fax: ....(212) 459-9201
www.merchantivory.com
Key Executives/Personnel:
Ismail Merchant, Owner
James Ivory, Owner
Richard Hawley, Executive VP & Executive Producer
Marla L. Shelton, Director of Planning & Production Management
Specialties: Independent
Credits: Howard's End; Remains of the Day; A Soldier's Daughter Never Cries; The Golden Bowl

METAFILMICS
4250 Wilshire Blvd.
Los Angeles, CA 90010
Phone: ....(818) 734-9320
Fax: ....(818) 345-2502
Key Executives/Personnel:
Stephen Simon, Co-Founder
Barnet Bain, Co-Founder
Specialties: Studio; Independent
Other Categories: TV; Interactive Multimedia
Credits: What Dreams May Come; Somewhere in Time; Bill & Ted's Excellent Adventure; Quantum Project

METRO-GOLDWYN-MAYER STUDIOS, INC.
2500 Broadway St.
Santa Monica, CA 90404
Phone: ....(310) 449-3000
www.mgm.com/motionpictures
Key Executives/Personnel:
Alex Yemenidijian, Chairman & CEO
Chris McGurk, Chairman & COO
Alex Gartner, President of Production
Dan Taylor, Sr. Executive VP & CFO
William Jones, Sr. Executive VP & Secretary
Jay Rakow, General Counsel
Michael Nathanson, President of MGM Pictures
Robert Relyen, President of Production, MGM Pictures/United Artists Films
Larry Gleason, President of Theatrical Distribution
Gerry Rich, President of Theatrical Marketing
Darcie Denkert, Sr. Executive VP of Business Affairs & Legal Affairs
Specialties: Studio; Independent
Credits: The World Is Not Enough; Autumn In New York; Thomas Crown Affair

MICHAEL/FINNEY PRODUCTIONS, INC.
8947 Hargis St.
Los Angeles, CA 90034
Phone: ....(310) 838-9350
Fax: ....(323) 801-2199
www.terencemichael.com
tm@terencemichael.com
Key Executives/Personnel:
Terence Michael, Producer
Richard Finney, Producer
Specialties: Studio; Independent
Credits: 100 Girls; Chill Factor; If Lucy Fell; Life In The Fast Lane

THE MILLER ENTERTAINMENT GROUP, INC.
5900 Wilshire Blvd., Ste. 540
Los Angeles, CA 90036
Phone: ....(323) 932-6500
Key Executives/Personnel:
Lawrence Miller, President
Ty Supancic, VP
Specialties: Independent; Direct-to-Video
Other Categories: Commercials; Music Video
Credits: Deadly Currency (feature); Sallie B - Baby Mama (music video); Nick Frost - Deep Love (music video); Regatta Condominium (infomercial)
Trade Assoc./Guilds/Unions: SAG

MILLER/BOYETT PRODUCTIONS
745 Fifth Ave., Ste. 3500
New York, NY 10151
Phone: ....(212) 702-9779
....(212) 702-8721
Fax: ....(212) 702-0899
Key Executives/Personnel:
Robert L. Boyett, Executive Producer
Thomas L. Miller, Executive Producer
Diane Murphy, Director of M/B Executive Offices
Specialties: Studio; Independent
Other Categories: TV
Credits: Full House; Family Matters; Step By Step; Two of A Kind
First Look/Development Deals: Warner Bros.
Trade Assoc./Guilds/Unions: DGA, PGA, WGAe
Additional Info: No unsolicited material accepted.

MINDFIRE ENTERTAINMENT
3740 Overland Ave., Ste. E
Los Angeles, CA 90034
Phone: ....(310) 204-4481
Fax: ....(310) 204-5882
www.mindfireentertainment.com
maltman@mindfireentertainment.com
Key Executives/Personnel:
Mark Gottwald, Chairman
Dan Bates, CEO
Mark A. Altman, COO
Ellie Gottwald, VP of Creative Affairs
Ann Kaesman, Director of Development
Carlos Rodriguez, Story Analyst
Specialties: Studio; Independent
Other Categories: TV; Interactive Multimedia
Credits: Free Enterprise; The Specials

MINDSTORM PRODUCTIONS, LLC
1434 6th St., Ste. 1
Santa Monica, CA 90401
Phone: ....(310) 393-1183
Fax: ....(310) 393-6622
www.mindstormprods.com

Production Companies – Feature Film

mind71@aol.com
Key Executives/Personnel:
    Karina Duffy, President
    Jacquenne Beaudette, Co-President
    Larry Leahy, Producer
Specialties: Independent
Other Categories: TV
Credits: Fanactic; Extra; Diaries - Love Hurts; Fox Files/Fox Undercover

MINERVISION
8000 Sunset Blvd., Ste. 301A
Los Angeles, CA 90046
Phone: ....(323) 848-3080
Fax: ....(323) 848-3085
Key Executives/Personnel:
    Steve Miner, Producer & Director
    Jessica Cunningham, VP of Production
    Kristy Scanlan, VP of Development
    Jeff Shapiro, Assistant to Mr. Miner
    Jimmy Bradley, Development Assistant
Specialties: Studio
Other Categories: TV
Credits: Dawson's Creek
First Look/Development Deals: Dimension Films

MIRAGE ENTERPRISES
10202 W. Washington Blvd., Lean Bldg.
Culver City, CA 90232
Phone: ....(310) 244-2044
Fax: ....(310) 244-0044
Key Executives/Personnel:
    Sydney Pollack, Producer & Director
    Anthony Minghella, Producer & Director
    William Horberg, Producer
    David Rubin, Producer
    Geoff Stier, Producer
    Jenny McLaren, Office Manager
Specialties: Studio; Independent
Credits: The Talented Mr. Ripley; Random Hearts; Sliding Doors; Sense and Sensibility
First Look/Development Deals: Sony Pictures Entertainment

MIRAMAX FILMS
375 Greenwich St.
New York, NY 10013
Phone: ....(212) 941-3800
....(323) 951-4200
Fax: ....(212) 941-3949
www.miramax.com
Key Executives/Personnel:
    Harvey Weinstein, Co-Chairman
    Bob Weinstein, Co-Chairman
    Robert Osher, Co-President, Production
    Meryl Poster, Co-President, Production
    Billy Campbell, President of Miramax TV
    Mark Gill, President of Miramax (LA)
    Bahman Naragi, CFO
    Randy Spendlove, President, Motion Picture Music
    Charles Layton, Executive VP
    Agnes Mentres, Executive VP of Acquisitions & Co-Production
    Irwin Reiter, Executive VP of Accounting
    Colin Vaines, Executive VP of Development
    Alan Friedman, General Counsel & Sr. VP of Business Affairs
    Vicki Cherkas, Sr. VP of Business & Legal Affairs
    Julie Goldstein, Sr. VP of Production & Development
    Jon Gordon, Sr. VP of Production
    John Hadity, Sr. VP of Production Finance
    Andrew Herwitz, Sr. VP of Acquisitions & Business Affairs
    Steven Hutensky, Sr. VP of Business & Legal Affairs
    Kevin Hyman, Sr. VP of Physical Production
    Jeremy Kramer, Sr. VP of Production
    Michael Luisi, Sr. VP of Business Affairs
    Scott Martin, Sr. VP of Post Production
    Jill Messisck, Sr. VP of Production
    Paula Simonetti, VP of Human Resources
Specialties: Studio; Independent
Credits: Bounce; The Cider House Rules; Good Will Hunting; The English Patient
Additional Info: 7966 Beverly Blvd., Los Angeles, CA 90048

MISS JONES
1558 Tenth St.
Santa Monica, CA 90401
Phone: ....(310) 576-9280
Fax: ....(310) 576-0515
www.missjones.com
tracy@missjones.com
Key Executives/Personnel:
    Tracy Hauser, Executive Producer
    Bronwen LaGrue, Executive Producer
Specialties: Trailers
Other Categories: Commercials
Credits: iCast.com; Arthritis Foundation (PSA); ESPN; Kleenex

MM2K
838 N. Doheny Dr., Ste. 904
West Hollywood, CA 90069
Phone: ....(310) 276-0750
Fax: ....(310) 276-0229
mm2k@earthlink.net
Key Executives/Personnel:
    William A. Levey, Executive Producer & Director
    Bob Manning, Head of Production
    Nancy Youngblood, Director of Creative Development
Specialties: Studio; Independent
Other Categories: TV; Commercials; Video; Music Video
Credits: Slumber Party 57; The Happy Hooker Goes To Washington; Skatetown U.S.A; White Stallion
Trade Assoc./Guilds/Unions: DGA, IATSE, WGAw

MO JO PRODUCTIONS, INC.
4224 Waialae Ave., Ste. 300
Honolulu, HI 96816
Phone: ....(808) 384-8460
....(626) 932-6432
Fax: ....(808) 733-4142
mojoproductions@juno.com
Key Executives/Personnel:
    Michael Pendell, President
Specialties: Trailers
Other Categories: TV; Commercials; Music Video
Credits: Baywatch: Hawaii; Extended list available upon request.
Trade Assoc./Guilds/Unions: DGA

MONAREX HOLLYWOOD CORPORATION
9421 1/2 W. Pico Blvd.
Los Angeles, CA 90035
Phone: ....(310) 552-1069
Fax: ....(310) 552-1724
Key Executives/Personnel:
    Chris D. Nebe, President
Specialties: Studio; Independent; Direct-to-Video; Documentaries
Other Categories: TV; Video
Credits: Heartbreaker; Rebels; The Inheritors; Last of The Caravans
Trade Assoc./Guilds/Unions: IDA

MONTAGE ENTERTAINMENT
2118 Wilshire Blvd., Ste. 297
Santa Monica, CA 90403

Production Companies – Feature Film

Phone: (310) 966-0222
Fax: (310) 966-0223
montage.ent@usa.net
Key Executives/Personnel:
   David Peters, Producer
   Bill Ewart, Producer
Specialties: Independent
Credits: Acting On Impulse; Blue Desert; Gas, Food, Lodging; Mi Vida Loca

THE MONTECITO PICTURE COMPANY
1482 East Valley Rd., Ste. 477
Montecito, CA 93108
Phone: (805) 565-8590
Fax: (805) 565-8661
Key Executives/Personnel:
   Ivan Reitman, Partner
   Tom Pollock, Partner
   Michael Chinich, Development/Casting Executive & Producer
   Joe Medjuck, Producer
   Dan M. Goldberg, Producer
   Sheldon Kahn, Producer & Editor
Specialties: Studio

MORGAN CREEK PRODUCTIONS
4000 Warner Blvd., Bldg. 76
Burbank, CA 91522
Phone: (818) 954-4800
Fax: (818) 954-4811
www.morgancreek.com
Key Executives/Personnel:
   James G. Robinson, Chairman & CEO
   Howard Kaplan, CFO
   Jonathan A. Zimbert, President of Production
Specialties: Independent
Other Categories: TV
Credits: Ace Ventura; Robin Hood; Wild America; American Outlaw
First Look/Development Deals: Warner Bros.

MORRA, BREZNER, STEINBERG & TENENBAUM
345 N. Maple Dr., Ste. 200
Beverly Hills, CA 90210
Phone: (310) 385-1820
Fax: (310) 385-1834
Key Executives/Personnel:
   Larry Brezner, Partner
   David Steinberg, Partner
   Stephen Tenenbaum, Partner
   Judy Apperson, no title
   Jonathan Brandstein, no title
   Scott Fedro, no title
   Walter Hamada, no title
   Andrew Tenenbaum, no title
Specialties: Studio
Other Categories: TV
Credits: Krippendorf's Tribe; Clifford; The Vanishing
First Look/Development Deals: Walt Disney Pictures/Touchstone Pictures

MOSTOW/LIEBERMAN
100 Universal City Plaza, Bungalow 4111
Universal City, CA 91608
Phone: (818) 777-4444
Fax: (818) 866-1328
Key Executives/Personnel:
   Hal Lieberman, Partner
   Jonathan Mostow, Partner
   Rick Silverman, President
   Jed Blaugrund, no title
Specialties: Studio

Credits: U-571; The Game; The Jackal
First Look/Development Deals: Universal Pictures

MOUSHEL PRODUCTIONS
66 Park St.
Andover, MA 01810
Phone: (978) 618-1933
Fax: (978) 475-1448
sstapo@aol.com
Key Executives/Personnel:
   Steve Stapinski, Producer
Specialties: Studio; Independent; Shorts
Credits: Sporting Dog

MOVING PICTURES
375 Greenwich St.
New York, NY 10013
Phone: (212) 219-4545
Fax: (212) 219-4546
Key Executives/Personnel:
   Demi Moore, Partner & Producer
   Daneen Conroy, Partner & President
   Andrea Asimow, Sr. VP of Production
   Ren Tucker, Creative Executive
Specialties: Studio
Other Categories: TV
Credits: Austin Powers 1 & 2; G. I. Jane; If These Walls Could Talk
First Look/Development Deals: Miramax Films

MOVING TARGET
1250 Sixth St., Ste. 201
Santa Monica, CA 90401
Phone: (310) 394-0110
Fax: (310) 394-4123
Specialties: Studio
Other Categories: TV; Commercials
Credits: Sleepy Hollow; The Others

MOZARK PRODUCTIONS
4024 Radford Ave., Bldg. 5, Ste. 104
Studio City, CA 91604
Phone: (818) 655-5779
Fax: (818) 655-5129
mozark@ix.netcom.com
Key Executives/Personnel:
   Linda Bloodworth-Thomason, Executive Producer & Writer
   Harry Thomason, Executive Producer & Director
Specialties: Independent
Other Categories: TV
Credits: Woman of the House; Evening Shade; Designing Women
First Look/Development Deals: CBS Entertainment, DreamWorks SKG

MR. MUDD PRODUCTIONS
5225 Wilshire Blvd., Ste. 604
Los Angeles, CA 90036
Phone: (323) 932-5656
Fax: (323) 932-5666
Key Executives/Personnel:
   John Malkovich, Partner
   Lianne Halfon, Partner
   Russ Smith, Partner
   Aileen Argentini, Head of Production
Specialties: Studio; Independent
Other Categories: TV
Credits: Ghost World; The Dancer Upstairs
First Look/Development Deals: Granada Film

MT. TABOR PRODUCTIONS
4974 N. Fresno St., PMB 544
Fresno, CA 93726

Phone: .... (559) 347-0835
Fax: .... (559) 347-0835
www.nextstopproductions.com
mttabor@lightspeed.net
Key Executives/Personnel:
  Joe Fawcett III, Producer
  Roger George, Producer
Specialties: Independent; Direct-to-Video
Credits: Academic Gameplan; The War Within; Demonhunter

MTV FILMS
5555 Melrose Ave., Modular Bldg., Ste. 213
Los Angeles, CA 90038
Phone: .... (323) 956-8023
Fax: .... (323) 862-1386
www.mtv.com
Key Executives/Personnel:
  Van Toffler, General Manager of MTV Networks/President of MTV Productions
  David M. Gale, Head of MTV Films/Sr. VP of MTV Films
  Momita Sengupta, MTV Films Production Manager
  Susan Lewis, Director of Development
Specialties: Studio
Credits: Varsity Blues; Election; The Wood
First Look/Development Deals: Paramount Pictures

MUSE PRODUCTIONS
15 Brooks Ave., Unit B
Venice, CA 90291
Phone: .... (310) 306-2001
Fax: .... (310) 574-2614
www.musefilm.com
Key Executives/Personnel:
  Chris Hanley, President & Producer
  Roberta Hanley, President & Director
  Jordan Gertner, VP
  Tim Peternel, VP of Creative Affairs
  Danny Vinik, VP of Digital Development
Specialties: Independent
Other Categories: TV
Credits: Bully; American Psycho; The Virgin Suicides; Trees Lounge

MUSIC ROOM PICTURES
P.O. Box 219
Redondo Beach, CA 90277
Phone: .... (310) 316-4551
Fax: .... (310) 540-3532
www.musicroomonline.com
mrp@aol.com
Key Executives/Personnel:
  John Reed, President
Specialties: Independent
Other Categories: Commercials; Video; Music Video

MUTANT ENEMY, INC.
P.O. Box 900
Beverly Hills, CA 90213
Phone: .... (310) 579-5180
Fax: .... (310) 579-5380
Key Executives/Personnel:
  Joss Whedon, CEO
  Tom Plotkin, Creative Executive
  George Synder, Director of Development
Specialties: Studio; Animation
Other Categories: TV
Credits: Buffy The Vampire Slayer; Angel
First Look/Development Deals: Twentieth Century Fox Television

MUTUAL FILM COMPANY
650 N. Bronson Ave., Clinton Bldg.
Los Angeles, CA 90004
Phone: .... (323) 871-5690
Fax: .... (323) 871-5689
Key Executives/Personnel:
  Marc Gordon, Principal
  Gary Levinsohn, Principal
  Betsy Beers, President of Production
  Tania Landau, Production Executive
  Suzanne Patmore, Production Executive
  Al Haferkamp, Controller
  Anthony Mosawi, Business & Legal Affairs
  Pamela Pickering, Mutual Film Int'l.
Specialties: Studio
Other Categories: TV
Credits: Saving Private Ryan; The Patriot; A Simple Plan; Wonder Boys
First Look/Development Deals: Paramount Pictures

MWG PRODUCTIONS
8075 W. Third St., Ste. 402
Los Angeles, CA 90048
Phone: .... (323) 937-8313
Fax: .... (323) 937-5239
Key Executives/Personnel:
  Max Goldenson, Owner & Producer
Specialties: Studio; Independent; Direct-to-Video; Shorts; Documentaries
Other Categories: TV
Credits: Nine; Saddlebags; The Tracy Bower Story; Cast No Shadow

NATIONAL GEOGRAPHIC FEATURE FILMS
501 S. Beverly Dr., Ste. 250
Beverly Hills, CA 90212
Phone: .... (310) 229-0990
Fax: .... (310) 229-0980
Key Executives/Personnel:
  Christine Whitaker, Head of Features
  Laura Kim Lodin, Story Editor
Specialties: Studio
Other Categories: TV

NATIONAL LAMPOON
10850 Wilshire Blvd., Ste. 1000
Los Angeles, CA 90024
Phone: .... (310) 474-5252
Fax: .... (310) 474-1219
www.nationallampoon.com
Key Executives/Personnel:
  James P. Jimirro, President & CEO
  Chris Trunkey, CFO
  Duncan Murray, VP of Marketing
Specialties: Studio
Other Categories: TV; Interactive Multimedia
Credits: Vacation; Animal House; National Lampoon's Senior Trip

NEILD STREET PROD., INC.
1932 Grace Ave., Ste. 12
Los Angeles, CA 90068
Phone: .... (323) 969-9447
Fax: .... (323) 512-4524
www.neildstreet.com
info@neildstreet.com
Key Executives/Personnel:
  Jacob Matthew Gerhardt, Writer & Producer
  Micah A. Hauptman, Producer
  David Keslick, Producer
  Jay Sefton, Producer
  Christine Tso, CFO
Specialties: Independent
Other Categories: TV

Production Companies – Feature Film

NELVANA ENTERTAINMENT
4500 Wilshire Blvd., 1st Fl.
Los Angeles, CA 90010
Phone: ....(323) 549-4222
Fax: ....(323) 549-4232
www.nelvana.com
Key Executives/Personnel:
    Michael Hirsh, Co-CEO
    Patrick Loubert, Co-CEO
    Toper Taylor, President
    Steven Galloway, VP of Development
    David Harleston, VP of Business Affairs
Specialties: Animation
Other Categories: TV
Credits: Babar; Rolie Polie Olie; Little Bear

NEMIROFF PRODUCTIONS
1506 Butler Ave., Ste. 1
Los Angeles, CA 90025
Phone: ....(310) 473-4100
                                                       (310) 917-5250
Fax: ....(310) 473-4100
Key Executives/Personnel:
    Steve Nemiroff, Producer & Assistant Director
Specialties: Independent; Direct-to-Video; Shorts; Documentaries; Large Format
Other Categories: TV; Commercials; Video; Music Video; Interactive Multimedia
Credits: The Real Deal; Miracles; Sparkletts; Kenny Kingston's Psychic Hotline III
Trade Assoc./Guilds/Unions: AFI; AICP; ITVA

NEO ART & LOGIC
8315 Beverly Blvd.
Los Angeles, CA 90048
Phone: ....(323) 653-6007
Fax: ....(323) 653-0409
neoartandlogic@neoartlogic.com
Key Executives/Personnel:
    Joel Soisson, Producer
    Wiki Border, Producer
    Michael Leahy, Producer
    Lauren Feige, Development
Specialties: Studio; Independent; Documentaries
Credits: Dracula 2000; Trekkies; The Prophecy; Phantoms

MACE NEUFELD PRODUCTIONS
10202 W. Washington Blvd., Tristar Bldg., Ste 220
Culver City, CA 90232
Phone: ....(310) 244-2555
Fax: ....(310) 244-0255
Key Executives/Personnel:
    Mace Neufeld, Producer
    Kel Symons, VP
    David Engle, Director of Development
    Jeff Kirschenbaum, Creative Executive
    Dax Phelan, Story Editor
    Kathy Day, Executive Assistant to Mr. Neufeld & Office Manager
Specialties: Studio
Other Categories: TV
Credits: No Way Out; Hunt For Red October; Clear and Present Danger; General's Daughter
First Look/Development Deals: Sony Pictures Entertainment

NEVERLAND FILMS, INC.
10323 Santa Monica Blvd., Ste. 106
Los Angeles, CA 90025
Phone: ....(310) 772-0008
Key Executives/Personnel:
    Al Corley, Producer
    Bart Rosenblatt, Producer
    Eugene Musso, Producer
Specialties: Independent
Credits: Drowning Mona; Ring of Fire; Palmetto; A Brother's Kiss

NEW CONCORDE
11600 San Vincente Blvd.
Los Angeles, CA 90049
Phone: ....(310) 820-6733
Fax: ....(310) 207-6816
www.newconcorde.com
Key Executives/Personnel:
    Roger Corman, President & CEO
    Gary Jones, President
    Julie Corman, Sr. VP & Producer
    Catherine Corman, Producer
    Frances Doel, VP of Development
    Goly Jamshidi, VP of Finance
    Doug Lowell, VP of Business Development
Specialties: Independent; Direct-to-Video
Other Categories: TV
Credits: The Suicide Club; Black Scorpion; Fire on the Amazon

NEW CRIME PRODUCTIONS
555 Rose Ave.
Venice, CA 90291
Phone: ....(310) 396-2199
Fax: ....(310) 396-4249
newcrime@aol.com
Key Executives/Personnel:
    John Cusack, Actor, Writer & Producer
    Steve Pink, Writer & Producer
    D. V. Devincentis, Writer & Producer
    Grace Loh, VP
Specialties: Studio
Credits: Grosse Pointe Blank; Jack Bull; High Fidelity
First Look/Development Deals: New Line Cinema, Inc.

NEW LINE CINEMA, INC.
116 N. Robertson Blvd., Ste. 200
Los Angeles, CA 90048
Phone: ....(310) 854-5811
Fax: ....(310) 967-6898
www.newline.com
Key Executives/Personnel:
    Robert K. Shaye, Chairman & CEO
    Michael Lynne, President & COO
    Stephen D. Abramson, CFO
    James Rosenthal, President of New Line Media
    Rolf Mittweg, Co-Chairman of Worldwide Theatrical Marketing/President of International Distribution
    Robert Friedman, Co-Chairman of Worldwide Theatrical Marketing
    Sara Risher, Chairperson of Production
    David Tuckerman, President of Theatrical Distribution
    Stephen Einhorn, President, Home Video
    Rolf Mittweg, President of International Distribution
    Joe Nimziki, President of Theatrical Marketing
    Michael De Luca, President & COO of Production
    Carla Fry, President of Physical Production
    Robert Friedman, President of Television Distribution
    Toby Emmerich, President of Music
    Benjamin Zinkin, Sr. Executive VP of Business & Legal Affairs
    Michael Spatt, Sr. Executive VP of Finance
    Richard Saperstein, Sr. Executive VP of Production
    Judd Funk, Executive VP of Business & Legal Affairs
    Tracy Adler, Executive VP of Finance
    Susanna Juni, Executive VP of Royalty & Contracts
    Marsha Hook Haygood, Executive VP of Administration
    Mary Donovan, Executive VP of Publicity & Promotions
    Lynn Harris, Executive VP of Production
    Claire Rudnick-Polstein, Executive VP of Production

Paul Prokop, Executive VP of Production Finance
Jay Stern, Executive VP of Production
David Imhoff, Executive VP of Licensing & Merchandising
Diane Keating, Executive VP of TV International
David Spiegelman, Executive VP of Distribution (Television)
Laura Armstrong, Executive VP of Production & Development
Jane H. Williams, Sr. VP & Business Development
Jonathan K. Beal, Sr. VP & Eastern Division Manager
David Keith, Sr. VP of Sales Administration
Lawrence Levy, Sr. VP & Western Division Manager
Donald Osley, Sr. VP of Southeastern Division Manager
John Trickett, Sr. VP & Southern Division Manager
Matt LaSorsa, Sr. VP of Marketing, Home Video
Steve Elzer, Sr. VP of Corporate Publicity
Mary Goss Robino, Sr. VP of National Publicity
Elissa Greer, Sr. VP of Publicity & Promotions
Marian Koltai-Levine, Sr. VP of Marketing
Gordon Paddison, Sr. VP of Interactive Media
Erik Holmberg, Sr. VP of Production
Jody A. Levin, Sr. VP of Post Production
Jayne Bieber, Sr. VP of Television Production
Amy Henkels, Sr. VP of Production & Development
Donna Langley, Sr. VP of Development
Steve Tao, Sr. VP of Television Production
Dana Sano, Sr. VP of Music
Paul Broucek, Sr. VP of Music
Arianna Bocco, VP of Acquisitions
Gisela Corcoran, VP of National Print Control
Ralpho Borgos, VP of International Distribution & Contracts
Christina S. Frantti, VP of International & Home Video Services
Clare A. Darragh, VP of National Publicity
Dana P. Laufer, VP of National Publicity
Ileen J. Reich, VP of Publicity
Richard Brener, VP of Development
Leon Dudevoir, VP of Production
Evan Edelist, VP of Post Production
Brent Kaviar, VP of Post Production
Sara Kaviar, VP of Post Production
Richard Keeley, VP of Post Production
Joshua Ravetch, VP of Production Resources
Lauren A. Ritchie, VP of Visual Effects
Charles J. Freericks, VP of Development & Production, Television
Mark S. Kaufman, VP of Music & Business
Mitch Rotter, VP of Soundtracks
Neal Rothman, VP of Business Development
Nevin I. Shalit, VP of New Media Projects
Emily Glatter, VP of Production
Jeff Behlendorf, Executive Director of Post Production
Janis Chaskin, Executive Director of Creative
Sandra Constantine, Executive Director of Production
Erica Beier, Director of Production Services
Jack Deutchman, Director of Post Production
Bobby L. Doyle, Director of Post Production
Michael Grembowicz, Director of Print Production
Jeffrey R. Halsey, Director of Home Video & Television Post Production
Renee W. Witt, Director of Development
Specialties: Studio; Independent
Credits: Lord of the Rings; Rush Hour 2; Austin Powers: The Spy Who Shagged Me
Additional Info: 888 Seventh Ave., New York, NY 10106

NEW MILLENNIUM STUDIOS
One New Millenium Dr.
Petersburg, VA 23805
Phone: ....(804) 957-4200
Fax: ....(804) 862-1200
www.nmstudios.com
martinj@nmstudios.com

Key Executives/Personnel:
Tim Reid, Producer
Daphne Maxwell Reid, Producer
Martin C. Jones, Producer
Specialties: Studio; Independent; Direct-to-Video
Other Categories: TV; Commercials; Music Video; Interactive Multimedia
Credits: Asunder; Out of Sync; Linc's; When We Were Colored

NEW REGENCY PRODUCTIONS
10201 W. Pico Blvd., Bldg. 12
Los Angeles, CA 90035
Phone: ....(310) 369-8300
Fax: ....(310) 969-0470
www.newregency.com
Key Executives/Personnel:
Arnon Milchan, Producer
David Matalon, President & CEO
Sanford Panitch, President of Production
Louis Santor, Executive VP & CFO
William S. Weiner, Executive VP of Business & Legal Affairs/General Council
Peter Cramer, Sr. VP of Production
Roy Matalon, Sr. VP of Distribution
Thomas Imperato, Sr. VP of Physical Production
Elissa Loparco, Sr. VP of Post Production
Kara Francis, VP of Creative Affairs
Alexandra Milchan, VP Production & Acquisitions
Jason Weiss, Director of Development
Alex Ort, Story Editor
Specialties: Studio; Independent
Other Categories: TV
Credits: L.A. Confidential; Entrapment; Fight Club; City of Angels
First Look/Development Deals: Twentieth Century Fox Television

NEWMARK FILMS, INC.
8222 Melrose Ave., Ste. 305
Los Angeles, CA 90046
Phone: ....(323) 782-4969
Fax: ....(323) 782-6866
andreamia@yahoo.com
Key Executives/Personnel:
Andrea Mia, VP of Development & Production
Isaac Eaton, Writer & Director
Pete McAlevey, Producer
Tim Swain, Producer
Specialties: Independent
Credits: Shadow Hours

NICKELODEON MOVIES
5555 Melrose Ave., Lubitsch Annex, Ste. 119
Hollywood, CA 90038
Phone: ....(323) 956-8663
Fax: ....(323) 862-1663
Key Executives/Personnel:
Albie Hecht, President
Julia Pistor, Sr. VP
Share Stallings, VP of Development, Animation
Ricki Spector, VP of Development, Live Action
Ramsey Naito, Sr. Producer, Animation
Damon Ross, Creative Executive
Specialties: Studio; Animation
Credits: Good Burger; Harriet The Spy; Snow Day; Rugrats I & II
First Look/Development Deals: Paramount Pictures

NITESTAR PRODUCTIONS
6671 Sunset Blvd., Bldg. 1509, Ste. 104
Los Angeles, CA 90028
Phone: ....(323) 468-8089
Fax: ....(323) 468-8094

Production Companies – Feature Film

www.nitestar.com
jvasilatos@nitestar.com
Key Executives/Personnel:
- Jerry A. Vasilatos, President, Producer, Director & Editor
- John O'Shaugnessy, Videographer & Cinematographer
- Kevin Leadingham, Associate Producer & Director

Specialties: Independent; Direct-to-Video; Documentaries
Other Categories: Commercials; Video
Credits: Shelter Me; A Refugee & Me; Solstice

NO PRISONERS
2260 S. Centinela Ave.
Los Angeles, CA 90064
Phone: (310) 979-9097
Fax: (310) 979-7097
www.noprisoners.net
info@noprisoners.net
Key Executives/Personnel:
- Todd Moyer, CEO & Producer
- Chris Brown, Visual Effects Supervisor
- Erik Strauss, Visual Effects Producer
- Bruce Martin, President of Commercials
- Nic Mathieu, Director
- Brian Scott Weber, Director
- Michael Abbott, Creative Executive
- Jim McCarthy, Controller

Specialties: Studio; Independent
Other Categories: Commercials; Music Video
Credits: Wing Commander (feature); Mercedes-Benz (commercial); The FireFlies (feature); Mai: The Psychic Girl (feature)

NOBLE PRODUCTIONS, INC.
1615 S. Crest Dr.
Los Angeles, CA 90035
Phone: (310) 552-2934
Fax: (310) 552-3508
nobleproductions@hotmail.com
Key Executives/Personnel:
- Ika Panajotovic, President
- Elena Panajotovic, VP & Secretary
- Sonja Panajotovic, Legal Affairs

Specialties: Independent
Other Categories: TV
Credits: Last Nazi; Day Of The Assassin; Cruise Missile; Hell River

NORAH FILMS
662 N. Van Ness Ave., Ste. 301
Los Angeles, CA 90004
Phone: (323) 960-3458
Fax: (323) 960-3456
norahfi@earthlink.net
Key Executives/Personnel:
- Rose Sharon, President

Specialties: Independent
Other Categories: TV
Credits: Nature Boy; Double Hang; Out Of The Cold
Trade Assoc./Guilds/Unions: DGA

NORTH HALL PRODUCTIONS
3000 S. Robertson Blvd., Ste. 240
Los Angeles, CA 90034
Phone: (310) 558-5040
Fax: (310) 558-5091
Key Executives/Personnel:
- Bill Nuss, Executive Producer

Specialties: Independent
Other Categories: TV
Credits: Booker; Pacific Blue; Raven

NOVA PICTURES
6496 Ivarene Ave.
Los Angeles, CA 90068
Phone: (323) 462-5502
Fax: (323) 467-1438
www.novapictures.com
pbarnett@novapictures.com
Key Executives/Personnel:
- Peter Barnett, Producer
- Chris Debie, Unit Production Manager

Specialties: Independent; Shorts
Other Categories: TV; Commercials
Credits: Extraordinary Visitor; Yellow Badge of Courage; Valley Clinic (commercial)
Trade Assoc./Guilds/Unions: ATAS, IFP

NUANCE PRODUCTIONS
345 N. Maple Dr., Ste. 208
Beverly Hills, CA 90210
Phone: (310) 247-1870
Fax: (310) 247-8150
Key Executives/Personnel:
- Paul Reiser, Partner
- Arthur Spivak, Partner
- Vernon Sanders, VP of Development

Specialties: Independent
Other Categories: TV
Credits: Mad About You
First Look/Development Deals: Columbia Pictures/Columbia Tristar Motion Picture Group

NXT ENTERTAINMENT
8639 Holloway Plaza Dr.
Los Angeles, CA 90069
Phone: (310) 289-9600
Fax: (310) 289-7383
www.wwwcine.com
nxt@wwwcine.com
Key Executives/Personnel:
- Klaus Lucka, Executive Producer

Specialties: Trailers
Other Categories: TV; Commercials; Video; Interactive Multimedia
Credits: www.cyberkidsplanet.com; www.neobodies.com
Trade Assoc./Guilds/Unions: DGA

O ENTERTAINMENT
31878 Camino Capistrano, Ste. 101
San Juan Capistrano, CA 92675
Phone: (949) 443-3222
Fax: (949) 443-3223
Key Executives/Personnel:
- Steve Oedekerk, Owner & Producer
- Paul Marshal, Producer

Specialties: Studio; Independent

OAK ISLAND FILMS, INC.
8581 Santa Monica Blvd.
Los Angeles, CA 90069
Phone: (310) 246-1466
Fax: (847) 557-1314
www.oakislandfilms.com
info@oakislandfilms.com
Key Executives/Personnel:
- Kenneth Schwenker, President
- Ronell Venter, Creative Executive
- Virginia Wilson, Acquisitions

Specialties: Studio; Independent
Credits: Cursed Part 3; Boys From Madrid; American Intellectuals; Evolution

LYNDA OBST PRODUCTIONS
5555 Melrose Ave., Bldg. 210
Hollywood, CA 90038
Phone: ....(323) 956-8744
Fax: ....(323) 862-2287
Key Executives/Personnel:
  Lynda Obst, Producer
  Elizabeth Hooper, VP of Physical Production
  Marc Rosen, Sr. VP of Development
  Mandy Safavi, VP of Development
  Kellie Bryce, Creative Executive
Specialties: Studio
Other Categories: TV
Credits: Animal Husbandry; Hope Floats; The Siege
First Look/Development Deals: Paramount Pictures

OCEAN PICTURES
10201 W. Pico Blvd., Bldg. 12, Rm. 123
Los Angeles, CA 90035
Phone: ....(310) 369-0093
Fax: ....(310) 369-7742
Key Executives/Personnel:
  Harold Ramis, Producer, Director & Writer
  Trevor Albert, Producer
  Suzanne Herrington, Director of Development
  Lisa Ullmann, Creative Executive
  Laurel Ward, Development Assistant
  Kym Bye, Development Assistant
Specialties: Studio
Credits: Bedazzled; Groundhog Day; Caddyshack; Multiplicity

LIN OLIVER PRODUCTIONS
8271 Beverly Blvd.
Los Angeles, CA 90048
Phone: ....(323) 782-1495
Fax: ....(323) 782-1892
www.linoliverproductions.com
lin@linoliverproductions.com
Key Executives/Personnel:
  Lin Oliver, Producer
  Mercedes Coats, Manager of Creative Affairs
Specialties: Direct-to-Video; Animation
Other Categories: TV
Credits: Trumpet of the Swan; Finding Buck McHenry; Corduroy; Harry and the Hendersons
First Look/Development Deals: Columbia TriStar Motion Picture Group, Kushner-Locke Company
Trade Assoc./Guilds/Unions: WGAw

OLMOS PRODUCTIONS, INC.
2020 Avenue of the Stars, Ste. 500
Century City, CA 90067
Phone: ....(310) 557-7010
....(914) 945-0566
Fax: ....(310) 557-6276
Key Executives/Personnel:
  Edward James Olmos, Chairman
  Nick Athas, Producer
  Danny Haro, Producer
  Javier Varon, Office Manager
Specialties: Studio; Documentaries
Credits: American Me; Lives in Hazard; It Ain't Love; Americanos: Latino Life in the U.S.

OMNIBUS
500 S. Buena Vista, Animation Bldg., 2E-3
Burbank, CA 91521
Phone: ....(818) 560-3611
Fax: ....(818) 972-2841
Key Executives/Personnel:
  Rob Scheidlinger, Producer & President
  Sean Jacques, Executive Assistant
Specialties: Studio
Other Categories: TV
Credits: Sports Night; Cousin Bette; Speaking of Sex
First Look/Development Deals: Walt Disney Pictures/Touchstone Pictures

ONE STEP PRODUCTIONS
12188 Laurel Terrace
Studio City, CA 91604
Phone: ....(818) 762-1624
Fax: ....(818) 763-1955
www.loop.com/~sister
sister@loop.com
Key Executives/Personnel:
  Judy Chaikin, Owner
  Nancy Kissock, Producer
Specialties: Independent; Shorts; Documentaries
Other Categories: TV; Video
Credits: Cotillion 65; Legacy of the Hollywood Blacklist FBI: Untold Stories; Stolen Innocence
Trade Assoc./Guilds/Unions: DGA

OPEN ROAD PRODUCTIONS, LTD.
6101 Morella Ave.
North Hollywood, CA 91606
Phone: ....(818) 980-1100
Fax: ....(818) 980-9862
openroad@i4f.com
Key Executives/Personnel:
  Robin Armstrong, Director & Producer
Specialties: Independent

ORBIT ENTERTAINMENT GROUP
714 N. La Brea Ave.
Hollywood, CA 90038
Phone: ....(323) 525-2626
Fax: ....(323) 525-2627
dror@orbiteg.com
Key Executives/Personnel:
  Dror Soref, Partner, President & Director
  Lee Nelson, Partner & Executive Producer
  Lynne Pateman, Executive Producer
  Kevin Moreton, VP of Orbit Pictures
  Jeremy White, Executive Creative Director
Specialties: Studio; Independent
Other Categories: Commercials; Interactive Multimedia
Credits: Oldsmobile (commercial); Sony (commercial); K-Swiss (commercial); The Seventh Coin (feature)

ORIGINAL FILM, INC.
2045 S. Barrington Ave., Ste. A
West Los Angeles, CA 90025
Phone: ....(310) 445-9000
Fax: ....(310) 445-9191
Key Executives/Personnel:
  Neal Moritz, Owner & Producer
  Mark Rossen, President of TV
  Stokely Chaffin, Sr. VP of Production
  Brad Luff, Sr. VP of Production
  Heather Zeegen, VP of Production
  Justin Rosenblatt, Creative Executive
  Brian Gefsky, Director of TV
  Jennifer Tuthill, Director of Development
  Amanda Cohen, Development Assistant
  Gretchen Douglass, Development Assistant
  Jennifer Grandy, Development Assistant
  Ross Brown, Development Assistant
  Jonah Barnes, Production Assistant
Specialties: Studio

Production Companies – Feature Film

Other Categories: TV
Credits: The Skulls; I Know What You Did Last Summer; I Still Know What You Did Last Summer; Cruel Intentions
First Look/Development Deals: Columbia Pictures/Columbia Tristar Motion Picture Group

ORIGINAL VOICES, INC.
2617 Third St.
Santa Monica, CA 90405
Phone: ....(310) 392-3479
Fax: ....(310) 392-3489
info@ovoices.com
Key Executives/Personnel:
  David Kirkpatrick, CEO
  Paul Harvey, President of Production
  Martin Svab, Development Executive
  Angela Bond, Business Affairs
Specialties: Independent
Credits: The Brady Bunch Movie; The Opposite of Sex; Bruno; Rasputin

OUR PRODUCTIONS, INC.
6255 Sunset Blvd., Ste. 2201
Hollywood, CA 90028
Phone: ....(323) 465-4197
       ....(818) 816-7332
Fax: ....(323) 465-6549
www.ourproduction.com
patricia@ourproduction.com
Key Executives/Personnel:
  Rick Munoz, Director & Producer
  Patricia Bolt, Director of Marketing & Production
Specialties: Studio; Independent; Direct-to-Video; Shorts; Documentaries
Other Categories: TV; Commercials; Video; Music Video
Credits: Natalie Cole Live at The Coliseum; The Miller Brewing Company; Winchell's Donuts

OUTERBANKS ENTERTAINMENT
8000 Sunset Blvd., Ste. 301A
Los Angeles, CA 90046
Phone: ....(323) 654-3700
Fax: ....(323) 654-3797
www.kevinwilliamson.com
Key Executives/Personnel:
  Kevin Williamson, Producer, Director & Writer
  Sherry Carnes, Development Executive
  Jennifer Breslow, Executive Assistant to Mr. Williamson
  Sara Kucserka, Development Assistant
  Mitch Ryan, Office Assistant
Specialties: Studio; Independent
Other Categories: TV
Credits: Scream 2 & 3; Halloween H20; Her Leading Man
First Look/Development Deals: Miramax Films
Additional Info: WMA - 151 El Camino Dr., Beverly Hills, CA 90212

OUTLAW PRODUCTIONS
9155 Sunset Blvd.
West Hollywood, CA 90069
Phone: ....(310) 777-2000
Fax: ....(310) 777-2010
Key Executives/Personnel:
  Robert Newmyer, Producer
  Jeffrey Silver, Producer
  Scott Strauss, President of Production
  Susan Novick, Associate Producer
  Brad Ley, Creative Executive
Specialties: Studio
Credits: Three to Tango; Ready to Rumble; The Santa Clause; Addicted to Love
First Look/Development Deals: Warner Bros., Intermedia Films

OVERBROOK ENTERTAINMENT
100 Universal City Plaza, Bldg. 6111
Universal City, CA 91608
Phone: ....(818) 777-2224
Fax: ....(818) 866-6206
Key Executives/Personnel:
  Will Smith, Partner
  James Lassiter, Partner
  Dale Ottley, General Manager
  John Dukakis, Executive VP of Music
  David Tochterman, Executive VP of TV
  Stacey Matthew, VP of TV
  Glendon Palmer, Creative Executive
  SoYun Roe, Film Executive
  Lori Zuker, Director of Development
  Omarr Rambert, A&R Executive of Music
  Anthony Demby, A&R Coordinator
Specialties: Studio
Other Categories: TV; Music Video
First Look/Development Deals: Universal Pictures

P.A.T. PRODUCTIONS
10202 W. Washington Blvd., David Lean Bldg., Ste. 230
Culver City, CA 90232
Phone: ....(310) 244-8811
Fax: ....(310) 244-1210
patprod@spe.sony.com
Key Executives/Personnel:
  Pat Sajak, President
  David Williger, Executive VP
  Gary Templeton, Director of Children's Programming
Specialties: Studio; Animation
Other Categories: TV; Video
Credits: Angus & the Ducks; Leo the Late Bloomer (animated); Merry Christmas; Space Case (animated)
First Look/Development Deals: Columbia TriStar Television

GEORGE PAIGE ASSOCIATES, INC.
3000 W. Olympic Blvd., Ste. 1407
Santa Monica, CA 90404
Phone: ....(310) 315-4835
Fax: ....(310) 315-4836
gpacorp@aol.com
Key Executives/Personnel:
  George Paige, Owner & President
  James R. Tumminia, Producer
Specialties: Independent; Direct-to-Video; Documentaries
Other Categories: TV; Commercials; Video; Music Video; Interactive Multimedia
Credits: Abbott & Costello Meet Jerry Seinfeld; 50 Years of Funny Females; Shafted
Trade Assoc./Guilds/Unions: ATAS

PARADOX PRODUCTIONS, INC.
11846 Ventura Blvd., Ste. 202
Studio City, CA 91604
Phone: ....(818) 623-2855
Fax: ....(818) 623-2856
Key Executives/Personnel:
  John Pasquin, President & Director
  Kimberly Brent, VP of Production
  Monica Gelardo, Story Editor
Specialties: Independent
Other Categories: TV
Credits: The Santa Clause; Small World; Roseanne; Home Improvement

PARAMOUNT CLASSICS
5555 Melrose Ave., Chevalier Bldg., 2nd Fl.
Los Angeles, CA 90038
Phone: ....(323) 956-2000

Production Companies – Feature Film

Fax: ....(323) 862-1212
www.PARAMOUNTCLASSICS.com
Key Executives/Personnel:
  David Dinerstein, Co-President
  Ruth Vitale, Co-President
  Michael Nash, VP of Acquisitions & Co-Production
  Justin Ring, Director of Acquisitions & Co-Production
Specialties: Studio; Independent

PARAMOUNT PICTURES - MOTION PICTURE GROUP
5555 Melrose Ave.
Los Angeles, CA 90038
Phone: ....(323) 956-5000
www.paramount.com
Key Executives/Personnel:
  Sherry Lansing, Chairman
  Robert G. Friedman, Vice Chairman
  John Goldwyn, President
  Joanna Johnson, Executive VP of Int'l. Motion Pictures
  Michelle Manning, President of Production
  Arthur Cohen, President of Worldwide Marketing
  Wayne Lewellen, President of Motion Picture Distribution
  Burt Berman, President of Music
  Fred Gallo, Executive VP of Feature Production Management Worldwide
  Donald Granger, Executive VP of Production
  Paul Haggar, Executive VP of Post Production
  Karen Rosenfelt, Executive VP of Production
  Brian Witten, Executive VP of Production
  E. Barry Haldeman, Executive VP of Business & Legal Affairs
  Nancy Goliger, Executive VP of Marketing & Creative Affairs
  Nancy Kirkpatrick, Executive VP of Worldwide Publicity
  Mark Bakshi, Sr. VP of Feature Production Management
  Chip Diggins, Sr. VP of Production
  Michael Hill, Sr. VP of Production Finance
  Gail Levin, Sr. VP of Features Casting
  Rochel Blachman, Sr. VP of Motion Picture Business Affairs
  Richard Fowkes, Sr. VP of Business Affairs
  Alan B. Heppel, Sr. VP of Legal Affairs
  Kevin Koloff, Sr. VP of Music Business Affairs
  Karen Magid, Sr. VP of Motion Picture Legal Affairs
  Scott Martin, Sr. VP of Intellectual Properties & Associate General Counsel
  Linda Wohl, Sr. VP of Music Legal Affairs
  Lisa Di Marzio, Sr. VP of Worldwide Marketing Partnerships
  Jasmine Madatian, Sr. VP of National Publicity
  Dede Gardner, VP of Production
  Brad Kessell, VP of Creative Affairs
  Nan Morales, VP of Feature Production Management
  Linda Springer, VP of Music Production
  Alex Young, VP of Production
  Eldridge Walker, VP of Music Clearance
  Brian Wensel, VP of Production Finance
  John Wiseman, VP of Post Production
Specialties: Studio
Other Categories: Feature Film

PARKWAY PRODUCTIONS
10202 W. Washington Blvd., Astaire Bldg., Ste. 2210
Culver City, CA 90232
Phone: ....(310) 244-4040
Fax: ....(310) 244-0240
Key Executives/Personnel:
  Penny Marshall, Executive Producer & Director
  Sean Corrigan, President
  Jessica Cox, VP of Development
  Amy Lemish, Producer
  Kinga Suto, Creative Executive
  Curt M. Pratt, Assistant to Ms. Marshall
Specialties: Studio; Independent

Credits: The Preacher's Wife; A League of Their Own; Awakenings; Big
First Look/Development Deals: Sony Pictures Entertainment

PATCHETT KAUFMAN ENTERTAINMENT
8621 Hayden Place
Culver City, CA 90232
Phone: ....(310) 838-7000
Fax: ....(310) 838-8430
Key Executives/Personnel:
  Kenneth Kaufman, President
  Tom Patchett, CEO
  Debra Smith-Cannold, VP of Production Services
Specialties: Independent
Other Categories: TV
Credits: Dean Koontz: Mr. Murder; Texas Justice; In The Line of Duty (TV series)

PATCHWORK PRODUCTIONS
1663 Euclid Street
Santa Monica, CA 90404
Phone: ....(310) 288-7488
Fax: ....(310) 288-7445
Key Executives/Personnel:
  Penny Finkelman Cox, Producer
  Sandra Rabins, Producer
  Jay Rifkin, Producer
  Hans Zimmer, Producer
  Craig Berenson, Development Executive
  Elizabeth Hackett, Development Executive
  Kirstie Field, Assistant to Ms. Cox
  Mike Lozano, Assistant to Mr. Rifkin
  Mo Nakamoto, Assistant to Mr. Zimmer
  Melissa Wylie, Assistant to Ms. Rabins
Specialties: Studio; Animation
Other Categories: TV
Credits: Antz; Prince of Egypt; 'Til There Was You; Dangerous Minds
First Look/Development Deals: DreamWorks SKG

PAVLIC/RAIMONDI PICTURES
3575 Cahuenga Blvd., Ste. 470
Los Angeles, CA 90068
Phone: ....(323) 850-0185
Fax: ....(323) 850-1264
Key Executives/Personnel:
  John Pavlic, Executive Producer
  Bobbie Pavlic, Executive Producer
  Paul Raimondi, Director
  Jane Raimondi, Producer
Specialties: Independent
Credits: Crosscut
Trade Assoc./Guilds/Unions: DGA

PEAK PRODUCTIONS
1780 Robinhood Rd.
Winston-Salem, NC 27104
Phone: ....(336) 761-5042
 ....(336) 813-0642
Fax: ....(336) 761-5043
peakprdns@aol.com
Key Executives/Personnel:
  Dale Pollock, Producer
Specialties: Studio; Independent
Other Categories: TV
Credits: Blaze; Midnight Clear; Set It Off
Trade Assoc./Guilds/Unions: AMPAS, PGA, WGAe

PENDRAGON FILM LTD.
Phone: ....(310) 828-1588
www.members.aol.com/jabwocky
jabwocky@aol.com

Production Companies – Feature Film

Key Executives/Personnel:
  Alain Silver, Writer & Producer
  Linda Brookover, Writer & Producer
Specialties: Independent; Direct-to-Video
Other Categories: TV
Credits: The Quickie; Beat; Bel-Air; Palmer's Pick-Up
Trade Assoc./Guilds/Unions: DGA, SAG

JAMES PENTECOST PRODUCTIONS
500 S. Buena Vista St., Animation Bldg., Ste. 2G6
Burbank, CA 91521
Phone: (818) 560-4965
Fax: (818) 845-7581
Key Executives/Personnel:
  James Pentecost, Producer
  Sheree Steiner, Office Manager
Specialties: Studio; Animation
Other Categories: TV
Credits: Pocahontas; Geppetto

PERMUT PRESENTATIONS
9150 Wilshire Blvd., Ste. 247
Beverly Hills, CA 90212
Phone: (310) 248-2792
Fax: (310) 248-2797
Key Executives/Personnel:
  David Permut, President
  Steven A. Longi, VP of Production
  David T. Mitchell, Development Associate
Specialties: Studio; Independent
Other Categories: TV
Credits: Double Take; Face/Off; Richard Pryor Live; Dragnet

PERSISTENT ENTERTAINMENT, INC.
9350 Wilshire Blvd., Ste. 328
Beverly Hills, CA 90212
Phone: (310) 777-1814
Fax: (310) 777-1824
www.persistentpictures.com
mail@persistentpictures.com
Key Executives/Personnel:
  Dan Stone, Producer
  Matthew Rhodes, Producer
  Lenny Bekerman, Manager & Producer
  Brian Dillingham, Story Editor
  Richard Williams, Assistant to Mr. Stone
  Nick Myles, Assistant to Mr. Rhodes
Specialties: Studio; Independent
Other Categories: TV
Credits: Auggie Rose; Alarmist (aka Life During Wartime); Star Struck (aka Starf*cker); Standoff

LESTER PERSKY PRODUCTIONS, INC.
9910 Tower Lane
Beverly Hills, CA 90210
Phone: (310) 278-1995
Fax: (310) 278-1910
lesterprods@aol.com
Key Executives/Personnel:
  Lester Persky, President
  Tomlinson Dean, Producer & VP
  Jonas Neilson, Director of Production
Specialties: Independent
Other Categories: TV
Credits: A Woman Named Jackie; Poor Little Rich Girl; Elizabeth Taylor Story; Hair

PERSPECTIVE FILMS
Phone: (310) 670-4030
(310) 261-8389
Fax: (310) 670-4031

Key Executives/Personnel:
  Debbie Pietsch, Executive Producer
Specialties: Shorts
Other Categories: TV; Commercials; Video; Music Video; Interactive Multimedia
Credits: Fast Point DSL; Mattel; Disney; Harman Kardan: MacWorld

PETERS ENTERTAINMENT
4000 Warner Blvd., Bldg. 15
Burbank, CA 91522
Phone: (818) 954-2441
Fax: (818) 954-4976
Key Executives/Personnel:
  Jon Peters, Chairman
  Brian D. Manis, Executive Producer
  Loretta Walsh-Gruber, Executive Assistant to Mr. Peters
  Jason Rogers, Second Assistant to Mr. Peters
Specialties: Independent
Credits: Wild Wild West; Batman; My Fellow Americans; Rosewood
First Look/Development Deals: Warner Bros.

PFEFFER FILM
500 S. Buena Vista Blvd., Animation Bldg., Ste. 2F-8
Burbank, CA 91521
Phone: (818) 560-3177
Fax: (818) 843-7485
pfefferfilm@aol.com
Key Executives/Personnel:
  Rachel Pfeffer, Producer
  Jess Siegler, VP
  Kathy Gerhard, Assistant
Specialties: Studio
Credits: A Civil Action; The Horse Whisperer; At Seventeen; A Few Good Men
First Look/Development Deals: Walt Disney Pictures/Touchstone Pictures

PHASE 1 PRODUCTIONS
3210 Club Dr.
Los Angeles, CA 90064
Phone: (310) 842-8401
Fax: (310) 280-0415
phase1prod@earthlink.net
Key Executives/Personnel:
  Joe Wizan, Producer
  Don Schneider, Producer
  Steve Wizan, President
  Dru Ransom, VP of Creative Affairs
Specialties: Studio; Independent
Other Categories: TV
Credits: Along Came A Spider; Kiss the Girls; Dunstin Checks In; Wrestling Ernest Hemingway

PHILMCO
P.O. Box 461783
Los Angeles, CA 90046
Phone: (213) 399-7624
philmco@earthlink.net
Key Executives/Personnel:
  Philip A. Mondello, Producer
Specialties: Trailers
Other Categories: Commercials

PHOENIX PICTURES
10125 W. Washington Blvd., Frankovich Bldg.
Culver City, CA 90232
Phone: (310) 244-6100
Fax: (310) 839-8915

Production Companies – Feature Film

Key Executives/Personnel:
- Mike Medavoy, Chairman & CEO
- Arnold Messer, President & COO
- Lindsey Bayman, Executive VP of Business & Legal Affairs
- Matt Bierman, Head of Production
- Judith Garinger, VP & Controller
- Eric Paquette, VP of Development
- Ian Smith, Publicity Consultant
- Amy Carr, Story Editor

Specialties: Studio
Credits: The People vs. Larry Flynt; The Thin Red Line; The Sixth Day; U-Turn

PICO CREEK PRODUCTIONS
409 Santa Monica Blvd., PH
Santa Monica, CA 90401
Phone: ....(310) 394-7522
Fax: ....(310) 394-5825
Key Executives/Personnel:
- Peter Horton, Director, Actor & Producer
- Julie Robinson, Director of Development

Specialties: Studio
Other Categories: TV
Credits: Brimstone; Murder Live
Trade Assoc./Guilds/Unions: DGA, SAG

PICTURE MILL
5620 Hollywood Blvd.
Los Angeles, CA 90028
Phone: ....(323) 465-8800
Fax: ....(323) 465-8875
www.picturemill.com
richard@picturemill.com
Key Executives/Personnel:
- Eric Ladd, President
- Rick Probst, Creative Director
- Richard Frank, Marketing & New Business
- Bill Cole, Digital Trailers

Specialties: Studio; Animation; Large Format; Trailers
Other Categories: Video
Credits: Godzilla (trailer); X-Files (trailer); Zorro (trailer); Fierce Creatures (trailer)

THE FREDERICK S. PIERCE COMPANY, INC.
5670 Wilshire Blvd., Ste. 1350
Los Angeles, CA 90036
Phone: ....(323) 964-7800
Fax: ....(323) 964-7818
www.piercefilms.com
piercefilms@earthlink.net
Key Executives/Personnel:
- Frederick S. Pierce, Owner & President
- Keith Pierce, Executive Producer
- Richard Pierce, Executive Producer

Specialties: Independent
Other Categories: TV
Credits: In a Heartbeat; 20,000 Leagues Under the Sea; The Absolute Truth; The Substitute Wife

PIXAR ANIMATION STUDIOS
1200 Park Avenue
Emeryville, CA 94608
Phone: ....(510) 752-3000
Fax: ....(510) 752-3151
www.pixar.com
webmaster@pixar.com
Key Executives/Personnel:
- Sarah McArthur, Executive VP of Production

Specialties: Animation
Credits: Toy Story 1 & 2; A Bug's Life; Gari's Game
First Look/Development Deals: Monsters, Inc.

PLASTERCITY PRODUCTIONS
5225 Wilshire Blvd., Ste. 1204
Los Angeles, CA 90036
Phone: ....(323) 938-0974
Fax: ....(323) 938-1189
www.plastercity.com
info@plastercity.com
Key Executives/Personnel:
- Christopher Coppola, President, Director & Producer
- Alain Silver, Producer
- Adrienne Coppola, VP

Specialties: Independent
Other Categories: TV
Credits: Bel Air; America's Most Wanted; I Survive; Gun Fighter
Trade Assoc./Guilds/Unions: DGA, SAG

PLEASANT PRODUCTIONS
P.O. Box 179
Beverly Hills, CA 90213
Phone: ....(213) 707-0500
www.pleasantproductions.com
Key Executives/Personnel:
- Mark Hibbard, Producer
- Ralph Pleasant, Producer

Specialties: Independent
Credits: Everything Relative; Best Enemies

POLESTAR ENTERTAINMENT GROUP, LLC
9454 Wilshire Blvd., Ste. 201
Beverly Hills, CA 90212
Phone: ....(310) 278-0080
Fax: ....(310) 278-0079
www.polestarentertainment.com
polestarentertainmentgroup@polestargroup.net
Key Executives/Personnel:
- Anthony Scala, CEO
- Catarina Conti, COO
- Dan Fantz, President of Releasing
- Terry White, President of Film & Television Production
- Russ Regan, President of Polestar Records
- Jeff Berk, Sr. VP of Production
- Jenifer Sorrow, Head of Management
- Jennifer Eatz, Literary Manager
- Rod Conti, VP of Production
- Jerry Conti, VP of Creative Affairs
- Stacy Hunter, Director of Operations

Specialties: Independent
Other Categories: TV
Credits: Hobb's End; Last Chance; Other Side of Monday; G-Saviour

PONGO PRODUCTIONS
Phone: ....(818) 562-3336
Fax: ....(818) 562-3337
www.gopongo.com
pongoprod@aol.com
Key Executives/Personnel:
- Thomas J. McGough, CEO
- Jon Mingle, Partner

Specialties: Trailers
Other Categories: Commercials

POP/ART FILM FACTORY
513 Wilshire Blvd., Ste. 215
Santa Monica, CA 90401
Phone: ....(310) 260-2868
....(310) 288-6815
dzpff@earthlink.net
Key Executives/Personnel:

Production Companies – Feature Film

Daniel Zirilli, Executive Producer & Director
Specialties: Independent
Other Categories: Commercials; Music Video
Credits: Winner Takes All; Rolling Stones - Voodoo Lounge; Avirex Clothing; Freddie Jackson - I Want to Thank You

POPULAR ARTS ENTERTAINMENT, INC.
2006 W. Olive Ave.
Burbank, CA 91506
Phone: ....(818) 562-6366
Fax: ....(818) 562-6373
contactus@populararts.com
Key Executives/Personnel:
Kevin Meagher, Co-President & Co-CEO
Gordon Braine, Co-President & Co-CEO
Thomas Guttry, VP of Business Affairs
Specialties: Independent
Other Categories: TV
Credits: Dr. Katz; Little Girls in Pretty Boxes; Jeff Corwin Experience
Additional Info: 53 W. 87th St., New York, NY 10024

PRODUCERS GROUP, LTD.
713 S. Pacific Coast Hwy., Ste. B
Redondo Beach, CA 90277
Phone: ....(310) 316-0481
Fax: ....(310) 316-1482
producers_group@csi.com
Key Executives/Personnel:
Lee Gluckman, President & Executive Producer
Ted Raynor, Executive VP of Legal Affairs & Executive Producer
Specialties: Independent; Direct-to-Video
Other Categories: TV; Commercials; Video
Credits: After The Red Star; Kids Are Cooking; Chicago Heist; San Miguel
Trade Assoc./Guilds/Unions: AFTRA, SAG

PRODUCTION ANALYSIS CORPORATION
Phone: ....(323) 876-6186
goodadvice@earthlink.net
Key Executives/Personnel:
Martin Pitts, Producer
Specialties: Shorts; Large Format
Other Categories: TV; Commercials; Video; Music Video
Credits: Wild California; The Full Moon Show with Robbie Robertson; The Bee Gees Live Concert Video

PROLETARIAT FILMWORKS
12165 Iredell St.
Studio City, CA 91604
Phone: ....(818) 763-8356
Fax: ....(818) 760-6584
proletfilm@aol.com
Key Executives/Personnel:
Terry Moloney, Executive Producer
Liam Kildare, Producer
Grant Gilmore, Line Producer
Specialties: Independent; Shorts; Documentaries
Other Categories: TV; Commercials; Video; Music Video
Credits: Tourette Syndrome Foundation (PSA); Elvis 2000: A Video Scrapbook; Warner Music: Wallstreet; Shout for Antz
Trade Assoc./Guilds/Unions: AFTRA, SAG

PROPAGANDA FILMS
940 N. Mansfield Ave
Los Angeles, CA 90038
Phone: ....(323) 462-6400
....(212) 982-1700
Fax: ....(323) 463-7874
www.propagandafilms.com
Key Executives/Personnel:
Rick Hess, President
Trevor Macy, COO
Severin White, CFO
Paul Schiff, Producer
Pat Dollard, Co-Head, Management Division
Lisa Franklin, Head of Legal Affairs
Beth Holden, Co-Head, Management Division
Brian Oliver, Director of Production
Sam Walsh, Head of Production
Specialties: Studio; Independent; Documentaries
Other Categories: Commercials; Music Video
Credits: Fight Club; Being John Malkovich; Seven; Portrait of a Lady
Additional Info: 902 Broadway, Ste. 1603, New York, NY 10010

PROUD MARY ENTERTAINMENT
433 N. Camden Dr., Ste. 600
Beverly Hills, CA 90210
Phone: ....(310) 288-1886
Fax: ....(310) 288-1801
proudmaryent@earthlink.net
Key Executives/Personnel:
Mary L. Aloe, Owner & Executive Producer
Todd Waxler, Executive Producer
Jay Jacobs, Director of Development
Specialties: Studio; Independent
Other Categories: TV; Commercials; Music Video
Credits: Caught in the Act; The Princess & The Private; Citizen Jane
Trade Assoc./Guilds/Unions: American Women in TV & Radio, CWA

PUNCH PRODUCTIONS
11661 San Vincente Blvd.
Los Angeles, CA 90049
Phone: ....(310) 442-4880
....(212) 595-8800
Fax: ....(310) 442-4884
Key Executives/Personnel:
Dustin Hoffman, Owner
Jay Cohen, Partner (LA)
Lee Gottsegen, President (NY)
Laura Gherardi, VP of Production (NY)
Murray Schisgal, Producer (NY)
Heather Waterman, Director of Development (LA)
Specialties: Studio; Independent
Credits: Tootsie; Wag the Dog; Outbreak; Swimming with Sharks
Additional Info: 1926 Broadway, Ste. 305, New York, NY 10023

QUASAR STUDIOS
P.O. Box 661266
Los Angeles, CA 90066
Phone: ....(310) 289-1547
....(818) 352-0908
Fax: ....(310) 289-1547
www.perufilmcommission.net
filmperu@gte.net
Key Executives/Personnel:
Marggie Castellano, Producer
Prudence Michael, Location Manager
Monica Leon, Designer
Specialties: Independent; Documentaries
Other Categories: TV; Video; Interactive Multimedia
Credits: Coyotes (feature); National Geographic: Ancient Graves; The Celestine Prophecy (miniseries); A&E: Ancient Mysteries

QUINN PRODUCTIONS
13816 Enadia Way
Van Nuys, CA 91405
Phone: ....(818) 787-5952
Fax: ....(818) 787-7146
johnmquinn@email.com
Key Executives/Personnel:
John Quinn, President

Production Companies – Feature Film

Kimberlee Duplechien, Director of Development
Specialties: Independent; Direct-to-Video
Credits: Cheerleader Camp; Magic of Golden Bear; Golden Bear Series 1, 2 & 3

RADAR PICTURES
10900 Wilshire Blvd., Ste. 1400
Los Angeles, CA 90024
Phone: ....(310) 208-8525
Fax: ....(310) 208-1764
Key Executives/Personnel:
   Ted Field, Chairman & CEO
   Scott Kroopf, President
   Erica Huggins, Executive VP & Producer
   Tom Engelman, Executive VP & Producer
   Monica Mullens, Production Executive
   Will Stubbs, Production Executive
   Derek Wilkins, Story Editor
Specialties: Studio; Independent
Credits: Truck 44; Jumanji; Runaway Bride; Mr. Holland's Opus
Additional Info: Formerly Interscope Communications

RADIANT PRODUCTIONS
914 Montana Ave., 2nd Fl.
Santa Monica, CA 90403
Phone: ....(310) 656-1400
Fax: ....(310) 656-1408
Key Executives/Personnel:
   Wolfgang Petersen, Director & Producer
   Gail Katz, President & Producer
   Samuel Dickerman, VP
   Rosemary Tarquinio, Head of TV
   Susan Stein, Director of Development
   David Markus, Story Editor
   Barbara Huber, Assistant to Mr. Petersen
   Aaron Huffman, Assistant to Ms. Katz
   Alicia Abatie, Assistant to Ms. Tarquinio
   Veronica Becker, Development Assistant
Specialties: Studio; Independent
Other Categories: TV
Credits: The Perfect Storm; Air Force One; Outbreak; In The Line of Fire

RAFFAELLA PRODUCTIONS, INC.
100 Universal City Plaza, Bungalow 5162
Universal City, CA 91608
Phone: ....(818) 777-2655
Fax: ....(818) 866-1571
Key Executives/Personnel:
   Raffaella DeLaurentiis, President & Producer
   Hester Hargett, VP & Co-Producer
   Steve O'Corr, VP of Operations
   Ed Wacek, Sr. VP of Production
   Erik Jessen, Story Editor
Specialties: Studio; Independent; Direct-to-Video
Other Categories: TV
Credits: Dragon Heart; Dragon: The Bruce Lee Story; Kull, The Conqueror; Daylight
First Look/Development Deals: Universal Pictures, Universal Television

RAINMAKER PRODUCTIONS
P.O. Box 5780
Beverly Hills, CA 90209
Phone: ....(323) 874-6770
Fax: ....(800) 858-0520
Key Executives/Personnel:
   Neal Edelstein, President
   Gaye Pope, Director of Development
Specialties: Studio; Independent
Other Categories: TV

RAINTREE PRODUCTIONS
666 N. Robertson Blvd.
West Hollywood, CA 90069
Phone: ....(310) 827-3336
Fax: ....(310) 301-3310
Key Executives/Personnel:
   Robert Wollin, Executive Producer
Specialties: Trailers
Other Categories: Commercials
Credits: Academy of Television Arts & Sciences; IHOP; 45th & 46th Creative Arts Emmy Awards
Trade Assoc./Guilds/Unions: DGA, EGA

RANDWELL PRODUCTIONS
11111 Santa Monica Blvd., Ste. 525
Los Angeles, CA 90025
Phone: ....(310) 996-6809
Fax: ....(310) 473-4376
Key Executives/Personnel:
   Randy Robinson, President & CEO
   Tom Kageff, VP
Specialties: Studio; Independent; Direct-to-Video
Other Categories: TV
Credits: See You In My Dreams; Come On Get Happy: Partridge Family; Sealed With A Kiss; Two Mother's For Zachary
First Look/Development Deals: Carlton America

MARTIN RANSOHOFF PRODUCTIONS, INC.
400 South Beverly Dr., Ste. 308
Beverly Hills, CA 90212
Phone: ....(310) 551-2680
Fax: ....(310) 551-2094
Key Executives/Personnel:
   Martin Ransohoff, Producer
   Bob Robinson, VP
   Heather Bowles, Creative Assistant & Operations
Specialties: Studio; Independent
Credits: Guilty As Sin; Jagged Edge; Switching Channels; Class

RASTAR PRODUCTIONS
10202 W. Washington Blvd., David Lean Bldg.
Culver City, CA 90232
Phone: ....(310) 244-7871
Fax: ....(310) 244-2331
Key Executives/Personnel:
   Ray Stark, Chairman
   Marykay Powell, President
   Janet Garrison, VP of Administration
   Don Safran, Consultant
   Michael Sudmeier, Consultant
   Theresa De La Paz, Executive Assistant to Mr. Stark
   Arden Doss, Assistant to Ms. Powell
Specialties: Studio
Credits: Lost in Yonkers; Random Hearts; Steel Magnolias; The Way We Were
First Look/Development Deals: Columbia Pictures/Columbia Tristar Motion Picture Group

PATRICK RAYMOND ENTERTAINMENT, INC.
1041 N. Formosa Ave., Formosa Bldg., Ste. 209
West Hollywood, CA 90046
Phone: ....(323) 850-2918
Fax: ....(323) 850-2920
praymondh@aol.com
Key Executives/Personnel:
   Patrick Raymond, Executive Producer
   Albert Frigone, Associate Producer
   Joey Estella, Assistant
Specialties: Independent
Other Categories: TV; Commercials; Video; Interactive Multimedia

Production Companies – Feature Film

REALITORY PRODUCTIONS
Phone: ....(818) 404-8711
Fax: ....(818) 702-8611
www.realitory.com
mac@realitory.com
Key Executives/Personnel:
  Michael Condro, Director, DP & VFX
  Monica Ramone, Producer & Partner
Specialties: Independent; Direct-to-Video; Documentaries
Other Categories: Video; Interactive Multimedia
Credits: World Championship: All Terrain Boards; Jousting, The First Extreme Sport; Strange and Weird Halloween Festivals
Trade Assoc./Guilds/Unions: IATSE, IFP

REARGUARD PRODUCTIONS, INC.
6030 Wilshire Blvd., Ste. 300
Los Angeles, CA 90036
Phone: ....(323) 937-1570
Fax: ....(323) 937-0564
Key Executives/Personnel:
  Julie G. Moldo Jones, Executive VP
Specialties: Studio; Independent
Other Categories: TV
Credits: Tales From The Crypt; The Land That Time Forgot; Rock, Rock, Rock!; The Birthday Party
Trade Assoc./Guilds/Unions: DGA, SAG

RED BIRD PRODUCTIONS
725 Arizona Ave., Ste. 200
Santa Monica, CA 90401
Phone: ....(310) 234-7234
Fax: ....(310) 234-7235
Key Executives/Personnel:
  Debbie Allen, President & Producer
  Joy Johnson, Director of Development
Specialties: Studio; Independent; Documentaries
Other Categories: TV
Credits: Amistad

RED HOTS ENTERTAINMENT
3105 Amigos Dr.
Burbank, CA 91504
Phone: ....(818) 954-0092
 ....(818) 607-8331
Fax: ....(818) 954-8421
pogmothon@earthlink.net
Key Executives/Personnel:
  Chip Miller, Director & Partner
  Sue Travis Miller, VP of Post Production & Editor
  Jane Gurtiza, Production Coordinator
  Dan Pomeroy, Director
  Mark St. Juste, Director
  Marvin "Young MC" Young, Director
  Kit Gleason, Production Manager
  Eileen Salgro, VP of Operations
  Vanessa Browne, Producer
  Marc Wolfson, Music Producer
  Theo Forster, Producer
Specialties: Studio; Independent; Shorts; Trailers
Other Categories: TV; Commercials; Video; Music Video
Credits: Four Day Shoot; Mortuary Academy; The Importance of Being Earnest; The Seven Fishes
Trade Assoc./Guilds/Unions: PGA, WGA

RED HOUR FILMS
193 N. Roberston Blvd.
Beverly Hills, CA 90211
Phone: ....(310) 289-2565
Fax: ....(310) 289-5988
www.redhourfilms.com
Key Executives/Personnel:
  Ben Stiller, Producer, Writer & Director
  Stuart Cornfeld, Feature Producer
  Erin Simon-Berenson, TV Producer
  Rhodes Rader, Creative Executive
  Stacy Fung, Assistant to Ms. Berenson
  Alan Griswold, Assistant to Mr. Cornfeld
  Will Klein, Assistant
Specialties: Studio; Independent
Other Categories: TV
Credits: Zoolander
First Look/Development Deals: New Line Cinema, Inc.

RED HOUSE ENTERTAINMENT
3400 Riverside Dr., Ste. 700
Burbank, CA 91505
Phone: ....(818) 977-1902
Fax: ....(818) 977-5287
Key Executives/Personnel:
  Tim Daly, Producer
  Steve Burleigh, Producer
  Amy Von Nostrand, Producer
  Aimee Flaherty, Development Associate & Story Editor
Specialties: Studio; Independent
Other Categories: TV
Credits: Execution of Justice; Rites of Passage; Seven Girlfriends; Urbania
First Look/Development Deals: Warner Bros. Television Productions
Additional Info: Formerly Daly-Harris Productions

RED WAGON
10202 W. Washington Blvd., Hepburn Bldg. West
Culver City, CA 90232
Phone: ....(310) 244-4466
Fax: ....(310) 244-1480
Key Executives/Personnel:
  Douglas Wick, Producer
  Lucy Fisher, Producer
  Gail Lyon, President
  Melissa Reid, VP of Development
  Tara Mark, Creative Executive
  Rachel Shane, Creative Executive
  David Schreiber & Jennifer Schurr, Assistants to Mr. Wick
  Amy Peltonen, Assistant to Ms. Lyon
  Meghan Simpson Snyder, Assistant Ms. Fisher
  Mariano Svidler, Assistant to Ms. Reid
Specialties: Studio
Credits: Gladiator; Girl, Interrupted; Stuart Little; Working Girl
First Look/Development Deals: Sony Pictures Entertainment

RED-HORSE PRODUCTIONS
6028 Calvin Ave.
Tarzana, CA 91356
Phone: ....(818) 705-2588
Fax: ....(818) 705-2523
www.naturallynative.com
redhorse88@aol.com
Key Executives/Personnel:
  Valerie Red-Horse, President, Producer, Writer, Actress & Director
  Dawn Jackson, Director of Development
  Yvonne Russo, VP, Producer & Actress
  Fabiane Carter, Executive Assistant
  Pam Aver, Business & Legal Affairs
Specialties: Independent; Documentaries
Other Categories: TV; Video
Credits: Naturally Native (feature); The Whispers (documentary); Windows on Mars (educational); My Indian Summer (TV)
First Look/Development Deals: Valhalla Motion Pictures
Trade Assoc./Guilds/Unions: HAPN, SAG, WGA, WIF

Production Companies – Feature Film

DAN REDLER ENTERTAINMENT
18730 Hatteras St., Ste. 8
Tarzana, CA 91356
Phone: ....(818) 776-0938
Fax: ....(818) 705-6870
dredler@pacbell.net
Key Executives/Personnel:
  Dan Redler, Producer
  Nadia Naili, Producer
Specialties: Studio; Independent; Direct-to-Video
Other Categories: TV; Commercials; Interactive Multimedia
Credits: In His Father's Shoes; Pygmalion; Tanks; Profile For Murder
First Look/Development Deals: Nu Image/Millenium

REGENT ENTERTAINMENT, INC.
1401 Ocean Ave., Ste. 300
Santa Monica, CA 90401
Phone: ....(310) 260-3333
....(310) 260-3343
Key Executives/Personnel:
  Paul Colichman, President & Partner
  Mark R. Harris, Partner
  Stephen P. Jarchow, Partner
  John Lambert, VP of Acquisitions & Theatrical Distribution
  Jeff Schenck, VP of Development
  Gene George, President of Int'l. Sales
  Megan Kimberly, VP of Int'l. Sales
  Chuck Speed, Business Affairs
  Lynn Di Paola, Assistant to Mr. Schenck
Specialties: Independent; Direct-to-Video
Other Categories: TV
Credits: Gods & Monsters; A Woman is a Hell of a Thing; I'll Remember April; The Twilight of the Golds

RICK REINERT PICTURES
1556 Covington Ave.
Westlake Village, CA 91361
Phone: ....(805) 494-0699
Fax: ....(805) 494-9780
Key Executives/Personnel:
  Rick Reinert, Producer & Director
  Tom Carter, Sales & Producer
  Carole Reinert, VP of Business Affairs
Specialties: Animation
Other Categories: TV; Video
Credits: Capn' O.G. Readmore; Precious Moments Videos; Winnie The Pooh and a Day for Eeyore
Trade Assoc./Guilds/Unions: AMPAS, ASIFA, ATAS

RENAISSANCE PICTURES
100 Universal City Plaza, Bldg. 5166, 3rd Fl.
Universal City, CA 91608
Phone: ....(818) 777-0088
Fax: ....(818) 866-0223
Key Executives/Personnel:
  Sam Raimi, Executive Producer & Director
  Rob Tapert, Executive Producer
  Patrick Moran, President of TV
  Michael McDonald, Producer
  Susan Binder, Business Manager
  Ali Rasul, Director of Marketing
  David Pollison, Assistant
  Tig Notaro, Assistant
Specialties: Studio; Direct-to-Video
Other Categories: TV
Credits: Evil Dead; Darkman; Quick and the Dead; Simple Plan
First Look/Development Deals: Studios USA

REVEAL ENTERTAINMENT
100 Universal Plaza, Bldg. 5171
Universal City, CA 91608
Phone: ....(818) 733-9818
Fax: ....(818) 733-9808
Key Executives/Personnel:
  Brad Silberling, no title
  Barry Isaacson, no title
  Minor Childers, no title
  Todd Hofacker, no title
  Valeska Ramet, no title
Specialties: Studio
Credits: City of Angels; Casper
First Look/Development Deals: DreamWorks SKG

REVELATIONS ENTERTAINMENT
301 Arizona Ave., Ste. 303
Santa Monica, CA 90401
Phone: ....(310) 394-3131
Fax: ....(310) 394-3133
www.revelationsent.com
Key Executives/Personnel:
  Morgan Freeman, President, Actor & Producer
  Lori McCreary, CEO & Producer
  Anne Marie Gillen, COO & Producer
  Janet M. Harrison, Director of East Coast Development
  Kelly Mendelsohn, Assistant to Ms. McCreary
  Meg Madison, Director of Accounting
  Alfonso Freeman, Director of Information Systems
  Martha Mitchell, Office Manager
  Stuart Hammer, Business Consultant
  Geanne Frank, Management Consultant
  Tonya Jones, Publicist for Morgan Freeman
Specialties: Studio
Other Categories: TV
Credits: Bopha!; Mutiny; Under Suspicion

REVOLUTION STUDIOS
Phone: ....(310) 264-4141
Key Executives/Personnel:
  Rob Moore, Partner
  Todd Gardner, Partner
  Joe Roth, Partner
  Tom Sherak, Partner
Specialties: Studio

REVOLVER FILMS, LLC
2022A Broadway
Santa Monica, CA 90404
Phone: ....(310) 829-2441
Fax: ....(310) 829-2661
Key Executives/Personnel:
  Mark Priola, Producer
  Jack Singman, Producer
Specialties: Independent; Shorts
Other Categories: TV; Commercials; Video
Credits: ATV Hardcore; Extended list available upon request.

RGH/LIONS SHARE PICTURES
8831 Sunset Blvd., Ste. 300
West Hollywood, CA 90069
Phone: ....(310) 652-2893
Fax: ....(310) 652-6237
www.lionssharepictures.com
rghlionssharepictures@hotmail.com
Key Executives/Personnel:
  Eric Louzil, President
  William Blake, Executive VP
  Erick Bryce, COO
  Anthony Tae-Jum Hong, VP Int'l. Sales
Specialties: Studio; Independent

Production Companies – Feature Film

RHYTHM & HUES STUDIOS
5404 Jandy Place
Los Angeles, CA 90066
Phone: (310) 448-7500
Fax: (310) 448-7603
gnolin@rhythm.com
Key Executives/Personnel:
  Gary Nolin, Head of Physical Production & Visual Effects Producer
Specialties: Studio
Other Categories: Commercials
Credits: End of Days; X-Files; McDonald's; ReMax

RICE & BEANS PRODUCTIONS
30 N. Raymond., Ste. 605
Pasadena, CA 91103
Phone: (626) 792-9171
Fax: (626) 792-9171
vin88@pacbell.net
Key Executives/Personnel:
  Vince Cheung, Writer & Producer
  Ben Montanio, Writer & Producer
Specialties: Studio; Independent
Other Categories: TV; Interactive Multimedia
Credits: The Steve Harvey Show; Married... with Children; In The House; Empty Nest
Trade Assoc./Guilds/Unions: ATAS, WGA

RIDINI ENTERTAINMENT CORPORATION
c/o Raleigh Studios, 650 N. Bronson Ave., Ste. B-152
Los Angeles, CA 90004
Phone: (323) 960-8071
www.ridinientertainment.com
maryann@ridinientertainment.com
Key Executives/Personnel:
  Mary Ann Ridini, no title
Specialties: Studio; Independent; Documentaries
Other Categories: TV; Video
Credits: Falling Fire; Convict 762; Future Fear; Shepherd
First Look/Development Deals: Third Millennium

RJ LAUREN
29395 Agoura Rd., Ste. 205
Agoura Hills, CA 91301
Phone: (818) 879-2200
www.rjlauren.com
info@rjlauren.com
Key Executives/Personnel:
  Robert Haukoos, Executive Producer
Specialties: Trailers
Other Categories: Commercials

RJN PRODUCTIONS, INC.
2934 1/2 Beverly Glen Circle, PMB 394
Bel Air, CA 90077
Phone: (310) 859-2770
Fax: (310) 859-2946
folksn@aol.com
Key Executives/Personnel:
  Richard Naegele, Producer & Director
  Nathan Folks, Producer
Specialties: Independent
Credits: Double Exposure; Executive Power

RKO PICTURES, INC.
1875 Century Park East, Ste. 2140
Los Angeles, CA 90067
Phone: (310) 277-0707
(212) 644-0600
Fax: (310) 226-2490
www.rko.com
info@rko.com
Key Executives/Personnel:
  Ted Hartley, Chairman & CEO
  Dina Merril, Vice Chairman
  Julia Halperin, Executive VP
  Adam W. Rosen, Sr. VP of Business Affairs
  Doris Schwartz, VP of Production
  Ron Gell, VP of Production & Development, Radio Pictures Division
  Laurel Lees-Gonzalez, VP of Finance & Administration
  Josh Schaer, Creative Executive
  Heather Carman, Rights Adminstration
Specialties: Studio
Credits: Mighty Joe Young; Milk & Money; Holiday Affair
Additional Info: 3 E. 54th St., 12th Fl., New York, NY 10022

ROADKILL FILMS
1604 Vista del Mar St.
Hollywood, CA 90028
Phone: (323) 962-0295
Fax: (323) 962-0372
sofagirl@aol.com
Key Executives/Personnel:
  Salomé Brezinér, Director
  Steven J. Wolfe, Producer
  Cory Neilson, Assistant to Mr. Brezinér
  Jon Cohen, Assistant to Mr. Wolfe
Specialties: Independent
Credits: Tollbooth; Fast Sofa; Relax...It's Just Sex; Twin Falls Idaho

ROADSIDE ATTRACTIONS, LLC
427 N. Cañon Dr., Ste. 216
Beverly Hills, CA 90210
Phone: (310) 860-1692
Fax: (310) 860-1693
www.roadsideattractions.com
mail@roadsideattractions.com
Key Executives/Personnel:
  Eric d'Arbeloff, Producer
  Chad Marting, Story Editor
Specialties: Studio; Independent; Shorts; Documentaries
Other Categories: TV
Credits: The Shoe; Trick; They Nest

DOLORES ROBINSON ENTERTAINMENT
112 S. Almont Dr.
Los Angeles, CA 90048
Phone: (310) 777-8777
Fax: (310) 777-8780
dorobent@aol.com
Key Executives/Personnel:
  Dolores Robinson, no title
  Ryan Babanzien, no title
Specialties: Studio; Independent
Other Categories: TV

STAN ROGOW PRODUCTIONS
846 N. Cahuenga Blvd., Bldg. D
Los Angeles, CA 90038
Phone: (323) 993-5644
Fax: (323) 993-5591
Key Executives/Personnel:
  Stan Rogow, Executive Producer
  Susan Jansen, Executive Producer
  Jill Danton, Line Producer
  Tom Lofaro, Line Producer
  Robin Lippin, Casting Director
Specialties: Independent

Production Companies – Feature Film

Other Categories: TV
Credits: None of the Above; State of Grace; Fame (TV series); Playing For Time
Trade Assoc./Guilds/Unions: DGA, WGAw

ROGUE ENTERTAINMENT
Phone: ....(801) 979-2229
....(818) 682-2152
Fax: ....(801) 263-0551
Key Executives/Personnel:
  Adam Smoot, Producer
  Kevin DeLullo, Producer, Director & Writer
Specialties: Independent
Other Categories: Video
Credits: Nightfall; Cage in Box Elder; Usher

PHIL ROMAN ENTERTAINMENT
4040 Vineland Ave., Ste. 205
Studio City, CA 91604
Phone: ....(818) 985-1200
Fax: ....(818) 985-2668
www.philromanent.com
phil@romanent.com
Key Executives/Personnel:
  Phil Roman, President & CEO
  Rick Ramirez, VP
Specialties: Studio; Independent; Direct-to-Video; Animation
Other Categories: TV; Interactive Multimedia
Credits: Grandma Got Run Over By A Reindeer; Christmas in Gaudinia

ALEX ROSE PRODUCTIONS
8291 Presson Pl.
Los Angeles, CA 90069
Phone: ....(323) 654-8662
Fax: ....(323) 654-0196
Key Executives/Personnel:
  Alex Rose, Executive Producer, President & CEO
  Giovanni Agnelli, Producer
  Mary Anderson, Development
Specialties: Studio; Independent
Credits: The Other Sister; Frankie and Johnny; Overboard; Nothing in Common
Trade Assoc./Guilds/Unions: AFI

HOWARD ROSENMAN PRODUCTIONS
635A Westbourne Dr.
Los Angeles, CA 90069
Phone: ....(310) 659-2100
Key Executives/Personnel:
  Howard Rosenman, Producer
Specialties: Studio; Independent; Documentaries; Large Format
Other Categories: TV
Credits: Common Threads: Stories From The Quilt; Father of the Bride; Buffy The Vampire Slayer (feature); Celluloid Closet

ROUNDTABLE INK
Phone: ....(323) 466-4646
Fax: ....(323) 466-4640
diedre@roundtableink.com
Key Executives/Personnel:
  Gina Matthews, Producer & Manager
  Diedre Nuwash, Story Editor & Assistant
Specialties: Studio; Animation
Other Categories: TV
Credits: What Women Want; Urban Legend; Popular

RUDDY MORGAN ORGANIZATION
9300 Wilshire Blvd., Ste. 508
Beverly Hills, CA 90212
Phone: ....(310) 271-7698
Fax: ....(310) 278-9978
ruddymorgan@earthlink.net
Key Executives/Personnel:
  Albert S. Ruddy, Producer
  André E. Morgan, Producer
  Douglas Nam, Executive Assistant
  Vivianne Kaplan, Executive Assistant
  Leslie Aurelio, Second Assistant
Specialties: Independent
Other Categories: TV
Credits: Martial Law; Walker, Texas Ranger; Running Mates

SCOTT RUDIN PRODUCTIONS
5555 Melrose Ave., DeMille Bldg., Ste. 100
Los Angeles, CA 90038
Phone: ....(323) 956-4600
....(212) 704-4600
Fax: ....(323) 862-0262
Key Executives/Personnel:
  Scott Rudin, Producer
  Scott Aversano, Sr. VP (LA)
  Jose Calleja Jr., Director of Development (LA)
  Carrie Cook, Director of Development (LA)
  Mark Roybal, Director of Development (NY)
  Melvin Amr, Development (LA)
  John Delaney, Director of Development (NY)
  Angelique Palozzi, Assistant to Mr. Rudin (LA)
  Eben Davidson, Assistant to Mr. Rudin (NY)
Specialties: Studio
Credits: Sleepy Hollow; South Park: Bigger, Longer, Uncut; The Truman Show; Clueless
Additional Info: 120 W. 45th St., 10th Fl., New York, NY 10036

RUMBALARA FILMS
7001 Melrose Ave.
Los Angeles, CA 90038
Phone: ....(323) 936-4436
Fax: ....(323) 936-4913
cory@rumbalara.com
Key Executives/Personnel:
  Kathleen McLaughlin, President
  Phillip Noyce, no title
Specialties: Studio; Independent
Credits: The Bone Collector; Clear and Present Danger; The Saint; Sliver

S.E.R. FILMWORKS
500 Botetourt St., Ste 401
Norfolk, VA 23510
Phone: ....(757) 625-7647
filmwrks@erols.com
Key Executives/Personnel:
  Susan Rohrer, Producer, Director & Writer
Specialties: Studio; Independent
Other Categories: TV
Credits: Never Say Goodbye; Terrible Things My Mother Told Me; For Jenny, With Love; Mother's Day
Trade Assoc./Guilds/Unions: ATAS, DGA, SAG, WGAw

SABAN ENTERTAINMENT
10960 Wilshire Blvd.
Los Angeles, CA 90024
Phone: ....(310) 235-5100
Fax: ....(310) 235-5102
Key Executives/Personnel:
  Haim Saban, Chairman & CEO
  Shuki Levy, President of Production
  Stan Golden, President of Int'l. Sales
  Cheryl McDermott, Sr. VP of Business & Legal Affairs
  Dana Booton, Sr. VP of Animation

Production Companies – Feature Film

   Mark Pinsker, Sr. VP of Special Projects
   Rodd Feingold, VP of Physical Production
   Robert Palmer, VP of Production
   Jacqui Grunfeld, VP of Business & Legal Affairs
Specialties: Studio; Animation
Other Categories: TV
Credits: Power Ranger; Rusty: A Dog's Tale; Sweet Valley High
Additional Info: A Division of Fox Family

ALAN SACKS PRODUCTIONS, INC.
11684 Ventura Blvd., Ste. 809
Studio City, CA 91604
Phone: (818) 752-6999
Fax: (818) 752-6985
asacks@pacbell.net
Key Executives/Personnel:
   Alan Sacks, Producer
   Teena Poiter, Assistant to Mr. Sacks
Specialties: Independent; Documentaries
Other Categories: TV
Credits: The Other Me; The Color of Friendship; Smart House; Welcome Back, Kotter

SAMUELSON PRODUCTIONS
10401 Wyton Dr.
Los Angeles, CA 90024
Phone: (310) 208-1000
Fax: (310) 208-2809
petersam@idt.net
Key Executives/Personnel:
   Marc Samuelson, Partner (UK)
   Peter Samuelson, Partner (LA)
Specialties: Studio; Independent; Large Format
Other Categories: TV
Credits: Jimmy Spud; Arlington Road; Wilde; Tom & Viv

SANFORD/PILLSBURY PRODUCTIONS
Phone: (310) 393-5225
Fax: (310) 393-8665
mssd@sanford-pillsbury.com
Key Executives/Personnel:
   Sarah Pillsbury, Partner & Producer
   Midge Sanford, Partner & Producer
   Rebecca Baldwin, Creative Executive
Specialties: Studio; Independent
Other Categories: TV
Credits: Desperately Seeking Susan; Eight Men Out; River's Edge; The Love Letter

SANTA MONICA PICTURES
3025 W. Olympic Blvd.
Santa Monica, CA 90404
Phone: (310) 264-5566
Fax: (310) 828-9183
infosmp@visionart.com
Key Executives/Personnel:
   David Rose, CEO & Producer
   Marina Muhlfriedel, VP of Development & Production
   Cindy Sison, Head of Int'l. Sales & Distribution
   Stasi McAteer, Executive Assistant
Specialties: Independent; Animation
Other Categories: TV; Interactive Multimedia
Credits: The Painting; Goldilocks and the Three Bears; Godiva; The Magic Forest

SARABANDE PRODUCTIONS
530 Wilshire Blvd., Ste. 308
Santa Monica, CA 90401
Phone: (310) 395-4842
Fax: (310) 395-7079
Key Executives/Personnel:
   David Manson, President
   Arla Sorkin Manson, Executive VP
   David Strohmeyer, Development Associate
Specialties: Studio
Other Categories: TV
Credits: Birdy; Bring on the Night; Nothing Sacred; Thicker Than Blood, Baby

SATURN FILMS
9000 Sunset Blvd., Ste. 911
West Hollywood, CA 90069
Phone: (310) 887-0900
Fax: (310) 248-2965
Key Executives/Personnel:
   Nicolas Cage, President
   Norm Golightly, Producer
   Clarke Anderson, Story Editor
   Christina Price, Assistant to Mr. Golightly & Office Manager
Specialties: Studio; Independent
Credits: Shadow of the Vampire; Tom Slick: Monster Hunter
First Look/Development Deals: Intermedia Films

SCHAPIRO ENTERTAINMENT GROUP
8840 Wilshire Blvd., 2nd Fl.
Beverly Hills, CA 90211
Phone: (310) 358-3215
Fax: (310) 358-3270
Key Executives/Personnel:
   Larry Schapiro, President
   Alex Murray, Head of Comedy Department
   Alex Pearl, Head of Development
Specialties: Independent
Credits: Playing Mona Lisa; Do It For Uncle Manny

EDGAR J. SCHERICK & ASSOCIATES, INC.
1950 Sawtelle Blvd., Ste. 282
Los Angeles, CA 90025
Phone: (310) 996-2376
Fax: (310) 996-2392
Key Executives/Personnel:
   Edgar T. Scherick, President
   Damon O'Daniel, Executive Assistant
   Dan Olsen, Assistant
Specialties: Studio; Independent
Other Categories: TV
Credits: The Heartbreak Kid; Sleuth; The Taking of Pelham 1, 2, 3; They Shoot Horses

PAUL SCHIFF PRODUCTIONS
940 N. Mansfield Ave.
Hollywood, CA 90038
Phone: (323) 462-6400
Key Executives/Personnel:
   Paul Schiff, President & Producer
   Jason Hawkins, Assistant
Specialties: Studio
Credits: Whatever It Takes; Rushmore; The Vanishing; My Cousin Vinny
First Look/Development Deals: Walt Disney Pictures/Touchstone Pictures

SCHOLASTIC ENTERTAINMENT
524 Broadway
New York, NY 10012
Phone: (212) 343-7500
Fax: (212) 343-7888

Production Companies – Feature Film

www.scholastic.com
ljackson@scholastic.com
Key Executives/Personnel:
    Deborah Forte, Executive VP & Division Head
    Martha Atwater, VP of Programming & Development
    Linda Kahn, VP of Int'l. Distribution
    Ginger McGuire, VP of Finance & Business Affairs
    Andrea Sporer, VP of Legal Affairs
Specialties: Independent; Animation
Other Categories: TV
Credits: Animorphs; Clifford the Big Red Dog; Indian in the Cupboard

JOEL SCHUMACHER PRODUCTIONS
4000 Warner Blvd., Bldg. 81, Rm. 207
Burbank, CA 91522
Phone: ....(818) 954-2508
Fax: ....(818) 954-2509
Key Executives/Personnel:
    Joel Schumacher, Owner
    Claire Baker, Executive Assistant to Mr. Schumacher
    Eli Richbourg, Assistant to Mr. Schumacher
Specialties: Studio
Credits: The Client; A Time to Kill; Batman & Robin; Flawless
Additional Info: Address changing beginning 2001.

BERNARD SCHWARTZ PRODUCTIONS
1900 Avenue of the Stars, Ste. 725
Los Angeles, CA 90067
Phone: ....(310) 277-3700
Fax: ....(310) 286-9700
Key Executives/Personnel:
    Bernard Schwartz, Producer
    Sandra Jones, Assistant
Specialties: Studio
Other Categories: TV
Credits: Coal Miner's Daughter; Sweet Dreams; Psycho II; St. Elmo's Fire

KRISTINE SCHWARZ PRODUCTIONS
Phone: ....(310) 393-0107
Fax: ....(310) 451-5454
www.kristineschwarzproductions.com
krisjs@aol.com
Key Executives/Personnel:
    Kristine Schwarz, Producer
Specialties: Studio; Independent
Other Categories: TV; Commercials; Interactive Multimedia
Credits: Raid Gauldises; Kalifornia; Another Stakeout

SCOTT FREE PRODUCTIONS
634 N. La Peer Dr.
West Hollywood, CA 90069
Phone: ....(310) 360-2250
Fax: ....(310) 360-2251
Key Executives/Personnel:
    Ridley Scott, Co-Chairman
    Tony Scott, Co-Chairman
    Lisa Ellzey, President
    Zach Schiff-Abrams, VP
    Anne Lai, Creative Executive
    Erin Upson, Story Editor
    Julie Payne, London Executive
    Beth Vitallo, Executive Assistant to Mr. Ridley Scott
    Peter Toumasis, Executive Assistant to Mr. Tony Scott
    Tom Moran, Executive Assistant to Mr. Tony Scott
    Ersin Pertan, Executive Assistant to Mr. Schiff-Abrams
    Milly Leigh, Executive Assistant to Ms. Payne
Specialties: Studio
Other Categories: TV
Credits: Hannibal; Gladiator; Enemy of the State; Top Gun
First Look/Development Deals: Intermedia Films, Jerry Bruckheimer Films
Additional Info: 42-44 Beak St., London, W1R 3DA England

SCOTTI PRODUCTIONS
Phone: ....(323) 654-3666
....(213) 500-1915
dscotti@earthlink.net
Key Executives/Personnel:
    Don Scotti, Owner
Specialties: Independent; Documentaries
Other Categories: Commercials; Video
Credits: Get Bruce! (documentary)
Trade Assoc./Guilds/Unions: AEA, SAG

SCREEN GEMS
10202 W. Washington Blvd.
Culver City, CA 90232
Phone: ....(310) 244-4000
Fax: ....(310) 244-2037
Key Executives/Personnel:
    Clint Culpepper, Executive VP of Acquisitions & Production
    Peter Schlessey, Executive VP of Business Affairs & Acquisitions
    Benedict Carver, VP of Acquisitions
    Stacy Kolker, VP of Production
    Linda Meadows, VP of Business Affairs
    Valerie van Galder, Executive VP of Marketing & Publicity
    Marc Weinstock, VP of Marketing
    Tracy McArdie, VP of Publicity
Specialties: Studio; Direct-to-Video
Credits: Girl Fight; The Opposite of Sex; Jaw Breaker

SECTION EIGHT PICTURES
4000 Warner Blvd., Bldg. 81, Rm. 117
Burbank, CA 91522
Phone: ....(818) 954-4840
Fax: ....(818) 954-4860
Key Executives/Personnel:
    George Clooney, Partner
    Steven Soderberg, Partner
    Ben Cosgrove, President
    Kevin Field, VP
    Amy Minda Cohen, Executive Assistant
Specialties: Studio; Independent
Additional Info: Formerly Maysville Entertainment

DYLAN SELLERS PRODUCTIONS
4000 Warner Blvd.
Burbank, CA 91522
Phone: ....(818) 954-4929
Key Executives/Personnel:
    Dylan Sellers, Owner & Producer
    Bonny Giardina, Director of Development
Specialties: Studio
Other Categories: TV
Credits: Valentine; Out to Sea; The Replacements; The Paper
First Look/Development Deals: Warner Bros.

SEVEN ARTS PICTURES
7080 Hollywood Blvd., Ste. 201
Hollywood, CA 90028
Phone: ....(323) 464-0225
Fax: ....(323) 464-8305
cinevision@aol.com
Key Executives/Personnel:
    Peter M. Hoffman, Chairman
    Colleen Camp, Producer & Partner
    Neil Canton, Producer & Partner
    Susan Hoffman, Producer & Partner
    Eric Sandys, President of Production
    Katie Hoffman, Creative Executive
    Brette Krinick, Creative Executive
    Erik Smith, Finance & Administration

Production Companies – Feature Film

Victor Teran, Creative Executive
Tori Crotts, Executive Assistant to Mr. Hoffman
Amber Aaseng, Executive Assistant to Ms. Camp
Andrea Ritigstein, Executive Assistant to Mr. Sandys
Specialties: Independent
Other Categories: TV
Credits: Rules of Engagement; Shattered Image; Duets; Never Talk To Strangers
First Look/Development Deals: Paramount Pictures

SHADY ACRES ENTERTAINMENT
100 Universal City Plaza, Bldg. 5225, 2nd Fl.
Universal City, CA 91608
Phone: ....(818) 777-4446
Fax: ....(818) 866-6612
Key Executives/Personnel:
Michael Bostick, no title
Jim Brubaker, no title
Ashley Cook, no title
Ginny Durkin, no title
Greg Messina, no title
Amanda Morgan Palmer, no title
Tom Shadyac, no title
Lindsay Smarz, no title
Winston Stromberg, no title
Gina Warendorp, no title
Jordan Wolfe, no title
Brook Worley, no title
Specialties: Independent
Other Categories: TV; Music Video
Credits: Patch Adams; The Nutty Professor; Liar Liar
First Look/Development Deals: Universal Pictures

SHANGHAI'D FILMS
2601 Colorado Ave.
Santa Monica, CA 90404
Phone: ....(310) 453-8337
Fax: ....(310) 453-3957
shanghfilm@aol.com
Key Executives/Personnel:
Ron Shelton, Partner
Stephen Chin, Partner
Specialties: Studio; Independent
Credits: Play It To The Bone

SHEARMAN ENTERTAINMENT, INC.
1541 Ocean Ave., Ste. 200
Santa Monica, CA 90401
Phone: ....(310) 860-0086
Fax: ....(310) 260-6336
jryan1111@aol.com
Key Executives/Personnel:
J. R. Shearman, Producer & Personal Manager
Specialties: Studio; Independent; Shorts; Documentaries
Other Categories: TV
Credits: Lie Down With Dogs; Never Met Picasso; The Casanovas

SHOELACE PRODUCTIONS, INC.
16 W. 19th St., 12th Fl.
New York, NY 10011
Phone: ....(212) 243-2900
Key Executives/Personnel:
Julia Roberts, Co-President & Producer
Deborah Schindler, Co-President & Producer
Mark James, Director of Literary Affairs
Mary Firestone, Story Editor
David Voila, Assistant to Ms. Schindler
Specialties: Studio

SHONKYTE PRODUCTIONS, INC.
11935 Kling St., Ste. 10
Valley Village, CA 91607
Phone: ....(818) 505-1332
Fax: ....(818) 505-1411
www.seanyoung.org
steffy@ix.netcom.com
Key Executives/Personnel:
Sean Young, Producer, Director & Actress
Stephany Hurkos, Producer
Specialties: Independent
Credits: Men; Mirage
First Look/Development Deals: Tricor Entertainment, FilmWorld, Inc.
Trade Assoc./Guilds/Unions: DGA, SAG, WGAw

SHORELINE ENTERTAINMENT
1875 Century Park East, Ste. 600
Los Angeles, CA 90067
Phone: ....(310) 551-2060
Fax: ....(310) 201-0729
www.shorelineentertainment.com
mruskin@shorelineentertainment.com
Key Executives/Personnel:
Vicky Pike, Producer
Morris Ruskin, Producer
Specialties: Studio; Independent
Other Categories: TV
Credits: Flight of Fancy; The King's Guard; The Visit

SIGNATURE ENTERTAINMENT
8306 Wilshire Blvd., Ste. 791
Beverly Hills, CA 90211
Phone: ....(213) 994-4695
Key Executives/Personnel:
Kelly Andrea Rubin, Producer
Specialties: Independent; Direct-to-Video; Shorts; Documentaries
Other Categories: TV; Commercials
Credits: The Third Wheel; Cotton Mouth; An Eye For Talent; Skippy
First Look/Development Deals: Indigo Entertainment

SIGNATURE FILMS
1875 Century Park East, Ste. 2000
Los Angeles, CA 90067
Phone: ....(310) 226-8374
Fax: ....(310) 226-8343
Key Executives/Personnel:
Moshe Diamant, CEO & Producer
Rudy Cohen, Producer
Limor Diamant, Producer
Victoria Lucas, VP of Production
James Portolese, Director of Development
Specialties: Studio; Independent
Credits: The Body; D'Artagnan; Time Cop

SILVER LINING PRODUCTIONS, INC.
8687 Melrose Ave., Ste. B300
West Hollywood, CA 90069
Phone: ....(310) 289-6650
Fax: ....(310) 289-6658
slpbozena@aol.com/silverliningp@aol.com
Key Executives/Personnel:
Bozena Armstrong, Executive Producer & Director
Randy Haberkamp, Producer
Specialties: Shorts; Trailers
Other Categories: TV; Commercials; Video; Interactive Multimedia
Credits: Cleopatra (promo); Forest Lawn (commercial); Reva: The Scarlet Years (video); The Unknown Tradition (documentary)
Trade Assoc./Guilds/Unions: DGA, SAG

SILVER LION FILMS
701 Santa Monica Blvd., Ste. 240
Santa Monica, CA 90401

Phone: ....(310) 393-9177
Fax: ....(310) 458-9372
www.silverlionfilms.com
slionfilms@aol.com
Key Executives/Personnel:
    Lance Hool, Producer
    Conrad Hool, Producer
    Chase Meilen, Business Affairs
    David Kohner-Zuckerman, Director of Development
Specialties: Studio
Credits: Crocodile Dundee in L.A.; One Man's Hero; Flipper; The Air Up There

SILVER PICTURES TELEVISION
c/o Warner Bros., 4000 Warner Blvd., Bldg. 90
Burbank, CA 91522
Phone: ....(818) 954-4490
Fax: ....(818) 954-3237
Key Executives/Personnel:
    Joel Silver, Chairman
    Steve Richards, CFO
    Dan Cracchiolo, Sr. VP of Production
    Susan Levin, VP of Production
    Pam Martin, VP of Operations
Specialties: Studio
Other Categories: TV
Credits: The Matrix; House on Haunted Hill; Romeo Must Die; Lethal Weapon Series

SILVEREYE PRODUCTIONS
4163 Murietta Ave.
Sherman Oaks, CA 91423
Phone: ....(818) 501-4232
Fax: ....(818) 990-9997
Key Executives/Personnel:
    Ahmed Lateef, Producer & Director
    Ashwin Joshi, Producer & VP
    Omer Mohamed, Producer & Treasurer
    Meher Tatna, Producer & Writer
    Subash Kundamal, Producer & Writer
    Sherwood Ho, Producer & Director
Specialties: Independent; Shorts; Documentaries
Other Categories: TV; Commercials
Credits: Pepsi; Changing Gears (feature); Locket (feature); Goodyear Tires
Trade Assoc./Guilds/Unions: DGA, FEU

SILVERLINE PICTURES
4410 Radford Ave.
North Hollywood, CA 91607
Phone: ....(818) 752-3730
Fax: ....(818) 752-3758
www.silverlinepictures.com
silverline@earthlink.net
Key Executives/Personnel:
    Axel Munch, President & Producer
    Leman Cetiner, CEO & Producer
    Christopher Tipton, Director of Production & Acquistions
    Robert Yap, Director of Development & Sales
Specialties: Studio; Independent
Other Categories: TV
Credits: Angels Don't Sleep Here; Traveling Bowls of Soup; Dusting Cliff Seven; Where Truth Lies

SIMEX DIGITAL STUDIOS
3250 Ocean Park Blvd., Ste. 100
Santa Monica, CA 90405
Phone: ....(310) 664-9500
Fax: ....(310) 664-9977
www.planetpoint.com
allen@simexds.com
Key Executives/Personnel:
    Allen Yamashita, Director
    Nick Bates, Director & Visual Effects Supervisor
    Jean Perramon, Director
    John Wash, Visual Effects Supervisor
Specialties: Studio; Shorts; Animation; Large Format
Other Categories: Commercials
Credits: Nintendo; Kellogg's Froot Loops; Anheuser-Busch; Keebler

SIMIAN FILMS
335 N. Maple Drive, Ste. 350
Beverly Hills, CA 90210
Phone: ....(310) 205-2724
Fax: ....(310) 888-3516
Key Executives/Personnel:
    Hugh Grant, Producer & Actor
    Elizabeth Hurley, Producer
    Lisa Reeve, Sr. VP of Production
Specialties: Studio
Credits: Mickey Blue Eyes; Extreme Measures
First Look/Development Deals: Castle Rock Entertainment

THE GENE SIMMONS COMPANY
P.O. Box 16075
Beverly Hills, CA 90210
Phone: ....(310) 859-1694
Fax: ....(310) 859-2631
Key Executives/Personnel:
    Gene Simmons, Producer
    David Slous, Assistant
Specialties: Studio
Other Categories: TV
Credits: Detroit Rock City; Neal Bogart Story; Sex, Drugs and Rock n' Roll; November Files

RANDY SIMON PRODUCTIONS
1113 N. Hillcrest Rd.
Beverly Hills, CA 90210
Phone: ....(310) 274-7440
Fax: ....(310) 274-9809
simonrandy@aol.com
Key Executives/Personnel:
    Randy Simon, Producer
Specialties: Studio; Independent
Other Categories: TV
Credits: Pi; Requiem For A Dream; Intern; Blue Ridge Fall

THE ROBERT SIMONDS COMPANY
100 Universal City Plaza, Bldg. 1320, PH.1A
Universal City, CA 91608
Phone: ....(818) 777-5445
Fax: ....(818) 866-1404
Key Executives/Personnel:
    Robert Simonds, Producer
    Tracey Trench, President of Creative Affairs
    Joy Gorman, VP of Creative Affairs
    Linda Cuevas, Executive Assistant to Mr. Simonds
    Alison Luzietti, Assistant to Ms. Trench
    Laura Millar, Assistant to Ms. Gorman
Specialties: Studio
Other Categories: TV
Credits: Little Nicky; The Water Boy; Big Daddy; Happy Gilmore
First Look/Development Deals: Universal Pictures

SINGLE SPARK PICTURES
3000 W. Olympic Blvd.
Santa Monica, CA 90404
Phone: ....(310) 315-4779
Fax: ....(310) 315-4773
Key Executives/Personnel:
    Mark Mori, President & Executive Producer
    Jim Hense, Producer

Production Companies – Feature Film

Specialties: Independent; Documentaries
Other Categories: TV
Credits: Kent State: The Day The War Came Home; Survivors; Raw Footage

SITTING DUCKS PRODUCTIONS
1532 Micheltorena St.
Los Angeles, CA 90026
Phone: ....(323) 660-0861
Fax: ....(323) 660-6021
sittingducks@earthlink.net
Key Executives/Personnel:
    Elizabeth Daro, Co-Owner
    Michael Bedard, Co-Owner
    Liz Bedard, Associate Producer
    Danielle Mentzer, Associate Producer
Specialties: Studio; Direct-to-Video; Animation
Other Categories: TV
Credits: Sitting Ducks; The Mouse and the Monster
First Look/Development Deals: Universal Pictures

SKYLARK ENTERTAINMENT, INC.
12405 Venice Blvd., Ste. 237
Los Angeles, CA 90066
Phone: ....(310) 390-2659
Fax: ....(310) 390-2759
skylarkinc@earthlink.net
Key Executives/Personnel:
    Jacobus Rose, Producer
Specialties: Studio; Independent; Animation
Other Categories: TV
Credits: Deadlocked; The Linda McCartney Story; Election; Steal This Movie
First Look/Development Deals: Robert Greenwald Productions

SKYLARK FILMS, LTD.
1123 Pacific St., Ste. G
Santa Monica, CA 90405
Phone: ....(310) 396-5753
Fax: ....(310) 396-5753
skyfilm@aol.com
Key Executives/Personnel:
    Brad Pollack, Producer
    Jasan Pagni, Development
Specialties: Independent
Other Categories: TV
Credits: The Styx; Coal of the Heart; Terminal Justice; Just One Look
First Look/Development Deals: Orly Adelson Productions

SLADEK ENTERTAINMENT CORPORATION
8306 Wilshire Blvd., Ste. 510
Beverly Hills, CA 90211
Phone: ....(323) 934-9268
Fax: ....(323) 934-7362
www.danielsladek.com
dansladek@aol.com
Key Executives/Personnel:
    Daniel Sladek, President
    Chris Taaffe, Producing Partner
Specialties: Independent
Other Categories: TV
Credits: Tale of the Mummy; Sub Down; Silent Trigger; Hidden Assassin

SNAPDRAGON FILMS, INC.
13428 Maxella Ave., Ste. 293
Marina Del Rey, CA 90292
Phone: ....(310) 822-2505
Fax: ....(310) 822-7054
Key Executives/Personnel:
    Bonnie Palef, Director, Producer & Writer
    Catherine Purchase, Assistant
    Manuel Granado, Jr., Assistant

Specialties: Studio; Independent; Shorts; Documentaries
Other Categories: TV; Video; Interactive Multimedia
Credits: Marvin's Room; Moonstruck; The Cemetary Club; Parents
First Look/Development Deals: Columbia Pictures/Columbia Tristar Motion Picture Group
Trade Assoc./Guilds/Unions: DGA, WGAw

SNEAK PREVIEW ENTERTAINMENT, INC.
1604 Vista del Mar
Hollywood, CA 90028
Phone: ....(323) 962-0295
Fax: ....(323) 962-0372
www.sneakpreviewentertain.com
sneakpreview@pacbell.net
Key Executives/Personnel:
    Steven J. Wolfe, Chairman, CEO & Producer
    Lynette Prucha Chavez, President & Writer
    David L. Cohn, Talent Manager
    Michael J. Roth, Director of Development
Specialties: Independent
Other Categories: TV; Video; Music Video
Credits: Fast Sofa; Twin Falls, Idaho; Relax...It's Just Sex; Tollbooth

SNL STUDIOS
5555 Melrose Ave., Dressing Room Bldg., Ste. 105
Los Angeles, CA 90038
Phone: ....(323) 956-5729
Fax: ....(323) 862-8605
Key Executives/Personnel:
    Lorne Michaels, Chairman
    Richard Feldman, President
    Mallory Eisenstein, Director of Development
    Abdul Williams, Assistant
Specialties: Studio
Other Categories: TV
Credits: Wayne's World 1 & 2; Ladies Man; Tommy Boy; Superstar
First Look/Development Deals: Paramount Pictures, NBC Entertainment, Inc.

SNOW LEOPARD PRODUCTIONS
Phone: ....(310) 827-1220
Fax: ....(310) 821-5251
www.snowleopard.net
snowcat711@mediaone.net
Key Executives/Personnel:
    C'esca Lawrence, Producer & Co-Owner
    Dan Tursi, Producer & Co-Owner
    Jan Monroe, VP of Creative Affairs
    Tim Merritt, Director of Development
Specialties: Studio; Independent; Documentaries
Other Categories: TV
Credits: A New View

SONNENFELD/JOSEPHSON WORLDWIDE ENTERTAINMENT
10202 W. Washington Blvd., Jimmy Stuart Bldg., Ste. 205
Culver City, CA 90232
Phone: ....(310) 244-8777
Fax: ....(310) 244-1977
Key Executives/Personnel:
    Barry Josephson, no title
    Barry Sonnenfeld, no title
    Brandon Chapnick, Assistant to Mr. Josephson & Mr. Sonnenfeld
Specialties: Studio
Other Categories: TV

SONY PICTURES CLASSICS
550 Madison Ave.
New York, NY 10022
Phone: ....(212) 833-8833
Fax: ....(212) 833-8844
www.spe.sony.com/classics/home.html

Production Companies – Feature Film

Key Executives/Personnel:
    Michael Barker, Co-President
    Tom Bernard, Co-President
    Marcie Bloom, Co-President
    Grace Murphy, Sr. VP of Operations
    Dylan Liner, Sr. VP of Acquisitions
    Carmelo Pirrone, VP of Advertising & Publicity
    Tom Prassis, VP of Sales
    Derzat Whelan, VP of Sales, Large Format Films
Specialties: Studio; Independent; Large Format
Credits: Run Lola Run; The Spanish Prisoner; Crouching Tiger, Hidden Dragon; Tao of Steve

SONY PICTURES ENTERTAINMENT
10202 W. Washington Blvd.
Culver City, CA 90232
Phone: (310) 244-4000
Fax: (310) 244-2626
www.spe.sony.com
Key Executives/Personnel:
    John Calley, Chairman & CEO
    Mel Harris, Co-President & COO
    Beth Berke, Executive VP & CAO
    Jerry Giaquinta, Executive VP of Corporate Communications
    Ronald Jacobi, Executive VP, General Counsel & Corporate Secretary
    Yari Landau, Executive VP
    Bedi A. Singh, Executive VP & CFO
    Suzanne Criley, Sr. VP of Human Resources
    Joe Kraft, Sr. VP & Treasurer
    Karen L. Halby, VP
    Robert Eichorn, Assistant Secretary
    Jared Jussim, Assistant Secretary
    Leah Well, Assistant Secretary
    Lynne R. Shulim, Assistant Treasurer
    Michael Winchester, Assistant Treasurer
Specialties: Studio; Direct-to-Video; Animation

SOUTH FORK PRODUCTIONS
P.O. Box 1935
Santa Monica, CA 90406
Phone: (310) 829-5029
Fax: (310) 829-5029
soforkprods@ireland.com
Key Executives/Personnel:
    Jim Sullivan, Producer & Director
    Greg Sullivan, Producer
Specialties: Studio; Independent; Documentaries
Other Categories: TV; Commercials; Video; Music Video
Credits: Making of Without Limits; Portraits of Courage; Those Who Dare
Trade Assoc./Guilds/Unions: AFI

SOUTHERN SKIES, INC.
1104 S. Holt Ave., Ste. 302
Los Angeles, CA 90035
Phone: (310) 855-9833
Fax: (310) 855-0220
www.southernskiesinc.com
soskies@aol.com
Key Executives/Personnel:
    Ed Markley, President
Specialties: Studio; Independent
Other Categories: TV
Credits: Major League 1 & 2; Alien 3; For The Boys; City Slickers
First Look/Development Deals: Octagon Productions, Inc.
Trade Assoc./Guilds/Unions: AFI, ATAS, DGA

THE SPARK FACTORY
710 Wilshire Blvd., Ste. 200
Santa Monica, CA 90401
Phone: (310) 395-6775
Fax: (310) 395-4595
www.sparkfactory.com
mailroom@sparkfactory.com
Key Executives/Personnel:
    Tim Street, President
    Gail Gillman, VP of Creative Affairs
Specialties: Trailers
Other Categories: Commercials; Interactive Multimedia
Credits: Entrapment (commercial); Out of Towners (commercial); Whoistylerdurden.com; Creepysites.com

SPIN PICTURES INTERTAINMENT, LLC
153 S. Maple Dr.
Beverly Hills, CA 90212
Phone: (310) 278-3569
Fax: (503) 217-1609
www.spinpics.com
spinpics@aol.com
Key Executives/Personnel:
    Jennifer Peckham, President
    Mark Buntzman, CFO
    Kurt Gurtman, Creative Executive
Specialties: Independent
Additional Info: Also a production financing company.

SPOKE FILM
11727 Mississippi Ave.
Los Angeles, CA 90025
Phone: (310) 477-2272
    (312) 640-0049
Fax: (310) 477-1372
www.spokefilm.com
Key Executives/Personnel:
    Dick Gillespie, Executive Producer
    Ed Amaya, Executive Producer
    Steve Farr, Director
    Barry Poltermann, Director
    Ron Lazzeretti, Director
    Jamie O'Malley, Director
    Christopher Yurkow, Director
Specialties: Studio
Credits: AT&T; McDonald's; Coca-Cola; Ford
Additional Info: 215 W. Superior St., Chicago, IL 60610

SPYGLASS ENTERTAINMENT
500 S. Buena Vista St.
Burbank, CA 91521
Phone: (818) 560-3458
Fax: (818) 563-1967
Key Executives/Personnel:
    Gary Barber, Co-Chairman & CEO
    Roger Birnbaum, Co-Chairman & CEO
    Jon Glickman, President of Production
    Drew Larner, Executive VP
    Paul Schwacke, CFO
    Ned Dowd, Sr. VP of Physical Production
    Derek Evans, VP of Production
    Megan Wolpert, VP of Production
    Paul Neinstein, VP of Business & Legal Affairs
    Rebekah Rudd, VP of Post Production
    Jeremy Steckler, Creative Executive
    Marlena Thomas, Executive Coordinator to Mr. Birnbaum
    Kim Buttlar, Executive Coordinator to Mr. Barber
Specialties: Studio; Independent; Documentaries
Other Categories: TV
Credits: The Sixth Sense; Keeping The Faith; Shanghai Noon; Instinct

ST. CLARE ENTERTAINMENT
8490 Sunset Blvd., Ste. 503
Los Angeles, CA 90069
Phone: (310) 360-0451

Production Companies – Feature Film

Fax: (310) 360-0421
Key Executives/Personnel:
  John Landis, Director
  Leslie Belzberg, Producer
Specialties: Studio; Independent
Other Categories: TV
Credits: Susan's Plan; Blues Brothers 2000; The Lost World (TV series); Honey I Shrunk The Kids (TV series)
Trade Assoc./Guilds/Unions: AMPAS, ATAS

J. STACK PRODUCTIONS
Phone: (310) 456-3272
Fax: (310) 456-3442
jmstack@aol.com
Key Executives/Personnel:
  Jeanne Stack, Producer
Specialties: Independent; Documentaries; Large Format
Other Categories: TV; Commercials; Music Video
Credits: Contact (2nd Unit); Kundun (2nd Unit); Eco-Challenge; Mild 7

STAGESCREEN PRODUCTIONS
2601 Nicholas Canyon Rd.
Los Angeles, CA 90046
Phone: (323) 969-1974
Fax: (323) 969-1975
stgescreen@aol.com
Key Executives/Personnel:
  Jeffrey Taylor, Producer
Specialties: Independent
Other Categories: TV
Credits: A Handful of Dust; Where Angels Fear to Tread; Foreign Affairs; What's Cooking
Additional Info: 12 Upper St. Martins Ln., London WC2H 9JY England

STAMPEDE ENTERTAINMENT
3000 W. Olympic Blvd.
Santa Monica, CA 90404
Phone: (310) 264-4229
Fax: (310) 264-4227
Key Executives/Personnel:
  Nancy Roberts, President & Partner
  Ron Underwood, Partner
  S. S. Wilson, Partner
  Brent Maddock, Partner
  Greg Stevens, Executive Story Editor
Specialties: Independent
Credits: Heart & Souls; Tremors; Tremors 2: Aftershocks

STAR ENTERTAINMENT GROUP, INC.
13547 Ventura Blvd., Ste. 140
Sherman Oaks, CA 91423
Phone: (818) 988-2200
Key Executives/Personnel:
  Lawrence D. Foldes, Chairman
  Victoria Paige Meyerink, President
Specialties: Independent
Credits: Finding Home; Prima Donnas; Young Warriors; Malibu High
Trade Assoc./Guilds/Unions: AMPAS

STARGAZER, INC.
2432 Seventh St., Ste. 1
Santa Monica, CA 90405
Phone: (310) 392-0392
www.stargazerproductions.com
paigerama@earthlink.net
Key Executives/Personnel:
  Paige Seidel, Producer
Specialties: Independent
Other Categories: Commercials; Music Video
Credits: United Airlines; Audi; monster.com; Jeep

JANE STARTZ PRODUCTIONS, INC.
244 Fifth Ave., 11th Fl.
New York, NY 10001
Phone: (212) 545-8910
Fax: (212) 545-8909
jsp@janestartzproductions.com
Key Executives/Personnel:
  Jane Startz, President & Producer
  Gillian Mackenzie, VP of Creative Affairs
  Billy Mulligan, Development Associate
Specialties: Studio; Independent
Other Categories: TV
Credits: Indian In The Cupboard; The Mighty; The Baby-Sitter's Club; The Magic School Bus

STATE STREET PICTURES
10201 W. Pico Blvd., Bldg. 50
Los Angeles, CA 90064
Phone: (310) 369-5099
Fax: (310) 369-8613
Key Executives/Personnel:
  Robert Teitel, Producer
  George Tillman, Director & Producer
Specialties: Studio
Other Categories: TV
Credits: Men of Honor; Soul Food (feature); Soul Food (TV series)

STEAMROLLER PRODUCTIONS
1041 N. Formosa Ave., Writer's Bldg., Ste. 11
West Hollywood, CA 90041
Phone: (323) 850-2940
Fax: (323) 850-2978
www.stevenseagal.com
Key Executives/Personnel:
  Steven Seagal, Co-CEO, Director, Writer, Producer & Actor
  Phillip Goldfine, President & COO
  Binh Dang, Assistant to Mr. Seagal
  Tracy Irvine, Executive Assistant
Specialties: Independent; Direct-to-Video; Shorts; Documentaries
Credits: Under Siege; Under Siege 2; The Path Beyond Thought; On Deadly Ground

STEFANINO PRODUCTIONS
15515 Sunset Blvd., Ste. 101
Pacific Palisades, CA 90272
Phone: (310) 454-0109
Fax: (310) 454-0109
www.stefanino.com
stefanino@earthlink.net
Key Executives/Personnel:
  Stuart Jemesen, Producer & Director
  Stefan Kendal Gordy, Director of Music
Specialties: Independent
Other Categories: TV; Commercials; Video; Music Video
Credits: Smokey Robinson; Michael Jackson Biography; Innerview (TV pilot)

THE HOWARD STERN PRODUCTION COMPANY
10 E. 44th St.
New York, NY 10017
Phone: (212) 867-1200
Fax: (212) 867-2434
www.howardstern.com
don@buchwald.com
Key Executives/Personnel:
  Howard Stern, President
  Don Buchwald, Agent
Specialties: Studio
Other Categories: TV
Credits: The Howard Stern Radio Show; Son of The Beach; The Howard Stern Show; Doomsday

Production Companies – Feature Film

STONE VS. STONE
189 Franklin St., 3rd Fl.
New York, NY 10013
Phone: ....(212) 941-1200
Fax: ....(212) 941-1115
stonesnyc@aol.com
Key Executives/Personnel:
  Robert Stone, Writer & Producer
  Webster Stone, Writer & Producer
Specialties: Studio
Credits: Gone in 60 Seconds; The Negotiator; Citizen X
Trade Assoc./Guilds/Unions: WGA

STONELOCK PICTURES
Phone: ....(818) 716-6356
....(818) 716-6356
Fax: ....(818) 716-6866
stonelock@aol.com
Key Executives/Personnel:
  Beni Atoori, Producer & Partner
  Heidi Crane, Partner
Specialties: Independent
Credits: In Dark Places; The Spreading Ground

STORM ENTERTAINMENT
225 Santa Monica Blvd., Ste. 601
Santa Monica, CA 90401
Phone: ....(310) 656-2500
Fax: ....(310) 656-2510
Key Executives/Personnel:
  H. Michael Heuser, President & CEO
Specialties: Independent
Credits: The Criminal; Hurlyburly; Modern Vampires; Lovelife

STRAW DOGS
8330 W. Third St.
Los Angeles, CA 90048
Phone: ....(323) 782-0777
Fax: ....(323) 782-9777
Key Executives/Personnel:
  Craig Rogers, Executive Producer
  Leslie Snow, Head of Production
  Jesse Dylan, Director
  Mike Rowles, Director
  Neil Burger, Director
  Deb Hagan, Director
  Stan Morse, Director
  Barry Sonnifeld, Director
Specialties: Studio
Other Categories: Commercials
Credits: Pepsi; Amazon.com; Pizza Hut; Vicks 44

STROM MAGALLON ENTERTAINMENT
3518 Cahuenga Blvd. West, Ste. 111
Los Angeles, CA 90068
Phone: ....(323) 969-1089
....(323) 969-1090
Fax: ....(323) 969-1091
strommagent@earthlink.net
Key Executives/Personnel:
  Gregory Strom, Director
  Douglas Magallon, Director
Specialties: Documentaries
Other Categories: Commercials; Video; Music Video
Credits: Dirt Devil (commercial); Pontiac (commercial)

MEL STUART PRODUCTIONS, INC.
1551 S. Robertson Blvd., Ste. 204
Los Angeles, CA 90035
Phone: ....(310) 785-9080
Fax: ....(310) 785-9179
melfilm@aol.com
Key Executives/Personnel:
  Mel Stuart, President, Producer & Director
  Chad Baron, Associate Producer
Specialties: Documentaries
Other Categories: TV; Video
Credits: Running on the Sun; AFI's 100 Years 100 Movies; The Rise & Fall of the Third Reich; Ripley's Believe It or Not
Trade Assoc./Guilds/Unions: DGA, WGAw

MIKE SULLIVAN PRODUCTIONS, INC.
2314 Michigan Ave.
Santa Monica, CA 90404
Phone: ....(310) 315-7315
Fax: ....(310) 582-0041
msp_inc@wgn.net
Key Executives/Personnel:
  Mike Sullivan, President & Executive Producer
  Polly Brown, Director of Creative Affairs
Specialties: Independent
Other Categories: TV
Credits: Growing Pains; Just The Ten Of Us; The Growing Pains Movie

SUMMERLAND ENTERTAINMENT
17939 Chatsworth St., Ste. 260
Granada Hills, CA 91344
Phone: ....(818) 363-4135
Fax: ....(818) 368-8227
sumrland47@aol.com
Key Executives/Personnel:
  Bruce A. Pobjoy, President & Producer
  Brianne Michelle, VP of Development
  Brooke Allison, Administrative Assistant
Specialties: Independent; Shorts
Other Categories: TV; Music Video
Credits: Fatal Memories; Baywatch Nights; Nightmare Cafe; In The Heat of The Night
Trade Assoc./Guilds/Unions: AAP

SUMMERS ENTERTAINMENT
5230 Linwood Dr.
Los Angeles, CA 90027
Phone: ....(323) 665-5400
Fax: ....(323) 663-6679
Key Executives/Personnel:
  Cathleen Summers, Producer
Specialties: Studio; Independent
Other Categories: TV
Credits: Stake Out; Dog Fight; The Sandlot; D.O.A
First Look/Development Deals: Twentieth Century Fox Pictures
Trade Assoc./Guilds/Unions: ACAD, PGA

SUNDOG PRODUCTIONS
1129 Highland Ave., Ste. 201
Manhattan Beach, CA 90266
Phone: ....(310) 564-9515
Fax: ....(310) 546-9516
laloula@aol.com
Key Executives/Personnel:
  Larry Carroll, Director
  Linda Agnelli, Producer
Specialties: Documentaries
Other Categories: TV
Credits: Sam Kinison: Why Did We Laugh?; The New American Heroes; Women Surfer Project
Trade Assoc./Guilds/Unions: DGA

Production Companies – Feature Film

MARTIN TAHSE PRODUCTIONS
360 South Burnside Ave., Ste. 5L
Los Angeles, CA 90036
Phone: (310) 652-3628
Fax: (310) 652-0538
www.newkidhomevideo.com
nkhv@aol.com
Key Executives/Personnel:
  Martin Tahse, President
  Michael Vodde, VP of Development
Specialties: Studio; Independent
Credits: Words By Heart; The Look-Alike; Matters of The Heart

TALENT ENTERTAINMENT GROUP
9111 Wilshire Blvd.
Beverly Hills, CA 90210
Phone: (323) 969-0700
 (310) 205-5525
Fax: (323) 969-9340
Key Executives/Personnel:
  Erwin More, Partner
  Brian Medavoy, Partner
  Suzan Bymel, Partner
  Evelyn O'Neill, Partner
  Cheryl Stanley, VP of Creative Affairs
  Bill Choi, Manager
  David Gardner, Manager
  Peter Kiernan, Manager
  Jill Littman, Manager
  Randi Siegel, Manager
  Louise Spinner, Manager
Specialties: Studio
Other Categories: TV
Credits: Just Shoot Me; Dharma & Greg; American High
First Look/Development Deals: Warner Bros. Television

TALISMAN PACIFIC
1351 Fourth St., Ste. 201
Santa Monica, CA 90401
Phone: (310) 260-1208
Fax: (310) 260-6116
talpacific@aol.com
Key Executives/Personnel:
  Scott Pennington, no title
  Steve Sherman, no title
Specialties: Independent
Credits: Rob Roy; Box Of Moonlight; The Tic Code

TALKING RINGS ENTERTAINMENT
P.O. Box 80141
Las Vegas, NV 89180
Phone: (702) 227-3433
www.scifisation.com
director@scifistation.com
Key Executives/Personnel:
  Arnold Leibovit, Director
  Barbara Schimpf, VP of Production
Specialties: Independent; Studio; Animation
Credits: The Fantasy Film Worlds of George Pal; The Puppetoon Movie

TAPESTRY FILMS, INC.
9328 Civic Center Dr.
Beverly Hills, CA 90210
Phone: (310) 275-1191
Fax: (310) 275-1266
tapestryfilms@tapestryfilms.com
Key Executives/Personnel:
  Robert Levy, Producer & Partner
  Peter Abrams, Producer & Partner
  Jennifer Gibgot, President of Production
  Andrew Panay, Sr. VP of Production
  Jonathon Komack Martin, Executive VP
  Michael K. Eitelman, Story Editor
  Natan Zahavi, Producer
  Sherwood Jones, Post Production Supervisor
  Alicia Hopkins, Controller
  Michelle Castillo, Executive Assistant
  Nichole Somers, Assistant to Mr. Levy & Mr. Abrams
  Jeremy Martin, Executive Assistant
Specialties: Studio; Independent; Direct-to-Video
Credits: Point Break; She's All That; Pay it Forward; The Wedding Planner

TAURUS ENTERTAINMENT COMPANY
5831 Sunset Blvd.
Hollywood, CA 90028
Phone: (323) 860-0807
Fax: (323) 860-0834
www.taurus-entertainment.com
taurusec@aol.com
Key Executives/Personnel:
  Stan Dudelson, Chairman
  James Dudelson, President & CEO
  Robert Dudelson, COO
  Ana Clevel, VP
  Steve Kripner, Stage Manager
  Kimberly Burch, Operations Manager
Specialties: Independent
Other Categories: TV
Credits: Horror 101; Morela; Mastermind; Hot Springs Hotel

TAVEL ENTERTAINMENT
9171 Wilshire Blvd., Ste. 406
Beverly Hills, CA 90210
Phone: (310) 278-6700
Fax: (310) 278-6770
Key Executives/Personnel:
  Connie Tavel, Owner, Manager & Producer
  Chris Ridenhour, Development for Features
  Vanessa Livingston, Development for TV
  Plato Wang, Development for Internet
  Vera Mihailovich, Talent Manager
  Mundi Male, Assistant to Ms. Tavel
  Marc Walker, Assistant to Mr. Ridenhour
  Courtney Adams, Assistant to Ms. Mihailovich
Specialties: Studio; Independent
Other Categories: TV; Interactive Multimedia
Credits: Judging Amy; Summer's End; Bill & Ted's Bogus Journey; Ride The Wind
First Look/Development Deals: Sony Pictures Entertainment

TAYLOR-BEDELL ENTERTAINMENT
9560 Wilshire Blvd., PH
Beverly Hills, CA 90212
Phone: (310) 859-9967
Fax: (310) 859-9965
tbe@earthlink.net
Key Executives/Personnel:
  Stephen Bedell, Partner & Producer
  Burton Taylor, Partner & Producer
  Chris Mock, Development
Specialties: Studio; Independent; Direct-to-Video; Animation
Other Categories: TV
Credits: The Westside Waltz; 1,000 Men and a Baby

TEAM TODD
9021 Melrose Ave., Ste. 301
Los Angeles, CA 90069
Phone: (310) 248-6001

Production Companies – Feature Film

Fax: ....(310) 385-8072
Key Executives/Personnel:
  Jennifer Todd, Partner & Producer
  Suzanne Todd, Partner & Producer
  Pamela Post, VP
  Lauren Tabach-Bank, Development Assistant
  Julie Ragland, Assistant to Producers
Specialties: Studio
Other Categories: TV
Credits: Momento; If These Walls Could Talk 2; Boiler Room; Austin Powers 1 & 2
First Look/Development Deals: New Line Cinema, Inc.

TELESCENE FILM GROUP, INC.
5705 Ferrier, Ste. 200
Montreal, QC H4P 1N3 Canada
Phone: ....(514) 737-5512
Fax: ....(514) 737-7945
www.telescene.ca
info@telescene.ca
Key Executives/Personnel:
  Robin Spry, President & CEO
  Bruce Moccia, President of Telescene Film Group, Inc. (USA)
  Michael Yudin, President of Telescene Entertainment, Inc.
  Claire Benoit, VP of Business & Legal Affairs/Secretary
  Daniel Proulx, VP of Finance & CEO
  Anita Simand, Head of Creative Affairs
  Diana Arcand, Head of Production
  Cynthia Lane, Manager of Public Relations
Specialties: Independent
Other Categories: TV
Credits: Hiroshima; Student Bodies; Big Wolf on Campus; Live Through This

TELLING PICTURES, INC.
121 Ninth St.
San Francisco, CA 94103
Phone: ....(415) 864-6714
Fax: ....(415) 864-4364
www.tellingpix.com
tellingpix@aol.com
Key Executives/Personnel:
  Rob Epstein, Director & Producer
  Jeffrey Friedman, Director & Producer
  Michael Ehrenzweig, Producer
  Whitney Saik, Production Manager
Specialties: Independent; Documentaries
Other Categories: TV; Video
Credits: The Times of Harvey Milk; Common Threads: Stories from the Quilt; The Celluloid Closet; Paragraph 175
Trade Assoc./Guilds/Unions: AMPAS, ATAS

TEN THIRTEEN PRODUCTIONS
P.O. Box 900
Beverly Hills, CA 90213
Phone: ....(310) 369-1100
Key Executives/Personnel:
  Chris Carter, Executive Producer
  Frank Spotnitz, President & Executive Producer
  Mary Astadourian, VP
Specialties: Studio
Other Categories: TV
Credits: The X Files; The Lone Gunman
First Look/Development Deals: Twentieth Century Fox Television

TEOCALLI ENTERTAINMENT, INC.
205 Timberline Court
Ruidoso, NM 88345
Phone: ....(505) 258-1373
Fax: ....(505) 258-1377
Key Executives/Personnel:
  Robert A. Nowotny, President
  Ed Callaway, Director of Development
Specialties: Independent; Direct-to-Video; Shorts; Documentaries
Other Categories: TV; Video
Credits: False River; The Top Of The Bottom Half; The Legend of Billy The Kid; The Radicals

TERRA BELLA ENTERTAINMENT
8170 Beverly Blvd., Ste. 102
Los Angeles, CA 90048
Phone: ....(323) 655-2311
Fax: ....(323) 655-0499
Key Executives/Personnel:
  Adam Leipzig, Producer
  Susanna Bieger, Research Associate
Specialties: Studio; Independent
Other Categories: TV
Credits: Titus; The Associate

THRESHOLD ENTERTAINMENT
1649 11th St.
Santa Monica, CA 90404
Phone: ....(310) 452-8899
Fax: ....(310) 452-0736
www.thethreshold.com
Key Executives/Personnel:
  Larry Kasanoff, Chairman & CEO
  Joshua Wexler, CIO
  George Johnsen, CTO
  Alison Savitch, President
Specialties: Studio; Independent; Animation
Other Categories: TV; Interactive Multimedia
Credits: Mortal Kombat: Annihilation; Beowulf; True Lies; Mortal Kombat

TIDEWATER ENTERTAINMENT
320 Mount Holyoke Ave.
Pacific Palisades, CA 90272
Phone: ....(310) 459-8711
Fax: ....(310) 459-0149
Key Executives/Personnel:
  Bill Ungar, President & Executive Producer
Specialties: Independent
Other Categories: TV
Credits: Excellent Cadavers; Crimson Tide; True Romance

THE STEVE TISCH COMPANY
3815 Hughes Ave.
Culver City, CA 90232
Phone: ....(310) 838-2500
Fax: ....(310) 204-2713
Key Executives/Personnel:
  Steve Tisch, Chairman
  Kim Skeeters, Controller & Business Affairs
  William Driver, Production Assistant
  Sharyn Steele, Assistant to Mr. Tisch
Specialties: Independent
Credits: Lock, Stock and Two Smoking Barrels; American History X; Forrest Gump; The Postman

TLC ENTERTAINMENT
c/o CBS Studio Center, 4024 Radford Ave., Edit Bldg. 2, Ste. 9
Studio City, CA 91604
Phone: ....(818) 655-6155
Fax: ....(818) 655-6254
tlce@aol.com
Key Executives/Personnel:
  George Taweel, Producer
  Rob Loos, Producer
  Jennifer Velasco, Assistant to Mr. Taweel & Mr. Loos
Specialties: Direct-to-Video

Production Companies – Feature Film

Other Categories: TV
Credits: Magee & Me; All New Captain Kangaroo Show; Secret Adventures
Trade Assoc./Guilds/Unions: ATAS, DGA, PGA, WGAw

TOLLIN/ROBBINS PRODUCTIONS
4133 Lankershim Blvd.
North Hollywood, CA 91602
Phone: (818) 766-5004
Fax: (818) 766-8488
Key Executives/Personnel:
   Mike Tollin, Executive Producer & Director
   Brian Robbins, Executive Producer & Director
   Joe Davola, Executive Producer
   Jonny Fink, Producer
   Jeff Blye, COO
   Chris Castallo, Director of Creative Affairs
   Michael Goldman, Talent Manager
   Virginie Lacoste, Office Manager & Bookkeeper
   Andre Burrell, Assistant to Mr. Davola & Mr. Costallo
   Jason Hutt, Assistant to Ms. Gray
   Alex Timchak, Assistant to Mr. Robbins & Mr. Davola
   Mark Warshaw, Assistant to Mr. Robbins
   Caleigh Vancata, Talent Maintenance
   Andrew Bennett, Office Production Assistant
   Susan Chan, Office Assistant
Specialties: Studio; Independent
Other Categories: TV
Credits: Summer Catch; Varsity Blues; Ready to Rumble; All That

TOTEM PRODUCTIONS
8009 Santa Monica Blvd.
Los Angeles, CA 90046
Phone: (323) 650-4994
Fax: (323) 650-1961
totempro@aol.com
Key Executives/Personnel:
   Tony Scott, Co-Chairman
   Peter Toumasis, Executive Assistant to Mr. Scott
   Tom Moran, Assistant to Mr. Scott
Specialties: Studio; Independent
Other Categories: Commercials
Credits: Enemy of the State; Top Gun; True Romance; Crimson Tide

TRIBE PICTURES
244 Main St.
Chatham, NJ 07928
Phone: (973) 635-2660
Fax: (973) 635-2654
www.tribepictures.com
mail@tribepictures.com
Key Executives/Personnel:
   Vera Oakley, Producer & Director
Specialties: Independent
Other Categories: Video

TRIBECA PRODUCTIONS
375 Greenwich St., 6th Fl.
New York, NY 10013
Phone: (212) 941-4000
Fax: (212) 941-4044
www.tribecafilm.com
Key Executives/Personnel:
   Robert DeNiro, Partner
   Jane Rosenthal, Partner
   Hardy Justice, VP of Creative Affairs
   Trina Wyatt, VP of Operations & Finance
   Elyse Klaits, Director of Production
   Scott Neustadler, Director of Development
   Kate Feeney, Assistant to Ms. Rosenthal
   Meghan Lyvers, Assistant to Ms. Rosenthal
   Tom Turner, Assistant to Ms. Wyatt
Specialties: Studio
Other Categories: TV
Credits: Meet the Parents; Analyze This; Wag the Dog; Thunderheart

THE TRIBUNAL
Phone: (323) 468-9300
Fax: (323) 936-1301
www.thetribunal.com
production@thetribunal.com
Key Executives/Personnel:
   Thomas Sammon, Producer & Partner
   Maria Bryant, Producer & Partner
Specialties: Studio; Independent
Other Categories: TV
Credits: High Caliber; Real Story

TRIOLOGY ENTERTAINMENT GROUP
2450 Broadway St., Ste. 675
Santa Monica, CA 90404
Phone: (310) 449-3095
Fax: (310) 449-3195
Key Executives/Personnel:
   Pen Densham, Founder
   John Watson, Founder
   Guy McElwaine, COO & Partner
   Mark Stern, President of TV & Partner
   Nora O'Brien, VP of Production
   Finley Glaize, Director of Development
   Jennifer Hare, Director of Production & Administration
   Kelly Stuart, Story Editor
   Rachel Leonard, Assistant to Mr. Watson
Specialties: Studio; Independent
Other Categories: TV
Credits: Backdraft; Outer Limits (TV series); Blown Away; Poltergeist

TRIUMPH PICTURES, INC.
6111 Shirley Ave.
Tarzana, CA 91356
Phone: (310) 234-9680
www.triumphpictures.com
triumphpictures@hotmail.com
Key Executives/Personnel:
   Yoram Benami, President
   Dean Wideman, Writer & Co-Producer
Specialties: Studio; Independent
Other Categories: TV
Credits: Lone Wolf McQuade; Jury Duty; The Man Who Broke A Thousand Chairs; 3 Ninjas: Kick Back
Trade Assoc./Guilds/Unions: AMPAS, DGA

TRUE BLUE PRODUCTIONS
P.O. Box 27127
Los Angeles, CA 90027
Phone: (323) 661-9191
Fax: (323) 661-9190
www.trueblueprod.com
info@trueblueprod.com
Key Executives/Personnel:
   Kirstie Alley, Producer
   Michael Wisner, Head of Creative Development
   Lee Ann Vasquez, Assistant to Ms. Alley
   Thora Magnusson, Office Manager
Specialties: Studio; Independent
Other Categories: TV
First Look/Development Deals: Warner Bros.

SIMON TSE PRODUCTIONS, INC.
9060 Santa Monica Blvd., Ste. 106
Los Angeles, CA 90069

Phone: ....(310) 385-9331
Fax: ....(310) 385-9347
stpwest@earthlink.net
Key Executives/Personnel:
Simon Tse, Producer & CEO
Specialties: Independent

THE TURMAN-MORRISSEY COMPANY
Phone: ....(310) 586-8649
Fax: ....(310) 586-8312
Key Executives/Personnel:
John Morrissey, Producer & Partner
Lawrence Turman, Producer & Partner
Matthew Waldman, Creative Executive
Devon Terrill, Assistant
Specialties: Studio; Independent
Other Categories: TV
Credits: American History X; Kingdom Come; What's The Worst That Could Happen?
Additional Info: Please call for current address.

JON TURTLE PRODUCTIONS
10880 Wilshire Blvd., Ste. 1101
Los Angeles, CA 90024
Phone: ....(310) 234-5347
Fax: ....(310) 234-5345
Key Executives/Personnel:
Jon Turtle, President
David Decker, VP & Head of Creative Affairs
Specialties: Studio; Independent
Other Categories: TV
Credits: Freak City; In a Class of His Own; Sirr; Fluke
First Look/Development Deals: Showtime Networks, Inc.
Trade Assoc./Guilds/Unions: PGA

TWENTIETH CENTURY FOX PICTURES
10201 W. Pico Blvd.
Los Angeles, CA 90035
Phone: ....(310) 369-1000
www.foxmovies.com
Key Executives/Personnel:
Peter Chernin, Chairman & CEO, Fox Group
Simon Bax, CFO & President of Studio Operations, Fox Filmed Entertainment
Hutch Parker, President of Production
Thomas Rothman, Chairman of Fox Filmed Entertainment
Robert Harper, Vice Chairman/Executive VP of Fox Filmed Entertainment
Robert Kraft, President of Fox Music, Inc.
Ted Gagliano, Executive VP of Post Production
Bob Cohen, Executive VP of Legal Affairs
Greg Gelfan, Executive VP of Business & Legal Affairs
Joe Hartwick, Executive VP of Features Production
Donna Isaacson, Executive VP of Casting
Mark Resnick, Executive VP of Business Affairs
Gary D. Roberts, Executive VP of Litigation
Michael Andreen, Sr. VP of Production
Josie Rosen, Sr. VP of Production
Fred Baron, Sr. VP of Features Production
Kimberly Cooper, Sr. VP of Features Production
Fred Chandler, Sr. VP of Post Production
John Amussen, Sr. VP of Finance
Steve Plum, Sr. VP of Business Affairs
Jim Dodson, VP of Features Production
Mike Hendrickson, VP of Features Production
Thomas Imperato, VP of Features Production
David Starke, VP of Features Production
Elysa Koplovitz, VP of Production
Vanessa Morrison, VP of Production
Ted Dodd, VP of Creative Affairs
Nate Hopper, Director of Production
Emma Watts, Director of Production
Specialties: Studio

TWILIGHT TIME FILMS
1875 Century Park East, 2nd Fl.
Los Angeles, CA 90067
Phone: ....(310) 284-7310
Fax: ....(310) 284-7317
Key Executives/Personnel:
Scott Winant, Producer & Director
Kelly McCarthy, VP of Production
Robert Keyghobad, Director of Development
Robyn Andrews, Production Associate
Specialties: Independent
Other Categories: TV
Credits: thirtysomething; My So Called Life; Cupid
First Look/Development Deals: Twentieth Century Fox Television

TWO STEPP PRODUCTIONS
15123 Sherman Way, Ste. 201
Van Nuys, CA 91405
Phone: ....(818) 908-4041
Fax: ....(818) 994-6483
asteppprod@aol.com
Key Executives/Personnel:
Alan Stepp, Producer
Specialties: Studio; Independent
Other Categories: TV
Credits: Willing To Kill; The Texas Cheerleading Story; Dancer, Texas Population 81

UBU PRODUCTIONS
4024 Radford Ave., Bungalow 14
Studio City, CA 91604
Phone: ....(818) 655-5850
Fax: ....(818) 655-8553
Key Executives/Personnel:
Gary David Goldberg, Executive Producer
Alex Maggioni, VP of Development
Heather Green, Assistant
Murray Miller, Assistant
Specialties: Studio
Other Categories: TV
Credits: Family Ties; Brooklyn Bridge; Battery Park; Spin City
First Look/Development Deals: DreamWorks SKG

UFLAND PRODUCTIONS
534 21st St.
Santa Monica, CA 90402
Phone: ....(310) 656-3031
Fax: ....(310) 656-3073
ufland@aol.com
Key Executives/Personnel:
Harry Ufland, Producer
Mary Jane Ufland, Producer
Bill Kravitz, Assistant
Specialties: Studio
Other Categories: TV
Credits: Snow Falling on Cedars; One True Thing; Not Without My Daughter

UNAPIX FILMS
200 Madison Ave., 24th Fl.
New York, NY 10016
Phone: ....(212) 252-7711
Fax: ....(212) 252-7626
www.unapixent.com
info@unapixent.com
Key Executives/Personnel:

Production Companies – Feature Film

Robert Baruc, President & CEO
Richard Abramowitz, President, Unapix Theatrical
Alicia Reilly-Larson, Sr. VP of Acquisitions & Development
Rebecca Glashow, Manager of Acquisitions & Development
Chris Valentini, Sr. VP of Production
Specialties: Independent; Direct-to-Video
Other Categories: TV
Credits: Ginger Snaps; Other Voices; Tangled; Jack Frost 1 & 2

UNDERGRACE PRODUCTIONS
14365 Foothill Blvd., Ste. 28
Sylmar, CA 91342
Phone: ....(818) 833-8666
....(818) 640-8698
Fax: ....(818) 833-8496
camanimal@hotmail.com
Key Executives/Personnel:
Cameron Baity, Producer, Director & Animator
Kathleen Lolley, Designer, Editor & Director
Jonathan Silsby, Animator
Ryan Streber, Composer
Jerry Summers, Sound Designer
Specialties: Independent; Animation
Other Categories: TV
Credits: Naropa; Questions and Answers

UNGER PRODUCTIONS, INC.
475 S. La Peer Dr.
Beverly Hills, CA 90211
Phone: ....(310) 859-1455
Fax: ....(310) 859-1048
tonyunger@exelonline.com
Key Executives/Personnel:
Anthony Unger, President
Will McElroy, Production Assistant
Specialties: Studio; Independent
Other Categories: TV
Credits: Dark Side of Hollywood; Silent Rage; Don't Look Now; Force 10 From Navarone
Trade Assoc./Guilds/Unions: BAFTA

UNITED ARTISTS FILMS
2500 Broadway
Santa Monica, CA 90404
Phone: ....(310) 449-3000
Fax: ....(310) 586-8358
Key Executives/Personnel:
Larry Gleason, Co-Head
Jerry Rich, Co-Head
Sara Rose, VP of Production & Acquisitions
Specialties: Independent
Credits: Tea With Mussolini; The Claim; All About My Mother; Ghostworld

UNIVERSAL PICTURES
100 Universal City Plaza
Universal City, CA 91608
Phone: ....(818) 777-1000
www.universalstudios.com
Key Executives/Personnel:
Stacey Snider, Chairman
David Kosse, Chairman, Universal Pictures UK Ltd.
Rick Finkelstein, President
Jon Gumpert, Executive VP
Frederick Huntsberry, CFO
Kevin Misher, President of Production
Marc Shmuger, President, Universal Pictures Marketing
Nadia Bronson, President of Int'l. Theatrical Marketing, Distribution & Operations
Nikki Rocco, President of Universal Pictures Distribution
Peter Smith, President of Universal Pictures Int'l. Video
Xavier Marchand, President of Distribution & Sales, Universal Pictures Int'l. Video
David Livingstone, President of Marketing, Universal Pictures Int'l. Video
Craig Kornblau, President, Universal Studios Home Video
Louis A. Feola, President, Universal Family & Home Entertainment
James M. Horowitz, Executive VP of Business & Legal Affairs
Allison Brecker, Executive VP of Production
Ron Lynch, Executive VP of Production
Mary Parent, Executive VP of Production
Scott Stuber, Executive VP of Production
Edward Egan, Executive VP of Marketing
Terry Curtin, Executive VP of National Publicity
Nick Carpou, Executive VP & National Sales Manager, Universal Pictures Distribution
Mark Gaines, Executive VP & National Sales Manager, Universal Pictures Distribution
Claudia Gray, Executive VP, Universal Focus
Nancy Steingard, Executive VP, Universal Cartoon Studios
Suzie Peterson, Executive VP of Direct-to-Video Programming, Universal Family & Home Entertainment
Mark Kristol, Sr. VP
Jim Burk, Sr. VP of International Operations
Harry Garfield, Sr. VP of Music, Universal Pictures Production
Andrew Given, Sr. VP of Physical Production
Leonard Kornberg, Sr. VP of Production
Pamela Blum, Sr. VP of Marketing & National Promotions
Hollace Davids, Sr. VP of Special Projects, Universal Pictures Marketing
Alan Sutton, Sr. VP of Distribution & Marketing
Paul Hardart, Sr. VP, Universal Focus
Lawrence Hariton, CFO, Universal Studios Home Video/Sr. VP of Direct Account Management, Universal Music & Video Distribution
Linda Pace-Alexander, VP of Special Projects
Joanna Colbert, VP of Feature Casting
Tony Grana, VP of Production Resources
Eric Hughes, VP of Production
Tim O'Hair, VP of Production
Bret Johnson, VP of Production Finance
Romy Kaufman, VP, Story Department
Kool Marder, VP of Physical Production
Dennis O'Connor, VP of Distribution, Universal Focus
Douglas Wood, VP of Animation Production & Creative Affairs
Deborah Johnson, VP of Physical Production
Jennifer Fox, VP of Production
Stephanie Kluft, VP of National Publicity
Michael Moses, VP of National Publicity
Thomas Castaneda, VP of International Publicity
Elizabeth Gaynes, VP of International Marketing
Eugene Amodeo, VP & General Manager, Universal Films Canada
Colleen Benn, VP of DVD Productions, Universal Studios Home Video
Specialties: Studio

UNIVERSAL STUDIOS, INC.
100 Universal City Plaza
Universal City, CA 91608
Phone: ....(818) 777-1000
www.universalstudios.com
Key Executives/Personnel:
Ron Meyer, President & COO
Jim Watters, President & General Manager, Universal Studios Operations Group
Kenton Low, President of Universal Studios Online
Hellene S. Runtagh, Executive VP
Karen Randall, Executive VP & General Counsel
Kenneth L. Kahrs, Executive VP of Human Resources
William A. Sutman, Sr. VP & CFO
Deborah Rosen, Sr. VP of Corporate Communications & Public Affairs
Ed Zeier, Sr. VP of Post Production, Universal Studios Operations Group
Don Skeoch, Sr. VP of Marketing
Janice Miller, VP of Business & Legal Affairs
Susan Nahley Fleishman, VP of Corporate Communications &

Production Companies – Feature Film

    Public Affairs
    Dave Beanes, VP of Production Services, Universal Studios Operations Group
    Brian Pope, VP of Marketing Services
Specialties: Studio
Other Categories: TV

UPSTART ENTERTAINMENT
10433 Wilshire Blvd., PH
Los Angeles, CA 90024
Phone: ....(310) 475-6025
Fax: ....(310) 475-9844
Key Executives/Personnel:
    Michael J. Nathanson, Producer & Writer
    Amy Graves, Director of Development
Specialties: Studio
Other Categories: TV
Credits: Mom's Got a Date With a Vampire; She's Out of Control; The Bulkin Trail

USA FILMS
65 Bleecker St., 2nd Fl.
New York, NY 10012
Phone: ....(212) 539-4002
....(310) 385-4400
Fax: ....(212) 539-4009
www.usafilms.net
Key Executives/Personnel:
    Scott Greenstein, Chairman (NY)
    Russell S. Schwartz, President (LA)
    Steve Flynn, Executive VP of Marketing (LA)
    Donna Gigliotti, President of Production (NY)
    Lawrence Bernstein, Executive VP & CFO
    Dan Leiblien, CFO (NY)
    Avy Eschenasy, Executive VP of Production (NY)
    Howard Meyers, Sr. VP of Business Affairs (LA)
    Randy Ostrow, Executive VP of Production (NY)
    Stephan Raphael, Sr. VP of Acquisitions & Co-Productions (NY)
    Matt Wall, Sr. VP of Production & Development (LA)
    Peter Kalmbach, VP of Acquisitions (NY)
    Amanda Klein, VP of Acquisitions (NY)
    Seth Nagel, Director of Theatrical & Ancillary Acquistions (LA)
Specialties: Independent
Credits: Nurse Betty; Traffic; Being John Malkovich; Topsy Turvy
First Look/Development Deals: Michael London Productions
Additional Info: 100 N. Crescent Dr., Beverly Hills, CA 90210 (310) 385-4408 fax

VAL D'ORO ENTERTAINMENT
1437 Seventh St., Ste. 200
Santa Monica, CA 90401
Phone: ....(310) 656-8555
Fax: ....(310) 656-8560
valdoro@aol.com
Key Executives/Personnel:
    Steven E. deSouza, President
    Jeri Barchilon deSouza, VP
    Scott Humphries, Apprentice
Specialties: Studio
Other Categories: TV; Interactive Multimedia
Trade Assoc./Guilds/Unions: DGA, WGAw

RENÉE VALENTE PRODUCTIONS
13547 Ventura Blvd., Ste. 195
Sherman Oaks, CA 91423
Phone: ....(323) 969-1541
Fax: ....(818) 788-0758
valenteprod@aol.com
Key Executives/Personnel:
    Renée Valente, Executive Producer
Specialties: Shorts; Independent
Other Categories: TV
Credits: A Storm In Summer; The Man From Left Field; The Man Upstairs; Loving Couple
Trade Assoc./Guilds/Unions: AFTRA, AMPAS, ATAS, PGA, WIF

VALHALLA MOTION PICTURES
3575 Cahuenga Blvd. West, Ste. 415
Los Angeles, CA 90068
Phone: ....(323) 969-4300
Fax: ....(323) 969-4301
vmp@valhallamotionpix.com
Key Executives/Personnel:
    Gale Anne Hurd, Chairman & Producer
    Barbara Boyle, President
    Julie Thomson, CFO
    Didi Gay, Controller
    Kelly Campbell, VP of Development
    Tracy Mercer, Director of Development
    Tim Reid, Assistant to Ms. Hurd
    Tiger Bela, Assistant to Ms. Boyle
    David Herrera, Development Assistant
Specialties: Studio; Independent; Documentaries
Other Categories: TV
Credits: Armageddon; Terminator 2; Dick; Dante's Peak
First Look/Development Deals: Kinowelt USA, Inc.

VANGUARD PRODUCTIONS
12111 Beatrice St.
Culver City, CA 90230
Phone: ....(310) 306-4910
Fax: ....(310) 306-4910
vangrdprod@earthlink.net
Key Executives/Personnel:
    Terence M. O'Keefe, Writer, Producer & Director
    Brent Huff, Writer & Director
    S. Drew Stotesbery, VP of Production
    Bruce Miyaki, Director of Development
    Bennett Fidlow, Director of Creative Affairs
Specialties: Studio; Independent; Direct-to-Video
Other Categories: TV; Commercials; Video; Music Video
Credits: We The People; Wanted; The Bad Pack; Closing The Deal

VAULT, INC., THE
1831 Centinela Ave., 2nd Fl.
Santa Monica, CA 90404
Phone: ....(310) 315-0012
Fax: ....(310) 315-9322
info@vaultfilms.com
Key Executives/Personnel:
    Matt Cooper, Producer & Director
    Lori Miller, Producer
    Carolyn Sivitz, Creative Executive
Specialties: Independent
Credits: The Last Supper; Campfire Tales; Panic

VCA PRODUCTIONS
Phone: ....(310) 489-3495
....(818) 986-5359
Fax: ....(818) 986-5359
vcaprod@hotmail.com
Key Executives/Personnel:
    Vincent Agostino, Producer
Specialties: Studio; Independent
Other Categories: Commercials
Trade Assoc./Guilds/Unions: DGA

Production Companies – Feature Film

VENTANA FILMS
Phone: . . . .(323) 876-3331
Fax: . . . .(323) 876-4666
lafilm@aol.com
Key Executives/Personnel:
  Arthur Gorson, President & Head of Production
  Bernard Nussbaumer, Executive Producer
  Julio Solorzano, VP
Specialties: Independent
Other Categories: Commercials; Music Video
Credits: Cronos (feature); Better Watch Out (feature); Cabeza De Vaca (feature)

VENTURE ENTERTAINMENT GROUP
P.O. Box 55113
Sherman Oaks, CA 91413
Phone: . . . .(818) 981-7813
. . . .(800) 981-8433
Fax: . . . .(818) 981-3466
www.venture818.com
venture818@aol.com
Key Executives/Personnel:
  Leigh Leshner, Producer
Specialties: Independent
Other Categories: TV; Commercials; Video
Credits: The Spa Workout (infomercial); Hidden Treasures (TV series); Zoofari; More Zoofari
Trade Assoc./Guilds/Unions: VSDA, WIF

VERDON-CEDRIC PRODUCTIONS
9255 Doheny Rd., Ste. 904
Los Angeles, CA 90069
Phone: . . . .(310) 274-7253
Fax: . . . .(310) 274-0697
Key Executives/Personnel:
  Sidney Poitier, Producer, Writer & Director
  Susan Garrison, Director of Development
  Marlene Perez, Assistant
Specialties: Independent
Credits: Free of Eden

VERHOEVEN/MARSHALL FILMS
10202 W. Washington Blvd., Astaire Bldg.
Culver City, CA 90232
Phone: . . . .(310) 244-5352
Fax: . . . .(310) 244-2034
Key Executives/Personnel:
  Paul Verhoeven, Director
  Alan Marshall, Producer
  Stacy Lumbrezer, Co-Producer
Specialties: Studio
Credits: Hollow Man; Starship Troopers; Showgirls
First Look/Development Deals: Sony Pictures Entertainment

VIACOM ENTERTAINMENT GROUP
5555 Melrose Ave.
Hollywood, CA 90038
Phone: . . . .(323) 956-5000
. . . .(212) 258-6000
www.viacom.com
Key Executives/Personnel:
  Jonathan L. Dolgen, Chairman
  Thomas McGrath, Executive VP
  David Molner, Sr. VP of Business Development
  Isaac Palmer, VP of Corporate Development
Specialties: Studio
Other Categories: TV
Additional Info: 1515 Broadway, New York, NY 10036

VIEW ASKEW PRODUCTIONS, INC.
3 Harding Rd.
Red Bank, NJ 07701
Phone: . . . .(732) 842-6933
Fax: . . . .(732) 842-3772
www.viewaskew.com
Key Executives/Personnel:
  Kevin Smith, President
  Scott Mosier, VP
Specialties: Studio
Other Categories: TV
Credits: Clerks; Dogma; Chasing Amy; Mallrats
First Look/Development Deals: Miramax Films

VILLAGE ROADSHOW PICTURES
3400 Riverside Dr., Ste. 900
Burbank, CA 91505
Phone: . . . .(818) 260-6000
Fax: . . . .(818) 260-6001
Key Executives/Personnel:
  Bruce Berman, CEO & Chairman
  Michael Lake, Executive VP of Worldwide Feature Productions
  Steve Krone, COO
  Reid Sullivan, CEO
  Bernie Goldman, President of Production
  Dana Goldberg, Sr. VP of Production
  William Heflin, Story Editor
Specialties: Studio
Credits: Space Cowboys; Three Kings; The Matrix; Analyze This
First Look/Development Deals: Warner Bros.

VISIONBOX
8800 Venice Blvd., Ste. 217
Los Angeles, CA 90034
Phone: . . . .(310) 204-4686
Fax: . . . .(310) 204-4603
www.visionboxpictures.com
info@visionboxpix.com
Key Executives/Personnel:
  Michael Kastenbaum, President
  John Manulis, CEO
  Brooke Dammkoehler, Development & Production
  Jenny Hinkey, Sales & Marketing
  Marc Ambrose, Executive in Charge of Production
Specialties: Independent
Other Categories: TV
Credits: Boyd's Out; Teddy Bears·Picnic; The Invisibles; Falling Like This

RAYMOND WAGNER PRODUCTIONS, INC.
10377 Rochester Ave.
Los Angeles, CA 90024
Phone: . . . .(310) 278-1970
Fax: . . . .(310) 274-2662
Key Executives/Personnel:
  Raymond Wagner, President
  Christine McBride, Development
Specialties: Studio; Animation; Large Format
Other Categories: TV
Credits: Snowday; Turner & Hooch; Code of Silence; Maniac Magee

KEN WALZ PRODUCTIONS
3000 Olympic Blvd.
Santa Monica, CA 90404
Phone: . . . .(310) 449-4001
Fax: . . . .(310) 449-4006
Key Executives/Personnel:
  Ken Walz, President
Specialties: Independent
Other Categories: TV
Credits: Like Father, Like Santa; Adventures of Pete & Pete; Gaudy, Bawdy, and Blue; Medusa, Dare to Be Truthful

Production Companies – Feature Film

WARNER BROS.
4000 Warner Blvd.
Burbank, CA 91522
Phone: ....(818) 954-6000
www.warnerbros.com
Key Executives/Personnel:
    Barry M. Meyer, Chairman & CEO
    Alan Horn, President & COO
    Veronika Kwan-Rubinek, President of Int'l. Distribution
    Edward A. Romano, Executive VP & CFO
    Patti Connolly, Executive VP of Business Affairs
    Chris Cookson, Executive VP & CTO
    Gary Credle, Executive VP of Administration & Studio Operations
    Richard J. Fox, Executive VP of Int'l.
    Bruce Rosenblum, Executive VP of TV
    John A. Schulman, Executive VP of General Counsel
    Kevin Tsujihara, Executive VP of New Media
    Barbara Brogliatti, Sr. VP & Chief Corporate Communications Officer
    Kiko Washington, Sr. VP of Worldwide Human Resources
    James L. Halsey, Sr. VP & CIO
    Reginald Harpur, Sr. VP & Controller
    Alan Raphael, Sr. VP of Industrial Relations
    Marisa O'Neil, VP of Corporate Services
    Lisa Mundt, VP of Int'l. Operations
Specialties: Studio

WARNER BROS. ANIMATION
15303 Ventura Blvd., Ste. 1200
Sherman Oaks, CA 91403
Phone: ....(818) 954-7670
Fax: ....(818) 954-7441
www.warnerbros.com
sarah.carragher@warnerbors.com
Key Executives/Personnel:
    Jean MacCurdy, President & Executive Producer
    Paul Dini, Producer & Writer
    Bruce Timm, Producer & Writer
    Alan Burnett, Producer
    Robert Goodman, Producer
    Liz Holzman, Producer
    Scott Jeralds, Producer
    Glen Murakami, Producer
    Denys Cowan, Animation Director
    Bob Doucette, Animation Director
    Curt Geda, Animation Director
    Butch Lukic, Animation Director
    Dan Riba, Animation Director
    James Tucker, Animation Director
    Leslie Lamers, Casting Director
    Andrea Romano, Voice Director
    Shaun McLaughlin, Associate Producer
    Kathy Page, Associate Producer
    Stan Berkowitz, Story Editor
    Rich Fogel, Story Editor
    Kevin Hopps, Story Editor
    Christopher Simmons, Story Editor
Specialties: Studio; Animation
Other Categories: TV
Credits: Batman Beyond; Static Shock!; The Zeta Project

WARNER BROS. PICTURES PRODUCTION
4000 Warner Blvd.
Burbank, CA 91522
Phone: ....(818) 954-6000
www.warnerbros.com
Key Executives/Personnel:
    Lorenzo di Bonaventura, President of Worldwide Production
    Kevin McCormick, Executive VP of Production
    Steve Papazian, Executive VP of Worldwide Feature Production
    Lora Kennedy, Sr. VP of Casting
    Jeff Robinov, Sr. VP of Production
    Marc Solomon, Sr. VP of Post Production
    Courtenay Valenti, Sr. VP of Production
    Lionel Wilgram, Sr. VP of Production
    William L. Young, Sr. VP of Feature Production
    Frank Vrioste, Sr. VP of Production Editing
    Polly Cohen, VP of Production
    Mark Scoon, VP of Features Production
    Fred Talmage, VP of Post Production
Specialties: Studio

WATERSHED FILMS
345 N. Maple Dr., Ste. 317
Beverly Hills, CA 90210
Phone: ....(310) 550-2175
Fax: ....(310) 550-2178
watershedfilms@pipeline.com
Key Executives/Personnel:
    James Brooke, Producer
    Neil DeGroot, Producer
    Wally Parks, Producer
Specialties: Studio; Independent; Large Format
Other Categories: TV
Credits: The Dinosaur Hunter; Plato's Run; Wind in the Wire
First Look/Development Deals: Backlot Productions

WEED ROAD PICTURES
4000 Warner Blvd., Bldg. 81, Ste. 115
Burbank, CA 91522
Phone: ....(818) 954-3771
Fax: ....(818) 954-3061
Key Executives/Personnel:
    Akiva Goldsman, Producer
    Varina Bleil, Executive VP
    Stephanie Gisondi, Director of Development
Specialties: Studio
Credits: Deep Blue Sea
First Look/Development Deals: Warner Bros.

JERRY WEINTRAUB PRODUCTIONS
4000 Warner Blvd., Bungalow 1
Burbank, CA 91522
Phone: ....(818) 954-2500
Fax: ....(818) 954-1399
Key Executives/Personnel:
    Jerry Weintraub, Producer
    John Tomko, Sr. VP of Production
    Susan Ekins, Sr. VP of Physical Production
    Kimberly Pinkstaff, Executive Assistant to Mr. Weintraub
    Jenny Lynn, Assistant to Mr. Tomko
Specialties: Studio
Credits: Nashville; The Specialist; The Avengers; Karate Kid Series
First Look/Development Deals: Warner Bros.

WEINTRAUB/KUHN PRODUCTIONS
1900 Avenue of the Stars, Ste. 1440
Los Angeles, CA 90067
Phone: ....(310) 788-9380
Fax: ....(310) 788-0476
Key Executives/Personnel:
    Fred Weintraub, Producer
    Tom Kuhn, Producer
    Chrissy Sherbanee, Assistant to Mr. Weintraub & Mr. Kuhn
Specialties: Direct-to-Video; Documentaries
Other Categories: TV; Video
Credits: High Road to China; The New Adventures of Robin Hood; Enter, the Dragon; Devil's Arithmetic

Production Companies – Feature Film

RONI WEISBERG PRODUCTIONS
Phone: ....(310) 286-1210
Fax: ....(310) 556-8248
rweisberg@earthlink.net
Key Executives/Personnel:
  Roni Weisberg, Producer
  Henry Tuggle, Director of Development
Specialties: Independent
Other Categories: TV; Commercials
Credits: Mermaid; Face Down; Death Dreams; Sharing Richard

JOHN WELLS PRODUCTIONS
4000 Warner Blvd., Bldg. 138, Rm. 1106
Burbank, CA 91522
Phone: ....(818) 954-1687
Fax: ....(818) 354-3657
Key Executives/Personnel:
  John Wells, Executive Producer & Writer
  Kristin Harms, President
  Ned Haspel, VP of Business Operations
  Andrew Stearn, VP of TV
  Laura Holstein, VP of Features
  Tracy Underwood, Director of Development, Features
  Randy Warner, Manager of TV
Specialties: Studio; Independent
Other Categories: TV
Credits: ER; The West Wing; Third Watch

BILL WHITE PRODUCTIONS
12423 Ventura Court, Ste. 200
Studio City, CA 91604
Phone: ....(818) 769-9090
Fax: ....(818) 769-1974
billwhitepro@earthlink.net
Key Executives/Personnel:
  Bill White, President
  Amy Shomer, Producer
Specialties: Independent; Documentaries
Other Categories: TV; Commercials; Video; Music Video
Credits: Globe Life Insurance (commercial); United American Insurance (commercial); Sanyo-Fisher (corp. video); Test Flights (TV)
Trade Assoc./Guilds/Unions: DGA

WHITEWATER FILMS
2232 Cotner Ave.
Los Angeles, CA 90064
Phone: ....(310) 575-5800
Fax: ....(310) 575-5802
Key Executives/Personnel:
  Rick Rosenthal, President
Specialties: Independent
Other Categories: TV
Credits: Bad Boy; Just a Little Harmless Sex; Distant Thunder; American Dreamer

WICKED MONKEY PRODUCTIONS
6404 Hollywood Blvd., Ste. 324
Hollywood, CA 90028
Phone: ....(323) 461-6665
Fax: ....(323) 461-6669
Key Executives/Personnel:
  Al Septien, Writer & Producer
  Turi Meyer, Writer & Director
Specialties: Studio; Independent; Direct-to-Video
Other Categories: TV
Credits: Sleepstalker; Candy Man III

WILD THINGS PRODUCTIONS
4500 Wilshire Blvd., 3rd Fl.
Los Angeles, CA 90010
Phone: ....(323) 954-4577
Key Executives/Personnel:
  Maurice Sendak, Partner
  John B. Carls, Partner
  Richard La Forge, Development Assistant
Specialties: Studio; Direct-to-Video; Animation
Other Categories: TV
Credits: Little Bear; George & Martha; Seven Little Monsters
First Look/Development Deals: Nelvana Entertainment

WILDWOOD ENTERPRISES, INC./SOUTH FORK PICTURES
1101 Montana Ave., Ste. E
Santa Monica, CA 90403
Phone: ....(310) 395-5155
Fax: ....(310) 395-3975
Key Executives/Personnel:
  Robert Redford, Owner
  Michael Nozik, President
  Karen Tenkhoff, Producer
  Leslie Urdang, Producer
  Per Saair, Creative Executive
  Miranda de Pencier, Director of Development
  Brad Simonsen, Director of Production
  Linda Davis, Story Editor
Specialties: Studio; Independent
Credits: The Legend of Bagger Vance; The Horse Whisperer; Quiz Show; Ordinary People

WIN VENTURES, LLC.
301 N. Cañon Dr., Ste. 300
Beverly Hills, CA 90210
Phone: ....(310) 859-2500
Fax: ....(310) 859-7500
winventures@win-11c.com
Key Executives/Personnel:
  Pierre David, Chairman of WIN Ventures & Producer
  Noel Zanitsch, President of Production & Producer
  Ken Sanders, VP of Production & Producer
  Rick Eyler, VP of Physical Production
Specialties: Independent
Other Categories: TV
Credits: The Perfect Wife; The Perfect Nanny; The Stepdaughter; Alone with a Stranger
Trade Assoc./Guilds/Unions: AFMA, AMPAS, IPA

WINCHESTER FILMS
Phone: ....(310) 458-1400
    ....(310) 458-1469
Fax: ....(310) 458-2106
www.winchesterfilms.com
winchester.la@gte.net
Key Executives/Personnel:
  Hadeel Reda, President
  Gary Smith, Chief Executive
  Billy Hurman, Sr. VP of Sales & Marketing
  Andrew Brown, Sr. VP of Sales & Marketing
Specialties: Independent
Credits: Wild About Harry; Another Life; Muggers; Shooting Fish

Production Companies – Feature Film

WIND DANCER PRODUCTION GROUP
1040 N. Las Palmas, Bldg. 2
Los Angeles, CA 90038
Phone: (323) 645-1200
Fax: (323) 645-1255
Key Executives/Personnel:
    Matt Williams, Principal
    David McFadzean, Principal
    Carmen Finestra, Principal
    Susan Cartsonis, President of Wind Dancer Films
    Dete Meserve, Executive VP
    Melissa Goddard, Sr. VP
    Roz Weisberg, Director of Development
    Robyn Frey-Monell, Office Manager
Specialties: Studio
Other Categories: TV
Credits: Where The Heart Is; Firelight; Home Improvement
Additional Info: 9 Desbrosses St., 2nd Fl., New York, NY 10013

WINKLER FILMS
211 S. Beverly Dr., Ste. 200
Beverly Hills, CA 90212
Phone: (310) 858-5780
Fax: (310) 858-5799
Key Executives/Personnel:
    Irwin Winkler, CEO
    Rob Cowan, President
    June Czerwinski, Assistant to Mr. Winkler
Specialties: Studio
Credits: At First Sight; The Net; Goodfellas; Rocky
First Look/Development Deals: Sony Pictures Entertainment

RALPH WINTER PRODUCTIONS, INC.
1201 W. 5th St., Maryland Bldg., Ste. M215
Los Angeles, CA 90017
Phone: (213) 534-3654
Fax: (213) 534-3078
Key Executives/Personnel:
    Ralph Winter, Producer
    David Gorder, Assistant to Mr. Winter
Specialties: Studio; Independent
Other Categories: TV
Credits: Planet of the Apes: aka The Visitor; X-Men; Inspector Gadget; Mighty Joe Young
Additional Info: Formerly Common Creed Entertainment

WITT/THOMAS/HARRIS PRODUCTIONS
1438 N. Gower St., Bldg. 35, Ste. 156
Hollywood, CA 90028
Phone: (323) 993-7000
Fax: (323) 957-9886
Key Executives/Personnel:
    Paul Junger Witt, Partner
    Tony Thomas, Partner
    Susan Harris, Partner
    Michael Feuerhelm, Assistant to Mr. Witt
    Marlene Fuentes, Assistant to Mr. Thomas
Specialties: Independent
Credits: Three Kings; Final Analysis; Dead Poets Society

WONDERLAND FILMS
8640 Wonderland Ave.
Los Angeles, CA 90046
Phone: (323) 656-6489
Key Executives/Personnel:
    Ava Lazar, Producer
    John Tarnoff, Producer
Specialties: Independent; Direct-to-Video; Documentaries
Other Categories: TV
Credits: Nature of the Beast; The Delinquents; Prisoners of the Sun

THE WOOFENILL WORKS, INC.
516 E. 81st St., Ste. 3
New York, NY 10028
Phone: (212) 734-2578
Fax: (212) 734-3186
home.earthlink.net/~woofenill/
woofenill@earthlink.net
Key Executives/Personnel:
    Joseph K. Landsman, Chairman & CEO
    Jan A. Koster, President & Creative Director
    Ronald Tanet, Executive Producer & Corporate Council
    Robert L. Cohen, Supervising Producer
    Robert J. Nichols, SCC Attorney
Specialties: Independent
Other Categories: TV

WORKING TITLE FILMS
9720 Wilshire Blvd., 4th Fl.
Beverly Hills, CA 90212
Phone: (310) 777-3100
Fax: (310) 777-5273
Key Executives/Personnel:
    Tim Bevan, Co-Chairman
    Eric Fellner, Co-Chairman
    Liza Chasin, President of Production (US)
    Debra Hayward, Head of Development (UK)
    Michelle Wright, Head of Production (UK)
    Amelia Granger, Literary Acquisitions Executive (UK)
    Sarah Harvey, Assistant to Mr. Bevan & Mr. Fellner
    Daniel Pipski, Assistant to Ms. Chasin
    Mark Simone, Assistant to Ms. Chasin
Specialties: Studio
First Look/Development Deals: Universal Studios
Additional Info: Oxford House, 76 Oxford St., London W1N 9FD England, (011) 171 307-3000 phone

WORLD OF WONDER PRODUCTIONS
6650 Hollywood Blvd., Ste. 400
Hollywood, CA 90028
Phone: (323) 463-7133
Fax: (323) 463-7134
www.worldofwonder.net
wow@worldofwonder.net
Key Executives/Personnel:
    Randy Barbato, Producer & Director
    Fenton Bailey, Producer & Director
Specialties: Documentaries
Other Categories: TV
Credits: The Eyes of Tammy Faye; 101 Rent Boys; Video Killed the Radio Star; Party Monster

MARVIN WORTH PRODUCTIONS
9784 Drake Lane
Beverly Hills, CA 90210
Phone: (310) 273-0181
Fax: (310) 274-7378
Key Executives/Personnel:
    Joan Worth, Producer
    Marty Binder, Assistant to Ms. Worth
Specialties: Studio
Other Categories: TV
Credits: Malcolm X; Lenny; Where's Poppa; See No Evil, Hear No Evil

Production Companies – Feature Film

NORTON WRIGHT PRODUCTIONS
13331 Moorpark St., Ste. 308
Sherman Oaks, CA 91423
Phone: ....(818) 990-3058
Key Executives/Personnel:
   Norton Wright, President
   Ygonabee Abigit, Production
   Reid Phat, Director of Development
Specialties: Independent
Other Categories: TV
Credits: Murderous Intent; Angel Flight Down; Crash Landing: Rescue Flight 237; Haunted By Her Past
Trade Assoc./Guilds/Unions: ATAS, DGA

WYCHWOOD PRODUCTIONS
940 N. Mansfield Ave.
Hollywood, CA 90038
Phone: ....(323) 462-6400
Fax: ....(323) 465-7903
jpolhemns@propagandafilms.com
Key Executives/Personnel:
   Simon West, Producer & Director
   Jib Polhemus, VP of Development
   Alex Close, Assistant
Specialties: Studio
Other Categories: TV
First Look/Development Deals: Propaganda Films

YAK YAK PICTURES
4000 Warner Blvd., Bldg. 138, Ste. 1202
Burbank, CA 91522
Phone: ....(818) 954-3861
Fax: ....(818) 954-1614
Key Executives/Personnel:
   Mimi Leder, Producer & Director
   Jill Arthur, VP of Development
   A. J. Marcantonio, Creative Executive
   Marit Weisenberg, Story Editor & Assistant to Ms. Arthur
   Bob Merrick, Assistant to Ms. Leder
Specialties: Studio
Other Categories: TV
Credits: Pay it Forward; The Beast; Casanova; Lazarus
First Look/Development Deals: John Wells Productions

MARK YELLEN PRODUCTIONS
419 N. Larchmont Blvd., Ste. 44
Los Angeles, CA 90004
Phone: ....(323) 935-5525
Fax: ....(323) 935-5755
Key Executives/Personnel:
   Mark Yellen, Producer
Specialties: Independent
Other Categories: Commercials; Music Video
Credits: Blast; Montana; Shiloh; The Big Squeeze

BUD YORKIN PRODUCTIONS
345 N. Maple Dr., Ste. 206
Beverly Hills, CA 90210
Phone: ....(310) 274-8111
Fax: ....(310) 274-8112
Key Executives/Personnel:
   Bud Yorkin, President
   Damon Carr, Associate Producer
Specialties: Studio
Other Categories: TV
Credits: Blade Runner; Intersection; Twice in a Lifetime
First Look/Development Deals: Paramount Pictures

YORKTOWN PRODUCTIONS, INC.
3000 Olympic Blvd., Bldg. 2, Ste. 2465
Santa Monica, CA 90404
Phone: ....(310) 264-4155
Fax: ....(310) 264-4167
Key Executives/Personnel:
   Norman Jewison, Director & Producer
   Dianne Hatlestad, Creative Executive
   Liz Broden, Assistant to Mr. Jewison
Specialties: Independent
Other Categories: TV
Credits: A Soldier's Story; The Hurricane; Moonstruck; Only You

ZALOOM FILM
1351 Fourth St., Ste. 400
Santa Monica, CA 90401
Phone: ....(310) 656-8400
Key Executives/Personnel:
   George Zaloom, Producer
   Bruno Fortuna, Executive VP of Development
   Robin Goodfellow, Creative Executive
Specialties: Studio; Independent
Other Categories: TV
Credits: Encino Man; Hearts of Darkness; The Sports Pages; The Whole Shebang

THE ZANUCK COMPANY
9465 Wilshire Blvd., Ste. 930
Beverly Hills, CA 90212
Phone: ....(310) 274-0261
Fax: ....(310) 273-9217
zanuckco@aol.com
Key Executives/Personnel:
   Richard D. Zanuck, Producer
   Lili Fini Zanuck, Producer & Director
   Dean Zanuck, VP
   Harrison Zanuck, VP
Specialties: Studio
Credits: Rules of Engagement; Deep Impact; Driving Miss Daisy; Jaws

ZEAL PICTURES
6605 Hollywood Blvd., Ste. 300
Los Angeles, CA 90028
Phone: ....(323) 871-4000
Fax: ....(323) 871-4004
www.zealpictures.com
info@zealpictures.com
Key Executives/Personnel:
   Timm Oberwelland, Producer
   Leon Melas, Producer
   Robert Biehn, Producer
   George Salden, CFO
Specialties: Independent; Documentaries
Other Categories: Commercials; Video; Music Video
Credits: Simpatico; Robbers; American Fighter Pilot; Werther's Originals
Trade Assoc./Guilds/Unions: SAG
Additional Info: Additional office in Berlin, Germany.

Production Companies – Feature Film

ZIDE/PERRY ENTERTAINMENT
9100 Wilshire Blvd., Ste. 615E
Beverly Hills, CA 90212
Phone: ....(310) 887-2999
Fax: ....(310) 887-2995
www.inzide.com
Key Executives/Personnel:
  Warren Zide, Producer & Manager
  Craig Perry, Producer
  Sheila Hanahan, VP of Production & Development
  Darby Parker, Manager & Executive
  Jennie Frankel, Manager & Director of Literary Acquisitions
  Zach Tann, Internet Executive
  Daniel Pancotto, Creative Associate
  Jim Sodini, Creative Associate
Specialties: Studio
Credits: American Pie; The Big Hit; Final Destination; Repli-Kate
First Look/Development Deals: New Line Cinema, Inc.

ZOOMA ZOOMA CORPORATION
11 Mercer St., 3rd Fl.
New York, NY 10013
Phone: ....(212) 941-7680
Fax: ....(212) 941-8179
www.zoomazooma.com
staff@zoomazooma.com
Key Executives/Personnel:
  Joseph Mantegna, Executive Producer
  Todd Bellanca, Director
  Eden Tyler, Director
  Sam Raimi, Director
  Michael Bellino, Director
  Tim Hamilton, Director
  Gavin O'Connor, Director
  Lori Vitale, East Coast Sales
Specialties: Independent; Shorts; Documentaries; Trailers
Other Categories: TV; Commercials; Music Video; Interactive Multimedia

ZUCKER PRODUCTIONS
1351 4th St., Ste. 300
Santa Monica, CA 90401
Phone: ....(310) 656-9202
Fax: ....(310) 656-9220
Key Executives/Personnel:
  Jerry Zucker, Director & Producer
  Janet Zucker, Producer
  Zooki Raphael, Assistant to Mr. Zucker
  Bannister Bergen, Assistant to Ms. Zucker
  Elizabeth McCarthy, no title
Specialties: Studio

ZUCKER/NETTER PRODUCTIONS
1411 Fifth St., Ste. 402
Santa Monica, CA 90401
Phone: ....(310) 394-1644
Fax: ....(310) 899-6722
Key Executives/Personnel:
  David Zucker, Producer, Director & Writer
  Gil Netter, President
  Lawrence Grey, VP
  Phil Dornfeld, Assistant to Mr. Zucker
  Mike Ades, Assistant to Mr. Netter
Specialties: Studio
Other Categories: TV
Credits: Dude Where's My Car; My Best Friends Wedding; Naked Gun Series; Ghost
First Look/Development Deals: Fox 2000 Productions, NBC Entertainment, Inc.

ZUCKERMAN ENTERTAINMENT
169 Pier Ave., 2nd Fl.
Santa Monica, CA 90405
Phone: ....(310) 452-4410
Fax: ....(310) 452-4006
donaldzucker@earthlink.net
Key Executives/Personnel:
  Donald Zuckerman, Producer
  Emily Mullen, Assistant
Specialties: Independent
Other Categories: TV
Credits: Beat; Big Brass Ring; Lowlife; Dogtown

ZYSTAR FILMS, INC.
330 Washington Blvd., Ste. 400
Marina Del Rey, CA 90292
Phone: ....(310) 301-3313
Fax: ....(310) 301-9433
www.zystar.com
mwallis@zystar.com
Key Executives/Personnel:
  Meryl Alison Wallis, Executive Producer
  Carmen Silva, Producer
  Scott Murphy, Assistant Director
  Howard Raishbrook, Production Manager
  Doug Mickel, Producer
Specialties: Independent
Other Categories: TV; Commercials; Video; Music Video
Credits: James Bond (behind the scenes); American Honda (commercial); Carrows Restaurants (commercial); Laurietta (feature)

featureFILMS

comMERCials

broadCAST

COMPUTERCAFE
3D animation - visual FX

santa **MONICA** california

310 **395-9013**   fax 310 **395-9814**

santa **MARIA** california

805 **922-9479**   fax 805 **922-3225**

www.computercafe.com

Production Companies - TV

21ST CENTURY MAN PRODUCTIONS
1950 N. Tamarind Ave., Ste. 323
Los Angeles, CA 90068
Phone: ....(323) 466-3227
....(310) 989-7353
Fax: ....(323) 466-3227
www.21stcman.com
future21@primenet.com
Key Executives/Personnel:
  Jane Linter, Producer & Director
  David May, Director & Editor
  Brian Bowie, Director & Director of Photography
  Andrea Fredrickson, Editor
Specialties: Network; Cable
Other Categories: Commercials; Video; Music Video; Interactive Multimedia
Credits: 21st CMAN; Sebastian Int.; Wella Alternative Hair Show; Stylezone 2000
Trade Assoc./Guilds/Unions: AEA, BAFTA, DGA, NATPE
Additional Info: 33 Limes Rd., Beckenham, Kent BR3 6N3 England

3 ARTS ENTERTAINMENT
9460 Wilshire Blvd., 7th Fl.
Beverly Hills, CA 90212
Phone: ....(310) 888-3200
....(212) 262-6565
Fax: ....(310) 888-3210
Key Executives/Personnel:
  Dave Becky, Manager
  Jeff Golenberg, Manager
  Howard Klein, Manager
  Molly Madden, Manager
  David Miner, Manager
  Daniel Rappaport, Manager
  Dave Rath, Manager
  Michael Rotenberg, Manager
  Mark Schulman, Manager
  Lainie Sorkin, Manager
  Erwin Stoff, Manager
  Kara Welker-Ryder, Manager
  Nick Frenkel, Manager
Specialties: Network; Cable
Other Categories: Feature Film
Credits: King of the Hill; The Chris Rock Show; The Hughleys
First Look/Development Deals: Twentieth Century Fox Television

30 SECOND FILMS
3019 Pico Blvd.
Santa Monica, CA 90405
Phone: ....(310) 315-1750
Fax: ....(310) 315-1757
www.30secondfilms.com
info@30secondfilms.com
Key Executives/Personnel:
  Alan Stamm, Executive Producer
  Bob Kronovet, Producer & Director
  Scott Baio, Director
  Debbie Allen, Director
  Tony Dow, Director
  Branscombe Richmond, Director
Specialties: Network; Cable; Documentaries; Made for TV Movies; Miniseries
Other Categories: Feature Film; Commercials; Video
Credits: American Tigers; Ghostown; Broken Bars; L.A. Task Force

A&E TELEVISION NETWORKS
235 E. 45th St.
New York, NY 10017
Phone: ....(212) 210-1400
Fax: ....(212) 210-1308
www.aande.com
Key Executives/Personnel:
  Nickolas Davatzes, President & CEO
  Gerard Gruosso, CFO & Sr. VP of Finance
  Whitney Goit, Executive VP of Sales & Marketing
  Dan Davids, Executive VP & General Manager
  Jim Greiner, Sr. VP of Operations & Business Development
  Delia Fine, VP of Drama & Film Programming
  Ed Hersh, VP of Documentary Programming
  Carol Anne Dolan, Director of Documentary Programming
Specialties: Network; Cable; Documentaries; Made for TV Movies; Miniseries
Other Categories: Feature Film; Video
Credits: Biography; American Justice; Investigative Reports

A BAND APART
7966 Beverly Blvd.
Los Angeles, CA 90048
Phone: ....(323) 951-4600
Fax: ....(323) 951-4601
Key Executives/Personnel:
  Lawrence Bender, Producer
  Quentin Tarantino, Writer & Director
  John Baldecchi, Producer
  Laura Bickford, Producer
  Julie Kirkham, Sr. VP of Production
  Kevin Brown, Executive Producer, TV
  Christian D'Andrea, VP of Production
  Janet Jeffries, Story Editor & Assistant to Ms. Kirkham
  Robin Reinhardt, Assistant to Mr. Brown

Morris Marketing Inc.
Global Strategists for the World of Entertainment
Public Relations-Strategic Planning-Marketing-Promotion
www.morrispr.com • (818)-487-9300 • info@morrispr.com

Production Companies – TV

David Zerr, Assistant to Mr. Baldecchi
Specialties: Network; Cable
Other Categories: Feature Film
Credits: Pulp Fiction; Anna And The King; Good Will Hunting; Jackie Brown
First Look/Development Deals: Miramax Films, Twentieth Century Fox

AB'-STRAKT PICTURES
100 N. Crescent Dr.
Beverly Hills, CA 90210
Phone: ....(310) 385-6611
....(310) 385-6608
Fax: ....(310) 385-4306
lupe_rilova@yahoo.com
Key Executives/Personnel:
 Gail Mutrux, Producer
 Valerie Dean, VP of Production
Specialties: Cable
Other Categories: Feature Film
Credits: Nurse Betty; Donnie Brasco; Quiz Show
First Look/Development Deals: USA Films

ABBY LOU ENTERTAINMENT
1411 Edgehill Pl.
Pasadena, CA 91103
Phone: ....(626) 795-7334
Fax: ....(626) 795-4013
ale@full-moon.com
Key Executives/Personnel:
 George LeFave, Executive Producer
 Chryl Pestor, Executive VP of Development
Specialties: Network; Cable; Animation; Made for TV Movies
Other Categories: Feature Film; Commercials; Video
Credits: Adventures in Whispering Gardens; A Christmas Whisper

ABC ENTERTAINMENT TELEVISION GROUP
2040 Avenue of the Stars
Los Angeles, CA 90067
Phone: ....(310) 557-7777
....(212) 456-7777
www.abc.go.com
Key Executives/Personnel:
 Stu Bloomberg, Co-Chairman
 Lloyd Braun, Co-Chairman
 Jeff Bader, Executive VP
 Mark Pedowitz, Executive VP
 Susan Lyne, Executive VP of Movies, Miniseries & The Wonderful World of Disney
 Alan Cohen, Executive VP of Marketing, Advertising & Promotion
 Steve McPherson, Executive VP, Touchtone Television
 Howard Davine, Sr. VP of Business & Legal Affairs
 Jim Hedges, Sr. VP of Finance & Planning
 Gene Blythe, Sr. VP of Casting
 Carolyn Ginsburg-Carlson, Sr. VP of Comedy Programming
 Mike Benson, Sr. VP of Advertising & Promotion
 Kevin Brockman, Sr. VP of Entertainment Communications
 Andrea Wong, Sr. VP of Alternative Series & Specials
 Thom Sherman, VP of Drama Programming
 Suzanne Bukinik, VP of Comedy Programming
 Glenn Adilman, VP of Comedy Programming
 Stephanie Leifer, VP of Comedy Programming
 Susan Leeper, VP of Current Comedy Series & Director, The Walt Disney Studios & ABC TV Writing Fellowship Program
 Jackie Lyons, VP of Drama Programming
 Quinn Taylor, VP of Movies for Television
 John Rose, VP of Human Resources
Specialties: Network; Made for TV Movies; Miniseries
Additional Info: 4151 Prospect Ave., Los Angeles, CA 90067
 77 W. 66th St., New York, NY 10023

ABC, INC./ABC TELEVISION NETWORK
2040 Avenue of The Stars
Los Angeles, CA 90067
Phone: ....(310) 557-7777
www.abc.go.com
Key Executives/Personnel:
 Robert F. Callahan, President, ABC Broadcast Group
 Lawrence J. Pollock, Chairman, ABC Owned Television Stations
 Walter C. Liss, President, ABC Owned Television Stations
 Alex Wallau, President, ABC Television Network
 Stu Bloomberg, Co-Chairman, ABC Entertainment Television Group
 Lloyd Braun, Co-Chairman, ABC Entertainment Television Group
 Janice Marinelli, President, Buena Vista Television
 John Hare, President, ABC Radio
 George Bodenheimer, President, ESPN, Inc.
 Preston A. Davis, President, Broadcast Operations & Engineering
 Howard Katz, President, ABC Sports
 Angela Shapiro, President, ABC Daytime
 Anne Sweeney, President, Disney-ABC Cable Networks
 David Westin, President, ABC News
 Alan N. Braverman, Executive VP & General Counsel, ABC, Inc.
 Michael Shaw, Executive VP & National Sales Manager
 John J. Wolters, Executive VP of Finance
 Jonathan Barzilay, Sr. VP & General Manager, Children's Programming
 Kevin Brockman, Sr. VP, Entertainment Communications
 Patricia J. Matson, Sr. VP of Communications, ABC, Inc.
 Robert Miller, Sr. VP & Managing Director, Hyperion
 John L. Rouse, Sr. VP of Affiliate Relations
 Laurie Younger, Sr. VP & CFO, ABC, Inc.
 Roger Goodman, VP of Special Projects
Specialties: Network

ACAPPELLA PICTURES
Phone: ....(323) 782-8200
Fax: ....(323) 782-8210
charlie@acapellapictures.com
Key Executives/Personnel:
 Charles Evans Jr., President & Producer
 Benjamin Sztajnkrycer, VP of Development & Production
 Scott Stein, Story Editor
 Jason Amos, Assistant
Specialties: Documentaries
Other Categories: Feature Film
Credits: The Brave

ACT III PRODUCTIONS
100 N. Crescent Dr., Ste. 250
Beverly Hills, CA 90210
Phone: ....(310) 385-4111
Fax: ....(310) 385-4148
Key Executives/Personnel:
 Norman Lear, Chairman & CEO
 John Baskin, President
 Rachel Davidson, VP of Feature & TV Development
Specialties: Network
Other Categories: Feature Film

THE AD-FILES
11465 Moorpark St., Ste. 1
North Hollywood, CA 91602
Phone: ....(213) 891-3784
Fax: ....(323) 460-6665
Key Executives/Personnel:
 Daniel W. Bolton, Executive Producer
 Chris Blackwood, Director
 Renard Muldrake, Director
 Vincent Rico, Director
 Mark Spring, Director
Specialties: Network; Cable
Other Categories: Commercials

Production Companies – TV

ADELSON ENTERTAINMENT
2601 Ocean Park Blvd., Ste. 112
Santa Monica, CA 90405
Phone: ....(310) 314-9151
Fax: ....(310) 314-9669
Key Executives/Personnel:
  Andrew Adelson, Producer & Partner
  Tracey Alexander, Executive Producer & Partner
  Laurie Arent, Director of Development
Specialties: Network; Cable; Made for TV Movies; Miniseries
Other Categories: Feature Film
Credits: Hiroshima; Her Own Rules; Critical Choices

ORLY ADELSON PRODUCTIONS
12304 Santa Monica Blvd., Ste. 115
Los Angeles, CA 90025
Phone: ....(310) 442-2012
Fax: ....(310) 442-2013
orly@orlyadelson.com
Key Executives/Personnel:
  Orly Adelson, President
  J. J. Jamieson, Executive Producer
  Jada Miranda, Story Editor
Specialties: Made for TV Movies
Other Categories: Feature Film
Credits: The Truth About Jane; On Hostile Ground; To Love, Honor & Betray; No Greater Love

AEI
9601 Wilshire Blvd., Ste. 1202
Beverly Hills, CA 90210
Phone: ....(323) 932-0407
www.aeionline.com
webaei@aol.com
Key Executives/Personnel:
  Ken Atchity, President
  Chi-Li Wong, VP
  Brenna Lui, Director of Development
  Gordon H. Lui, Development Executive
  Jennifer Pope, Submissions Coordinator
Specialties: Network; Cable; Made for TV Movies
Other Categories: Feature Film
Credits: Me; Henry's List of Wrongs; The Kill Martin Club

AERIAL FOCUS PRODUCTIONS
8 Camino Verde
Santa Barbara, CA 93103
Phone: ....(805) 962-9911
Fax: ....(805) 962-9536
www.aerialfocus.com
aerialfcs@aol.com
Key Executives/Personnel:
  Tom Sanders, Executive Producer
  David Stanfield, Segment Producer
Specialties: Documentaries
Other Categories: Feature Film; Video
Credits: Over The Edge; The Best Boogie Continues; Royal Sky Celebration
Trade Assoc./Guilds/Unions: AFTRA, SAG

AFRA-FILM ENTERPRISES, INC.
137 S. Robertson Blvd., Ste. 254
Beverly Hills, CA 90211
Phone: ....(323) 882-6193
Fax: ....(323) 882-6032
sidazfor@earthlink.net
Key Executives/Personnel:
  Anatoly A. Fradis, President
  Jeff Ratner, VP of Finance
  Felix Kleiman, VP of Development
  Olga Fradis, VP of Production
Specialties: Cable; Made for TV Movies; Miniseries
Other Categories: Feature Film
Credits: Arena; Iron Maiden; Red Shoe Diaries; Business For Pleasure

ALBRECHT & ASSOCIATES, INC.
3442 Dorothy Rd.
Topanga, CA 90290
Phone: ....(818) 222-4836
jaalbrecht@yahoo.com
Specialties: Network; Cable; Animation; Documentaries
Credits: Carol King One to One; Mickey's 60th Birthday
Trade Assoc./Guilds/Unions: DGA, SAG, WGA

ALCHEMY ENTERTAINMENT
73 Market St.
Venice, CA 90291
Phone: ....(310) 396-5937
Fax: ....(310) 450-4988
Key Executives/Personnel:
  Andy Tennant, Writer & Director
  Jon Jashni, Producer
  Wink Mordaunt, Producer
Specialties: Network
Other Categories: Feature Film
Credits: Anna and the King; Ever After

ALL GIRL PRODUCTIONS
4024 Radford Ave., Bungalow 20
Studio City, CA 91604
Phone: ....(818) 655-6000
Fax: ....(818) 655-8380
Key Executives/Personnel:
  Bette Midler, Actress & Producer
  Bonnie Bruckheimer, Producer
  Yvette Taylor, Executive VP
  Julia Eisenman, Sr. VP
  Laura Mueller, Development Assistant
  Robert Nguyen, Assistant to Ms. Bruckheimer
Specialties: Network; Cable; Animation; Made for TV Movies; Miniseries
Other Categories: Feature Film
Credits: Bette; Beaches; Diva Las Vegas; Man of the House
First Look/Development Deals: Sony Pictures Entertainment

ALLEN & ASSOCIATES
5304 Ballone Ln.
Culver City, CA 90230
Phone: ....(310) 390-5522
sportstape@aol.com
Key Executives/Personnel:
  Donald V. Allen, Producer
Specialties: Network; Cable; Documentaries; Made for TV Movies; Miniseries
Other Categories: Feature Film; Commercials
Credits: The Home Show; Suburbia; Car Wash; Super Picnic
Trade Assoc./Guilds/Unions: AFTRA, NARAS, SAG

ALLIANCE ATLANTIS
121 Bloor St. East, Ste. 800
Toronto, ON M4W 3M5
Phone: ....(416) 967-1174
       ....(310) 899-8000
Fax: ....(310) 899-8100
www.allianceatlantis.com
Key Executives/Personnel:
  Peter Sussman, President
  John Morayniss, Executive VP of TV Production
  Ed Gernon, VP of TV Movies & Miniseries
  Janine Coughlin, VP of TV Series Production

Production Companies – TV

Noreen Halpern, VP of TV Series Production
Specialties: Network; Cable; Animation; Made for TV Movies; Miniseries
Other Categories: Feature Film
Credits: Joan of Arc; Beastmaster (TV series); Sunshine; The Sweet Hereafter

ALTA VISTA PRODUCTIONS
11805 Mississippi Ave., Ste. 102
West Los Angeles, CA 90025
Phone: ....(310) 444-2050
Fax: ....(310) 444-2055
altvista@earthlink.net
Key Executives/Personnel:
David Lozano, Executive Producer
Michael Lozano, Producer
Astrid Steel, Producer
Colleen Steckloff, Casting Director
Yves Douville, Post Production Supervisor
Specialties: Animation
Other Categories: Commercials; Music Video

AM PRODUCTIONS & MANAGEMENT
8899 Beverly Blvd., Ste. 713
Los Angeles, CA 90048
Phone: ....(310) 275-9081
Fax: ....(310) 275-9082
Key Executives/Personnel:
Ann Margret, Executive Producer & Actor
Burt Reynolds, Executive Producer, Director & Actor
Alan Margulies, Executive Producer
Roger Smith, Executive Producer & Writer
Christina King, Administration
Specialties: Network; Cable; Made for TV Movies; Miniseries
Other Categories: Feature Film
Credits: Mystery Alaska; Hard Time; Life of the Party

AMALGAMATED, INC.
6565 Sunset Blvd., Ste. 525
Los Angeles, CA 90028
Phone: ....(323) 466-5400
Fax: ....(323) 960-9283
Key Executives/Personnel:
Erik Feig, Producer
Dawn Ebert-Byrnes, Assistant
Specialties: Network
Other Categories: Feature Film
Credits: I Know What You Did Last Summer; I Still Know What You Did Last Summer; Slackers

AMBITIOUS ENTERTAINMENT
Phone: ....(818) 990-8993
Fax: ....(818) 990-8994
ambitious1@earthlink.net
Key Executives/Personnel:
Paul M. Addis, Producer
Specialties: Network; Cable; Documentaries
Other Categories: Commercials; Video
Credits: Muhammad Ali: King of the World (promo); Talk To Me (promo); Wolfgang Puck Cafe (commercial); Sony PlayStation (commercial)

AMEN RA FILMS
301 N. Cañon Dr., Ste. 228
Beverly Hills, CA 90210
Phone: ....(310) 246-6510
Fax: ....(310) 550-1932
firstname@amenraflims.com
Key Executives/Personnel:
Wesley Snipes, Producer & Actor
Kimiko Fox, President & Producer

Victor McGauley, Sr. VP & Producer
Carmen Baker, Comptroller
Julian Chang Zolkin, Creative Executive
Clay Rivers, Director of Design & Marketing
Glennis Bastien, Physical Production
Trudy Snipes Baylock, Human Resources
Rachelle L. Thomas, Special Projects
Lori Davis, Executive Assistant to Mr. Snipes
Jeanie Lee, Assistant to Ms. Fox
Waraine Boswell, Executive Assistant to Mr. McGauley
Specialties: Cable; Documentaries; Made for TV Movies; Miniseries
Other Categories: Feature Film
Credits: Blade; Disappearing Acts; Money Train; The Art of War

AMERICAN ENTERTAINMENT CO.
5225 Wilshire Blvd., Ste. 615
Los Angeles, CA 90036
Phone: ....(323) 939-6746
Fax: ....(323) 939-6747
Key Executives/Personnel:
Bill Paxton, Producer & President
Tom Huckabee, Producer & VP
Xander Maksik, Creative Executive
Mike Culbert, Creative Executive
Specialties: Documentaries
Other Categories: Feature Film
Credits: Traveller; Mexicali; Frailty; Beer Ban

AMERICAN MOVIE CLASSICS/ROMANCE CLASSICS
1111 Stewart Ave.
Bethpage, NY 11714
Phone: ....(516) 803-4300
Fax: ....(516) 803-3044
www.romanceclassics.com
Key Executives/Personnel:
Katie McEnroe, President, AMC/Romance
Marc Juns, Sr. VP of Original Programming, Packaging & Production, AMC
Martin von Ruden, Sr. VP & General Manager, Romance
Jeff Eisenberg, Executive in Charge of Production, Romance
David Sehring, Sr. VP of Acquisitions & Programming, AMC
Paula Connelly Skorka, VP of Original Program Development Series, AMC
Pat Davis, VP of Programming, AMC
Jessica Falcon, VP of Documentaries, AMC
Nancy McKenna, VP of Production, AMC
Laura Masse, VP of Marketing
Ellen Kroner, VP of Public Relations
Laura Messano, Associate Producer, Romance
Judith Orlowski, Director of Aquisitions, Romance
Vlad Wolynetz, Manager of Development, AMC
Specialties: Cable; Documentaries; Miniseries
Credits: Blacklist: Hollywood on Trial; Backstory; The Lot; Remember WENN

AMERICAN SPORTS NETWORK, INC.
P.O. Box 6100
Rosemead, CA 91770
Phone: ....(626) 292-2222
Fax: ....(626) 292-2221
Key Executives/Personnel:
Louis Zwick, President
Robin Chang, Director
Steve Roguet, Producer
Specialties: Cable
Other Categories: Video; Music Video
Credits: ESPN; Eurosport; Star Sport Asia; TSN-Canada

AMERICAN VIDEO GROUP
12020 Pico Blvd.
Los Angeles, CA 90064

Production Companies – TV

Phone: .... (310) 477-1535
Fax: .... (310) 473-5299
www.americanvideogroup.com
amervideo@earthlink.net
Key Executives/Personnel:
   John Berzner, Executive Producer
   Fred Goldey, Production Manager
   Christopher Meisel, Production Supervisor
Specialties: Documentaries
Other Categories: Commercials; Video
Credits: DirecTV; AT&T Wireless; Dali Lama: Message for New Millenium; Bob Mann's Automatic Golf
Trade Assoc./Guilds/Unions: AICP, ERA, ITVA

AMERICAN WORLD PICTURES
21700 Oxnard St., Ste. 660
Woodland Hills, CA 91367
Phone: .... (818) 715-1480
Fax: .... (818) 715-1081
awpics@earthlink.net
Key Executives/Personnel:
   Mark L. Lester, President & CEO
   Dana Dubovsky, President of Production
   Brian R. Etting, VP of Production
   Terese Linden Kohn, VP of Int'l. Sales & Acquisitions
   Jenny Dillon, Director, Int'l.
   Anna Montgomery, Production Executive
Specialties: Cable
Other Categories: Feature Film
Credits: Blowback; Sacrifice; The Ex; Misbegotten

AMERICAN ZOETROPE
808 Wilshire Blvd., 3rd Fl.
Santa Monica, CA 90401
Phone: .... (310) 899-8000
.... (415) 788-7500
Fax: .... (310) 899-8100
www.zoetrope.com
Key Executives/Personnel:
   Francis Ford Coppola, no title
   Linda Reisman, President (NY)
   Jay Shoemaker, CEO (SF)
   Tara McCann, Sr. VP, Head of TV & Producer (LA)
   Bobby Rock, VP of Features Production & Acquisitions (LA)
   Aude Soichet, Creative Executive, TV (LA)
   Shannon Lail, Assistant to Mr. Coppola
Specialties: Network; Cable
Other Categories: Feature Film
Credits: The Virgin Suicides; The Godfather I, II, III; The Third Miracle; Sleepy Hollow
First Look/Development Deals: MGM, Inc., Alliance Atlantis

CRAIG ANDERSON PRODUCTIONS
9696 Culver Blvd., Meralta Plaza, Ste. 208
Culver City, CA 90232
Phone: .... (310) 841-2555
Fax: .... (310) 841-5934
Key Executives/Personnel:
   Craig Anderson, Owner & Executive Producer
   Phil Kruner, VP of Development
   Chris St. George, Creative Executive
   Noah Jones, Creative Development Executive
   Marty Schwartz, Production Supervisor
Specialties: Network; Cable; Made for TV Movies; Miniseries
Other Categories: Feature Film
Credits: The Piano Lesson

ANGEL ARK PRODUCTIONS
12711 Ventura Blvd., Ste. 330
Studio City, CA 91604
Phone: .... (818) 508-3338
Fax: .... (818) 508-2009
Key Executives/Personnel:
   Jason Alexander, Partner
   Jenny Birchfield-Eick, Partner
   Michael A. Jackman, Partner
   Christopher May, VP of TV
   Colin Martin, Assistant
   Vera Wagman, Assistant
Specialties: Network; Cable; Made for TV Movies; Miniseries
Other Categories: Feature Film
Credits: Just Looking; Rocky & Bullwinkle; On Edge

APATOW PRODUCTIONS
1438 N. Gower, Bldg. 38, Ste. 557
Hollywood, CA 90028
Phone: .... (323) 860-7825
Fax: .... (323) 860-7849
Key Executives/Personnel:
   Judd Apatow, Producer & Writer
   Maureen Jennings, Internet
   John Hayes, Assistant
Specialties: Network; Cable
Other Categories: Feature Film
Credits: The Cable Guy; Freaks & Geeks; The Larry Sanders Show
First Look/Development Deals: DreamWorks SKG

APOSTLE PICTURES
1697 Broadway, Ste. 906
New York, NY 10019
Phone: .... (212) 541-4323
Fax: .... (212) 541-4330
Key Executives/Personnel:
   Dennis Leary, Producer & Director
   Jim Serpico, President
   Tom Sellitti, Creative Executive
   Barstow Church, Assistant to Producers
   Steve Hochmuth, Assistant to Mr. Leary
Specialties: Network; Cable
Other Categories: Feature Film
Credits: Blow
First Look/Development Deals: DreamWorks SKG

MARK ARCHER ENTERTAINMENT
1910 St. Joe Center Rd., Ste. 22
Fort Wayne, IN 46825
Phone: .... (219) 486-8831
Fax: .... (219) 486-8971
www.markarcherentertainment.com
development@markarcherentertainment.com
Key Executives/Personnel:
   Mark Archer, President & CEO
   Johnathan Brouwer, VP Production & Operations
Specialties: Cable; Documentaries
Other Categories: Feature Film
Credits: In the Company of Men; American Reel; The Life Between

THE ARNET/KERNER CO.
3815 Hughes Ave.
Culver City, CA 90232
Phone: .... (310) 838-2500
Key Executives/Personnel:
   Jon Avnet, Director & Producer
   Jordan Kerner, Producer
   Carol Chacamaty, Sr. VP of Finance
   Lisa Lindstrom, Sr. VP of Feature Development & Production
   Paul Neesan, Sr. VP of Development & Production
   Marsha Oglesby, VP of Development & Production
   Sandra Hodges, VP of Operations
   Jason Abril, Story Editor
Specialties: Network; Made for TV Movies; Miniseries

Production Companies – TV

Other Categories: Feature Film
Credits: Inspector Gadget; George of the Jungle; Fried Green Tomatoes; Red Corner
Trade Assoc./Guilds/Unions: DGA, SAG, WGAw

ARTISAN ENTERTAINMENT
2700 Colorado Ave., 2nd Fl.
Santa Monica, CA 90404
Phone: ....(310) 449-9200
....(212) 577-2400
Fax: ....(310) 255-3920
www.artisanent.com
Key Executives/Personnel:
  Amir Malin, CEO
  Bill Block, President
  John Shestack, President of Production & Development
  Steve Beeks, President of Home Entertainment
  Glenn Ross, President of Family Home Entertainment
  Ken Schapiro, COO of Artisan Pictures
  Jim Keegan, Executive VP & CFO
  Nick Van Dyk, Executive VP of Corporate Development & Strategic Planning
  Caitlin Scanlon, Executive VP of Production
  Meltem Demirer, Executive VP of Production
  Andrew Golov, Executive VP of Production
  Patrick Gunn, Sr. VP
  Gary Rubin, Sr. VP of TV
  Nancy V. Coleman, Sr. VP of Human Resources
  Rachel Cohen, VP of Acquisitions & Production (NY)
  Leilani Forby, VP of Film Acquisitions
  Cybelle Greenman, VP of Development & Production
  Marc Danon, Manager of Production
Specialties: Network; Cable; Animation; Made for TV Movies; Miniseries
Other Categories: Feature Film
Credits: Blair Witch I & II; The Way of the Gun; The Limey; Reservoir Dogs

THE ARTISTS' COLONY
7421 Beverly Blvd., Ste. 13
Los Angeles, CA 90036
Phone: ....(323) 930-7900
Fax: ....(323) 930-7919
www.theartistscolony.com
las@theartistscolony.com
Key Executives/Personnel:
  Lloyd A. Silverman, President & Producer
  Ginnina d'Orazio, Development Executive
  Julian Bernard, Urban Markets
  Caelyn Smith, Assistant
Specialties: Network; Cable; Documentaries; Made for TV Movies; Miniseries
Other Categories: Feature Film
Credits: Snow Falling On Cedars; Shattered Image; Solid Ones; Till The End of Time

ARTISTS TELEVISION GROUP
9465 Wilshire Blvd., Ste. 510
Beverly Hills, CA 90212
Phone: ....(310) 860-8200
Fax: ....(310) 860-8100
Key Executives/Personnel:
  Eric Tannenbaum, President & CEO
  Sandra Stern, Executive VP & COO
  Kim Haswell, Executive VP of Creative Affairs
  Tom Patricia, Executive VP of TV Movies & Miniseries
  Gary Gradinger, Sr. VP of Business Affairs
  Larry Levin, Sr. VP of Post Production
  Dawn Steinberg, Sr. VP of Casting & Talent
  Nina Lederman, Sr. VP of Creative Affairs
  Jamie Erlicht, VP of Creative Affairs
  Marc Korman, VP of Business Affairs
  Carl Beverly, VP of Creative Affairs
  Bill Phillips, Executive in Charge of Production
  Kathleen Mawhinney, Director of Creative Affairs
  Toby Midgen, Director of Business Affairs
  Brett Weitz, Manager of Creative Affairs
Specialties: Network; Made for TV Movies; Miniseries
Credits: The Street; Cursed; Grosse Pointe (TV series)

ASSET PICTURES
526 W. 26th St., Ste. 813
New York, NY 10001
Phone: ....(212) 255-6187
Fax: ....(212) 242-8345
www.fivewives.com
asetpix@aol.com
Key Executives/Personnel:
  Tessa Blake, President
  Jason Lyon, Producer
Specialties: Cable; Documentaries
Other Categories: Feature Film
Credits: Five Wives; Three Secretaries & Me
Trade Assoc./Guilds/Unions: AIVF, IDA, IFP
Additional Info: LA Partner: Joe Messian, 1218 N. Bronson Ave., Hollywood, CA 90038

THE ASSOCIATION, INC.
135 N. Screenland Dr.
Burbank, CA 91505
Phone: ....(818) 841-9660
Fax: ....(818) 841-8370
theassoc@aol.com
Key Executives/Personnel:
  Randy Stith, Producer
  Tim Melchior, Producer
  Fletch Murray, Producer
  Jeff Murphy, Production Manager
  Maureen Bernal, Sales Representative
Specialties: Documentaries
Other Categories: Commercials; Video
Credits: Quake Ready (PSA's); Hyundai (commercial); PAX TV (promos); Demin Bank (commercial)
First Look/Development Deals: PaxTV/Paxson Communications

ATKINSON WAY FILMS
6121 Santa Monica Blvd., Ste. 100
Los Angeles, CA 90038
Phone: ....(323) 465-3350
Fax: ....(323) 465-3344
Key Executives/Personnel:
  Sam Waterson, Owner
  Beth Colt, Owner
  Andew Myler, Director of Development
  Erika Coleman, Development
Specialties: Network; Cable; Made for TV Movies
Other Categories: Feature Film
Credits: Chuck & Buck; A House Divided; Star Maps; Journey of August King
First Look/Development Deals: NBC Entertainment, Inc.

AVENUE PICTURES
11111 Santa Monica Blvd., Ste. 525
Los Angeles, CA 90025
Phone: ....(310) 996-6800
Fax: ....(310) 473-4376
www.avepix.com
Key Executives/Personnel:
  Cary Brokaw, President & CEO
  Sheri Halfon, Sr. VP & CFO

Judy Geletko, Controller
David Tellefsen, Assistant to Mr. Brokaw
Geoff Goodman, Office Manager & Assistant
Specialties: Network; Cable; Animation; Documentaries; Made for TV Movies; Miniseries
Other Categories: Feature Film
Credits: Drugstore Cowboy; The Player; Short Cuts; Restoration
First Look/Development Deals: Pearson Television, Intermedia Films

AXELROD ENTERTAINMENT
5555 Melrose Ave., B Annex 1
Hollywood, CA 90038
Phone: (323) 956-3705
Fax: (323) 862-0079
Key Executives/Personnel:
Jonathan Axelrod, Executive Producer
Stacey Ackman, Assistant to Mr. Axelrod
Specialties: Network
Other Categories: Feature Film
Credits: Kiss Me Guido; Dave's World; Brother's Keeper; Movie Stars
First Look/Development Deals: Paramount Pictures
Additional Info: Formerly Axelrod/Widdoes Entertainment

AXELSON-WEINTRAUB PRODUCTIONS
4421 Riverside Dr., Ste. 208
Burbank, CA 91505
Phone: (818) 954-8661
Fax: (818) 954-0468
aw-prods@earthlink.net
Key Executives/Personnel:
John Axelson, Producer & Director
Barbara Weintraub, Executive Producer
Specialties: Network; Cable; Documentaries
Other Categories: Feature Film
Credits: An Affectionate Look at Fatherhood; The Really Naked Truth; The New Adventures of Robin Hood; Strip Poker

THE BADHAM COMPANY
3344 Clerendon Rd.
Beverly Hills, CA 90210
Phone: (818) 990-9495
Fax: (818) 981-9163
www.badhamcompany.com
Key Executives/Personnel:
John Badham, Director & Producer
Cammie Crier-Herbert, Co-Producer & Development
Specialties: Cable; Made for TV Movies
Other Categories: Feature Film
Credits: Saturday Night Fever; War Games; The Jack Bull
First Look/Development Deals: HBO, Paramount Pictures

BALLPARK PRODUCTIONS
P.O. Box 508
Venice, CA 90294
Phone: (310) 827-1328
Fax: (310) 577-9626
Key Executives/Personnel:
Michael Schiffer, Producer & Writer
Sally Allen, VP of Development
Specialties: Network; Made for TV Movies; Miniseries
Credits: Very Bad Things; Lean on Me

BALLYHOO, INC.
6738 Wedgewood Place
Los Angeles, CA 90068
Phone: (323) 874-3396
Fax: (323) 883-0265
mbesman@wgn.net
Key Executives/Personnel:
Michael Besman, President
Brian Cosgrove, Story Editor
Specialties: Made for TV Movies
Other Categories: Feature Film
Credits: Seven Years In Tibet; The Opposite of Sex; Bounce; About Schmidt

BANDEIRA ENTERTAINMENT
8447 Wilshire Blvd., Ste. 212
Beverly Hills, CA 90211
Phone: (323) 866-3535
Fax: (323) 866-3599
Key Executives/Personnel:
Beau Flynn, Producer
Christine Johnson, Director of Development
Specialties: Cable
Other Categories: Feature Film
Credits: Fear (TV series); The Love Letter; Judas Kiss
First Look/Development Deals: DreamWorks SKG

BARNSTORM FILMS
73 Market St.
Venice, CA 90291
Phone: (310) 396-5937
Fax: (310) 450-4988
Key Executives/Personnel:
Tony Bill, Producer & Director
Helen Bartlett, Producer
Specialties: Network; Cable; Made for TV Movies; Miniseries
Other Categories: Feature Film
Credits: Harlan County War; Taxi Driver; The Sting; Untamed Heart

BARWOOD FILMS
330 W. 58th St., Ste. 301
New York, NY 10019
Phone: (212) 765-7191
Fax: (212) 765-6988
Key Executives/Personnel:
Barbra Streisand, Owner, Producer & Director
Cis Corman, President
Evan Cohen, VP of Development
Jane Mendle, Story Editor
Specialties: Network; Cable; Documentaries; Made for TV Movies; Miniseries
Other Categories: Feature Film
Credits: What Makes A Family; Prince of Tides; Serving in Silence

SUZANNE BAUMAN PRODUCTIONS
21901 Velicata St.
Woodland Hills, CA 91364
Phone: (818) 348-4342
Fax: (818) 348-6482
Key Executives/Personnel:
Suzanne Bauman, Producer & Director
Toni Pace, Producer
John Marzilli, Director of Development
Specialties: Network; Cable; Documentaries; Made for TV Movies; Miniseries
Other Categories: Feature Film; Video; Music Video
Credits: Jackie: Behind the Myth; Jack Hanna's Animal Adventures; La Belle Epoque; Women of Summer
Trade Assoc./Guilds/Unions: DGA, WGAw

BARBARA L. BAUMANN INC.
13428 Maxella Ave., Ste. 460
Marina Del Rey, CA 90292
Phone: (310) 821-2429
(310) 569-7991
Fax: (310) 821-1429
skyenm@aol.com

Production Companies – TV

Specialties: Documentaries
Other Categories: Feature Film; Commercials
Credits: A Displaced Person (documentary); One River, Many Voices (documentary); Toyota (commercial); Visa (commercial)

BAUMGARTEN/PROPHET ENTERTAINMENT
1640 S. Sepulveda Blvd., Ste. 218
Los Angeles, CA 90025
Phone: (310) 996-1885
Fax: (310) 996-1892
Key Executives/Personnel:
  Craig Baumgarten, Producer
  Melissa Prophet, Manager
  Adam Merims, Producer
  Jessica Berlinski, Manager
  Ruth Vester, Assistant to Mr. Baumgarten
  Jackie Tallarido, Assistant to Ms. Prophet
  Eric Morris, Assistant to Mr. Merims
  Shawn Minton, Second Assistant to Mr. Baumgarten & Ms. Prophet
Specialties: Cable; Made for TV Movies
Other Categories: Feature Film
Credits: Universal Soldier: The Return; Love Stinks; Blank Check; Hook

BAY FILMS
2110 Broadway
Santa Monica, CA 90404
Phone: (310) 829-7799
Fax: (310) 829-7099
Key Executives/Personnel:
  Michael Bay, Director & Partner
  Jennifer Klein, VP
  Mathew Cohan, Creative Executive
  Scott Windhauser, Story Editor
Specialties: Network
Other Categories: Feature Film
Credits: Armageddon; Pearl Harbor; The Rock
First Look/Development Deals: The Walt Disney Company

BCPRODUCTIONS, INC./BCTV PRODUCTIONS
Phone: (949) 495-1500
Fax: (949) 495-4954
budconnell@aol.com
Key Executives/Personnel:
  Bud W. Connell, Executive Producer
  John G. Connell, Art Director
  Ann Maré, Marketing Manager
Specialties: Cable
Other Categories: Commercials; Video
Credits: Goodwill; JCPenney; Hilton Hotels; Amercian Heart Association

JUNE BEALLOR PRODUCTIONS
100 Universal City Plaza, Bldg. 477
Universal City, CA 91608
Phone: (818) 777-9000
Fax: (818) 866-2161
Key Executives/Personnel:
  June Beallor, Producer
  Susan M. Baker, Associate Producer
  Dawn Spiwak, Development Associate
  Vanessa Lee, Assistant to Ms. Beallor
Specialties: Network; Cable; Made for TV Movies; Miniseries
Other Categories: Feature Film
Credits: Survivors of the Holocaust; The Lost Children of Berlin; The Last Days
First Look/Development Deals: DreamWorks SKG

THE BEDFORD FALLS COMPANY
8660 Hayden Pl.
Culver City, CA 90232
Phone: (310) 394-5022
Fax: (310) 394-5825
Key Executives/Personnel:
  Marshall Herskovitz, Executive Producer, Writer & Director
  Edward Zwick, Executive Producer, Writer & Director
  Richard Solomon, President
  Lisa Moiselle, Sr. VP of Production
  Robin Budd, Director of Development
Specialties: Network
Other Categories: Feature Film
Credits: Shakespeare in Love; Once and Again; Dangerous Beauty; thirtysomething
First Look/Development Deals: ABC Entertainment Television Group

BELISARIUS PRODUCTIONS
5555 Melrose Ave., Clara Bow Bldg., Ste. 204
Los Angeles, CA 90038
Phone: (323) 956-8660
Fax: (323) 862-0250
Key Executives/Personnel:
  Donald P. Bellisario, Executive Producer, Director & Writer
  Floyd Johnson, Co-Executive Producer
  Ed Zuckerman, Co-Executive Producer
  Steven Zito, Co-Executive Producer & Writer
  Mark Saraceni, Producer
  David Bellisario, Producer
  Dana Coen, Producer
  Avery Drewe, Producer
  Mark M. Horowitz, Producer
  Julie Watson, Producer
  Paul Levine, Executive Story Editor
Specialties: Network
Other Categories: Feature Film
Credits: JAG
First Look/Development Deals: Paramount Pictures

BELL-PHILLIP TELEVISION PRODUCTIONS, INC.
7800 Beverly Blvd., Ste. 3371
Los Angeles, CA 90036
Phone: (323) 575-4138
Fax: (323) 655-8760
Key Executives/Personnel:
  Bradley Bell, Executive Producer & Head Writer
  Rhonda Friedman, Supervising Producer
  Ron Weaver, Sr. Producer
  Cynthia J. Popp, Producer
  Christy Dooley, Casting Director
Specialties: Network
Credits: The Bold and the Beautiful

BELLA PRODUCTIONS
4250 Beethoven St.
Los Angeles, CA 90066
Phone: (310) 823-3115
Fax: (310) 823-8366
bella1@earthlnk.net
Key Executives/Personnel:
  Cami Taylor, Executive Producer
  Bill Hayden, Executive Producer
  Herb Ritts, Director
  Mark Story, Director
  Peter Abraham, Executive Producer
  Audrey Pask, Executive Producer
Specialties: Cable
Other Categories: Feature Film; Commercials; Music Video
Credits: Nike (commercial); Little Caesar's (commercial); Pac Bell (commercial)
Trade Assoc./Guilds/Unions: DGA

BENDER-SPINK
1149 N. Poinsettia Place
West Hollywood, CA 90046
Phone: (323) 845-1640

Fax: ....(323) 512-5347
Key Executives/Personnel:
  Chris Bender, no title
  J. C. Spink, no title
  Charlie Gogolak, no title
  Roy Lee, no title
  Jim Valdes, no title
  Shane Thueson, no title
  Nicole Harb, no title
  Bryan O'Donnell, no title
  Brian Spink, no title
Specialties: Network
Other Categories: Feature Film; Interactive Multimedia
Credits: American Pie; Cheaters; Like Cats and Dogs
First Look/Development Deals: Twentieth Century Fox Television, New Line Cinema, Inc.

ROBERT BENEDETTI PRODUCTIONS, INC.
Phone: ....(310) 664-0912
Fax: ....(310) 664-0932
Key Executives/Personnel:
  Robert Benedetti, President
Specialties: Network; Cable; Made for TV Movies; Miniseries
Credits: A Lesson Before Dying; Aldrich Ames: Traitor Within; Miss Evers Boys; The Canterville Ghost
Trade Assoc./Guilds/Unions: PGA, SAG, WGA

BENJAMIN PRODUCTIONS, INC.
10451 Valley Spring Ln.
North Hollywood, CA 91602
Phone: ....(818) 752-8500
Fax: ....(818) 752-4928
Key Executives/Personnel:
  Stuart Benjamin, Producer
  Alise Benjamin, Producer
Specialties: Network; Cable; Animation; Made for TV Movies; Miniseries
Other Categories: Feature Film

RICK BERMAN PRODUCTIONS
5555 Melrose Ave., Cooper Bldg., Rm. 232
Los Angeles, CA 90038
Phone: ....(323) 956-5037
Fax: ....(323) 862-1076
Key Executives/Personnel:
  Rick Berman, Executive Producer
  Dave Rossi, Supervisor, Star Trek Projects
  Joanna Fuller, Assistant to Mr. Berman
Specialties: Network
Other Categories: Feature Film
Credits: Star Trek (features & TV series)
First Look/Development Deals: Paramount Pictures

JAY BERNSTEIN PRODUCTIONS
P.O. Box 1148
Beverly Hills, CA 90213
Phone: ....(310) 851-2126
Fax: ....(310) 858-1607
Specialties: Network; Cable
Other Categories: Feature Film
Credits: Mickey Spillane's Mike Hammer; Double Jeopardy; Diamond Trap
Trade Assoc./Guilds/Unions: AFTRA, DGA, PGA, SAG, WGAw

BETTINA PRODUCTIONS, LTD.
624 S. June St.
Los Angeles, CA 90005
Phone: ....(323) 937-2101
Fax: ....(323) 937-2103
Key Executives/Personnel:
  Walter Doniger, President
Specialties: Network; Made for TV Movies; Miniseries

Other Categories: Feature Film
Credits: Rope of Sand; Kentucky Woman; Stone Cold

BIG DADDY PRODUCTIONS
3605 W. Pacific Ave.
Burbank, CA 91505
Phone: ....(818) 845-0161
Fax: ....(818) 729-7817
Key Executives/Personnel:
  Kerri Friedland, Executive Producer
  Scott Friedland, Executive Producer
  Julie Ward, Head of Development
Specialties: Cable; Made for TV Movies; Miniseries
Credits: My Indian Summer

BIG TICKET TELEVISION
1438 N. Gower St., Bldg. 35, 3rd Fl., Box 45
Los Angeles, CA 90028
Phone: ....(323) 860-7400
Fax: ....(323) 468-4176
Key Executives/Personnel:
  Larry Lyttle, President
  Bill Sanders, Executive VP
  Deborah Curtan, Sr. VP of Current Programming
  Bruce Kerner, Sr. VP of Production
  Roger Kirman, Sr. VP of Business Affairs
  Mark S. Johnson, Sr. VP of Production
  Laura Schrock, Sr. VP, Series Development
  Fred Paccone, Sr. VP & Controller
  Rob Morhaim, VP of First Run Programming
  Paul Shapiro, VP of Series Development
  Donna Ekholdt, VP of Talent Development & Casting
  Warren Coulter, Manager of Production
  Susan Edelist, Director of Business Affairs
  John Westphal, Creative Affairs
  Meredith Layne, Talent
Specialties: Network
Credits: Judge Judy; The Parkers; Gary & Mike; Moesha

BLACK & BLU ENTERTAINMENT
10202 W. Washington Blvd., Lean Bldg., Rm. 333
Culver City, CA 90232
Phone: ....(310) 244-8833
Fax: ....(310) 244-2151
Key Executives/Personnel:
  Todd Black, Producer
  Jason Blumenthal, Producer
  Brian Morewitz, Sr. VP
  Chrissy Blumenthal, VP of Development
Specialties: Network
Other Categories: Feature Film
Credits: A Knight's Tale
First Look/Development Deals: Sony Pictures Entertainment

BLACK ENTERTAINMENT TELEVISION (BET)
811 S. San Fernando Rd.
Burbank, CA 91502
Phone: ....(818) 566-9948
....(202) 608-2000
Fax: ....(818) 566-1655
www.bet.com
Key Executives/Personnel:
  Robert Johnson, Chairman & CEO
  Debra Lee, President & COO
  Curtis Gadson, Sr. VP of Entertainment, Programming & Network Operations
  Andre Barnwell, VP of Development
  Stephen Hill, VP of Music
  Gina Holland, VP of Production & Technical Operations
  Philip Johnson, VP of Network Operations & Business Administration
  Veronica Hatchinson, VP of Programming

Production Companies – TV

Specialties: Cable; Made for TV Movies; Miniseries
Other Categories: Feature Film
Additional Info: 1 B.E.T. Plaza, 1900 W. Place, NE, Washington, DC 20018

BLACK SHEEP ENTERTAINMENT
4063 Radford Ave., Ste. 203-A
Studio City, CA 91604
Phone: (818) 769-2227
Fax: (818) 769-2228
blacksheepent@aol.com
Key Executives/Personnel:
  Steven Feder, Owner, Producer, Director & Writer
  Jeff Mazzola, Producer
  Mark Groubert, Producer
  Tracey Morton, Development Executive
Specialties: Network; Cable; Made for TV Movies
Other Categories: Feature Film
Credits: The Big Gig; The Cottonwood; It Had To Be You; With A Bullet
Trade Assoc./Guilds/Unions: WGAw

BLEECKER STREET FILMS
1438 N. Gower St., Ste. 22
Los Angeles, CA 90028
Phone: (323) 993-7386
Fax: (323) 993-7387
bleeckerfilms@aol.com
Key Executives/Personnel:
  Lois Bonfiglio, President
  Simone Study, Director of Development
Specialties: Cable
Other Categories: Feature Film
Credits: Boss of Bosses; Broken Trust; A Bright Shining Lie; Old Gringo
First Look/Development Deals: Turner Network Television (TNT)

BLUE RELIEF
301 N. Cañon Dr., Ste. 205
Beverly Hills, CA 90210
Phone: (310) 275-7900
Fax: (310) 724-5820
Key Executives/Personnel:
  Diane Keaton, Producer & Director
  Bill Robinson, Producer
  Jennifer Glianna, Assistant to Ms. Keaton
  Erin Corzine, Assistant to Mr. Robinson
Specialties: Network; Cable; Miniseries
Other Categories: Feature Film
Credits: Hanging Up; Northern Lights; Plan B
First Look/Development Deals: USA Films, Brillstein-Grey Entertainment

BLUE TULIP PRODUCTIONS
1658 10th St.
Santa Monica, CA 90404
Phone: (310) 752-7900
Fax: (310) 752-7920
Key Executives/Personnel:
  Jan De Bont, Producer & Director
  Lucas Foster, Producer & Partner
  Jessica Borsiceky, Head of Production & Development
  Erin Davis, Creative Executive
Specialties: Network; Cable
Other Categories: Feature Film
Credits: Librium; Minority Report; Speed 2; SLC-Punk
First Look/Development Deals: Twentieth Century Fox Pictures

BLUMBERG PRODUCTIONS & MANAGEMENT
833 Moraga Dr., Ste. 12
Los Angeles, CA 90049
Phone: (310) 472-6410
Fax: (310) 472-5705
mgblumberg@earthlink.net
Key Executives/Personnel:
  Mitch Blumberg, Producer
Specialties: Network; Made for TV Movies
Other Categories: Feature Film
Credits: Sensation; West Side Waltz; Plato's Run

BOB BOOKER PRODUCTIONS
2 Yankee Beach Way
Carmel, CA 93923
Phone: (831) 626-6505
(310) 914-1441
Fax: (831) 626-6505
Key Executives/Personnel:
  Bob Booker, CEO
  Barbara Booker, Executive Producer
Specialties: Network
Credits: Out of This World; Foul-Ups, Bleeps, & Blunders; Anything for A Laugh; World's Funniest Foul-Ups
Trade Assoc./Guilds/Unions: DGA, WGAw

STEVEN BOCHCO PRODUCTIONS
10201 W. Pico Blvd., Bldg. 1
Los Angeles, CA 90035
Phone: (310) 369-2400
Fax: (310) 369-3236
Key Executives/Personnel:
  Steven Bochco, Chairman & CEO
  Dayna Kalins, President
  Franklin B. Rohner, President & CFO
  Julie Waxman, Sr. VP of Business Affairs
  James A. Roach, VP of Finance
  Maureen Milligan, VP of Human Resources & Administration
Specialties: Network
Credits: NYPD Blue; City of Angels

CAROL BODIE ENTERTAINMENT
9465 Wilshire Blvd., Ste. 420
Beverly Hills, CA 90212
Phone: (310) 247-8181
Fax: (310) 247-8555
entcbe@aol.com
Key Executives/Personnel:
  Carol Bodie, CEO & Producer
  Steven Dubin, COO
  Jennifer Choi, Executive Assistant
Specialties: Cable
Other Categories: Feature Film
Credits: Girl, Interrupted

BONFIRE FILMS OF AMERICA
4655 Kingswell Ave., Ste. 213
Los Angeles, CA 90027
Phone: (323) 953-6815
Fax: (323) 953-0623
Key Executives/Personnel:
  Shirley Moyers, Executive Producer
  A. J. Schnack, Executive Producer
  John McGinnis, Director's Rep
Specialties: Cable
Other Categories: Feature Film; Commercials; Music Video

BOZ PRODUCTIONS
1632 N. Sierra Bonita Ave.
Los Angeles, CA 90046

Phone: ....(323) 876-3232
Fax: ....(323) 876-3231
boz51@aol.com
Key Executives/Personnel:
  Bo Zenga, Producer & Writer
  Jeff Monarch, Director of Development
Specialties: Network; Cable; Made for TV Movies; Miniseries
Other Categories: Feature Film
Credits: Scary Movie; Everything's Jake

BRAGA PRODUCTIONS
5555 Melrose Ave., Hart Bldg., Ste. 205
Hollywood, CA 90038
Phone: ....(323) 956-5799
Fax: ....(323) 862-8503
Key Executives/Personnel:
  Brannon Braga, President
  Michael O'Halloran, VP of Production & Development
  Robert Gillan, Story & Script Reader
Specialties: Network
Other Categories: Feature Film
Credits: Star Trek (TV series); Star Trek: Voyager
First Look/Development Deals: Paramount Pictures

BRAYTON/CARLUCCI PRODUCTIONS
1640 S. Sepulveda Blvd., 4th Fl.
Los Angeles, CA 90025
Phone: ....(310) 478-1700
Fax: ....(310) 478-2202
Key Executives/Personnel:
  Anne Carlucci, Executive Producer
  Marian Brayton, Executive Producer
  Larry Grimaldi, Director of Development & Co-Producer
Specialties: Network; Cable; Made for TV Movies; Miniseries
Other Categories: Feature Film
Credits: Out-of-Sync; Sex and Mrs. X; The Soul Collector; Dangerous Evidence
First Look/Development Deals: Hearst Entertainment Productions

PAULETTE BREEN PRODUCTIONS
6920 Texhoma Ave., Ste. 101
Van Nuys, CA 91406
Phone: ....(818) 342-0228
Fax: ....(818) 342-0228
breenpg@aol.com
Key Executives/Personnel:
  Paulette Breen, President & Producer
  Diane Biederbeck, VP of Creative Affairs
  Kathy Page, Creative Assistant
Specialties: Network; Cable
Other Categories: Feature Film
Credits: Haven; Down Will Come Baby; Separated by Murder; Stranger Within

THE BREGMAN ENTERTAINMENT COMPANY
1950 Sawtelle Blvd., Ste. 360
Los Angeles, CA 90025
Phone: ....(213) 833-6207
Fax: ....(323) 876-1957
budboy@worldnet.att.net
Key Executives/Personnel:
  Buddy Bregman, President
  Marie DePuthod, Writer, Director & Producer
Specialties: Network; Cable; Made for TV Movies; Miniseries
Other Categories: Feature Film; Music Video
Credits: Ain't Misbehavin'; The American Civil War; Olivia Newton John; Nancy Wilson Show
First Look/Development Deals: Gen X Entertainment, Int'l. Filmed Entertainment
Trade Assoc./Guilds/Unions: AFM, DGA, PGA, WGAw

BRIGHT-KAUFFMAN-CRANE PRODUCTIONS
4000 Warner Blvd., Bldg. 160, Ste. 750
Burbank, CA 91522
Phone: ....(818) 977-7777
Fax: ....(818) 977-7999
Key Executives/Personnel:
  Kevin S. Bright, Executive Producer
  Marta Kauffman, Executive Producer
  David Crane, Executive Producer
Specialties: Network
Credits: Friends

BRILLSTEIN-GREY ENTERTAINMENT
9150 Wilshire Blvd., Ste. 350
Beverly Hills, CA 90212
Phone: ....(310) 275-6135
Fax: ....(310) 275-6180
Key Executives/Personnel:
  Bernie Brillstein, Consultant
  Brad Grey, Chairman & CEO
  Kevin Reilly, President of BGTV
  Steve Blume, CFO
  Matthew Baer, Head of Motion Picture Division
  Sandy Wernick, Sr. Executive VP
  Jonathan Liebman, Executive VP
  Marc Gurvitz, Executive VP of Management
  Peter Travgott, Executive VP of BGTV
  Susie Fitzgerald, Sr. VP of TV
  Tony Carey, VP of TV Production
  Laura Hopper, VP of Motion Pictures
  Denise Stewart, VP of Motion Pictures
Specialties: Network; Cable
Other Categories: Feature Film
Credits: The Sopranos; Scary Movie; Just Shoot Me
First Look/Development Deals: Miramax Films

BROADWAY VIDEO
1619 Broadway, Brill Bldg., 9th Fl.
New York, NY 10019
Phone: ....(212) 265-7621
www.broadwayvideo.com
Key Executives/Personnel:
  Lorne Michaels, Chairman
  Jack Sullivan, COO
  Quise Shapiro, Producer
  Ron Yassen, Producer
  Erin Fraser, Producer
  John Irwin, VP of Production & Development
  David Long, VP of Creative Group
Specialties: Network; Cable
Credits: Saturday Night Live; Late Night with Conan O'Brien; Kids in the Hall
First Look/Development Deals: NBC Entertainment, Inc., Paramount Pictures

BROOKWELL MCNAMARA ENTERTAINMENT
5433 Beethoven St.
Los Angeles, CA 90066
Phone: ....(310) 306-2151
Fax: ....(310) 823-7026
Key Executives/Personnel:
  David Brookwell, Executive Producer
  Sean McNamara, Executive Producer
Specialties: Network; Cable; Animation; Documentaries; Made for TV Movies; Miniseries

Production Companies – TV

Other Categories: Feature Film
Credits: Even Stevens; Race to Space; The Trial Of Old Drum; Wild Grizzly

JERRY BRUCKHEIMER FILMS
1631 10th St.
Santa Monica, CA 90404
Phone: ....(310) 664-6260
Key Executives/Personnel:
    Jerry Bruckheimer, Producer
    Mike Stenson, President
    Chad Oman, President of Production
    Jonathan Littman, Executive VP of TV
    Kristie Anne Groelinger, Director of Production
Specialties: Network
Other Categories: Feature Film
Credits: Gone in 60 Seconds; Remember the Titans; Armageddon; Coyote Ugly
First Look/Development Deals: Touchstone Pictures

BUENA VISTA TELEVISION
500 S. Buena Vista St., Team Disney Bldg.
Burbank, CA 91521
Phone: ....(818) 560-5000
www.bvtv.com
Key Executives/Personnel:
    Janice Marinelli, President
    Dan Cohen, Sr. VP & General Manager
    Jed Cohen, Sr. VP of Western Region
    Mary Kellogg-Joslyn, Sr. VP of Current Programming
    Lloyd Komesar, Sr. VP of Strategic Planning
    Tom Malanga, Sr. VP of Finance
    Lori Bernstein, VP of Business Affairs
    Sandra Brewer, VP of Affiliate Relations
    Brooke Karzan, VP of Development
    Mike Henry, VP of Creative Services
    Julie Piepenkotter, VP of Research
    Carlos Torres, VP of Production
Specialties: Network; Cable

BUNGALOW 78 PRODUCTIONS
5555 Melrose Ave., Lasky Bldg., Ste. 200
Los Angeles, CA 90038
Phone: ....(323) 956-4440
Fax: ....(323) 862-2090
Key Executives/Personnel:
    Barry Kemp, Executive Producer & Writer
    Devorah Moos-Hankin, President of Feature Production
    Bess Walkes, Director of Development
Specialties: Network
Other Categories: Feature Film
Credits: Catch Me If You Can; Patch Adams; Romy & Michelle's High Reunion
First Look/Development Deals: Paramount Pictures

BUNIM-MURRAY PRODUCTIONS
6007 Sepulveda Blvd.
Van Nuys, CA 91411
Phone: ....(818) 756-5100
Fax: ....(818) 756-5140
www.bunim-murray.com
Key Executives/Personnel:
    Mary-Ellis Bunim, Executive Producer
    Jonathan Murray, Executive Producer
    Scott Freeman, VP of Creative Affairs & Development
    Bonnie Bogard, VP of Creative Affairs
    Joyce Corrington, VP of Creative Affairs
    Ricardo de Oliveira, VP of Creative Affairs
    Andrew Hoegl, VP of Creative Affairs
    Bruce Toms, VP of Development
Specialties: Network; Cable; Documentaries; Made for TV Movies
Credits: The Real World; Road Rules; Making the Band; Personally Yours

BURRUD PRODUCTIONS
16351 Gothard St., Unit D
Huntington Beach, CA 92647
Phone: ....(714) 842-8422
Fax: ....(714) 842-0433
www.burrud.com
burrudprod@aol.com
Key Executives/Personnel:
    John Burrud, President & CEO
    Linda Karabin, VP of Adminitration
    Drew Horton, VP of Production
    Stan Green, VP of Business Affairs
    Kurt Porter, VP of Post Production
    Gita Patel, Producer
    Gerry Wright, Producer
    Shannon Mead, Assistant to Mr. Burrud
Specialties: Network; Cable; Documentaries
Other Categories: Video
Credits: Weird World; Beyond Bizarre; Yoga for Children

AL BURTON PRODUCTIONS
468 N. Camden Dr., Ste. 200
Beverly Hills, CA 90210
Phone: ....(310) 858-5511
Key Executives/Personnel:
    Al Burton, President & Executive Producer
    Rachel Reiss, Director of Development
    Hilary Holmes, Production
Specialties: Network; Cable
Credits: Turn Ben Stein On; Win Ben Stein's Money; Charles In Charge; The New Lassie
First Look/Development Deals: Comedy Central, Twentieth Century Fox Television, The Buena Vista Motion Pictures Group
Trade Assoc./Guilds/Unions: AFTRA, ATAS, DGA, WGAw

BUSHWOOD PICTURES
320 S. Irving Blvd.
Los Angeles, CA 90020
Phone: ....(323) 936-1659
Fax: ....(323) 936-1977
Key Executives/Personnel:
    Sandy Isaac, Producer & Writer
    Margaret French Isaac, Producer
Specialties: Network
Other Categories: Feature Film
Credits: Jack and Jill; Never Been Kissed; Stepmom; To Die For

CAIRO/SIMPSON ENTERTAINMENT, INC.
9255 Sunset Blvd., Ste. 507
West Hollywood, CA 90069
Phone: ....(310) 888-1262
Fax: ....(310) 887-1813
judycairo@aol.com
Key Executives/Personnel:
    Judy Cairo, Executive Producer
    Michael Simpson, Producer, Director & Writer
Specialties: Network; Cable; Made for TV Movies; Miniseries
Other Categories: Feature Film; Interactive Multimedia
Credits: Her Deadly Rival; Twisted Desire; Perfect Body; What We Did That Night

CALAR
335 N. Maple Dr., Ste. 245
Beverly Hills, CA 90210
Phone: ....(310) 271-2202
Fax: ....(310) 271-8990
Key Executives/Personnel:
    Caylyn E. Morris, Executive Producer
    Alex Muñoz, Director

Specialties: Documentaries
Other Categories: Feature Film; Commercials; Video

CALICO WORLD ENTERTAINMENT
10200 Riverside Dr., Ste. 203
North Hollywood, CA 91602
Phone: ....(818) 755-3800
Fax: ....(818) 755-4643
www.calicoworld.com
tom@calicoworld.com
Key Executives/Personnel:
    Tom Burton, Executive Director & Producer
    Claudia Zeitlin Burton, Managing Director
    Ken Leonard, Art Director
    Joel Fajnor, Producer & Director
    Mary Cim, Producer & Director
    Jim Livolsi, Executive Producer & Marketing
    Pedram Shohadai, Digital Animator
Specialties: Animation
Other Categories: Feature Film; Commercials; Interactive Multimedia
Credits: Denver, The Lost Dinosaur; Bad Baby; Kid's Songs of Woody Guthrie; Ghosts Legends of the Queen Mary

CALM DOWN PRODUCTIONS, INC.
1360 N. Crescent Heights Blvd., Ste. 3B
Los Angeles, CA 90046
Phone: ....(323) 650-4027
Fax: ....(323) 654-1104
Key Executives/Personnel:
    Kevin Pollak, CEO
    Lucy Webb, President & Producer
    Lana Estrada, Executive Assistant
    Amy Barnes, Creative Development
Specialties: Network; Cable
Other Categories: Feature Film
Credits: Work With Me; Grant & Lee; The Underworld; Stop With The Kicking

CANNELL STUDIOS
7083 Hollywood Blvd., Ste. 600
Hollywood, CA 90028
Phone: ....(323) 465-5800
Fax: ....(323) 856-7390
www.cannell.com
Key Executives/Personnel:
    Stephen J. Cannell, CEO
    Wayne S. Williams, VP of Development
Specialties: Network; Cable; Made for TV Movies; Miniseries
Other Categories: Feature Film
Credits: Dawg; Terror.net; Director's Cut

THE CANTON COMPANY
4000 Warner Blvd., Bldg. 81, Ste. 200
Burbank, CA 91522
Phone: ....(818) 954-2130
Fax: ....(818) 954-2967
Key Executives/Personnel:
    Mark Canton, CEO & President
    Chris Carter, no title
    Anna DeRoy, no title
    Nathan Kahane, no title
    Barbara Kalish, no title
    Ben Hurivtz, no title
    Scott Coleman, no title
    Nicole Fitzpatrick, no title
    Michael Gordon, no title
    Jim Miller, no title
    Sabrina Steele, no title
Specialties: Network; Cable; Made for TV Movies; Miniseries
Other Categories: Feature Film
Credits: Get Carter; Red Planet; Angel Eyes; Jack & Jill

CANVAS HOUSE FILMS
3671 Bear St., Ste. E
Santa Ana, CA 92704
Phone: ....(714) 850-1964
....(323) 459-0609
teteemley@aol.com
Key Executives/Personnel:
    Mitch Teemley, Writer & Producer
    Elizabeth Gray, Associate Producer
Specialties: Network; Cable; Made for TV Movies; Miniseries
Other Categories: Feature Film; Commercials; Music Video
Credits: Out Of Time (TV series); Lennar Homes (commercial); The Limited (feature); Kragira (feature)

CAPITAL ARTS ENTERTAINMENT
Phone: ....(310) 581-3020
Fax: ....(310) 581-3023
www.capitalarts.com
capartsent@aol.com
Key Executives/Personnel:
    Mike Elliott, Co-President
    Rob Kerchner, Co-President
Specialties: Cable
Other Categories: Feature Film
Credits: Skipped Parts; After The Storm; Northface; Rocket's Red Glare
First Look/Development Deals: Fox Family Channel, Trimark Pictures, Saban Entertainment

CAPO PRODUCTIONS, INC.
Phone: ....(310) 477-4234
capoprod@aol.com
Key Executives/Personnel:
    Deborah Capogresso, President
Specialties: Made for TV Movies; Miniseries
Other Categories: Feature Film
Credits: Just a Little Harmless Sex; The Hot Spot; Other Voices

MARK CARLINER PRODUCTIONS
4121 1/2 Radford Ave
Studio City, CA 91604
Phone: ....(818) 763-4783
mcarliner@aol.com
Key Executives/Personnel:
    Mark Carliner, Producer
    B. J. Heath, Assistant to Mr. Carliner
Specialties: Made for TV Movies; Miniseries
Other Categories: Feature Film
Credits: Rose Red; Storm of the Century; The Shining (miniseries); Stalin

CARLYLE PRODUCTIONS & MANAGEMENT
2050 Laurel Canyon Rd.
Los Angeles, CA 90046
Phone: ....(323) 848-4960
Fax: ....(323) 650-8249
carlyle@earthlink.net
Key Executives/Personnel:
    Phyllis Carlyle, Producer & Manager
    Devin Klein, Manager
    Joseph O'Connor, Creative Executive
Specialties: Cable
Other Categories: Feature Film
Credits: Seven; The Accidental Tourist; Mean Streak

CARRIE PRODUCTIONS
4444 Riverside Dr., Ste. 110
Burbank, CA 91505
Phone: ....(818) 567-3292

Production Companies – TV

Fax: .... (818) 567-3296
Key Executives/Personnel:
- Danny Glover, Executive Producer
- Carolyn McDonald, Executive Producer
- Judith Alonso, Creative Executive

Specialties: Cable
Other Categories: Feature Film
Credits: Freedom Song; America's Dream; Buffalo Soldiers

THE CARSEY-WERNER, LLC.
4024 Radford Ave., Bldg. 3
Studio City, CA 91604
Phone: .... (818) 655-5598
www.carseywerner.com
Key Executives/Personnel:
- Marcy Carsey, Executive Producer
- Tom Werner, Executive Producer
- Bill Martin, Executive Producer
- Mike Schiff, Executive Producer
- Caryn Mandabach, Executive Producer
- David Isreal, Co-Executive Producer
- Jim O'Doherty, Co-Executive Producer
- Tracey Ormandy, Line Producer
- Ned Goldreyer, Producer
- Tyrone Finch, Producer
- Tom Purcell, Producer
- Chris Kelly, Producer

Specialties: Network
Credits: 3rd Rock From the Sun; Normal, Ohio; That '70s Show; Grounded for Life

CASTLE ROCK ENTERTAINMENT
335 N. Maple Dr., Ste. 135
Beverly Hills, CA 90210
Phone: .... (310) 285-2300
Fax: .... (310) 285-2345
Key Executives/Personnel:
- Rob Reiner, Producer & Director
- Andrew Scheinman, Producer & Director
- Martin Shafer, President, Castle Rock Pictures
- Glenn Padnick, President, Castle Rock TV
- Greg Paul, COO
- Liz Glotzer, President of Production, Features
- Jeffrey Stott, Executive VP of Production Management
- Jess Wittenberg, Executive VP
- Brady Thomas, Creative Executive

Specialties: Network; Miniseries
Other Categories: Feature Film
Credits: The Green Mile; The Shawshank Redemption; A Few Good Men; Seinfeld
First Look/Development Deals: Warner Bros.

CATES/DOTY PRODUCTIONS
10920 Wilshire Blvd., Ste. 830
Los Angeles, CA 90024
Phone: .... (310) 208-2134
Fax: .... (310) 208-3980
Key Executives/Personnel:
- Gilbert Cates, Producer & Director
- Dennis Doty, Producer
- Peggy Griffin, Associate Producer

Specialties: Network; Cable; Made for TV Movies; Miniseries
Credits: Tom Clancy's: Net Force; Innocent Victims; Confessions: Two Faces of Evil; In My Daughter's Name

CBS ENTERPRISES
51 W. 52nd St.
New York, NY 10019
Phone: .... (212) 975-4321
Fax: .... (212) 653-8266
www.cbs.com
Key Executives/Personnel:
- Roger King, Chairman & CEO
- Ed Wilson, President & COO
- Armando Nuñez Jr., President of CBS Broadcast Int'l.
- Bob Cook, Executive VP
- Barry Wallach, Executive VP of Syndication
- Joe DiSalvo, Sr. VP & General Sales Manager
- John Holdridge, Sr. VP of Southern Sales
- Robb Dalton, Sr. VP of Business & Program Development
- Jim Dauphinee, Sr. VP of Programming & Development
- Jon Hookstratten, Sr. VP of Business Affairs
- Bill Kunkel, Sr. VP of Int'l. Media Sales
- Andi Sporkin, VP of Communications
- Joanne Burns, VP of Marketing Research & Strategic Planning
- Barry Chamberlain, VP of Sales
- Scott Michaels, VP of Sales Operations & Administration
- Suni Deskin, VP of Sales Services
- Sid Beighley, VP of Eastern Sales
- Frances Manfredi, VP of Cable Sales & Special Markets
- Sean O'Boyle, VP of Midwestern Sales
- Elaine Bauer, VP of Programming & Development
- Sam Cue, VP of Operations
- Mary Beth McAdaragh, VP of Marketing Services
- Judith Bass, VP of Business Affairs & Operations
- Harvey Rappaport, VP of Production & Operations
- Kenneth Ross, VP of Marketing & GM, CBS Video

Specialties: Network

CBS ENTERTAINMENT
7800 Beverly Blvd.
Los Angeles, CA 90036
Phone: .... (323) 575-2345
www.cbs.com
Key Executives/Personnel:
- Nancy Tellem, President
- Maria Crenna, Executive VP of CBS Productions
- Kelly Kahl, Sr. VP of Program Planning & Scheduling
- David Stapf, Sr. VP of Current Programming
- Chris Ender, Sr. VP of Communications
- Peter Golden, Sr. VP of Talent & Casting
- Sunta Izzicupo, Sr. VP of Movies for Television & Miniseries
- Lucy Johnson, Sr. VP of Daytime, Children's Programs & Special Projects
- Mitchell R. Semel, Sr. VP of Programming (East Coast)
- Wendi Goldstein, Sr. VP of Comedy Series Development
- Nina Tassler, Sr. VP of Drama Series Development
- Robert Gros, Sr. VP of Production, CBS Productions
- Jim McKairnes, VP of Program Planning & Scheduling
- Laurie Zaks, VP of Current Programs
- Chris Davidson, VP of Current Programs
- Jack Sussman, VP of Specials
- Ghen Maynard, VP of Alternative Programming
- Nancy Carr, VP of Communications
- Fern Orenstein, VP of Casting
- Lucy Cavallo, VP of Casting
- Martin Garcia, VP of Business Affairs, Programs & Rights Negotiations
- Gary Silver, VP of Business Affairs
- Sam Semon, VP of Business Affairs
- Ericka Rockler, VP of Business Affairs
- Anne Nelson, VP of Business Affairs
- Leola Gorius, VP of Business Affairs, Talent & Guild Negotiations, CBS Productions
- Sidney H. Lyons, VP of Business Affairs, Long Form Contracts & Acquisitions
- Michael Wright, VP of Movies for Television, CBS Productions
- Joan Yee, VP of Sponsor Programming, Movies & Miniseries
- Brian O'Neal, VP of Children's Programs
- Madeline Peerce, VP of Creative Services & Artist Relations
- Julie Pemworth, VP of Comedy Series Development
- Kevin Berg, VP of Production, CBS Productions
- Mark Saks, VP of Casting, CBS Productions

Production Companies – TV

Specialties: Network; Animation; Documentaries; Made for TV Movies; Miniseries

CBS TELEVISION
51 W. 52th St.
New York, NY 10019
Phone: .... (212) 975-4321
Fax: .... (212) 653-8266
www.cbs.com
Key Executives/Personnel:
  Leslie Moonves, President & CEO
  Nancy Tellem, President of CBS Entertainment
  Andrew Heyward, President of CBS News
  Sean McManus, President of CBS Sports
  John Severino, President & General Manager of CBS Television
  Roger King, Chairman & CEO of CBS Enterprises
  Ed Wilson, President & COO of CBS Enterprises
  Peter K. Schruth, President of Affiliate Relations
  Joseph Abruzzese, President of Sales
  Martin Franks, Executive VP, CBS Television/CFO, Viacom Inc.
  Fred Reynolds, Executive VP, CBS Television/CFO, Viacom Inc.
  Gil Schwartz, Executive VP of Communications
  Louis Briskman, Executive VP & General Counsel
  Jo Ann Ross, Executive VP of Sales
  David Poltrack, Executive VP of Planning & Research
  George Schweitzer, Executive VP of Marketing & Communications
  Martin P. Messinger, Sr. VP & Deputy General Counsel
  Susan J. Holliday, Sr. VP & Deputy General Counsel
  Bob Ross, Sr. VP of Broadcast Operations
  Bruce Taub, Sr. VP of Financial Planning & CFO
  Chris Ender, Sr. VP of Communications, CBS Entertainment
  Joseph Flaherty, Sr. VP of Technology
  Charles Cappleman, Sr. VP of West Coast Operations & Engineering
  William Cecil, Sr. VP of Program Sales
  Dean Kaplan, Sr. VP of Sales Planning & Administration
  John Gray, Sr. VP of Business Development
  Preston Farr, Sr. VP & Director of Affiliate Relations
  Frances Eigendorff, Sr. VP & Director of Affiliate Relations
  Ron Scalera, Sr. VP & Creative Director of Advertising & Promotions
  Anne O'Grady, Sr. VP of Marketing & Events
  Robert Freedline, VP & Controller
  Gary McCarthy, VP of Finance (West Coast)
  Dana McClintock, VP of Communications
  Gail Plautz, VP of Photography
  Sandra Genelius, VP of Communications, CBS News
  Leslie Anne Wade, VP of Communications, CBS Sports
  Nancy Carr, VP of Communications, CBS Entertainment
  Andi Sporkin, VP of Communications, CBS Enterprises
  Matthew Margo, VP of Program Practices (East Coast)
  Carol Altieri, VP of Program Practices (West Coast)
  Howell Mette, VP of Engineering
  Robert Seidel, VP of Engineering & Advanced Technology
  Shane O'Donoghue, VP of Technical Services
  David Conant, VP of Entertainment Production Services
  Brent Stranathan, VP of Broadcast Distribution
  Ray Potter, VP of Sports Production Systems
  Louis Jerome, VP of Sales for Movies & Mini-Series
  Russell Behrman, VP & Director of Sales Planning & Proposals
  Ann Harkins, VP of Sales Services
  Robert Shellard, VP of Planning & Administration
  Jack Parmeter, VP of On-Air Promotion
  Kathleen Culleton, VP of Marketing Operations
  Ileene Mittleman, VP of Advertising & Creative Services
Specialties: Network

CELLULOID
2128 15th St.
Denver, CO 80202
Phone: .... (303) 595-3152
.... (303) 595-4908
www.celluliodstudio.com
jan@celluloidstudios.com
Key Executives/Personnel:
  Olivier Katz, President
  Jan Johnson, Executive Producer
Specialties: Animation
Other Categories: Commercials
Credits: PBS; Fox Kids; Denver Art Museum; Drug Free America

CHANCELLOR ENTERTAINMENT
10600 Holman Ave., Ste. 1
Los Angeles, CA 90024
Phone: .... (310) 474-4521
Fax: .... (310) 470-9273
chaent@aol.com
Key Executives/Personnel:
  Bob Marcucci, President & CEO
Specialties: Made for TV Movies; Miniseries
Other Categories: Feature Film
Credits: The Razor's Edge; Letter to Three Wives; Stitches
Trade Assoc./Guilds/Unions: AMPAS, ASCAP, BMI, NARAS, PGA, WGAw

CHARLES BROS. PRODUCTIONS
5555 Melrose Ave., Bungalow 1
Los Angeles, CA 90038
Phone: .... (323) 956-5962
Fax: .... (323) 862-3407
Key Executives/Personnel:
  Glen Charles, Executive Producer
  Les Charles, Executive Producer
  Jim Burrows, Executive Producer & Director
Specialties: Network
First Look/Development Deals: Paramount Pictures

STANLEY CHASE PRODUCTIONS, INC.
1937 S. Beverly Glen Blvd.
Los Angeles, CA 90025
Phone: .... (310) 475-4236
Fax: .... (310) 474-5720
chaseprods@aol.com
Key Executives/Personnel:
  Stanley Chase, President
  Dorothy Rice, VP
Specialties: Network; Cable; Made for TV Movies; Miniseries
Credits: Mack The Knife; The Guardian; American Xmas Carol; Colossus: The Forbin Project
Trade Assoc./Guilds/Unions: AMPAS

CHERRY ALLEY PRODUCTIONS
1250 Sixth St., Ste. 200
Santa Monica, CA 90401
Phone: .... (310) 458-8886
Key Executives/Personnel:
  Goldie Hawn, CEO
  Deloris Horn, Assistant
  Patty Davis, Assistant
Specialties: Network; Cable; Made for TV Movies; Miniseries
Other Categories: Feature Film
Credits: The Out of Towners; Hope

CHESLER/PERLMUTTER PRODUCTIONS
1045 Gayley Ave., Ste. 200
Los Angeles, CA 90024
Phone: .... (310) 443-9650
Fax: .... (310) 443-9524
chesper1@aol.com
Key Executives/Personnel:
  Lewis B. Chesler, CEO
  David Perlmutter, CEO (Toronto)

Production Companies – TV

    Kevin Commins, VP of Development
    Rob Vaughn, VP of Production
    Hank McCann, VP of Talent
    Michael Cote, Director of Finance (Toronto)
    Gaille LeDrew, Development Executive (Toronto)
    Roberta Harron, Administrative Executive (Toronto)
    Beth Blum, Office Coordinator
    Edie Monroe, Accounting (Toronto)
    Rob Carpio, Development Assistant
    Steve Stromberg, Assistant
Specialties: Network; Cable; Made for TV Movies
Other Categories: Feature Film
Credits: Hostile Intent; The Hidden Room; The Hitchhiker; Undertow
First Look/Development Deals: HBO, Canal +
Additional Info: 129 Yorkville Ave, Ste. 200, Toronto, ON M5R IC4 Canada, (416) 927-0016 phone, (416) 960-8447 fax

CHICAGOFILMS
250 W. 57th St., Ste. 2217
New York, NY 10107
Phone: (212) 307-0050
Fax: (212) 307-9066
Key Executives/Personnel:
    Bob Balaban, Producer & Director
    Allison Shigo, Director of Development
Specialties: Cable
Other Categories: Feature Film

CHIODO BROS. PRODUCTIONS, INC.
110 W. Providencia Ave.
Burbank, CA 91502
Phone: (818) 842-5656
Fax: (818) 848-0891
www.chiodobros.com
klowns@chiodobros.com
Key Executives/Personnel:
    Edward Chiodo, Producer & Development
    Stephen Chiodo, Director & Development
    Charles Chiodo, Design & Development
    Paul Kemp, COO & Development
Specialties: Network; Cable; Animation; Made for TV Movies; Miniseries
Other Categories: Feature Film; Commercials
Credits: Killer Klowns from Outer Space (feature); Amazing Live Sea Monkeys (TV series); The Crayon Box (TV series); Skwid Zone (TV pilot)

CHRIS/ROSE PRODUCTIONS
10202 W. Washington Blvd., Gable Bldg., Ste. 304
Culver City, CA 90232
Phone: (310) 244-2833
Fax: (310) 244-0133
Key Executives/Personnel:
    Robert W. Christiansen, Executive Producer
    Rick Rosenberg, Executive Producer
    Corina A. Sandru, Assistant
Specialties: Network; Cable; Made for TV Movies; Miniseries
Credits: The Crossing; Down in the Delta; Long Island Incident; Kingfish: A Story of Huey P. Long
First Look/Development Deals: Columbia TriStar Television

CINEMAGIC PRODUCTIONS
537 Jones St., Ste. 898
San Francisco, CA 94102
Phone: (510) 233-2002
(415) 207-5300
Fax: (510) 233-2247
cdupont@ureach.com
Key Executives/Personnel:
    Colyer Dupont, Producer & Director
    Catherine Lee, Production Manager
    Steve Young, Production Assistant
Specialties: Documentaries
Credits: MTV Music News; Office of the Future; Computer Magic; Computer Animation Magic
First Look/Development Deals: PBS

CIRCLE ASSOCIATES LTD.
P.O. Box 5730
Santa Monica, CA 90409
Phone: (310) 823-4024
Fax: (310) 574-1950
Key Executives/Personnel:
    Mike Kaplan, President
Specialties: Documentaries
Other Categories: Feature Film
Credits: Luck Trust & Ketchup; The Whales of August

DICK CLARK PRODUCTIONS, INC.
3003 W. Olive Ave.
Burbank, CA 91505
Phone: (818) 841-3003
Fax: (818) 954-8609
www.dickclarkproductions.com
Key Executives/Personnel:
    Dick Clark, CEO
    Francis La Maina, President
    Al Schwartz, Producer
    Barry Adelman, Producer & Writer
    Larry Klein, Producer
Specialties: Network; Cable
Credits: American Music Awards; Dick Clark's New Years Rockin' Eve; Golden Globe Awards; Your Big Break

CLIFDEN PRODUCTIONS
10880 Wilshire Blvd., Ste. 1101
Los Angeles, CA 90024
Phone: (310) 234-5074
Fax: (310) 234-5094
Key Executives/Personnel:
    Patricia Clifford, Executive Producer
    Brian Dennehy, Executive Producer
    Peter Karabats, Development Assistant
    Brian Farrah, Assistant
Specialties: Made for TV Movies; Miniseries
Credits: The Warden; Arthur Miller's Death of A Salesman; To Dance With the White Dog
First Look/Development Deals: Viacom Productions

COAST MEDIA TELEPRODUCTIONS, INC.
17062 Murphy Ave., Bldg. B
Irvine, CA 92614
Phone: (949) 417-0300
www.coastmedia.com
digipost@earthlink.net
Key Executives/Personnel:
    Art Royce, President, CEO & Producer
    Brian Ferguson, Director of Photography
    Joyce D. Smith, VP
    Donovan Smith, Audio Engineer
    Curtis Matovich, Editor & Composer
    Steve Hirai, Production Manager
    Becky Fisher, Account Manager
Specialties: Network; Cable; Documentaries
Other Categories: Commercials; Video; Music Video; Interactive Multimedia
Credits: Simple Green (infomercial); Milk Advisory Board (commercial); Meguiar's Wax (corp. video & commercial); Disney (corp. video)

COLLABORATIVE ARTISTS
445 S. Beverly Dr., Ste. 100
Beverly Hills, CA 90212

Production Companies – TV

Phone: ....(310) 274-4800
Fax: ....(310) 274-4803
www.collaborativeartists.com
labird@mindspring.com
Key Executives/Personnel:
  Steve Leon, no title
  Leslie A. Bird, no title
Specialties: Network; Cable; Made for TV Movies; Miniseries
Other Categories: Feature Film

COLOMBY/KEATON PRODUCTIONS
2110 Main St., Ste. 302
Santa Monica, CA 90405
Phone: ....(310) 399-8881
Fax: ....(310) 392-1323
www.colombykeaton.com
Key Executives/Personnel:
  Harry Colomby, Partner
  Michael Keaton, Partner
  Jennifer Keohane, Producer
  Helen Baines, Story Editor
  Ford Delman, Creative Associate
Specialties: Network; Cable; Animation; Documentaries; Made for TV Movies; Miniseries
Other Categories: Feature Film
Credits: Body Shots

COLUMBIA TRISTAR TELEVISION
9336 W. Washington Blvd.
Culver City, CA 90232
Phone: ....(310) 202-1234
www.spe.sony.com
Key Executives/Personnel:
  Len Gross, President
  Tom Mazza, President of Network Production
  Jeanie Bradley, Executive VP of Programming
  Edward Lammi, Executive VP of Production
  Don Loughery, Executive VP of Business Affairs
  Justin Pierce, Executive VP of Media Relations
  Sarah Timberman, Executive VP of Development
  Helen Verno, Executive VP of Movies & Miniseries
  Robert Hunka, Sr. VP of Music
  Joanne Mazzo, Sr. VP of Business Affairs
  Vicki Rosenberg, Sr. VP of Talent & Casting
  Steve Tann, Sr. VP of Programming
  Christina Friedgen, VP of Post Production
Specialties: Network; Cable; Documentaries; Made for TV Movies; Miniseries

COMEDY CENTRAL
2049 Century Park East, Ste. 2295
Los Angeles, CA 90067
Phone: ....(212) 767-8600
 ....(310) 201-9515
Fax: ....(212) 767-8592
Key Executives/Personnel:
  Larry Divney, President & CEO
  John Cucci, CFO & Sr. VP
  Bill Hilary, General Manager
  Shari Patrick, Sr. VP & General Counsel, Business & Legal Affairs
  Deborah Liebling, Sr. VP of Original Programming & Development
  Michele Ganeless, Sr. VP of Programming
  Joan Aceste, Sr. VP of Programming
  Richard de Croce, VP of Int'l.
  Beth Hisler, Sr. VP of Human Resources
  Lou Wallach, VP of Development
  Debbie Drimmer, VP of Talent
  Lauren Gray, VP of Production
  David Epstein, VP of Planning & Operations
Specialties: Cable; Animation

Credits: Dr. Katz; South Park; The Daily Show with Jon Stewart; The Man Show
Additional Info: 2049 Century Park East, Ste. 4170, Los Angeles, CA 90067

CONNECTION III ENTERTAINMENT CORP.
8489 W. 3rd St.
Los Angeles, CA 90048
Phone: ....(323) 653-3400
www.connection3.com
Key Executives/Personnel:
  Cleveland O'Neal, Producer
Specialties: Cable
Other Categories: Feature Film; Interactive Multimedia
Credits: What About Your Friends; The Garage Club; Phat Beach
Trade Assoc./Guilds/Unions: PGA

CORNICE ENTERTAINMENT
190 N. Cañon Dr., PH
Beverly Hills, CA 90210
Phone: ....(310) 777-0200
Fax: ....(310) 777-0357
Key Executives/Personnel:
  Michael Marcus, no title
  Carroll Kemp, no title
  Marcie Hartley, no title
Specialties: Network; Cable
Other Categories: Feature Film
First Look/Development Deals: The Buena Vista Motion Pictures Group

THE CORT/MADDEN COMPANY
5555 Melrose Ave., Marx Bros. Bldg., Ste. 107
Hollywood, CA 90038
Phone: ....(323) 956-5884
Fax: ....(323) 862-1408
Key Executives/Personnel:
  Robert Cort, Producer
  Scarlett Lacey, VP
  Eric Hertzel, Creative Executive
Specialties: Cable
Other Categories: Feature Film
Credits: Save The Last Dance; Runaway Bride; Out of Towners; Harlen County War
First Look/Development Deals: Paramount Pictures

COSGROVE-MEURER PRODUCTIONS
4303 W. Verdugo Ave.
Burbank, CA 91505
Phone: ....(818) 843-5600
Fax: ....(818) 843-8585
Key Executives/Personnel:
  Terry Meurer, Partner & President
  John Cosgrove, Partner & CEO
  Stuart Schwartz, VP of Reality Development
  Rebecca Whittington, VP of Development
  Joe Levi, Director of Feature Development
Specialties: Network; Cable; Made for TV Movies
Other Categories: Feature Film
Credits: Yesterday's Children; Unsolved Mysteries; The Inheritance

COSSETTE PRODUCTIONS
8899 Beverly Blvd., Ste. 100
Los Angeles, CA 90048
Phone: ....(310) 278-3366
Fax: ....(310) 278-6587
Key Executives/Personnel:
  Pierre Cossette, Chairman
  John Cossette, President
  Mary Cossette, VP

Production Companies – TV

Andrea Dossa, Coordinator
Specialties: Network; Cable
Credits: 1st Latin Grammy Awards; BET 20th Anniversary Special
Additional Info: Also produces Broadway Theater

CINDY COWAN ENTERTAINMENT, INC.
8265 Sunset Blvd., Ste. 205
Los Angeles, CA 90046
Phone: ....(323) 822-1082
Fax: ....(323) 822-1086
jjaggars@cowanent.com
Key Executives/Personnel:
  Cindy Cowan, President & Producer
  Carole McGorrian, Head of Production
  Josh R. Jaggars, Director of Development
Specialties: Network; Cable
Other Categories: Feature Film
Credits: Very Bad Things; Savior; Little City; Dr. T and the Women

CPC ENTERTAINMENT
840 N. Larrabee St., Ste. 2322
West Hollywood, CA 90069
Phone: ....(310) 652-8194
Fax: ....(310) 652-4998
www.cpcentertainment.com
chane@compuserve.com
Key Executives/Personnel:
  Peggy Chane, President, Producer & Director
  Clayton Herzog, Development Associate
  Louis Farber, Development Associate
  Sylvia De La Riviere, Development Associate
Specialties: Made for TV Movies
Other Categories: Feature Film
Credits: Eyes of a Stranger; River to Greyrock; Under the Mummy's Spell; Zero Hour
Trade Assoc./Guilds/Unions: ATAS, IFP, PGA, WIF

CRANE WEXELBLATT ENTERTAINMENT
6061 Galahad Dr.
Malibu, CA 90265
Phone: ....(310) 457-4821
Fax: ....(310) 457-3888
twomoguls@aol.com
Key Executives/Personnel:
  Peter Crane, Producer & Director
  Linda Curran Wexelblatt, Producer
Specialties: Cable; Made for TV Movies
Other Categories: Feature Film
Credits: Lily Dale; The Passion of Ayn Rand
Trade Assoc./Guilds/Unions: DGA

WES CRAVEN FILMS
11846 Ventura Blvd., Ste. 208
Studio City, CA 91604
Phone: ....(818) 752-0197
Fax: ....(818) 752-1789
Key Executives/Personnel:
  Wes Craven, Director & Producer
  Marianne Maddalena, President & Producer
  Rene Garcia, President of Production
  Alix Taylor, VP of Development
Specialties: Network
Other Categories: Feature Film
Credits: Scream 1, 2 & 3; Music of the Heart
First Look/Development Deals: Miramax Films

CREATIVE IMPULSE ENTERTAINMENT
4524 Tujunga Ave., Ste. 15
Studio City, CA 91602
Phone: ....(818) 623-8260

Key Executives/Personnel:
  Rockne S. O'Bannon, Executive Producer, Director & Writer
  Robin Johannsen, VP of Development
Specialties: Network; Cable; Made for TV Movies
Other Categories: Feature Film
Credits: Farscape; Seaquest

CRUSADER ENTERTAINMENT
132B Laskey Dr.
Beverly Hills, CA 90212
Phone: ....(310) 248-6360
Fax: ....(310) 248-6370
Key Executives/Personnel:
  Howard Baldwin, President
  Stuart Benjamin, Executive VP
  Karen Baldwin, Executive VP of Creative Affairs
  Jennifer Smith, VP of Television
Specialties: Network; Cable; Made for TV Movies
Other Categories: Feature Film
Credits: Mystery Alaska; Gidion; La Bamba; Everybody's All American

CRYSTAL PYRAMID PRODUCTIONS
7323 Rondel Ct.
San Diego, CA 92119
Phone: ....(619) 644-3000
....(619) 293-9500
www.crystalpyramid.com
cpp@newuniquevideos.com
Key Executives/Personnel:
  Mark Schulze, CEO
  Patty Mooney, COO
  Mike Freeman, Producer
  Michael Sterner, Producer
Specialties: Network; Cable
Other Categories: Video
Credits: IBM; Coca-Cola

D.L.T. ENTERTAINMENT LTD.
1888 Century Park East, Ste. 1900
Los Angeles, CA 90067
Phone: ....(323) 937-1144
Fax: ....(323) 937-5095
Key Executives/Personnel:
  Don Taffner Jr., Executive VP
  Emmet G. Lavery Jr., VP of Business Affairs
Specialties: Network; Cable
Credits: Three's Company; Too Close For Comfort; As Time Goes By; Wanted

DALRYMPLE PRODUCTIONS
150 E. Meda Ave., Ste. 100
Glendora, CA 91741
Phone: ....(626) 963-5588
www.dalpro.com
james@dalpro.com
Key Executives/Personnel:
  James Dalrymple, Producer
Specialties: Animation; Documentaries
Other Categories: Commercials; Video

DAPTV ASSOCIATES
9080 Santa Monica Blvd.
West Hollywood, CA 90069
Phone: ....(310) 860-9001
....(877) 860-9003
Fax: ....(310) 860-9003
www.daptv.com
info@daptv.com
Key Executives/Personnel:
  Don Azars, Writer, Director & Executive Producer

Production Companies – TV

Michael Berman, Producer
Specialties: Cable; Documentaries
Other Categories: Commercials; Video; Music Video
Credits: The Edge and Beyond; Crisis Counselor; Carroll, Her First Special

DARK HORSE ENTERTAINMENT
100 Universal City Plaza, John Ford Bldg., Ste. 3G
Universal City, CA 91608
Phone: (818) 777-5830
Fax: (818) 866-5939
www.dhorse.com
Key Executives/Personnel:
Mike Richardson, President & Producer
Steven Gilder, VP of Production
Kevin Hageman, Creative Executive
Specialties: Network; Cable; Animation; Miniseries
Other Categories: Feature Film
Credits: The Mask; Time Cop; Mystery Men; Big Guy & Rusty
First Look/Development Deals: Universal Pictures

DAVIS CLASSICS
c/o Davis Entertainment, 2121 Ave. of the Stars, Ste. 2900
Los Angeles, CA 90067
Phone: (310) 551-2266
Fax: (310) 556-3760
Key Executives/Personnel:
J. Todd Harris, Producer
Jourdan Krauss, VP of Development
Craig Roth, VP of Production
Corey Witte, Creative Executive
Nichols Thurkettle, Story Editor
Specialties: Network; Cable
Other Categories: Feature Film
Credits: Urbania; Digging to China; Bad Manners; Denise Calls Up

DAVIS ENTERTAINMENT CO.
2121 Ave. of the Stars, Ste. 2900
Los Angeles, CA 90067
Phone: (310) 556-3550
Fax: (310) 556-3688
Key Executives/Personnel:
John A. Davis, Chairman
Paul Spadone, President of Series TV
Teddy Zee, President of Features
Brooke Brooks, Executive VP of Administration
Wyck Godfrey, Executive VP of Production & Development
Liz Phillips, Creative Executive
Amy Palmer, Director of Development, TV
Chris Aldrich, Assistant to Mr. Davis
Specialties: Network; Cable; Made for TV Movies
Other Categories: Feature Film
Credits: Predator; Courage Under Fire; Grumpy Old Men; Breakers
First Look/Development Deals: Twentieth Century Fox Television

DAYBREAK PRODUCTIONS
100 Universal City Plaza, Bungalow 4172
Universal City, CA 91608
Phone: (818) 777-0277
Fax: (818) 866-0285
Key Executives/Personnel:
Charles Gordon, Producer
Marc Sternberg, President
James Abraham, Assistant to Mr. Gordon
Andrew Hong, Assistant to Mr. Sternberg
Specialties: Network
Other Categories: Feature Film
Credits: Die Hard 1 & 2; Waterworld; Field of Dreams; October Sky
First Look/Development Deals: Universal Pictures

DEJA VIEW PRODUCTIONS, INC.
7603 Atron Ave.
West Hills, CA 91304
Phone: (818) 704-9185
Fax: (818) 704-6001
dejavprods@aol.com
Key Executives/Personnel:
Robyn Evans-Jones, Producer & Partner
Dennis E. Jones, Producer, UPM & Partner
Specialties: Network; Cable
Other Categories: Feature Film
Credits: The Flintstones in Viva Rock Vegas; Glory, Glory (TV pilot); OutBreak; Pacific Heights
Trade Assoc./Guilds/Unions: DGA

DENALI PRODUCTIONS, INC.
Studio One, 6743 Fernhill Dr.
Malibu, CA 90265
Phone: (310) 457-7566
Fax: (310) 457-5789
www.denaliproductions.com
bcarmic@earthlink.net
Key Executives/Personnel:
Doug Millington, Executive Producer
Bobby Carmichael, Director
Specialties: Documentaries
Other Categories: Feature Film; Commercials; Video
Credits: Merrill-Lynch (commercial); Sprite (commercial); Cadillac (commercial); Dayton 500 (documentary)

DESERT HEART PRODUCTIONS
685 Venice Blvd.
Venice, CA 90291
Phone: (310) 399-0013
Fax: (310) 396-4047
ddietchco@aol.com
Key Executives/Personnel:
Donna Deitch, Director & Producer
Scott Foundas, Assistant to Ms. Deitch
Specialties: Network; Cable; Made for TV Movies; Miniseries
Other Categories: Feature Film
Credits: Desert Hearts; Angel on My Shoulder

DI NOVI PICTURES
3110 Main St., Ste. 220
Santa Monica, CA 90405
Phone: (310) 581-1355
Fax: (310) 399-0499
Key Executives/Personnel:
Denise Di Novi, Producer
Ed McDonnell, President
Alison Greenspan, VP of Development
Specialties: Network; Miniseries
Other Categories: Feature Film
Credits: Little Women; Ed Wood; Edward Scissorhands

DIC ENTERTAINMENT
303 N. Glenoaks Blvd., 4th Fl.
Burbank, CA 91502
Phone: (818) 955-5400
Fax: (818) 955-5696
Key Executives/Personnel:
Andy Heyward, President & CEO
Jeff Wernick, Executive VP of Operations & COO
Robby London, Executive VP of Creative Affairs
Kaaren Brown, Executive Director of Creative Affairs
Michael Maliani, Executive VP of Development
Stacey Gallishaw, VP of Production
Specialties: Network; Cable; Animation
Other Categories: Feature Film

Production Companies – TV

Credits: Meet the Deedles; Carmen San Diego; Inspector Gadget; Madeline

LOUIS DIGIAIMO & ASSOCIATES
214 Sullivan St., Ste. 2C
New York, NY 10012
Phone: ....(212) 253-5510
Fax: ....(212) 253-5540
l.digiaimo@att.net
Key Executives/Personnel:
    Louis DiGiaimo, Producer
    Lou DiGiaimo Jr., Producer
    Stephanie Corsalini, Director of Development
Specialties: Network; Made for TV Movies
Other Categories: Feature Film
Credits: Donnie Brasco; Falcone; Everlasting Piece; Dinner Rush
Additional Info: Also casting director

DISCOVERY NETWORKS/DISCOVERY COMMUNICATIONS, INC.
7700 Wisconsin Ave.
Bethesda, MD 20814
Phone: ....(301) 986-1999
www.discovery.com
Key Executives/Personnel:
    John S. Hendricks, Founder, Chairman & CEO
    Judith A. McHale, President & COO
    Greg Durig, Executive VP & CFO
    Michela English, President & COO, Discovery.com
    Johnathan Rodgers, President
    Dawn L. McCall, President, Discovery Int'l.
    Donald D. Wear, President, Int'l. Policy
    Donald A. Baer, Executive VP
    Daniel Fischer, Executive VP of Corporate Technology & Content Services
    Mark Hollinger, Executive VP & General Counsel
    Pandit Wright, Executive VP of Human Resources & Administration
Specialties: Cable; Documentaries
Credits: Walking With Dinosaurs; Raising the Mammoth

WALT DISNEY TELEVISION ANIMATION
500 S. Buena Vista Street
Burbank, CA 91521
Phone: ....(818) 560-5000
www.disney.com
Key Executives/Personnel:
    Barry Blumberg, Executive VP
    Sharon Morrill, Executive VP
    David Stainton, Executive VP
    Lenora Hume, Sr. VP of Production
    Matt Walker, Sr. VP of Music
    Mark Kenchelian, Sr. VP of Business & Legal Affairs
    Joanna Spak, Sr. VP of Finance
    Lisa Salamone, VP of Television Production
    Ellen Gurney, VP of Video Premieres
    Brian Snedeker, VP of Video Premieres
    Cheryl Murphy, VP of Post Production
    Roy Price, VP of Television Series
    Paul Rappaport, VP of Finance
    Lori Tellez, VP of Publicity
    Joyce Miller, Video Premieres Production
Specialties: Network; Cable; Animation

THE DISNEY CHANNEL
3800 W. Alameda Ave.
Burbank, CA 91505
Phone: ....(818) 569-7500
Fax: ....(818) 842-7611
www.disneychannel.com
Key Executives/Personnel:
    Anne Sweeney, President
    Eleo Hensleigh, Executive VP of Marketing
    Frederick Kuperberg, Executive VP of Business & Legal Affairs
    Gary K. Marsh, Executive VP of Original Programming
    Rich Ross, General Manager & Executive VP of Programming & Production
    Ben Pyne, Sr. VP of Affiliate Sales & Marketing (NY)
    Jill Casagrande, VP of Program Planning & Scheduling
    Jewel Engstrom, VP of Planning & Control
    Michael Healy, VP of Original Movies
    Susette Hsiung, VP of Production
    Chuck Kent, VP of Business Affairs
    Maria T. Mason, VP of Creative Services
    Patricia Wilber, VP of New Business Development (NY)
    Vincent H. Roberts, VP of Engineering & Operations
    Adina Savin, VP of Business & Legal Affairs
    Carol Sussman, VP of Acquired Programming
    Tina Treadwell, VP of Talent & Alternative Programming
    Sandra Wax, VP of Research & Planning
    Susie Norris-Epstein, Creative Executive
Specialties: Cable

DISNEY TELEFILMS
2020 Avenue of the Stars
Los Angeles, CA 90067
Phone: ....(310) 557-7777
Fax: ....(310) 557-6747
www.disney.com
Key Executives/Personnel:
    Nancy D. Bennett, VP of Production
    Joe Del Hierro, VP of Development & Production
    Donna Ebbs, VP of Development & Production
Specialties: Network
Credits: The Wonderful World of Disney

DISTANT HORIZON
8282 Sunset Blvd., Ste. A
Los Angeles, CA 90046
Phone: ....(323) 848-4140
Fax: ....(323) 848-4144
www.distant-horizon.com
distanth@pacbell.net
Key Executives/Personnel:
    Avant Singh, President
    Brian Cox, Producer
    Tyler Steele, Production Coordinator
Specialties: Network; Documentaries
Other Categories: Feature Film
Credits: The Theory of Flight; Twin Dragons; Cry The Beloved Country; Get Real

THE DONNERS' COMPANY
Phone: ....(818) 954-3611
................................(818) 954-3961
Fax: ....(818) 954-3475
Key Executives/Personnel:
    Lauren Shuler Donner, Producer
    Richard Donner, Producer & Director
    Julie Durk, Development Executive
    Michael Aguilar, Development Executive
Specialties: Network
Other Categories: Feature Film
Credits: Leathal Weapon 1, 2 & 3; Free Willy 1, 2 & 3; X-Men; Dave
First Look/Development Deals: Warner Bros., NBC Entertainment, Inc.

DOUBLE WHAMMY PRODUCTIONS
345 N. Maple Dr., Ste. 280
Beverly Hills, CA 90210
Phone: ....(310) 859-8853
Fax: ....(310) 859-2490
wickeddest@aol.com
Key Executives/Personnel:
    Pamela Beck, Producer & Writer
Specialties: Network; Animation; Documentaries; Made for TV Movies; Miniseries

Credits: Rich Men, Single Women
Trade Assoc./Guilds/Unions: WGAw

JEAN DOUMANIAN PRODUCTIONS
595 Madison Ave., Ste. 2200
New York, NY 10022
Phone: ....(212) 486-2626
Fax: ....(212) 688-6236
Key Executives/Personnel:
  Jean Doumanian, Producer & President
  John Logigian, VP of Business Affairs
  Adam Schlesinger, Director of Development
  Kimberly Jose, Story Editor
Specialties: Network; Cable; Made for TV Movies
Other Categories: Feature Film
Credits: Small Time Crooks; Sweet & Lowdown; The Spanish Prisoner; Everyone Says I Love You

DREAMWORKS SKG
100 Universal Plaza, Bldg. 10
Universal City, CA 91608
Phone: ....(818) 733-7000
Fax: ....(848) 733-7574
www.dreamworks.com
Key Executives/Personnel:
  Steven Spielberg, Principal
  Jeffrey Katzenberg, Principal
  David Geffen, Principal
  Helene Hahn, Legal
  Ron Nelson, Finance
  Laurie MacDonald, Production
  Walter Parkers, Production
  Ann Daly, Animation & Home Video
  Adam Goodman, Theatrical Production
  Marc Haimes, Theatrical Production
  Leah Keith, Theatrical Production
  Damien Stevenson, Theatrical Production
  Mark Sourian, Theatrical Production
  Paul Lister, Theatrical Production
  Glenn Williamson, Theatrical Production
  Michael Grillo, Production
  Andrea McCall, Production
  Leslee Feldman, Production
  Steve Molen, Production
  Terry Press, Marketing
  Jim Tharp, Theatrical Distribution
  Brian Edwards, Legal Affairs, Motion Pictures
  Andy Spahn, Corporate Affairs
  Dan McDermott, TV
  Justin Falvey, TV
  Darryl Frank, TV
  Hal Richardson, TV Worldwide & Pay TV
  Michael Ostin, Music
  Mo Ostin, Music
  Lenny Waronker, Music
  Tony Hull, Finance
  Laura Fox, Theatrical Business Affairs
  Art Frazier, Theatrical Business Affairs
  Alan Myerson, Animation Business Affairs
  Barbara Zipperman, Animation Business Affairs
  Pamela Baron, TV Business Affairs
  Anne Globe, Consumer Products
  Brad Globe, Consumer Products
Specialties: Network; Cable; Animation
Other Categories: Feature Film

DREYFUSS/JAMES PRODUCTIONS
1041 Formosa Ave., Pickford Bldg., Rm. 110
West Hollywood, CA 90046
Phone: ....(323) 850-3140
Fax: ....(323) 850-3141
Key Executives/Personnel:
  Richard Dreyfuss, Partner & Executive Producer
  Judith James, Partner & Executive Producer
  Greg Szimonisz, Director of Development
  Audrey Bamber, Assistant
Specialties: Network; Cable; Made for TV Movies
Other Categories: Feature Film
Credits: Having Our Say; Mr. Holland's Opus; Quiz Show

E! ENTERTAINMENT TELEVISION
5750 Wilshire Blvd.
Los Angeles, CA 90036
Phone: ....(323) 954-2400
Fax: ....(323) 954-2660
www.eonline.com
Key Executives/Personnel:
  Greg Brannan, Executive VP of Programming
  Jon Helmrich, Sr. VP of Int'l. Development
  John Rieber, Sr. VP of Original Programming
  Marta Tracy, Sr. VP, Style Network
  Jeff Lai, Sr. VP of Business & Legal Affairs
  Lisa Kaye, Sr. VP of Human Resources
  Lynn Deegan, VP of Development
  Bill Lee, VP of Int'l. Development
  Betsy Rott, VP of Original Programming
  Gary Snegaroff, VP of Original Programming
  Jennifer Davis, VP of Advertising Sales
  Gail McClellan, Director of Corporate Planning
Specialties: Cable; Documentaries; Made for TV Movies

E.M.E., INC.
Phone: ....(310) 330-8841
emeinc@earthlink.net
Specialties: Animation; Made for TV Movies
Other Categories: Feature Film; Commercials; Music Video; Interactive Multimedia

EDMONDS ENTERTAINMENT
1635 N. Cahuenga Blvd., 5th Fl.
Los Angeles, CA 90028
Phone: ....(416) 630-3825
Fax: ....(323) 860-1554
Key Executives/Personnel:
  Tracey Edmonds, President & CEO
  Kenneth "Babyface" Edmonds, President & CEO
  Bridget D. Davis, VP of Film
  Patrick-Ian Polk, VP of E2 Filmworks
  Shelia Ducksworth, Director of Development
Specialties: Network; Cable
Other Categories: Feature Film
Credits: Soul Food (feature); Hav Plenty; Light It Up; Soul Food (TV series)
First Look/Development Deals: Fox 2000 Productions

RONA EDWARDS PRODUCTIONS
264 S. La Cienega Blvd., Ste. 1052
Beverly Hills, CA 90211
Phone: ....(323) 466-3013
Fax: ....(323) 467-1258
Key Executives/Personnel:
  Rona Edwards, Producer & Manager
Specialties: Network; Cable; Made for TV Movies; Miniseries
Other Categories: Feature Film
Credits: Out of Sync; I Know What You Did; The Companion; One Special Victory

RALPH EDWARDS/STU BILLETT PRODUCTIONS
6922 Hollywood Blvd., Ste. 415
Hollywood, CA 90028
Phone: ....(323) 462-2212

Production Companies – TV

Fax: ....(323) 461-1224
Key Executives/Personnel:
 Ralph Edwards, Partner & Executive Producer
 Stu Billett, Partner & Executive Producer
 Gary Edwards, VP & Executive Producer
 James B. Pollock, COO & General Counsel
 Barbara Dunn-Leonard, Executive Producer
Specialties: Network; Cable
Other Categories: Feature Film
Credits: The People's Court

EL NORTE PRODUCTIONS
8701 W. Olympic Blvd.
Los Angeles, CA 90035
Phone: ....(310) 360-1194
Fax: ....(310) 360-1199
Key Executives/Personnel:
 Gregory Nava, Director & Producer
 Barbara Martinez-Jitner, VP of TV
 Darlene Caamano, Sr. VP of Development & Production
 Laura Flores, Production & Development Assistant
Specialties: Network; Documentaries
Other Categories: Feature Film
Credits: El Norte; Selena; Mi Familia; Why Do Fools Fall in Love
First Look/Development Deals: New Line Cinema, Inc.

ELEPHANT WALK ENTERTAINMENT
Phone: ....(310) 887-3977
elephantwalk@earthlink.net
Key Executives/Personnel:
 Doug McHenry, Producer & Director
 Lana Campbell, Director of Development
Specialties: Network; Cable; Made for TV Movies
Other Categories: Feature Film
Credits: The Brothaz; Mr. Murder; Malcolm & Eddie; Thin Line Between Love and Hate
Additional Info: Office address subject to change.

ELEVENTH DAY ENTERTAINMENT
17003 Ventura Blvd., Ste. 200
Encino, CA 91316
Phone: ....(818) 784-6403
Fax: ....(818) 784-6421
www.eleventhday.com
mail@eleventhday.com
Key Executives/Personnel:
 Frank Martin, Producer & Director
 Rudy Poe, Producer & Director
Specialties: Network; Cable; Documentaries
Other Categories: Commercials; Video
Credits: CBS: The First Fifty Years; John Houston: The Man, The Movies, The Maverick; US Department of Defense; Balance Bars

EMK PRODUCTIONS
1401 Ocean Ave., Ste. 300
Santa Monica, CA 90401
Phone: ....(310) 260-3362
Fax: ....(310) 260-3343
aweiss@regententertainment.com
Key Executives/Personnel:
 Ellen Krass, President
 Karen Frost, Director of Development
Specialties: Cable; Documentaries; Made for TV Movies; Miniseries
Other Categories: Feature Film
Credits: Lesson Before Dying; Other People's Money; Intimate Portrait: Jackie Onassis; The Kathy & Mo Show
First Look/Development Deals: Regent Entertainment, Inc.

PETER ENGEL PRODUCTIONS
330 Bob Hope Dr., Ste. C-113
Burbank, CA 91523
Phone: ....(818) 840-7780
Key Executives/Personnel:
 Peter Engel, Chairman & CEO
 Lisa Mancuso, President & COO
 Kerry Holmwood, VP
 Brittany Levin, Manager
 Rebecca McGill, Coordinator
 Elaine Metaxas, Talent Coordinator
Specialties: Network; Cable
Credits: Malibu, CA; Saved by the Bell; California Dreams; Hang Time

ENSEMBLE ENTERTAINMENT
10474 Santa Monica Blvd., Ste. 380
Los Angeles, CA 90025
Phone: ....(310) 882-8900
Fax: ....(310) 882-8901
jbdead@aol.com
Key Executives/Personnel:
 Jon Brown, Producer & Manager
 Brian Jarvis, Assistant
Specialties: Cable; Made for TV Movies
Other Categories: Feature Film
Credits: The Tie That Binds
First Look/Development Deals: Showtime, Warner Bros. Television Productions

ENTERAKTION, INC.
2401 E. Atlantic Blvd., Ste. 410
Pompano Beach, FL 33062
Phone: ....(954) 785-5070
Fax: ....(954) 785-5042
www.enteraktion.com
enteraktion@enteraktion.com
Key Executives/Personnel:
 Tom Walsh, Producer, Co-Chairman & CEO
 Ronald Hilton, Producer & Co-Chairman
 Adriana Walsh, Producer & Sr. VP
 Claire Le Covac, Director of Marketing
 Michael Laughlin, Digital Director
 Lloyd Gross, Producer
Specialties: Network; Animation
Other Categories: Feature Film; Interactive Multimedia
Credits: Denial; We Dare You!; House to House; Mismatch

ENTERTAINMENT TELEVISION SERVICES, INC.
930 S. Bedford St., Ste. 2
Los Angeles, CA 90035
Phone: ....(310) 360-9600
Fax: ....(310) 360-9696
www.celebrityfootage.com
etsgoldberg@mediaone.net
Key Executives/Personnel:
 Michael Goldberg, no title
Specialties: Network; Cable; Documentaries

EPIPHANY PRODUCTIONS, INC.
10625 Esther Ave.
Los Angeles, CA 90064
Phone: ....(310) 815-1266
 ....(310) 505-1133
Fax: ....(310) 815-1269
roadog@concentric.net
Key Executives/Personnel:
 Dan Halperin, Producer
 Mark Frazel, Director of Development
 Scott JT Frank, Producer
 Karen Anderson, Line Producer
Specialties: Documentaries

Other Categories: Feature Film; Video
First Look/Development Deals: Liberty International Entertainment

ERRATIC ENTERTAINMENT, INC.
1131 Alta Loma Rd., Ste. 331
Los Angeles, CA 90069
Phone: ....(310) 657-0922
Fax: ....(310) 657-1360
erraticent@aol.com
Key Executives/Personnel:
  Graham Ludlow, Producer & Partner
  Sam Okun, Producer & Partner
  Matt Miller, Creative Executive
  Tom Damien, Director of Development
  Arlene Pachasa, Assistant to Producers
Specialties: Network; Cable; Documentaries; Made for TV Movies; Miniseries
Other Categories: Feature Film
Credits: The Call of the Wild; Anya's Bell

ESPARZA-KATZ PRODUCTIONS
8899 Beverly Blvd., Ste. 506
Los Angeles, CA 90048
Phone: ....(310) 281-3770
Fax: ....(310) 281-3770
esparzakatz@msn.com
Key Executives/Personnel:
  Moctesuma Esparza, Producer
  Robert Katz, Producer
Specialties: Network; Cable; Documentaries; Made for TV Movies; Miniseries
Other Categories: Feature Film
Credits: Gettysberg; Selena; Introducing Dorothy Dandridge

EVOLUTION FILM
Phone: ....(805) 386-1285
Fax: ....(805) 386-1295
ifilmr@aol.com
Key Executives/Personnel:
  Anita Untersee, Producer
  Chuck Untersee, Director & Cameraman
Specialties: Cable
Credits: National Geographic: International Kidnapping

FACE BROADCAST PRODUCTIONS
3921 W. Magnolia Blvd.
Burbank, CA 91505
Phone: ....(818) 842-9081
Fax: ....(818) 842-3708
www.facebroadcast.com
face@facebroadcast.com
Key Executives/Personnel:
  Jamie Celeste Tullo, Partner
  Ron Malvin, Partner
  Keith Leon, Audio & Video Engineer
  Ellen Rubel, Graphics
Specialties: Network; Cable; Documentaries
Other Categories: Video
Credits: The Alameda Corridor (LA County); Totally Cool Business News
Trade Assoc./Guilds/Unions: ATAS, NATPE

FAIR DINKUM PRODUCTIONS
2500 Broadway St., Bldg. E-5018
Santa Monica, CA 90404
Phone: ....(310) 586-8471
Fax: ....(310) 586-8469
Key Executives/Personnel:
  Henry Winkler, Executive Producer, Director & Actor
  Michele McCole Moss, Executive Assistant to Mr. Winkler
Specialties: Network; Cable
Other Categories: Feature Film
Credits: MacGyver; Sightings; Dead Man's Gun; So Weird

FAST CARRIER PICTURES
c/o Showtime, 10880 Wilshire Blvd., Ste. 1500
Los Angeles, CA 90024
Phone: ....(310) 234-5376
Fax: ....(310) 234-5393
steve.rubin@showtime.net
Key Executives/Personnel:
  Steven Jay Rubin, President
  Rory J. Aylward, VP of Development
Specialties: Network; Cable; Made for TV Movies
Other Categories: Feature Film
Credits: Combat!; The Errand Boy; The Battle of Hollywood

FAT CHANCE FILMS
3751 Motor Ave., Ste. 928
Los Angeles, CA 90034
Phone: ....(323) 882-4130
bobmardis2@aol.com
Key Executives/Personnel:
  Bobby Mardis, Producer & Director
Specialties: Cable
Other Categories: Feature Film; Video; Music Video
Credits: Midnight Blue; Circle of Pain; Why Colors; One Last Time
Trade Assoc./Guilds/Unions: DGA, WGAw

THE EDWARD S. FELDMAN CO.
500 S. Buena Vista St.
Burbank, CA 91521
Phone: ....(818) 972-3304
Fax: ....(818) 972-3309
esfeldman@aol.com
Key Executives/Personnel:
  Winship Cook, Creative Associate
Specialties: Made for TV Movies
Other Categories: Feature Film
Credits: 102 Dalmations; The Truman Show; Witness; The Doctor

FENADY ASSOCIATES, INC.
249 N. Larchmont Blvd., Ste. 6
Los Angeles, CA 90004
Phone: ....(323) 466-6375
Fax: ....(323) 466-6376
Key Executives/Personnel:
  Andrew J. Fenady, President
  Duke Fenady, VP of Creative Affairs
Specialties: Network; Cable; Made for TV Movies
Other Categories: Feature Film
Credits: The Man With Bogart's Face; The Love She Sought; Yes Virginia, There is a Santa Claus; The Sea Wolf

ADAM FIELDS PRODUCTIONS
10390 Santa Monica Blvd., Ste. 350
Los Angeles, CA 90025
Phone: ....(310) 552-8244
Fax: ....(310) 552-8247
Key Executives/Personnel:
  Adam Fields, President
  John Harman, VP of Creative Affairs
Specialties: Network; Cable
Other Categories: Feature Film
Credits: Ravenous; Money Train; Brokedown Palace; Great Balls of Fire
First Look/Development Deals: Twentieth Century Fox

FILM ROMAN, INC.
12020 Chandler Blvd., Ste. 300
North Hollywood, CA 91607
Phone: ....(818) 761-2544
Fax: ....(818) 985-2973
www.filmroman.com

Production Companies – TV

John Hyde, CEO
Michael Minchester, CFO
Peter Schankowitz, President of TV Programming & Development
Mitch Solomon, President of Features
Uriel Sigala, CTO
Sidney Clifton, VP of TV
Kathee Schneider, VP of Commercial Division
Eric Radomski, Creative Director
Mike Wolf, Head of Animation Production
Specialties: Network; Animation
Other Categories: Feature Film
Credits: The Simpsons; King of the Hill; My First Mister (feature); Level13.net

THE FILM SYNDICATE
7214 Melrose Ave.
Los Angeles, CA 90046
Phone: ....(323) 938-8080
Fax: ....(323) 938-8183
fsyndicate@aol.com
Key Executives/Personnel:
Bryan Johnson, Executive Producer & Director
Specialties: Network; Cable
Other Categories: Commercials; Music Video
Credits: Fox (promos); Dr. Pepper; Melrose Place Specials; U2 - Streets Have No Name
Trade Assoc./Guilds/Unions: DGA

FIREWORKS TELEVISION
1041 N. Formosa Ave.
Los Angeles, CA 90046
Phone: ....(323) 850-2470
Fax: ....(323) 850-2462
Key Executives/Personnel:
Jay Firestone, Chairman & CEO
Adam Haight, President & COO
Robb Dalton, President
David Tibbets, VP
Erika Grenadier, Manager
Specialties: Network; Cable; Made for TV Movies; Miniseries
Credits: RoboCop: Prime Directives; Queen of Swords; Poison; Relic Hunter
Additional Info: A division of Fireworks Entertainment, 111 George St., 3rd Fl., Toronto, ON M5A 2N4 Canada

FIRST AVENUE FILMS
567 MossHill Rd.
Orcas, WA 98280
Phone: ....(360) 376-3737
www.firstavenuefilms.com
info@firstavenuefilms.com
Key Executives/Personnel:
John G. Ginnes, Executive Producer
Leslie Kahan, Executive Producer
Specialties: Documentaries
Other Categories: Feature Film; Commercials
Credits: Madonna - You Must Love Me; Out Of The Silence; Anheuser-Busch
Trade Assoc./Guilds/Unions: AICP, DGA

FLIP YOUR LID, INC.
23501 Park Sorrento, Ste. 207
Calabasas, CA 91302
Phone: ....(818) 222-0700
Fax: ....(818) 222-9166
www.flipyourlid.com
jay@flipyourlid.com
Key Executives/Personnel:
Steve Soffer, Co-President & Executive Producer
Jay Jacoby, Co-President & Creative Director

Gay Murdock, Controller
John Kokum, Producer
Specialties: Animation
Other Categories: Feature Film; Interactive Multimedia
Credits: Forty & Shorty; Undercover Brother; Shapes

FLOWER FILMS, INC.
9220 Sunset Blvd., Ste. 309
Los Angeles, CA 90069
Phone: ....(310) 285-0200
Fax: ....(310) 285-0827
Key Executives/Personnel:
Drew Barrymore, Partner
Nancy Juvonen, Partner
Stephanie Savage, VP of Development
Linda McDonough, Director of Development, TV & New Media
Specialties: Network; Cable
Other Categories: Feature Film
Credits: Charlie's Angels; Never Been Kissed; Donnie Darko; Olive, the Other Reindeer
First Look/Development Deals: Fox 2000 Productions

FOREST HILLS PICTURES
P.O. Box 49694
Los Angeles, CA 90049
Phone: ....(310) 207-6462
www.foresthillspictures.com
howeis@aol.com
Key Executives/Personnel:
Howard Weisman, President & Executive Producer
Specialties: Network; Cable; Made for TV Movies; Miniseries
Other Categories: Feature Film; Video
Credits: Lovestruck

FORWARD PASS, INC.
12233 W. Olympic Blvd., Ste. 340
Los Angeles, CA 90064
Phone: ....(310) 571-3443
Key Executives/Personnel:
Michael Mann, Writer, Producer & Director
Michael Schulman, VP of Development & Production
Nancy Peardon, VP of Business Affairs
Specialties: Network; Made for TV Movies; Miniseries
Other Categories: Feature Film
Credits: Insider; Heat; Last of the Mohicans; Ali
First Look/Development Deals: The Walt Disney Pictures/ Touchstone Pictures

DAVID FOSTER PRODUCTIONS
4000 Warner Blvd., Producers Bldg. 1, Ste. 211
Burbank, CA 91522
Phone: ....(818) 954-4113
Fax: ....(818) 954-4449
Key Executives/Personnel:
David Foster, Producer
Pierre Weidemann, Director of Development
Specialties: Network; Cable
Other Categories: Feature Film
Credits: Hearts War; The Mask of Zorro; The River Wild; The Getaway 1 & 2

FOUNDATION ENTERTAINMENT
8800 Venice Blvd., Ste. 217
Los Angeles, CA 90034
Phone: ....(310) 204-4686
Fax: ....(310) 204-4603
www.foundent.com
Key Executives/Personnel:
John Manulis, President
Steve Przybylowski, Development
Specialties: Network; Cable; Made for TV Movies

Production Companies – TV

Other Categories: Feature Film
Credits: Daybreak; Swing Kids

FOUNTAINHEAD PICTURES
8670 Burton Way, Ste. 319
Los Angeles, CA 90048
Phone: ....(310) 276-5583
Fax: ....(310) 276-5583
fountpix@pacbell.net
Key Executives/Personnel:
    Aaron J. Shuster, Director, Writer & Producer
    Kimberly Norton, Producer & Manager
    Jonathan King, Creative Affairs
    Morgan Richards, Assistant
Specialties: Network
Other Categories: Feature Film
Credits: Pictures At The Beach; Straight & Narrow; Sandor; Baraba

FOUR SQUARE PRODUCTIONS, INC.
5205 Kearny Villa Way
San Diego, CA 92123
Phone: ....(858) 874-1900
www.foursq.com
Key Executives/Personnel:
    John DeBello, Director
    Scott Sorensen, Sr. Producer
    David Craven, Sr. Producer
Specialties: Cable; Animation
Other Categories: Feature Film; Commercials; Video
Credits: This Week in Sports; SPA War (video); SignOnSanDiego.com; The Guide

FOX BROADCASTING COMPANY
10201 W. Pico Blvd.
Los Angeles, CA 90035
Phone: ....(310) 369-1000
www.fox.com
Key Executives/Personnel:
    Rupert Murdoch, Chairman & CEO, News Corp.
    Peter Chernin, President & COO, News Corp./Chairman & CEO, Fox Group
    Chase Carey, COO, News Corp./Chairman & CEO, Fox Television
    Sandy Grushow, Chairman, Fox Television Group
    Mitch Stern, Chairman & CEO, Fox Television Stations
    Gail Berman, President of Entertainment
    David Nevins, Executive VP of Comedy & Drama Series
    Marci Pool, Executive VP of Movies & Miniseries
    Mike Darnell, Executive VP of Specials & Alternative Programming
    Ira Kurgan, Executive VP of Network Business Operations
    Preston Beckman, Executive VP of Strategic Program Planning
    Eric Yeldell, Executive VP of Legal Affairs
    Del Mayberry, Sr. VP & CFO
    Danielle Gelber, Sr. VP of Drama Series Programming
    Karen Fox, Sr. VP of Business Affairs
    Minna Taylor, Sr. VP of Legal Affairs
    Suzanne Horenstein, Sr. VP of Scheduling
    Robert Harbin, Sr. VP of Talent & Casting
    Missy Halperin, Sr. VP of Talent Relations
    Charles Kennedy, VP of Programming
    Craig Erwich, VP of Current Drama Programming
    Lance Taylor, VP of Current Comedy Programming
    Cheryl Bloch, VP of Drama Development
    Kelly Kulchak, VP of Comedy Development
    Kary McHoul, VP of Alternative Programming & Late Night Development
    Tom Sheets, VP of Special Programming
    MJ LaVaccare, VP of Scheduling
    Marisa Fermin, VP of Business Affairs
    Sandy Gong, VP of Finance
    Mindy Hahn, VP of Program & Market Research
Specialties: Network

FOX FAMILY CHANNEL
10960 Wilshire Blvd.
Los Angeles, CA 90024
Phone: ....(310) 235-9700
Fax: ....(310) 235-5102
www.foxfamilychannel.com
Key Executives/Personnel:
    Haim Saban, Chairman
    Mel Woods, President & COO
    Maureen Smith, President of Fox Family Channel & Fox Kids Network
    Lance H. Robbins, President of TV Movies & Mini-Series
    Eytan Keller, Executive VP of Reality Programming & Specials
    Cori Stern, Executive Producer of Special Projects
    Joel Andryc, Sr. VP of Children's Programming & Development
    Abbie A. Charette, Sr. VP of Production
    Tom Cosgrove, Sr. VP of Planning & Scheduling
    Amy Goldberg, Sr. VP of Motion Pictures
    Stacy Lifton, Sr. VP of Business & Legal Affairs
    Yvonne Bennett, VP of Business & Legal Affairs
    Kim Christianson, VP of Development & Current Programming
    Susan Cooper, VP of Acquisitions
    Stephen Fisch, VP of Business Affairs
    Julia Gilbert, VP of Reality Programming & Production
    Jill Goldfarb, VP of Planning & Scheduling
    Tom Halleen, VP of Primetime Acquisitions
    Nancy Redford, VP of Programming
    Julie Resh, VP of Development
    Dan Smith, VP of Specials Development
Specialties: Network

FOX KIDS NETWORK
10960 Wilshire Blvd.
Los Angeles, CA 90024
Phone: ....(310) 235-9600
Fax: ....(310) 225-9513
www.foxkids.com
Key Executives/Personnel:
    Haim Saban, Chairman & CEO
    Mel Woods, President & COO
    Maureen Smith, President
    Lance Robbins, President of Development
    Donna Cunningham, Executive VP of Business & Legal Affairs
    Joel Andryc, Executive VP of Programming & Development
    David McDermott, Executive Director of Programming & Development
    Tom Cosgrove, Sr. VP of Planning & Scheduling
    Stacy Lifton, Sr. VP of Business Affairs
    Donna Mitroff, Sr. VP of Educational Policies
    Jonathan Rosenthal, VP of Development
Specialties: Network; Cable; Animation

FOX TELEVISION STUDIOS
10201 W. Pico Blvd.
Los Angeles, CA 90035
Phone: ....(310) 369-1000
www.fox.com
Key Executives/Personnel:
    David A. Grant, President
    Rich Vokulich, Executive VP
    Lisa Berger, Executive VP of Creative Affairs
    David Madden, Executive VP of Fox Television Pictures, Movies & Miniseries
    Kaki Kirby, Sr. VP of Foxstar Productions
    Bob Lemchen, Sr. VP of Production, Movies and Miniseries
    Daniela Welteke, Sr. VP of International Programming & Co-Production
    Jim Sharp, Sr. VP of Production
    Donna Redier Linsk, VP of Business & Legal Affairs
    Edward Sabin, VP of Business & Legal Affairs
    Martin Carlson, VP of Business & Legal Affairs
    Naomi Martinez, VP of Finance & Administration
    Nissa Diederich, Director of Production Accounting
    Gary Hall, Director of Post Production
    Livia Hanich, Director of Physical Production, Foxstar

Production Companies – TV

Zig Gauthier, Director of Creative Affairs
Marney Hochman, Director of Creative Affairs
Sue Bugden, Director of Production, Movie and Miniseries
Eric Poticha, Director of Development, Movies and Miniseries
Susan Lindheim, Director of Business Development
Andrew Durham, Director of Physical Production
Specialties: Network

WOODY FRASER PRODUCTIONS
1239 S. Glendale Ave.
Glendale, CA 91205
Phone: ....(818) 550-6102
Fax: ....(818) 550-6104
woodyfraserpdtns@yahoo.com
Key Executives/Personnel:
Woody Fraser, Executive Producer
Cathy Masamitsu, Producer
Specialties: Network; Cable
Other Categories: Interactive Multimedia
Credits: Mike Douglas Show; Good Morning America; The Home Show; Home & Family

FRIED FILMS
4503 Glencoe Ave.
Marina Del Rey, CA 90292
Phone: ....(310) 754-2676
Fax: ....(310) 778-9596
Key Executives/Personnel:
Robert Fried, Producer
Richard Zinman, Producer
Marisa Forrest, Creative Executive
Specialties: Cable
Other Categories: Feature Film
Credits: Rudy; Godzilla; Winchell; So I Married an Axe Murder
First Look/Development Deals: HBO

MARK FROST PRODUCTIONS
5700 Wilshire Blvd.
Los Angeles, CA 90036
Phone: ....(323) 965-5785
Key Executives/Personnel:
Mark Frost, Executive Producer
Susie Putnam, Assistant
Specialties: Network; Cable; Made for TV Movies
Other Categories: Feature Film
Credits: The Repair Shop; Buddy Faro; Twin Peaks: Fire Walk With Me

FURMAN FILMS, INC.
4754 La Villa Marina, Ste. J
Marina Del Rey, CA 90292
Phone: ....(310) 306-2700
....(415) 350-8107
willfurman@aol.com
Key Executives/Personnel:
Will Furman, Producer
Specialties: Documentaries; Made for TV Movies
Other Categories: Video
Credits: Beyond Courage: Surviving Vietnam as a P.O.W.; The Best You Can Be; The Other Side of the Island; The Stones of Eden
Additional Info: 115 Stanley Ave., Pacifica, CA 94044, (650) 557-1550 phone

FX NETWORKS, LLC
1440 S. Sepulveda Blvd.
Los Angeles, CA 90025
Phone: ....(310) 444-8123
Fax: ....(310) 231-1621
www.fxnetworks.com
Key Executives/Personnel:
Peter Liguori, President
Kevin Reilly, President of Development
Michael Sakin, Sr. VP & National Sales Manager
Chris Carlisle, Sr. VP of Marketing
Chuck Saftler, Sr. VP of Programming & Acquisitions
Mark De Vitre, Sr. VP of Operations
Patrice Callahan, VP of Business & Legal Affairs
Mike Middeleer, VP of On Air Promotion
John Luma, VP of On Air Promotion
Steve Le Blang, VP of Strategic Planning & Research
Elena Gutierrez, VP of Entertainment Sales
Eric Shiu, VP of Marketing & Advertising
Ruben Burgess, Director of Production, Marketing & On Air Promotion
Specialties: Cable; Made for TV Movies; Miniseries
Credits: Deliberate Intent (TV movie); The Sight; Son of the Beach; The X Show

GALLO & GALLO, INC.
1421 Ambassador St., Ste. 101
Los Angeles, CA 90035
Phone: ....(310) 277-8107
....(310) 277-1828
Key Executives/Personnel:
Lillian B. Gallo, Producer
Specialties: Network; Cable; Made for TV Movies; Miniseries
Credits: The Life Force Experiment; The Look Alike; Hustling; Princess Daisy

GEARS COMMUNICATIONS
315 W. Verdugo Ave.
Burbank, CA 91502
Phone: ....(818) 840-9333
Fax: ....(818) 840-9358
www.gearscom.com
maureen@gearscom.com
Key Executives/Personnel:
Greg Gears, Producer
Steven Kovner, VP of Production
Maureen English, VP of Sales
Specialties: Documentaries
Other Categories: Video; Music Video; Interactive Multimedia

GENREBEND PRODUCTIONS, INC.
1875 Century Park East, 2nd Fl.
Los Angeles, CA 90067
Phone: ....(310) 284-7312
Fax: ....(310) 284-7317
Key Executives/Personnel:
David Nutter, President & Director
Tom Lavagnino, Writer & VP of Creative Affairs
Brian Vanderwilt, Director of Development
Specialties: Network; Cable; Made for TV Movies
Other Categories: Feature Film
Credits: Dark Angel; Millennium; Roswell
First Look/Development Deals: Twentieth Century Fox

ROGER GIMBEL PRODUCTIONS, INC.
1675 Old Oak Rd.
Los Angeles, CA 90049
Phone: ....(310) 459-3838
gimpix1@ix.netcom.com
Key Executives/Personnel:
Roger Gimbel, Producer
Mark Trabulus, Producer
Stephanie Young, Development
Specialties: Network; Cable; Made for TV Movies; Miniseries
Other Categories: Feature Film
Credits: The Amazing Howard Hughes; Chernobyl, The Final Warning; A Perfect Mother; Murder Between Friends

Production Companies – TV

First Look/Development Deals: Showtime
Trade Assoc./Guilds/Unions: PGA

GINTY FILMS
16255 Ventura Blvd., Ste. 625
Encino, CA 91436
Phone: ....(310) 274-9691
....(310) 277-1408
Fax: ....(310) 274-9692
www.robertginty.com
rwginty@aol.com
Key Executives/Personnel:
- Robert Ginty, CEO
- Skip Heinecke, (Ireland)
- Shira Zeltzer, Executive Assistant
- Layla Bennett, Executive Assistant
- Lyndi Vanderhout, (Paris)
- Moira Proletti, (Rome)
- Jean Diamond, (London)
- John Gallagher, (New York)
- John Mein, (Vancouver)

Specialties: Network; Cable; Made for TV Movies
Other Categories: Feature Film; Commercials; Music Video; Interactive Multimedia
Credits: Bounty Hunter; Woman of Desire; Day of Reckoning
Trade Assoc./Guilds/Unions: BAFTA, DGA, SAG, WGAw

GMR PRODUCTIONS
1333 Sixth Ave.
Venice, CA 90291
Phone: ....(310) 401-1400
Fax: ....(310) 401-1200
Key Executives/Personnel:
- Gina Resnick, Executive Producer

Specialties: Network
Other Categories: Feature Film
Credits: Female Perversions; Clockwatchers; 13 Conversations About One Thing

GOEPP CIRCLE PRODUCTIONS
5555 Melrose Ave., Cooper Bldg., Ste. 116
Los Angeles, CA 90049
Phone: ....(323) 956-4620
Fax: ....(323) 862-1119
Key Executives/Personnel:
- Jonathan Frakes, Director & Producer
- Lisa J. Olin, Producer
- Daisy Gardner, Story Editor

Specialties: Network; Cable; Made for TV Movies
Other Categories: Feature Film
Credits: Roswell; Dying to Live
First Look/Development Deals: Paramount Pictures

JEFF GOLD PRODUCTIONS, INC.
13900 Panay Way, Ste. 309
Marina Del Rey, CA 90292
Phone: ....(310) 827-9165
j47737@yahoo.com
Specialties: Made for TV Movies
Other Categories: Feature Film; Commercials; Video; Music Video
Credits: The Alpha Section; Talking Heads; Career Bed; Changing Times
Trade Assoc./Guilds/Unions: DGA

GOLD'N HEN PRODUCTIONS
12301 Wilshire Blvd., Ste. 402
Los Angeles, CA 90024
Phone: ....(310) 820-1308
Fax: ....(310) 820-1398
judy@groupmsi.com
Key Executives/Personnel:
- Joel Goldstein, Chairman
- Judy Henry, President
- Dale Eldridge Kaye, VP
- Jamie Goldstein, VP

Specialties: Network; Cable; Made for TV Movies
Other Categories: Feature Film; Commercials
Credits: Replacing Dad; Nelson Diebel Story; Spy Girl

GOLDEN EAGLE PIX
475 Ravensbury St.
Thousand Oaks, CA 91361
Phone: ....(805) 381-9095
....(805) 907-1860
Fax: ....(805) 381-9096
www.goldeneaglepix.com
goldeneaglepix@hotmail.com
Key Executives/Personnel:
- Peter B. Good, Producer

Specialties: Documentaries
Other Categories: Feature Film; Commercials
Credits: Roller Coasters; Fireworks; Beyond Bizarre; Death Valley

GOLDENRING PRODUCTIONS
11271 Ventura Blvd., Rm. 506
Studio City, CA 91604
Phone: ....(323) 969-0354
Fax: ....(323) 969-8581
Key Executives/Personnel:
- Jane Goldenring, President
- Victoria R. Farwell, Associate

Specialties: Network; Cable; Documentaries; Made for TV Movies; Miniseries
Other Categories: Feature Film
Credits: On The Second Day Of Christmas; Widows; My First Mister
First Look/Development Deals: Von Zerneck-Sertner Films

GOODMAN/ROSEN PRODUCTIONS
4063 Radford Ave., Ste. 201
Studio City, CA 91604
Phone: ....(818) 505-6603
Fax: ....(818) 505-6606
Key Executives/Personnel:
- Barry Rosen, Partner & Producer
- Gary Goodman, Partner & Producer
- Ford Gilmore, VP
- Andrew Combs, Assistant

Specialties: Cable; Made for TV Movies
Credits: Highlander; Wagons East; The Virginian; Zorro
First Look/Development Deals: Fireworks Entertainment, Inc.

GRACIE FILMS
10202 W. Washington Blvd., Sidney Poitier Bldg.
Culver City, CA 90232
Phone: ....(310) 244-4222
Fax: ....(310) 244-1530
Key Executives/Personnel:
- James L. Brooks, Producer, Director & Writer
- Richard Sakai, President
- Julie Ansell, President of Motion Pictures
- Denise Sirkot, Executive VP

Specialties: Network; Animation
Other Categories: Feature Film; Interactive Multimedia
Credits: As Good As It Gets; Jerry Maguire; Bottle Rocket; Riding in Cars with Boys
First Look/Development Deals: Columbia Pictures/Columbia Tristar Motion Picture Group
Additional Info: Simpson's Production Office: 10201 W. Pico Blvd., Los Angeles, CA 90035

Production Companies – TV

GRADE A ENTERTAINMENT
368 N. La Cienega Blvd.
Los Angeles, CA 90048
Phone: ....(310) 358-8600
Fax: ....(310) 652-0718
gradeaprod@aol.com
Key Executives/Personnel:
    Andy Cohen, Producer
Specialties: Network; Cable; Made for TV Movies; Miniseries
Other Categories: Feature Film; Interactive Multimedia
Credits: Captain Ron; It Takes Two; A Chance of Snow; Billboard Dad

GRAMMNET PRODUCTIONS (TV)
5555 Melrose Ave., Lucy Bungalow, 2nd Fl.
Los Angeles, CA 90038
Phone: ....(323) 956-5547
Fax: ....(323) 862-1774
Key Executives/Personnel:
    Kelsey Grammer, Producer & CEO
    Mark Ganshirt, Sr. VP
    Karyn Lamb, Director of Development
    Xochitl Olivas, Production Manager
    Jon Norwood, Development Assistant
Specialties: Network; Cable; Made for TV Movies; Miniseries
Credits: Girlfriends; Frasier; Fired-Up

GRANADA ENTERTAINMENT USA
11812 San Vicente Blvd., Ste. 500
Los Angeles, CA 90049
Phone: ....(310) 689-4777
Fax: ....(310) 689-4789
Key Executives/Personnel:
    Antony Root, Acting President
    Craig McNeil, Executive VP of Production
    Bill Hamm, Sr. VP of Series Programming
    Gary Robinson, Sr. VP of Business & Legal Affairs
    Ann Johnson, VP of Creative Affairs
Specialties: Network; Cable; Made for TV Movies; Miniseries
Credits: Longitude; The John Denver Story; Cracker; Dash & Lilly

GRAZKA TAYLOR PRODUCTIONS
9899 Santa Monica Blvd., Ste. 206
Beverly Hills, CA 90212
Phone: ....(310) 201-0806
Fax: ....(310) 201-0711
grazkat@aol.com
Key Executives/Personnel:
    Grazka Taylor, Producer
Specialties: Cable
Other Categories: Feature Film
Credits: Tricks; Mahalia Jackson; Prophecies; The Operation

GREEN COMMUNICATIONS
303 N. Glen Oaks, Ste. 605
Burbank, CA 91502
Phone: ....(818) 557-0050
Fax: ....(818) 557-0056
www.greenfilms.com
tcaptan@greenfilms.com
Key Executives/Personnel:
    Talaat Captan, President
Specialties: Network; Cable; Made for TV Movies
Other Categories: Feature Film; Commercials
Credits: Ground Control; Living in Peril; Apex; Space Marines

GREEN MOON PRODUCTIONS
3110 Main St., Ste. 205
Santa Monica, CA 90405
Phone: ....(310) 450-6111
Fax: ....(310) 450-1333
name@greenmoon.com
Key Executives/Personnel:
    Antonio Banderas, Producer & Actor
    Melanie Griffith, Producer & Actor
    Diane Sillan Isaacs, President
Specialties: Network; Cable; Animation; Documentaries; Made for TV Movies; Miniseries
Other Categories: Feature Film
Credits: Crazy In Alabama; The Body; Loving Lulu; Tart
First Look/Development Deals: HBO

THE GREIF COMPANY/A DAY WITH, INC.
9233 W. Pico Blvd., Ste. 218
Los Angeles, CA 90035
Phone: ....(310) 385-1200
Fax: ....(310) 385-1207
leslie@greifco.cncdsl.com
Key Executives/Personnel:
    Leslie Greif, Executive Producer
    Tiffany Mclinn Lore, Producer
    Kristen Stabile, Executive in Charge of Production
Specialties: Cable; Documentaries; Made for TV Movies
Other Categories: Feature Film
Credits: Meet Wally Sparks; Keys to Tulsa; Lifetime, Intimate Portraits

GREYSTONE COMMUNICATION GROUP, INC./GREYSTONE FILMS
5161 Lankershim Blvd., Ste. 280
North Hollywood, CA 91601
Phone: ....(818) 762-2900
Fax: ....(818) 762-1626
www.ghistory.com
Key Executives/Personnel:
    Craig Haffner, Chairman, CEO & President of Greystone Films
    Shinaan Krakowsky, COO & General Counsel
    Rick Brookwell, CFO & Corporate Counsel
    Donna E. Lusitana, President of Greystone TV
    Nicholas Stein, VP of Greystone TV
    Melanie Blythe-Moreau, VP of Greystone TV
    Raymond Bridgers, VP of Greystone TV
    Glenn Kirschbaum, VP of Greystone TV
Specialties: Cable; Documentaries
Other Categories: Video
Credits: Prophecies; Ancient Mysteries
First Look/Development Deals: A&E Television Networks

MERV GRIFFIN ENTERTAINMENT
9860 Wilshire Blvd.
Beverly Hills, CA 90210
Phone: ....(310) 385-3160
Fax: ....(310) 385-3162
Key Executives/Personnel:
    Merv Griffin, Chairman
    Lawrence Cohen, CEO
    Ernest Chambers, Sr. VP of Production
    Robert Kosberg, Producer
    Scott Manville, Manager of Development
    Rick Upshaw, Director of Multimedia Development
    Jim Bradley, Executive Producer
    Kira Mason, Development Executive
    Diana Redman, Contract Administrator
Specialties: Network; Cable; Made for TV Movies
Other Categories: Feature Film

KEN GROSS MANAGEMENT
7919 Sunset Blvd., 2nd Fl.
Los Angeles, CA 90046
Phone: ....(323) 512-2999
Fax: ....(323) 512-2699
kgrossm@msn.com
Key Executives/Personnel:
    Ken Gross, President

Stephanie Gaines, VP
Jenz Bergren, Coordinator
Specialties: Network; Cable; Made for TV Movies; Miniseries
Other Categories: Feature Film

GROSS PRODUCTIONS
1 Skyline Dr.
Burbank, CA 91501
Phone: ....(818) 557-7335
Fax: ....(818) 557-7336
www.grosspro.com
callgross@aol.com
Key Executives/Personnel:
Chris Gross, Producer & Director
Specialties: Cable
Other Categories: Feature Film; Commercials
Credits: Gloria Estefan & Carribean Soul; La Femme Nikita; Duckman
Trade Assoc./Guilds/Unions: ASCAP

BETH GROSSBARD PRODUCTIONS
10202 W. Washington Blvd., Meralta Bldg., Ste. 308
Culver City, CA 90232
Phone: ....(310) 841-2555
Fax: ....(310) 841-5934
bethgcap@aol.com
Key Executives/Personnel:
Beth Grossbard, Producer
K. Jacobs, Development Associate
Specialties: Network; Cable; Made for TV Movies; Miniseries
Other Categories: Feature Film
Credits: No One Could Protect Her; Range of Motion
First Look/Development Deals: Craig Anderson Productions

GRUB STREET PRODUCTIONS
5555 Melrose Ave., Wilder Bldg., Ste. 101
Los Angeles, CA 90038
Phone: ....(323) 956-4657
Key Executives/Personnel:
David Angell, Creator & Executive Producer
Peter Casey, Creator & Executive Producer
David Lee, Creator & Executive Producer
Dan O'Shannon, Executive Producer
Mark Reisman, Executive Producer
Specialties: Network
Credits: Frasier
First Look/Development Deals: Paramount Pictures

GULLANE PICTURES
1351 Third St., Ste. 200
Santa Monica, CA 90401
Phone: ....(310) 451-5111
Fax: ....(310) 451-5321
Key Executives/Personnel:
Britt Allcroft, Co-Chairman
Charles Falzon, Co-Chairman
Meredith Metz, Head of Development & Packaging
Jesse Stovin, Development Executive
Specialties: Cable; Animation; Documentaries; Made for TV Movies; Miniseries
Other Categories: Feature Film
Credits: Thomas & The Magic Railroad; Thomas the Tank Engine & Friends; What Katy Did

H-GUN LABS
587 Shotwell St.
San Francisco, CA 94110
Phone: ....(415) 648-4386
....(773) 561-5354
Fax: ....(415) 920-3911
www.hgun.com

info@hgun.com
Key Executives/Personnel:
James Deloye, Executive Producer
Sara Kraft, Producer
Nancy Williams, Lab Manager
Specialties: Network; Cable; Animation
Other Categories: Feature Film; Commercials; Music Video; Interactive Multimedia

HALLMARK ENTERTAINMENT
1325 Avenue of the Americas, 21st Fl.
New York, NY 10019
Phone: ....(212) 977-9001
....(323) 634-3000
Fax: ....(212) 977-9049
www.hallmarkent.com
Key Executives/Personnel:
Robert Halmi, Sr., Chairman
Robert Halmi, Jr., President & CEO
Peter Von Gal, Executive VP & COO
Bill Aliber, CFO
David V. Picker, President of Production Worldwide
Dan Martin, Executive VP of Production
Lynn Holst, Sr. VP of Development
Janet Jacobson, Sr. VP & Co-Production Programming
Tony Guido, Sr. VP of Legal & Business Affairs
Kelly Coogan Swanson, VP of Marketing
Specialties: Network; Cable; Made for TV Movies; Miniseries
Other Categories: Video
Credits: Arabian Nights; Merlin; Dinotopia; Animal Farm
Additional Info: 4201 Wilshire Blvd., Ste. 304, Los Angeles, CA 90010

HALLMARK HALL OF FAME PRODUCTIONS, INC.
12001 Ventura Place, Ste. 300
Studio City, CA 91604
Phone: ....(818) 505-9191
Fax: ....(818) 505-9842
Key Executives/Personnel:
Brad R. Moore, President
Jan Parkinson, VP
Kathleen Straub, Executive of Production
Richard E. Welsh, Executive Producer
Brent Shields, Producer & Director
Karen Mayeda Vranek, Post Production Supervisor
Cameron Johann, Director of Development
Shawn McClaren, Manager of Development
Specialties: Network; Made for TV Movies
Credits: Missing Pieces; Cupid & Cate

HALSTED PICTURES
15 Brooks Ave., Unit B
Venice, CA 90291
Phone: ....(310) 450-7804
Fax: ....(310) 450-8174
Key Executives/Personnel:
Dan Halsted, Executive Producer
David Scheer, Creative Executive
Ryan Lewis, Story Editor
Specialties: Network; Cable; Documentaries
Other Categories: Feature Film
Credits: Servicing Sarah; The Art of War; Any Given Sunday; The Virgin Suicides
First Look/Development Deals: Mandalay Pictures

HANDPRINT ENTERTAINMENT
1100 Glendon Ave., Ste. 1000
Los Angeles, CA 90024
Phone: ....(310) 481-4400
Fax: ....(310) 481-4419
Key Executives/Personnel:

Production Companies – TV

David Guillod, Partner
Benny Medina, Partner
Jeff Pollack, Partner
Jay Polstein, Producer
Specialties: Network; Cable
Other Categories: Feature Film
Credits: Standoff; Eve's Bayou; Above the Rim; Fresh Prince of Bel Air
First Look/Development Deals: Miramax Films

HARBOR LIGHTS PRODUCTIONS
8634 Oak Park Ave.
Northridge, CA 91325
Phone: ....(818) 993-5255
Fax: ....(818) 993-5266
movierock@aol.com
Key Executives/Personnel:
Rocky Lang, Producer & Director
Specialties: Network; Cable; Documentaries
Other Categories: Feature Film
Credits: White Squall; Titanic (miniseries)

DEAN HARGROVE PRODUCTIONS
10202 W. Washington Blvd.
Culver City, CA 90232
Phone: ....(310) 244-8383
Fax: ....(310) 244-0303
Key Executives/Personnel:
Dean Hargrove, Executive Producer
Doris Stockstill, Executive Assistant to Mr. Hargrove
Specialties: Network; Made for TV Movies; Miniseries
Credits: Diagnosis Murder; Matlock; Perry Mason
First Look/Development Deals: Columbia TriStar Television

HARPO FILMS
345 N. Maple Dr., Ste. 315
Beverly Hills, CA 90210
Phone: ....(310) 278-5559
....(312) 633-1000
Key Executives/Personnel:
Oprah Winfrey, Chairman & CEO
Kate Forte, President
Lisa Halliday, Director of Media & Corporate Relations
Susan Heyer, Director of Development, TV
Valerie Scoon, Director of Development, Features
Tim Tortora, Director of Production
Specialties: Network; Made for TV Movies
Other Categories: Feature Film
Credits: Tuesday's With Morrie; Beloved; David & Lisa; Before Women Had Wings
First Look/Development Deals: ABC Entertainment Television Group, The Walt Disney Company
Additional Info: Oprah Winfrey Show Office: 110 N. Carpenter, Chicago, IL 60607

DAVID HAUGLAND PRODUCTIONS
8961 Sunset Blvd., Ste. 2D
West Hollywood, CA 90069
Phone: ....(310) 550-1556
Fax: ....(310) 550-1584
dkhaugland@earthlink.net
Key Executives/Personnel:
David Haugland, Producer & Director
Christopher Miller, Assistant
Specialties: Network; Cable; Documentaries
Other Categories: Feature Film; Video; Music Video
Credits: Changing Our Minds; World and Time Enough; The Oscar Legacy; The Portrait
Trade Assoc./Guilds/Unions: DGA, WGAw

HAWK ENTERTAINMENT
8888 W. 3rd St., Ste. 306
Los Angeles, CA 90048

Phone: ....(310) 859-7779
Fax: ....(310) 859-7797
Key Executives/Personnel:
John Crededio, Partner
Paul Pompian, Partner
Ron DeRosa, Producer
Specialties: Network; Cable; Made for TV Movies; Miniseries
Other Categories: Feature Film; Interactive Multimedia
Credits: The Watcher; Time Served; Vincent Verelli

HBO
1100 Avenue of the Americas
New York, NY 10036
Phone: ....(212) 512-1000
www.hbo.com
Key Executives/Personnel:
Jeff Bewkes, Chairman & CEO
Chris Albrecht, President of HBO Original Programming
John Billock, President of US Network Group
Colin Callender, President of HBO Films
Ross Greenburg, President of HBO Sports
Henry McGee, President of HBO Home Video
Steve Rosenberg, President of HBO International
Steve Scheffer, President of Film Programming, Video & Enterprises
Charles Schreger, President of HBO Enterprises
Specialties: Cable

HBO FILMS
2049 Century Park East, Ste. 3600
Los Angeles, CA 90067
Phone: ....(310) 201-9200
....(212) 512-1000
www.hbo.com
Key Executives/Personnel:
Colin Callender, President
Kerith Putnam, Sr. VP
Kary Antholis, VP
Jonathan Krauss, VP
Maud Nadler, VP
Carrie Frazier, VP of Casting
Specialties: Cable; Made for TV Movies
Credits: RKO 281; If These Walls Could Talk 2; Introducing Dorothy Dandridge; The Last of the Blonde Bombshells
Additional Info: 1100 Ave. of the Americas, New York, NY 10036

HBO INDEPENDENT PRODUCTIONS/HBO DOWNTOWN PRODUCTIONS
1100 Avenue of the Americas
New York, NY 10036
Phone: ....(212) 512-1000
www.hbo.com
Key Executives/Personnel:
Chris Albrecht, President
Russell Schwartz, Executive VP of Business & Planning
Nancy Geller, Sr. VP
John Fisher, VP of Production
Specialties: Network
Credits: Everybody Loves Raymond

HBO ORIGINAL PROGRAMMING
1100 Avenue of the Americas
New York, NY 10036
Phone: ....(212) 512-1000
....(310) 201-9300
www.hbo.com
Key Executives/Personnel:
Chris Albrecht, President
Sheila Nevins, Executive VP
Nancy Geller, Sr. VP

Production Companies – TV

Carolyn Strauss, Sr. VP (West Coast)
Anne Thomopoulos, Sr. VP (West Coast)
Susan Ennis, Sr. VP of Planning & Operations
Nancy Abraham, VP of Documentaries
Sarah Condon, VP of Comedy Series, Late Night & Specials
Dolores Morris, VP of HBO Family Channel
Bruce Richmond, VP of Production
Specialties: Cable; Documentaries; Made for TV Movies; Miniseries
Credits: The Sopranos; Sex and the City; Oz; Arli$$
Additional Info: 2049 Century Park East, Ste. 4200, Los Angeles, CA 90067

HEARST ENTERTAINMENT PRODUCTIONS
1640 S. Sepulveda Blvd., 4th Fl.
Los Angeles, CA 90025
Phone: ....(310) 478-1700
Fax: ....(310) 478-2202
Key Executives/Personnel:
Glenda Grant, President
Gideon Amir, Executive VP
Ronald Ulloa, Executive VP of Business Affairs
Paul Goldman, Sr. VP of Production & Post Production
Jerry Shevick, Sr. VP of Reality & Documentary Programming
Mary Ann Spero, Sr. VP of Movies & Miniseries
Specialties: Network; Cable; Documentaries; Made for TV Movies
Credits: Crash Course; Out of Sync; House Beautiful; Intimate Portrait

HELLER HIGHWATER
5917 Foothill Dr.
Los Angeles, CA 90068
Phone: ....(323) 467-9490
Fax: ....(323) 468-8074
Key Executives/Personnel:
Peter Heller, Producer
Specialties: Cable
Other Categories: Feature Film
Credits: Bones; Caught Up; Hotel De Love; Barb Wire

HENNESSEY ENTERTAINMENT, LTD.
P.O. Box 481164
Los Angeles, CA 90048
Phone: ....(323) 876-2400
Fax: ....(323) 876-2444
www.hennesseyentertainment.com
a_sleuth@hotmail.com
Key Executives/Personnel:
Ellis A. Cohen, Producer, Writer & CEO
Leonard H. Cohen, Creative Executive
Jerome Cohen, Creative Executive
Specialties: Cable; Made for TV Movies; Miniseries
Other Categories: Feature Film; Interactive Multimedia
Credits: Dangerous Evidence; Love, Mary; First Steps; Aunt Mary
Trade Assoc./Guilds/Unions: ATAS, PGA, WGAw

THE JIM HENSON COMPANY
1416 N. La Brea Ave.
Los Angeles, CA 90028
Phone: ....(323) 802-1500
Fax: ....(323) 802-1825
www.henson.com
Key Executives/Personnel:
Brian Henson, Chairman
Charles H. Rivkin, President & CEO
Linda Govreau, Executive VP of Corporate Finance & CFO
Lisa Henson, President, Jim Henson Pictures
John Stephenson, Executive VP & Creative Supervisor, Jim Henson's Creature Shop
Juliet Blake, Executive VP & Co-Head, Jim Henson Television Group Worldwide
Angus Fletcher, Executive VP & Co-Head, Jim Henson Television Group Worldwide
Peter Schube, General Counsel/Executive VP of Business & Legal Affairs
Michael Bolingbroke, Sr. VP of Finance & Operations, Jim Henson's Creature Shop
Craig Allen, Sr. VP & General Manager, Jim Henson Interactive
Robert Norton, Sr. VP of Business & Legal Affairs
Ritamarie Peruggi, Sr. VP of Production Worldwide
Robert Wozniak, VP of Production Administration & Finance/Production Executive
Kristine Belson, Production, Jim Henson Pictures
Louis Philips, VP of Production Administration
Halle Stanford Grossman, VP of Creative Affairs, Jim Henson Television
Ruth Caruso, VP of Development, Jim Henson Television
Michele Martell, VP of Business Affairs & Interactive Business Development
Antonia Downey, VP of International Legal & Business Affairs
Pete Coogan, VP of Physical Production
David Barrington-Holt, Creative Supervisor, Jim Henson's Creature Shop
Debbie McClellan, Sr. Director of Corporate Communications & Special Projects
Omar Camacho, Director of Current Programming, Jim Henson Television
Specialties: Network; Cable; Made for TV Movies; Miniseries
Other Categories: Feature Film; Commercials; Video; Music Video; Interactive Multimedia
Credits: Farscape; Story Telling with Tomie de Paola; Rat; Muppets From Space

DEBRA HILL PRODUCTIONS
1250 Sixth St., Ste. 205
Santa Monica, CA 90401
Phone: ....(310) 319-0052
Fax: ....(310) 260-8502
Key Executives/Personnel:
Debra Hill, Producer, Writer & Director
Barri Evins, President
Patrick List, Director of Development
Specialties: Network; Cable
Other Categories: Feature Film
Credits: The Fisher King; Halloween; Crazy in Alabama; Escape From New York

THE HISTORY CHANNEL
235 E. 45th St.
New York, NY 10017
Phone: ....(212) 210-1400
Fax: ....(212) 210-9016
www.historychannel.com
Key Executives/Personnel:
Abbe Raven, Executive VP & General Manager
Joe La Polla, VP of Program Acquisitions & Scheduling
Charles Maday, VP of Historical Programming
Specialties: Cable; Documentaries; Made for TV Movies; Miniseries
Credits: Modern Marvels; Time Machine; History Undercover

HODGE FILM & VIDEO
10770 Esther Ave.
Los Angeles, CA 90064
Phone: ....(310) 441-9773
Fax: ....(310) 474-7611
hodge@pacbell.net
Key Executives/Personnel:
David Hodge, President
Stacey Freeman, Producer
Specialties: Network; Cable; Documentaries
Other Categories: Commercials; Video; Music Video
Credits: Carly Simon - Every Time We Say Goodbye; Bank One (corp. video); Human Rights Campaign; Carlos Santana - Supernatural

Production Companies – TV

HOFFLUND-POLONE
9465 Wilshire Blvd., Ste 820
Beverly Hills, CA 90212
Phone: ....(310) 859-1971
Fax: ....(310) 859-7250
Key Executives/Personnel:
　Judy Hofflund, Partner
　Gavin Polone, Partner
　Vivian Cannon, Production Executive
Specialties: Network
Other Categories: Feature Film
Credits: Stir of Echoes; Drop Dead Gorgeous; 8mm; The Gilmore Girls (TV series)

HOLLANE CORP./MARTIN POLL FILMS, LTD.
P.O. Box 17137
Beverly Hills, CA 90209
Phone: ....(323) 876-8873
Fax: ....(323) 876-8892
Key Executives/Personnel:
　Martin Poll, President
　Shirley Mellner, VP
Specialties: Network
Other Categories: Feature Film
Credits: Nighthawks; The Lion In Winter; My Heroes Have Always Been Cowboys; Diana: Her True Story (miniseries)

HORSESHOE BAY PRODUCTIONS
500 S. Buena Vista St., Animation Bldg., Ste. 1G
Burbank, CA 91521
Phone: ....(818) 560-3229
Fax: ....(818) 848-6832
Key Executives/Personnel:
　Greg S. Foster, Producer
　Mark Steven Johnson, Producer, Writer & Director
　Julia Dray, President of Production
　Erik Baiers, Director of Development
Specialties: Network
Other Categories: Feature Film
Credits: The Score; Simon Birch; Sleepless in Seattle
First Look/Development Deals: Touchstone Pictures

HY-TONE PRODUCTIONS
26349 Fairside Rd.
Malibu, CA 90265
Phone: ....(310) 456-3052
Fax: ....(310) 456-9659
www.notelvis.com
hytone@aol.com
Key Executives/Personnel:
　Robert Jaye, Producer, Director & Cinematographer
　Walter Hoylman, Producer, Director & Editor
Specialties: Documentaries
Other Categories: Feature Film; Video; Interactive Multimedia
Credits: Some of the King's Men; Mustang America; Art and Sex; Fire Engine

ICON PRODUCTIONS INC.
5555 Melrose Ave., Wilder Bldg.
Los Angeles, CA 90038
Phone: ....(323) 956-2100
Fax: ....(323) 862-2121
Key Executives/Personnel:
　Bruce Davey, President
　Jim Lemley, President of TV
　Michael Lustig, President of Music
　Vicki Christianson, Sr. VP of Business
　Eveleen Bandy, VP of TV
　Karen J. Glasser, VP of Creative Affairs
Specialties: Network
Other Categories: Feature Film
Credits: Bless the Child; Payback; Three Stooges; Braveheart
First Look/Development Deals: Paramount Pictures

IMAGE G
10900 Ventura Blvd.
Studio City, CA 91604
Phone: ....(818) 761-6644
Fax: ....(818) 761-8397
www.imageg.com
Key Executives/Personnel:
　Nick Paine, Producer
　Tom Barron, Producer
Specialties: Network
Other Categories: Feature Film; Commercials
Credits: Nestle; Del Monte; Spy Kids

IMAGINE ENTERTAINMENT
9465 Wilshire Blvd., 7th Fl.
Beverly Hills, CA 90212
Phone: ....(310) 858-2000
Fax: ....(310) 858-2020
www.imagine-entertainment.com
Key Executives/Personnel:
　Brian Grazer, Co-Chairman
　Ron Howard, Co-Chairman
　Tony Krantz, Co-Chairman & CEO
　Michael Rosenberg, President
　Karen Kehela, Co-Chair of Imagine Films
　Skip Chasey, Executive VP of Business Affairs, TV
　Robin Barris, Sr. VP of Administration & Operations
　Maureen Peyrot, Sr. VP of Motion Pictures
　Jim Whitaker, Sr. VP of Motion Pictures
　Jan Geniesse, VP of Motion Pictures
　Kim Roth, VP of Motion Pictures
　Suszy Barbieri, VP of Motion Pictures
　Gayle Pillsbury, VP of Talent & Casting, TV
　Katie O'Connell, VP of Current TV Programming & Development
　Jennifer Robinson, VP of Current TV Programming & Development
　Mike Vorndian, Creative Executive
　Barry Jossen, Production Consultant
Specialties: Network
Other Categories: Feature Film
Credits: The Grinch; Bowfinger; Felicity; Sports Night

IN-FINN-ITY PRODUCTIONS, INC.
11400 W. Olympic Blvd., 16th Fl.
Los Angeles, CA 90064
Phone: ....(310) 444-6300
Fax: ....(310) 444-6310
www.infinnity.com
Key Executives/Personnel:
　Pat Finn, Executive Producer
　Ann Marie Griffith, Executive in Charge of Production
　Jana Morgan, Director of Development
Specialties: Network; Cable
Other Categories: Commercials; Music Video
Credits: Instant Comedy with the Groundlings; Soulmates
First Look/Development Deals: Universal Television & Networks Group

INDIEGAL PRODUCTIONS, LLC
14350 Little Tujunga Canyon Rd.
San Fernando, CA 91342
Phone: ....(818) 890-6111
Fax: ....(818) 890-5851
indiegal_prods@hotmail.com
Key Executives/Personnel:
　Angela P. Schapiro, Partner

Production Companies – TV

Laura Keats, Partner
Gail Harris, Partner
Jan Marlyn Reesman, VP of Creative Affairs
Deborah Zimmerly, VP of Development
Susanna Midnight, Director of Creative Affairs
Jeanne Yu, Director of Development
Specialties: Network; Made for TV Movies
Other Categories: Feature Film
Credits: To Protect and Serve; The Iron Triangle; He's My Girl

INFRONT PRODUCTIONS
10201 W. Pico Blvd., Bldg. 3 North
Los Angeles, CA 90035
Phone: ....(310) 369-5890
Fax: ....(310) 369-8356
Key Executives/Personnel:
   Danny Jacobson, Writer & Producer
   Marjorie Weitzman, Producer
   Jennifer Hertrich, VP of Feature Development
Specialties: Network
Other Categories: Feature Film
Credits: Mad About You; Two Guys and a Girl; Roseanne
First Look/Development Deals: Twentieth Century Fox

INTELLISCAPE FILMS, LLC
11601 Wilshire Blvd., 5th Fl.
Los Angeles, CA 90025
Phone: ....(310) 235-1422
....(800) 422-5996
Fax: ....(800) 828-4330
www.intelliscapefilms.com
info@intelliscapefilms.com
Key Executives/Personnel:
   Bruce Caulk, Writer & Director
   Jeff Teitelman, Writer
Specialties: Documentaries
Other Categories: Commercials; Video
Credits: San Diego Convention Visitors Bureau; Konami; National Financial Partners; Royal Family of Saudi Arabia (documentary)

INTERNATIONAL TELEVISION GROUP (ITG)
1322 Second St., Ste. 6
Santa Monica, CA 90401
Phone: ....(310) 656-9100
Fax: ....(310) 656-9104
intvg@aol.com
Key Executives/Personnel:
   Teresa Campbell, VP of Production & Development
   Lou La Monte, Producer
Specialties: Network; Cable; Made for TV Movies
Other Categories: Feature Film; Commercials; Video
Credits: Cat on a Hot Tin Roof (1985); Uncle Wally's General Store

ITASCA PICTURES, INC.
345 N. Maple Dr., Ste. 278
Beverly Hills, CA 90210
Phone: ....(310) 273-6505
Fax: ....(310) 273-1475
Key Executives/Personnel:
   Robert Snukal, Producer & Chairman
   Dan Grudnik, CEO & Producer
   Kandia Stroh, Associate Producer
Specialties: Network; Cable
Other Categories: Feature Film
Credits: Morton Orwell; Cletis Tout; Higher Love; Powder

ITB CINEGROUP/TELEVISION
3839 Brilliant Dr.
Los Angeles, CA 90065
Phone: ....(323) 258-5564
Fax: ....(323) 258-6634

quixotic@att.net
Key Executives/Personnel:
   Mark Byers, Writer & Producer
   Frank Antonelli, Writer & Producer
   Heather Ashley, Development
Specialties: Cable
Other Categories: Feature Film
Credits: The Treatment; Criminal Act; Deception; Race, Religion, & Racism
First Look/Development Deals: Timeless Entertainment

MICHAEL JACOBS PRODUCTIONS
4024 Radford Ave., Administration Bldg., Ste. 310
Studio City, CA 91604
Phone: ....(818) 655-5765
Fax: ....(818) 655-8746
Key Executives/Personnel:
   Michael Jacobs, Executive Producer
   Geralyn Schaefer, Director of Development
Specialties: Network
Credits: Boy Meets World; My 2 Dads; Dinosaurs
First Look/Development Deals: NBC Entertainment, Inc.

JARET ENTERTAINMENT
2017 Pacific Ave., Ste. 2
Venice, CA 90291
Phone: ....(310) 883-8807
Fax: ....(310) 822-0916
www.jaretentertainment.com
sjaret@jaretentertainment.com
Key Executives/Personnel:
   Seth Jaret, CEO & Producer
   Susan Sullivan, Development Associate & Story Editor
   Amy O'Brien, Assistant
Specialties: Network; Animation; Made for TV Movies; Miniseries
Other Categories: Feature Film; Interactive Multimedia
Credits: Rounders; 10 Things I Hate About You

JERSEY FILMS
10351 Santa Monica Blvd., Ste. 200
Los Angeles, CA 90025
Phone: ....(310) 203-1000
Fax: ....(310) 203-1010
Key Executives/Personnel:
   Danny DeVito, Co-Chairman
   Michael Shamberg, Co-Chairman
   Stacey Sher, Co-Chairman
   John Landgraf, President of TV
   Richard Klubeck, COO
   Pamela Abdy, Sr. VP of Production
   Carla Santos Shamberg, VP of Special Projects
   Adrienne Biddle, Story Editor
   Sindy Lin, Story Editor
   David Kurs, Assistant Story Editor
   Monica Hall, Manager of Finance
   Amy Hurdelbrink, Office Manager
Specialties: Network
Other Categories: Feature Film
Credits: Man on the Moon; Erin Brockovich; Get Shorty; Out of Sight

JKR PRODUCTIONS, INC.
12140 W. Olympic Blvd., Ste. 21
Los Angeles, CA 90064
Phone: ....(310) 826-3666
jimruxin@aol.com
Key Executives/Personnel:
   Jim Ruxin, Producer
Specialties: Network; Cable; Documentaries
Other Categories: Feature Film; Commercials; Video
Credits: Stoogemania; Defense Play; In God We Trust
Trade Assoc./Guilds/Unions: DGA, IALocal700

Production Companies – TV

DON JOHNSON PRODUCTIONS
3400 Riverside Dr., Ste. 100
Burbank, CA 91505
Phone: ....(818) 238-2200
Key Executives/Personnel:
  Don Johnson, Executive Producer & CEO
  Marc Granirer, COO
  Nick Kelley, President
  David Buelow, Executive VP of Creative Affairs
Specialties: Network; Cable; Made for TV Movies; Miniseries
Other Categories: Feature Film
Credits: Nash Bridges; The Marshall; In The Company of Darkness

MARK JOHNSON PRODUCTIONS
8490 Sunset Blvd., Ste. 700
West Hollywood, CA 90069
Phone: ....(310) 777-0007
Fax: ....(310) 777-0008
Key Executives/Personnel:
  Mark Johnson, Producer
  Tiffany Daniel, President
Specialties: Network
Credits: Rain Man; Good Morning Vietnam; Galaxy Quest; The Little Princess

QUINCY JONES MEDIA GROUP, INC.
3800 Barham Blvd., 5th Fl.
Los Angeles, CA 90068
Phone: ....(323) 874-2009
Fax: ....(323) 874-3364
Key Executives/Personnel:
  Quincy Jones, CEO
  Joel Simon, President
  Jill Tanner, VP
  Debborah Foreman, Executive Assistant to Mr. Jones
Specialties: Network; Cable
Other Categories: Feature Film
Credits: Passing Glory
First Look/Development Deals: Warner Bros.

JUMBO PICTURES, INC.
161 Avenue of the Americas, 15th Fl.
New York, NY 10013
Phone: ....(212) 337-0077
Fax: ....(212) 337-0437
Key Executives/Personnel:
  Jim Jinkins, President
  David Campbell, Executive VP
  Jack Spillum, VP of Production
  Ellie Copland, VP of Finance
  Beldeen Fortunato, VP of Adminitration
Specialties: Network; Cable; Animation
Other Categories: Feature Film
Credits: Doug's First Movie; PB & J Otter; Doug (TV series)

JUST SINGER ENTERTAINMENT
4242 Tujunga Ave.
Studio City, CA 91604
Phone: ....(818) 506-2400
Fax: ....(818) 506-2409
Key Executives/Personnel:
  Georgene Smith, VP of Development
  Sheri Singer, Executive Producer
Specialties: Network; Cable; Made for TV Movies; Miniseries
Credits: Jackie, Ethel, Joan: Women of Camelot; Halloweentown; Tempting Fate

KAHN POWER PICTURES
818 N. Doheny Dr.
Los Angeles, CA 90049
Phone: ....(310) 550-0770
....(310) 967-6566
Fax: ....(310) 550-6292
Ilene.kahn@newline.com
Key Executives/Personnel:
  Ilene Kahn Power, President & Producer
  Derek Power, Partner
  Mark McCoy, Director of Development
  Jeremy Kahn, VP of New Media
Specialties: Network; Cable; Made for TV Movies; Miniseries
Other Categories: Feature Film
Credits: Gia (1998); Stalin; Roswell; Fatherland
First Look/Development Deals: New Line Cinema, Inc.
Trade Assoc./Guilds/Unions: ATAS, BAFTA

KATIE FACE PRODUCTIONS
10202 W. Washington Blvd., Lean Bldg., Ste. 103
Culver City, CA 90232
Phone: ....(310) 244-6788
Fax: ....(310) 244-1828
Key Executives/Personnel:
  Tony Danza, Principal
  Tamara Holmes, Sr. VP of TV
  George Sealey, VP of Development
Specialties: Network; Cable; Made for TV Movies; Miniseries
Credits: Hudson Street; Before They Were Stars; Bermuda Triangle; Crowned and Dangerous
First Look/Development Deals: Sony Pictures Entertainment

THE KAUFMAN COMPANY
808 Wilshire Blvd., 3rd Fl.
Santa Monica, CA 90401
Phone: ....(310) 899-8080
Fax: ....(818) 899-8081
www.thekaufmancompany.com
info@thekaufmancompany.com
Key Executives/Personnel:
  Paul Kaufman, Executive Producer
  Helene Lynn-Nash, VP of Creative Affairs
  Gregg Tilson, Director of Development
  Erin Tierneu, Executive Assistant
Specialties: Network; Cable; Made for TV Movies; Miniseries
Other Categories: Feature Film
Credits: Jewel; Run the Wild Fields; Emma's Wish; Thirst
Trade Assoc./Guilds/Unions: DGA, WGAw

KEDZIE PRODUCTIONS
8615 Tamarack Ave.
Sun Valley, CA 91352
Phone: ....(818) 252-6129
Fax: ....(818) 504-3508
Key Executives/Personnel:
  Deborah Joy Levine, Executive Producer
  Sasheen Artis, Assistant
Specialties: Network; Cable; Made for TV Movies
Credits: Lois & Clark: The New Adventures of Superman; Dawson's Creek; Any Day Now; Courthouse
First Look/Development Deals: Viacom Productions

DAVID E. KELLEY PRODUCTIONS
1600 Rosecrans Ave., Bldg. 4B
Manhattan Beach, CA 90266
Phone: ....(310) 727-2200
Fax: ....(310) 727-2423
Key Executives/Personnel:
  David E. Kelley, CEO, Writer & Executive Producer
  Pamela Wisne, Executive VP & Producer
  Rick Silverman, COO
  Veronica Wilson, VP of Legal Affairs

Roseann M. Keris, Director of Marketing & Publicity
Neely Swanson, Director of Business Affairs
Bob Breech, Executive Producer
Gary M. Strangis, Co-Executive Producer
Bill D'Elia, Executive Producer
Alice West, Co-Executive Producer
Mike Listo, Supervising Producer
Jonathan Pontell, Co-Executive Producer
Shea Farrell, Manager of Creative Affairs
Elisa Todd, Manager of Creative Affairs
Specialties: Network
Other Categories: Feature Film
Credits: The Practice; Ally McBeal; Boston Public; Mystery Alaska
First Look/Development Deals: Twentieth Century Fox

KELLEY PRODUCTIONS INTERNATIONAL
2047 Caminito Capa
La Jolla, CA 92037
Phone: ....(858) 456-6609
Fax: ....(858) 459-5876
www.globalcuisine.com
Key Executives/Personnel:
Marie G. Kelley, President
Specialties: Cable; Documentaries
Other Categories: Commercials; Video
Trade Assoc./Guilds/Unions: ATAS, IDA, ITVA

THE KENNEDY/MARSHALL COMPANY
1351 Fourth St., 4th Fl.
Santa Monica, CA 90401
Phone: ....(310) 656-8400
Fax: ....(310) 656-8430
Key Executives/Personnel:
Zanne Devine, President
Kathleen Kennedy, Producer
Frank Marshall, Producer & Director
Mark Ross, Development Executive
Nancy Cavello, Story Editor
Mary Radford, Assistant to Mr. Marshall
Crissy Thomas-Taylor & Henrik Knudsen, Assistants to Ms. Kennedy
John Tantillo, Assistant to Ms. Devine
Specialties: Network
Other Categories: Feature Film
Credits: Milk Money; Congo; Snow Falling On Cedars; The Sixth Sense
First Look/Development Deals: Universal Pictures

DIANA KEREW PRODUCTIONS
c/o Alliance Atlantis, 808 Wilshire Blvd.
Santa Monica, CA 90401
Phone: ....(310) 899-8000
Fax: ....(310) 899-8100
Key Executives/Personnel:
Diana Kerew, President & Executive Producer
Linda Carolei, Director of Development
Chiara Frenquellucci, Executive Assistant
Specialties: Network; Cable; Made for TV Movies; Miniseries
Credits: Stepsister From the Planet Weird; 15 and Pregnant; Paris Trout; 87th Precinct
First Look/Development Deals: Alliance Atlantis

KINGSGATE FILMS
8954 W. Pico Blvd., 2nd Fl.
Los Angeles, CA 90035
Phone: ....(310) 281-5880
Key Executives/Personnel:
Nick Nolte, Producer
Greg Shapiro, Producer
Heather Edison, Executive Assistant
Specialties: Network; Cable

Other Categories: Feature Film
Credits: Affliction; Simpatico; Investigating Sex

DAVID KIRSCHNER PRODUCTIONS
400 S. June St.
Los Angeles, CA 90020
Phone: ....(323) 939-0230
Fax: ....(323) 930-0753
dkps@pacbell.net
Key Executives/Personnel:
David Kirschner, Producer
Corey Sienega, VP
Karen Loop, Director of Development
Specialties: Cable; Miniseries
Other Categories: Feature Film
Credits: The Flintstones; Hocus Pocus; Child's Play 1-4; An American Tail

KLASKY CSUPO, INC.
6353 Sunset Blvd.
Los Angeles, CA 90028
Phone: ....(323) 463-0145
www.klaskycsupo.com
Key Executives/Personnel:
Gabor Csupo, Founder & Co-Chair
Arlene Klasky, Founder & Co-Chair
Terry Thoren, President & CEO
Specialties: Network; Cable; Animation
Other Categories: Feature Film; Commercials
Credits: Rugrats; Duckman; The Simpsons; The Rugrats Movie

KONTRAST FILMS
315 W. Verdugo Ave.
Burbank, CA 91502
Phone: ....(818) 840-9333
Fax: ....(818) 840-9358
www.kontrastfilms.com
maureen@kontrastfilms.com
Key Executives/Personnel:
Greg Gears, Producer
Steven Kovner, VP of Production
Maureen English, VP of Sales
Valerio Ventura, Director
Specialties: Network; Cable; Animation; Documentaries; Made for TV Movies; Miniseries
Other Categories: Feature Film; Commercials
Credits: Cart Racing (commercial)

KOPELSON ENTERTAINMENT
2121 Avenue of the Stars, Ste. 1400
Los Angeles, CA 90067
Phone: ....(310) 369-7555
Fax: ....(310) 369-7501
Key Executives/Personnel:
Arnold Kopelson, Producer & Co-Chairperson
Anne Kopelson, Producer & Co-Chairperson
Nana Greenwald, President of Creative Affairs
Matthew Gross, Executive VP of Production
David Goldman, Sr. VP
Sherryl Clark, VP of Creative Affairs
Mark Stein, Creative Executive
Lara Wood, Creative Executive
Claudia O'Hehir, Executive Assistant to Ms. Kopelson
Elaine Mongeon, Executive Assistant to Mr. Kopelson
Specialties: Network
Other Categories: Feature Film
Credits: Platoon; The Fugitive (feature & TV series); Seven; A Perfect Murder

Production Companies – TV

KOUF-BIGELOW PRODUCTIONS
10061 Riverside Dr., PMB 1024
Toluca Lake, CA 91602
Phone: ....(818) 508-1010
Fax: ....(818) 508-1079
Key Executives/Personnel:
  Jim Kouf, Producer, Writer & Director
  Lynn Bigelow-Kouf, Producer
Specialties: Network; Made for TV Movies
Other Categories: Feature Film
Credits: Gang Related; Stakeout; Rush Hour
Additional Info: No unsolicited material accepted.

KRAININ PRODUCTIONS, INC.
8 Century Rd.
Palisades, NY 10964
Phone: ....(914) 359-0445
Fax: ....(914) 359-0446
krainin@rockland.net
Key Executives/Personnel:
  Julian Krainin, President, Producer & Director
  Michael Lawrence, Producer
  Todd Philips, Development
  Martye Wayne, VP
  Jason Hart, Special Projects
Specialties: Network; Cable; Documentaries; Made for TV Movies; Miniseries
Other Categories: Feature Film
Credits: Quiz Show; George Wallace; Disaster At Silo Seven; To America

SID & MARTY KROFFT PICTURES
14144 Ventura Blvd., Ste. 110
Sherman Oaks, CA 91423
Phone: ....(818) 386-1918
Fax: ....(818) 386-9790
Key Executives/Personnel:
  Marty Krofft, President
  Sid Krofft, Executive VP
  Randy Pope, Sr. VP of Production
Specialties: Network
Other Categories: Feature Film
Credits: H.R. Pufnstuf; The Bugaloos; Land of the Lost

KURTZ & FRIENDS
2312 W. Olive Ave.
Burbank, CA 91506
Phone: ....(818) 841-8188
Fax: ....(818) 841-6263
www.kurtzandfriends.com
bobkurtz@aol.com
Key Executives/Personnel:
  Bob Kurtz, Director, Writer & Designer
  Boo Lopez, Producer
  Robert Peluce, Designer & Director
Specialties: Animation
Other Categories: Feature Film; Commercials
Credits: Smokey the Bear (commercial)

KUSHNER-LOCKE COMPANY
11601 Wilshire Blvd., 21st Fl.
Los Angeles, CA 90025
Phone: ....(818) 841-8188
Fax: ....(818) 841-6263
www.kushner-locke.com
Key Executives/Personnel:
  Donald Kushner, Co-Chairman
  Peter Locke, Co-Chairman
  Bruce Lilliston, President & COO
  Rob Aft, President of Int'l. Distribution
  Richard Marks, Executive VP of Business Affairs
  Adam Moss, Executive VP of Production
  Steve Rosen, Executive VP of Operations & Finance
  Brett Robinson, Senior VP/CFO
  Cynthia Griffith, VP of Int'l. Distribution
  Bob Wenokur, VP of Post Production
  Dana Scanlan, VP of Feature Films
Specialties: Network; Cable; Made for TV Movies
Other Categories: Feature Film
Credits: They Nest; Mambo Cafe; Beowolf

KUZUI ENTERPRISES, INC.
1041 N. Formosa Ave., Ste. B
Los Angeles, CA 90046
Phone: ....(323) 850-1195
Fax: ....(323) 850-5465
uskuzui@earthlink.net
Key Executives/Personnel:
  Kaz Kuzui, President
  Fran Kuzui, Co-President
  Dawn Haber, Director of Creative Affairs
Specialties: Network
Other Categories: Feature Film
Credits: Tokyo Pop; Buffy The Vampire Slayer; Telling Lies in America; Orgazmo

LA PRODUCTIONS
Phone: ....(323) 874-9487
....(323) 871-1982
Fax: ....(323) 874-9487
Key Executives/Personnel:
  Herb Linsey, Executive Producer
  John Arnow, Executive Producer
  Stephen Paul, Executive Producer
  Thomas Cost, Executive Producer
Specialties: Network; Cable; Made for TV Movies; Miniseries
Other Categories: Feature Film; Commercials; Music Video
Credits: Curad Bandages; Goodyear Tires; Johnson & Johnson; Wrangler Clothes

THE LADD COMPANY
9465 Wilshire Blvd., Ste. 910
Beverly Hills, CA 90212
Phone: ....(310) 777-2060
Fax: ....(310) 777-2061
Key Executives/Personnel:
  Alan Ladd Jr., President
  Keiliann Ladd, Producer
  Natalia Chydzik, Creative Executive
  Peter Bisanz, Assistant to Mr. Ladd
  Lucy Rimalower, Assistant to Mr. Ladd
Specialties: Network; Cable
Other Categories: Feature Film
Credits: Chariots of Fire; Bladerunner; The Brady Bunch Movie; Braveheart

LANGLEY PRODUCTIONS
2225 Colorado Ave.
Santa Monica, CA 90404
Phone: ....(310) 449-5300
Key Executives/Personnel:
  John Langley, President, Executive Producer, Director & Writer
  Murray Jordan, Producer
  Doug Waterman, Producer
  Elie Cohn, Producer
  Karen Hori, VP of TV Development
Specialties: Network; Cable; Documentaries
Other Categories: Feature Film; Interactive Multimedia
Credits: Cops; Anatomy of a Crime; Code 3; Wild Side
First Look/Development Deals: Twentieth Century Fox

Production Companies – TV

LAWTON ENTERTAINMENT
419 N. Larchmont, PMB 27
Los Angeles, CA 90004
Phone: ....(323) 467-5677
Fax: ....(323) 467-5755
lawtonenter@earthlink.net
Key Executives/Personnel:
    J. F. Lawton, President
Specialties: Network; Cable
Other Categories: Feature Film
Credits: V.I.P.; Under Seige

LE MONDE ENTERTAINMENT
808 Wilshire Blvd., 3rd Fl.
Santa Monica, CA 90404
Phone: ....(310) 899-8000
....(416) 967-1174
Fax: ....(310) 899-8100
www.allianceatlantis.com
Key Executives/Personnel:
    Marc Forby, Director of Creative Affairs
Specialties: Cable
Other Categories: Feature Film
Credits: Second Skin; Cara Cara; Teacher's Pet; Falling Through

MALCOLM LEO PRODUCTIONS
6536 Sunset Blvd.
Los Angeles, CA 90028
Phone: ....(323) 464-4448
Fax: ....(323) 856-8755
Key Executives/Personnel:
    Malcolm Leo, Executive Producer & Director
    David Fairfield, Producer
    Nat Segaloff, Producer
    Edick Hossepian, Editorial
    Lionel Banes, Operations Manager
Specialties: Network; Cable; Documentaries
Other Categories: Feature Film
Credits: Rock 'n Roll Moments; Laverne & Shirley Reunion; This Is Elvis; Rolling Stone - 20 Years of Rock 'n Roll
First Look/Development Deals: Discovery Network, Selznick Properties, Paramount Pictures
Trade Assoc./Guilds/Unions: AFTRA, BMI, DGA, SAG, WGAw

LET THERE BE LIGHT PRODUCTIONS
4240 Lost Hills Rd., Ste. 2801
Agoura Hills, CA 91301
Phone: ....(818) 880-4717
Fax: ....(818) 880-4717
littnet@cs.com
Key Executives/Personnel:
    Robert Litt, Producer
Specialties: Cable
Other Categories: Feature Film; Commercials; Video; Music Video
Credits: Jenny Craig; WorldFreeNet.com; MPI/LA Tourism Bureau; Turbo - Take It To The Limit
First Look/Development Deals: Summer Storm Pictures

THE LEVINSON/FONTANA COMPANY
448 W. 16th St., 6th Fl.
New York, NY 10011
Phone: ....(212) 633-0440
Fax: ....(212) 633-7008
www.levinson.com
Key Executives/Personnel:
    Barry Levinson, Executive Producer, Writer & Director
    Tom Fontana, Executive Producer & Writer
    James Finnerty, Executive Producer
    Amy Solan, CFO & Business Affairs
Specialties: Network; Cable; Made for TV Movies
Credits: Oz

MICHAEL I. LEVY ENTERPRISES
6404 Wilshire Blvd., Ste. 520
Los Angeles, CA 90048
Phone: ....(323) 866-1802
Fax: ....(323) 866-1820
Key Executives/Personnel:
    Michael I. Levy, Producer
    Stephen Macias, VP of Creative Affairs
    Mark Saffian, Director of Development
    Georgette Waas, Creative Assistant
Specialties: Network; Cable
Other Categories: Feature Film
Credits: Prelude to a Kiss; Article 99; O

SIMON LEWIS PRODUCTIONS, INC.
16002 Meadowcrest Rd.
Sherman Oaks, CA 91403
Phone: ....(818) 906-7677
Fax: ....(818) 906-2836
Key Executives/Personnel:
    Simon R. Lewis, President
Specialties: Network; Cable
Other Categories: Feature Film
Credits: Look Who's Talking; The Chocolate War; Age Old Friends; Howie From Maui

LICHT/MUELLER FILMS
132A S. Lasky Dr., Ste. 200
Beverly Hills, CA 90212
Phone: ....(310) 205-5500
Fax: ....(310) 205-5590
Key Executives/Personnel:
    Andrew Licht, Producer & Partner
    Jeffery Mueller, Producer & Partner
    Ben Sitzer, Director of Development
    Doug Hammond, Creative Assistant
Specialties: Network; Cable
Other Categories: Feature Film
Credits: Idle Hands; License to Drive; The Cable Guy; Waterworld

LIFETIME TELEVISION (EAST COAST)
309 W. 49th St.
New York, NY 10019
Phone: ....(212) 424-7000
www.lifetimetv.com
Key Executives/Personnel:
    Carole Black, President & CEO
    Rick Haskins, Executive VP of Marketing & Creative Services
    Patricia Langer, Executive VP of Business, Legal Affairs & Human Resources
    Dawn Tarnofsky-Ostroff, Executive VP of Entertainment
    James Wesley, Executive VP of Finance & CFO
    Tim Brooks, Executive VP of Research
    Rick Basso, Sr. VP of Pricing & Planning
    Jessica Marshall, Sr. VP of Online Department
    Meredith Wagner, Sr. VP of Public Affairs
    Dorian Winship, VP of Production
    Amy Introcaso-Davis, VP of Series
    Marilyn McAleer, VP of Creative Services
    Kevin Moran, VP of Business Development
    Michael Tedone, VP of Sales
    Steve Warner, VP of Programming & Acquisitions
Specialties: Cable; Made for TV Movies
Credits: Oh Baby; Any Day Now

LIFETIME TELEVISION (WEST COAST)
2049 Century Park East, Ste. 840
Los Angeles, CA 90067
Phone: ....(310) 556-7500
Fax: ....(310) 557-8964

Production Companies – TV

www.lifetimetv.com
Key Executives/Personnel:
  Carole Black, President & CEO
  Louise Henry-Bryson, Executive VP of Business Affairs
  Aviva Bergman, Sr. VP of Business Affairs
  Laurette Hayden, VP of Original Movies
  Kelly Goode, VP of Series
  Rick Jacobs, VP of Talent
  Colleen McCormick, VP of Production
  Kelly Abugov, VP of Series
  Marian Effinger, VP of Reality Series
Specialties: Cable; Movie of the Week
Credits: Oh Baby; Any Day Now

LIGHTMOTIVE, INC.
10351 Santa Monica Blvd., Ste. 402
Los Angeles, CA 90025
Phone: ....(310) 282-0660
Fax: ....(310) 282-0990
Key Executives/Personnel:
  Roland Joffe, Chairman & CEO
  Ethan Markowitz, Creative Director
  Brian Lhee, Executive Assistant to Mr. Joffe
Specialties: Network; Cable; Made for TV Movies
Other Categories: Feature Film
Credits: Fat Man and Little Boy; City of Joy; Undressed (TV series); Goodbye Lover

LIGHTNING BOLT PIX: BARNYARD PRODUCTIONS
1653 18th St., Ste. 3B
Santa Monica, CA 90404
Phone: ....(310) 828-8239
Fax: ....(310) 828-1923
www.boltpix.com
mwbfield@aol.com
Key Executives/Personnel:
  Michael Barnard, Owner, Producer & Director
  Morgan Barnard, Co-Owner, Director & Editor
  Philip DeVellis, Production Coordinator & Designer
Specialties: Cable; Documentaries
Other Categories: Commercials; Video; Music Video
Credits: Bringing The Light; Chihuly River of Glass; Edgar.com; National Labor Life

LION ROCK PRODUCTIONS
2450 Broadway, Ste. 590
Santa Monica, CA 90404
Phone: ....(310) 449-3205
Fax: ....(310) 449-3512
Key Executives/Personnel:
  John Woo, Director & Producer
  Terence Chang, Producer
  Caroline Bruce, VP
  Suzanne Zizzi, VP
  Annie Hughes, Creative Associate
Specialties: Network; Cable
Other Categories: Feature Film
Credits: Windtalkers; The Big Hit; Broken Arrow; Face Off
First Look/Development Deals: MGM, Inc.

LIONS GATE ENTERTAINMENT
5750 Wilshire Blvd., Ste. 501
Los Angeles, CA 90036
Phone: ....(323) 692-7300
          ....(310) 314-2000
Fax: ....(323) 692-7395
www.lionsgate.ent.com
Key Executives/Personnel:
  Michael Paseornek, President of Production
  Mark Amin, Board of Directors
  Mark Urman, Co-President of Releasing
  Tom Ortenberg, Co-President of Releasing
  Cami Winikoff, Executive VP
  Peter Block, Executive VP of Distribution, Acquisitions & New Media
  Kevin Beggs, Executive VP of TV Series
  Doug Shwartz, Executive Producer
  Sergei Yershov, Sr. VP of Int'l. Sales
  Ellen Burditt, Sr. VP of TV Series
  Andy Reimer, Sr. VP of Worldwide Television
  Robin Schorr, Sr. VP of Production
  Ron Schwartz, Sr. VP of Home Video
  Richard Jordan, Sr. VP of Physical Operations
  Joella West, Sr. VP of Business Affairs
  James L. Zemelman, Sr. VP of Business Affairs
  Peter Marshall, VP of TV Production
  Guy Stodel, VP of Acquisitions
  Tracy Ames, VP of Worldwide Home Video Marketing
  Sarah Lash, Director of Acquisitions & Development
Specialties: Network; Cable; Miniseries
Other Categories: Feature Film
Credits: American Psycho; Buffalo 66; Shadow of the Vampire; Jerry & Tom
Additional Info: Recently merged with Trimark Pictures. Personnel titles subject to change.

SI LITVINOFF PRODUCTIONS
2825 Woodstock Rd.
Los Angeles, CA 90046
Phone: ....(323) 848-6907
Fax: ....(323) 848-6908
slitvinoff@aol.com
Key Executives/Personnel:
  Si Litvinoff, President
  Paul Madden, VP of Development
  Ian Litvinoff, VP
Specialties: Cable
Other Categories: Feature Film
Credits: A Clockwork Orange; The Man Who Fell To Earth; Walkabout; The Queen
Trade Assoc./Guilds/Unions: AMPAS

WARREN LOCKHART PRODUCTIONS, INC.
P.O. Box 11629
Marina Del Rey, CA 90295
Phone: ....(310) 821-1414
Fax: ....(310) 301-0536
warren@lockhartproductions.com
Key Executives/Personnel:
  Warren Lockhart, Producer & Writer
  Mackenzie Allen, VP of Development
Specialties: Network; Cable; Animation; Documentaries
Other Categories: Feature Film
Trade Assoc./Guilds/Unions: MPAA

LOGO ENTERTAINMENT
1888 Century Park East, Ste. 1900
Los Angeles, CA 90067
Phone: ....(310) 276-6700
Fax: ....(310) 284-3290
logoent@earthlink.net
Key Executives/Personnel:
  Louis Gossett Jr., President
  Dennis Considine, Executive Producer
  Laurie Ferneau, Development
Specialties: Network; Cable; Made for TV Movies
Other Categories: Feature Film
Credits: The Color of Love: Jacey's Story; For Love of Olivia; The Inspectors; The Inspectors 2: A Shred of Evidence
First Look/Development Deals: TeleVest, Inc.

Production Companies – TV

LUCASFILM LTD.
5858 Lucas Valley Rd.
Nicasio, CA 94946
Phone: ....(415) 662-1800
Specialties: Network; Cable
Other Categories: Feature Film
Additional Info: P.O. Box 2009, San Rafael, CA 94912

LUCID FILM
8490 Sunset Blvd., Ste. 700
West Hollywood, CA 90069
Phone: ....(310) 777-0007
Fax: ....(310) 360-8613
www.lucidfilm.com
Key Executives/Personnel:
    Ryan Phillippe, Producer
    David E. Siegel, Producer
Specialties: Cable; Animation
Other Categories: Feature Film; Interactive Multimedia
First Look/Development Deals: Intermedia Films

LUCID MEDIA
Phone: ....(818) 764-8580
www.loop.com/~macbravo
macbravo@loop.com
Key Executives/Personnel:
    Marino Colmano, Producer
Specialties: Cable; Documentaries; Made for TV Movies
Other Categories: Feature Film; Commercials; Video
Credits: Reservoirs of Strength; End of the Rainbow

LUMINATION INC.
12356 Laurel Terrace Dr.
Studio City, CA 91604
Phone: ....(818) 766-1868
Fax: ....(818) 762-4866
lumin8ion@email.msn.com
Key Executives/Personnel:
    Alvin Mori, Executive Producer
    Meg Okura, Producer
Specialties: Miniseries
Other Categories: Commercials
Credits: Honda; Big John Jeans

M.H.S. PRODUCTIONS
9336 W. Washington Blvd., Bldg. 0, Rm. 202
Culver City, CA 90232
Phone: ....(310) 202-3336
Fax: ....(310) 202-3320
Key Executives/Personnel:
    Joan Hyler, Producer
    Alfred Molina, Producer & Actor
    Larry Scissors, Business Affairs
    Adam Gascoine, Director of Development
    Joey Chang, Development Assistant
Specialties: Network
Other Categories: Feature Film
Credits: Ladies Man
First Look/Development Deals: Columbia Pictures/Columbia Tristar Motion Picture Group

WILLIAM J. MACDONALD PRODUCTIONS
3100 Donald Douglas Loop North, Box 17, Hangar 5
Santa Monica, CA 90405
Phone: ....(310) 581-4840
Fax: ....(310) 581-6111
wjmprods@aol.com
Key Executives/Personnel:
    Bill MacDonald, Producer
    Erik Mountain, Development
Specialties: Cable; Made for TV Movies; Miniseries

Other Categories: Feature Film
Credits: Sliver; The Saint; Jade; Molly

MAKE IT HAPPEN PRODUCTIONS, INC.
Phone: ....(323) 851-6444
Fax: ....(323) 851-6465
www.billyfrank.com
mihpi@aol.com
Key Executives/Personnel:
    Billy Frank, President & Producer
    Todd Denkin, Director & Producer
    Mark Eberle, Director of Photography
    Caroline Hileman, Assistant to President & Coordinator
Specialties: Network; Cable; Documentaries
Other Categories: Feature Film; Commercials; Video; Music Video
Credits: Wap!; Toughman (specials); Australian Experience
First Look/Development Deals: ABC Entertainment Television Group, FX Networks, LLC
Trade Assoc./Guilds/Unions: SAG, WGAw

MANDALAY TELEVISION
9229 Sunset Blvd., Ste. 410
Los Angeles, CA 90069
Phone: ....(310) 205-9800
Fax: ....(310) 205-9006
www.mandalay.com
Key Executives/Personnel:
    Joe Voci, Executive VP, TV Series
    Nancy Cotton, VP, TV Series
    Chris Selak, Director of Development, TV Series
    Elizabeth Stephen, President, TV Pictures
    Shirley Lima, Creative Executive, TV Pictures
Specialties: Network; Made for TV Movies; Miniseries
Credits: Rude Awakening; Young Americans; Linda McCartney Story; First Daughter

MANDOLIN ENTERTAINMENT
1741 Ivar Ave.
Los Angeles, CA 90028
Phone: ....(323) 802-6950
Fax: ....(323) 802-6951
Key Executives/Personnel:
    Mimi Polk Gitlin, Producer
    Tanna Thompson, Director of Development
    Lisa Kelly, Story Editor & Assistant
Specialties: Made for TV Movies; Miniseries
Other Categories: Feature Film
Credits: Thelma & Louise; White Squall; Black Rain; The Browning Version
First Look/Development Deals: Propaganda Films
Trade Assoc./Guilds/Unions: AMPAS

THE MANHATTAN PROJECT
1775 Broadway, Ste. 410
New York, NY 10019
Phone: ....(212) 258-2541
Fax: ....(212) 258-2546
Key Executives/Personnel:
    David Brown, President & Producer
    Kit Golden, Sr. VP of Production
    Doris Wood, Executive Assistant
Specialties: Made for TV Movies; Miniseries
Other Categories: Feature Film
Credits: Enigma; Angela's Ashes; Deep Impact; A Few Good Men

MARCH HARE ENTERTAINMENT AT JAFFE-BRAUNSTEIN
7920 Sunset Blvd., Ste. 444
Los Angeles, CA 90046
Phone: ....(323) 464-4100
Fax: ....(323) 878-0871
ellynw@earthlink.net

Production Companies – TV

Key Executives/Personnel:
  Sally Jessy Raphael, CEO
  Ellyn Williams, President
Specialties: Network; Made for TV Movies; Miniseries
Credits: Sally Jessy Raphael Show; The Third Twin; Bootcamp; Rivals
First Look/Development Deals: USA Network, Jaffe/Braunstein Films, Ltd.

JEFF MARGOLIS PRODUCTIONS
1401 Westwood Blvd., 3rd Fl.
Los Angeles, CA 90024
Phone: ....(310) 235-1030
Fax: ....(310) 235-1032
jmp@jmprod.net
Key Executives/Personnel:
  Jeff Margolis, Producer & Director
  Gloria Fujita-O'Brien, Producer
  Mick McCullough, Producer
Specialties: Network
Credits: Screen Actors Guild Awards; Miss America Pageant; A Gala for the President at Ford's Theatre; Quincy Jones: The First 50 Years

LAURENCE MARK PRODUCTIONS
10202 W. Washington Blvd., Poitier Bldg., Ste. 3111
Culver City, CA 90232
Phone: ....(310) 244-5239
Key Executives/Personnel:
  Laurence Mark, Producer
  Jonathon King, President of Production
  John McNamara, VP of Development & Film
  Ilene Berg, VP of Development & TV
Specialties: Network; Made for TV Movies
Other Categories: Feature Film
Credits: Finding Forrester; Center Stage; As Good As It Gets; Jerry Maguire
First Look/Development Deals: Columbia Pictures/Columbia Tristar Motion Picture Group

MARVEL CHARACTERS, INC.
10474 Santa Monica Blvd., Ste. 206
Los Angeles, CA 90025
Phone: ....(310) 234-8991
Fax: ....(310) 234-8481
www.marvel.com
Key Executives/Personnel:
  Stan Lee, Chairman Emeritus
  Avi Arad, President & CEO
  Rich Ungar, President of Marvel Characters Group
  Carlos Lopez, Executive Director of Creative Development
  Matt Sullivan, Director of Development
  Michael Kelly, Executive Assistant to Mr. Lee
  Amy Lewis, Executive Assistant to Mr. Ungar
  Victoria Tapscott, Executive Assistant to Mr. Arad
Specialties: Network; Cable; Animation
Other Categories: Feature Film
Credits: Spiderman; X-Men; Blade

NIKI MARVIN PRODUCTIONS
8919 Harratt St., Ste. 304
Los Angeles, CA 90069
Phone: ....(310) 274-6320
Key Executives/Personnel:
  Niki Marvin, President
Specialties: Network; Cable; Documentaries; Made for TV Movies
Other Categories: Feature Film; Video
Credits: Nightmare On Elm Street 3; Buried Alive 1 & 2; The Shawshank Redemption

JOHN MASIUS PRODUCTIONS, INC.
100 Universal City Plaza, Bldg. 2128, Ste. E
Universal City, CA 91608
Phone: ....(310) 395-1572
Key Executives/Personnel:
  John Masius, Executive Producer
Specialties: Network
Credits: Providence; St. Elsewhere
First Look/Development Deals: NBC Entertainment, Inc.

MATADOR PICTURES
12424 Wilshire Blvd., Ste. 770
Los Angeles, CA 90025
Phone: ....(310) 820-5866
Fax: ....(310) 207-2275
www.matadorpictures.com
lauri@matadorpictures.com
Key Executives/Personnel:
  Lauri Apelian, Producer
  Nigel Thomas, Producer
  Peter Watson-Wood, Producer
Specialties: Made for TV Movies
Other Categories: Feature Film
Credits: Mad Dogs & Englishmen; The Fall; Dead Funny; Mortal Kombat
Trade Assoc./Guilds/Unions: IFPW, PGA

THE MATTHAU COMPANY, INC.
11661 San Vicente Blvd., Ste. 609
Los Angeles, CA 90049
Phone: ....(310) 454-3300
Key Executives/Personnel:
  Charles Matthau, President
  Michael McDavitt, President of Management Division
  Lana Morgan, Director of Creative Affairs
  Kristina Jeffers, Director of Business Affairs
  Jessica Cooper, Office Manager
Specialties: Network; Cable; Made for TV Movies
Other Categories: Feature Film
Credits: Hanging up; Mrs. Lambert Remembers Love; The Grass Harp; Grumpy Old Men

MESITA
11005 Wrightwood Pl.
Studio City, CA 91604
Phone: ....(818) 760-8707
Fax: ....(818) 760-0925
mesitafilms@aol.com
Key Executives/Personnel:
  Richard Black, Director & Cameraman
  Jeremy Hammond, Executive Producer
  Darr Hawthorne, Representative
Specialties: Documentaries
Other Categories: Commercials
Credits: California Tourism Board; Hawaii Tourism Board; Celebrity Cruises; American Express

METAFILMICS
4250 Wilshire Blvd.
Los Angeles, CA 90010
Phone: ....(818) 734-9320
Fax: ....(818) 345-2502
Key Executives/Personnel:
  Stephen Simon, Co-Founder
  Barnet Bain, Co-Founder
Specialties: Network; Cable; Made for TV Movies; Miniseries
Other Categories: Feature Film; Interactive Multimedia
Credits: What Dreams May Come; Somewhere in Time; Bill & Ted's Excellent Adventure; Quantum Project

METRO-GOLDWYN-MAYER/WORLDWIDE TV
2500 Broadway
Santa Monica, CA 90404
Phone: ....(310) 449-3000
www.mgm.com

Key Executives/Personnel:
- Alex Yemenidijian, Chairman & CEO
- Chris McGurk, Vice Chairman & COO
- Dan Taylor, Sr. Executive VP & CFO
- William Jones, Sr. Executive VP & Secretary
- Jay Rakow, General Counsel
- Hank Cohen, President of MGM TV Group
- Jim Griffiths, President of TV Distribution
- Jules Haimovitz, President of MGM Networks

Specialties: Network; Cable; Made for TV Movies
Credits: Outer Limits; Stargate SG-1

MILLER/BOYETT PRODUCTIONS
745 Fifth Ave., Ste. 3500
New York, NY 10151
Phone: ...(212) 702-9779
...(212) 702-8721
Fax: ...(212) 702-0899

Key Executives/Personnel:
- Robert L. Boyett, Executive Producer
- Thomas L. Miller, Executive Producer
- Diane Murphy, Director of M/B Executive Offices

Specialties: Network
Other Categories: Feature Film
Credits: Full House; Family Matters; Step By Step; Two of A Kind
First Look/Development Deals: Warner Bros.
Trade Assoc./Guilds/Unions: DGA, PGA, WGAe
Additional Info: No unsolicited material accepted.

MINDFIRE ENTERTAINMENT
3740 Overland Ave., Ste. E
Los Angeles, CA 90034
Phone: ...(310) 204-4481
Fax: ...(310) 204-5882
www.mindfireentertainment.com
maltman@mindfireentertainment.com

Key Executives/Personnel:
- Mark Gottwald, Chairman
- Dan Bates, CEO
- Mark A. Altman, COO
- Ellie Gottwald, VP of Creative Affairs
- Ann Kaesman, Director of Development
- Carlos Rodriguez, Story Analyst

Specialties: Cable; Animation
Other Categories: Feature Film; Interactive Multimedia
Credits: Free Enterprise; The Specials

MINDSTORM PRODUCTIONS, LLC
1434 6th St., Ste. 1
Santa Monica, CA 90401
Phone: ...(310) 393-1183
Fax: ...(310) 393-6622
www.mindstormprods.com
mind71@aol.com

Key Executives/Personnel:
- Karina Duffy, President
- Jacquenne Beaudette, Co-President
- Larry Leahy, Producer

Specialties: Network; Cable
Other Categories: Feature Film
Credits: Fanatic; Extra; Diaries - Love Hurts; Fox Files/Fox Undercover

MINERVISION
8000 Sunset Blvd., Ste. 301A
Los Angeles, CA 90046
Phone: ...(323) 848-3080
Fax: ...(323) 848-3085

Key Executives/Personnel:
- Steve Miner, Producer & Director
- Jessica Cunningham, VP of Production
- Kristy Scanlan, VP of Development
- Jeff Shapiro, Assistant to Mr. Miner
- Jimmy Bradley, Development Assistant

Specialties: Network; Cable
Other Categories: Feature Film
Credits: Dawson's Creek
First Look/Development Deals: Dimension Films

MM2K
838 N. Doheny Dr., Ste. 904
West Hollywood, CA 90069
Phone: ...(310) 276-0750
Fax: ...(310) 276-0229
mm2k@earthlink.net

Key Executives/Personnel:
- William A. Levey, Executive Producer & Director
- Bob Manning, Head of Production
- Nancy Youngblood, Director of Creative Development

Specialties: Cable
Other Categories: Feature Film; Commercials; Video; Music Video
Credits: Slumber Party 57; The Happy Hooker Goes To Washington; Skatetown U.S.A.; White Stallion
Trade Assoc./Guilds/Unions: DGA, IATSE, WGAw

MO JO PRODUCTIONS, INC.
4224 Waialae Ave., Ste. 300
Honolulu, HI 96816
Phone: ...(808) 384-8460
...(626) 932-6432
Fax: ...(808) 733-4142
mojoproductions@juno.com

Key Executives/Personnel:
- Michael Pendell, President

Specialties: Cable; Made for TV Movies; Miniseries
Other Categories: Feature Film; Commercials; Music Video
Credits: Baywatch: Hawaii; Extended list available upon request.
Trade Assoc./Guilds/Unions: DGA

MONAREX HOLLYWOOD CORPORATION
9421 1/2 W. Pico Blvd.
Los Angeles, CA 90035
Phone: ...(310) 552-1069
Fax: ...(310) 552-1724

Key Executives/Personnel:
- Chris D. Nebe, President

Specialties: Network; Cable; Documentaries; Made for TV Movies
Other Categories: Feature Film; Video
Credits: Heartbreaker; Rebels; The Inheritors; Last of The Caravans
Trade Assoc./Guilds/Unions: IDA

MORGAN CREEK PRODUCTIONS
4000 Warner Blvd., Bldg. 76
Burbank, CA 91522
Phone: ...(818) 954-4800
Fax: ...(818) 954-4811
www.morgancreek.com

Key Executives/Personnel:
- James G. Robinson, Chairman & CEO
- Howard Kaplan, CFO
- Jonathan A. Zimbert, President of Production

Specialties: Animation
Other Categories: Feature Film
Credits: Ace Ventura; Robin Hood; Wild America; American Outlaw
First Look/Development Deals: Warner Bros.

MORRA, BREZNER, STEINBERG & TENENBAUM
345 N. Maple Dr., Ste. 200
Beverly Hills, CA 90210

Production Companies – TV

Phone: (310) 385-1820
Fax: (310) 385-1834
Key Executives/Personnel:
- Larry Brezner, Partner
- David Steinberg, Partner
- Stephen Tenenbaum, Partner
- Judy Apperson, no title
- Jonathan Brandstein, no title
- Scott Fedro, no title
- Walter Hamada, no title
- Andrew Tenenbaum, no title

Specialties: Network; Cable; Made for TV Movies
Other Categories: Feature Film
Credits: Krippendorf's Tribe; Clifford; The Vanishing
First Look/Development Deals: Walt Disney Pictures/Touchstone Pictures

MOVING PICTURES
375 Greenwich St.
New York, NY 10013
Phone: (212) 219-4545
Fax: (212) 219-4546
Key Executives/Personnel:
- Demi Moore, Partner & Producer
- Daneen Conroy, Partner & President
- Andrea Asimow, Sr. VP of Production
- Ren Tucker, Creative Executive

Specialties: Made for TV Movies
Other Categories: Feature Film
Credits: Austin Powers 1 & 2; G. I. Jane; If These Walls Could Talk
First Look/Development Deals: Miramax Films

MOVING TARGET
1250 Sixth St., Ste. 201
Santa Monica, CA 90401
Phone: (310) 394-0110
Fax: (310) 394-4123
Specialties: Network; Cable
Other Categories: Feature Film; Commercials
Credits: Sleepy Hollow; The Others

MOZARK PRODUCTIONS
4024 Radford Ave., Bldg. 5, Ste. 104
Studio City, CA 91604
Phone: (818) 655-5779
Fax: (818) 655-5129
mozark@ix.netcom.com
Key Executives/Personnel:
- Linda Bloodworth-Thomason, Executive Producer & Writer
- Harry Thomason, Executive Producer & Director

Specialties: Network
Other Categories: Feature Film
Credits: Woman of the House; Evening Shade; Designing Women
First Look/Development Deals: CBS Entertainment, DreamWorks SKG

MR. MUDD PRODUCTIONS
5225 Wilshire Blvd., Ste. 604
Los Angeles, CA 90036
Phone: (323) 932-5656
Fax: (323) 932-5666
Key Executives/Personnel:
- John Malkovich, Partner
- Lianne Halfon, Partner
- Russ Smith, Partner
- Aileen Argentini, Head of Production

Specialties: Network; Cable
Other Categories: Feature Film
Credits: Ghost World; The Dancer Upstairs
First Look/Development Deals: Granada Film

MTV NETWORKS (EAST COAST)
1515 Broadway Ave.
New York, NY 10036
Phone: (212) 258-8000
www.mtv.com
Key Executives/Personnel:
- Thomas E. Freston, Chairman & CEO
- Judith McGarth, President of MTV/Chairman of Interactive Music
- Mark Rosenthal, President & COO
- Brian Graden, President of Programming
- Van Teffler, President of MTV Productions & MTV2
- Abby Turkuhle, President of MTV Animation
- Bob Kusbit, Sr. VP of MTV Productions
- Tony DiSanto, VP of Development
- Paul Benedettis, VP of Program Scheduling

Specialties: Cable; Animation; Documentaries; Made for TV Movies; Miniseries
Credits: Real World; Road Rules; The Tom Green Show; Daria

MTV NETWORKS (WEST COAST)
2600 Colorado Ave.
Santa Monica, CA 90404
Phone: (310) 752-8000
www.mtv.com
Key Executives/Personnel:
- Thomas E. Freston, Chairman & CEO
- Judith McGrath, President of MTV/Chairman of Interactive Music
- Mark Rosenthal, President & COO
- Brian Graden, President of Programming
- Leslie Leventman, Executive VP of Creative Services, Special Events & Travel Services
- Lois Clark Curren, Sr. VP of Music Development
- John Miller, Sr. VP of Original Series Development & Current Programming
- Salli Frantini, Sr. VP of Production

Specialties: Cable; Animation; Documentaries; Made for TV Movies; Miniseries
Credits: Real World; Road Rules; The Tom Green Show; Daria

MUSE PRODUCTIONS
15 Brooks Ave., Unit B
Venice, CA 90291
Phone: (310) 306-2001
Fax: (310) 574-2614
www.musefilm.com
Key Executives/Personnel:
- Chris Hanley, President & Producer
- Roberta Hanley, President & Director
- Jordan Gertner, VP
- Tim Peternel, VP of Creative Affairs
- Danny Vinik, VP of Digital Development

Specialties: Cable
Other Categories: Feature Film
Credits: Bully; American Psycho; The Virgin Suicides; Trees Lounge

MUTANT ENEMY, INC.
P.O. Box 900
Beverly Hills, CA 90213
Phone: (310) 579-5180
Fax: (310) 579-5380
Key Executives/Personnel:
- Joss Whedon, CEO
- Tom Plotkin, Creative Executive
- George Synder, Director of Development

Specialties: Network; Animation
Other Categories: Feature Film
Credits: Buffy The Vampire Slayer; Angel
First Look/Development Deals: Twentieth Century Fox Television

Production Companies – TV

MUTUAL FILM COMPANY
650 N. Bronson Ave., Clinton Bldg.
Los Angeles, CA 90004
Phone: (323) 871-5690
Fax: (323) 871-5689
Key Executives/Personnel:
    Marc Gordon, Principal
    Gary Levinsohn, Principal
    Betsy Beers, President of Production
    Tania Landau, Production Executive
    Suzanne Patmore, Production Executive
    Al Haferkamp, Controller
    Anthony Mosawi, Business & Legal Affairs
    Pamela Pickering, Mutual Film Int'l.
Specialties: Cable
Other Categories: Feature Film
Credits: Saving Private Ryan; The Patriot; A Simple Plan; Wonder Boys
First Look/Development Deals: Paramount Pictures

MWG PRODUCTIONS
8075 W. Third St., Ste. 402
Los Angeles, CA 90048
Phone: (323) 937-8313
Fax: (323) 937-5239
Key Executives/Personnel:
    Max Goldenson, Owner & Producer
Specialties: Network; Cable; Documentaries; Made for TV Movies; Miniseries
Other Categories: Feature Film
Credits: Nine; Saddlebags; The Tracy Bower Story; Cast No Shadow

NATIONAL GEOGRAPHIC FEATURE FILMS
501 S. Beverly Dr., Ste. 250
Beverly Hills, CA 90212
Phone: (310) 229-0990
Fax: (310) 229-0980
Key Executives/Personnel:
    Christine Whitaker, Head of Features
    Laura Kim Lodin, Story Editor
Specialties: Network; Cable; Made for TV Movies; Miniseries
Other Categories: Feature Film

NATIONAL LAMPOON
10850 Wilshire Blvd., Ste. 1000
Los Angeles, CA 90024
Phone: (310) 474-5252
Fax: (310) 474-1219
www.nationallampoon.com
Key Executives/Personnel:
    James P. Jimirro, President & CEO
    Chris Trunkey, CFO
    Duncan Murray, VP of Marketing
Specialties: Network; Cable
Other Categories: Feature Film; Interactive Multimedia
Credits: Vacation; Animal House; National Lampoon's Senior Trip

NBC ENTERTAINMENT, INC.
30 Rockefeller Plaza
New York, NY 10112
Phone: (212) 664-4444
www.nbc.com
Key Executives/Personnel:
    Robert Wright, President & CEO
    Mark Begor, Executive VP & CFO, President of NBC Business Development & Interactive Media
    Dick Ebersol, Chairman of NBC Sports & NBC Olympics
    John Eck, President of Broadcast & Network Operations
    Randy Falco, President of NBC Television Network
    Jay Ireland, President of NBC Television Stations
    Andrew Lack, President of NBC News
    Kenneth Schanzer, President of NBC Sports
    Keith Turner, President of Sales, NBC Television Network
    Alan Wurtzel, President of Research & Media Development
    David M. Zaslav, President of Cable Distribution, NBC
    Martin J. Yudkovitz, President of NBC Digital Media
Specialties: Network; Made for TV Movies; Miniseries

NBC ENTERTAINMENT (WEST COAST)
3000 W. Alameda Ave.
Burbank, CA 91523
Phone: (818) 840-4444
www.nbc.com
Key Executives/Personnel:
    Scott Sassa, President of NBC West Coast
    Garth Ancier, President of NBC Entertainment
    Ted Harbert, President of NBC Studios
    John Miller, President of The NBC Agency
    Ed Wilson, President of NBC Enterprises & Syndication
    Susan Weiner, Executive VP & General Counsel
    Marc J. Graboff, Executive VP of Business Affairs
    Harold Brook, Executive VP of Business Affairs, NBC Entertainment & NBC Studios
    Karey Burke, Executive VP of Primetime Series Development, NBC Entertainment
    Gary Considine, Executive Producer of NBC Studios
    Marc Hirschfeld, Executive VP of Casting, NBC Entertainment
    Vince Manze, Executive VP & Creative Director, The NBC Agency
    Jerry Petry, Executive VP of NBC Enterprises
    Steve White, Executive VP of Movies & Miniseries, NBC Entertainment
    JoAnn Alfano, Sr. VP of Comedy Development
    Tom Cairns, Sr. VP of Employee Relations, NBC West Coast
    Christopher Conti, Sr. VP of Drama Development, NBC Entertainment
    Anne Egerton, Sr. VP & General Counsel, NBC West Coast
    Linda Finneli, Sr. VP of Non-Fiction Daytime Programs, NBC Entertainment
    Ted Frank, Sr. VP of Current Series and Program Scheduling, NBC Entertainment
    Patti Hutton, Sr. VP of Finance, NBC West Coast
    Sheraton Kalouria, Sr. VP of Daytime Programming
    Rick Ludwin, Sr. VP of Late Night and Primetime Series, NBC Entertainment
    Shelley McCrory, Sr. VP of NBC Studios
    Mitch Metcalf, Sr. VP of Program Research, NBC West Coast
    Shirley Powell, Sr. VP of Publicity, NBC Entertainment
    Lee Gaither, VP of Saturday Morning Programs, NBC Entertainment
    Curt Sharp, VP of Alternative Programs, NBC Entertainment
    Cory Shields, VP of Corporate Communications
Specialties: Network; Made for TV Movies; Mini Series

NEILD STREET PROD., INC.
1932 Grace Ave., Ste. 12
Los Angeles, CA 90068
Phone: (323) 969-9447
Fax: (323) 512-4524
www.neildstreet.com
info@neildstreet.com
Key Executives/Personnel:
    Jacob Matthew Gerhardt, Writer & Producer
    Micah A. Hauptman, Producer
    David Keslick, Producer
    Jay Sefton, Producer
    Christine Tso, CFO
Specialties: Network; Cable
Other Categories: Feature Film

NELVANA ENTERTAINMENT
4500 Wilshire Blvd., 1st Fl.
Los Angeles, CA 90010
Phone: (323) 549-4222
Fax: (323) 549-4232
www.nelvana.com
Key Executives/Personnel:

Production Companies – TV

Michael Hirsh, Co-CEO
Patrick Loubert, Co-CEO
Toper Taylor, President
Steven Galloway, VP of Development
David Harleston, VP of Business Affairs
Specialties: Network; Cable; Animation
Other Categories: Feature Film
Credits: Babar; Rolie Polie Olie; Little Bear

NEMIROFF PRODUCTIONS
1506 Butler Ave., Ste. 1
Los Angeles, CA 90025
Phone: (310) 473-4100
          (310) 917-5250
Fax: (310) 473-4100
Key Executives/Personnel:
Steve Nemiroff, Producer & Assistant Director
Specialties: Cable; Documentaries
Other Categories: Feature Film; Commercials; Video; Music Video; Interactive Multimedia
Credits: The Real Deal; Miracles; Sparkletts; Kenny Kingston's Psychic Hotline III
Trade Assoc./Guilds/Unions: AFI, AICP, ITVA

MACE NEUFELD PRODUCTIONS
10202 W. Washington Blvd., Tristar Bldg., Ste 220
Culver City, CA 90232
Phone: (310) 244-2555
Fax: (310) 244-0255
Key Executives/Personnel:
Mace Neufeld, Producer
Kel Symons, VP
David Engle, Director of Development
Jeff Kirschenbaum, Creative Executive
Dax Phelan, Story Editor
Kathy Day, Executive Assistant to Mr. Neufeld & Office Manager
Specialties: Network; Cable
Other Categories: Feature Film
Credits: No Way Out; Hunt For Red October; Clear and Present Danger; General's Daughter
First Look/Development Deals: Sony Pictures Entertainment

NEW CONCORDE
11600 San Vincente Blvd.
Los Angeles, CA 90049
Phone: (310) 820-6733
Fax: (310) 207-6816
www.newconcorde.com
Key Executives/Personnel:
Roger Corman, President & CEO
Gary Jones, President
Julie Corman, Sr. VP & Producer
Catherine Corman, Producer
Frances Doel, VP of Development
Goly Jamshidi, VP of Finance
Doug Lowell, VP of Business Development
Specialties: Cable; Made for TV Movies
Other Categories: Feature Film
Credits: The Suicide Club; Black Scorpion; Fire on the Amazon

NEW MILLENNIUM STUDIOS
One New Millenium Dr.
Petersburg, VA 23805
Phone: (804) 957-4200
Fax: (804) 862-1200
www.nmstudios.com
martinj@nmstudios.com
Key Executives/Personnel:
Tim Reid, Producer
Daphne Maxwell Reid, Producer

Martin C. Jones, Producer
Specialties: Network; Cable; Documentaries; Made for TV Movies
Other Categories: Feature Film; Commercials; Music Video; Interactive Multimedia
Credits: Asunder; Out of Sync; Linc's; When We Were Colored

NEW REGENCY PRODUCTIONS
10201 W. Pico Blvd., Bldg. 12
Los Angeles, CA 90035
Phone: (310) 369-8300
Fax: (310) 969-0470
www.newregency.com
Key Executives/Personnel:
Arnon Milchan, Producer
David Matalon, President & CEO
Sanford Panitch, President of Production
Louis Santor, Executive VP & CFO
William S. Weiner, Executive VP of Business & Legal Affairs/ General Council
Peter Cramer, Sr. VP of Production
Roy Matalon, Sr. VP of Distribution
Elissa Loparco, Sr. VP of Physical Production
Thomas Imperato, Sr. VP of Physical Production
Kara Francis, VP of Creative Affairs
Alexandra Milchan, VP of Production & Acquisitions
Jason Weiss, Director of Development
Alex Ort, Story Editor
Specialties: Network
Other Categories: Feature Film
Credits: L.A. Confidential; Entrapment; Fight Club; City of Angels
First Look/Development Deals: Twentieth Century Fox Television

NEW SCREEN CONCEPTS, INC.
84 W. Park Place
Stamford, CT 06901
Phone: (203) 961-0670
          (310) 557-7486
Fax: (203) 961-0831
www.newscreenconcepts.com
newscren@aol.com
Key Executives/Personnel:
Charles A. Bangert, Chairman
Louis H. Gorfain, President
Hank O'Karma, Producer & Director
Mitchell Horn, Producer
Janis Biewend, Co-Producer
Luana Barzon, Co-Producer
Curt Northrup, Director of Development
Josie Roxas, Finance & Business Affairs
Specialties: Network; Cable; Documentaries
Credits: Body Human 2000 Series; I Am Your Child; Brazelton On Parenting; Armageddon: Target Earth
First Look/Development Deals: ABC Entertainment Television Group
Additional Info: 2020 Avenue Of The Stars, Ste. 500 Century City, CA 90067, (310) 557-7487 fax

NICKELODEON/NICK AT NITE
1515 Broadway, 38th Fl.
New York, NY 10036
Phone: (212) 258-7500
          (818) 736-3911
Fax: (212) 258-7705
www.nick.com
Key Executives/Personnel:
Herb Scannell, President
Albie Hecht, President of Film and TV Entertainment
Jeff Dunn, COO
Larry W. Jones, Executive VP & General Manager, TV Land
Andra Shapiro, Executive VP of Business Affairs & General Counsel
Cyma Zarghami, Executive VP & General Manager, Nickelodeon

Jim Burns, Sr. VP of Programming, Nick at Nite
Margorie Cohn, Sr. VP of Current Series
Alison Dexter, Sr. VP of Operations
Brown Johnson, Sr. VP of Production & Development
Lisa Judson, Sr. Creative VP
Kevin Kay, Sr. VP of Production
Dan Martinsen, Sr. VP of Corporate Communications
Diane Robina, Sr. VP & Assoc. General Manager of Programming
Paul Ward, Sr. VP, Nick at Night Communications
Laura Wendt, Sr. VP of Research & Planning
Adrian Lopez, VP of Casting
Specialties: Network; Cable; Animation
Additional Info: 231 W. Olive Ave., Burbank, CA 91502

NOBLE PRODUCTIONS, INC.
1615 S. Crest Dr.
Los Angeles, CA 90035
Phone: ....(310) 552-2934
Fax: ....(310) 552-3508
nobleproductions@hotmail.com
Key Executives/Personnel:
 Ika Panajotovic, President
 Elena Panajotovic, VP & Secretary
 Sonja Panajotovic, Legal Affairs
Specialties: Documentaries
Other Categories: Feature Film
Credits: Last Nazi; Day Of The Assassin; Cruise Missile; Hell River

NORAH FILMS
662 N. Van Ness Ave., Ste. 301
Los Angeles, CA 90004
Phone: ....(323) 960-3458
Fax: ....(323) 960-3456
norahfi@earthlink.net
Key Executives/Personnel:
 Rose Sharon, President
Specialties: Network
Other Categories: Feature Film
Credits: Nature Boy; Double Hang; Out Of The Cold
Trade Assoc./Guilds/Unions: DGA

NORTH HALL PRODUCTIONS
3000 S. Robertson Blvd., Ste. 240
Los Angeles, CA 90034
Phone: ....(310) 558-5040
Fax: ....(310) 558-5091
Key Executives/Personnel:
 Bill Nuss, Executive Producer
Specialties: Network; Cable; Made for TV Movies; Miniseries
Other Categories: Feature Film
Credits: Booker; Pacific Blue; Raven

NOVA PICTURES
6496 Ivarene Ave.
Los Angeles, CA 90068
Phone: ....(323) 462-5502
Fax: ....(323) 467-1438
www.novapictures.com
pbarnett@novapictures.com
Key Executives/Personnel:
 Peter Barnett, Producer
 Chris Debie, Unit Production Manager
Specialties: Cable
Other Categories: Feature Film; Commercials
Credits: Extraordinary Visitor; Yellow Badge of Courage; Valley Clinic (commercial)
Trade Assoc./Guilds/Unions: ATAS, IFP

NUANCE PRODUCTIONS
345 N. Maple Dr., Ste. 208
Beverly Hills, CA 90210
Phone: ....(310) 247-1870
Fax: ....(310) 247-8150
Key Executives/Personnel:
 Paul Reiser, Partner
 Arthur Spivak, Partner
 Vernon Sanders, VP of Development
Specialties: Network; Cable
Other Categories: Feature Film
Credits: Mad About You
First Look/Development Deals: Columbia Pictures/Columbia Tristar Motion Picture Group

NXT ENTERTAINMENT
8639 Holloway Plaza Dr.
Los Angeles, CA 90069
Phone: ....(310) 289-9600
Fax: ....(310) 289-7383
www.wwwcine.com
nxt@wwwcine.com
Key Executives/Personnel:
 Klaus Lucka, Executive Producer
Specialties: Network
Other Categories: Feature Film; Commercials; Video; Interactive Multimedia
Credits: www.cyberkidsplanet.com; www.neobodies.com
Trade Assoc./Guilds/Unions: DGA

LYNDA OBST PRODUCTIONS
5555 Melrose Ave., Bldg. 210
Hollywood, CA 90038
Phone: ....(323) 956-8744
Fax: ....(323) 862-2287
Key Executives/Personnel:
 Lynda Obst, Producer
 Marc Rosen, Sr. VP of Development
 Elizabeth Hooper, VP of Physical Production
 Mandy Safavi, VP of Development
 Kellie Bryce, Creative Executive
Specialties: Cable
Other Categories: Feature Film
Credits: Animal Husbandry; Hope Floats; The Siege
First Look/Development Deals: Paramount Pictures

OCTOBER PRODUCTIONS
122 E. Arrellaga
Santa Barbara, CA 93101
Phone: ....(805) 962-2523
Fax: ....(805) 650-0704
octprod@pacbell.net
Key Executives/Personnel:
 Richard Hughes, Producer, Writer & Director
Specialties: Animation; Documentaries
Other Categories: Commercials; Video
Credits: G.M.; Toshiba; JCPenney; Mentor
Trade Assoc./Guilds/Unions: DGA

LIN OLIVER PRODUCTIONS
8271 Beverly Blvd.
Los Angeles, CA 90048
Phone: ....(323) 782-1495
Fax: ....(323) 782-1892
www.linoliverproductions.com
lin@linoliverproductions.com
Key Executives/Personnel:
 Lin Oliver, Producer
 Mercedes Coats, Manager of Creative Affairs
Specialties: Cable; Animation; Made for TV Movies
Other Categories: Feature Film
Credits: Trumpet of the Swan; Finding Buck McHenry; Corduroy; Harry and the Hendersons

Production Companies – TV

First Look/Development Deals: Columbia TriStar Motion Picture Group, Kushner-Locke Company
Trade Assoc./Guilds/Unions: WGAw

OMNIBUS
500 S. Buena Vista, Animation Bldg., 2E-3
Burbank, CA 91521
Phone: ....(818) 560-3611
Fax: ....(818) 972-2841
Key Executives/Personnel:
    Rob Scheidlinger, Producer & President
    Sean Jacques, Executive Assistant
Specialties: Network
Other Categories: Feature Film
Credits: Sports Night; Cousin Bette; Speaking of Sex
First Look/Development Deals: Walt Disney Pictures/Touchstone Pictures

ONE STEP PRODUCTIONS
12188 Laurel Terrace
Studio City, CA 91604
Phone: ....(818) 762-1624
Fax: ....(818) 763-1955
www.loop.com/~sister
sister@loop.com
Key Executives/Personnel:
    Judy Chaikin, Owner
    Nancy Kissock, Producer
Specialties: Network; Documentaries; Made for TV Movies
Other Categories: Feature Film; Video
Credits: Cotillion 65; Legacy of the Hollywood Blacklist FBI: Untold Stories; Stolen Innocence
Trade Assoc./Guilds/Unions: DGA

ORIGINAL FILM, INC.
2045 S. Barrington Ave., Ste. A
West Los Angeles, CA 90025
Phone: ....(310) 445-9000
Fax: ....(310) 445-9191
Key Executives/Personnel:
    Neal Moritz, Owner & Producer
    Mark Rossen, President of TV
    Stokely Chaffin, Sr. VP of Production
    Brad Luff, Sr. VP of Production
    Heather Zeegen, VP of Production
    Justin Rosenblatt, Creative Executive
    Brian Gefsky, Director of TV
    Jennifer Tuthill, Director of Development
    Amanda Cohen, Development Assistant
    Gretchen Douglass, Development Assistant
    Jennifer Grandy, Development Assistant
    Ross Brown, Development Assistant
    Jonah Barnes, Production Assistant
Specialties: Network; Cable
Other Categories: Feature Film
Credits: The Skulls; I Know What You Did Last Summer; I Still Know What You Did Last Summer; Cruel Intentions
First Look/Development Deals: Columbia Pictures/Columbia Tristar Motion Picture Group

OUR GANG PRODUCTIONS
8522 National Blvd., Ste. 107
Culver City, CA 90232
Phone: ....(310) 300-1010
Fax: ....(310) 636-8304
ourgangproductions@earthlink.net
Key Executives/Personnel:
    Gayle Gluck, President
    Kevin Miller, Sr. VP & Creative Director
    Chris Conway, Audio Production
    Matt Fisher, Supervising Editor
    Ron Mesa, Chief Audio Engineer
    Rachel Burkes, Production Assistant
Specialties: Network; Cable; Animation; Documentaries; Made for TV Movies; Miniseries
Other Categories: Commercials; Music Video; Interactive Multimedia

OUR PRODUCTIONS, INC.
6255 Sunset Blvd., Ste. 2201
Hollywood, CA 90028
Phone: ....(323) 465-4197
    ....(818) 816-7332
Fax: ....(323) 465-6549
www.ourproduction.com
patricia@ourproduction.com
Key Executives/Personnel:
    Rick Munoz, Director & Producer
    Patricia Bolt, Director of Marketing & Production
Specialties: Cable; Documentaries; Made for TV Movies
Other Categories: Feature Film; Commercials; Video; Music Video
Credits: Natalie Cole Live at The Coliseum; The Miller Brewing Company; Winchell's Donuts

OUTERBANKS ENTERTAINMENT
8000 Sunset Blvd., Ste. 301A
Los Angeles, CA 90046
Phone: ....(323) 654-3700
Fax: ....(323) 654-3797
www.kevinwilliamson.com
Key Executives/Personnel:
    Kevin Williamson, Producer, Director & Writer
    Sherry Carnes, Development Executive
    Jennifer Breslow, Executive Assistant to Mr. Williamson
    Sara Kucserka, Development Assistant
    Mitch Ryan, Office Assistant
Specialties: Network
Other Categories: Feature Film
Credits: Scream 2 & 3; Halloween H20; Her Leading Man
First Look/Development Deals: Miramax Films
Additional Info: WMA, 151 El Camino Dr., Beverly Hills, CA 90212

OVERBROOK ENTERTAINMENT
100 Universal City Plaza, Bldg. 6111
Universal City, CA 91608
Phone: ....(818) 777-2224
Fax: ....(818) 866-6206
Key Executives/Personnel:
    Will Smith, Partner
    James Lassiter, Partner
    Dale Ottley, General Manager
    John Dukakis, Executive VP of Music
    David Tochterman, Executive VP of TV
    Stacey Matthew, VP of TV
    Glendon Palmer, Creative Executive
    SoYun Roe, Film Executive
    Lori Zuker, Director of Development
    Omarr Rambert, A&R Executive of Music
    Anthony Demby, A&R Coordinator
Specialties: Network; Made for TV Movies
Other Categories: Feature Film; Music Video
First Look/Development Deals: Universal Pictures

P.A.T. PRODUCTIONS
10202 W. Washington Blvd., David Lean Bldg., Ste. 230
Culver City, CA 90232
Phone: ....(310) 244-8811
Fax: ....(310) 244-1210
patprod@spe.sony.com
Key Executives/Personnel:
    Pat Sajak, President

Production Companies – TV

David Williger, Executive VP
Gary Templeton, Director of Children's Programming
Specialties: Cable; Animation
Other Categories: Feature Film; Video
Credits: Angus & the Ducks; Leo the Late Bloomer (animated); Merry Christmas; Space Case (animated)
First Look/Development Deals: Columbia TriStar Television

GEORGE PAIGE ASSOCIATES, INC.
3000 W. Olympic Blvd., Ste. 1407
Santa Monica, CA 90404
Phone: ....(310) 315-4835
Fax: ....(310) 315-4836
gpacorp@aol.com
Key Executives/Personnel:
George Paige, Owner & President
James R. Tumminia, Producer
Specialties: Network; Cable; Animation; Documentaries; Made for TV Movies
Other Categories: Feature Film; Commercials; Video; Music Video; Interactive Multimedia
Credits: Abbott & Costello Meet Jerry Seinfeld; 50 Years of Funny Females; Shafted
Trade Assoc./Guilds/Unions: ATAS

PARADOX PRODUCTIONS, INC.
11846 Ventura Blvd., Ste. 202
Studio City, CA 91604
Phone: ....(818) 623-2855
Fax: ....(818) 623-2856
Key Executives/Personnel:
John Pasquin, President & Director
Kimberly Brent, VP of Production
Monica Gelardo, Story Editor
Specialties: Network
Other Categories: Feature Film
Credits: The Santa Clause; Small World; Roseanne; Home Improvement

PARAMOUNT DOMESTIC TELEVISION
5555 Melrose Ave.
Los Angeles, CA 90038
Phone: ....(323) 956-5000
www.paramount.com
Key Executives/Personnel:
Joel Berman, Co-President
Frank Kelly, Co-President
John Nogawski, President of Distribution
Michael Mischler, Executive VP of Marketing
Bobbee Gabelmann, Executive VP of Current Programming
Bruce Pottash, Executive VP of Business & Legal Affairs
Dennis Emerson, Sr. VP of Off-Network Sales
Robert Mendez, Sr. VP of Business & Legal Affairs
Mark Dvornik, Sr. VP & General Sales Manager
David Lafountaine, Sr. VP of Advertising & Promotion
Robert Friedman, Sr. VP of Cable Sales
Dawn Abel, VP of Sales & Special Projects
Linda Carrasquillo, VP of Programming
Lou Dennig, VP of Programming
Lynn Fero, VP of Business Affairs Administration
Gary Holland, VP of Advertising & Promotion
Lisa Fimiani, VP of Sales Administration & Program Lineups
Stan Justice, VP & Western Division Manager
Peter Kane, VP of Business Affairs & Legal
Cynthia Lieberman, VP of Off-Network & Special Projects
Cynthia Teele, VP of Legal
David Theodosopoulos, VP of Legal
David Thomas, VP of Creative Services & Design
Terry Wood, VP of Programming
Rob Wussler, VP & Western Regional Manager

John Kohler, VP of Programming
Christopher Gerondale, VP of Research
Specialties: Network; Cable

PARAMOUNT INTERNATIONAL TELEVISION
c/o Paramount Pictures, 5555 Melrose Ave.
Los Angeles, CA 90038
Phone: ....(323) 956-5000
www.paramount.com
Key Executives/Personnel:
Gary Marenzi, President
Joe Lucas, Executive VP of Sales & Marketing
Susan Akens, Sr. VP of Business Affairs
Javier Avitia, VP of Business Affairs
Chris Ottinger, VP of Business Development
Jim Brehm, VP of Finance
Isis Moussa, VP of Marketing
James Dowaliby, VP of Production
Mina Patel, VP of Sales Planning & Administration
Stefani Deoul, Executive Director of Creative Affairs
Christopher Heisen, Director of Business Affairs
Mark Manuel, Director of Business Development
Chris Alchermes, Director of Contracts
Michael Keller, Director of Creative Affairs
Russell Kolody, Director of Publicity
Annette Warren, Director of Sales Administration
Steve Lindsey, Director of Sales Planning
Renee Westergaard, Manager of Finance
Marlene Johnson, Manager of Int'l. Rights
Teri Fleming, Manager of Marketing & New Media
Christine Kay, Manager of Sales Administration
Michelle Youngblood, Manager of Operations
Karen Johnson, Sr. Contract Coordinator
Monica Garcia, Assistant Manager of Advertising & Marketing
Laura Marks, Assistant Manager of Publicity
Specialties: Network

PARAMOUNT NETWORK TELEVISION
5555 Melrose Ave.
Los Angeles, CA 90038
Phone: ....(323) 956-5000
www.paramount.com
Key Executives/Personnel:
Garry Hart, President of Network Television
Tom Mazza, Executive VP of Creative Affairs
Jake Jacobson, Executive VP of Business Affairs
Milinda McNeely, Executive VP of Legal Network TV
Dan Fauci, Sr. VP of Comedy Development
Trisha Cardoso, Sr. VP of Advertising, Publicity & Promotions
Hal Harrison, Sr. VP of Post Production
Kathy Lingg, Sr. VP of Drama Development
Helen Mossler, Sr. VP of Talent & Casting
Tom Russo, Sr. VP of TV Movies & Miniseries
Reid Shane, Sr. VP of Production
Steve Stark, Sr. VP of Current Programs
David Grossman, Sr. VP of Television Music
Marshall Coben, VP of Current Programs
Brett King, VP of Current Programs Network
J. R. McGinnis, VP of Business Affairs Network TV
Rose Catherine Pinkney, VP of Comedy Development
Sandra Delaney, VP of Business Affairs
Mark Weissman, VP of Production Finance
Craig Wagner, Director of Business
Specialties: Network; Cable

PARAMOUNT TELEVISION GROUP
5555 Melrose Ave.
Los Angeles, CA 90038
Phone: ....(323) 956-5000
www.paramount.com

Production Companies – TV

Key Executives/Personnel:
- Kerry McCluggage, Chairman of Paramount TV Group
- Steve Goldman, Executive VP & CAO of Television Group
- Robert Sheehan, Executive VP of Business Affairs & Finance
- John A. Wentworth, Executive VP of Marketing & Media Relations
- Michelle Hunt, Sr. VP of Media Relations
- Michael Mellon, Sr. VP of Research

Specialties: Network; Cable

PATCHETT KAUFMAN ENTERTAINMENT
8621 Hayden Place
Culver City, CA 90232
Phone: (310) 838-7000
Fax: (310) 838-8430
Key Executives/Personnel:
- Kenneth Kaufman, President
- Tom Patchett, CEO
- Debra Smith-Cannold, VP of Production Services

Specialties: Made for TV Movies; Miniseries
Other Categories: Feature Film
Credits: Dean Koontz: Mr. Murder; Texas Justice; In The Line of Duty (TV series)

PATCHWORK PRODUCTIONS
1663 Euclid Street
Santa Monica, CA 90404
Phone: (310) 288-7488
Fax: (310) 288-7445
Key Executives/Personnel:
- Penny Finkelman Cox, Producer
- Sandra Rabins, Producer
- Jay Rifkin, Producer
- Hans Zimmer, Producer
- Craig Berenson, Development Executive
- Elizabeth Hackett, Development Executive
- Kirstie Field, Assistant to Ms. Finkelman Cox
- Mike Lozano, Assistant to Mr. Rifkin
- Mo Nakamoto, Assistant to Mr. Zimmer
- Melissa Wylie, Assistant to Ms. Rabins

Specialties: Network; Cable; Animation
Other Categories: Feature Film
Credits: Antz; Prince of Egypt; 'Til There Was You; Dangerous Minds
First Look/Development Deals: DreamWorks SKG

PAXTV/PAXSON COMMUNICATIONS
10880 Wilshire Blvd., Ste. 1200
Los Angeles, CA 90024
Phone: (310) 234-2200
Fax: (310) 234-3427
www.pax.net
Key Executives/Personnel:
- Bud Paxon, Chairman
- Jeff Sagansky, President & CEO
- Dean Goodman, President of TV
- Tim Johnson, Sr. VP of West Coast Productions
- Steve Appel, VP of National Sales
- David Macaione, Associate General Counsel

Specialties: Cable

PBS
1320 Braddock Place
Alexandria, VA 22314
Phone: (703) 739-5000
Fax: (703) 739-0775
www.pbs.org
Key Executives/Personnel:
- Pat Mitchell, President & CEO
- Beth Wolfe, Executive VP & CAO
- Gregory Ferenbach, Sr. VP & General Counsel
- Jim Guerra, Sr. VP of Program Business Affairs
- Cindy Johanson, Sr. VP of Internet & Broadband Services
- John F. Wilson, Sr. VP of Programming Services
- Michael Diefenbach, VP of Sponsor Development
- Patricia DiRuggiero, VP, Associate General Counsel & Corporate Secretary
- Alan Foster, VP of Fundraising & Syndicated Programming
- Steven Gray, VP of Program Scheduling & PBS Channels
- Pat Hunter, VP of Programming Administration & Communication
- Andre Mendes, VP & CIO
- Annette Pocica, VP of Finance
- Jack Dougherty, VP of Program Business Affairs
- Glenn DuBose, Sr. Director of Drama, Performance & Arts
- Sandy Heberer, Sr. Director of News & Information
- Mary Jane McKinven, Sr. Director of Science, Natural History & Exploration
- Pat Nugent, Sr. Director of Children's Programming
- Dick Hanratty, Director of PBS Plus & PBS Select
- Lauren Kalos, Director of Program Operations

Specialties: Network

PEAK PRODUCTIONS
1780 Robinhood Rd.
Winston-Salem, NC 27104
Phone: (336) 761-5042
(336) 813-0642
Fax: (336) 761-5043
peakprdns@aol.com
Key Executives/Personnel:
- Dale Pollock, Producer

Specialties: Network; Cable; Made for TV Movies
Other Categories: Feature Film
Credits: Blaze; Midnight Clear; Set It Off
Trade Assoc./Guilds/Unions: AMPAS, PGA, WGAe

PEARSON TELEVISION
2700 Colorado Ave., Ste. 450
Santa Monica, CA 90404
Phone: (310) 656-1100
(415) 856-8089
Fax: (310) 255-4800
Key Executives/Personnel:
- Brian Harris, President & CEO, Pearson TV North America/CEO, Pearson TV Int'l.
- Bill Lincoln, COO
- Joseph Abrams, President, Pearson TV Int'l.
- Matthew Loze, President of Production, Drama & Long-Form
- Sara Rutenberg, President of Business Development & Strategy
- Catherine Mackay, President of Pearson Television Enterprises (NY)
- Syd Vinnedge, Sr. Executive VP of North American Productions
- Lou Festa, CFO (NY)
- David Lyle, Executive VP of Entertainment
- Rand Stoll, Executive VP of Programming (NY)
- Cecile Frot-Coutaz, Executive VP of Digital Media (San Francisco)
- Paul Pavlis, Executive VP & General Counsel
- Gaby Johnston, Sr. Vice President of Light Entertainment
- Dana Walker, VP of Business & Legal Affairs
- Dan Watanabe, VP of Current Programming
- Kim Stratton, Director of Clip Licensing

Specialties: Network; Cable
Additional Info: 444 Spear St., San Francisco, CA 94105
1330 Avenue of the Americas, New York, NY 10019

PENDRAGON FILM LTD.
Phone: (310) 828-1588
www.members.aol.com/jabwocky
jabwocky@aol.com
Key Executives/Personnel:
- Alain Silver, Writer & Producer
- Linda Brookover, Writer & Producer

Specialties: Documentaries
Other Categories: Feature Film
Credits: The Quickie; Beat; Bel-Air; Palmer's Pick-Up
Trade Assoc./Guilds/Unions: DGA, SAG

Production Companies – TV

JAMES PENTECOST PRODUCTIONS
500 S. Buena Vista St., Animation Bldg., Ste. 2G6
Burbank, CA 91521
Phone: ....(818) 560-4965
Fax: ....(818) 845-7581
Key Executives/Personnel:
    James Pentecost, Producer
    Sheree Steiner, Office Manager
Specialties: Network; Cable
Other Categories: Feature Film
Credits: Pocahontas; Geppetto

PERMUT PRESENTATIONS
9150 Wilshire Blvd., Ste. 247
Beverly Hills, CA 90212
Phone: ....(310) 248-2792
Fax: ....(310) 248-2797
Key Executives/Personnel:
    David Permut, President
    Steven A. Longi, VP of Production
    David T. Mitchell, Development Associate
Specialties: Network; Cable; Made for TV Movies; Miniseries
Other Categories: Feature Film
Credits: Double Take; Face/Off; Richard Pryor Live; Dragnet

PERSISTENT ENTERTAINMENT, INC.
9350 Wilshire Blvd., Ste. 328
Beverly Hills, CA 90212
Phone: ....(310) 777-1814
Fax: ....(310) 777-1824
www.persistentpictures.com
mail@persistentpictures.com
Key Executives/Personnel:
    Dan Stone, Producer
    Matthew Rhodes, Producer
    Lenny Bekerman, Manager & Producer
    Brian Dillingham, Story Editor
    Richard Williams, Assistant to Mr. Stone
    Nick Myles, Assistant to Mr. Rhodes
Specialties: Network; Cable; Made for TV Movies
Other Categories: Feature Film
Credits: Auggie Rose; Alarmist (aka Life During Wartime); Star Struck (aka Starf*cker); Standoff

LESTER PERSKY PRODUCTIONS, INC.
9910 Tower Lane
Beverly Hills, CA 90210
Phone: ....(310) 278-1995
Fax: ....(310) 278-1910
lesterprods@aol.com
Key Executives/Personnel:
    Lester Persky, President
    Tomlinson Dean, Producer & VP
    Jonas Neilson, Director of Production
Specialties: Network; Cable; Miniseries
Other Categories: Feature Film
Credits: A Woman Named Jackie; Poor Little Rich Girl; Elizabeth Taylor Story; Hair

PERSPECTIVE FILMS
Phone: ....(310) 670-4030
    ....(310) 261-8389
Fax: ....(310) 670-4031
Key Executives/Personnel:
    Debbie Pietsch, Executive Producer
Specialties: Documentaries
Other Categories: Feature Film; Commercials; Video; Music Video; Interactive Multimedia
Credits: Fast Point DSL; Mattel; Disney; Harman Kardan: MacWorld

DOROTHEA G. PETRIE PRODUCTIONS, INC.
13201 Haney Place
Los Angeles, CA 90049
Phone: ....(310) 394-2608
Fax: ....(310) 395-8530
Key Executives/Personnel:
    Dorothea G. Petrie, Executive Producer
    June Petrie, Producer
    Ashli Stepp, Development
Specialties: Network; Cable; Made for TV Movies; Miniseries
Credits: Song of the Lark; Echo of Thunder; Captive Heart; Face on the Milk Carton
Trade Assoc./Guilds/Unions: PGA

PHASE 1 PRODUCTIONS
3210 Club Dr.
Los Angeles, CA 90064
Phone: ....(310) 842-8401
Fax: ....(310) 280-0415
phase1prod@earthlink.net
Key Executives/Personnel:
    Joe Wizan, Producer
    Don Schneider, Producer
    Steve Wizan, President
    Dru Ransom, VP of Creative Affairs
Specialties: Network; Cable
Other Categories: Feature Film
Credits: Along Came A Spider; Kiss the Girls; Dunstin Checks In; Wrestling Ernest Hemingway

PICO CREEK PRODUCTIONS
409 Santa Monica Blvd., PH
Santa Monica, CA 90401
Phone: ....(310) 394-7522
Fax: ....(310) 394-5825
Key Executives/Personnel:
    Peter Horton, Director, Actor & Producer
    Julie Robinson, Director of Development
Specialties: Network; Made for TV Movies
Other Categories: Feature Film
Credits: Brimstone; Murder Live
Trade Assoc./Guilds/Unions: DGA, SAG

PIE TOWN PRODUCTIONS
3255 Cahuenga Blvd. West, Ste. 300
Los Angeles, CA 90068
Phone: ....(323) 851-2333
Fax: ....(323) 851-2334
www.pietownprods.com
pietown@pietownprods.com
Key Executives/Personnel:
    Tara Sandler, Executive Producer
    Jennifer Davidson, Executive Producer
    Scott Templeton, Co-Executive Producer
    Robin Facer, Supervising Producer
    Eric Black, Supervising Producer
    Marisa Johnston, Supervising Producer
    Lesley Taylor, Supervising Producer
    Kristine Davis, Supervising Producer
    Stacy Schneider Malvino, Supervising Producer
    Susan Seide, Supervising Producer
    Roberta White, Supervising Producer
Specialties: Network; Cable; Documentaries
Credits: A Baby Town; Designing for the Sexes; Cooking School Stories; Househunters

Production Companies – TV

THE FREDERICK S. PIERCE COMPANY, INC.
5670 Wilshire Blvd., Ste. 1350
Los Angeles, CA 90036
Phone: ....(323) 964-7800
Fax: ....(323) 964-7818
www.piercefilms.com
piercefilms@earthlink.net
Key Executives/Personnel:
    Frederick S. Pierce, Owner & President
    Keith Pierce, Executive Producer
    Richard Pierce, Executive Producer
Specialties: Cable; Made for TV Movies; Miniseries
Other Categories: Feature Film
Credits: In a Heartbeat; 20,000 Leagues Under the Sea; The Absolute Truth; The Substitute Wife

PIRATES' COVE ENTERTAINMENT, INC.
Phone: ....(310) 288-2001
    ....(310) 288-2000
Fax: ....(310) 288-2020
Key Executives/Personnel:
    Paul G. Stupin, Executive Producer
    Nicole Ranadive, Director of Development
Specialties: Network; Cable
Credits: Dawson's Creek; Fortune Hunter; Real Life
First Look/Development Deals: Columbia TriStar Television

PLASTERCITY PRODUCTIONS
5225 Wilshire Blvd., Ste. 1204
Los Angeles, CA 90036
Phone: ....(323) 938-0974
Fax: ....(323) 938-1189
www.plastercity.com
info@plastercity.com
Key Executives/Personnel:
    Christopher Coppola, President, Producer & Director
    Alain Silver, Producer
    Adrienne Coppola, VP
Specialties: Network; Cable
Other Categories: Feature Film
Credits: Bel Air; America's Most Wanted; I Survive; Gun Fighter
Trade Assoc./Guilds/Unions: DGA, SAG

POINT OF VIEW PRODUCTIONS
2477 Folsom St.
San Francisco, CA 94110
Phone: ....(415) 821-0435
    ....(415) 227-9292
Fax: ....(415) 931-0948
www.wenet.net/~karil/about.html
karil@wenet.net
Key Executives/Personnel:
    Karil Daniels, Producer & Director
Specialties: Documentaries
Other Categories: Commercials; Video

POLESTAR ENTERTAINMENT GROUP, LLC
9454 Wilshire Blvd., Ste. 201
Beverly Hills, CA 90212
Phone: ....(310) 278-0080
Fax: ....(310) 278-0079
www.polestarentertainment.com
polestarentertainmentgroup@polestargroup.net
Key Executives/Personnel:
    Anthony Scala, CEO
    Catarina Conti, COO
    Dan Fantz, President of Releasing
    Terry White, President of Film & Television Production
    Russ Regan, President of Polestar Records
    Jeff Berk, Sr. VP of Production
    Jenifer Sorrow, Head of Management
    Jennifer Eatz, Literary Manager
    Rod Conti, VP of Production
    Jerry Conti, VP of Creative Affairs
    Stacy Hunter, Director of Operations
Specialties: Network; Cable
Other Categories: Feature Film
Credits: Hobb's End; Last Chance; Other Side of Monday; G-Saviour

POPULAR ARTS ENTERTAINMENT, INC.
2006 W. Olive Ave.
Burbank, CA 91506
Phone: ....(818) 562-6366
Fax: ....(818) 562-6373
contactus@populararts.com
Key Executives/Personnel:
    Kevin Meagher, Co-President & Co-CEO
    Gordon Braine, Co-President & Co-CEO
    Thomas Guttry, VP of Business Affairs
Specialties: Network; Cable; Animation; Documentaries; Made for TV Movies; Miniseries
Other Categories: Feature Film
Credits: Dr. Katz; Little Girls in Pretty Boxes; Jeff Corwin Experience
Additional Info: 53 W. 87th St., New York, NY 10024

PRODUCERS GROUP, LTD.
713 S. Pacific Coast Hwy., Ste. B
Redondo Beach, CA 90277
Phone: ....(310) 316-0481
Fax: ....(310) 316-1482
producers_group@csi.com
Key Executives/Personnel:
    Lee Gluckman, President & Executive Producer
    Ted Raynor, Executive VP of Legal & Executive Producer
Specialties: Network; Cable; Documentaries; Made for TV Movies; Miniseries
Other Categories: Feature Film; Commercials; Video
Credits: After The Red Star; Kids Are Cooking; Chicago Heist; San Miguel
Trade Assoc./Guilds/Unions: AFTRA, SAG

PRODUCTION ANALYSIS CORPORATION
Phone: ....(323) 876-6186
goodadvice@earthlink.net
Key Executives/Personnel:
    Martin Pitts, Producer
Specialties: Network; Cable; Documentaries
Other Categories: Feature Film; Commercials; Video; Music Video
Credits: Wild California; The Full Moon Show with Robbie Robertson; The Bee Gees Live Concert Video

PRODUCTION PARTNERS, INC.
4421 Riverside Dr., Ste. 206
Burbank, CA 91505
Phone: ....(818) 556-5065
Fax: ....(818) 556-5069
Key Executives/Personnel:
    Sandy Chanley, President & Executive Producer
    Tom Bull, Producer
    Keith Truesdell, Director
Specialties: Network; Cable
Credits: Larry David: Curb Your Enthusiasm; Chris Rock: Bring the Pain; Bill Maher: Be More Cynical; Chris Rock: Bigger & Blacker

PROLETARIAT FILMWORKS
12165 Iredell St.
Studio City, CA 91604
Phone: ....(818) 763-8356
Fax: ....(818) 760-6584
proletfilm@aol.com
Key Executives/Personnel:

Terry Moloney, Executive Producer
Grant Gilmore, Line Producer
Liam Kildare, Producer
Specialties: Documentaries
Other Categories: Feature Film; Commercials; Video; Music Video
Credits: Tourette Syndrome Foundation (PSA); Elvis 2000: A Video Scrapbook; Warner Music: Wallstreet; Shout for Antz
Trade Assoc./Guilds/Unions: AFTRA, SAG

PROUD MARY ENTERTAINMENT
433 N. Camden Dr., Ste. 600
Beverly Hills, CA 90210
Phone: ....(310) 288-1886
Fax: ....(310) 288-1801
proudmaryent@earthlink.net
Key Executives/Personnel:
Mary L. Aloe, Owner & Executive Producer
Todd Waxler, Executive Producer
Jay Jacobs, Director of Development
Specialties: Network; Cable; Made for TV Movies; Miniseries
Other Categories: Feature Film; Commercials; Music Video
Credits: Caught in the Act; The Princess & The Private; Citizen Jane
Trade Assoc./Guilds/Unions: American Women in TV & Radio, CWA

QUASAR STUDIOS
P.O. Box 661266
Los Angeles, CA 90066
Phone: ....(310) 289-1547
....(818) 352-0908
Fax: ....(310) 289-1547
www.perufilmcommission.net
filmperu@gte.net
Key Executives/Personnel:
Marggie Castellano, Producer
Prudence Michael, Location Manager
Monica Leon, Designer
Specialties: Documentaries
Other Categories: Feature Film; Video; Interactive Multimedia
Credits: Coyotes (feature); National Geographic: Ancient Graves; The Celestine Prophecy (miniseries); A&E: Ancient Mysteries

RADIANT PRODUCTIONS
914 Montana Ave., 2nd Fl.
Santa Monica, CA 90403
Phone: ....(310) 656-1400
Fax: ....(310) 656-1408
Key Executives/Personnel:
Wolfgang Petersen, Director & Producer
Gail Katz, President & Producer
Samuel Dickerman, VP
Rosemary Tarquinio, Head of TV
Susan Stein, Director of Development
David Markus, Story Editor
Barbara Huber, Assistant to Mr. Petersen
Aaron Huffman, Assistant to Ms. Katz
Alicia Abatie, Assistant to Ms. Tarquinio
Veronica Becker, Development Assistant
Specialties: Network
Other Categories: Feature Film
Credits: The Perfect Storm; Air Force One; Outbreak; In The Line of Fire

RAFFAELLA PRODUCTIONS, INC.
100 Universal City Plaza, Bungalow 5162
Universal City, CA 91608
Phone: ....(818) 777-2655
Fax: ....(818) 866-1571
Key Executives/Personnel:
Raffaella DeLaurentiis, President & Producer
Hester Hargett, VP & Co-Producer
Steve O'Corr, VP of Operations
Ed Wacek, Sr. VP of Production
Erik Jessen, Story Editor
Specialties: Network; Cable
Other Categories: Feature Film
Credits: Dragon Heart; Dragon: The Bruce Lee Story; Kull, The Conqueror; Daylight
First Look/Development Deals: Universal Pictures, Universal Television

RAIMONDI FILMS, INC.
3575 Cahuenga Blvd. West, Ste. 470
Los Angeles, CA 90068
Phone: ....(323) 850-0185
Fax: ....(323) 850-1264
raimondica@aol.com
Key Executives/Personnel:
Jane Raimondi, Producer
Paul Raimondi, Director
Specialties: Documentaries
Other Categories: Commercials
Credits: L.A. Times (theater trailers); Lucky's; Jockey; Hecht's Department Stores
Trade Assoc./Guilds/Unions: DGA

RAINMAKER PRODUCTIONS
P.O. Box 5780
Beverly Hills, CA 90209
Phone: ....(323) 874-6770
Fax: ....(800) 858-0520
Key Executives/Personnel:
Neal Edelstein, President
Gaye Pope, Director of Development
Specialties: Network
Other Categories: Feature Film

RANDWELL PRODUCTIONS
11111 Santa Monica Blvd., Ste. 525
Los Angeles, CA 90025
Phone: ....(310) 996-6809
Fax: ....(310) 473-4376
Key Executives/Personnel:
Randy Robinson, President & CEO
Tom Kageff, VP
Specialties: Network; Cable; Made for TV Movies; Miniseries
Other Categories: Feature Film
Credits: See You In My Dreams; Come On Get Happy: Partridge Family; Sealed With A Kiss; Two Mother's For Zachary
First Look/Development Deals: Carlton America

KEN RASKOFF PRODUCTIONS
2700 Colorado Ave., Ste. 450
Santa Monica, CA 90404
Phone: ....(310) 255-4707
Fax: ....(310) 255-4809
douglas.fronk@pearsontv.com
Key Executives/Personnel:
Ken Raskoff, Executive Producer
Douglas Fronk, Development
Specialties: Network; Cable; Made for TV Movies; Miniseries
Credits: The Moving Of Sophia Myles; Labor Of Love; Saved By The Light; Futuresport
First Look/Development Deals: Pearson Television

RAVEN PRODUCTIONS, INC.
1053 S. Palm Canyon Dr.
Palm Springs, CA 92264
Phone: ....(760) 325-7191
Fax: ....(760) 325-7258

Production Companies – TV

raventv1@aol.com
Key Executives/Personnel:
    Mitchell Sussman, Executive Producer
    Joni Ravenna, Producer & Writer
    Steve Peyton, Producer
    Mike Lestico, Writer
Specialties: Network; Cable; Documentaries
Other Categories: Commercials
Credits: Desert Magazine; Great Sports Vacations; Outdoors; The Aging of America
First Look/Development Deals: PBS

PATRICK RAYMOND ENTERTAINMENT, INC.
1041 N. Formosa Ave., Formosa Bldg., Ste. 209
West Hollywood, CA 90046
Phone: ....(323) 850-2918
Fax: ....(323) 850-2920
praymondh@aol.com
Key Executives/Personnel:
    Patrick Raymond, Executive Producer
    Albert Frigone, Associate Producer
    Joey Estella, Assistant
Specialties: Cable; Documentaries
Other Categories: Feature Film; Commercials; Video; Interactive Multimedia

REARGUARD PRODUCTIONS, INC.
6030 Wilshire Blvd., Ste. 300
Los Angeles, CA 90036
Phone: ....(323) 937-1570
Fax: ....(323) 937-0564
Key Executives/Personnel:
    Julie G. Moldo Jones, Executive VP
Specialties: Network; Cable; Made for TV Movies
Other Categories: Feature Film
Credits: Tales From The Crypt; The Land That Time Forgot; Rock, Rock, Rock!; The Birthday Party
Trade Assoc./Guilds/Unions: DGA, SAG

RED BIRD PRODUCTIONS
725 Arizona Ave., Ste. 200
Santa Monica, CA 90401
Phone: ....(310) 234-7234
Fax: ....(310) 234-7235
Key Executives/Personnel:
    Debbie Allen, President & Producer
    Joy Johnson, Director of Development
Specialties: Network; Cable
Other Categories: Feature Film
Credits: Amistad

RED HOTS ENTERTAINMENT
3105 Amigos Dr.
Burbank, CA 91504
Phone: ....(818) 954-0092
....(818) 607-8331
Fax: ....(818) 954 8421
pogmothon@earthlink.net
Key Executives/Personnel:
    Chip Miller, Director & Partner
    Sue Travis Miller, VP of Post Production & Editor
    Jane Gurtiza, Production Coordinator
    Dan Pomeroy, Director
    Marvin "Young MC" Young, Director
    Mark St. Juste, Director
    Kit Gleason, Production Manager
    Eileen Salgro, VP of Operations
    Vanessa Browne, Producer
    Marc Wolfson, Music Producer
    Theo Forster, Producer
Specialties: Network; Cable; Made for TV Movies
Other Categories: Feature Film; Commercials; Video; Music Video
Credits: Four Day Shoot; Mortuary Academy; The Importance of Being Earnest; The Seven Fishes
Trade Assoc./Guilds/Unions: PGA, WGA

RED HOUR FILMS
193 N. Roberston Blvd.
Beverly Hills, CA 90211
Phone: ....(310) 289-2565
Fax: ....(310) 289-5988
www.redhourfilms.com
Key Executives/Personnel:
    Ben Stiller, Producer, Writer & Director
    Stuart Cornfeld, Feature Producer
    Erin Simon-Berenson, TV Producer
    Rhodes Rader, Creative Executive
    Stacy Fung, Assistant to Ms. Berenson
    Alan Griswold, Assistant to Mr. Cornfeld
    Will Klein, Assistant
Specialties: Network
Other Categories: Feature Film
Credits: Zoolander
First Look/Development Deals: New Line Cinema

RED HOUSE ENTERTAINMENT
3400 Riverside Dr., Ste. 700
Burbank, CA 91505
Phone: ....(818) 977-1902
Fax: ....(818) 977-5287
Key Executives/Personnel:
    Tim Daly, Producer
    Steve Burleigh, Producer
    Amy Von Nostrand, Producer
    Aimee Flaherty, Development Associate & Story Editor
Specialties: Network; Cable; Made for TV Movies; Miniseries
Other Categories: Feature Film
Credits: Execution of Justice; Rites of Passage; Seven Girlfriends; Urbania
First Look/Development Deals: Warner Bros. Television Productions
Additional Info: Formerly Daly-Harris Productions

RED-HORSE PRODUCTIONS
6028 Calvin Ave.
Tarzana, CA 91356
Phone: ....(818) 705-2588
Fax: ....(818) 705-2523
www.naturallynative.com
redhorse88@aol.com
Key Executives/Personnel:
    Valerie Red-Horse, President, Producer, Writer, Actress & Director
    Dawn Jackson, Director of Development
    Yvonne Russo, VP, Producer & Actress
    Fabiane Carter, Executive Assistant
    Pam Aver, Business & Legal Affairs
Specialties: Network; Cable; Documentaries
Other Categories: Feature Film; Video
Credits: Naturally Native (feature); The Whispers (documentary); Windows on Mars (educational); My Indian Summer (TV)
First Look/Development Deals: Valhala Motion Pictures
Trade Assoc./Guilds/Unions: HAPN, SAG, WGA, WIF

DAN REDLER ENTERTAINMENT
18730 Hatteras St., Ste. 8
Tarzana, CA 91356
Phone: ....(818) 776-0938
Fax: ....(818) 705-6870
dredler@pacbell.net
Key Executives/Personnel:
    Dan Redler, Producer
    Nadia Naili, Producer
Specialties: Network; Cable; Made for TV Movies; Miniseries

Other Categories: Feature Film; Commercials; Interactive Multimedia
Credits: In His Father's Shoes; Pygmalion; Tanks; Profile For Murder
First Look/Development Deals: Nu Image/Millenium

REEL ORANGE
316 La Jolla Dr.
Newport Beach, CA 92663
Phone: ....(949) 548-4524
..................................(714) 349-6322
Fax: ....(949) 548-0749
reelorange@aol.com
Key Executives/Personnel:
  Art Vitarelli, Producer
Specialties: Cable; Documentaries
Other Categories: Commercials; Video
Credits: Call of The Cangon; Mitsubishi Corp. (corp. video); Voices from the Stone

MARIAN REES ASSOCIATES
3708 Vantage Ave.
Studio City, CA 91604
Phone: ....(818) 508-5599
Fax: ....(818) 508-8012
Key Executives/Personnel:
  Marian Rees, CEO
  Anne Hopkins, President
  Dyan Austin Conway, Business Affairs
  Sue Revitz, Development
Specialties: Cable; Network; Made for TV Movies
Credits: Ruby Bridges; In Pursuit of Honor; Miss Rose White; Decoration Day

REGENT ENTERTAINMENT, INC.
1401 Ocean Ave., Ste. 300
Santa Monica, CA 90401
Phone: ....(310) 260-3333
..................................(310) 260-3343
Key Executives/Personnel:
  Paul Colichman, President & Partner
  Mark R. Harris, Partner
  Stephen P. Jarchow, Partner
  John Lambert, VP of Acquisitions & Theatrical Distribution
  Jeff Schenck, VP of Development
  Gene George, President of Int'l. Sales
  Megan Kimberly, VP of Int'l. Sales
  Chuck Speed, Business Affairs
  Lynn Di Paola, Assistant to Mr. Schenck
Specialties: Network; Cable; Made for TV Movies; Miniseries
Other Categories: Feature Film
Credits: Gods & Monsters; A Woman is a Hell of a Thing; I'll Remember April; The Twilight of the Golds

TIM REID PRODUCTIONS, INC.
One New Millennium Dr.
Petersburg, VA 23805
Phone: ....(804) 957-4200
Fax: ....(804) 862-1200
Key Executives/Personnel:
  Tim Reid, President
  Jarene Fleming, Production Executive
  Tori Reid, Executive Assistant
Specialties: Network; Cable; Documentaries; Made for TV Movies
Credits: Blue Moon; About Sarah; The Contender; Linc's

RICK REINERT PICTURES
1556 Covington Ave.
Westlake Village, CA 91361
Phone: ....(805) 494-0699
Fax: ....(805) 494-9780
Key Executives/Personnel:
  Rick Reinert, Producer & Director
  Tom Carter, Sales & Producer
  Carole Reinert, VP of Business Affairs
Specialties: Animation
Other Categories: Feature Film; Video
Credits: Capn' O.G. Readmore; Precious Moments Videos; Winnie The Pooh and a Day for Eeyore
Trade Assoc./Guilds/Unions: AMPAS, ASIFA, ATAS

REVELATIONS ENTERTAINMENT
301 Arizona Ave., Ste. 303
Santa Monica, CA 90401
Phone: ....(310) 394-3131
Fax: ....(310) 394-3133
www.revelationsent.com
Key Executives/Personnel:
  Morgan Freeman, President, Actor & Producer
  Lori McCreary, CEO & Producer
  Anne Marie Gillen, COO & Producer
  Janet M. Harrison, Director of East Coast Development
  Meg Madison, Director of Accounting
  Alfonso Freeman, Director of Information Systems
  Martha Mitchell, Office Manager
  Stuart Hammes, Business Consultant
  Geanne Frank, Management Consultant
  Tonya Jones, Publicist for Morgan Freeman
  Kelly Mendelsohn, Assistant to Ms. McCreary
Specialties: Network; Cable
Other Categories: Feature Film
Credits: Bopha!; Mutiny; Under Suspicion

REVOLVER FILMS, LLC
2022A Broadway
Santa Monica, CA 90404
Phone: ....(310) 829-2441
Fax: ....(310) 829-2661
Key Executives/Personnel:
  Mark Priola, Producer
  Jack Singman, Producer
Specialties: Network; Cable; Documentaries
Other Categories: Feature Film; Commercials; Video
Credits: ATV Hardcore; Extended list available upon request.

RICE & BEANS PRODUCTIONS
30 N. Raymond., Ste. 605
Pasadena, CA 91103
Phone: ....(626) 792-9171
Fax: ....(626) 792-9171
vin88@pacbell.net
Key Executives/Personnel:
  Vince Cheung, Writer & Producer
  Ben Montanio, Writer & Producer
Specialties: Network; Cable; Animation
Other Categories: Feature Film; Interactive Multimedia
Credits: The Steve Harvey Show; Married... with Children; In The House; Empty Nest
Trade Assoc./Guilds/Unions: ATAS, WGA

RIDINI ENTERTAINMENT CORPORATION
c/o Raleigh Studios, 650 N. Bronson Ave., Ste. B-152
Los Angeles, CA 90004
Phone: ....(323) 960-8071
www.ridinientertainment.com
maryann@ridinientertainment.com
Key Executives/Personnel:
  Mary Ann Ridini, no title
Specialties: Network; Cable; Documentaries; Made for TV Movies; Miniseries
Other Categories: Feature Film; Video
Credits: Falling Fire; Convict 762; Future Fear; Shepherd
First Look/Development Deals: Third Millennium

Production Companies – TV

ROADSIDE ATTRACTIONS, LLC
427 N. Cañon Dr., Ste. 216
Beverly Hills, CA 90210
Phone: ....(310) 860-1692
Fax: ....(310) 860-1693
www.roadsideattractions.com
mail@roadsideattractions.com
Key Executives/Personnel:
  Eric d'Arbeloff, Producer
  Chad Marting, Story Editor
Specialties: Cable; Made for TV Movies
Other Categories: Feature Film
Credits: The Shoe; Trick; They Nest

DOLORES ROBINSON ENTERTAINMENT
112 S. Almont Dr.
Los Angeles, CA 90048
Phone: ....(310) 777-8777
Fax: ....(310) 777-8780
dorobent@aol.com
Key Executives/Personnel:
  Dolores Robinson, no title
  Ryan Babanzien, no title
Specialties: Network; Cable
Other Categories: Feature Film

STAN ROGOW PRODUCTIONS
846 N. Cahuenga Blvd., Bldg. D
Los Angeles, CA 90038
Phone: ....(323) 993-5644
Fax: ....(323) 993-5591
Key Executives/Personnel:
  Stan Rogow, Executive Producer
  Susan Jansen, Executive Producer
  Jill Danton, Line Producer
  Tom Lofaro, Line Producer
  Robin Lippin, Casting Director
Specialties: Network; Cable; Made for TV Movies; Miniseries
Other Categories: Feature Film
Credits: None of the Above; State of Grace; Fame (TV series); Playing For Time
Trade Assoc./Guilds/Unions: DGA, WGAw

PHIL ROMAN ENTERTAINMENT
4040 Vineland Ave., Ste. 205
Studio City, CA 91604
Phone: ....(818) 985-1200
Fax: ....(818) 985-2668
www.philromanent.com
phil@romanent.com
Key Executives/Personnel:
  Phil Roman, President & CEO
  Rick Ramirez, VP
Specialties: Network; Cable; Animation
Other Categories: Feature Film; Interactive Multimedia
Credits: Grandma Got Run Over By A Reindeer; Christmas in Gaudinia

HOWARD ROSENMAN PRODUCTIONS
635A Westbourne Dr.
Los Angeles, CA 90069
Phone: ....(310) 659-2100
Key Executives/Personnel:
  Howard Rosenman, Producer
Specialties: Network; Cable; Documentaries; Made for TV Movies; Miniseries
Other Categories: Feature Film
Credits: Common Threads: Stories From The Quilt; Father of the Bride; Buffy The Vampire Slayer (feature); Celluloid Closet

FREYDA ROTHSTEIN PRODUCTIONS
9255 Doheny Rd., Ste. 805
West Hollywood, CA 90069
Phone: ....(310) 859-4750
Fax: ....(310) 859-8875
Key Executives/Personnel:
  Freyda Rothstein, Executive Producer
  Deborah Wolsh, VP of Creative Affairs
Specialties: Made for TV Movies
Credits: Blue Valley Songbird; Change of Heart; In Broad Daylight; Passions Way

ROUNDTABLE INK
Phone: ....(323) 466-4646
Fax: ....(323) 466-4640
diedre@roundtableink.com
Key Executives/Personnel:
  Gina Matthews, Producer & Manager
  Diedre Nuwash, Story Editor & Assistant
Specialties: Network; Cable; Animation; Made for TV Movies; Miniseries
Other Categories: Feature Film
Credits: What Women Want; Urban Legend; Popular

RUDDY MORGAN ORGANIZATION
9300 Wilshire Blvd., Ste. 508
Beverly Hills, CA 90212
Phone: ....(310) 271-7698
Fax: ....(310) 278-9978
ruddymorgan@earthlink.net
Key Executives/Personnel:
  Albert S. Ruddy, Producer
  André E. Morgan, Producer
  Douglas Nam, Executive Assistant
  Vivianne Kaplan, Executive Assistant
  Leslie Aurelio, Second Assistant
Specialties: Network; Cable; Made for TV Movies; Miniseries
Other Categories: Feature Film
Credits: Martial Law; Walker, Texas Ranger; Running Mates

RUMRUNNER CINE SERVICE
469 26th St.
Manhattan Beach, CA 90266
Phone: ....(310) 540-8411
....(310) 901-5515
Fax: ....(310) 545-0136
omara@earthlink.net
Key Executives/Personnel:
  Cay Mohr, Executive Producer & Owner
  Gerry Trafficanda, Director & Owner
  Kevin Van Fleet, Agency Owner
  Lee Tirce, Director
  Ron Dexter, Owner & Director
  Mel Hall, Owner & Director
  Andrew Gallerani, Director
  Aaron Spelling, Executive Producer
  James Row, Owner & Producer
  Judy Trotter, Producer
  Marilyn Penn, Producer
  Paulette Glassman, Producer
Specialties: Documentaries; Miniseries
Other Categories: Commercials; Video
Credits: The State of Energy (documentary); E-I Carrier (training video); Dynasty (miniseries); Toyota (commercial)
Trade Assoc./Guilds/Unions: DGA

S.E.R. FILMWORKS
500 Botetourt St., Ste 401
Norfolk, VA 23510
Phone: ....(757) 625-7647
filmwrks@erols.com

Production Companies – TV

Key Executives/Personnel:
    Susan Rohrer, Producer, Director & Writer
Specialties: Made for TV Movies
Other Categories: Feature Film
Credits: Never Say Goodbye; Terrible Things My Mother Told Me; For Jenny, With Love; Mother's Day
Trade Assoc./Guilds/Unions: ATAS, DGA, SAG, WGAw

SABAN ENTERTAINMENT
10960 Wilshire Blvd.
Los Angeles, CA 90024
Phone: ....(310) 235-5100
Fax: ....(310) 235-5102
Key Executives/Personnel:
    Haim Saban, Chairman & CEO
    Shuki Levy, President of Production
    Stan Golden, President of Int'l. Services
    Cheryl McDermott, Sr. VP of Business & Legal Affairs
    Dana Booton, Sr. VP of Animation
    Mark Pinsker, Sr. VP of Special Projects
    Rodd Feingold, VP of Physical Production
    Robert Palmer, VP of Production
    Jacqui Grunfeld, VP of Business & Legal Affairs
Specialties: Cable; Made for TV Movies; Miniseries
Other Categories: Feature Film
Credits: Power Ranger; Rusty: A Dog's Tale; Sweet Valley High
Additional Info: A Division of Fox Family

ALAN SACKS PRODUCTIONS, INC.
11684 Ventura Blvd., Ste. 809
Studio City, CA 91604
Phone: ....(818) 752-6999
Fax: ....(818) 752-6985
asacks@pacbell.net
Key Executives/Personnel:
    Alan Sacks, Producer
    Teena Poiter, Assistant to Mr. Sacks
Specialties: Network; Cable; Made for TV Movies
Other Categories: Feature Film
Credits: The Other Me; The Color of Friendship; Smart House; Welcome Back, Kotter

SAMUELSON PRODUCTIONS
10401 Wyton Dr.
Los Angeles, CA 90024
Phone: ....(310) 208-1000
Fax: ....(310) 208-2809
petersam@idt.net
Key Executives/Personnel:
    Marc Samuelson, Partner (UK)
    Peter Samuelson, Partner (LA)
Specialties: Network; Cable; Made for TV Movies
Other Categories: Feature Film
Credits: Jimmy Spud; Arlington Road; Wilde; Tom & Viv

SANFORD/PILLSBURY PRODUCTIONS
Phone: ....(310) 393-5225
Fax: ....(310) 393-8665
mssd@sanford-pillsbury.com
Key Executives/Personnel:
    Sarah Pillsbury, Partner & Producer
    Midge Sanford, Partner & Producer
    Rebecca Baldwin, Creative Executive
Specialties: Cable
Other Categories: Feature Film
Credits: Desperately Seeking Susan; Eight Men Out; River's Edge; The Love Letter

SANTA MONICA PICTURES
3025 W. Olympic Blvd.
Santa Monica, CA 90404
Phone: ....(310) 264-5566
Fax: ....(310) 828-9183
infosmp@visionart.com
Key Executives/Personnel:
    David Rose, CEO & Producer
    Marina Muhlfriedel, VP of Development & Production
    Cindy Sison, Head of Int'l. Sales & Distribution
    Stasi McAteer, Executive Assistant
Specialties: Animation; Made for TV Movies
Other Categories: Feature Film; Interactive Multimedia
Credits: The Painting; Goldilocks and the Three Bears; Godiva; The Magic Forest

SARABANDE PRODUCTIONS
530 Wilshire Blvd., Ste. 308
Santa Monica, CA 90401
Phone: ....(310) 395-4842
Fax: ....(310) 395-7079
Key Executives/Personnel:
    David Manson, President
    Arla Sorkin Manson, Executive VP
    David Strohmeyer, Development Associate
Specialties: Network; Cable; Made for TV Movies; Miniseries
Other Categories: Feature Film
Credits: Birdy; Bring on the Night; Nothing Sacred; Thicker Than Blood, Baby

EDGAR J. SCHERICK & ASSOCIATES, INC.
1950 Sawtelle Blvd., Ste. 282
Los Angeles, CA 90025
Phone: ....(310) 996-2376
Fax: ....(310) 996-2392
Key Executives/Personnel:
    Edgar T. Scherick, President
    Damon O'Daniel, Executive Assistant
    Dan Olsen, Assistant
Specialties: Network; Cable; Made for TV Movies; Miniseries
Other Categories: Feature Film
Credits: The Heartbreak Kid; Sleuth; The Taking of Pelham 1, 2, 3; They Shoot Horses

GEORGE SCHLATTER PRODUCTIONS
8321 Beverly Blvd.
Los Angeles, CA 90048
Phone: ....(323) 655-1400
Fax: ....(323) 852-1640
Key Executives/Personnel:
    George Schlatter, Executive Producer
    Gary Necessary, Executive in Charge of Production
Specialties: Network; Cable
Credits: Laugh-In; AFI Life Achievement in Honor of Dustin Hoffman; American Comedy Honors; Frank Sinatra: 80 Years My Way

SCHOLASTIC ENTERTAINMENT
524 Broadway
New York, NY 10012
Phone: ....(212) 343-7500
Fax: ....(212) 343-7888
www.scholastic.com
ljackson@scholastic.com
Key Executives/Personnel:
    Deborah Forte, Executive VP & Division Head
    Linda Kahn, VP of Int'l. Distribution
    Martha Atwater, VP of Programming & Development
    Ginger McGuire, VP of Finance & Business Affairs
    Andrea Sporer, VP of Legal Affairs

Production Companies – TV

Specialties: Network; Cable; Animation
Other Categories: Feature Film
Credits: Animorphs; Clifford the Big Red Dog; Indian in the Cupboard

BERNARD SCHWARTZ PRODUCTIONS
1900 Avenue of the Stars, Ste. 725
Los Angeles, CA 90067
Phone: ....(310) 277-3700
Fax: ....(310) 286-9700
Key Executives/Personnel:
  Bernard Schwartz, Producer
  Sandra Jones, Assistant
Specialties: Network; Cable; Made for TV Movies; Miniseries
Other Categories: Feature Film
Credits: Coal Miner's Daughter; Sweet Dreams; Psycho II; St. Elmo's Fire

KRISTINE SCHWARZ PRODUCTIONS
Phone: ....(310) 393-0107
Fax: ....(310) 451-5454
www.kristineschwarzproductions.com
krisjs@aol.com
Key Executives/Personnel:
  Kristine Schwarz, Producer
Specialties: Network; Cable; Made for TV Movies; Miniseries
Other Categories: Feature Film; Commercials; Interactive Multimedia
Credits: Raid Gauldises; Kalifornia; Another Stakeout

SCOTT FREE PRODUCTIONS
634 N. La Peer Dr.
West Hollywood, CA 90069
Phone: ....(310) 360-2250
Fax: ....(310) 360-2251
Key Executives/Personnel:
  Ridley Scott, Co-Chairman
  Tony Scott, Co-Chairman
  Lisa Ellzey, President
  Zach Schiff-Abrams, VP
  Anne Lai, Creative Executive
  Erin Upson, Story Editor
  Julie Payne, London Executive
  Beth Vitallo, Executive Assistant to Mr. Tony Scott
  Peter Toumasis, Executive Assistant to Mr. Ridley Scott
  Tom Moran, Executive Assistant to Mr. Tony Scott
  Ersin Pertan, Executive Assistant to Mr. Schiff-Abrams
  Milly Leigh, Executive Assistant to Ms. Payne
Specialties: Network; Cable
Other Categories: Feature Film
Credits: Hannibal; Gladiator; Enemy of the State; Top Gun
First Look/Development Deals: Intermedia Films, Jerry Bruckheimer Films
Additional Info: 42-44 Beak St., London, W1R 3DA England

DYLAN SELLERS PRODUCTIONS
4000 Warner Blvd.
Burbank, CA 91522
Phone: ....(818) 954-4929
Key Executives/Personnel:
  Dylan Sellers, Owner & Producer
  Bonny Giardina, Director of Development
Specialties: Network; Made for TV Movies
Other Categories: Feature Film
Credits: Valentine; Out to Sea; The Replacements; The Paper
First Look/Development Deals: Warner Bros.

SEVEN ARTS PICTURES
7080 Hollywood Blvd., Ste. 201
Hollywood, CA 90028
Phone: ....(323) 464-0225
Fax: ....(323) 464-8305
cinevision@aol.com
Key Executives/Personnel:
  Peter M. Hoffman, Chairman
  Colleen Camp, Producer & Partner
  Neil Canton, Producer & Partner
  Susan Hoffman, Producer & Partner
  Eric Sandys, President of Production
  Katie Hoffman, Creative Executive
  Brette Krinick, Creative Executive
  Erik Smith, Finance & Administration
  Victor Teran, Creative Executive
  Tori Crotts, Executive Assistant to Mr. Hoffman
  Amber Aaseng, Executive Assistant to Ms. Camp
  Andrea Ritigstein, Executive Assistant to Mr. Sandys
Specialties: Cable
Other Categories: Feature Film
Credits: Rules of Engagement; Shattered Image; Duets; Never Talk To Strangers
First Look/Development Deals: Paramount Pictures

SHADY ACRES ENTERTAINMENT
100 Universal City Plaza, Bldg. 5225, 2nd Fl.
Universal City, CA 91608
Phone: ....(818) 777-4446
Fax: ....(818) 866-6612
Key Executives/Personnel:
  Michael Bostick, no title
  Jim Brubaker, no title
  Ashley Cook, no title
  Ginny Durkin, no title
  Greg Messina, no title
  Amanda Morgan Palmer, no title
  Tom Shadyac, no title
  Lindsay Smarz, no title
  Winston Stromberg, no title
  Gina Warendorp, no title
  Jordan Wolfe, no title
  Brook Worley, no title
Specialties: Network
Other Categories: Feature Film; Music Video
Credits: Patch Adams; The Nutty Professor; Liar Liar
First Look/Development Deals: Universal Pictures

SHEARMAN ENTERTAINMENT, INC.
1541 Ocean Ave., Ste. 200
Santa Monica, CA 90401
Phone: ....(310) 860-0086
Fax: ....(310) 260-6336
jryan1111@aol.com
Key Executives/Personnel:
  J. R. Shearman, Producer & Personal Manager
Specialties: Documentaries; Made for TV Movies
Other Categories: Feature Film
Credits: Lie Down With Dogs; Never Met Picasso; The Casanovas

SHORELINE ENTERTAINMENT
1875 Century Park East, Ste. 600
Los Angeles, CA 90067
Phone: ....(310) 551-2060
Fax: ....(310) 201-0729
www.shorelineentertainment.com
mruskin@shorelineentertainment.com
Key Executives/Personnel:
  Vicky Pike, Producer
  Morris Ruskin, Producer
Specialties: Cable
Other Categories: Feature Film
Credits: Flight of Fancy; The King's Guard; The Visit

Production Companies – TV

SHOWTIME NETWORKS, INC.
10880 Wilshire Blvd., Ste. 1500 & 1600
Los Angeles, CA 90024
Phone: ....(310) 234-5200
www.sho.com
Key Executives/Personnel:
  Matthew C. Blank, President & CEO
  Jerry Offsay, President of Programming
  Mark Zakarin, Executive VP of Original Programming
  Ann Foley, Executive VP of East Coast Programming
  Melinda Benedek, Executive VP of Business Affairs
  Jerry Cooper, Executive VP of Finance & Operations
  Matthew Duda, Executive VP of Program Acquisitions & Planning
  Matthew Riklin, Executive VP of Program Enterprises & Distribution
  Joan Boorstein, Sr. VP of Creative Affairs
  Peter Keramidas, Sr. VP of Programming & New Media Content
  Anne Kurrasch, Sr. VP of Business Affairs
  Pancho Mansfield, Sr. VP of Development & Original Programming
  Frank Pintauro, Sr. VP of Family Programming
  Judith Pless, Sr. VP of Business Development
  Mike Rauch, Sr. VP of Motion Picture Production
  David Stern, Sr. VP of Business Affairs
  Monica Foster, VP of Motion Pictures & Series Development (NY)
  Lori Kahn, VP of Family & Childrens Programming
  Cynthia Bell, VP of Comedy Programming
  Sharon Byrens, VP of Motion Picture Development
  Katy Coyle, VP of Development
  Pearlena Igbokwe, VP of Original Programming
  Vicky Letizia, VP of Creative Affairs, Motion Pictures
  Jamie Padnos, VP of Program Planning
  Deborah Scott-Spera, VP of Motion Picture Development
  John Vasey, VP of Original Programming
  Tom Christine, Sundance Channel
  Ann Gilmore, Director of Series & Original Programming
  John Moser, Director of Family Programming
  Dominique Telson, Director of Development
  Vince Porter, Supervisor of Motion Picture Production
Specialties: Cable; Documentaries; Made for TV Movies

SHUKOVSKY ENGLISH ENTERTAINMENT
4605 Lankershim Blvd., Ste. 510
North Hollywood, CA 91602
Phone: ....(818) 763-9191
Fax: ....(818) 763-9878
Key Executives/Personnel:
  Diane English, Executive Producer & Writer
  Joel Shukovsky, Executive Producer
  Erica Nasser, Executive Assistant to Ms. English & Mr. Shukovsky
Specialties: Network
Credits: Love & War; Murphy Brown; Living in Captivity; Double Rush

SÍ TV
8322 Beverly Blvd., Ste. 304
Los Angeles, CA 90048
Phone: ....(323) 651-2242
Fax: ....(323) 651-2238
www.sitv.com
sitv@aol.com
Key Executives/Personnel:
  Jeff Valdez, Co-Chairman
  Bruce Barshop, Co-Chairman
  Bob Owen, CEO
  Leo Perez, COO
Specialties: Network; Cable
Credits: Brothers Garcia; Funny is Funny; Cafe Olé; Latino Laugh Festival

SIGNATURE ENTERTAINMENT
8306 Wilshire Blvd., Ste. 791
Beverly Hills, CA 90211
Phone: ....(213) 994-4695
Key Executives/Personnel:
  Kelly Andrea Rubin, Producer
Specialties: Cable; Documentaries; Made for TV Movies
Other Categories: Feature Film; Commercials
Credits: The Third Wheel; Cotton Mouth; An Eye For Talent; Skippy
First Look/Development Deals: Indigo Entertainment

SILVER LINING PRODUCTIONS, INC.
8687 Melrose Ave., Ste. B300
West Hollywood, CA 90069
Phone: ....(310) 289-6650
Fax: ....(310) 289-6658
slpbozena@aol.com/silverliningp@aol.com
Key Executives/Personnel:
  Bozena Armstrong, Executive Producer & Director
  Randy Haberkamp, Producer
Specialties: Network; Cable
Other Categories: Feature Film; Commercials; Video; Interactive Multimedia
Credits: Cleopatra (promo); Forest Lawn (commercial); Reva: The Scarlet Years (video); The Unknown Tradition (documentary)
Trade Assoc./Guilds/Unions: DGA, SAG

SILVER PICTURES TELEVISION
c/o Warner Bros., 4000 Warner Blvd., Bldg. 90
Burbank, CA 91522
Phone: ....(818) 954-4490
Fax: ....(818) 954-3237
Key Executives/Personnel:
  Joel Silver, Chairman
  Steve Richards, CFO
  Dan Cracchiolo, Sr. VP of Production
  Susan Levin, VP of Production
  Pam Martin, VP of Operations
Specialties: Network
Other Categories: Feature Film
Credits: The Matrix; House on Haunted Hill; Romeo Must Die; Lethal Weapon Series

SILVEREYE PRODUCTIONS
4163 Murietta Ave.
Sherman Oaks, CA 91423
Phone: ....(818) 501-4232
Fax: ....(818) 990-9997
Key Executives/Personnel:
  Ahmed Lateef, Producer & Director
  Ashwin Joshi, Producer & VP
  Omer Mohamed, Producer & Treasurer
  Meher Tatna, Producer & Writer
  Subash Kundamal, Producer & Writer
  Sherwood Ho, Producer & Director
Specialties: Made for TV Movies
Other Categories: Feature Film; Commercials
Credits: Pepsi; Changing Gears (feature); Locket (feature); Goodyear Tires
Trade Assoc./Guilds/Unions: DGA, FEU

SILVERLINE PICTURES
4410 Radford Ave.
North Hollywood, CA 91607
Phone: ....(818) 752-3730
Fax: ....(818) 752-3758
www.silverlinepictures.com
silverline@earthlink.net
Key Executives/Personnel:
  Axel Munch, Producer & President
  Leman Cetiner, CEO & Producer
  Christopher Tipton, Director of Production & Acquistions
  Robert Yap, Director of Development & Sales
Specialties: Cable

Production Companies – TV

Other Categories: Feature Film
Credits: Angels Don't Sleep Here; Traveling Bowls of Soup; Dusting Cliff Seven; Where Truth Lies

THE FRED SILVERMAN COMPANY
1648 Mandeville Canyon Rd.
Los Angeles, CA 90049
Phone: (310) 234-5000
Fax: (310) 471-6536
Key Executives/Personnel:
  Fred Silverman, President
  Kelly Perkins, Executive Assistant
Specialties: Network; Cable; Made for TV Movies; Miniseries
Credits: Diagnosis Murder

THE GENE SIMMONS COMPANY
P.O. Box 16075
Beverly Hills, CA 90210
Phone: (310) 859-1694
Fax: (310) 859-2631
Key Executives/Personnel:
  Gene Simmons, Producer
  David Slous, Assistant
Specialties: Network; Cable; Animation; Documentaries; Made for TV Movies; Miniseries
Other Categories: Feature Film
Credits: Detroit Rock City; Neal Bogart Story; Sex, Drugs and Rock 'n Roll; November Files

RANDY SIMON PRODUCTIONS
1113 N. Hillcrest Rd.
Beverly Hills, CA 90210
Phone: (310) 274-7440
Fax: (310) 274-9809
simonrandy@aol.com
Key Executives/Personnel:
  Randy Simon, Producer
Specialties: Network; Cable
Other Categories: Feature Film
Credits: Pi; Requiem For A Dream; Intern; Blue Ridge Fall

THE ROBERT SIMONDS COMPANY
100 Universal City Plaza, Bldg. 1320, PH.1A
Universal City, CA 91608
Phone: (818) 777-5445
Fax: (818) 866-1404
Key Executives/Personnel:
  Robert Simonds, Producer
  Tracey Trench, President of Creative Affairs
  Joy Gorman, VP of Creative Affairs
  Linda Cuevas, Executive Assistant
  Alison Luzietti, Assistant to Ms. Trench
  Laura Millar, Assistant to Ms. Gorman
Specialties: Network
Other Categories: Feature Film
Credits: Little Nicky; The Water Boy; Big Daddy; Happy Gilmore
First Look/Development Deals: Universal Pictures

DAVID A. SIMONS PRODUCTIONS
5301 Parion Ct.
Woodland Hills, CA 91367
Phone: (818) 884-7823
Fax: (818) 884-8553
dav4all@aol.com
Key Executives/Personnel:
  David A. Simons, Writer & Producer
Specialties: Network; Cable; Documentaries; Made for TV Movies; Miniseries
Credits: Locked In Silence; American Detective; Equal Justice
Trade Assoc./Guilds/Unions: WGAw

SINGLE SPARK PICTURES
3000 W. Olympic Blvd.
Santa Monica, CA 90404
Phone: (310) 315-4779
Fax: (310) 315-4773
Key Executives/Personnel:
  Mark Mori, President & Executive Producer
  Jim Hense, Producer
Specialties: Cable; Documentaries
Other Categories: Feature Film
Credits: Kent State: The Day The War Came Home; Survivors; Raw Footage

SITTING DUCKS PRODUCTIONS
1532 Micheltorena St.
Los Angeles, CA 90026
Phone: (323) 660-0861
Fax: (323) 660-6021
sittingducks@earthlink.net
Key Executives/Personnel:
  Elizabeth Daro, Co-Owner
  Michael Bedard, Co-Owner
  Liz Bedard, Associate Producer
  Danielle Mentzer, Associate Producer
Specialties: Network; Cable; Animation; Made for TV Movies
Other Categories: Feature Film
Credits: Sitting Ducks; The Mouse and the Monster
First Look/Development Deals: Universal Pictures

SKYLARK ENTERTAINMENT, INC.
12405 Venice Blvd., Ste. 237
Los Angeles, CA 90066
Phone: (310) 390-2659
Fax: (310) 390-2759
skylarkinc@earthlink.net
Key Executives/Personnel:
  Jacobus Rose, Producer
Specialties: Network; Cable; Animation
Other Categories: Feature Film
Credits: Deadlocked; The Linda McCartney Story; Election; Steal This Movie
First Look/Development Deals: Robert Greenwald Productions

SKYLARK FILMS, LTD.
1123 Pacific St., Ste. G
Santa Monica, CA 90405
Phone: (310) 396-5753
Fax: (310) 396-5753
skyfilm@aol.com
Key Executives/Personnel:
  Brad Pollack, Producer
  Jasan Pagni, Development
Specialties: Cable; Made for TV Movies; Miniseries
Other Categories: Feature Film
Credits: The Styx; Coal of the Heart; Terminal Justice; Just One Look
First Look/Development Deals: Orly Adelson Productions

SLADEK ENTERTAINMENT CORPORATION
8306 Wilshire Blvd., Ste. 510
Beverly Hills, CA 90211
Phone: (323) 934-9268
Fax: (323) 934-7362
www.danielsladek.com
dansladek@aol.com
Key Executives/Personnel:
  Daniel Sladek, President
  Chris Taaffe, Producing Partner
Specialties: Network; Cable; Made for TV Movies; Miniseries
Other Categories: Feature Film
Credits: Tale of the Mummy; Sub Down; Silent Trigger; Hidden Assassin

SNAPDRAGON FILMS, INC.
13428 Maxella Ave., Ste. 293
Marina Del Rey, CA 90292
Phone: ....(310) 822-2505
Fax: ....(310) 822-7054
Key Executives/Personnel:
  Bonnie Palef, Director, Producer & Writer
  Catherine Purchase, Assistant
  Manuel Granado, Jr., Assistant
Specialties: Cable; Documentaries; Made for TV Movies
Other Categories: Feature Film; Video; Interactive Multimedia
Credits: Marvin's Room; Moonstruck; The Cemetary Club; Parents
First Look/Development Deals: Columbia Pictures/Columbia Tristar Motion Picture Group
Trade Assoc./Guilds/Unions: DGA, WGAw

SNEAK PREVIEW ENTERTAINMENT, INC.
1604 Vista del Mar
Hollywood, CA 90028
Phone: ....(323) 962-0295
Fax: ....(323) 962-0372
www.sneakpreviewentertain.com
sneakpreview@pacbell.net
Key Executives/Personnel:
  Steven J. Wolfe, Chairman, CEO & Producer
  Lynette Prucha Chavez, President & Writer
  David L. Cohn, Talent Manager
  Michael J. Roth, Director of Development
Specialties: Made for TV Movies
Other Categories: Feature Film; Video; Music Video
Credits: Fast Sofa; Twin Falls, Idaho; Relax...It's Just Sex; Tollbooth

SNL STUDIOS
5555 Melrose Ave., Dressing Room Bldg., Ste. 105
Los Angeles, CA 90038
Phone: ....(323) 956-5729
Fax: ....(323) 862-8605
Key Executives/Personnel:
  Lorne Michaels, Chairman
  Richard Feldman, President
  Mallory Eisenstein, Director of Development
  Abdul Williams, Assistant
Specialties: Network; Cable
Other Categories: Feature Film
Credits: Wayne's World 1 & 2; Ladies Man; Tommy Boy; Superstar
First Look/Development Deals: Paramount Pictures, NBC Entertainment, Inc.

SNOW LEOPARD PRODUCTIONS
Phone: ....(310) 827-1220
Fax: ....(310) 821-5251
www.snowleopard.net
snowcat711@mediaone.net
Key Executives/Personnel:
  C'esca Lawrence, Producer & Co-Owner
  Dan Tursi, Producer & Co-Owner
  Jan Monroe, VP of Creative Affairs
  Tim Merritt, Director of Development
Specialties: Network; Cable; Documentaries; Made for TV Movies; Miniseries
Other Categories: Feature Film
Credits: A New View

SOFRONSKI PRODUCTIONS
10202 W. Washington Blvd., Tristar Bldg., Ste. 204
Culver City, CA 90232
Phone: ....(310) 244-5412
Fax: ....(310) 244-2472
Key Executives/Personnel:
  Bernard Sofronski, Executive Producer
Specialties: Made for TV Movies; Miniseries
Credits: Too Rich: The Secret Life of Doris Duke; Into Thin Air: Death on Everest; Mandela & Deklerk

SONNENFELD/JOSEPHSON WORLDWIDE ENTERTAINMENT
10202 W. Washington Blvd., Jimmy Stuart Bldg., Ste. 205
Culver City, CA 90232
Phone: ....(310) 244-8777
Fax: ....(310) 244-1977
Key Executives/Personnel:
  Barry Josephson, no title
  Barry Sonnenfeld, no title
  Brandon Chapnick, Assistant to Mr. Josephson & Mr. Sonnenfeld
Specialties: Network; Cable
Other Categories: Feature Film

SONY PICTURES ENTERTAINMENT
10202 W. Washington Blvd.
Culver City, CA 90232
Phone: ....(310) 244-4000
Fax: ....(310) 244-2626
www.spe.sony.com
Key Executives/Personnel:
  John Calley, Chairman & CEO
  Mel Harris, Co-President & COO
  Beth Berke, Executive VP & CAO
  Jerry Giaquinta, Executive VP of Corporate Communications
  Ronald Jacobi, Executive VP, General Counsel & Corporate Secretary
  Yari Landau, Executive VP
  Bedi A. Singh, Executive VP & CFO
  Suzanne Criley, Sr. VP of Human Resources
  Joe Kraft, Sr. VP & Treasurer
  Karen L. Halby, VP
  Robert Eichorn, Assistant Secretary
  Jared Jussim, Assistant Secretary
  Leah Well, Assistant Secretary
  Lynne R. Shulim, Assistant Treasurer
  Michael Winchester, Assistant Treasurer
Specialties: Network; Cable; Animation

SOUTH FORK PRODUCTIONS
P.O. Box 1935
Santa Monica, CA 90406
Phone: ....(310) 829-5029
Fax: ....(310) 829-5029
soforkprods@ireland.com
Key Executives/Personnel:
  Jim Sullivan, Producer & Director
  Greg Sullivan, Producer
Specialties: Cable; Documentaries
Other Categories: Feature Film; Commercials; Video; Music Video
Credits: Making of Without Limits; Portraits of Courage; Those Who Dare
Trade Assoc./Guilds/Unions: AFI

SOUTHERN SKIES, INC.
1104 S. Holt Ave., Ste. 302
Los Angeles, CA 90035
Phone: ....(310) 855-9833
Fax: ....(310) 855-0220
www.southernskiesinc.com
soskies@aol.com
Key Executives/Personnel:
  Ed Markley, President
Specialties: Network; Cable; Made for TV Movies; Miniseries
Other Categories: Feature Film
Credits: Major League 1 & 2; Alien 3; For The Boys; City Slickers
First Look/Development Deals: Octagon Productions, Inc.
Trade Assoc./Guilds/Unions: AFI, ATAS, DGA

Production Companies – TV

SPELLING TELEVISION, INC.
5700 Wilshire Blvd., 5th Fl.
Los Angeles, CA 90036
Phone: ....(323) 965-5700
Fax: ....(323) 965-5895
Key Executives/Personnel:
  Aaron Spelling, Chairman & CEO
  E. Duke Vincent, Vice Chairman
  Jonathan C. Levin, President
  James Conway, Executive VP
  Renate Kamer, Sr. VP
  Kenneth Miller, Sr. VP of Post Production
  Jennifer Nicholson-Salke, Sr. VP of Series Development
  Gail Patterson, Sr. VP of Production
  Pamela Shae, Sr. VP of Talent
  Kristina Espinoza, VP of Current Programming
  Ted Gold, VP of Series Development
  Lougenia Patrick, VP of Series Business Affairs
  Robert Zinser, VP of Business & Legal Affairs
  Jennifer Grisanti, Executive Director of Current Programming
Specialties: Network
Credits: 7th Heaven; Charmed; Titans; All Souls

SPLENDIDLIGHT MEDIA PRODUCTIONS
177 Riverside St., PMB 151
Newport Beach, CA 92663
Phone: ....(949) 722-8485
Fax: ....(949) 722-7896
www.splendidlight.com
lsplendid@splendidlight.com
Key Executives/Personnel:
  Lynn Splendid, Producer & Director
  Clayton Light, Producer & Editor
Specialties: Cable; Documentaries
Other Categories: Commercials; Video
Additional Info: 2801 Pacific Coast Hwy., Ste. 325
  Newport Beach, CA 92663

SPRING CREEK PRODUCTIONS
4000 Warner Blvd., Bldg. 76
Burbank, CA 91522
Phone: ....(818) 954-1210
Fax: ....(818) 954-2737
Key Executives/Personnel:
  Robin Forman, President
  Barry Levinson, Director, Writer & Producer
  Paula Weinstein, Producer
  Amy Solan, CFO & Business Affairs
  Rhonda Bloom, VP
  Robyn Snyder, Director of Development
Specialties: Made for TV Movies; Miniseries

SPYGLASS ENTERTAINMENT
500 S. Buena Vista St.
Burbank, CA 91521
Phone: ....(818) 560-3458
Fax: ....(818) 563-1967
Key Executives/Personnel:
  Gary Barber, Co-Chairman & CEO
  Roger Birnbaum, Co-Chairman & CEO
  Jon Glickman, President of Production
  Drew Larner, Executive VP
  Paul Schwacke, CFO
  Ned Dowd, Sr. VP of Physical Production
  Derek Evans, VP of Production
  Megan Wolpert, VP of Production
  Paul Neinstein, VP of Business & Legal Affairs
  Rebekah Rudd, VP of Post Production
  Jeremy Steckler, Creative Executive
  Marlena Thomas, Executive Coordinator to Mr. Birnbaum
  Kim Buttlar, Executive Coordinator to Mr. Barber
Specialties: Network
Other Categories: Feature Film
Credits: The Sixth Sense; Keeping The Faith; Shanghai Noon; Instinct

ST. CLARE ENTERTAINMENT
8490 Sunset Blvd., Ste. 503
Los Angeles, CA 90069
Phone: ....(310) 360-0451
Fax: ....(310) 360-0421
Key Executives/Personnel:
  John Landis, Director
  Leslie Belzberg, Producer
Specialties: Network; Cable
Other Categories: Feature Film
Credits: Susan's Plan; Blues Brothers 2000; The Lost World (TV series);
  Honey I Shrunk The Kids (TV series)
Trade Assoc./Guilds/Unions: AMPAS, ATAS

J. STACK PRODUCTIONS
Phone: ....(310) 456-3272
Fax: ....(310) 456-3442
jmstack@aol.com
Key Executives/Personnel:
  Jeanne Stack, Producer
Specialties: Network; Cable; Documentaries; Made for TV Movies
Other Categories: Feature Film; Commercials; Music Video
Credits: Contact (2nd Unit); Kundun (2nd Unit); Eco-Challenge; Mild 7

STAGESCREEN PRODUCTIONS
2601 Nicholas Canyon Rd.
Los Angeles, CA 90046
Phone: ....(323) 969-1974
Fax: ....(323) 969-1975
stgescreen@aol.com
Key Executives/Personnel:
  Jeffrey Taylor, Producer
Specialties: Cable; Made for TV Movies; Miniseries
Other Categories: Feature Film
Credits: A Handful of Dust; Where Angels Fear to Tread; Foreign Affairs;
  What's Cooking
Additional Info: 12 Upper St. Martins Ln., London, WC2H 9DL England

STARTOONS INTERNATIONAL, LLC.
18147 Harwood Ave.
Homewood, IL 60430
Phone: ....(708) 335-3535
Fax: ....(708) 335-3999
www.startoons.net
ravi@startoons.net
Key Executives/Personnel:
  Jon McClenahan, President
  Raui Yanamadula, VP
  Harold Dempsey, General Manager
  Caroline Manalo, Producer
  Dave Pryor, Director
  John Griffin, Director
  Katie Fry, Production Coordinator
Specialties: Animation
Credits: Fat Cats; Animaniacs; Historia; Little Dogs On The Prairie

JANE STARTZ PRODUCTIONS, INC.
244 Fifth Ave., 11th Fl.
New York, NY 10001
Phone: ....(212) 545-8910
Fax: ....(212) 545-8909
jsp@janestartzproductions.com
Key Executives/Personnel:
  Jane Startz, President & Producer
  Gillian Mackenzie, VP of Creative Affairs

Billy Mulligan, Development Associate
Specialties: Network; Cable
Other Categories: Feature Film
Credits: Indian In The Cupboard; The Mighty; The Baby-Sitter's Club; The Magic School Bus

STARZ ENCORE ENTERTAINMENT GROUP
5445 DTC Parkway, Ste. 600
Englewood, CO 80111
Phone: ....(303) 771-7700
....(310) 550-7172
Fax: ....(303) 267-4092
www.encoremedia.com
Key Executives/Personnel:
John Si, Chairman & CEO
Robert Leighton, Sr. VP of Programming
Stephan Shelanski, Sr. VP of Program Acquisitions & Planning
Andrea Levitt-Stein, VP of Business Affairs
Paige Orloff, VP of Original Movies
Specialties: Cable; Documentaries

STATE STREET PICTURES
10201 W. Pico Blvd., Bldg. 50
Los Angeles, CA 90064
Phone: ....(310) 369-5099
Fax: ....(310) 369-8613
Key Executives/Personnel:
Robert Teitel, Producer
George Tillman, Director & Producer
Specialties: Cable
Other Categories: Feature Film
Credits: Men of Honor; Soul Food (feature); Soul Food (TV series)

STEFANINO PRODUCTIONS
15515 Sunset Blvd., Ste. 101
Pacific Palisades, CA 90272
Phone: ....(310) 454-0109
Fax: ....(310) 454-0109
www.stefanino.com
stefanino@earthlink.net
Key Executives/Personnel:
Stuart Jemesen, Producer & Director
Stefan Kendal Gordy, Director of Music
Specialties: Documentaries
Other Categories: Feature Film; Commercials; Video; Music Video
Credits: Smokey Robinson; Michael Jackson Biography; Innerview (TV pilot)

THE HOWARD STERN PRODUCTION COMPANY
10 E. 44th St.
New York, NY 10017
Phone: ....(212) 867-1200
Fax: ....(212) 867-2434
www.howardstern.com
don@buchwald.com
Key Executives/Personnel:
Howard Stern, President
Don Buchwald, Agent
Specialties: Network; Cable; Animation
Other Categories: Feature Film
Credits: The Howard Stern Radio Show; Son of The Beach; The Howard Stern Show; Doomsday

MEL STUART PRODUCTIONS, INC.
1551 S. Robertson Blvd., Ste. 204
Los Angeles, CA 90035
Phone: ....(310) 785-9080
Fax: ....(310) 785-9179
melfilm@aol.com
Key Executives/Personnel:
Mel Stuart, President, Producer & Director

Chad Baron, Associate Producer
Specialties: Network; Cable; Documentaries
Other Categories: Feature Film; Video
Credits: Running on the Sun; AFI's 100 Years 100 Movies; The Rise & Fall of the Third Reich; Ripley's Believe It or Not
Trade Assoc./Guilds/Unions: DGA, WGAw

STUDIOS USA
8800 Sunset Blvd.
West Hollywood, CA 90069
Phone: ....(310) 360-2300
Fax: ....(310) 360-2517
www.studiosusa.com
Key Executives/Personnel:
Bob Fleming, Group President
David Kissinger, President of Network Programming
Steven Rosenberg, President of Domestic Syndication
Charles Engel, Executive VP of Programming
Valerie Schaer, Executive VP of Programming & Development
Matthew N. Herman, Executive VP of Production
Lonnie Burstein, Sr. VP of First Run Development
Juliana Carnesale, Sr. VP of Business Affairs
Daniel Pasternack, Sr. VP of Drama Development
Marcy Ross, Sr. VP of Comedy Programming
Neil Strum, Sr. VP of Business & Legal Affairs
Nancy Perkins, Sr. VP of Casting
Soheila Ataei, VP of Human Resources
Specialties: Network; Cable; Animation; Documentaries; Made for TV Movies; Miniseries

MIKE SULLIVAN PRODUCTIONS, INC.
2314 Michigan Ave.
Santa Monica, CA 90404
Phone: ....(310) 315-7315
Fax: ....(310) 582-0041
msp_inc@wgn.net
Key Executives/Personnel:
Mike Sullivan, President & Executive Producer
Polly Brown, Director of Creative Affairs
Specialties: Network; Made for TV Movies
Other Categories: Feature Film
Credits: Growing Pains; Just The Ten Of Us; The Growing Pains Movie

SUMMERLAND ENTERTAINMENT
17939 Chatsworth St., Ste. 260
Granada Hills, CA 91344
Phone: ....(818) 363-4135
Fax: ....(818) 368-8227
sumrland47@aol.com
Key Executives/Personnel:
Bruce A. Pobjoy, President & Producer
Brianne Michelle, VP of Development
Brooke Allison, Administrative Assistant
Specialties: Network; Cable; Made for TV Movies; Miniseries
Other Categories: Feature Film; Music Video
Credits: Fatal Memories; Baywatch Nights; Nightmare Cafe; In The Heat of The Night
Trade Assoc./Guilds/Unions: AAP

SUMMERS ENTERTAINMENT
5230 Linwood Dr.
Los Angeles, CA 90027
Phone: ....(323) 665-5400
Fax: ....(323) 663-6679
Key Executives/Personnel:
Cathleen Summers, Producer
Specialties: Network; Cable; Made for TV Movies; Miniseries
Other Categories: Feature Film
Credits: Stake Out; Dog Fight; The Sandlot; D.O.A

Production Companies – TV

First Look/Development Deals: Twentieth Century Fox
Trade Assoc./Guilds/Unions: ACAD, PGA

SUNDOG PRODUCTIONS
1129 Highland Ave., Ste. 201
Manhattan Beach, CA 90266
Phone: ....(310) 564-9515
Fax: ....(310) 546-9516
laloula@aol.com
Key Executives/Personnel:
 Larry Carroll, Director
 Linda Agnelli, Producer
Specialties: Network; Documentaries
Other Categories: Feature Film
Credits: Sam Kinison: Why Did We Laugh?; The New American Heroes; Women Surfer Project
Trade Assoc./Guilds/Unions: DGA

SWEET LORRAINE PRODUCTIONS, INC.
2001 Barrington Ave., Ste. 215
Los Angeles, CA 90025
Phone: ....(310) 575-3066
Fax: ....(310) 575-9388
lvanlowe@blackboardkids.com
Key Executives/Personnel:
 Ehrich Van Lowe, President
 Kaj Goldberg, TV & Theatrical Production
 Robin Claire, TV & Theatrical Production
 Michael Davis, TV & Theatrical Production
 Kevin Wafford, Reality TV
 Corey Crimson, Music & Theatrical Production
 Latif Van Lowe, TV & Theatrical Production
Specialties: Network; Cable
Credits: Homeboys In Outer Space; ROC; Where I Live; Cosby Show

TAFFNER ENTERTAINMENT
31 W. 56th St.
New York, NY 10019
Phone: ....(323) 937-1144
Fax: ....(323) 937-5095
Key Executives/Personnel:
 Don Taffner Jr., Executive VP
 Emmet G. Lavery Jr., VP of Business Affairs
Specialties: Network; Cable
Credits: Three's Company; As Time Goes By; Too Close for Comfort;
First Look/Development Deals: Twentieth Century Fox Television

TALENT ENTERTAINMENT GROUP
9111 Wilshire Blvd.
Beverly Hills, CA 90210
Phone: ....(323) 969-0700
 ....(310) 205-5525
Fax: ....(323) 969-9340
Key Executives/Personnel:
 Erwin More, Partner
 Brian Medavoy, Partner
 Suzan Bymel, Partner
 Evelyn O'Neill, Partner
 Cheryl Stanley, VP of Creative Affairs
 Bill Choi, Manager
 David Gardner, Manager
 Peter Kiernan, Manager
 Jill Littman, Manager
 Randi Siegel, Manager
 Louise Spinner, Manager
Specialties: Network
Other Categories: Feature Film

Credits: Just Shoot Me; Dharma & Greg; American High
First Look/Development Deals: Warner Bros. Television

TAURUS ENTERTAINMENT COMPANY
5831 Sunset Blvd.
Hollywood, CA 90028
Phone: ....(323) 860-0807
Fax: ....(323) 860-0834
www.taurus-entertainment.com
taurusec@aol.com
Key Executives/Personnel:
 Stan Dudelson, Chairman
 James Dudelson, President & CEO
 Robert Dudelson, COO
 Ana Clevel, VP
 Steve Kripner, Stage Manager
 Kimberly Burch, Operations Manager
Specialties: Cable
Other Categories: Feature Film
Credits: Horror 101; Morela; Mastermind; Hot Springs Hotel

TAVEL ENTERTAINMENT
9171 Wilshire Blvd., Ste. 406
Beverly Hills, CA 90210
Phone: ....(310) 278-6700
Fax: ....(310) 278-6770
Key Executives/Personnel:
 Connie Tavel, Owner, Manager & Producer
 Chris Ridenhour, Development for Features
 Vanessa Livingston, Development for TV
 Plato Wang, Development for Internet
 Vera Mihailovich, Talent Scout
 Mundi Male, Assistant to Ms. Tavel
 Marc Walker, Assistant to Mr. Ridenhour
 Courtney Adams, Assistant to Ms. Mihailovich
Specialties: Network; Cable
Other Categories: Feature Film; Interactive Multimedia
Credits: Judging Amy; Summer's End; Bill & Ted's Bogus Journey; Ride The Wind
First Look/Development Deals: Sony Pictures Entertainment

TAYLOR-BEDELL ENTERTAINMENT
9560 Wilshire Blvd., PH
Beverly Hills, CA 90212
Phone: ....(310) 859-9967
Fax: ....(310) 859-9965
tbe@earthlink.net
Key Executives/Personnel:
 Stephen Bedell, Partner & Producer
 Burton Taylor, Partner & Producer
 Chris Mock, Development
Specialties: Network; Cable; Animation; Made for TV Movies
Other Categories: Feature Film
Credits: The Westside Waltz; 1,000 Men and a Baby

TBS SUPERSTATION
1050 Techwood Dr. NW
Atlanta, GA 30318
Phone: ....(404) 827-1717
 ....(310) 788-6800
www.tbssuperstation.com
tbssuperstation@turner.com
Key Executives/Personnel:
 Brad Siegel, President
 Dennis Quinn, Executive VP & General Manager
 Jim Head, Sr. VP of Development
 Tana Jamleson, VP of Original Programming, Movies (LA)
 Christy Kreisberg, VP of Original Programming, Series (LA)
 Susan Birell, Legal Affairs (LA)

Production Companies – TV

    Margie Moreno, Manager of Original Programming (LA)
    Debbie Stasson, Business Affairs (LA)
    Barbara Lancaster, Assistant to Mr. Head
    Sara Anspitz, Assistant to Ms. Kriesberg (LA)
    Adam Silverman, Assistant to Ms. Jamieson (LA)
Specialties: Cable; Made for TV Movies
Credits: Nuremberg; Witchblade; Bull; Running Mates
Additional Info: 1888 Century Park East, 14th Fl., Los Angeles, CA 90067

TEAM TODD
9021 Melrose Ave., Ste. 301
Los Angeles, CA 90069
Phone: ....(310) 248-6001
Fax: ....(310) 385-8072
Key Executives/Personnel:
    Jennifer Todd, Partner & Producer
    Suzanne Todd, Partner & Producer
    Pamela Post, VP
    Lauren Tabach-Bank, Development Assistant
    Julie Ragland, Assistant to Producers
Specialties: Made for TV Movies
Other Categories: Feature Film
Credits: Momento; If These Walls Could Talk 2; Boiler Room; Austin Powers 1 & 2
First Look/Development Deals: New Line Cinema

TELESCENE FILM GROUP, INC.
5705 Ferrier, Ste. 200
Montreal, QC H4P 1N3 Canada
Phone: ....(514) 737-5512
Fax: ....(514) 737-7945
www.telescene.ca
info@telescene.ca
Key Executives/Personnel:
    Robin Spry, President & CEO
    Bruce Moccia, President of Telescene Film Group Inc. (USA)
    Michael Yudin, President of Telescene Entertainment Inc.
    Claire Benoit, VP of Business & Legal Affairs/Secretary
    Daniel Proulx, VP of Finance & CEO
    Anita Simand, Head of Creative Affairs
    Diana Arcand, Head of Production
    Cynthia Lane, Manager of Public Relations
Specialties: Network; Cable; Documentaries; Made for TV Movies; Miniseries
Other Categories: Feature Film
Credits: Hiroshima; Student Bodies; Big Wolf on Campus; Live Through This

TELLING PICTURES, INC.
121 Ninth St.
San Francisco, CA 94103
Phone: ....(415) 864-6714
Fax: ....(415) 864-4364
www.tellingpix.com
tellingpix@aol.com
Key Executives/Personnel:
    Rob Epstein, Director & Producer
    Jeffrey Friedman, Director & Producer
    Michael Ehrenzweig, Producer
    Whitney Saik, Production Manager
Specialties: Cable; Documentaries
Other Categories: Feature Film; Video
Credits: The Times of Harvey Milk; Common Threads: Stories from the Quilt; The Celluloid Closet; Paragraph 175
Trade Assoc./Guilds/Unions: AMPAS, ATAS

TEN THIRTEEN PRODUCTIONS
P.O. Box 900
Beverly Hills, CA 90213
Phone: ....(310) 369-1100
Key Executives/Personnel:
    Chris Carter, Executive Producer
    Frank Spotnitz, President & Executive Producer
    Mary Astadourian, VP
Specialties: Network
Other Categories: Feature Film
Credits: The X Files; The Lone Gunman
First Look/Development Deals: Twentieth Century Fox Television

TEOCALLI ENTERTAINMENT, INC.
205 Timberline Court
Ruidoso, NM 88345
Phone: ....(505) 258-1373
Fax: ....(505) 258-1377
Key Executives/Personnel:
    Robert A. Nowotny, President
    Ed Callaway, Director of Development
Specialties: Documentaries; Cable
Other Categories: Feature Film; Video
Credits: False River; The Top Of The Bottom Half; The Legend of Billy The Kid; The Radicals

TERRA BELLA ENTERTAINMENT
8170 Beverly Blvd., Ste. 102
Los Angeles, CA 90048
Phone: ....(323) 655-2311
Fax: ....(323) 655-0499
Key Executives/Personnel:
    Adam Leipzig, Producer
    Susanna Bieger, Research Associate
Specialties: Cable
Other Categories: Feature Film
Credits: Titus; The Associate

THRESHOLD ENTERTAINMENT
1649 11th St.
Santa Monica, CA 90404
Phone: ....(310) 452-8899
Fax: ....(310) 452-0736
www.thethreshold.com
Key Executives/Personnel:
    Larry Kasanoff, Chairman & CEO
    Joshua Wexler, CIO
    George Johnsen, CTO
    Alison Savitch, President
Specialties: Network; Cable; Animation
Other Categories: Feature Film; Interactive Multimedia
Credits: Mortal Kombat: Annihilation; Beowulf; True Lies; Mortal Kombat

TIDEWATER ENTERTAINMENT
320 Mount Holyoke Ave.
Pacific Palisades, CA 90272
Phone: ....(310) 459-8711
Fax: ....(310) 459-0149
Key Executives/Personnel:
    Bill Ungar, President & Executive Producer
Specialties: Network; Cable; Made for TV Movies
Other Categories: Feature Film
Credits: Excellent Cadavers; Crimson Tide; True Romance

TLC ENTERTAINMENT
c/o CBS Studio Center, 4024 Radford Ave., Edit Bldg. 2, Ste. 9
Studio City, CA 91604
Phone: ....(818) 655-6155
Fax: ....(818) 655-6254
tlce@aol.com
Key Executives/Personnel:

Production Companies – TV

George Taweel, Producer
Rob Loos, Producer
Jennifer Velasco, Assistant to Mr. Taweel & Mr. Loos
Specialties: Animation
Other Categories: Feature Film
Credits: Magee & Me; All New Captain Kangaroo Show; Secret Adventures
Trade Assoc./Guilds/Unions: ATAS, DGA, PGA, WGAw

TOLLIN/ROBBINS PRODUCTIONS
4133 Lankershim Blvd.
North Hollywood, CA 91602
Phone: ....(818) 766-5004
Fax: ....(818) 766-8488
Key Executives/Personnel:
  Mike Tollin, Executive Producer & Director
  Brian Robbins, Executive Producer & Director
  Joe Davola, Executive Producer
  Jonny Fink, Producer
  Jeff Blye, COO
  Chris Castallo, Director of Creative Affairs
  Michael Goldman, Talent Manager
  Virginie Lacoste, Office Manager & Bookkeeper
  Andre Burrell, Assistant to Mr. Davola & Mr. Costallo
  Jason Hutt, Assistant to Ms. Gray
  Alex Timchak, Assistant to Mr. Robbins & Mr. Davola
  Mark Warshaw, Assistant to Mr. Robbins
  Caleigh Vancata, Talent Maintenance
  Andrew Bennett, Office Production Assistant
  Susan Chan, Office Assistant
Specialties: Network
Other Categories: Feature Film
Credits: Summer Catch; Varsity Blues; Ready to Rumble; All That

TRIBECA PRODUCTIONS
375 Greenwich St., 6th Fl.
New York, NY 10013
Phone: ....(212) 941-4040
Fax: ....(212) 941-4044
www.tribecafilm.com
Key Executives/Personnel:
  Robert DeNiro, Partner
  Jane Rosenthal, Partner
  Hardy Justice, VP of Creative Affairs
  Trina Wyatt, VP of Operations & Finance
  Elyse Klaits, Director of Production
  Scott Neustadler, Director of Development
  Kate Feeney, Assistant to Ms. Rosenthal
  Meghan Lyvers, Assistant to Ms. Rosenthal
  Angela Robinson, Assistant to Mr. Epstein
  Tom Turner, Assistant to Ms. Wyatt
Specialties: Network; Cable
Other Categories: Feature Film
Credits: Meet the Parents; Analyze This; Wag the Dog; Thunderheart

THE TRIBUNAL
Phone: ....(323) 468-9300
Fax: ....(323) 936-1301
www.thetribunal.com
production@thetribunal.com
Key Executives/Personnel:
  Thomas Sammon, Producer & Partner
  Maria Bryant, Producer & Partner
Specialties: Network; Cable
Other Categories: Feature Film
Credits: High Caliber; Real Story

TRIBUNE ENTERTAINMENT COMPANY
5800 Sunset Blvd., TEC Bldg.
Los Angeles, CA 90028
Phone: ....(323) 460-5800
Fax: ....(323) 460-3858
www.tribtv.com
Key Executives/Personnel:
  Richard H. Askin, Jr., President & CEO
  David Berson, Sr. VP of Business Affairs
  Philip Segal, Sr. VP of Scripted Programming & Development
  Richard Inouye, VP of Finance & Administration
  Fern Field, Creative Consultant, Programming & Development
  Gina Brittle-Mackey, Director of Development, Reality
  Seth Howard, Director of Programming & Development
  George NeJame, Director of Operations & Production
  Paul Jensen, Facilities Manager
  Jim Toten, Director of Engineering
  Cindie Zimmerman, Manager of Programming & Development
Specialties: Network
Credits: Judge Joe Brown; Judge Judy; Kids Say the Darndest Things; Who's Line is it Anyway?

TRIOLOGY ENTERTAINMENT GROUP
2450 Broadway St., Ste. 675
Santa Monica, CA 90404
Phone: ....(310) 449-3095
Fax: ....(310) 449-3195
Key Executives/Personnel:
  Pen Densham, Founder
  John Watson, Founder
  Guy McElwaine, COO & Partner
  Mark Stern, President of TV & Partner
  Nora O'Brien, VP of Production
  Finley Glaize, Director of Development
  Jennifer Hare, Director of Production & Administration
  Kelly Stuart, Story Editor
  Rachel Leonard, Assistant to Mr. Watson
Specialties: Cable
Other Categories: Feature Film
Credits: Backdraft; Outer Limits (TV series); Blown Away; Poltergeist

TRIUMPH PICTURES, INC.
6111 Shirley Ave.
Tarzana, CA 91356
Phone: ....(310) 234-9680
www.triumphpictures.com
triumphpictures@hotmail.com
Key Executives/Personnel:
  Yoram Benami, President
  Dean Wideman, Writer & Co-Producer
Specialties: Network; Cable
Other Categories: Feature Film
Credits: Lone Wolf McQuade; Jury Duty; The Man Who Broke A Thousand Chairs; 3 Ninjas: Kick Back
Trade Assoc./Guilds/Unions: AMPAS, DGA

TRUE BLUE PRODUCTIONS
P.O. Box 27127
Los Angeles, CA 90027
Phone: ....(323) 661-9191
Fax: ....(323) 661-9190
www.trublueprod.com
info@trueblueprod.com
Key Executives/Personnel:
  Kirstie Alley, Producer
  Michael Wisner, Head of Creative Development
  Lee Ann Vasquez, Assistant to Ms. Alley
  Thora Magnusson, Office Manager
Specialties: Network; Made for TV Movies; Miniseries

Production Companies – TV

Other Categories: Feature Film
First Look/Development Deals: Warner Bros.

THE TURMAN-MORRISSEY COMPANY
Phone: ....(310) 586-8649
Fax: ....(310) 586-8312
Key Executives/Personnel:
  John Morrissey, Producer & Partner
  Lawrence Turman, Producer & Partner
  Matthew Waldman, Creative Executive
  Devon Terrill, Assistant
Specialties: Network; Cable; Made for TV Movies
Other Categories: Feature Film
Credits: American History X; Kingdom Come; What's The Worst That Could Happen?
Additional Info: Please call for current address

TURNER ENTERTAINMENT GROUP
1050 Techwood Dr., NW
Atlanta, GA 30318
Phone: ....(404) 827-1500
www.turner.com
Key Executives/Personnel:
  Terence McGuirk, Chairman & CEO
  Steven J. Heyer, President & CEO
  Bob Levi, President of Worldwide Programming, Planning & Acquisitions
  Wayne H. Pace, Executive VP, CFO & Administration
  Julia W. Sprunt, Corporate VP, Public Relations, Human Resources & Corporate Resources
  Vicky Miller, Executive VP of Finance & Planning
  Louise Sams, Sr. VP & General Counsel
  Terri Tingle, Sr. VP of Standards & Practices
  Jonathan Katz, Sr. VP of Worldwide Planning & Acquisitions
Specialties: Cable; Animation; Miniseries

TURNER NETWORK TELEVISION (TNT)
1888 Century Park East, 14th Fl.
Los Angeles, CA 90067
Phone: ....(310) 551-6300
Fax: ....(310) 551-6344
www.turner.com
Key Executives/Personnel:
  Robert DeBitetto, President of Original Programming
  Julie Weitz, Executive VP of Original Programming
  Susan O. Gross, Sr. VP of Business Affairs
  Iris Grossman, Sr. VP of Talent & Casting
  Kim Long, Sr. VP of Production
  Nicholas Bogner, VP of Original Programming
  Michael Borza, VP of On Air Promotion
  Sandra Dewey, VP of Business Affairs
  Teri Fournier, VP & Deputy General Counsel, TNT
  Jonathan Harris, VP of Business Affairs
  Aaron Khristeus, VP of Production & Finanace
  Jeffrey Levine, VP of Original Programming
  Betsy Newman, VP of Original Programming
  Candace Snyder, VP of Post Production
  Jim Wilberger, VP of Production
  Cathy Wischner-Sola, VP of Development
  Catherine George, Director of Production
  Kat Slonaker, Director of Production
  Gloria Teshner, Assistant to Mr. DeBitetto
  Brian Hardwick, Assistant to Ms. Weitz
  Dori Fram, Assistant to Ms. Grossman
  Kathleen Behun, Assistant to Ms. Long
  Walter J. Harris, Assistant to Mr. Khristeus
  Sharon Nelson, Assistant to Ms. Newman
  Mick LeGrande, Assistant to Mr. Wilberger
Specialties: Network

JON TURTLE PRODUCTIONS
10880 Wilshire Blvd., Ste. 1101
Los Angeles, CA 90024
Phone: ....(310) 234-5347
Fax: ....(310) 234-5345
Key Executives/Personnel:
  Jon Turtle, President
  David Decker, VP & Head of Creative Affairs
Specialties: Network; Cable; Miniseries
Other Categories: Feature Film
Credits: Freak City; In a Class of His Own; Sirr; Fluke
First Look/Development Deals: Showtime Networks
Trade Assoc./Guilds/Unions: PGA

TVA PRODUCTIONS
10900 Ventura Blvd.
Studio City, CA 91604
Phone: ....(818) 505-8300
Fax: ....(818) 505-8370
www.tvaproductions.com
jgoddard@businessworldnews.com
Key Executives/Personnel:
  Jeffery Goddard, Executive Producer
  Andrea Goodstein, Executive VP of Production
  Geno Brunton, Sr. Producer
Specialties: Cable; Animation; Documentaries
Other Categories: Commercials; Video
Credits: Business World News
Trade Assoc./Guilds/Unions: AMPAS, IAAPA, TEA

TVP STUDIOS
1539 Magnolia Blvd.
Burbank, CA 91506
Phone: ....(818) 843-3188
Fax: ....(818) 843-3189
www.tvpstudios.cc
tvprich@aol.com
Key Executives/Personnel:
  Richard Tamayo, Producer
  Meredith Day, Producer
Specialties: Network; Cable; Animation
Other Categories: Commercials; Video; Music Video
Credits: Bank of America; Panasonic; Golden Globe Awards; etvhollywood.com

TWENTIETH CENTURY FOX TELEVISION
10201 W. Pico Blvd.
Los Angeles, CA 90035
Phone: ....(310) 369-1000
Fax: ....(310) 369-4339
www.fox.com
Key Executives/Personnel:
  Sandy Grushow, Chairman, Fox Television Entertainment Group
  Gary S. Newman, President
  Dana Walden, President
  Charlie Goldstein, Executive VP of Production & Finance
  Howard Kurtzman, Executive VP of Business & Legal Affairs
  Robert Barton, Executive VP & CFO
  Brad Johnson, Sr. VP of Comedy Development
  Steven Kuo, Sr. VP of Business Development
  Edward Nassour, Sr. VP of Post Production
  Marcia Shulman, Sr. VP of Talent & Casting
  Scott Vila, Sr. VP of Drama Development
  Steven Melnick, VP of Advertising & Media Relations
  Jeremy Gold, VP
  Jamie Wagner, Director, Comedy Dept.
Specialties: Network

Production Companies – TV

TWILIGHT TIME FILMS
1875 Century Park East, 2nd Fl.
Los Angeles, CA 90067
Phone: (310) 284-7310
Fax: (310) 284-7317
Key Executives/Personnel:
- Scott Winant, Producer & Director
- Kelly McCarthy, VP of Production
- Robert Keyghobad, Director of Development
- Robyn Andrews, Production Associate

Specialties: Network
Other Categories: Feature Film
Credits: thirtysomething; My So Called Life; Cupid
First Look/Development Deals: Twentieth Century Fox Television

TWO OCEANS ENTERTAINMENT
15250 Ventura Blvd., Ste. 800
Sherman Oaks, CA 91403
Phone: (818) 501-6550
Fax: (818) 501-6558
Key Executives/Personnel:
- Meryl Marshall, President
- Susan Whittaker, VP

Specialties: Network; Cable; Animation; Documentaries; Made for TV Movies

TWO STEPP PRODUCTIONS
15123 Sherman Way, Ste. 201
Van Nuys, CA 91405
Phone: (818) 908-4041
Fax: (818) 994-6483
asteppprod@aol.com
Key Executives/Personnel:
- Alan Stepp, Producer

Specialties: Network; Cable; Made for TV Movies
Other Categories: Feature Film
Credits: Willing To Kill; The Texas Cheerleading Story; Dancer, Texas Population 81

UBU PRODUCTIONS
4024 Radford Ave., Bungalow 14
Studio City, CA 91604
Phone: (818) 655-5850
Fax: (818) 655-8553
Key Executives/Personnel:
- Gary David Goldberg, Executive Producer
- Alex Maggioni, VP of Development
- Heather Green, Assistant
- Murray Miller, Assistant

Specialties: Network
Other Categories: Feature Film
Credits: Family Ties; Brooklyn Bridge; Battery Park; Spin City
First Look/Development Deals: DreamWorks SKG

UFLAND PRODUCTIONS
534 21st St.
Santa Monica, CA 90402
Phone: (310) 656-3031
Fax: (310) 656-3073
ufland@aol.com
Key Executives/Personnel:
- Harry Ufland, Producer
- Mary Jane Ufland, Producer
- Bill Kravitz, Assistant

Specialties: Network
Other Categories: Feature Film
Credits: Snow Falling on Cedars; One True Thing; Not Without My Daughter

UNAPIX FILMS
200 Madison Ave., 24th Fl.
New York, NY 10016
Phone: (212) 252-7711
Fax: (212) 252-7626
www.unapixent.com
info@unapixent.com
Key Executives/Personnel:
- Robert Baruc, President & CEO
- Richard Abramowitz, President, Unapix Theatrical
- Alicia Reilly-Larson, Sr. VP of Acquisitions & Development
- Rebecca Glashow, Manager of Acquisitions & Development
- Chris Valentini, Sr. VP of Production

Specialties: Cable; Documentaries; Made for TV Movies
Other Categories: Feature Film
Credits: Ginger Snaps; Other Voices; Tangled; Jack Frost 1 & 2

UNDERGRACE PRODUCTIONS
14365 Foothill Blvd., Ste. 28
Sylmar, CA 91342
Phone: (818) 833-8666
(818) 640-8698
Fax: (818) 833-8496
camanimal@hotmail.com
Key Executives/Personnel:
- Cameron Baity, Producer, Director & Animator
- Kathleen Lolley, Designer, Editor & Director
- Jonathan Silsby, Animator
- Ryan Streber, Composer
- Jerry Summers, Sound Designer

Specialties: Animation
Other Categories: Feature Film
Credits: Naropa; Questions and Answers

UNGER PRODUCTIONS, INC.
475 S. La Peer Dr.
Beverly Hills, CA 90211
Phone: (310) 859-1455
Fax: (310) 859-1048
tonyunger@exelonline.com
Key Executives/Personnel:
- Anthony Unger, President
- Will McElroy, Production Assistant

Specialties: Documentaries
Other Categories: Feature Film
Credits: Dark Side of Hollywood; Silent Rage; Don't Look Now; Force 10 From Navarone
Trade Assoc./Guilds/Unions: BAFTA

UNIVERSAL STUDIOS, INC.
100 Universal City Plaza
Universal City, CA 91608
Phone: (818) 777-1000
www.universalstudios.com
Key Executives/Personnel:
- Ron Meyer, President & COO
- Jim Watters, President & General Manager, Universal Studios Operations Group
- Kenton Low, President of Universal Studios Online
- Hellene S. Runtagh, Executive VP
- Karen Randall, Executive VP & General Counsel
- Kenneth L. Kahrs, Executive VP of Human Resources
- William A. Sutman, Sr. VP & CFO
- Deborah Rosen, Sr. VP of Corporate Communications & Public Affairs
- Ed Zeier, Sr. VP of Post Production, Universal Studios Operations Group
- Don Skeoch, Sr. VP of Marketing
- Susan Nahley Fleishman, VP of Corporate Communications & Public Affairs
- Dave Beanes, VP of Production Services, Universal Studios Operations Group
- Janice Miller, VP of Business & Legal Affairs
- Brian Pope, VP of Marketing Services

Production Companies – TV

Specialties: Network
Other Categories: Feature Film

UNIVERSAL TELEVISION
100 Universal City Plaza, Bldg. 9128-02
Universal City, CA 91608
Phone: ....(818) 777-5300
www.universalstudios.com
Key Executives/Personnel:
- Blair Westlake, Chairman
- Tony Garland, President, Universal Studios Networks
- Ned Nalle, President of Production
- Beverly Thelander, Executive VP & CFO
- Peter Schoenfeld, Executive VP & Group Strategic Director
- Philip Schuman, Executive VP of Business & Legal Affairs
- Steven Jarmus, Executive VP, Universal Int'l. Television
- Dan Fillie, Executive VP of Dramatic Production, Universal Worldwide Television
- Lori Shackel, Sr. VP of Marketing
- Matt Cooperstein, Sr. VP of Syndicated Distribution
- Holly Leff-Pressman, Sr. VP of Worldwide Pay-Per-View
- Pascal Somarriba, Managing Director, France
- Wolfram Winter, Managing Director, Germany
- Alessandra Zingales, Managing Director, Italy
- Carina Pardavila, Managing Director, Spain
- Janet Goldsmith, Managing Director of Sci-Fi, UK
- Maurcio Gerson, VP, Latin America
- David Ellender, Managing Director, Europe, Universal Int'l. Television
- Lloyd Scott, VP of Programming
- Valerie Spiller, VP of Production, Universal Worldwide Television

Specialties: Network; Cable; Made for TV Movies
Credits: Total Recall; Motown Live; Blind Date

UPN (UNITED PARAMOUNT NETWORK)
11800 Wilshire Blvd.
West Los Angeles, CA 90025
Phone: ....(310) 575-7000
Fax: ....(310) 575-7280
www.upn.com
Key Executives/Personnel:
- Thomas Nunan, President of Entertainment
- Dean Valentine, President & CEO
- Adam Ware, COO
- Eric Cardinal, Sr. VP of Research
- Kelly Edwards, Sr. VP of Comedy
- Barbara Mannina, Sr. VP of Finance & Administration
- Nicole Ungerman, Sr. VP of Business Affairs
- Judith Weiner, Sr. VP of Talent & Casting
- Danielle Greene, VP of Programming & Alternative Development
- John Levoff, VP of Movies
- Patrick Moran, VP of Drama Development
- Todd Lituchy, VP of Scheduling
- Kevin Levy, Manager of Scheduling
- Robin Gurney, Director of Drama Development
- Darren Maddern, Director of Current Programming
- Brad Sterling, Director of Current Programming
- Steve Veisel, Director of Current Programming
- Jon Alon Walz, Manager of Movies
- Traci Lynn Blackwell, Assistant to Mr. Nunan
- Christina Mack, Assistant to Mr. Valentine
- Richard Remppel, Assistant to Mr. Valentine
- Patrick Dixon, Assistant to Casting
- Eric Kim, Assistant to Ms. Edwards
- Merete Stockman, Assistant to Ms. Greene
- Tifani Vernon, Assistant to Current Programming

Specialties: Network

UPSTART ENTERTAINMENT
10433 Wilshire Blvd., PH
Los Angeles, CA 90024
Phone: ....(310) 475-6025
Fax: ....(310) 475-9844
Key Executives/Personnel:
- Michael J. Nathanson, Producer & Writer
- Amy Graves, Director of Development

Specialties: Network; Cable; Documentaries; Made for TV Movies; Miniseries
Other Categories: Feature Film
Credits: Mom's Got a Date With a Vampire; She's Out of Control; The Bulkin Trail

USA NETWORK
1230 Avenue of the Americas
New York, NY 10020
Phone: (212) 413-5000
................................(310) 360-2300
www.usanetwork.com
Key Executives/Personnel:
- Stephen Chao, President, USA Cable
- Jim Miller, Sr. VP of Original Programming
- Jackie Lyons, Sr. VP
- Sarah Beatty, Sr. VP of Marketing
- Adam Shapiro, VP of USA Long Form Original Programming
- Cari Esta-Albert, VP of Original Series Development
- Tim Krubsack, VP of Alternative Programming
- Dara Cohen, Director of Long Form Development
- Kate McArdle, Director of Original Pictures Development
- Michael Thorn, Director of Drama Development
- Stefani Relles, Director of Current Programming & Creative Affairs
- Christof Bove, Manager of Long Form Programming
- Bill McGoldrick, Manager of Series Development
- Gary Shapiro, Manager of Series Development
- Michael Sluchan, Creative Executive, Long Form Programming

Specialties: Cable; Made for TV Movies
Credits: Cover Me; Huntress; Dark Prince: The True Story of Dracula; Attila
Additional Info: 8800 Sunset Blvd., 4th Fl., West Hollywood, CA 90069

VAL D'ORO ENTERTAINMENT
1437 Seventh St., Ste. 200
Santa Monica, CA 90401
Phone: ....(310) 656-8555
Fax: ....(310) 656-8560
valdoro@aol.com
Key Executives/Personnel:
- Steven E. deSouza, President
- Jeri Barchilon deSouza, VP
- Scott Humphries, Apprentice

Specialties: Cable; Animation; Made for TV Movies; Miniseries
Other Categories: Feature Film; Interactive Multimedia
Trade Assoc./Guilds/Unions: DGA, WGAw

RENÉE VALENTE PRODUCTIONS
13547 Ventura Blvd., Ste. 195
Sherman Oaks, CA 91423
Phone: ....(323) 969-1541
Fax: ....(818) 788-0758
valenteprod@aol.com
Key Executives/Personnel:
- Renée Valente, Executive Producer

Specialties: Network; Cable; Made for TV Movies; Miniseries
Other Categories: Feature Film
Credits: A Storm In Summer; The Man From Left Field; The Man Upstairs; Loving Couple
Trade Assoc./Guilds/Unions: AFTRA, AMPAS, ATAS, PGA, WIF

VALHALLA MOTION PICTURES
3575 Cahuenga Blvd. West, Ste. 415
Los Angeles, CA 90068
Phone: ....(323) 969-4300
Fax: ....(323) 969-4301

Production Companies – TV

vmp@valhallamotionpix.com
Key Executives/Personnel:
    Gale Anne Hurd, Chairman & Producer
    Barbara Boyle, President
    Julie Thomson, CFO
    Didi Gay, Controller
    Kelly Campbell, VP of Development
    Tracy Mercer, Director of Development
    Tim Reid, Assistant to Ms. Hurd
    Tiger Bela, Assistant to Ms. Boyle
    David Herrera, Development Assistant
Specialties: Cable; Documentaries
Other Categories: Feature Film
Credits: Armageddon; Terminator 2; Dick; Dante's Peak
First Look/Development Deals: Kinowelt USA, Inc.

VANGUARD PRODUCTIONS
12111 Beatrice St.
Culver City, CA 90230
Phone: ....(310) 306-4910
Fax: ....(310) 306-4910
vangrdprod@earthlink.net
Key Executives/Personnel:
    Terence M. O'Keefe, Writer, Producer & Director
    Brent Huff, Writer & Director
    S. Drew Stotesbery, VP of Production
    Bruce Miyaki, Director of Development
    Bennett Fidlow, Director of Creative Affairs
Specialties: Network; Cable; Made for TV Movies
Other Categories: Feature Film; Commercials; Video; Music Video
Credits: We The People; Wanted; The Bad Pack; Closing The Deal

VENTURE ENTERTAINMENT GROUP
P.O. Box 55113
Sherman Oaks, CA 91413
Phone: ....(818) 981-7813
....(800) 981-8433
Fax: ....(818) 981-3466
www.venture818.com
venture818@aol.com
Key Executives/Personnel:
    Leigh Leshner, Producer
Specialties: Network; Cable
Other Categories: Feature Film; Commercials; Video
Credits: The Spa Workout (infomercial); Hidden Treasures (TV series); Zoofari; More Zoofari
Trade Assoc./Guilds/Unions: VSDA, WIF

VERITÉ PRODUCTIONS
3762 S. Hughes Ave., Ste. 306
Los Angeles, CA 90034
Phone: ....(310) 838-3119
www.craigforrest.com
craigforrest@earthlink.net
Key Executives/Personnel:
    Craig Forrest, Creative Director
Specialties: Cable; Documentaries
Other Categories: Video
Credits: In Concert; Strange Universe; World of Wonder; Travelling Life

VH1
1515 Broadway
New York, NY 10036
Phone: ....(212) 846-7800
....(310) 752-8000
www.vh1.com
Key Executives/Personnel:
    John Sykes, President
    Jeff Gaspin, Executive VP of Programming & Development
    Wayne Isaak, Executive VP of Talent Relations & Music Programming
    Ann Sarnoff, Executive VP of Business Strategy & Program Enterprises
    Eddie Dalva, Sr. VP of Programming Aquisitions & Co-Productions
    Colleen Fahey Rush, Sr. VP of Research & Planning
    Robert S. Katz, VP of East Coast Production
    George Moll, VP of West Coast Productions
Specialties: Cable
Additional Info: 2600 Colorado Ave., Santa Monica, CA 90404
(404) 814-7800, phone (Atlanta), (312) 755-0310, phone (Chicago)

VIACOM ENTERTAINMENT GROUP
5555 Melrose Ave.
Hollywood, CA 90038
Phone: ....(323) 956-5000
....(212) 258-6000
www.viacom.com
Key Executives/Personnel:
    Jonathan L. Dolgen, Chairman
    Thomas McGrath, Executive VP
    David Molner, Sr. VP of Business Development
    Isaac Palmer, VP of Corporate Development
Specialties: Network
Other Categories: Feature Film
Additional Info: 1515 Broadway, New York, NY 10036

VIACOM PRODUCTIONS
10880 Wilshire Blvd., Ste. 1101
Los Angeles, CA 90024
Phone: ....(310) 234-5000
....(212) 258-6000
Fax: ....(310) 234-5059
Key Executives/Personnel:
    Perry Simon, President of Viacom TV
    Steven Gordon, Executive VP of Creative Affairs
    Michele Conklin, Sr. VP of Creative Affairs
    Beth Klein, Sr. VP of Casting & Talent
    Paul Mason, Sr. VP of Production
    Lorna Shepard, Sr. VP of Business Affairs
    James Goodman, VP of Business Affairs
    Janell Gorham, VP of Finance & Operations
    David Lavia, VP of Business Affairs
    Chris Sangustin, Executive Director of Creative Affairs
    Jim Fuller, Manager of Creative Affairs
Specialties: Network; Cable
Credits: Ressurection Blvd.; Ed; Sabrina the Teenage Witch; Diagnosis Murder
Additional Info: 1515 Broadway, New York, NY 10036

VIDEO HOLLYWOOD PRODUCTIONS
P.O. Box 19336
Encino, CA 91416
Phone: ....(888) 368-7347
....(310) 890-0066
Fax: ....(805) 583-8809
pcsinc@dotregs.com
Key Executives/Personnel:
    Kirk Van Houten, President
    Bob Telford, VP of Post Production
    Alfred Powers, VP
    Steven Piper, VP
Specialties: Cable; Documentaries
Credits: El Monte Police (promo)

VIDEOWERKS
3435 Ocean Park Blvd., Ste. 112
Santa Monica, CA 90405
Phone: ....(310) 393-8754
Fax: ....(310) 399-1829
www.videowerks.com

videowerks@earthlink.net
Key Executives/Personnel:
David M. Werk, Owner, Cameraman & DP
Specialties: Network; Cable; Documentaries
Other Categories: Commercials; Video; Interactive Multimedia
Credits: The Directors; History's Lost & Found; Investigative Reports; Headliners & Legends
Trade Assoc./Guilds/Unions: IDA, ITVA

VIDEOX
18034 Ventura Blvd., Ste. 291
Encino, CA 91316
Phone: ....(818) 761-0704
....(818) 679-6160
Fax: ....(818) 509-1805
egaynes@pacbell.net
Key Executives/Personnel:
Edmund Gaynes, Producer
Pamela Hall, Associate Producer
Specialties: Cable
Credits: They Made Movie Magic
Additional Info: Developing Film & TV adaptations of stage productions.

VIEW ASKEW PRODUCTIONS, INC.
3 Harding Rd.
Red Bank, NJ 07701
Phone: ....(732) 842-6933
Fax: ....(732) 842-3772
www.viewaskew.com
Key Executives/Personnel:
Kevin Smith, President
Scott Mosier, VP
Specialties: Network
Other Categories: Feature Film
Credits: Clerks; Dogma; Chasing Amy; Mallrats
First Look/Development Deals: Miramax Films

VIHLENE & ASSOCIATES, INC.
26941 Cabot Rd., Ste. 120
Laguna Hills, CA 92653
Phone: ....(949) 582-0937
Fax: ....(949) 582-0978
www.vihlene.com
vern@vihlene.com
Key Executives/Personnel:
Vern Vihlene, President
Vicki Wellnitz, Producer
Betty McBurnie, Accountant
George Adams, Post Supervisor
Brent Loefke, Director
Specialties: Documentaries
Other Categories: Commercials; Video
Credits: Mailbox etc.; American Honda Motor Co.; AT&T; American Suzuki Motor Co.

VIN DI BONA PRODUCTIONS
12233 W. Olympic Blvd., Ste. 170
Los Angeles, CA 90064
Phone: ....(310) 442-5600
Fax: ....(310) 442-5605
Key Executives/Personnel:
Vin Di Bona, Chairman
Richard Brustein, President & CEO
Lloyd Weintraub, Executive VP of Creative Affairs
Houston Curtis, Executive VP of Series Development
Terry Moore, Executive VP of Development & Production
Paul La Pointe, Head of Accounting
Margaret O'Reilly, Manager of Development
Specialties: Network; Cable; Made for TV Movies; Miniseries
Credits: America's Funniest Home Videos

VISIONBOX
8800 Venice Blvd., Ste. 217
Los Angeles, CA 90034
Phone: ....(310) 204-4686
Fax: ....(310) 204-4603
www.visionboxpictures.com
info@visionboxpix.com
Key Executives/Personnel:
Michael Kastenbaum, President
John Manulis, CEO
Brooke Dammkoehler, Development & Production
Jenny Hinkey, Sales & Marketing
Marc Ambrose, Executive in Charge of Production
Specialties: Network; Cable; Made for TV Movies
Other Categories: Feature Film
Credits: Boyd's Out; Teddy Bears Picnic; The Invisibles; Falling Like This

RAYMOND WAGNER PRODUCTIONS, INC.
10377 Rochester Ave.
Los Angeles, CA 90024
Phone: ....(310) 278-1970
Fax: ....(310) 274-2662
Key Executives/Personnel:
Raymond Wagner, President
Christine McBride, Development
Specialties: Network; Cable; Made for TV Movies
Other Categories: Feature Film
Credits: Snowday; Turner & Hooch; Code of Silence; Maniac Magee

JEFF WALD ENTERTAINMENT
3000 W. Olympic Blvd., Bldg. 2, Ste. 1400
Santa Monica, CA 90404
Phone: ....(310) 264-4156
Fax: ....(310) 264-4157
Key Executives/Personnel:
Jeff Wald, President & CEO
Steven Thomas, Sr. VP
Dana Gonshor, Creative Associate
Specialties: Network; Cable; Made for TV Movies; Miniseries
Other Categories: Feature Film
Credits: 2 Days in the Valley; Pensacola: Wings of Gold; The Roseanne Show

WALLACH ENTERTAINMENT
1400 Braeridge Dr.
Beverly Hills, CA 90210
Phone: ....(310) 278-4574
Fax: ....(310) 273-0548
wallach@prodigy.net
Key Executives/Personnel:
George Wallach, President
Specialties: Network; Cable
Credits: Gramblings White Tiger; Super Dogs; Super Jocks; Scripps Howard National Spelling Bee

KEN WALZ PRODUCTIONS
3000 Olympic Blvd.
Santa Monica, CA 90404
Phone: ....(310) 449-4001
Fax: ....(310) 449-4006
Key Executives/Personnel:
Ken Walz, President
Specialties: Network; Cable; Made for TV Movies
Other Categories: Feature Film
Credits: Like Father, Like Santa; Adventures of Pete & Pete; Gaudy, Bawdy, and Blue; Medusa, Dare to Be Truthful

Production Companies – TV

WARNER BROS. ANIMATION
15303 Ventura Blvd., Ste. 1200
Sherman Oaks, CA 91403
Phone: ....(818) 954-7670
Fax: ....(818) 954-7441
www.warnerbros.com
sarah.carragher@warnerbors.com
Key Executives/Personnel:
  Jean MacCurdy, President & Executive Producer
  Paul Dini, Producer & Writer
  Bruce Timm, Producer & Writer
  Alan Burnett, Producer
  Robert Goodman, Producer
  Liz Holzman, Producer
  Scott Jeralds, Producer
  Glen Murakami, Producer
  Denys Cowan, Animation Director
  Bob Doucette, Animation Director
  Curt Geda, Animation Director
  Butch Lukic, Animation Director
  Dan Riba, Animation Director
  James Tucker, Animation Director
  Leslie Lamers, Casting Director
  Andrea Romano, Voice Director
  Shaun McLaughlin, Associate Producer
  Kathy Page, Associate Producer
  Stan Berkowitz, Story Editor
  Rich Fogel, Story Editor
  Kevin Hopps, Story Editor
  Christopher Simmons, Story Editor
Specialties: Network; Animation
Other Categories: Feature Film
Credits: Batman Beyond; Static Shock!; The Zeta Project

WARNER BROS. INTERNATIONAL TELEVISION
4000 W. Alameda, 6th Fl.
Burbank, CA 91505
Phone: ....(818) 977-8255
Fax: ....(818) 977-8077
www.wbitv.com
Key Executives/Personnel:
  Jeffrey R. Schlesinger, President
  Mauro A. Sardi, Sr. VP of Int'l. Administration & Operations
Specialties: Network; Cable; Animation
Additional Info: 4001 W. Olive Ave., Burbank, CA 91505, (818) 977-5491 phone, (818) 977-4040 fax

WARNER BROS. TELEPICTURES PRODUCTION
4000 Warner Blvd.
Burbank, CA 91522
Phone: ....(818) 972-0777
Fax: ....(818) 972-0864
www.warnerbros.com
Key Executives/Personnel:
  Jim Paratore, President of Production
  Alan Saxe, Executive VP of Business & Legal Affairs
  David Auerbach, Sr. VP of Development
  Hilary Estey-McLoughlin, Sr. VP of Programming & Development
  Kevin Fortson, Sr. VP of Production
  Lisa Hackner-Goldberg, VP of Development
Specialties: Network

WARNER BROS. TELEVISION
4000 Warner Blvd.
Burbank, CA 91522
Phone: ....(818) 954-6000
Fax: ....(818) 954-7367
www.warnerbros.com
Key Executives/Personnel:
  Peter Roth, President
  Andrew Ackerman, Executive VP of Television Production
  Steve Pearlman, Executive VP of Drama & Comedy Development
  Trent Jones, Sr. VP of Current Programming
  Gregg Maday, Sr. VP of Movies & Miniseries
  David Sacks, Sr. VP of Current Programming
  Judith Zaylor, Sr. VP of TV Production
Specialties: Network

WATERSHED FILMS
345 N. Maple Dr., Ste. 317
Beverly Hills, CA 90210
Phone: ....(310) 550-2175
Fax: ....(310) 550-2178
watershedfilms@pipeline.com
Key Executives/Personnel:
  James Brooke, Producer
  Neil DeGroot, Producer
  Wally Parks, Producer
Specialties: Network; Cable; Made for TV Movies; Miniseries
Other Categories: Feature Film
Credits: The Dinosaur Hunter; Plato's Run; Wind in the Wire
First Look/Development Deals: Backlot Productions

WB TELEVISION NETWORK
3701 W. Oak St., Bldg. 34R
Burbank, CA 91505
Phone: ....(818) 977-5000
Fax: ....(818) 977-6336
www.wb.com
Key Executives/Personnel:
  Jamie Kellner, CEO
  Susanne Daniels, President of Entertainment
  Sue Kroll, President of Int'l. Marketing
  Jordan Levin, Executive VP of Programming
  Mitchell Nedick, Executive VP of Finance & Operations
  Michael Ross, Executive VP of Business Affairs
  Carolyn Bernstein, Sr. VP of Alt. Programming & VP of Drama Development
  Donna Friedman, Sr. VP of Kids' WB! Programming
  Kate Juergens, Sr. VP of Comedy & Drama Development
  Kathleen Letterie, Sr. VP of Talent & Casting
  John Litvack, Sr. VP of Current Programming
  John Maata, Sr. VP of Legal & General Counsel
  Rick Mater, Sr. VP of Broadcast Standards
  Rusty Mintz, Sr. VP of Scheduling & Director of Current Programming
  Jack Wakshlag, Sr. VP of Research
  Nancie Martin, Sr. VP of New Media
  Dana Abel, VP of Finance
  Michael Clements, VP of Current Programming & VP of Michigan J. Frog Productions
  Phil Gonzales, VP of Publicity
  Jody Horwitz, VP of Human Resources
  Tracey Pakosta, VP of Comedy Development
Specialties: Network

ED WEINBERGER PRODUCTIONS
5300 Melrose Ave.
Los Angeles, CA 90038
Phone: ....(323) 960-4506
Fax: ....(323) 960-4920
Key Executives/Personnel:
  Ed Weinberger, Producer, Writer & Director
  Darrell Straight, Executive Assistant
Specialties: Network
Credits: Sparks; The Good News

WEINTRAUB/KUHN PRODUCTIONS
1900 Avenue of the Stars, Ste. 1440
Los Angeles, CA 90067
Phone: ....(310) 788-9380
Fax: ....(310) 788-0476

Production Companies – TV

Key Executives/Personnel:
 Fred Weintraub, Producer
 Tom Kuhn, Producer
 Chrissy Sherbanee, Assistant to Mr. Weintraub & Mr. Kuhn
Specialties: Network; Made for TV Movies; Miniseries
Other Categories: Feature Film; Video
Credits: High Road to China; The New Adventures of Robin Hood; Enter the Dragon; Devil's Arithmetic

RONI WEISBERG PRODUCTIONS
1644 Warnall Ave.
Los Angeles, CA 90024
Phone: ....(310) 286-1210
Fax: ....(310) 556-8248
rweisberg@earthlink.net
Key Executives/Personnel:
 Roni Weisberg, Producer
 Henry Tuggle, Director of Development
Specialties: Network; Cable; Made for TV Movies; Miniseries
Other Categories: Feature Film; Commercials
Credits: Mermaid; Face Down; Death Dreams; Sharing Richard

WELLER/GROSSMAN PRODUCTIONS
14144 Ventura Blvd., Ste. 200
Sherman Oaks, CA 91423
Phone: ....(818) 755-4800
Fax: ....(818) 755-4820
Key Executives/Personnel:
 Gary H. Grossman, Executive Producer
 Robb Weller, Executive Producer
 Noel Poole, CFO
 Joel Rizor, Director of Programming
 Debbie Supnik, Development
 Steve Lange, General Manager
Specialties: Cable; Documentaries
Other Categories: Video
Credits: Food 911; Wolfgang Puck; The Most; National Geographic Program

JOHN WELLS PRODUCTIONS
4000 Warner Blvd., Bldg. 138, Rm. 1106
Burbank, CA 91522
Phone: ....(818) 954-1687
Fax: ....(818) 354-3657
Key Executives/Personnel:
 John Wells, Executive Producer & Writer
 Kristin Harms, President
 Ned Haspel, VP of Business Operations
 Andrew Stearn, VP of TV
 Laura Holstein, VP of Features
 Tracy Underwood, Director of Development, Features
 Randy Warner, Manager of TV
Specialties: Network; Cable
Other Categories: Feature Film
Credits: ER; The West Wing; Third Watch

WESTERN BRANCH PRODUCTIONS, INC.
4231 Beck Ave.
Studio City, CA 91604
Phone: ....(818) 762-3810
....(818) 642-3810
Fax: ....(818) 769-2847
www.western-branch.com
pvan@western-branch.com
Key Executives/Personnel:
 Pete Vanlaw, President
Specialties: Cable; Documentaries
Other Categories: Commercials; Video

Credits: Memories of a Millenium (documentary); Night at the Pote (TV pilot)
Trade Assoc./Guilds/Unions: DGA

BILL WHITE PRODUCTIONS
12423 Ventura Court, Ste. 200
Studio City, CA 91604
Phone: ....(818) 769-9090
Fax: ....(818) 769-1974
billwhitepro@earthlink.net
Key Executives/Personnel:
 Bill White, President
 Amy Shomer, Producer
Specialties: Network; Cable; Documentaries
Other Categories: Feature Film; Commercials; Video; Music Video
Credits: Globe Life Insurance (commercial); United American Insurance (commercial); Sanyo-Fisher (corp. video); Test Flights (TV)
Trade Assoc./Guilds/Unions: DGA

WHITEWATER FILMS
2232 Cotner Ave.
Los Angeles, CA 90064
Phone: ....(310) 575-5800
Fax: ....(310) 575-5802
Key Executives/Personnel:
 Rick Rosenthal, President
Specialties: Network; Cable
Other Categories: Feature Film
Credits: Bad Boy; Just a Little Harmless Sex; Distant Thunder; American Dreamer

WICKED MONKEY PRODUCTIONS
6404 Hollywood Blvd., Ste. 324
Hollywood, CA 90028
Phone: ....(323) 461-6665
Fax: ....(323) 461-6669
Key Executives/Personnel:
 Al Septien, Writer & Producer
 Turi Meyer, Writer & Director
Specialties: Network; Cable; Made for TV Movies; Miniseries
Other Categories: Feature Film
Credits: Sleepstalker; Candy Man III

WILD THINGS PRODUCTIONS
4500 Wilshire Blvd., 3rd Fl.
Los Angeles, CA 90010
Phone: ....(323) 954-4577
Key Executives/Personnel:
 Maurice Sendak, Partner
 John B. Carls, Partner
 Richard La Forge, Development Assistant
Specialties: Network; Cable; Animation; Made for TV Movies
Other Categories: Feature Film
Credits: Little Bear; George & Martha; Seven Little Monsters
First Look/Development Deals: Nelvana Entertainment

WILDRICE PRODUCTIONS
4400 Coldwater Canyon, Ste. 321
Studio City, CA 91604
Phone: ....(818) 623-2898
Fax: ....(818) 623-2890
wildrice@aol.com
Key Executives/Personnel:
 Joel Rice, Executive Producer
 Amanda Moore, VP of Development
 Gabriel Gazoul, Development Associate
Specialties: Network; Cable; Made for TV Movies; Miniseries
Credits: One Kill; Half A Dozen Babies; About Sarah; Dare To Love

Production Companies – TV

WILSHIRE COURT PRODUCTIONS
1840 Century Park East, Ste. 400
Los Angeles, CA 90067
Phone: ....(310) 557-2444
Fax: ....(310) 557-0017
Key Executives/Personnel:
- John J. McMahon, President
- Jack Angeles, VP of Business & Legal Affairs
- Stacy Mandelberg, VP of Development
- Ed Milkovich, VP of Production
- Ken Weikel, VP of Finance & Administration

Specialties: Network; Cable; Made for TV Movies
Credits: Sweet Water

WIN VENTURES, LLC.
301 N. Cañon Dr., Ste. 300
Beverly Hills, CA 90210
Phone: ....(310) 859-2500
Fax: ....(310) 859-7500
winventures@win-11c.com
Key Executives/Personnel:
- Pierre David, Chairman of WIN Ventures & Producer
- Noel Zanitsch, President of Production & Producer
- Ken Sanders, VP of Production & Producer
- Rick Eyler, VP of Physical Production

Specialties: Network; Cable; Made for TV Movies
Other Categories: Feature Film
Credits: The Perfect Wife; The Perfect Nanny; The Stepdaughter; Alone with a Stranger
Trade Assoc./Guilds/Unions: AFMA, AMPAS, IPA

WIND DANCER PRODUCTION GROUP
1040 N. Las Palmas, Bldg. 2
Los Angeles, CA 90038
Phone: ....(323) 645-1200
Fax: ....(323) 645-1255
Key Executives/Personnel:
- Matt Williams, Principal
- David McFadzean, Principal
- Carmen Finestra, Principal
- Susan Cartsonis, President of Wind Dancer Films
- Dete Meserve, Executive VP
- Melissa Goddard, Sr. VP
- Roz Weisberg, Director of Development
- Robyn Frey-Monell, Office Manager

Specialties: Network
Other Categories: Feature Film
Credits: Where The Heart Is; Firelight; Home Improvement
Additional Info: 9 Desbrosses St., 2nd Fl., New York, NY 10013

RALPH WINTER PRODUCTIONS, INC.
1201 W. 5th St., Maryland Bldg., Ste. M215
Los Angeles, CA 90017
Phone: ....(213) 534-3654
Fax: ....(213) 534-3078
Key Executives/Personnel:
- Ralph Winter, Producer
- David Gorder, Assistant to Mr. Winter

Specialties: Network
Other Categories: Feature Film
Credits: Planet of the Apes: aka The Visitor; X-Men; Inspector Gadget; Mighty Joe Young

WOLF FILMS, INC.
100 Universal City Plaza, Bldg. 2252
Universal City, CA 91608
Phone: ....(818) 777-1236
Key Executives/Personnel:
- Dick Wolf, Executive Producer
- Peter Jankowski, President
- John L. Roman, Producer

Specialties: Network; Cable
Credits: Law & Order; Law & Order Special Victims Unit; Deadline
First Look/Development Deals: USA Films

THE WOLPER ORGANIZATION
4000 Warner Blvd., Bldg. 14, Rm. X
Burbank, CA 91522
Phone: ....(818) 954-1421
Fax: ....(818) 954-1593
Key Executives/Personnel:
- David L. Wolper, Chairman
- Mark Wolper, President
- Kevin Nicklaus, VP of Development
- Murad Hussain, Story Editor
- Hilary Winston, Assistant to Mr. Wolper

Specialties: Network; Cable; Made for TV Movies; Miniseries
Credits: L.A. Confidential; Murder in the First; Mists of Avalon; Roots
First Look/Development Deals: Warner Bros.

WONDERLAND FILMS
8640 Wonderland Ave.
Los Angeles, CA 90046
Phone: ....(323) 656-6489
Key Executives/Personnel:
- Ava Lazar, Producer
- John Tarnoff, Producer

Specialties: Network; Cable; Miniseries
Other Categories: Feature Film
Credits: Nature of the Beast; The Delinquents; Prisoners of the Sun

THE WOOFENILL WORKS, INC.
516 E. 81st St., Ste. 3
New York, NY 10028
Phone: ....(212) 734-2578
Fax: ....(212) 734-3186
home.earthlinke.net/~woofenill/
woofenill@earthlink.net
Key Executives/Personnel:
- Joseph K. Landsman, Chairman & CEO
- Jan A. Koster, President & Creative Director
- Ronald Tanet, Executive Producer & Corporate Council
- Robert L. Cohen, Supervising Producer
- Robert J. Nichols, SCC Attorney

Specialties: Cable; Made for TV Movies
Other Categories: Feature Film

WORLD OF WONDER PRODUCTIONS
6650 Hollywood Blvd., Ste. 400
Hollywood, CA 90028
Phone: ....(323) 463-7133
Fax: ....(323) 463-7134
www.worldofwonder.net
wow@worldofwonder.net
Key Executives/Personnel:
- Randy Barbato, Producer & Director
- Fenton Bailey, Producer & Director

Specialties: Documentaries
Other Categories: Feature Film
Credits: The Eyes of Tammy Faye; 101 Rent Boys; Video Killed the Radio Star; Party Monster

WORLD WIDE PANTS, INC
1697 Broadway
New York, NY 10019
Phone: ....(212) 975-5300
....(323) 575-5600
Fax: ....(212) 975-4780

Key Executives/Personnel:
  Rob Burnett, President & CEO
  James Peterson, Executive VP & COO
  David Letterman, Comptroller
  Dave Wolthoff, Creative Affairs
Specialties: Network
Credits: The Late Show with David Letterman; The Late Late Show with Craig Kilborn; Everybody Loves Raymond; Welcome to New York

MARVIN WORTH PRODUCTIONS
9784 Drake Lane
Beverly Hills, CA 90210
Phone: ....(310) 273-0181
Fax: ....(310) 274-7378
Key Executives/Personnel:
  Joan Worth, Producer
  Marty Binder, Assistant to Ms. Worth
Specialties: Cable
Other Categories: Feature Film
Credits: Malcolm X; Lenny; Where's Poppa; See No Evil, Hear No Evil

LINDA WRIGHT PRODUCTIONS
28947 Thousand Oaks Blvd., Ste. 220
Agoura Hills, CA 91301
Phone: ....(818) 879-4647
Fax: ....(818) 879-4647
Lin5280@aol.com
Key Executives/Personnel:
  Linda Wright, Producer & Writer
  Robyn Haddad, Story Editor
Specialties: Network; Made for TV Movies; Miniseries
Credits: A Champion's Flight

NORTON WRIGHT PRODUCTIONS
13331 Moorpark St., Ste. 308
Sherman Oaks, CA 91423
Phone: ....(818) 990-3058
Key Executives/Personnel:
  Norton Wright, President
  Ygonabee Abigit, Production
  Reid Phat, Director of Development
Specialties: Network; Cable; Made for TV Movies; Miniseries
Other Categories: Feature Film
Credits: Murderous Intent; Angel Flight Down; Crash Landing: Rescue Flight 237; Haunted By Her Past
Trade Assoc./Guilds/Unions: ATAS, DGA

WYCHWOOD PRODUCTIONS
940 N. Mansfield Ave.
Hollywood, CA 90038
Phone: ....(323) 462-6400
Fax: ....(323) 465-7903
jpolhemns@propagandafilms.com
Key Executives/Personnel:
  Simon West, Producer & Director
  Jib Polhemus, VP of Development
  Alex Close, Assistant
Specialties: Network
Other Categories: Feature Film
First Look/Development Deals: Propaganda Films

YAK YAK PICTURES
4000 Warner Blvd., Bldg. 138, Ste. 1202
Burbank, CA 91522
Phone: ....(818) 954-3861
Fax: ....(818) 954-1614
Key Executives/Personnel:
  Mimi Leder, Producer & Director
  Jill Arthur, VP of Development
  A.J. Marcantonio, Creative Executive
  Marit Weisenberg, Story Editor & Assistant to Ms. Arthur
  Bob Merrick, Assistant to Ms. Leder
Specialties: Network
Other Categories: Feature Film
Credits: Pay it Forward; The Beast; Casanova; Lazarus
First Look/Development Deals: John Wells Productions

BUD YORKIN PRODUCTIONS
345 N. Maple Dr., Ste. 206
Beverly Hills, CA 90210
Phone: ....(310) 274-8111
Fax: ....(310) 274-8112
Key Executives/Personnel:
  Bud Yorkin, President
  Damon Carr, Associate Producer
Specialties: Network
Other Categories: Feature Film
Credits: Blade Runner; Intersection; Twice in a Lifetime
First Look/Development Deals: Paramount Pictures

YORKTOWN PRODUCTIONS, INC.
3000 Olympic Blvd., Bldg. 2, Ste. 2465
Santa Monica, CA 90404
Phone: ....(310) 264-4155
Fax: ....(310) 264-4167
Key Executives/Personnel:
  Norman Jewison, Director & Producer
  Dianne Hatlestad, Creative Executive
  Liz Broden, Assistant to Mr. Jewison
Specialties: Cable
Other Categories: Feature Film
Credits: A Soldier's Story; The Hurricane; Moonstruck; Only You

ZALOOM FILM
1351 Fourth St., Ste. 400
Santa Monica, CA 90401
Phone: ....(310) 656-8400
Key Executives/Personnel:
  George Zaloom, Producer
  Bruno Fortuna, Executive VP of Development
  Robin Goodfellow, Creative Executive
Specialties: Cable; Made for TV Movies
Other Categories: Feature Film
Credits: Encino Man; Hearts of Darkness; The Sports Pages; The Whole Shebang

ZOOMA ZOOMA CORPORATION
11 Mercer St., 3rd Fl.
New York, NY 10013
Phone: ....(212) 941-7680
Fax: ....(212) 941-8179
www.zoomazooma.com
staff@zoomazooma.com
Key Executives/Personnel:
  Joseph Mantegna, Executive Producer
  Todd Bellanca, Director
  Eden Tyler, Director
  Sam Raimi, Director
  Michael Bellino, Director
  Tim Hamilton, Director
  Gavin O'Connor, Director
  Lori Vitale, East Coast Sales
Specialties: Network; Cable; Documentaries
Other Categories: Feature Film; Commercials; Music Video; Interactive Multimedia

Production Companies – TV

ZUCKER/NETTER PRODUCTIONS
1411 Fifth St., Ste. 402
Santa Monica, CA 90401
Phone: ....(310) 394-1644
Fax: ....(310) 899-6722
Key Executives/Personnel:
  David Zucker, Producer, Director & Writer
  Gil Netter, President
  Lawrence Grey, VP
  Phil Dornfeld, Assistant to Mr. Zucker
  Mike Ades, Assistant to Mr. Netter
Specialties: Network
Other Categories: Feature Film
Credits: Dude Where's My Car; My Best Friends Wedding; Naked Gun Series; Ghost
First Look/Development Deals: Fox 2000 Productions, NBC Entertainment, Inc.

ZUCKERMAN ENTERTAINMENT
169 Pier Ave., 2nd Fl.
Santa Monica, CA 90405
Phone: ....(310) 452-4410
Fax: ....(310) 452-4006
donaldzucker@earthlink.net
Key Executives/Personnel:
  Donald Zuckerman, Producer

  Emily Mullen, Assistant
Specialties: Cable
Other Categories: Feature Film
Credits: Beat; Big Brass Ring; Lowlife; Dogtown

ZYSTAR FILMS, INC.
330 Washington Blvd., Ste. 400
Marina Del Rey, CA 90292
Phone: ....(310) 301-3313
Fax: ....(310) 301-9433
www.zystar.com
mwallis@zystar.com
Key Executives/Personnel:
  Meryl Alison Wallis, Executive Producer
  Carmen Silva, Producer
  Scott Murphy, Assistant Director
  Howard Raishbrook, Production Manager
  Doug Mickel, Producer
Specialties: Cable
Other Categories: Feature Film; Commercials; Video; Music Video
Credits: James Bond (behind the scenes); American Honda (commercial); Carrows Restaurants (commercial); Laurietta (feature)

Environmentally Controlled, State-of-the-art Secure Storage for Film, Video and Audio Tape

★

High Security

★

Pick-up and Delivery

★

Internet Access

Pacific Title Archives Locations

4800 San Vicente Blvd.	10717 Vanowen	900 Grand Central
Los Angeles, CA 90019	N. Hollywood, CA 91605	Glendale, CA 91201
Tel (323) 938-3711	Tel (818) 760-4223	Tel (818) 547-0090
Fax (323) 938-6364	Fax (818) 760-1704	Fax (818) 548-7990

www.pacifictitlearchives.com - (800) 968-9111

Production Companies – Commercials

1171 PRODUCTION GROUP
303 S. Sweetzer Ave.
Los Angeles, CA 90048
Phone: (323) 655-1171
             (213) 247-7424
Fax: (323) 655-1135
www.1171.com
film1171@aol.com
Key Executives/Personnel:
  Grant Cihlar, Owner & Executive Producer
  Bruce Martin, Owner & Executive Producer
Specialties: Television
Other Categories: Music Video
Credits: Bloodhound Gang - Mope; Alice DeeJay - Better Off Alone; Coca-Cola

21ST CENTURY MAN PRODUCTIONS
1950 N. Tamarind Ave., Ste. 323
Los Angeles, CA 90068
Phone: (323) 466-3227
             (310) 989-7353
Fax: (323) 466-3227
www.21stcman.com
future21@primenet.com
Key Executives/Personnel:
  Jane Linter, Producer & Director
  David May, Director & Editor
  Brian Bowie, Director & Director of Photography
  Andrea Fredrickson, Editor
Specialties: Television; Infomercials/Direct Response; Promos
Other Categories: TV; Video; Music Video; Interactive Multimedia
Credits: 21st CMAN; Sebastian Int.; Wella Alternative Hair Show; Stylezone 2000
Trade Assoc./Guilds/Unions: AEA, BAFTA, DGA, NATPE
Additional Info: 21st Century Man Productions, 33 Limes Rd., Beckenham, Kent BR3 6NS England

2EZ, LLC
5531 Venice Blvd.
Los Angeles, CA 90019
Phone: (323) 939-9975
             (213) 494-7404
Fax: (323) 939-9480
www.filmbiz.com/2ez
la2ez@hotmail.com
Key Executives/Personnel:
  Christopher McKinnon, Producer
  John Bell, Producer
Specialties: Television; Promos
Credits: Toyota; Nissan; Maki Jewelry

30 SECOND FILMS
3019 Pico Blvd.
Santa Monica, CA 90405
Phone: (310) 315-1750
Fax: (310) 315-1757
www.30secondfilms.com
info@30secondfilms.com
Key Executives/Personnel:
  Alan Stamm, Executive Producer
  Bob Kronovet, Producer & Director
  Scott Baio, Director
  Debbie Allen, Director
  Tony Dow, Director
  Branscombe Richmond, Director
Specialties: Television; Infomercials/Direct Response; Promos
Other Categories: Feature Film; TV; Video
Credits: American Tigers; Ghostown; Broken Bars; L.A. Task Force

40 ACRES & A MULE FILMWORKS, INC.
124 Dekalb Ave.
Brooklyn, NY 11217
Phone: (718) 624-3703
Fax: (718) 624-2008
Key Executives/Personnel:
  Spike Lee, CEO
  Sam Kitt, President of Production
  Andre Hereford, Director of Development
  Heather Parish, Business Manager
Specialties: Television
Other Categories: Feature Film; Video; Music Video
Credits: Bamboozled; Summer of Sam; He Got Game; Malcolm X
Additional Info: NY Development Office:
  75 S. Elliot Pl., 3rd Fl., Brooklyn, NY 11217

A BAND APART COMMERCIALS
7966 Beverly Blvd., 2nd Fl.
Los Angeles, CA 90048
Phone: (323) 951-4400
Fax: (323) 951-4401
www.abandapart.com
info@abandapart.com
Key Executives/Personnel:
  Michael Bodnarchek, President & CEO
  Eric Bonniot, Executive Producer
  Kim Dellara, Executive Producer, Music Videos
  Mike Sarkissian, Head of Production, Music Videos
  Susan Boothby, Production Manager, Commercials
  Brian Rackohn, Controller
  Josh Goldstein, Assistant to Mr. Bodnarchek
Specialties: Television
Other Categories: Music Video

ABBY LOU ENTERTAINMENT
1411 Edgehill Pl.
Pasadena, CA 91103
Phone: (626) 795-7334
Fax: (626) 795-4013
ale@full-moon.com
Key Executives/Personnel:
  George LeFave, Executive Producer
  Chryl Pestor, Executive VP of Development
Specialties: Television
Other Categories: Feature Film; TV; Video
Credits: Adventures in Whispering Gardens; A Christmas Whisper

ABSOLUTEFILMS.NET
1441 Huntington Dr., Ste. 3010
South Pasadena, CA 91030
Phone: (626) 442-6454
Fax: (626) 448-1930
www.absolutefilms.net
info@absolute.net
Key Executives/Personnel:
  Ty Thompson, Producer
  Byron Jost, Producer
  Josh Ochoa, Producer
  Robert Villalobos, Producer
  Tom Franklin, Producer
  Romeo Carey, Producer
Specialties: Television; Radio; Infomercials/Direct Response; Promos
Other Categories: Video; Music Video; Interactive Multimedia
Credits: Juan-A-Be.com; Mr. Fab

ACCESS FILM
4030 Sumac Dr.
Sherman Oaks, CA 91403
Phone: (818) 990-3389
Fax: (818) 990-3379

Production Companies – Commercials

accessca@earthlink.net
Key Executives/Personnel:
  Jonathan Gilson, Executive Producer
  Alan Pierce, Executive Producer
  Jill Rosenblum, Producer
Specialties: Television
Credits: Disney; Holiday Inn; Burger King; Crowne Plaza
Additional Info: 31 W. 26th St., 5th Fl., New York, NY 10010 (212) 696-9200

ACME FILMWORKS, INC.
6525 Sunset Blvd., Ste. G-10
Hollywood, CA 90028
Phone: (323) 464-7805
Fax: (323) 464-6614
www.acmefilmworks.com
acmeinfo@acmefilmworks.com
Key Executives/Personnel:
  Ron Diamond, Executive Producer
  Libby Simon, Producer
Specialties: Television
Credits: Whiskas; Charmin; Rally's/Checker's

THE AD-FILES
11465 Moorpark St., Ste. 1
North Hollywood, CA 91602
Phone: (213) 891-3784
Fax: (323) 460-6665
Key Executives/Personnel:
  Daniel W. Bolton, Executive Producer
  Chris Blackwood, Director
  Renard Muldrake, Director
  Vincent Rico, Director
  Mark Spring, Director
Specialties: Television
Other Categories: TV

AD-LIB MARKETING & ADVERTISING
One Blacksmith Circle
Phillips Ranch, CA 91766
Phone: (909) 629-1995
Fax: (909) 629-1995
ad-lib@2-hot.com
Key Executives/Personnel:
  Keith Underwood, Executive Producer
  Brenda Underwood, Associate Producer
Specialties: Television; Radio; Infomercials/Direct Response; Promos
Other Categories: Video; Music Video
Credits: Titan Business Solutions; P. Joseph, A Law Corp.; Ben & Jerry's; Perferred Financial Corp.

ALAMEDA FILMWORKS, INC.
Phone: (818) 846-4074
afwinc@att.net
Key Executives/Personnel:
  Wendy Yorkshire, Producer
Specialties: Television; Promos
Other Categories: Feature Film; Video
Trade Assoc./Guilds/Unions: AICP, DGA

ALBRECHT & ASSOCIATES, INC.
3442 Dorothy Rd.
Topanga, CA 90290
Phone: (818) 222-4836
jaalbrecht@yahoo.com
Key Executives/Personnel:
  Joie Albrecht, President
Specialties: Infomercials/Direct Response
Credits: Carol King One to One; Mickey's 60th Birthday
Trade Assoc./Guilds/Unions: DGA, SAG, WGA

ALLEN & ASSOCIATES
5304 Ballone Ln.
Culver City, CA 90230
Phone: (310) 390-5522
sportstape@aol.com
Key Executives/Personnel:
  Donald V. Allen, Producer
Specialties: Television; Radio; Infomercials/Direct Response; Promos
Other Categories: Feature Film; TV
Credits: The Home Show; Suburbia; Car Wash; Super Picnic
Trade Assoc./Guilds/Unions: AFTRA, NARAS, SAG

ALTA VISTA PRODUCTIONS
11805 Mississippi Ave., Ste. 102
West Los Angeles, CA 90025
Phone: (310) 444-2050
Fax: (310) 444-2055
altvista@earthlink.net
Key Executives/Personnel:
  David Lozano, Executive Producer
  Michael Lozano, Producer
  Astrid Steel, Producer
  Colleen Steckloff, Casting Director
  Yves Douville, Post Production Supervisor
Specialties: Television; Radio; Infomercials/Direct Response; Promos
Other Categories: TV; Music Video

AMBITIOUS ENTERTAINMENT
Phone: (818) 990-8993
Fax: (818) 990-8994
ambitious1@earthlink.net
Key Executives/Personnel:
  Paul M. Addis, Producer
Specialties: Television; Promos
Other Categories: TV; Video
Credits: Muhammad Ali: King of the World (promo); Talk To Me (promo); Wolfgang Puck Cafe (commercial); Sony PlayStation (commercial)

AMERICAN VIDEO GROUP
12020 Pico Blvd.
Los Angeles, CA 90064
Phone: (310) 477-1535
Fax: (310) 473-5299
www.americanvideogroup.com
amervideo@earthlink.net
Key Executives/Personnel:
  John Berzner, Executive Producer
  Fred Goldey, Production Manager
  Christopher Meisel, Production Supervisor
Specialties: Television; Radio; Infomercials/Direct Response; Promos
Other Categories: TV; Video
Credits: DirecTV; AT&T Wireless; Dali Lama: Message for New Millenium; Bob Mann's Automatic Golf
Trade Assoc./Guilds/Unions: AICP, ERA, ITVA

ANGEL CITY PRODUCTIONS
7000 Romaine St.
Los Angeles, CA 90038
Phone: (323) 465-6802
Fax: (323) 850-5398
Key Executives/Personnel:
  Stephen Netburn, Executive Producer
Specialties: Television
Credits: Tylenol; AT&T; Acura; California Anti-Smoking
Trade Assoc./Guilds/Unions: DGA

ANOTHER DIVERSION
Phone: (818) 763-0338
  (818) 802-0758
Fax: (818) 763-0504
omokyra@aol.com

Production Companies – Commercials

Key Executives/Personnel:
   Kyra Shelgren, Executive Producer
Specialties: Television
Other Categories: Feature Film
Credits: Motorola; Gatorade; Dodge; Jeep
Trade Assoc./Guilds/Unions: DGA

ANOTHER LARGE PRODUCTION
5750 Wilshire Blvd., Ste 600
Los Angeles, CA 90036
Phone: ....(323) 954-8500
Fax: ....(323) 954-8510
www.anotherlarge.com
phillipl@anotherlarge.com
Key Executives/Personnel:
   Phillip Large, President
   Alan Skinner, Sr. VP
   Ron Cohen, VP & Director
   Marilyn Higgins, Sr. Producer
Specialties: Television; Radio; Promos
Other Categories: Video
Credits: Colombia TriStar (corp. video); Curious World (documentary); V.I.P. (commercial); Martha Stewart (commercial)
Trade Assoc./Guilds/Unions: CTAM, DGA, NATPE, PROMAX

AREA 51 FILMS
1501 Colorado Ave.
Santa Monica, CA 90404
Phone: ....(310) 395-5151
Fax: ....(310) 395-5102
Key Executives/Personnel:
   Mark Thomas, Executive Producer
   John Adams, Director
   James Dalthorp, Director
   Scotty Bergstein, Director
   Toby Phillips, Director & Cameraman
Specialties: Television
Trade Assoc./Guilds/Unions: AICP

ARSENAL, INC.
1103 N. El Centro Ave.
Hollywood, CA 90038
Phone: ....(323) 957-5100
Fax: ....(323) 957-5101
arsenlfilm@aol.com
Key Executives/Personnel:
   Larry Perel, Executive Producer
Specialties: Television
Other Categories: Music Video
Credits: Live - They Stood Up For Love; Estevan Oriol - Heart of a Rebel; Wes Cunningham - Not Enough

THE ARTISTS COMPANY/THE A&R GROUP
1015 N. Fairfax Ave.
Los Angeles, CA 90046
Phone: ....(323) 650-4722
Fax: ....(323) 650-4706
Key Executives/Personnel:
   Roberto Cecchini, Executive Producer & President
   Lori Lober, Executive Producer
   Susan Burton, Head of Production
Specialties: Television
Other Categories: Music Video

ASHLEY PRODUCTIONS
5225 Canyon Crest Dr., Ste. 71-340
Riverside, CA 92507
Phone: ....(909) 781-6597
www.ashleyproductions.com
info@ashleyproductions.com
Key Executives/Personnel:
   Jacqueline Ashley, President & CEO
   William Ashley II, VP & CFO
Specialties: Promos
Other Categories: Feature Film; Music Video
Credits: Between Friends; Stolen Moments; The Right Crowd

THE ASSOCIATION, INC.
135 N. Screenland Dr.
Burbank, CA 91505
Phone: ....(818) 841-9660
Fax: ....(818) 841-8370
theassoc@aol.com
Key Executives/Personnel:
   Randy Stith, Producer
   Tim Melchior, Producer
   Fletch Murray, Producer
   Jeff Murphy, Production Manager
   Maureen Bernal, Sales Representative
Specialties: Television; Promos
Other Categories: TV; Video
Credits: Quake Ready (PSA's); Hyundai (commercial); PAX TV (promos); Demin Bank (commercial)
First Look/Development Deals: PaxTV/Paxson Communications

ATLAS PICTURES
201 Wilshire Blvd., 2nd Fl.
Santa Monica, CA 90401
Phone: ....(310) 587-2376
Fax: ....(310) 587-2389
atlas@atlas-pictures.com
Key Executives/Personnel:
   Sterling Ray, President
   Eric Barrett, Executive Producer
Specialties: Television
Credits: McDonald's; Toyota; Clairol; Sears
Trade Assoc./Guilds/Unions: AICP

AVALANCHE! ENTERTAINMENT
506 Santa Monica Blvd., Ste. 322
Santa Monica, CA 90401
Phone: ....(310) 395-3660
Fax: ....(310) 395-8322
info@avalanche-ent.com
Key Executives/Personnel:
   Richard Hull, President
   Anthony Ross, Director of Development
   Rodney Lee Conover, Co-President of New Media
   Jeff Hause, Co-President of New Media
   Ken Dupuis, Director
Specialties: Television
Other Categories: Feature Film
Credits: She's All That; Getting Over Allison; Jekyll Island; Within The Lines

AVD PRODUCTIONS, INC./AV DESIGNS
Phone: ....(310) 379-5818
dondavol@pacbell.net
Key Executives/Personnel:
   Genie Davis, Producer, Writer & Director
   Don Davis, Producer
Specialties: Television; Promos
Other Categories: Feature Film; Video
Credits: Relentless; IHOP; Taco Bell
First Look/Development Deals: Smith Hemion Productions
Trade Assoc./Guilds/Unions: WGAw

BACK HOME PICTURES
6918 Santa Monica Blvd.
Los Angeles, CA 90038
Phone: ....(323) 962-8500
bhpictures@aol.com
Key Executives/Personnel:

Production Companies – Commercials

Charles Abehsera, Director
Shelley O'Connor, Producer
Diona Pavinsky, Producer
Moshe Abehsera, Sales Representative
Specialties: Television
Other Categories: Feature Film
Credits: Viatel Communications; Econophone; Destia; AC Transit

BACKYARD PRODUCTIONS
248 Main St.
Venice, CA 90291
Phone: ....(310) 314-1122
Fax: ....(310) 314-1123
www.backyard.com
mail@backyard.com
Key Executives/Personnel:
Blair Stribley, President & Executive Producer
Roy Skillicorn, Head of Sales
Sheila Stepanek, Executive Producer
Peter Steinzeig, Head of Production
Ann Edgar, VP of Development
Kevin Smith, Director
Rob Pritts, Director
Don Rase, Director
Shaun Conrad, Director
Chace Strickland, Director
Eddy Chu, Director
Peter Keenan, Producer
Kris Mathur, Producer
Specialties: Television
Other Categories: Feature Film; Music Video
Credits: American Express; Anheuser-Busch; AT&T; Delta Airlines

THE BAER ANIMATION COMPANY, INC.
7743 Woodrow Wilson Dr.
Los Angeles, CA 90046
Phone: ....(323) 874-9122
....(818) 760-8666
Fax: ....(323) 874-7690
www.baeranimation.com
baer@baeranimation.com
Key Executives/Personnel:
Jane Baer, President & Executive Producer
Hope Parker, VP & Director of Administration & Marketing
Milt Vallas, Producer
Specialties: Television
Other Categories: Feature Film; Music Video
Credits: Annabelle's Wish (feature); Coca-Cola (commercial); Chevrolet (commercial); Disney World (commercial)
Trade Assoc./Guilds/Unions: AMPAS, ATAS, IATSE
Additional Info: Production of all styles of animation. Specializes in integrating with live action.

BANDOLERO FILMS
409 Santa Monica Blvd.
Santa Monica, CA 90401
Phone: ....(310) 434-1231
Fax: ....(310) 395-8224
djbemphfilms.com
Key Executives/Personnel:
Donna Distefano, Executive Producer
Marù Benjamin, Producer
Specialties: Television

BARKING WEASEL PRODUCTIONS, INC.
1040 N. Las Palmas Ave., Bldg. 7
Hollywood, CA 90038
Phone: ....(323) 464-2275
....(323) 816-3242
Fax: ....(323) 461-4993
la464bark@aol.com

Key Executives/Personnel:
Bill Hewes, Executive Producer
Dolores Dolan, Controller
Samantha Condello, Production Coordinator
Specialties: Television
Credits: Toyota Motor Sports; Puffs; Dodge; Crest

BASSETT PRODUCTIONS
125 Primose Rd.
Burlingame, CA 94010
Phone: ....(650) 579-1313
Fax: ....(650) 579-4414
www.bassettproductions.com
debra@bassettproductions.com
Key Executives/Personnel:
Debra Bassett, Executive Producer
Specialties: Television
Other Categories: Feature Film
Credits: Wisdom of the Elders, The Last Owl (feature); Epinions.com (commercial); Wall St. Journal (commercial); HBO (commercial)

BARBARA L. BAUMANN, INC.
13428 Maxella Ave., Ste. 460
Marina Del Rey, CA 90292
Phone: ....(310) 821-2429
....(310) 569-7991
Fax: ....(310) 821-1429
skyenm@aol.com
Specialties: Television
Other Categories: Feature Film; TV
Credits: A Displaced Person (documentary); One River, Many Voices (documentary); Toyota (commercial); Visa (commercial)

BCPRODUCTIONS, INC./BCTV PRODUCTIONS
8 Seascape
Laguna Niguel, CA 92677
Phone: ....(949) 495-1500
Fax: ....(949) 495-4954
budconnell@aol.com
Key Executives/Personnel:
Bud W. Connell, Executive Producer
John G. Connell, Art Director
Ann Maré, Marketing Manager
Specialties: Television; Radio; Infomercials/Direct Response; Promos
Other Categories: TV; Video
Credits: Goodwill; JCPenney; Hilton Hotels; Amercian Heart Association

BEANTOWN PRODUCTIONS, INC.
9220 Sunset Blvd., Ste. 106
West Hollywood, CA 90069
Phone: ....(310) 278-1007
Fax: ....(310) 278-1009
www.beantownprod.com
mail@beantownprod.com
Key Executives/Personnel:
David Carr, Executive Producer
David Comtois, Executive Producer
Jon Gottlieb, Executive Producer
Judie Stillman, Executive Producer
Specialties: Promos
Credits: Just Shoot Me; The Simpsons; Seinfeld; Cops

BEARD BOY PRODUCTIONS
728 Via Otono Ave.
San Clemente, CA 92672
Phone: ....(949) 458-2305
Fax: ....(949) 458-2410
beardboy@earthlink.net
Key Executives/Personnel:
Mike Smith, Executive Producer
Rob Wagner, Executive Producer

Production Companies – Commercials

Marya Reed, Producer
Specialties: Television; Radio
Other Categories: Video
Credits: Blue Cross; Lexus; Hunt Wesson
Trade Assoc./Guilds/Unions: AFTRA, SAG

BELLA PRODUCTIONS
4250 Beethoven St.
Los Angeles, CA 90066
Phone: (310) 823-3115
Fax: (310) 823-8366
bella1@earthlnk.net
Key Executives/Personnel:
Cami Taylor, Executive Producer
Bill Hayden, Executive Producer
Herb Ritts, Director
Mark Story, Director
Peter Abraham, Executive Producer
Audrey Pask, Executive Producer
Specialties: Television
Other Categories: Feature Film; TV; Music Video
Credits: Nike (commercial); Little Caesar's (commercial); Pac Bell (commercial)
Trade Assoc./Guilds/Unions: DGA

BJOIN FILMS
146 N. La Brea Ave.
Los Angeles, CA 90036
Phone: (323) 937-4097
(310) 995-1840
Fax: (323) 936-8037
hbfilms@pacbell.net
Key Executives/Personnel:
Henry Bjoin, Director & Cameraman
Philip J. Brown, Executive Producer
Specialties: Television
Credits: Coca-Cola; McDonald's; Denny's; Anheuser-Busch

BRIAN BLEAK FILMS
73 Market St.
Venice, CA 90291
Phone: (310) 396-5500
Fax: (310) 396-7423
bleakfilms@earthlink.net
Key Executives/Personnel:
Brian Bleak, Director & Cameraman
David Stoltz, Executive Producer
John Moore, Western Sales
Lauren McNamara, Midwest Sales
Specialties: Television; Promos
Credits: Vans; Quicksilver.com; Ford; Volcom Clothing

CHRISTAL BLUE PRODUCTIONS
5723 Melrose Ave.
Los Angeles, CA 90038
Phone: (323) 466-9083
Fax: (323) 466-9583
www.christalblue.com
christalblucast@aol.com
Key Executives/Personnel:
Christal Blue, Producer
Specialties: Television; Promos
Other Categories: Feature Film; Video
Credits: Smart & Final (corp. video); Airwalk (commercial); Spanish Entertainment (educational video); English Education (educational video)

BLUE GOOSE PRODUCTIONS
8350 Melrose Ave., Ste. 11
West Hollywood, CA 90069
Phone: (323) 658-6893
(206) 232-4075
Fax: (323) 658-7409
planetpoint.com/bluegoose
blugoos1@aol.com
Key Executives/Personnel:
Ron Gross, Director
Specialties: Television
Other Categories: Music Video
Credits: Nike (commercial); Pearl Jam - Single Video Theory; Seattle Mariners (commercial); Motorola (commercial)

BOB INDUSTRIES
811 Hampton Dr.
Venice, CA 90291
Phone: (310) 396-7333
Fax: (310) 396-0202
www.bobcentral.com
Key Executives/Personnel:
T. K. Knowles, Executive Producer
John O'Grady, Executive Producer
Chuck Ryant, Executive Producer
Specialties: Television
Other Categories: Music Video
Credits: PlayStation; Georgia Pacific; Gap Kids; Snickers
Trade Assoc./Guilds/Unions: AICP

BONFIRE FILMS OF AMERICA
4655 Kingswell Ave., Ste. 213
Los Angeles, CA 90027
Phone: (323) 953-6815
Fax: (323) 953-0623
Key Executives/Personnel:
Shirley Moyers, Executive Producer
A. J. Schnack, Executive Producer
John McGinnis, Director's Rep
Specialties: Television
Other Categories: Feature Film; TV; Music Video

BOYINGTON STUDIOS, INC.
17 Galleon St.
Marina Del Rey, CA 90292
Phone: (310) 822-2360
Fax: (310) 822-0430
www.boyingtonfilms.com
pboy@gte.net
Key Executives/Personnel:
Paul Boyington, Producer, Director & Effects Supervisor
Tibor Takacs, Director
Foster Corder, Director
Anthony Mabin, Director & Effects Supervisor
Robert Scopinich, Director & Effects Supervisor
Specialties: Television
Other Categories: Feature Film; Music Video
Credits: Sweet Talk; Fox Sports (Promo); Megadeath - Hangar 18; Keith Richards - Take It So Hard

BROWNSTONE FILMS
621 Broadway
Santa Monica, CA 90401
Phone: (310) 319-6136
Key Executives/Personnel:
Michael Degan, Executive Producer
Barry Dukoff, Director
Alan Arkin, Director
Adam Arkin, Director
Specialties: Television
Credits: Bryan Foods; Via Christi Medical; Detrol
Trade Assoc./Guilds/Unions: AICP

BUNGALOW 3
10220-B Riverside Dr.
Toluca Lake, CA 91602

Production Companies – Commercials

Phone: ....(818) 760-1333
Fax: ....(818) 760-2334
mailbox@bungalow3.com
Key Executives/Personnel:
    Sherry Hodge, Partner
    Siobhan Murphy, Partner
    Rosemond Cranner, Partner
Specialties: Television; Radio; Promos
Credits: Sony Pictures Entertainment; Columbia TriStar International TV; Game Show Network; Tribune Entertainment
Trade Assoc./Guilds/Unions: NATPE, PROMAX

BURKE/TRIOLO PRODUCTIONS
8755 Washington Blvd.
Culver City, CA 90232
Phone: ....(310) 837-9900
Fax: ....(310) 837-1341
www.burkertriolo.com
burketriolo@burketriolo.com
Key Executives/Personnel:
    Jeff Burke, Director of Photography
    Lorraine Triolo, Stylist & Director
    Lew Robertson, Photographer
    Tim Hawley, Photographer
    Bruce James, Photographer
Specialties: Television
Credits: Progresso Soup; Subway; Lucky Supermarket

C.2K ENTERTAINMENT
1067 Gayley Ave.
Los Angeles, CA 90024
Phone: ....(310) 208-2324
Fax: ....(310) 208-2414
www.c-2k.com
info@c-2k.com
Key Executives/Personnel:
    Jennifer Silver Nieman, Executive Producer
    Ken Musen, Director
    Rod Findley, Director
    Pierre de Lespinois, Director
    Doug Lay, Director
    Yasushi Matsuura, Director
Specialties: Television
Credits: La Victoria; Toshiba; H20 Cosmetics; Ricoh
Trade Assoc./Guilds/Unions: AICP

C'EST TOUT PRODUCTIONS
10792 Rochester Ave.
Los Angeles, CA 90024
Phone: ....(310) 475-5615
zensat@aol.com
Key Executives/Personnel:
    Nancy Kissock, Producer
Specialties: Television; Promos
Other Categories: Feature Film
Credits: Catillion 65 (feature); Shelter (feature); Mission Impossible (trailer); Frasier (promo)

CALAR
335 N. Maple Dr., Ste. 245
Beverly Hills, CA 90210
Phone: ....(310) 271-2202
Fax: ....(310) 271-8990
Key Executives/Personnel:
    Caylyn E. Morris, Executive Producer
    Alex Muñoz, Director
Specialties: Television
Other Categories: Feature Film; TV; Video

CALICO WORLD ENTERTAINMENT
10200 Riverside Dr., Ste. 203
North Hollywood, CA 91602

Phone: ....(818) 755-3800
Fax: ....(818) 755-4643
www.calicoworld.com
tom@calicoworld.com
Key Executives/Personnel:
    Tom Burton, Executive Director & Producer
    Claudia Zeitlin Burton, Managing Director
    Ken Leonard, Art Director
    Joel Fajnor, Producer & Director
    Mary Cim, Producer & Director
    Jim Livolsi, Executive Producer & Marketing
    Pedram Shohadai, Digital Animator
Other Categories: Feature Film; TV; Interactive Multimedia
Credits: Denver, The Lost Dinosaur; Bad Baby; Kid's Songs of Woody Guthrie; Ghosts Legends of the Queen Mary

CANVAS HOUSE FILMS
3671 Bear St., Ste. E
Santa Ana, CA 92704
Phone: ....(714) 850-1964
    ....(323) 459-0609
teteemley@aol.com
Key Executives/Personnel:
    Mitch Teemley, Writer & Producer
    Elizabeth Gray, Associate Producer
Specialties: Television; Promos
Other Categories: Feature Film; TV; Music Video
Credits: Out Of Time (TV series); Lennar Homes (commercial); The Limited (feature); Kragira (feature)

CANYON PICTURES, INC.
2925 Seabreeze Dr.
Malibu, CA 90265
Phone: ....(310) 456-1331
    ....(310) 880-1269
Fax: ....(310) 456-2255
Key Executives/Personnel:
    Beau Gooliak, Executive Producer
    Peter Yacavone, Producer
    Amber Dawn, Production Manager
Specialties: Television
Credits: McDonald's; Toyota; Ford
Trade Assoc./Guilds/Unions: DGA

CARBO FILMS
2032 Broadway Ave.
Santa Monica, CA 90404
Phone: ....(310) 586-1969
Fax: ....(310) 586-0061
www.carbofilms.com
carbofilms@carbofilms.com
Key Executives/Personnel:
    Javier Carbo, Executive Producer
    Dora Medrano, Executive Producer
    Nicholas Vayonis, Head of Production
    Juan Luis Arruga, Director
    Miguel Navarro, Director
    Isabel Coixet, Director
    Basil, Director
    Pedro Avila, Director
    Andrew Orci, Director
    Marinet Quinones, Sales Representative
    Miller/Nadler, Sales Representative
    Rachel Finn & Mary Saxon, Sales Representatives
    Lauren McNamara, Sales Representative
Specialties: Television
Trade Assoc./Guilds/Unions: AICP

KATIE CARLSON KASTING
P.O. Box 6892
Laguna Niguel, CA 92677

Production Companies – Commercials

Phone: .... (714) 364-6160
Fax: .... (714) 364-6160
katecast00@aol.com
Specialties: Television; Radio; Infomercials/Direct Response; Promos
Credits: Pringles; Gravy Train; Pampers

CELLULOID
2128 15th St.
Denver, CO 80202
Phone: .... (303) 595-3152
.... (303) 595-4908
www.celluliodstudio.com
jan@celluloidstudios.com
Key Executives/Personnel:
  Olivier Katz, President
  Jan Johnson, Executive Producer
Specialties: Television
Other Categories: TV
Credits: PBS; Fox Kids; Denver Art Museum; Drug Free America

THE CHELMAR GROUP
PMB# 345, 411 E. Huntington Dr., Bldg. 107
Arcadia, CA 91006
Phone: .... (626) 358-4001
chelmar@earthlink.net
Key Executives/Personnel:
  Richard James, Executive Producer
  Michelle Palmer, Producer
Specialties: Television; Infomercials/Direct Response; Promos
Other Categories: Feature Film; Video; Music Video
Credits: Renewable Power (documentary); The View From Malabar (documentary); Salvation Army (commercial); Coca-Cola (commercial)

CHELSEA PICTURES
1040 N. Las Palmas Ave., Bldg. 15
Hollywood, CA 90038
Phone: .... (323) 860-8030
Fax: .... (323) 860-8035
info@chelsea.com
Key Executives/Personnel:
  Steve Wax, President (NY)
  Lisa Mehling, Executive Producer (NY)
  Allison Amon, Executive Producer (LA)
  Stacy Wolberg, Head of Production (NY)
  Sandra Penfield, Head of Production (LA)
Specialties: Television

CHIARI COOK COMPANY, INC.
5822 W. Washington Blvd.
Culver City, CA 90232
Phone: .... (323) 937-1272
Fax: .... (323) 937-1274
chiaricook@earthlink.net
Key Executives/Personnel:
  Jared Cook, Executive Producer
  Chiari Endo, Executive Producer
Specialties: Television
Credits: McDonald's; Coca-Cola; Sony; Honda

CHICAGO STORY
401 W. Superior, 2nd Fl.
Chicago, IL 60610
Phone: .... (312) 642-3173
Fax: .... (312) 642-3149
androw@thestory.companies.com
Key Executives/Personnel:
  Mark Androw, Executive Producer
Specialties: Television
Additional Info: L.A. Story, 1501 Colorado Ave., Santa Monica, CA 90404, (310) 917-4462 phone, (310) 395-5102 fax

CHIODO BROS. PRODUCTIONS, INC.
110 W. Providencia Ave.
Burbank, CA 91502
Phone: .... (818) 842-5656
Fax: .... (818) 848-0891
www.chiodobros.com
klowns@chiodobros.com
Key Executives/Personnel:
  Edward Chiodo, Producer & Development
  Stephen Chiodo, Director & Development
  Charles Chiodo, Design & Development
  Paul Kemp, COO & Development
Specialties: Television
Other Categories: Feature Film; TV
Credits: Killer Klowns from Outer Space (feature); Amazing Live Sea Monkeys (TV series); The Crayon Box (TV series); Skwid Zone (TV pilot)

CINEMANIX
22627 Hatteras St.
Woodland Hills, CA 91367
Phone: .... (818) 999-2229
Fax: .... (818) 999-3188
cinemanix@aol.com
Key Executives/Personnel:
  Paul Manix, Producer
Specialties: Television
Credits: United Airlines; Big Shot; Kahlua; Sam Adams

COAST MEDIA TELEPRODUCTIONS, INC.
17062 Murphy Ave., Bldg. B
Irvine, CA 92614
Phone: .... (949) 417-0300
www.coastmedia.com
digipost@earthlink.net
Key Executives/Personnel:
  Art Royce, President, CEO & Producer
  Brian Ferguson, Director of Photography
  Joyce D. Smith, VP
  Donovan Smith, Audio Engineer
  Curtis Matovich, Editor & Composer
  Steve Hirai, Production Manager
  Becky Fisher, Account Manager
Specialties: Television; Radio; Infomercials/Direct Response; Promos
Other Categories: TV; Video; Music Video; Interactive Multimedia
Credits: Simple Green (infomercial); Milk Advisory Board (commercial); Meguiar's Wax (corp. video & commercial); Disney (corp. video)

COHN & COMPANY
1313 Fifth St.
Santa Monica, CA 90401
Phone: .... (310) 899-6979
Fax: .... (310) 394-7212
lasseron@aol.com
Key Executives/Personnel:
  Jack Cohn, Owner & CEO
  Tony Cunningham, Executive Producer
  Randi Arnold, Head of Sales
  David Lasseron, Executive Producer
  Heather Poll, Office Manager
  Elena Schuber, Staff
  Joaquin Pineda, Staff
  Mark Raymon Bennett, Director
  Olivier Venturini, Director
  Paul Golman, Director
  Martin Bell, Director & Documentarian
  Paul Cade, Director
  Ray Lawrence, Director
  Ron Blair, Rep (West Coast)
Specialties: Television
Credits: McDonald's; Ford; Mitsubishi; Vauxhall
Trade Assoc./Guilds/Unions: PGA

Production Companies – Commercials

COMMERCIALS WHILE-U-WAIT, INC.
218 Grand Blvd.
Venice, CA 90291
Phone: ....(310) 399-3456
Fax: ....(310) 396-1614
info@cwuw.com
Key Executives/Personnel:
    Rene Kock, Executive Producer & Director
Specialties: Television
Credits: West Cigarettes; R1 Cigarettes; Kinder Country Chocolate Bar

COPPOS FILMS
118 N. Larchmont Blvd.
Los Angeles, CA 90004
Phone: ....(323) 463-0764
Fax: ....(323) 463-5366
www.copposfilms.com
Key Executives/Personnel:
    Bill Bratkowski, Chairman
    Michael Appel, Executive Producer
    Mark Coppos, Director
    Virginia Lee, Director
    Brian Aldrich, Director
    Scott Gillen, Director
    Lucy Campos, Controller & Head of Operations
    Alexandra Chamberlain, Head of Production
    Joanne Ferraro, National Head of Sales & East Coast Managing Director
Specialties: Television
Credits: Apple; Earthlink; Time Warner; GMC
Additional Info: 22 W. 21st St., Ste. 1204, New York, NY 10010

MICHAEL COWAN, INC.
3756 Effingham Pl.
Los Angeles, CA 90027
Phone: ....(323) 666-0600
Key Executives/Personnel:
    Michael Cowan, Director & Executive Producer
    Teresa Flores, Producer
Specialties: Television
Credits: Ford; Dodge; Toyota; Mitsubishi

CPPRODS
Phone: ....(310) 441-9211
Fax: ....(310) 441-9211
cpprods@earthlink.net
Key Executives/Personnel:
    Cindy Pierson, Producer
Specialties: Television; Infomercials/Direct Response; Promos
Other Categories: Music Video
Credits: Brandy & Monica - The Boy is Mine; Monster Magnet - Space Lord; Foxy Brown - Hot Spot; Smokey Brown - Sleeping In

CREATIVE CHAOS
425 19th St.
Santa Monica, CA 90402
Phone: ....(310) 451-4112
....(310) 451-8019
Fax: ....(310) 451-8069
chaos@home.com
Key Executives/Personnel:
    Adam Bleibtreu, Director
    Suzanne Bleibtreu, Executive Producer
Specialties: Television; Radio; Promos
Credits: The Rio Hotel Casino; Sportspage.com; Station Casinos; The Bachelor

THE CREATIVE DEPARTMENT, LLC
26403 Emerald Dove Dr.
Valencia, CA 91355
Phone: ....(661) 288-1155
....(661) 609-2492
Fax: ....(661) 288-1166
mborchetta@mediaone.net
Key Executives/Personnel:
    Mark Borchetta, Director & Producer
Specialties: Television
Other Categories: Video; Music Video
Credits: Bushnell Sports Optics Worldwide; Mercedes-Benz; S. California Volvo Dealers; SAAB
Trade Assoc./Guilds/Unions: ASCAP

CRONENWETH FILMS
633 N. La Brea Ave., Ste. 200
Los Angeles, CA 90036
Phone: ....(323) 964-4888
Fax: ....(323) 964-4887
cronenweth@filmfortv.com
Key Executives/Personnel:
    Tim Cronenweth, Director
    Patricia Friedman, Executive Producer
Specialties: Television
Credits: Energizer; Kozyhome.com; Twinlab; PBS
Trade Assoc./Guilds/Unions: DGA

CROSSROADS FILMS
8630 Pine Tree Pl.
West Hollywood, CA 90069
Phone: ....(310) 659-6880
Key Executives/Personnel:
    Cami Taylor, Executive Producer
    Carole Hughes, Executive Producer
    Charlie Curran, Executive Producer
Specialties: Television; Promos
Trade Assoc./Guilds/Unions: AICP
Additional Info: 136 W. 21st St., New York, NY 10011

CYLO
5540 Hollywood Blvd., 2nd Fl.
Los Angeles, CA 90028
Phone: ....(323) 957-7824
Fax: ....(323) 957-8531
www.cylo.com
catalaine@cylo.com
Key Executives/Personnel:
    Julie Atherton, President
    Cindy Akins, Executive Producer
    Catalaine Knell, Producer
Specialties: Television
Other Categories: Music Video; Interactive Multimedia
Additional Info: Previously Atherton

DALRYMPLE PRODUCTIONS
150 E. Meda Ave., Ste. 100
Glendora, CA 91741
Phone: ....(626) 963-5588
www.dalpro.com
james@dalpro.com
Key Executives/Personnel:
    James Dalrymple, Producer
Specialties: Television; Radio; Infomercials/Direct Response; Promos
Other Categories: TV; Video

DAPTV ASSOCIATES
9080 Santa Monica Blvd.
West Hollywood, CA 90069
Phone: ....(310) 860-9001
....(877) 860-9003
Fax: ....(310) 860-9003
www.daptv.com
info@daptv.com
Key Executives/Personnel:
    Don Azars, Writer, Director & Executive Producer

Production Companies – Commercials

Michael Berman, Producer
Specialties: Television; Radio; Infomercials/Direct Response
Other Categories: TV; Video; Music Video
Credits: The Edge and Beyond; Crisis Counselor; Carroll, Her First Special

DEKTOR FILM
1151 N. Highland Ave.
Hollywood, CA 90038
Phone: ....(323) 466-3455
Fax: ....(323) 856-8187
dh4663455@aol.com
Key Executives/Personnel:
 Leslie Dektor, Director & DP
 Paul Dektor, Director
 Mark Dektor, Director & DP
 Eugene Yelchin, Director
 Faith Dektor, Executive Producer
 Sven Shelgren, Executive Producer
Specialties: Television
Credits: TXV; Compaq; Hewlett Packard; IdeaExchange.com

DENALI PRODUCTIONS, INC.
Studio One, 6743 Fernhill Dr.
Malibu, CA 90265
Phone: ....(310) 457-7566
Fax: ....(310) 457-5789
www.denaliproductions.com
bcarmic@earthlink.net
Key Executives/Personnel:
 Doug Millington, Executive Producer
 Bobby Carmichael, Director
Specialties: Infomercials/Direct Response
Other Categories: Feature Film; TV; Video
Credits: Merrill-Lynch (commercial); Sprite (commercial); Cadillac (commercial); Dayton 500 (documentary)

DNA, INC.
6535 Santa Monica Blvd.
Hollywood, CA 90038
Phone: ....(323) 463-2826
Fax: ....(323) 463-2535
www.dnala.com
mailbox@dnala.com
Key Executives/Personnel:
 David Naylor, President
 Patricia Judice, Executive Producer, Commercials
 Sam Aslanian, Executive Producer, Music Videos
 Francis Lawrence, Director
 Liz Friedlander, Director
 Yuki, Director
 Marco Brambilla, Director
 Steve Willis, Director
 Marc Webb, Director
 Rocky Schenck, Director
 Lili Fini Zanuck, Director
 Jean-Baptiste Mondino, Director
Specialties: Television
Other Categories: Music Video
Credits: Target; Bacardi; Footlocker; McDonald's
Trade Assoc./Guilds/Unions: AICP, MVPA

DOOM, INC.
355 N. Maple St., Ste. 112
Burbank, CA 91505
Phone: ....(818) 972-2007
Fax: ....(818) 972-2008
www.doominc.com
Key Executives/Personnel:
 Thomas Mignone, Director & Executive Producer
 Darci Oltman, Producer
 Peter Davison, Office Manager

Specialties: Television
Other Categories: Video; Music Video; Interactive Multimedia
Credits: Slipknot - Spit it Out (music video); American Red Cross (corp. video); Mudvayne - Dig (music video); Donald Trump: Trump Organization (corp. video)

BRUCE DORN FILMS
466-A Foothill Blvd., PMB 319
La Cañada, CA 91011
Phone: ....(818) 790-3080
Key Executives/Personnel:
 Bruce Dorn, Owner
Specialties: Television; Promos
Other Categories: Feature Film

BRUCE DOWAD ASSOCIATES
8085 Selma Ave.
Los Angeles, CA 90046
Phone: ....(323) 654-8855
Fax: ....(323) 654-8775
www.bda-la.com
info@bda-la.com
Key Executives/Personnel:
 Bruce Dowad, President & Director
 Heidi Nolting Sturges, Executive Producer
 Robert Logevall, Director
 Alain Gourrier, Director
Specialties: Television
Credits: Mercedes-Benz; Audi; Lexus; Coca-Cola
Trade Assoc./Guilds/Unions: AICP

DRIVE MEDIA
123 Market St.
Venice, CA 90291
Phone: ....(310) 392-6920
Fax: ....(310) 392-8710
Key Executives/Personnel:
 Jeff Armstrong, Executive Producer
 Charlie Love, Sales Coordinator
 Nicole Sacker, Office Manager
 Jennifer Pyper, Assistant to Mr. Armstrong
Specialties: Television; Promos
Credits: Nike; Levi's; Coca-Cola; G.M.
Trade Assoc./Guilds/Unions: AICP, DGA

DUCK SOUP STUDIOS
2205 Stoner Ave.
Los Angeles, CA 90064
Phone: ....(310) 478-0771
Fax: ....(310) 478-0773
www.ducksoupla.com
ducksoupla@aol.net
Key Executives/Personnel:
 Mark Medernach, Executive Producer
 Carolyn Bates, Producer
Specialties: Television; Promos
Other Categories: Feature Film; Music Video; Interactive Multimedia
Credits: Starkist; Dean's Milk; Bell Atlantic; McDonald's

E.M.E., INC.
Phone: ....(310) 330-8841
emeinc@earthlink.net
Specialties: Television
Other Categories: Feature Film; TV; Music Video; Interactive Multimedia

ELEVENTH DAY ENTERTAINMENT
17003 Ventura Blvd., Ste. 200
Encino, CA 91316
Phone: ....(818) 784-6403
Fax: ....(818) 784-6421
www.eleventhday.com

Production Companies – Commercials

mail@eleventhday.com
Key Executives/Personnel:
  Frank Martin, Producer & Director
  Rudy Poe, Producer & Director
Specialties: Television; Infomercials/Direct Response
Other Categories: TV; Video
Credits: CBS: The First Fifty Years; John Houston: The Man, The Movies, The Maverick; US Department of Defense; Balance Bars

EVIL TWIN PRODUCTIONS
5201 Fulton Ave.
Sherman Oaks, CA 91401
Phone: ....(818) 986-8551
Fax: ....(818) 986-8582
www.eviltwinproductions.com
info@eviltwinproductions.com
Key Executives/Personnel:
  Harri Mark, Producer
  Kristin Armfield, Producer
Specialties: Television; Radio; Promos
Credits: Aqua

FATE JUNKIE FILMS, INC.
4555 Matilija Ave.
Sherman Oaks, CA 91423
Phone: ....(818) 905-1333
....(818) 929-7500
Fax: ....(818) 907-1333
stacey33@pacbell.net
Key Executives/Personnel:
  Stacy Schachter, Owner & Producer
Specialties: Television
Other Categories: Feature Film; Music Video
Credits: Politically Incorrect (commercial); Frito Lay (commercial); Mattel (commercial); Tupac (music video)
Trade Assoc./Guilds/Unions: DGA

FDG
32 W. 22nd St., 3rd Fl.
New York, NY 10010
Phone: ....(212) 624-1446
Fax: ....(212) 624-1448
www.fdg3.com
david@fdg3.com
Key Executives/Personnel:
  David Edelstein, Executive Producer
  Michael Uman, Creative Director
  Adam Kagan, Head of Production
Specialties: Television; Promos
Credits: HBO (promos); MSNBC (promos); BET (promos); USA Network (promos)

FILM PLANET
1317 Innes Pl.
Venice, CA 90291
Phone: ....(310) 581-1100
Fax: ....(310) 581-1130
www.filmplanet.com
la@filmplanet.com
Key Executives/Personnel:
  Robyn Bensinger, Executive Producer
  Karin Stuckenschmidt, Executive Producer
Specialties: Television
Credits: Miller Lite; Crest; McDonald's; MCI
Trade Assoc./Guilds/Unions: AICP

THE FILM SYNDICATE
7214 Melrose Ave.
Los Angeles, CA 90046
Phone: ....(323) 938-8080
Fax: ....(323) 938-8183

fsyndicate@aol.com
Key Executives/Personnel:
  Bryan Johnson, Executive Producer & Director
Specialties: Television; Promos
Other Categories: TV; Music Video
Credits: Fox (promos); Dr. Pepper; Melrose Place Specials; U2 - Streets Have No Name
Trade Assoc./Guilds/Unions: DGA

FIRST AVENUE FILMS
567 MossHill Rd.
Orcas, WA 98280
Phone: ....(360) 376-3737
www.firstavenuefilms.com
info@firstavenuefilms.com
Key Executives/Personnel:
  John G. Ginnes, Executive Producer
  Leslie Kahan, Executive Producer
Specialties: Television; Infomercials/Direct Response; Promos
Other Categories: Feature Film; TV
Credits: Madonna - You Must Love Me; Out Of The Silence; Anheuser-Busch
Trade Assoc./Guilds/Unions: AICP, DGA

FLYING TIGER FILMS
2828 Donald Douglas Loop North
Santa Monica, CA 90405
Phone: ....(310) 664-9171
....(212) 832-4600
Fax: ....(310) 664-9177
www.ftfilms.com
production@ftfilms.com
Key Executives/Personnel:
  Skip Short, President
  Lance O'Connor, Executive Producer
  Ken Arlidge, Director
  Robert Gordon, Director
  James Holt, Director
  Klaus Obermeyer, Director
  Mikael Salomon, Director
  Henrik Hansen, Director
  Jeff Devlin, Sales Representative
  Ron Hoffman, Sales Representative
  Deborah Marlowe, Sales Representative
  Richard Latarewicz, Production Manager
Specialties: Television
Credits: Visa; Mazda; Anheuser-Busch
Trade Assoc./Guilds/Unions: AICP, DGA

FM ROCKS
1351 Third St., Ste. 201
Santa Monica, CA 90401
Phone: ....(310) 587-1501
....(310) 664-3615
Fax: ....(310) 587-1502
www.fmrocks.com
etlove@fmrocks.com
Key Executives/Personnel:
  Dave Meyers, Director
  F. Gary Gray, Director
  Gregory Dark, Director
  Tim Story, Director
  Eileen Terry, Executive Producer
Specialties: Television
Other Categories: Music Video
Credits: Pringles; Sprite; Britney Spears - Lucky; 'NSync - Drive Myself Crazy
Trade Assoc./Guilds/Unions: AFI, AICP, American Cinematheque, DGA, IFP, WIF

Production Companies – Commercials

FOUR SISTERS PRODUCTION
11324 Emelita St., Ste. 1
North Hollywood, CA 91601
Phone: ....(818) 755-1815
....(818) 819-1789
Fax: ....(818) 755-1815
www.castingnotices.com
filmcast@pacbell.net
Key Executives/Personnel:
   Tom Daniels, Producer
Specialties: Television
Credits: San Manuel Casino; BadCreditNoCredit.com

FOUR SQUARE PRODUCTIONS, INC.
5205 Kearny Villa Way
San Diego, CA 92123
Phone: ....(858) 874-1900
www.foursq.com
Key Executives/Personnel:
   John DeBello, Director
   Scott Sorensen, Sr. Producer
   David Craven, Sr. Producer
Specialties: Television; Promos
Other Categories: Feature Film; TV; Video
Credits: This Week in Sports; SPA War (video); SignOnSanDiego.com; The Guide

FUEL
1914 Main St., Ste. 212
Santa Monica, CA 90405
Phone: ....(310) 314-1644
Fax: ....(310) 314-1640
david.mcginley@razorfish.com
Key Executives/Personnel:
   Matthew Marquis, Executive Producer
   David McGinley, Head of Production
   Seth Epstein, Director
   John Lindauer, Director
   Jarl Olsen, Director
   Neil Tardio Jr., Director
   Mark Andrews, Sales Representative
   Tracy Bernard, Sales Representative
   Nancy Workman, Sales Representative
Specialties: Television
Other Categories: Music Video
Credits: Gatorade; HBO; AT&T; United Way
Trade Assoc./Guilds/Unions: AICP

FUSION FILMS
1548 18th St.
Santa Monica, CA 90404
Phone: ....(310) 449-1300
Fax: ....(310) 449-1301
www.fusionfilms.com
peter@fusionfilms.com
Key Executives/Personnel:
   Peter Abraham, Executive Producer
   Kristy Wilson, Producer
Specialties: Television
Credits: Honda Motorcross; LegoLand; Union Bank; Ford Outfitters
Trade Assoc./Guilds/Unions: AICP

GALANTY & COMPANY, INC.
1640 Fifth St., Ste. 202
Santa Monica, CA 90401
Phone: ....(310) 451-2525
galantyco@juno.com
Key Executives/Personnel:
   Sidney Galanty, Director
   Mark Galanty, Executive Producer
   Sanja Brizic, Associate Producer & Writer
Specialties: Television; Radio; Infomercials/Direct Response

Other Categories: Video; Music Video
Credits: TIAA: Cref Mutual Funds; America's Workout; Jane Fonda Workout Series
Trade Assoc./Guilds/Unions: AAPC

GARTNER
1531 Colorado Ave.
Santa Monica, CA 90404
Phone: ....(310) 899-1700
Fax: ....(310) 899-1710
christieb@gartnerfilms.com
Key Executives/Personnel:
   Don Block, Executive Producer
   Rich Carter, Executive Producer
   Christine Berges, Production Executive
Specialties: Television

GINTY FILMS
16255 Ventura Blvd., Ste. 625
Encino, CA 91436
Phone: ....(310) 274-9691
....(310) 277-1408
Fax: ....(310) 274-9692
www.robertginty.com
rwginty@aol.com
Key Executives/Personnel:
   Robert Ginty, CEO
   Skip Heinecke, (Ireland)
   Shira Zeltzer, Executive Assistant
   Layla Bennett, Executive Assistant
   Lyndi Vanderhout, (Paris)
   Moira Proletti, (Rome)
   Jean Diamond, (London)
   John Gallagher, (New York)
   John Mein, (Vancouver)
Specialties: Television
Other Categories: Feature Film; TV; Music Video; Interactive Multimedia
Credits: Bounty Hunter; Woman of Desire; Day of Reckoning
Trade Assoc./Guilds/Unions: BAFTA, DGA, SAG, WGAw

GLASS GUNS
7280 Melrose Ave., 2nd Fl.
Los Angeles, CA 90046
Phone: ....(323) 938-0729
Fax: ....(323) 938-7007
www.glassguns.com
jeff@glassguns.com
Key Executives/Personnel:
   Jeff Clark, Executive Producer
Specialties: Television
Other Categories: Music Video; Interactive Multimedia
Credits: General Mills; Nescafe; Sky TV; Backstreet Boys - Get Down
Trade Assoc./Guilds/Unions: AICP, MVPA

GO FILM
51 E. 12th St., 6th Fl.
New York, NY 10003
Phone: ....(212) 677-7500
Fax: ....(212) 677-7555
www.gofilm.net
Key Executives/Personnel:
   Jonathan Weinstein, Partner
   Robert Wherry, Partner
   Preston Lee, Executive Producer
   Caitlin Felton, Director
   Gary McKendry, Director
   Frank W. Ockenfels 3, Director
   Nick Rafter, Director
   Rad-ish, Director
Specialties: Television
Other Categories: Feature Film; Music Video

Production Companies – Commercials

Additional Info: 1103 Abbot Kinney Blvd., Venice, CA 90291
(310) 581-1992 phone, (310) 581-4994 fax

JEFF GOLD PRODUCTIONS, INC.
13900 Panay Way, Ste. 309
Marina Del Rey, CA 90292
Phone: ....(310) 827-9165
j47737@yahoo.com
Specialties: Television; Radio; Infomercials/Direct Response
Other Categories: Feature Film; TV; Video; Music Video
Credits: The Alpha Section; Talking Heads; Career Bed; Changing Times
Trade Assoc./Guilds/Unions: DGA

GOLD'N HEN PRODUCTIONS
12301 Wilshire Blvd., Ste. 402
Los Angeles, CA 90024
Phone: ....(310) 820-1308
Fax: ....(310) 820-1398
judy@groupmsi.com
Key Executives/Personnel:
    Joel Goldstein, Chairman
    Judy Henry, President
    Dale Eldridge Kaye, VP
    Jamie Goldstein, VP
Specialties: Television
Other Categories: Feature Film; TV
Credits: Replacing Dad; Nelson Diebel Story; Spy Girl

GOLDEN EAGLE PIX
475 Ravensbury St.
Thousand Oaks, CA 91361
Phone: ....(805) 381-9095
 ....(805) 907-1860
Fax: ....(805) 381-9096
www.goldeneaglepix.com
goldeneaglepix@hotmail.com
Key Executives/Personnel:
    Peter B. Good, Producer
Specialties: Promos
Other Categories: Feature Film; TV
Credits: Roller Coasters; Fireworks; Beyond Bizarre; Death Valley

GRAYING & BALDING, INC.
924 Colorado Ave.
Santa Monica, CA 90401
Phone: ....(310) 587-2330
Fax: ....(310) 587-2340
Key Executives/Personnel:
    Jim Gable, Director
    Ann Kim, Executive Producer
    Jason Barager, Producer
Specialties: Television
Other Categories: Music Video

GREEN COMMUNICATIONS
303 N. Glen Oaks, Ste. 605
Burbank, CA 91502
Phone: ....(818) 557-0050
Fax: ....(818) 557-0056
www.greenfilms.com
tcaptan@greenfilms.com
Key Executives/Personnel:
    Talaat Captan, President
Specialties: Television
Other Categories: Feature Film; TV
Credits: Ground Control; Living in Peril; Apex; Space Marines

GREEN DOT FILMS, INC.
1554 16th St.
Santa Monica, CA 90404
Phone: ....(310) 656-4900

Fax: ....(310) 656-0444
mail@greendotfilms.com
Key Executives/Personnel:
    Brent Thomas, Owner & Director
    Rick Fishbein, Executive Producer
    Alex Anderson, Head of Sales
    Dan Appel, Director
    Mark Reber, Director
    Garry Sato, Director
    Moira Shenlin, West Coast & Texas Sales
Specialties: Television

GREENWATER PICTURES
3940 Laurel Canyon Blvd., Ste. 736
Studio City, CA 91604
Phone: ....(323) 655-9585
Fax: ....(323) 655-9025
www.greenwaterpictures.com
tlowe@greenwaterpictures.com
Key Executives/Personnel:
    Tom Lowe, President & Producer
    Barbara Cordis, VP of Development
Specialties: Television; Promos
Other Categories: Video; Music Video; Interactive Multimedia
Credits: Fireball (webisodes); Nick Forester (webisodes)
Trade Assoc./Guilds/Unions: DGA

GROSS PRODUCTIONS
1 Skyline Dr.
Burbank, CA 91501
Phone: ....(818) 557-7335
Fax: ....(818) 557-7336
www.grosspro.com
callgross@aol.com
Key Executives/Personnel:
    Chris Gross, Producer & Director
Specialties: Promos
Other Categories: Feature Film; TV
Credits: Gloria Estefan & Carribean Soul; La Femme Nikita; Duckman
Trade Assoc./Guilds/Unions: ASCAP

H-GUN LABS
587 Shotwell St.
San Francisco, CA 94110
Phone: ....(415) 648-4386
 ....(773) 561-5354
Fax: ....(415) 920-3911
www.hgun.com
info@hgun.com
Key Executives/Personnel:
    James Deloye, Executive Producer
    Sara Kraft, Producer
    Nancy Williams, Lab Manager
Specialties: Television; Promos
Other Categories: Feature Film; TV; Music Video; Interactive Multimedia

HALLOWES PRODUCTIONS
11260 Regent St.
Los Angeles, CA 90066
Phone: ....(310) 390-4767
adjim@aol.com
Key Executives/Personnel:
    Jim Hallowes, Director & Producer
    Harry Mathias, Producer
    Mark Oppenheimer, Producer
Specialties: Television
Credits: Pac Bell; CareUnit; Volkswagen; HeadStart Computers

HEADQUARTERS
3015 Main St., 4th Fl.
Santa Monica, CA 90405
Phone: ....(310) 752-5200

Fax: ....(310) 752-5220
hesh@hqfilm.com
Key Executives/Personnel:
  Alex Blum, Partner
  Tom Mooney, Partner
  Andrew Denyer, Executive Producer
  Philip Fox-Mills, Head of Sales
  Hesh Rephun, West Coast Sales & Public Relations
  Jared Shapiro, Midwest Sales
  David Cornell, Director & Cinematographer
  John Moore, Director
  Sean Mullens, Director
  Joe Public, Director
  Lloyd Stein, Director
  Eric Steinman, Director
  Craig Champion, Director
  Neil Harris, Director
Specialties: Television
Other Categories: Feature Film
Credits: Capitol One; Southwest Bell; G.M.; Visa
Additional Info: 7 West 18th St., 6th Fl., New York, NY 10011 (212) 255-9000 phone, (212) 255-9009 fax

THE JIM HENSON COMPANY
1416 N. La Brea Ave.
Los Angeles, CA 90028
Phone: ....(323) 802-1500
Fax: ....(323) 802-1825
www.henson.com
Key Executives/Personnel:
  Brian Henson, Chairman
  Charles H. Rivkin, President & CEO
  Linda Govreau, Executive VP of Corporate Finance & CFO
  Lisa Henson, President, Jim Henson Pictures
  John Stephenson, Executive VP & Creative Supervisor, Jim Henson's Creature Shop
  Juliet Blake, Executive VP & Co-Head, Jim Henson Television Group Worldwide
  Angus Fletcher, Executive VP & Co-Head, Jim Henson Television Group Worldwide
  Peter Schube, General Counsel & Executive VP of Business & Legal Affairs
  Michael Bolingbroke, Sr. VP of Finance & Operations, Jim Henson's Creature Shop
  Craig Allen, Sr. VP & General Manager, Jim Henson Interactive
  Robert Norton, Sr. VP of Business & Legal Affairs
  Ritamarie Peruggi, Sr. VP of Production Worldwide
  Robert Wozniak, VP of Production Administration & Finance, Production Executive
  Kristine Belson, Production, Jim Henson Pictures
  Louis Philips, VP of Production Administration
  Halle Stanford Grossman, VP of Creative Affairs, Jim Henson Television
  Ruth Caruso, VP of Development, Jim Henson Television
  Michele Martell, VP of Business Affairs & Interactive Business Development
  Antonia Downey, VP of International Legal & Business Affairs
  Pete Coogan, VP of Physical Production
  David Barrington-Holt, Creative Supervisor, Jim Henson's Creature Shop
  Debbie McClellan, Sr. Director of Corporate Communications & Special Projects
  Omar Camacho, Director of Current Programming, Jim Henson Television
Specialties: Television; Promos
Other Categories: Feature Film; TV; Video; Music Video; Interactive Multimedia
Credits: Farscape; Story Telling with Tomie de Paola; Rat; Muppets From Space

HKM PRODUCTIONS
1641 N. Ivar Ave.
Hollywood, CA 90028
Phone: ....(323) 465-9494
Fax: ....(323) 465-4203
Key Executives/Personnel:
  Tom Mickel, President
  Lisa Prentis Margulis, Executive Producer
  Carl Swan, Head of Production
  Jordan Brady, Director
  Michele Civetta, Director
  Graham Henman, Director
  Michael Patrick Jann, Director
  Michael Karbelnikoff, Director
  Christian Loubek, Director
  Richard Sears, Director
  Alex Madero, Sales Representative
Specialties: Television

HODGE FILM & VIDEO
10770 Esther Ave.
Los Angeles, CA 90064
Phone: ....(310) 441-9773
Fax: ....(310) 474-7611
hodge@pacbell.net
Key Executives/Personnel:
  David Hodge, President
  Stacey Freeman, Producer
Specialties: Television; Promos
Other Categories: TV; Video; Music Video
Credits: Carly Simon - Every Time We Say Goodbye; Bank One (corp. video); Human Rights Campaign; Carlos Santana - Supernatural

HOKUS POKUS PRODUCTIONS, INC.
29395 Agoura Rd., Ste. 205
Agoura Hills, CA 91301
Phone: ....(818) 879-2200
www.tvadvertising.com
Specialties: Television
Credits: atrade USA; Castric Brick; E Street Access; Wall Street Attack

HORIZON SHINE, INC.
8621 Hayden Pl.
Culver City, CA 90232
Phone: ....(310) 990-6532
Fax: ....(310) 280-9776
www.horizonshine.com
info@horizonshine.com
Key Executives/Personnel:
  Robert Nackman, Executive Producer
Specialties: Television
Other Categories: Video; Music Video
Credits: Kodak Film; American Eagle; Burger King (corp. video)

HOT SPOTS TELEVISION
880 Apollo St., Ste. 347
El Segundo, CA 90245
Phone: ....(310) 606-5700
....(310) 606-5703
Fax: ....(310) 606-5705
www.hot4spots.com
fkilpatrick@hot4spots.com
Key Executives/Personnel:
  Linda Hendricks, Producer
  Frank Kilpatrick, Executive Producer
Specialties: Television; Radio; Infomercials/Direct Response
Credits: Johnson & Johnson; Nokia; Novartis; Duke's Fast Food

THE HOUSE PRODUCTION COMPANY
1429 N. Spaulding Ave.
Los Angeles, CA 90046
Phone: ....(323) 851-5151

Production Companies – Commercials

....(323) 697-3830
Fax: ....(323) 851-9598
Key Executives/Personnel:
  Bonnie Matchinga, Executive Producer
  Alleda Harrison, Marketing Director
  Bob Schwartz, Director
Specialties: Television; Infomercials/Direct Response; Promos
Other Categories: Feature Film; Video
Credits: Poligrip; Total Telcom Media; Birds and the Bees
Trade Assoc./Guilds/Unions: DGA

HSI PRODUCTIONS, INC.
3630 Eastham Dr.
Culver City, CA 90232
Phone: ....(310) 452-9999
Fax: ....(310) 396-2128
Key Executives/Personnel:
  Stavros Merjos, President
  Bill Sandwick, Executive Producer
  Kerstin Emhoff, Executive Producer
  Maddi Carlton, Executive Producer
  Steve Ross, Executive Producer
  Tracie Norfleet, Head of Production
  Jessica Thomas, Sales
Specialties: Television
Trade Assoc./Guilds/Unions: AICP, DGA

IMAGE G
10900 Ventura Blvd.
Studio City, CA 91604
Phone: ....(818) 761-6644
Fax: ....(818) 761-8397
www.imageg.com
Key Executives/Personnel:
  Nick Paine, Producer
  Tom Barron, Producer
Specialties: Television
Other Categories: Feature Film; TV
Credits: Nestle; Del Monte; Spy Kids

IMAGINARY FORCES
6526 Sunset Blvd.
Los Angeles, CA 90028
Phone: ....(323) 957-6868
Fax: ....(323) 957-9577
www.imaginaryforces.com
information@imaginaryforces.com
Key Executives/Personnel:
  Kyle Cooper, Creative Director & Managing Partner
  Chip Houghton, Executive Producer & Managing Partner
  Peter Frankfurt, Creative Director & Managing Partner
  Saffron Kenny, Head of Production & Partner
  Mikon Van Gastel, Creative Director & Partner
  Karin Fong, Creative Director & Partner
  Kurt Mattila, Creative Director & Partner
  Michael Riley, Creative Director & Partner
  Linda Nakagawa, CFO & Partner
Specialties: Television
Other Categories: Feature Film
Credits: Blade; Blade 2; Coors Lite; Janus

IMPACT PSA, INC.
1429 N. Spaulding Ave.
Los Angeles, CA
Phone: ....(323) 851-5151
....(323) 697-3830
Fax: ....(323) 851-9598
Key Executives/Personnel:
  Bonnie Matchinga, Executive Producer
  Alleda Harrison, Director of Marketing
Specialties: Television; Infomercials/Direct Response; Promos; PSA's

Other Categories: Feature Film; Video
Credits: Spilled Milk (PSA); A Place For Me (documentary)
Trade Assoc./Guilds/Unions: DGA

IN PLAY MEDIA ARTS
4174 Ince Blvd.
Culver City, CA 90232
Phone: ....(310) 839-7497
....(800) 260-6580
Fax: ....(310) 839-5365
www.inplaymediaarts.com
dutydukes@aol.com
Key Executives/Personnel:
  Gary Hoffman, no title
Specialties: Television; Infomercials/Direct Response; Promos
Other Categories: Feature Film; Video

IN-FINN-ITY PRODUCTIONS, INC.
11400 W. Olympic Blvd., 16th Fl.
Los Angeles, CA 90064
Phone: ....(310) 444-6300
Fax: ....(310) 444-6310
www.infinnity.com
Key Executives/Personnel:
  Pat Finn, Executive Producer
  Ann Marie Griffith, Executive in Charge of Production
  Jana Morgan, Director of Development
Specialties: Television; Infomercials/Direct Response
Other Categories: TV; Music Video
Credits: Instant Comedy with the Groundlings; Soulmates
First Look/Development Deals: Universal Television & Networks Group

INDUSTRIAL LIGHT + MAGIC COMMERCIAL PRODUCTIONS
732 N. Highland Ave.
Hollywood, CA 90038
Phone: ....(323) 957-2002
Fax: ....(323) 464-8373
www.ilmcp.com
Key Executives/Personnel:
  Marcie Malooly, Executive Producer & Division Manager
  John Denis, Executive Producer
  Paul Grimshaw, Head of Production
Specialties: Television
Other Categories: Music Video; Interactive Multimedia
Credits: First Union; Toyota; Gatorade; Armor All

INFOMERCIAL SOLUTIONS, INC.
5512 Meadow Vista Way
Agoura Hills, CA 91301
Phone: ....(818) 879-1140
Fax: ....(818) 879-1148
www.infomercialsolutions.com
infosol2@aol.com
Key Executives/Personnel:
  David Schwartz, President
  Rosemary Kavanaugh, CEO
Specialties: Television; Infomercials/Direct Response
Other Categories: Video
Credits: HT Beauty System; Ashley of Beverly Hills; Jenny Craig Weight Loss; Psychic Friends Network; Cambridge Credit Corporation

INSTINCT PICTURES
520 Washington Blvd., Ste. 257
Marina Del Rey, CA 90292
Phone: ....(310) 578-9778
....(213) 426-7211
zenueg@yahoo.com
Specialties: Television
Other Categories: Feature Film; Music Video
Credits: The Shelter (feature); Best Buddies (PSA); APLA (PSA)

Production Companies – Commercials

INTELLISCAPE FILMS, LLC
11601 Wilshire Blvd., 5th Fl.
Los Angeles, CA 90025
Phone: ....(310) 235-1422
....(800) 422-5996
Fax: ....(800) 828-4330
www.intelliscapefilms.com
info@intelliscapefilms.com
Key Executives/Personnel:
   Bruce Caulk, Writer & Director
   Jeff Teitelman, Writer
Specialties: Television; Infomercials/Direct Response
Other Categories: TV; Video
Credits: San Diego Convention Visitors Bureau; Konami; National Financial Partners; Royal Family of Saudi Arabia (documentary)

INTERNATIONAL TELEVISION GROUP (ITG)
1322 Second St., Ste. 6
Santa Monica, CA 90401
Phone: ....(310) 656-9100
Fax: ....(310) 656-9104
intvg@aol.com
Key Executives/Personnel:
   Teresa Campbell, VP of Development & Production
   Lou La Monte, Producer
Specialties: Television
Other Categories: Feature Film; TV; Video
Credits: Cat on a Hot Tin Roof (1985); Uncle Wally's General Store

IPS PRODUCTIONS
3518 Cahuenga Blvd. West, Ste. 100
Los Angeles, CA 90068
Phone: ....(323) 851-3595
Fax: ....(323) 851-4679
oneips@aol.com
Key Executives/Personnel:
   Jim Sommers, President & Executive Producer
   Dennis McCullough, Producer
Specialties: Television
Other Categories: Video
Credits: Ford; Pontiac

JGF
1145 N. McCadden Pl.
Los Angeles, CA 90038
Phone: ....(323) 462-1500
Fax: ....(323) 462-1666
www.jgf.com
production@jgf.com
Key Executives/Personnel:
   Jeff Gorman, Director
   Gayleen Sharon, Executive Producer
   Laura Macauley, Head of Production
   Holly Ross, Sales Rep (LA)
   Messiler & Associates, Sales Rep (NY)
   Rabin, Moran & Rashford, Sales Reps (Chicago)
Specialties: Television
Credits: Reebok; ESPN; Staples; American Legacy (Anti-Tabacco)
Trade Assoc./Guilds/Unions: AICP

JKR PRODUCTIONS, INC.
12140 W. Olympic Blvd., Ste. 21
Los Angeles, CA 90064
Phone: ....(310) 826-3666
jimruxin@aol.com
Key Executives/Personnel:
   Jim Ruxin, Producer
Specialties: Promos
Other Categories: Feature Film; TV; Video
Credits: Stoogemania; Defense Play; In God We Trust
Trade Assoc./Guilds/Unions: DGA, IALocal700

THE JONESES
1501 Colorado Ave.
Santa Monica, CA 90404
Phone: ....(310) 656-8300
Fax: ....(310) 395-5102
Key Executives/Personnel:
   Dan Bryant, Executive Producer
   Ali Selim, Director
   Jim Manera, Director
Specialties: Television
Trade Assoc./Guilds/Unions: AICP

CAROLYN JUDD & ASSOCIATES, INC.
1332 3/4 Miller Dr.
West Hollywood, CA 90069
Phone: ....(323) 654-2571
Fax: ....(323) 654-7904
cjuddnow@aol.com
Key Executives/Personnel:
   Carolyn Judd, Producer & Director
Specialties: Television
Credits: Levi Jeans; Coca-Cola; Jeep; Chevy
Trade Assoc./Guilds/Unions: DGA

KABOOM
Phone: ....(415) 434-2666
Fax: ....(415) 837-0295
lauren@kaboomproductions.com
Key Executives/Personnel:
   Lauren Schwartz, Executive Producer
   Jim Barton, Director
   Mo Husseini, Director
   Liz Garman, Producer
   Jim Taylor, Office Manager
Specialties: Television
Credits: Milk Advisory Board; Storehouse Furniture; Cellular One; Dunkin' Donuts
Trade Assoc./Guilds/Unions: AICP

KANDOO FILMS, INC.
4515 Van Nuys Blvd., Ste. 100
Sherman Oaks, CA 91403
Phone: ....(818) 789-6777
Fax: ....(818) 789-2299
www.kandoofilms.com
info@kandoofilms.com
Specialties: Promos
Other Categories: Feature Film
Credits: CBS (promo); Mad About You (promo); Friends (promo)

KELLEY PRODUCTIONS INTERNATIONAL
2047 Caminito Capa
La Jolla, CA 92037
Phone: ....(858) 456-6609
Fax: ....(858) 459-5876
www.globalcuisine.com
Key Executives/Personnel:
   Marie G. Kelley, President
Specialties: Television
Other Categories: TV; Video
Trade Assoc./Guilds/Unions: ATAS, IDA, ITVA

KLASKY CSUPO, INC.
6353 Sunset Blvd.
Los Angeles, CA 90028
Phone: ....(323) 463-0145
www.klaskycsupo.com
Key Executives/Personnel:
   Gabor Csupo, Founder & Co-Chair
   Arlene Klasky, Founder & Co-Chair
   Terry Thoren, President & CEO
Specialties: Television

Production Companies – Commercials

Other Categories: Feature Film; TV
Credits: Rugrats; Duckman; The Simpsons; The Rugrats Movie

KONTRAST FILMS
315 W. Verdugo Ave.
Burbank, CA 91502
Phone: .... (818) 840-9333
Fax: .... (818) 840-9358
www.kontrastfilms.com
maureen@kontrastfilms.com
Key Executives/Personnel:
    Greg Gears, Producer
    Steven Kovner, VP of Production
    Maureen English, VP of Sales
    Valerio Ventura, Director
Specialties: Television; Infomercials/Direct Response; Promos
Other Categories: Feature Film; TV
Credits: Cart Racing (commercial)

KURTZ & FRIENDS
2312 W. Olive Ave.
Burbank, CA 91506
Phone: .... (818) 841-8188
Fax: .... (818) 841-6263
www.kurtzandfriends.com
bobkurtz@aol.com
Key Executives/Personnel:
    Bob Kurtz, Director, Writer & Designer
    Boo Lopez, Producer
    Robert Peluce, Designer & Director
Specialties: Television; Infomercials/Direct Response; Promos
Other Categories: Feature Film; TV
Credits: Smokey the Bear (commercial)

LA PRODUCTIONS
Phone: .... (323) 874-9487
.... (323) 871-1982
Fax: .... (323) 874-9487
Key Executives/Personnel:
    Herb Linsey, Executive Producer
    John Arnow, Executive Producer
    Stephen Paul, Executive Producer
    Thomas Cost, Executive Producer
Specialties: Television; Radio; Infomercials/Direct Response
Other Categories: Feature Film; TV; Music Video
Credits: Curad Bandages; Goodyear Tires; Johnson & Johnson; Wrangler Clothes

LEGACY FILMS
6311 Romaine St., Ste. 7204
Los Angeles, CA 90038
Phone: .... (323) 856-8888
Fax: .... (323) 856-8880
www.legacyfilms.net
legacyfm@pacbell.net
Key Executives/Personnel:
    Michelle Colbert, Executive Producer
    Mauricio Kuri, Director
    Bill Orisich, Director
    Eric Haywood, Director
    Bernard Gourley, Director
Specialties: Television
Other Categories: Music Video
Credits: The Athletes Foot; Pontiac; KMART; Dominos Pizza
Trade Assoc./Guilds/Unions: ACLA, MVPA

LET THERE BE LIGHT PRODUCTIONS
4240 Lost Hills Rd., Ste. 2801
Agoura Hills, CA 91301
Phone: .... (818) 880-4717
Fax: .... (818) 880-4717
littnet@cs.com

Key Executives/Personnel:
    Robert Litt, Producer
Specialties: Television; Radio; Infomercials/Direct Response; Promos
Other Categories: Feature Film; TV; Video; Music Video
Credits: Jenny Craig; WorldFreeNet.com; MPI/LA Tourism Bureau; Turbo - Take It To The Limit
First Look/Development Deals: Summer Storm Pictures

LEVEL 7 PRODUCTIONS
12307 Ventura Blvd., Ste. B
Studio City, CA 91604
Phone: .... (818) 754-0074
.... (213) 703-5555
Fax: .... (818) 754-0068
www.level7productions.com
levelseven@earthlink.net
Key Executives/Personnel:
    Larry Serraino, Executive Producer
    Rob Thomas, Director
    James Wvinner, Director
    Jon Fauer, Director
    Robert Starchfield, Director
Specialties: Television
Trade Assoc./Guilds/Unions: DGA

THE LIEBERMAN COMPANY
8330 W. Third St.
Los Angeles, CA 90048
Phone: .... (323) 782-0881
Fax: .... (323) 782-0777
Key Executives/Personnel:
    Craig Rodgers, Executive Producer
    Leslie Snow, Head of Production
Specialties: Television
Credits: Chevy; McDonald's; Disney

LIFE OF RILEY, INC.
845 Via De La Paz, Ste. 9
Pacific Palisades, CA 90272
Phone: .... (310) 230-7798
Fax: .... (310) 230-4552
lifeofriley@earthlink.net
Key Executives/Personnel:
    Dave Kleinman, Head of Production
    Paige Kamin, Executive Producer
    Duncan Sharp, Director
    Glenn Miller, Director
Specialties: Television
Credits: LA Cellular; Mitsubishi; Toyota Dealers

LIGHTNING BOLT PIX: BARNYARD PRODUCTIONS
1653 18th St., Ste. 3B
Santa Monica, CA 90404
Phone: .... (310) 828-8239
Fax: .... (310) 828-1923
www.boltpix.com
mwbfield@aol.com
Key Executives/Personnel:
    Michael Barnard, Owner, Producer & Director
    Morgan Barnard, Co-Owner, Director & Editor
    Philip DeVellis, Production Coordinator & Designer
Specialties: Television; Promos
Other Categories: TV; Video; Music Video
Credits: Bringing The Light; Chihuly River of Glass; Edgar.com; National Labor Life

LITTLE T TELEVISION
Phone: .... (323) 933-8733
Fax: .... (323) 933-8734
Key Executives/Personnel:
    Patricia Priest, Producer
Specialties: Television; Promos

Production Companies – Commercials

Trade Assoc./Guilds/Unions: DGA

LONG COAT PRODUCTIONS
10625 Esther Ave.
Los Angeles, CA 90064
Phone: ....(310) 815-8897
Fax: ....(310) 815-1269
serendip@concentric.net
Key Executives/Personnel:
    Karen Anderson, Producer
Specialties: Television
Credits: Anheuser-Busch; McDonald's; Ralston Purina; Mountain Dew

LONGBOARD PRODUCTIONS, INC.
P.O. Box 2130
Elk Grove, CA 95759
Phone: ....(916) 684-5085
 ....(916) 825-5390
Fax: ....(916) 684-5085
longboardproductions.com
fbernhardt@jps.net
Key Executives/Personnel:
    Ernie Cabral, President, Producer & Screenwriter
    Fred Bernhardt, VP, CFO & Producer
    Roland Ozzie Smith, VP, DP & Producer
    Michael Dryhurst, Producer
Specialties: Television
Other Categories: Feature Film
First Look/Development Deals: Digital Magic Company

LOTUS FILMS
6063 Sunset Blvd.
Los Angeles, CA 90028
Phone: ....(626) 292-1015
 ....(626) 695-1112
Fax: ....(626) 292-1002
www.lotusfilms.com
lotusfilms@excite.com
Key Executives/Personnel:
    Dawn Fanning, Producer
    Mark Taylor, Director
    Gail Brooks, Director
    Paul McIlvaine, Director of Photography
Specialties: Television
Other Categories: Feature Film
Credits: Room (short); Forever (short); McDonald's

LUCID MEDIA
Phone: ....(818) 764-8580
www.loop.com/~macbravo
macbravo@loop.com
Key Executives/Personnel:
    Marino Colmano, Producer
Specialties: Television; Infomercials/Direct Response
Other Categories: Feature Film; TV; Video
Credits: Reservoirs of Strength; End of the Rainbow

LUMINATION INC.
12356 Laurel Terrace Dr.
Studio City, CA 91604
Phone: ....(818) 766-1868
Fax: ....(818) 762-4866
lumin8ion@email.msn.com
Key Executives/Personnel:
    Alvin Mori, Executive Producer
    Meg Okura, Producer
Specialties: Television
Other Categories: TV
Credits: Honda; Big John Jeans

LUMINOSITY PRODUCTIONS
4220 Lankershim Blvd., 3rd Fl.
North Hollywood, CA 91602
Phone: ....(818) 752-3318
 ....(310) 620-0403
Fax: ....(818) 752-3311
www.luminosityprod.com
marla@luminosityprod.com
Key Executives/Personnel:
    Marla Friedler, Executive Producer
    Debbie Pinckes, Production Rep.
    Michael Kahn, Director
    Johnathan Kahn, Director
    Gregg Marquette, Director
    Pascal Franchot, Director
    Matthew Curry, Director
    David Kennedy, Director
Specialties: Television; Radio
Other Categories: Feature Film
Credits: Planned Parenthood; Apponline; Protest Clothing
Additional Info: 219 Broadway, Ste. 209, Laguna Beach, CA 92651

LUX PICTURES, INC.
120 Mildred Ave.
Venice, CA 90291
Phone: ....(310) 301-0101
Fax: ....(310) 301-0153
www.luxpix.com
Key Executives/Personnel:
    James Magowan, President & Executive Producer
    Fiona Banister, Sr. Executive Producer & Partner
    Martin Kistler, Sr. Producer
    Mark Ching, Producer
Specialties: Television; Promos
Other Categories: Feature Film
Credits: Charles E. Merril: An American Tycoon

LYON STUDIOS
Phone: ....(949) 723-0657
 ....(949) 640-6246
Fax: ....(949) 640-6518
wwiles1430@aol.com
Key Executives/Personnel:
    William C. Wiles, Producer
Specialties: Television
Other Categories: Video
Credits: National Car Rental; Valvoline Motor Oil; Canon Copiers; Giant Foods

M-80 FILMS
409 Santa Monica Blvd.
Santa Monica, CA 90401
Phone: ....(310) 899-9100
Fax: ....(310) 394-2903
gstern@m80films.com
Key Executives/Personnel:
    Greg Stern, Executive Producer
    Glenn Rudolph, Producer (freelance)
    Tony Mosa, Producer (freelance)
    Mathew McManus, Head of Production
    Vanessa Hadibrata, Production Manager
Specialties: Television
Credits: Rice Krispies Treats; Arizona Jeans; Lipton; Sony Playstation

MAD HEART
P.O. Box 17652
Beverly Hills, CA 90209
Phone: ....(323) 938-1488
madheart@mediaone.net
Key Executives/Personnel:
    Lisa Phillips, Producer
Specialties: Television
Credits: BMW; Pantene; Goodyear Tires; Ikea

Production Companies – Commercials

MAKE IT HAPPEN PRODUCTIONS, INC.
Phone: ....(323) 851-6444
Fax: ....(323) 851-6465
www.billyfrank.com
mihpi@aol.com
Key Executives/Personnel:
　Billy Frank, President & Producer
　Todd Denkin, Director & Producer
　Mark Eberle, Director of Photography
　Caroline Hileman, Assistant to President & Coordinator
Specialties: Television; Radio; Infomercials/Direct Response; Promos
Other Categories: Feature Film; TV; Video; Music Video
Credits: Wap!; Toughman (specials); Australian Experience
First Look/Development Deals: ABC Entertainment Television Group, FX Networks, LLC
Trade Assoc./Guilds/Unions: SAG, WGAw

CHARLES MALCOLM VIDEO PRODUCTIONS
P.O. Box 1772
Newport Beach, CA 92646
Phone: ....(714) 963-4222
charlesmalcolm@yahoo.com
Key Executives/Personnel:
　Charles Malcolm, Owner
Specialties: Television
Other Categories: Feature Film; Video

JOHN MARIAS PRODUCTIONS
709 21st St.
Santa Monica, CA 90402
Phone: ....(310) 394-4214
　...(310) 245-4204
Fax: ....(310) 395-2590
johnmarias@aol.com
Key Executives/Personnel:
　John Marias, Producer
Specialties: Television
Credits: Mercedes-Benz; Coca-Cola; Chevrolet; Levi's
Trade Assoc./Guilds/Unions: DGA

MARIPOSA
Phone: ....(805) 527-9990
Fax: ....(805) 527-9990
www.surfbit.com
nadar@pacbell.net
Key Executives/Personnel:
　Bridget Gardner, Director & Producer
　Carole Gardner, Production Manager
Specialties: Television; PSA's
Other Categories: Feature Film; Interactive Multimedia
Credits: American Cancer Society; NAMES Project; MADD; SurfBit.com

MARS MEDIA, INC.
3630 Eastham Blvd.
Culver City, CA 90232
Phone: ....(310) 664-6760
Fax: ....(310) 396-2128
Key Executives/Personnel:
　Stavros Merjos, President
　Bill Sandwich, Executive Producer
　Kerstin Emhott, Executive Producer
　Steve Ross, Executive Producer
　Tracie Norfleet, Executive Producer
　Rebecca Skinner, Sr. Executive Producer of Music Videos
　Ericka Panko, Executive Producer of Music Videos
　Alisa Ratner, Head of Production, Music Videos
　Jessica Thomas, Sales
　Inga Veronique, Sales (NY)
Specialties: Television
Other Categories: Music Video

MATRIX COMMUNICATIONS
2522 Torrance Blvd.
Torrance, CA 90503
Phone: ....(310) 782-8400
Key Executives/Personnel:
　Marta Houske, Executive Producer & Director
Specialties: Television
Other Categories: Feature Film; Video; Music Video; Interactive Multimedia
Credits: Zimbabwe Legit (music video); A Stitch in Time (documentary); Times Mirror (commercial); In Search of ... (TV series)

ROSS MCCANSE & ASSOCIATES, INC.
3315 Oakdell Rd.
Studio City, CA 91604
Phone: ....(818) 506-4715
Fax: ....(818) 506-4587
Key Executives/Personnel:
　Ross McCanse, Director
Specialties: Television; Radio
Credits: Dianne Feinstein For U.S Senate (CA); Richard Riordian For L.A. Mayor; Chuck Schumer For U.S. Senate (NY); Tom Menino For Mayor (Boston, MA)

MEGAHERTZ PICTURES
1600 Rosecrans Ave., Bldg. 2B, 1st. Fl.
Manhattan Beach, CA 90266
Phone: ....(310) 727-2600
Fax: ....(310) 727-2601
www.directorsite.com
megahertz@directorsite.com
Key Executives/Personnel:
　John Harris, Executive Producer
　Francis Mohajerin, Executive Producer
　Suzanne O'Keefe, Producer & Writer
　Masashi Nagadoi, Producer & Writer
Specialties: Television; Infomercials/Direct Response; Promos
Other Categories: Feature Film; Video
Credits: She Said I Love You

MEKANISM
600 Townsend, Ste. 300
San Francisco, CA 94103
Phone: ....(415) 252-5331
　...(415) 412-7545
Fax: ....(415) 621-6780
www.mekanism.tv
tmeans@mekanism.tv
Key Executives/Personnel:
　Tommy Means, Executive Producer
　Ken Solomon, Business Development
　Tuesday McGowen, Creative Director
　Jim Bartel, CTO
　Kurt Noble, Technical Director
Specialties: Television
Other Categories: Interactive Multimedia
Credits: Rock The Vote Yes/No 2000

CAREY MELCHER PRODUCTIONS, INC.
639 N. Larchmont Blvd., Ste. 202
Los Angeles, CA 90004
Phone: ....(323) 962-7020
Fax: ....(323) 962-7511
Key Executives/Personnel:
　Carey Melcher, Producer
Specialties: Television
Credits: Albertsons; Sears; Williams Communication; Coors

MESITA
11005 Wrightwood Pl.
Studio City, CA 91604

Production Companies – Commercials

Phone: (818) 760-8707
Fax: (818) 760-0925
mesitafilms@aol.com
Key Executives/Personnel:
  Richard Black, Director & Cameraman
  Jeremy Hammond, Executive Producer
  Darr Hawthorne, Representative
Specialties: Television
Other Categories: TV
Credits: California Tourism Board; Hawaii Tourism Board; Celebrity Cruises; American Express

METRO PICTURES
3409 Strongs Dr.
Marina Del Rey, CA 90292
Phone: (310) 301-7890
Fax: (310) 301-7891
www.metropics.com
metropic@aol.com
Key Executives/Personnel:
  Craig Farkas, Executive Producer
  Tracy Bowser, Office Manager
  Larry Shiu, Director & Cameraman
  Brian Lai, Director & Cameraman
  David Lena, Director & Cameraman
  Phil Brown, Director
  Richard Lowenstein, Director
  Lynn-Maree Milburn, Director
  Spencer Antle, Director
  Paul Loosely, Director
  Steven Ang, Director
Specialties: Television
Credits: Panasonic; Hyundai; Coca-Cola; Virgin Records
Trade Assoc./Guilds/Unions: AICP, DGA

THE MILLER ENTERTAINMENT GROUP, INC.
5900 Wilshire Blvd., Ste. 540
Los Angeles, CA 90036
Phone: (323) 932-6500
Key Executives/Personnel:
  Lawrence Miller, President
  Ty Supancic, VP
Specialties: Infomercials/Direct Response
Other Categories: Feature Film; Music Video
Credits: Deadly Currency (feature); Sallie B - Baby Mama (music video); Nick Frost - Deep Love (music video); Regatta Condominium (infomercial)
Trade Assoc./Guilds/Unions: SAG

MIRELLA FILM CO.
6561 Franklin Ave.
Los Angeles, CA 90028
Phone: (323) 850-5522
Fax: (323) 850-5527
mirellafilm@earthlink.net
Key Executives/Personnel:
  Kelli McDowell, Executive Producer
  Robin White, Office Manager
  Michael Cerny, Director
  Michael Sitzer, East Coast Rep
  Tim Hanwood, Midwest Rep
  Patty Everett, West Coast Rep
Specialties: Television
Credits: Pillsbury; Ford; Blue Cross; State Farm
Trade Assoc./Guilds/Unions: AICP

MISS JONES
1558 Tenth St.
Santa Monica, CA 90401
Phone: (310) 576-9280
Fax: (310) 576-0515
www.missjones.com
tracy@missjones.com
Key Executives/Personnel:
  Tracy Hauser, Executive Producer
  Bronwen LaGrue, Executive Producer
Specialties: Television
Other Categories: Feature Film
Credits: iCast.com; Arthritis Foundation (PSA); ESPN; Kleenex

MM2K
838 N. Doheny Dr., Ste. 904
West Hollywood, CA 90069
Phone: (310) 276-0750
Fax: (310) 276-0229
mm2k@earthlink.net
Key Executives/Personnel:
  William A. Levey, Executive Producer & Director
  Bob Manning, Head of Production
  Nancy Youngblood, Director of Creative Development
Specialties: Promos
Other Categories: Feature Film; TV; Video; Music Video
Credits: Slumber Party 57; The Happy Hooker Goes To Washington; Skatetown U.S.A; White Stallion
Trade Assoc./Guilds/Unions: DGA, IATSE, WGAw

MO JO PRODUCTIONS, INC.
4224 Waialae Ave., Ste. 300
Honolulu, HI 96816
Phone: (808) 384-8460
 (626) 932-6432
Fax: (808) 733-4142
mojoproductions@juno.com
Key Executives/Personnel:
  Michael Pendell, President
Specialties: Television; Infomercials/Direct Response; Promos
Other Categories: Feature Film; TV; Music Video
Credits: Baywatch: Hawaii; Extended list available upon request.
Trade Assoc./Guilds/Unions: DGA

MORTON JANKEL ZANDER, INC.
2201 Carmelina Ave.
Los Angeles, CA 90064
Phone: (310) 826-6200
Fax: (310) 826-6219
saranda@mjz.com
Key Executives/Personnel:
  David Zander, President
  Jeff Scruton, Sr. Executive Producer
  Lisa Rich, Executive Producer
  Rocky Morton, Director
  Annabel Jankel, Director
  Irv Blitz, Director
  Jonathan David, Director
  Robert Richardson, Director
  Sean Thonson, Director
  Kieran Walsh, Director
  Tom DeCerchio, Director
  Victor Garcia, Director
  Marcus Nispel, Director
  Craig Gillespie, Director
Specialties: Television
Credits: Fox Sports; Burger King; Hallmark; Mercedes-Benz
Trade Assoc./Guilds/Unions: DGA, IATSE

MOVING IMAGE
8748 Holloway Dr.
West Hollywood, CA 90069
Phone: (310) 659-8022
Fax: (310) 659-8095
production@moving-image.net
Key Executives/Personnel:
  Orlando Leal, Owner & Director
  Luis Aira, Owner & Director

Production Companies – Commercials

Pavel Cantù, Owner & Director
Francisco Pugliese, Director
Angel, Director
Specialties: Television
Credits: AT&T; McDonald's; Honda; Toyota
Additional Info: Hispanic & Latin Commercials

MOVING TARGET
1250 Sixth St., Ste. 201
Santa Monica, CA 90401
Phone: ...(310) 394-0110
Fax: ...(310) 394-4123
Specialties: Television
Other Categories: Feature Film; TV
Credits: Sleepy Hollow; The Others

MOXIE PICTURES
1040 N. Sycamore Ave.
Hollywood, CA 90038
Phone: ...(323) 957-5420
Fax: ...(323) 466-1343
www.moxiepictures.com
moxiepictures@moxiepictures.com
Key Executives/Personnel:
Gary Rose, Executive Producer
Dan Levinson, President
Kristen Wageman, Head of Production
Lizzie Schwartz, Executive Producer
Specialties: Television; Radio; Infomercials/Direct Response; Promos
Other Categories: Music Video
Credits: Coca-Cola; McDonald's; Levi's; Savage Garden

MPH FILMS
409 Santa Monica Blvd.
Santa Monica, CA 90401
Phone: ...(310) 395-9952
Fax: ...(310) 395-8224
djb@mphfilms.com
Key Executives/Personnel:
Diane Leuci, Producer
Gabrielle Yuro-Vickers, Producer
Janie Walter, Producer
Janice Doskey, Producer
Donna DiStefano, Executive Producer
Specialties: Television
Credits: Hyundai; Volvo; Citracal; Nicoderm

MUSIC ROOM PICTURES
P.O. Box 219
Redondo Beach, CA 90277
Phone: ...(310) 316-4551
Fax: ...(310) 540-3532
www.musicroomonline.com
mrp@aol.com
Key Executives/Personnel:
John Reed, President
Specialties: Television; Promos
Other Categories: Feature Film; Video; Music Video

NEMIROFF PRODUCTIONS
1506 Butler Ave., Ste. 1
Los Angeles, CA 90025
Phone: ...(310) 473-4100
...(310) 917-5250
Fax: ...(310) 473-4100
Key Executives/Personnel:
Steve Nemiroff, Producer & Assistant Director
Specialties: Television; Infomercials/Direct Response; Promos
Other Categories: Feature Film; TV; Video; Music Video; Interactive Multimedia
Credits: The Real Deal; Miracles; Sparkletts; Kenny Kingston's Psychic Hotline III

Trade Assoc./Guilds/Unions: AFI; AICP; ITVA

NEW MILLENNIUM STUDIOS
One New Millenium Dr.
Petersburg, VA 23805
Phone: ...(804) 957-4200
Fax: ...(804) 862-1200
www.nmstudios.com
martinj@nmstudios.com
Key Executives/Personnel:
Tim Reid, Producer
Daphne Maxwell Reid, Producer
Martin C. Jones, Producer
Specialties: Television
Other Categories: Feature Film; TV; Music Video; Interactive Multimedia
Credits: Asunder; Out of Sync; Linc's; When We Were Colored

NITESTAR PRODUCTIONS
6671 Sunset Blvd., Bldg. 1509, Ste. 104
Los Angeles, CA 90028
Phone: ...(323) 468-8089
Fax: ...(323) 468-8094
www.nitestar.com
jvasilatos@nitestar.com
Key Executives/Personnel:
Jerry A. Vasilatos, President, Producer, Director & Editor
John O'Shaugnessy, Videographer & Cinematographer
Kevin Leadingham, Associate Producer & Director
Specialties: Promos
Other Categories: Feature Film; Video
Credits: Shelter Me; A Refugee & Me; Solstice

NO PRISONERS
2260 S. Centinela Ave.
Los Angeles, CA 90064
Phone: ...(310) 979-9097
Fax: ...(310) 979-7097
www.noprisoners.net
info@noprisoners.net
Key Executives/Personnel:
Todd Moyer, CEO & Producer
Chris Brown, Visual Effects Supervisor
Erik Strauss, Visual Effects Producer
Bruce Martin, President of Commercials
Nic Mathieu, Director
Brian Scott Weber, Director
Michael Abbott, Creative Executive
Jim McCarthy, Controller
Specialties: Television
Other Categories: Feature Film; Music Video
Credits: Wing Commander (feature); Mercedes-Benz (commercial); The FireFlies (feature); Mai: The Psychic Girl (feature)

NONFICTION SPOTS
621 Broadway
Santa Monica, CA 90401
Phone: ...(310) 319-6140
Fax: ...(310) 656-9881
www.nonfictionspots.com
nonfiction@spots.net
Key Executives/Personnel:
Loretta Jeneski, Executive Producer
Michael Degan, Executive Producer
Specialties: Television
Credits: Madison Square Garden Network; Ford/Susan Kemen Foundation; Fox Sports Networks; Reebok

NOVA PICTURES
6496 Ivarene Ave.
Los Angeles, CA 90068
Phone: ...(323) 462-5502

Production Companies – Commercials

Fax: ....(323) 467-1438
www.novapictures.com
pbarnett@novapictures.com
Key Executives/Personnel:
  Peter Barnett, Producer
  Chris Debie, Unit Production Manager
Specialties: Television
Other Categories: Feature Film; TV
Credits: Extraordinary Visitor; Yellow Badge of Courage; Valley Clinic (commercial)
Trade Assoc./Guilds/Unions: ATAS, IFP

NXT ENTERTAINMENT
8639 Holloway Plaza Dr.
Los Angeles, CA 90069
Phone: ....(310) 289-9600
Fax: ....(310) 289-7383
www.wwwcine.com
nxt@wwwcine.com
Key Executives/Personnel:
  Klaus Lucka, Executive Producer
Specialties: Television; Promos
Other Categories: Feature Film; TV; Video; Interactive Multimedia
Credits: www.cyberkidsplanet.com; www.neobodies.com
Trade Assoc./Guilds/Unions: DGA

NYDRLE
670 N. La Peer Dr.
West Hollywood, CA 90069
Phone: ....(310) 659-8844
Fax: ....(310) 659-7733
www.nydrle.com
nydrle@nydrle.com
Key Executives/Personnel:
  Laura Heflin, Executive Producer
  Peter Nydrle, Director
Specialties: Television
Trade Assoc./Guilds/Unions: AICP

OCTOBER PRODUCTIONS
122 E. Arrellaga
Santa Barbara, CA 93101
Phone: ....(805) 962-2523
Fax: ....(805) 650-0704
octprod@pacbell.net
Key Executives/Personnel:
  Richard Hughes, Producer, Writer & Director
Specialties: Television; Infomercials/Direct Response
Other Categories: TV; Video
Credits: G.M.; Toshiba; JCPenney; Mentor
Trade Assoc./Guilds/Unions: DGA

OMAHA PICTURES
1658 Tenth St.
Santa Monica, CA 90404
Phone: ....(310) 396-4333
Fax: ....(310) 396-4323
omahala@omahapictures.com
Key Executives/Personnel:
  Greg Ferguson, Executive Producer
  Diane McArter, Managing Director
  Paul Gay, Director
  David McNally, Director
  Michael Grasso, Director
  Robin Armstrong, Director
  Rupert Sanders, Director
  Peter Goldschmidt, Director
  Pia Alexander, Sales Representative
Specialties: Television
Credits: Nike; American Express; Anheuser-Busch; BlueNile.com
Trade Assoc./Guilds/Unions: AICP

ONESUCH FILMS
425 N. Robertson Blvd.
Los Angeles, CA 90048
Phone: ....(310) 273-3200
Fax: ....(310) 273-0868
info@onesuch.com
Key Executives/Personnel:
  Brian Donnelly, Executive Producer
  Fran Wall, Head of Production
  Bruce Nadel, Director
  Bill Scarlet, Director
  John St. Clair, Director
  Debra Roberts Sher, Sales Representative
Specialties: Television

ONYX PRODUCTIONS, INC.
5550 Wilshire Blvd., Ste. 301
Los Angeles, CA 90036
Phone: ....(323) 692-9830
Fax: ....(323) 692-9832
onyxprod@aol.com
Key Executives/Personnel:
  Joan Renfrow, President
Specialties: Television; Infomercials/Direct Response
Other Categories: Video
Credits: Ron Popeil's Automatic Pasta Maker; Hoover; Thighmaster Plus; Gary Player Gran Prix Irons
Additional Info: Specializes in DRTV

ORBIT ENTERTAINMENT GROUP
714 N. La Brea Ave.
Hollywood, CA 90038
Phone: ....(323) 525-2626
Fax: ....(323) 525-2627
dror@orbiteg.com
Key Executives/Personnel:
  Dror Soref, Partner, President & Director
  Lee Nelson, Partner & Executive Producer
  Lynne Pateman, Executive Producer
  Kevin Moreton, VP of Orbit Pictures
  Jeremy White, Executive Creative Director
Specialties: Television; Infomercials/Direct Response; Promos
Other Categories: Feature Film; Interactive Multimedia
Credits: Oldsmobile (commercial); Sony (commercial); K-Swiss (commercial); The Seventh Coin (feature)

OUR GANG PRODUCTIONS
8522 National Blvd., Ste. 107
Culver City, CA 90232
Phone: ....(310) 300-1010
Fax: ....(310) 636-8304
ourgangproductions@earthlink.net
Key Executives/Personnel:
  Gayle Gluck, President
  Kevin Miller, Sr. VP & Creative Director
  Chris Conway, Audio Production
  Matt Fisher, Supervising Editor
  Ron Mesa, Chief Audio Engineer
  Rachel Burkes, Production Assistant
Specialties: Television; Promos
Other Categories: TV; Music Video; Interactive Multimedia

OUR PRODUCTIONS, INC.
6255 Sunset Blvd., Ste. 2201
Hollywood, CA 90028
Phone: ....(323) 465-4197
....(818) 816-7332
Fax: ....(323) 465-6549
www.ourproduction.com
patricia@ourproduction.com
Key Executives/Personnel:
  Rick Munoz, Director & Producer

Production Companies – Commercials

Patricia Bolt, Director of Marketing & Production
Specialties: Television; Infomercials/Direct Response; Promos
Other Categories: Feature Film; TV; Video; Music Video
Credits: Natalie Cole Live at The Coliseum; The Miller Brewing Company; Winchell's Donuts

OVATION ENTERTAINMENT
Phone: ....(310) 344-1442
ovationmail@yahoo.com
Key Executives/Personnel:
   Steve Woroniecki, Producer
Specialties: Television
Other Categories: Video; Music Video

PACIFIC STAR PRODUCTIONS
146 N. La Brea Ave.
Los Angeles, CA 90036
Phone: ....(310) 450-5258
  ....(310) 995-1840
Fax: ....(323) 936-8037
pacifstr@aol.com
Key Executives/Personnel:
   Philip J. Brown, Executive Producer
Specialties: Television
Credits: Ford; Dodge; Lincoln/Mercury; Chevrolet
Trade Assoc./Guilds/Unions: AICP

EDWARD PACIO & ASSOCIATES
Phone: ....(818) 880-1586
  ....(310) 560-9221
Fax: ....(818) 880-1001
epacio@earthlink.net
Key Executives/Personnel:
   Edward Pacio, Producer & Director
   Chip Payne, Producer & DP
   Kevin Ford, Art Director
Specialties: Television; Radio; Infomercials/Direct Response; Promos
Other Categories: Video
Credits: Prevent-A-Theft; Lasik Vision; Healthy Hair
Additional Info: P.O. Box 1363, Pacific Palisades, CA 90272

GEORGE PAIGE ASSOCIATES, INC.
3000 W. Olympic Blvd., Ste. 1407
Santa Monica, CA 90404
Phone: ....(310) 315-4835
Fax: ....(310) 315-4836
gpacorp@aol.com
Key Executives/Personnel:
   George Paige, Owner & President
   James R. Tumminia, Producer
Specialties: Television; Infomercials/Direct Response
Other Categories: Feature Film; TV; Video; Music Video; Interactive Multimedia
Credits: Abbott & Costello Meet Jerry Seinfeld; 50 Years of Funny Females; Shafted
Trade Assoc./Guilds/Unions: ATAS

PEARSON TELEVISION
2700 Colorado Ave., Ste. 450
Santa Monica, CA 90404
Phone: ....(310) 656-1100
  ....(415) 856-8089
Fax: ....(310) 255-4800
Key Executives/Personnel:
   Brian Harris, President & CEO, Pearson TV North America/
      CEO, Pearson TV Int'l.
   Bill Lincoln, COO
   Matthew Loze, President of Production, Drama & Long-Form
   Sara Rutenberg, President of Business Development & Strategy
   Catherine Mackay, President of Pearson Television Enterprises (NY)
   Syd Vinnedge, Sr. Executive VP of North American Productions
   Lou Festa, CFO (NY)
   Rand Stoll, Executive VP of Programming (NY)
   Cecile Frot-Coutaz, Executive VP of Digital Media (San Francisco)
   Paul Pavlis, Executive VP & General Counsel
   Gaby Johnston, Sr. VP of Light Entertainment
   Dana Walker, VP of Business & Legal Affairs
   Dan Watanabe, VP of Current Programming
   Kim Stratton, Director of Clip Licensing
Specialties: Television
Additional Info: 444 Spear St., San Francisco, CA 94105
   1330 Avenue of the Americas, New York, NY 10019

PERSEVERANCE PRODUCTIONS
Phone: ....(310) 306-1960
Fax: ....(310) 306-1820
buddywins@aol.com
Specialties: Television; Promos
Other Categories: Video; Music Video
Credits: Ford; Pfizer; Alamo; Rite Aid
Trade Assoc./Guilds/Unions: DGA

PERSPECTIVE FILMS
Phone: ....(310) 670-4030
  ....(310) 261-8389
Fax: ....(310) 670-4031
Key Executives/Personnel:
   Debbie Pietsch, Executive Producer
Specialties: Television; Radio; Infomercials/Direct Response; Promos
Other Categories: Feature Film; TV; Video; Music Video; Interactive Multimedia
Credits: Fast Point DSL; Mattel; Disney; Harman Kardan: MacWorld

PHILMCO
P.O. Box 461783
Los Angeles, CA 90046
Phone: ....(213) 399-7624
philmco@earthlink.net
Key Executives/Personnel:
   Philip A. Mondello, Producer
Specialties: Television; Promos
Other Categories: Feature Film

PICTURE PARK
2940 Nebraska Ave.
Santa Monica, CA 90404
Phone: ....(310) 315-1949
  ....(617) 536-1949
Fax: ....(310) 315-9749
www.picturepk.com
Key Executives/Personnel:
   Mark Hawkey, Executive Producer & Owner
   Bill Near, Executive Producer
   Rosser Goodman, Production Manager
Specialties: Television
Credits: Fighting Force 2; Blue Shield of California; Shell Oil; McDonald's

PIPER PRODUCTIONS
2017 Pacific Ave., Ste. 6
Venice, CA 90291
Phone: ....(310) 883-8822
  ....(212) 352-1999
Fax: ....(310) 822-8597
www.piperproductions.com
piperla@earthlink.net
Key Executives/Personnel:
   Sarah Jenks, Managing Director
   Katy Greene, Executive Producer
   Nick Hippisley-Coxe, Executive Producer
   Paul Arden, Director
   Jonathan Darby, Director
   Hugh Hudson, Director
   Ian Leech, Director & Cameraman
   Kristian Levering, Director

Production Companies – Commercials

Iain MacKenzie, Director
Kevin Molony, Director
Pelle Seth, Director
Eric Yealland, Director
Specialties: Television
Trade Assoc./Guilds/Unions: AICP

PLUM PRODUCTIONS
2202 Main St.
Santa Monica, CA 90405
Phone: ....(310) 450-1942
Fax: ....(310) 450-9424
www.plumprod.com
plum@plumprod.com
Key Executives/Personnel:
Chuck Sloan, Executive Producer & Owner
Eric Saarinen, Owner & Director
Thom Tyson, Executive Producer
Shelby Sexton, Production Executive
Jan De Bont, Director
Nick Broomfield, Director
Nick Piper, Director
Bob Rice, Director
Alisa Allen, Controller
Specialties: Television
Credits: Chevrolet; Pepsi/Mountain Dew; Dodge; Canon

PMC PICTURES
710 Wilshire Blvd., Ste. 500
Santa Monica, CA 90401
Phone: ....(310) 656-3255
Fax: ....(310) 656-3261
doug@pmcglobal.com
Key Executives/Personnel:
Doug Dilge, Executive Producer (LA)
Specialties: Television; Promos

POINT OF VIEW PRODUCTIONS
2477 Folsom St.
San Francisco, CA 94110
Phone: ....(415) 821-0435
....(415) 227-9292
Fax: ....(415) 931-0948
www.wenet.net/~karil/about.html
karil@wenet.net
Key Executives/Personnel:
Karil Daniels, Producer & Director
Specialties: Television; Infomercials/Direct Response; Promos
Other Categories: TV; Video

POLESTAR FILM & PHOTOGRAPHIC PRODUCTION
P.O. Box 2269
Los Angeles, CA 90078
Phone: ....(323) 851-5488
....(323) 791-7204
Fax: ....(323) 851-9006
polstar@att.net
Key Executives/Personnel:
James Peters, Producer
Specialties: Television; Promos
Other Categories: Video
Credits: BMW; L & M Cigarettes; Ford; Chevrolet

PONGO PRODUCTIONS
Phone: ....(818) 562-3336
Fax: ....(818) 562-3337
www.gopongo.com
pongoprod@aol.com
Key Executives/Personnel:
Thomas J. McGough, CEO
Jon Mingle, Partner
Specialties: Promos

Other Categories: Feature Film

POP/ART FILM FACTORY
513 Wilshire Blvd., Ste. 215
Santa Monica, CA 90401
Phone: ....(310) 260-2868
....(310) 288-6815
www.home.earthlink.net
dzpff@earthlink.net
Key Executives/Personnel:
Daniel Zirilli, Executive Producer & Director
Specialties: Television
Other Categories: Feature Film; Music Video
Credits: Winner Takes All; Rolling Stones - Voodoo Lounge; Avirex Clothing; Freddie Jackson - I Want to Thank You

PORTER FILM COMPANY
6427 Sunset Blvd.
Los Angeles, CA 90066
Phone: ....(323) 962-7855
Fax: ....(323) 962-8028
www.porterfilm.com
pfc@porterfilm.com
Key Executives/Personnel:
Fred Porter, Executive Producer
J. Brown, Director
Matt Murphy, Director
Carlo Sigon, Director
Kimble Rendall, Director
Specialties: Television

POST MODERN EDIT
1211 E. Dyer Rd., Ste. 110
Santa Ana, CA 92705
Phone: ....(714) 751-2681
Fax: ....(714) 751-2686
www.postmodernedit.com
info@postmodernedit.com
Key Executives/Personnel:
Scott Cain, Director of Production
Tim Pendergrass, Sr. Producer
Jim Reed, Sr. Staff Editor
Rick Warren, Executive VP of Marketing & Operations
Janice Daniello, VP of Sales
Jason Syzmanski, VP of Operations
Tony Kost, Director of Axillary Marketing
Specialties: Television; Infomercials/Direct Response
Other Categories: Video
Credits: Canon Computer Systems; Rockwell Collins Passenger Systems; Dominion Alarm; Orange Co. Water District
Trade Assoc./Guilds/Unions: Media Alliance of Orange County

PRODUCERS GROUP, LTD.
713 S. Pacific Coast Hwy., Ste. B
Redondo Beach, CA 90277
Phone: ....(310) 316-0481
Fax: ....(310) 316-1482
producers_group@csi.com
Key Executives/Personnel:
Lee Gluckman, President & Executive Producer
Ted Raynor, Executive VP of Legal Affairs & Executive Producer
Specialties: Television
Other Categories: Feature Film; TV; Video
Credits: After The Red Star; Kids Are Cooking; Chicago Heist; San Miguel
Trade Assoc./Guilds/Unions: AFTRA, SAG

PRODUCTION ANALYSIS CORPORATION
Phone: ....(323) 876-6186
goodadvice@earthlink.net
Key Executives/Personnel:
Martin Pitts, Producer
Specialties: Television; Radio; Promos

Production Companies – Commercials

Other Categories: Feature Film; TV; Video; Music Video
Credits: Wild California; The Full Moon Show with Robbie Robertson; The Bee Gees Live Concert Video

THE PRODUCTION ASYLUM
Phone: ....(760) 599-5494
Fax: ....(760) 439-6688
productionsasylum@aol.com
Key Executives/Personnel:
  Amy Krause, Producer & President
  Cat Sautter, Producer, VP & Treasurer
Specialties: Television; Radio
Other Categories: Video
Trade Assoc./Guilds/Unions: AFTRA, SAG

PROLETARIAT FILMWORKS
12165 Iredell St.
Studio City, CA 91604
Phone: ....(818) 763-8356
Fax: ....(818) 760-6584
proletfilm@aol.com
Key Executives/Personnel:
  Terry Moloney, Executive Producer
  Grant Gilmore, Line Producer
  Liam Kildare, Producer
Specialties: Television; Infomercials/Direct Response; Promos
Other Categories: Feature Film; TV; Video; Music Video
Credits: Tourette Syndrome Foundation (PSA); Elvis 2000: A Video Scrapbook; Warner Music: Wallstreet; Shout for Antz
Trade Assoc./Guilds/Unions: AFTRA, SAG

PROPAGANDA FILMS
940 N. Mansfield Ave
Los Angeles, CA 90038
Phone: ....(323) 462-6400
....(212) 982-1700
Fax: ....(323) 463-7874
www.propagandafilms.com
Key Executives/Personnel:
  Rick Hess, President
  Trevor Macy, COO
  Severin White, CFO
  Paul Schiff, Producer
  Pat Dollard, Co-Head, Management Division
  Lisa Franklin, Head of Legal Affairs
  Beth Holden, Co-Head, Management Division
  Brian Oliver, Director of Production
  Sam Walsh, Head of Production
Specialties: Television
Other Categories: Feature Film; Music Video
Credits: Fight Club; Being John Malkovich; Seven; Portrait of a Lady
Additional Info: 902 Broadway, Ste. 1603, New York, NY 10010

PROUD MARY ENTERTAINMENT
433 N. Camden Dr., Ste. 600
Beverly Hills, CA 90210
Phone: ....(310) 288-1886
Fax: ....(310) 288-1801
proudmaryent@earthlink.net
Key Executives/Personnel:
  Mary L. Aloe, Owner & Executive Producer
  Todd Waxler, Executive Producer
  Jay Jacobs, Director of Development
Specialties: Television
Other Categories: Feature Film; TV; Music Video
Credits: Caught in the Act; The Princess & The Private; Citizen Jane
Trade Assoc./Guilds/Unions: American Women in TV & Radio, CWA

JOSEPH PYTKA PRODUCTIONS, INC.
916 Main St.
Venice, CA 90291
Phone: ....(310) 392-9571
Fax: ....(310) 392-9571
Key Executives/Personnel:
  Tracie Heileson, Controller
  Tara Fitzpatrick, Head of Special Projects
  Kathy Rhodes, Executive Producer
Specialties: Television

@RADICAL.MEDIA
1630 12th St.
Santa Monica, CA 90404
Phone: ....(310) 664-4500
Fax: ....(310) 664-4600
www.radicalmedia.com
info@radicalmedia.com
Key Executives/Personnel:
  Jon Kamen, Co-Proprietor (NY)
  Robert Fernandez, Executive Producer (NY)
  Donna Portaio, Executive Producer (LA)
  Frank Scherma, Co-Proprietor (LA)
Specialties: Television
Credits: Jack in the Box

RAIMONDI FILMS, INC.
3575 Cahuenga Blvd. West, Ste. 470
Los Angeles, CA 90068
Phone: ....(323) 850-0185
Fax: ....(323) 850-1264
raimondica@aol.com
Key Executives/Personnel:
  Jane Raimondi, Producer
  Paul Raimondi, Director
Specialties: Television
Other Categories: TV
Credits: L.A. Times (theater trailers); Lucky's; Jockey; Hecht's Department Stores
Trade Assoc./Guilds/Unions: DGA

RAINTREE PRODUCTIONS
666 N. Robertson Blvd.
West Hollywood, CA 90069
Phone: ....(310) 827-3336
Fax: ....(310) 301-3310
Key Executives/Personnel:
  Robert Wollin, Executive Producer
Specialties: Promos
Other Categories: Feature Film
Credits: Academy of Television Arts & Sciences; IHOP; 45th & 46th Creative Arts Emmy Awards
Trade Assoc./Guilds/Unions: DGA, EGA

RANCH EXIT FILMS, INC.
146 N. Gunston Dr.
Los Angeles, CA 90049
Phone: ....(310) 471-0157
Fax: ....(310) 476-1925
www.ranchexitfilms.com
ranchexitfilms@aol.com
Key Executives/Personnel:
  Christopher Raser, President & Executive Producer
  Sarah Schoessler, Sr. Producer
  Alan Rich, Sr. Producer
Specialties: Television
Credits: Lincoln Mercury; Suzuki; carsdirect.com; Ford

RAPPORT FILMS, INC.
Phone: ....(818) 980-4483
Key Executives/Personnel:
  D. Cassidy, Producer
Specialties: Television; Promos
Credits: Taco Bell; McDonald's; Oldsmobile; Kraft

Production Companies – Commercials

RAVEN PRODUCTIONS, INC.
1053 S. Palm Canyon Dr.
Palm Springs, CA 92264
Phone: ....(760) 325-7191
Fax: ....(760) 325-7258
raventv1@aol.com
Key Executives/Personnel:
    Mitchell Sussman, Executive Producer
    Joni Ravenna, Producer & Writer
    Steve Peyton, Producer
    Mike Lestico, Writer
Specialties: Television
Other Categories: TV
Credits: Desert Magazine; Great Sports Vacations; Outdoors; The Aging of America
First Look/Development Deals: PBS

PATRICK RAYMOND ENTERTAINMENT, INC.
1041 N. Formosa Ave., Formosa Bldg., Ste. 209
West Hollywood, CA 90046
Phone: ....(323) 850-2918
Fax: ....(323) 850-2920
praymondh@aol.com
Key Executives/Personnel:
    Patrick Raymond, Executive Producer
    Albert Frigone, Associate Producer
    Joey Estella, Assistant
Specialties: Television; Infomercials/Direct Response; Promos
Other Categories: Feature Film; TV; Video; Interactive Multimedia

KEN RAYZOR SOUND DESIGN
1608 Argyle Ave.
Los Angeles, CA 90028
Phone: ....(323) 466-9221
....(213) 307-7006
Fax: ....(323) 462-8463
www.kenrayzor.com
kenrayzor@pacbell.net
Key Executives/Personnel:
    Ken Rayzor, President & Chief Creative Officer
    Mark Bauserman, Engineer
Specialties: Radio
Credits: Nordstrom; Blue Cross; Pacificare; Edison

RED HOTS ENTERTAINMENT
3105 Amigos Dr.
Burbank, CA 91504
Phone: ....(818) 954-0092
....(818) 607-8331
Fax: ....(818) 954-8421
pogmothon@earthlink.net
Key Executives/Personnel:
    Chip Miller, Director & Partner
    Sue Travis Miller, VP of Post Production & Editor
    Jane Gurtiza, Production Coordinator
    Dan Pomeroy, Director
    Marvin "Young MC" Young, Director
    Mark St. Juste, Director
    Kit Gleason, Production Manager
    Eileen Salgro, VP of Operations
    Vanessa Browne, Producer
    Marc Wolfson, Music Producer
    Theo Forster, Producer
Specialties: Infomercials/Direct Response; Promos
Other Categories: Feature Film; TV; Video; Music Video
Credits: Four Day Shoot; Mortuary Academy; The Importance of Being Earnest; The Seven Fishes
Trade Assoc./Guilds/Unions: PGA, WGA

DAN REDLER ENTERTAINMENT
18730 Hatteras St., Ste. 8
Tarzana, CA 91356
Phone: ....(818) 776-0938
Fax: ....(818) 705-6870
dredler@pacbell.net
Key Executives/Personnel:
    Dan Redler, Producer
    Nadia Naili, Producer
Specialties: Infomercials/Direct Response
Other Categories: Feature Film; TV; Interactive Multimedia
Credits: In His Father's Shoes; Pygmalion; Tanks; Profile For Murder
First Look/Development Deals: Nu Image/Millenium

REEL ORANGE
316 La Jolla Dr.
Newport Beach, CA 92663
Phone: ....(949) 548-4524
....(714) 349-6322
Fax: ....(949) 548-0749
reelorange@aol.com
Key Executives/Personnel:
    Art Vitarelli, Producer
Specialties: Television; Infomercials/Direct Response
Other Categories: TV; Video
Credits: Call of The Cangon; Mitsubishi Corp. (corp. video); Voices from the Stone

REGENT FILMS, INC.
4030 Sumac Dr.
Sherman Oaks, CA 91403
Phone: ....(818) 990-3377
....(212) 696-1010
Fax: ....(818) 990-3379
Key Executives/Personnel:
    Alan Pierce, Executive Producer
    Jill Rosenblum, Producer
Specialties: Television
Credits: Nerf; 3DO; Next Electronics; Buena Vista
Additional Info: 31 W. 26th St., 5th Fl., New York, NY 10010

RENEGADE ANIMATION, INC.
204 N. San Fernando Blvd.
Burbank, CA 91502
Phone: ....(818) 556-3395
Fax: ....(818) 556-3398
www.renegadeanimation.com
ashley@renegadeanimation.com
Key Executives/Personnel:
    Ashley Postlewaite, Executive Producer
    Darrell Van Citters, Director
Specialties: Television
Other Categories: Interactive Multimedia
Credits: Nike; Carl's Jr.; Chester Cheetah; Mattel
Additional Info: Full service animation house.

REVOLVER FILMS, LLC
2022A Broadway
Santa Monica, CA 90404
Phone: ....(310) 829-2441
Fax: ....(310) 829-2661
Key Executives/Personnel:
    Mark Priola, Producer
    Jack Singman, Producer
Specialties: Television; Infomercials/Direct Response; Promos
Other Categories: Feature Film; TV; Video
Credits: ATV Hardcore; Extended list available upon request.

KAVICH REYNOLDS PRODUCTIONS, INC.
6381 Hollywood Blvd., Ste. 580
Hollywood, CA 90028
Phone: ....(323) 466-2490
Fax: ....(323) 466-3655
www.kavichreynolds.com
Key Executives/Personnel:

Production Companies – Commercials

Steve Kavich, Executive Producer
John Reynolds, Executive Producer
Specialties: Television
Other Categories: Video
Credits: Harley Davidson; Suzuki; Namco; Yamaha

RHYTHM & HUES STUDIOS
5404 Jandy Place
Los Angeles, CA 90066
Phone: (310) 448-7500
Fax: (310) 448-7603
gnolin@rhythm.com
Specialties: Television
Other Categories: Feature Film
Credits: End of Days; X-Files; McDonald's; ReMax

RJ LAUREN
29395 Agoura Rd., Ste. 205
Agoura Hills, CA 91301
Phone: (818) 879-2200
www.rjlauren.com
info@rjlauren.com
Key Executives/Personnel:
Robert Haukoos, Executive Producer
Specialties: Television; Infomercials/Direct Response; Promos
Other Categories: Feature Film

ROARING TIGER FILMS
1475 Folsom St., Ste. 100
San Francisco, CA 94103
Phone: (415) 241-7125
Fax: (415) 241-7135
www.roaringtigerfilms.com
carey_crosby@roaringtigerfilms.com
Key Executives/Personnel:
Carey Crosby, Executive Producer
Specialties: Television
Credits: Union Bank; Saturn; California Tourism Board; Amtrak

RUMRUNNER CINE SERVICE
469 26th St.
Manhattan Beach, CA 90266
Phone: (310) 540-8411
(310) 901-5515
Fax: (310) 545-0136
omara@earthlink.net
Key Executives/Personnel:
Cay Mohr, Executive Producer & Owner
Gerry Trafficanda, Director & Owner
Kevin Van Fleet, Agency Owner
Lee Tirce, Director
Ron Dexter, Owner & Director
Mel Hall, Owner & Director
Scott Manville, Director
Andrew Gallerani, Director
Aaron Spelling, Executive Producer
James Row, Owner & Producer
Judy Trotter, Producer
Marilyn Penn, Producer
Paulette Glassman, Producer
Specialties: Television; Infomercials/Direct Response; Promos
Other Categories: TV; Video
Credits: The State of Energy (documentary); E-I Carrier (training video); Dynasty (miniseries); Toyota (commercial)
Trade Assoc./Guilds/Unions: DGA

SATELLITE FILMS
940 N. Mansfield Ave.
Hollywood, CA 90038
Phone: (323) 465-9300
Fax: (323) 465-8860
www.satellitefilms.net
info@satellitefilms.net
Key Executives/Personnel:
Phillip Detchmendy, Executive Producer, Commercials
Janet Haase, Executive Producer, Music Videos
Brian Carmody, West Coast Sales
Susan Murphy, East Coast Sales
Dawn Rao, Midwest Sales
Specialties: Television
Other Categories: Music Video
Credits: Whitney Houston - Heartbreak Hotel; 'NSync - Promise; Energizer 2; Nike
Trade Assoc./Guilds/Unions: AICP, MVPA

KRISTINE SCHWARZ PRODUCTIONS
Phone: (310) 393-0107
Fax: (310) 451-5454
www.kristineschwarzproductions.com
krisjs@aol.com
Key Executives/Personnel:
Kristine Schwarz, Producer
Specialties: Television
Other Categories: Feature Film; TV; Interactive Multimedia
Credits: Raid Gauldises; Kalifornia; Another Stakeout

SCOTTI PRODUCTIONS
Phone: (323) 654-3666
(213) 500-1915
dscotti@earthlink.net
Key Executives/Personnel:
Don Scotti, Owner
Specialties: Television
Other Categories: Feature Film; Video
Credits: Get Bruce! (documentary)
Trade Assoc./Guilds/Unions: AEA, SAG

SCREAM, LLC.
629 N. La Brea Ave.
Los Angeles, CA 90036
Phone: (323) 930-5900
Fax: (323) 930-5909
www.screamusa.com
info@screamusa.com
Key Executives/Personnel:
Charles Salice, Executive Producer
Mishel Cali, Controller
Rika Osenberg, Production Manager
Specialties: Television
Credits: Coca-Cola; Pennzoil; Noxzema
Trade Assoc./Guilds/Unions: AICP

SHARPCUT PRODUCTIONS
9000 Cynthia Street, Ste. 410
West Hollywood, CA 90069
Phone: (310) 247-0088
Fax: (310) 858-2254
www.sharpcut.com
sharpcutprods@aol.com
Key Executives/Personnel:
Gary Robinson, Producer & Director
Specialties: Television; Promos
Other Categories: Music Video
Credits: Mets Corp.; Blind Date (promo); Stephen King: The Stand (promo)

SIGNATURE ENTERTAINMENT
8306 Wilshire Blvd., Ste. 791
Beverly Hills, CA 90211
Phone: (213) 994-4695
Key Executives/Personnel:
Kelly Andrea Rubin, Producer
Specialties: Radio; Infomercials/Direct Response; Promos
Other Categories: Feature Film; TV
Credits: The Third Wheel; Cotton Mouth; An Eye For Talent; Skippy

Production Companies – Commercials

First Look/Development Deals: Indigo Entertainment

SILVER LINING PRODUCTIONS, INC.
8687 Melrose Ave., Ste. B300
West Hollywood, CA 90069
Phone: (310) 289-6650
Fax: (310) 289-6658
slpbozena@aol.com/silverliningp@aol.com
Key Executives/Personnel:
  Bozena Armstrong, Executive Producer & Director
  Randy Haberkamp, Producer
Specialties: Television; Radio; Promos
Other Categories: Feature Film; TV; Video; Interactive Multimedia
Credits: Cleopatra (promo); Forest Lawn (commercial); Reva: The Scarlet Years (video); The Unknown Tradition (documentary)
Trade Assoc./Guilds/Unions: DGA, SAG

SILVEREYE PRODUCTIONS
4163 Murietta Ave.
Sherman Oaks, CA 91423
Phone: (818) 501-4232
Fax: (818) 990-9997
Key Executives/Personnel:
  Ahmed Lateef, Producer & Director
  Ashwin Joshi, Producer & VP
  Omer Mohamed, Producer & Treasurer
  Meher Tatna, Producer & Writer
  Subash Kundamal, Producer & Writer
  Sherwood Ho, Producer & Director
Specialties: Infomercials/Direct Response
Other Categories: Feature Film; TV
Credits: Pepsi; Changing Gears (feature); Locket (feature); Goodyear Tires
Trade Assoc./Guilds/Unions: DGA, FEU

JAY SILVERMAN PRODUCTIONS
1541 N. Cahuenga Blvd.
Los Angeles, CA 90028
Phone: (323) 466-6030
Fax: (323) 466-7139
www.jaysilverman.com
gabriel@jaysilverman.com
Key Executives/Personnel:
  Neil Gabriel, Producer
  Jay Silverman, Director
Specialties: Television; Promos
Credits: Cadillac; Greyhound; WWF Smackdown (promo); Doctor Laura (promo)

SIMEX DIGITAL STUDIOS
3250 Ocean Park Blvd., Ste. 100
Santa Monica, CA 90405
Phone: (310) 664-9500
Fax: (310) 664-9977
www.planetpoint.com
allen@simexds.com
Key Executives/Personnel:
  Allen Yamashita, Director
  Nick Bates, Director & Visual Effects Supervisor
  Jean Perramon, Director
  John Wash, Visual Effects Supervisor
Specialties: Television
Other Categories: Feature Film
Credits: Nintendo; Kellogg's Froot Loops; Anheuser-Busch; Keebler

SMILLIE FILMS
1421 Abbot Kinney Blvd.
Venice, CA 90291
Phone: (310) 314-0072
Fax: (310) 314-1349
smilliefilms@earthlink.net
Key Executives/Personnel:
  Peter Smillie, Director
  Stephanie Swor, Executive Producer
  Linda Livingston, Head of Production
Specialties: Television

SODAS & SHOES
5550 Wilshire Blvd., Ste. 301
Los Angeles, CA 90036
Phone: (323) 692-9848
Fax: (323) 692-9832
sodasshoes@aol.com
Key Executives/Personnel:
  Scott Mellini, Partner
  Louis Mellini, Partner
  Joan Renfrow, Partner
Specialties: Television
Other Categories: Music Video
Credits: Mattel; Saturn; Suzuki; Circus Circus Casino

SONIC FILMS, INC.
73 Market St.
Venice, CA 90291
Phone: (310) 785-9100
           (212) 744-5333
Fax: (310) 396-7423
Key Executives/Personnel:
  David Stoltz, Executive Producer
Specialties: Television; Promos
Credits: BMW; Hardee's Restaurants; Chi Chi's Restaurants; Bank 121

SOUND CONCEPTS, INC.
3485 Meier St.
Los Angeles, CA 90066
Phone: (800) 451-8560
Fax: (310) 391-1165
www.soundconceptsinc.com
sndcpts@aol.com
Key Executives/Personnel:
  Mark McIntyre, President
  John Knoerle, VP & Creative Director
Specialties: Radio
Credits: Capitol-EMI Records; U.S. Army Recruiting; Edgewater Hotel; Yamaha Motor Sports

SOUTH FORK PRODUCTIONS
P.O. Box 1935
Santa Monica, CA 90406
Phone: (310) 829-5029
Fax: (310) 829-5029
soforkprods@ireland.com
Key Executives/Personnel:
  Jim Sullivan, Producer & Director
  Greg Sullivan, Producer
Specialties: Television; Promos
Other Categories: Feature Film; TV; Video; Music Video
Credits: Making of Without Limits; Portraits of Courage; Those Who Dare
Trade Assoc./Guilds/Unions: AFI

THE SPARK FACTORY
710 Wilshire Blvd., Ste. 200
Santa Monica, CA 90401
Phone: (310) 395-6775
Fax: (310) 395-4595
www.sparkfactory.com
mailroom@sparkfactory.com
Key Executives/Personnel:
  Tim Street, President
  Gail Gillman, VP of Creative Affairs
Specialties: Television; Radio; Promos
Other Categories: Feature Film; Interactive Multimedia
Credits: Entrapment (commercial); Out of Towners (commercial); Whoistylerdurden.com; Creepysites.com

Production Companies – Commercials

SPLENDIDLIGHT MEDIA PRODUCTIONS
177 Riverside St., PMB 151
Newport Beach, CA 92663
Phone: ....(949) 722-8485
Fax: ....(949) 722-7896
www.splendidlight.com
lsplendid@splendidlight.com
Key Executives/Personnel:
    Lynn Splendid, Producer & Director
    Clayton Light, Producer & Editor
Specialties: Television; Infomercials/Direct Response
Other Categories: TV; Video
Additional Info: 2801 Pacific Coast Hwy., Ste. 325, Newport Beach, CA 92663

SPORTS' CINEMATOGRAPHY GROUP
73 Market St.
Venice, CA 90291
Phone: ....(310) 785-9100
....(212) 744-5333
Fax: ....(310) 396-7423
www.sportscinema.net
sportscinema@earthlink.net
Key Executives/Personnel:
    David Stoltz, Executive Producer
Specialties: Television; Promos
Other Categories: Music Video
Credits: Quik Silver; Kawasaki; Qxygen Snowboards; Polo Sport

J. STACK PRODUCTIONS
Phone: ....(310) 456-3272
Fax: ....(310) 456-3442
jmstack@aol.com
Key Executives/Personnel:
    Jeanne Stack, Producer
Specialties: Television; Promos
Other Categories: Feature Film; TV; Music Video
Credits: Contact (2nd Unit); Kundun (2nd Unit); Eco-Challenge; Mild 7

STARBOARD PRODUCTIONS
50 Bulkley Ave.
Sausalito, CA 94965
Phone: ....(415) 332-6462
....(415) 740-2924
Fax: ....(415) 332-6462
riko2@ix.netcom.com
Key Executives/Personnel:
    Rick Whiting, Producer
Specialties: Television; Radio; Infomercials/Direct Response; Promos
Credits: Fox NFL (promo); Aquafresh Toothpaste; Albertsons; Next Card

STARGAZER, INC.
2432 Seventh St., Ste. 1
Santa Monica, CA 90405
Phone: ....(310) 392-0392
www.stargazerproductions.com
paigerama@earthlink.net
Key Executives/Personnel:
    Paige Seidel, Producer
Specialties: Television
Other Categories: Feature Film; Music Video
Credits: United Airlines; Audi; monster.com; Jeep

STEAM
3021 Airport Ave., Ste. 201
Santa Monica, CA 90405
Phone: ....(310) 636-4620
Fax: ....(310) 636-4621
www.steamshow.com
info@steamshow.com
Key Executives/Personnel:
    Tammy Kimbler, Executive Producer
    Jim Brykit, Director
    Scott Bryant, Creative Director
Specialties: Television; Promos
Credits: Intel; KCRW; Mattel; Fisher-Price

STEFANINO PRODUCTIONS
15515 Sunset Blvd., Ste. 101
Pacific Palisades, CA 90272
Phone: ....(310) 454-0109
Fax: ....(310) 454-0109
www.stefanino.com
stefanino@earthlink.net
Key Executives/Personnel:
    Stuart Jemesen, Producer & Director
    Stefan Kendal Gordy, Director of Music
Specialties: Infomercials/Direct Response
Other Categories: Feature Film; TV; Video; Music Video
Credits: Smokey Robinson; Michael Jackson Biography; Innerview (TV pilot)

KRIS STEVENS ENTERPRISES, INC.
22362 Dardenne St.
Calabasas, CA 91302
Phone: ....(818) 225-7585
Fax: ....(818) 225-8485
www.kriserikstevens.com
kris@kriserikstevens.com
Key Executives/Personnel:
    Kris Erik Stevens, Executive Producer
Specialties: Radio

STIEFEL + COMPANY
1620 Euclid St.
Santa Monica, CA 90404
Phone: ....(310) 581-7000
....(800) 950-7843
Fax: ....(310) 581-7929
www.stiefelco.com
production@stiefelco.com
Key Executives/Personnel:
    Frank Stiefel, Executive Producer
    Marie Perry, Executive Producer
    Phyllis Koenig, Executive Producer
    SueEllen Clair, Head of Production
    Brett Froomer, Director
    Marc Greenfield, Director
    Craig Henderson, Director
    Andrews Jenkins, Director
    Peter Kagan, Director
    Peter Darley Miller, Director
    Peter Ziegler, East Coast Rep
    Steven Monkarsh, West Coast Rep
    Gay Guthrey, Midwest Rep
Specialties: Television
Credits: Honda; Kellogg's Raisin Bran Crunch; American Century; Carnival Cruise Lines
Trade Assoc./Guilds/Unions: AICP

STRAW DOGS
8330 W. Third St.
Los Angeles, CA 90048
Phone: ....(323) 782-0777
Fax: ....(323) 782-9777
Key Executives/Personnel:
    Craig Rogers, Executive Producer
    Leslie Snow, Head of Production
    Jesse Dylan, Director
    Mike Rowles, Director
    Neil Burger, Director
    Deb Hagan, Director
    Stan Morse, Director
    Barry Sonnifeld, Director

Specialties: Television
Other Categories: Feature Film
Credits: Pepsi; Amazon.com; Pizza Hut; Vicks 44

STROM MAGALLON ENTERTAINMENT
3518 Cahuenga Blvd. West, Ste. 111
Los Angeles, CA 90068
Phone: ....(323) 969-1089
....(323) 969-1090
Fax: ....(323) 969-1091
strommagent@earthlink.net
Key Executives/Personnel:
  Gregory Strom, Director
  Douglas Magallon, Director
Specialties: Television
Other Categories: Feature Film; Video; Music Video
Credits: Dirt Devil (commercial); Pontiac (commercial)

SUN SPOTS
5358 Melrose Ave., Ste. 100W
Hollywood, CA 90038
Phone: ....(323) 960-4000
Fax: ....(323) 960-4080
www.sunspotsmedia.com
sunspotsla@aol.com
Key Executives/Personnel:
  David Dryer, Director
  Linda Dryer, Executive Producer
  Carlton Ashley, Executive Producer
  Craig Worsham, Director
  Kevin Dole, Director
  Jonathan Frakes, Director
Specialties: Television
Credits: Dodge; Orkin; Toyota; Mattel
Trade Assoc./Guilds/Unions: AICP, DGA, IATSE

TAG TEAM
1334 Westwood Blvd., Ste. 9
Los Angeles, CA 90024
Phone: ....(310) 470-0491
Fax: ....(310) 475-9041
wbfilms@aol.com
Key Executives/Personnel:
  Cynthia Wright-Banks, Executive Producer
Specialties: Television
Credits: Hasbro Toy Group; Mattel; Rose Art
Trade Assoc./Guilds/Unions: AICP, DGA, IATSE

TANGO FILMS
1334 Westwood Blvd., Ste. 6
Los Angeles, CA 90024
Phone: ....(310) 470-4908
Fax: ....(310) 475-9041
thebank@aol.com
Key Executives/Personnel:
  Steve Banks, Executive Producer
  Greg Weinschenker, Director
  Lauren McNamara, Midwest Sales
Specialties: Television; Infomercials/Direct Response; Promos
Other Categories: Music Video
Credits: Polident; MCI; Vicks Vaporub; Keystone Financial
Trade Assoc./Guilds/Unions: AICP, DGA

TOOL OF NORTH AMERICA
2210 Broadway
Santa Monica, CA 90404
Phone: ....(310) 453-9244
....(888) 877-8665
Fax: ....(310) 453-4185
info@toolofna.com
Key Executives/Personnel:
  Dierdre Harrington, Executive Producer
  Jennifer Siegel, Head of Production
  Amy De Lossa, Producer
  Erich Joiner, Owner & Director
  Scott Burns, Owner & Director
  Chris Hooper, Director
  Tom Routson, Director
  David Jellison, Director
  David Jellison, Director
  Peter Berg, Director
  Clint Clemens, Director
Specialties: Television

TOTEM PRODUCTIONS
8009 Santa Monica Blvd.
Los Angeles, CA 90046
Phone: ....(323) 650-4994
Fax: ....(323) 650-1961
totempro@aol.com
Key Executives/Personnel:
  Tony Scott, Co-Chairman
  Peter Toumasis, Executive Assistant to Mr. Scott
  Tom Moran, Assistant to Mr. Scott
Specialties: Television
Other Categories: Feature Film
Credits: Enemy of the State; Top Gun; True Romance; Crimson Tide

TRAFFICANDA STUDIOS, INC.
1111 N. Beachwood Dr.
Hollywood, CA 90038
Phone: ....(323) 466-1111
Fax: ....(323) 466-2028
Key Executives/Personnel:
  Gerry Trafficanda, Director
  Paul J. Harder, Executive Producer
Specialties: Television; Promos
Credits: Safeway Stores; Tech Deck; Universal (promo); Nestlé

TROPIX FILMS
201 Wilshire Blvd, 2nd Fl.
Santa Monica, CA 90401
Phone: ....(310) 393-9956
Fax: ....(310) 587-2389
dcoulter@tropixfilms.com
Key Executives/Personnel:
  David Coulter, Executive Producer
  Patti Coulter, Head of Production
  Richard Taylor, Director
  Larry Carroll, Director
  Martin Shewchuk, Director
  Martin Brierley, Director
  Mark Rowen, Director
Specialties: Television
Credits: Coca-Cola; Disney Cruise Lines; Dodge; AT&T
Trade Assoc./Guilds/Unions: AICP, DGA

TUESDAY FILMS
532 Colorado Ave.
Santa Monica, CA 90401
Phone: ....(310) 899-0335
Fax: ....(310) 899-9845
production@tuesdayfilms.com
Key Executives/Personnel:
  Mardi Minogue, Executive Producer
  Jonathan Yarbrough, Director
  Anita Grant, Controller
  Neil Daniels, Production Supervisor
  Jennifer Lebsack, Production Coordinator
Specialties: Television
Credits: Honda; Arco/AmPm

Production Companies – Commercials

TVA PRODUCTIONS
10900 Ventura Blvd.
Studio City, CA 91604
Phone: ....(818) 505-8300
Fax: ....(818) 505-8370
www.tvaproductions.com
jgoddard@businessworldnews.com
Key Executives/Personnel:
  Jeffery Goddard, Executive Producer
  Andrea Goodstein, Executive VP of Production
  Geno Brunton, Sr. Producer
Specialties: Television; Infomercials/Direct Response
Other Categories: TV; Video
Credits: Business World News
Trade Assoc./Guilds/Unions: AMPAS, IAAPA, TEA

TVP STUDIOS
1539 Magnolia Blvd.
Burbank, CA 91506
Phone: ....(818) 843-3188
Fax: ....(818) 843-3189
www.tvpstudios.cc
tvprich@aol.com
Key Executives/Personnel:
  Richard Tamayo, Producer
  Meredith Day, Producer
Specialties: Television; Infomercials/Direct Response
Other Categories: TV; Video; Music Video
Credits: Bank of America; Panasonic; Golden Globe Awards; etvhollywood.com

VANGUARD PRODUCTIONS
12111 Beatrice St.
Culver City, CA 90230
Phone: ....(310) 306-4910
Fax: ....(310) 306-4910
vangrdprod@earthlink.net
Key Executives/Personnel:
  Terence M. O'Keefe, Writer, Producer & Director
  Brent Huff, Writer & Director
  S. Drew Stotesbery, VP of Production
  Bruce Miyaki, Director of Development
  Bennett Fidlow, Director of Creative Affairs
Specialties: Television; Infomercials/Direct Response; Promos
Other Categories: Feature Film; TV; Video; Music Video
Credits: We The People; Wanted; The Bad Pack; Closing The Deal

VCA PRODUCTIONS
851 N. Kings Rd., Ste. 112
West Hollywood, CA 90069
Phone: ....(310) 489-3495
....(818) 986-5359
Fax: ....(818) 986-5359
vcaprod@hotmail.com
Key Executives/Personnel:
  Vincent Agostino, Producer
Specialties: Television
Other Categories: Feature Film
Trade Assoc./Guilds/Unions: DGA

VENTANA FILMS
7440 Palo Vista Dr.
Los Angeles, CA 90046
Phone: ....(323) 876-3331
Fax: ....(323) 876-4666
lafilm@aol.com
Key Executives/Personnel:
  Arthur Gorson, President & Head of Production
  Bernard Nussbaumer, Executive Producer
  Julio Solorzano, VP
Specialties: Television
Other Categories: Feature Film; Music Video

Credits: Cronos (feature); Better Watch Out (feature); Cabeza De Vaca (feature)

VENTURE ENTERTAINMENT GROUP
P.O. Box 55113
Sherman Oaks, CA 91413
Phone: ....(818) 981-7813
....(800) 981-8433
Fax: ....(818) 981-3466
www.venture818.com
venture818@aol.com
Key Executives/Personnel:
  Leigh Leshner, Producer
Specialties: Infomercials/Direct Response
Other Categories: Feature Film; TV; Video
Credits: The Spa Workout (infomercial); Hidden Treasures (TV series); Zoofari; More Zoofari
Trade Assoc./Guilds/Unions: VSDA, WIF

VENUS ENTERTAINMENT
3630 Eastham Blvd.
Culver City, CA 90232
Phone: ....(310) 581-4236
Fax: ....(310) 396-2128
Key Executives/Personnel:
  Stavros Merjos, President
  Kerstin Emhoff, Executive Producer
  Jessica Thomas, Sales
Specialties: Television

VIDEO HOLLYWOOD PRODUCTIONS
P.O. Box 19336
Encino, CA 91416
Phone: ....(888) 368-7347
....(310) 890-0066
Fax: ....(805) 583-8809
pcsinc@dotregs.com
Key Executives/Personnel:
  Kirk Van Houten, President
  Bob Telford, VP of Post Production
  Alfred Powers, VP
  Steven Piper, VP
Specialties: Promos
Credits: El Monte Police (promo)

VIDEOWERKS
3435 Ocean Park Blvd., Ste. 112
Santa Monica, CA 90405
Phone: ....(310) 393-8754
....(800) 356-6541
Fax: ....(310) 399-1829
www.videowerks.com
videowerks@earthlink.net
Key Executives/Personnel:
  David M. Werk, Owner, Cameraman & DP
Specialties: Television; Infomercials/Direct Response; Promos
Other Categories: TV; Video; Interactive Multimedia
Credits: The Directors; History's Lost & Found; Investigative Reports; Headliners & Legends
Trade Assoc./Guilds/Unions: IDA, ITVA

VIHLENE & ASSOCIATES, INC.
26941 Cabot Rd., Ste. 120
Laguna Hills, CA 92653
Phone: ....(949) 582-0937
Fax: ....(949) 582-0978
www.vihlene.com
vern@vihlene.com
Key Executives/Personnel:
  Vern Vihlene, President
  Vicki Wellnitz, Producer
  Betty McBurnie, Accountant

Production Companies – Commercials

George Adams, Post Supervisor
Brent Loefke, Director
Specialties: Television; Infomercials/Direct Response
Other Categories: TV; Video
Credits: Mailbox etc.; American Honda Motor Co.; AT&T; American Suzuki Motor Co.

VILLAINS
9247 Alden Dr.
Beverly Hills, CA 90210
Phone: ....(310) 888-8900
Fax: ....(310) 888-8444
www.villains.com
Key Executives/Personnel:
John Marshall, President
Robin Benson, Executive Producer
Joby Barnhart, Head of Production
Bo McDonald, Executive Producer of Music Videos
Bill Mather, Director
Scott Bibo, Director
Jeffrey Fleisig, Director
Brett Ratner, Director
Steve Carr, Director
Daniela Federici, Director
Jim Giddens, Director
Specialties: Television
Other Categories: Music Video
Credits: Madonna - Beautiful Stranger; Mariah Carey - Heart Breaker; Sprite; Nike

VISITOR, LLC
1323 Ocean Ave.
Santa Monica, CA 90401
Phone: ....(310) 828-8255
Fax: ....(310) 828-8911
vistorllc@earthlink.net
Key Executives/Personnel:
Oliver Katz, Executive Producer
Michael Brady, Executive Producer
Specialties: Television
Credits: Anheuser-Busch; Nintendo; Earthshare; Gain
Trade Assoc./Guilds/Unions: AICP

RONI WEISBERG PRODUCTIONS
1644 Warnall Ave.
Los Angeles, CA 90024
Phone: ....(310) 286-1210
Fax: ....(310) 556-8248
rweisberg@earthlink.net
Key Executives/Personnel:
Roni Weisberg, Producer
Henry Tuggle, Director of Development
Specialties: Television
Other Categories: Feature Film; TV
Credits: Mermaid; Face Down; Death Dreams; Sharing Richard

WESTERN BRANCH PRODUCTIONS, INC.
4231 Beck Ave.
Studio City, CA 91604
Phone: ....(818) 762-3810
....(818) 642-3810
Fax: ....(818) 769-2847
www.western-branch.com
pvan@western-branch.com
Key Executives/Personnel:
Pete Vanlaw, President
Specialties: Television
Other Categories: TV; Video
Credits: Memories of a Millenium (documentary); Night at the Pote (TV pilot)
Trade Assoc./Guilds/Unions: DGA

BILL WHITE PRODUCTIONS
12423 Ventura Court, Ste. 200
Studio City, CA 91604
Phone: ....(818) 769-9090
Fax: ....(818) 769-1974
billwhitepro@earthlink.net
Key Executives/Personnel:
Bill White, President
Amy Shomer, Producer
Specialties: Television; Radio; Infomercials/Direct Response
Other Categories: Feature Film; TV; Video; Music Video
Credits: Globe Life Insurance (commercial); United American Insurance (commercial); Sanyo-Fisher (corp. video); Test Flights (TV)
Trade Assoc./Guilds/Unions: DGA

WILDLIFE MANAGEMENT
425 N. Robertson Blvd.
Los Angeles, CA 90048
Phone: ....(310) 276-8008
Fax: ....(310) 273-0868
Key Executives/Personnel:
Brian Donnelly, Executive Producer
Fran Wall, Head of Production
Mark Celentano, Director
Paul Freedman, Director
Molly O'Brien, Director
Max Da-Yung Wang, Director
Jay Torres, Director
Debra Roberts Sher, Sales Representative
Specialties: Television

WINDMILL LANE PRODUCTIONS
1558 Tenth St.
Santa Monica, CA 90401
Phone: ....(310) 576-1344
Fax: ....(310) 576-0515
www.windmill-lane.com
ben@windmill-lane.com
Key Executives/Personnel:
Ben Dossett, Executive Producer
Meiert Avis, Director
Rupert Wainwright, Director
Richard Bowen, Director
Specialties: Television
Other Categories: Music Video
Credits: Toyota; Sprite; LA Times; Kawasaki

WYLD SPOTS
606 N. Larchmont Blvd., Ste. 100
Los Angeles, CA 90004
Phone: ....(323) 960-2633
Fax: ....(323) 461-2288
www.wyldspots.com
film@wyldspots.com
Key Executives/Personnel:
Michael Hartog, Director
Burt DuBois, Director
Frank Furlong, Director
Specialties: Television
Credits: Toyota; Oracle; Media One

X-1 FILMS
8630 Pine Tree Pl.
West Hollywood, CA 90069
Phone: ....(310) 659-6220
Key Executives/Personnel:
Cami Taylor, Executive Producer
Charlie Curran, Executive Producer
Carole Hughes, Executive Producer
Specialties: Television; Promos
Additional Info: 136 W. 21st St., New York, NY 10011

X-RAY PRODUCTIONS
8630 Pine Tree Pl.
West Hollywood, CA 90069
Phone: ....(310) 659-7659
Key Executives/Personnel:
    Cami Taylor, Executive Producer
    Joanne Thrailkill, Executive Producer
    Carole Hughes, Executive Producer
    Charlie Curran, Executive Producer
Specialties: Television; Promos
Other Categories: Music Video
Trade Assoc./Guilds/Unions: AICP
Additional Info: 136 W. 21st St., New York, NY 10011

YADA/LEVINE PRODUCTIONS
606 N. Larchmont Blvd., Ste. 100
Los Angeles, CA 90004
Phone: ....(323) 461-1616
Fax: ....(323) 461-2288
www.yadalevine.com
video@yadalevine.com
Key Executives/Personnel:
    Michael Yada, Executive Producer
Specialties: Television
Other Categories: Video
Credits: ABC; Disney; Toyota

MARK YELLEN PRODUCTIONS
419 N. Larchmont Blvd., Ste. 44
Los Angeles, CA 90004
Phone: ....(323) 935-5525
Fax: ....(323) 935-5755
Key Executives/Personnel:
    Mark Yellen, Producer
Specialties: Television
Other Categories: Feature Film; Music Video
Credits: Blast; Montana; Shiloh; The Big Squeeze

ZEAL PICTURES
6605 Hollywood Blvd., Ste. 300
Los Angeles, CA 90028
Phone: ....(323) 871-4000
Fax: ....(323) 871-4004
www.zealpictures.com
info@zealpictures.com
Key Executives/Personnel:
    Timm Oberwelland, Producer
    Leon Melas, Producer
    Robert Biehn, Producer
    George Salden, CFO
Specialties: Television; Promos
Other Categories: Feature Film; Video; Music Video
Credits: Simpatico; Robbers; American Fighter Pilot; Werther's Originals
Trade Assoc./Guilds/Unions: SAG
Additional Info: Additional office in Berlin, Germany.

ZOOMA ZOOMA CORPORATION
11 Mercer St., 3rd Fl.
New York, NY 10013
Phone: ....(212) 941-7680
Fax: ....(212) 941-8179
www.zoomazooma.com
staff@zoomazooma.com
Key Executives/Personnel:
    Joseph Mantegna, Executive Producer
    Todd Bellanca, Director
    Eden Tyler, Director
    Sam Raimi, Director
    Michael Bellino, Director
    Tim Hamilton, Director
    Gavin O'Connor, Director
    Lori Vitale, East Coast Sales
Specialties: Television; Promos
Other Categories: Feature Film; TV; Music Video; Interactive Multimedia

ZYSTAR FILMS, INC.
330 Washington Blvd., Ste. 400
Marina Del Rey, CA 90292
Phone: ....(310) 301-3313
Fax: ....(310) 301-9433
www.zystar.com
mwallis@zystar.com
Key Executives/Personnel:
    Meryl Alison Wallis, Executive Producer
    Carmen Silva, Producer
    Scott Murphy, Assistant Director
    Howard Raishbrook, Production Manager
    Doug Mickel, Producer
Specialties: Television
Other Categories: Feature Film; TV; Video; Music Video
Credits: James Bond (behind the scenes); American Honda (commercial); Carrows Restaurants (commercial); Laurietta (feature)

Pacific Soundwaves
post sound services

Sound Design ~ Editorial ~ Mixing

A Professional Boutique-Style Facility

Specializing in Short Form and Episodic TV

Commercials and Promos

Voice Over and ADR recording

Avid Offline and Online Editing

Transfers and Duplication

ISDN and Signatory Services

OMFI and multi format compatible

10807 Fruitland Dr., Studio City, CA 91604
(818) 487-5677 ph ~ **(818) 487-2870** fax

w w w . p a c i f i c s o u n d w a v e s . c o m

featureFILMS

comMERCials

broadCAST

COMPUTERCAFE
3D animation - visual FX

santa **MONICA** california

310 395-9013   fax 310 395-9814

santa **MARIA** california

805 922-9479   fax 805 922-3225

www.computercafe.com

Production Companies – Video

21ST CENTURY MAN PRODUCTIONS
1950 N. Tamarind Ave., Ste. 323
Los Angeles, CA 90068
Phone: ....(323) 466-3227
................................(310) 989-7353
Fax: ....(323) 466-3227
www.21stcman.com
future21@primenet.com
Key Executives/Personnel:
 Jane Linter, Producer & Director
 David May, Director & Editor
 Brian Bowie, Director & Director of Photography
 Andrea Fredrickson, Editor
Specialties: Industrial/Corporate; Educational
Other Categories: TV; Commercials; Music Video; Interactive Multimedia
Credits: 21st CMAN; Sebastian Int.; Wella Alternative Hair Show; Stylezone 2000
Trade Assoc./Guilds/Unions: AEA, BAFTA, DGA, NATPE
Additional Info: 33 Limes Rd., Beckenham, Kent BR3 6NS England

30 SECOND FILMS
3019 Pico Blvd.
Santa Monica, CA 90405
Phone: ....(310) 315-1750
Fax: ....(310) 315-1757
www.30secondfilms.com
info@30secondfilms.com
Key Executives/Personnel:
 Alan Stamm, Executive Producer
 Bob Kronovet, Producer & Director
 Scott Baio, Director
 Debbie Allen, Director
 Tony Dow, Director
 Branscombe Richmond, Director
Specialties: Industrial/Corporate; Documentaries
Other Categories: Feature Film; TV; Commercials
Credits: American Tigers; Ghostown; Broken Bars; L.A. Task Force

40 ACRES & A MULE FILMWORKS, INC.
124 Dekalb Ave.
Brooklyn, NY 11217
Phone: ....(718) 624-3703
Fax: ....(718) 624-2008
Key Executives/Personnel:
 Spike Lee, CEO
 Sam Kitt, President of Production
 Andre Hereford, Director of Development
 Heather Parish, Business Manager
Specialties: Industrial/Corporate; Documentaries
Other Categories: Feature Film; Commercials; Music Video
Credits: Bamboozled; Summer of Sam; He Got Game; Malcolm X
Additional Info: NY Development Office: 75 S. Elliot Pl., 3rd Fl. Brooklyn, NY 11217

A&E TELEVISION NETWORKS
235 E. 45th St.
New York, NY 10017
Phone: ....(212) 210-1400
Fax: ....(212) 210-1308
www.aande.com
Key Executives/Personnel:
 Nickolas Davatzes, President & CEO
 Gerard Gruosso, CFO & Sr. VP of Finance
 Whitney Goit, Executive VP of Sales & Marketing
 Dan Davids, Executive VP & General Manager
 Jim Greiner, Sr. VP of Operations & Business Development
 Delia Fine, VP of Drama & Film Programming
 Ed Hersh, VP of Documentary Programming
 Carol Anne Dolan, Director of Documentary Programming
Specialties: Documentaries
Other Categories: Feature Film; TV
Credits: Biography; American Justice; Investigative Reports

A STORY UNTOLD PRODUCTIONS
15395 Saranac Dr.
Whittier, CA 90604
Phone: ....(562) 943-7505
communities.msn.com
georgeangelo@hotmail.com
Key Executives/Personnel:
 George Angelo, Producer
Specialties: Documentaries
Credits: Whispers; Los Angeles History Project
Trade Assoc./Guilds/Unions: ATAS

ABBY LOU ENTERTAINMENT
1411 Edgehill Pl.
Pasadena, CA 91103
Phone: ....(626) 795-7334
Fax: ....(626) 795-4013
ale@full-moon.com
Key Executives/Personnel:
 George LeFave, Executive Producer
 Chryl Pestor, Executive VP of Development
Specialties: Educational
Other Categories: Feature Film; TV; Commercials
Credits: Adventures in Whispering Gardens; A Christmas Whisper

ABSOLUTEFILMS.NET
1441 Huntington Dr., Ste. 3010
South Pasadena, CA 91030
Phone: ....(626) 442-6454
Fax: ....(626) 448-1930
www.absolutefilms.net
info@absolute.net
Key Executives/Personnel:
 Ty Thompson, Producer
 Byron Jost, Producer
 Josh Ochoa, Producer
 Robert Villalobos, Producer
 Tom Franklin, Producer
 Romeo Carey, Producer
Specialties: Industrial/Corporate; Educational; Documentaries
Other Categories: Commercials; Music Video; Interactive Multimedia
Credits: Juan-A-Be.com; Mr. Fab

AD-LIB MARKETING & ADVERTISING
One Blacksmith Circle
Phillips Ranch, CA 91766
Phone: ....(909) 629-1995
Fax: ....(909) 629-1995
ad-lib@2-hot.com
Key Executives/Personnel:
 Keith Underwood, Executive Producer
 Brenda Underwood, Associate Producer
Specialties: Industrial/Corporate; Educational; Documentaries
Other Categories: Commercials; Music Video
Credits: Titan Business Solutions; P. Joseph, A Law Corp.; Ben & Jerry's; Perferred Financial Corp.

AERIAL FOCUS PRODUCTIONS
8 Camino Verde
Santa Barbara, CA 93103
Phone: ....(805) 962-9911
Fax: ....(805) 962-9536
www.aerialfocus.com
aerialfcs@aol.com

Production Companies – Video

Key Executives/Personnel:
    Tom Sanders, Executive Producer
    David Stanfield, Segment Producer
Specialties: Documentaries
Other Categories: Feature Film; TV
Credits: Over The Edge; The Best Boogie Continues; Royal Sky Celebration
Trade Assoc./Guilds/Unions: AFTRA, SAG

ALAMEDA FILMWORKS, INC.
1713 W. Alameda Ave.
Burbank, CA 91506
Phone: ....(818) 846-4074
afwinc@att.net
Key Executives/Personnel:
    Wendy Yorkshire, Producer
Specialties: Industrial/Corporate
Other Categories: Feature Film; Commercials
Trade Assoc./Guilds/Unions: AICP, DGA

ALBRECHT & ASSOCIATES, INC.
3442 Dorothy Rd.
Topanga, CA 90290
Phone: ....(818) 222-4836
jaalbrecht@yahoo.com
Specialties: Documentaries; Educational; Industrial/Corporate
Credits: Carol King One to One; Mickey's 60th Birthday
Trade Assoc./Guilds/Unions: DGA, SAG, WGA

AMBITIOUS ENTERTAINMENT
Phone: ....(818) 990-8993
Fax: ....(818) 990-8994
ambitious1@earthlink.net
Key Executives/Personnel:
    Paul M. Addis, Producer
Specialties: Industrial/Corporate
Other Categories: TV; Commercials
Credits: Muhammad Ali: King of the World (promo); Talk To Me (promo); Wolfgang Puck Cafe (commercial); Sony PlayStation (commercial)

AMERICAN SPORTS NETWORK, INC.
P.O. Box 6100
Rosemead, CA 91770
Phone: ....(626) 292-2222
Fax: ....(626) 292-2221
Key Executives/Personnel:
    Louis Zwick, President
    Robin Chang, Director
    Steve Roguet, Producer
Specialties: Documentaries
Other Categories: TV; Music Video
Credits: ESPN; Eurosport; Star Sport Asia; TSN-Canada

AMERICAN VIDEO GROUP
12020 Pico Blvd.
Los Angeles, CA 90064
Phone: ....(310) 477-1535
Fax: ....(310) 473-5299
www.americanvideogroup.com
amervideo@earthlink.net
Key Executives/Personnel:
    John Berzner, Executive Producer
    Fred Goldey, Production Manager
    Christopher Meisel, Production Supervisor
Specialties: Industrial/Corporate; Educational; Documentaries
Other Categories: TV; Commercials
Credits: DirecTV; AT&T Wireless; Dali Lama: Message for New Millenium; Bob Mann's Automatic Golf
Trade Assoc./Guilds/Unions: AICP, ERA, ITVA

ANOTHER LARGE PRODUCTION
5750 Wilshire Blvd., Ste 600
Los Angeles, CA 90036
Phone: ....(323) 954-8500
Fax: ....(323) 954-8510
www.anotherlarge.com
phillipl@anotherlarge.com
Key Executives/Personnel:
    Phillip Large, President
    Alan Skinner, Sr. VP
    Ron Cohen, VP & Director
    Marilyn Higgins, Sr. Producer
Specialties: Industrial/Corporate; Documentaries
Other Categories: Commercials
Credits: Colombia TriStar (corp. video); Curious World (documentary); V.I.P. (commercial); Martha Stewart (commercial)
Trade Assoc./Guilds/Unions: CTAM, DGA, NATPE, PROMAX

JOEL ASHER STUDIO
13448 Albers St.
Sherman Oaks, CA 91401
Phone: ....(818) 785-1551
Fax: ....(818) 785-1902
Key Executives/Personnel:
    Joel Asher, Producer & Director
    T. Michael, Producer
    Jeff Doucette, Teacher
Specialties: Educational; Documentaries
Credits: Getting The Part; Casting Directors; Agents: Tell It Like It Is!
Trade Assoc./Guilds/Unions: DGA, SAG, WGAw

THE ASSOCIATION, INC.
135 N. Screenland Dr.
Burbank, CA 91505
Phone: ....(818) 841-9660
Fax: ....(818) 841-8370
theassoc@aol.com
Key Executives/Personnel:
    Randy Stith, Producer
    Tim Melchior, Producer
    Fletch Murray, Producer
    Jeff Murphy, Production Manager
    Maureen Bernal, Sales Representative
Specialties: Industrial/Corporate
Other Categories: TV; Commercials
Credits: Quake Ready (PSA's); Hyundai (commercial); PAX TV (promos); Demin Bank (commercial)
First Look/Development Deals: PaxTV/Paxson Communications

AVD PRODUCTIONS, INC./AV DESIGNS
1738 Speyer Ln.
Redondo Beach, CA 90278
Phone: ....(310) 379-5818
dondavol@pacbell.net
Key Executives/Personnel:
    Genie Davis, Producer, Writer & Director
    Don Davis, Producer
Specialties: Industrial/Corporate; Educational
Other Categories: Feature Film; Commercials
Credits: Relentless; IHOP; Taco Bell
First Look/Development Deals: Smith Hemion Productions
Trade Assoc./Guilds/Unions: WGAw

BCPRODUCTIONS, INC./BCTV PRODUCTIONS
8 Seascape
Laguna Niguel, CA 92677
Phone: ....(949) 495-1500
Fax: ....(949) 495-4954
budconnell@aol.com
Key Executives/Personnel:
    Bud W. Connell, Executive Producer

Production Companies – Video

John G. Connell, Art Director
Ann Maré, Marketing Manager
Specialties: Industrial/Corporate; Educational; Documentaries
Other Categories: TV; Commercials
Credits: Goodwill; JCPenney; Hilton Hotels; Amercian Heart Association

BEARD BOY PRODUCTIONS
728 Via Otono Ave.
San Clemente, CA 92672
Phone: ....(949) 458-2305
Fax: ....(949) 458-2410
beardboy@earthlink.net
Key Executives/Personnel:
Mike Smith, Executive Producer
Rob Wagner, Executive Producer
Marya Reed, Producer
Specialties: Industrial/Corporate
Other Categories: Commercials
Credits: Blue Cross; Lexus; Hunt Wesson
Trade Assoc./Guilds/Unions: AFTRA, SAG

PAT BLESSING PRODUCTIONS
755 N. Lafayette Park Pl.
Los Angeles, CA 90026
Phone: ....(213) 413-4158
................................(213) 705-6978
Fax: ....(213) 413-4158
Key Executives/Personnel:
Pat Blessing, Owner
Specialties: Industrial/Corporate; Educational; Documentaries

CHRISTAL BLUE PRODUCTIONS
5723 Melrose Ave.
Los Angeles, CA 90038
Phone: ....(323) 466-9083
Fax: ....(323) 466-9583
www.christalblue.com
christalblucast@aol.com
Key Executives/Personnel:
Christal Blue, Producer
Specialties: Industrial/Corporate; Educational; Documentaries
Other Categories: Feature Film; Commercials
Credits: Smart & Final (corp. video); Airwalk (commercial); Spanish Entertainment (educational video); English Education (educational video)

BURRUD PRODUCTIONS
16351 Gothard St., Unit D
Huntington Beach, CA 92647
Phone: ....(714) 842-8422
Fax: ....(714) 842-0433
www.burrud.com
burrudprod@aol.com
Key Executives/Personnel:
John Burrud, President & CEO
Linda Karabin, VP of Administration
Drew Horton, VP of Production
Stan Green, VP of Business Affairs
Kurt Porter, VP of Post Production
Gita Patel, Producer
Gerry Wright, Producer
Shannon Mead, Assistant to Mr. Burrud
Specialties: Educational
Other Categories: TV
Credits: Weird World; Beyond Bizarre; Yoga for Children

CALAR
335 N. Maple Dr., Ste. 245
Beverly Hills, CA 90210
Phone: ....(310) 271-2202
Fax: ....(310) 271-8990

Key Executives/Personnel:
Caylyn E. Morris, Executive Producer
Alex Muñoz, Director
Specialties: Documentaries
Other Categories: Feature Film; TV; Commercials

CBIE, INC.
5723 Melrose Ave.
Los Angeles, CA 90038
Phone: ....(323) 466-9083
Fax: ....(323) 466-9583
www.christalblue.com
christalblucast@aol.com
Key Executives/Personnel:
Christal Blue, Producer
Specialties: Industrial/Corporate; Educational; Documentaries
First Look/Development Deals: CSD Entertainment, LLC.

THE CHELMAR GROUP
PMB# 345, 411 E. Huntington Dr., Bldg. 107
Arcadia, CA 91006
Phone: ....(626) 358-4001
chelmar@earthlink.net
Key Executives/Personnel:
Richard James, Executive Producer
Michelle Palmer, Producer
Specialties: Industrial/Corporate; Educational; Documentaries
Other Categories: Feature Film; Commercials; Music Video
Credits: Renewable Power (documentary); The View From Malabar (documentary); Salvation Army (commercial); Coca-Cola (commercial)

COAST MEDIA TELEPRODUCTIONS, INC.
17062 Murphy Ave., Bldg. B
Irvine, CA 92614
Phone: ....(949) 417-0300
www.coastmedia.com
digipost@earthlink.net
Key Executives/Personnel:
Art Royce, President, CEO & Producer
Brian Ferguson, Director of Photography
Joyce D. Smith, VP
Donovan Smith, Audio Engineer
Curtis Matovich, Editor & Composer
Steve Hirai, Production Manager
Becky Fisher, Account Manager
Specialties: Industrial/Corporate; Educational; Documentaries
Other Categories: TV; Commercials; Music Video; Interactive Multimedia
Credits: Simple Green (infomercial); Milk Advisory Board (commercial); Meguiar's Wax (corp. video & commercial); Disney (corp. video)

THE CREATIVE DEPARTMENT, LLC
26403 Emerald Dove Dr.
Valencia, CA 91355
Phone: ....(661) 288-1155
Fax: ....(661) 288-1166
mborchetta@mediaone.net
Key Executives/Personnel:
Mark Borchetta, Director & Producer
Specialties: Industrial/Corporate
Other Categories: Commercials; Music Video
Credits: Bushnell Sports Optics Worldwide; Mercedes-Benz; S. California Volvo Dealers; SAAB
Trade Assoc./Guilds/Unions: ASCAP

CRYSTAL PYRAMID PRODUCTIONS
7323 Rondel Ct.
San Diego, CA 92119
Phone: ....(619) 644-3000
................................(619) 293-9500
www.crystalpyramid.com

Production Companies – Video

cpp@newuniquevideos.com
Key Executives/Personnel:
- Mark Schulze, CEO
- Patty Mooney, COO
- Mike Freeman, Producer
- Michael Sterner, Producer

Specialties: Industrial/Corporate; Educational; Documentaries
Other Categories: TV
Credits: IBM; Coca-Cola

DALRYMPLE PRODUCTIONS
150 E. Meda Ave., Ste. 100
Glendora, CA 91741
Phone: (626) 963-5588
www.dalpro.com
james@dalpro.com
Key Executives/Personnel:
- James Dalrymple, Producer

Specialties: Industrial/Corporate; Educational; Documentaries
Other Categories: TV; Commercials

DAPTV ASSOCIATES
9080 Santa Monica Blvd.
West Hollywood, CA 90069
Phone: (310) 860-9001
(877) 860-9003
Fax: (310) 860-9003
www.daptv.com
info@daptv.com
Key Executives/Personnel:
- Don Azars, Writer, Director & Executive Producer
- Michael Berman, Producer

Specialties: Industrial/Corporate; Documentaries
Other Categories: TV; Commercials; Music Video
Credits: The Edge and Beyond; Crisis Counselor; Carroll, Her First Special

DENALI PRODUCTIONS, INC.
Studio One, 6743 Fernhill Dr.
Malibu, CA 90265
Phone: (310) 457-7566
Fax: (310) 457-5789
www.denaliproductions.com
bcarmic@earthlink.net
Key Executives/Personnel:
- Doug Millington, Executive Producer
- Bobby Carmichael, Director

Specialties: Industrial/Corporate
Other Categories: Feature Film; TV; Commercials
Credits: Merrill-Lynch (commercial); Sprite (commercial); Cadillac (commercial); Dayton 500 (documentary)

DIGITAL VISIONARIES
14009 Barner St.
Sylmar, CA 91342
Phone: (818) 364-0397
(800) 538-7800
Fax: (818) 364-0397
www.dvhome.com
richard@dvhome.com
Key Executives/Personnel:
- Richard Wainess, Founder & President

Specialties: Industrial/Corporate
Other Categories: Interactive Multimedia
Credits: MGM; Kowai America; Farmer's Insurance

DIGIVISION PRODUCTIONS
7164 Melrose Ave.
Los Angeles, CA 90046
Phone: (323) 937-3348
(323) 937-3349
Fax: (323) 937-3334
www.digivisionproductions.com
dvinfo@digivisionproductions.com
Key Executives/Personnel:
- Sam Mollo, Producer
- David Morris, Director

Specialties: Industrial/Corporate; Educational
Credits: Ball Park Franks; Domino's Pizza; Lincoln Mercury; Bank of Amercia

DOOM, INC.
355 N. Maple St., Ste. 112
Burbank, CA 91505
Phone: (818) 972-2007
Fax: (818) 972-2008
www.doominc.com
Key Executives/Personnel:
- Thomas Mignone, Director & Executive Producer
- Darci Oltman, Producer
- Peter Davison, Office Manager

Specialties: Industrial/Corporate
Other Categories: Commercials; Music Video; Interactive Multimedia
Credits: Slipknot - Spit it Out (music video); American Red Cross (corp. video); Mudvayne - Dig (music video); Donald Trump: Trump Organization (corp. video)

ELEVENTH DAY ENTERTAINMENT
17003 Ventura Blvd., Ste. 200
Encino, CA 91316
Phone: (818) 784-6403
Fax: (818) 784-6421
www.eleventhday.com
mail@eleventhday.com
Key Executives/Personnel:
- Frank Martin, Producer & Director
- Rudy Poe, Producer & Director

Specialties: Industrial/Corporate; Educational
Other Categories: TV; Commercials
Credits: CBS: The First Fifty Years; John Houston: The Man, The Movies, The Maverick; US Department of Defense; Balance Bars

EPIPHANY PRODUCTIONS, INC.
10625 Esther Ave.
Los Angeles, CA 90064
Phone: (310) 815-1266
(310) 505-1133
Fax: (310) 815-1269
roadog@concentric.net
Key Executives/Personnel:
- Dan Halperin, Producer
- Mark Frazel, Director of Development
- Scott JT Frank, Producer
- Karen Anderson, Line Producer

Specialties: Educational
Other Categories: Feature Film; TV
First Look/Development Deals: Liberty International Entertainment

FACE BROADCAST PRODUCTIONS
3921 W. Magnolia Blvd.
Burbank, CA 91505
Phone: (818) 842-9081
Fax: (818) 842-3708
www.facebroadcast.com
face@facebroadcast.com
Key Executives/Personnel:
- Jamie Celeste Tullo, Partner
- Ron Malvin, Partner
- Keith Leon, Audio & Video Engineer
- Ellen Rubel, Graphics

Specialties: Industrial/Corporate; Educational; Documentaries

Production Companies – Video

Other Categories: TV
Credits: The Alameda Corridor (LA County); Totally Cool Business News
Trade Assoc./Guilds/Unions: ATAS, NATPE

FAT CHANCE FILMS
3751 Motor Ave., Ste. 928
Los Angeles, CA 90034
Phone: ....(323) 882-4130
bobmardis2@aol.com
Key Executives/Personnel:
　Bobby Mardis, Producer & Director
Specialties: Industrial/Corporate
Other Categories: Feature Film; TV; Music Video
Credits: Midnight Blue; Circle of Pain; Why Colors; One Last Time
Trade Assoc./Guilds/Unions: DGA, WGAw

FOREST HILLS PICTURES
P.O. Box 49694
Los Angeles, CA 90049
Phone: ....(310) 207-6462
www.foresthillspictures.com
howeis@aol.com
Key Executives/Personnel:
　Howard Weisman, President & Executive Producer
Specialties: Industrial/Corporate
Other Categories: Feature Film; TV
Credits: Lovestruck

FOUR SQUARE PRODUCTIONS, INC.
5205 Kearny Villa Way
San Diego, CA 92123
Phone: ....(858) 874-1900
www.foursq.com
Key Executives/Personnel:
　John DeBello, Director
　Scott Sorensen, Sr. Producer
　David Craven, Sr. Producer
Specialties: Industrial/Corporate; Educational
Other Categories: Feature Film; TV; Commercials
Credits: This Week in Sports; SPA War (video); SignOnSanDiego.com; The Guide

FURMAN FILMS, INC.
4754 La Villa Marina, Ste. J
Marina Del Rey, CA 90292
Phone: ....(310) 306-2700
....(415) 350-8107
willfurman@aol.com
Key Executives/Personnel:
　Will Furman, Producer
Specialties: Documentaries
Other Categories: TV
Credits: Beyond Courage: Surviving Vietnam as a P.O.W.; The Best You Can Be; The Other Side of the Island; The Stones of Eden
Additional Info: 115 Stanley Ave., Pacifica., CA 94044, (650) 557-1550 phone

GALANTY & COMPANY, INC.
1640 Fifth St., Ste. 202
Santa Monica, CA 90401
Phone: ....(310) 451-2525
galantyco@juno.com
Key Executives/Personnel:
　Sidney Galanty, Director
　Mark Galanty, Executive Producer
　Sanja Brizic, Associate Producer & Writer
Specialties: Industrial/Corporate; Educational; Documentaries
Other Categories: Commercials; Music Video
Credits: TIAA: Cref Mutual Funds; America's Workout; Jane Fonda Workout Series
Trade Assoc./Guilds/Unions: AAPC

GEARS COMMUNICATIONS
315 W. Verdugo Ave.
Burbank, CA 91502
Phone: ....(818) 840-9333
Fax: ....(818) 840-9358
www.gearscom.com
maureen@gearscom.com
Key Executives/Personnel:
　Greg Gears, Producer
　Steven Kovner, VP of Production
　Maureen English, VP of Sales
Specialties: Industrial/Corporate; Educational; Documentaries
Other Categories: TV; Music Video; Interactive Multimedia

GERONIMO FILM PRODUCTIONS, INC.
8205 Santa Monica Blvd., Ste. 428
Los Angeles, CA 90046
Phone: ....(323) 965-0200
Fax: ....(323) 634-7337
www.geronimofilms.com
geronimofilm@earthlink.net
Key Executives/Personnel:
　Philip Atwell, Owner & Executive Producer
Specialties: Documentaries
Other Categories: Music Video
Credits: Eminem - The Real Slim Shady; Dr. Dre - The Next Episode; Dr. Dre - Forgot about Dre; Dr. Dre - Up in Smoke Tour (documentary)

JEFF GOLD PRODUCTIONS, INC.
13900 Panay Way, Ste. 309
Marina Del Rey, CA 90292
Phone: ....(310) 827-9165
j47737@yahoo.com
Specialties: Industrial/Corporate
Other Categories: Feature Film; TV; Commercials; Music Video
Credits: The Alpha Section; Talking Heads; Career Bed; Changing Times
Trade Assoc./Guilds/Unions: DGA

GREENWATER PICTURES
3940 Laurel Canyon Blvd., Ste. 736
Studio City, CA 91604
Phone: ....(323) 655-9585
Fax: ....(323) 655-9025
www.greenwaterpictures.com
tlowe@greenwaterpictures.com
Key Executives/Personnel:
　Tom Lowe, President & Producer
　Barbara Cordis, VP of Development
Specialties: Industrial/Corporate
Other Categories: Commercials; Music Video; Interactive Multimedia
Credits: Fireball (webisodes); Nick Forester (webisodes)
Trade Assoc./Guilds/Unions: DGA

GREYSTONE COMMUNICATION GROUP, INC./GREYSTONE FILMS
5161 Lankershim Blvd., Ste. 280
North Hollywood, CA 91601
Phone: ....(818) 762-2900
Fax: ....(818) 762-1626
www.ghistory.com
Key Executives/Personnel:
　Craig Haffner, Chairman, CEO & President of Greystone Films
　Shinaan Krakowsky, COO & General Counsel
　Rick Brookwell, CFO & Corporate Counsel
　Donna E. Lusitana, President of Greystone TV
　Nicholas Stein, VP of Greystone TV
　Melanie Blythe-Moreau, VP of Greystone TV
　Raymond Bridgers, VP of Greystone TV
　Glenn Kirschbaum, VP of Greystone TV
Specialties: Documentaries
Other Categories: TV

Production Companies – Video

Credits: Prophecies; Ancient Mysteries
First Look/Development Deals: A&E Television Networks

HALLMARK ENTERTAINMENT
1325 Avenue of the Americas, 21st Fl.
New York, NY 10019
Phone: ....(212) 977-9001
....(323) 634-3000
Fax: ....(212) 977-9049
www.hallmarkent.com
Key Executives/Personnel:
  Robert Halmi, Sr., Chairman
  Robert Halmi, Jr., President & CEO
  Peter Von Gal, Executive VP & COO
  Bill Aliber, CFO
  David V. Picker, President of Production Worldwide
  Dan Martin, Executive VP of Production
  Lynn Holst, Sr. VP of Development
  Janet Jacobson, Sr. VP & Co-Production Programming
  Tony Guido, Sr. VP of Legal & Business Affairs
  Kelly Coogan Swanson, VP of Marketing
Specialties: Educational; Documentaries
Other Categories: TV
Credits: Arabian Nights; Merlin; Dinotopia; Animal Farm
Additional Info: 4201 Wilshire Blvd., Ste. 304, Los Angeles, CA 90010

DAVID HAUGLAND PRODUCTIONS
8961 Sunset Blvd., Ste. 2D
West Hollywood, CA 90069
Phone: ....(310) 550-1556
Fax: ....(310) 550-1584
dkhaugland@earthlink.net
Key Executives/Personnel:
  David Haugland, Producer & Director
  Christopher Miller, Assistant
Specialties: Industrial/Corporate; Educational; Documentaries
Other Categories: Feature Film; TV; Music Video
Credits: Changing Our Minds; World and Time Enough; The Oscar Legacy; The Portrait
Trade Assoc./Guilds/Unions: DGA, WGAw

THE JIM HENSON COMPANY
1416 N. La Brea Ave.
Los Angeles, CA 90028
Phone: ....(323) 802-1500
Fax: ....(323) 802-1825
www.henson.com
Key Executives/Personnel:
  Brian Henson, Chairman
  Charles H. Rivkin, President & CEO
  Linda Govreau, Executive VP of Corporate Finance & CFO
  Lisa Henson, President, Jim Henson Pictures
  John Stephenson, Executive VP & Creative Supervisor,
    Jim Henson's Creature Shop
  Juliet Blake, Executive VP & Co-Head, Jim Henson
    Television Group Worldwide
  Angus Fletcher, Executive VP & Co-Head, Jim Henson
    Television Group Worldwide
  Peter Schube, General Counsel & Executive VP of Business
    & Legal Affairs
  Michael Bolingbroke, Sr. VP of Finance & Operations,
    Jim Henson's Creature Shop
  Craig Allen, Sr. VP & General Manager, Jim Henson Interactive
  Robert Norton, Sr. VP of Business & Legal Affairs
  Ritamarie Peruggi, Sr. VP of Production Worldwide
  Robert Wozniak, VP of Production Administration & Finance,
    Production Executive
  Kristine Belson, Production, Jim Henson Pictures
  Louis Philips, VP of Production Administration
  Halle Stanford Grossman, VP of Creative Affairs, Jim Henson Television
  Ruth Caruso, VP of Development, Jim Henson Television
  Michele Martell, VP of Business Affairs & Interactive
    Business Development
  Antonia Downey, VP of Int'l. Legal & Business Affairs
  Pete Coogan, VP of Physical Production
  David Barrington-Holt, Creative Supervisor, Jim Henson's
    Creature Shop
  Debbie McClellan, Sr. Director of Corporate Communications
    & Special Projects
  Omar Camacho, Director of Current Programming,
    Jim Henson Television
Specialties: Educational
Other Categories: Feature Film; TV; Commercials; Music Video;
  Interactive Multimedia
Credits: Farscape; Story Telling with Tomie de Paola; Rat; Muppets From Space

HODGE FILM & VIDEO
10770 Esther Ave.
Los Angeles, CA 90064
Phone: ....(310) 441-9773
Fax: ....(310) 474-7611
hodge@pacbell.net
Key Executives/Personnel:
  David Hodge, President
  Stacey Freeman, Producer
Specialties: Industrial/Corporate; Documentaries
Other Categories: TV; Commercials; Music Video
Credits: Carly Simon - Every Time We Say Goodbye; Bank One (corp. video); Human Rights Campaign; Carlos Santana - Supernatural

HORIZON SHINE, INC.
8621 Hayden Pl.
Culver City, CA 90232
Phone: ....(310) 990-6532
Fax: ....(310) 280-9776
www.horizonshine.com
info@horizonshine.com
Key Executives/Personnel:
  Robert Nackman, Executive Producer
Specialties: Industrial/Corporate
Other Categories: Commercials; Music Video
Credits: Kodak Film; American Eagle; Burger King (corp. video)

THE HOUSE PRODUCTION COMPANY
1429 N. Spaulding Ave.
Los Angeles, CA 90046
Phone: ....(323) 851-5151
....(323) 697-3830
Fax: ....(323) 851-9598
Key Executives/Personnel:
  Bonnie Matchinga, Executive Producer
  Alleda Harrison, Marketing Director
  Bob Schwartz, Director
Specialties: Industrial/Corporate; Educational; Documentaries
Other Categories: Feature Film; Commercials
Credits: Poligrip; Total Telcom Media; Birds and the Bees
Trade Assoc./Guilds/Unions: DGA

HY-TONE PRODUCTIONS
26349 Fairside Rd.
Malibu, CA 90265
Phone: ....(310) 456-3052
Fax: ....(310) 456-9659
www.notelvis.com
hytone@aol.com
Key Executives/Personnel:
  Robert Jaye, Producer, Director & Cinematographer
  Walter Hoylman, Producer, Director & Editor
Specialties: Industrial/Corporate; Educational; Documentaries
Other Categories: Feature Film; TV; Interactive Multimedia

Credits: Some of the King's Men; Mustang America; Art and Sex; Fire Engine

IMPACT PSA, INC.
1429 N. Spaulding Ave.
Los Angeles, CA
Phone: ....(323) 851-5151
....(323) 697-3830
Fax: ....(323) 851-9598
Key Executives/Personnel:
  Bonnie Matchinga, Executive Producer
  Alleda Harrison, Director of Marketing
Specialties: Industrial/Corporate; Educational; Documentaries
Other Categories: Feature Film; Commercials
Credits: Spilled Milk (PSA); A Place For Me (documentary)
Trade Assoc./Guilds/Unions: DGA

IN PLAY MEDIA ARTS
4174 Ince Blvd.
Culver City, CA 90232
Phone: ....(310) 839-7497
....(800) 260-6580
Fax: ....(310) 839-5365
www.inplaymediaarts.com
dutydukes@aol.com
Key Executives/Personnel:
  Gary Hoffman, no title
Specialties: Industrial/Corporate
Other Categories: Feature Film; Commercials

INFOMERCIAL SOLUTIONS, INC.
5512 Meadow Vista Way
Agoura Hills, CA 91301
Phone: ....(818) 879-1140
Fax: ....(818) 879-1148
www.infomercialsolutions.com
infosol2@aol.com
Key Executives/Personnel:
  David Schwartz, President
  Rosemary Kavanaugh, CEO
Specialties: Industrial/Corporate; Educational
Other Categories: Commercials
Credits: HT Beauty System, Ashley of Beverly Hills; Jenny Craig Weight Loss; Psychic Friends Network; Cambridge Credit Corporation

INTELLISCAPE FILMS, LLC
11601 Wilshire Blvd., 5th Fl.
Los Angeles, CA 90025
Phone: ....(310) 235-1422
....(800) 422-5996
Fax: ....(800) 828-4330
www.intelliscapefilms.com
info@intelliscapefilms.com
Key Executives/Personnel:
  Bruce Caulk, Writer & Director
  Jeff Teitelman, Writer
Specialties: Industrial/Corporate
Other Categories: TV; Commercials
Credits: San Diego Convention Visitors Bureau; Konami; National Financial Partners; Royal Family of Saudi Arabia (documentary)

INTERNATIONAL TELEVISION GROUP (ITG)
1322 Second St., Ste. 6
Santa Monica, CA 90401
Phone: ....(310) 656-9100
Fax: ....(310) 656-9104
intvg@aol.com
Key Executives/Personnel:
  Teresa Campbell, VP of Development & Production
  Lou La Monte, Producer
Specialties: Industrial/Corporate

Other Categories: Feature Film; TV; Commercials
Credits: Cat on a Hot Tin Roof (1985); Uncle Wally's General Store

IPS PRODUCTIONS
3518 Cahuenga Blvd. West, Ste. 100
Los Angeles, CA 90068
Phone: ....(323) 851-3595
Fax: ....(323) 851-4679
oneips@aol.com
Key Executives/Personnel:
  Jim Sommers, President & Executive Producer
  Dennis McCullough, Producer
Specialties: Industrial/Corporate
Other Categories: Commercials
Credits: Ford; Pontiac

JKR PRODUCTIONS, INC.
12140 W. Olympic Blvd., Ste. 21
Los Angeles, CA 90064
Phone: ....(310) 826-3666
Fax: ....(310) 471-8438
jimruxin@aol.com
Key Executives/Personnel:
  Jim Ruxin, Producer
Specialties: Industrial/Corporate; Educational; Documentaries
Other Categories: Feature Film; TV; Commercials
Credits: Stoogemania; Defense Play; In God We Trust
Trade Assoc./Guilds/Unions: DGA, IALocal700

KAVICH REYNOLDS PRODUCTIONS, INC.
6381 Hollywood Blvd., Ste. 580
Hollywood, CA 90028
Phone: ....(323) 466-2490
Fax: ....(323) 466-3655
www.kavichreynolds.com
Key Executives/Personnel:
  Steve Kavich, Executive Producer
  John Reynolds, Executive Producer
Specialties: Industrial/Corporate
Other Categories: Commercials
Credits: Harley Davidson; Suzuki; Namco; Yamaha

KELLEY PRODUCTIONS INTERNATIONAL
2047 Caminito Capa
La Jolla, CA 92037
Phone: ....(858) 456-6609
Fax: ....(858) 459-5876
www.globalcuisine.com
Key Executives/Personnel:
  Marie G. Kelley, President
Specialties: Industrial/Corporate; Educational; Documentaries
Other Categories: TV; Commercials
Trade Assoc./Guilds/Unions: ATAS, IDA, ITVA

LET THERE BE LIGHT PRODUCTIONS
4240 Lost Hills Rd., Ste. 2801
Agoura Hills, CA 91301
Phone: ....(818) 880-4717
Fax: ....(818) 880-4717
littnet@cs.com
Key Executives/Personnel:
  Robert Litt, Producer
Specialties: Industrial/Corporate
Other Categories: Feature Film; TV; Commercials; Music Video
Credits: Jenny Craig; WorldFreeNet.com; MPI/LA Tourism Bureau; Turbo - Take It To The Limit
First Look/Development Deals: Summer Storm Pictures

Production Companies – Video

LIGHTNING BOLT PIX: BARNYARD PRODUCTIONS
1653 18th St., Ste. 3B
Santa Monica, CA 90404
Phone: ....(310) 828-8239
Fax: ....(310) 828-1923
www.boltpix.com
mwbfield@aol.com
Key Executives/Personnel:
  Michael Barnard, Owner, Producer & Director
  Morgan Barnard, Co-Owner, Director & Editor
  Philip DeVellis, Production Coordinator & Designer
Specialties: Industrial/Corporate; Educational; Documentaries
Other Categories: TV; Commercials; Music Video
Credits: Bringing The Light; Chihuly River of Glass; Edgar.com; National Labor Life

LUCID MEDIA
7120 Alcove Ave.
North Hollywood, CA 91605
Phone: ....(818) 764-8580
www.loop.com/~macbravo
macbravo@loop.com
Key Executives/Personnel:
  Marino Colmano, Producer
Specialties: Documentaries
Other Categories: Feature Film; TV; Commercials
Credits: Reservoirs of Strength; End of the Rainbow

LYON STUDIOS
Phone: ....(949) 723-0657
....(949) 640-6246
Fax: ....(949) 640-6518
wwiles1430@aol.com
Key Executives/Personnel:
  William C. Wiles, Producer
Specialties: Industrial/Corporate; Documentaries
Other Categories: Commercials
Credits: National Car Rental; Valvoline Motor Oil; Canon Copiers; Giant Foods

MAKE IT HAPPEN PRODUCTIONS, INC.
Phone: ....(323) 851-6444
Fax: ....(323) 851-6465
www.billyfrank.com
mihpi@aol.com
Key Executives/Personnel:
  Billy Frank, President & Producer
  Todd Denkin, Director & Producer
  Mark Eberle, Director of Photography
  Caroline Hileman, Assistant to President & Coordinator
Specialties: Industrial/Corporate; Educational; Documentaries
Other Categories: Feature Film; TV; Commercials; Music Video
Credits: Wap!; Toughman (specials); Australian Experience
First Look/Development Deals: ABC Entertainment Television Group, FX Networks, LLC
Trade Assoc./Guilds/Unions: SAG, WGAw

CHARLES MALCOLM VIDEO PRODUCTIONS
P.O. Box 1772
Newport Beach, CA 92646
Phone: ....(714) 963-4222
charlesmalcolm@yahoo.com
Key Executives/Personnel:
  Charles Malcolm, Owner
Specialties: Industrial/Corporate
Other Categories: Feature Film; Commercials

NIKI MARVIN PRODUCTIONS
8919 Harratt St., Ste. 304
Los Angeles, CA 90069
Phone: ....(310) 274-6320
Key Executives/Personnel:
  Niki Marvin, President
Specialties: Documentaries
Other Categories: Feature Film; TV
Credits: Nightmare On Elm Street 3; Buried Alive 1 & 2; The Shawshank Redemption

MATRIX COMMUNICATIONS
2522 Torrance Blvd.
Torrance, CA 90503
Phone: ....(310) 782-8400
Key Executives/Personnel:
  Marta Houske, Executive Producer & Director
Specialties: Industrial/Corporate; Educational; Documentaries
Other Categories: Feature Film; Commercials; Music Video; Interactive Multimedia
Credits: Zimbabwe Legit (music video); A Stitch in Time (documentary); Times Mirror (commercial); In Search of … (TV series)

MEGAHERTZ PICTURES
1600 Rosecrans Ave., Bldg. 2B, 1st. Fl.
Manhattan Beach, CA 90266
Phone: ....(310) 727-2600
Fax: ....(310) 727-2601
www.directorsite.com
megahertz@directorsite.com
Key Executives/Personnel:
  John Harris, Executive Producer
  Francis Mohajerin, Executive Producer
  Masashi Nagadoi, Producer & Writer
  Suzanne O'Keefe, Producer & Writer
Specialties: Industrial/Corporate
Other Categories: Feature Film; Commercials
Credits: She Said I Love You

MM2K
838 N. Doheny Dr., Ste. 904
West Hollywood, CA 90069
Phone: ....(310) 276-0750
Fax: ....(310) 276-0229
mm2k@earthlink.net
Key Executives/Personnel:
  William A. Levey, Executive Producer & Director
  Bob Manning, Head Producer
  Nancy Youngblood, Director of Creative Development
Specialties: Industrial/Corporate
Other Categories: Feature Film; TV; Commercials; Music Video
Credits: Slumber Party 57; The Happy Hooker Goes To Washington; Skatetown U.S.A; White Stallion
Trade Assoc./Guilds/Unions: DGA, IATSE, WGAw

MONAREX HOLLYWOOD CORPORATION
9421 1/2 W. Pico Blvd.
Los Angeles, CA 90035
Phone: ....(310) 552-1069
Fax: ....(310) 552-1724
Key Executives/Personnel:
  Chris D. Nebe, President
Specialties: Educational; Documentaries
Other Categories: Feature Film; TV
Credits: Heartbreaker; Rebels; The Inheritors; Last of The Caravans
Trade Assoc./Guilds/Unions: IDA

MUSIC ROOM PICTURES
P.O. Box 219
Redondo Beach, CA 90277
Phone: ....(310) 316-4551

Production Companies – Video

Fax: ....(310) 540-3532
www.musicroomonline.com
mrp@aol.com
Key Executives/Personnel:
  John Reed, President
Specialties: Documentaries
Other Categories: Feature Film; Commercials; Music Video

NEMIROFF PRODUCTIONS
1506 Butler Ave., Ste. 1
Los Angeles, CA 90025
Phone: ....(310) 473-4100
....(310) 917-5250
Fax: ....(310) 473-4100
Key Executives/Personnel:
  Steve Nemiroff, Producer & Assistant Director
Specialties: Industrial/Corporate; Educational; Documentaries
Other Categories: Feature Film; TV; Commercials; Music Video; Interactive Multimedia
Credits: The Real Deal; Miracles; Sparkletts; Kenny Kingston's Psychic Hotline III
Trade Assoc./Guilds/Unions: AFI, AICP, ITVA

NEW & UNIQUE VIDEOS
7323 Rondel Ct.
San Diego, CA 92119
Phone: ....(619) 644-3000
....(619) 293-9500
Fax: ....(619) 644-3001
www.newuniquevideos.com
video@newuniquevideos.com
Key Executives/Personnel:
  Mark Schulze, CEO
  Patty Mooney, COO
Specialties: Industrial/Corporate; Educational; Documentaries

NITESTAR PRODUCTIONS
6671 Sunset Blvd., Bldg. 1509, Ste. 104
Los Angeles, CA 90028
Phone: ....(323) 468-8089
Fax: ....(323) 468-8094
www.nitestar.com
jvasilatos@nitestar.com
Key Executives/Personnel:
  Jerry A. Vasilatos, President, Producer, Director & Editor
  John O'Shaugnessy, Videographer & Cinematographer
  Kevin Leadingham, Associate Producer & Director
Specialties: Documentaries
Other Categories: Feature Film; Commercials
Credits: Shelter Me; A Refugee & Me; Solstice

NXT ENTERTAINMENT
8639 Holloway Plaza Dr.
Los Angeles, CA 90069
Phone: ....(310) 289-9600
Fax: ....(310) 289-7383
www.wwwcine.com
nxt@wwwcine.com
Key Executives/Personnel:
  Klaus Lucka, Executive Producer
Specialties: Industrial/Corporate
Other Categories: Feature Film; TV; Commercials; Interactive Multimedia
Credits: www.cyberkidsplanet.com; www.neobodies.com
Trade Assoc./Guilds/Unions: DGA

OCTOBER PRODUCTIONS
122 E. Arrellaga
Santa Barbara, CA 93101
Phone: ....(805) 962-2523
Fax: ....(805) 650-0704
octprod@pacbell.net

Key Executives/Personnel:
  Richard Hughes, Producer, Writer & Director
Specialties: Industrial/Corporate; Educational; Documentaries
Other Categories: TV; Commercials
Credits: G.M.; Toshiba; JCPenney; Mentor
Trade Assoc./Guilds/Unions: DGA

ONE STEP PRODUCTIONS
12188 Laurel Terrace
Studio City, CA 91604
Phone: ....(818) 762-1624
Fax: ....(818) 763-1955
www.loop.com/~sister
sister@loop.com
Key Executives/Personnel:
  Judy Chaikin, Owner
  Nancy Kissock, Producer
Specialties: Industrial/Corporate; Educational; Documentaries
Other Categories: Feature Film; TV
Credits: Cotillion 65; Legacy of the Hollywood Blacklist FBI: Untold Stories; Stolen Innocence
Trade Assoc./Guilds/Unions: DGA

ONYX PRODUCTIONS, INC.
5550 Wilshire Blvd., Ste. 301
Los Angeles, CA 90036
Phone: ....(323) 692-9830
Fax: ....(323) 692-9832
onyxprod@aol.com
Key Executives/Personnel:
  Joan Renfrow, President
Specialties: Industrial/Corporate; Educational
Other Categories: Commercials
Credits: Ron Popeil's Automatic Pasta Maker; Hoover; Thighmaster Plus; Gary Player Gran Prix Irons
Additional Info: Specializes in DRTV

OUR PRODUCTIONS, INC.
6255 Sunset Blvd., Ste. 2201
Hollywood, CA 90028
Phone: ....(323) 465-4197
....(818) 816-7332
Fax: ....(323) 465-6549
www.ourproduction.com
patricia@ourproduction.com
Key Executives/Personnel:
  Rick Munoz, Director & Producer
  Patricia Bolt, Director of Marketing & Production
Specialties: Industrial/Corporate; Educational; Documentaries
Other Categories: Feature Film; TV; Commercials; Music Video
Credits: Natalie Cole Live at The Coliseum; The Miller Brewing Company; Winchell's Donuts

OVATION ENTERTAINMENT
Phone: ....(310) 344-1442
ovationmail@yahoo.com
Key Executives/Personnel:
  Steve Woroniecki, Producer
Specialties: Industrial/Corporate; Educational; Documentaries
Other Categories: Commercials; Music Video

P.A.T. PRODUCTIONS
10202 W. Washington Blvd., David Lean Bldg., Ste. 230
Culver City, CA 90232
Phone: ....(310) 244-8811
Fax: ....(310) 244-1210
patprod@spe.sony.com
Key Executives/Personnel:
  Pat Sajak, President
  David Williger, Executive VP
  Gary Templeton, Director of Children's Programming

Production Companies – Video

Specialties: Educational
Other Categories: Feature Film; TV
Credits: Angus & the Ducks; Leo the Late Bloomer (animated); Merry Christmas; Space Case (animated)
First Look/Development Deals: Columbia TriStar Television

EDWARD PACIO & ASSOCIATES
Phone: (818) 880-1586
(310) 560-9221
Fax: (818) 880-1001
epacio@earthlink.net
Key Executives/Personnel:
Edward Pacio, Producer & Director
Chip Payne, Producer & DP
Kevin Ford, Art Director
Specialties: Industrial/Corporate; Educational
Other Categories: Commercials
Credits: Prevent-A-Theft; Lasik Vision; Healthy Hair
Additional Info: P.O. Box 1363, Pacific Palisades, CA 90272

GEORGE PAIGE ASSOCIATES, INC.
3000 W. Olympic Blvd., Ste. 1407
Santa Monica, CA 90404
Phone: (310) 315-4835
Fax: (310) 315-4836
gpacorp@aol.com
Key Executives/Personnel:
George Paige, Owner & President
James R. Tumminia, Producer
Specialties: Educational
Other Categories: Feature Film; TV; Commercials; Music Video; Interactive Multimedia
Credits: Abbott & Costello Meet Jerry Seinfeld; 50 Years of Funny Females; Shafted
Trade Assoc./Guilds/Unions: ATAS

PERSEVERANCE PRODUCTIONS
Phone: (310) 306-1960
Fax: (310) 306-1820
buddywins@aol.com
Specialties: Industrial/Corporate; Educational; Documentaries
Other Categories: Commercials; Music Video
Credits: Ford; Pfizer; Alamo; Rite Aid
Trade Assoc./Guilds/Unions: DGA

PERSPECTIVE FILMS
Phone: (310) 670-4030
(310) 261-8389
Fax: (310) 670-4031
Key Executives/Personnel:
Debbie Pietsch, Executive Producer
Specialties: Industrial/Corporate; Educational; Documentaries
Other Categories: Feature Film; TV; Commercials; Music Video; Interactive Multimedia
Credits: Fast Point DSL; Mattel; Disney; Harman Kardan: MacWorld

PICTURE MILL
5620 Hollywood Blvd.
Los Angeles, CA 90028
Phone: (323) 465-8800
Fax: (323) 465-8875
www.picturemill.com
richard@picturemill.com
Key Executives/Personnel:
Eric Ladd, President
Rick Probst, Creative Director
Richard Frank, Marketing & New Business
Bill Cole, Digital Trailers
Specialties: Industrial/Corporate
Other Categories: Feature Film
Credits: Godzilla (trailer); X-Files (trailer); Zorro (trailer); Fierce Creatures (trailer)

POINT OF VIEW PRODUCTIONS
2477 Folsom St.
San Francisco, CA 94110
Phone: (415) 821-0435
(415) 227-9292
Fax: (415) 931-0948
www.wenet.net/~karil/about.html
karil@wenet.net
Key Executives/Personnel:
Karil Daniels, Producer & Director
Specialties: Industrial/Corporate; Educational; Documentaries
Other Categories: TV; Commercials

POLESTAR FILM & PHOTOGRAPHIC PRODUCTION
P.O. Box 2269
Los Angeles, CA 90078
Phone: (323) 851-5488
(323) 791-7204
Fax: (323) 851-9006
polstar@att.net
Key Executives/Personnel:
James Peters, Producer
Specialties: Industrial/Corporate
Other Categories: Commercials
Credits: BMW; L & M Cigarettes; Ford; Chevrolet

POST MODERN EDIT
1211 E. Dyer Rd., Ste. 110
Santa Ana, CA 92705
Phone: (714) 751-2681
Fax: (714) 751-2686
www.postmodernedit.com
info@postmodernedit.com
Key Executives/Personnel:
Scott Cain, Director of Production
Tim Pendergrass, Sr. Producer
Jim Reed, Sr. Staff Editor
Rick Warren, Executive VP of Marketing & Operations
Janice Daniello, VP of Sales
Jason Syzmanski, VP of Operations
Tony Kost, Director of Axillary Marketing
Specialties: Industrial/Corporate
Other Categories: Commercials
Credits: Canon Computer Systems; Rockwell Collins Passenger Systems; Dominion Alarm; Orange Co. Water District
Trade Assoc./Guilds/Unions: Media Alliance of Orange County

PRODUCERS GROUP, LTD.
713 S. Pacific Coast Hwy., Ste. B
Redondo Beach, CA 90277
Phone: (310) 316-0481
Fax: (310) 316-1482
producers_group@csi.com
Key Executives/Personnel:
Lee Gluckman, President & Executive Producer
Ted Raynor, Executive VP of Legal Affairs & Executive Producer
Specialties: Documentaries
Other Categories: Feature Film; TV; Commercials
Credits: After The Red Star; Kids Are Cooking; Chicago Heist; San Miguel
Trade Assoc./Guilds/Unions: AFTRA, SAG

PRODUCTION ANALYSIS CORPORATION
Phone: (323) 876-6186
goodadvice@earthlink.net
Key Executives/Personnel:
Martin Pitts, Producer
Specialties: Industrial/Corporate; Documentaries
Other Categories: Feature Film; TV; Commercials; Music Video
Credits: Wild California; The Full Moon Show with Robbie Robertson; The Bee Gees Live Concert Video

Production Companies – Video

THE PRODUCTION ASYLUM
P.O. Box 360
Carlsbad, CA 92018
Phone: ....(760) 599-5494
Fax: ....(760) 439-6688
productionsasylum@aol.com
Key Executives/Personnel:
    Amy Krause, Producer & President
    Cat Sautter, Producer, VP & Treasurer
Specialties: Industrial/Corporate; Educational
Other Categories: Commercials
Trade Assoc./Guilds/Unions: AFTRA, SAG

PROLETARIAT FILMWORKS
12165 Iredell St.
Studio City, CA 91604
Phone: ....(818) 763-8356
Fax: ....(818) 760-6584
proletfilm@aol.com
Key Executives/Personnel:
    Terry Moloney, Executive Producer
    Grant Gilmore, Line Producer
    Liam Kildare, Producer
Specialties: Industrial/Corporate; Educational; Documentaries
Other Categories: Feature Film; TV; Commercials; Music Video
Credits: Tourette Syndrome Foundation (PSA); Elvis 2000: A Video Scrapbook; Warner Music: Wallstreet; Shout for Antz
Trade Assoc./Guilds/Unions: AFTRA, SAG

QUASAR STUDIOS
P.O. Box 661266
Los Angeles, CA 90066
Phone: ....(310) 289-1547
    ....(818) 352-0908
Fax: ....(310) 289-1547
www.perufilmcommission.net
filmperu@gte.net
Key Executives/Personnel:
    Marggie Castellano, Producer
    Prudence Michael, Location Manager
    Monica Leon, Designer
Specialties: Documentaries
Other Categories: Feature Film; TV; Interactive Multimedia
Credits: Coyotes (feature); National Geographic: Ancient Graves; The Celestine Prophecy (miniseries); A&E: Ancient Mysteries

PATRICK RAYMOND ENTERTAINMENT, INC.
1041 N. Formosa Ave., Formosa Bldg., Ste. 209
West Hollywood, CA 90046
Phone: ....(323) 850-2918
Fax: ....(323) 850-2920
praymondh@aol.com
Key Executives/Personnel:
    Patrick Raymond, Executive Producer
    Albert Frigone, Associate Producer
    Joey Estella, Assistant
Specialties: Industrial/Corporate; Documentaries
Other Categories: Feature Film; TV; Commercials; Interactive Multimedia

REALITORY PRODUCTIONS
Phone: ....(818) 404-8711
Fax: ....(818) 702-8611
www.realitory.com
mac@realitory.com
Key Executives/Personnel:
    Michael Condro, Director, DP & VFX
    Monica Ramone, Producer & Partner
Specialties: Documentaries
Other Categories: Feature Film; Interactive Multimedia

Credits: World Championship: All Terrain Boards; Jousting, The First Extreme Sport; Strange and Weird Halloween Festivals
Trade Assoc./Guilds/Unions: IATSE, IFP

RED HOTS ENTERTAINMENT
3105 Amigos Dr.
Burbank, CA 91504
Phone: ....(818) 954-0092
    ....(818) 607-8331
Fax: ....(818) 954-8421
pogmothon@earthlink.net
Key Executives/Personnel:
    Chip Miller, Director & Partner
    Sue Travis Miller, VP of Post Production & Editor
    Jane Gurtiza, Production Coordinator
    Dan Pomeroy, Director
    Marvin "Young MC" Young, Director
    Mark St. Juste, Director
    Kit Gleason, Production Manager
    Eileen Salgro, VP of Operations
    Vanessa Browne, Producer
    Marc Wolfson, Music Producer
    Theo Forster, Producer
Specialties: Industrial/Corporate; Documentaries
Other Categories: Feature Film; TV; Commercials; Music Video
Credits: Four Day Shoot; Mortuary Academy; The Importance of Being Earnest; The Seven Fishes
Trade Assoc./Guilds/Unions: PGA, WGA

RED-HORSE PRODUCTIONS
6028 Calvin Ave.
Tarzana, CA 91356
Phone: ....(818) 705-2588
Fax: ....(818) 705-2523
www.naturallynative.com
redhorse88@aol.com
Key Executives/Personnel:
    Valerie Red-Horse, President, Producer, Writer, Actress & Director
    Dawn Jackson, Director of Development
    Yvonne Russo, VP, Producer & Actress
    Fabiane Carter, Executive Assistant
    Pam Aver, Business & Legal Affairs
Specialties: Educational; Documentaries
Other Categories: Feature Film; TV
Credits: Naturally Native (feature); The Whispers (documentary); Windows on Mars (educational); My Indian Summer (TV)
First Look/Development Deals: Valhala Motion Pictures
Trade Assoc./Guilds/Unions: HAPN, SAG, WGA, WIF

REEL ORANGE
316 La Jolla Dr.
Newport Beach, CA 92663
Phone: ....(949) 548-4524
    ....(714) 349-6322
Fax: ....(949) 548-0749
reelorange@aol.com
Key Executives/Personnel:
    Art Vitarelli, Producer
Specialties: Industrial/Corporate; Educational; Documentaries
Other Categories: TV; Commercials
Credits: Call of The Cangon; Mitsubishi Corp. (corp. video); Voices from the Stone

RICK REINERT PICTURES
1556 Covington Ave.
Westlake Village, CA 91361
Phone: ....(805) 494-0699
Fax: ....(805) 494-9780
Key Executives/Personnel:
    Rick Reinert, Producer & Director
    Tom Carter, Sales & Producer

Production Companies – Video

Carole Reinert, VP of Business Affairs
Specialties: Industrial/Corporate; Educational
Other Categories: Feature Film; TV
Credits: Capn' O.G. Readmore; Precious Moments Videos; Winnie The Pooh and a Day for Eeyore
Trade Assoc./Guilds/Unions: AMPAS, ASIFA, ATAS

REVOLVER FILMS, LLC
2022A Broadway
Santa Monica, CA 90404
Phone: (310) 829-2441
Fax: (310) 829-2661
Key Executives/Personnel:
Mark Priola, Producer
Jack Singman, Producer
Specialties: Industrial/Corporate; Documentaries
Other Categories: Feature Film; TV; Commercials
Credits: ATV Hardcore; Extended list available upon request.

RIDINI ENTERTAINMENT CORPORATION
c/o Raleigh Studios, 650 N. Bronson Ave., Ste. B-152
Los Angeles, CA 90004
Phone: (323) 960-8071
www.ridinientertainment.com
maryann@ridinientertainment.com
Key Executives/Personnel:
Mary Ann Ridini, no title
Specialties: Educational; Documentaries
Other Categories: Feature Film; TV
Credits: Falling Fire; Convict 762; Future Fear; Shepherd
First Look/Development Deals: Third Millennium

ROGUE ENTERTAINMENT
Phone: (801) 979-2229
(818) 682-2152
Fax: (801) 263-0551
Key Executives/Personnel:
Adam Smoot, Producer
Kevin DeLullo, Producer, Director & Writer
Specialties: Industrial/Corporate
Other Categories: Feature Film
Credits: Nightfall; Cage in Box Elder; Usher

RUMRUNNER CINE SERVICE
469 26th St.
Manhattan Beach, CA 90266
Phone: (310) 540-8411
(310) 901-5515
Fax: (310) 545-0136
omara@earthlink.net
Key Executives/Personnel:
Cay Mohr, Executive Producer & Owner
Gerry Trafficanda, Director & Owner
Kevin Van Fleet, Agency Owner
Lee Tirce, Director
Ron Dexter, Owner & Director
Mel Hall, Owner & Director
Andrew Gallerani, Director
Aaron Spelling, Executive Producer
James Row, Owner & Producer
Judy Trotter, Producer
Marilyn Penn, Producer
Paulette Glassman, Producer
Specialties: Industrial/Corporate; Educational; Documentaries
Other Categories: TV; Commercials
Credits: The State of Energy (documentary); E-I Carrier (training video); Dynasty (miniseries); Toyota (commercial)
Trade Assoc./Guilds/Unions: DGA

SCOTTI PRODUCTIONS
Phone: (323) 654-3666
(213) 500-1915
dscotti@earthlink.net
Key Executives/Personnel:
Don Scotti, Owner
Specialties: Documentaries
Other Categories: Feature Film; Commercials
Credits: Get Bruce! (documentary)
Trade Assoc./Guilds/Unions: AEA, SAG

SILVER LINING PRODUCTIONS, INC.
8687 Melrose Ave., Ste. B300
West Hollywood, CA 90069
Phone: (310) 289-6650
Fax: (310) 289-6658
slpbozena@aol.com/silverliningp@aol.com
Key Executives/Personnel:
Bozena Armstrong, Executive Producer & Director
Randy Haberkamp, Producer
Specialties: Industrial/Corporate
Other Categories: Feature Film; TV; Commercials; Interactive Multimedia
Credits: Cleopatra (promo); Forest Lawn (commercial); Reva: The Scarlet Years (video); The Unknown Tradition (documentary)
Trade Assoc./Guilds/Unions: DGA, SAG

SNAPDRAGON FILMS, INC.
13428 Maxella Ave., Ste. 293
Marina Del Rey, CA 90292
Phone: (310) 822-2505
Fax: (310) 822-7054
Key Executives/Personnel:
Bonnie Palef, Director, Producer & Writer
Catherine Purchase, Assistant
Manuel Granado, Jr., Assistant
Specialties: Documentaries
Other Categories: Feature Film; TV; Interactive Multimedia
Credits: Marvin's Room; Moonstruck; The Cemetary Club; Parents
First Look/Development Deals: Columbia Pictures/Columbia Tristar Motion Picture Group
Trade Assoc./Guilds/Unions: DGA, WGAw

SNEAK PREVIEW ENTERTAINMENT, INC.
1604 Vista del Mar
Hollywood, CA 90028
Phone: (323) 962-0295
Fax: (323) 962-0372
www.sneakpreviewentertain.com
sneakpreview@pacbell.net
Key Executives/Personnel:
Steven J. Wolfe, Chairman, CEO & Producer
Lynette Prucha Chavez, President & Writer
David L. Cohn, Talent Manager
Michael J. Roth, Director of Development
Specialties: Industrial/Corporate
Other Categories: Feature Film; TV; Music Video
Credits: Fast Sofa; Twin Falls, Idaho; Relax...It's Just Sex; Tollbooth

SOUTH FORK PRODUCTIONS
P.O. Box 1935
Santa Monica, CA 90406
Phone: (310) 829-5029
Fax: (310) 829-5029
soforkprods@ireland.com
Key Executives/Personnel:
Jim Sullivan, Producer & Director
Greg Sullivan, Producer
Specialties: Industrial/Corporate; Educational; Documentaries
Other Categories: Feature Film; TV; Commercials; Music Video

Production Companies – Video

Credits: Making of Without Limits; Portraits of Courage; Those Who Dare
Trade Assoc./Guilds/Unions: AFI

SPLENDIDLIGHT MEDIA PRODUCTIONS
177 Riverside St., PMB 151
Newport Beach, CA 92663
Phone: ....(949) 722-8485
Fax: ....(949) 722-7896
www.splendidlight.com
lsplendid@splendidlight.com
Key Executives/Personnel:
 Lynn Splendid, Producer & Director
 Clayton Light, Producer & Editor
Specialties: Industrial/Corporate; Educational; Documentaries
Other Categories: TV; Commercials
Additional Info: 2801 Pacific Coast Hwy., Ste. 325, Newport Beach, CA 92663

STEFANINO PRODUCTIONS
15515 Sunset Blvd., Ste. 101
Pacific Palisades, CA 90272
Phone: ....(310) 454-0109
Fax: ....(310) 454-0109
www.stefanino.com
stefanino@earthlink.net
Key Executives/Personnel:
 Stuart Jemesen, Producer & Director
 Stefan Kendal Gordy, Director of Music
Specialties: Documentaries
Other Categories: Feature Film; TV; Commercials; Music Video
Credits: Smokey Robinson; Michael Jackson Biography; Innerview (TV pilot)

STEREOMEDIA 3D VIDEO PRODUCTIONS
2307 W. Olive St.
Burbank, CA 91506
Phone: ....(818) 559-6515
Fax: ....(818) 559-6598
stereo3DTV@aol.com
Key Executives/Personnel:
 Anthony Coogan, Executive Producer
 Eric Bakke, CTO & Director of 3D Videography
 Patrick Dunauan, Producer
Specialties: Industrial/Corporate; Educational; Documentaries
Other Categories: Music Video; Interactive Multimedia

STROM MAGALLON ENTERTAINMENT
3518 Cahuenga Blvd. West, Ste. 111
Los Angeles, CA 90068
Phone: ....(323) 969-1089
 ....(323) 969-1090
Fax: ....(323) 969-1091
strommagent@earthlink.net
Key Executives/Personnel:
 Gregory Strom, Director
 Douglas Magallon, Director
Specialties: Documentaries
Other Categories: Feature Film; Commercials; Music Video
Credits: Dirt Devil (commercial); Pontiac (commercial)

MEL STUART PRODUCTIONS, INC.
1551 S. Robertson Blvd., Ste. 204
Los Angeles, CA 90035
Phone: ....(310) 785-9080
Fax: ....(310) 785-9179
melfilm@aol.com
Key Executives/Personnel:
 Mel Stuart, President, Producer & Director
 Chad Baron, Associate Producer
Specialties: Documentaries
Other Categories: Feature Film; TV

Credits: Running on the Sun; AFI's 100 Years 100 Movies; The Rise & Fall of the Third Reich; Ripley's Believe It or Not
Trade Assoc./Guilds/Unions: DGA, WGAw

SUZANNE BAUMAN PRODUCTIONS
21901 Velicata St.
Woodland Hills, CA 91364
Phone: ....(818) 348-4342
Fax: ....(818) 348-6482
suz557@aol.com
Key Executives/Personnel:
 Suzanne Bauman, Producer & Director
 Toni Pace, Producer & Editor
 John Marzilli, Director of Development
Other Categories: Feature Film; TV; Music Video
Credits: Jackie: Behind the Myth; Jack Hanna's Animal Adventures; La Belle Epoque; Women of Summer
Trade Assoc./Guilds/Unions: DGA; WGAw

TELLING PICTURES, INC.
121 Ninth St.
San Francisco, CA 94103
Phone: ....(415) 864-6714
Fax: ....(415) 864-4364
www.tellingpix.com
tellingpix@aol.com
Key Executives/Personnel:
 Rob Epstein, Director & Producer
 Jeffrey Friedman, Director & Producer
 Michael Ehrenzweig, Producer
 Whitney Saik, Production Manager
Specialties: Industrial/Corporate; Educational; Documentaries
Other Categories: Feature Film; TV
Credits: The Times of Harvey Milk; Common Threads: Stories from the Quilt; The Celluloid Closet; Paragraph 175
Trade Assoc./Guilds/Unions: AMPAS, ATAS

TEOCALLI ENTERTAINMENT, INC.
205 Timberline Court
Ruidoso, NM 88345
Phone: ....(505) 258-1373
Fax: ....(505) 258-1377
Key Executives/Personnel:
 Robert A. Nowotny, President
 Ed Callaway, Director of Development
Specialties: Documentaries
Other Categories: Feature Film; TV
Credits: False River; The Top Of The Bottom Half; The Legend of Billy The Kid; The Radicals

TIME-LIFE VIDEO
2000 Duke St.
Alexandria, VA 22314
Phone: ....(703) 838-7000
www.timelife.com
Key Executives/Personnel:
 Martin Shampaine, President
 Lisa Kauffman, Sr. VP
 Harvey Becker, VP of Business Development
 Sally Adams, Director of New Product Development
Specialties: Educational; Documentaries

TRIBE PICTURES
244 Main St.
Chatham, NJ 07928
Phone: ....(973) 635-2660
Fax: ....(973) 635-2654
www.tribepictures.com
mail@tribepictures.com

Production Companies – Video

Key Executives/Personnel:
    Vera Oakley, Producer & Director
Specialties: Industrial/Corporate
Other Categories: Feature Film

TVA PRODUCTIONS
10900 Ventura Blvd.
Studio City, CA 91604
Phone: ....(818) 505-8300
Fax: ....(818) 505-8370
www.tvaproductions.com
jgoddard@businessworldnews.com
Key Executives/Personnel:
    Jeffery Goddard, Executive Producer
    Andrea Goodstein, Executive VP of Production
    Geno Brunton, Sr. Producer
Specialties: Industrial/Corporate; Educational; Documentaries
Other Categories: TV; Commercials
Credits: Business World News
Trade Assoc./Guilds/Unions: AMPAS, IAAPA, TEA

TVP STUDIOS
1539 Magnolia Blvd.
Burbank, CA 91506
Phone: ....(818) 843-3188
Fax: ....(818) 843-3189
www.tvpstudios.cc
tvprich@aol.com
Key Executives/Personnel:
    Richard Tamayo, Producer
    Meredith Day, Producer
Specialties: Industrial/Corporate; Educational; Documentaries
Other Categories: TV; Commercials; Music Video
Credits: Bank of America; Panasonic; Golden Globe Awards; etvhollywood.com

VANGUARD PRODUCTIONS
12111 Beatrice St.
Culver City, CA 90230
Phone: ....(310) 306-4910
Fax: ....(310) 306-4910
vangrdprod@earthlink.net
Key Executives/Personnel:
    Terence M. O'Keefe, Writer, Producer & Director
    Brent Huff, Writer & Director
    S. Drew Stotesbery, VP of Production
    Bruce Miyaki, Director of Development
    Bennett Fidlow, Director of Creative Affairs
Specialties: Industrial/Corporate
Other Categories: Feature Film; TV; Commercials; Music Video
Credits: We The People; Wanted; The Bad Pack; Closing The Deal

VENTURE ENTERTAINMENT GROUP
P.O. Box 55113
Sherman Oaks, CA 91413
Phone: ....(818) 981-7813
....(800) 981-8433
Fax: ....(818) 981-3466
www.venture818.com
venture818@aol.com
Key Executives/Personnel:
    Leigh Leshner, Producer
Specialties: Industrial/Corporate; Educational; Documentaries
Other Categories: Feature Film; TV; Commercials
Credits: The Spa Workout (infomercial); Hidden Treasures (TV series); Zoofari; More Zoofari
Trade Assoc./Guilds/Unions: VSDA, WIF

VERITÉ PRODUCTIONS
3762 S. Hughes Ave., Ste. 306
Los Angeles, CA 90034
Phone: ....(310) 838-3119
www.craigforrest.com
craigforrest@earthlink.net
Key Executives/Personnel:
    Craig Forrest, Creative Director
Specialties: Documentaries
Other Categories: TV
Credits: In Concert; Strange Universe; World of Wonder; Travelling Life

VIDEO HOLLYWOOD PRODUCTIONS
P.O. Box 19336
Encino, CA 91416
Phone: ....(888) 368-7347
....(310) 890-0066
Fax: ....(805) 583-8809
pcsinc@dotregs.com
Key Executives/Personnel:
    Kirk Van Houten, President
    Bob Telford, VP of Post Production
    Alfred Powers, VP
    Steven Piper, VP
Specialties: Industrial/Corporate; Educational; Documentaries
Credits: El Monte Police (promo)

VIDEOWERKS
3435 Ocean Park Blvd., Ste. 112
Santa Monica, CA 90405
Phone: ....(310) 393-8754
....(800) 356-6541
Fax: ....(310) 399-1829
www.videowerks.com
videowerks@earthlink.net
Key Executives/Personnel:
    David M. Werk, Owner, Cameraman & DP
Specialties: Industrial/Corporate; Educational; Documentaries
Other Categories: TV; Commercials; Interactive Multimedia
Credits: The Directors; History's Lost & Found; Investigative Reports; Headliners & Legends
Trade Assoc./Guilds/Unions: IDA, ITVA

VIHLENE & ASSOCIATES, INC.
26941 Cabot Rd., Ste. 120
Laguna Hills, CA 92653
Phone: ....(949) 582-0937
Fax: ....(949) 582-0978
www.vihlene.com
vern@vihlene.com
Key Executives/Personnel:
    Vern Vihlene, President
    Vicki Wellnitz, Producer
    Betty McBurnie, Accountant
    George Adams, Post Supervisor
    Brent Loefke, Director
Specialties: Industrial/Corporate; Documentaries
Other Categories: TV; Commercials
Credits: Mailbox etc.; American Honda Motor Co.; AT&T; American Suzuki Motor Co.

WEINTRAUB/KUHN PRODUCTIONS
1900 Avenue of the Stars, Ste. 1440
Los Angeles, CA 90067
Phone: ....(310) 788-9380
Fax: ....(310) 788-0476
Key Executives/Personnel:
    Fred Weintraub, Producer
    Tom Kuhn, Producer
    Chrissy Sherbanee, Assistant to Mr. Weintraub & Mr. Kuhn
Specialties: Documentaries

Production Companies – Video

Other Categories: Feature Film; TV
Credits: High Road to China; The New Adventures of Robin Hood; Enter the Dragon; Devil's Arithmetic

WELLER/GROSSMAN PRODUCTIONS
14144 Ventura Blvd., Ste. 200
Sherman Oaks, CA 91423
Phone: ....(818) 755-4800
Fax: ....(818) 755-4820
Key Executives/Personnel:
  Garry H. Grossman, Executive Producer
  Robb Weller, Executive Producer
  Noel Poole, CFO
  Joel Rizor, Director of Programming
  Debbie Supnik, Development
  Steve Lange, General Manager
Specialties: Documentaries
Other Categories: TV
Credits: Food 911; Wolfgang Puck; The Most; National Geographic Program

WESTERN BRANCH PRODUCTIONS, INC.
4231 Beck Ave.
Studio City, CA 91604
Phone: ....(818) 762-3810
 ....(818) 642-3810
Fax: ....(818) 769-2847
www.western-branch.com
pvan@western-branch.com
Key Executives/Personnel:
  Pete Vanlaw, President
Specialties: Documentaries
Other Categories: TV; Commercials
Credits: Memories of a Millenium (documentary); Night at the Pote (TV pilot)
Trade Assoc./Guilds/Unions: DGA

BILL WHITE PRODUCTIONS
12423 Ventura Court, Ste. 200
Studio City, CA 91604
Phone: ....(818) 769-9090
Fax: ....(818) 769-1974
billwhitepro@earthlink.net
Key Executives/Personnel:
  Bill White, President
  Amy Shomer, Producer
Specialties: Industrial/Corporate; Educational; Documentaries
Other Categories: Feature Film; TV; Commercials; Music Video
Credits: Globe Life Insurance (commercial); United American Insurance (commercial); Sanyo-Fisher (corp. video); Test Flights (TV)
Trade Assoc./Guilds/Unions: DGA

YADA/LEVINE PRODUCTIONS
606 N. Larchmont Blvd., Ste. 100
Los Angeles, CA 90004
Phone: ....(323) 461-1616
Fax: ....(323) 461-2288
www.yadalevine.com
video@yadalevine.com
Key Executives/Personnel:
  Michael Yada, Executive Producer
Specialties: Industrial/Corporate
Other Categories: Commercials
Credits: ABC; Disney; Toyota

ZEAL PICTURES
6605 Hollywood Blvd., Ste. 300
Los Angeles, CA 90028
Phone: ....(323) 871-4000
Fax: ....(323) 871-4004
www.zealpictures.com
info@zealpictures.com
Key Executives/Personnel:
  Timm Oberwelland, Producer
  Leon Melas, Producer
  Robert Biehn, Producer
  George Salden, CFO
Specialties: Industrial/Corporate
Other Categories: Feature Film; Commercials; Music Video
Credits: Simpatico; Robbers; American Fighter Pilot; Werther's Originals
Trade Assoc./Guilds/Unions: SAG
Additional Info: Additional office in Berlin, Germany.

ZYSTAR FILMS, INC.
330 Washington Blvd., Ste. 400
Marina Del Rey, CA 90292
Phone: ....(310) 301-3313
Fax: ....(310) 301-9433
www.zystar.com
mwallis@zystar.com
Key Executives/Personnel:
  Meryl Alison Wallis, Executive Producer
  Carmen Silva, Producer
  Scott Murphy, Assistant Director
  Howard Raishbrook, Production Manager
  Doug Mickel, Producer
Specialties: Industrial/Corporate
Other Categories: Feature Film; TV; Commercials; Music Video
Credits: James Bond (behind the scenes); American Honda (commercial); Carrows Restaurants (commercial); Laurietta (feature)

Production Companies – Music Video

1171 PRODUCTION GROUP
303 S. Sweetzer Ave.
Los Angeles, CA 90048
Phone: ....(323) 655-1171
....(213) 247-7424
Fax: ....(323) 655-1135
www.1171.com
film1171@aol.com
Key Executives/Personnel:
  Grant Cihlar, Owner & Executive Producer
  Bruce Martin, Owner & Executive Producer
Specialties: Short Form; Long Form
Other Categories: Commercials
Credits: Bloodhound Gang - Mope; Alice DeeJay - Better Off Alone; Coca-Cola

21ST CENTURY MAN PRODUCTIONS
1950 N. Tamarind Ave., Ste. 323
Los Angeles, CA 90068
Phone: ....(323) 466-3227
....(310) 989-7353
Fax: ....(323) 466-3227
www.21stcman.com
future21@primenet.com
Key Executives/Personnel:
  Jane Linter, Producer & Director
  David May, Director & Editor
  Brian Bowie, Director & Director of Photography
  Andrea Fredrickson, Editor
Specialties: Short Form; Long Form
Other Categories: TV; Commercials; Video; Interactive Multimedia
Credits: 21st CMAN; Sebastian Int.; Wella Alternative Hair Show; Stylezone 2000
Trade Assoc./Guilds/Unions: AEA, BAFTA, DGA, NATPE
Additional Info: 33 Limes Rd., Beckenham, Kent BR3 6NS England

40 ACRES & A MULE FILMWORKS, INC.
124 Dekalb Ave.
Brooklyn, NY 11217
Phone: ....(718) 624-3703
Fax: ....(718) 624-2008
Key Executives/Personnel:
  Spike Lee, CEO
  Sam Kitt, President of Production
  Andre Hereford, Director of Development
  Heather Parish, Business Manager
Specialties: Short Form; Long Form
Other Categories: Feature Film; Commercials; Video
Credits: Bamboozled; Summer of Sam; He Got Game; Malcolm X
Additional Info: NY Development Office:
  75 S. Elliot Pl. 3rd Fl., Brooklyn, NY 11217

5TH GEAR ENTERTAINMENT
5657 Wilshire Blvd., Ste. 230
Los Angeles, CA 90036
Phone: ....(323) 954-0555
Fax: ....(323) 936-9421
centralhq@aol.com
Key Executives/Personnel:
  Carl Craig, Executive Producer
Specialties: Short Form; Long Form
Other Categories: Feature Film
Credits: Players Club; Hollywood Shuffle; Book of Love

A BAND APART COMMERCIALS
7966 Beverly Blvd., 2nd Fl.
Los Angeles, CA 90048
Phone: ....(323) 951-4400
Fax: ....(323) 951-4401
www.abandapart.com
info@abandapart.com
Key Executives/Personnel:
  Michael Bodnarchek, President & CEO
  Eric Bonniot, Executive Producer
  Kim Dellara, Executive Producer, Music Videos
  Mike Sarkissian, Head of Production, Music Videos
  Susan Boothby, Production Manager, Commercials
  Brian Rackohn, Controller
  Josh Goldstein, Assistant of Mr. Bodnarchek
Specialties: Short Form
Other Categories: Commercials

A FEW MILES NORTH
1507 Abbot Kinney Blvd.
Venice, CA 90291
Phone: ....(310) 399-6366
Fax: ....(310) 399-2632
Key Executives/Personnel:
  Brent Coert, Producer
  Scott Pourroy, Producer
Specialties: Short Form
Credits: Lucy Pearl - Without You; Veruca Salt - Born Entertainer; Luis Miguel - Amartees un Placer; Face To Face - God is a Man

ABSOLUTEFILMS.NET
1441 Huntington Dr., Ste. 3010
South Pasadena, CA 91030
Phone: ....(626) 442-6454
Fax: ....(626) 448-1930
www.absolutefilms.net
info@absolute.net
Key Executives/Personnel:
  Ty Thompson, Producer
  Byron Jost, Producer
  Josh Ochoa, Producer
  Robert Villalobos, Producer
  Tom Franklin, Producer
  Romeo Carey, Producer
Specialties: Short Form; Long Form
Other Categories: Commercials; Video; Interactive Multimedia
Credits: Juan-A-Be.com; Mr. Fab

AD-LIB MARKETING & ADVERTISING
One Blacksmith Circle
Phillips Ranch, CA 91766
Phone: ....(909) 629-1995
Fax: ....(909) 629-1995
ad-lib@2-hot.com
Key Executives/Personnel:
  Keith Underwood, Executive Producer
  Brenda Underwood, Associate Producer
Specialties: Short Form
Other Categories: Commercials; Video
Credits: Titan Business Solutions; P. Joseph, A Law Corp.; Ben & Jerry's; Perferred Financial Corp.

ALBRECHT & ASSOCIATES, INC.
3442 Dorothy Rd.
Topanga, CA 90290
Phone: ....(818) 222-4836
jaalbrecht@yahoo.com
Key Executives/Personnel:
  Joie Albrecht, President

Production Companies – Music Video

Specialties: Short Form; Long Form
Credits: Carol King One to One; Mickey's 60th Birthday
Trade Assoc./Guilds/Unions: DGA, SAG, WGA

ALTA VISTA PRODUCTIONS
11805 Mississippi Ave., Ste. 102
West Los Angeles, CA 90025
Phone: .... (310) 444-2050
Fax: .... (310) 444-2055
altvista@earthlink.net
Key Executives/Personnel:
  David Lozano, Executive Producer
  Michael Lozano, Producer
  Astrid Steel, Producer
  Colleen Steckloff, Casting Director
  Yves Douville, Post Production Supervisor
Specialties: Short Form
Other Categories: TV; Commercials

AMERICAN SPORTS NETWORK, INC.
P.O. Box 6100
Rosemead, CA 91770
Phone: .... (626) 292-2222
Fax: .... (626) 292-2221
Key Executives/Personnel:
  Louis Zwick, President
  Robin Chang, Director
  Steve Roguet, Producer
Specialties: Short Form; Long Form
Other Categories: TV; Video
Credits: ESPN; Eurosport; Star Sport Asia; TSN-Canada

ARSENAL, INC.
1103 N. El Centro Ave.
Hollywood, CA 90038
Phone: .... (323) 957-5100
Fax: .... (323) 957-5101
arsenlfilm@aol.com
Key Executives/Personnel:
  Larry Perel, Executive Producer
Specialties: Short Form; Long Form
Other Categories: Commercials
Credits: Live - They Stood Up For Love; Estevan Oriol - Heart of a Rebel; Wes Cunningham - Not Enough

THE ARTISTS COMPANY/THE A&R GROUP
1015 N. Fairfax Ave.
Los Angeles, CA 90046
Phone: .... (323) 650-4722
Fax: .... (323) 650-4706
Key Executives/Personnel:
  Roberto Cecchini, Executive Producer & President
  Lori Lober, Executive Producer
  Susan Burton, Head of Production
Specialties: Short Form
Other Categories: Commercials

ASHLEY PRODUCTIONS
5225 Canyon Crest Dr., Ste. 71-340
Riverside, CA 92507
Phone: .... (909) 781-6597
www.ashleyproductions.com
info@ashleyproductions.com
Key Executives/Personnel:
  Jacqueline Ashley, President & CEO
  William Ashley II, VP & CFO
Specialties: Short Form; Long Form
Other Categories: Feature Film; Commercials
Credits: Between Friends; Stolen Moments; The Right Crowd

BACKYARD PRODUCTIONS
248 Main St.
Venice, CA 90291
Phone: .... (310) 314-1122
Fax: .... (310) 314-1123
www.backyard.com
mail@backyard.com
Key Executives/Personnel:
  Blair Stribley, President & Executive Producer
  Roy Skillicorn, Head of Sales
  Sheila Stepanek, Executive Producer
  Peter Steinzeig, Head of Production
  Ann Edgar, VP of Development
  Kevin Smith, Director
  Rob Pritts, Director
  Don Rase, Director
  Shaun Conrad, Director
  Chace Strickland, Director
  Eddy Chu, Director
  Peter Keenan, Producer
  Kris Mathur, Producer
Specialties: Short Form
Other Categories: Feature Film; Commercials
Credits: American Express; Anheuser-Busch; AT&T; Delta Airlines

THE BAER ANIMATION COMPANY, INC.
7743 Woodrow Wilson Dr.
Los Angeles, CA 90046
Phone: .... (323) 874-9122
.... (818) 760-8666
Fax: .... (323) 874-7690
www.baeranimation.com
baer@baeranimation.com
Key Executives/Personnel:
  Jane Baer, President & Executive Producer
  Hope Parker, VP & Director of Administration & Marketing
  Milt Vallas, Producer
Specialties: Short Form; Long Form
Other Categories: Feature Film; Commercials
Credits: Annabelle's Wish (feature); Coca-Cola (commercial); Chevrolet (commercial); Disney World (commercial)
Trade Assoc./Guilds/Unions: AMPAS, ATAS, IATSE
Additional Info: Production of all styles of animation. Specializes in integrating live action.

SUZANNE BAUMAN PRODUCTIONS
21901 Velicata St.
Woodland Hills, CA 91364
Phone: .... (818) 348-4342
Fax: .... (818) 348-6482
Key Executives/Personnel:
  Suzanne Bauman, Producer & Director
  Toni Pace, Producer
  John Marzilli, Director of Development
Specialties: Industrial/Corporate; Educational; Documentaries
Other Categories: Feature Film; TV; Video
Credits: Jackie: Behind the Myth; Jack Hanna's Animal Adventures; La Belle Epoque; Women of Summer
Trade Assoc./Guilds/Unions: DGA, WGAw

BELLA PRODUCTIONS
4250 Beethoven St.
Los Angeles, CA 90066
Phone: .... (310) 823-3115
Fax: .... (310) 823-8366
bella1@earthlnk.net
Key Executives/Personnel:
  Cami Taylor, Executive Producer
  Bill Hayden, Executive Producer

Production Companies – Music Video

Herb Ritts, Director
Mark Story, Director
Peter Abraham, Executive Producer
Audrey Pask, Executive Producer
Specialties: Short Form
Other Categories: Feature Film; TV; Commercials
Credits: Nike (commercial); Little Caesar's (commercial); Pac Bell (commercial)
Trade Assoc./Guilds/Unions: DGA

BLACK DOG FILMS (RSA USA)
634 N. La Peer Dr.
West Hollywood, CA 90069
Phone: ....(310) 659-1017
Fax: ....(310) 659-1671
Key Executives/Personnel:
Jules Daly, Managing Director
Angel, Director
Cassius Colman, Director
James Cox, Director
Christopher Erskin, Director
Jake Scott, Director
Luke Scott, Director
Jordan Scott, Director
Dawn Shadforth, Director
Spencer Susser, Director
Tom Dey, Director
Specialties: Short Form

BLUE GOOSE PRODUCTIONS
8350 Melrose Ave., Ste. 11
West Hollywood, CA 90069
Phone: ....(323) 658-6893
....(206) 232-4075
Fax: ....(323) 658-7409
planetpoint.com/bluegoose
blugoos1@aol.com
Key Executives/Personnel:
Ron Gross, Director
Specialties: Short Form; Long Form
Other Categories: Commercials
Credits: Nike (commercial); Pearl Jam - Single Video Theory; Seattle Mariners (commercial); Motorola (commercial)

BOB INDUSTRIES
811 Hampton Dr.
Venice, CA 90291
Phone: ....(310) 396-7333
Fax: ....(310) 396-0202
www.bobcentral.com
Key Executives/Personnel:
T. K. Knowles, Executive Producer
John O'Grady, Executive Producer
Chuck Ryant, Executive Producer
Specialties: Short Form
Other Categories: Commercials
Credits: PlayStation; Georgia Pacific; Gap Kids; Snickers
Trade Assoc./Guilds/Unions: AICP

BONFIRE FILMS OF AMERICA
4655 Kingswell Ave., Ste. 213
Los Angeles, CA 90027
Phone: ....(323) 953-6815
Fax: ....(323) 953-0623
Key Executives/Personnel:
Shirley Moyers, Executive Producer
A. J. Schnack, Executive Producer
John McGinnis, Director's Rep
Specialties: Short Form; Long Form
Other Categories: Feature Film; TV; Commercials

BOYINGTON STUDIOS, INC.
17 Galleon St.
Marina Del Rey, CA 90292
Phone: ....(310) 822-2360
Fax: ....(310) 822-0430
www.boyingtonfilms.com
pboy@gte.net
Key Executives/Personnel:
Paul Boyington, Producer, Director & Effects Supervisor
Tibor Takacs, Director
Foster Corder, Director
Anthony Mabin, Director & Effects Supervisor
Robert Scopinich, Director & Effects Supervisor
Specialties: Commercials; Feature Film; Short Form
Other Categories: Feature; Commercial
Credits: Sweet Talk; Fox Sports (Promo); Megadeath - Hangar 18; Keith Richards - Take It So Hard

THE BREGMAN ENTERTAINMENT COMPANY
1950 Sawtelle Blvd., Ste. 360
Los Angeles, CA 90025
Phone: ....(213) 833-6207
Fax: ....(323) 876-1957
budboy@worldnet.att.net
Key Executives/Personnel:
Buddy Bregman, President
Marie DePuthod, Writer, Director & Producer
Specialties: Long Form
Other Categories: Feature Film; TV
Credits: Ain't Misbehavin'; The American Civil War; Olivia Newton John; Nancy Wilson Show
First Look/Development Deals: Gen X Entertainment, Int'l. Filmed Entertainment
Trade Assoc./Guilds/Unions: AFM, DGA, PGA, WGAw

CANVAS HOUSE FILMS
3671 Bear St., Ste. E
Santa Ana, CA 92704
Phone: ....(714) 850-1964
....(323) 459-0609
teteemley@aol.com
Key Executives/Personnel:
Mitch Teemley, Writer & Producer
Elizabeth Gray, Associate Producer
Specialties: Short Form; Long Form
Other Categories: Feature Film; TV; Commercials
Credits: Out Of Time (TV series); Lennar Homes (commercial); The Limited (feature); Kragira (feature)

THE CHELMAR GROUP
PMB# 345, 411 E. Huntington Dr., Bldg. 107
Arcadia, CA 91006
Phone: ....(626) 358-4001
chelmar@earthlink.net
Key Executives/Personnel:
Richard James, Executive Producer
Michelle Palmer, Producer
Specialties: Short Form
Other Categories: Feature Film; Commercials; Video
Credits: Renewable Power (documentary); The View From Malabar (documentary); Salvation Army (commercial); Coca-Cola (commercial)

COAST MEDIA TELEPRODUCTIONS, INC.
17062 Murphy Ave., Bldg. B
Irvine, CA 92614
Phone: ....(949) 417-0300
www.coastmedia.com
digipost@earthlink.net
Key Executives/Personnel:
Art Royce, President, CEO & Producer
Brian Ferguson, Director of Photography

Joyce D. Smith, VP
Donovan Smith, Audio Engineer
Curtis Matovich, Editor & Composer
Steve Hirai, Production Manager
Becky Fisher, Account Manager
Specialties: Short Form; Long Form
Other Categories: TV; Commercials; Video; Interactive Multimedia
Credits: Simple Green (infomercial); Milk Advisory Board (commercial); Meguiar's Wax (corp. video & commercial); Disney (corp. video)

CPPRODS
Phone: ....(310) 441-9211
Fax: ....(310) 441-9211
cpprods@earthlink.net
Key Executives/Personnel:
Cindy Pierson, Producer
Specialties: Short Form; Long Form
Other Categories: Commercials
Credits: Brandy & Monica - The Boy is Mine; Monster Magnet - Space Lord; Foxy Brown - Hot Spot; Smokey Brown - Sleeping In

THE CREATIVE DEPARTMENT, LLC
26403 Emerald Dove Dr.
Valencia, CA 91355
Phone: ....(661) 288-1155
Fax: ....(661) 288-1166
mborchetta@mediaone.net
Key Executives/Personnel:
Mark Borchetta, Director & Producer
Specialties: Short Form
Other Categories: Commercials; Video
Credits: Bushnell Sports Optics Worldwide; Mercedes-Benz; S. California Volvo Dealers; SAAB
Trade Assoc./Guilds/Unions: ASCAP

CYLO
5540 Hollywood Blvd., 2nd Fl.
Los Angeles, CA 90028
Phone: ....(323) 957-7824
Fax: ....(323) 957-8531
www.cylo.com
catalaine@cylo.com
Key Executives/Personnel:
Julie Atherton, President
Cindy Akins, Executive Producer
Catalaine Knell, Producer
Specialties: Short Form
Other Categories: Commercials; Interactive Multimedia
Additional Info: Previously Atherton

DAPTV ASSOCIATES
9080 Santa Monica Blvd.
West Hollywood, CA 90069
Phone: ....(310) 860-9001
....(877) 860-9003
Fax: ....(310) 860-9003
www.daptv.com
info@daptv.com
Key Executives/Personnel:
Don Azars, Writer, Director & Executive Producer
Michael Berman, Producer
Specialties: Short Form; Long Form
Other Categories: TV; Commercials; Video
Credits: The Edge and Beyond; Crisis Counselor; Carroll, Her First Special

DAYTON/FARIS, INC.
811 Hampton Dr.
Venice, CA 90291
Phone: ....(310) 396-7333
Fax: ....(310) 396-0202
Key Executives/Personnel:
Jonathan Dayton, Director & Executive Producer
Valerie Faris, Director & Executive Producer
Specialties: Short Form
Credits: Janes Addiction - Gift; The Decline of Western Civilization Pt.2; Beck - The New Pollution; Smashing Pumpkin - Thirty-Three

DNA, INC.
6535 Santa Monica Blvd.
Hollywood, CA 90038
Phone: ....(323) 463-2826
Fax: ....(323) 463-2535
www.dnala.com
mailbox@dnala.com
Key Executives/Personnel:
David Naylor, President
Patricia Judice, Executive Producer, Commercials
Sam Aslanian, Executive Producer, Music Videos
Francis Lawrence, Director
Liz Friedlander, Director
Yuki, Director
Marco Brambilla, Director
Steve Willis, Director
Marc Webb, Director
Rocky Schenck, Director
Lili Fini Zanuck, Director
Jean-Baptiste Mondino, Director
Specialties: Short Form
Other Categories: Commercials
Credits: Target; Bacardi; Footlocker; McDonald's
Trade Assoc./Guilds/Unions: AICP, MVPA

DOOM, INC.
355 N. Maple St., Ste. 112
Burbank, CA 91505
Phone: ....(818) 972-2007
Fax: ....(818) 972-2008
www.doominc.com
Key Executives/Personnel:
Thomas Mignone, Director & Executive Producer
Darci Oltman, Producer
Peter Davison, Office Manager
Specialties: Short Form; Long Form
Other Categories: Commercials; Video; Interactive Multimedia
Credits: Slipknot - Spit it Out (music video); American Red Cross (corp. video); Mudvayne - Dig (music video); Donald Trump: Trump Organization (corp. video)

DUCK SOUP STUDIOS
2205 Stoner Ave.
Los Angeles, CA 90064
Phone: ....(310) 478-0771
Fax: ....(310) 478-0773
www.ducksoupla.com
ducksoupla@aol.net
Key Executives/Personnel:
Mark Medernach, Executive Producer
Carolyn Bates, Producer
Specialties: Short Form
Other Categories: Feature Film; Commercials; Interactive Multimedia
Credits: Starkist; Dean's Milk; Bell Atlantic; McDonald's

E.M.E., INC.
Phone: ....(310) 330-8841
emeinc@earthlink.net
Specialties: Short Form
Other Categories: Feature Film; TV; Commercials; Interactive Multimedia

Production Companies – Music Video

FAT CHANCE FILMS
3751 Motor Ave., Ste. 928
Los Angeles, CA 90034
Phone: .... (323) 882-4130
bobmardis2@aol.com
Key Executives/Personnel:
Bobby Mardis, Producer & Director
Specialties: Long Form
Other Categories: Feature Film; TV; Video
Credits: Midnight Blue; Circle of Pain; Why Colors; One Last Time
Trade Assoc./Guilds/Unions: DGA, WGAw

FATE JUNKIE FILMS, INC.
4555 Matilija Ave.
Sherman Oaks, CA 91423
Phone: .... (818) 905-1333
.... (818) 929-7500
Fax: .... (818) 907-1333
stacey33@pacbell.net
Key Executives/Personnel:
Stacy Schachter, Owner & Producer
Specialties: Short Form
Other Categories: Feature Film; Commercials
Credits: Politically Incorrect (commercial); Frito Lay (commercial); Mattel (commercial); Tupac (music video)
Trade Assoc./Guilds/Unions: DGA

THE FILM SYNDICATE
7214 Melrose Ave.
Los Angeles, CA 90046
Phone: .... (323) 938-8080
Fax: .... (323) 938-8183
fsyndicate@aol.com
Key Executives/Personnel:
Bryan Johnson, Executive Producer & Director
Specialties: Short Form; Long Form
Other Categories: TV; Commercials
Credits: Fox (promos); Dr. Pepper; Melrose Place Specials; U2 - Streets Have No Name
Trade Assoc./Guilds/Unions: DGA

FM ROCKS
1351 Third St., Ste. 201
Santa Monica, CA 90401
Phone: .... (310) 587-1501
.... (310) 664-3615
Fax: .... (310) 587-1502
www.fmrocks.com
etlove@fmrocks.com
Key Executives/Personnel:
Dave Meyers, Director
F. Gary Gray, Director
Gregory Dark, Director
Tim Story, Director
Eileen Terry, Executive Producer
Specialties: Short Form
Other Categories: Commercials
Credits: Pringles; Sprite; Britney Spears - Lucky; 'NSync - Drive Myself Crazy
Trade Assoc./Guilds/Unions: AFI, AICP, American Cinematheque, DGA, IFP, WIF

FUEL
1914 Main St., Ste. 212
Santa Monica, CA 90405
Phone: .... (310) 314-1644
Fax: .... (310) 314-1640
david.mcginley@razorfish.com
Key Executives/Personnel:
Matthew Marquis, Executive Producer
David McGinley, Head of Production

Seth Epstein, Director
John Lindauer, Director
Jarl Olsen, Director
Neil Tardio Jr., Director
Mark Andrews, Sales Representative
Tracy Bernard, Sales Representative
Nancy Workman, Sales Representative
Specialties: Short Form; Long Form
Other Categories: Commercials
Credits: Gatorade; HBO; AT&T; United Way
Trade Assoc./Guilds/Unions: AICP

GALANTY & COMPANY, INC.
1640 Fifth St., Ste. 202
Santa Monica, CA 90401
Phone: .... (310) 451-2525
galantyco@juno.com
Key Executives/Personnel:
Sidney Galanty, Director
Mark Galanty, Executive Producer
Sanja Brizic, Associate Producer & Writer
Specialties: Short Form
Other Categories: Commercials; Video
Credits: TIAA: Cref Mutual Funds; America's Workout; Jane Fonda Workout Series
Trade Assoc./Guilds/Unions: AAPC

GEARS COMMUNICATIONS
315 W. Verdugo Ave.
Burbank, CA 91502
Phone: .... (818) 840-9333
Fax: .... (818) 840-9358
www.gearscom.com
maureen@gearscom.com
Key Executives/Personnel:
Greg Gears, Producer
Steven Kovner, VP of Production
Maureen English, VP of Sales
Specialties: Short Form; Long Form
Other Categories: TV; Video; Interactive Multimedia

GERONIMO FILM PRODUCTIONS, INC.
8205 Santa Monica Blvd., Ste. 428
Los Angeles, CA 90046
Phone: .... (323) 965-0200
Fax: .... (323) 634-7337
www.geronimofilms.com
geronimofilm@earthlink.net
Key Executives/Personnel:
Philip Atwell, Owner & Executive Producer
Specialties: Short Form
Other Categories: Video
Credits: Eminem - The Real Slim Shady; Dr. Dre - The Next Episode; Dr. Dre - Forgot about Dre; Dr. Dre - Up in Smoke Tour (documentary)

GINTY FILMS
16255 Ventura Blvd., Ste. 625
Encino, CA 91436
Phone: .... (310) 274-9691
.... (310) 277-1408
Fax: .... (310) 274-9692
www.robertginty.com
rwginty@aol.com
Key Executives/Personnel:
Robert Ginty, CEO
Skip Heinecke, (Ireland)
Shira Zeltzer, Executive Assistant
Layla Bennett, Executive Assistant
Lyndi Vanderhout, (Paris)
Moira Proletti, (Rome)

Production Companies – Music Video

Jean Diamond, (London)
John Gallagher, (New York)
John Mein, (Vancouver)
Specialties: Short Form; Long Form
Other Categories: Feature Film; TV; Commercials; Interactive Multimedia
Credits: Bounty Hunter; Woman of Desire; Day of Reckoning
Trade Assoc./Guilds/Unions: BAFTA, DGA, SAG, WGAw

GLASS GUNS
7280 Melrose Ave., 2nd Fl.
Los Angeles, CA 90046
Phone: (323) 938-0729
Fax: (323) 938-7007
www.glassguns.com
jeff@glassguns.com
Key Executives/Personnel:
 Jeff Clark, Executive Producer
Specialties: Short Form
Other Categories: Commercials; Interactive Multimedia
Credits: General Mills; Nescafe; Sky TV; Backstreet Boys - Get Down
Trade Assoc./Guilds/Unions: AICP, MVPA

GO FILM
51 E. 12th St., 6th Fl.
New York, NY 10003
Phone: (212) 677-7500
Fax: (212) 677-7555
www.gofilm.net
Key Executives/Personnel:
 Jonathan Weinstein, Partner
 Robert Wherry, Partner
 Preston Lee, Executive Producer
 Caitlin Felton, Director
 Gary McKendry, Director
 Frank W. Ockenfels 3, Director
 Nick Rafter, Director
 Rad-ish, Director
Specialties: Short Form
Other Categories: Feature Film; Commercials
Additional Info: 1103 Abbot Kinney Blvd., Venice CA 90291 (310) 581-1992 phone, (310) 581-4994 fax

JEFF GOLD PRODUCTIONS, INC.
13900 Panay Way, Ste. 309
Marina Del Rey, CA 90292
Phone: (310) 827-9165
j47737@yahoo.com
Specialties: Short Form; Long Form
Other Categories: Feature Film; TV; Commercials; Video
Credits: The Alpha Section; Talking Heads; Career Bed; Changing Times
Trade Assoc./Guilds/Unions: DGA

GRAYING & BALDING, INC.
924 Colorado Ave.
Santa Monica, CA 90401
Phone: (310) 587-2330
Fax: (310) 587-2340
Key Executives/Personnel:
 Jim Gable, Director
 Ann Kim, Executive Producer
 Jason Barager, Producer
Specialties: Short Form; Long Form
Other Categories: Commercials

GREENWATER PICTURES
3940 Laurel Canyon Blvd., Ste. 736
Studio City, CA 91604
Phone: (323) 655-9585
Fax: (323) 655-9025
www.greenwaterpictures.com
tlowe@greenwaterpictures.com
Key Executives/Personnel:
 Tom Lowe, President & Producer
 Barbara Cordis, VP of Development
Specialties: Short Form
Other Categories: Commercials; Video; Interactive Multimedia
Credits: Fireball (webisodes); Nick Forester (webisodes)
Trade Assoc./Guilds/Unions: DGA

H-GUN LABS
587 Shotwell St.
San Francisco, CA 94110
Phone: (415) 648-4386
(773) 561-5354
Fax: (415) 920-3911
www.hgun.com
info@hgun.com
Key Executives/Personnel:
 James Deloye, Executive Producer
 Sara Kraft, Producer
 Nancy Williams, Lab Manager
Specialties: Short Form; Long Form
Other Categories: Feature Film; TV; Commercials; Interactive Multimedia

DAVID HAUGLAND PRODUCTIONS
8961 Sunset Blvd., Ste. 2D
West Hollywood, CA 90069
Phone: (310) 550-1556
Fax: (310) 550-1584
dkhaugland@earthlink.net
Key Executives/Personnel:
 David Haugland, Producer & Director
 Christopher Miller, Assistant
Specialties: Short Form; Long Form
Other Categories: Feature Film; TV; Video
Credits: Changing Our Minds; World and Time Enough; The Oscar Legacy; The Portrait
Trade Assoc./Guilds/Unions: DGA, WGAw

THE JIM HENSON COMPANY
1416 N. La Brea Ave.
Los Angeles, CA 90028
Phone: (323) 802-1500
Fax: (323) 802-1825
www.henson.com
Key Executives/Personnel:
 Brian Henson, Chairman
 Charles H. Rivkin, President & CEO
 Linda Govreau, Executive VP of Corporate Finance & CFO
 Lisa Henson, President, Jim Henson Pictures
 John Stephenson, Executive VP & Creative Supervisor, Jim Henson's Creature Shop
 Juliet Blake, Executive VP & Co-Head, Jim Henson Television Group Worldwide
 Angus Fletcher, Executive VP & Co-Head, Jim Henson Television Group Worldwide
 Peter Schube, General Counsel & Executive VP of Business & Legal Affairs
 Michael Bolingbroke, Sr. VP of Finance & Operations, Jim Henson's Creature Shop
 Craig Allen, Sr. VP & General Manager, Jim Henson Interactive
 Robert Norton, Sr. VP of Business & Legal Affairs
 Ritamarie Peruggi, Sr. VP of Production Worldwide
 Robert Wozniak, VP of Production Administration & Finance, Production Executive
 Kristine Belson, Production, Jim Henson Pictures
 Louis Philips, VP of Production Administration
 Halle Stanford Grossman, VP of Creative Affairs, Jim Henson Television
 Ruth Caruso, VP of Development, Jim Henson Television
 Michele Martell, VP of Business Affairs & Interactive Business Development

Production Companies – Music Video

Antonia Downey, VP of International Legal & Business Affairs
Pete Coogan, VP of Physical Production
David Barrington-Holt, Creative Supervisor,
  Jim Henson's Creature Shop
Debbie McClellan, Sr. Director of Corporate Communications
  & Special Projects
Omar Camacho, Director of Current Programming,
  Jim Henson Television
Specialties: Short Form; Long Form
Other Categories: Feature Film; TV; Commercials; Video; Interactive Multimedia
Credits: Farscape; Story Telling with Tomie de Paola; Rat; Muppets From Space

HODGE FILM & VIDEO
10770 Esther Ave.
Los Angeles, CA 90064
Phone: ....(310) 441-9773
Fax: ....(310) 474-7611
hodge@pacbell.net
Key Executives/Personnel:
  David Hodge, President
  Stacey Freeman, Producer
Specialties: Short Form; Long Form
Other Categories: TV; Commercials; Video
Credits: Carly Simon - Every Time We Say Goodbye; Bank One (corp. video); Human Rights Campaign; Carlos Santana - Supernatural

HORIZON SHINE, INC.
8621 Hayden Pl.
Culver City, CA 90232
Phone: ....(310) 990-6532
Fax: ....(310) 280-9776
www.horizonshine.com
info@horizonshine.com
Key Executives/Personnel:
  Robert Nackman, Executive Producer
Specialties: Short Form
Other Categories: Commercials; Video
Credits: Kodak Film; American Eagle; Burger King (corp. video)

IN-FINN-ITY PRODUCTIONS, INC.
11400 W. Olympic Blvd., 16th Fl.
Los Angeles, CA 90064
Phone: ....(310) 444-6300
Fax: ....(310) 444-6310
www.infinnity.com
Key Executives/Personnel:
  Pat Finn, Executive Producer
  Ann Marie Griffith, Executive in Charge of Production
  Jana Morgan, Director of Development
Specialties: Short Form; Long Form
Other Categories: TV; Commercials
Credits: Instant Comedy with the Groundlings; Soulmates
First Look/Development Deals: Universal Television & Networks Group

INDUSTRIAL LIGHT + MAGIC COMMERCIAL PRODUCTIONS
732 N. Highland Ave.
Hollywood, CA 90038
Phone: ....(323) 957-2002
Fax: ....(323) 464-8373
www.ilmcp.com
Key Executives/Personnel:
  Marcie Malooly, Executive Producer & Division Manager
  John Denis, Executive Producer
  Paul Grimshaw, Head of Production
Specialties: Short Form
Other Categories: Commercials; Interactive Multimedia
Credits: First Union; Toyota; Gatorade; Armor All

INSTINCT PICTURES
520 Washington Blvd., Ste. 257
Marina Del Rey, CA 90292
Phone: ....(310) 578-9778
....(213) 426-7211
zenueg@yahoo.com
Specialties: Short Form
Other Categories: Feature Film; Commercials
Credits: The Shelter (feature); Best Buddies (PSA); APLA (PSA)

LA PRODUCTIONS
Phone: ....(323) 874-9487
....(323) 871-1982
Fax: ....(323) 874-9487
Key Executives/Personnel:
  Herb Linsey, Executive Producer
  John Arnow, Executive Producer
  Stephen Paul, Executive Producer
  Thomas Cost, Executive Producer
Specialties: Short Form
Other Categories: Feature Film; TV; Commercials
Credits: Curad Bandages; Goodyear Tires; Johnson & Johnson; Wrangler Clothes

LEGACY FILMS
6311 Romaine St., Ste. 7204
Los Angeles, CA 90038
Phone: ....(323) 856-8888
Fax: ....(323) 856-8880
www.legacyfilms.net
legacyfm@pacbell.net
Key Executives/Personnel:
  Michelle Colbert, Executive Producer
  Mauricio Kuri, Director
  Bill Orisich, Director
  Eric Haywood, Director
  Bernard Gourley, Director
Specialties: Short Form; Long Form
Other Categories: Commercials
Credits: The Athletes Foot; Pontiac; KMART; Dominos Pizza
Trade Assoc./Guilds/Unions: ACLA, MVPA

LET THERE BE LIGHT PRODUCTIONS
4240 Lost Hills Rd., Ste. 2801
Agoura Hills, CA 91301
Phone: ....(818) 880-4717
Fax: ....(818) 880-4717
littnet@cs.com
Key Executives/Personnel:
  Robert Litt, Producer
Specialties: Short Form; Long Form
Other Categories: Feature Film; TV; Commercials; Video
Credits: Jenny Craig; WorldFreeNet.com; MPI/LA Tourism Bureau; Turbo - Take It To The Limit
First Look/Development Deals: Summer Storm Pictures

LIGHTNING BOLT PIX: BARNYARD PRODUCTIONS
1653 18th St., Ste. 3B
Santa Monica, CA 90404
Phone: ....(310) 828-8239
Fax: ....(310) 828-1923
www.boltpix.com
mwbfield@aol.com
Key Executives/Personnel:
  Michael Barnard, Owner, Producer & Director
  Morgan Barnard, Co-Owner, Director & Editor
  Philip DeVellis, Production Coordinator & Designer
Specialties: Short Form
Other Categories: TV; Commercials; Video
Credits: Bringing The Light; Chihuly River of Glass; Edgar.com; National Labor Life

Production Companies – Music Video

MAKE IT HAPPEN PRODUCTIONS, INC.
Phone: ....(323) 851-6444
Fax: ....(323) 851-6465
www.billyfrank.com
mihpi@aol.com
Key Executives/Personnel:
   Billy Frank, President & Producer
   Todd Denkin, Director & Producer
   Mark Eberle, Director of Photography
   Carolina Hileman, Assistant to President & Coordinator
Specialties: Short Form; Long Form
Other Categories: Feature Film; TV; Commercials; Video
Credits: Wap!; Toughman (specials); Australian Experience
First Look/Development Deals: ABC Entertainment Television Group, FX Networks, LLC
Trade Assoc./Guilds/Unions: SAG, WGAw

MARS MEDIA, INC.
3630 Eastham Blvd.
Culver City, CA 90232
Phone: ....(310) 664-6760
Fax: ....(310) 396-2128
Key Executives/Personnel:
   Stavros Merjos, President
   Bill Sandwick, Executive Producer
   Kerstin Emhott, Executive Producer
   Steve Ross, Executive Producer
   Tracie Norfleet, Executive Producer
   Rebecca Skinner, Sr. Executive Producer of Music Videos
   Ericka Panko, Executive Producer of Music Videos
   Alisa Ratner, Head of Production, Music Videos
   Jessica Thomas, Sales
   Inga Veronique, Sales (NY)
Specialties: Short Form
Other Categories: Commercials

MATRIX COMMUNICATIONS
2522 Torrance Blvd.
Torrance, CA 90503
Phone: ....(310) 782-8400
Key Executives/Personnel:
   Marta Houske, Executive Producer & Director
Specialties: Short Form
Other Categories: Feature Film; Commercials; Video; Interactive Multimedia
Credits: Zimbabwe Legit (music video); A Stitch in Time (documentary); Times Mirror (commercial); In Search of ... (TV series)

THE MILLER ENTERTAINMENT GROUP, INC.
5900 Wilshire Blvd., Ste. 540
Los Angeles, CA 90036
Phone: ....(323) 932-6500
Key Executives/Personnel:
   Lawrence Miller, President
   Ty Supancic, VP
Specialties: Short Form
Other Categories: Feature Film; Commercials
Credits: Deadly Currency (feature); Sallie B - Baby Mama (music video); Nick Frost - Deep Love (music video); Regatta Condominium (infomercial)
Trade Assoc./Guilds/Unions: SAG

MM2K
838 N. Doheny Dr., Ste. 904
West Hollywood, CA 90069
Phone: ....(310) 276-0750
Fax: ....(310) 276-0229
mm2k@earthlink.net
Key Executives/Personnel:
   William A. Levey, Executive Producer & Director
   Bob Manning, Head Producer
   Nancy Youngblood, Director of Creative Development
Specialties: Short Form
Other Categories: Feature Film; TV; Commercials; Video
Credits: Slumber Party 57; The Happy Hooker Goes To Washington; Skatetown U.S.A; White Stallion
Trade Assoc./Guilds/Unions: DGA, IATSE, WGAw

MO JO PRODUCTIONS, INC.
4224 Waialae Ave., Ste. 300
Honolulu, HI 96816
Phone: ....(808) 384-8460
....(626) 932-6432
Fax: ....(808) 733-4142
mojoproductions@juno.com
Key Executives/Personnel:
   Michael Pendell, President
Specialties: Short Form; Long Form
Other Categories: Feature Film; TV; Commercials
Credits: Baywatch: Hawaii; Extended list available upon request.
Trade Assoc./Guilds/Unions: DGA

MOXIE PICTURES
1040 N. Sycamore Ave.
Hollywood, CA 90038
Phone: ....(323) 957-5420
Fax: ....(323) 466-1343
www.moxiepictures.com
moxiepictures@moxiepictures.com
Key Executives/Personnel:
   Gary Rose, Executive Producer
   Dan Levinson, President
   Kristen Wageman, Head of Production
   Lizzie Schwartz, Executive Producer
Specialties: Short Form; Long Form
Other Categories: Commercials
Credits: Coca-Cola; McDonald's; Levi's; Savage Garden

MUSIC ROOM PICTURES
P.O. Box 219
Redondo Beach, CA 90277
Phone: ....(310) 316-4551
Fax: ....(310) 540-3532
www.musicroomonline.com
mrp@aol.com
Key Executives/Personnel:
   John Reed, President
Specialties: Short Form
Other Categories: Feature Film; Commercials; Video

NEMIROFF PRODUCTIONS
1506 Butler Ave., Ste. 1
Los Angeles, CA 90025
Phone: ....(310) 473-4100
....(310) 917-5250
Fax: ....(310) 473-4100
Key Executives/Personnel:
   Steve Nemiroff, Producer & Assistant Director
Specialties: Long Form
Other Categories: Feature Film; TV; Commercials; Video; Interactive Multimedia
Credits: The Real Deal; Miracles; Sparkletts; Kenny Kingston's Psychic Hotline III
Trade Assoc./Guilds/Unions: AFI, AICP, ITVA

NEW MILLENNIUM STUDIOS
One New Millenium Dr.
Petersburg, VA 23805
Phone: ....(804) 957-4200
Fax: ....(804) 862-1200
www.nmstudios.com

Production Companies – Music Video

martinj@nmstudios.com
Key Executives/Personnel:
   Tim Reid, Producer
   Daphne Maxwell Reid, Producer
   Martin C. Jones, Producer
Specialties: Short Form
Other Categories: Feature Film; TV; Commercials; Interactive Multimedia
Credits: Asunder; Out of Sync; Linc's; When We Were Colored

NO PRISONERS
2260 S. Centinela Ave.
Los Angeles, CA 90064
Phone: (310) 979-9097
Fax: (310) 979-7097
www.noprisoners.net
info@noprisoners.net
Key Executives/Personnel:
   Todd Moyer, CEO & Producer
   Chris Brown, Visual Effects Supervisor
   Erik Strauss, Visual Effects Producer
   Bruce Martin, President of Commercials
   Nic Mathieu, Director
   Brian Scott Weber, Director
   Michael Abbott, Creative Executive
   Jim McCarthy, Controller
Specialties: Short Form
Other Categories: Feature Film; Commercials
Credits: Wing Commander (feature); Mercedes-Benz (commercial); The FireFlies (feature); Mai: The Psychic Girl (feature)

ORANGE SODA
5657 Wilshire Blvd., 4th Fl.
Los Angeles, CA 90036
Phone: (323) 634-4375
Fax: (323) 525-2912
Key Executives/Personnel:
   Joseph Kahn, CEO & Director
   Greg Tharp, President & Producer
   Brian Cooperman, Head of Production
   Lanette Phillips, Executive Producer & Rep
   Jolie Klein, Director
   Super America, Director
Specialties: Short Form
Credits: Janet Jackson - Doesn't Really Matter; Destiny's Child - Say My Name; Sisqo - Thong Song; Backstreet Boys - Larger Than Life

OUR GANG PRODUCTIONS
8522 National Blvd., Ste. 107
Culver City, CA 90232
Phone: (310) 300-1010
Fax: (310) 636-8304
ourgangproductions@earthlink.net
Key Executives/Personnel:
   Gayle Gluck, President
   Kevin Miller, Sr. VP & Creative Director
   Chris Conway, Audio Production
   Matt Fisher, Supervising Editor
   Ron Mesa, Chief Audio Engineer
   Rachel Burkes, Production Assistant
Specialties: Short Form; Long Form
Other Categories: TV; Commercials; Interactive Multimedia

OUR PRODUCTIONS, INC.
6255 Sunset Blvd., Ste. 2201
Hollywood, CA 90028
Phone: (323) 465-4197
(818) 816-7332
Fax: (323) 465-6549
www.ourproduction.com
patricia@ourproduction.com
Key Executives/Personnel:
   Rick Munoz, Director & Producer
   Patricia Bolt, Director of Marketing & Production
Specialties: Short Form; Long Form
Other Categories: Feature Film; TV; Commercials; Video
Credits: Natalie Cole Live at The Coliseum; The Miller Brewing Company; Winchell's Donuts

OVATION ENTERTAINMENT
Phone: (310) 344-1442
ovationmail@yahoo.com
Key Executives/Personnel:
   Steve Woroniecki, Producer
Specialties: Long Form
Other Categories: Commercials; Video

OVERBROOK ENTERTAINMENT
100 Universal City Plaza, Bldg. 6111
Universal City, CA 91608
Phone: (818) 777-2224
Fax: (818) 866-6206
Key Executives/Personnel:
   Will Smith, Partner
   James Lassiter, Partner
   Dale Ottley, General Manager
   John Dukakis, Executive VP of Music
   David Tochterman, Executive VP of TV
   Stacey Matthew, VP of TV
   Glendon Palmer, Creative Executive
   SoYun Roe, Film Executive
   Lori Zuker, Director of Development
   Omarr Rambert, A&R Executive of Music
   Anthony Demby, A&R Coordinator
Specialties: Short Form
Other Categories: Feature Film; TV
First Look/Development Deals: Universal Pictures

GEORGE PAIGE ASSOCIATES, INC.
3000 W. Olympic Blvd., Ste. 1407
Santa Monica, CA 90404
Phone: (310) 315-4835
Fax: (310) 315-4836
gpacorp@aol.com
Key Executives/Personnel:
   George Paige, Owner & President
   James R. Tumminia, Producer
Specialties: Long Form
Other Categories: Feature Film; TV; Commercials; Video; Interactive Multimedia
Credits: Abbott & Costello Meet Jerry Seinfeld; 50 Years of Funny Females; Shafted
Trade Assoc./Guilds/Unions: ATAS

PERSEVERANCE PRODUCTIONS
Phone: (310) 306-1960
Fax: (310) 306-1820
buddywins@aol.com
Specialties: Short Form
Other Categories: Commercials; Video
Credits: Ford; Pfizer; Alamo; Rite Aid
Trade Assoc./Guilds/Unions: DGA

PERSPECTIVE FILMS
Phone: (310) 670-4030
(310) 261-8389
Fax: (310) 670-4031
Key Executives/Personnel:
   Debbie Pietsch, Executive Producer
Specialties: Short Form
Other Categories: Feature Film; TV; Commercials; Video; Interactive Multimedia
Credits: Fast Point DSL; Mattel; Disney; Harman Kardan; MacWorld

Production Companies – Music Video

PLANET, INC.
6311 Romaine St., Ste. 7235
Hollywood, CA 90038
Phone: ....(323) 461-2695
Fax: ....(323) 461-0899
Key Executives/Personnel:
    Gerry Wenner, Owner & Director
    Jim Shea, Owner & Director
    Amy Reeves, Director's Rep
    Ann Richman, Executive Producer
Specialties: Short Form

POP/ART FILM FACTORY
513 Wilshire Blvd., Ste. 215
Santa Monica, CA 90401
Phone: ....(310) 260-2868
....(310) 288-6815
www.home.earthlink.net
dzpff@earthlink.net
Key Executives/Personnel:
    Daniel Zirilli, Executive Producer & Director
Specialties: Short Form
Other Categories: Feature Film; Commercials
Credits: Winner Takes All; Rolling Stones - Voodoo Lounge; Avirex Clothing; Freddie Jackson - I Want to Thank You

PRODUCTION ANALYSIS CORPORATION
Phone: ....(323) 876-6186
goodadvice@earthlink.net
Key Executives/Personnel:
    Martin Pitts, Producer
Specialties: Short Form; Long Form
Other Categories: Feature Film; TV; Commercials; Video
Credits: Wild California; The Full Moon Show with Robbie Robertson; The Bee Gees Live Concert Video

PROLETARIAT FILMWORKS
12165 Iredell St.
Studio City, CA 91604
Phone: ....(818) 763-8356
Fax: ....(818) 760-6584
proletfilm@aol.com
Key Executives/Personnel:
    Terry Moloney, Executive Producer
    Grant Gilmore, Line Producer
    Liam Kildare, Producer
Specialties: Short Form
Other Categories: Feature Film; TV; Commercials; Video
Credits: Tourette Syndrome Foundation (PSA); Elvis 2000: A Video Scrapbook; Warner Music: Wallstreet; Shout for Antz
Trade Assoc./Guilds/Unions: AFTRA, SAG

PROPAGANDA FILMS
940 N. Mansfield Ave
Los Angeles, CA 90038
Phone: ....(323) 462-6400
....(212) 982-1700
Fax: ....(323) 463-7874
www.propagandafilms.com
Key Executives/Personnel:
    Rick Hess, President
    Trevor Macy, COO
    Severin White, CFO
    Paul Schiff, Producer
    Pat Dollard, Co-Head, Management Division
    Lisa Franklin, Head of Legal Affairs
    Beth Holden, Co-Head, Management Division
    Brian Oliver, Director of Production
    Sam Walsh, Head of Production
Specialties: Short Form
Other Categories: Feature Film; Commercials
Credits: Fight Club; Being John Malkovich; Seven; Portrait of a Lady
Additional Info: 902 Broadway, Ste. 1603, New York, NY 10010

PROUD MARY ENTERTAINMENT
433 N. Camden Dr., Ste. 600
Beverly Hills, CA 90210
Phone: ....(310) 288-1886
Fax: ....(310) 288-1801
proudmaryent@earthlink.net
Key Executives/Personnel:
    Mary L. Aloe, Owner & Executive Producer
    Todd Waxler, Executive Producer
    Jay Jacobs, Director of Development
Specialties: Short Form
Other Categories: Feature Film; TV; Commercials
Credits: Caught in the Act; The Princess & The Private; Citizen Jane
Trade Assoc./Guilds/Unions: American Women in TV & Radio, CWA

RED HOTS ENTERTAINMENT
3105 Amigos Dr.
Burbank, CA 91504
Phone: ....(818) 954-0092
....(818) 607-8331
Fax: ....(818) 954-8421
pogmothon@earthlink.net
Key Executives/Personnel:
    Chip Miller, Director & Partner
    Sue Travis Miller, VP of Post Production & Editor
    Jane Gurtiza, Production Coordinator
    Dan Pomeroy, Director
    Marvin "Young MC" Young, Director
    Mark St. Juste, Director
    Kit Gleason, Production Manager
    Eileen Salgro, VP of Operations
    Vanessa Browne, Producer
    Marc Wolfson, Music Producer
    Theo Forster, Producer
Specialties: Short Form; Long Form
Other Categories: Feature Film; TV; Commercials; Video
Credits: Four Day Shoot; Mortuary Academy; The Importance of Being Earnest; The Seven Fishes
Trade Assoc./Guilds/Unions: PGA, WGA

SATELLITE FILMS
940 N. Mansfield Ave.
Hollywood, CA 90038
Phone: ....(323) 465-9300
Fax: ....(323) 465-8860
www.satellitefilms.net
info@satellitefilms.net
Key Executives/Personnel:
    Phillip Detchmendy, Executive Producer, Commercials
    Janet Haase, Executive Producer, Music Videos
    Brian Carmody, West Coast Sales
    Susan Murphy, East Coast Sales
    Dawn Rao, Midwest Sales
Specialties: Short Form
Other Categories: Commercials
Credits: Whitney Houston - Heartbreak Hotel; 'NSync - Promise; Energizer 2; Nike
Trade Assoc./Guilds/Unions: AICP, MVPA

SHADY ACRES ENTERTAINMENT
100 Universal City Plaza, Bldg. 5225, 2nd Fl.
Universal City, CA 91608
Phone: ....(818) 777-4446
Fax: ....(818) 866-6612
Key Executives/Personnel:
    Michael Bostick, no title
    Jim Brubaker, no title

Production Companies – Music Video

   Ashley Cook, no title
   Ginny Durkin, no title
   Greg Messina, no title
   Amanda Morgan Palmer, no title
   Tom Shadyac, no title
   Lindsay Smarz, no title
   Winston Stromberg, no title
   Gina Warendorp, no title
   Jordan Wolfe, no title
   Brook Worley, no title
Specialties: Short Form
Other Categories: Feature Film; TV
Credits: Patch Adams; The Nutty Professor; Liar Liar
First Look/Development Deals: Universal Pictures

SHARPCUT PRODUCTIONS
9000 Cynthia Street, Ste. 410
West Hollywood, CA 90069
Phone: ....(310) 247-0088
Fax: ....(310) 858-2254
www.sharpcut.com
sharpcutprods@aol.com
Key Executives/Personnel:
   Gary Robinson, Producer & Director
Specialties: Short Form
Other Categories: Commercials
Credits: Mets Corp.; Blind Date (promo); Stephen King: The Stand (promo)

SNEAK PREVIEW ENTERTAINMENT, INC.
1604 Vista del Mar
Hollywood, CA 90028
Phone: ....(323) 962-0295
Fax: ....(323) 962-0372
www.sneakpreviewentertain.com
sneakpreview@pacbell.net
Key Executives/Personnel:
   Steven J. Wolfe, Chairman, CEO & Producer
   Lynette Prucha Chavez, President & Writer
   David L. Cohn, Talent Manager
   Michael J. Roth, Director of Development
Specialties: Short Form
Other Categories: Feature Film; TV; Video
Credits: Fast Sofa; Twin Falls, Idaho; Relax...It's Just Sex; Tollbooth

SODAS & SHOES
5550 Wilshire Blvd., Ste. 301
Los Angeles, CA 90036
Phone: ....(323) 692-9848
Fax: ....(323) 692-9832
sodasshoes@aol.com
Key Executives/Personnel:
   Scott Mellini, Partner
   Louis Mellini, Partner
   Joan Renfrow, Partner
Specialties: Short Form; Long Form
Other Categories: Commercials
Credits: Mattel; Saturn; Suzuki; Circus Circus Casino

SOUTH FORK PRODUCTIONS
P.O. Box 1935
Santa Monica, CA 90406
Phone: ....(310) 829-5029
Fax: ....(310) 829-5029
soforkprods@ireland.com
Key Executives/Personnel:
   Jim Sullivan, Producer & Director
   Greg Sullivan, Producer
Specialties: Short Form; Long Form
Other Categories: Feature Film; TV; Commercials; Video
Credits: Making of Without Limits; Portraits of Courage; Those Who Dare
Trade Assoc./Guilds/Unions: AFI

SPORTS' CINEMATOGRAPHY GROUP
73 Market St.
Venice, CA 90291
Phone: ....(310) 785-9100
....(212) 744-5333
Fax: ....(310) 396-7423
www.sportscinema.net
sportscinema@earthlink.net
Key Executives/Personnel:
   David Stoltz, Executive Producer
Specialties: Short Form; Long Form
Other Categories: Commercials
Credits: Quik Silver; Kawasaki; Qxygen Snowboards; Polo Sport

J. STACK PRODUCTIONS
Phone: ....(310) 456-3272
Fax: ....(310) 456-3442
jmstack@aol.com
Key Executives/Personnel:
   Jeanne Stack, Producer
Specialties: Short Form; Long Form
Other Categories: Feature Film; TV; Commercials
Credits: Contact (2nd Unit); Kundun (2nd Unit); Eco-Challenge; Mild 7

STARGAZER, INC.
2432 Seventh St., Ste. 1
Santa Monica, CA 90405
Phone: ....(310) 392-0392
www.stargazerproductions.com
paigerama@earthlink.net
Key Executives/Personnel:
   Paige Seidel, Producer
Specialties: Short Form
Other Categories: Feature Film; Commercials
Credits: United Airlines; Audi; monster.com; Jeep

STEFANINO PRODUCTIONS
15515 Sunset Blvd., Ste. 101
Pacific Palisades, CA 90272
Phone: ....(310) 454-0109
Fax: ....(310) 454-0109
www.stefanino.com
stefanino@earthlink.net
Key Executives/Personnel:
   Stuart Jemesen, Producer & Director
   Stefan Kendal Gordy, Director of Music
Specialties: Short Form
Other Categories: Feature Film; TV; Commercials; Video
Credits: Smokey Robinson; Michael Jackson Biography; Innerview (TV pilot)

STEREOMEDIA 3D VIDEO PRODUCTIONS
2307 W. Olive St.
Burbank, CA 91506
Phone: ....(818) 559-6515
Fax: ....(818) 559-6598
stereo3DTV@aol.com
Key Executives/Personnel:
   Anthony Coogan, Executive Producer
   Eric Bakke, CTO & Director of 3D Videography
   Patrick Dunauan, Producer
Specialties: Long Form; Short Form
Other Categories: Video; Interactive Multimedia

STROM MAGALLON ENTERTAINMENT
3518 Cahuenga Blvd. West, Ste. 111
Los Angeles, CA 90068
Phone: ....(323) 969-1089
....(323) 969-1090
Fax: ....(323) 969-1091
strommagent@earthlink.net

Production Companies – Music Video

Key Executives/Personnel:
- Gregory Strom, Director
- Douglas Magallon, Director

Specialties: Short Form
Other Categories: Feature Film; Commercials; Video
Credits: Dirt Devil (commercial); Pontiac (commercial)

SUMMERLAND ENTERTAINMENT
17939 Chatsworth St., Ste. 260
Granada Hills, CA 91344
Phone: (818) 363-4135
Fax: (818) 368-8227
sumrland47@aol.com
Key Executives/Personnel:
- Bruce A. Pobjoy, President & Producer
- Brianne Michelle, VP of Development
- Brooke Allison, Administrative Assistant

Specialties: Short Form
Other Categories: Feature Film; TV
Credits: Fatal Memories; Baywatch Nights; Nightmare Cafe; In The Heat of The Night
Trade Assoc./Guilds/Unions: AAP

TANGO FILMS
1334 Westwood Blvd., Ste. 6
Los Angeles, CA 90024
Phone: (310) 470-4908
Fax: (310) 475-9041
thebank@aol.com
Key Executives/Personnel:
- Steve Banks, Executive Producer
- Greg Weinschenker, Director
- Lauren McNamara, Midwest Sales

Specialties: Short Form; Long Form
Other Categories: Commercials
Credits: Polident; MCI; Vicks Vaporub; Keystone Financial
Trade Assoc./Guilds/Unions: AICP, DGA

TVP STUDIOS
1539 Magnolia Blvd.
Burbank, CA 91506
Phone: (818) 843-3188
Fax: (818) 843-3189
www.tvpstudios.cc
tvprich@aol.com
Key Executives/Personnel:
- Richard Tamayo, Producer
- Meredith Day, Producer

Specialties: Short Form
Other Categories: TV; Commercials; Video
Credits: Bank of America; Panasonic; Golden Globe Awards; etvhollywood.com

VANGUARD PRODUCTIONS
12111 Beatrice St.
Culver City, CA 90230
Phone: (310) 306-4910
Fax: (310) 306-4910
vangrdprod@earthlink.net
Key Executives/Personnel:
- Terence M. O'Keefe, Writer, Producer & Director
- Brent Huff, Writer & Director
- S. Drew Stotesbery, VP of Production
- Bruce Miyaki, Director of Development
- Bennett Fidlow, Director of Creative Affairs

Specialties: Short Form; Long Form
Other Categories: Feature Film; TV; Commercials; Video
Credits: We The People; Wanted; The Bad Pack; Closing The Deal

VENTANA FILMS
7440 Palo Vista Dr.
Los Angeles, CA 90046
Phone: (323) 876-3331
Fax: (323) 876-4666
lafilm@aol.com
Key Executives/Personnel:
- Arthur Gorson, President & Head of Production
- Bernard Nussbaumer, Executive Producer
- Julio Solorzano, VP

Specialties: Short Form
Other Categories: Feature Film; Commercials
Credits: Cronos (feature); Better Watch Out (feature); Cabeza De Vaca (feature)

VIDE-U
9976 W. Wanda Dr.
Beverly Hills, CA 90210
Phone: (310) 276-5509
Fax: (310) 276-1183
Key Executives/Personnel:
- Bradley Friedman, Director & Producer
- David T., Producer
- Ann Marie Donahue, Producer

Specialties: Short Form
Credits: Berlin - Metro; Duran Duran - Rio on Modern Music; Ramones - Live at the Whiskey; The Step Dykes - The Step Dykes

VILLAINS
9247 Alden Dr.
Beverly Hills, CA 90210
Phone: (310) 888-8900
Fax: (310) 888-8444
www.villains.com
Key Executives/Personnel:
- John Marshall, President
- Robin Benson, Executive Producer
- Joby Barnhart, Head of Production
- Bo McDonald, Executive Producer of Music Videos
- Bill Mather, Director
- Scott Bibo, Director
- Jeffrey Fleisig, Director
- Brett Ratner, Director
- Steve Carr, Director
- Daniela Federici, Director
- Jim Giddens, Director

Specialties: Short Form
Other Categories: Commercials
Credits: Madonna - Beautiful Stranger; Mariah Carey - Heart Breaker; Sprite; Nike

BILL WHITE PRODUCTIONS
12423 Ventura Court, Ste. 200
Studio City, CA 91604
Phone: (818) 769-9090
Fax: (818) 769-1974
billwhitepro@earthlink.net
Key Executives/Personnel:
- Bill White, President
- Amy Shomer, Producer

Specialties: Short Form
Other Categories: Feature Film; TV; Commercials; Video
Credits: Globe Life Insurance (commercial); United American Insurance (commercial); Sanyo-Fisher (corp. video); Test Flights (TV)
Trade Assoc./Guilds/Unions: DGA

Production Companies – Music Video

WINDMILL LANE PRODUCTIONS
1558 Tenth St.
Santa Monica, CA 90401
Phone: (310) 576-1344
Fax: (310) 576-0515
www.windmill-lane.com
ben@windmill-lane.com
Key Executives/Personnel:
  Ben Dossett, Executive Producer
  Meiert Avis, Director
  Rupert Wainwright, Director
  Richard Bowen, Director
Specialties: Short Form
Other Categories: Commercials
Credits: Toyota; Sprite; LA Times; Kawasaki

X-RAY PRODUCTIONS
8630 Pine Tree Pl.
West Hollywood, CA 90069
Phone: (310) 659-7659
Key Executives/Personnel:
  Cami Taylor, Executive Producer
  Joanne Thrailkill, Executive Producer
  Carole Hughes, Executive Producer
  Charlie Curran, Executive Producer
Specialties: Short Form
Other Categories: Commercials
Trade Assoc./Guilds/Unions: AICP
Additional Info: 136 W. 21st St., New York, NY 10011

MARK YELLEN PRODUCTIONS
419 N. Larchmont Blvd., Ste. 44
Los Angeles, CA 90004
Phone: (323) 935-5525
Fax: (323) 935-5755
Key Executives/Personnel:
  Mark Yellen, Producer
Specialties: Short Form; Long Form
Other Categories: Feature Film; Commercials
Credits: Blast; Montana; Shiloh; The Big Squeeze

ZEAL PICTURES
6605 Hollywood Blvd., Ste. 300
Los Angeles, CA 90028
Phone: (323) 871-4000
Fax: (323) 871-4004
www.zealpictures.com
info@zealpictures.com
Key Executives/Personnel:
  Timm Oberwelland, Producer
  Leon Melas, Producer
  Robert Biehn, Producer
  George Salden, CFO
Specialties: Short Form
Other Categories: Feature Film; Commercials; Video
Credits: Simpatico; Robbers; American Fighter Pilot; Werther's Originals
Trade Assoc./Guilds/Unions: SAG
Additional Info: Additional Office in Berlin, Germany.

ZOOMA ZOOMA CORPORATION
11 Mercer St., 3rd Fl.
New York, NY 10013
Phone: (212) 941-7680
Fax: (212) 941-8179
www.zoomazooma.com
staff@zoomazooma.com
Key Executives/Personnel:
  Joseph Mantegna, Executive Producer
  Todd Bellanca, Director
  Eden Tyler, Director
  Sam Raimi, Director
  Michael Bellino, Director
  Tim Hamilton, Director
  Gavin O'Connor, Director
  Lori Vitale, East Coast Sales Rep
Specialties: Short Form; Long Form
Other Categories: Feature Film; TV; Commercials; Interactive Multimedia

ZYSTAR FILMS, INC.
330 Washington Blvd., Ste. 400
Marina Del Rey, CA 90292
Phone: (310) 301-3313
Fax: (310) 301-9433
www.zystar.com
mwallis@zystar.com
Key Executives/Personnel:
  Meryl Alison Wallis, Executive Producer
  Carmen Silva, Producer
  Scott Murphy, Assistant Director
  Howard Raishbrook, Production Manager
  Doug Mickel, Producer
Specialties: Short Form
Other Categories: Feature Film; TV; Commercials; Video
Credits: James Bond (behind the scenes); American Honda (commercial); Carrows Restaurants (commercial); Laurietta (feature)

Production Companies – Interactive Multimedia

21ST CENTURY MAN PRODUCTIONS
1950 N. Tamarind Ave., Ste. 323
Los Angeles, CA 90068
Phone: ....(323) 466-3227
....(310) 989-7353
Fax: ....(323) 466-3227
www.21stcman.com
future21@primenet.com
Key Executives/Personnel:
  Jane Linter, Producer & Director
  David May, Director & Editor
  Brian Bowie, Director & Director of Photography
  Andrea Fredrickson, Editor
Specialties: Television; Infomercials/Direct Response; Promos
Other Categories: TV; Video; Music Video; Interactive Multimedia
Credits: 21st CMAN; Sebastian Int.; Wella Alternative Hair Show; Stylezone 2000
Trade Assoc./Guilds/Unions: AEA, BAFTA, DGA, NATPE
Additional Info: 21st Century Man Productions, 33 Limes Rd., Beckenham, Kent BR3 6NS England

ABSOLUTEFILMS.NET
1441 Huntington Dr., Ste. 3010
South Pasadena, CA 91030
Phone: ....(626) 442-6454
Fax: ....(626) 448-1930
www.absolutefilms.net
info@absolute.net
Key Executives/Personnel:
  Ty Thompson, Producer
  Bryon Jost, Producer
  Josh Ochoa, Producer
  Robert Villalobos, Producer
  Tom Franklin, Producer
  Romeo Carey, Producer
Specialties: Web Content
Other Categories: Commercials; Video; Music Video
Credits: Juan-A-Be.com; Mr. Fab

ANTEYE.COM
11925 Wilshire Blvd., Ste. 102
Los Angeles, CA 90025
Phone: ....(310) 312-4884
Fax: ....(310) 312-4885
www.anteye.com
info@anteye.com
Specialties: Webcasting

ATOM FILMS
10 E. Colorado
Pasadena, CA 91105
Phone: ....(626) 793-4950
Fax: ....(626) 796-0987
www.atomfilms.com
info@atomfilms.com
Key Executives/Personnel:
  Mika Salmi, Founder & CEO
  Matt Hulett, Chief Marketing Officer
  Michael Comish, Managing Director
  John Marcom, Sr. VP of Worldwide Revenue & Media Strategies
  Heather Redman, Sr. VP of Development
  Dean Terry, Sr. VP of Creative Development
  Eric D. Cansler, VP of Finance & Operations
  Adam Flick, VP of New Platforms
  Jannat Gargi, VP of Acquisitions
  Seth Levenson, VP of Online Services
  Irl Nathan, VP of Technology
Specialties: Webcasting

BENDER-SPINK
1149 N. Poinsettia Place
West Hollywood, CA 90046
Phone: ....(323) 845-1640
Fax: ....(323) 512-5347
Key Executives/Personnel:
  Chris Bender, no title
  J. C. Spink, no title
  Charlie Gogolak, no title
  Roy Lee, no title
  Jim Valdes, no title
  Shane Thueson, no title
  Nicole Harb, no title
  Bryan O'Donnell, no title
  Brian Spink, no title
Specialties: Web Content
Other Categories: Feature Film; TV
Credits: American Pie; Cheaters; Like Cats and Dogs
First Look/Development Deals: Twentieth Century Fox Television, New Line Cinema, Inc.

BUNNYGRENADE
2128 15th St.
Denver, CO 80202
Phone: ....(303) 595-3152
Fax: ....(303) 595-4908
www.bunnygrenade.com
krist@bunnygrenade.com
Key Executives/Personnel:
  Kristi Westphal, Director of Marketing
  Olivier Katz, President of Celluloid
  Rich Moyer, Creative Director
Specialties: Web Content; Animation

CAIRO/SIMPSON ENTERTAINMENT, INC.
9255 Sunset Blvd., Ste. 507
West Hollywood, CA 90069
Phone: ....(310) 888-1262
Fax: ....(310) 887-1813
judycairo@aol.com
Key Executives/Personnel:
  Judy Cairo, Executive Producer
  Michael Simpson, Producer, Director & Writer
Specialties: Web Content
Other Categories: Feature Film; TV
Credits: Her Deadly Rival; Twisted Desire; Perfect Body; What We Did That Night

CALICO WORLD ENTERTAINMENT
10200 Riverside Dr., Ste. 203
North Hollywood, CA 91602
Phone: ....(818) 755-3800
Fax: ....(818) 755-4643
www.calicoworld.com
tom@calicoworld.com
Key Executives/Personnel:
  Tom Burton, Executive Director & Producer
  Claudia Zeitlin Burton, Managing Director
  Ken Leonard, Art Director
  Joel Fajnor, Producer & Director
  Mary Cim, Producer & Director
  Jim Livolsi, Executive Producer & Marketing
  Pedram Shohadai, Digital Animator
Specialties: Web Content; Animation
Other Categories: Feature Film; TV; Commercials
Credits: Denver, The Lost Dinosaur; Bad Baby; Kid's Songs of Woody Guthrie; Ghosts Legends of the Queen Mary

Production Companies – Interactive Multimedia

CANNED INTERACTIVE
6834 Hollywood Blvd., 3rd Fl.
Los Angeles, CA 90028
Phone: ....(323) 308-4200
....(323) 308-4226
Fax: ....(323) 463-8075
www.cannery.com
info@cannery.com
Key Executives/Personnel:
  Doug Textor, CEO
  A. J. Cosgrove, Director of Accounts
  Eliot Arnold, Sales & Business Development
Specialties: Web Content

CINEMANOW
4553 Glencoe Ave., Ste. 380
Marina Del Rey, CA 90292
Phone: ....(310) 314-2000
www.cinemanow.com
Key Executives/Personnel:
  Curt Marvis, President & CEO
  Bruce David Eisen, Executive VP
  Brad Serling, CTO
Specialties: Webcasting

CINEMAPOP
3303 Harbor Blvd., F-3
Costa Mesa, CA 92626
Phone: ....(714) 444-0530
Fax: ....(714) 549-8970
www.cinemapop.com
Key Executives/Personnel:
  Alex Kanakaris, Chairman & CEO
  Branch Lotspeich, Director & Vice Chairman
  John McKay, Director & Webmaster
  David Shomaker, CFO
Specialties: Webcasting

CINEVILLE, INC.
225 Santa Monica Blvd., 7th Fl.
Santa Monica, CA 90401
Phone: ....(310) 394-4699
Fax: ....(310) 394-3052
www.cineville.com
cineville@aol.com
Key Executives/Personnel:
  Bob Joyce, VP of Production
  Mavrizio Bizzarri, VP of Marketing & Sales, Cineville.com
  Annabelle Frankl, Director of Development
  Gina Carollo, Controller
  Carl-Jan Colpaert, Administration
  Christoph Henkel, Administration
Specialties: Web Content; Animation; Movies/Films; Webisodes
Other Categories: Feature Film
Credits: Swimming With Sharks; Hurlyburly; Gas Food Lodging; The Whole Wide World

COAST MEDIA TELEPRODUCTIONS, INC.
17062 Murphy Ave., Bldg. B
Irvine, CA 92614
Phone: ....(949) 417-0300
www.coastmedia.com
digipost@earthlink.net
Key Executives/Personnel:
  Art Royce, President, CEO & Producer
  Brian Ferguson, Director of Photography
  Joyce D. Smith, VP
  Donovan Smith, Audio Engineer
  Curtis Matovich, Editor & Composer
  Steve Hirai, Production Manager
  Becky Fisher, Account Manager

Specialties: Web Content
Other Categories: TV; Commercials; Video; Music Video
Credits: Simple Green (infomercial); Milk Advisory Board (commercial); Meguiar's Wax (corp. video & commercial); Disney (corp. video)

CONNECTION III ENTERTAINMENT CORP.
8489 W. 3rd St.
Los Angeles, CA 90048
Phone: ....(323) 653-3400
www.connection3.com
Key Executives/Personnel:
  Cleveland O'Neal, Producer
Specialties: Web Content
Other Categories: Feature Film; TV
Credits: What About Your Friends; The Garage Club; Phat Beach
Trade Assoc./Guilds/Unions: PGA

CRAPTV
4935 McConnell Ave., Unit 1
Los Angeles, CA 90066
Phone: ....(310) 823-6640
Fax: ....(310) 823-9080
www.craptv.com
Key Executives/Personnel:
  Paul Rosenberg, Chairman
  Jason McHugh, President
  Glasgow Phillips, CEO
  Brody McHugh, COO
  Jolon Bankey, CTO
  Ward Robinson, Director of Acquisitions
Specialties: Webcasting

CTONIC FLIKZ
5540 Hollywood Blvd., 2nd Fl.
Los Angeles, CA 90028
Phone: ....(323) 957-7824
Fax: ....(323) 957-8531
ctonic@aol.com
Key Executives/Personnel:
  Catalaine Knell, Executive Producer
Specialties: Web Content
Other Categories: Feature Film

CYLO
5540 Hollywood Blvd., 2nd Fl.
Los Angeles, CA 90028
Phone: ....(323) 957-7824
Fax: ....(323) 957-8531
www.cylo.com
catalaine@cylo.com
Key Executives/Personnel:
  Julie Atherton, President
  Cindy Akins, Executive Producer
  Catalaine Knell, Producer
Specialties: Web Content
Other Categories: Commercials; Music Video
Additional Info: Previously Atherton

D.FILM
7095 Hollywood Blvd., Ste. 1001
Los Angeles, CA 90028
www.dfilm.com
Specialties: Webcasting

DIGITAL PLANET
9909 Jefferson Blvd.
Culver City, CA 90232
Phone: ....(310) 733-5300
Fax: ....(310) 733-5301

Production Companies – Interactive Multimedia

www.digitalplanet.com
info@digitalplanet.com
Specialties: Webcasting

DIGITAL VISIONARIES
14009 Barner St.
Sylmar, CA 91342
Phone: ...(818) 364-0397
...(800) 538-7800
Fax: ...(818) 364-0397
www.dvhome.com
richard@dvhome.com
Key Executives/Personnel:
    Richard Wainess, Founder & President
Specialties: Web Content; Movies/Films
Other Categories: Video
Credits: MGM; Kowai America; Farmer's Insurance

DOOM, INC.
355 N. Maple St., Ste. 112
Burbank, CA 91505
Phone: ...(818) 972-2007
Fax: ...(818) 972-2008
www.doominc.com
Key Executives/Personnel:
    Thomas Mignone, Director & Executive Producer
    Darci Oltman, Producer
    Peter Davison, Office Manager
Specialties: Web Content
Other Categories: Commercials; Video; Music Video
Credits: Slipknot - Spit it Out (music video); American Red Cross (corp. video); Mudvayne - Dig (music video); Donald Trump: Trump Organization (corp. video)

DOTCOMIX
2727 Mariposa, Studio 100
San Francisco, CA 94110
Phone: ...(415) 522-6500
Fax: ...(415) 522-6522
www.dotcomix.com
Key Executives/Personnel:
    Brad deGraf, Founder & CCO
    Damon Danielson, President & CEO
    Eric Gregory, Founder & CTO
    Jane White, Sr. VP of Development
    Buzz Hays, Executive Producer
    Marc Scaparro, Founder & Head of Production
Specialties: Webcasting

DUCK SOUP STUDIOS
2205 Stoner Ave.
Los Angeles, CA 90064
Phone: ...(310) 478-0771
Fax: ...(310) 478-0773
www.ducksoupla.com
ducksoupla@aol.net
Key Executives/Personnel:
    Mark Medernach, Executive Producer
    Carolyn Bates, Producer
Specialties: Web Content
Other Categories: Feature Film; Commercials; Music Video
Credits: Starkist; Dean's Milk; Bell Atlantic; McDonald's

E.M.E., INC.
Phone: ...(310) 330-8841
emeinc@earthlink.net
Specialties: Web Content
Other Categories: Feature Film; TV; Commercials; Music Video

ENTERAKTION, INC.
2401 E. Atlantic Blvd., Ste. 410
Pompano Beach, FL 33062
Phone: ...(954) 785-5070
Fax: ...(954) 785-5042
www.enteraktion.com
enteraktion@enteraktion.com
Key Executives/Personnel:
    Tom Walsh, Producer, Co-Chairman & CEO
    Ronald Hilton, Producer & Co-Chairman
    Adriana Walsh, Producer & Sr. VP
    Claire Le Covac, Director of Marketing
    Michael Laughlin, Digital Director
    Lloyd Gross, Producer
Specialties: Web Content; Movies/Films; Webcasting; Webisodes; Animation
Other Categories: Feature Film; TV
Credits: Denial; We Dare You!; House to House; Mismatch

FDG INTERNET
8330 W. Third St.
Los Angeles, CA 90048
Phone: ...(310) 251-7026
Fax: ...(801) 382-1848
www.fdg3.com
matt@fdg3.com
Key Executives/Personnel:
    Matthew Diamond, Executive Producer & Head of Development
Specialties: Web Content; Movies/Films
Credits: Cornbread & Coyote; Go; Glyph; Whore!
First Look/Development Deals: CRAPtv, Neurotrash

FLIP YOUR LID, INC.
23501 Park Sorrento, Ste. 207
Calabasas, CA 91302
Phone: ...(818) 222-0700
Fax: ...(818) 222-9166
www.flipyourlid.com
jay@flipyourlid.com
Key Executives/Personnel:
    Steve Soffer, Co-President & Executive Producer
    Jay Jacoby, Co-President & Creative Director
    Gay Murdock, Controller
    John Kokum, Producer
Specialties: Web Content; Webcasting; Animation
Other Categories: Feature Film; TV
Credits: Forty & Shorty; Undercover Brother; Shapes

WOODY FRASER PRODUCTIONS
1239 S. Glendale Ave.
Glendale, CA 91205
Phone: ...(818) 550-6102
Fax: ...(818) 550-6104
woodyfraserpdtns@yahoo.com
Key Executives/Personnel:
    Woody Fraser, Executive Producer
    Cathy Masamitsu, Producer
Specialties: Web Content
Other Categories: TV
Credits: Mike Douglas Show; Good Morning America; The Home Show; Home & Family

GEARS COMMUNICATIONS
315 W. Verdugo Ave.
Burbank, CA 91502
Phone: ...(818) 840-9333
Fax: ...(818) 840-9358
www.gearscom.com
maureen@gearscom.com

Production Companies – Interactive Multimedia

Key Executives/Personnel:
  Greg Gears, Producer
  Steven Kovner, VP of Production
  Maureen English, VP of Sales
Specialties: Web Content
Other Categories: TV; Video; Music Video

GINTY FILMS
16255 Ventura Blvd., Ste. 625
Encino, CA 91436
Phone: ....(310) 274-9691
....(310) 277-1408
Fax: ....(310) 274-9692
www.robertginty.com
rwginty@aol.com
Key Executives/Personnel:
  Robert Ginty, CEO
  Skip Heinecke, (Ireland)
  Shira Zeltzer, Executive Assistant
  Layla Bennett, Executive Assistant
  Lyndi Vanderhout, (Paris)
  Moira Proletti, (Rome)
  Jean Diamond, (London)
  John Gallagher, (New York)
  John Mein, (Vancouver)
Specialties: Web Content
Other Categories: Feature Film; TV; Commercials; Music Video
Credits: Bounty Hunter; Woman of Desire; Day of Reckoning
Trade Assoc./Guilds/Unions: BAFTA, DGA, SAG, WGAw

GLASS GUNS
7280 Melrose Ave., 2nd Fl.
Los Angeles, CA 90046
Phone: ....(323) 938-0729
Fax: ....(323) 938-7007
www.glassguns.com
jeff@glassguns.com
Key Executives/Personnel:
  Jeff Clark, Executive Producer
Specialties: Web Content
Other Categories: Commercials; Music Video
Credits: General Mills; Nescafe; Sky TV; Backstreet Boys - Get Down
Trade Assoc./Guilds/Unions: AICP, MVPA

GRACIE FILMS
10202 W. Washington Blvd., Sidney Poitier Bldg.
Culver City, CA 90232
Phone: ....(310) 244-4222
Fax: ....(310) 244-1530
Key Executives/Personnel:
  James L. Brooks, Producer, Director & Writer
  Richard Sakai, President
  Julie Ansell, President of Motion Pictures
  Denise Sirkot, Executive VP
Specialties: Animation
Other Categories: Feature Film; TV
Credits: As Good As It Gets; Jerry Maguire; Bottle Rocket; Riding in Cars with Boys
First Look/Development Deals: Columbia Pictures/Columbia Tristar Motion Picture Group
Additional Info: Simpson's Production Office: 10201 W. Pico Blvd., Los Angeles, CA 90035

GRADE A ENTERTAINMENT
368 N. La Cienega Blvd.
Los Angeles, CA 90048
Phone: ....(310) 358-8600
Fax: ....(310) 652-0718
gradeaprod@aol.com

Key Executives/Personnel:
  Andy Cohen, Producer
Specialties: Web Content; Webcasting; Webisodes
Other Categories: Feature Film; TV
Credits: Captain Ron; It Takes Two; A Chance of Snow; Billboard Dad

GREENWATER PICTURES
3940 Laurel Canyon Blvd., Ste. 736
Studio City, CA 91604
Phone: ....(323) 655-9585
Fax: ....(323) 655-9025
www.greenwaterpictures.com
tlowe@greenwaterpictures.com
Key Executives/Personnel:
  Tom Lowe, President & Producer
  Barbara Cordis, VP of Development
Specialties: Animation; Movies/Films; Webisodes
Other Categories: Commercials; Video; Music Video
Credits: Fireball (webisodes); Nick Forester (webisodes)
Trade Assoc./Guilds/Unions: DGA

H-GUN LABS
587 Shotwell St.
San Francisco, CA 94110
Phone: ....(415) 648-4386
....(773) 561-5354
Fax: ....(415) 920-3911
www.hgun.com
info@hgun.com
Key Executives/Personnel:
  James Deloye, Executive Producer
  Sara Kraft, Producer
  Nancy Williams, Lab Manager
Specialties: Web Content
Other Categories: Feature Film; TV; Commercials; Music Video

HAWK ENTERTAINMENT
8888 W. 3rd St., Ste. 306
Los Angeles, CA 90048
Phone: ....(310) 859-7779
Fax: ....(310) 859-7797
hawkentertain@aol.com
Key Executives/Personnel:
  John Crededio, Partner
  Paul Pompian, Partner
  Ron DeRosa, Producer
Specialties: Web Content
Other Categories: Feature Film; TV
Credits: The Watcher; Time Served; Vincent Verelli

HENNESSEY ENTERTAINMENT, LTD.
P.O. Box 481164
Los Angeles, CA 90048
Phone: ....(323) 876-2400
Fax: ....(323) 876-2444
www.hennesseyentertainment.com
a_sleuth@hotmail.com
Key Executives/Personnel:
  Ellis A. Cohen, Producer, Writer & CEO
  Leonard H. Cohen, Creative Executive
  Jerome Cohen, Creative Executive
Specialties: Web Content
Other Categories: Feature Film; TV
Credits: Dangerous Evidence; Love, Mary; First Steps; Aunt Mary
Trade Assoc./Guilds/Unions: ATAS, PGA, WGAw

THE JIM HENSON COMPANY
1416 N. La Brea Ave.
Los Angeles, CA 90028
Phone: ....(323) 802-1500
Fax: ....(323) 802-1825
www.henson.com
Key Executives/Personnel:
    Brian Henson, Chairman
    Charles H. Rivkin, President & CEO
    Linda Govreau, Executive VP of Corporate Finance & CFO
    Lisa Henson, President, Jim Henson Pictures
    John Stephenson, Executive VP & Creative Supervisor,
      Jim Henson's Creature Shop
    Juliet Blake, Executive VP & Co-Head, Jim Henson
      Television Group Worldwide
    Angus Fletcher, Executive VP & Co-Head, Jim Henson
      Television Group Worldwide
    Peter Schube, General Counsel & Executive VP of Business
      & Legal Affairs
    Michael Bolingbroke, Sr. VP of Finance & Operations,
      Jim Henson's Creature Shop
    Craig Allen, Sr. VP & General Manager, Jim Henson Interactive
    Robert Norton, Sr. VP of Business & Legal Affairs
    Ritamarie Peruggi, Sr. VP of Production Worldwide
    Robert Wozniak, VP of Production Administration & Finance,
      Production Executive
    Kristine Belson, Production, Jim Henson Pictures
    Louis Philips, VP of Production Administration
    Halle Stanford Grossman, VP of Creative Affairs, Jim Henson Television
    Ruth Caruso, VP of Development, Jim Henson Television
    Michele Martell, VP of Business Affairs & Interactive
      Business Development
    Antonia Downey, VP of Int'l. Legal & Business Affairs
    Pete Coogan, VP of Physical Production
    David Barrington-Holt, Creative Supervisor,
      Jim Henson's Creature Shop
    Debbie McClellan, Sr. Director of Corporate Communications
      & Special Projects
    Omar Camacho, Director of Current Programming,
      Jim Henson Television
Specialties: Web Content
Other Categories: Feature Film; TV; Commercials; Video; Music Video
Credits: Farscape; Story Telling with Tomie de Paola; Rat; Muppets From Space

HY-TONE PRODUCTIONS
26349 Fairside Rd.
Malibu, CA 90265
Phone: ....(310) 456-3052
Fax: ....(310) 456-9659
www.notelvis.com
hytone@aol.com
Key Executives/Personnel:
    Robert Jaye, Producer, Director & Cinematographer
    Walter Hoylman, Producer, Director & Editor
Specialties: Web Content; Animation; Movies/Films
Other Categories: Feature Film; TV; Video
Credits: Some of the King's Men; Mustang America; Art and Sex; Fire Engine

ICEBOX
3453 S. La Cienega Blvd.
Los Angeles, CA 90016
Phone: ....(310) 202-5000
www.icebox.com
Key Executives/Personnel:
    Steve Stanford, Co-Founder & CEO
    Jonathan Collier, Co-Founder & Co-President of Production
    Howard Gordon, Co-Founder & Co-President of Production
    Rob Lazebnik, Co-Founder & Co-President of Production
    Gary Levine, President
Specialties: Webcasting

INDUSTRIAL LIGHT + MAGIC COMMERCIAL PRODUCTIONS
732 N. Highland Ave.
Hollywood, CA 90038
Phone: ....(323) 957-2002
Fax: ....(323) 464-8373
www.ilmcp.com
Key Executives/Personnel:
    Marcie Malooly, Executive Producer & Division Manager
    John Denis, Executive Producer
    Paul Grimshaw, Head of Production
Specialties: Web Content
Other Categories: Commercials; Music Video
Credits: First Union; Toyota; Gatorade; Armor All

JARET ENTERTAINMENT
2017 Pacific Ave., Ste. 2
Venice, CA 90291
Phone: ....(310) 883-8807
Fax: ....(310) 822-0916
www.jaretentertainment.com
sjaret@jaretentertainment.com
Key Executives/Personnel:
    Seth Jaret, CEO & Producer
    Susan Sullivan, Development Associate & Story Editor
    Amy O'Brien, Assistant
Specialties: Web Content
Other Categories: Feature Film; TV
Credits: Rounders; 10 Things I Hate About You

KILLER FILMS
380 Lafayette St., Ste. 302
New York, NY 10003
Phone: ....(212) 473-3950
Fax: ....(212) 473-6152
www.killerfilms.com
dwagner@killerfilms.com
Key Executives/Personnel:
    Christine Vachon, Producer & President
    Pamela Koffler, Producer & President
    Katie Roumel, Head of Production
    Jon Marcus, Production Executive
    Brad Simpson, Head of Development
    Jocelyn Hayes, Development Executive
    Laird Adamson, Director of Creative Affairs
    Daniel Wagner, Office Manager
Specialties: Web Content
Other Categories: Feature Film
Credits: Boys Don't Cry; Velvet Goldmine; Officer Killer; Kiss Me Guido
First Look/Development Deals: John Wells Productions, Clear Blue Sky Productions

Production Companies – Interactive Multimedia

LANGLEY PRODUCTIONS
2225 Colorado Ave.
Santa Monica, CA 90404
Phone: ....(310) 449-5300
Key Executives/Personnel:
    John Langley, President, Executive Producer, Director & Writer
    Murray Jordan, Producer
    Doug Waterman, Producer
    Elie Cohn, Producer
    Karen Hori, VP of TV Development
Specialties: Web Content
Other Categories: Feature Film; TV
Credits: Cops; Anatomy of a Crime; Code 3; Wild Side
First Look/Development Deals: Twentieth Century Fox

STAN LEE MEDIA, INC.
15821 Ventura Blvd., Ste. 675
Encinco, CA 91436
Phone: ....(818) 461-1757
Fax: ....(818) 461-1760
www.stanleemedia.com
info@stanleemedia.com
Key Executives/Personnel:
    Stan Lee, Chairman & CCO
    Ken Williams, President & CEO
    Peter Paul, Co-Founder
    Stephen Brain, Executive VP of Production
    Stephen Gordon, Executive VP of Operations
    Jamie Wilkenson, Executive VP of Internet Strategy
    George Hamilton, President of Global Branded Entertainment
    Dana Moreshead, VP of Creative Services
Specialties: Web Content; Animation; Webisodes; Movies/Films
Other Categories: Feature Film
Credits: 7th Portal (feature); The Drifter (multimedia); The Backstreet Project (multimedia)
First Look/Development Deals: Shockwave.com, The Mark Canton Company

LINEUP TECHNOLOGIES, INC.
2329 S. Purdue St.
Los Angeles, CA 90064
Phone: ....(310) 473-8890
Fax: ....(310) 444-9454
www.lineup.com
info@lineup.com
Key Executives/Personnel:
    Jeffrey A. Stern, CEO
    Jonathan Snyder, VP of Business Development
    Joe Mauro, VP of Business Development
    Jim Bunte, VP of Content & Production
    Peter Phillips, VP of Advertising & Marketing
Specialties: Webcasting

LUCID FILM
8490 Sunset Blvd., Ste. 700
West Hollywood, CA 90069
Phone: ....(310) 777-0007
Fax: ....(310) 360-8613
www.lucidfilm.com
Key Executives/Personnel:
    Ryan Phillippe, Producer
    David E. Siegel, Producer
Specialties: Web Content
Other Categories: Feature Film; TV
First Look/Development Deals: Intermedia Films

MARIPOSA
Phone: ....(805) 527-9990
Fax: ....(805) 527-9990
www.surfbit.com
nadar@pacbell.net
Key Executives/Personnel:
    Bridget Gardner, Director & Producer
    Carole Gardner, Production Manager
Specialties: Web Content; Movies/Films; Webisodes
Other Categories: Feature Film; Commercials
Credits: American Cancer Society; NAMES Project; MADD; SurfBit.com

MATRIX COMMUNICATIONS
2522 Torrance Blvd.
Torrance, CA 90503
Phone: ....(310) 782-8400
Key Executives/Personnel:
    Marta Houske, Executive Producer & Director
Specialties: Web Content
Other Categories: Feature Film; Commercials; Video; Music Video
Credits: Zimbabwe Legit (music video); A Stitch in Time (documentary); Times Mirror (commercial); In Search of ... (TV series)
Additional Info: www.potentialsmedia.com

MEDIATRIP
11111 Santa Monica Blvd., Ste. 300
Los Angeles, CA 90025
Phone: ....(310) 445-1888
Fax: ....(310) 445-3310
www.mediatrip.com
Specialties: Webcasting

MEKANISM
600 Townsend, Ste. 300
San Francisco, CA 94103
Phone: ....(415) 252-5331
    ....(415) 412-7545
Fax: ....(415) 621-6780
www.mekanism.tv
tmeans@mekanism.tv
Key Executives/Personnel:
    Tommy Means, Executive Producer
    Ken Solomon, Business Development
    Tuesday McGowen, Creative Director
    Jim Bartel, CTO
    Kurt Noble, Technical Director
Specialties: Web Content; Movies/Films; Webcasting; Webisodes
Other Categories: Commercials
Credits: Rock The Vote Yes/No 2000

METAFILMICS
4250 Wilshire Blvd.
Los Angeles, CA 90010
Phone: ....(818) 734-9320
Fax: ....(818) 345-2502
Key Executives/Personnel:
    Stephen Simon, Co-Founder
    Barnet Bain, Co-Founder
Specialties: Movies/Films
Other Categories: Feature Film; TV
Credits: What Dreams May Come; Somewhere in Time; Bill & Ted's Excellent Adventure; Quantum Project

MINDFIRE ENTERTAINMENT
3740 Overland Ave., Ste. E
Los Angeles, CA 90034
Phone: ....(310) 204-4481
Fax: ....(310) 204-5882
www.mindfireentertainment.com
maltman@mindfireentertainment.com
Key Executives/Personnel:
    Mark Gottwald, Chairman
    Dan Bates, CEO
    Mark A. Altman, COO
    Ellie Gottwald, VP of Creative Affairs
    Ann Kaesman, Director of Development
    Carlos Rodriguez, Story Analyst
Specialties: Web Content; Animation; Movies/Films; Webisodes
Other Categories: Feature Film; TV
Credits: Free Enterprise; The Specials

NATIONAL LAMPOON
10850 Wilshire Blvd., Ste. 1000
Los Angeles, CA 90024
Phone: ....(310) 474-5252
Fax: ....(310) 474-1219
www.nationallampoon.com
Key Executives/Personnel:
    James P. Jimirro, President & CEO
    Chris Trunkey, CFO
    Duncan Murray, VP of Marketing
Specialties: Web Content
Other Categories: Feature Film; TV
Credits: Vacation; Animal House; National Lampoon's Senior Trip

NEMIROFF PRODUCTIONS
1506 Butler Ave., Ste. 1
Los Angeles, CA 90025
Phone: ....(310) 473-4100
....(310) 917-5250
Fax: ....(310) 473-4100
Key Executives/Personnel:
    Steve Nemiroff, Producer & Assistant Director
Specialties: Web Content
Other Categories: Feature Film; TV; Commercials; Video; Music Video
Credits: The Real Deal; Miracles; Sparkletts; Kenny Kingston's Psychic Hotline III
Trade Assoc./Guilds/Unions: AFI, AICP, ITVA

NEW MILLENNIUM STUDIOS
One New Millenium Dr.
Petersburg, VA 23805
Phone: ....(804) 957-4200
Fax: ....(804) 862-1200
www.nmstudios.com
martinj@nmstudios.com
Key Executives/Personnel:
    Tim Reid, Producer
    Daphne Maxwell Reid, Producer
    Martin C. Jones, Producer
Specialties: Web Content; Animation; Movies/Films; Webisodes
Other Categories: Feature Film; TV; Commercials; Music Video
Credits: Asunder; Out of Sync; Linc's; When We Were Colored

NXT ENTERTAINMENT
8639 Holloway Plaza Dr.
Los Angeles, CA 90069
Phone: ....(310) 289-9600
Fax: ....(310) 289-7383
www.wwwcine.com
nxt@wwwcine.com
Key Executives/Personnel:
    Klaus Lucka, Executive Producer
Specialties: Web Content; Webcasting
Other Categories: Feature Film; TV; Commercials; Video
Credits: www.cyberkidsplanet.com; www.neobodies.com
Trade Assoc./Guilds/Unions: DGA

ORBIT ENTERTAINMENT GROUP
714 N. La Brea Ave.
Hollywood, CA 90038
Phone: ....(323) 525-2626
Fax: ....(323) 525-2627
dror@orbiteg.com
Key Executives/Personnel:
    Dror Soref, Partner, President & Director
    Lee Nelson, Partner & Executive Producer
    Lynne Pateman, Executive Producer
    Kevin Moreton, VP of Orbit Pictures
    Jeremy White, Executive Creative Director
Specialties: Web Content
Other Categories: Feature Film; Commercials
Credits: Oldsmobile (commercial); Sony (commercial); K-Swiss (commercial); The Seventh Coin (feature)

Production Companies – Interactive Multimedia

OUR GANG PRODUCTIONS
8522 National Blvd., Ste. 107
Culver City, CA 90232
Phone: (310) 300-1010
Fax: (310) 636-8304
ourgangproductions@earthlink.net
Key Executives/Personnel:
   Gayle Gluck, President
   Kevin Miller, Sr. VP & Creative Director
   Chris Conway, Audio Production
   Matt Fisher, Supervising Editor
   Ron Mesa, Chief Audio Engineer
   Rachel Burkes, Production Assistant
Specialties: Web Content
Other Categories: TV; Commercials; Music Video

GEORGE PAIGE ASSOCIATES, INC.
3000 W. Olympic Blvd., Ste. 1407
Santa Monica, CA 90404
Phone: (310) 315-4835
Fax: (310) 315-4836
gpacorp@aol.com
Key Executives/Personnel:
   George Paige, Owner & President
   James R. Tumminia, Producer
Specialties: Web Content
Other Categories: Feature Film; TV; Commercials; Video; Music Video
Credits: Abbott & Costello Meet Jerry Seinfeld; 50 Years of Funny Females; Shafted
Trade Assoc./Guilds/Unions: ATAS

PERSPECTIVE FILMS
Phone: (310) 670-4030
             (310) 261-8389
Fax: (310) 670-4031
Key Executives/Personnel:
   Debbie Pietsch, Executive Producer
Specialties: Web Content
Other Categories: Feature Film; TV; Commercials; Video; Music Video
Credits: Fast Point DSL; Mattel; Disney; Harman Kardan: MacWorld

QUASAR STUDIOS
P.O. Box 661266
Los Angeles, CA 90066
Phone: (310) 289-1547
            (818) 352-0908
Fax: (310) 289-1547
www.perufilmcommission.net
filmperu@gte.net
Key Executives/Personnel:
   Marggie Castellano, Producer
   Prudence Michael, Location Manager
   Monica Leon, Designer
Specialties: Web Content
Other Categories: Feature Film; TV; Video
Credits: Coyotes (feature); National Geographic: Ancient Graves; The Celestine Prophecy (miniseries); A&E: Ancient Mysteries

PATRICK RAYMOND ENTERTAINMENT, INC.
1041 N. Formosa Ave., Formosa Bldg., Ste. 209
West Hollywood, CA 90046
Phone: (323) 850-2918
Fax: (323) 850-2920
praymondh@aol.com
Key Executives/Personnel:
   Patrick Raymond, Executive Producer
   Albert Frigone, Associate Producer
   Joey Estella, Assistant
Specialties: Web Content
Other Categories: Feature Film; TV; Commercials; Video

REALITORY PRODUCTIONS
Phone: (818) 404-8711
Fax: (818) 702-8611
www.realitory.com
mac@realitory.com
Key Executives/Personnel:
   Michael Condro, Director, DP & VFX
   Monica Ramone, Producer & Partner
Specialties: Web Content
Other Categories: Feature Film; Video
Credits: World Championship: All Terrain Boards; Jousting, The First Extreme Sport; Strange and Weird Halloween Festivals
Trade Assoc./Guilds/Unions: IATSE, IFP

Production Companies – Interactive Multimedia

DAN REDLER ENTERTAINMENT
18730 Hatteras St., Ste. 8
Tarzana, CA 91356
Phone: ....(818) 776-0938
Fax: ....(818) 705-6870
dredler@pacbell.net
Key Executives/Personnel:
  Dan Redler, Producer
  Nadia Naili, Producer
Specialties: Web Content
Other Categories: Feature Film; TV; Commercials
Credits: In His Father's Shoes; Pygmalion; Tanks; Profile For Murder
First Look/Development Deals: Nu Image/Millenium

RENEGADE ANIMATION, INC.
204 N. San Fernando Blvd.
Burbank, CA 91502
Phone: ....(818) 556-3395
Fax: ....(818) 556-3398
www.renegadeanimation.com
ashley@renegadeanimation.com
Key Executives/Personnel:
  Ashley Postlewaite, Executive Producer
  Darrell Van Citters, Director
Specialties: Web Content; Animation
Other Categories: Commercials
Credits: Nike; Carl's Jr.; Chester Cheetah; Mattel
Additional Info: Full-service animation house

RICE & BEANS PRODUCTIONS
30 N. Raymond., Ste. 605
Pasadena, CA 91103
Phone: ....(626) 792-9171
Fax: ....(626) 792-9171
vin88@pacbell.net
Key Executives/Personnel:
  Vince Cheung, Writer, Director, Producer & Owner
  Ben Montanio, Writer, Director, Producer & Owner
Specialties: Web Content
Other Categories: Feature Film; TV
Credits: The Steve Harvey Show; Married... with Children; In The House; Empty Nest
Trade Assoc./Guilds/Unions: ATAS, WGA

PHIL ROMAN ENTERTAINMENT
4040 Vineland Ave., Ste. 205
Studio City, CA 91604
Phone: ....(818) 985-1200
Fax: ....(818) 985-2668
www.philromanent.com
phil@romanent.com
Key Executives/Personnel:
  Phil Roman, President & CEO
  Rick Ramirez, VP
Specialties: Web Content
Other Categories: Feature Film; TV
Credits: Grandma Got Run Over By A Reindeer; Christmas in Gaudinia

SANTA MONICA PICTURES
3025 W. Olympic Blvd.
Santa Monica, CA 90404
Phone: ....(310) 264-5566
Fax: ....(310) 828-9183
infosmp@visionart.com
Key Executives/Personnel:
  David Rose, CEO & Producer
  Marina Muhlfriedel, VP of Development & Production
  Cindy Sison, Head of Int'l. Sales & Distribution
  Stasi McAteer, Executive Assistant
Specialties: Web Content
Other Categories: Feature Film; TV
Credits: The Painting; Goldilocks and the Three Bears; Godiva; The Magic Forest

KRISTINE SCHWARZ PRODUCTIONS
Phone: ....(310) 393-0107
Fax: ....(310) 451-5454
www.kristineschwarzproductions.com
krisjs@aol.com
Key Executives/Personnel:
  Kristine Schwarz, Producer
Specialties: Web Content
Other Categories: Feature Film; TV; Commercials
Credits: Raid Gauldises; Kalifornia; Another Stakeout

SIGHTSOUND.COM
733 Washington Rd., Ste. 400
Mount Lebanon, PA 15228
Phone: ....(412) 341-1001
Fax: ....(412) 341-2442
www.sightsound.com
Specialties: Webcasting

Production Companies – Interactive Multimedia

SILVER LINING PRODUCTIONS, INC.
8687 Melrose Ave., Ste. B300
West Hollywood, CA 90069
Phone: ....(310) 289-6650
Fax: ....(310) 289-6658
slpbozena@aol.com/silverliningp@aol.com
Key Executives/Personnel:
  Bozena Armstrong, Executive Producer & Director
  Randy Haberkamp, Producer
Specialties: Web Content
Other Categories: Feature Film; TV; Commercials; Video
Credits: Cleopatra (promo); Forest Lawn (commercial); Reva: The Scarlet Years (video); The Unknown Tradition (documentary)
Trade Assoc./Guilds/Unions: DGA, SAG

SNAPDRAGON FILMS, INC.
13428 Maxella Ave., Ste. 293
Marina Del Rey, CA 90292
Phone: ....(310) 822-2505
Fax: ....(310) 822-7054
Key Executives/Personnel:
  Bonnie Palef, Director, Producer & Writer
  Catherine Purchase, Assistant
  Manuel Granado, Jr., Assistant
Specialties: Web Content
Other Categories: Feature Film; TV; Video
Credits: Marvin's Room; Moonstruck; The Cemetary Club; Parents
First Look/Development Deals: Columbia Pictures/Columbia Tristar Motion Picture Group
Trade Assoc./Guilds/Unions: DGA, WGAw

THE SPARK FACTORY
710 Wilshire Blvd., Ste. 200
Santa Monica, CA 90401
Phone: ....(310) 395-6775
Fax: ....(310) 395-4595
www.sparkfactory.com
mailroom@sparkfactory.com
Key Executives/Personnel:
  Tim Street, President
  Gail Gillman, VP of Creative Affairs
Specialties: Web Content; Animation; Movies/Films; Webisodes
Other Categories: Feature Film; Commercials
Credits: Entrapment (commercial); Out of Towners (commercial); Whoistylerdurden.com; Creepysites.com

STEREOMEDIA 3D VIDEO PRODUCTIONS
2307 W. Olive St.
Burbank, CA 91506
Phone: ....(818) 559-6515
Fax: ....(818) 559-6598
stereo3DTV@aol.com
Key Executives/Personnel:
  Anthony Coogan, Executive Producer
  Eric Bakke, CTO & Director of 3D Videography
  Patrick Dunauan, Producer
Specialties: Web Content
Other Categories: Video; Music Video

STREAMEDIA.NET
244-250 W. 54th St., 12th Fl.
New York, NY 10019
Phone: ....(212) 445-1700
Fax: ....(212) 445-1099
www.streamedia.net
info@streamedia.net
Key Executives/Personnel:
  James D. Rupp, President & CEO
  Nicholas Malino, Executive VP, CFO & COO
  Gayle Essary, VP of Strategic Development
  Mark D. Smith, VP of Content Sales
Specialties: Webcasting
Additional Info: www.bijoucafe.com

TAVEL ENTERTAINMENT
9171 Wilshire Blvd., Ste. 406
Beverly Hills, CA 90210
Phone: ....(310) 278-6700
Fax: ....(310) 278-6770
Key Executives/Personnel:
  Connie Tavel, Owner, Manager & Producer
  Chris Ridenhour, Development for Features
  Vanessa Livingston, Development for TV
  Plato Wang, Development for Internet
  Vera Mihailovich, Talent Scout
  Mundi Male, Assistant to Ms. Tavel
  Marc Walker, Assistant to Mr. Ridenhour
  Courtney Adams, Assistant to Ms. Mihailovich
Specialties: Web Content
Other Categories: Feature Film; TV
Credits: Judging Amy; Summer's End; Bill & Ted's Bogus Journey; Ride The Wind
First Look/Development Deals: Sony Pictures Entertainment

Production Companies – Interactive Multimedia

THRESHOLD ENTERTAINMENT
1649 11th St.
Santa Monica, CA 90404
Phone: ....(310) 452-8899
Fax: ....(310) 452-0736
www.thethreshold.com
Key Executives/Personnel:
 Larry Kasanoff, Chairman & CEO
 Joshua Wexler, CIO
 George Johnsen, CTO
 Alison Savitch, President
Specialties: Web Content; Animation; Movies/Films; Webcasting; Webisodes
Other Categories: Feature Film; TV
Credits: Mortal Kombat: Annihilation; Beowulf; True Lies; Mortal Kombat

UNDERGROUNDFILM.COM
137 W. 14th St., Ste. 202
New York, NY 10011
Phone: ....(212) 206-1995
Fax: ....(212) 206-1997
www.undergroundfilm.com
Key Executives/Personnel:
 Mike Kelly, Co-Founder & CEO
 Adrien Glover, Co-Founder & Executive Content Editor
 Bradford Smith, Director of Technology
Specialties: Webcasting

VAL D'ORO ENTERTAINMENT
1437 Seventh St., Ste. 200
Santa Monica, CA 90401
Phone: ....(310) 656-8555
Fax: ....(310) 656-8560
valdoro@aol.com
Key Executives/Personnel:
 Steven E. deSouza, President
 Jeri Barchilon deSouza, VP
 Scott Humphries, Apprentice
Specialties: Web Content
Other Categories: Feature Film; TV
Trade Assoc./Guilds/Unions: DGA, WGAw

VIDEOWERKS
3435 Ocean Park Blvd., Ste. 112
Santa Monica, CA 90405
Phone: ....(310) 393-8754
....(800) 356-6541
Fax: ....(310) 399-1829
www.videowerks.com
videowerks@earthlink.net
Key Executives/Personnel:
 David M. Werk, Owner, Cameraman & DP
Specialties: Web Content
Other Categories: TV; Commercials; Video
Credits: The Directors; History's Lost & Found; Investigative Reports; Headliners & Legends
Trade Assoc./Guilds/Unions: IDA, ITVA

Z.COM
2919 West Empire Ave.
Burbank, CA 91504
Phone: ....(323) 762-1600
Fax: ....(323) 762-1601
www.z.com
pr@corpz.com
Specialties: Webcasting

ZEROONEFILMS.COM
438 Broome St., Ste. 5S
New York, NY 10013
Phone: ....(212) 941-1993
Fax: ....(212) 334-1168
www.01films.com
Key Executives/Personnel:
 Tarrick Wahba, President
 Johnny Wahba, VP
 Keith Abrahamsson, Director of Acquisitions
Specialties: Webcasting

ZOOMA ZOOMA CORPORATION
11 Mercer St., 3rd Fl.
New York, NY 10013
Phone: ....(212) 941-7680
Fax: ....(212) 941-8179
www.zoomazooma.com
staff@zoomazooma.com
Key Executives/Personnel:
 Joseph Mantegna, Executive Producer
 Todd Bellanca, Director
 Eden Tyler, Director
 Sam Raimi, Director
 Michael Bellino, Director
 Tim Hamilton, Director
 Gavin O'Connor, Director
 Lori Vitale, East Coast Sales
Specialties: Web Content
Other Categories: Feature Film; TV; Commercials; Music Video

Notes

Freelance Producer Category Key

Feature Film
Albanese, Paul
Amemiya, Emie H.
Anthony, Beth
Barlow, Louise
Basile, Tony
Bernard, Yvonne M.
Bishop, Kathryn
Brooks, John
Castro, Mark
Cooper, Jessica
Corser, John
Curran, Bill
Curtis, Madelyn
Dear, Heather
Doskey, Janice
Fauntleroy, Tom
Ferrari, Janet
Fink, Barry
Fritzberg, Bruce
Ginnes, John G.
Goldfarb, Bonnie
Haukoos, Robert
Hollingshead, Lisa
Jones, Bronston
Kahan, Leslie A.
Kaye, Dessa
Leimbrook, Jenny
Leonard, Mary
MacBain, Don
Martin, Sandy
McCrary, Colleen
Peterson, Susie
Priest, Patricia
Rapiel, Ron
Respol, Craig
Reynolds, Lynn
Robinson, Phil Alden
Scott, Jan
Stevenson, Brad
Tassone, Sal
Vogelfang, Susan
West, Jaki
Ziga, Jack
Zurla, Leslie

TV
Amemiya, Emie H.
Barlow, Louise
Bedell, Stephanie
Bernard, Yvonne M.
Brooks, John
Cooper, Jessica
Corser, John
Curran, Bill
Dear, Heather
Fritzberg, Bruce
Ginnes, John G.
Haukoos, Robert
Kahan, Leslie A.
Kaye, Dessa
Leimbrook, Jenny
Leonard, Mary
McCrary, Colleen
Priest, Patricia
Respol, Craig
Robinson, Phil Alden
Schmidt, Robert
Simon, Denise
Tassone, Sal
Tobin, Joseph P.
Vogelfang, Susan
Zommers, Anita

Commercials
Albanese, Paul
Amato, Kelly
Amemiya, Emie H.
Anthony, Beth
Barlow, Louise
Barry-Goldman, LuAnn
Basile, Tony
Bedell, Stephanie
Bernard, Yvonne M.
Bishop, Kathryn
Black, Stuart
Bolois, Hope Grossman
Brook, Terri Lee
Brooks, John
Bukrey-Lloyd, Shirley
Butcher, Marol
Castro, Mark
Christensen, Kim
Cooper, Jessica
Corser, John
Craig, Scott
Curran, Bill
Curtis, Madelyn
Davis, Beverly
Days, Rick
Dear, Heather
Demopoulos, Diana
Dietrich, Steve
Dillon, Kat
Donald, Carr
Doskey, Janice
Dow, Helen
Druckman, Valerie
Evers, Leslie M.
Faull-La Violette, Franny
Fauntleroy, Tom
Ferrari, Janet
Fink, Barry
Fisher, Debbie A.
Forsyth, Fiona
Fox, J.P.
Franklin, Tammy A.
Frazier, Ruth
Freiberger, Franny
Friedman, Nona Sue
Fritzberg, Bruce
Fulton-Rogers, Nancy
Galloway, Debbie
Gates, Kent
Ginnes, John G.
Glass, Leora
Goldfarb, Bonnie
Goto, Janice K.
Greene, Katy
Haak, Carol
Hall-West, Naia
Haukoos, Robert
Hettler, Paul
Hill, Cynthia
Hollingshead, Lisa
Houchin, Craig
Houle, Chantal
Jones, Bronston
Kahan, Leslie A.
Katz, Jan
Kauper, Doron
Kaye, Dessa
Lancaster, Patti
Leimbrook, Jenny
Leonard, Mary
Lowe, Sonny
Lucas, Martha
Maier, Jeffrey
Martin, Sandy
McClelland, Lisa
McCrary, Colleen
Mills, Roger
Monico, Alison
Morov, Sharon
Murov, Tommy
Nayer, Jack
Newman, Merilee
Oltman, Darcy
Papanek, Paul
Pearson, Beth
Penfield, Sandra
Persoff, David
Peterson, Susie
Piazzie
Pollock-Barish, Sadie
Powers, Rick
Provost, Jack
Rapiel, Ron
Respol, Craig
Reynolds, Lynn
Rhodes, Kathryn L.
Ritzmann, Christina

Freelance Producer Category Key

Rocchietti, Denise
Samuelson, Amy M.
Schmidt, Robert
Schoessler, Sarah
Schreiner, Larry
Scott, Jan
Shapiro, Harvey
Shine, Dona
Sidoti, Thom
Siegal, Scott
Siegel, Marc
Silver, Karen
Simon, Denise
Skutch, Lindsay
Smith, Al
Stevenson, Brad
Strachan, Steven
Tassone, Sal
Tietjen, Debbie
Timmons, Debby
Trask, Lee
Troop, Clarissa
Tuttle, Jeffrey S.
Vogelfang, Susan
Walter, Janie
Weiner, Francine
West, Jaki
Whitford, Ree
Yacavone, Peter
Young, Diana
Yuro-Vickers, Gabrielle
Zarro, Raymond
Ziga, Jack
Zimmerman, Joel R.
Zommers, Anita
Zurla, Leslie

Video
Bernard, Yvonne M.
Brooks, John
Castro, Mark
Corser, John
Curtis, Madelyn
Doskey, Janice
Fritzberg, Bruce
Hettler, Paul
Leimbrook, Jenny
Martin, Sandy
McCrary, Colleen
Oltman, Darcy
Priest, Patricia
Respol, Craig
Schoessler, Sarah
Simon, Denise
Zurla, Leslie

Music Video
Albanese, Paul
Barlow, Louise
Bedell, Stephanie
Bernard, Yvonne M.
Castro, Mark
Christensen, Kim
Cooper, Jessica
Demopoulos, Diana
Evers, Leslie M.
Ferrari, Janet
Fink, Barry
Fox, J.P.
Frazier, Ruth
Freiberger, Franny
Hall-West, Naia
Hettler, Paul
Hill, Cynthia
Hollingshead, Lisa
Jones, Bronston
Lowe, Sonny
McCrary, Colleen
Morov, Sharon
Oltman, Darcy
Piazzie
Respol, Craig
Sidoti, Thom
Stevenson, Brad
Tuttle, Jeffrey S.
Weiner, Francine

Interactive Media
Black, Stuart
Christensen, Kim
Fritzberg, Bruce
Hettler, Paul
Leonard, Mary
Martin, Sandy
McCrary, Colleen
Oltman, Darcy

Freelance Producers – Feature Film

PAUL ALBANESE
Phone: ....(323) 653-7243
....(310) 428-7285
paulbanese@aol.com
Specialties: Independent
Other Categories: Commercials; Music Video
Credits: Nike; ESPN; Dixie Chicks; Don Henley

EMIE H. AMEMIYA
Phone: ....(323) 463-3033
Specialties: Documentaries
Other Categories: TV; Commercials

BETH ANTHONY
Phone: ....(323) 654-3390
....(310) 486-2235
babell@aol.com
Specialties: Trailers
Other Categories: Commercials

LOUISE BARLOW
Phone: ....(310) 391-0142
....(213) 206-0282
Fax: ....(310) 397-8835
louisebarlow@earthlink.net
Specialties: Independent
Other Categories: TV; Commercials; Music Video
Credits: Pontiac; Xerox; Savagegarden - Crash & Burn; OffSpring - The Kids Aren't Alright

TONY BASILE
Phone: ....(323) 935-5481
....(213) 324-5481
ynotbasile@hotmail.com
Specialties: Shorts; Documentaries
Credits: DirecTV; Saturn; Wrigley's; State Farm Insurance

YVONNE M. BERNARD
Phone: ....(310) 318-0884
....(310) 353-4568
Fax: ....(310) 318-3955
yvonne3@aol.com
Specialties: Studio; Independent; Shorts; Documentaries; Animation; Trailers
Other Categories: TV; Commercials; Video; Music Video
Credits: Anheuser-Busch; McDonald's; Dodge; Nike

KATHRYN BISHOP
Phone: ....(818) 980-4483
Specialties: Independent
Other Categories: Commercials
Trade Assoc./Guilds/Unions: DGA

JOHN BROOKS
217 Third Pl.
Manhattan Beach, CA 90266
Phone: ....(310) 418-6708
....(310) 717-6593
www.johnbrooks.cc
jbrooks@alohababy.cc
Specialties: Documentaries
Other Categories: TV; Commercials; Video

MARK CASTRO
2275 Huntington Dr., Ste. 320
San Marino, CA 91108
Phone: ....(626) 564-8195
....(213) 309-7680
Fax: ....(626) 564-8195
castrodel@aol.com
Specialties: Independent
Other Categories: Commercials; Video; Music Video
Credits: WashingtonPost.com; Kevon Edmonds; Chili's

JESSICA COOPER
Phone: ....(323) 655-3255
Fax: ....(323) 655-3250
carlsncoop@aol.com
Specialties: Independent
Other Categories: TV; Commercials; Music Video
Credits: Coca-Cola; Levi's; Intel; Xerox

JOHN CORSER
827 S. Muirfield Rd.
Los Angeles, CA 90005
Phone: ....(323) 934-6346
....(213) 200-1477
Fax: ....(323) 934-1641
jcorser@earthlink.net
Specialties: Shorts
Other Categories: TV; Commercials; Video
Credits: ED TV (promo); Isuzu; Texas Pete Hot Sauce; Universal Studios

BILL CURRAN
Phone: ....(310) 392-1035
Fax: ....(310) 392-2694
billcurran@hotmail.com
Specialties: Independent; Trailers
Other Categories: TV; Commercials
Credits: KIA; Universal Studios; Mattel; Albertsons
Trade Assoc./Guilds/Unions: DGA

MADELYN CURTIS
Phone: ....(310) 459-8976
....(310) 663-3481
Fax: ....(310) 459-9256
madelyn459@aol.com
Specialties: Independent; Direct-to-Video
Other Categories: Commercials; Video

HEATHER DEAR
Phone: ....(310) 915-9570
Fax: ....(310) 915-9670
dear@web.com
Specialties: Independent; Shorts; Animation
Other Categories: TV; Commercials
Trade Assoc./Guilds/Unions: DGA

JANICE DOSKEY
Phone: ....(323) 663-6355
....(914) 232-4407
doskey@mindspring.com
Specialties: Documentaries
Other Categories: Commercials; Video
Credits: MCI; A Circle of Women; Mastercard; Nike
Trade Assoc./Guilds/Unions: DGA, IDA, IFP, SAG

Freelance Producers – Feature Film

TOM FAUNTLEROY
1326 Estrella Dr.
Santa Barbara, CA 93110
Phone: ....(805) 898-1035
Specialties: Studio; Independent; Trailers
Other Categories: Commercials
Credits: List available upon request.
Trade Assoc./Guilds/Unions: DGA

JANET FERRARI
Phone: ....(310) 546-2376
....(310) 203-6060
Specialties: Shorts
Other Categories: Commercials; Music Video
Credits: Nissan (commercial); IFP (promo); Oreos (commercial); Burning Passion (short)

BARRY FINK
Phone: ....(323) 654-6523
....(310) 345-7474
Fax: ....(323) 654-6537
barryfink@hotmail.com
Specialties: Shorts
Other Categories: Commercials; Music Video

BRUCE FRITZBERG
4127 Via Marina, Apt. 104
Marina Del Rey, CA 90292
Phone: ....(310) 823-9668
....(415) 995-2366
Fax: ....(310) 823-9074
brukf@earthlink.net
Specialties: Studio; Independent; Documentaries; Trailers
Other Categories: TV; Commercials; Video; Interactive Multimedia
Credits: Credit Roll (TV series); First and Ten (TV series); McDonald's; Jack in the Box
Trade Assoc./Guilds/Unions: ATAS, DGA

JOHN G. GINNES
NSN Moss Hill Rd.
Orcas, WA 98280
Phone: ....(360) 376-3737
johng@firstavenuefilms.com
Specialties: Independent
Other Categories: TV; Commercials
Credits: When We Were Kings (documentary); Out of the Silence (documentary); Anheuser-Busch (commercial)
Trade Assoc./Guilds/Unions: DGA

BONNIE GOLDFARB
23852 Pacific Coast Hwy., PMB 770
Malibu, CA 90265
Phone: ....(310) 456-5153
cattlecrk@aol.com
Specialties: Documentaries
Other Categories: Commercials
Credits: Hollywood Video; Saturn; Nike
Trade Assoc./Guilds/Unions: DGA

ROBERT HAUKOOS
29395 Agoura Rd.
Agoura Hills, CA 91301
Phone: ....(818) 879-2200
rjlauren.com
info@rjlauren.com
Specialties: Trailers
Other Categories: TV; Commercials

LISA HOLLINGSHEAD
Phone: ....(323) 953-0281
....(323) 646-0646
lisa123102@aol.com
Specialties: Independent
Other Categories: Commercials; Music Video
Credits: Nike; RCA; Coca-Cola; Honda

BRONSTON JONES
Phone: ....(310) 828-0050
....(310) 345-9805
Fax: ....(310) 315-0021
Specialties: Independent
Other Categories: Commercials; Music Video
Credits: Playing Politics; NBC (promos); EBE - What Y'all Want; Mary Jay Blige - Give Me You

LESLIE A. KAHAN
NSN Moss Hill Road
Orcas, WA 98280
Phone: ....(360) 376-3737
leslie@firstavenuefilms.com
Specialties: Independent
Other Categories: TV; Commercials
Credits: Anheuser-Busch; Madonna - You Must Love Me

DESSA KAYE
P.O. Box 1397
Studio City, CA 91614
Phone: ....(818) 766-7318
Specialties: Independent
Other Categories: TV; Commercials
Credits: Win Ben Stein's Money; Richard Simmons' Dream Maker; Vital Signs; Silk Stalkings
Trade Assoc./Guilds/Unions: DGA

JENNY LEIMBROOK
Phone: ....(213) 209-6302
poire@aol.com
Specialties: Documentaries
Other Categories: TV; Commercials; Video
Credits: Test Pilots (TV series); A Day In The Life of Cinema; Prodigy (commercial); Mercury 13: The Secret Astronauts
Trade Assoc./Guilds/Unions: BAFTA

MARY LEONARD
Phone: ....(626) 791-9790
Fax: ....(626) 791-8727
leonard63@earthlink.net
Specialties: Independent
Other Categories: TV; Commercials; Interactive Multimedia
Credits: Kablam!; Boys and Girls; Disney TV; Volkswagen
Trade Assoc./Guilds/Unions: DGA

DON MACBAIN
Phone: ....(650) 846-8100
....(310) 655-8800
Specialties: Shorts; Animation; Large Format
Credits: Fire (large format); Special Effects (large format)

SANDY MARTIN
Phone: ....(323) 851-3755
....(213) 509-7722
Fax: ....(323) 851-4359
sandyem@martingallery.com
Specialties: Shorts; Documentaries
Other Categories: Commercials; Video; Interactive Multimedia
Trade Assoc./Guilds/Unions: DGA

Freelance Producers – Feature Film

COLLEEN MCCRARY
Phone: ....(626) 357-5160
Specialties: Independent; Direct-to-Video; Documentaries
Other Categories: TV; Commercials; Video; Music Video; Interactive Multimedia

SUSIE PETERSON
Phone: ....(310) 376-3288
Fax: ....(310) 376-3288
r-s-peterson@juno.com
Specialties: Studio
Other Categories: Commercials
Credits: Nick of Time (feature); Drop Zone (feature); Virginia Lottery (commercial); Carnation Instant Breakfast (commercial)

PATRICIA PRIEST
Phone: ....(323) 933-8733
Specialties: Independent
Other Categories: TV; Video
Trade Assoc./Guilds/Unions: DGA

RON RAPIEL
Phone: ....(310) 390-5454
Specialties: Studio; Independent
Other Categories: Commercials
Credits: Toyota; Visa; Pepsi; E*Trade
Trade Assoc./Guilds/Unions: DGA

CRAIG RESPOL
Phone: ....(818) 346-4641
....(818) 801-2524
Fax: ....(818) 346-4641
Specialties: Independent; Direct-to-Video
Other Categories: TV; Commercials; Video; Music Video
Credits: Lexus (commercial); Detour (feature)

LYNN REYNOLDS
Phone: ....(323) 254-5455
....(541) 601-7913
lynn@wherewelive.com
Specialties: Direct-to-Video
Other Categories: Commercials
Credits: BellSouth; AT&T; Coca-Cola; Ruby Princess Runs Away (feature)

PHIL ALDEN ROBINSON
100 Universal City Plaza, Bungalow 4132
Universal City, CA 91608
Phone: ....(818) 777-5055
Key Executives/Personnel:
  Phil Robinson, Producer, Writer & Director
  Lale Arpaci, Assistant to Mr. Robinson
Specialties: Studio
Other Categories: TV
Credits: Field of Dreams; All of Me; Freedom Song; Band of Brothers
First Look/Development Deals: Universal Pictures
Additional Info: Address subject to change.

JAN SCOTT
Phone: ....(310) 993-5574
Fax: ....(310) 833-5226
Specialties: Documentaries; Trailers
Other Categories: Commercials
Credits: McDonald's; Mattel; Coca-Cola; Home Depot
Trade Assoc./Guilds/Unions: DGA

BRAD STEVENSON
23852 Pacific Coast Hwy., Ste. 546
Malibu, CA 90265
Phone: ....(310) 455-1752
sog85@aol.com
Specialties: Trailers
Other Categories: Commercials; Music Video

SAL TASSONE
Phone: ....(310) 455-7822
....(310) 403-0007
Fax: ....(310) 455-7822
zenmasterfilms@earthlink.net
Specialties: Independent
Other Categories: TV; Commercials
Credits: Carl's Jr.; Milk Advisory Board; Wells Fargo; Celebrations: A Malibu Christmas (TV special)
Trade Assoc./Guilds/Unions: SAG

SUSAN VOGELFANG
Phone: ....(310) 306-2648
jazztomato@aol.com
Specialties: Studio; Independent
Other Categories: TV; Commercials

JAKI WEST
Phone: ....(310) 374-2082
Fax: ....(310) 798-1493
jakiwest@aol.com
Specialties: Independent
Other Categories: Commercials
Credits: GM; Kodak; Nike
Trade Assoc./Guilds/Unions: AFI, IFPW

JACK ZIGA
P.O. Box 389
Los Angeles, CA 90078
Phone: ....(323) 664-9862
....(323) 465-9862
Specialties: Studio; Independent
Other Categories: Commercials
Credits: The Independent; Vegas Vacation; The Birch Street Gym; Take This Job & Shove It
Trade Assoc./Guilds/Unions: DGA

LESLIE ZURLA
Phone: ....(818) 762-4346
Fax: ....(818) 506-8483
lzurla2000@aol.com
Specialties: Independent; Trailers
Other Categories: Commercials; Video
Credits: Toyota; American Airlines; Silent Scream; Dirty Mouth
Trade Assoc./Guilds/Unions: DGA

Freelance Producers – TV

Freelance Producers – TV

EMIE H. AMEMIYA
Phone: ....(323) 463-3033
Specialties: Documentaries
Other Categories: Feature Film; Commercials

LOUISE BARLOW
Phone: ....(310) 391-0142
....(213) 206-0282
Fax: ....(310) 397-8835
louisebarlow@earthlink.net
Specialties: Cable
Other Categories: Feature Film; Commercials; Music Video
Credits: Pontiac; Xerox; Savagegarden - Crash & Burn; OffSpring - The Kids Aren't Alright

STEPHANIE BEDELL
Phone: ....(818) 784-0446
....(213) 991-9965
Specialties: Movie of the Week
Other Categories: Commercials; Music Video
Credits: Breath-Assure; Delco Electronics; Levi's; Century 21

YVONNE M. BERNARD
Phone: ....(310) 318-0884
....(310) 353-4568
Fax: ....(310) 318-3955
yvonne3@aol.com
Specialties: Network; Cable; Animation; Documentaries; Made for TV Movies; Miniseries
Other Categories: Feature Film; Commercials; Video; Music Video
Credits: Anheuser-Busch; McDonald's; Dodge; Nike

JOHN BROOKS
217 Third Pl.
Manhattan Beach, CA 90266
Phone: ....(310) 418-6708
....(310) 717-6593
www.johnbrooks.cc
jbrooks@alohababy.cc
Specialties: Documentaries
Other Categories: Feature Film; Commercials; Video

JESSICA COOPER
Phone: ....(323) 655-3255
Fax: ....(323) 655-3250
carlsncoop@aol.com
Specialties: Cable
Other Categories: Feature Film; Commercials; Music Video
Credits: Coca-Cola; Levi's; Intel; Xerox

JOHN CORSER
827 S. Muirfield Rd.
Los Angeles, CA 90005
Phone: ....(323) 934-6346
....(213) 200-1477
Fax: ....(323) 934-1641
jcorser@earthlink.net
Specialties: Documentaries
Other Categories: Feature Film; Commercials; Video
Credits: ED TV (promo); Isuzu; Texas Pete Hot Sauce; Universal Studios

BILL CURRAN
Phone: ....(310) 392-1035
Fax: ....(310) 392-2694
billcurran@hotmail.com
Specialties: Cable
Other Categories: Feature Film; Commercials
Credits: KIA; Universal Studios; Mattel; Albertsons
Trade Assoc./Guilds/Unions: DGA

HEATHER DEAR
Phone: ....(310) 915-9570
....(805) 882-3435
Fax: ....(310) 915-9670
dear@web.com
Specialties: Animation
Other Categories: Feature Film; Commercials
Trade Assoc./Guilds/Unions: DGA

BRUCE FRITZBERG
4127 Via Marina, Apt. 104
Marina Del Rey, CA 90292
Phone: ....(310) 823-9668
....(415) 995-2366
Fax: ....(310) 823-9074
brukf@earthlink.net
Specialties: Network; Cable; Documentaries; Made for TV Movies
Other Categories: Feature Film; Commercials; Video; Interactive Multimedia
Credits: Credit Roll (TV series); First and Ten (TV series); McDonald's; Jack in the Box
Trade Assoc./Guilds/Unions: ATAS, DGA

JOHN G. GINNES
NSN Moss Hill Rd.
Orcas, WA 98280
Phone: ....(360) 376-3737
johng@firstavenuefilms.com
Specialties: Documentaries
Other Categories: Feature Film; Commercials
Credits: When We Were Kings (documentary); Out of the Silence (documentary); Anheuser-Busch (commercial)
Trade Assoc./Guilds/Unions: DGA

ROBERT HAUKOOS
29395 Agoura Rd.
Agoura Hills, CA 91301
Phone: ....(818) 879-2200
rjlauren.com
info@rjlauren.com
Specialties: Made for TV Movies
Other Categories: Feature Film; Commercials

LESLIE A. KAHAN
NSN Moss Hill Road
Orcas, WA 98280
Phone: ....(360) 376-3737
leslie@firstavenuefilms.com
Specialties: Documentaries
Other Categories: Feature Film; Commercials
Credits: Anheuser-Busch; Madonna - You Must Love Me

Freelance Producers – TV

DESSA KAYE
P.O. Box 1397
Studio City, CA 91614
Phone: ....(818) 766-7318
Specialties: Network; Cable; Made for TV Movies
Other Categories: Feature Film; Commercials
Credits: Win Ben Stein's Money; Richard Simmons' Dream Maker; Vital Signs; Silk Stalkings
Trade Assoc./Guilds/Unions: DGA

JENNY LEIMBROOK
Phone: ....(213) 209-6302
poire@aol.com
Specialties: Documentaries
Other Categories: Feature Film; Commercials; Video
Credits: Test Pilots (TV series); A Day In The Life of Cinema; Prodigy (commercial); Mercury 13: The Secret Astronauts
Trade Assoc./Guilds/Unions: BAFTA

MARY LEONARD
Phone: ....(626) 791-9790
Fax: ....(626) 791-8727
leonard63@earthlink.net
Specialties: Animation
Other Categories: Feature Film; Commercials; Interactive Multimedia
Credits: Kablam!; Boys and Girls; Disney TV; Volkswagen
Trade Assoc./Guilds/Unions: DGA

COLLEEN MCCRARY
Phone: ....(626) 357-5160
Specialties: Cable
Other Categories: Feature Film; Commercials; Video; Music Video; Interactive Multimedia

PATRICIA PRIEST
Phone: ....(323) 933-8733
Specialties: Network
Other Categories: Feature Film; Video
Trade Assoc./Guilds/Unions: DGA

CRAIG RESPOL
Phone: ....(818) 346-4641
....(818) 801-2524
Fax: ....(818) 346-4641
Specialties: Network
Other Categories: Feature Film; Commercials; Video; Music Video
Credits: Lexus (commercial); Detour (feature)

PHIL ALDEN ROBINSON
Phone: ....(818) 777-5055
Key Executives/Personnel:
    Phil Robinson, Producer, Writer & Director
Specialties: Cable; Network
Other Categories: Feature Film
Credits: Field of Dreams; All of Me; Freedom Song; Band of Brothers
First Look/Development Deals: Universal Pictures
Additional Info: Address subject to change.

ROBERT SCHMIDT
336 E. Verdugo Ave, Ste. 208
Burbank, CA 91502
Phone: ....(818) 842-1929
Specialties: Network; Cable
Other Categories: Commercials
Credits: Lords of the Mafia (TV series); NRA (commercial)

DENISE SIMON
Phone: ....(561) 758-3197
....(800) 520-0592
deniseasimon@aol.com
Specialties: Cable; Animation; Documentaries
Other Categories: Commercials; Video
Credits: Coca-Cola; MCI; AT&T; Anheuser-Busch
Trade Assoc./Guilds/Unions: DGA

SAL TASSONE
Phone: ....(310) 455-7822
....(310) 403-0007
Fax: ....(310) 455-7822
zenmasterfilms@earthlink.net
Specialties: Documentaries
Other Categories: Feature Film; Commercials
Credits: Carl's Jr.; Milk Advisory Board; Wells Fargo; Celebrations: A Malibu Christmas (TV special)
Trade Assoc./Guilds/Unions: SAG

JOSEPH P. TOBIN
Phone: ....(818) 769-7697
jooeet@aol.com
Specialties: Network
Credits: A&E Biography (TV series)
Trade Assoc./Guilds/Unions: DGA, WGAw

SUSAN VOGELFANG
Phone: ....(310) 306-2648
jazztomato@aol.com
Specialties: Cable
Other Categories: Feature Film; Commercials

ANITA ZOMMERS
Phone: ....(310) 456-6042
Fax: ....(310) 456-0468
Specialties: Miniseries
Other Categories: Commercials
Credits: Denny's; Chrysler; Ikea; GTE

Freelance Producers – Commercials

PAUL ALBANESE
Phone: .... (323) 653-7243
.... (310) 428-7285
paulbanese@aol.com
Specialties: Television
Other Categories: Feature Film; Music Video
Credits: Nike; ESPN; Dixie Chicks; Don Henley

KELLY AMATO
Phone: .... (310) 374-2786
.... (310) 600-8224
Fax: .... (310) 374-0826
kngamato@earthlink.net
Specialties: Television
Credits: Nissan; Anheuser-Busch; ESPN

EMIE H. AMEMIYA
Phone: .... (323) 463-3033
Specialties: Television; Promos
Other Categories: Feature Film; TV

BETH ANTHONY
Phone: .... (323) 654-3390
.... (310) 486-2235
babell@aol.com
Specialties: Television
Other Categories: Feature Film

LOUISE BARLOW
Phone: .... (310) 391-0142
.... (213) 206-0282
Fax: .... (310) 397-8835
louisebarlow@earthlink.net
Specialties: Television; Promos
Other Categories: Feature Film; TV; Music Video
Credits: Pontiac; Xerox; Savagegarden - Crash & Burn; OffSpring - The Kids Aren't Alright

LUANN BARRY-GOLDMAN
Phone: .... (310) 474-2439
lwebee@worldnet.att.net
Specialties: Television; Promos
Credits: Fox Family Channel; American Express; Mattel; Coca-Cola
Trade Assoc./Guilds/Unions: DGA

TONY BASILE
Phone: .... (323) 935-5481
.... (213) 324-5481
ynotbasile@hotmail.com
Specialties: Television
Credits: DirecTV; Saturn; Wrigley's; State Farm Insurance

STEPHANIE BEDELL
Phone: .... (818) 784-0446
.... (213) 991-9965
Specialties: Television; Promos
Other Categories: TV; Music Video
Credits: Breath-Assure; Delco Electronics; Levi's; Century 21

YVONNE M. BERNARD
Phone: .... (310) 318-0884
.... (310) 353-4568
Fax: .... (310) 318-3955
yvonne3@aol.com
Specialties: Television; Radio; Infomercials/Direct Response; Promos
Other Categories: Feature Film; TV; Video; Music Video
Credits: Anheuser-Busch; McDonald's; Dodge; Nike

KATHRYN BISHOP
Phone: .... (818) 980-4483
Specialties: Television
Other Categories: Feature Film
Trade Assoc./Guilds/Unions: DGA

STUART BLACK
Phone: .... (310) 821-2221
Fax: .... (310) 821-4106
Specialties: Television
Other Categories: Interactive Multimedia
Credits: Chrysler; Mobil; U.S. Army

HOPE GROSSMAN BOLOIS
Phone: .... (818) 905-7972
.... (818) 607-7537
Specialties: Television

TERRI LEE BROOK
Phone: .... (818) 559-8656
Specialties: Television

JOHN BROOKS
217 Third Pl.
Manhattan Beach, CA 90266
Phone: .... (310) 418-6708
.... (310) 717-6593
www.johnbrooks.cc
jbrooks@alohababy.cc
Specialties: Television; Radio; Infomercials/Direct Response; Promos
Other Categories: Feature Film; TV; Video

SHIRLEY BUKREY-LLOYD
Phone: .... (310) 306-1502
Specialties: Television

MAROL BUTCHER
Phone: .... (323) 906-9088
Fax: .... (323) 906-9089
weeegee@aol.com
Specialties: Television; Promos
Trade Assoc./Guilds/Unions: DGA

MARK CASTRO
2275 Huntington Dr., Ste. 320
San Marino, CA 91108
Phone: .... (626) 564-8195
.... (213) 309-7680
Fax: .... (626) 564-8195
castrodel@aol.com
Specialties: Television; Promos
Other Categories: Feature Film; Video; Music Video
Credits: WashingtonPost.com; Kevon Edmonds; Chili's

KIM CHRISTENSEN
Phone: .... (310) 396-1122
Fax: .... (310) 396-2030
kimmyx10@yahoo.com
Specialties: Television
Other Categories: Music Video; Interactive Multimedia

JESSICA COOPER
Phone: .... (323) 655-3255
Fax: .... (323) 655-3250
carlsncoop@aol.com
Specialties: Television
Other Categories: Feature Film; TV; Music Video
Credits: Coca-Cola; Levi's; Intel; Xerox

Freelance Producers – Commercials

JOHN CORSER
827 S. Muirfield Rd.
Los Angeles, CA 90005
Phone: (323) 934-6346
(213) 200-1477
Fax: (323) 934-1641
jcorser@earthlink.net
Specialties: Television; Promos
Other Categories: Feature Film; TV; Video
Credits: ED TV (promo); Isuzu; Texas Pete Hot Sauce; Universal Studios

SCOTT CRAIG
Phone: (323) 665-2069
(213) 364-4894
Fax: (323) 665-2069
scraig@aol.com
Specialties: Television; Promos
Credits: Pac Bell; Burger King; NBC (promo); Toyota

BILL CURRAN
Phone: (310) 392-1035
Fax: (310) 392-2694
billcurran@hotmail.com
Specialties: Television; Radio; Promos
Other Categories: Feature Film; TV
Credits: KIA; Universal Studios; Mattel; Albertsons
Trade Assoc./Guilds/Unions: DGA

MADELYN CURTIS
Phone: (310) 459-8976
(310) 663-3481
Fax: (310) 459-9256
madelyn459@aol.com
Specialties: Television
Other Categories: Feature Film; Video

BEVERLY DAVIS
Phone: (818) 780-6767
Specialties: Television
Credits: Levi's; BMW; Campbell's Soup

RICK DAYS
Phone: (323) 221-9003
Specialties: Television
Trade Assoc./Guilds/Unions: DGA

HEATHER DEAR
Phone: (310) 915-9570
(805) 882-3435
Fax: (310) 915-9670
dear@web.com
Specialties: Television; Infomercials/Direct Response; Promos
Other Categories: Feature Film; TV
Trade Assoc./Guilds/Unions: DGA

DIANA DEMOPOULOS
Phone: (323) 650-3831
(323) 821-8217
Specialties: Television; Promos
Other Categories: Music Video
Credits: Visa; Clairol; Mercedes-Benz; Gatorade

STEVE DIETRICH
Phone: (818) 760-2915
(800) 877-2597
Fax: (818) 980-2028
axnfaxn@aol.com
Specialties: Television
Credits: Ford; Sears; Cellular One; Hundai

KAT DILLON
Phone: (310) 399-7839
(212) 924-0945
Specialties: Television
Credits: Coca-Cola; Dodge

CARR DONALD
4373 Clybourn Ave.
Toluca Lake, CA 91602
Phone: (818) 506-0888
(888) 861-4551
Fax: (818) 508-1193
carrmug@earthlink.net
Specialties: Television
Credits: Honda; Visa; Mobil Oil; Coors

JANICE DOSKEY
Phone: (323) 663-6355
(914) 232-4407
doskey@mindspring.com
Specialties: Television
Other Categories: Feature Film; Video
Credits: MCI; A Circle of Women; Mastercard; Nike
Trade Assoc./Guilds/Unions: DGA, IDA, IFP, SAG

HELEN DOW
Phone: (310) 396-8840
(818) 567-7176
Fax: (310) 581-6651
hsquidly@aol.com
Specialties: Television
Credits: Bell Atlantic; May Co.; Lexus; Pizza Hut

VALERIE DRUCKMAN
Phone: (323) 654-5402
Fax: (323) 654-3934
valgal333@earthlink.net
Specialties: Television

LESLIE M. EVERS
Phone: (310) 600-7373
Specialties: Television
Other Categories: Music Video
Trade Assoc./Guilds/Unions: DGA

FRANNY FAULL-LA VIOLETTE
4222 Coolidge Ave.
Los Angeles, CA 90066
Phone: (310) 391-6960
(310) 614-0992
Fax: (310) 915-0966
frannyf@webtv.net
Specialties: Television

TOM FAUNTLEROY
1326 Estrella Dr.
Santa Barbara, CA 93110
Phone: (805) 898-1035
Specialties: Television
Other Categories: Feature Film
Credits: List available upon request.
Trade Assoc./Guilds/Unions: DGA

JANET FERRARI
Phone: (310) 546-2376
(310) 203-6060
Specialties: Television; Infomercials/Direct Response; Promos
Other Categories: Feature Film; Music Video
Credits: Nissan (commercial); IFP (promo); Oreos (commercial); Burning Passion (short)

Freelance Producers – Commercials

BARRY FINK
Phone: ....(323) 654-6523
....(310) 345-7474
Fax: ....(323) 654-6537
barryfink@hotmail.com
Specialties: Television; Infomercials/Direct Response; Promos
Other Categories: Feature Film; Music Video

DEBBIE A. FISHER
Phone: ....(310) 475-8767
Specialties: Television
Credits: Uniroyal Tires; Windex; Target; IHOP

FIONA FORSYTH
Phone: ....(310) 395-8300
Specialties: Television
Credits: Coca-Cola; Jack in the Box

J.P. FOX
Phone: ....(310) 207-8855
Specialties: Television
Other Categories: Music Video
Credits: Madonna - American Pie; No Doubt - A Simple Kind of Life; Bush - Letting the Cables Sleep; Everclear - Wonderful

TAMMY A. FRANKLIN
Phone: ....(323) 533-3354
nannyson@aol.com
Specialties: Television
Credits: MCI; Census 2000; McDonald's; JCPenney

RUTH FRAZIER
Phone: ....(818) 848-9129
....(818) 637-1575
ruthlesgang@mindspring.com
Specialties: Television; Infomercials/Direct Response; Promos
Other Categories: Music Video
Credits: Jeep; Motorola; Cotton; Fannie Mae
Trade Assoc./Guilds/Unions: DGA

FRANNY FREIBERGER
Phone: ....(818) 371-7100
frannyfry@aol.com
Specialties: Television
Other Categories: Music Video

NONA SUE FRIEDMAN
Phone: ....(323) 933-6367
Specialties: Television
Credits: AT&T; E*Trade; Gallo Wines; CBS Marketwatch

BRUCE FRITZBERG
4127 Via Marina, Apt. 104
Marina Del Rey, CA 90292
Phone: ....(310) 823-9668
....(415) 995-2366
Fax: ....(310) 823-9074
brukf@earthlink.net
Specialties: Television; Radio; Promos
Other Categories: Feature Film; TV; Video; Interactive Multimedia
Credits: Credit Roll (TV series); First and Ten (TV series); McDonald's; Jack in the Box
Trade Assoc./Guilds/Unions: ATAS, DGA

NANCY FULTON-ROGERS
Phone: ....(310) 376-7757
....(818) 776-6847
Fax: ....(310) 376-1363
Specialties: Television
Credits: Gateway Computers; Mazda; The Learning Channel; Disneyland

DEBBIE GALLOWAY
4600 Willis Ave., Ste. 202
Sherman Oaks, CA 91403
Phone: ....(818) 386-2157
....(800) 646-0941
Fax: ....(818) 386-2857
debgalloway@earthlink.net
Specialties: Television; Radio; Promos
Credits: Rhythms; 20th Century Insurance; DiTech Funding; MCI

KENT GATES
Phone: ....(661) 294-8694
....(818) 667-5368
Fax: ....(661) 294-8693
dgakent@ca.freei.net
Specialties: Television
Credits: Taco Bell; Mitsubishi; Mattel; Cheerios

JOHN G. GINNES
NSN Moss Hill Rd.
Orcas, WA 98280
Phone: ....(360) 376-3737
johng@firstavenuefilms.com
Specialties: Television; Infomercials/Direct Response; Promos
Other Categories: Feature Film; TV
Credits: When We Were Kings (documentary); Out of the Silence (documentary); Anheuser-Busch (commercial)
Trade Assoc./Guilds/Unions: DGA

LEORA GLASS
6436 Moore Dr.
Los Angeles, CA 90048
Phone: ....(323) 938-9553
....(213) 705-6718
Fax: ....(323) 938-9010
lglass3335@aol.com
Specialties: Television
Credits: Mercury Sable; Audi; People Soft; GTE

BONNIE GOLDFARB
23852 Pacific Coast Hwy., PMB 770
Malibu, CA 90265
Phone: ....(310) 456-5153
cattlecrk@aol.com
Specialties: Television
Other Categories: Feature Film
Credits: Hollywood Video; Saturn; Nike
Trade Assoc./Guilds/Unions: DGA

JANICE K. GOTO
Phone: ....(415) 383-1225
....(800) 606-4689
Fax: ....(415) 383-1625
jkgotowong@aol.com
Specialties: Television
Credits: Mattel; Toyota; Ford
Trade Assoc./Guilds/Unions: DGA

KATY GREENE
Phone: ....(310) 374-2827
Specialties: Television

CAROL HAAK
Phone: ....(818) 762-8979
....(888) 515-4058
Fax: ....(818) 788-3645
chaak@earthlink.net
Specialties: Television
Credits: Nissan; Lexus; Air National Guard; Jeep

Freelance Producers – Commercials

NAIA HALL-WEST
Phone: (323) 650-4893
          (323) 855-9400
Fax: (323) 650-8214
naia@wwdb.org
Specialties: Television
Other Categories: Music Video
Credits: Pepsi; Nike; Visa

ROBERT HAUKOOS
29395 Agoura Rd.
Agoura Hills, CA 91301
Phone: (818) 879-2200
rjlauren.com
info@rjlauren.com
Specialties: Television; Infomercials/Direct Response; Promos
Other Categories: Feature Film; TV

PAUL HETTLER
405 Pine St.
Mill Valley, CA 94941
Phone: (415) 381-1606
         (415) 277-8523
Fax: (415) 381-1606
phettler@flashcom.net
Specialties: Television
Other Categories: Video; Music Video; Interactive Multimedia
Credits: First Union Bank; Harry's Island

CYNTHIA HILL
Phone: (310) 398-2224
cynister1@earthlink.net
Specialties: Television
Other Categories: Music Video
Credits: Nike; Converse; Paul Young - I Wish You Love; Asahi Beer

LISA HOLLINGSHEAD
Phone: (323) 953-0281
         (323) 646-0646
lisa123102@aol.com
Specialties: Television
Other Categories: Feature Film; Music Video
Credits: Nike; RCA; Coca-Cola; Honda

CRAIG HOUCHIN
Phone: (323) 661-7828
         (213) 812-4555
Fax: (323) 661-7828
houchins@earthlink.net
Specialties: Television; Infomercials/Direct Response
Credits: Miller Ice House Beer; U.S. West; Coca-Cola; Toyota

CHANTAL HOULE
Phone: (818) 762-9822
         (310) 299-6787
Fax: (818) 762-9823
www.chantalhoule.com
chantal@chantalhoule.com
Specialties: Television; Radio
Credits: Ralston Purina; Mitsubishi; Power Deck; Adidas

BRONSTON JONES
Phone: (310) 828-0050
         (310) 345-9805
Fax: (310) 315-0021
Specialties: Television
Other Categories: Feature Film; Music Video
Credits: Playing Politics; NBC (promos); EBE - What Y'all Want; Mary Jay Blige - Give Me You

LESLIE A. KAHAN
NSN Moss Hill Road
Orcas, WA 98280
Phone: (360) 376-3737
leslie@firstavenuefilms.com
Specialties: Television; Infomercials/Direct Response; Promos
Other Categories: Feature Film; TV
Credits: Anheuser-Busch; Madonna - You Must Love Me

JAN KATZ
Phone: (310) 821-2221
Fax: (310) 821-4106
sjqblack@aol.com
Specialties: Television
Credits: Chrysler; GMC; Milk Advisory Board

DORON KAUPER
3662 Ventura Canyon Ave.
Sherman Oaks, CA 91423
Phone: (818) 907-6028
Fax: (818) 907-6029
www.hookups.com
doronk@hookups.com
Specialties: Television

DESSA KAYE
P.O. Box 1397
Studio City, CA 91614
Phone: (818) 766-7318
Specialties: Television; Infomercials/Direct Response
Other Categories: Feature Film; TV
Credits: Win Ben Stein's Money; Richard Simmons' Dream Maker; Vital Signs; Silk Stalkings
Trade Assoc./Guilds/Unions: DGA

PATTI LANCASTER
Phone: (310) 450-2213
Fax: (310) 450-2355
Specialties: Television
Credits: Bellagio; Capital One; Kraft; Pontiac

JENNY LEIMBROOK
834 S. Orange Grove Ave., Ste. 8
Los Angeles, CA 90036
Phone: (213) 209-6302
poire@aol.com
Specialties: Television
Other Categories: Feature Film; TV; Video
Credits: Test Pilots (TV series); A Day In The Life of Cinema; Prodigy (commercial); Mercury 13: The Secret Astronauts
Trade Assoc./Guilds/Unions: BAFTA

MARY LEONARD
Phone: (626) 791-9790
Fax: (626) 791-8727
leonard63@earthlink.net
Specialties: Television; Promos
Other Categories: Feature Film; TV; Interactive Multimedia
Credits: Kablam!; Boys and Girls; Disney TV; Volkswagen
Trade Assoc./Guilds/Unions: DGA

SONNY LOWE
Phone: (310) 994-8097
yeehafilms@aol.com
Specialties: Television; Promos
Other Categories: Music Video
Credits: Toyota; Mitsubishi; Pringles; Mattel

Freelance Producers – Commercials

MARTHA LUCAS
Phone: .... (323) 663-6739
Specialties: Television
Credits: Macy's; Nokia; Blue Cross; Bounce

JEFFREY MAIER
1317 First St.
Manhattan Beach, CA 90266
Phone: .... (310) 318-9924
.... (310) 797-0236
Fax: .... (310) 318-9924
cambren1@gte.net
Specialties: Television; Radio; Infomercials/Direct Response
Trade Assoc./Guilds/Unions: SAG

SANDY MARTIN
Phone: .... (323) 851-3755
.... (213) 509-7722
Fax: .... (323) 851-4359
sandyem@martingallery.com
Specialties: Television; Infomercials/Direct Response; Promos
Other Categories: Feature Film; Video; Interactive Multimedia
Trade Assoc./Guilds/Unions: DGA

LISA MCCLELLAND
Phone: .... (310) 457-7294
.... (310) 991-7294
Fax: .... (310) 589-1594
Specialties: Television
Credits: AT&T; Nike; Pepsi; Jaguar

COLLEEN MCCRARY
311 Meadow Ln.
Monrovia, CA 91016
Phone: .... (626) 357-5160
Specialties: Television; Promos
Other Categories: Feature Film; TV; Video; Music Video; Interactive Multimedia

ROGER MILLS
Phone: .... (818) 242-0532
Specialties: Television
Credits: Carnival Cruise Line; New York Stock Exchange; Mattel; McDonald's
Trade Assoc./Guilds/Unions: DGA, WGAw

ALISON MONICO
Phone: .... (323) 938-3881
Fax: .... (323) 938-3882
alimonico@earthlink.net
Specialties: Television
Credits: Harvard Health; National City Bank; LuckySurf.com
Trade Assoc./Guilds/Unions: DGA

SHARON MOROV
Phone: .... (310) 399-4868
sharonmorov@earthlink.net
Specialties: Television
Other Categories: Music Video
Credits: Mountain Dew; Coca-Cola; Jeep; BellSouth
Trade Assoc./Guilds/Unions: DGA

TOMMY MUROV
Phone: .... (323) 465-0404
Fax: .... (323) 465-0499
tcm910@aol.com
Specialties: Television; Radio
Credits: Honda; BMW; United Airlines

JACK NAYER
Phone: .... (310) 301-3020
.... (917) 874-7079
jjjjn@hotmail.com
Specialties: Television
Credits: Chrysler; BellSouth; MTA; NCR
Trade Assoc./Guilds/Unions: DGA

MERILEE NEWMAN
Phone: .... (310) 399-7463
Fax: .... (310) 399-2392
Specialties: Television
Credits: Kodak; American Express; Organ Donation (PSA); MTV (promo)

DARCY OLTMAN
355 N. Maple St., Ste. 112
Burbank, CA 91505
Phone: .... (818) 841-8601
.... (213) 303-1339
Fax: .... (818) 972-2008
darci_o@yahoo.com
Specialties: Television
Other Categories: Video; Music Video; Interactive Multimedia

PAUL PAPANEK
Phone: .... (323) 732-0776
.... (213) 989-8070
paulpap@earthlink.net
Specialties: Television
Credits: Toyota; Visa; Windows 95; Honda

BETH PEARSON
Phone: .... (310) 457-6195
.... (310) 567-5725
Fax: .... (818) 889-2193
Specialties: Television
Credits: Dodge; Chrysler; Anheuser-Busch; Subway
Trade Assoc./Guilds/Unions: DGA

SANDRA PENFIELD
Phone: .... (323) 661-3532
.... (213) 949-3532
Fax: .... (213) 949-3532
sam@chelsea.com
Specialties: Television
Credits: Coca-Cola; Nissan; Bank of America

DAVID PERSOFF
3648 Cadman Dr.
Los Angeles, CA 90027
Phone: .... (323) 669-0141
www.birchbarkfilms.com
birchbark@earthlink.net
Specialties: Television; Infomercials/Direct Response; Promos
Credits: Blockbuster; Six Flags; Mars; McDonald's

SUSIE PETERSON
Phone: .... (310) 376-3288
Fax: .... (310) 376-3288
r-s-peterson@juno.com
Specialties: Television
Other Categories: Feature Film
Credits: Nick of Time (feature); Drop Zone (feature); Virginia Lottery (commercial); Carnation Instant Breakfast (commercial)

Freelance Producers – Commercials

PIAZZIE
Phone: ....(310) 996-1096
Fax: ....(310) 996-1056
piaz212@earthlink.net
Specialties: Television
Other Categories: Music Video
Trade Assoc./Guilds/Unions: DGA

SADIE POLLOCK-BARISH
Phone: ....(310) 457-6858
sadiemlp@aol.com
Specialties: Television
Credits: Soloman Smith Barney; Lee Jeans; Anheuser-Busch; Adidas

RICK POWERS
Phone: ....(310) 542-9397
....(310) 960-5535
Fax: ....(310) 793-7790
rpowers6@pacbell.net
Specialties: Television
Credits: Sizzler; Coffee Mate; Little Caesars; HealthNet

JACK PROVOST
4570 Van Nuys Blvd., Ste. 122
Sherman Oaks, CA 91403
Phone: ....(818) 988-8150
Fax: ....(818) 988-8152
provostjax@aol.com
Specialties: Television
Credits: Chanel; Reebok
Trade Assoc./Guilds/Unions: DGA

RON RAPIEL
Phone: ....(310) 390-5454
Specialties: Television
Other Categories: Feature Film
Credits: Toyota; Visa; Pepsi; E*Trade
Trade Assoc./Guilds/Unions: DGA

CRAIG RESPOL
Phone: ....(818) 346-4641
....(818) 801-2524
Fax: ....(818) 346-4641
Specialties: Television; Infomercials/Direct Response
Other Categories: Feature Film; TV; Video; Music Video
Credits: Lexus (commercial); Detour (feature)

LYNN REYNOLDS
Phone: ....(323) 254-5455
....(541) 601-7913
lynn@wherewelive.com
Specialties: Television
Other Categories: Feature Film
Credits: BellSouth; AT&T; Coca-Cola; Ruby Princess Runs Away (feature)

KATHRYN L. RHODES
Phone: ....(310) 475-0709
Fax: ....(310) 475-3509
Specialties: Television
Credits: Pepsi; Anheuser-Busch; Federal Express; HBO

CHRISTINA RITZMANN
Phone: ....(310) 823-7867
Fax: ....(310) 827-8137
critzmann@earthlink.net
Specialties: Television
Credits: MCI; AT&T; Chrysler

DENISE ROCCHIETTI
Phone: ....(818) 783-3214
Fax: ....(818) 783-6358
Specialties: Television
Credits: S.A.P.com; Toyota; Adidas; Pac Bell

AMY M. SAMUELSON
2111 Pearl St.
Santa Monica, CA 90405
Phone: ....(310) 396-4133
....(310) 463-1238
Fax: ....(310) 392-1842
amesala@aol.com
Specialties: Television; Radio; Promos
Credits: ESPN; KIA; Chevrolet

ROBERT SCHMIDT
336 E. Verdugo Ave., Ste. 208
Burbank, CA 91502
Phone: ....(818) 842-1929
Specialties: Television
Other Categories: TV
Credits: Lords of the Mafia (TV series); NRA (commercial)

SARAH SCHOESSLER
Phone: ....(310) 577-0877
....(310) 259-0600
Fax: ....(310) 577-9207
tootallpod@aol.com
Specialties: Television; Infomercials/Direct Response; Promos
Other Categories: Video
Credits: Suzuki; Wheel of Fortune; Certs; Mercedes-Benz

LARRY SCHREINER
Phone: ....(310) 643-7322
....(310) 847-2164
Specialties: Television; Infomercials/Direct Response; Promos
Credits: KFC; Anheuser-Busch; Chrysler; Mattel
Trade Assoc./Guilds/Unions: DGA

JAN SCOTT
Phone: ....(310) 993-5574
Fax: ....(310) 833-5226
Specialties: Television; Radio; Infomercials/Direct Response; Promos
Other Categories: Feature Film
Credits: McDonald's; Mattel; Coca-Cola; Home Depot
Trade Assoc./Guilds/Unions: DGA

HARVEY SHAPIRO
Phone: ....(310) 395-4546
....(310) 702-9855
Fax: ....(310) 395-7117
ticker@gte.net
Specialties: Television; Promos

DONA SHINE
Phone: ....(818) 708-2403
Fax: ....(818) 343-3681
Specialties: Television
Credits: Meryl Lynch; U.S. Army; AT&T; Anheuser-Busch

THOM SIDOTI
Phone: ....(818) 752-0356
Fax: ....(818) 752-0341
thomsidoti@aol.com
Specialties: Television
Other Categories: Music Video
Credits: Mountain Dew; Pepsi; Nike; Milk Advisory Board
Trade Assoc./Guilds/Unions: DGA

Freelance Producers – Commercials

SCOTT SIEGAL
Phone: ....(626) 794-7760
....(213) 713-0154
Specialties: Television
Credits: Gatorade; Visa; Expedia.com; Lynx
Trade Assoc./Guilds/Unions: DGA

MARC SIEGEL
Phone: ....(323) 653-3550
Fax: ....(323) 653-3553
nalkdmarc@aol.com
Specialties: Television
Credits: Hewlett-Packard; IBM; Levi's; Lincoln-Mercury
Trade Assoc./Guilds/Unions: DGA

KAREN SILVER
Phone: ....(416) 861-1204
Fax: ....(416) 861-0220
www.treenorth.com
thnorth@interlog.com
Specialties: Television
Credits: Volkswagen; Lee Jeans; Sony Wega

DENISE SIMON
Phone: ....(561) 758-3197
....(800) 520-0592
deniseasimon@aol.com
Specialties: Television
Other Categories: TV; Video
Credits: Coca-Cola; MCI; AT&T; Anheuser-Busch
Trade Assoc./Guilds/Unions: DGA

LINDSAY SKUTCH
2628 Clinton Terrace
Santa Barbara, CA 93105
Phone: ....(805) 687-9852
Fax: ....(805) 687-7880
lindsayskutch@earthlink.net
Specialties: Television
Credits: USAF; Cadillac; Price Waterhouse; United Airlines

AL SMITH
2109 Tenth St.
Santa Monica, CA 90405
Phone: ....(310) 452-3751
Fax: ....(310) 392-5313
a1smith11@aol.com
Specialties: Television; Promos
Credits: Rent-A-Center; U.S.G.A.; Old Country Buffet; America On-Line
Trade Assoc./Guilds/Unions: DGA

BRAD STEVENSON
23852 Pacific Coast Hwy., Ste. 546
Malibu, CA 90265
Phone: ....(310) 455-1752
sog85@aol.com
Specialties: Television
Other Categories: Feature Film; Music Video

STEVEN STRACHAN
Phone: ....(310) 459-1299
....(310) 200-5582
Specialties: Television
Credits: Oldsmobile; Deutsche Post; The Mony Group; Asic.com

SAL TASSONE
Phone: ....(310) 455-7822
....(310) 403-0007
Fax: ....(310) 455-7822
zenmasterfilms@earthlink.net
Specialties: Television; Promos
Other Categories: Feature Film; TV
Credits: Carl's Jr.; Milk Advisory Board; Wells Fargo; Celebrations: A Malibu Christmas (TV special)
Trade Assoc./Guilds/Unions: SAG

DEBBIE TIETJEN
6851 Fernhill Dr.
Malibu, CA 90265
Phone: ....(310) 457-6488
....(310) 418-3632
Specialties: Television; Infomercials/Direct Response; Promos
Credits: Volkswagen; Toyota; Bluenile.com
Trade Assoc./Guilds/Unions: DGA

DEBBY TIMMONS
Phone: ....(818) 906-2093
Fax: ....(818) 788-8106
dtinc@earthlink.net
Specialties: Television; Promos
Trade Assoc./Guilds/Unions: DGA

LEE TRASK
Phone: ....(310) 396-5023
....(310) 871-1551
Specialties: Television
Credits: McDonald's; Chrysler; Volkswagon; Hewlett Packard

CLARISSA TROOP
Phone: ....(323) 463-7933
Fax: ....(323) 462-5710
oldcow99@aol.com
Specialties: Television
Credits: Sprite; Mercedes-Benz; US Army

JEFFREY S. TUTTLE
211 S. Wilson Ave., Ste. 306
Pasadena, CA 91106
Phone: ....(626) 666-1211
....(626) 932-4826
Fax: ....(626) 666-1212
sybertuts@aol.com
Specialties: Television; Infomercials/Direct Response; Promos
Other Categories: Music Video
Credits: Logix; Time Computer; Dodge Durango/Dakota; HealthNet
Trade Assoc./Guilds/Unions: DGA

Freelance Producers – Commercials

SUSAN VOGELFANG
Phone: ....(310) 306-2648
jazztomato@aol.com
Specialties: Television
Other Categories: Feature Film; TV

JANIE WALTER
Phone: ....(323) 665-6009
Specialties: Television
Credits: BMW; Mercedes-Benz; American Airlines; Northwest Airlines

FRANCINE WEINER
Phone: ....(818) 592-0455
....(818) 558-0775
Fax: ....(818) 348-7312
francineweiner@aol.com
Specialties: Television; Radio; Infomercials/Direct Response; Promos
Other Categories: Music Video
Credits: Carl's Jr.; DirecTV; Samson; Toyota

JAKI WEST
Phone: ....(310) 374-2082
Fax: ....(310) 798-1493
jakiwest@aol.com
Specialties: Television
Other Categories: Feature Film
Credits: GM; Kodak; Nike
Trade Assoc./Guilds/Unions: AFI, IFPW

REE WHITFORD
Phone: ....(818) 505-1060
....(818) 424-9988
reewit@aol.com
Specialties: Television; Radio; Promos
Credits: Anheuser-Busch; CarOrder.com; Hyundai; Acura
Trade Assoc./Guilds/Unions: DGA

PETER YACAVONE
Phone: ....(818) 991-5775
....(213) 470-2040
yacsmac@earthlink.net
Specialties: Television
Credits: Toyota; E-Gain.com; Hyundai; Virgin Atlantic

DIANA YOUNG
Phone: ....(310) 391-2400
Fax: ....(310) 397-6556
Specialties: Television
Credits: Hallmark; Chevrolet; Sprint

GABRIELLE YURO-VICKERS
Phone: ....(818) 760-2155
Fax: ....(818) 760-2095
Specialties: Television
Credits: Mountain Dew; Motorola; Pepsi; McDonald's

RAYMOND ZARRO
Phone: ....(310) 821-8473
....(310) 420-7795
Fax: ....(310) 823-3149
rayzarro@earthlink.net
Specialties: Television
Credits: Mattel; Inspop.com; Hasbro; Nickelodeon
Trade Assoc./Guilds/Unions: DGA

JACK ZIGA
P.O. Box 389
Los Angeles, CA 90078
Phone: ....(323) 664-9862
....(323) 465-9862
Specialties: Television
Other Categories: Feature Film
Credits: The Independent; Vegas Vacation; The Birch Street Gym; Take This Job & Shove It
Trade Assoc./Guilds/Unions: DGA

JOEL R. ZIMMERMAN
Phone: ....(310) 399-9906
Fax: ....(310) 399-9907
Specialties: Television; Promos
Credits: First Union Bank; Gatorade; Dodge

ANITA ZOMMERS
Phone: ....(310) 456-6042
Fax: ....(310) 456-0468
Specialties: Television
Other Categories: TV
Credits: Denny's; Chrysler; Ikea; GTE

LESLIE ZURLA
Phone: ....(818) 762-4346
Fax: ....(818) 506-8483
lzurla2000@aol.com
Specialties: Television; Radio; Infomercials/Direct Response; Promos
Other Categories: Feature Film; Video
Credits: Toyota; American Airlines; Silent Scream; Dirty Mouth
Trade Assoc./Guilds/Unions: DGA

Freelance Producers – Video

YVONNE M. BERNARD
Phone: ....(310) 318-0884
....(310) 353-4568
Fax: ....(310) 318-3955
yvonne3@aol.com
Specialties: Industrial/Corporate; Educational; Documentaries
Other Categories: Feature Film; TV; Commercials; Music Video
Credits: Anheuser-Busch; McDonald's; Dodge; Nike

JOHN BROOKS
217 Third Pl.
Manhattan Beach, CA 90266
Phone: ....(310) 418-6708
....(310) 717-6593
www.johnbrooks.cc
jbrooks@alohababy.cc
Specialties: Industrial/Corporate; Educational; Documentaries
Other Categories: Feature Film; TV; Commercials

MARK CASTRO
2275 Huntington Dr., Ste. 320
San Marino, CA 91108
Phone: ....(626) 564-8195
....(213) 309-7680
Fax: ....(626) 564-8195
castrodel@aol.com
Specialties: Documentaries
Other Categories: Feature Film; Commercials; Music Video
Credits: WashingtonPost.com; Kevon Edmonds; Chili's

JOHN CORSER
827 S. Muirfield Rd.
Los Angeles, CA 90005
Phone: ....(323) 934-6346
....(213) 200-1477
Fax: ....(323) 934-1641
jcorser@earthlink.net
Specialties: Industrial/Corporate; Educational; Documentaries
Other Categories: Feature Film; TV; Commercials
Credits: ED TV (promo); Isuzu; Texas Pete Hot Sauce; Universal Studios

MADELYN CURTIS
Phone: ....(310) 459-8976
....(310) 663-3481
Fax: ....(310) 459-9256
madelyn459@aol.com
Specialties: Industrial/Corporate
Other Categories: Feature Film; Commercials

JANICE DOSKEY
Phone: ....(323) 663-6355
....(914) 232-4407
doskey@mindspring.com
Specialties: Documentaries
Other Categories: Feature Film; Commercials
Credits: MCI; A Circle of Women; Mastercard; Nike
Trade Assoc./Guilds/Unions: DGA, IDA, IFP, SAG

BRUCE FRITZBERG
4127 Via Marina, Apt. 104
Marina Del Rey, CA 90292
Phone: ....(310) 823-9668
....(415) 995-2366
Fax: ....(310) 823-9074
brukf@earthlink.net
Specialties: Industrial/Corporate; Educational
Other Categories: Feature Film; TV; Commercials; Interactive Multimedia
Credits: Credit Roll (TV series); First and Ten (TV series); McDonald's; Jack in the Box
Trade Assoc./Guilds/Unions: ATAS, DGA

PAUL HETTLER
405 Pine St.
Mill Valley, CA 94941
Phone: ....(415) 381-1606
....(415) 277-8523
Fax: ....(415) 381-1606
phettler@flashcom.net
Specialties: Industrial/Corporate; Educational
Other Categories: Commercials; Music Video; Interactive Multimedia
Credits: First Union Bank; Harry's Island

Freelance Producers – Video

JENNY LEIMBROOK
834 S. Orange Grove Ave., Ste. 8
Los Angeles, CA 90036
Phone: ....(213) 209-6302
poire@aol.com
Specialties: Documentaries
Other Categories: Feature Film; TV; Commercials
Credits: Test Pilots (TV series); A Day In The Life of Cinema; Prodigy (commercial); Mercury 13: The Secret Astronauts
Trade Assoc./Guilds/Unions: BAFTA

SANDY MARTIN
Phone: ....(323) 851-3755
................................(213) 509-7722
Fax: ....(323) 851-4359
sandyem@martingallery.com
Specialties: Industrial/Corporate; Educational; Documentaries
Other Categories: Feature Film; Commercials; Interactive Multimedia
Trade Assoc./Guilds/Unions: DGA

COLLEEN MCCRARY
Phone: ....(626) 357-5160
Specialties: Documentaries
Other Categories: Feature Film; TV; Commercials; Music Video; Interactive Multimedia

DARCY OLTMAN
355 N. Maple St., Ste. 112
Burbank, CA 91505
Phone: ....(818) 841-8601
................................(213) 303-1339
Fax: ....(818) 972-2008
darci_o@yahoo.com
Specialties: Industrial/Corporate; Documentaries
Other Categories: Commercials; Music Video; Interactive Multimedia

PATRICIA PRIEST
Phone: ....(323) 933-8733
Specialties: Industrial/Corporate
Other Categories: Feature Film; TV
Trade Assoc./Guilds/Unions: DGA

CRAIG RESPOL
Phone: ....(818) 346-4641
................................(818) 801-2524
Fax: ....(818) 346-4641
Specialties: Industrial/Corporate
Other Categories: Feature Film; TV; Commercials; Music Video
Credits: Lexus (commercial); Detour (feature)

SARAH SCHOESSLER
Phone: ....(310) 577-0877
................................(310) 259-0600
Fax: ....(310) 577-9207
tootallpod@aol.com
Specialties: Industrial/Corporate
Other Categories: Commercials
Credits: Suzuki; Wheel of Fortune; Certs; Mercedes-Benz

DENISE SIMON
Phone: ....(561) 758-3197
................................(800) 520-0592
deniseasimon@aol.com
Specialties: Industrial/Corporate; Educational; Documentaries
Other Categories: TV; Commercials
Credits: Coca-Cola; MCI; AT&T; Anheuser-Busch
Trade Assoc./Guilds/Unions: DGA

LESLIE ZURLA
Phone: ....(818) 762-4346
Fax: ....(818) 506-8483
lzurla2000@aol.com
Specialties: Industrial/Corporate; Educational
Other Categories: Feature Film; Commercials
Credits: Toyota; American Airlines; Silent Scream; Dirty Mouth
Trade Assoc./Guilds/Unions: DGA

Freelance Producers – Music Video

PAUL ALBANESE
Phone: ....(323) 653-7243
....(310) 428-7285
paulbanese@aol.com
Specialties: Short Form
Other Categories: Feature Film; Commercials
Credits: Nike; ESPN; Dixie Chicks; Don Henley

LOUISE BARLOW
Phone: ....(310) 391-0142
....(213) 206-0282
Fax: ....(310) 397-8835
louisebarlow@earthlink.net
Specialties: Short Form; Long Form
Other Categories: Feature Film; TV; Commercials
Credits: Pontiac; Xerox; Savagegarden - Crash & Burn; OffSpring - The Kids Aren't Alright

STEPHANIE BEDELL
Phone: ....(818) 784-0446
....(213) 991-9965
Specialties: Short Form; Long Form
Other Categories: TV; Commercials
Credits: Breath-Assure; Delco Electronics; Levi's; Century 21

YVONNE M. BERNARD
Phone: ....(310) 318-0884
....(310) 353-4568
Fax: ....(310) 318-3955
yvonne3@aol.com
Specialties: Short Form; Long Form
Other Categories: Feature Film; TV; Commercials; Video
Credits: Anheuser-Busch; McDonald's; Dodge; Nike

MARK CASTRO
2275 Huntington Dr., Ste. 320
San Marino, CA 91108
Phone: ....(626) 564-8195
....(213) 309-7680
Fax: ....(626) 564-8195
castrodel@aol.com
Specialties: Short Form; Long Form
Other Categories: Feature Film; Commercials; Video
Credits: WashingtonPost.com; Kevon Edmonds; Chili's

KIM CHRISTENSEN
Phone: ....(310) 396-1122
Fax: ....(310) 396-2030
kimmyx10@yahoo.com
Specialties: Short Form
Other Categories: Commercials; Interactive Multimedia

JESSICA COOPER
Phone: ....(323) 655-3255
Fax: ....(323) 655-3250
carlsncoop@aol.com
Specialties: Short Form; Long Form
Other Categories: Feature Film; TV; Commercials
Credits: Coca-Cola; Levi's; Intel; Xerox

DIANA DEMOPOULOS
Phone: ....(323) 650-3831
....(323) 821-8217
Specialties: Short Form
Other Categories: Commercials
Credits: Visa; Clairol; Mercedes-Benz; Gatorade

LESLIE M. EVERS
Phone: ....(310) 600-7373
Specialties: Short Form; Long Form
Other Categories: Commercials
Trade Assoc./Guilds/Unions: DGA

Freelance Producers – Music Video

JANET FERRARI
Phone: ....(310) 546-2376
....(310) 203-6060
Specialties: Short Form; Long Form
Other Categories: Feature Film; Commercials
Credits: Nissan (commercial); IFP (promo); Oreos (commercial); Burning Passion (short)

BARRY FINK
Phone: ....(323) 654-6523
....(310) 345-7474
Fax: ....(323) 654-6537
barryfink@hotmail.com
Specialties: Short Form; Long Form
Other Categories: Feature Film; Commercials

J.P. FOX
Phone: ....(310) 207-8855
Specialties: Short Form
Other Categories: Commercials
Credits: Madonna - American Pie; No Doubt - A Simple Kind of Life; Bush - Letting the Cables Sleep; Everclear - Wonderful

RUTH FRAZIER
Phone: ....(818) 848-9129
....(818) 637-1575
ruthlesgang@mindspring.com
Specialties: Short Form; Long Form
Other Categories: Commercials
Credits: Jeep; Motorola; Cotton; Fannie Mae
Trade Assoc./Guilds/Unions: DGA

FRANNY FREIBERGER
Phone: ....(818) 371-7100
frannyfry@aol.com
Specialties: Short Form
Other Categories: Commercials

NAIA HALL-WEST
Phone: ....(323) 650-4893
....(323) 855-9400
Fax: ....(323) 650-8214
naia@wwdb.org
Specialties: Short Form; Long Form
Other Categories: Commercials
Credits: Pepsi; Nike; Visa

PAUL HETTLER
405 Pine St.
Mill Valley, CA 94941
Phone: ....(415) 381-1606
....(415) 277-8523
Fax: ....(415) 381-1606
phettler@flashcom.net
Specialties: Short Form; Long Form
Other Categories: Commercials; Video; Interactive Multimedia
Credits: First Union Bank; Harry's Island

CYNTHIA HILL
Phone: ....(310) 398-2224
cynister1@earthlink.net
Specialties: Short Form; Long Form
Other Categories: Commercials
Credits: Nike; Converse; Paul Young - I Wish You Love; Asahi Beer

LISA HOLLINGSHEAD
Phone: ....(323) 953-0281
....(323) 646-0646
lisa123102@aol.com
Specialties: Short Form; Long Form
Other Categories: Feature Film; Commercials
Credits: Nike; RCA; Coca-Cola; Honda

BRONSTON JONES
1255 Princeton St., Ste. 202
Santa Monica, CA 90404
Phone: ....(310) 828-0050
....(310) 345-9805
Fax: ....(310) 315-0021
Specialties: Short Form
Other Categories: Feature Film; Commercials
Credits: Playing Politics; NBC (promos); EBE - What Y'all Want; Mary Jay Blige - Give Me You

SONNY LOWE
Phone: ....(310) 994-8097
yeehafilms@aol.com
Specialties: Short Form
Other Categories: Commercials
Credits: Toyota; Mitsubishi; Pringles; Mattel

Freelance Producers – Music Video

COLLEEN MCCRARY
Phone: .... (626) 357-5160
Specialties: Short Form; Long Form
Other Categories: Feature Film; TV; Commercials; Video; Interactive Multimedia

SHARON MOROV
Phone: .... (310) 399-4868
sharonmorov@earthlink.net
Specialties: Short Form; Long Form
Other Categories: Commercials
Credits: Mountain Dew; Coca-Cola; Jeep; BellSouth
Trade Assoc./Guilds/Unions: DGA

DARCY OLTMAN
355 N. Maple St., Ste. 112
Burbank, CA 91505
Phone: .... (818) 841-8601
.... (213) 303-1339
Fax: .... (818) 972-2008
darci_o@yahoo.com
Specialties: Short Form; Long Form
Other Categories: Commercials; Video; Interactive Multimedia

PIAZZIE
Phone: .... (310) 996-1096
Fax: .... (310) 996-1056
piaz212@earthlink.net
Specialties: Short Form
Other Categories: Commercials
Trade Assoc./Guilds/Unions: DGA

CRAIG RESPOL
Phone: .... (818) 346-4641
.... (818) 801-2524
Fax: .... (818) 346-4641
Specialties: Short Form
Other Categories: Feature Film; TV; Commercials; Video
Credits: Lexus (commercial); Detour (feature)

THOM SIDOTI
Phone: .... (818) 752-0356
Fax: .... (818) 752-0341
thomsidoti@aol.com
Specialties: Short Form; Long Form
Other Categories: Commercials
Credits: Mountain Dew; Pepsi; Nike; Milk Advisory Board
Trade Assoc./Guilds/Unions: DGA

BRAD STEVENSON
23852 Pacific Coast Hwy., Ste. 546
Malibu, CA 90265
Phone: .... (310) 455-1752
sog85@aol.com
Specialties: Short Form
Other Categories: Feature Film; Commercials

JEFFREY S. TUTTLE
211 S. Wilson Ave., Ste. 306
Pasadena, CA 91106
Phone: .... (626) 666-1211
.... (626) 932-4826
Fax: .... (626) 666-1212
sybertuts@aol.com
Specialties: Short Form
Other Categories: Commercials
Credits: Logix; Time Computer; Dodge Durango/Dakota; HealthNet
Trade Assoc./Guilds/Unions: DGA

FRANCINE WEINER
Phone: .... (818) 592-0455
.... (818) 558-0775
Fax: .... (818) 348-7312
francineweiner@aol.com
Specialties: Long Form
Other Categories: Commercials
Credits: Carl's Jr.; DirecTV; Samson; Toyota

Freelance Producers – Interactive Multimedia

STUART BLACK
Phone: .... (310) 821-2221
Fax: .... (310) 821-4106
Specialties: Web Content
Other Categories: Commercials
Credits: Chrysler; Mobil; U.S. Army

KIM CHRISTENSEN
Phone: .... (310) 396-1122
Fax: .... (310) 396-2030
kimmyx10@yahoo.com
Specialties: Web Content
Other Categories: Commercials; Music Video

BRUCE FRITZBERG
4127 Via Marina, Apt. 104
Marina Del Rey, CA 90292
Phone: .... (310) 823-9668
.... (415) 995-2366
Fax: .... (310) 823-9074
brukf@earthlink.net
Specialties: Web Content
Other Categories: Feature Film; TV; Commercials; Video
Credits: Credit Roll (TV series); First and Ten (TV series); McDonald's; Jack in the Box
Trade Assoc./Guilds/Unions: ATAS, DGA

PAUL HETTLER
405 Pine St.
Mill Valley, CA 94941
Phone: .... (415) 381-1606
.... (415) 277-8523
Fax: .... (415) 381-1606
phettler@flashcom.net
Specialties: Web Content
Other Categories: Commercials; Video; Music Video
Credits: First Union Bank; Harry's Island

MARY LEONARD
544 E. Poppyfield Dr.
Altadena, CA 91001
Phone: .... (626) 791-9790
Fax: .... (626) 791-8727
leonard63@earthlink.net
Specialties: Web Content
Other Categories: Feature Film; TV; Commercials
Credits: Kablam!; Boys and Girls; Disney TV; Volkswagen
Trade Assoc./Guilds/Unions: DGA

SANDY MARTIN
Phone: .... (323) 851-3755
.... (213) 509-7722
Fax: .... (323) 851-4359
sandyem@martingallery.com
Specialties: Web Content
Other Categories: Feature Film; Commercials; Video
Trade Assoc./Guilds/Unions: DGA

COLLEEN MCCRARY
Phone: .... (626) 357-5160
Specialties: Web Content
Other Categories: Feature Film; TV; Commercials; Video; Music Video

DARCY OLTMAN
355 N. Maple St., Ste. 112
Burbank, CA 91505
Phone: .... (818) 841-8601
.... (213) 303-1339
Fax: .... (818) 972-2008
darci_o@yahoo.com
Specialties: Web Content
Other Categories: Commercials; Video; Music Video

Notes

TV Shows

2GETHER
c/o Alliance Atlantis, 808 Wilshire Blvd., 3rd Fl.
Santa Monica, CA 90401
Phone: ....(310) 899-8000
Production Company: Alliance Atlantis
121 Bloor St. East, Ste. 800
Toronto, ON M4W 3M5 Canada
Phone: (416) 967-1174
Key Executives/Personnel:
   Roger Schulman, Executive Producer
   Brian Gunn, Executive Producer
   Mark Gunn, Executive Producer
Casting Director: Heike Brandstatter & Correen Mayrs
Produced in Assn. With: MTV Networks, (310) 752-8000
Cast: Noah Bastian, Kevin Farley, Evan Farmer, Alex Solowitz, Michael Cuccione
Network: MTV
Show Type: Comedy
Show Length: 30 mins.

3RD ROCK FROM THE SUN
4024 Radford Ave., Bldg. 1, Rm. 111
Studio City, CA 91604
Phone: ....(818) 655-6057
Production Company: Carsey-Werner Productions
4024 Radford Ave., Bldg. 3
Studio City, CA 91604
Phone: (818) 655-5598
Key Executives/Personnel:
   Marcy Carsey, Executive Producer
   Tom Werner, Executive Producer
   Caryn Mandabach, Executive Producer
   Bonnie Turner, Executive Producer
   Terry Turner, Executive Producer
   Christine Zander, Executive Producer
Casting Director: Cami Patton & Tara Johnson
Cast: John Lithgow, Kristen Johnson, French Stewart, Jane Curtin, Joseph Gordon-Levitt, Simbi Khali, Elmarie Wendel, Wayne Knight, Lansa Oleynik
Network: NBC
Syndicated: Yes
Show Type: Comedy
Show Length: 30 mins.

7 DAYS
3100 N. Burbank Blvd., Ste. 200
Burbank, CA 91505
Phone: ....(818) 526-0270
Production Company: Christopher Crowe Entertainment
5555 Melrose Ave., Marx Bros. Bldg., Ste. 110
Los Angeles, CA 90038
Phone: (323) 956-5000
Key Executives/Personnel:
   Christopher Crowe, Executive Producer
   Tom Ropelewski, Executive Producer
Casting Director: Tory Herald
Produced in Assn. With: Paramount Network Television, (323) 956-5000
Cast: Jonathan LaPaglia, Don Franklin, Justina Vail, Nick Searcy, Alan Scarfe, Kevin Christy
Network: UPN
Show Type: Drama
Show Length: 60 mins.

7TH HEAVEN
3401 Exposition Blvd.
Santa Monica, CA 90404
Phone: ....(310) 998-5700
Production Company: Spelling Television, Inc.
5700 Wilshire Blvd., 5th Fl.
Los Angeles, CA 90036
Phone: (323) 965-5700
Key Executives/Personnel:
   Aaron Spelling, Executive Producer
   E. Duke Vincent, Executive Producer
   Brenda Hampton, Executive Producer
Casting Director: Vicki Huff & Associates
Cast: Stephen Collins, Catherine Hicks, Barry Watson, David Gallagher, Jessica Biel, Beverly Mitchell, Mackenzie Rosman
Network: WB
Show Type: Drama
Show Length: 60 mins.

ALL MY CHILDREN
c/o ABC Television, 77 W. 66th St.
New York, NY 10023
Phone: ....(212) 456-7777
Production Company: ABC Television
77 W. 66th St.
New York, NY 10023
Phone: (212) 456-7777
Key Executives/Personnel:
   Jean Dadario Burke, Executive Producer
Casting Director: Judy Wilson
Network: ABC
Show Type: Soap
Show Length: 60 mins.

ALL SOULS
1 Provost St., Ste. 400
Lachine, QC H8S 4H2 Canada
Phone: ....(514) 634-2005
Production Company: Spelling Television, Inc.
5700 Wilshire Blvd., 5th Fl.
Los Angeles, CA 90036
Phone: (323) 965-5700
Key Executives/Personnel:
   Aaron Spelling, Executive Producer
   E. Duke Vincent, Executive Producer
   Steven Tolkin, Executive Producer
   Stuart Gillard, Executive Producer
   Mark Frost, Executive Producer
Casting Director: Leslee Dennis
Cast: Grayson McCouch, Reiko Aylesworth, Serena Scott Thomas, Daniel Cosgrove, Irma P. Hall, Adam Rodriguez
Network: UPN
Show Type: Drama
Show Length: 60 mins.

TV Shows

ALLY MCBEAL
1600 Rosecrans Ave., Bldg. 4B
Manhattan Beach, CA 90266
Phone: ....(310) 727-2100
Production Company: David E. Kelley Productions
1600 Rosecrans Ave., Bldg. 4B
Manhattan Beach, CA 90266
Phone: (310) 727-2200
Key Executives/Personnel:
   David E. Kelley, Executive Producer
   Bill D'Elia, Executive Producer
Casting Director: Nikki Valko & Ken Miller, C.S.A.
Produced in Assn. With: Twentieth Century Fox Television, (310) 369-1000
Cast: Calista Flockhart, Greg Germann, Lisa Nicole Carson, Jane Krakowski, Portia de Rossi, Lucy Lui, Peter MacNicol, Vonda Shepard
Network: Fox
Show Type: Comedy
Show Length: 60 mins.

ANGEL
5555 Melsose Ave., Bungalow 11
Hollywood, CA 90038
Phone: ....(323) 956-2300
Production Company: Mutant Enemy, Inc., Greenwalt Corporation, Kuzui Enterprises, Inc.
P.O. Box 900
Beverly Hills, CA 90213
Phone: (310) 579-5180
Key Executives/Personnel:
   Joss Whedon, Executive Producer
   David Greenwalt, Executive Producer
   Sandy Gallin, Executive Producer
   Gail Berman, Executive Producer
   Fran Rubel Kuzui, Executive Producer
   Kaz Kuzui, Executive Producer
Casting Director: Amy McIntyre Britt, Anya Coloff & Jennifer Fishman
Produced in Assn. With: Twentieth Century Fox Television, (310) 369-1000
Cast: David Boreanaz, Charisma Carpenter, Alexis Denisof, J. August Richards
Network: WB
Show Type: Drama
Show Length: 60 mins.

ANY DAY NOW
27420 Ave. Scott, Stage A
Santa Clarita, CA 91355
Phone: ....(661) 295-4400
Production Company: Grammar Productions
27420 Ave. Scott, Stage A
Santa Clarita, CA 91355
Phone: (661) 295-4400
Key Executives/Personnel:
   Nancy Miller, Executive Producer
   Gary A. Randall, Executive Producer
Casting Director: Carol Kritzer & Andy Henry
Produced in Assn. With: Spelling Entertainment, (323) 965-5700
Cast: Annie Potts, Lorraine Toussaint, Mae Middelton, Shari Perry, Chris Mulkey
Network: Lifetime
Show Type: Drama
Show Length: 60 mins.

ARLI$$
c/o Tollin/Robbins Production, 4133 Lankershim Blvd.
North Hollywood, CA 91602
Phone: ....(818) 766-5004
Production Company: Tollin/Robbins Productions
4133 Lankershim Blvd.
North Hollywood, CA 91602
Phone: (818) 766-5004
Key Executives/Personnel:
   Robert Wuhl, Executive Producer
   Mike Tollin, Executive Producer
   Brian Robbins, Executive Producer
Casting Director: Lisa London & Catherine Stroud
Cast: Robert Wuhl, Sandra Oh, Jim Turner, Michael Boatman
Network: HBO
Show Type: Comedy
Show Length: 30 mins.

AS THE WORLD TURNS
1268 E. 14th St.
Brooklyn, NY 11230
Phone: ....(718) 780-6464
Production Company: Televest Daytime Programming
1268 E. 14th St.
Brooklyn, NY 11230
Key Executives/Personnel:
   Chris Goutman, Executive Producer
Casting Director: Jimmy Bohr
Produced in Assn. With: Proctor Gamble Productions, Inc.
Network: CBS
Show Type: Soap
Show Length: 60 mins.

BABY BLUES
15477 Ventura Blvd., Ste. 200
Sherman Oaks, CA 91403
Phone: ....(818) 977-0720
Production Company: Warner Bros. Television
4000 Warner Blvd.
Burbank, CA 91522
Phone: (818) 954-6000
Key Executives/Personnel:
   Pete Ocko, Executive Producer
   Jeff Martin, Executive Producer
Casting Director: Barbara Miller
Produced in Assn. With: Split the Difference Productions, (818) 977-0720
Cast: Julie Sweeney, Michael O'Malley, Kath Soucie, Arabella Field, Joel Murray, Diedrich Bader, Nicole Sullivan, E.G. Daily, Phil Lamarr
Network: WB
Show Type: Animated Comedy
Show Length: 30 mins.

BAYWATCH HAWAII
510 18th Ave.
Honolulu, HI 96816
Phone: ....(808) 733-4141
Production Company: Pearson Television
2700 Colorado Ave., Ste. 450
Santa Monica, CA 90404
Phone: (310) 656-1100
Key Executives/Personnel:
   Greg Bonann, Executive Producer
Casting Director: Margret Dover Sola
Cast: Jason Brooks, Michael Bergin, Jason Momoa, Stacy Kamano, Brande Roderick, Krista Allen, Charlie Brumbly, Alicia Rickter, Brooke Burns
Network: UPN
Syndicated: Yes
Show Type: Drama
Show Length: 60 mins.

BEASTMASTER

c/o Alliance Atlantis, 121 Bloor St. East, Ste. 800
Toronto, ON M4W 3M5 Canada
Phone: ....(416) 967-1174
Production Company: Alliance Atlantis
121 Bloor St. East, Ste. 800
Toronto, ON M4W 3M5 Canada
Phone: (416) 967-1174
Key Executives/Personnel:
  Steve Feke, Executive Producer
  Jefferey M. Hayes, Executive Producer
  Sylvio Tabet, Executive Producer
Casting Director: Maura Fay
Produced in Assn. With: Tribune Entertainment
Cast: Daniel Goodard, Jackson Raine, Emilie de Ravin, Tayler Kane, Danielle Carter, Jefferey M. Hayes, Sylvio Tabet
Syndicated: Yes
Show Type: Action
Show Length: 60 mins.

BECKER

c/o Paramount Pictures, 5555 Melrose Ave., Hope Bldg., Ste. 100
Los Angeles, CA 90038
Phone: ....(323) 956-8822
Production Company: David Hackel Productions, Industry Entertainment
c/o Paramount Pictures, 5555 Melrose Ave., Hope Bldg., Ste. 100
Los Angeles, CA 90038
Phone: (323) 956-5000
Key Executives/Personnel:
  Dave Hackel, Executive Producer
  Ian Gurvitz, Executive Producer
Casting Director: Sheila Guthrie
Produced in Assn. With: Paramount Network Television, (323) 956-5000
Cast: Ted Danson, Terry Farrell, Hattie Winston, Shawnee Smith, Alex Desert, Saverio Guerra
Network: CBS
Show Type: Comedy
Show Length: 30 mins.

BEGGARS & CHOOSERS

11812 San Vincente Blvd., Ste. 503
Los Angeles, CA 90049
Phone: ....(310) 826-7431
Production Company: Granada Entertainment
11812 San Vicente Blvd., Ste. 500
Los Angeles, CA 90049
Phone: (310) 689-4777
Key Executives/Personnel:
  Peter Lefcourt, Executive Producer
  Antony Root, Executive Producer
  Kim Fleary, Executive Producer
  Lilly Tartikoff, Executive Producer
Casting Director: Joel Thurm
Cast: Brian Kerwin, Charlotte Ross, Tuc Watkins, Billy McNamara, James Belushi
Network: Showtime
Show Type: Comedy
Show Length: 60 mins.

BETTE

c/o Culver Studios, 9336 W. Washington Blvd., Stage 11, Ste. 3
Culver City, CA 90232
Phone: ....(310) 202-2788
Production Company: D-Train Productions, All Girl Productions, CBS Productions
9336 W. Washington Blvd.
Culver City, CA 90232
Phone: (310) 836-5537
Key Executives/Personnel:
  Jeffrey Lane, Executive Producer
  Bonnie Bruckheimer, Executive Producer
  Bette Midler, Executive Producer
  Andrew D. Weyman, Executive Producer
Casting Director: Lori Openden
Produced in Assn. With: Colombia Tristar Television, (310) 202-1234
Cast: Bette Midler, Kevin Dunn, Joanna Gleason, James Dreyfus, Marina Molota
Network: CBS
Show Type: Comedy
Show Length: 30 mins.

THE BOLD AND THE BEAUTIFUL

c/o Bell-Phillip Television, 7800 Beverly Blvd., Ste. 3371
Los Angeles, CA 90036
Phone: ....(323) 575-4138
Production Company: Bell-Phillip Television Productions, Inc.
7800 Beverly Blvd., Ste. 3371
Los Angeles, CA 90036
Phone: (323) 575-4138
Key Executives/Personnel:
  Bradley Bell, Executive Producer
Casting Director: Christy Dooley
Network: CBS
Show Type: Soap
Show Length: 30 mins.

BOSTON PUBLIC

1600 Rosecrans Ave, Bldg. 4B
Manhattan Beach, CA 90266
Phone: ....(310) 727-2912
Production Company: David E. Kelley Productions
1600 Rosecrans Ave., Bldg. 4B
Manhattan Beach, CA 90266
Phone: (310) 727-2200
Key Executives/Personnel:
  David E. Kelley, Executive Producer
Casting Director: Janet Gilmore & Megan McConnell
Produced in Assn. With: Twentieth Century Fox Television, (310) 369-1000
Cast: Anothy Heald, Jessalyn Gilsig, Fyvush Finkel, Nicky Katt, Chi McBride, Joey Slotnick, Sharon Leal, Rashida Jones, Thomas McCarthy
Network: Fox
Show Type: Drama
Show Length: 60 mins.

TV Shows

BUFFY THE VAMPIRE SLAYER
P.O. Box 900
Beverly Hills, CA 90213
Phone: ....(310) 579-5100
Production Company: Twentieth Century Fox Television
10201 W. Pico Blvd.
Los Angeles, CA 90035
Phone: (310) 369-1000
Key Executives/Personnel:
    Joss Whedon, Executive Producer
    Gail Berman, Executive Producer
    Sandy Gallin, Executive Producer
    Fran Rubel Kuzui, Executive Producer
    Kaz Kuzui, Executive Producer
Casting Director: Amy McIntyre Britt, Anya Coloff & Jennifer Fishman
Produced in Assn. With: Mutant Enemy, Kuzui Enterprises & Sandollar Television
Cast: Sarah Michelle Geller, Nicholas Brendon, Alyson Hannigan, James Marsters, Anthony Stewart Head, Seth Green, Marc Blucas
Network: WB
Show Type: Drama
Show Length: 60 mins.

BULL
3701 W. Oak St., Bldg. 218
Burbank, CA 91522
Phone: ....(818) 977-2001
Production Company: Michael S. Chernuchin Productions
4000 Warner Blvd., Bldg. 36, Ste. 140
Burbank, CA 91522
Phone: (818) 954-2426
Key Executives/Personnel:
    Michael S. Chernuchin, Executive Producer
    Eric Laneuville, Executive Producer
    Ken Horton, Executive Producer
Casting Director: Barbara Miller & Megan Branman
Produced in Assn. With: Warner Bros. Television, (818) 954-6000
Cast: George Newbern, Malik Yoba, Alicia Coppola, Elizabeth Rohm, Christopher Wiehl, Ian Kahn
Network: TNT
Show Type: Drama
Show Length: 60 mins.

DREW CAREY SHOW, THE
c/o Warner Bros. Television, 4000 Warner Blvd., Bldg. 19
Burbank, CA 91522
Phone: ....(818) 954-3878
Production Company: Mohawk Productions
c/o Warner Bros. Television, 4000 Warner Blvd., Bldg. 19
Burbank, CA 91522
Phone: (818) 954-7442
Key Executives/Personnel:
    Bruce Helford, Executive Producer
    Drew Carey, Executive Producer
    Robert Borden, Executive Producer
    Deborah Oppenheimer, Executive Producer
Casting Director: Bonnie Zane Casting
Produced in Assn. With: Warner Bros. Television, (818) 954-6000
Cast: Drew Carey, Diedrich Bader, Christa Miller, Kathy Kinney, Craig Ferguson, Ryan Stiles
Network: ABC
Show Type: Comedy
Show Length: 30 mins.

C.S.I.
25100 Rye Canyon Rd., Bldg. 31
Santa Clarita, CA 91355
Phone: ....(661) 257-7200
Production Company: CBS Productions, Alliance Atlantis
7800 Beverly Blvd.
Los Angeles, CA 90036
Phone: (323) 575-2345
Key Executives/Personnel:
    Jerry Bruckheimer, Executive Producer
    Ann Donahue, Executive Producer
    Carol Mendelsohn, Executive Producer
Casting Director: April Webster
Cast: William Petersen, Marg Helgenberger, Gary Dourdan, George Eads, Jorja Fox, Paul Guilfoyle
Network: CBS
Show Type: Drama
Show Length: 60 mins.

CHARMED
6625 Variel Ave.
Canoga Park, CA 91303
Phone: ....(818) 673-1100
Production Company: Spelling Television, Inc.
5700 Wilshire Blvd., 5th Fl.
Los Angeles, CA 90036
Phone: (323) 965-5700
Key Executives/Personnel:
    Aaron Spelling, Executive Producer
    E. Duke Vincent, Executive Producer
    Brad Kern, Executive Producer
Casting Director: Stacey Alexander
Cast: Shannen Doherty, Holly Marie Combs, Alyssa Milano, Brian Krause, Julian MacMahon
Network: WB
Show Type: Drama
Show Length: 60 mins.

THE CHRIS ISAAK SHOW
26 Southwest Marine Dr.
Vancouver, BC V5X 2P9 Canada
Phone: ....(604) 321-7229
Production Company: Viacom Productions
10880 Wilshire Blvd., Ste. 1101
Los Angeles, CA 90024
Phone: (310) 234-5000
Key Executives/Personnel:
    Diane Frolov, Executive Producer
    Andrew Schneider, Executive Producer
Casting Director: Trish Robinson & Bonnie Zane
Produced in Assn. With: C. I. Productions, Inc., (604) 321-7229
Cast: Chris Issak, Kristin Dattilo, Jed Rees, Kenneth Johnson, Hershel Yatovitz, Gerg Winter, Rowland Salley, Bobby Jo Moore
Network: Showtime
Show Type: Comedy
Show Length: 60 mins.

CITY GUYS
c/o Sunset-Gower Studios, 1438 N. Gower St.
Hollywood, CA 90028
Phone: ....(323) 468-3366
Production Company: Peter Engel Productions
330 Bob Hope Dr., Ste. C-113
Burbank, CA 91523
Phone: (818) 840-7780
Key Executives/Personnel:
    Peter Engel, Executive Producer
Casting Director: Patricia Noland
Produced in Assn. With: NBC Entertainment, Inc.,
    (818) 840-4444
Cast: Dion Basco, Steven Daniel, Marissa Dyan, Wesley Jonathan, Marcella Lowery, Caitlin Mourey, Scott Whyte
Network: NBC
Show Type: Comedy
Show Length: 30 mins.

CITY OF ANGELS
c/o Steven Bochco Productions, 10201 W. Pico Blvd., Bldg. 1
Los Angeles, CA 90035
Phone: ....(310) 202-4433
Production Company: Steven Bochco Productions
10201 W. Pico Blvd., Bldg. 1
Los Angeles, CA 90035
Phone: (310) 369-2400
Key Executives/Personnel:
    Steven Bochco, Supervising Executive Producer
    Kevin Hooks, Supervising Executive Producer
Casting Director: Junie Lowry-Johnson & Scott Genringer
Cast: Blair Underwood, Michael Warren, Phil Buckman, Hill Harper, T. E. Russell, Viola Davis, Kyle Secor, Gabrielle Union
Network: CBS
Show Type: Drama
Show Length: 60 mins.

CLEOPATRA 2525
100 Universal City Plaza, Bldg. 5166
Universal City, CA 91608
Phone: ....(818) 777-0088
Production Company: Renaissance Pictures
100 Universal City Plaza, Bldg. 5166, 3rd Fl.
Universal City, CA 91608
Phone: (818) 777-0088
Key Executives/Personnel:
    Rob Tapert, Executive Producer
    Sam Raimi, Executive Producer
    R. J. Stewart, Executive Producer
Casting Director: Marie Adams
Produced in Assn. With: Studio , (310) 360-2300
Cast: Gina Torres, Jennifer Sky, Victoria Pratt
Syndicated: Yes
Show Type: Action
Show Length: 60 mins.

COMICVIEW
811 S. San Fernando Blvd.
Burbank, CA 91502
Phone: ....(818) 566-9948
Production Company: Black Entertainment Television (BET)
811 S. San Fernando Rd.
Burbank, CA 91502
Phone: (818) 566-9948
Key Executives/Personnel:
    Andre Barnwell, Executive Producer
    Boogeyman, Executive Producer
Casting Director: Rhonda & Tony Spires
Cast: Tyler Bearde, Mercedes Bey, Gigi Bolden, LeVan Davis, Chole Gadson, Darrell Heath, Emil Johnson, Scruncho
Network: BET
Show Type: Comedy
Show Length: 60 mins.

CURSED
c/o NBC Studios, 3000 W. Alameda Ave.
Burbank, CA 91523
Phone: ....(818) 655-6501
Production Company: NBC Entertainment, Inc.
3000 W. Alameda Ave.
Burbank, CA 91523
Phone: (818) 840-4444
Casting Director: Gilda Stratton
Produced in Assn. With: Artist Television Group, (310) 860-8000
Cast: Steven Weber, Amy Pietz, Wendell Pierce, Chris Elliot
Network: NBC
Show Type: Comedy
Show Length: 30 mins.

D.A.G
4024 Radford Ave., Bungalow 15
Studio City, CA 91604
Phone: ....(818) 655-5561
Production Company: NBC Entertainment, Inc.
30 Rockefeller Plaza
New York, NY 10112
Phone: (212) 664-4444
Key Executives/Personnel:
    Jack Burditt, Executive Producer
    Eileen Conn, Executive Producer
    Andrew Gordon, Executive Producer
Casting Director: Jeff Greenberg
Cast: David Allen Grier, Delta Burke, Stephen Dunham, Lauren Tom, Mel Jackson, Emmy Laybourne, Paul F. Tompkins
Network: NBC
Show Type: Comedy
Show Length: 30 mins.

DARK ANGEL
555 Brooksbank Ave., Bldg. 10, Ste. 210
North Vancouver, BC V7J 3S5 Canada
Phone: ....(604) 983-5993
Production Company: Cameron-Eglee Productions, Twentieth Century Fox Television
919 Santa Monica Blvd., 3rd Fl.
Santa Monica, CA 90401
Phone: (310) 656-6100
Key Executives/Personnel:
    James Cameron, Executive Producer
    Charles Eglee, Executive Producer
Casting Director: Robert Ulrich (U.S.) & Coreen Mayrs (Canada)
Cast: Jessica Alba, J. C. Mackenzie, Allimi Ballard, Michael Weatherly, Valarie Ray Miller, Jennifer Blanc, Richard Gunn, John Savage
Network: Fox
Show Type: Drama
Show Length: 60 mins.

TV Shows

DAWSON'S CREEK
9255 Sunset Blvd., Ste. 1000
Los Angeles, CA 90069
Phone: ....(310) 288-2000
Production Company: Granville Productions
9255 Sunset Blvd., Ste. 1000
West Hollywood, CA 90069
Phone: (310) 288-2000
Key Executives/Personnel:
    Paul Stupin, Executive Producer
    Greg Berlanti, Executive Producer
    Gerg Prange, Executive Producer
Casting Director: Patrick Rush & Sharon Klein
Produced in Assn. With: Columbia Tristar Television, (310) 244-4000
Cast: James Van Der Beek, Katie Holmes, Joshua Jackson, Michelle Williams
Network: WB
Show Type: Drama
Show Length: 60 mins.

DAYS OF OUR LIVES
3400 Riverside Dr., Ste. 780
Burbank, CA 91505
Phone: ....(818) 972-0917
Production Company: Columbia TriStar Television
9336 W. Washington Blvd.
Culver City, CA 90232
Phone: (310) 202-1234
Key Executives/Personnel:
    Ken Corday, Executive Producer
    Tom Langan, Executive Producer
Casting Director: Fran Bascom
Produced in Assn. With: Corday Productions, Inc., (818) 972-0917
Network: NBC
Show Type: Soap
Show Length: 60 mins.

DHARMA & GREG
10201 W. Pico Blvd., Bldg. 38, Rm. 125
Los Angeles, CA 90035
Phone: ....(310) 369-7174
Production Company: Twentieth Century Fox Television
10201 W. Pico Blvd.
Los Angeles, CA 90035
Phone: (310) 369-1000
Key Executives/Personnel:
    Chuck Lorre, Executive Producer
    Bill Prady, Executive Producer
    Erwin More, Executive Producer
    Brian Medavoy, Executive Producer
Casting Director: Nikki Valko & Ken Miller, C.S.A.
Produced in Assn. With: Chuck Lorre Productions
Cast: Jenna Elfman, Thomas Gibson, Shae D'lyn, Mimi Kennedy, Joel Murray, Alan Rachins, Mitchell Ryan, Susan Sullivan
Network: ABC
Show Type: Comedy
Show Length: 30 mins.

DIAGNOSIS MURDER
7700 Balboa Blvd.
Van Nuys, CA 91406
Phone: ....(818) 756-1260
Production Company: The Fred Silverman Company, Dean Hargrove Productions
c/o Viacom Productions, 10880 Wilshire Blvd., Ste. 1101
Los Angeles, CA 90024
Phone: (310) 234-5000
Key Executives/Personnel:
    Dean Hargrove, Executive Producer
    Fred Silverman, Executive Producer
    Dick Van Dyke, Executive Producer
    Chris Abbott, Executive Producer
Casting Director: Penny Ellers
Produced in Assn. With: Viacom Productions, (310) 234-5000
Cast: Dick Van Dyke, Barry Van Dyke, Victoria Rowell, Charlie Schlatter
Network: CBS
Show Type: Drama
Show Length: 60 mins.

THE DISTRICT
12636 Beatrice St.
Los Angeles, CA 90066
Phone: ....(310) 577-3400
Production Company: CBS Television
7800 Beverly Blvd.
Los Angeles, CA 90036
Phone: (323) 575-2345
Key Executives/Personnel:
    Terry George, Executive Producer
    Denise Di Novi, Executive Producer
Casting Director: Karen Rea
Produced in Assn. With: Studios USA, (310) 360-2300
Cast: Craig T. Nelson, Jayne Brook, Lynn Thigoen, Sean Patrick Thomas, Justin Theroux, Roger Aaron Brown, David O'Hara, Elizabeth Marvel
Network: CBS
Show Type: Drama
Show Length: 60 mins.

ED
c/o Viacom Productions, 10880 Wilshire Blvd., Ste. 1101
Los Angeles, CA 90024
Phone: ....(201) 767-4007
Production Company: Viacom Productions
10880 Wilshire Blvd., Ste. 1101
Los Angeles, CA 90024
Phone: (310) 234-5000
Key Executives/Personnel:
    Rob Burnett, Executive Producer
    Jon Beckerman, Executive Producer
    David Letterman, Executive Producer
Casting Director: Todd Phaler
Produced in Assn. With: NBC Entertainment, Inc. & Worldwide Pants, (818) 840-4444
Cast: Thomas Cavanagh, Julie Bowen, Josh Randall, Lesley Boone, Jana Marie Hupp
Network: NBC
Show Type: Drama
Show Length: 60 mins.

ER
4000 Warner Blvd., Bldg. 133, Rm. 204
Burbank, CA 91522
Phone: ....(818) 954-3830
Production Company: John Wells Productions, Constant c,
 Amblin Television
4000 Warner Blvd., Bldg. 138, Rm. 1106
Burbank, CA 91522
Phone: (818) 954-6000
Key Executives/Personnel:
 John Wells, Executive Producer
 Michael Crichton, Executive Producer
 Lydia Woodward, Executive Producer
Casting Director: John Frank Levey
Produced in Assn. With: Warner Bros. Television, (818) 954-6000
Cast: Anthony Edwards, Eriq La Salle, Noah Wyle, Laura Innes, Alex Kingston, Goran Visnjic, Maura Tierney, Paul McCrane, Michael Michele, Erik Palladino, Ming-Na
Network: NBC
Show Type: Drama
Show Length: 60 mins.

EVERYBODY LOVES RAYMOND
4000 Warner Blvd., Bldg. 131
Burbank, CA 91522
Phone: ....(818) 954-7770
Production Company: Where's the Lunch Productions, Talk Productions, Worldwide Pants, Inc.
4000 Warner Blvd., Bldg. 131
Burbank, CA 91522
Phone: (818) 954-7770
Key Executives/Personnel:
 Phil Rosenthal, Executive Producer
 Rory Rosegarten, Executive Producer
 Stu Smiley, Executive Producer
Casting Director: Lisa Miller Katz
Produced in Assn. With: HBO Independent Productions, (310) 201-9300
Cast: Ray Romano, Patricia Heaton, Brad Garrett, Doris Roberts, Peter Boyle
Network: CBS
Show Type: Comedy
Show Length: 30 mins.

FAMILY LAW
10202 W. Washington Blvd., Tracy Bldg.
Culver City, CA 90232
Phone: ....(310) 244-8333
Production Company: Paul Haggis Productions
10202 W. Washington Blvd., David Lean Bldg., Ste. 103
Culver City, CA 90232
Phone: (310) 244-4915
Key Executives/Personnel:
 Paul Haggis, Executive Producer
Casting Director: Lisa London & Catherine Stroud
Produced in Assn. With: CBS Productions & Columbia Tristar Television, (323) 575-2345
Cast: Kathleen Quinlan, Christopher McDonald, Julie Warner, Dixie Carter, Tony Danza, Salli Richardson, Christian de la Fuente, Merrilee McCommas
Network: CBS
Show Type: Drama
Show Length: 60 mins.

FELICITY
3322 La Cienega Place
Los Angeles, CA 90016
Phone: ....(310) 558-5200
Production Company: Imagine Television Productions
9465 Wilshire Blvd., 7th Fl.
Beverly Hills, CA 90212
Phone: (310) 858-2000
Key Executives/Personnel:
 Brian Grazer, Executive Producer
 Ron Howard, Executive Producer
 Tony Krantz, Executive Producer
 J. J. Abrams, Executive Producer
 Matt Reeves, Executive Producer
 John Eisendrath, Executive Producer
Casting Director: Megan McConnell & Janet Gilmore
Produced in Assn. With: Touchstone Television, (818) 560-1000
Cast: Keri Russel, Scott Speedman, Scott Foley, Amy Jo Johnson, Tangi Miller, Greg Grunberg, Amanda Foreman
Network: WB
Show Type: Drama
Show Length: 60 mins.

FOR YOUR LOVE
300 Television Plaza, Bldg. 136, Rm. 143
Burbank, CA 91522
Phone: ....(818) 954-3638
Production Company: Sister Lee Productions, Inc.
300 Television Plaza
Burbank, CA 91522
Phone: (818) 954-3638
Key Executives/Personnel:
 Yvette Bowser, Executive Producer
Casting Director: Leah Daniels-Butler
Produced in Assn. With: Warner Bros. Television, (818) 954-6000
Cast: Holly Robinson Peete, Tamala Jones, James Lesure, Edafe Blackmon, Deedee Pfeiffer, D. W. Moffett
Network: WB
Show Type: Comedy
Show Length: 30 mins.

FRASIER
c/o Paramount Studios, 5555 Melrose Ave., Lucille Ball Bldg., Ste. 101
Hollywood, CA 90038
Phone: ....(323) 956-3100
Production Company: Grub Street Productions
5555 Melrose Ave., Wilder Bldg., Ste. 101
Los Angeles, CA 90038
Phone: (323) 956-4657
Key Executives/Personnel:
 David Angell, Executive Producer
 Peter Casey, Executive Producer
 David Lee, Executive Producer
 Christopher Lloyd, Executive Producer
 Joe Keenan, Executive Producer
 Kelsey Grammer, Executive Producer
Casting Director: Jeff Greenberg
Produced in Assn. With: Paramount Network Television, (323) 956-5000
Cast: Kelsey Grammer, Jane Leeves, David Hyde Pierce, Peri Gilpin, John Mahoney
Network: NBC
Syndicated: Yes
Show Type: Comedy
Show Length: 30 mins.

TV Shows

FREAKY STORIES
126 York St., Ste. 219
Ottawa, ON K1N 5T5 Canada
Phone: ....(613) 241-5111
Production Company: Decode Entertainment
512 King St. East, Ste. 104
Toronto, ON M5A 1M1 Canada
Phone: (416) 363-8034
Key Executives/Personnel:
   Steve De Nure, Executive Producer
   Neil Court, Executive Producer
   John A. Delmage, Executive Producer
   Curtis Crawford, Executive Producer
   Neil Bregman, Executive Producer
Casting Director: Joanne Boreham
Produced in Assn. With: Sound Venture Productions, (613) 241-5111
Cast: James Rankin, Dan Redican
Syndicated: Yes
Show Type: Drama
Show Length: 30 mins.

FREEDOM
3645 Grandview Highway
Vancouver, BC V5M 2J7 Canada
Phone: ....(604) 419-9000
Production Company: Silver Pictures Television
c/o Warner Bros., 4000 Warner Blvd., Bldg. 90
Burbank, CA 91522
Phone: (818) 954-4490
Key Executives/Personnel:
   Joel Silver, Executive Producer
   Hans Tobeason, Executive Producer
   Dan Cracchiolo, Executive Producer
Casting Director: Geraldine Leder
Produced in Assn. With: Pandemonium Pictures Limited & Warner Bros. Television, (818) 954-6000
Cast: Holt McCallany, Bodhi Elfman, Scarlett Chorvat, Darius McCrary
Network: UPN
Show Type: Drama
Show Length: 60 mins.

FRIENDS
4000 Warner Blvd., Bldg. 160, Ste. 750
Burbank, CA 91522
Phone: ....(818) 977-7943
Production Company: Bright-Kauffman-Crane Productions
4000 Warner Blvd., Bldg. 160, Ste. 750
Burbank, CA 91522
Phone: (818) 977-7777
Key Executives/Personnel:
   Kevin Bright, Executive Producer
   Marta Kauffman, Executive Producer
   David Crane, Executive Producer
   Greg Malins, Executive Producer
Casting Director: Leslie Litt Casting
Produced in Assn. With: Warner Bros. Television, (818) 954-6000
Cast: Jennifer Aniston, Courtney Cox Arquette, Lisa Kudrow, Matt LeBlanc, Matthew Perry, David Schwimmer
Network: NBC
Syndicated: Yes
Show Type: Comedy
Show Length: 30 mins.

THE FUGITIVE
3400 Riverside Dr., Ste. 200
Burbank, CA 91505
Phone: ....(818) 977-4050
Production Company: Kopelson Entertainment, McNamara Paper Products
2121 Avenue of the Stars, Ste. 1400
Los Angeles, CA 90067
Phone: (310) 369-7555
Key Executives/Personnel:
   John McNamara, Executive Producer
   Arnold Kopelson, Executive Producer
   Anne Kopelson, Executive Producer
   Roy Huggins, Executive Producer
   R. W. Goodwin, Executive Producer
Casting Director: Barbara Miller & Pamela Basker (LA), Jodi Rothfield & Heidi Walker (Seattle)
Produced in Assn. With: Warner Bros. Television, (818) 954-6000
Cast: Tim Daly, Mykelti Williamson
Network: CBS
Show Type: Drama
Show Length: 60 mins.

FUTURAMA
c/o Twentieth Century Fox Television, 10201 W. Pico Blvd.
Los Angeles, CA 90035
Phone: ....(310) 444-6165
Production Company: Twentieth Century Fox Television
10201 W. Pico Blvd.
Los Angeles, CA 90035
Phone: (310) 369-1000
Key Executives/Personnel:
   Matt Groening, Executive Producer
   David Cohen, Executive Producer
Casting Director: Julie Mossberg & Jill Anthony
Produced in Assn. With: The Curiosity Company
Cast: Billy West, Kate Sagal, John DiMaggio, Lauren Tom, Phil LaMarr, Maurice LaMarche, David Herman, Tress MacNeille
Network: Fox
Show Type: Animated Comedy
Show Length: 30 mins.

GARY & MIKE
1438 N. Gower St., Bldg. 35, 3rd Fl., Box 45
Los Angeles, CA 90028
Phone: ....(323) 860-7430
Production Company: Big Ticket Television
1438 N. Gower St., Bldg. 35, 3rd Fl., Box 45
Los Angeles, CA 90028
Phone: (323) 860-7400
Key Executives/Personnel:
   Fax Bahr, Executive Producer
   Adam Small, Executive Producer
   Tom Turpin, Executive Producer
   Will Vinton, Executive Producer
Casting Director: Donna Ekholdt
Cast: Harland Williams, Chris Moynihan
Network: UPN
Show Type: Comedy
Show Length: 30 mins.

THE GEENA DAVIS SHOW
c/o Touchstone Television Productions, 500 S. Buena Vista St.
Burbank, CA 91521
Phone: ....(818) 560-6363
Production Company: Touchstone Television Productions
500 S. Buena Vista St.
Burbank, CA 91521
Phone: (818) 560-1000
Key Executives/Personnel:
  Nina Wass, Executive Producer
  Gene Stein, Executive Producer
  Terri Minsky, Executive Producer
  David Flebotte, Executive Producer
  Geena Davis, Executive Producer
Casting Director: Lisa Miller Katz
Cast: Geena Davis, Peter Horton, Mimi Rogers, Kim Coles, John Daley, Esther Scott, Mackenzie Vega, Harland Williams
Network: ABC
Show Type: Comedy
Show Length: 30 mins.

GENE RODDENBERRY: EARTH FINAL CONFLICT
4450 Lakeside Dr., Ste. 350
Burbank, CA 91505
Phone: ....(818) 843-7730
Production Company: David Kirschner Productions, Lost Script IV Productions
629 Eastern Ave., Bldg. B, 2nd Fl.
Toronto, ON M4M 1E4 Canada
Phone: (416) 778-4171
Key Executives/Personnel:
  Paul Gertz, Supervising Executive Producer
  David Kirschner, Executive Producer
  Majel Roddenberry, Executive Producer
Casting Director: John Comerford
Produced in Assn. With: Tribune Entertainment & Alliance Atlantis, (416) 967-1174
Cast: Robert Leeshock, Jayne Heitmeyer, Von Flores, Leni Parker, Anita Le Selva, Melinda Deines, Richard Chervolleau, Lisa Howard, Majel Roddenberg
Syndicated: Yes
Show Type: Drama
Show Length: 60 mins.

GENERAL HOSPITAL
4151 Prospect Ave., Stage 54
Los Angeles, CA 90027
Phone: ....(310) 557-5563
Production Company: ABC Television
2040 Avenue of Stars, 5th Fl.
Los Angeles, CA 90067
Phone: (310) 557-7777
Key Executives/Personnel:
  Wendy Riche, Executive Producer
Casting Director: Mark Teschner & Gwen Hillier
Network: ABC
Show Type: Soap
Show Length: 60 mins.

GIDEON'S CROSSING
c/o Raliegh Studios, 5300 Melrose Ave., Support Bldg., 3rd Fl.
Los Angeles, CA 90038
Phone: ....(323) 960-8006
Production Company: Touchstone Television Productions
500 S. Buena Vista St.
Burbank, CA 91521
Phone: (818) 560-1000
Key Executives/Personnel:
  Paul Attanasio, Executive Producer
  Katie Jacobs, Executive Producer
  Eric Overmyer, Executive Producer
  Randy Zisk, Executive Producer
Casting Director: Mali Finn
Cast: Andre Braugher, Ruben Blades, Rhona Mitra, Harnish Linklatter, Ravi Kapoor, Sophie Keller, Russel Hornsby, Jascha Washington, Megan Gregory, Brian Wiltshire, Eric Dane, Kevin J. O'Connor
Network: ABC
Show Type: Drama
Show Length: 60 mins.

GILMORE GIRLS
4000 Warner Blvd., Trailer 22
Burbank, CA 91522
Phone: ....(818) 954-5898
Production Company: Dorthy Parker Drank Here Productions, Hofflund-Polone
4000 Warner Blvd., Trailer 22
Burbank, CA 91522
Phone: (818) 954-5898
Key Executives/Personnel:
  Amy Sherman-Palladino, Executive Producer
  Gavin Polone, Executive Producer
Casting Director: Mara Casey & Jami Rudofsky
Produced in Assn. With: Warner Bros. Television, (818) 954-6000
Cast: Lauren Graham, Alexis Bledel, Alex Borstein, Keiko Agena, Yanic Truesdale, Kelly Bishop, Edward Herrmann, Melissa McCarthy, Scott Patterson, Liz Torres
Network: WB
Show Type: Drama
Show Length: 60 mins.

GIRLFRIENDS
5555 Melrose Ave., Balaban Bldg., Ste. 120
Hollywood, CA 90038
Phone: ....(323) 956-1803
Production Company: Grammnet Productions (TV)
5555 Melrose Ave., Lucy Bungalow, 2nd Fl.
Los Angeles, CA 90038
Phone: (323) 956-5547
Key Executives/Personnel:
  Mara Brock Akil, Executive Producer & Creator
  Kelsey Grammer, Executive Producer
  Rudy Hornish, Executive Producer
  Dee La Duke, Executive Producer
  Mark Brown, Executive Producer
Casting Director: Eileen Knight
Produced in Assn. With: Paramount Network Television, (323) 956-5000
Cast: Tracee Ellis Ross, Golden Brooks, Reggie Hayes, Jill Jones, Persia White
Network: UPN
Show Type: Comedy
Show Length: 30 mins.

TV Shows

GROSS POINTE
c/o Sony Pictures Entertainment, 10202 W. Washington Blvd.,
Gable Bldg., Ste. 120
Culver City, CA 90232
Phone: ....(310) 244-4168
Production Company: Artists Television Group
9465 Wilshire Blvd., Ste. 212
Beverly Hills, CA 90212
Phone: (310) 860-8200
Key Executives/Personnel:
  Darren Star, Executive Producer
  Robin Schiff, Executive Producer
Casting Director: Greg Orson
Produced in Assn. With: Darren Star Productions
Cast: Irene Molloy, Lindsay Sloane, Kyle Howard, Al Santos, Kohl Sudduth, Bonnie Sommerville, William Ragsdale
Network: WB
Show Type: Comedy
Show Length: 30 mins.

GROUNDED FOR LIFE
4024 Radford Ave., Bldg. 4, Ste. 101
Studio City, CA 91604
Phone: ....(818) 655-5967
Production Company: Carsey-Werner Productions
4024 Radford Ave., Bldg. 3
Studio City, CA 91604
Phone: (818) 655-5598
Key Executives/Personnel:
  Marcy Carsey, Executive Producer
  Tom Werner, Executive Producer
  Caryn Mandabach, Executive Producer
  Bill Martin, Executive Producer
  Mike Schiff, Executive Producer
Casting Director: Cami Patton & Cheryl Kloner
Cast: Donal Logue, Megyn Price, Kevin Corrigan, Lynsey Bartilson, Griffin Frazen, Jake Burbage, Richard Riehle
Network: Fox
Show Type: Comedy
Show Length: 30 mins.

GUIDING LIGHT
222 E. 44th St.
New York, NY 10017
Phone: ....(212) 975-4321
Production Company: Televest Daytime Programming
222 E. 44th St.
New York, NY 10017
Key Executives/Personnel:
  Paul Rauch, Executive Producer
Casting Director: Rob Decina
Produced in Assn. With: Proctor Gamble Productions, Inc.
Network: CBS
Show Type: Soap
Show Length: 60 mins.

THE HUGHLEYS
c/o Hollywood Center Studios, 1040 N. Las Palmas Ave., Bldg. 33, 2nd Fl.
Los Angeles, CA 90038
Phone: ....(323) 860-8484
Production Company: Greenblatt Janollari Studios
9346 Civic Center Dr., Garden Level
Beverly Hills, CA 90210
Phone: (310) 860-3600
Key Executives/Personnel:
  Robert Greenblatt, Executive Producer
  David Janollari, Executive Producer
  Kim Friese, Executive Producer
  D. L. Hughley, Executive Producer
  Chris Rock, Executive Producer
  Michael Rotenberg, Executive Producer
  Dave Becky, Executive Producer
Casting Director: Carol Goldwasser
Cast: D. L. Hughley, Elise Neal, Eric Allan Kramer, John Henton, Ashley Monique Clark, Dee Jay Daniels, Marietta De Prima
Network: UPN
Show Type: Comedy
Show Length: 30 mins.

HYPE
4000 Warner Blvd., Bldg. 136, Ste. 213
Burbank, CA 91522
Phone: ....(818) 954-3352
Production Company: Tollin/Robbins Productions
4133 Lankershim Blvd.
North Hollywood, CA 91602
Phone: (818) 766-5004
Key Executives/Personnel:
  Joe Devola, Executive Producer
  Scott King, Executive Producer
  Lanier Laney, Executive Producer
  Terry Sweeney, Executive Producer
Casting Director: Barbara Miller
Produced in Assn. With: Warner Bros. Television, (818) 954-6000
Cast: Frank Caliendo, Daniele Gaither, Steve Kramer, Jennifer Elise Cox, Nadya Ginsburg, Michael Roof, Gavin Crawford, Shayma Tash, Chris Williams, Christen Nelson
Network: WB
Show Type: Comedy
Show Length: 30 mins.

JACK & JILL
4000 Warner Blvd., Bldg. 136, Ste. 101
Burbank, CA 91522
Phone: ....(818) 954-3115
Production Company: Warner Bros. Television
4000 Warner Blvd.
Burbank, CA 91522
Phone: (818) 954-6000
Key Executives/Personnel:
  Mark Cauton, Executive Producer & Creator
  Mike Pavone, Executive Producer & Creator
Casting Director: Elizabeth Rudolph
Cast: Amanda Peet, Ivan Sergei, Sarah Paulson, Jamie Pressley, Justin Kirk, Simon Rex
Network: WB
Show Type: Drama
Show Length: 60 mins.

JAG
28343 Crocker Ave., Ste. 1
Valencia, CA 91355
Phone: ....(661) 294-5500
Production Company: Belisarius Productions
5555 Melrose Ave., Clara Bow Bldg., Ste. 204
Los Angeles, CA 90038
Phone: (323) 956-8660
Key Executives/Personnel:
 Don Bellisario, Executive Producer
Casting Director: Melissa Skoff
Produced in Assn. With: Paramount Network Television, (323) 956-5000
Cast: David James Elliot, Catherine Bell, Patrick Labyorteaux, John M. Jackson, Karri Turner
Network: CBS
Show Type: Drama
Show Length: 60 mins.

JUDGING AMY
10201 W. Pico Blvd., Ste. 773
Los Angeles, CA 90035
Phone: ....(310) 369-0704
Production Company: Barbara Hall/Joseph Stern Productions
10201 W. Pico Blvd.
Los Angeles, CA 90035
Phone: (310) 369-4220
Key Executives/Personnel:
 Barbara Hall, Executive Producer
 Joseph Stern, Executive Producer
 Amy Brenneman, Executive Producer
 Connie Tavel, Executive Producer
Casting Director: Jeannie Bacharach & Gillian O'Neill
Produced in Assn. With: CBS Productions & Twentieth Century Fox Television, (323) 369-1000
Cast: Amy Brenneman, Dan Futterman, Richard T. Jones, Jessica Tuck, Marcus Giamatti, Karle Warren, Tyne Daly, Jillian Armenante
Network: CBS
Show Type: Drama
Show Length: 60 mins.

JUST SHOOT ME
c/o Universal Studios Network Programming, 100 Universal City Plaza
Universal City, CA 91608
Phone: ....(818) 655-5760
Production Company: Universal Studios Network Programming
100 Universal City Plaza
Universal City, CA 91608
Phone: (818) 777-1000
Key Executives/Personnel:
 Marsh McCall, Executive Producer
 Tom Maxwell, Executive Producer
 Don Woodward, Executive Producer
 Brad Grey, Executive Producer
 Bernie Brillstein, Executive Producer
 Steven Levitan, Executive Producer
Casting Director: Brian Meyers Casting
Cast: Laura San Giacomo, George Segal, Wendie Malick, Enrico Colantoni, David Spade
Network: NBC
Show Type: Comedy
Show Length: 30 mins.

THE KING OF QUEENS
10202 W. Washington Blvd., David Lane Bldg., Ste. 410
Culver City, CA 90232
Phone: ....(310) 244-3343
Production Company: Hanley Productions, CBS Productions
7800 Beverly Blvd.
Los Angeles, CA 90036
Phone: (323) 575-2345
Key Executives/Personnel:
 Michael J. Weithorn, Executive Producer
 David Litt, Executive Producer
Casting Director: Cami Patton & Cheryl Kloner
Produced in Assn. With: Columbia Tristar Television, (310) 202-1234
Cast: Kevin James, Leah Remini, Jerry Stiller
Network: CBS
Show Type: Comedy
Show Length: 30 mins.

KING OF THE HILL
1875 Century Park East, 4th Fl.
Los Angeles, CA 90067
Phone: ....(310) 229-2476
Production Company: Twentieth Century Fox Television
10201 W. Pico Blvd.
Los Angeles, CA 90035
Phone: (310) 369-1000
Key Executives/Personnel:
 Greg Daniels, Executive Producer
 Mike Judge, Executive Producer
 Michael Rotenberg, Executive Producer
 Howard Klein, Executive Producer
 Richard Appel, Executive Producer
Casting Director: Julie Mossberg
Produced in Assn. With: Deedle-Dee Productions, Judgemental Films, 3 Arts Entertainment & Film Roman, Inc.
Cast: Mike Judge, Kathy Najimy, Pamela Segall, Brittany Murphy, Johnny Hardwick, Stephen Root, Toby Huss
Network: Fox
Show Type: Animated Comedy
Show Length: 30 mins.

KISS ME GUIDO
c/o Paramount Pictures, 5555 Melrose Ave., Annex 1
Los Angeles, CA 90038
Phone: ....(323) 956-1800
Production Company: Paramount Pictures
Key Executives/Personnel:
 Jonathan Axelrod, Executive Producer
 James Widdoes, Executive Producer
 Marc Cherry, Executive Producer
 Judd Pillot, Executive Producer
 John Peaslee, Executive Producer
Casting Director: Dara Waite
Produced in Assn. With: Axelrod-Widdoes Entertainment, (323) 956-5000
Cast: Jason Bateman, Danny Nucci, Alec Mapa, Michael DeLuise, Jessica Lundy
Network: CBS
Show Type: Comedy
Show Length: 30 mins.

TV Shows

KRISTIN
5555 Melrose Ave., Mae West Bldg., Ste. 152
Los Angeles, CA 90038
Phone: ....(323) 956-4700
Production Company: Markus Farms Productions
5555 Melrose Ave., Mae West Bldg., Ste. 152
Los Angeles, CA 90038
Phone: (323) 956-5000
Key Executives/Personnel:
  John Markus, Executive Producer
  Earl Pomerantz, Executive Producer
Casting Director: Susan Vash
Produced in Assn. With: Paramount Network Television,
  (323) 956-5000
Cast: Kristin Chenoweth, Larry Romano, Christopher Durang, Jon Tenney, Mindy Sterling, Ana Ortiz, Dale Godboldo
Network: NBC
Show Type: Comedy
Show Length: 30 mins.

LADIES MAN
9336 W. Washington Blvd., Ste. 318
Culver City, CA 90232
Phone: ....(310) 202-3334
Production Company: CBS Productions, Columbia TriStar Television
7800 Beverly Blvd.
Los Angeles, CA 90036
Phone: (323) 575-2345
Key Executives/Personnel:
  Victor Levin, Executive Producer
Casting Director: Andrea Cohen
Cast: Alfred Molina, Sharon Lawrence, Betty White, Stephen Root, Alexa Vega, Kaley Cuoco
Network: CBS
Show Type: Comedy
Show Length: 30 mins.

LAW & ORDER
Pier 62, W. 23rd St.
New York, NY 10011
Phone: ....(212) 627-0088
Production Company: Wolf Films, Inc.
100 Universal City Plaza, Bldg. 2252
Universal City, CA 91608
Phone: (818) 777-1236
Key Executives/Personnel:
  Dick Wolf, Executive Producer
  Arthur Penn, Executive Producer
  Bill Finkelstein, Executive Producer
Casting Director: Lynn Kressel & Suzanne Ryan
Produced in Assn. With: Studios USA, (310) 360-2300
Cast: Jerry Orbach, Jesse L. Martin, Epatha Merkson, Sam Waterson, Angie Harmon, Diane Wiest
Network: NBC
Show Type: Drama
Show Length: 60 mins.

LAW & ORDER: SPECIAL VICTIMS UNIT
5801 Westside Ave.
North Bergen, NJ 07047
Phone: ....(201) 662-7170
Production Company: Wolf Films, Inc.
100 Universal City Plaza, Bldg. 2252
Universal City, CA 91608
Phone: (818) 777-1236
Key Executives/Personnel:
  Dick Wolf, Executive Producer
  Ted Kotcheff, Executive Producer
  David Burke, Executive Producer
Casting Director: Lynn Kressel & Julie Tucker
Produced in Assn. With: Studios USA, (310) 360-2300
Cast: Dann Florek, Mariska Hargitay, Richard Belzer, Michelle Hurd, Ice-T, Stephanie March, Christopher Meloni
Network: NBC
Show Type: Drama
Show Length: 60 mins.

LEVEL 9
2820 Bentall St.
Vancouver, BC V5M 4H4 Canada
Phone: ....(604) 412-9150
Production Company: Samoset Productions
409 Santa Monica Blvd., 2nd Fl.
Santa Monica, CA 90401
Phone: (310) 393-5210
Key Executives/Personnel:
  John Sacret Young, Executive Producer
Casting Director: Debi Manwiller & Peggy Kennedy
Produced in Assn. With: Paramount Network Television,
  (323) 956-5000
Cast: Max Martini, Kate Hodge, Michael Kelley, Romany Malco, Fabrizio Flippo, Esteban Powell, Kim Murphy, Susie Park
Network: UPN
Show Type: Drama
Show Length: 60 mins.

MALCOLM IN THE MIDDLE
4024 Radford Ave, Bldg. 4
Studio City, CA 91604
Phone: ....(818) 655-5562
Production Company: Regency Television
10201 W. Pico Blvd., Bldg. 12
Los Angeles, CA 90035
Phone: (310) 369-7593
Key Executives/Personnel:
  Linwood Boomer, Executive Producer
Casting Director: Nikki Valko & Ken Miller
Produced in Assn. With: Twentieth Century Fox Television
  (310) 369-1000
Cast: Frankie Muniz, Christopher Kennedy Masterson, Jane Kaczmarek, Bryan Cranston, Justin Berfield, Erik Per Sullivan
Network: Fox
Show Type: Comedy
Show Length: 30 mins.

MOESHA
1438 N. Gower St., Bldg. 13, 3rd Fl.
Hollywood, CA 90028
Phone: ....(323) 468-4800
Production Company: Big Ticket Television
1438 N. Gower St., Bldg. 35, 3rd Fl., Box 45
Los Angeles, CA 90028
Phone: (323) 860-7400
Key Executives/Personnel:
    Jacque Edmonds, Executive Producer
    Warren Hutcherson, Executive Producer
    Fred Johnson, Executive Producer
Casting Director: Chemin Bernard Casting
Cast: Brandy, William Allen Young, Marcus T. Paulk, Lamont Bentley, Shar Jackson, Sheryl Lee Ralph, Ray J. Norwood
Network: UPN
Show Type: Comedy
Show Length: 30 mins.

MYSTERIOUS WAYS
555 Brooksbank Ave., Bldg. 9, Ste. 240
North Vancouver, BC V7J 3S5 Canada
Phone: ....(310) 234-2200
Production Company: PaxTV/Paxson Communications
10880 Wilshire Blvd., Ste. 1200
Los Angeles, CA 90024
Phone: (310) 234-2200
Key Executives/Personnel:
    Carl Binder, Executive Producer
    Peter O'Fallon, Executive Producer
    Harold Tichenor, Executive Producer
Casting Director: Eve Brandstein (LA) & Corinne Clark (Vancouver)
Produced in Assn. With: Lions Gate Entertainment
Cast: Adrian Pasdar, Rae Daion Chong, Alisen Down
Network: NBC
Show Type: Drama
Show Length: 60 mins.

NASH BRIDGES
Treasure Island, 440 California Ave., Bldg. 2
San Francisco, CA 94130
Phone: ....(415) 782-4100
Production Company: Don Johnson Productions, Carlton Cuse Productions
3400 Riverside Dr., Ste. 100
Burbank, CA 91505
Phone: (818) 238-2200
Key Executives/Personnel:
    Don Johnson, Executive Producer
    Carlton Cuse, Executive Producer
    John Wirth, Executive Producer
Casting Director: Nan Dutton (LA) & Nina Henniger (SF)
Produced in Assn. With: Rysher Entertainment & Paramount Network Telelvision, (323) 956-5000
Cast: Don Johnson, Cheech Marin, James Gammon, Jodi Lyn O'Keefe, Jeff Perry, Cress Williams, Wendy Moniz
Network: CBS
Show Type: Drama
Show Length: 60 mins.

NIGHT VISIONS
c/o Shank Visions Productions, 1416 N. La Brea Ave.
Los Angeles, CA 90028
Phone: ....(323) 802-1535
Production Company: Shank Visions Productions
1416 N. La Brea Ave.
Los Angeles, CA 90028
Phone: (323) 802-1535
Key Executives/Personnel:
    Dan Angel, Executive Producer
    Billy Brown, Executive Producer
Casting Director: Tony Sepulveda
Produced in Assn. With: Warner Bros. Television, (818) 954-6000
Network: Fox
Show Type: Drama
Show Length: 30 mins.

NIKKI
4000 Warner Blvd., Bldg. 19, Ste. 239
Burbank, CA 91522
Phone: ....(818) 954-3332
Production Company: Mohawk Productions
c/o Warner Bros. Television, 4000 Warner Blvd., Bldg. 19
Burbank, CA 91522
Phone: (818) 954-7442
Key Executives/Personnel:
    Deborah Oppenheimer, Executive Producer
    Bob Myer, Executive Producer
    Bruce Helford, Executive Producer
Casting Director: Tammy Billik Casting
Produced in Assn. With: Warner Bros. Television, (818) 954-6000
Cast: Nikki Cox, Nick von Esmarch, Toby Huss, Marina Benedict, Susan Egan, Christine Estabrook
Network: WB
Show Type: Comedy
Show Length: 30 mins.

NORM
4000 Warner Blvd., Bldg. 19
Burbank, CA 91522
Phone: ....(818) 954-7542
Production Company: Mohawk Productions
c/o Warner Bros. Television, 4000 Warner Blvd., Bldg. 19
Burbank, CA 91522
Phone: (818) 954-7442
Key Executives/Personnel:
    Bruce Helford, Executive Producer
    Bruce Rassmussen, Executive Producer
    Rob Ulin, Executive Producer
    Deborah Oppenheimer, Executive Producer
    Norm MacDonald, Executive Producer
Casting Director: Bonnie Zane Casting
Produced in Assn. With: Warner Bros. Production, (818) 954-6000
Cast: Norm MacDonald, Laurie Metcalf, Ian Gomez, Max Wright, Faith Ford, Artie Lange
Network: ABC
Show Type: Comedy
Show Length: 30 mins.

TV Shows

NYPD BLUE
10201 W. Pico Blvd., Bldg. 1, Ste. 232
Los Angeles, CA 90035
Phone: ....(310) 369-1404
Production Company: Steven Bochco Productions
10201 W. Pico Blvd., Bldg. 1
Los Angeles, CA 90035
Phone: (310) 369-2400
Key Executives/Personnel:
  Steven Bochco, Executive Producer
  David Milch, Executive Producer
  Mark Tinker, Executive Producer
  Bill Clark, Executive Producer
Casting Director: Junie Lowry-Johnson
Cast: Dennis Franz, Rick Schroder, James McDaniel, Kim Delaney, Gordon Clapp, Bill Brochtrup, Henry Simmons
Network: ABC
Show Type: Drama
Show Length: 60 mins.

ONCE AND AGAIN
8660 Hayden Pl.
Culver City, CA 90232
Phone: ....(310) 840-7477
Production Company: The Bedford Falls Company
8660 Hayden Pl.
Culver City, CA 90232
Phone: (310) 394-5022
Key Executives/Personnel:
  Marshall Herskovitz, Executive Producer
  Edward Zwick, Executive Producer
Casting Director: Amy Lippens
Produced in Assn. With: Touchstone Television, (818) 560-1000
Cast: Sela Ward, Billy Campbell, Susanna Thompson, Jeffery Nording, Shane West, Julia Whelan, Evan Rachel Wood, Meredith Deane, Marin Hinkle, Todd Field, Jennifer Crystal, David Clennon
Network: ABC
Show Type: Drama
Show Length: 60 mins.

ONE LIFE TO LIVE
56 W. 66th St.
New York, NY 10023
Phone: ....(212) 456-7777
Production Company: ABC Television
77 W. 66th St.
New York, NY 10023
Phone: (212) 456-7777
Key Executives/Personnel:
  Jill Farren Phelps, Executive Producer
Casting Director: Julie Madison
Network: ABC
Show Type: Soap
Show Length: 60 mins.

OUT OF BOUNDS
c/o Artists Television Group, 9465 Wilshire Blvd., Ste. 212
Beverly Hills, CA 90212
Phone: ....(310) 244-2929
Production Company: Artists Television Group
9465 Wilshire Blvd., Ste. 212
Beverly Hills, CA 90212
Phone: (310) 860-8200
Key Executives/Personnel:
  Michael Wilson, Executive Producer
  Al Haymon, Executive Producer
Produced in Assn. With: United Paramount Network, (323) 956-5000
Network: UPN
Show Type: Comedy
Show Length: 30 mins.

OZ
c/o Viacom Productions, 10880 Wilshire Blvd., Ste. 1101
Los Angeles, CA 90024
Phone: ....(212) 352-1755
Production Company: Viacom Productions
10880 Wilshire Blvd., Ste. 1101
Los Angeles, CA 90024
Phone: (310) 234-5000
Key Executives/Personnel:
  Barry Levinson, Executive Producer
  Tom Fontana, Executive Producer
  Jim Finnerty, Executive Producer
Casting Director: Alexa Fogel
Produced in Assn. With: The Levinson/Fontana Company, (212) 633-0440
Cast: (Revolving Cast)
Network: HBO
Show Type: Drama
Show Length: 60 mins.

THE PARKERS
1438 N. Gower St., Courtyard Box 44
Los Angeles, CA 90028
Phone: ....(323) 860-7100
Production Company: Big Ticket Television
1438 N. Gower St., Bldg. 35, 3rd Fl., Box 45
Los Angeles, CA 90028
Phone: (323) 860-7400
Key Executives/Personnel:
  Sara Finney, Executive Producer
Casting Director: Monica Swann
Produced in Assn. With: Saradipity Productions
Cast: Countess Vaughn, Mo' Nique, Dorien Wilson, Jenna Von Oy, Yvette Wilson
Network: UPN
Show Type: Comedy
Show Length: 30 mins.

PASSIONS
4024 Radford Ave., Administration Bldg., Ste. 240
Studio City, CA 91604
Phone: ....(818) 840-4444
Production Company: NBC Studios, Outpost Farm Productions, Inc.
4024 Radford Ave.
Studio City, CA 91604
Phone: (818) 840-4444
Key Executives/Personnel:
  Lisa Hesser, Executive Producer
Casting Director: Jackie Briskey & Don Philip-Smith
Network: NBC
Show Type: Soap
Show Length: 60 mins.

TV Shows

THE PJ'S
3701 West Oak, Trailer 219
Burbank, CA 91505
Phone: ....(818) 977-2146
Production Company: Imagine Television Productions, Murphy Company, Will Vinton Studios
9465 Wilshire Blvd., 7th Fl.
Beverly Hills, CA 90212
Phone: (310) 858-2000
Key Executives/Personnel:
  Steve Tompkins, Executive Producer
  Larry Wilmore, Executive Producer
  Tony Krantz, Executive Producer
  Brian Grazer, Executive Producer
  Ron Howard, Executive Producer
  Eddie Murphy, Executive Producer
  Will Vinton, Executive Producer
  Tom Turpin, Executive Producer
Casting Director: Barbara Miller & Gayle Pillsbury
Produced in Assn. With: One Thirty Seven Productions
Cast: Eddie Murphy, Loretta Devine, James Black, Michael Paul Chan, Cassi Davis, Ja'Net DuBois, Cheryl Francis Harrington
Network: WB
Show Type: Comedy
Show Length: 30 mins.

POPULAR
500 S. Buena Vista St., Bldg. 21
Burbank, CA 91521
Phone: ....(818) 560-7565
Production Company: Touchstone Television Productions
500 S. Buena Vista St.
Burbank, CA 91521
Phone: (818) 560-1000
Key Executives/Personnel:
  Greer Shephard, Executive Producer
  Michael Robin, Executive Producer
  Ryan Murphy, Executive Producer
Casting Director: Ulrich/Dawson/Kritzer Casting
Produced in Assn. With: Shepard-Robin Productions, Ryan Murphy Productions & Roundtable Ink
Cast: Leslie Bibb, Carly Pope, Tamara Mello, Christopher Gorham, Sara Rue, Bryce Johnson, Tammy Lynn Michaels, Ron Lester, Leslie Grossman, Lisa Darr, Scott Bryce
Network: WB
Show Type: Drama
Show Length: 60 mins.

PORT CHARLES
4151 Prospect Ave., Stage 54
Los Angeles, CA 90027
Phone: ....(310) 557-5561
Production Company: ABC Television
2040 Avenue of Stars, 5th Fl.
Los Angeles, CA 90067
Phone: (310) 557-7777
Key Executives/Personnel:
  Julie Carruthers, Executive Producer
Casting Director: Mark Teschner
Network: ABC
Show Type: Soap
Show Length: 30 mins.

THE PRACTICE
1600 Rosecrans Ave., Bldg. 4B
Manhattan Beach, CA 90266
Phone: ....(310) 727-2303
Production Company: David E. Kelley Productions
1600 Rosecrans Ave., Bldg. 4B
Manhattan Beach, CA 90266
Phone: (310) 727-2200
Key Executives/Personnel:
  David E. Kelley, Executive Producer
  Bob Breech, Executive Producer
Casting Director: Janet Gilmore & Megan McConnell
Produced in Assn. With: Twentieth Century Fox Television, (310) 369-1000
Cast: Dylan McDermott, Michael Badalucco, Lisa Gay Hamilton, Steve Harris, Camryn Manheim, Marla Sokoloff, Kelli Williams, Lara Flynn Boyle, Jason Kravits
Network: ABC
Show Type: Drama
Show Length: 60 mins.

PROVIDENCE
100 Universal City Plaza, Bldg. 2128, Ste. E
Universal City, CA 91608
Phone: ....(818) 733-3400
Production Company: John Masius Productions, Inc.
100 Universal City Plaza, Bldg. 2128, Ste. E
Universal City, CA 91608
Phone: (310) 395-1572
Key Executives/Personnel:
  John Masius, Executive Producer
  Bob DeLaurentis, Executive Producer
Casting Director: Susan Bluestein
Produced in Assn. With: NBC Entertainment, Inc., (818) 840-4444
Cast: Melina Kanakaredes, Mike Farrel, Paula Cale, Seth Peterson, Concetta Tomei
Network: NBC
Syndicated: Yes
Show Type: Drama
Show Length: 60 mins.

ROSWELL
P.O. Box 900
Beverly Hills, CA 90213
Phone: ....(323) 956-1700
Production Company: Regency Television
10201 W. Pico Blvd., Bldg. 12
Los Angeles, CA 90035
Phone: (310) 369-7593
Key Executives/Personnel:
  Jason Katims, Executive Producer
  Ron Moore, Executive Producer
  Jonathan Frakes, Executive Producer
  Kevin Brown, Executive Producer
  Lisa J. Olin, Executive Producer
Casting Director: Michael Testa & Dan Shaner
Produced in Assn. With: Twentieth Century Fox Television, (310) 369-1000
Cast: Shiri Appleby, Jason Behr, Katherine Heigl, Majandra Delfino, Brendan Fehr, Colin Hanks, Emile de Ravin
Network: WB
Show Type: Sci-Fi
Show Length: 60 mins.

TV Shows

SABRINA, THE TEENAGE WITCH
5555 Melrose Ave., Modular Bldg., Ste. 100
Hollywood, CA 90038
Phone: ....(323) 956-2600
Production Company: Hartbreak Films
5555 Melrose Ave., Hart Bldg., 3rd Fl.
Los Angeles, CA 90038
Phone: (323) 956-8595
Key Executives/Personnel:
  Paula Hart, Executive Producer
  Bruce Ferber, Executive Producer
Casting Director: Rick Millikan
Cast: Melissa Joan Hart, Caroline Rhea, Beth Broderick, Nick Bakay, Elisa Donovan, Trevor Lissauer, Soleil Moon Frye, David Lascher
Network: WB
Show Type: Comedy
Show Length: 30 mins.

SEX AND THE CITY
Silver Cup Studios, 42-22, 22nd St.
Long Island City, NY 11101
Phone: ....(718) 937-4527
Production Company: Darren Star Productions,
HBO Original Programming
1100 Avenue of the Americas
New York, NY 10036
Phone: (212) 512-1000
Key Executives/Personnel:
  Darren Star, Executive Producer
  Michael Patrick King, Executive Producer
Casting Director: Jennifer McNamara
Cast: Sarah Jessica Parker, Kristin Davis, Cynthia Nixon, Kim Cattrall, Chris Noth, John Corbett, David Eigenberg, Kyle MacLachlan
Network: HBO
Show Type: Comedy
Show Length: 30 mins.

THE SIMPSONS
c/o Twentieth Century Fox Television, 10201 W. Pico Blvd.
Los Angeles, CA 90035
Phone: ....(310) 369-3959
Production Company: Twentieth Century Fox Television
10201 W. Pico Blvd.
Los Angeles, CA 90035
Phone: (310) 369-1000
Key Executives/Personnel:
  Mike Scully, Executive Producer
  James L. Brooks, Executive Producer
  Matt Groening, Executive Producer
  George Meyer, Executive Producer
  Al Jean, Executive Producer
Casting Director: Bonnie Pietila
Produced in Assn. With: Gracie Films & Film Roman, Inc.
Cast: Dan Castellaneta, Julie Kavner, Nancy Cartwright, Yeardley Smith, Hank Azaria, Harry Shearer
Network: Fox
Syndicated: Yes
Show Type: Animated Comedy
Show Length: 30 mins.

SIR ARTHUR CONAN DOYLE'S THE LOST WORLD
WRM Studios, Pacific Highway
Oxford, Queensland 4210 Australia
Phone: ....(011) + (617) 5588-6753
Production Company: Telescene Film Group, Inc.
5705 Ferrier, Ste. 200
Montreal, QC H4P 1N3 Canada
Phone: (514) 737-5512
Key Executives/Personnel:
  Robin Spry, Executive Producer
  Paul Painter, Executive Producer
  Greg Coote, Executive Producer
  Jeffrey Hayes, Executive Producer
  Leslie Belzberg, Executive Producer
  John Landis, Executive Producer
Casting Director: Maura Fay
Produced in Assn. With: Coote-Hayes Productions, (011) + (617) 5588-6753
Cast: Peter McCauley, Michael Sinelnikoff, David Orth, Rachel Blakely, William Snow, Jennifer O'Dell, Laura Vazquez, George Henare, Lani John Tupu
Syndicated: Yes
Show Type: Action
Show Length: 60 mins.

SIX FEET UNDER
1438 N. Gower St., Bldg. 48, Box 32
Los Angeles, CA 90028
Phone: ....(323) 993-7070
Production Company: HBO Independent Productions
2049 Century Park East, 42nd Fl.
Los Angeles, CA 90067
Phone: (310) 201-9300
Key Executives/Personnel:
  Alan Ball, Executive Producer
  Robert Greenblatt, Executive Producer
  David Janollari, Executive Producer
Casting Director: Junie Lowry-Johnson & Libby Goldstein
Produced in Assn. With: Greenblatt-Janollari Studio, (310) 860-3600
Cast: Peter Krause, Michael Hall, Frances Conroy, Lauren Ambrose, Rachel Griffiths, Freddy Rodriguez, Matthew St. Patrick
Network: HBO
Show Type: Comedy
Show Length: 60 mins.

THE SOPRANOS
Silver Cup Studios, 42-22, 22nd St.
Long Island City, NY 11101
Phone: ....(718) 906-2323
Production Company: HBO Independent Productions
1100 Avenue of the Americas, 10th Fl.
New York, NY 10036
Phone: (212) 512-1000
Key Executives/Personnel:
  David Chase, Executive Producer
Casting Director: Shelia Jaffe & Georgianne Walken
Cast: James Gandolfini, Edie Falco, Nancy Marchand, Lorraine Bracco, Dominic Chianese, Michael Imperioli, Jamie-Lynn Sigler, Robert Iler, Tony Sirico, Steve Van Zandt, Vincent Pastore, Aida Turturro, Drea de Matteo, David Proval
Network: HBO
Show Type: Drama
Show Length: 60 mins.

TV Shows

SOUL FOOD
40 Carl-Hall Rd., Bldg. 151, 2nd Fl.
Toronto, ON M3K 2B8 Canada
Phone: ....(416) 630-3828
Production Company: Edmonds Entertainment, State Street Pictures
40 Carl-Hall Rd., Bldg. 151, 2nd Fl.
Toronto, ON M3K 2B8 Canada
Phone: (416) 630-3825
Key Executives/Personnel:
 Kenneth "Babyface" Edmonds, Executive Producer
 Tracey Edmonds, Executive Producer
 George Tillman, Executive Producer
 Robert Teitel, Executive Producer
 Kevin Arkadie, Executive Producer
Casting Director: Monica Swann & Clare Walker
Produced in Assn. With: Paramount Network Television, (323) 956-5000
Cast: Nicole Ari Parker, Vanessa Williams, Melinda Williams, Darrin Henson, Rockmond Dunbar, Aaron Meeks
Network: Showtime
Show Type: Drama
Show Length: 60 mins.

SOUTH PARK
2049 Century Park East, Ste. 9340
Los Angeles, CA 90067
Phone: ....(310) 201-9515
Production Company: Comedy Central
2049 Century Park East, Ste. 2295
Los Angeles, CA 90067
Key Executives/Personnel:
 Trey Parker, Executive Producer
 Matt Stone, Executive Producer
 Anne Garefino, Executive Producer
 Deborah Liebling, Executive Producer
Cast: Matt Stone, Trey Parker
Network: Comedy Central
Show Type: Animated Comedy
Show Length: 30 mins.

SPIN CITY
100 Universal City Plaza, Bldg. 10
Universal City, CA 91608
Phone: ....(818) 655-5335
Production Company: DreamWorks Television
100 Universal City Plaza, Bldg. 10
Universal City, CA 91608
Phone: (818) 695-5000
Key Executives/Personnel:
 Michael J. Fox, Executive Producer
 David Rosenthal, Executive Producer
Casting Director: Allison Jones
Produced in Assn. With: UBU Productions & Lottery Hill Entertainment
Cast: Charlie Sheen, Richard Kind, Heather Locklear, Alan Ruck, Michael Boatman, Barry Bostwick, Lana Parrilla
Network: ABC
Show Type: Comedy
Show Length: 30 mins.

STAR TREK: VOYAGER
5555 Melrose Ave., Cooper Bldg., Ste. 205
Hollywood, CA 90038
Phone: ....(323) 956-5951
Production Company: Paramount Network Television
5555 Melrose Ave.
Los Angeles, CA 90038
Phone: (323) 956-5000
Key Executives/Personnel:
 Rick Berman, Executive Producer
 Brannon Braga, Executive Producer
 Ken Biller, Executive Producer
Casting Director: Junie Lowry-Johnson & Ron Surma
Cast: Kate Mulgrew, Robert Beltran, Roxanne Dawson, Robert Duncan McNeill, Ethan Phillips, Robert Picardo, Tim Russ, Garrett Wang, Jeri Ryan
Network: UPN
Show Type: Drama
Show Length: 60 mins.

STARGATE SG-1
2400 Boundary Rd.
Burnaby, BC V5M 3Z3 Canada
Phone: ....(604) 292-8500
Production Company: Stargate Production IV Limited Partnership
2400 Boundary Rd.
Burnaby, BC V5M 3Z3 Canada
Phone: (604) 292-8500
Key Executives/Personnel:
 Brad Wright, Executive Producer
 Richard Dean Anderson, Executive Producer
 Michael Greenberg, Executive Producer
 Robert Cooper, Executive Producer
Casting Director: Paul Webber (US) & Carol Kelsay (Canada)
Produced in Assn. With: MGM Television Distribution & Showtime Network, Inc.
Cast: Richard Dean Anderson, Amanda Tapping, Michael Shanks, Christopher Judge, Don S. Davis
Network: Showtime
Show Type: Sci-Fi
Show Length: 60 mins.

THE STEVE HARVEY SHOW
100 Universal City Plaza, Bldg. 3213
Universal City, CA 91608
Phone: ....(818) 733-2875
Production Company: Universal Studios, Winifred Harvey Productions, Stan Lathan Television
100 Universal City Plaza
Universal City, CA 91608
Phone: (818) 777-1000
Key Executives/Personnel:
 Winifred Hervey, Executive Producer
 Stan Latham, Executive Producer
Casting Director: Monica Swann
Produced in Assn. With: Columbia Tristar Television, (310) 202-1234
Cast: Steve Harvey, Merlin Santana, William Lee Scott, Terri J. Vangh, Wendy Raquel Robinson, Lori Beth Denberg, Cedric "The Entertainer"
Network: USA
Show Type: Comedy
Show Length: 30 mins.

TV Shows

THAT 70'S SHOW
4024 Radford Ave., Bldg. 1, Ste. 111
Studio City, CA 91604
Phone: ....(818) 655-5161
Production Company: Carsey-Werner Productions
4024 Radford Ave., Bldg. 3
Studio City, CA 91604
Phone: (818) 655-5598
Key Executives/Personnel:
  Marcy Carsey, Executive Producer
  Tom Werner, Executive Producer
  Caryn Mandabach, Executive Producer
  Bonnie Turner, Executive Producer
  Terry Turner, Executive Producer
  Mark Brazil, Executive Producer
  Joshua Sternin, Executive Producer
Casting Director: Cecily Adams
Cast: Topher Grace, Laura Prepon, Ashton Kutcher, Mila Kunis, Wilmer Valderrama, Kurtwood Smith, Debra Jo Rupp, Don Stark, Tanya Roberts, Lisa Robin Kelley, Danny Masterson
Network: Fox
Show Type: Comedy
Show Length: 30 mins.

THAT'S LIFE
c/o Paramount Pictures, 5555 Melrose Ave., Bungalow 6
Los Angeles, CA 90038
Phone: ....(323) 956-8865
Production Company: Paramount Network Television
5555 Melrose Ave.
Los Angeles, CA 90038
Phone: (323) 956-5000
Key Executives/Personnel:
  Anita Addison, Executive Producer
  Maddy Horne, Executive Producer
  Frank Renzulli, Executive Producer
Casting Director: Nan Dutton
Cast: Heather Paige Kent, Ellen Burstyn, Paul Sorvino, Debi Mazar, Kristen Bauer, Kevin Dillon, Peter Firth
Network: CBS
Show Type: Drama
Show Length: 60 mins.

THIRD WATCH
196 Diamond St., 2nd Fl.
Brooklyn, NY 11222
Phone: ....(718) 609-9616
Production Company: John Wells Productions
4000 Warner Blvd., Bldg. 138, Rm. 1106
Burbank, CA 91522
Phone: (818) 954-1687
Key Executives/Personnel:
  John Wells, Executive Producer
  Christopher Chulack, Executive Producer
Casting Director: Jeff Block & John Frank Levey
Produced in Assn. With: Warner Bros. Television, (818) 954-6000
Cast: Michael Beach, Coby Bell, Bobby Cannavale, Eddie Cibrian, Molly Price, Kim Raver, Anthony Ruivivar, Skipp Sudduth, Jason Wiles
Network: NBC
Show Type: Drama
Show Length: 60 mins.

TITUS
4024 Radford Ave., Norvet Bldg., Ste. 301
Studio City, CA 91604
Phone: ....(818) 655-4030
Production Company: Twentieth Century Fox Television
10201 W. Pico Blvd.
Los Angeles, CA 90035
Phone: (310) 369-1000
Key Executives/Personnel:
  Brian Hargrove, Executive Producer
  Jack Kenny, Executive Producer
  Christopher Titus, Executive Producer
Casting Director: Sheila Guthrie
Produced in Assn. With: Kenny & Hargrove & Deranged Entertainment
Cast: Christopher Titus, Cynthia Watros, Zack Ward, David Shatraw, Stacey Keach
Network: Fox
Show Type: Comedy
Show Length: 30 mins.

TOUCHED BY AN ANGEL
12711 Ventura Blvd., Ste. 210
Studio City, CA 91604
Phone: ....(818) 508-3420
Production Company: CBS Productions
7800 Beverly Blvd.
Los Angeles, CA 90036
Phone: (323) 575-2345
Key Executives/Personnel:
  Martha Williamson, Executive Producer
Casting Director: David Giella
Produced in Assn. With: Moon Water Productions
Cast: Roma Downey, Della Reese, John Dye
Network: CBS
Show Type: Drama
Show Length: 60 mins.

THE TROUBLE WITH NORMAL
5555 Melrose Ave., Balaban Bldg., Ste. B
Los Angeles, CA 90035
Phone: ....(323) 956-4200
Production Company: Garfield Grove Productions
5555 Melrose Ave., Balaban Bldg., Ste. B
Los Angeles, CA 90035
Phone: (323) 956-4260
Key Executives/Personnel:
  Victor Fresco, Executive Producer
Casting Director: Julie Mossberg & Jill Anthony
Produced in Assn. With: Paramount Network Television, (323) 956-5000
Cast: David Krumholtz, Jon Cryer, Brad Raider, Paget Brewster, Larry Joe Campbell
Network: ABC
Show Type: Comedy
Show Length: 30 mins.

TV Shows

TWO GUYS AND A GIRL
4024 Radford Ave., Editorial Bldg., Rm. 1
Studio City, CA 91604
Phone: ....(818) 655-5008
Production Company: InFront Productions
10201 W. Pico Blvd., Bldg. 3 North
Los Angeles, CA 90035
Phone: (310) 369-5890
Key Executives/Personnel:
  Kevin Abbott, Executive Producer
  Danny Jacobson, Executive Producer
Casting Director: Sally Stiner & Barbie Block
Produced in Assn. With: Twentieth Century Fox Television, (310) 369-1000
Cast: Traylor Howard, Ryan Reynolds, Richard Ruccolo, Nathan Fillion, Suzanne Cryer
Network: ABC
Show Type: Comedy
Show Length: 30 mins.

WALKER: TEXAS RANGER
11969 Ventura Blvd., 3rd Fl.
Studio City, CA 91604
Phone: ....(818) 752-9292
Production Company: Amadea Film Productions, Norris Brothers Entertainment
11969 Ventura Blvd., 3rd Fl.
Studio City, CA 91604
Phone: (818) 752-9292
Key Executives/Personnel:
  Aaron Norris, Executive Producer
  Chuck Norris, Executive Producer
  Gordon Dawson, Executive Producer
Casting Director: Shana Landsburg
Produced in Assn. With: CBS Productions, (323) 575-2345
Cast: Chuck Norris, Clarence Gilyard, Sheree J. Wilson, Judson Mills, Nia Peeples, Noble Willingham
Network: CBS
Show Type: Drama
Show Length: 60 mins.

WELCOME TO NEW YORK
3402 Star Ave., 1st Fl.
Long Island City, NY 11101
Phone: ....(718) 906-3100
Production Company: Studios USA
8800 Sunset Blvd.
West Hollywood, CA 90069
Phone: (310) 360-2300
Key Executives/Personnel:
  Barbara Wallace, Executive Producer
  Tom Wolfe, Executive Producer
  Eric Gilliland, Executive Producer
  Christine Baranski, Executive Producer
Casting Director: Mark Sacks
Produced in Assn. With: Worldwide Pants & CBS Productions, (323) 575-2345
Cast: Christine Baranski, Jim Gaffigan, Rocky Caroll, Sara Gilbert, Mary Birdsong, Anthony De Sando
Network: CBS
Show Type: Comedy
Show Length: 30 mins.

THE WEST WING
4000 Warner Blvd., Trailer 8
Burbank, CA 91522
Phone: ....(818) 954-7303
Production Company: John Wells Productions
4000 Warner Blvd., Bldg. 138, Rm. 1106
Burbank, CA 91522
Phone: (818) 954-1687
Key Executives/Personnel:
  Aaron Sorkin, Executive Producer
  Thomas Schlamme, Executive Producer
  John Wells, Executive Producer
Casting Director: Barbara Miller, John Frank Levey & Kevin Scott
Produced in Assn. With: Warner Bros. Television, (818) 954-6000
Cast: Rob Lowe, Dule Hill, Allison Janney, Janal Moloney, Richard Schiff, John Spencer, Bradley Whitford, Martin Sheen
Network: NBC
Show Type: Drama
Show Length: 60 mins.

WHOSE LINE IS IT ANYWAY?
5300 Melrose Ave., Ste. 231 E
Los Angeles, CA 90038
Phone: ....(323) 960-3447
Production Company: Riverside Productions
5300 Melrose Ave., Ste. 231 E
Los Angeles, CA 90038
Phone: (323) 960-3447
Key Executives/Personnel:
  Denise O'Donoghue, Executive Producer
  Jim Mulville, Executive Producer
  Dan Patterson, Executive Producer
  Drew Carey, Executive Producer
  Ryan Stiles, Executive Producer
Produced in Assn. With: Hat Trick Productions & Warner Bros. Television
Cast: Drew Carey, Ryan Stiles, Colin Mochrio, Wayne Brady
Network: ABC
Show Type: Comedy
Show Length: 60 mins.

WILL & GRACE
4024 Radford Ave., Bungalow 3
Studio City, CA 91604
Phone: ....(818) 655-5642
Production Company: Komut Entertainment
4024 Radford Ave., Bungalow 3
Studio City, CA 91604
Phone: (818) 655-5563
Key Executives/Personnel:
  David Kohan, Executive Producer
  Max Mutchnick, Executive Producer
  James Burrows, Executive Producer
Casting Director: Tracy Lilienfield
Produced in Assn. With: Three Sisters Entertainment & NBC Entertainment, Inc.
Cast: Eric McCormack, Debra Messing, Megan Mullaly, Sean P. Hayes
Network: NBC
Show Type: Comedy
Show Length: 30 mins.

TV Shows

THE X-FILES
P.O. Box 900
Beverly Hills, CA 90213
Phone: ....(310) 369-1130
Production Company: Twentieth Century Fox Television
10201 W. Pico Blvd.
Los Angeles, CA 90035
Phone: (310) 369-1000
Key Executives/Personnel:
    Chris Carter, Executive Producer
    Frank Spotnitz, Executive Producer
    Vince Gilligan, Executive Producer
Casting Director: Rick Millikan
Produced in Assn. With: Ten Thirteen Productions,
    (310) 369-1130
Cast: David Duchovny, Gillian Anderson, Robert Patrick, Mitch Pileggi
Network: Fox
Show Type: Drama
Show Length: 60 mins.

YES, DEAR
4024 Radford Ave., Bldg. 7, 2nd Fl.
Studio City, CA 91604
Phone: ....(818) 655-5121
Production Company: Twentieth Century Fox Television
10201 W. Pico Blvd.
Los Angeles, CA 90035
Phone: (310) 369-1000
Key Executives/Personnel:
    Alan Kirschenbaum, Executive Producer
    Greg Garcia, Executive Producer
Casting Director: Dara Waite
Produced in Assn. With: CBS Productions, (323) 575-2345
Cast: Anthony Clark, Mike O'Malley, Jean Louisa Kelly, Liza Snyder
Network: CBS
Show Type: Comedy
Show Length: 30 mins.

THE YOUNG AND THE RESTLESS
7800 Beverly Blvd., Ste. 3305
Los Angeles, CA 90036
Phone: ....(323) 575-2532
Production Company: Columbia TriStar Television
9336 W. Washington Blvd.
Culver City, CA 90232
Phone: (310) 202-1234
Key Executives/Personnel:
    William J. Bell, Executive Producer
    Edward Scott, Executive Producer
Casting Director: Marnie Saitta
Produced in Assn. With: Bell Dramatic Serial Co. & Corday Productions
Network: CBS
Show Type: Soap
Show Length: 60 mins.

Studio & Network Quick Reference

A&E
235 E. 45th St.
New York, NY 10017
Ph: (212) 210-1400
www.aande.com

ABC, Inc./ABC Network Television
ABC Entertainment Television Group (LA)
2040 Avenue of the Stars
Los Angeles, CA 90067
Ph: (310) 557-7777
Ph2: (212) 456-7777
www.abc.go.com

ABC Entertainment Television Group (NY)
77 West 66th St.
New York, NY 10023
Ph: (212) 456-7777
Ph2: (310) 557-7777
www.abc.go.com

American Movie Classics/Romance Channel
1111 Stewart Ave.
Bethpage, NY 11714
Ph: (516) 803-4300
www.romanceclassics.com

Black Entertainment Television (BET)
811 S. San Fernando Rd.
Burbank, CA 91502
Ph: (818) 566-9948
Ph2: (202) 608-2000
www.bet.com

The Buena Vista Motion Pictures Group
500 South Buena Vista St.
Burbank, CA 91521
Ph: (818) 560-1000
www.buenavista.com

Buena Vista Television
500 S. Buena Vista St., Team Disney Bldg.
Burbank, CA 91521
Ph: (818) 560-5000
www.bvtv.com

CBS Entertainment (LA)
7800 Beverly Blvd.
Los Angeles, CA 90036
Ph: (323) 575-2345
www.cbs.com

CBS Enterprises
CBS Network Television (NY)
51 West 52nd St.
New York, NY 10019
Ph: (212) 975-4321
www.cbs.com

Columbia Pictures/Columbia Tristar Motion Picture Group
10202 W. Washington Blvd.
Culver City, CA 90232
Ph: (310) 244-4000
www.spe.sony.com

Columbia Tristar Television
9336 W. Washington Blvd.
Culver City, CA 90232
Ph: (310) 202-1234
www.spe.sony.com

Comedy Central (LA)
2049 Century Park East, Ste. 2295
Los Angeles, CA 90067
Ph: (310) 201-9515
www.comedycentral.com

Comedy Central (NY)
1775 Broadway
New York, NY 10019
Ph: (212) 767-8600
www.comedycentral.com

Discovery Networks/Discovery Communications, Inc.
7700 Wisconsin Ave.
Bethesda, MD 20814
Ph: (301) 986-1999
www.discovery.com

The Disney Channel
3800 W. Alameda Ave.
Burbank, CA 91505
Ph: (818) 569-7500
www.disneychannel.com

The Walt Disney Company
Walt Disney Pictures/Touchstone Pictures
500 S. Buena Vista St.
Burbank, CA 91521
Ph: (818) 560-1000
www.disney.com

DreamWorks SKG
100 Universal Plaza, Bldg.10
Universal City, CA 91608
Ph: (818) 733-7000
www.dreamworks.com

E! Entertainment Television (LA)
5750 Wilshire Blvd.
Los Angeles, CA 90036
Ph: (323) 954-2400
www.eonline.com

E! Entertainment Television (NY)
11 W 42nd St., 19th Fl.
New York, NY 10036
Ph: (212) 852-5100
www.eonline.com

Fox Broadcasting Company
10201 W. Pico Blvd.
Los Angeles, CA 90035
Ph: (310) 369-1000
www.fox.com

Fox Family Channel
10960 Wilshire Blvd.
Los Angeles, CA 90024
Ph: (310) 235-4700
www.foxfamilychannel.com

Studio & Network Quick Reference

Fox Kids Network
10960 Wilshire Blvd.
Los Angeles, CA 90024
Ph: (310) 235-9600
www.foxkids.com

Fox Searchlight Pictures
10201 W. Pico Blvd., Bldg. 38
Los Angeles, CA 90035
Ph: (310) 369-4402
www.foxsearchlight.com

Fox Television Studios
10201 W. Pico Blvd., Bldg. 41
Los Angeles, CA 90035
Ph: (310) 369-1000
www.fox.com

FX Networks, LLC
1440 S. Sepulveda Blvd.
Los Angeles, CA 90025
Ph: (310) 444-8123
www.fxnetworks.com

HBO
HBO Original Programming
HBO Independent Productions/Downtown Productions
1100 Avenue of the Americas
New York, NY 10036
Ph: (212) 512-1000
www.hbo.com

HBO Films
2049 Century Park East, Ste. 3600
Los Angeles, CA 90067
Ph: (310) 201-9200
www.hbo.com

The History Channel
235 E. 45th St.
New York, NY 10017
Ph.: (212) 210-1400
www.historychannel.com

Lifetime Television (LA)
2049 Century Park East, Ste. 840
Los Angeles, CA 90067
Ph: (310) 556-7500
www.lifetimetv.com

Lifetime Television (NY)
309 W. 49th St.
New York, NY 10019
Ph: (212) 424-7000
www.lifetimetv.com

Metro-Goldwyn-Mayer Studios, Inc.
Metro-Goldwyn-Mayer Worldwide TV
2500 Broadway
Santa Monica, CA 90404
Ph: (310) 449-3000
www.mgm.com

MTV Networks (LA)
2600 Colorado Ave.
Santa Monica, CA 90404
Ph: (310) 752-8000
www.mtv.com

MTV Networks (NY)
1515 Broadway Ave.
New York, NY 10036
Ph: (212) 258-8000
www.mtv.com

NBC
30 Rockefeller Plaza
New York, NY 10112
Ph: (212) 664-4444
www.nbc.com

NBC Entertainment (LA)
3000 W. Alameda Ave.
Burbank, CA 91523
Ph: (818) 840-4444
www.nbc.com

Nickelodeon/Nick At Night
1515 Broadway, 38th Fl.
New York, NY 10036
Ph: (212) 258-7500
www.nick.com

Paramount Classics
Paramount Pictures-Motion Picture Group
Paramount Television Group
5555 Melrose Ave.
Los Angeles, CA 90038
Ph: (323) 956-5000
www.paramount.com

PAX TV/Paxon Communications (HQ)
Clearwater Park Rd.
West Palm Beach, FL 33401
Ph: (516) 659-4122
www.pax.net

PAX TV/Paxon Communications (LA)
10880 Wilshire Blvd., Ste. 1200
Los Angeles, CA 90024
Ph: (310) 234-2200
www.pax.net

PAX TV/Paxon Communications (NY)
1330 Avenue of the Americas, 32nd Fl.
New York, NY 10019
Ph: (212) 757-3100
www.pax.net

PBS
1320 Braddock Place
Alexandria, VA 22314
Ph: (703) 739-5000
Fax: (703) 739-0775
www.pbs.org

Showtime Networks, Inc. (LA)
10880 Wilshire Blvd., Ste. 1600
Los Angeles, CA 90024
Ph: (310) 234-5200
www.showtimeonline.com

Showtime Networks, Inc. (NY)
1633 Broadway
New York, NY 10019
Ph: (212) 708-1600
www.showtimeonline.com

Studio & Network Quick Reference

Sony Pictures Classics
550 Madison Ave.
New York, NY 10022
Ph: (212) 833-8833
www.spe.sony.com/classics/home

Sony Pictures Entertainment
10202 W. Washington Blvd.
Culver City, CA 90232
Ph: (310) 244-4000
www.spe.sony.com

Starz Encore Entertainment Group
5445 DTC Pkwy., Ste. 600
Englewood, CO 80111
Ph: (303) 771-7700
Ph2: (310) 550-7172
www.encoremedia.com

TBS Superstation (HQ)
1050 Techwood Dr., NW
Atlanta, GA 30318
Ph: (404) 827-1717
www.tbssuperstation@turner.com

TBS Superstation (LA)
1888 Century Park East, 12th Fl.
Los Angeles, CA 90067
Ph: (310) 788-6800
www.tbssuperstation@turner.com

TLC
7700 Wisconsin Ave.
Bethesda, MD 20814
Ph: (301) 986-0444
Ph2: (888) 404-5969
www.tlc.discovery.com

Turner Entertainment Group
1050 Techwood Dr., NW
Atlanta, GA 30318
Ph: (404) 827-1500
www.turner.com

Turner Network Television (TNT)
1888 Century Park East, 12th Fl.
Los Angeles, CA 90067
Ph: (310) 551-6300
www.turner.com

Twentieth Century Fox
Twentieth Century Fox Television
10201 W. Pico Blvd.
Los Angeles, CA 90035
Ph: (310) 369-1000
www.fox.com

UPN (United Paramount Network)
11800 Wilshire Blvd.
Los Angeles, CA 90025
Ph: (310) 575-7000
www.upn.com

Universal Pictures
Universal Studios, Inc.
100 Universal City Plaza
Universal City, CA 91608
Ph: (818) 777-1000
www.universalstudios.com

Universal Television & Networks Group
100 Universal City Plaza, Bldg. 9128-02
Universal City, CA 91608
(818) 777-5300
www.universalstudios.com

USA Network (LA)
8800 Sunset Blvd., 4th Fl.
W. Hollywood, CA 90069
Ph: (310) 360-2300
www.usanetwork.com

USA Network (NY)
1230 Avenue of the Americas
New York, NY 10020
Ph: (212) 413-5000
www.usanetwork.com

VH1 (LA)
2600 Colorado Ave.
Santa Monica, CA 90404
Ph: (310) 752-8000
www.vh1.com

VH1 (NY)
1515 Broadway
New York, NY 10036
Ph: (212) 846-7800
www.vh1.com

Viacom Entertainment Group
5555 Melrose Ave.
Los Angeles, CA 90038
Ph: (323) 956-5000
www.viacom.com

Viacom Productions
10880 Wilshire Blvd., Ste. 1101
Los Angeles, CA 90024
Ph: (310) 234-5000
www.viacom.com

Warner Bros.
Warner Bros. Telepictures Production
4000 Warner Blvd.
Burbank, CA 91522
Ph: (818) 954-6000
www.warnerbros.com

Warner Bros. International Television
4000 W. Alameda Blvd., 6th Fl.
Burbank, CA 91505
Ph: (818) 954-6012
www.warnerbros.com

Warner Bros. Television
300 Television Plaza
Burbank, CA 91505
Ph: (818) 954-6000
www.warnerbros.com

WB Television Network (LA)
4000 Warner Blvd.
Burbank, CA 91522
Ph: (818) 954-6000
www.thewb.com

WB Television Network (NY)
1325 Avenue of the Americas
New York, NY 10019
Ph: (212) 636-5000
www.thewb.com

Notes

Trade Associations/Unions/Guilds

ACADEMY OF MOTION PICTURE ARTS & SCIENCES (AMPAS)
8949 Wilshire Blvd.
Beverly Hills, CA 90211
Phone: ....(310) 247-3000
Fax: ....(310) 859-9351
www.oscars.org

ACADEMY OF TELEVISION ARTS & SCIENCES (ATAS)
5220 Lankershim Blvd., 2nd Fl.
North Hollywood, CA 91601
Phone: ....(818) 754-2800
Fax: ....(818) 761-2827
www.emmys.org

ACTORS EQUITY ASSOCIATION (AEA)
5757 Wilshire Blvd., Ste. 1
Los Angeles, CA 90036
Phone: ....(323) 634-1750
Fax: ....(323) 634-1777
www.actorsequity.org

ADVERTISING CLUB OF LOS ANGELES (ACLA)
6404 Wilshire Blvd., Ste. 1111
Los Angeles, CA 90048
Phone: ....(323) 782-1044
Fax: ....(323) 655-8627
www.la-adclub.com
acla@goldenmanagement.com

AMERICAN ASSOCIATION OF PRODUCERS (AAP)
15030 Ventura Blvd., PMB 675
Sherman Oaks, CA 91403
Phone: ....(818) 503-6102
Fax: ....(818) 981-6491
www.tvproducers.org
info@tvproducers.org

AMERICAN CINEMATHEQUE
1800 N. Highland Ave., Ste. 717
Los Angeles, CA 90028
Phone: ....(323) 461-2020
....(323) 466-FILM
Fax: ....(323) 461-9737
www.americancinematheque.com
amcin@msn.com

AMERICAN FEDERATION OF MUSICIANS (AFM)
817 N. Vine St.
Los Angeles, CA 90038
Phone: ....(323) 462-2161
Fax: ....(323) 461-3090
www.afm.org
local47@afm.org

AMERICAN FEDERATION OF TV & RADIO ARTISTS (AFTRA)
5757 Wilshire Blvd., Ste. 900
Los Angeles, CA 90036
Phone: ....(323) 634-8100
Fax: ....(323) 634-8246
www.aftra.org

AMERICAN FILM INSTITUTE (AFI)
2021 N. Western Ave.
Los Angeles, CA 90027
Phone: ....(323) 856-7600
Fax: ....(323) 467-4578
www.afionline.org

AMERICAN GUILD OF MUSICAL ARTISTS (AGMA)
1727 Broadway
New York, NY 10019
Phone: ....(212) 265-3687
Fax: ....(212) 262-9088
www.agmanatl.com
agma@agmanatl.com

AMERICAN GUILD OF VARIETY ARTISTS (AGVA)
184 Fifth Ave., 6th Fl.
New York, NY 10010
Phone: ....(212) 675-1003

AMERICAN SOCIETY OF CINEMATOGRAPHERS (ASC)
1782 N. Orange Dr.
Hollywood, CA 90028
Phone: ....(323) 969-4333
Fax: ....(323) 882-6391
www.cinematographer.com
office@theasc.com

AMERICAN SOCIETY OF COMPOSERS, AUTHORS & PUBLISHERS (ASCAP)
7920 Sunset Blvd., Ste. 300
Los Angeles, CA 90046
Phone: ....(323) 883-1000
Fax: ....(323) 883-1049
www.ascap.com
info@ascap.com

ASSOCIATION OF INDEPENDENT COMMERCIAL PRODUCERS (AICP)
650 N. Bronson Ave., Ste. 223B
Los Angeles, CA 90004
Phone: ....(323) 960-4763
Fax: ....(323) 960-4766
www.aicp.com

ASSOCIATION OF INDEPENDENT VIDEO & FILMMAKERS (AIVF)
304 Hudson St., 6th Fl.
New York, NY 10013
Phone: ....(212) 807-1400
Fax: ....(212) 463-8519
www.aivf.org

BRITISH ACADEMY OF FILM & TELEVISION ARTS (BAFTA)
195 Piccadilly,
London W1V OLN England
Phone: ....(011) 44 20 7734 0022
Fax: ....(011) 44 20 7734 1792
www.bafta.org

BROADCAST MUSIC, INC. (BMI)
8730 Sunset Blvd., 3rd Fl. West
Los Angeles, CA 90069
Phone: ....(310) 659-9109
Fax: ....(310) 657-6947
www.bmi.com
writerpublisher@bmi.com

CASTING SOCIETY OF AMERICA (CSA)
606 N. Larchmont Blvd., Ste. 4B
Los Angeles, CA 90004
Phone: ....(323) 463-1925
www.castingsociety.com

Trade Associations/Unions/Guilds

**COMMERCIAL CASTING
DIRECTORS ASSOCIATION (CCDA)**
c/o Big House Studios, 4420 Lankershim Blvd.
North Hollywood, CA 91602
Phone: ....(818) 752-7100
Fax: ....(818) 752-7101

CREATIVE WOMEN OF THE ARTS (CWA)
171 Pier Ave., Ste. 249
Santa Monica, CA 90405
Phone: ....(323) 856-6200
www.cwa-la.org

CTAM
201 N. Union St., Ste. 440
Alexandria, VA 22314
Phone: ....(703) 549-4200
Fax: ....(703) 684-1167
www.ctam.com
ctam@ctam.com

DIRECTORS GUILD OF AMERICA (DGA)
7920 Sunset Blvd.
Los Angeles, CA 90046
Phone: ....(310) 289-5333
Fax: ....(310) 289-2029
www.dga.org

INDEPENDENT FEATURE PROJECT WEST (IFPw)
1964 Westwood Blvd., Ste. 205
Los Angeles, CA 90025
Phone: ....(310) 475-4379
....(310) 475-0840
Fax: ....(310) 441-5676
www.ifp.org
dearifpwest@earthlink.net

**INTERNATIONAL ALLIANCE OF THEATRICAL
STAGE EMPLOYEES (IATSE)**
1515 Broadway, Ste. 601
New York, NY 10036
Phone: ....(212) 730-1770
Fax: ....(212) 730-7809
www.iatse.com

**INTERNATIONAL ASSOCIATION OF
AMUSEMENT PARKS AND ATTRACTIONS (IAAPA)**
1448 Duke St.
Alexandria, VA 22314
Phone: ....(703) 836-4800
....(703) 836-9678
Fax: ....(703) 836-4801
www.iaapa.org
mparsont@iaapa.org

**INTERNATIONAL ASSOCIATION OF TELEVISION PROGRAM
EXECUTIVES (NATPE)**
2425 Olympic Blvd., Ste. 600E
Santa Monica, CA 90404
Phone: ....(310) 453-4440
Fax: ....(310) 453-5258
www.natpe.com

JAPANESE US PRODUCERS ASSOCIATION (JUSPA)
6630 Sunset Blvd.
Los Angeles, CA 90028
Phone: ....(213) 463-9929
Fax: ....(213) 464-8048
www.juspa.org

MEDIA COMMUNICATIONS ASSOCIATION INTERNATIONAL
9202 N. Meridan St., Ste. 200
Indianapolis, IN 46260
Phone: ....(317) 816-6269
Fax: ....(800) 801-8926
www.itva.com

**MOTION PICTURE ASSOCIATION OF
AMERICA (MPAA)**
15503 Ventura Blvd.
Encino, CA 91436
Phone: ....(818) 995-6600
Fax: ....(818) 382-1799
www.mpaa.org

MOTION PICTURE EDITORS GUILD (IA LOCAL 700)
7715 Sunset Blvd., Ste 200
Los Angeles, CA 90046
Phone: ....(323) 876-4770
Fax: ....(323) 876-0861
www.editorsguild.com
mail@editorsguild.com

**MOTION PICTURE SCREEN
CARTOONISTS (IA LOCAL 839)**
4729 Lankershim Blvd.
North Hollywood, CA 91602
Phone: ....(818) 766-7151
Fax: ....(818) 506-4805
www.mpsc839.org/mpsc839
mpsc839@primenet.com

MUSIC VIDEO PRODUCERS ASSOCIATION
940 N. Orange Dr., Ste. 104
Los Angeles, CA 90038
Phone: ....(323) 469-9494
Fax: ....(323) 469-9445
www.mvpa.com

Trade Associations/Unions/Guilds

**NATIONAL ACADEMY OF
RECORDING ARTS & SCIENCES (NARAS)**
3402 Pico Blvd.
Santa Monica, CA 90405
Phone: ....(310) 392-3777
Fax: ....(310) 392-2778
www.grammys.com

**NATIONAL CONFERENCE OF
PERSONAL MANAGERS (NCOPN)**
964 Second Ave.
New York, NY 10022
Phone: ....(212) 421-2670
www.ncopm.com

PRODUCERS GUILD OF AMERICA (PGA)
6363 Sunset Blvd., 9th Fl.
Los Angeles, CA 90028
Phone: ....(323) 960-2590
Fax: ....(323) 960-2591
www.producersguild.com
thepga@pacbell.net

PROMAX & BDA
2029 Century Park East, Ste. 555
Los Angeles, CA 90067
Phone: ....(310) 788-7600
Fax: ....(310) 788-7616
www.promax.org

SCREEN ACTORS GUILD (SAG)
5757 Wilshire Blvd.
Los Angeles, CA 90036
Phone: ....(323) 954-1600
Fax: ....(323) 549-6656
www.sag.org

THE SOCIETY OF STAGE DIRECTORS & CHOREOGRAPHERS (SSDC)
1501 Broadway, Ste. 1701
New York, NY 10036
Phone: ....(212) 391-1070
Fax: ....(212) 302-6195
www.ssdc.org

SUNDANCE INSTITUTE
8857 W. Olympic Blvd.
Beverly Hills, CA 90211
Phone: ....(310) 360-1981
Fax: ....(310) 360-1969
www.sundance.org
la@sundance.org
Additional Info: P.O. Box 3630, Salt Lake City, UT 84110

THEMED ENTERTAINMENT ASSOCIATION (TEA)
P.O. Box 11148
Burbank, CA 91510
Phone: ....(818) 843-8497
Fax: ....(818) 843-8477
www.themeit.com

WOMEN IN ANIMATION (WIA)
P.O. Box 17706
Encino, CA 91416
Phone: ....(818) 759-9596
www.womeninanimation.org

WOMEN IN FILM (WIF)
6464 Sunset Blvd., Ste. 1080
Hollywood, CA 90028
Phone: ....(323) 463-6040
Fax: ....(323) 463-0963
www.wif.org

WRITERS GUILD OF AMERICA WEST (WGAW)
7000 W. Third St.
Los Angeles, CA 90048
Phone: ....(323) 951-4000
Fax: ....(323) 782-4800
www.wga.org

Notes

Awards/Expos/Festivals

Acadamy Awards
(310) 247-3000
www.oscar.com
March 25

AFI Los Angeles International Film Festival
(323) 856-7707
www.afifest.com
October TBA

AICP Show
(323) 960-4763
www.aicp.com
July TBA

Annie Awards
(818) 842-8330
www.asifa-hollywood.org
November TBA

Austin Film Festival
(512) 478-4795
October 4-12
www.austinfilmfestival.org

Berlin International Film Festival
(49 30) 25 9 20202
www.berlinale.de
February 7-18

Billboard Music Video Awards
(646) 654-5500
www.billboard.com
November TBA

Cannes Film Festival
(33) 1 4561 6600
www.cannes-fest.com
May 9-20

Chicago International Childrens Film Festival
(773) 281-9075
www.cicff.org
October TBA

Chicago International Film Festival
(312) 425-9400
www.chicago.ddbn.com
October 4-18

Clio Awards
(800) 946-2546
www.clioawards.com
May 22

CMJ Music Marathon, Musicfest & Filmfest
(646) 485-6600
www.cmj.com
October TBA

Digital Film Festival
(323) 993-6008
www.dfilm.com
February TBA

Emmys
(818) 754-2800
www.emmys.org
September TBA

Flanders International Film Festival
(32 9) 221 8946
www.filmfestival.be
October 9-20

Grammy Awards
(310) 392-3777
www.grammy.com
February 28

Heartland Film Festival
(317) 464-9405
www.heartlandfilmfest.org
October 17-25

Hollywood Film Festival
(310) 288-1882
www.hollywoodfestival.com
August 2-6

Hong Kong Film Festival
(852) 2734 2903
www.hkiff.org.hk
April 6-21

Independent Feature Film Market
(212) 465-8200
www.ifp.org
September TBA

The Independent Spirit Awards
(310) 475-4379
www.ifpwest.org
March TBA

The International Advertising Festival/Lions
(212) 715-5389
www.canneslions.com
June 18-23

International CINDY Competition
(619) 461-1600
www.cindys.com
March & September TBA

International Monitor Awards
(703) 319-0800
www.itsnet.org
July 21

Locations '99 Trade Show
(323) 852-4747
February 23-24

London Film Festival
(44 20) 7815 1322
www.lff.org.uk
November TBA

Los Angeles Independent Film Festival
(323) 937-9155
www.laiff.com
April 20-28

Awards/Expos/Festivals

MIFED (Milan)
(39 02) 4801 2912
www.fmd.it/mifed
October TBA

Mill Valley Film Festival
(415) 383-5256
www.finc.org/mvff.html
October 4-14

Mobius Advertising Awards
(630) 834-7773
www.mobiusawards.com
February 8

Montreal World Film Festival
(514) 848-3883
www.ffm-montreal.org
August 23-September 3

MTV Music Video Awards
(310) 752-8000
www.mtv.com
September TBA

Music Video Production Association Awards
(323) 469-9464
www.mvpa.com
April TBA

New York Exposition of Short Film and Video
(212) 505-7742
www.yrd.com/nyexpo
November TBA

New York Festivals Television Advertising Awards
(914) 238-4481
www.nyfests.com
February TBA

New York Film Festival
(212) 875-5600
www.filmlinc.com/nyff/nyff.htm
September TBA

New York Underground Film Festival
(212) 675-1137
www.nyuff.com
March 7-13

The One Show
(212) 979-1900
www.oneclub.com
May 9

Res-Fest Digital Film Festival
(212) 217-1154
www.resfest.com
November TBA

San Francisco International Film Festival
(415) 561-5000
www.sfiff.org
April 19-May 3

Santa Monica Film Festival & Moxie! Awards
(310) 264-4274
www.smff.com
February 14-19

Short Pictures International Film Festival
(310) 558-6691
www.spiffest.com
October TBA

Showbiz Expo (West)
(203) 840-4800
showbiz.reedexpo.com
May 31-June 2

SIGGRAPH
(312) 321-6830
www.siggraph.org/s99
August 12-14

Slamdance International Film Festival
(323) 466-1786
www.slamdance.com
January 20-27

South By Southwest Music & Madia Conference
(512) 467-7979
www.sxsw.com
March 15-19

Sundance Film Festival
(801) 328-3456
www.sundance.org
January 9-18

Sydney Film Festival
(9) 9660-3844
www.sydfilm-fest.com.au
June 8-22

Telluride Film Festival
(603) 433-9202
www.telluridefilmfestival.com
August 31-September 3

U.S. International Film & Video Festival
(630) 834-7773
www.filmfestawards.com
June 7-8

Vancouver International Film Festival
(604) 685-0269
www.viff.org
September 27-October 12

Venice Film Festival
(39 041) 521-8711
www.labiennale.org
August 28-September 8

Executives/Personnel Alphabetical Key

Bob Aaronson	Fireworks Pictures	(310) 854-2429
Amber Aaseng	Seven Arts Pictures	(323) 464-0225
Michael Abbott	No Prisoners	(310) 979-9097
Michelle Abbrecht	Columbia Pictures	(310) 244-4000
Pamela Abdy	Jersey Films	(310) 203-1000
Charles Abehsera	Back Home Pictures	(323) 962-8500
Moshe Abehsera	Back Home Pictures	(323) 962-8500
Ygonabee Abigit	Norton Wright Prod.	(818) 990-3058
Marc Abraham	Beacon Communications	(310) 260-7000
Peter Abraham	Bella Prod.	(310) 823-3115
Richard Abramowitz	Unapix Films	(212) 252-7711
Joseph Abrams	Pearson Television	(310) 656-1100
Peter Abrams	Tapestry Films	(310) 275-1191
Lawrence Abramson	Incognito Ent.	(310) 246-1500
Stephen D. Abramson	New Line Cinema	(310) 854-5811
Jason Abril	The Arnet/Kerner Co.	(310) 838-2500
Joan Aceste	Comedy Central	(212) 767-8600
Mario Acosta	Baer Ent. Grp.	(310) 777-3680
Joed W. Adair	Adobe Pictures	(818) 955-8345
John Adams	Area 51 Films	(310) 395-5151
Laird Adamson	Killer Films	(212) 473-3950
Paul M. Addis	Ambitious Ent.	(818) 990-8993
Andrew Adelson	Adelson Ent.	(310) 314-9151
Orly Adelson	Orly Adelson Prod.	(310) 442-2012
Glenn Adilman	ABC Entertainment	(310) 557-7777
Tracy Adler	New Line Cinema	(310) 854-5811
Rob Aft	Kushner-Locke Company	(818) 841-8188
Giovanni Agnelli	Alex Rose Prod.	(323) 654-8662
Linda Agnelli	Sundog Prod.	(310) 564-9515
Vincent Agostino	VCA Prod.	(310) 489-3495
Michael Aguilar	The Donners' Company	(818) 954-3611
Luis Aira	Moving Image	(310) 659-8022
Cindy Akins	Cylo	(323) 957-7824
Trevor Albert	Ocean Pictures	(310) 369-0093
Chris Albrecht	HBO	(212) 512-1000
Joie Albrecht	Albrecht & Assoc.	(818) 222-4836
Brian Aldrich	Coppos Films	(323) 463-0764
Jason Alexander	Angel Ark Prod.	(818) 508-3338
Pia Alexander	Omaha Pictures	(310) 396-4333
Tracey Alexander	Adelson Ent.	(310) 314-9151
Bill Aliber	Hallmark Ent.	(212) 977-9001
Britt Allcroft	Gullane Pictures	(310) 451-5111
Craig Allen	The Jim Henson Company	(323) 802-1500
Debbie Allen	30 Second Films	(310) 315-1750
Debbie Allen	Red Bird Prod.	(310) 234-7234
Donald V. Allen	Allen & Assoc.	(310) 390-5522
Sally Allen	BallPark Prod.	(310) 827-1328
Stephanie Allen	Fox Searchlight Pictures	(310) 369-4402
Tim Allen	Boxing Cat Prod.	(818) 765-4870
Kirstie Alley	True Blue Prod.	(323) 661-9191
Jeanne Allgood	Konrad Pictures	(310) 244-3555
Mary L. Aloe	Proud Mary Ent.	(310) 288-1886
Judith Alonso	Carrie Prod.	(310) 567-3292
Robin Alper	Echo Lake Prod.	(310) 399-9164
Mark A. Altman	Mindfire Ent.	(310) 204-4481
Len Amato	Baltimore/Spring Creek Pictures	(818) 954-1210
Ed Amaya	Spoke Film	(310) 477-2272
Marc Ambrose	Visionbox	(310) 204-4686
Tracy Ames	Lions Gate Ent.	(323) 692-7300
Mark Amin	Lions Gate Ent.	(323) 692-7300
Eugene Amodeo	Universal Pictures	(818) 777-1000
Allison Amon	Chelsea Pictures	(323) 860-8030
Melvin Amr	Scott Rudin Prod.	(323) 956-4600
John Amussen	20th Century Fox Pictures	(310) 369-1000
Alex Anderson	Green Dot Films	(310) 656-4900
Bobby Anderson	Good Machine	(212) 343-9230
Clarke Anderson	Saturn Films	(310) 887-0900
Craig Anderson	Craig Anderson Prod.	(310) 841-2555
Karen Anderson	Epiphany Prod.	(310) 815-1266
Mark Anderson	Enchantment Films	(818) 506-5249
Mary Anderson	Alex Rose Prod.	(323) 654-8662
Steve Anderson	Enchantment Films	(818) 506-5249
Michael Andreen	20th Century Fox Pictures	(310) 369-1000
Mark Andrews	Fuel	(310) 314-1644
Robyn Andrews	Twilight Time Films	(310) 284-7310
Mark Androw	Chicago Story	(312) 642-3173
Joel Andryc	Fox Family Channel	(310) 235-9700
Steven Ang	Metro Pictures	(310) 301-7890
Angel	Moving Image	(310) 659-8022
Julie Ansell	Gracie Films	(310) 244-4222
Spencer Antle	Metro Pictures	(310) 301-7890
Frank Antonelli	ITB CineGrp./Television	(323) 258-5564
Judd Apatow	Apatow Prod.	(323) 860-7825
Lauri Apelian	Matador Pictures	(310) 820-5866
Dan Appel	Green Dot Films	(310) 656-4900
Michael Appel	Coppos Films	(323) 463-0764
Judy Apperson	Morra, Brezner, Steinberg & Tenenbaum	(310) 385-1820
Avi Arad	Marvel Characters	(310) 234-8991
Diana Arcand	Telescene Film Grp.	(514) 737-5512
Mark Archer	Mark Archer Ent.	(219) 486-8831
Paul Arden	Piper Prod.	(310) 883-8822
Laurie Arent	Adelson Ent.	(310) 314-9151
Aileen Argentini	Mr. Mudd Prod.	(323) 932-5656
Adam Arkin	Brownstone Films	(310) 319-6136
Alan Arkin	Brownstone Films	(310) 319-6136
Ken Arlidge	Flying Tiger Films	(310) 664-9171
Tobin Armbrust	Intermedia Films	(310) 777-0007
Kristin Armfield	Evil Twin Prod.	(818) 986-8551
Bozena Armstrong	Silver Lining Prod.	(310) 289-6650
Jeff Armstrong	Drive Media	(310) 392-6920
Laura Armstrong	New Line Cinema	(310) 854-5811
Robin Armstrong	Open Road Prod.	(818) 980-1100
Randi Arnold	Cohn & Company	(310) 899-6979
John Arnow	LA Prod.	(323) 874-9487
Craig Arrington	Capella Films	(310) 247-4700
Juan Luis Arruga	Carbo Films	(310) 586-1969
Jill Arthur	Yak Yak Pictures	(818) 954-3861
William Ashley II	Ashley Prod.	(909) 781-6597
Carlton Ashley	Sun Spots	(323) 960-4000
Heather Ashley	ITB CineGrp./Television	(323) 258-5564
Jacqueline Ashley	Ashley Prod.	(909) 781-6597
Andrea Asimow	Moving Pictures	(212) 219-4545
Sam Aslanian	DNA	(323) 463-2826
Mary Astadourian	Ten Thirteen Prod.	(310) 369-1100
Ken Atchity	AEI	(323) 932-0407
Nick Athas	Olmos Prod.	(310) 557-7010
Julie Atherton	Cylo	(323) 957-7824
Beni Atoori	Stonelock Pictures	(818) 716-6356
Martha Atwater	Scholastic Ent.	(212) 343-7500
Philip Atwell	Geronimo Film Prod.	(323) 965-0200
Pam Aver	Red-Horse Prod.	(818) 705-2588
Scott Aversano	Scott Rudin Prod.	(323) 956-4600
Pedro Avila	Carbo Films	(310) 586-1969
Meiert Avis	Windmill Lane Prod.	(310) 576-1344
Oren Aviv	Buena Vista Motion Pictures	(818) 560-1000
Jon Avnet	The Arnet/Kerner Co.	(310) 838-2500
Jonathan Axelrod	Axelrod Ent.	(323) 956-3705
John Axelson	Axelson-Weintraub Prod.	(818) 954-8661
Rory J. Aylward	Fast Carrier Pictures	(310) 234-5376
Don Azars	dapTV associates	(310) 860-9001
Ryan Babanzien	Dolores Robinson Ent.	(310) 777-8777
John Badham	The Badham Company	(818) 990-9495
Amy Baer	Columbia Pictures	(310) 244-4000
Donald A. Baer	Discovery Networks	(301) 986-1999
Jane Baer	The Baer Animation Company	(323) 874-9122
Matthew Baer	Brillstein-Grey Ent.	(310) 275-6135
Thomas Baer	Baer Ent. Grp.	(310) 777-3680
Erik Baiers	Horseshoe Bay Prod.	(818) 560-3229
Fenton Bailey	World of Wonder Prod.	(323) 463-7133
Barnet Bain	Metafilmics	(818) 734-9320
Helen Baines	Colomby/Keaton Prod.	(310) 399-8881
Scott Baio	30 Second Films	(310) 315-1750
Cameron Baity	Undergrace Prod.	(818) 833-8666
Carmen Baker	Amen Ra Films	(310) 246-6510
Susan M. Baker	June Beallor Prod.	(818) 777-9000
Eric Bakke	Stereomedia 3D Video Prod.	(818) 559-6515
Mark Bakshi	Paramount Pictures	(323) 956-5000
Bob Balaban	Chicagofilms	(212) 307-0050
John Baldecchi	A Band Apart	(323) 951-4600
Howard Baldwin	Crusader Ent.	(310) 248-6360

Executives/Personnel Alphabetical Key

Karen Baldwin	Crusader Ent.	(310) 248-6360
Rebecca Baldwin	Sanford/Pillsbury Prod.	(310) 393-5225
Antonio Banderas	Green Moon Prod.	(310) 450-6111
Eveleen Bandy	Icon Prod. Inc.	(323) 956-2100
Lionel Banes	Malcolm Leo Prod.	(323) 464-4448
Fiona Banister	Lux Pictures	(310) 301-0101
Steve Banks	Tango Films	(310) 470-4908
Jason Barager	Graying & Balding	(310) 587-2330
Randy Barbato	World of Wonder Prod.	(323) 463-7133
Gary Barber	Spyglass Ent.	(818) 560-3458
Suzy Barbier	Imagine Ent.	(310) 858-2000
Steve Bardwil	Walt Disney Pictures	(818) 560-1000
Michael Barker	Sony Pictures Classics	(212) 833-8833
Phil Barlow	Walt Disney Pictures	(818) 560-1000
Michael Barnard	Lightning Bolt PIX	(310) 828-8239
Morgan Barnard	Lightning Bolt PIX	(310) 828-8239
Amy Barnes	Calm Down Prod.	(323) 650-4027
Jonah Barnes	Original Film	(310) 445-9000
Peter Barnett	Nova Pictures	(323) 462-5502
Joby Barnhart	Villains	(310) 888-8900
Barry Barnholtz	Barnholtz Ent.	(310) 457-7484
Andre Barnwell	BET	(818) 566-9948
Chad Baron	Mel Stuart Prod.	(310) 785-9080
Fred Baron	20th Century Fox Pictures	(310) 369-1000
Nina Baron	Fine Line Features	(310) 854-5811
Eric Barrett	Atlas Pictures	(310) 587-2376
David Barrington-Holt	The Jim Henson Company	(323) 802-1500
Robin Barris	Imagine Ent.	(310) 858-2000
Tom Barron	Image G	(818) 761-6644
Drew Barrymore	Flower Films	(310) 285-0200
Bruce Barshop	Si TV	(323) 651-2242
Helen Bartlett	Barnstorm Films	(310) 396-5937
Gerald S. Barton	The Bubble Factory	(310) 358-3000
Helena Bartuccio	Incognito Ent.	(310) 246-1500
Robert Baruc	Unapix Films	(212) 252-7711
Basil	Carbo Films	(310) 586-1969
John Baskin	Act III Prod.	(310) 385-4111
Glen Basner	Good Machine	(212) 343-9230
Judith Bass	CBS Enterprises	(212) 975-4321
Debra Bassett	Bassett Prod.	(650) 579-1313
Glennis Bastien	Amen Ra Films	(310) 246-6510
Carolyn Bates	Duck Soup Studios	(310) 478-0771
Dan Bates	Mindfire Ent.	(310) 204-4481
Nick Bates	SimEx Digital Studios	(310) 664-9500
Brent Baum	Destination Films	(310) 434-2700
Suzanne Bauman	Suzanne Bauman Prod.	(818) 348-4342
Craig Baumgarten	Baumgarten/Prophet Ent.	(310) 996-1885
Simon Bax	20th Century Fox Pictures	(310) 369-1000
Michael Bay	Bay Films	(310) 829-7799
Trudy Snipes Baylock	Amen Ra Films	(310) 246-6510
Lindsey Bayman	Phoenix Pictures	(310) 244-6100
Jonathan K. Beal	New Line Cinema	(310) 854-5811
June Beallor	June Beallor Prod.	(818) 777-9000
Dave Beanes	Universal Studios	(818) 777-1000
Jacquenne Beaudette	MindStorm Prod.	(310) 393-1183
Veronica Becker	Radiant Prod.	(310) 656-1400
Dave Becky	3 Arts Ent.	(310) 888-3200
Liz Bedard	Sitting Ducks Prod.	(323) 660-0861
Michael Bedard	Sitting Ducks Prod.	(323) 660-0861
Frank Beddor	Automatic Pictures	(323) 935-1800
Stephen Bedell	Taylor-Bedell Ent.	(310) 859-9967
Steve Beeks	Artisan Ent.	(310) 449-9200
Betsy Beers	Mutual Film Company	(323) 871-5690
Kevin Beggs	Lions Gate Ent.	(323) 692-7300
Jeff Behlendorf	New Line Cinema	(310) 854-5811
Erica Beier	New Line Cinema	(310) 854-5811
Lenny Bekerman	Persistent Ent.	(310) 777-1814
Karen Belanger	Intermedia Films	(310) 777-0007
Doug Belgrad	Columbia Pictures	(310) 244-4000
Bradley Bell	Bell-Phillip Television Prod.	(323) 575-4138
John Bell	2EZ	(323) 939-9975
Martin Bell	Cohn & Company	(310) 899-6979
Todd Bellanca	Zooma Zooma Corp.	(212) 941-7680
Michael Bellino	Zooma Zooma Corp.	(212) 941-7680
Donald P. Bellisario	Belisarius Prod.	(323) 956-8660
Kristine Belson	The Jim Henson Company	(323) 802-1500
Leslie Belzberg	St. Clare Ent.	(310) 360-0451
Yoram Benami	Triumph Pictures	(310) 234-9680
Chris Bender	Bender-Spink	(323) 845-1640
Lawrence Bender	A Band Apart	(323) 951-4600
Alise Benjamin	Benjamin Prod.	(818) 752-8500
Marù Benjamin	Bandolero Films	(310) 434-1231
Stewart Benjamin	Crusader Ent.	(310) 248-6360
Stuart Benjamin	Benjamin Prod.	(818) 752-8500
Colleen Benn	Universal Pictures	(818) 777-1000
Bill Bennett	MacGillivray Freeman Films	(949) 494-1055
Mark Raymon Bennett	Cohn & Company	(310) 899-6979
Yvonne Bennett	Fox Family Channel	(310) 235-9700
Claire Benoit	Telescene Film Grp.	(514) 737-5512
Robyn Bensinger	Film Planet	(310) 581-1100
Robin Benson	Villains	(310) 888-8900
Robert Benun	Lakeshore Ent. Corp.	(323) 956-4222
Craig Berenson	Patchwork Prod.	(310) 288-7488
Ilene Berg	Laurence Mark Prod.	(310) 244-5239
Kevin Berg	CBS Ent.	(323) 575-2345
Peter Berg	Tool of North America	(310) 453-9244
Albert Berger	Bona Fide Prod.	(310) 273-6782
Christine Berges	Gartner	(310) 899-1700
Jenz Bergren	Ken Gross Management	(323) 512-2999
Jeff Berk	Polestar Ent. Grp.	(310) 278-0080
Beth Berke	Sony Pictures Ent.	(310) 244-4000
Stan Berkowitz	Warner Bros. Animation	(818) 954-7670
Jessica Berlinski	Baumgarten/Prophet Ent.	(310) 996-1885
Bruce Berman	Village Roadshow Pictures	(818) 260-6000
Burt Berman	Paramount Pictures	(323) 956-5000
Michael Berman	dapTV associates	(310) 860-9001
Rick Berman	Rick Berman Prod.	(323) 956-5037
Maureen Bernal	The Association	(818) 841-9660
Julian Bernard	The Artists' Colony	(323) 930-7900
Tom Bernard	Sony Pictures Classics	(212) 833-8833
Tracy Bernard	Fuel	(310) 314-1644
Fred Bernhardt	Longboard Prod.	(916) 684-5085
Armyan Bernstein	Beacon Communications	(310) 260-7000
Lawrence Bernstein	USA Films	(212) 539-4002
John Bertolli	Destination Films	(310) 434-2700
John Berzner	American Video Grp.	(310) 477-1535
Michael Besman	Ballyhoo	(323) 874-3396
Tim Bevan	Working Title Films	(310) 777-3100
Carl Beverly	Artists Television Grp.	(310) 860-8200
Scott Bibo	Villains	(310) 888-8900
Laura Bickford	A Band Apart	(323) 951-4600
Adrienne Biddle	Jersey Films	(310) 203-1000
Jayne Bieber	New Line Cinema	(310) 854-5811
Diane Biederbeck	Paulette Breen Prod.	(818) 342-0228
Susanna Bieger	Terra Bella Ent.	(323) 655-2311
Robert Biehn	Zeal Pictures	(323) 871-4000
Matt Bierman	Phoenix Pictures	(310) 244-6100
Lynn Bigelow-Kouf	Kouf-Bigelow Prod.	(818) 508-1010
Maggie Biggar	Fortis Films	(310) 659-4533
Tony Bill	Barnstorm Films	(310) 396-5937
Stu Billett	Ralph Edwards/Stu Billett Prod.	(323) 462-2212
Susan Binder	Renaissance Pictures	(818) 777-0088
Gary Binkow	FilmColony	(323) 951-4650
Christine Birch	Columbia Pictures	(310) 244-4000
Jenny Birchfield-Eick	Angel Ark Prod.	(818) 508-3338
Leslie A. Bird	Collaborative Artists	(310) 274-4800
Roger Birnbaum	Spyglass Ent.	(818) 560-3458
Mavrizio Bizzarri	Cineville	(310) 394-4699
Henry Bjoin	Bjoin Films	(323) 937-4097
Rochel Blachman	Paramount Pictures	(323) 956-5000
Carole Black	Lifetime Television	(310) 556-7500
Richard Black	Mesita	(818) 760-8707
Todd Black	Black & Blu Ent.	(310) 244-8833
Chris Blackwood	The Ad-Files	(213) 891-3784
Ron Blair	Cohn & Company	(310) 899-6979
Juliet Blake	The Jim Henson Company	(323) 802-1500
Tessa Blake	Asset Pictures	(212) 255-6187
William Blake	RGH/Lions Share Pictures	(310) 652-2893
Matthew C. Blank	Showtime Networks	(310) 234-5200
Jed Blaugrund	Mostow/Lieberman	(818) 777-4444
Brian Bleak	Brian Bleak Films	(310) 396-5500
Adam Bleibtreu	Creative Chaos	(310) 451-4112
Suzanne Bleibtreu	Creative Chaos	(310) 451-4112
Varina Bleil	Weed Road Pictures	(818) 954-3771
Pat Blessing	Pat Blessing Prod.	(213) 413-4158
Steve Blinn	Marca-Relli Prod.	(310) 457-8867

Executives/Personnel Alphabetical Key

Thomas Bliss	Beacon Communications	(310) 260-7000
Irv Blitz	Morton Jankel Zander	(310) 826-6200
Bill Block	Artisan Ent.	(310) 449-9200
Don Block	Gartner	(310) 899-1700
Peter Block	Lions Gate Ent.	(323) 692-7300
Linda Bloodworth-Thomason	Mozark Prod.	(818) 655-5779
Marcie Bloom	Sony Pictures Classics	(212) 833-8833
Stu Bloomberg	ABC Entertainment	(310) 557-7777
Christal Blue	Christal Blue Prod.	(323) 466-9083
Alex Blum	Headquarters	(310) 752-5200
Pamela Blum	Universal Pictures	(818) 777-1000
Barry Blumberg	Blumberg Prod. & Management	(310) 472-6410
Steve Blume	Brillstein-Grey Ent.	(310) 275-6135
Chrissy Blumenthal	Black & Blu Ent.	(310) 244-8833
Jason Blumenthal	Black & Blu Ent.	(310) 244-8833
Jeff Blye	Tollin/Robbins Prod.	(818) 766-5004
Gene Blythe	ABC Entertainment	(310) 557-7777
Melanie Blythe-Moreau	Greystone Communication Grp.	(818) 762-2900
Gerald Bocaccio	The Bubble Factory	(310) 358-3000
Arianna Bocco	New Line Cinema	(310) 854-5811
George Bodenheimer	ABC Inc./ABC Television	(310) 557-7777
Carol Bodie	Carol Bodie Ent.	(310) 247-8181
Michael Bolingbroke	The Jim Henson Company	(323) 802-1500
Anthony Bolinsky	Fine Line Features	(310) 854-5811
Patricia Bolt	Our Prod.	(323) 465-4197
Daniel W. Bolton	The Ad-Files	(213) 891-3784
Angela Bond	Original Voices	(310) 392-3479
Lois Bonfiglio	Bleecker Street Films	(323) 993-7386
Dana Booton	Saban Ent.	(310) 235-5100
Kirk Borcherding	Bel-Air Ent.	(818) 954-4040
Mark Borchetta	The Creative Department	(661) 288-1155
Wiki Border	Neo Art & Logic	(323) 653-6007
Ralpho Borgos	New Line Cinema	(310) 854-5811
Jessica Borsiceky	Blue Tulip Prod.	(310) 752-7900
Michael Bostick	Shady Acres Ent.	(818) 777-4446
Richard Bowen	Windmill Lane Prod.	(310) 576-1344
Brian Bowie	21st Century Man	(323) 466-3227
Heather Bowles	Martin Ransohoff Prod.	(310) 551-2680
Steven Boyd	Image Movers	(818) 733-8313
Robert L. Boyett	Miller/Boyett Prod.	(212) 702-9779
Paul Boyington	Boyington Studios	(310) 822-2360
Barbara Boyle	Valhalla Motion Pictures	(323) 969-4300
Jim Bradley	Merv Griffin Ent.	(310) 385-3160
Jimmy Bradley	Minervision	(323) 848-3080
Jordan Brady	HKM Prod.	(323) 465-9494
Michael Brady	Visitor	(310) 828-8255
Brannon Braga	Braga Prod.	(323) 956-5799
Stephen Brain	Stan Lee Media	(818) 461-1757
Gordon Braine	Popular Arts Ent.	(818) 562-6366
Marco Brambilla	DNA	(323) 463-2826
Bernadine Brandis	Buena Vista Motion Pictures	(818) 560-1000
Jonathan Brandstein	Morra, Brezner, Steinberg & Tenenbaum	(310) 385-1820
Lloyd Braun	ABC Entertainment	(310) 557-7777
Marian Brayton	Brayton/Carlucci Prod.	(310) 478-1700
Allison Brecker	Universal Pictures	(818) 777-1000
Bob Breech	David E. Kelley Prod.	(310) 727-2200
Kevin W. Breen	Walt Disney Pictures	(818) 560-1000
Paulette Breen	Paulette Breen Prod.	(818) 342-0228
Anthony Bregman	Good Machine	(212) 343-9230
Buddy Bregman	Bregman Ent.	(213) 833-6207
Richard Brener	New Line Cinema	(310) 854-5811
Tom Brennan	Atlas Ent.	(310) 724-7350
Kimberly Brent	Paradox Prod.	(818) 623-2855
Salomé Breziner	RoadKill Films	(323) 962-0295
Larry Brezner	Morra, Brezner, Steinberg & Tenenbaum	(310) 385-1820
Raymond Bridgers	Greystone Communication Grp.	(818) 762-2900
Martin Brierley	Tropix Films	(310) 393-9956
Kevin S. Bright	Bright-Kauffman-Crane Prod.	(818) 977-7777
Bernie Brillstein	Brillstein-Grey Ent.	(310) 275-6135
Gina Brittle-Mackey	Tribune Ent. Company	(323) 460-5800
Sanja Brizic	Galanty & Company	(310) 451-2525
Barbara Broccoli	Danjaq	(310) 449-3185
Dana Broccoli	Danjaq	(310) 449-3185
Kevin Brockman	ABC Inc./ABC Television	(310) 557-7777
Barbara Brogliatti	Warner Bros.	(818) 954-6000
Cary Brokaw	Avenue Pictures	(310) 996-6800
Nadia Bronson	Universal Pictures	(818) 777-1000
James Brooke	Watershed Films	(310) 550-2175
Linda Brookover	Pendragon Film	(310) 828-1588
Brooke Brooks	Davis Ent. Co.	(310) 556-3550
Gail Brooks	Lotus Films	(626) 292-1015
James L. Brooks	Gracie Films	(310) 244-4222
Mel Brooks	Brooksfilms	(310) 202-3292
David Brookwell	Brookwell McNamara Ent.	(310) 306-2151
Nick Broomfield	Plum Prod.	(310) 450-1942
Pierce Brosnan	Irish DreamTime	(310) 449-3411
Paul Broucek	New Line Cinema	(310) 854-5811
Johnathan Brouwer	Mark Archer Ent.	(219) 486-8831
Andrew Brown	Winchester Films	(310) 458-1400
Chris Brown	Lakeshore Ent. Corp.	(323) 956-4222
Chris Brown	No Prisoners	(310) 979-9097
David Brown	The Manhattan Project	(212) 258-2541
Jon Brown	Ensemble Ent.	(310) 882-8900
Kaaren Brown	DIC Ent.	(818) 955-5400
Phil Brown	Metro Pictures	(310) 301-7890
Philip J. Brown	Bjoin Films	(323) 937-4097
Polly Brown	Mike Sullivan Prod.	(310) 315-7315
Ross Brown	Original Film	(310) 445-9000
Vanessa Browne	Red Hots Ent.	(818) 954-0092
Scott Browning	Dino De Laurentiis	(818) 777-2111
Jim Brubaker	Shady Acres Ent.	(818) 777-4446
Caroline Bruce	Lion Rock Prod.	(310) 449-3205
Bonnie Bruckheimer	All Girl Prod.	(818) 655-6000
Jerry Bruckheimer	Jerry Bruckheimer Films	(310) 664-6260
Dan Bryant	The Joneses	(310) 656-8300
Maria Bryant	The Tribunal	(323) 468-9300
Scott Bryant	Steam	(310) 636-4620
Erick Bryce	RGH/Lions Share Pictures	(310) 652-2893
Kellie Bryce	Lynda Obst Prod.	(323) 956-8744
Christine Buckley	Lakeshore Ent. Corp.	(323) 956-4222
Robin Budd	The Bedford Falls Company	(310) 394-5022
David Buelow	Don Johnson Prod.	(818) 238-2200
Suzanne Bukinik	ABC Entertainment	(310) 557-7777
Gesine Bullock	Fortis Films	(310) 659-4533
Sandra Bullock	Fortis Films	(310) 659-4533
Mark Buntzman	Spin Pictures Intertainment	(310) 278-3569
Lisa Buono	Egg Pictures	(323) 956-8400
Kimberly Burch	Taurus Ent. Company	(323) 860-0807
Ellen Burditt	Lions Gate Ent.	(323) 692-7300
Neil Burger	Straw Dogs	(323) 782-0777
Jim Burk	Universal Pictures	(818) 777-1000
Rachel Burkes	Our Gang Prod.	(310) 300-1010
Steve Burleigh	Red House Ent.	(818) 977-1902
Alan Burnett	Warner Bros. Animation	(818) 954-7670
Rob Burnett	World Wide Pants, Inc	(212) 975-5300
Jim Burns	Nickelodeon/Nick at Nite	(212) 258-7500
Scott Burns	Tool of North America	(310) 453-9244
Jim Burrows	Charles Bros. Prod.	(323) 956-5962
John Burrud	Burrud Prod.	(714) 842-8422
Al Burton	Al Burton Prod.	(310) 858-5511
Claudia Zeitlin Burton	Calico World Ent.	(818) 755-3800
Susan Burton	The Artists Company	(323) 650-4722
Tom Burton	Calico World Ent.	(818) 755-3800
Kym Bye	Ocean Pictures	(310) 369-0093
Mark Byers	ITB CineGrp./Television	(323) 258-5564
Suzan Bymel	Talent Ent. Grp.	(323) 969-0700
Darlene Caamano	El Norte Prod.	(310) 360-1194
Ernie Cabral	Longboard Prod.	(916) 684-5085
Paul Cade	Cohn & Company	(310) 899-6979
Nicolas Cage	Saturn Films	(310) 887-0900
Dwight Caines	Columbia Pictures	(310) 244-4000
Judy Cairo	Cairo/Simpson Ent.	(310) 888-1262
Robert F. Callahan	ABC Inc./ABC Television	(310) 557-7777
Ed Callaway	Teocalli Ent.	(505) 258-1373
Jose Calleja Jr.	Scott Rudin Prod.	(323) 956-4600
Colin Callender	HBO	(212) 512-1000
John Calley	Sony Pictures Ent.	(310) 244-4000
Omar Camacho	The Jim Henson Company	(323) 802-1500
Breena Camden	Fox Searchlight Pictures	(310) 369-4402
James Cameron	Lightstorm Ent.	(310) 656-6100
Colleen Camp	Seven Arts Pictures	(323) 464-0225
Billy Campbell	Miramax Films	(212) 941-3800
David Campbell	Jumbo Pictures	(212) 337-0077

Executives/Personnel Alphabetical Key

Diane Campbell	Belladonna Prod.	(310) 452-0399
Kelly Campbell	Valhalla Motion Pictures	(323) 969-4300
Lana Campbell	Elephant Walk Ent.	(310) 887-3977
Teresa Campbell	Int'l. Television Grp. (ITG)	(310) 656-9100
Stephen J. Cannell	Cannell Studios	(323) 465-5800
Vivian Cannon	Hofflund-Polone	(310) 859-1971
Mark Canton	The Canton Company	(818) 954-2130
Neil Canton	Lakota Prod.	(323) 464-8462
Neil Canton	Seven Arts Pictures	(323) 464-0225
Pavel Cantù	Moving Image	(310) 659-8022
Deborah Capogresso	Capo Prod.	(310) 477-4234
Talaat Captan	Green Communications	(818) 557-0050
Andre Caraco	Columbia Pictures	(310) 244-4000
Javier Carbo	Carbo Films	(310) 586-1969
Kim Carey	Columbia Pictures	(310) 244-4000
Romeo Carey	AbsoluteFilms.net	(626) 442-6454
Tony Carey	Brillstein-Grey Ent.	(310) 275-6135
Mark Carliner	Mark Carliner Prod.	(818) 763-4783
Rob Carliner	Butchers Run Films	(310) 246-4630
John B. Carls	Wild Things Prod.	(323) 954-4577
Sandra Carlso	Green Grass Blue Sky Company	(818) 760-8243
Cori Carlson	Hogan Moorhouse Pictures	(310) 319-9299
Maddi Carlton	HSI Prod.	(310) 452-9999
Anne Carlucci	Brayton/Carlucci Prod.	(310) 478-1700
Phyllis Carlyle	Carlyle Prod.	(323) 848-4960
Heather Carman	RKO Pictures	(310) 277-0707
Bobby Carmichael	Denali Prod.	(310) 457-7566
Brian Carmody	Satellite Films	(323) 465-9300
Sherry Carnes	Outerbanks Ent.	(323) 654-3700
Gina Carollo	Cineville	(310) 394-4699
Rob Carpio	Chesler/Perlmutter Prod.	(310) 443-9650
Nick Carpou	Universal Pictures	(818) 777-1000
Amy Carr	Phoenix Pictures	(310) 244-6100
Damon Carr	Bud Yorkin Prod.	(310) 274-8111
David Carr	Beantown Prod.	(310) 278-1007
Nancy Carr	CBS Ent.	(323) 575-2345
Steve Carr	Villains	(310) 888-8900
Larry Carroll	Sundog Prod.	(310) 564-9515
Matt Carroll	Boxing Cat Prod.	(818) 765-4870
Marcy Carsey	The Carsey-Werner.	(818) 655-5598
Matthew Carson	MDP Worldwide	(310) 226-8300
Chris Carter	Ten Thirteen Prod.	(310) 369-1100
Chris Carter	The Canton Company	(818) 954-2130
Doug Carter	Walt Disney Pictures	(818) 560-1000
Kathy Carter	Incognito Ent.	(310) 246-1500
Rich Carter	Gartner	(310) 899-1700
Tom Carter	Rick Reinert Pictures	(805) 494-0699
Susan Cartsonis	Wind Dancer Prod. Grp.	(323) 645-1200
Ruth Caruso	The Jim Henson Company	(323) 802-1500
Benedict Carver	Screen Gems	(310) 244-4000
D. Cassidy	Rapport Films	(818) 980-4483
Chris Castallo	Tollin/Robbins Prod.	(818) 766-5004
Thomas Castaneda	Universal Pictures	(818) 777-1000
Marggie Castellano	Quasar Studios	(310) 289-1547
Anthony Catalano	Green Grass Blue Sky Company	(818) 760-8243
Frank Catalano	Green Grass Blue Sky Company	(818) 760-8243
Gilbert Cates	Cates/Doty Prod.	(310) 208-2134
Bruce Caulk	Intelliscape Films	(310) 235-1422
Liz Cavalier	Automatic Pictures	(323) 935-1800
Lucy Cavallo	CBS Ent.	(323) 575-2345
Sue Cazen	Dockry Prod.	(310) 274-0761
Lila Cazes	Lumiere Films	(323) 650-6773
Roberto Cecchini	The Artists Company	(323) 650-4722
Mark Celentano	WildLife Management	(310) 276-8008
Leman Cetiner	Silverline Pictures	(818) 752-3730
Carol Chacamaty	The Arnet/Kerner Co.	(310) 838-2500
Stokely Chaffin	Original Film	(310) 445-9000
Judy Chaikin	One Step Prod.	(818) 762-1624
Alexandra Chamberlain	Coppos Films	(323) 463-0764
Ernest Chambers	Merv Griffin Ent.	(310) 385-3160
Craig Champion	Headquarters	(310) 752-5200
Fred Chandler	20th Century Fox Pictures	(310) 369-1000
Peggy Chane	CPC Ent.	(310) 652-8194
Joey Chang	M.H.S. Prod.	(310) 202-3336
Robin Chang	American Sports Network	(626) 292-2222
Terence Chang	Lion Rock Prod.	(310) 449-3205
Les Charles	Charles Bros. Prod.	(323) 956-5962
Mark Charpentier	Conundrum Ent.	(310) 319-2800
Robert Chartoff	Chartoff Prod.	(310) 319-1960
Stanley Chase	Stanley Chase Prod.	(310) 475-4236
Skip Chasey	Imagine Ent.	(310) 858-2000
Liza Chasin	Working Title Films	(310) 777-3100
Janis Chaskin	New Line Cinema	(310) 854-5811
Lynette Prucha Chavez	Sneak Preview Ent.	(323) 962-0295
Vicki Cherkas	Miramax Films	(212) 941-3800
Peter Chernin	20th Century Fox Pictures	(310) 369-1000
Peter Chernin	Fox Broadcasting Company	(310) 369-1000
Lewis B. Chesler	Chesler/Perlmutter Prod.	(310) 443-9650
Vince Cheung	Rice & Beans Prod.	(626) 792-9171
Minor Childers	Reveal Ent.	(818) 733-9818
Stephen Chin	Shanghai'd Films	(310) 453-8337
Mark Ching	Lux Pictures	(310) 301-0101
Michael Chinich	The Montecito Picture Company	(805) 565-8590
Charles Chiodo	Chiodo Bros. Prod.	(818) 842-5656
Edward Chiodo	Chiodo Bros. Prod.	(818) 842-5656
Stephen Chiodo	Chiodo Bros. Prod.	(818) 842-5656
Bill Choi	Talent Ent. Grp.	(323) 969-0700
Vicki Christianson	Icon Prod. Inc.	(323) 956-2100
Tom Christine	Showtime Networks	(310) 234-5200
Eddy Chu	Backyard Prod.	(310) 314-1122
Caldecot Chubb	Alphaville	(323) 956-4803
Natalia Chydzik	The Ladd Company	(310) 777-2060
Grant Cihlar	1171 Prod. Grp.	(323) 655-1171
Mary Cim	Calico World Ent.	(818) 755-3800
Michele Civetta	HKM Prod.	(323) 465-9494
SueEllen Clair	Stiefel + Company	(310) 581-7000
Jeff Clark	Glass Guns	(323) 938-0729
Sherryl Clark	Kopelson Ent.	(310) 369-7555
William Clark	Walt Disney Pictures	(818) 560-1000
Clint Clemens	Tool of North America	(310) 453-9244
Ana Clevel	Taurus Ent. Company	(323) 860-0807
Jeff Clifford	Buena Vista Motion Pictures	(818) 560-1000
Sidney Clifton	Film Roman	(818) 761-2544
Paige Cline	Chapter 10 Prod.	(323) 460-6665
George Clooney	Section Eight Pictures	(818) 954-4840
Mercedes Coats	Lin Oliver Prod.	(323) 782-1495
Dana Coen	Belisarius Prod.	(323) 956-8660
Matthew Cohan	Bay Films	(310) 829-7799
Amanda Cohen	Original Film	(310) 445-9000
Amy Minda Cohen	Section Eight Pictures	(818) 954-4840
Andy Cohen	Grade A Ent.	(310) 358-8600
Arthur Cohen	Paramount Pictures	(323) 956-5000
Bob Cohen	20th Century Fox Pictures	(310) 369-1000
Bobby Cohen	Cohen Pictures	(323) 951-4250
Bruce Cohen	The Jinks/Cohen Company	(818) 733-9880
Ellis A. Cohen	Hennessey Ent.	(323) 876-2400
Evan Cohen	Barwood Films	(212) 765-7191
Hank Cohen	Metro-Goldwyn-Mayer	(310) 449-3000
Jay Cohen	Punch Prod.	(310) 442-4880
Jerome Cohen	Hennessey Ent.	(323) 876-2400
Lawrence Cohen	Merv Griffin Ent.	(310) 385-3160
Leonard H. Cohen	Hennessey Ent.	(323) 876-2400
Polly Cohen	Warner Bros. Pictures Prod.	(818) 954-6000
Rachel Cohen	Artisan Ent.	(310) 449-9200
Robert L. Cohen	The Woofenill Works	(212) 734-2578
Ron Cohen	Another Large Prod.	(323) 954-8500
Rudy Cohen	Signature Films	(310) 226-8374
Tom Cohen	Lightstorm Ent.	(310) 656-6100
David L. Cohn	Sneak Preview Ent.	(323) 962-0295
Elie Cohn	Langley Prod.	(310) 449-5300
Jack Cohn	Cohn & Company	(310) 899-6979
Isabel Coixet	Carbo Films	(310) 586-1969
Joanna Colbert	Universal Pictures	(818) 777-1000
Michelle Colbert	Legacy Films	(323) 856-8888
Erika Coleman	Atkinson Way Films	(323) 465-3350
Nancy V. Coleman	Artisan Ent.	(310) 449-9200
Scott Coleman	The Canton Company	(818) 954-2130
Paul Colichman	Regent Ent.	(310) 260-3333
Cassius Colman	Black Dog Films (RSA USA)	(310) 659-1017
Marino Colmano	Lucid Media	(818) 764-8580
Harry Colomby	Colomby/Keaton Prod.	(310) 399-8881
Beth Colt	Atkinson Way Films	(323) 465-3350
Kevin Commins	Chesler/Perlmutter Prod.	(310) 443-9650
David Comtois	Beantown Prod.	(310) 278-1007
Sarah Condon	HBO Original Programming	(212) 512-1000
Michael Condro	Reality Prod.	(818) 404-8711

Executives/Personnel Alphabetical Key

Angela Congelose	Further Films	(818) 777-6700
Bud W. Connell	BCProd./BCTV Prod.	(949) 495-1500
John G. Connell	BCProd./BCTV Prod.	(949) 495-1500
Sean Connery	Fountainbridge Films	(310) 244-8080
Patti Connolly	Warner Bros.	(818) 954-6000
Rodney Lee Conover	Avalanche! Ent.	(310) 395-3660
Shaun Conrad	Backyard Prod.	(310) 314-1122
Daneen Conroy	Moving Pictures	(212) 219-4545
Dennis Considine	Logo Ent.	(310) 276-6700
Sandra Constantine	New Line Cinema	(310) 854-5811
Victor Constantino	Junction Ent.	(818) 560-2800
Catarina Conti	Polestar Ent. Grp.	(310) 278-0080
Jerry Conti	Polestar Ent. Grp.	(310) 278-0080
Rod Conti	Polestar Ent. Grp.	(310) 278-0080
Chris Conway	Our Gang Prod.	(310) 300-1010
Anthony Coogan	Stereomedia 3D Video Prod.	(818) 559-6515
Pete Coogan	The Jim Henson Company	(323) 802-1500
Ashley Cook	Shady Acres Ent.	(818) 777-4446
Carrie Cook	Scott Rudin Prod.	(323) 956-4600
Jared Cook	Chiari Cook Company	(323) 937-1272
Richard Cook	Buena Vista Motion Pictures	(818) 560-1000
Winship Cook	The Edward S. Feldman Co.	(818) 972-3304
Chris Cookson	Warner Bros.	(818) 954-6000
Jerry Cooper	Showtime Networks	(310) 234-5200
Jessica Cooper	The Matthau Company	(310) 454-3300
Kimberly Cooper	20th Century Fox Pictures	(310) 369-1000
Kyle Cooper	Imaginary Forces	(323) 957-6868
Matt Cooper	The Vault	(310) 315-0012
Susan Cooper	Fox Family Channel	(310) 235-9700
Ellie Copland	Jumbo Pictures	(212) 337-0077
Adrienne Coppola	PlasterCITY Prod.	(323) 938-0974
Christopher Coppola	PlasterCITY Prod.	(323) 938-0974
Francis Ford Coppola	American Zoetrope	(310) 899-8000
Mark Coppos	Coppos Films	(323) 463-0764
Gisela Corcoran	New Line Cinema	(310) 854-5811
Foster Corder	Boyington Studios	(310) 822-2360
Barbara Cordis	GreenWater Pictures	(323) 655-9585
Al Corley	Neverland Films	(310) 772-0008
Catherine Corman	New Concorde	(310) 820-6733
Cis Corman	Barwood Films	(212) 765-7191
Julie Corman	New Concorde	(310) 820-6733
Roger Corman	New Concorde	(310) 820-6733
David Cornell	Headquarters	(310) 752-5200
Stuart Cornfeld	Red Hour Films	(310) 289-2565
Peter Corral	Columbia Pictures	(310) 244-4000
Sean Corrigan	Parkway Prod.	(310) 244-4040
Joyce Corrington	Bunim-Murray Prod.	(818) 756-5100
Stephanie Corsalini	Louis DiGiaimo & Assoc.	(212) 253-5510
Robert Cort	The Cort/Madden Company	(323) 956-5884
A. J. Cosgrove	Canned Interactive	(323) 308-4200
Ben Cosgrove	Section Eight Pictures	(818) 954-4840
Brian Cosgrove	Ballyhoo	(323) 874-3396
John Cosgrove	Cosgrove-Meurer Prod.	(818) 843-5600
Tom Cosgrove	Fox Family Channel	(310) 235-9700
Thomas Cost	LA Prod.	(323) 874-9487
Michael Costigan	Columbia Pictures	(310) 244-4000
Michael Cote	Chesler/Perlmutter Prod.	(310) 443-9650
Colin Cotter	Initial Ent. Grp.	(310) 315-1722
Janine Coughlin	Alliance Atlantis	(310) 899-8000
David Coulter	Tropix Films	(310) 393-9956
Patti Coulter	Tropix Films	(310) 393-9956
Heather Courtney	Bel-Air Ent.	(818) 954-4040
Cindy Cowan	Cindy Cowan Ent.	(323) 822-1082
Denys Cowan	Warner Bros. Animation	(818) 954-7670
Michael Cowan	Michael Cowan	(323) 666-0600
Rob Cowan	Winkler Films	(310) 858-5780
Brian Cox	Distant Horizon	(323) 848-4140
James Cox	Black Dog Films (RSA USA)	(310) 659-1017
Jessica Cox	Parkway Prod.	(310) 244-4040
Penny Finkelman Cox	Patchwork Prod.	(310) 288-7488
Dan Cracchiolo	Silver Pictures Television	(818) 954-4490
Carl Craig	5th Gear Ent.	(323) 954-0555
Peter Cramer	New Regency Prod.	(310) 369-8300
Cherie Crane	Columbia Pictures	(310) 244-4000
Heidi Crane	Stonelock Pictures	(818) 716-6356
Peter Crane	Crane Wexelblatt Ent.	(310) 457-4821
David Craven	Four Square Prod.	(858) 874-1900
Wes Craven	Wes Craven Films	(818) 752-0197
John Crededio	Hawk Ent.	(310) 859-7779
Gary Credle	Warner Bros.	(818) 954-6000
Maria Crenna	CBS Ent.	(323) 575-2345
Cammie Crier-Herbert	The Badham Company	(818) 990-9495
Suzanne Criley	Sony Pictures Ent.	(310) 244-4000
Tim Cronenweth	Cronenweth Films	(323) 964-4888
Tori Crotts	Seven Arts Pictures	(323) 464-0225
Billy Crystal	Face Prod.	(310) 285-2300
Gabor Csupo	Klasky Csupo	(323) 463-0145
Mike Culbert	American Ent. Co.	(323) 939-6746
Clint Culpepper	Screen Gems	(310) 244-4000
Emily Cummins	Franchise Pictures	(323) 822-0730
Jessica Cunningham	Minervision	(323) 848-3080
Tony Cunningham	Cohn & Company	(310) 899-6979
Bryan Cuprill	Chapter 10 Prod.	(323) 460-6665
Charlie Curran	Crossroads Films	(310) 659-6880
Matthew Curry	Luminosity Prod.	(818) 752-3318
Terry Curtin	Universal Pictures	(818) 777-1000
Beverly Cusack	Cinergi Pictures	(310) 315-6000
John Cusack	New Crime Prod.	(310) 396-2199
Devin Cutler	MDP Worldwide	(310) 226-8300
Jeff Daitch	Walt Disney Pictures	(818) 560-1000
James Dalrymple	Dalrymple Prod.	(626) 963-5588
James Dalthorp	Area 51 Films	(310) 395-5151
Robb Dalton	Fireworks Television	(323) 850-2470
Ann Daly	DreamWorks SKG	(818) 733-7000
John Daly	FilmWorld	(323) 655-7705
Jules Daly	Black Dog Films (RSA USA)	(310) 659-1017
Tim Daly	Red House Ent.	(818) 977-1902
Tom Damien	Erratic Ent.	(310) 657-0922
Brooke Dammkoehler	Visionbox	(310) 204-4686
Mark Damon	MDP Worldwide	(310) 226-8300
Christian D'Andrea	A Band Apart	(323) 951-4600
Sean Daniel	Alphaville	(323) 956-4803
Tiffany Daniel	Mark Johnson Prod.	(310) 777-0007
Janice Daniello	Post Modern Edit	(714) 751-2681
Karil Daniels	Point of View Prod.	(415) 821-0435
Neil Daniels	Tuesday Films	(310) 899-0335
Marc Danon	Artisan Ent.	(310) 449-9200
Jill Danton	Stan Rogow Prod.	(323) 993-5644
Carol Dantuono	Bel-Air Ent.	(818) 954-4040
Eric d'Arbeloff	Roadside Attractions	(310) 860-1692
Jonathan Darby	Piper Prod.	(310) 883-8822
Gregory Dark	FM Rocks	(310) 587-1501
Elizabeth Daro	Sitting Ducks Prod.	(323) 660-0861
Clare A. Darragh	New Line Cinema	(310) 854-5811
Nickolas Davatzes	A&E Television Networks	(212) 210-1400
Bruce Davey	Icon Prod. Inc.	(323) 956-2100
Jonathan David	Morton Jankel Zander	(310) 826-6200
Lorena David	Kingsize Ent.	(323) 467-7199
Pierre David	WIN Ventures	(310) 859-2500
Dan Davids	A&E Television Networks	(212) 210-1400
Hollace Davids	Universal Pictures	(818) 777-1000
Chris Davidson	CBS Ent.	(323) 575-2345
John Davidson	IMAX Corp.	(310) 255-5500
Rachel Davidson	Act III Prod.	(310) 385-4111
Bridget D. Davis	Edmonds Ent.	(416) 630-3825
Don Davis	AVD Prod./AV Designs	(310) 379-5818
Erin Davis	Blue Tulip Prod.	(310) 752-7900
Genie Davis	AVD Prod./AV Designs	(310) 379-5818
John A. Davis	Davis Ent. Co.	(310) 556-3550
Linda Davis	Wildwood Enterprises	(310) 395-5155
Michael Davis	Sweet Lorraine Prod.	(310) 575-3066
Preston A. Davis	ABC Inc./ABC Television	(310) 557-7777
Doug Davison	Mad Chance	(818) 954-3803
Joe Davola	Tollin/Robbins Prod.	(818) 766-5004
Meredith Day	TVP Studios	(818) 843-3188
Jonathan Dayton	Dayton/Faris	(310) 396-7333
Jan De Bont	Blue Tulip Prod.	(310) 752-7900
Jan De Bont	Plum Prod.	(310) 450-1942
Sylvia De La Riviere	CPC Ent.	(310) 652-8194
Dino De Laurentiis	Dino De Laurentiis	(818) 777-2111
Martha Di Laurentiis	Dino De Laurentiis	(818) 777-2111
Pierre de Lespinois	c.2K Ent.	(310) 208-2324
Michael De Luca	New Line Cinema	(310) 854-5811
Joseph De Marco	Fox Searchlight Pictures	(310) 369-4402
Ricardo de Oliveira	Bunim-Murray Prod.	(818) 756-5100
Miranda de Pencier	Wildwood Enterprises	(310) 395-5155

Executives/Personnel Alphabetical Key

Lillian Dean	Fortis Films	(310) 659-4533
Tomlinson Dean	Lester Persky Prod.	(310) 278-1995
Valerie Dean	Ab'-strakt Pictures	(310) 385-6611
John DeBello	Four Square Prod.	(858) 874-1900
Chris Debie	Nova Pictures	(323) 462-5502
Tom DeCerchio	Morton Jankel Zander	(310) 826-6200
David Decker	Jon Turtle Prod.	(310) 234-5347
Michael Degan	Nonfiction Spots	(310) 319-6140
Neil DeGroot	Watershed Films	(310) 550-2175
Joshua Deighton	Fox Searchlight Pictures	(310) 369-4402
Donna Deitch	Desert Heart Prod.	(310) 399-0013
Faith Dektor	Dektor Film	(323) 466-3455
Leslie Dektor	Dektor Film	(323) 466-3455
Mark Dektor	Dektor Film	(323) 466-3455
Paul Dektor	Dektor Film	(323) 466-3455
John Delaney	Scott Rudin Prod.	(323) 956-4600
Pamela Delaney	Fireworks Pictures	(310) 854-2429
Raffaella DeLaurentiis	Raffaella Prod.	(818) 777-2655
Bill D'Elia	David E. Kelley Prod.	(310) 727-2200
Ford Delman	Colomby/Keaton Prod.	(310) 399-8881
James Deloye	H-Gun Labs	(415) 648-4386
Kevin DeLullo	Rogue Ent.	(801) 979-2229
Anthony Demby	Overbrook Ent.	(818) 777-2224
Meltem Demirer	Artisan Ent.	(310) 449-9200
Mark Dempsey	Echo Lake Prod.	(310) 399-9164
Robert DeNiro	Tribeca Prod.	(212) 941-4000
John Denis	Industrial Light + Magic Commercial Prod.	(323) 957-2002
Darcie Denkert	Metro-Goldwyn-Mayer Studios	(310) 449-3000
Todd Denkin	Make It Happen Prod.	(323) 851-6444
Pen Densham	Triology Ent. Grp.	(310) 449-3095
Andrew Denyer	Headquarters	(310) 752-5200
Marie DePuthod	Bregman Ent.	(213) 833-6207
Ron DeRosa	Hawk Ent.	(310) 859-7779
Anna DeRoy	The Canton Company	(818) 954-2130
Jeri Barchilon deSouza	Val D'Oro Ent.	(310) 656-8555
Steven E. deSouza	Val D'Oro Ent.	(310) 656-8555
Naomi Despres	Manifest Film Company	(310) 899-5554
Phillip Detchmendy	Satellite Films	(323) 465-9300
Jack Deutchman	New Line Cinema	(310) 854-5811
Philip DeVellis	Lightning Bolt PIX	(310) 828-8239
D. V. Devincentis	New Crime Prod.	(310) 396-2199
Danny DeVito	Jersey Films	(310) 203-1000
Dean Devlin	Centropolis Ent.	(310) 244-4300
Jeff Devlin	Flying Tiger Films	(310) 664-9171
Tom Dey	Black Dog Films (RSA USA)	(310) 659-1017
Lorenzo di Bonaventura	Warner Bros. Pictures Prod.	(818) 954-6000
Lisa Di Marzio	Paramount Pictures	(323) 956-5000
Denise Di Novi	Di Novi Pictures	(310) 581-1355
Limor Diamant	Signature Films	(310) 226-8374
Moshe Diamant	Signature Films	(310) 226-8374
Daniel Diamond	Fireworks Pictures	(310) 854-2429
Jean Diamond	Ginty Films	(310) 274-9691
Ron Diamond	Acme	(323) 464-7805
Neil Dick	Columbia Pictures	(310) 244-4000
Samuel Dickerman	Radiant Prod.	(310) 656-1400
Chip Diggins	Paramount Pictures	(323) 956-5000
Lou DiGiaimo Jr.	Louis DiGiaimo & Assoc.	(212) 253-5510
Louis DiGiaimo	Louis DiGiaimo & Assoc.	(212) 253-5510
Doug Dilge	PMC Pictures	(310) 656-3255
Brian Dillingham	Persistent Ent.	(310) 777-1814
Jenny Dillon	American World Pictures	(818) 715-1480
David Dinerstein	Paramount Classics	(323) 956-2000
Paul Dini	Warner Bros. Animation	(818) 954-7670
Roy E. Disney	The Walt Disney Company	(818) 560-1000
Donna Distefano	MPH Films	(310) 395-9952
Nancy Dockry	Dockry Prod.	(310) 274-0761
Ted Dodd	20th Century Fox Pictures	(310) 369-1000
Jim Dodson	20th Century Fox Pictures	(310) 369-1000
Frances Doel	New Concorde	(310) 820-6733
Carol Anne Dolan	A&E Television Networks	(212) 210-1400
Dolores Dolan	Barking Weasel Prod.	(323) 464-2275
Kevin Dole	Sun Spots	(323) 960-4000
Jonathan L. Dolgen	Viacom Ent. Grp.	(323) 956-5000
Pat Dollard	Propaganda Films	(323) 462-6400
Walter Doniger	Bettina Prod.	(323) 937-2101
Brian Donnelly	OneSuch Films	(310) 273-3200
Lauren Shuler Donner	The Donners' Company	(818) 954-3611
Richard Donner	The Donners' Company	(818) 954-3611
Mary Donovan	New Line Cinema	(310) 854-5811
Ginnina d'Orazio	The Artists' Colony	(323) 930-7900
Ben Dossett	Windmill Lane Prod.	(310) 576-1344
Bob Doucette	Warner Bros. Animation	(818) 954-7670
Michael Douglas	Further Films	(818) 777-6700
Gretchen Douglass	Original Film	(310) 445-9000
Jean Doumanian	Jean Doumanian Prod.	(212) 486-2626
Kendra Dousette	FilmWorld	(323) 655-7705
Tony Dow	30 Second Films	(310) 315-1750
Bruce Dowad	Bruce Dowad Assoc.	(323) 654-8855
Ned Dowd	Spyglass Ent.	(818) 560-3458
Samuel Dowe-Sanders	The Robert Evans Company	(323) 956-8800
Antonia Downey	The Jim Henson Company	(323) 802-1500
Bobby L. Doyle	New Line Cinema	(310) 854-5811
Julia Dray	Horseshoe Bay Prod.	(818) 560-3229
Lori Drazen	Franchise Pictures	(323) 822-0730
Avery Drewe	Belisarius Prod.	(323) 956-8660
Richard Dreyfuss	Dreyfuss/James Prod.	(323) 850-3140
William Driver	The Steve Tisch Company	(310) 838-2500
Marcy Drogin	Further Films	(818) 777-6700
David Dryer	Sun Spots	(323) 960-4000
Linda Dryer	Sun Spots	(323) 960-4000
Michael Dryhurst	Longboard Prod.	(916) 684-5085
Lloyd D'Souza	Hallway Pictures	(323) 850-2680
Steven Dubin	Carol Bodie Ent.	(310) 247-8181
Burt DuBois	Wyld Spots	(323) 960-2633
Dana Dubovsky	American World Pictures	(818) 715-1480
Shelia Ducksworth	Edmonds Ent.	(323) 860-1550
James Dudelson	Taurus Ent. Company	(323) 860-0807
Robert Dudelson	Taurus Ent. Company	(323) 860-0807
Stan Dudelson	Taurus Ent. Company	(323) 860-0807
Leon Dudevoir	New Line Cinema	(310) 854-5811
Karina Duffy	MindStorm Prod.	(310) 393-1183
John Dukakis	Overbrook Ent.	(818) 777-2224
Barry Dukoff	Brownstone Films	(310) 319-6136
Patrick Dunauan	Stereomedia 3D Video Prod.	(818) 559-6515
Barbara Dunn-Leonard	Ralph Edwards/Stu Billett Prod.	(323) 462-2212
Kimberlee Duplechien	Quinn Prod.	(818) 787-5952
Colyer Dupont	Cinemagic Prod.	(510) 233-2002
Ken Dupuis	Avalanche! Ent.	(310) 395-3660
Greg Durig	Discovery Networks	(301) 986-1999
Julie Durk	The Donners' Company	(818) 954-3611
Ann L. Duval	Bel-Air Ent.	(818) 954-4040
Robert Duvall	Butchers Run Films	(310) 246-4630
Jesse Dylan	Straw Dogs	(323) 782-0777
Guy East	Intermedia Films	(310) 777-0007
Clint Eastwood	Malpaso Prod.	(818) 954-3367
Isaac Eaton	Newmark Films	(323) 782-4969
Jennifer Eatz	Polestar Ent. Grp.	(310) 278-0080
Donna Ebbs	Disney Telefilms	(310) 557-7777
Mark Eberle	Make It Happen Prod.	(323) 851-6444
Evan Edelist	New Line Cinema	(310) 854-5811
David Edelstein	FDG	(212) 624-1446
Neal Edelstein	Rainmaker Prod.	(323) 874-6770
Ann Edgar	Backyard Prod.	(310) 314-1122
Heather Edison	Kingsgate Films	(310) 281-5880
K. Babyface Edmonds	Edmonds Ent.	(323) 860-1550
Tracey Edmonds	Edmonds Ent.	(323) 860-1550
Brian Edwards	DreamWorks SKG	(818) 733-7000
Gary Edwards	Ralph Edwards/Stu Billett Prod.	(323) 462-2212
Ralph Edwards	Ralph Edwards/Stu Billett Prod.	(323) 462-2212
Rona Edwards	Rona Edwards Prod.	(323) 466-3013
Walter Edwards	Dockry Prod.	(310) 274-0761
Edward Egan	Universal Pictures	(818) 777-1000
Michael Ehrenzweig	Telling Pictures	(415) 864-6714
Bernd Eichinger	Constantin Film	(310) 247-0300
Frances Eigendorff	CBS Television	(212) 975-4321
Stephen Einhorn	New Line Cinema	(310) 854-5811
Julia Eisenman	All Girl Prod.	(818) 655-6000
Mallory Eisenstein	SNL Studios	(323) 956-5729
Michael D. Eisner	The Walt Disney Company	(818) 560-1000
Michael K. Eitelman	Tapestry Films	(310) 275-1191
Donna Ekholdt	Big Ticket Television	(323) 860-7400
Susan Ekins	Jerry Weintraub Prod.	(818) 954-2500
Liza-Maria el Khazen	Franchise Pictures	(323) 822-0730
David Ellender	Universal Television	(818) 777-5300
Kjose Elliot	Lakeshore Ent. Corp.	(323) 956-4222

Executives/Personnel Alphabetical Key

Mike Elliott	Capital Arts Ent.	(310) 581-3020
Suzann Ellis	Beacon Communications	(310) 260-7000
Lisa Ellzey	Scott Free Prod.	(310) 360-2250
Philip Elway	Bel-Air Ent.	(818) 954-4040
Steve Elzer	New Line Cinema	(310) 854-5811
Kerstin Emhoff	Venus Ent.	(310) 581-4236
Kerstin Emhott	Mars Media	(310) 664-6760
Roland Emmerich	Centropolis Ent.	(310) 244-4300
Toby Emmerich	New Line Cinema	(310) 854-5811
Chris Ender	CBS Ent.	(323) 575-2345
Chiari Endo	Chiari Cook Company	(323) 937-1272
Tim Engel	Walt Disney Pictures	(818) 560-1000
Tom Engelman	Radar Pictures	(310) 208-8525
David Engle	Mace Neufeld Prod.	(310) 244-2555
Maureen English	Gears Communications	(818) 840-9333
Susan Ennis	HBO Original Programming	(212) 512-1000
Rob Epstein	Telling Pictures	(415) 864-6714
Seth Epstein	Fuel	(310) 314-1644
Tiffany Ericksen	Wendy Finerman Prod.	(310) 369-8800
Jamie Erlicht	Artists Television Grp.	(310) 860-8200
Christopher Erskin	Black Dog Films (RSA USA)	(310) 659-1017
Avy Eschenasy	USA Films	(212) 539-4002
Moctesuma Esparza	Esparza-Katz Prod.	(310) 281-3770
Anthony Esposito	Leading Pictures	(310) 385-0951
Hilary Estey-McLoughlin	Warner Bros. Telepictures Prod.	(818) 972-0777
Brian R. Etting	American World Pictures	(818) 715-1480
Charles Evans Jr.	Acappella Pictures	(323) 782-8200
Derek Evans	Spyglass Ent.	(818) 560-3458
Jane Evans	Dimension Films	(212) 941-3800
Robert Evans	The Robert Evans Company	(323) 956-8800
Robyn Evans-Jones	Deja View Prod.	(818) 704-9185
Patty Everett	Mirella Film Co.	(323) 850-5522
Barri Evins	Debra Hill Prod.	(310) 319-0052
Bill Ewart	Montage Ent.	(310) 966-0222
Bill Ewing	Columbia Pictures	(310) 244-4000
Rick Eyler	WIN Ventures.	(310) 859-2500
Robin Facer	Pie Town Prod.	(323) 851-2333
David Fairfield	Malcolm Leo Prod.	(323) 464-4448
Joel Fajnor	Calico World Ent.	(818) 755-3800
Samuel Falconello	Cinergi Pictures	(310) 315-6000
Justin Falvey	DreamWorks SKG	(818) 733-7000
Charles Falzon	Gullane Pictures	(310) 451-5111
Gloria Fan	Atlas Ent.	(310) 724-7350
Dawn Fanning	Lotus Films	(626) 292-1015
Dan Fantz	Polestar Ent. Grp.	(310) 278-0080
Louis Farber	CPC Ent.	(310) 652-8194
Valerie Faris	Dayton/Faris	(310) 396-7333
Craig Farkas	Metro Pictures	(310) 301-7890
Steve Farr	Spoke Film	(310) 477-2272
Shea Farrell	David E. Kelley Prod.	(310) 727-2200
Bobby Farrelly	Conundrum Ent.	(310) 319-2800
Peter Farrelly	Conundrum Ent.	(310) 319-2800
Victoria R. Farwell	Goldenring Prod.	(323) 969-0354
Joe Fawcett III	MT. Tabor Prod.	(559) 347-0835
William Fay	Centropolis Ent.	(310) 244-4300
Steven Feder	Black Sheep Ent.	(818) 769-2227
Daniela Federici	Villains	(310) 888-8900
Scott Fedro	Morra, Brezner, Steinberg & Tenenbaum	(310) 385-1820
Erik Feig	Amalgamated	(323) 466-5400
Lauren Feige	Neo Art & Logic	(323) 653-6007
Rodd Feingold	Saban Ent.	(310) 235-5100
Leslee Feldman	DreamWorks SKG	(818) 733-7000
Richard Feldman	SNL Studios	(323) 956-5729
Sherri Feldman	Walt Disney Pictures	(818) 560-1000
Eric Fellner	Working Title Films	(310) 777-3100
Caitlin Felton	Go Film	(212) 677-7500
Andrew J. Fenady	Fenady Assoc.	(323) 466-6375
Duke Fenady	Fenady Assoc.	(323) 466-6375
Louis A. Feola	Universal Pictures	(818) 777-1000
Robert Fernandez	@radical.media	(310) 664-4500
Laurie Ferneau	Logo Ent.	(310) 276-6700
Joanne Ferraro	Coppos Films	(323) 463-0764
Dominique Fichera	Junction Ent.	(818) 560-2800
Bennett Fidlow	Vanguard Prod.	(310) 306-4910
Kevin Field	Section Eight Pictures	(818) 954-4840
Ted Field	Radar Pictures	(310) 208-8525
Adam Fields	Adam Fields Prod.	(310) 552-8244
Tyrone Finch	The Carsey-Werner.	(818) 655-5598
Delia Fine	A&E Television Networks	(212) 210-1400
Wendy Finerman	Wendy Finerman Prod.	(310) 369-8800
Carmen Finestra	Wind Dancer Prod. Grp.	(323) 645-1200
Jonny Fink	Tollin/Robbins Prod.	(818) 766-5004
Rick Finkelstein	Universal Pictures	(818) 777-1000
Pat Finn	In-Finn-Ity Prod.	(310) 444-6300
Rachel Finn	Carbo Films	(310) 586-1969
Richard Finney	Michael/Finney Prod.	(310) 838-9350
Jay Firestone	Fireworks Pictures	(310) 854-2429
Mary Firestone	Shoelace Prod.	(212) 243-2900
Rick Fishbein	Green Dot Films	(310) 656-4900
Lucy Fisher	Red Wagon	(310) 244-4466
Susie Fitzgerald	Brillstein-Grey Ent.	(310) 275-6135
Nicole Fitzpatrick	The Canton Company	(818) 954-2130
Matthew Fladell	Barnholtz Ent.	(310) 457-7484
Aimee Flaherty	Red House Ent.	(818) 977-1902
Susan Nahley Fleishman	Universal Studios	(818) 777-1000
Jeffrey Fleisig	Villains	(310) 888-8900
Angus Fletcher	The Jim Henson Company	(323) 802-1500
Teresa Flores	Michael Cowan	(323) 666-0600
Chris Floyd	Walt Disney Pictures	(818) 560-1000
Steve Flynn	USA Films	(212) 539-4002
Rich Fogel	Warner Bros. Animation	(818) 954-7670
Lawrence D. Foldes	Star Ent. Grp.	(818) 988-2200
Joseph Foley	Columbia Pictures	(310) 244-4000
Nathan Folks	RJN Prod.	(310) 859-2770
Karin Fong	Imaginary Forces	(323) 957-6868
Tom Fontana	The Levinson/Fontana Company	(212) 633-0440
Leilani Forby	Artisan Ent.	(310) 449-9200
Marc Forby	Le Monde Ent.	(310) 899-8000
Kevin Ford	Edward Pacio & Assoc.	(818) 880-1586
Kevin D. Forester	The Bubble Factory	(310) 358-3000
Craig Forrest	Verité Prod.	(310) 838-3119
Marisa Forrest	Fried Films	(310) 754-2676
Theo Forster	Red Hots Ent.	(818) 954-0092
Christine Forsyth-Peters	The Robert Evans Company	(323) 956-8800
Deborah Forte	Scholastic Ent.	(212) 343-7500
Kate Forte	Harpo Films	(310) 278-5559
Bruno Fortuna	Zaloom Film	(310) 656-8400
Beldeen Fortunato	Jumbo Pictures	(212) 337-0077
David Foster	David Foster Prod.	(818) 954-4113
Greg S. Foster	Horseshoe Bay Prod.	(818) 560-3229
Jodi Foster	Egg Pictures	(323) 956-8400
Lucas Foster	Blue Tulip Prod.	(310) 752-7900
Richard Fowkes	Paramount Pictures	(323) 956-5000
Jennifer Fox	Universal Pictures	(818) 777-1000
Kimiko Fox	Amen Ra Films	(310) 246-6510
Laura Fox	DreamWorks SKG	(818) 733-7000
Richard J. Fox	Warner Bros.	(818) 954-6000
Philip Fox-Mills	Headquarters	(310) 752-5200
Anatoly A. Fradis	Afra-Film Enterprises	(323) 882-6193
Olga Fradis	Afra-Film Enterprises	(323) 882-6193
Jonathan Frakes	Goepp Circle Prod.	(323) 956-4620
Pascal Franchot	Luminosity Prod.	(818) 752-3318
Kara Francis	New Regency Prod.	(310) 369-8300
Billy Frank	Make It Happen Prod.	(323) 851-6444
Darryl Frank	DreamWorks SKG	(818) 733-7000
Geanne Frank	Revelations Ent.	(310) 394-3131
Richard Frank	Picture Mill	(323) 465-8800
Scott JT Frank	Epiphany Prod.	(310) 815-1266
Jennie Frankel	Zide/Perry Ent.	(310) 887-2999
Peter Frankfurt	Imaginary Forces	(323) 957-6868
Annabelle Frankl	Cineville	(310) 394-4699
Lisa Franklin	Propaganda Films	(323) 462-6400
Tom Franklin	AbsoluteFilms.net	(626) 442-6454
Christina S. Frantti	New Line Cinema	(310) 854-5811
Erin Fraser	Broadway Video	(212) 265-7621
Woody Fraser	Woody Fraser Prod.	(818) 550-6102
Mark Frazel	Epiphany Prod.	(310) 815-1266
Art Frazier	DreamWorks SKG	(818) 733-7000
Paul Freedman	WildLife Management	(310) 276-8008
Alfonso Freeman	Revelations Ent.	(310) 394-3131
Betty Freeman	Joel Freeman Prod.	(818) 995-1189
Joel Freeman	Joel Freeman Prod.	(818) 995-1189
Mike Freeman	Crystal Pyramid Prod.	(619) 644-3000
Morgan Freeman	Revelations Ent.	(310) 394-3131
Scott Freeman	Bunim-Murray Prod.	(818) 756-5100

Executives/Personnel Alphabetical Key

Stacey Freeman	Hodge Film & Video	(310) 441-9773
Charles J. Freericks	New Line Cinema	(310) 854-5811
Margaret French Isaac	Bushwood Pictures	(323) 936-1659
Clemens Frenek	Conundrum Ent.	(310) 319-2800
Nick Frenkel	3 Arts Ent.	(310) 888-3200
Thomas E. Freston	MTV Networks	(310) 752-8000
Robyn Frey-Monell	Wind Dancer Prod. Grp.	(323) 645-1200
Daniel Fried	Daniel Fried Prod.	(310) 452-7646
Robert Fried	Fried Films	(310) 754-2676
Liz Friedlander	DNA	(323) 463-2826
Steve Friedlander	Fine Line Features	(310) 854-5811
Marla Friedler	Luminosity Prod.	(818) 752-3318
Alan Friedman	Miramax Films	(212) 941-3800
Andrew Friedman	Marty Katz Prod.	(310) 260-8501
Bradley Friedman	Vide-U	(310) 276-5509
Jeffrey Friedman	Telling Pictures	(415) 864-6714
Robert Friedman	New Line Cinema	(310) 854-5811
Robert G. Friedman	Paramount Pictures	(323) 956-5000
David T. Friendly	Friendly Prod.	(310) 369-3973
Albert Frigone	Patrick Raymond Ent.	(323) 850-2918
Brett Froomer	Stiefel + Company	(310) 581-7000
Karen Frost	EMK Prod.	(310) 260-3362
Mark Frost	Mark Frost Prod.	(323) 965-5785
Carla Fry	New Line Cinema	(310) 854-5811
Marc Frydman	Camera Marc	(818) 753-9901
Judd Funk	New Line Cinema	(310) 854-5811
Frank Furlong	Wyld Spots	(323) 960-2633
Will Furman	Furman Films	(310) 306-2700
Jim Gable	Graying & Balding	(310) 587-2330
Neil Gabriel	Jay Silverman Prod.	(323) 466-6030
Curtis Gadson	BET	(818) 566-9948
Ted Gagliano	20th Century Fox Pictures	(310) 369-1000
Mark Gaines	Universal Pictures	(818) 777-1000
Stephanie Gaines	Ken Gross Management	(323) 512-2999
Mark Galanty	Galanty & Company	(310) 451-2525
Sidney Galanty	Galanty & Company	(310) 451-2525
David M. Gale	MTV Films	(323) 956-8023
John Gallagher	Ginty Films	(310) 274-9691
Andrew Gallerani	RumRunner Cine Service	(310) 540-8411
Stacey Gallishaw	DIC Ent.	(818) 955-5400
Fred Gallo	Paramount Pictures	(323) 956-5000
Steven Galloway	Nelvana Ent.	(323) 549-4222
John J. Garand	The Walt Disney Company	(818) 560-1000
Jennifer Garces Cerchiai	Blue Wolf Prod.	(415) 561-6655
Martin Garcia	CBS Ent.	(323) 575-2345
Rene Garcia	Wes Craven Films	(818) 752-0197
Victor Garcia	Morton Jankel Zander	(310) 826-6200
Bridget Gardner	Mariposa	(805) 527-9990
Carole Gardner	Mariposa	(805) 527-9990
Daisy Gardner	Goepp Circle Prod.	(323) 956-4620
David Gardner	Talent Ent. Grp.	(323) 969-0700
Dede Gardner	Paramount Pictures	(323) 956-5000
Todd Gardner	Revolution Studios	(310) 264-4141
Harry Garfield	Universal Pictures	(818) 777-1000
Jannat Gargi	Atom Films	(626) 793-4950
Judith Garinger	Phoenix Pictures	(310) 244-6100
Tony Garland	Universal Television	(818) 777-5300
Jane Garnett	Longfellow Pictures	(212) 431-5550
Janet Garrison	Rastar Prod.	(310) 244-7871
Susan Garrison	Verdon-Cedric Prod.	(310) 274-7253
Alex Gartner	Metro-Goldwyn-Mayer Studios	(310) 449-3000
Adam Gascoine	M.H.S. Prod.	(310) 202-3336
Didi Gay	Valhalla Motion Pictures	(323) 969-4300
Paul Gay	Omaha Pictures	(310) 396-4333
David Gaynes	MDP Worldwide	(310) 226-8300
Elizabeth Gaynes	Universal Pictures	(818) 777-1000
Greg Gears	Gears Communications	(818) 840-9333
Robert Geary	Columbia Pictures	(310) 244-4000
Curt Geda	Warner Bros. Animation	(818) 954-7670
David Geffen	DreamWorks SKG	(818) 733-7000
Brian Gefsky	Original Film	(310) 445-9000
Monica Gelardo	Paradox Prod.	(818) 623-2855
Judy Geletko	Avenue Pictures	(310) 996-6800
Greg Gelfan	20th Century Fox Pictures	(310) 369-1000
Richard L. Gelfond	IMAX Corp.	(310) 255-5500
Ron Gell	RKO Pictures	(310) 277-0707
Jamie Geller Hawtof	Columbia Pictures	(310) 244-4000
Nancy Geller	HBO Original Programming	(212) 512-1000
Andrew Gellis	IMAX Corp.	(310) 255-5500
Jan Geniesse	Imagine Ent.	(310) 858-2000
Gene George	Regent Ent.	(310) 260-3333
Roger George	MT. Tabor Prod.	(559) 347-0835
Jacob Matthew Gerhardt	Neild Street Prod.	(323) 969-9447
Ed Gernon	Alliance Atlantis	(310) 899-8000
Steven W. Gerse	Walt Disney Pictures	(818) 560-1000
Jordan Gertner	Muse Prod.	(310) 306-2001
Laura Gherardi	Punch Prod.	(310) 442-4880
Andrea Giannetti	Columbia Pictures	(310) 244-4000
Jerry Giaquinta	Sony Pictures Ent.	(310) 244-4000
Bonny Giardina	Dylan Sellers Prod.	(818) 954-4929
Jennifer Gibgot	Tapestry Films	(310) 275-1191
Cori Gibson	Kandice King Prod.	(310) 822-9502
Jon Gibson	Columbia Pictures	(310) 244-4000
Jim Giddens	Villains	(310) 888-8900
Donna Gigliotti	USA Films	(212) 539-4002
Jill Gilbert	Love Spell Ent.	(310) 244-6040
Murray Gilden	Barnholtz Ent.	(310) 457-7484
Steven Gilder	Dark Horse Ent.	(818) 777-5830
Mark Gill	Miramax Films	(212) 941-3800
Robert Gillan	Braga Prod.	(323) 956-5799
Anne Marie Gillen	Revelations Ent.	(310) 394-3131
Scott Gillen	Coppos Films	(323) 463-0764
Craig Gillespie	Morton Jankel Zander	(310) 826-6200
Dick Gillespie	Spoke Film	(310) 477-2272
Gail Gillman	The Spark Factory	(310) 395-6775
Grant Gilmore	Proletariat	(818) 763-8356
Roger Gimbel	Roger Gimbel Prod.	(310) 459-3838
John G. Ginnes	First Avenue Films	(360) 376-3737
Robert Ginty	Ginty Films	(310) 274-9691
Stephanie Gisondi	Weed Road Pictures	(818) 954-3771
Mimi Polk Gitlin	Mandolin Ent.	(323) 802-6950
Harry Gittes	Gittes	(310) 244-4333
Andrew Given	Universal Pictures	(818) 777-1000
Richard Gladstein	FilmColony	(323) 951-4650
Finley Glaize	Triology Ent. Grp.	(310) 449-3095
Jim Glander	Dimension Films	(212) 941-3800
Rebecca Glashow	Unapix Films	(212) 252-7711
Karen Glass	Buena Vista Motion Pictures	(818) 560-1000
Karen J. Glasser	Icon Prod. Inc.	(323) 956-2100
Emily Glatter	New Line Cinema	(310) 854-5811
Alan Glazer	Atlas Ent.	(310) 724-7350
Kit Gleason	Red Hots Ent.	(818) 954-0092
Larry Gleason	Metro-Goldwyn-Mayer Studios	(310) 449-3000
Larry Gleason	United Artists Films	(310) 449-3000
Jon Glickman	Spyglass Ent.	(818) 560-3458
Anne Globe	DreamWorks SKG	(818) 733-7000
Brad Globe	DreamWorks SKG	(818) 733-7000
Liz Glotzer	Castle Rock Ent.	(310) 285-2300
Danny Glover	Carrie Prod.	(818) 567-3292
Gayle Gluck	Our Gang Prod.	(310) 300-1010
Lee Gluckman	Producers Grp.	(310) 316-0481
Jeffery Goddard	TVA Prod.	(818) 505-8300
Melissa Goddard	Wind Dancer Prod. Grp.	(323) 645-1200
Wyck Godfrey	Davis Ent. Co.	(310) 556-3550
Charlie Gogolak	Bender-Spink	(323) 845-1640
Whitney Goit	A&E Television Networks	(212) 210-1400
Menahem Golan	FilmWorld	(323) 655-7705
Jeremy Gold	20th Century Fox Television	(310) 369-1000
Amy Goldberg	Fox Family Channel	(310) 235-9700
Dan M. Goldberg	The Montecito Picture Company	(805) 565-8590
Dana Goldberg	Village Roadshow Pictures	(818) 260-6000
Gail Goldberg	Buena Vista Motion Pictures	(818) 560-1000
Gary David Goldberg	UBU Prod.	(818) 655-5850
Julie Golden	Intermedia Films	(310) 777-0007
Kit Golden	The Manhattan Project	(212) 258-2541
Stan Golden	Saban Ent.	(310) 235-5100
Jane Goldenring	Goldenring Prod.	(323) 969-0354
Max Goldenson	MWG Prod.	(323) 937-8313
Fred Goldey	American Video Grp.	(310) 477-1535
Phillip Goldfine	Steamroller Prod.	(323) 850-2940
Lori Goldklang-Furie	Columbia Pictures	(310) 244-4000
Bernie Goldman	Village Roadshow Pictures	(818) 260-6000
David Goldman	Kopelson Ent.	(310) 369-7555
Michael Goldman	Tollin/Robbins Prod.	(818) 766-5004
Paul Goldman	Hearst Ent. Prod.	(310) 478-1700
Peter Goldschmidt	Omaha Pictures	(310) 396-4333

Executives/Personnel Alphabetical Key

Akiva Goldsman	Weed Road Pictures	(818) 954-3771
Charlie Goldstein	20th Century Fox Television	(310) 369-1000
Gary W. Goldstein	The Goldstein Company	(310) 659-9511
Jamie Goldstein	Gold'N Hen Prod.	(310) 820-1308
Jennifer Goldstein	Wendy Finerman Prod.	(310) 369-8800
Joel Goldstein	Gold'N Hen Prod.	(310) 820-1308
Julie Goldstein	Miramax Films	(212) 941-3800
Josh Goldstine	Columbia Pictures	(310) 244-4000
Samuel Goldwyn Jr.	Samuel Goldwyn Films	(310) 860-3100
John Goldwyn	Paramount Pictures	(323) 956-5000
Jeff Golenberg	3 Arts Ent.	(310) 888-3200
Nancy Goliger	Paramount Pictures	(323) 956-5000
Norm Golightly	Saturn Films	(310) 887-0900
Andrew Golov	Artisan Ent.	(310) 449-9200
Dana Gonshor	Jeff Wald Ent.	(310) 264-4156
Peter B. Good	Golden Eagle Pix	(805) 381-9095
Robin Goodfellow	Zaloom Film	(310) 656-8400
Adam Goodman	DreamWorks SKG	(818) 733-7000
Geoff Goodman	Avenue Pictures	(310) 996-6800
Kathy Goodman	Intermedia Films	(310) 777-0007
Robert Goodman	Warner Bros. Animation	(818) 954-7670
Roger Goodman	ABC Inc./ABC Television	(310) 557-7777
Beau Gooliak	Canyon Pictures	(310) 456-1331
Leslie Goott	Bel-Air Ent.	(818) 954-4040
Charles Gordon	Daybreak Prod.	(818) 777-0277
Jon Gordon	Miramax Films	(212) 941-3800
Lawrence Gordon	Lawrence Gordon Prod.	(818) 777-7933
Marc Gordon	Mutual Film Company	(323) 871-5690
Michael Gordon	The Canton Company	(818) 954-2130
Robert Gordon	Flying Tiger Films	(310) 664-9171
Stephen Gordon	Stan Lee Media	(818) 461-1757
Stefan Kendal Gordy	Stefanino Prod.	(310) 454-0109
Leola Gorius	CBS Ent.	(323) 575-2345
Jeff Gorman	JGF	(323) 462-1500
Joy Gorman	The Robert Simonds Company	(818) 777-5445
Arthur Gorson	Ventana Films	(323) 876-3331
Louis Gossett Jr.	Logo Ent.	(310) 276-6700
Meyer Gottlieb	Samuel Goldwyn Films	(310) 860-3100
Lee Gottsegen	Punch Prod.	(310) 442-4880
Ellie Gottwald	Mindfire Ent.	(310) 204-4481
Mark Gottwald	Mindfire Ent.	(310) 204-4481
Bernard Gourley	Legacy Films	(323) 856-8888
Alain Gourrier	Bruce Dowad Assoc.	(323) 654-8855
Linda Govreau	The Jim Henson Company	(323) 802-1500
Marc J. Graboff	NBC Ent.	(818) 840-4444
Brian Graden	MTV Networks	(310) 752-8000
Gary Gradinger	Artists Television Grp.	(310) 860-8200
Tracie Graham	Graham/Rosenzweig Films	(310) 264-3956
Kelsey Grammer	Grammnet Prod. (Film)	(323) 956-5840
Tony Grana	Universal Pictures	(818) 777-1000
Jennifer Grandy	Original Film	(310) 445-9000
Amelia Granger	Working Title Films	(310) 777-3100
Donald Granger	Paramount Pictures	(323) 956-5000
Marc Granirer	Don Johnson Prod.	(818) 238-2200
Hugh Grant	Simian Films	(310) 205-2724
Michael Grasso	Omaha Pictures	(310) 396-4333
Amy Graves	Upstart Ent.	(310) 475-6025
Claudia Gray	Universal Pictures	(818) 777-1000
Elizabeth Gray	Canvas House Films	(714) 850-1964
F. Gary Gray	FM Rocks	(310) 587-1501
Brian Grazer	Imagine Ent.	(310) 858-2000
Paul Green	Beacon Communications	(310) 260-7000
Stan Green	Burrud Prod.	(714) 842-8422
Katy Greene	Piper Prod.	(310) 883-8822
Marc Greenfield	Stiefel + Company	(310) 581-7000
Cybelle Greenman	Artisan Ent.	(310) 449-9200
Alison Greenspan	Di Novi Pictures	(310) 581-1355
Scott Greenstein	USA Films	(212) 539-4002
Nana Greenwald	Kopelson Ent.	(310) 369-7555
Elissa Greer	New Line Cinema	(310) 854-5811
Leslie Greif	The Greif Company	(310) 385-1200
Jim Greiner	A&E Television Networks	(212) 210-1400
Michael Grembowicz	New Line Cinema	(310) 854-5811
Brad Grey	Brillstein-Grey Ent.	(310) 275-6135
Lawrence Grey	Zucker/Netter Prod.	(310) 394-1644
John Griffin	StarToons Int'l..	(708) 335-3535
Merv Griffin	Merv Griffin Ent.	(310) 385-3160
Ann Marie Griffith	In-Finn-Ity Prod.	(310) 444-6300
Cynthia Griffith	Kushner-Locke Company	(818) 841-8188
Melanie Griffith	Green Moon Prod.	(310) 450-6111
Jim Griffiths	Metro-Goldwyn-Mayer	(310) 449-3000
Michael Grillo	DreamWorks SKG	(818) 733-7000
Larry Grimaldi	Brayton/Carlucci Prod.	(310) 478-1700
Paul Grimshaw	Industrial Light + Magic Commercial Prod.	(323) 957-2002
Kristie Anne Groelinger	Jerry Bruckheimer Films	(310) 664-6260
Robert Gros	CBS Ent.	(323) 575-2345
Chay Gross	Franchise Pictures	(323) 822-0730
Chris Gross	Gross Prod.	(818) 557-7335
Ken Gross	Ken Gross Management	(323) 512-2999
Kim Gross	The Bubble Factory	(310) 358-3000
Lloyd Gross	Enteraktion	(954) 785-5070
Matthew Gross	Kopelson Ent.	(310) 369-7555
Ron Gross	Blue Goose Prod.	(323) 658-6893
Beth Grossbard	Beth Grossbard Prod.	(310) 841-2555
Halle Stanford Grossman	The Jim Henson Company	(323) 802-1500
Mark Groubert	Black Sheep Ent.	(818) 769-2227
Jud Grubbs	Flying Freehold Prod.	(323) 956-8838
Dan Grudnik	Itasca Pictures	(310) 273-6505
Jacqui Grunfeld	Saban Ent.	(310) 235-5100
Gerard Gruosso	A&E Television Networks	(212) 210-1400
Sandy Grushow	20th Century Fox Television	(310) 369-1000
Peter Guber	Mandalay Pictures	(323) 956-2400
Tony Guido	Hallmark Ent.	(212) 977-9001
David Guillod	Handprint Ent.	(310) 481-4400
Andrew Gumpert	Dimension Films	(212) 941-3800
Jon Gumpert	Universal Pictures	(818) 777-1000
Dianne Gunn	Atlas Ent.	(310) 724-7350
Patrick Gunn	Artisan Ent.	(310) 449-9200
Jane Gurtiza	Red Hots Ent.	(818) 954-0092
Kurt Gurtman	Spin Pictures Intertainment	(310) 278-3569
Marc Gurvitz	Brillstein-Grey Ent.	(310) 275-6135
Gay Guthrey	Stiefel + Company	(310) 581-7000
Robin Guthrie	The Robert Evans Company	(323) 956-8800
Thomas Guttry	Popular Arts Ent.	(818) 562-6366
Jill Gwen	Fox Searchlight Pictures	(310) 369-4402
Janet Haase	Satellite Films	(323) 465-9300
Dawn Haber	Kuzui Enterprises	(323) 850-1195
Randy Haberkamp	Silver Lining Prod.	(310) 289-6650
Elizabeth Hackett	Patchwork Prod.	(310) 288-7488
Robyn Haddad	Linda Wright Prod.	(818) 879-4647
John Hadity	Miramax Films	(212) 941-3800
Al Haferkamp	Mutual Film Company	(323) 871-5690
Craig Haffner	Greystone Communication Grp.	(818) 762-2900
Deb Hagan	Straw Dogs	(323) 782-0777
Kevin Hageman	Dark Horse Ent.	(818) 777-5830
Paul Haggar	Paramount Pictures	(323) 956-5000
Helene Hahn	DreamWorks SKG	(818) 733-7000
Adam Haight	Fireworks Pictures	(310) 854-2429
Marc Haimes	DreamWorks SKG	(818) 733-7000
Jules Haimovitz	Metro-Goldwyn-Mayer	(310) 449-3000
Karen L. Halby	Sony Pictures Ent.	(310) 244-4000
E. Barry Haldeman	Paramount Pictures	(323) 956-5000
Lianne Halfon	Mr. Mudd Prod.	(323) 932-5656
Sheri Halfon	Avenue Pictures	(310) 996-6800
Monica Hall	Jersey Films	(310) 203-1000
Paul Hall	Hallway Pictures	(323) 850-2680
Dean Hallett	Buena Vista Motion Pictures	(818) 560-1000
Lisa Halliday	Harpo Films	(310) 278-5559
Jim Hallowes	Hallowes Prod.	(310) 390-4767
Robert Halmi, Jr.	Hallmark Ent.	(212) 977-9001
Robert Halmi, Sr.	Hallmark Ent.	(212) 977-9001
Dan Halperin	Epiphany Prod.	(310) 815-1266
Julia Halperin	RKO Pictures	(310) 277-0707
Marc Halperin	Fine Line Features	(310) 854-5811
Noreen Halpern	Alliance Atlantis	(310) 899-8000
James L. Halsey	Warner Bros.	(818) 954-6000
Jeffrey R. Halsey	New Line Cinema	(310) 854-5811
Dan Halsted	Halsted Pictures	(310) 450-7804
Walter Hamada	Morra, Brezner, Steinberg & Tenenbaum	(310) 385-1820
George Hamilton	Stan Lee Media	(818) 461-1757
Tim Hamilton	Zooma Zooma Corp.	(212) 941-7680
Stuart Hammer	Revelations Ent.	(310) 394-3131
Jeremy Hammond	Mesita	(818) 760-8707
Sheila Hanahan	Zide/Perry Ent.	(310) 887-2999

Executives/Personnel Alphabetical Key

Chris Hanley	Muse Prod.	(310) 306-2001
Roberta Hanley	Muse Prod.	(310) 306-2001
Henrik Hansen	Flying Tiger Films	(310) 664-9171
Nicole Harb	Bender-Spink	(323) 845-1640
Paul Hardart	Universal Pictures	(818) 777-1000
Paul J. Harder	Trafficanda Studios	(323) 466-1111
Jennifer Hare	Triology Ent. Grp.	(310) 449-3095
John Hare	ABC Inc./ABC Television	(310) 557-7777
Hester Hargett	Raffaella Prod.	(818) 777-2655
Lawrence Hariton	Universal Pictures	(818) 777-1000
David Harleston	Nelvana Ent.	(323) 549-4222
John Harman	Adam Fields Prod.	(310) 552-8244
Kristin Harms	John Wells Prod.	(818) 954-1687
Danny Haro	Olmos Prod.	(310) 557-7010
Robert Harper	20th Century Fox Pictures	(310) 369-1000
Reginald Harpur	Warner Bros.	(818) 954-6000
Dierdre Harrington	Tool of North America	(310) 453-9244
Gail Harris	IndieGal Prod.	(818) 890-6111
J. Todd Harris	Davis Classics	(310) 551-2266
John Harris	Megahertz Pictures	(310) 727-2600
Lynn Harris	New Line Cinema	(310) 854-5811
Mark R. Harris	Regent Ent.	(310) 260-3333
Mel Harris	Sony Pictures Ent.	(310) 244-4000
Neil Harris	Headquarters	(310) 752-5200
Stephanie J. Harris	Walt Disney Pictures	(818) 560-1000
Susan Harris	Witt/Thomas/Harris Prod.	(323) 993-7000
Alleda Harrison	Impact PSA	(323) 851-5151
Alleda Harrison	The House Prod. Company	(323) 851-5151
Janet M. Harrison	Revelations Ent.	(310) 394-3131
Jason Hart	Krainin Prod.	(914) 359-0445
Marcie Hartley	Cornice Ent.	(310) 777-0200
Ted Hartley	RKO Pictures	(310) 277-0707
Michael Hartog	Wyld Spots	(323) 960-2633
Joe Hartwick	20th Century Fox Pictures	(310) 369-1000
Paul Harvey	Original Voices	(310) 392-3479
Ned Haspel	John Wells Prod.	(818) 954-1687
Kim Haswell	Artists Television Grp.	(310) 860-8200
June Hatch	Kandice King Prod.	(310) 822-9502
Veronica Hatchinson	BET	(818) 566-9948
Dianne Hatlestad	Yorktown Prod.	(310) 264-4155
David Haugland	David Haugland Prod.	(310) 550-1556
Robert Haukoos	RJ Lauren	(818) 879-2200
Micah A. Hauptman	Neild Street Prod.	(323) 969-9447
Jeff Hause	Avalanche! Ent.	(310) 395-3660
Tracy Hauser	Miss Jones	(310) 576-9280
Diana Hawkins	Columbia Pictures	(310) 244-4000
Richard Hawley	Merchant-Ivory Prod.	(212) 582-8049
Tim Hawley	Burke/Triolo Prod.	(310) 837-9900
Goldie Hawn	Cherry Alley Prod.	(310) 458-8886
Darr Hawthorne	Mesita	(818) 760-8707
Bill Hayden	Bella Prod.	(310) 823-3115
Laurette Hayden	Lifetime Television	(310) 556-7500
Jocelyn Hayes	Killer Films	(212) 473-3950
Marsha Hook Haygood	New Line Cinema	(310) 854-5811
Debra Hayward	Working Title Films	(310) 777-3100
Eric Haywood	Legacy Films	(323) 856-8888
Albie Hecht	Nickelodeon Movies	(323) 956-8663
Jim Hedges	ABC Entertainment	(310) 557-7777
Laura Heflin	Nydrle	(310) 659-8844
William Heflin	Village Roadshow Pictures	(818) 260-6000
Jody Heiden	Mad Chance	(818) 954-3803
Skip Heinecke	Ginty Films	(310) 274-9691
Michael Helfant	Dimension Films	(212) 941-3800
Peter Heller	Heller Highwater	(323) 467-9490
Lynn Hendee	Chartoff Prod.	(310) 319-1960
Clark Henderson	Dimension Films	(212) 941-3800
Craig Henderson	Stiefel + Company	(310) 581-7000
Bruce Hendricks	Buena Vista Motion Pictures	(818) 560-1000
Bruce Hendricks	Walt Disney Pictures	(818) 560-1000
John S. Hendricks	Discovery Networks	(301) 986-1999
Mike Hendrickson	20th Century Fox Pictures	(310) 369-1000
Amy Henkels	New Line Cinema	(310) 854-5811
Graham Henman	HKM Prod.	(323) 465-9494
Carol Henry	Lightstorm Ent.	(310) 656-6100
Judy Henry	Gold'N Hen Prod.	(310) 820-1308
Jim Hense	Single Spark Pictures	(310) 315-4779
Brian Henson	The Jim Henson Company	(323) 802-1500
Lisa Henson	Manifest Film Company	(310) 899-5554
Alan B. Heppel	Paramount Pictures	(323) 956-5000
Andre Hereford	40 Acres & A Mule	(718) 624-3703
David Herrera	Valhalla Motion Pictures	(323) 969-4300
Suzanne Herrington	Ocean Pictures	(310) 369-0093
Elayne Herscovici	Matovich Prod.	(661) 250-0644
Ed Hersh	A&E Television Networks	(212) 210-1400
Marshall Herskovitz	The Bedford Falls Company	(310) 394-5022
Jennifer Hertrich	InFront Prod.	(310) 369-5890
Eric Hertzel	The Cort/Madden Company	(323) 956-5884
Andrew Herwitz	Miramax Films	(212) 941-3800
Clayton Herzog	CPC Ent.	(310) 652-8194
Rick Hess	Propaganda Films	(323) 462-6400
H. Michael Heuser	Storm Ent.	(310) 656-2500
Bill Hewes	Barking Weasel Prod.	(323) 464-2275
Jennifer Love Hewitt	Love Spell Ent.	(310) 244-6040
Susan Heyer	Harpo Films	(310) 278-5559
Andy Heyward	DIC Ent.	(818) 955-5400
Mark Hibbard	Pleasant Prod.	(213) 707-0500
Noessa Higa	Friendly Prod.	(310) 369-3973
Angelique Higgins	Irish DreamTime	(310) 449-3411
David W. Higgins	Friendly Prod.	(310) 369-3973
Dennis P. Higgins	Columbia Pictures	(310) 244-4000
Marilyn Higgins	Another Large Prod.	(323) 954-8500
Debra Hill	Debra Hill Prod.	(310) 319-0052
Michael Hill	Paramount Pictures	(323) 956-5000
Stephen Hill	BET	(818) 566-9948
Ronald Hilton	Enteraktion	(954) 785-5070
Jenny Hinkey	Visionbox	(310) 204-4686
Michael Hirsh	Nelvana Ent.	(323) 549-4222
Sherwood Ho	Silvereye Prod.	(818) 501-4232
Jessica Hochman	Grammnet Prod. (Film)	(323) 956-5840
David Hodge	Hodge Film & Video	(310) 441-9773
Sandra Hodges	The Arnet/Kerner Co.	(310) 838-2500
Andrew Hoegl	Bunim-Murray Prod.	(818) 756-5100
Todd Hofacker	Reveal Ent.	(818) 733-9818
Judy Hofflund	Hofflund-Polone	(310) 859-1971
Dustin Hoffman	Punch Prod.	(310) 442-4880
Gary Hoffman	In Play Media Arts	(310) 839-7497
Katie Hoffman	Seven Arts Pictures	(323) 464-0225
Peter M. Hoffman	Seven Arts Pictures	(323) 464-0225
Ron Hoffman	Flying Tiger Films	(310) 664-9171
Susan Hoffman	Seven Arts Pictures	(323) 464-0225
Tom Hoffman	The Jacobson Company	(818) 560-1600
P. J. Hogan	Hogan Moorhouse Pictures	(310) 319-9299
Beth Holden	Propaganda Films	(323) 462-6400
John Holdridge	CBS Enterprises	(212) 975-4321
Gina Holland	BET	(818) 566-9948
Susan J. Holliday	CBS Television	(212) 975-4321
Mark Hollinger	Discovery Networks	(301) 986-1999
Erik Holmberg	New Line Cinema	(310) 854-5811
Lynn Holst	Hallmark Ent.	(212) 977-9001
Laura Holstein	John Wells Prod.	(818) 954-1687
James Holt	Flying Tiger Films	(310) 664-9171
James Holt	Franchise Pictures	(323) 822-0730
Scott Holtzman	Walt Disney Pictures	(818) 560-1000
Liz Holzman	Warner Bros. Animation	(818) 954-7670
Anthony Tae-Jum Hong	RGH/Lions Share Pictures	(310) 652-2893
James Honore	Columbia Pictures	(310) 244-4000
Conrad Hool	Silver Lion Films	(310) 393-9177
Lance Hool	Silver Lion Films	(310) 393-9177
Chris Hooper	Tool of North America	(310) 453-9244
Elizabeth Hooper	Lynda Obst Prod.	(323) 956-8744
Ted Hope	Good Machine	(212) 343-9230
Alicia Hopkins	Tapestry Films	(310) 275-1191
Laura Hopper	Brillstein-Grey Ent.	(310) 275-6135
Nate Hopper	20th Century Fox Pictures	(310) 369-1000
Kevin Hopps	Warner Bros. Animation	(818) 954-7670
William Horberg	Mirage Enterprises	(310) 244-2044
Karen Hori	Langley Prod.	(310) 449-5300
Alan Horn	Warner Bros.	(818) 954-6000
Rachel Horovitz	Fine Line Features	(310) 854-5811
James M. Horowitz	Universal Pictures	(818) 777-1000
Mark Horowitz	Columbia Pictures	(310) 244-4000
Mark M. Horowitz	Belisarius Prod.	(323) 956-8660
Drew Horton	Burrud Prod.	(714) 842-8422
Peter Horton	Pico Creek Prod.	(310) 394-7522
Wittney Horton	Cohen Pictures	(323) 951-4250
Mitch Horwits	Constantin Film	(310) 247-0300

Executives/Personnel Alphabetical Key

Chip Houghton	Imaginary Forces	(323) 957-6868
Marta Houske	Matrix Communications	(310) 782-8400
Andrew Howard	Incognito Ent.	(310) 246-1500
Ron Howard	Imagine Ent.	(310) 858-2000
Maura T. Hoy	Fireworks Pictures	(310) 854-2429
Walter Hoylman	Hy-Tone Prod.	(310) 456-3052
Ellen Huang	Hunt-Tavel Prod.	(310) 244-3144
Tom Huckabee	American Ent. Co.	(323) 939-6746
Hugh Hudson	Piper Prod.	(310) 883-8822
David Huey	Cine Excel Ent.	(818) 848-4478
Julie Huey	Samuel Goldwyn Films	(310) 860-3100
Brent Huff	Vanguard Prod.	(310) 306-4910
Erica Huggins	Radar Pictures	(310) 208-8525
Annie Hughes	Lion Rock Prod.	(310) 449-3205
Carole Hughes	Crossroads Films	(310) 659-6880
Eric Hughes	Universal Pictures	(818) 777-1000
Jennifer Hughes	Blue Bay Prod.	(310) 440-9904
Richard Hughes	October Prod.	(805) 962-2523
Richard Hull	Avalanche! Ent.	(310) 395-3660
Tony Hull	DreamWorks SKG	(818) 733-7000
Scott Humphries	Val D'Oro Ent.	(310) 656-8555
Helen Hunt	Hunt-Tavel Prod.	(310) 244-3144
Stacy Hunter	Polestar Ent. Grp.	(310) 278-0080
Frederick Huntsberry	Universal Pictures	(818) 777-1000
Gale Anne Hurd	Valhalla Motion Pictures	(323) 969-4300
Ben Hurivtz	The Canton Company	(818) 954-2130
Stephany Hurkos	Shonkyte Prod.	(818) 505-1332
Elizabeth Hurley	Simian Films	(310) 205-2724
Billy Hurman	Winchester Films	(310) 458-1400
Mo Husseini	kaboom	(415) 434-2666
Steven Hutensky	Miramax Films	(212) 941-3800
John Hyde	Film Roman	(818) 761-2544
Joan Hyler	M.H.S. Prod.	(310) 202-3336
Kevin Hyman	Dimension Films	(212) 941-3800
Bob Iger	The Walt Disney Company	(818) 560-1000
David Imhoff	New Line Cinema	(310) 854-5811
Thomas Imperato	20th Century Fox Pictures	(310) 369-1000
Thomas Imperato	New Regency Prod.	(310) 369-8300
Beth Irizarry	Barry Mendel Prod.	(818) 733-3076
Tracy Irvine	Steamroller Prod.	(323) 850-2940
John Irwin	Broadway Video	(212) 265-7621
Sandy Isaac	Bushwood Pictures	(323) 936-1659
Barry Isaacson	Reveal Ent.	(818) 733-9818
Donna Isaacson	20th Century Fox Pictures	(310) 369-1000
David Isreal	The Carsey-Werner.	(818) 655-5598
James Ivory	Merchant-Ivory Prod.	(212) 582-8049
Sunta Izzicupo	CBS Ent.	(323) 575-2345
Michael A. Jackman	Angel Ark Prod.	(818) 508-3338
Jim Jacks	Alphaville	(323) 956-4803
Dana Jackson	Hunt-Tavel Prod.	(310) 244-3144
Dawn Jackson	Red-Horse Prod.	(818) 705-2588
Ronald Jacobi	Sony Pictures Ent.	(310) 244-4000
Jay Jacobs	Proud Mary Ent.	(310) 288-1886
K. Jacobs	Beth Grossbard Prod.	(310) 841-2555
Rick Jacobs	Lifetime Television	(310) 556-7500
Danny Jacobson	InFront Prod.	(310) 369-5890
Janet Jacobson	Hallmark Ent.	(212) 977-9001
Mark Jacobson	Destination Films	(310) 434-2700
Nina Jacobson	Buena Vista Motion Pictures	(818) 560-1000
Tom Jacobson	The Jacobson Company	(818) 560-1600
Jay Jacoby	Flip Your Lid	(818) 222-0700
Sean Jacques	OMNIBUS	(818) 560-3611
Bob Jaffe	Jaffilms	(310) 820-2200
Stanley Jaffe	Jaffilms	(310) 820-2200
Josh R. Jaggars	Cindy Cowan Ent.	(323) 822-1082
Bruce James	Burke/Triolo Prod.	(310) 837-9900
Judith James	Dreyfuss/James Prod.	(323) 850-3140
Mark James	Shoelace Prod.	(212) 243-2900
Richard James	The Chelmar Grp.	(626) 358-4001
J. J. Jamieson	Orly Adelson Prod.	(310) 442-2012
Goly Jamshidi	New Concorde	(310) 820-6733
Annabel Jankel	Morton Jankel Zander	(310) 826-6200
Michael Patrick Jann	HKM Prod.	(323) 465-9494
Susan Jansen	Stan Rogow Prod.	(323) 993-5644
Stephen P. Jarchow	Regent Ent.	(310) 260-3333
Seth Jaret	Jaret Ent.	(310) 883-8807
Steven Jarmus	Universal Television	(818) 777-5300
Jon Jashni	Alchemy Ent.	(310) 396-5937
Robert Jaye	Hy-Tone Prod.	(310) 456-3052
Kristina Jeffers	The Matthau Company	(310) 454-3300
David Jellison	Tool of North America	(310) 453-9244
Stuart Jemesen	Stefanino Prod.	(310) 454-0109
Loretta Jeneski	Nonfiction Spots	(310) 319-6140
Brad Jenkel	Destination Films	(310) 434-2700
Andrews Jenkins	Stiefel + Company	(310) 581-7000
Sarah Jenks	Piper Prod.	(310) 883-8822
Maureen Jennings	Apatow Prod.	(323) 860-7825
Scott Jeralds	Warner Bros. Animation	(818) 954-7670
Erik Jessen	Raffaella Prod.	(818) 777-2655
Norman Jewison	Yorktown Prod.	(310) 264-4155
James P. Jimirro	National Lampoon	(310) 474-5252
Jim Jinkins	Jumbo Pictures	(212) 337-0077
Dan Jinks	The Jinks/Cohen Company	(818) 733-9880
Roland Joffe	Lightmotive	(310) 282-0660
Tatyana Joffe	MDP Worldwide	(310) 226-8300
Robin Johannsen	Creative Impulse Ent.	(818) 623-8260
George Johnsen	Threshold Ent.	(310) 452-8899
Brad Johnson	20th Century Fox Television	(310) 369-1000
Bret Johnson	Universal Pictures	(818) 777-1000
Bryan Johnson	The Film Syndicate	(323) 938-8080
Deborah Johnson	Universal Pictures	(818) 777-1000
Don Johnson	Don Johnson Prod.	(818) 238-2200
Floyd Johnson	Belisarius Prod.	(323) 956-8660
Jan Johnson	Celluloid	(303) 595-3152
Joanna Johnson	Paramount Pictures	(323) 956-5000
Joy Johnson	Red Bird Prod.	(310) 234-7234
Lucy Johnson	CBS Ent.	(323) 575-2345
Mark Johnson	Mark Johnson Prod.	(310) 777-0007
Mark S. Johnson	Big Ticket Television	(323) 860-7400
Mark Steven Johnson	Horseshoe Bay Prod.	(818) 560-3229
Philip Johnson	BET	(818) 566-9948
Robert Johnson	BET	(818) 566-9948
Robert W. Johnson	Walt Disney Pictures	(818) 560-1000
Tim Johnson	PaxTV/Paxson Communications	(310) 234-2200
Erich Joiner	Tool of North America	(310) 453-9244
David A. Jones	Initial Ent. Grp.	(310) 315-1722
Dennis E. Jones	Deja View Prod.	(818) 704-9185
Gary Jones	New Concorde	(310) 820-6733
Martin C. Jones	New Millennium Studios	(804) 957-4200
Noah Jones	Craig Anderson Prod.	(310) 841-2555
Quincy Jones	Quincy Jones Media Grp.	(323) 874-2009
William Jones	Metro-Goldwyn-Mayer	(310) 449-3000
Murray Jordan	Langley Prod.	(310) 449-5300
Richard Jordan	Lions Gate Ent.	(323) 692-7300
Kimberly Jose	Jean Doumanian Prod.	(212) 486-2626
Rick Joseph	Destination Films	(310) 434-2700
Barry Josephson	Sonnenfeld/Josephson	(310) 244-8777
Ashwin Joshi	Silvereye Prod.	(818) 501-4232
Barry Jossen	Imagine Ent.	(310) 858-2000
Byron Jost	AbsoluteFilms.net	(626) 442-6454
Bob Joyce	Cineville	(310) 394-4699
Carolyn Judd	Carolyn Judd & Assoc.	(323) 654-2571
Patricia Judice	DNA	(323) 463-2826
Stephen Judson	MacGillivray Freeman Films	(949) 494-1055
Kate Juergens	WB Television Network	(818) 977-5000
Susanna Juni	New Line Cinema	(310) 854-5811
Hardy Justice	Tribeca Prod.	(212) 941-4000
Nancy Juvonen	Flower Films	(310) 285-0200
Adolph Kaczynski	Dockry Prod.	(310) 274-0761
Ann Kaesman	Mindfire Ent.	(310) 204-4481
Peter Kagan	Stiefel + Company	(310) 581-7000
Tom Kageff	Randwell Prod.	(310) 996-6809
Leslie Kahan	First Avenue Films	(360) 376-3737
Nathan Kahane	The Canton Company	(818) 954-2130
Jeremy Kahn	Kahn Power Pictures	(310) 550-0770
Johnathan Kahn	Luminosity Prod.	(818) 752-3318
Joseph Kahn	Orange Soda	(323) 634-4375
Linda Kahn	Scholastic Ent.	(212) 343-7500
Michael Kahn	Luminosity Prod.	(818) 752-3318
Sheldon Kahn	The Montecito Picture Company	(805) 565-8590
Kenneth L. Kahrs	Universal Studios	(818) 777-1000
Peter Kalmbach	USA Films	(212) 539-4002
Sheraton Kalouria	NBC Ent.	(818) 840-4444
Jon Kamen	@radical.media	(310) 664-4500
Paige Kamin	Life of Riley	(310) 230-7798
Howard Kaplan	Morgan Creek Prod.	(818) 954-4800

Executives/Personnel Alphabetical Key

Mike Kaplan	Circle Assoc.	(310) 823-4024
Vivianne Kaplan	Ruddy Morgan Organization	(310) 271-7698
Peter Karabats	Clifden Prod.	(310) 234-5074
Linda Karabin	Burrud Prod.	(714) 842-8422
Michael Karbelnikoff	HKM Prod.	(323) 465-9494
Andrew Karsch	Longfellow Pictures	(212) 431-5550
Larry Kasanoff	Threshold Ent.	(310) 452-8899
Michael Kastenbaum	Visionbox	(310) 204-4686
Campbell Katz	Marty Katz Prod.	(310) 260-8501
Gail Katz	Radiant Prod.	(310) 656-1400
Howard Katz	ABC Inc./ABC Television	(310) 557-7777
Marty Katz	Marty Katz Prod.	(310) 260-8501
Olivier Katz	Celluloid	(303) 595-3152
Perry Katz	Perry Katz Prod.	(818) 981-0232
Robert Katz	Esparza-Katz Prod.	(310) 281-3770
Ross Katz	Good Machine	(212) 343-9230
Jeffrey Katzenberg	DreamWorks SKG	(818) 733-7000
Kenneth Kaufman	Patchett Kaufman Ent.	(310) 838-7000
Mark S. Kaufman	New Line Cinema	(310) 854-5811
Romy Kaufman	Universal Pictures	(818) 777-1000
Rosemary Kavanaugh	Infomercial Solutions	(818) 879-1140
Brent Kaviar	New Line Cinema	(310) 854-5811
Sara Kaviar	New Line Cinema	(310) 854-5811
Steve Kavich	Kavich Reynolds Prod.	(323) 466-2490
Dale Eldridge Kaye	Gold'N Hen Prod.	(310) 820-1308
Diane Keating	New Line Cinema	(310) 854-5811
Diane Keaton	Blue Relief	(310) 275-7900
Michael Keaton	Colomby/Keaton Prod.	(310) 399-8881
Laura Keats	IndieGal Prod.	(818) 890-6111
Jim Keegan	Artisan Ent.	(310) 449-9200
Richard Keeley	New Line Cinema	(310) 854-5811
Peter Keenan	Backyard Prod.	(310) 314-1122
Karen Kehela	Imagine Ent.	(310) 858-2000
David Keighley	IMAX Corp.	(310) 255-5500
David Keith	New Line Cinema	(310) 854-5811
Leah Keith	DreamWorks SKG	(818) 733-7000
Eytan Keller	Fox Family Channel	(310) 235-9700
Michael Keller	Paramount Int'l. Television	(323) 956-5000
David E. Kelley	David E. Kelley Prod.	(310) 727-2200
Marie G. Kelley	Kelley Prod.	(858) 456-6609
Nick Kelley	Don Johnson Prod.	(818) 238-2200
Jamie Kellner	WB Television Network	(818) 977-5000
Barry Kemp	Bungalow 78 Prod.	(323) 956-4440
Carroll Kemp	Cornice Ent.	(310) 777-0200
Paul Kemp	Chiodo Bros. Prod.	(818) 842-5656
David Kennedy	Luminosity Prod.	(818) 752-3318
Donald Kennedy	Columbia Pictures	(310) 244-4000
Lora Kennedy	Warner Bros. Pictures Prod.	(818) 954-6000
Saffron Kenny	Imaginary Forces	(323) 957-6868
Jennifer Keohane	Colomby/Keaton Prod.	(310) 399-8881
Rob Kerchner	Capital Arts Ent.	(310) 581-3020
Roseann M. Keris	David E. Kelley Prod.	(310) 727-2200
Bruce Kerner	Big Ticket Television	(323) 860-7400
Jordan Kerner	The Arnet/Kerner Co.	(310) 838-2500
David Keslick	Neild Street Prod.	(323) 969-9447
Brad Kessell	Paramount Pictures	(323) 956-5000
Jerry Ketcham	Buena Vista Motion Pictures	(818) 560-1000
Robert Keyghobad	Twilight Time Films	(310) 284-7310
Peter Kiernan	Talent Ent. Grp.	(323) 969-0700
Liam Kildare	Proletariat	(818) 763-8356
Frank Kilpatrick	Hot Spots Television	(310) 606-5700
Ann Kim	Graying & Balding	(310) 587-2330
Scott Kimball	Enchantment Films	(818) 506-5249
Megan Kimberly	Regent Ent.	(310) 260-3333
Graham King	Initial Ent. Grp.	(310) 315-1722
Jonathan King	Fountainhead Pictures	(310) 276-5583
Jonathon King	Laurence Mark Prod.	(310) 244-5239
Kandice King	Kandice King Prod.	(310) 822-9502
Roger King	CBS Enterprises	(212) 975-4321
Dick Kiratsonlis	MDP Worldwide	(310) 226-8300
Julie Kirkham	A Band Apart	(323) 951-4600
David Kirkpatrick	Original Voices	(310) 392-3479
Nancy Kirkpatrick	Paramount Pictures	(323) 956-5000
Glenn Kirschbaum	Greystone Communication Grp.	(818) 762-2900
Jeff Kirschenbaum	Mace Neufeld Prod.	(310) 244-2555
David Kirschner	David Kirschner Prod.	(323) 939-0230
Nancy Kissock	C'est Tout Prod.	(310) 475-5615
Martin Kistler	Lux Pictures	(310) 301-0101
Sam Kitt	40 Acres & A Mule	(718) 624-3703
Arlene Klasky	Klasky Csupo	(323) 463-0145
Felix Kleiman	Afra-Film Enterprises	(323) 882-6193
Amanda Klein	USA Films	(212) 539-4002
Devin Klein	Carlyle Prod.	(323) 848-4960
Howard Klein	3 Arts Ent.	(310) 888-3200
J. J. Klein	Destination Films	(310) 434-2700
Jennifer Klein	Bay Films	(310) 829-7799
Larry Klein	Dick Clark Prod.	(818) 841-3003
Dave Kleinman	Life of Riley	(310) 230-7798
Richard Klubeck	Jersey Films	(310) 203-1000
Stephanie Kluft	Universal Pictures	(818) 777-1000
Catalaine Knell	Ctonic Flikz	(323) 957-7824
Kelly Knight	Ideal Ent.	(323) 939-3399
T. K. Knowles	Bob Industries	(310) 396-7333
Kristine Knudson	MDP Worldwide	(310) 226-8300
Howard Hawk Koch Jr.	The Koch Company	(818) 954-7964
Rene Kock	Commercials While-U-Wait	(310) 399-3456
Phyllis Koenig	Stiefel + Company	(310) 581-7000
Pamela Koffler	Killer Films	(212) 473-3950
David Kohner-Zuckerman	Silver Lion Films	(310) 393-9177
Larry Kohorn	Columbia Pictures	(310) 244-4000
John Kokum	Flip Your Lid	(818) 222-0700
Stacy Kolker	Screen Gems	(310) 244-4000
Kevin Koloff	Paramount Pictures	(323) 956-5000
Marian Kolta	Fine Line Features	(310) 854-5811
Marian Koltai-Levine	New Line Cinema	(310) 854-5811
Jonathon Komack Martin	Tapestry Films	(310) 275-1191
Cathy Konrad	Konrad Pictures	(310) 244-3555
Anne Kopelson	Kopelson Ent.	(310) 369-7555
Arnold Kopelson	Kopelson Ent.	(310) 369-7555
Elysa Koplovitz	20th Century Fox Pictures	(310) 369-1000
David Korda	Capella Films	(310) 247-4700
Rosanne Korenberg	Fox Searchlight Pictures	(310) 369-4402
Leonard Kornberg	Universal Pictures	(818) 777-1000
Craig Kornblau	Universal Pictures	(818) 777-1000
Robert Kosberg	Merv Griffin Ent.	(310) 385-3160
David Kosse	Universal Pictures	(818) 777-1000
Tony Kost	Post Modern Edit	(714) 751-2681
Jan A. Koster	The Woofenill Works	(212) 734-2578
Jim Kouf	Kouf-Bigelow Prod.	(818) 508-1010
Steven Kovner	Gears Communications	(818) 840-9333
Joe Kraft	Sony Pictures Ent.	(310) 244-4000
Robert Kraft	20th Century Fox Pictures	(310) 369-1000
Sara Kraft	H-Gun Labs	(415) 648-4386
Julian Krainin	Krainin Prod.	(914) 359-0445
Shinaan Krakowsky	Greystone Communication Grp.	(818) 762-2900
Andrew Kramer	Franchise Pictures	(323) 822-0730
Jeremy Kramer	Miramax Films	(212) 941-3800
Jonathan Krane	The Jonathan Krane Grp.	(310) 278-0142
Tony Krantz	Imagine Ent.	(310) 858-2000
Sylvia J. Krask	Walt Disney Pictures	(818) 560-1000
Ellen Krass	EMK Prod.	(310) 260-3362
Amy Krause	The Prod. Asylum	(760) 599-5494
Jourdan Krauss	Davis Classics	(310) 551-2266
Debbie Kreger	Columbia Pictures	(310) 244-4000
Lisa Kregness	Constantin Film	(310) 247-0300
Alan Krieger	Columbia Pictures	(310) 244-4000
Brette Krinick	Seven Arts Pictures	(323) 464-0225
Steve Kripner	Taurus Ent. Company	(323) 860-0807
Mark Kristol	Universal Pictures	(818) 777-1000
Marty Krofft	Sid & Marty Krofft Pictures	(818) 386-1918
Sid Krofft	Sid & Marty Krofft Pictures	(818) 386-1918
Steve Krone	Village Roadshow Pictures	(818) 260-6000
Bob Kronovet	30 Second Films	(310) 315-1750
Scott Kroopf	Radar Pictures	(310) 208-8525
Phil Kruner	Craig Anderson Prod.	(310) 841-2555
Sara Kucserka	Outerbanks Ent.	(323) 654-3700
Tom Kuhn	Weintraub/Kuhn Prod.	(310) 788-9380
Robert Kulzer	Constantin Film	(310) 247-0300
Subash Kundamal	Silvereye Prod.	(818) 501-4232
Mauricio Kuri	Legacy Films	(323) 856-8888
David Kurs	Jersey Films	(310) 203-1000
Bob Kurtz	Kurtz & Friends	(818) 841-8188
Howard Kurtzman	20th Century Fox Television	(310) 369-1000
Donald Kushner	Kushner-Locke Company	(818) 841-8188
Fran Kuzui	Kuzui Enterprises	(323) 850-1195
Kaz Kuzui	Kuzui Enterprises	(323) 850-1195

Executives/Personnel Alphabetical Key

Veronika Kwan-Rubinek	Warner Bros.	(818) 954-6000
Richard La Forge	Wild Things Prod.	(323) 954-4577
Lou La Monte	Int'l. Television Grp. (ITG)	(310) 656-9100
Scarlett Lacey	The Cort/Madden Company	(323) 956-5884
Virginie Lacoste	Tollin/Robbins Prod.	(818) 766-5004
Alan Ladd Jr.	The Ladd Company	(310) 777-2060
Eric Ladd	Picture Mill	(323) 465-8800
Keiliann Ladd	The Ladd Company	(310) 777-2060
Bronwen LaGrue	Miss Jones	(310) 576-9280
Anne Lai	Scott Free Prod.	(310) 360-2250
Brian Lai	Metro Pictures	(310) 301-7890
Michael Lake	Village Roadshow Pictures	(818) 260-6000
Andre Lamal	Lakeshore Ent. Corp.	(323) 956-4222
Bob Lambert	Walt Disney Pictures	(818) 560-1000
John Lambert	Regent Ent.	(310) 260-3333
Leslie Lamers	Warner Bros. Animation	(818) 954-7670
Jon Landau	Lightstorm Ent.	(310) 656-6100
Tania Landau	Mutual Film Company	(323) 871-5690
Yari Landau	Sony Pictures Ent.	(310) 244-4000
John Landgraf	Jersey Films	(310) 203-1000
Kristin Landholt	Bona Fide Prod.	(310) 273-6782
John Landis	St. Clare Ent.	(310) 360-0451
Joseph K. Landsman	The Woofenill Works	(212) 734-2578
Cynthia Lane	Telescene Film Grp.	(514) 737-5512
Rocky Lang	Harbor Lights Prod.	(818) 993-5255
Steve Lange	Weller/Grossman Prod.	(818) 755-4800
Patricia Langer	Lifetime Television	(212) 424-7000
Donna Langley	New Line Cinema	(310) 854-5811
John Langley	Langley Prod.	(310) 449-5300
Sherry Lansing	Paramount Pictures	(323) 956-5000
Phillip Large	Another Large Prod.	(323) 954-8500
Drew Larner	Spyglass Ent.	(818) 560-3458
Sarah Lash	Lions Gate Ent.	(323) 692-7300
Matt LaSorsa	New Line Cinema	(310) 854-5811
David Lasseron	Cohn & Company	(310) 899-6979
James Lassiter	Overbrook Ent.	(818) 777-2224
Richard Latarewicz	Flying Tiger Films	(310) 664-9171
Ahmed Lateef	Silvereye Prod.	(818) 501-4232
Dana P. Laufer	New Line Cinema	(310) 854-5811
Tom Lavagnino	Genrebend Prod.	(310) 284-7312
Emmet G. Lavery Jr.	D.L.T. Ent.	(323) 937-1144
C'esca Lawrence	Snow Leopard Prod.	(310) 827-1220
Francis Lawrence	DNA	(323) 463-2826
Michael Lawrence	Krainin Prod.	(914) 359-0445
Ray Lawrence	Cohn & Company	(310) 899-6979
J. F. Lawton	Lawton Ent.	(323) 467-5677
Doug Lay	c.2K Ent.	(310) 208-2324
Charles Layton	Miramax Films	(212) 941-3800
Andrew Lazar	Mad Chance	(818) 954-3803
Ava Lazar	Wonderland Films	(323) 656-6489
Rob Lazebnik	Icebox	(310) 202-5000
Ron Lazzeretti	Spoke Film	(310) 477-2272
Claire Le Covac	Enteraktion	(954) 785-5070
Kevin Leadingham	Nitestar Prod.	(323) 468-8089
Larry Leahy	MindStorm Prod.	(310) 393-1183
Michael Leahy	Neo Art & Logic	(323) 653-6007
Orlando Leal	Moving Image	(310) 659-8022
Norman Lear	Act III Prod.	(310) 385-4111
Dennis Leary	Apostle Pictures	(212) 541-4323
Mimi Leder	Yak Yak Pictures	(818) 954-3861
Nina Lederman	Artists Television Grp.	(310) 860-8200
Gaille LeDrew	Chesler/Perlmutter Prod.	(310) 443-9650
Bill Lee	E! Ent. Television	(323) 954-2400
Debra Lee	BET	(818) 566-9948
Preston Lee	Go Film	(212) 677-7500
Raymond Lee	Leading Pictures	(310) 385-0951
Roy Lee	Bender-Spink	(323) 845-1640
Spike Lee	40 Acres & A Mule	(718) 624-3703
Stan Lee	Marvel Characters	(310) 234-8991
Virginia Lee	Coppos Films	(323) 463-0764
Ian Leech	Piper Prod.	(310) 883-8822
Laurel Lees-Gonzalez	RKO Pictures	(310) 277-0707
Meg LeFauve	Egg Pictures	(323) 956-8400
George LeFave	Abby Lou Ent.	(626) 795-7334
Dan Leiblien	USA Films	(212) 539-4002
Arnold Leibovit	Talking Rings Ent.	(702) 227-3433
Stephanie Leifer	ABC Entertainment	(310) 557-7777
Adam Leipzig	Terra Bella Ent.	(323) 655-2311
Kenneth Lemberger	Columbia Pictures	(310) 244-4000
Amy Lemish	Parkway Prod.	(310) 244-4040
Jim Lemley	Icon Prod. Inc.	(323) 956-2100
David Lena	Metro Pictures	(310) 301-7890
Malcolm Leo	Malcolm Leo Prod.	(323) 464-4448
George Leon	Columbia Pictures	(310) 244-4000
Monica Leon	Quasar Studios	(310) 289-1547
Steve Leon	Collaborative Artists	(310) 274-4800
Ken Leonard	Calico World Ent.	(818) 755-3800
Leigh Leshner	Venture Ent. Grp.	(818) 981-7813
Diana Lesmez	Atlantic Streamline	(310) 319-9366
Mark L. Lester	American World Pictures	(818) 715-1480
Mike Lestico	Raven Prod.	(760) 325-7191
Leslie Leventman	MTV Networks	(310) 752-8000
William A. Levey	MM2K	(310) 276-0750
Joe Levi	Cosgrove-Meurer Prod.	(818) 843-5600
Gail Levin	Paramount Pictures	(323) 956-5000
Jody A. Levin	New Line Cinema	(310) 854-5811
Robert Levin	Columbia Pictures	(310) 244-4000
Susan Levin	Columbia Pictures	(310) 244-4000
Susan Levin	Silver Pictures Television	(818) 954-4490
Dan Levine	Jersey Shore Films	(212) 333-3377
Jackie Levine	Further Films	(818) 777-6700
Paul Levine	Belisarius Prod.	(323) 956-8660
Gary Levinsohn	Mutual Film Company	(323) 871-5690
Barry Levinson	Baltimore/Spring Creek Pictures	(818) 954-1210
Barry Levinson	Spring Creek Prod.	(818) 954-1210
Barry Levinson	The Levinson/Fontana Company	(212) 633-0440
Dan Levinson	Moxie Pictures	(323) 957-5420
Frederick Levy	Marty Katz Prod.	(310) 260-8501
John Levy	Columbia Pictures	(310) 244-4000
Lawrence Levy	New Line Cinema	(310) 854-5811
Michael I. Levy	Michael I. Levy Enterprises	(323) 866-1802
Robert Levy	Tapestry Films	(310) 275-1191
Shuki Levy	Saban Ent.	(310) 235-5100
Wayne Lewellen	Paramount Pictures	(323) 956-5000
Claudia Lewis	Fox Searchlight Pictures	(310) 369-4402
Ryan Lewis	Halsted Pictures	(310) 450-7804
Simon R. Lewis	Simon Lewis Prod.	(818) 906-7677
Susan Lewis	MTV Films	(323) 956-8023
Brad Ley	Outlaw Prod.	(310) 777-2000
Rodney Liber	Blue Bay Prod.	(310) 440-9904
Andrew Licht	Licht/Mueller Films	(310) 205-5500
Mickey Liddell	Banner Ent.	(323) 848-2880
Cory M. Lidschin	The Bubble Factory	(310) 358-3000
Hal Lieberman	Mostow/Lieberman	(818) 777-4444
Jonathan Liebman	Brillstein-Grey Ent.	(310) 275-6135
Stacy Lifton	Fox Family Channel	(310) 235-9700
Clayton Light	SplendidLight Media Prod.	(949) 722-8485
Bruce Lilliston	Kushner-Locke Company	(818) 841-8188
Sindy Lin	Jersey Films	(310) 203-1000
John Lindauer	Fuel	(310) 314-1644
David Linde	Good Machine	(212) 343-9230
Terese Linden Kohn	American World Pictures	(818) 715-1480
Lisa Lindstrom	The Arnet/Kerner Co.	(310) 838-2500
Dylan Liner	Sony Pictures Classics	(212) 833-8833
Herb Linsey	LA Prod.	(323) 874-9487
Jane Linter	21st Century Man	(323) 466-3227
Robin Lippin	Stan Rogow Prod.	(323) 993-5644
Walter C. Liss	ABC Inc./ABC Television	(310) 557-7777
Patrick List	Debra Hill Prod.	(310) 319-0052
Paul Lister	DreamWorks SKG	(818) 733-7000
Mike Listo	David E. Kelley Prod.	(310) 727-2200
Robert Litt	Let There Be Light Prod.	(818) 880-4717
Jill Littman	Talent Ent. Grp.	(323) 969-0700
Jonathan Littman	Jerry Bruckheimer Films	(310) 664-6260
Ian Litvinoff	Si Litvinoff Prod.	(323) 848-6907
Si Litvinoff	Si Litvinoff Prod.	(323) 848-6907
Linda Livingston	Smillie Films	(310) 314-0072
Vanessa Livingston	Tavel Ent.	(310) 278-6700
David Livingstone	Universal Pictures	(818) 777-1000
Jim Livolsi	Calico World Ent.	(818) 755-3800
Lori Lober	The Artists Company	(323) 650-4722
Peter Locke	Kushner-Locke Company	(818) 841-8188
Warren Lockhart	Warren Lockhart Prod.	(310) 821-1414
Laura Kim Lodin	National Geographic Films	(310) 229-0990
Brent Loefke	Vihlene & Assoc.	(949) 582-0937
Phil Lofarno	Walt Disney Pictures	(818) 560-1000

349

Executives/Personnel Alphabetical Key

Tom Lofaro	Stan Rogow Prod.	(323) 993-5644
Robert Logevall	Bruce Dowad Assoc.	(323) 654-8855
John Logigian	Jean Doumanian Prod.	(212) 486-2626
Grace Loh	New Crime Prod.	(310) 396-2199
Kathleen Lolley	Undergrace Prod.	(818) 833-8666
Barry London	Destination Films	(310) 434-2700
Robby London	DIC Ent.	(818) 955-5400
David Long	Broadway Video	(212) 265-7621
Steven A. Longi	Permut Presentations	(310) 248-2792
Karen Loop	David Kirschner Prod.	(323) 939-0230
Rob Loos	TLC Ent.	(818) 655-6155
Elissa Loparco	New Regency Prod.	(310) 369-8300
Boo Lopez	Kurtz & Friends	(818) 841-8188
Carlos Lopez	Marvel Characters	(310) 234-8991
Sarah Lopez	Conundrum Ent.	(310) 319-2800
Tiffany Mclinn Lore	The Greif Company	(310) 385-1200
Alec Lorimore	MacGillivray Freeman Films	(949) 494-1055
Christian Loubek	HKM Prod.	(323) 465-9494
Patrick Loubert	Nelvana Ent.	(323) 549-4222
Eric Louzil	RGH/Lions Share Pictures	(310) 652-2893
Kenton Low	Universal Studios	(818) 777-1000
Tom Lowe	GreenWater Pictures	(323) 655-9585
Doug Lowell	New Concorde	(310) 820-6733
Richard Lowenstein	Metro Pictures	(310) 301-7890
David Lozano	Alta Vista Prod.	(310) 444-2050
Michael Lozano	Alta Vista Prod.	(310) 444-2050
Victoria Lucas	Signature Films	(310) 226-8374
Gary Lucchesi	Lakeshore Ent. Corp.	(323) 956-4222
Fran Lucci	Atlantic Streamline	(310) 319-9366
Klaus Lucka	NXT Ent.	(310) 289-9600
Graham Ludlow	Erratic Ent.	(310) 657-0922
Brad Luff	Original Film	(310) 445-9000
Brenna Lui	AEI	(323) 932-0407
Gordon H. Lui	AEI	(323) 932-0407
Michael Luisi	Miramax Films	(212) 941-3800
Butch Lukic	Warner Bros. Animation	(818) 954-7670
John Luma	FX Networks	(310) 444-8123
Stacy Lumbrezer	Verhoeven/Marshall Films	(310) 244-5352
Donna E. Lusitana	Greystone Communication Grp.	(818) 762-2900
Michael Lustig	Icon Prod. Inc.	(323) 956-2100
Ron Lynch	Buena Vista Motion Pictures	(818) 560-1000
Ron Lynch	Universal Pictures	(818) 777-1000
Susan Lyne	ABC Entertainment	(310) 557-7777
Michael Lynne	New Line Cinema	(310) 854-5811
Gail Lyon	Red Wagon	(310) 244-4466
Jason Lyon	Asset Pictures	(212) 255-6187
Jackie Lyons	USA Network	(212) 413-5000
Sidney H. Lyons	CBS Ent.	(323) 575-2345
Anthony Mabin	Boyington Studios	(310) 822-2360
Laura Macauley	JGF	(323) 462-1500
Jean MacCurdy	Warner Bros. Animation	(818) 954-7670
Bill MacDonald	William I. MacDonald Prod.	(310) 581-4840
Laurie MacDonald	DreamWorks SKG	(818) 733-7000
Greg MacGillivray	MacGillivray Freeman Films	(949) 494-1055
Stephen Macias	Michael I. Levy Enterprises	(323) 866-1802
Gillian Mackenzie	Jane Startz Prod.	(212) 545-8910
Iain MacKenzie	Piper Prod.	(310) 883-8822
Trevor Macy	Propaganda Films	(323) 462-6400
Jasmine Madatian	Paramount Pictures	(323) 956-5000
Marianne Maddalena	Wes Craven Films	(818) 752-0197
Molly Madden	3 Arts Ent.	(310) 888-3200
Paul Madden	Si Litvinoff Prod.	(323) 848-6907
Brent Maddock	Stampede Ent.	(310) 264-4229
Alex Madero	HKM Prod.	(323) 465-9494
Meg Madison	Revelations Ent.	(310) 394-3131
Madonna	Maverick Films	(310) 276-6177
Stacy Maes	Lightstorm Ent.	(310) 656-6100
Douglas Magallon	Strom Magallon Ent.	(323) 969-1089
Heather Magee	Barry Mendel Prod.	(818) 733-3076
Alex Maggioni	UBU Prod.	(818) 655-5850
Karen Magid	Paramount Pictures	(323) 956-5000
Thora Magnusson	True Blue Prod.	(323) 661-9191
James Magowan	Lux Pictures	(310) 301-0101
Philippe Maigret	Centropolis Ent.	(310) 244-4300
Juliana Maio	Lighthouse Prod.	(310) 859-4923
Ileen Maisel	Fine Line Features	(310) 854-5811
Xander Maksik	American Ent. Co.	(323) 939-6746
Charles Malcolm	Charles Malcolm Video Prod.	(714) 963-4222
Michael Maliani	DIC Ent.	(818) 955-5400
Amir Malin	Artisan Ent.	(310) 449-9200
John Malkovich	Mr. Mudd Prod.	(323) 932-5656
Lorielle Mallue	Egg Pictures	(323) 956-8400
Marcie Malooly	Industrial Light + Magic Commercial Prod.	(323) 957-2002
Ron Malvin	Face Broadcast Prod.	(818) 842-9081
Caroline Manalo	StarToons Int'l..	(708) 335-3535
Renee Mancuso	Lakeshore Ent. Corp.	(323) 956-4222
Frank Mancuso, Jr.	FGM Ent.	(310) 358-1370
Jim Manera	The Joneses	(310) 656-8300
Stephanie Mangano	Buena Vista Motion Pictures	(818) 560-1000
Brian D. Manis	Peters Ent.	(818) 954-2441
Doug Mankoff	Echo Lake Prod.	(310) 399-9164
Michael Mann	Forward Pass	(310) 571-3443
Bob Manning	MM2K	(310) 276-0750
Michelle Manning	Paramount Pictures	(323) 956-5000
David Manson	Sarabande Prod.	(310) 395-4842
Joseph Mantegna	Zooma Zooma Corp.	(212) 941-7680
John Manulis	Foundation Ent.	(310) 204-4686
John Manulis	Visionbox	(310) 204-4686
Scott Manville	Merv Griffin Ent.	(310) 385-3160
A. J. Marcantonio	Yak Yak Pictures	(818) 954-3861
Rob Marcarelli	Marca-Relli Prod.	(310) 457-8867
Xavier Marchand	Universal Pictures	(818) 777-1000
Gina Marcheschi	Everyman Pictures	(310) 244-1686
John Marcom	Atom Films	(626) 793-4950
Bob Marcucci	Chancellor Ent.	(310) 474-4521
Jon Marcus	Killer Films	(212) 473-3950
Michael Marcus	Cornice Ent.	(310) 777-0200
Kool Marder	Universal Pictures	(818) 777-1000
Bobby Mardis	Fat Chance Films	(323) 882-4130
Ann Maré	BCProd./BCTV Prod.	(949) 495-1500
Gary Marenzi	Paramount Int'l. Television	(323) 956-5000
Cyndi Margolis	Blue Wolf Prod.	(415) 561-6655
Ann Margret	AM Prod.	(310) 275-9081
Alan Margulies	AM Prod.	(310) 275-9081
Lisa Prentis Margulis	HKM Prod.	(323) 465-9494
Janice Marinelli	Buena Vista Television	(818) 560-5000
Harri Mark	Evil Twin Prod.	(818) 986-8551
James Mark	Dockry Prod.	(310) 274-0761
Laurence Mark	Laurence Mark Prod.	(310) 244-5239
Tara Mark	Red Wagon	(310) 244-4466
Ed Markley	Southern Skies	(310) 855-9833
Ethan Markowitz	Lightmotive	(310) 282-0660
Richard Marks	Kushner-Locke Company	(818) 841-8188
David Markus	Radiant Prod.	(310) 656-1400
Deborah Marlowe	Flying Tiger Films	(310) 664-9171
Andrea Marozas	Walt Disney Pictures	(818) 560-1000
Gregg Marquette	Luminosity Prod.	(818) 752-3318
Matthew Marquis	Fuel	(310) 314-1644
Joe Marroquin	Marca-Relli Prod.	(310) 457-8867
Paul Marshal	O Ent.	(949) 443-3222
Alan Marshall	Verhoeven/Marshall Films	(310) 244-5352
John Marshall	Villains	(310) 888-8900
Penny Marshall	Parkway Prod.	(310) 244-4040
Peter Marshall	Lions Gate Ent.	(323) 692-7300
Michele Martell	The Jim Henson Company	(323) 802-1500
Bruce Martin	1171 Prod. Grp.	(323) 655-1171
Bruce Martin	No Prisoners	(310) 979-9097
Dan Martin	Hallmark Ent.	(212) 977-9001
Frank Martin	Eleventh Day Ent.	(818) 784-6403
Gary Martin	Columbia Pictures	(310) 244-4000
Pam Martin	Silver Pictures Television	(818) 954-4490
Scott Martin	Paramount Pictures	(323) 956-5000
Barbara Martinez-Jitner	El Norte Prod.	(310) 360-1194
Chad Marting	Roadside Attractions	(310) 860-1692
Niki Marvin	Niki Marvin Prod.	(310) 274-6320
John Marzilli	Suzanne Bauman Prod.	(818) 348-4342
Cathy Masamitsu	Woody Fraser Prod.	(818) 550-6102
Kira Mason	Merv Griffin Ent.	(310) 385-3160
David Matalon	New Regency Prod.	(310) 369-8300
Roy Matalon	New Regency Prod.	(310) 369-8300
Bonnie Matchinga	The House Prod. Company	(323) 851-5151
Bill Mather	Villains	(310) 888-8900
Annette Mathews	Face Prod.	(310) 285-2300
Harry Mathias	Hallowes Prod.	(310) 390-4767
Nic Mathieu	No Prisoners	(310) 979-9097

Executives/Personnel Alphabetical Key

Kris Mathur	Backyard Prod.	(310) 314-1122
Mitchel Matovich	Matovich Prod.	(661) 250-0644
Patricia J. Matson	ABC Inc./ABC Television	(310) 557-7777
Yasushi Matsuura	c.2K Ent.	(310) 208-2324
Charles Matthau	The Matthau Company	(310) 454-3300
Stacey Matthew	Overbrook Ent.	(818) 777-2224
Gina Matthews	Roundtable Ink	(323) 466-4646
Kurt Mattila	Imaginary Forces	(323) 957-6868
Cynthia Matzeger	The Robert Evans Company	(323) 956-8800
Joe Mauro	Lineup Technologies	(310) 473-8890
Daphne Maxwell Reid	New Millennium Studios	(804) 957-4200
Christopher May	Angel Ark Prod.	(818) 508-3338
Tom Mazza	Columbia TriStar Television	(310) 202-1234
Jeff Mazzola	Black Sheep Ent.	(818) 769-2227
Marilyn McAleer	Lifetime Television	(212) 424-7000
Pete McAlevey	Newmark Films	(323) 782-4969
Alessandra McAliley	Capella Films	(310) 247-4700
Tracy McArdie	Screen Gems	(310) 244-4000
Kate McArdle	USA Network	(212) 413-5000
Diane McArter	Omaha Pictures	(310) 396-4333
Sarah McArthur	Pixar Animation Studios	(510) 752-3000
Stasi McAteer	Santa Monica Pictures	(310) 264-5566
Christine McBride	Raymond Wagner Prod.	(310) 278-1970
Betty McBurnie	Vihlene & Assoc.	(949) 582-0937
Andrea McCall	DreamWorks SKG	(818) 733-7000
David McCann	Walt Disney Pictures	(818) 560-1000
Hank McCann	Chesler/Perlmutter Prod.	(310) 443-9650
Tara McCann	American Zoetrope	(310) 899-8000
Ross McCanse	Ross McCanse & Assoc.	(818) 506-4715
Jim McCarthy	No Prisoners	(310) 979-9097
Kelly McCarthy	Twilight Time Films	(310) 284-7310
Debbie McClellan	The Jim Henson Company	(323) 802-1500
Gail McClellan	E! Ent. Television	(323) 954-2400
Kevin McCormick	Warner Bros. Pictures Prod.	(818) 954-6000
Mark McCoy	Kahn Power Pictures	(310) 550-0770
Lori McCreary	Revelations Ent.	(310) 394-3131
Dennis McCullough	IPS Prod.	(323) 851-3595
Pilar McCurry	Columbia Pictures	(310) 244-4000
Michael McDavitt	The Matthau Company	(310) 454-3300
Cheryl McDermott	Saban Ent.	(310) 235-5100
Dan McDermott	DreamWorks SKG	(818) 733-7000
Kathy McDermott	Columbia Pictures	(310) 244-4000
Bo McDonald	Villains	(310) 888-8900
Carolyn McDonald	Carrie Prod.	(818) 567-3292
Michael McDonald	Renaissance Pictures	(818) 777-0088
Ed McDonnell	Di Novi Pictures	(310) 581-1355
Linda McDonough	Flower Films	(310) 285-0200
Will McElroy	Unger Prod.	(310) 859-1455
Guy McElwaine	Triology Ent. Grp.	(310) 449-3095
Katie McEnroe	American Movie Classics	(516) 803-4300
Rob McEntegart	Intermedia Films	(310) 777-0007
David McFadzean	Wind Dancer Prod. Grp.	(323) 645-1200
Michael McGahey	Friendly Prod.	(310) 369-3973
Mark McGarry	Franchise Pictures	(323) 822-0730
Victor McGauley	Amen Ra Films	(310) 246-6510
David McGinley	Fuel	(310) 314-1644
J. R. McGinnis	Paramount Network Television	(323) 956-5000
John McGinnis	Bonfire Films of America	(323) 953-6815
Carole McGorrian	Cindy Cowan Ent.	(323) 822-1082
Thomas J. McGough	Pongo Prod.	(818) 562-3336
Thomas McGrath	Viacom Ent. Grp.	(323) 956-5000
Ginger McGuire	Scholastic Ent.	(212) 343-7500
Terence McGuirk	Turner Ent. Grp.	(404) 827-1500
Chris McGurk	Metro-Goldwyn-Mayer Studios	(310) 449-3000
Judith A. McHale	Discovery Networks	(301) 986-1999
Doug McHenry	Elephant Walk Ent.	(310) 887-3977
Paul McIlvaine	Lotus Films	(626) 292-1015
John McKay	CinemaPop	(714) 444-0530
Gary McKendry	Go Film	(212) 677-7500
Christopher McKinnon	2EZ	(323) 939-9975
Jenny McLaren	Mirage Enterprises	(310) 244-2044
Kathleen McLaughlin	Rumbalara Films	(323) 936-4436
Shaun McLaughlin	Warner Bros. Animation	(818) 954-7670
John J. McMahon	Wilshire Court Prod.	(310) 557-2444
Bob McMinn	Lakeshore Ent. Corp.	(323) 956-4222
David McNally	Omaha Pictures	(310) 396-4333
John McNamara	Laurence Mark Prod.	(310) 244-5239
Lauren McNamara	Carbo Films	(310) 586-1969
Sean McNamara	Brookwell McNamara Ent.	(310) 306-2151
Cynthia McWethy	Beacon Communications	(310) 260-7000
Linda Meadows	Screen Gems	(310) 244-4000
Kevin Meagher	Popular Arts Ent.	(818) 562-6366
Brian Medavoy	Talent Ent. Grp.	(323) 969-0700
Mike Medavoy	Phoenix Pictures	(310) 244-6100
Mark Medernach	Duck Soup Studios	(310) 478-0771
Benny Medina	Handprint Ent.	(310) 481-4400
Joe Medjuck	The Montecito Picture Company	(805) 565-8590
Dora Medrano	Carbo Films	(310) 586-1969
Lisa Mehling	Chelsea Pictures	(323) 860-8030
Chase Meilen	Silver Lion Films	(310) 393-9177
John Mein	Ginty Films	(310) 274-9691
Christopher Meisel	American Video Grp.	(310) 477-1535
Louis M. Meisenger	The Walt Disney Company	(818) 560-1000
Leon Melas	Zeal Pictures	(323) 871-4000
Carey Melcher	Carey Melcher Prod.	(323) 962-7020
Tim Melchior	The Association	(818) 841-9660
Louis Mellini	Sodas & Shoes	(323) 692-9848
Scott Mellini	Sodas & Shoes	(323) 692-9848
Shirley Mellner	Hollane Corp./Martin Poll Films	(323) 876-8873
Michael Mellon	Paramount Television Grp.	(323) 956-5000
Steven Melnick	20th Century Fox Television	(310) 369-1000
Barry Mendel	Barry Mendel Prod.	(818) 733-3076
Michael Mendenhall	Walt Disney Pictures	(818) 560-1000
Robert Mendez	Paramount Domestic Television	(323) 956-5000
Jane Mendle	Barwood Films	(212) 765-7191
Agnes Mentres	Miramax Films	(212) 941-3800
Danielle Mentzer	Sitting Ducks Prod.	(323) 660-0861
Tracy Mercer	Valhalla Motion Pictures	(323) 969-4300
Ismail Merchant	Merchant-Ivory Prod.	(212) 582-8049
Adam Merims	Baumgarten/Prophet Ent.	(310) 996-1885
Stavros Merjos	Mars Media	(310) 664-6760
Dina Merril	RKO Pictures	(310) 277-0707
Tim Merritt	Snow Leopard Prod.	(310) 827-1220
Ron Mesa	Our Gang Prod.	(310) 300-1010
Dete Meserve	Wind Dancer Prod. Grp.	(323) 645-1200
Arnold Messer	Phoenix Pictures	(310) 244-6100
Greg Messina	Shady Acres Ent.	(818) 777-4446
Jill Messisck	Miramax Films	(212) 941-3800
Mitch Metcalf	NBC Ent.	(818) 840-4444
Marsha Metz	Constantin Film	(310) 247-0300
Meredith Metz	Gullane Pictures	(310) 451-5111
Terry Meurer	Cosgrove-Meurer Prod.	(818) 843-5600
Barry M. Meyer	Warner Bros.	(818) 954-6000
Kris Meyer	Conundrum Ent.	(310) 319-2800
Ron Meyer	Universal Studios	(818) 777-1000
Turi Meyer	Wicked Monkey Prod.	(323) 461-6665
Victoria Paige Meyerink	Star Ent. Grp.	(818) 988-2200
Dave Meyers	FM Rocks	(310) 587-1501
Howard Meyers	USA Films	(212) 539-4002
Andrea Mia	Newmark Films	(323) 782-4969
Prudence Michael	Quasar Studios	(310) 289-1547
T. Michael	Joel Asher Studio	(818) 785-1551
Terence Michael	Michael/Finney Prod.	(310) 838-9350
Lorne Michaels	Broadway Video	(212) 265-7621
Brianne Michelle	Summerland Ent.	(818) 363-4135
Doug Mickel	Zystar Films	(310) 301-3313
Tom Mickel	HKM Prod.	(323) 465-9494
Linda Middleton	Columbia Pictures	(310) 244-4000
Toby Midgen	Artists Television Grp.	(310) 860-8200
Bette Midler	All Girl Prod.	(818) 655-6000
Susanna Midnight	IndieGal Prod.	(818) 890-6111
Thomas Mignone	Doom	(818) 972-2007
Vera Mihailovich	Tavel Ent.	(310) 278-6700
Lynn-Maree Milburn	Metro Pictures	(310) 301-7890
Alexandra Milchan	New Regency Prod.	(310) 369-8300
Arnon Milchan	New Regency Prod.	(310) 369-8300
Matt Milich	Kinowelt USA	(310) 205-9600
Chip Miller	Red Hots Ent.	(818) 954-0092
Dawn Miller	Franchise Pictures	(323) 822-0730
Glenn Miller	Life of Riley	(310) 230-7798
Janice Miller	Universal Studios	(818) 777-1000
Jason Miller	Barry Mendel Prod.	(818) 733-3076
Jeffrey Miller	Buena Vista Motion Pictures	(818) 560-1000
Jim Miller	The Canton Company	(818) 954-2130
Jim Miller	USA Network	(212) 413-5000
John Miller	MTV Networks	(310) 752-8000

Executives/Personnel Alphabetical Key

John Miller	NBC Ent.	(818) 840-4444
Katherine L. Miller	Barnholtz Ent.	(310) 457-7484
Kevin Miller	Our Gang Prod.	(310) 300-1010
Lawrence Miller	Miller Ent. Grp.	(323) 932-6500
Lori Miller	The Vault	(310) 315-0012
Matt Miller	Erratic Ent.	(310) 657-0922
Peter Darley Miller	Stiefel + Company	(310) 581-7000
Robert Miller	ABC Inc./ABC Television	(310) 557-7777
Thomas L. Miller	Miller/Boyett Prod.	(212) 702-9779
Vicky Miller	Turner Ent. Grp.	(404) 827-1500
David Miner	3 Arts Ent.	(310) 888-3200
Steve Miner	Minervision	(323) 848-3080
Anthony Minghella	Mirage Enterprises	(310) 244-2044
Jon Mingle	Pongo Prod.	(818) 562-3336
Mardi Minogue	Tuesday Films	(310) 899-0335
Wendi Mirabella	IMAX Corp.	(310) 255-5500
Jada Miranda	Orly Adelson Prod.	(310) 442-2012
Kevin Misher	Universal Pictures	(818) 777-1000
David T. Mitchell	Permut Presentations	(310) 248-2792
Martha Mitchell	Revelations Ent.	(310) 394-3131
Rolf Mittweg	New Line Cinema	(310) 854-5811
Bruce Miyaki	Vanguard Prod.	(310) 306-4910
Bruce Moccia	Telescene Film Grp.	(514) 737-5512
Chris Mock	Taylor-Bedell Ent.	(310) 859-9967
Francis Mohajerin	Megahertz Pictures	(310) 727-2600
Omer Mohamed	Silvereye Prod.	(818) 501-4232
Cay Mohr	RumRunner Cine Service	(310) 540-8411
Lisa Moiselle	The Bedford Falls Company	(310) 394-5022
Julie G. Moldo Jones	Rearguard Prod.	(323) 937-1570
Steve Molen	DreamWorks SKG	(818) 733-7000
Alfred Molina	M.H.S. Prod.	(310) 202-3336
George Moll	VH1	(212) 846-7800
Sam Mollo	Digivision Prod.	(323) 937-3348
David Molner	Viacom Ent. Grp.	(323) 956-5000
Terry Moloney	Proletariat	(818) 763-8356
Kevin Molony	Piper Prod.	(310) 883-8822
Jeff Monarch	Boz Prod.	(323) 876-3232
Philip A. Mondello	Philmco	(213) 399-7624
Jean-Baptiste Mondino	DNA	(323) 463-2826
Steven Monkarsh	Stiefel + Company	(310) 581-7000
Jan Monroe	Snow Leopard Prod.	(310) 827-1220
Ben Montanio	Rice & Beans Prod.	(626) 792-9171
Anna Montgomery	American World Pictures	(818) 715-1480
Patty Mooney	Crystal Pyramid Prod.	(619) 644-3000
Tom Mooney	Headquarters	(310) 752-5200
Greg Mooradian	Wendy Finerman Prod.	(310) 369-8800
Bryan Moore	Fortis Films	(310) 659-4533
Demi Moore	Moving Pictures	(212) 219-4545
John Moore	Brian Bleak Films	(310) 396-5500
John Moore	Headquarters	(310) 752-5200
Liza Moore	Hogan Moorhouse Pictures	(310) 319-9299
Rob Moore	Revolution Studios	(310) 264-4141
Jocelyn Moorhouse	Hogan Moorhouse Pictures	(310) 319-9299
Devorah Moos-Hankin	Bungalow 78 Prod.	(323) 956-4440
Nan Morales	Paramount Pictures	(323) 956-5000
Patrick Moran	Renaissance Pictures	(818) 777-0088
Patrick Moran	UPN	(310) 575-7000
John Morayniss	Alliance Atlantis	(310) 899-8000
Wink Mordaunt	Alchemy Ent.	(310) 396-5937
Erwin More	Talent Ent. Grp.	(323) 969-0700
Dana Moreshead	Stan Lee Media	(818) 461-1757
Kevin Moreton	Orbit Ent. Grp.	(323) 525-2626
Brian Morewitz	Black & Blu Ent.	(310) 244-8833
Amanda Morgan Palmer	Shady Acres Ent.	(818) 777-4446
André E. Morgan	Ruddy Morgan Organization	(310) 271-7698
Jana Morgan	In-Finn-Ity Prod.	(310) 444-6300
Lana Morgan	The Matthau Company	(310) 454-3300
Mark Morgan	Destination Films	(310) 434-2700
Alvin Mori	Lumination Inc.	(818) 766-1868
Mark Mori	Single Spark Pictures	(310) 315-4779
Neal Moritz	Original Film	(310) 445-9000
Donna Morong	Buena Vista Motion Pictures	(818) 560-1000
Sharon Morrill	Walt Disney TV Animation	(818) 560-5000
Caylyn E. Morris	Calar	(310) 271-2202
David Morris	Digivision Prod.	(323) 937-3348
Vanessa Morrison	20th Century Fox Pictures	(310) 369-1000
John Morrissey	The Turman-Morrissey Company	(310) 586-8649
Stan Morse	Straw Dogs	(323) 782-0777
Rocky Morton	Morton Jankel Zander	(310) 826-6200
Tracey Morton	Black Sheep Ent.	(818) 769-2227
Tony Mosa	M-80 Films	(310) 899-9100
Anthony Mosawi	Mutual Film Company	(323) 871-5690
John Moser	Showtime Networks	(310) 234-5200
Michael Moses	Universal Pictures	(818) 777-1000
Scott Mosier	View Askew Prod.	(732) 842-6933
Adam Moss	Kushner-Locke Company	(818) 841-8188
Jonathan Mostow	Mostow/Lieberman	(818) 777-4444
Erik Mountain	William J. MacDonald Prod.	(310) 581-4840
Karen Moy	Columbia Pictures	(310) 244-4000
Jennifer Moyer	Alphaville	(323) 956-4803
Todd Moyer	No Prisoners	(310) 979-9097
Shirley Moyers	Bonfire Films of America	(323) 953-6815
Jeffery Mueller	Licht/Mueller Films	(310) 205-5500
Laura Mueller	All Girl Prod.	(818) 655-6000
Phillip Muhl	Walt Disney Pictures	(818) 560-1000
Marina Muhlfriedel	Santa Monica Pictures	(310) 264-5566
Renard Muldrake	The Ad-Files	(213) 891-3784
Monica Mullens	Radar Pictures	(310) 208-8525
Billy Mulligan	Jane Startz Prod.	(212) 545-8910
Axel Munch	Silverline Pictures	(818) 752-3730
Lisa Mundt	Warner Bros.	(818) 954-6000
Alex Muñoz	Calar	(310) 271-2202
Rick Munoz	Our Prod.	(323) 465-4197
Glen Murakami	Warner Bros. Animation	(818) 954-7670
Gay Murdock	Flip Your Lid	(818) 222-0700
Diane Murphy	Miller/Boyett Prod.	(212) 702-9779
Grace Murphy	Sony Pictures Classics	(212) 833-8833
Jeff Murphy	The Association	(818) 841-9660
Matt Murphy	Porter Film Company	(323) 962-7855
Peter E. Murphy	The Walt Disney Company	(818) 560-1000
Scott Murphy	Zystar Films	(310) 301-3313
Susan Murphy	Satellite Films	(323) 465-9300
Alex Murray	Schapiro Ent. Grp.	(310) 358-3215
Duncan Murray	National Lampoon	(310) 474-5252
Fletch Murray	The Association	(818) 841-9660
Jonathan Murray	Bunim-Murray Prod.	(818) 756-5100
Patrick Murray	IMAX Corp.	(310) 255-5500
Ken Musen	c.2K Ent.	(310) 208-2324
Eugene Musso	Neverland Films	(310) 772-0008
Gail Mutrux	Ab'-strakt Pictures	(310) 385-6611
Alan Myerson	DreamWorks SKG	(818) 733-7000
Andrew Myler	Atkinson Way Films	(323) 465-3350
Robert Nackman	Horizon Shine	(310) 990-6532
Bruce Nadel	OneSuch Films	(310) 273-3200
Richard Naegele	RJN Prod.	(310) 859-2770
Masashi Nagadoi	Megahertz Pictures	(310) 727-2600
Seth Nagel	USA Films	(212) 539-4002
Nadia Naili	Dan Redler Ent.	(818) 776-0938
Ramsey Naito	Nickelodeon Movies	(323) 956-8663
Linda Nakagawa	Imaginary Forces	(323) 957-6868
Douglas Nam	Ruddy Morgan Organization	(310) 271-7698
Stephanie Napoli	Columbia Pictures	(310) 244-4000
Bahman Naragi	Miramax Films	(212) 941-3800
Michael Nash	Paramount Classics	(323) 956-2000
Michael J. Nathanson	Upstart Ent.	(310) 475-6025
Michael Nathanson	Metro-Goldwyn-Mayer Studios	(310) 449-3000
Gregory Nava	El Norte Prod.	(310) 360-1194
Miguel Navarro	Carbo Films	(310) 586-1969
David Naylor	DNA	(323) 463-2826
Bill Near	Picture Park	(310) 315-1949
Chris D. Nebe	Monarex Hollywood Corp.	(310) 552-1069
Paul Neesan	The Arnet/Kerner Co.	(310) 838-2500
Jonas Neilson	Lester Persky Prod.	(310) 278-1995
Paul Neinstein	Spyglass Ent.	(818) 560-3458
George NeJame	Tribune Ent. Company	(323) 460-5800
Anne Nelson	CBS Ent.	(323) 575-2345
Kathy Nelson	Buena Vista Motion Pictures	(818) 560-1000
Kori Nelson	Friendly Prod.	(310) 369-3973
Lee Nelson	Orbit Ent. Grp.	(323) 525-2626
Ron Nelson	DreamWorks SKG	(818) 733-7000
Steve Nemiroff	Nemiroff Prod.	(310) 473-4100
Stephen Netburn	Angel City Prod.	(323) 465-6802
Gil Netter	Zucker/Netter Prod.	(310) 394-1644
Mace Neufeld	Mace Neufeld Prod.	(310) 244-2555
Wendy Neuss	Flying Freehold Prod.	(323) 956-8838
Scott Neustadler	Tribeca Prod.	(212) 941-4000

Executives/Personnel Alphabetical Key

Sheila Nevins	HBO Original Programming	(212) 512-1000
Betsy Newman	Turner Network Television	(310) 551-6300
Eric Newman	Beacon Communications	(310) 260-7000
Robert Newmyer	Outlaw Prod.	(310) 777-2000
Thi Ngyuen	FR Prod.	(310) 470-9212
Robert J. Nichols	The Woofenill Works	(212) 734-2578
Jennifer Nicholson-Salke	Spelling Television	(323) 965-5700
Jennifer Silver Nieman	c.2K Ent.	(310) 208-2324
Joe Nimziki	New Line Cinema	(310) 854-5811
Marcus Nispel	Morton Jankel Zander	(310) 826-6200
Gary Nolin	Rhythm & Hues Studios	(310) 448-7500
Nick Nolte	Kingsgate Films	(310) 281-5880
Tracie Norfleet	HSI Prod.	(310) 452-9999
Tracie Norfleet	Mars Media	(310) 664-6760
Susie Norris-Epstein	The Disney Channel	(818) 569-7500
Kimberly Norton	Fountainhead Pictures	(310) 276-5583
Robert Norton	The Jim Henson Company	(323) 802-1500
Blaise Noto	Columbia Pictures	(310) 244-4000
Susan Novick	Outlaw Prod.	(310) 777-2000
Robert A. Nowotny	Teocalli Ent.	(505) 258-1373
Phillip Noyce	Rumbalara Films	(323) 936-4436
Michael Nozik	Wildwood Enterprises	(310) 395-5155
Armando Nuñez Jr.	CBS Enterprises	(212) 975-4321
Bill Nuss	North Hall Prod.	(310) 558-5040
Bernard Nussbaumer	Ventana Films	(323) 876-3331
David Nutter	Genrebend Prod.	(310) 284-7312
Peter Nydrle	Nydrle	(310) 659-8844
Vera Oakley	Tribe Pictures	(973) 635-2660
Rockne S. O'Bannon	Creative Impulse Ent.	(818) 623-8260
Klaus Obermeyer	Flying Tiger Films	(310) 664-9171
Timm Oberwelland	Zeal Pictures	(323) 871-4000
Molly O'Brien	WildLife Management	(310) 276-8008
Nora O'Brien	Triology Ent. Grp.	(310) 449-3095
Lynda Obst	Lynda Obst Prod.	(323) 956-8744
Josh Ochoa	AbsoluteFilms.net	(626) 442-6454
Frank W. Ockenfels 3	Go Film	(212) 677-7500
Katie O'Connell	Imagine Ent.	(310) 858-2000
Dennis O'Connor	Universal Pictures	(818) 777-1000
Gavin O'Connor	Zooma Zooma Corp.	(212) 941-7680
Joseph O'Connor	Carlyle Prod.	(323) 848-4960
Lance O'Connor	Flying Tiger Films	(310) 664-9171
Shelley O'Connor	Back Home Pictures	(323) 962-8500
Steve O'Corr	Raffaella Prod.	(818) 777-2655
Jim O'Doherty	The Carsey-Werner.	(818) 655-5598
Bryan O'Donnell	Bender-Spink	(323) 845-1640
Erin O'Donnell	Egg Pictures	(323) 956-8400
Steve Oedekerk	O Ent.	(949) 443-3222
Jerry Offsay	Showtime Networks	(310) 234-5200
Marsha Oglesby	The Arnet/Kerner Co.	(310) 838-2500
John O'Grady	Bob Industries	(310) 396-7333
Tim O'Hair	Universal Pictures	(818) 777-1000
Michael O'Halloran	Braga Prod.	(323) 956-5799
Suzanne O'Keefe	Megahertz Pictures	(310) 727-2600
Terence M. O'Keefe	Vanguard Prod.	(310) 306-4910
Stuart Oken	Walt Disney Pictures	(818) 560-1000
Sam Okun	Erratic Ent.	(310) 657-0922
Meg Okura	Lumination Inc.	(818) 766-1868
Lisa J. Olin	Goepp Circle Prod.	(323) 956-4620
Xochitl Olivas	Grammnet Prod. (Film)	(323) 956-5840
Brian Oliver	Propaganda Films	(323) 462-6400
Lin Oliver	Lin Oliver Prod.	(323) 782-1495
Edward James Olmos	Olmos Prod.	(310) 557-7010
Jarl Olsen	Fuel	(310) 314-1644
Todd Olsson	MDP Worldwide	(310) 226-8300
Darci Oltman	Doom	(818) 972-2007
Jamie O'Malley	Spoke Film	(310) 477-2272
Chad Oman	Jerry Bruckheimer Films	(310) 664-6260
Cleveland O'Neal	Connection III Ent.	(323) 653-3400
Marisa O'Neil	Warner Bros.	(818) 954-6000
Evelyn O'Neill	Talent Ent. Grp.	(323) 969-0700
Mark Oppenheimer	Hallowes Prod.	(310) 390-4767
Andrew Orci	Carbo Films	(310) 586-1969
Mark Ordesky	Fine Line Features	(310) 854-5811
Fern Orenstein	CBS Ent.	(323) 575-2345
Bill Orisich	Legacy Films	(323) 856-8888
Alex Ort	New Regency Prod.	(310) 369-8300
Tom Ortenberg	Lions Gate Ent.	(323) 692-7300
Gwen Osborne	The Bubble Factory	(310) 358-3000
Guy Oseary	Maverick Films	(310) 276-6177
Dan O'Shannon	Grub Street Prod.	(323) 956-4657
John O'Shaugnessy	Nitestar Prod.	(323) 468-8089
Robert Osher	Miramax Films	(212) 941-3800
Donald Osley	New Line Cinema	(310) 854-5811
Anna Osso	Fine Line Features	(310) 854-5811
Michael Ostin	DreamWorks SKG	(818) 733-7000
Mo Ostin	DreamWorks SKG	(818) 733-7000
Randy Ostrow	USA Films	(212) 539-4002
Dale Ottley	Overbrook Ent.	(818) 777-2224
Toni Pace	Suzanne Bauman Prod.	(818) 348-4342
Linda Pace-Alexander	Universal Pictures	(818) 777-1000
Edward Pacio	Edward Pacio & Assoc.	(818) 880-1586
Gordon Paddison	New Line Cinema	(310) 854-5811
Glenn Padnick	Castle Rock Ent.	(310) 285-2300
Albert Page	The Jinks/Cohen Company	(818) 733-9880
Kathy Page	Warner Bros. Animation	(818) 954-7670
Jasan Pagni	Skylark Films	(310) 396-5753
George Paige	George Paige Assoc.	(310) 315-4835
Nick Paine	Image G	(818) 761-6644
Bonnie Palef	Snapdragon Films	(310) 822-2505
Amy Palmer	Davis Ent. Co.	(310) 556-3550
Chris Palmer	Alphaville	(323) 956-4803
Glendon Palmer	Overbrook Ent.	(818) 777-2224
Isaac Palmer	Viacom Ent. Grp.	(323) 956-5000
Michelle Palmer	The Chelmar Grp.	(626) 358-4001
Robert Palmer	Saban Ent.	(310) 235-5100
Cynthia Palormo	Irish DreamTime	(310) 449-3411
Elena Panajotovic	Noble Prod.	(310) 552-2934
Ika Panajotovic	Noble Prod.	(310) 552-2934
Sonja Panajotovic	Noble Prod.	(310) 552-2934
Andrew Panay	Tapestry Films	(310) 275-1191
Daniel Pancotto	Zide/Perry Ent.	(310) 887-2999
Sanford Panitch	New Regency Prod.	(310) 369-8300
Ericka Panko	Mars Media	(310) 664-6760
Steve Papazian	Warner Bros. Pictures Prod.	(818) 954-6000
Eric Paquette	Phoenix Pictures	(310) 244-6100
Mary Parent	Universal Pictures	(818) 777-1000
Russ Paris	Columbia Pictures	(310) 244-4000
Heather Parish	40 Acres & A Mule	(718) 624-3703
Wendy Park	Hallway Pictures	(323) 850-2680
Darby Parker	Zide/Perry Ent.	(310) 887-2999
Hope Parker	The Baer Animation Company	(323) 874-9122
Hutch Parker	20th Century Fox Pictures	(310) 369-1000
Walter Parkers	DreamWorks SKG	(818) 733-7000
Wally Parks	Watershed Films	(310) 550-2175
Amy Pascal	Columbia Pictures	(310) 244-4000
Michael Paseornek	Lions Gate Ent.	(323) 692-7300
Audrey Pask	Bella Prod.	(310) 823-3115
John Pasquin	Paradox Prod.	(818) 623-2855
Tom Patchett	Patchett Kaufman Ent.	(310) 838-7000
Gita Patel	Burrud Prod.	(714) 842-8422
Lynne Pateman	Orbit Ent. Grp.	(323) 525-2626
Suzanne Patmore	Mutual Film Company	(323) 871-5690
Tom Patricia	Artists Television Grp.	(310) 860-8200
Greg Paul	Castle Rock Ent.	(310) 285-2300
Peter Paul	Stan Lee Media	(818) 461-1757
Stephen Paul	LA Prod.	(323) 874-9487
Bobbie Pavlic	Pavlic/Raimondi Pictures	(323) 850-0185
John Pavlic	Pavlic/Raimondi Pictures	(323) 850-0185
Bill Paxton	American Ent. Co.	(323) 939-6746
Chip Payne	Edward Pacio & Assoc.	(818) 880-1586
Julie Payne	Scott Free Prod.	(310) 360-2250
Nancy Peardon	Forward Pass	(310) 571-3443
Alex Pearl	Schapiro Ent. Grp.	(310) 358-3215
Jennifer Peckham	Spin Pictures Intertainment	(310) 278-3569
Mark Pedowitz	ABC Entertainment	(310) 557-7777
Madeline Peerce	CBS Ent.	(323) 575-2345
Robert Peluce	Kurtz & Friends	(818) 841-8188
Michael Pendell	Mo Jo Prod.	(808) 384-8460
Tim Pendergrass	Post Modern Edit	(714) 751-2681
Sandra Penfield	Chelsea Pictures	(323) 860-8030
Nicole Pennington	A Band Apart	(323) 951-4600
Scott Pennington	Talisman Pacific	(310) 260-1208
James Pentecost	James Pentecost Prod.	(818) 560-4965
Larry Perel	Arsenal	(323) 957-5100
Raul Perez	Columbia Pictures	(310) 244-4000
Jennifer Perini	Image Movers	(818) 733-8313

353

Executives/Personnel Alphabetical Key

David Perlmutter	Chesler/Perlmutter Prod.	(310) 443-9650
David Permut	Permut Presentations	(310) 248-2792
Jean Perramon	SimEx Digital Studios	(310) 664-9500
Craig Perry	Zide/Perry Ent.	(310) 887-2999
Lester Persky	Lester Persky Prod.	(310) 278-1995
Ritamarie Peruggi	The Jim Henson Company	(323) 802-1500
Chryl Pestor	Abby Lou Ent.	(626) 795-7334
Tim Peternel	Muse Prod.	(310) 306-2001
David Peters	Montage Ent.	(310) 966-0222
James Peters	Polestar Film	(323) 851-5488
Jon Peters	Peters Ent.	(818) 954-2441
Wolfgang Petersen	Radiant Prod.	(310) 656-1400
James Peterson	World Wide Pants, Inc	(212) 975-5300
Suzie Peterson	Universal Pictures	(818) 777-1000
Maureen Peyrot	Imagine Ent.	(310) 858-2000
Steve Peyton	Raven Prod.	(760) 325-7191
Rachel Pfeffer	Pfeffer Film	(818) 560-3177
Reid Phat	Norton Wright Prod.	(818) 990-3058
Dax Phelan	Mace Neufeld Prod.	(310) 244-2555
Louis Philips	The Jim Henson Company	(323) 802-1500
Todd Philips	Krainin Prod.	(914) 359-0445
Ryan Phillippe	Lucid Film	(310) 777-0007
Liz Phillips	Davis Ent. Co.	(310) 556-3550
Michael Phillips	Lighthouse Prod.	(310) 859-4923
Toby Phillips	Area 51 Films	(310) 395-5151
Joe Pichirallo	Fox Searchlight Pictures	(310) 369-4402
David V. Picker	Hallmark Ent.	(212) 977-9001
Pamela Pickering	Mutual Film Company	(323) 871-5690
Alan Pierce	Access Film	(818) 990-3389
Frederick S. Pierce	The Frederick S. Pierce Company	(323) 964-7800
Keith Pierce	The Frederick S. Pierce Company	(323) 964-7800
Richard Pierce	The Frederick S. Pierce Company	(323) 964-7800
Cindy Pierson	CPProds	(310) 441-9211
Debbie Pietsch	Perspective Films	(310) 670-4030
Vicky Pike	Shoreline Ent.	(310) 551-2060
Gayle Pillsbury	Imagine Ent.	(310) 858-2000
Sarah Pillsbury	Sanford/Pillsbury Prod.	(310) 393-5225
Debbie Pinckes	Luminosity Prod.	(818) 752-3318
Steve Pink	New Crime Prod.	(310) 396-2199
Mark Pinsker	Saban Ent.	(310) 235-5100
Nick Piper	Plum Prod.	(310) 450-1942
Steven Piper	Video Hollywood Prod.	(888) 368-7347
Carmelo Pirrone	Sony Pictures Classics	(212) 833-8833
Julia Pistor	Nickelodeon Movies	(323) 956-8663
Martin Pitts	Prod. Analysis Corp.	(323) 876-6186
Irina Piyevsky	Barnholtz Ent.	(310) 457-7484
Tim Plant	Kandice King Prod.	(310) 822-9502
Adam Platnick	Mandalay Pictures	(323) 956-2400
Ralph Pleasant	Pleasant Prod.	(213) 707-0500
Tom Plotkin	Mutant Enemy	(310) 579-5180
Steve Plum	20th Century Fox Pictures	(310) 369-1000
Bruce A. Pobjoy	Summerland Ent.	(818) 363-4135
Annette Pocica	PBS	(703) 739-5000
Rudy Poe	Eleventh Day Ent.	(818) 784-6403
Sidney Poitier	Verdon-Cedric Prod.	(310) 274-7253
Jib Polhemus	Wychwood Prod.	(323) 462-6400
Patrick-Ian Polk	Edmonds Ent.	(416) 630-3825
Martin Poll	Hollane /Martin Poll Films	(323) 876-8873
Brad Pollack	Skylark Films	(310) 396-5753
Jeff Pollack	Handprint Ent.	(310) 481-4400
Sydney Pollack	Mirage Enterprises	(310) 244-2044
Kevin Pollak	Calm Down Prod.	(323) 650-4027
Dale Pollock	Peak Prod.	(336) 761-5042
James B. Pollock	Ralph Edwards/Stu Billett Prod.	(323) 462-2212
Lawrence J. Pollock	ABC Inc./ABC Television	(310) 557-7777
Tom Pollock	The Montecito Picture Company	(805) 565-8590
Gavin Polone	Hofflund-Polone	(310) 859-1971
Jay Polstein	Handprint Ent.	(310) 481-4400
Barry Poltermann	Spoke Film	(310) 477-2272
Dan Pomeroy	Red Hots Ent.	(818) 954-0092
Paul Pompian	Hawk Ent.	(818) 859-7779
Jonathan Pontell	David E. Kelley Prod.	(310) 727-2200
Noel Poole	Weller/Grossman Prod.	(818) 755-4800
Brian Pope	Universal Studios	(818) 777-1000
David Pope	Danjaq	(310) 449-3185
Gaye Pope	Rainmaker Prod.	(323) 874-6770
Jennifer Pope	AEI	(323) 932-0407
Randy Pope	Sid & Marty Krofft Pictures	(818) 386-1918
Donna Portaio	@radical.media	(310) 664-4500
Fred Porter	Porter Film Company	(323) 962-7855
Kurt Porter	Burrud Prod.	(714) 842-8422
James Portolese	Signature Films	(310) 226-8374
Pamela Post	Team Todd	(310) 248-6001
Meryl Poster	Miramax Films	(212) 941-3800
Ashley Postlewaite	Renegade Animation	(818) 556-3395
Marykay Powell	Rastar Prod.	(310) 244-7871
Derek Power	Kahn Power Pictures	(310) 550-0770
Ilene Kahn Power	Kahn Power Pictures	(310) 550-0770
Alfred Powers	Video Hollywood Prod.	(888) 368-7347
Tom Prassis	Sony Pictures Classics	(212) 833-8833
Dana Precious	Columbia Pictures	(310) 244-4000
Terry Press	DreamWorks SKG	(818) 733-7000
Adam Prince	Butchers Run Films	(310) 246-4630
Tom Prince	The Bubble Factory	(310) 358-3000
Mark Priola	Revolver Films	(310) 829-2441
Rob Pritts	Backyard Prod.	(310) 314-1122
Danielle Probst	Leading Pictures	(310) 385-0951
Rick Probst	Picture Mill	(323) 465-8800
Paul Prokop	New Line Cinema	(310) 854-5811
Moira Proletti	Ginty Films	(310) 274-9691
Melissa Prophet	Baumgarten/Prophet Ent.	(310) 996-1885
Daniel Proulx	Telescene Film Grp.	(514) 737-5512
Cynthia Pruett	Constantin Film	(310) 247-0300
Steve Przybylowski	Foundation Ent.	(310) 204-4686
Joe Public	Headquarters	(310) 752-5200
Francisco Pugliese	Moving Image	(310) 659-8022
John Quinn	Quinn Prod.	(818) 787-5952
Tom Quinn	Samuel Goldwyn Films	(310) 860-3100
Marinet Quinones	Carbo Films	(310) 586-1969
Sandra Rabins	Patchwork Prod.	(310) 288-7488
Rhodes Rader	Red Hour Films	(310) 289-2565
Rad-ish	Go Film	(212) 677-7500
Eric Radomski	Film Roman	(818) 761-2544
Nick Rafter	Go Film	(212) 677-7500
Sam Raimi	Renaissance Pictures	(818) 777-0088
Sam Raimi	Zooma Zooma Corp.	(212) 941-7680
Jane Raimondi	Pavlic/Raimondi Pictures	(323) 850-0185
Paul Raimondi	Pavlic/Raimondi Pictures	(323) 850-0185
Howard Raishbrook	Zystar Films	(310) 301-3313
Jay Rakow	Metro-Goldwyn-Mayer Studios	(310) 449-3000
Omarr Rambert	Overbrook Ent.	(818) 777-2224
Lynnette Ramirez	Fountainbridge Films	(310) 244-8080
Rick Ramirez	Phil Roman Ent.	(818) 985-1200
Harold Ramis	Ocean Pictures	(310) 369-0093
Monica Ramone	Reality Prod.	(818) 404-8711
Karen Randall	Universal Studios	(818) 777-1000
Marjorie Randolph	Walt Disney Pictures	(818) 560-1000
Martin Ransohoff	Martin Ransohoff Prod.	(310) 551-2680
Dru Ransom	Phase I Prod.	(310) 842-8401
Dawn Rao	Satellite Films	(323) 465-9300
Alan Raphael	Warner Bros.	(818) 954-6000
Stephan Raphael	USA Films	(212) 539-4002
Jack Rapke	Image Movers	(818) 733-8313
Daniel Rappaport	3 Arts Ent.	(310) 888-3200
Don Rase	Backyard Prod.	(310) 314-1122
Christopher Raser	Ranch Exit Films	(310) 471-0157
Ali Rasul	Renaissance Pictures	(818) 777-0088
Dave Rath	3 Arts Ent.	(310) 888-3200
Alisa Ratner	Mars Media	(310) 664-6760
Brett Ratner	Villains	(310) 888-8900
Jeff Ratner	Afra-Film Enterprises	(323) 882-6193
Joni Ravenna	Raven Prod.	(760) 325-7191
Joshua Ravetch	New Line Cinema	(310) 854-5811
Sterling Ray	Atlas Pictures	(310) 587-2376
Patrick Raymond	Patrick Raymond Ent.	(323) 850-2918
Ted Raynor	Producers Grp.	(310) 316-0481
Mark Reber	Green Dot Films	(310) 656-4900
Timothy Record	Wendy Finerman Prod.	(310) 369-8800
Hadeel Reda	Winchester Films	(310) 458-1400
Robert Redford	Wildwood Enterprises	(310) 395-5155
Valerie Red-Horse	Red-Horse Prod.	(818) 705-2588
Dan Redler	Dan Redler Ent.	(818) 776-0938
Jason Reed	Buena Vista Motion Pictures	(818) 560-1000
John Reed	Music Room Pictures	(310) 316-4551
Marsha L. Reed	The Walt Disney Company	(818) 560-1000
Nikki Reed	Junction Ent.	(818) 560-2800

Executives/Personnel Alphabetical Key

Jan Marlyn Reesman	IndieGal Prod.	(818) 890-6111
Lisa Reeve	Simian Films	(310) 205-2724
Amy Reeves	Planet	(323) 461-2695
Russ Regan	Polestar Ent. Grp.	(310) 278-0080
Ileen J. Reich	New Line Cinema	(310) 854-5811
Eric Reid	Lakeshore Ent. Corp.	(323) 956-4222
Melissa Reid	Red Wagon	(310) 244-4466
Tim Reid	New Millennium Studios	(804) 957-4200
Brian Reilly	Boxing Cat Prod.	(818) 765-4870
Kevin Reilly	Brillstein-Grey Ent.	(310) 275-6135
Alicia Reilly-Larson	Unapix Films	(212) 252-7711
Andy Reimer	Lions Gate Ent.	(323) 692-7300
Rob Reiner	Castle Rock Ent.	(310) 285-2300
Carole Reinert	Rick Reinert Pictures	(805) 494-0699
Rick Reinert	Rick Reinert Pictures	(805) 494-0699
Paul Reiser	Nuance Prod.	(310) 247-1870
Linda Reisman	American Zoetrope	(310) 899-8000
Irwin Reiter	Miramax Films	(212) 941-3800
Ivan Reitman	The Montecito Picture Company	(805) 565-8590
Robert Relyen	Metro-Goldwyn-Mayer Studios	(310) 449-3000
Kimble Rendall	Porter Film Company	(323) 962-7855
Joan Renfrow	Onyx Prod.	(323) 692-9830
Joan Renfrow	Sodas & Shoes	(323) 692-9848
Hesh Rephun	Headquarters	(310) 752-5200
Art Repola	Buena Vista Motion Pictures	(818) 560-1000
Gina Resnick	GMR Prod.	(310) 401-1400
Mark Resnick	20th Century Fox Pictures	(310) 369-1000
Steve Reuther	Bel-Air Ent.	(818) 954-4040
Joseph A. Revitte	Fine Line Features	(310) 854-5811
Burt Reynolds	AM Prod.	(310) 275-9081
John Reynolds	Kavich Reynolds Prod.	(323) 466-2490
Kathy Rhodes	Joseph Pytka Prod.	(310) 392-9571
Matthew Rhodes	Persistent Ent.	(310) 777-1814
Dan Riba	Warner Bros. Animation	(818) 954-7670
Bob Rice	Plum Prod.	(310) 450-1942
Dorothy Rice	Stanley Chase Prod.	(310) 475-4236
Peter Rice	Fox Searchlight Pictures	(310) 369-4402
Alan Rich	Ranch Exit Films	(310) 471-0157
Gerry Rich	Metro-Goldwyn-Mayer Studios	(310) 449-3000
Jerry Rich	United Artists Films	(310) 449-3000
Steve Richards	Silver Pictures Television	(818) 954-4490
Hal Richardson	DreamWorks SKG	(818) 733-7000
Mike Richardson	Dark Horse Ent.	(818) 777-5830
Robert Richardson	Morton Jankel Zander	(310) 826-6200
Carrie Richman	Columbia Pictures	(310) 244-4000
Branscombe Richmond	30 Second Films	(310) 315-1750
Vincent Rico	The Ad-Files	(213) 891-3784
Chris Ridenhour	Tavel Ent.	(310) 278-6700
Mary Ann Ridini	Ridini Ent. Corp.	(323) 960-8071
Jay Rifkin	Patchwork Prod.	(310) 288-7488
Michael Riley	Imaginary Forces	(323) 957-6868
Justin Ring	Paramount Classics	(323) 956-2000
Sara Risher	New Line Cinema	(310) 854-5811
Lauren A. Ritchie	New Line Cinema	(310) 854-5811
Andrea Ritigstein	Seven Arts Pictures	(323) 464-0225
Herb Ritts	Bella Prod.	(310) 823-3115
Clay Rivers	Amen Ra Films	(310) 246-6510
Charles H. Rivkin	The Jim Henson Company	(323) 802-1500
Joel Rizor	Weller/Grossman Prod.	(818) 755-4800
Jay Roach	Everyman Pictures	(310) 244-1686
Brian Robbins	Tollin/Robbins Prod.	(818) 766-5004
Lance H. Robbins	Fox Family Channel	(310) 235-9700
Tim Robbins	Havoc Inc.	(212) 924-1629
Gary D. Roberts	20th Century Fox Pictures	(310) 369-1000
Julia Roberts	Shoelace Prod.	(212) 243-2900
Mark Roberts	Kingsize Ent.	(323) 467-7199
Nancy Roberts	Stampede Ent.	(310) 264-4229
Mary Goss Robino	New Line Cinema	(310) 854-5811
Jeff Robinov	Warner Bros. Pictures Prod.	(818) 954-6000
Adam Robinson	Flying Freehold Prod.	(323) 956-8838
Bill Robinson	Blue Relief	(310) 275-7900
Bob Robinson	Martin Ransohoff Prod.	(310) 551-2680
Brett Robinson	Kushner-Locke Company	(818) 841-8188
Dolores Robinson	Dolores Robinson Ent.	(310) 777-8777
Gary Robinson	Sharpcut Prod.	(310) 247-0088
James G. Robinson	Morgan Creek Prod.	(818) 954-4800
Jennifer Robinson	Imagine Ent.	(310) 858-2000
Julie Robinson	Pico Creek Prod.	(310) 394-7522
Phil Robinson	Phil Alden Robinson	(818) 777-5055
Randy Robinson	Randwell Prod.	(310) 996-6809
Marc Rocco	Camera Marc	(818) 753-9901
Nikki Rocco	Universal Pictures	(818) 777-1000
Bobby Rock	American Zoetrope	(310) 899-8000
Ericka Rockler	CBS Ent.	(323) 575-2345
Craig Rodgers	The Lieberman Company	(323) 782-0881
Johnathan Rodgers	Discovery Networks	(301) 986-1999
Carlos Rodriguez	Mindfire Ent.	(310) 204-4481
SoYun Roe	Overbrook Ent.	(818) 777-2224
Craig Rogers	Straw Dogs	(323) 782-0777
Peter Rogers	Lakeshore Ent. Corp.	(323) 956-4222
Stan Rogow	Stan Rogow Prod.	(323) 993-5644
Steve Roguet	American Sports Network	(626) 292-2222
Susan Rohrer	S.E.R.	(757) 625-7647
Phil Roman	Phil Roman Ent.	(818) 985-1200
Andrea Romano	Warner Bros. Animation	(818) 954-7670
Edward A. Romano	Warner Bros.	(818) 954-6000
Andrew Rona	Dimension Films	(212) 941-3800
Melissa Rooker	Malpaso Prod.	(818) 954-3367
Fred Roos	FR Prod.	(310) 470-9212
Alex Rose	Alex Rose Prod.	(323) 654-8662
David Rose	Santa Monica Pictures	(310) 264-5566
Gary Rose	Moxie Pictures	(323) 957-5420
Jacobus Rose	Skylark Ent.	(310) 390-2659
Merry Rose	Beacon Communications	(310) 260-7000
Sara Rose	United Artists Films	(310) 449-3000
Adam W. Rosen	RKO Pictures	(310) 277-0707
Deborah Rosen	Universal Studios	(818) 777-1000
Josie Rosen	20th Century Fox Pictures	(310) 369-1000
Marc Rosen	Lynda Obst Prod.	(323) 956-8744
Steve Rosen	Kushner-Locke Company	(818) 841-8188
Michael Rosenberg	Imagine Ent.	(310) 858-2000
Rick Rosenberg	Chris/Rose Prod.	(310) 244-2833
Tom Rosenberg	Lakeshore Ent. Corp.	(323) 956-4222
Bart Rosenblatt	Neverland Films	(310) 772-0008
Justin Rosenblatt	Original Film	(310) 445-9000
Bruce Rosenblum	Warner Bros.	(818) 954-6000
Jill Rosenblum	Regent Films	(818) 990-3377
John Frank Rosenblum	Lighthouse Prod.	(310) 859-4923
Karen Rosenfelt	Paramount Pictures	(323) 956-5000
Howard Rosenman	Howard Rosenman Prod.	(310) 659-2100
James Rosenthal	New Line Cinema	(310) 854-5811
Jane Rosenthal	Tribeca Prod.	(212) 941-4000
Mark Rosenthal	MTV Networks	(310) 752-8000
Rick Rosenthal	Whitewater Films	(310) 575-5800
Alison Rosenzweig	Graham/Rosenzweig Films	(310) 264-3956
Marc Roskin	Centropolis Ent.	(310) 244-4300
Anthony Ross	Avalanche! Ent.	(310) 395-3660
Damon Ross	Nickelodeon Movies	(323) 956-8663
Glenn Ross	Artisan Ent.	(310) 449-9200
Holly Ross	JGF	(323) 462-1500
Marcia Ross	Buena Vista Motion Pictures	(818) 560-1000
Mark Ross	The Kennedy/Marshall Company	(310) 656-8400
Michael Ross	WB Television Network	(818) 977-5000
Rich Ross	The Disney Channel	(818) 569-7500
Steve Ross	Mars Media	(310) 664-6760
Mark Rossen	Original Film	(310) 445-9000
Dave Rossi	Rick Berman Prod.	(323) 956-5037
Michael Rotenberg	3 Arts Ent.	(310) 888-3200
Craig Roth	Davis Classics	(310) 551-2266
Joe Roth	Revolution Studios	(310) 264-4141
Kim Roth	Imagine Ent.	(310) 858-2000
Michael J. Roth	Sneak Preview Ent.	(323) 962-0295
Neal Rothman	New Line Cinema	(310) 854-5811
Thomas Rothman	20th Century Fox Pictures	(310) 369-1000
Betsy Rott	E! Ent. Television	(323) 954-2400
Mitch Rotter	New Line Cinema	(310) 854-5811
Katie Roumel	Killer Films	(212) 473-3950
Kelly Rouse	Echo Lake Prod.	(310) 399-9164
Tom Routson	Tool of North America	(310) 453-9244
Charles Roven	Atlas Ent.	(310) 724-7350
Will Rowbotham	Friendly Prod.	(310) 369-3973
Chris Rowe	Samuel Goldwyn Films	(310) 860-3100
Mark Rowen	Tropix Films	(310) 393-9956
Mike Rowles	Straw Dogs	(323) 782-0777
Mark Roybal	Scott Rudin Prod.	(323) 956-4600
David Rubin	Mirage Enterprises	(310) 244-2044

Executives/Personnel Alphabetical Key

Gary Rubin	Artisan Ent.	(310) 449-9200
Jean-Louis Rubin	Capella Films	(310) 247-4700
Kelly Andrea Rubin	Signature Ent.	(213) 994-4695
Steven Jay Rubin	Fast Carrier Pictures	(310) 234-5376
Rebekah Rudd	Spyglass Ent.	(818) 560-3458
Albert S. Ruddy	Ruddy Morgan Organization	(310) 271-7698
Scott Rudin	Scott Rudin Prod.	(323) 956-4600
Claire Rudnick-Polstein	New Line Cinema	(310) 854-5811
Glenn Rudolph	M-80 Films	(310) 899-9100
Hellene S. Runtagh	Universal Studios	(818) 777-1000
Morris Ruskin	Shoreline Ent.	(310) 551-2060
Yvonne Russo	Red-Horse Prod.	(818) 705-2588
Jim Ruxin	JKR Prod.	(310) 826-3666
Chuck Ryant	Bob Industries	(310) 396-7333
Per Saair	Wildwood Enterprises	(310) 395-5155
Eric Saarinen	Plum Prod.	(310) 450-1942
Haim Saban	Fox Family Channel	(310) 235-9700
Alan Sacks	Alan Sacks Prod.	(818) 752-6999
Mandy Safavi	Lynda Obst Prod.	(323) 956-8744
Howard Safenowitz	Walt Disney Pictures	(818) 560-1000
Mark Saffian	Michael I. Levy Enterprises	(323) 866-1802
Tony Safford	Fox Searchlight Pictures	(310) 369-4402
Don Safran	Rastar Prod.	(310) 244-7871
Whitney Saik	Telling Pictures	(415) 864-6714
Pat Sajak	P.A.T. Prod.	(310) 244-8811
Richard Sakai	Gracie Films	(310) 244-4222
Mark Saks	CBS Ent.	(323) 575-2345
George Salden	Zeal Pictures	(323) 871-4000
Eileen Salgro	Red Hots Ent.	(818) 954-0092
Charles Salice	Scream	(323) 930-5900
Mika Salmi	Atom Films	(626) 793-4950
Mikael Salomon	Flying Tiger Films	(310) 664-9171
Elie Samaha	Franchise Pictures	(323) 822-0730
Thomas Sammon	The Tribunal	(323) 468-9300
Marc Samuelson	Samuelson Prod.	(310) 208-1000
Peter Samuelson	Samuelson Prod.	(310) 208-1000
Rae Sanchini	Lightstorm Ent.	(310) 656-6100
Jay Sanders	Lightstorm Ent.	(310) 656-6100
Ken Sanders	WIN Ventures.	(310) 859-2500
Rupert Sanders	Omaha Pictures	(310) 396-4333
Tom Sanders	Aerial Focus Prod.	(805) 962-9911
Vernon Sanders	Nuance Prod.	(310) 247-1870
Bill Sandwick	Mars Media	(310) 664-6760
Eric Sandys	Seven Arts Pictures	(323) 464-0225
Midge Sanford	Sanford/Pillsbury Prod.	(310) 393-5225
Dana Sano	New Line Cinema	(310) 854-5811
Louis Santor	New Regency Prod.	(310) 369-8300
Carla Santos Shamberg	Jersey Films	(310) 203-1000
Richard Saperstein	New Line Cinema	(310) 854-5811
Mark Saraceni	Belisarius Prod.	(323) 956-8660
Cat Sautter	The Prod. Asylum	(760) 599-5494
Stephanie Savage	Flower Films	(310) 285-0200
Alison Savitch	Threshold Ent.	(310) 452-8899
Liz Sayre	Fox Searchlight Pictures	(310) 369-4402
Anthony Scala	Polestar Ent. Grp.	(310) 278-0080
Dana Scanlan	Kushner-Locke Company	(818) 841-8188
Kristy Scanlan	Minervision	(323) 848-3080
Caitlin Scanlon	Artisan Ent.	(310) 449-9200
Amanda Scarano	Irish DreamTime	(310) 449-3411
Bill Scarlet	OneSuch Films	(310) 273-3200
Stacy Schachter	Fate Junkie Films	(818) 905-1333
Paul Schaeffer	Mandalay Pictures	(323) 956-2400
Josh Schaer	RKO Pictures	(310) 277-0707
James Schamus	Good Machine	(212) 343-9230
Peter Schankowitz	Watershed Films	(310) 550-2175
Ken Schapiro	Artisan Ent.	(310) 449-9200
Larry Schapiro	Schapiro Ent. Grp.	(310) 358-3215
David Scheer	Halsted Pictures	(310) 450-7804
Steve Scheffer	HBO	(212) 512-1000
Beth R. Scheffres	Fine Line Features	(310) 854-5811
Rob Scheidlinger	OMNIBUS	(818) 560-3611
Andrew Scheinman	Castle Rock Ent.	(310) 285-2300
Jeff Schenck	Regent Ent.	(310) 260-3333
Rocky Schenck	DNA	(323) 463-2826
Edgar T. Scherick	Edgar J. Scherick & Assoc.	(310) 996-2376
Frank Scherma	@radical.media	(310) 664-4500
Paul Schiff	Paul Schiff Prod.	(323) 462-6400
Paul Schiff	Propaganda Films	(323) 462-6400
Zach Schiff-Abrams	Scott Free Prod.	(310) 360-2250
Michael Schiffer	BallPark Prod.	(310) 827-1328
John Schimmel	Bel-Air Ent.	(818) 954-4040
Barbara Schimpf	Talking Rings Ent.	(702) 227-3433
Deborah Schindler	Shoelace Prod.	(212) 243-2900
Murray Schisgal	Punch Prod.	(310) 442-4880
Adam Schlesinger	Jean Doumanian Prod.	(212) 486-2626
Peter Schlessel	Columbia Pictures	(310) 244-4000
Peter Schlessey	Screen Gems	(310) 244-4000
A. J. Schnack	Bonfire Films of America	(323) 953-6815
Don Schneider	Phase I Prod.	(310) 842-8401
Kathee Schneider	Film Roman	(818) 761-2544
Peter Schneider	Walt Disney Pictures	(818) 560-1000
Bennett Schneir	Image Movers	(818) 733-8313
Sarah Schoessler	Ranch Exit Films	(310) 471-0157
Robin Schorr	Lions Gate Ent.	(323) 692-7300
Peter Schube	The Jim Henson Company	(323) 802-1500
John A. Schulman	Warner Bros.	(818) 954-6000
Mark Schulman	3 Arts Ent.	(310) 888-3200
Michael Schulman	Forward Pass	(310) 571-3443
Mark Schulze	Crystal Pyramid Prod.	(619) 644-3000
Joel Schumacher	Joel Schumacher Prod.	(818) 954-2508
Thomas Schumacher	Walt Disney Pictures	(818) 560-1000
Paul Schwacke	Spyglass Ent.	(818) 560-3458
Bernard Schwartz	Bernard Schwartz Prod.	(310) 277-3700
Bob Schwartz	The House Prod. Company	(323) 851-5151
David Schwartz	Infomercial Solutions	(818) 879-1140
Doris Schwartz	RKO Pictures	(310) 277-0707
Marty Schwartz	Craig Anderson Prod.	(310) 841-2555
Ron Schwartz	Lions Gate Ent.	(323) 692-7300
Russell S. Schwartz	USA Films	(212) 539-4002
Stuart Schwartz	Cosgrove-Meurer Prod.	(818) 843-5600
Kristine Schwarz	Kristine Schwarz Prod.	(310) 393-0107
Joyce Schweickert	Fresh Produce Company	(323) 931-3700
Kenneth Schwenker	Oak Island Films	(310) 246-1466
Peter Schwerin	Dimension Films	(212) 941-3800
Larry Scissors	M.H.S. Prod.	(310) 202-3336
Mark Scoon	Warner Bros. Pictures Prod.	(818) 954-6000
Valerie Scoon	Harpo Films	(310) 278-5559
Robert Scopinich	Boyington Studios	(310) 822-2360
Martin Scorsese	Cappa Prod.	(212) 906-8800
Jake Scott	Black Dog Films (RSA USA)	(310) 659-1017
Jason D. Scott	Hunt-Tavel Prod.	(310) 244-3144
Jordan Scott	Black Dog Films (RSA USA)	(310) 659-1017
Luke Scott	Black Dog Films (RSA USA)	(310) 659-1017
Ridley Scott	Scott Free Prod.	(310) 360-2250
Tony Scott	Totem Prod.	(323) 650-4994
Don Scotti	Scotti Prod.	(323) 654-3666
Jeff Scruton	Morton Jankel Zander	(310) 826-6200
Bob Scwartz	The House Prod. Company	(323) 851-5151
Steven Seagal	Steamroller Prod.	(323) 850-2940
Richard Sears	HKM Prod.	(323) 465-9494
Jay Sefton	Neild Street Prod.	(323) 969-9447
Douglas Segal	Atlas Ent.	(310) 724-7350
Philip Segal	Tribune Ent. Company	(323) 460-5800
Nat Segaloff	Malcolm Leo Prod.	(323) 464-4448
Allison Segan	Further Films	(818) 777-6700
Paige Seidel	Stargazer	(310) 392-0392
Beth Sekul	Lakeshore Ent. Corp.	(323) 956-4222
Keri Selig	Bel-Air Ent.	(818) 954-4040
Dylan Sellers	Dylan Sellers Prod.	(818) 954-4929
Tom Sellitti	Apostle Pictures	(212) 541-4323
Allison Semenza	Franchise Pictures	(323) 822-0730
Sam Semon	CBS Ent.	(323) 575-2345
Maurice Sendak	Wild Things Prod.	(323) 964-4577
Momita Sengupta	MTV Films	(323) 956-8023
Al Septien	Wicked Monkey Prod.	(323) 461-6665
Jim Serpico	Apostle Pictures	(212) 541-4323
Larry Serraino	Level 7 Prod.	(818) 754-0074
Pelle Seth	Piper Prod.	(310) 883-8822
Shelby Sexton	Plum Prod.	(310) 450-1942
Dawn Shadforth	Black Dog Films (RSA USA)	(310) 659-1017
Tom Shadyac	Shady Acres Ent.	(818) 777-4446
Martin Shafer	Castle Rock Ent.	(310) 285-2300
Nevin I. Shalit	New Line Cinema	(310) 854-5811
Michael Shamberg	Jersey Films	(310) 203-1000
Rachel Shane	Red Wagon	(310) 244-4466
Allen Shapiro	Atlas Ent.	(310) 724-7350

Executives/Personnel Alphabetical Key

Angela P. Shapiro	IndieGal Prod.	(818) 890-6111
Angela Shapiro	ABC Inc./ABC Television	(310) 557-7777
Gary Shapiro	USA Network	(212) 413-5000
Greg Shapiro	Kingsgate Films	(310) 281-5880
Jared Shapiro	Headquarters	(310) 752-5200
Jon Shapiro	Ideal Ent.	(323) 939-3399
Paul Shapiro	Big Ticket Television	(323) 860-7400
Pete Shapiro	Ideal Ent.	(323) 939-3399
Far Shariat	Mad Chance	(818) 954-3803
Gayleen Sharon	JGF	(323) 462-1500
Rose Sharon	Norah Films	(323) 960-3458
Duncan Sharp	Life of Riley	(310) 230-7798
Michael Shaw	ABC Inc./ABC Television	(310) 557-7777
Robert K. Shaye	New Line Cinema	(310) 854-5811
Jim Shea	Planet	(323) 461-2695
J. R. Shearman	Shearman Ent.	(310) 860-0086
Steve Shedd	Lumiere Films	(323) 650-6773
Bill Sheinberg	The Bubble Factory	(310) 358-3000
Jon Sheinberg	The Bubble Factory	(310) 358-3000
Sid Sheinberg	The Bubble Factory	(310) 358-3000
Kyra Shelgren	Another Diversion	(818) 763-0338
Sven Shelgren	Dektor Film	(323) 466-3455
Marla L. Shelton	Merchant-Ivory Prod.	(212) 582-8049
Ron Shelton	Shanghai'd Films	(310) 453-8337
Debra Roberts Sher	WildLife Management	(310) 276-8008
Stacey Sher	Jersey Films	(310) 203-1000
Tom Sherak	Revolution Studios	(310) 264-4141
Steve Sherman	Talisman Pacific	(310) 260-1208
John Shestack	Artisan Ent.	(310) 449-9200
Martin Shewchuk	Tropix Films	(310) 393-9956
Allison Shigo	Chicagofilms	(212) 307-0050
Larry Shiu	Metro Pictures	(310) 301-7890
Marc Shmuger	Universal Pictures	(818) 777-1000
Jay Shoemaker	American Zoetrope	(310) 899-8000
Amy Shomer	Bill White Prod.	(818) 769-9090
Skip Short	Flying Tiger Films	(310) 664-9171
Dan Shotz	Junction Ent.	(818) 560-2800
Marcia Shulman	20th Century Fox Television	(310) 369-1000
Aaron J. Shuster	Fountainhead Pictures	(310) 276-5583
Doug Shwartz	Lions Gate Ent.	(323) 692-7300
David E. Siegel	Lucid Film	(310) 777-0007
Jennifer Siegel	Tool of North America	(310) 453-9244
Randi Siegel	Talent Ent. Grp.	(323) 969-0700
Jess Siegler	Pfeffer Film	(818) 560-3177
Corey Sienega	David Kirschner Prod.	(323) 939-0230
Chris Sievernich	Kinowelt USA	(310) 205-9600
Uriel Sigala	Film Roman	(818) 761-2544
Carlo Sigon	Porter Film Company	(323) 962-7855
Brad Silberling	Reveal Ent.	(818) 733-9818
Diane Sillan Isaacs	Green Moon Prod.	(310) 450-6111
Jonathan Silsby	Undergrace Prod.	(818) 833-8666
Carmen Silva	Zystar Films	(310) 301-3313
Alain Silver	Pendragon Film	(310) 828-1588
Alain Silver	PlasterCITY Prod.	(323) 938-0974
Jeffrey Silver	Outlaw Prod.	(310) 777-2000
Joel Silver	Silver Pictures Television	(818) 954-4490
Jay Silverman	Jay Silverman Prod.	(323) 466-6030
Lloyd A. Silverman	The Artists' Colony	(323) 930-7900
Rick Silverman	David E. Kelley Prod.	(310) 727-2200
Rick Silverman	Mostow/Lieberman	(818) 777-4444
Anita Simand	Telescene Film Grp.	(514) 737-5512
Christopher Simmons	Warner Bros. Animation	(818) 954-7670
Gene Simmons	The Gene Simmons Company	(310) 859-1694
Joel Simon	Quincy Jones Media Grp.	(323) 874-2009
Randy Simon	Randy Simon Prod.	(310) 274-7440
Stephen Simon	Metafilmics	(818) 734-9320
Erin Simon-Berenson	Red Hour Films	(310) 289-2565
Robert Simonds	The Robert Simonds Company	(818) 777-5445
Paula Simonetti	Miramax Films	(212) 941-3800
Brad Simonsen	Wildwood Enterprises	(310) 395-5155
Brad Simpson	Killer Films	(212) 473-3950
Jennifer Simpson	Barry Mendel Prod.	(818) 733-3076
Michael Simpson	Cairo/Simpson Ent.	(310) 888-1262
Nigel Sinclair	Intermedia Films	(310) 777-0007
Avant Singh	Distant Horizon	(323) 848-4140
Bedi A. Singh	Sony Pictures Ent.	(310) 244-4000
Jack Singman	Revolver Films	(310) 829-2441
Denise Sirkot	Gracie Films	(310) 244-4222
Cindy Sison	Santa Monica Pictures	(310) 264-5566
Ben Sitzer	Licht/Mueller Films	(310) 205-5500
Michael Sitzer	Mirella Film Co.	(323) 850-5522
Carolyn Sivitz	The Vault	(310) 315-0012
Kim Skeeters	The Steve Tisch Company	(310) 838-2500
Don Skeoch	Universal Studios	(818) 777-1000
Roy Skillicorn	Backyard Prod.	(310) 314-1122
Alan Skinner	Another Large Prod.	(323) 954-8500
Rebecca Skinner	Mars Media	(310) 664-6760
Daniel Sladek	Sladek Ent. Corp.	(323) 934-9268
Chuck Sloan	Plum Prod.	(310) 450-1942
Kat Slonaker	Turner Network Television	(310) 551-6300
Lindsay Smarz	Shady Acres Ent.	(818) 777-4446
Peter Smillie	Smillie Films	(310) 314-0072
Erik Smith	Seven Arts Pictures	(323) 464-0225
Gary Smith	Winchester Films	(310) 458-1400
Ian Smith	Phoenix Pictures	(310) 244-6100
James Smith	The Robert Evans Company	(323) 956-8800
Jennifer Smith	Crusader Ent.	(310) 248-6360
Kevin Smith	Backyard Prod.	(310) 314-1122
Kevin Smith	View Askew Prod.	(732) 842-6933
Matthew Smith	Conundrum Ent.	(310) 319-2800
Maureen Smith	Fox Family Channel	(310) 235-9700
Mike Smith	Beard Boy Prod.	(949) 458-2305
Paul Smith	Columbia Pictures	(310) 244-4000
Peter Smith	Universal Pictures	(818) 777-1000
Roger Smith	AM Prod. & Management	(310) 275-9081
Roland Ozzie Smith	Longboard Prod.	(916) 684-5085
Russ Smith	Mr. Mudd Prod.	(323) 932-5656
Todd Smith	Atlas Ent.	(310) 724-7350
Will Smith	Overbrook Ent.	(818) 777-2224
Debra Smith-Cannold	Patchett Kaufman Ent.	(310) 838-7000
Kelley Smith-Wait	Atlas Ent.	(310) 724-7350
Adam Smoot	Rogue Ent.	(801) 979-2229
Brian Snedeker	Walt Disney TV Animation	(818) 560-5000
Gary Snegaroff	E! Ent. Television	(323) 954-2400
Gregory Snegoff	Green Grass Blue Sky Company	(818) 760-8243
Stacey Snider	Universal Pictures	(818) 777-1000
Wesley Snipes	Amen Ra Films	(310) 246-6510
Leslie Snow	Straw Dogs	(323) 782-0777
Robert Snukal	Itasca Pictures	(310) 273-6505
Steven Soderberg	Section Eight Pictures	(818) 954-4840
Jim Sodini	Zide/Perry Ent.	(310) 887-2999
Steve Soffer	Flip Your Lid	(818) 222-0700
Aude Soichet	American Zoetrope	(310) 899-8000
Joel Soisson	Neo Art & Logic	(323) 653-6007
Amy Solan	Baltimore/Spring Creek Pictures	(818) 954-1210
Marc Solomon	Warner Bros. Pictures Prod.	(818) 954-6000
Mitch Solomon	Film Roman	(818) 761-2544
Richard Solomon	The Bedford Falls Company	(310) 394-5022
Julio Solorzano	Ventana Films	(323) 876-3331
Jim Sommers	IPS Prod.	(323) 851-3595
Barry Sonnifeld	Straw Dogs	(323) 782-0777
Dror Soref	Orbit Ent. Grp.	(323) 525-2626
Scott Sorensen	Four Square Prod.	(858) 874-1900
Arla Sorkin Manson	Sarabande Prod.	(310) 395-4842
Lainie Sorkin	3 Arts Ent.	(310) 888-3200
Jenifer Sorrow	Polestar Ent. Grp.	(310) 278-0080
Mark Sourian	DreamWorks SKG	(818) 733-7000
Paul Spadone	Davis Ent. Co.	(310) 556-3550
Michael Spatt	New Line Cinema	(310) 854-5811
Ricki Spector	Nickelodeon Movies	(323) 956-8663
Chuck Speed	Regent Ent.	(310) 260-3333
Aaron Spelling	RumRunner Cine Service	(310) 540-8411
Clark Spencer	Walt Disney Pictures	(818) 560-1000
Daniel Spencer	Blue Wolf Prod.	(415) 561-6655
Randy Spendlove	Miramax Films	(212) 941-3800
David Spiegelman	New Line Cinema	(310) 854-5811
Steven Spielberg	DreamWorks SKG	(818) 733-7000
Jack Spillum	Jumbo Pictures	(212) 337-0077
Brian Spink	Bender-Spink	(323) 845-1640
J. C. Spink	Bender-Spink	(323) 845-1640
Louise Spinner	Talent Ent. Grp	(323) 969-0700
Arthur Spivak	Nuance Prod.	(310) 247-1870
Dawn Spiwak	June Beallor Prod.	(818) 777-9000
Lynn Splendid	SplendidLight Media Prod.	(949) 722-8485
Andrea Sporer	Scholastic Ent.	(212) 343-7500
Andi Sporkin	CBS Enterprises	(212) 975-4321

Executives/Personnel Alphabetical Key

Frank Spotnitz	Ten Thirteen Prod.	(310) 369-1100
Samantha Sprecher	Face Prod.	(310) 285-2300
Mark Spring	The Ad-Files	(213) 891-3784
Linda Springer	Paramount Pictures	(323) 956-5000
Robin Spry	Telescene Film Grp.	(514) 737-5512
Beau St. Clair	Irish DreamTime	(310) 449-3411
John St. Clair	OneSuch Films	(310) 273-3200
Chris St. George	Craig Anderson Prod.	(310) 841-2555
Mark St. Juste	Red Hots Ent.	(818) 954-0092
Kristen Stabile	The Greif Company	(310) 456-1200
Jeanne Stack	J. Stack Prod.	(310) 456-3272
Thomas Stack	Columbia Pictures	(310) 244-4000
Thomas O. Staggs	The Walt Disney Company	(818) 560-1000
Share Stallings	Nickelodeon Movies	(323) 956-8663
Alan Stamm	30 Second Films	(310) 315-1750
David Stanfield	Aerial Focus Prod.	(805) 962-9911
Cheryl Stanley	Talent Ent. Grp.	(323) 969-0700
Trancee Stanley	Franchise Pictures	(323) 822-0730
Steve Stapinski	Moushel Prod.	(978) 618-1933
Robert Starchfield	Level 7 Prod.	(818) 754-0074
Ray Stark	Rastar Prod.	(310) 244-7871
Steve Stark	Paramount Network Television	(323) 956-5000
David Starke	20th Century Fox Pictures	(310) 369-1000
Steve Starkey	Image Movers	(818) 733-8313
Jane Startz	Jane Startz Prod.	(212) 545-8910
Andrew Stearn	John Wells Prod.	(818) 954-1687
Jeremy Steckler	Spyglass Ent.	(818) 560-3458
Colleen Steckloff	Alta Vista Prod.	(310) 444-2050
Astrid Steel	Alta Vista Prod.	(310) 444-2050
Sabrina Steele	The Canton Company	(818) 954-2130
Tyler Steele	Distant Horizon	(323) 848-4140
Lloyd Stein	Headquarters	(310) 752-5200
Mark Stein	Kopelson Ent.	(310) 369-7555
Nicholas Stein	Greystone Communication Grp.	(818) 762-2900
Scott Stein	Acappella Pictures	(323) 782-8200
Susan Stein	Radiant Prod.	(310) 656-1400
Christina Steinberg	Junction Ent.	(818) 560-2800
David Steinberg	Morra, Brezner, Steinberg & Tenenbaum	(310) 385-1820
Sheree Steiner	James Pentecost Prod.	(818) 560-4965
Nancy Steingard	Universal Pictures	(818) 777-1000
Michael Steinhardt	Baer Ent. Grp.	(310) 777-3680
Paul Steinke	Walt Disney Pictures	(818) 560-1000
Eric Steinman	Headquarters	(310) 752-5200
Peter Steinzeig	Backyard Prod.	(310) 314-1122
Mike Stenson	Jerry Bruckheimer Films	(310) 664-6260
Sheila Stepanek	Backyard Prod.	(310) 314-1122
David Stephanov	Wendy Finerman Prod.	(310) 369-8800
John Stephenson	The Jim Henson Company	(323) 802-1500
Alan Stepp	Two Stepp Prod.	(818) 908-4041
Brad Sterling	UPN	(310) 575-7000
Cori Stern	Fox Family Channel	(310) 235-9700
Greg Stern	M-80 Films	(310) 899-9100
Howard Stern	Howard Stern Prod.	(212) 867-1200
Jay Stern	New Line Cinema	(310) 854-5811
Mark Stern	Triology Ent. Grp.	(310) 449-3095
Marc Sternberg	Daybreak Prod.	(818) 777-0277
Michael Sterner	Crystal Pyramid Prod.	(619) 644-3000
Andrew Stevens	Franchise Pictures	(323) 822-0730
Greg Stevens	Stampede Ent.	(310) 264-4229
Damien Stevenson	DreamWorks SKG	(818) 733-7000
Allyn Stewart	Bel-Air Ent.	(818) 954-4040
Denise Stewart	Brillstein-Grey Ent.	(310) 275-6135
Patrick Stewart	Flying Freehold Prod.	(323) 956-8838
Frank Stiefel	Stiefel + Company	(310) 581-7000
Geoff Stier	Mirage Enterprises	(310) 244-2044
Ben Stiller	Red Hour Films	(310) 289-2565
Randy Stith	The Association	(818) 841-9660
Guy Stodel	Lions Gate Ent.	(323) 692-7300
Erwin Stoff	3 Arts Ent.	(310) 888-3200
David Stoltz	Brian Bleak Films	(310) 396-5500
Dan Stone	Persistent Ent.	(310) 777-1814
Nancy Rae Stone	Beacon Communications	(310) 260-7000
Robert Stone	Stone vs. Stone	(212) 941-1200
Webster Stone	Stone vs. Stone	(212) 941-1200
Andrew Storms	Konrad Pictures	(310) 244-3555
Mark Story	Bella Prod.	(310) 823-3115
Tim Story	FM Rocks	(310) 587-1501
S. Drew Stotesbery	Vanguard Prod.	(310) 306-4910
Jeffrey Stott	Castle Rock Ent.	(310) 285-2300
Jennifer Stott	Fine Line Features	(310) 854-5811
Jesse Stovin	Gullane Pictures	(310) 451-5111
Gary M. Strangis	David E. Kelley Prod.	(310) 727-2200
Erik Strauss	No Prisoners	(310) 979-9097
Scott Strauss	Outlaw Prod.	(310) 777-2000
Ryan Streber	Undergrace Prod.	(818) 833-8666
Tim Street	The Spark Factory	(310) 395-6775
Barbra Streisand	Barwood Films	(212) 765-7191
Blair Stribley	Backyard Prod.	(310) 314-1122
Chace Strickland	Backyard Prod.	(310) 314-1122
Kandia Stroh	Itasca Pictures	(310) 273-6505
David Strohmeyer	Sarabande Prod.	(310) 395-4842
Gregory Strom	Strom Magallon Ent.	(323) 969-1089
Winston Stromberg	Shady Acres Ent.	(818) 777-4446
Kelly Stuart	Triology Ent. Grp.	(310) 449-3095
Mel Stuart	Mel Stuart Prod.	(310) 785-9080
Will Stubbs	Radar Pictures	(310) 208-8525
Scott Stuber	Universal Pictures	(818) 777-1000
Karin Stuckenschmidt	Film Planet	(310) 581-1100
Simone Study	Bleecker Street Films	(323) 993-7386
Richard Suckle	Atlas Ent.	(310) 724-7350
Michael Sudmeier	Rastar Prod.	(310) 244-7871
Greg Sullivan	South Fork Prod.	(310) 829-5029
Jim Sullivan	South Fork Prod.	(310) 829-5029
Matt Sullivan	Marvel Characters	(310) 234-8991
Mike Sullivan	Mike Sullivan Prod.	(310) 315-7315
Reid Sullivan	Village Roadshow Pictures	(818) 260-6000
Susan Sullivan	Jaret Ent.	(310) 883-8807
Jerry Summers	Undergrace Prod.	(818) 833-8666
Ty Supancic	Miller Ent. Grp.	(323) 932-6500
Debbie Supnik	Weller/Grossman Prod.	(818) 755-4800
Spencer Susser	Black Dog Films (RSA USA)	(310) 659-1017
Mitchell Sussman	Raven Prod.	(760) 325-7191
Peter Sussman	Alliance Atlantis	(310) 899-8000
William A. Sutman	Universal Studios	(818) 777-1000
Kinga Suto	Parkway Prod.	(310) 244-4040
Alan Sutton	Universal Pictures	(818) 777-1000
Martin Svab	Original Voices	(310) 392-3479
Tim Swain	Newmark Films	(323) 782-4969
Carl Swan	HKM Prod.	(323) 465-9494
Kelly Coogan Swanson	Hallmark Ent.	(212) 977-9001
Neely Swanson	David E. Kelley Prod.	(310) 727-2200
Cynthia Swartz	Columbia Pictures	(310) 244-4000
Anne Sweeney	ABC Inc./ABC Television	(310) 557-7777
Stephanie Swor	Smillie Films	(310) 314-0072
Kel Symons	Mace Neufeld Prod.	(310) 244-2555
George Synder	Mutant Enemy	(310) 579-5180
Jason Syzmanski	Post Modern Edit	(714) 751-2681
Greg Szimonisz	Dreyfuss/James Prod.	(323) 850-3140
Benjamin Sztajnkrycer	Acappella Pictures	(323) 782-8200
Chris Taaffe	Sladek Ent. Corp.	(323) 934-9268
Lauren Tabach-Bank	Team Todd	(310) 248-6001
Alia Tabet	Lighthouse Prod.	(310) 859-4923
Don Taffner Jr.	D.L.T. Ent.	(323) 937-1144
Martin Tahse	Martin Tahse Prod.	(310) 652-3628
Tibor Takacs	Boyington Studios	(310) 822-2360
Fred Talmage	Warner Bros. Pictures Prod.	(818) 954-6000
Richard Tamayo	TVP Studios	(818) 843-3188
Ronald Tanet	The Woofenill Works	(212) 734-2578
Zach Tann	Zide/Perry Ent.	(310) 887-2999
Ted Tannebaum	Lakeshore Ent. Corp.	(323) 956-4222
Jill Tanner	Quincy Jones Media Grp.	(323) 874-2009
Steve Tao	New Line Cinema	(310) 854-5811
Rob Tapert	Renaissance Pictures	(818) 777-0088
Dana Taprogge	Atlantic Streamline	(310) 319-9366
Quentin Tarantino	A Band Apart	(323) 951-4600
Neil Tardio Jr.	Fuel	(310) 314-1644
John Tarnoff	Wonderland Films	(323) 656-6489
Dawn Tarnofsky-Ostroff	Lifetime Television	(212) 424-7000
Rosemary Tarquinio	Radiant Prod.	(310) 656-1400
Meher Tatna	Silvereye Prod.	(818) 501-4232
Connie Tavel	Tavel Ent.	(310) 278-6700
George Taweel	TLC Ent.	(818) 655-6155
Alix Taylor	Wes Craven Films	(818) 752-0197
Burton Taylor	Taylor-Bedell Ent.	(310) 859-9967
Cami Taylor	Bella Prod.	(310) 823-3115

Executives/Personnel Alphabetical Key

Dan Taylor	Metro-Goldwyn-Mayer Studios	(310) 449-3000
Grazka Taylor	Grazka Taylor Prod.	(310) 201-0806
Jamie Taylor	Fox Searchlight Pictures	(310) 369-4402
Jeffrey Taylor	Stagescreen Prod.	(323) 969-1974
Jim Taylor	kaboom	(415) 434-2666
Mark Taylor	Lotus Films	(626) 292-1015
Richard Taylor	Tropix Films	(310) 393-9956
Toper Taylor	Nelvana Ent.	(323) 549-4222
Yvette Taylor	All Girl Prod.	(818) 655-6000
Michael Tedone	Lifetime Television	(212) 424-7000
Cynthia Teele	Paramount Domestic Television	(323) 956-5000
Mitch Teemley	Canvas House Films	(714) 850-1964
Karen Teicher	Mandalay Pictures	(323) 956-2400
Robert Teitel	State Street Pictures	(310) 369-5099
Jeff Teitelman	Intelliscape Films	(310) 235-1422
Bob Telford	Video Hollywood Prod.	(888) 368-7347
Nancy Tellem	CBS Ent.	(323) 575-2345
Gary Templeton	P.A.T. Prod.	(310) 244-8811
Andrew Tenenbaum	Morra, Brezner, Steinberg & Tenenbaum	(310) 385-1820
Stephen Tenenbaum	Morra, Brezner, Steinberg & Tenenbaum	(310) 385-1820
Karen Tenkhoff	Wildwood Enterprises	(310) 395-5155
Andy Tennant	Alchemy Ent.	(310) 396-5937
Victor Teran	Seven Arts Pictures	(323) 464-0225
Eileen Terry	FM Rocks	(310) 587-1501
Jim Tharp	DreamWorks SKG	(818) 733-7000
Beverly Thelander	Universal Television	(818) 777-5300
Bradley Thomas	Conundrum Ent.	(310) 319-2800
Brady Thomas	Castle Rock Ent.	(310) 285-2300
Brent Thomas	Green Dot Films	(310) 656-4900
Jessica Thomas	Mars Media	(310) 664-6760
Mark Thomas	Area 51 Films	(310) 395-5151
Nigel Thomas	Matador Pictures	(310) 820-5866
Rachelle L. Thomas	Amen Ra Films	(310) 246-6510
Rob Thomas	Level 7 Prod.	(818) 754-0074
Steven Thomas	Jeff Wald Ent.	(310) 264-4156
Tony Thomas	Witt/Thomas/Harris Prod.	(323) 993-7000
Harry Thomason	Mozark Prod.	(818) 655-5779
Tanna Thompson	Mandolin Ent.	(323) 802-6950
Ty Thompson	21st Century Man	(323) 466-3227
Julie Thomson	Valhalla Motion Pictures	(323) 969-4300
Sean Thonson	Morton Jankel Zander	(310) 826-6200
Terry Thoren	Klasky Csupo	(323) 463-0145
Joanne Thrailkill	X-Ray Prod.	(310) 659-7659
Shane Thueson	Bender-Spink	(323) 845-1640
Nichols Thurkettle	Davis Classics	(310) 551-2266
Susan Tick	Columbia Pictures	(310) 244-4000
George Tillman	State Street Pictures	(310) 369-5099
Bruce Timm	Warner Bros. Animation	(818) 954-7670
Terri Tingle	Turner Ent. Grp.	(404) 827-1500
Fred Tio	Buena Vista Motion Pictures	(818) 560-1000
Christopher Tipton	Silverline Pictures	(818) 752-3730
Lee Tirce	RumRunner Cine Service	(310) 540-8411
Steve Tisch	The Steve Tisch Company	(310) 838-2500
David Tochterman	Overbrook Ent.	(818) 777-2224
Elisa Todd	David E. Kelley Prod.	(310) 727-2200
Jennifer Todd	Team Todd	(310) 248-6001
Suzanne Todd	Team Todd	(310) 248-6001
Van Toffler	MTV Films	(323) 956-8023
Joyce Tollefson	Fountainbridge Films	(310) 244-8080
Rhonda Tollefson	Fountainbridge Films	(310) 244-8080
Mike Tollin	Tollin/Robbins Prod.	(818) 766-5004
Matt Tolmach	Columbia Pictures	(310) 244-4000
Mark Tolner	FilmWorld	(323) 655-7705
Sandra Tomita	The Goldstein Company	(310) 659-9511
John Tomko	Jerry Weintraub Prod.	(818) 954-2500
Jay Torres	WildLife Management	(310) 276-8008
Peter Torres	Fresh Produce Company	(323) 931-3700
Tim Tortora	Harpo Films	(310) 278-5559
Mark Trabulus	Roger Gimbel Prod.	(310) 459-3838
Gerry Trafficanda	Trafficanda Studios	(323) 466-1111
Bic Tran	Lakeshore Ent. Corp.	(323) 956-4222
Peter Travgott	Brillstein-Grey Ent.	(310) 275-6135
Sue Travis Miller	Red Hots Ent.	(818) 954-0092
Tracey Trench	The Robert Simonds Company	(818) 777-5445
John Trickett	New Line Cinema	(310) 854-5811
Lorraine Triolo	Burke/Triolo Prod.	(310) 837-9900
Chris Trunkey	National Lampoon	(310) 474-5252
Simon Tse	Simon Tse Prod.	(310) 385-9331
Christine Tso	Neild Street Prod.	(323) 969-9447
Kevin Tsujihara	Warner Bros.	(818) 954-6000
James Tucker	Warner Bros. Animation	(818) 954-7670
Ren Tucker	Moving Pictures	(212) 219-4545
David Tuckerman	New Line Cinema	(310) 854-5811
Jenny Lew Tugend	JLT Prod.	(323) 993-7093
Henry Tuggle	Roni Weisberg Prod.	(310) 286-1210
Jamie Celeste Tullo	Face Broadcast Prod.	(818) 842-9081
James R. Tumminia	George Paige Assoc.	(310) 315-4835
Lawrence Turman	The Turman-Morrissey Company	(310) 586-8649
Hans Turner	Franchise Pictures	(323) 822-0730
Dan Tursi	Snow Leopard Prod.	(310) 827-1220
Jon Turteltaub	Junction Ent.	(818) 560-2800
Jon Turtle	Jon Turtle Prod.	(310) 234-5347
Jennifer Tuthill	Original Film	(310) 445-9000
Eden Tyler	Zooma Zooma Corp.	(212) 941-7680
Thom Tyson	Plum Prod.	(310) 450-1942
Harry Ufland	Ufland Prod.	(310) 656-3031
Mary Jane Ufland	Ufland Prod.	(310) 656-3031
Lisa Ullmann	Ocean Pictures	(310) 369-0093
Brenda Underwood	Ad-Lib	(909) 629-1995
Ron Underwood	Stampede Ent.	(310) 264-4229
Tracy Underwood	John Wells Prod.	(818) 954-1687
Bill Ungar	Tidewater Ent.	(310) 459-8711
Rich Ungar	Marvel Characters	(310) 234-8991
Anthony Unger	Unger Prod.	(310) 859-1455
Anita Untersee	Evolution Film	(805) 386-1285
Chuck Untersee	Evolution Film	(805) 386-1285
Rick Upshaw	Merv Griffin Ent.	(310) 385-3160
Erin Upson	Scott Free Prod.	(310) 360-2250
Leslie Urdang	Wildwood Enterprises	(310) 395-5155
Mark Urman	Lions Gate Ent.	(323) 692-7300
Nancy Utley	Fox Searchlight Pictures	(310) 369-4402
Christine Vachon	Killer Films	(212) 473-3950
Colin Vaines	Miramax Films	(212) 941-3800
Annette Vait	Fresh Produce Company	(323) 931-3700
Andrew Vajna	Cinergi Pictures	(310) 315-6000
Jim Valdes	Bender-Spink	(323) 845-1640
Renée Valente	Renée Valente Prod.	(323) 969-1541
Courtenay Valenti	Warner Bros. Pictures Prod.	(818) 954-6000
Chris Valentini	Unapix Films	(212) 252-7711
Milt Vallas	The Baer Animation Company	(323) 874-9122
Darrell Van Citters	Renegade Animation	(818) 556-3395
Nick Van Dyk	Artisan Ent.	(310) 449-9200
Valerie van Galder	Screen Gems	(310) 244-4000
Mikon Van Gastel	Imaginary Forces	(323) 957-6868
Kirk Van Houten	Video Hollywood Prod.	(888) 368-7347
Caleigh Vancata	Tollin/Robbins Prod.	(818) 766-5004
Lyndi Vanderhout	Ginty Films	(310) 274-9691
Brian Vanderwilt	Genrebend Prod.	(310) 284-7312
Pete Vanlaw	Western Branch Prod.	(818) 762-3810
Javier Varon	Olmos Prod.	(310) 557-7010
Jerry A. Vasilatos	Nitestar Prod.	(323) 468-8089
Rob Vaughn	Chesler/Perlmutter Prod.	(310) 443-9650
Nicholas Vayonis	Carbo Films	(310) 586-1969
Steve Veisel	UPN	(310) 575-7000
Ronell Venter	Oak Island Films	(310) 246-1466
Gary Ventimiglia	Maverick Films	(310) 276-6177
Valerio Ventura	Kontrast Films	(818) 840-9333
Olivier Venturini	Cohn & Company	(310) 899-6979
Paul Verhoeven	Verhoeven/Marshall Films	(310) 244-5352
Lori Imbler Vernon	Chartoff Prod.	(310) 319-1960
Inga Veronique	Mars Media	(310) 664-6760
Rino Vetrone	The Jonathan Krane Grp.	(310) 278-0142
Vern Vihlene	Vihlene & Assoc.	(949) 582-0937
Scott Vila	20th Century Fox Television	(310) 369-1000
Robert Villalobos	AbsoluteFilms.net	(626) 442-6454
Danny Vinik	Muse Prod.	(310) 306-2001
Lori Vitale	Zooma Zooma Corp.	(212) 941-7680
Ruth Vitale	Paramount Classics	(323) 956-2000
Art Vitarelli	Reel Orange	(949) 548-4524
Michael Vodde	Martin Tahse Prod.	(310) 652-3628
Lia Vollack	Columbia Pictures	(310) 244-4000
Peter Von Gal	Hallmark Ent.	(212) 977-9001
Amy Von Nostrand	Red House Ent.	(818) 977-1902
Mike Vorndian	Imagine Ent.	(310) 858-2000

Executives/Personnel Alphabetical Key

Frank Vrioste	Warner Bros. Pictures Prod.	(818) 954-6000
Ed Wacek	Raffaella Prod.	(818) 777-2655
Daniel Wagner	Killer Films	(212) 473-3950
Raymond Wagner	Raymond Wagner Prod.	(310) 278-1970
Rob Wagner	Beard Boy Prod.	(949) 458-2305
Richard Wainess	Digital Visionaries	(818) 364-0397
Rupert Wainwright	Windmill Lane Prod.	(310) 576-1344
Jeff Wald	Jeff Wald Ent.	(310) 264-4156
Dana Walden	20th Century Fox Television	(310) 369-1000
Matthew Waldman	The Turman-Morrissey Company	(310) 586-8649
Alexander Walker Jr.	FilmWorld	(323) 655-7705
Darrell Walker	Mandalay Pictures	(323) 956-2400
Eldridge Walker	Paramount Pictures	(323) 956-5000
Bess Walkes	Bungalow 78 Prod.	(323) 956-4440
Fran Wall	OneSuch Films	(310) 273-3200
Matt Wall	USA Films	(212) 539-4002
Meryl Alison Wallis	Zystar Films	(310) 301-3313
Adriana Walsh	Enteraktion	(954) 785-5070
Kieran Walsh	Morton Jankel Zander	(310) 826-6200
Sam Walsh	Propaganda Films	(323) 462-6400
Tom Walsh	Enteraktion	(954) 785-5070
Kal Walthers	Walt Disney Pictures	(818) 560-1000
Ken Walz	Ken Walz Prod.	(310) 449-4001
Elizabeth Wang Lee	Constantin Film	(310) 247-0300
Edward C. Wang	Gittes	(310) 244-4333
Max Da-Yung Wang	WildLife Management	(310) 276-8008
Plato Wang	Tavel Ent.	(310) 278-6700
Laurel Ward	Ocean Pictures	(310) 369-0093
Noreen Ward	Good Machine	(212) 343-9230
Gina Warendorp	Shady Acres Ent.	(818) 777-4446
Randy Warner	John Wells Prod.	(818) 954-1687
Steve Warner	Lifetime Television	(212) 424-7000
Lenny Waronker	DreamWorks SKG	(818) 733-7000
Rick Warren	Post Modern Edit	(714) 751-2681
John Wash	SimEx Digital Studios	(310) 664-9500
Kiko Washington	Warner Bros.	(818) 954-6000
Dan Watanabe	Pearson Television	(310) 656-1100
Doug Waterman	Langley Prod.	(310) 449-5300
Heather Waterman	Punch Prod.	(310) 442-4880
Sam Waterson	Atkinson Way Films	(323) 465-3350
John Watson	Triology Ent. Grp.	(310) 449-3095
Julie Watson	Belisarius Prod.	(323) 956-8660
Peter Watson-Wood	Matador Pictures	(310) 820-5866
Jim Watters	Universal Studios	(818) 777-1000
Emma Watts	20th Century Fox Pictures	(310) 369-1000
Steve Wax	Chelsea Pictures	(323) 860-8030
Todd Waxler	Proud Mary Ent.	(310) 288-1886
Martye Wayne	Krainin Prod.	(914) 359-0445
Donald D. Wear	Discovery Networks	(301) 986-1999
Lucy Webb	Calm Down Prod.	(323) 650-4027
Marc Webb	DNA	(323) 463-2826
Brian Scott Weber	No Prisoners	(310) 979-9097
Marco Weber	Atlantic Streamline	(310) 319-9366
Bradley J. Wechsler	IMAX Corp.	(310) 255-5500
Jim Wedaa	The Jacobson Company	(818) 560-1600
Pierre Weidemann	David Foster Prod.	(818) 954-4113
Larry Weinberg	Incognito Ent.	(310) 246-1500
William S. Weiner	New Regency Prod.	(310) 369-8300
Greg Weinschenker	Tango Films	(310) 470-4908
Bob Weinstein	Dimension Films	(212) 941-3800
Harvey Weinstein	Miramax Films	(212) 941-3800
Jonathan Weinstein	Go Film	(212) 677-7500
Paula Weinstein	Baltimore/Spring Creek Pictures	(818) 954-1210
Marc Weinstock	Screen Gems	(310) 244-4000
Barbara Weintraub	Axelson-Weintraub Prod.	(818) 954-8661
Fred Weintraub	Weintraub/Kuhn Prod.	(310) 788-9380
Jerry Weintraub	Jerry Weintraub Prod.	(818) 954-2500
Roni Weisberg	Roni Weisberg Prod.	(310) 286-1210
Roz Weisberg	Wind Dancer Prod. Grp.	(323) 645-1200
Howard Weisman	Forest Hills Pictures	(310) 207-6462
Jason Weiss	New Regency Prod.	(310) 369-8300
Joanne Weiss	Grammnet Prod. (Film)	(323) 956-5840
Marjorie Weitzman	InFront Prod.	(310) 369-5890
Kara Welker-Ryder	3 Arts Ent.	(310) 888-3200
Robb Weller	Weller/Grossman Prod.	(818) 755-4800
Vicki Wellnitz	Vihlene & Assoc.	(949) 582-0937
Gerry Wenner	Planet	(323) 461-2695
Bob Wenokur	Kushner-Locke Company	(818) 841-8188
Brian Wensel	Paramount Pictures	(323) 956-5000
John A. Wentworth	Paramount Television Grp.	(323) 956-5000
David M. Werk	Videowerks	(310) 393-8754
Jeff Wernick	DIC Ent.	(818) 955-5400
Sandy Wernick	Brillstein-Grey Ent.	(310) 275-6135
Alice West	David E. Kelley Prod.	(310) 727-2200
Joella West	Lions Gate Ent.	(323) 692-7300
Simon West	Wychwood Prod.	(323) 462-6400
David Westin	ABC Inc./ABC Television	(310) 557-7777
Brad Weston	Dimension Films	(212) 941-3800
Peter Wetherell	Echo Lake Prod.	(310) 399-9164
Linda Curran Wexelblatt	Crane Wexelblatt Ent.	(310) 457-4821
Joshua Wexler	Threshold Ent.	(310) 452-8899
Joss Whedon	Mutant Enemy	(310) 579-5180
Derzat Whelan	Sony Pictures Classics	(212) 833-8833
Robert Wherry	Go Film	(212) 677-7500
Christine Whitaker	National Geographic Films	(310) 229-0990
Jim Whitaker	Imagine Ent.	(310) 858-2000
Bill White	Bill White Prod.	(818) 769-9090
Jeremy White	Orbit Ent. Grp.	(323) 525-2626
Severin White	Propaganda Films	(323) 462-6400
Steve White	NBC Ent.	(818) 840-4444
Terry White	Polestar Ent. Grp.	(310) 278-0080
Rebecca Whittington	Cosgrove-Meurer Prod.	(818) 843-5600
Douglas Wick	Red Wagon	(310) 244-4466
Dean Wideman	Triumph Pictures	(310) 234-9680
Gareth Wigan	Columbia Pictures	(310) 244-4000
William C. Wiles	Lyon Studios	(949) 723-0657
Lionel Wilgram	Warner Bros. Pictures Prod.	(818) 954-6000
Jamie Wilkenson	Stan Lee Media	(818) 461-1757
Derek Wilkins	Radar Pictures	(310) 208-8525
Jane H. Williams	New Line Cinema	(310) 854-5811
Ken Williams	Stan Lee Media	(818) 461-1757
Marsha Williams	Blue Wolf Prod.	(415) 561-6655
Matt Williams	Wind Dancer Prod. Grp.	(323) 645-1200
Robin Williams	Blue Wolf Prod.	(415) 561-6655
Victor Williams	Dockry Prod.	(310) 274-0761
Vikki Williams	FGM Ent.	(310) 358-1370
Wayne S. Williams	Cannell Studios	(323) 465-5800
Glenn Williamson	DreamWorks SKG	(818) 733-7000
Kevin Williamson	Outerbanks Ent.	(323) 654-3700
David Williger	P.A.T. Prod.	(310) 244-8811
Steve Willis	DNA	(323) 463-2826
Ed Wilson	CBS Television	(212) 975-4321
Lisa Wilson	Franchise Pictures	(323) 822-0730
Michael Wilson	Danjaq	(310) 449-3185
S. S. Wilson	Stampede Ent.	(310) 264-4229
Veronica Wilson	David E. Kelley Prod.	(310) 727-2200
Virginia Wilson	Oak Island Films	(310) 246-1466
Scott Winant	Twilight Time Films	(310) 284-7310
Michael Winchester	Film Roman	(818) 761-2544
Scott Windhauser	Bay Films	(310) 829-7799
Oprah Winfrey	Harpo Films	(310) 278-5559
Cami Winikoff	Lions Gate Ent.	(323) 692-7300
Henry Winkler	Fair Dinkum Prod.	(310) 586-8471
Irwin Winkler	Winkler Films	(310) 858-5780
Dorian Winship	Lifetime Television	(212) 424-7000
Ralph Winter	Ralph Winter Prod.	(213) 534-3654
Peter Winther	Centropolis Ent.	(310) 244-4300
John Wiseman	Paramount Pictures	(323) 956-5000
Pamela Wisne	David E. Kelley Prod.	(310) 727-2200
Michael Wisner	True Blue Prod.	(323) 661-9191
Paul Junger Witt	Witt/Thomas/Harris Prod.	(323) 993-7000
Renee W. Witt	New Line Cinema	(310) 854-5811
Corey Witte	Davis Classics	(310) 551-2266
Brian Witten	Paramount Pictures	(323) 956-5000
Jess Wittenberg	Castle Rock Ent.	(310) 285-2300
Joe Wizan	Phase 1 Prod.	(310) 842-8401
Steve Wizan	Phase 1 Prod.	(310) 842-8401
Linda Wohl	Paramount Pictures	(323) 956-5000
Stacy Wolberg	Chelsea Pictures	(323) 860-8030
Mike Wolf	Film Roman	(818) 761-2544
Jordan Wolfe	Shady Acres Ent.	(818) 777-4446
Steven J. Wolfe	RoadKill Films	(323) 962-0295
Steven J. Wolfe	Sneak Preview Ent.	(323) 962-0295
Marc Wolfson	Red Hots Ent.	(818) 954-0092
Robert Wollin	Raintree Prod.	(310) 827-3336
Megan Wolpert	Spyglass Ent.	(818) 560-3458

Executives/Personnel Alphabetical Key

John J. Wolters	ABC Inc./ABC Television	(310) 557-7777
Andrea Wong	ABC Entertainment	(310) 557-7777
Chi-Li Wong	AEI	(323) 932-0407
Ronald J. Wong	Green Grass Blue Sky Company	(818) 760-8243
John Woo	Lion Rock Prod.	(310) 449-3205
Amy Wood	Longfellow Pictures	(212) 431-5550
Doris Wood	The Manhattan Project	(212) 258-2541
Douglas Wood	Universal Pictures	(818) 777-1000
Lara Wood	Kopelson Ent.	(310) 369-7555
Terry Wood	Paramount Domestic Television	(323) 956-5000
Mel Woods	Fox Family Channel	(310) 235-9700
Nancy Workman	Fuel	(310) 314-1644
Brook Worley	Shady Acres Ent.	(818) 777-4446
Steve Woroniecki	Ovation Ent.	(310) 344-1442
Craig Worsham	Sun Spots	(323) 960-4000
Joan Worth	Marvin Worth Prod.	(310) 273-0181
Robert Wozniak	The Jim Henson Company	(323) 802-1500
Gerry Wright	Burrud Prod.	(714) 842-8422
Michael Wright	CBS Ent.	(323) 575-2345
Michelle Wright	Working Title Films	(310) 777-3100
Norton Wright	Norton Wright Prod.	(818) 990-3058
Pandit Wright	Discovery Networks	(301) 986-1999
Richard Wright	Lakeshore Ent. Corp.	(323) 956-4222
James Wvinner	Level 7 Prod.	(818) 754-0074
Trina Wyatt	Tribeca Prod.	(212) 941-4000
Mark Wyman	Columbia Pictures	(310) 244-4000
Michael Yada	Yada/Levine Prod.	(323) 461-1616
Jennifer Yale	Brooksfilms	(310) 202-3292
Allen Yamashita	SimEx Digital Studios	(310) 664-9500
Janet Yang	Manifest Film Company	(310) 899-5554
Paul Yanover	Walt Disney Pictures	(818) 560-1000
Robert Yap	Silverline Pictures	(818) 752-3730
Jonathan Yarbrough	Tuesday Films	(310) 899-0335
Ron Yassen	Broadway Video	(212) 265-7621
Eric Yealland	Piper Prod.	(310) 883-8822
Eugene Yelchin	Dektor Film	(323) 466-3455
Mark Yellen	Mark Yellen Prod.	(323) 935-5525
Alex Yemenidijian	Metro-Goldwyn-Mayer Studios	(310) 449-3000
Sergei Yershov	Lions Gate Ent.	(323) 692-7300
Ron Yerxa	Bona Fide Prod.	(310) 273-6782
Bud Yorkin	Bud Yorkin Prod.	(310) 274-8111
Wendy Yorkshire	Alameda	(818) 846-4074
Alex Young	Paramount Pictures	(323) 956-5000
Marvin Young MC Young	Red Hots Ent.	(818) 954-0092
Sean Young	Shonkyte Prod.	(818) 505-1332
Stephanie Young	Roger Gimbel Prod.	(310) 459-3838
Steve Young	Cinemagic Prod.	(510) 233-2002
William L. Young	Warner Bros. Pictures Prod.	(818) 954-6000
Nancy Youngblood	MM2K	(310) 276-0750
Laurie Younger	ABC Inc./ABC Television	(310) 557-7777
Jeanne Yu	IndieGal Prod.	(818) 890-6111
Michael Yudin	Telescene Film Grp.	(514) 737-5512
Martin J. Yudkovitz	NBC Ent.	(212) 664-4444
Yuki	DNA	(323) 463-2826
Christopher Yurkow	Spoke Film	(310) 477-2272
John Zabel	Mandalay Pictures	(323) 956-2400
Natan Zahavi	Tapestry Films	(310) 275-1191
Rita Zak	Columbia Pictures	(310) 244-4000
Mark Zakarin	Showtime Networks	(310) 234-5200
George Zaloom	Zaloom Film	(310) 656-8400
Stacy Zand	FilmColony	(323) 951-4650
David Zander	Morton Jankel Zander	(310) 826-6200
Noel Zanitsch	WIN Ventures.	(310) 859-2500
Dean Zanuck	The Zanuck Company	(310) 274-0261
Harrison Zanuck	The Zanuck Company	(310) 274-0261
Lili Fini Zanuck	DNA	(323) 463-2826
Lili Fini Zanuck	The Zanuck Company	(310) 274-0261
Richard D. Zanuck	The Zanuck Company	(310) 274-0261
Leah Zappy	Brooksfilms	(310) 202-3292
Teddy Zee	Davis Ent. Co.	(310) 556-3550
Heather Zeegen	Original Film	(310) 445-9000
Ed Zeier	Universal Studios	(818) 777-1000
David Zelon	Mandalay Pictures	(323) 956-2400
Shira Zeltzer	Ginty Films	(310) 274-9691
Robert Zemeckis	Image Movers	(818) 733-8313
James L. Zemelman	Lions Gate Ent.	(323) 692-7300
Bo Zenga	Boz Prod.	(310) 876-3232
Warren Zide	Zide/Perry Ent.	(310) 887-2999
Jonathan A. Zimbert	Morgan Creek Prod.	(818) 954-4800
Hans Zimmer	Patchwork Prod.	(310) 288-7488
Deborah Zimmerly	IndieGal Prod.	(818) 890-6111
Ray Zimmerman	Columbia Pictures	(310) 244-4000
Benjamin Zinkin	New Line Cinema	(310) 854-5811
Richard Zinman	Fried Films	(310) 754-2676
Barbara Zipperman	DreamWorks SKG	(818) 733-7000
Daniel Zirilli	Pop/Art Film Factory	(310) 260-2868
Steven Zito	Belisarius Prod.	(323) 956-8660
Suzanne Zizzi	Lion Rock Prod.	(310) 449-3205
Julian Chang Zolkin	Amen Ra Films	(310) 246-6510
Mark Zoradi	Buena Vista Motion Pictures	(818) 560-1000
Karim Zreik	Junction Ent.	(818) 560-2800
David Zucker	Zucker/Netter Prod.	(310) 394-1644
Janet Zucker	Zucker Prod.	(310) 656-9202
Jerry Zucker	Zucker Prod.	(310) 656-9202
Donald Zuckerman	Zuckerman Ent.	(310) 452-4410
Ed Zuckerman	Belisarius Prod.	(323) 956-8660
Lori Zuker	Overbrook Ent.	(818) 777-2224
Louis Zwick	American Sports Network	(626) 292-2222

Notes

Freelance Producer & Production Company Alpha Index

1171 Production Group 211, 260
21st Century Man Productions 137, 211, 245, 260, 273
2EZ, LLC 211
3 Arts Entertainment 53, 137
30 Second Films 53, 137, 211, 245
40 Acres & A Mule Filmworks, Inc. 53, 211, 245, 260
5th Gear Entertainment 53, 260
A&E Television Networks. 53, 137, 245
A Band Apart 53, 137, 211, 260
A Band Apart Commercials 211, 260
A Few Miles North 260
A Story Untold Productions. 245
Ab'-strakt Pictures 53, 138
Abby Lou Entertainment 53, 138, 211, 245
ABC Entertainment Television Group 138
ABC, Inc./ABC Television Network 138
AbsoluteFilms.net. 211, 245, 260, 273
Acappella Pictures 54, 138
Access Film. 211
Acme Filmworks, Inc.. 213
Act III Productions 54, 138
Adelson Entertainment 54, 139
Orly Adelson Productions 54, 139
The Ad-Files 138, 213
Ad-Lib Marketing & Advertising. 213, 245, 260
Adobe Pictures 54
AEI 54, 139
Aerial Focus Productions. 54, 139, 245
Afra-Film Enterprises, Inc. 54, 139
Alameda Filmworks, Inc.. . . . . 55, 213, 246
Paul Albanese 287, 292, 302
Albrecht & Associates, Inc. 55, 139, 213, 246, 260
Alchemy Entertainment. 55, 139
All Girl Productions 55, 139
Allen & Associates 55, 139, 213
Alliance Atlantis 55, 139
Alphaville. 55
Alta Vista Productions. 140, 213, 261
AM Productions & Management 55, 140
Amalgamated, Inc. 55, 140
Kelly Amato 292
Ambitious Entertainment 140, 213, 246
Amblin Entertainment. 55
Emie H. Amemiya 287, 290, 292
Amen Ra Films 56, 140
American Entertainment Co.. . . . . 56, 140
American Movie Classics/Romance Classics 140
American Sports Network, Inc. 140, 246, 261
American Video Group. 140, 213, 246
American World Pictures 56, 141
American Zoetrope 56, 141
Craig Anderson Productions 56, 141
Angel Ark Productions 56, 141
Angel City Productions. 213
Another Diversion 56, 213
Another Large Production 214, 246
AntEye.com 273
Beth Anthony 287, 292
Apatow Productions. 56, 141
Apostle Pictures. 56, 141
Mark Archer Entertainment 57, 141
Area 51 Films. 214
The Arnet/Kerner Co. 57, 141
Arsenal, Inc. 214, 261
Artisan Entertainment. 57, 142
The Artists' Colony. 57, 142
The Artists Company/The A&R Group 214, 261
Artists Television Group 142
Joel Asher Studio 246
Ashley Productions. 57, 214, 261
Asset Pictures 58, 142
The Association, Inc.. . . . . 142, 214, 246
Atkinson Way Films 58, 142
Atlantic Streamline 58
Atlas Entertainment 58
Atlas Pictures 214
Atom Films 273
Automatic Pictures, Inc. 58
Avalanche! Entertainment 58, 214
AVD Productions, Inc./AV Designs 58, 214, 246
Avenue Pictures. 58, 142
Axelrod Entertainment 59, 143
Axelson-Weintraub Productions. 59, 143
Back Home Pictures 59, 214
Backyard Productions 59, 215, 261
The Badham Company. 59, 143
The Baer Animation Company, Inc. 59, 215, 261
Baer Entertainment Group 59
BallPark Productions. 59, 143
Ballyhoo, Inc. 59, 143
Baltimore/Spring Creek Pictures, LLC 59
Bandeira Entertainment 60, 143
Bandolero Films 215
Banner Entertainment. 60
Barking Weasel Productions, Inc.. 215
Louise Barlow 287, 290, 292, 302
Barnholtz Entertainment 60
Barnstorm Films 60, 143
LuAnn Barry-Goldman 292
Barwood Films 60, 143
Tony Basile 287, 292
Bassett Productions. 60, 215
Suzanne Bauman Productions 60, 143, 261
Barbara L. Baumann, Inc. 60, 143, 215
Baumgarten/Prophet Entertainment 60, 144
Bay Films 60, 144
BCProductions, Inc./BCTV Productions 144, 215, 246
Beacon Communications, LLC 61
June Beallor Productions. 61, 144
Beantown Productions, Inc.. 215
Beard Boy Productions 215, 247
Stephanie Bedell 290, 292, 302

363

Freelance Producer & Production Company Alpha Index

The Bedford Falls Company	61, 144
Bel-Air Entertainment	61
Belisarius Productions	61, 144
Bella Productions	62, 144, 216, 261
Belladonna Productions	62
Bell-Phillip Television Productions, Inc.	144
Bender-Spink	62, 144, 273
Robert Benedetti Productions, Inc.	145
Benjamin Productions, Inc.	62, 145
Rick Berman Productions	62, 145
Yvonne M. Bernard	287, 290, 292, 300, 302
Jay Bernstein Productions	62, 145
Bettina Productions, Ltd.	62, 145
Big Daddy Productions	145
Big Ticket Television	145
Kathryn Bishop	287, 292
Bjoin Films	216
Black & Blu Entertainment	62, 145
Black Dog Films (RSA USA)	262
Black Entertainment Television (BET)	62, 145
Black Sheep Entertainment	62, 146
Stuart Black	292, 305
Brian Bleak Films	216
Bleecker Street Films	63, 146
Pat Blessing Productions	247
Blue Bay Productions	63
Blue Goose Productions	216, 262
Blue Relief	63, 146
Blue Tulip Productions	63, 146
Blue Wolf Productions	63
Christal Blue Productions	63, 216, 247
Blumberg Productions & Management	63, 146
Bob Booker Productions	146
Bob Industries	216, 262
Steven Bochco Productions	146
Carol Bodie Entertainment	63, 146
Hope Grossman Bolois	292
Bona Fide Productions	63
Bonfire Films of America	63, 146, 216, 262
Boxing Cat Productions	64
Boyington Studios, Inc.	64, 216, 262
Boz Productions	64, 146
Braga Productions	64, 147
Brayton/Carlucci Productions	64, 147
Paulette Breen Productions	64, 147
The Bregman Entertainment Company	64, 147, 262
Bright-Kauffman-Crane Productions	147
Brillstein-Grey Entertainment	64, 147
Broadway Video	147
Terri Lee Brook	292
John Brooks	287, 290, 292, 300
Brooksfilms, Ltd.	64
Brookwell McNamara Entertainment	65, 147
Brownstone Films	216
Jerry Bruckheimer Films	65, 148
The Bubble Factory	65
The Buena Vista Motion Pictures Group	65, 148
Buena Vista Television	148
Shirley Bukrey-Lloyd	292
Bungalow 3	216
Bungalow 78 Productions	65, 148
Bunim-Murray Productions	148
Bunnygrenade	273
Burke/Triolo Productions	217
Burrud Productions	148, 247
Al Burton Productions	148
Bushwood Pictures	65, 148
Marol Butcher	292
Butchers Run Films	65
c.2K Entertainment	217
C'est Tout Productions	65, 217
Cairo/Simpson Entertainment, Inc.	66, 148, 273
Calar	66, 148, 217, 247
Calico World Entertainment	66, 149, 217, 273
Calm Down Productions, Inc.	66, 149
Camera Marc	66
Canned Interactive	274
Cannell Studios	66, 149
The Canton Company	66, 149
Canvas House Films	66, 149, 217, 262
Canyon Pictures, Inc.	217
Capella Films, Inc.	66
Capital Arts Entertainment	66, 149
Capo Productions, Inc.	67, 149
Cappa Productions	67
Carbo Films	217
Mark Carliner Productions	67, 149
Katie Carlson Kasting	217
Carlyle Productions & Management	67, 149
Carrie Productions	67, 149
The Carsey-Werner, LLC	150
Castle Rock Entertainment	67, 150
Mark Castro	287, 292, 300, 302
Cates/Doty Productions	150
CBIE, Inc.	247
CBS Enterprises	150
CBS Entertainment	150
CBS Television	151
Celluloid	151, 218, 273
Centropolis Entertainment	67
Chancellor Entertainment	67, 151
Chapter 10 Productions	67
Charles Bros. Productions	151
Chartoff Productions	67
Stanley Chase Productions, Inc.	68, 151
The Chelmar Group	68, 218, 247, 262
Chelsea Pictures	218
Cherry Alley Productions	68, 151
Chesler/Perlmutter Productions	68, 151
Chiari Cook Company, Inc.	218
Chicago Story	218
Chicagofilms	68, 152
Chiodo Bros. Productions, Inc.	68, 152, 218
Chris/Rose Productions	152
Kim Christensen	292, 302, 305
Cine Excel Entertainment	68
Cinemagic Productions	152
Cinemanix	218

Name	Pages
CinemaNow	274
CinemaPop	274
Cinergi Pictures	68
Cineville, Inc.	68, 274
Circle Associates Ltd.	69, 152
Dick Clark Productions, Inc.	152
Clifden Productions	152
Coast Media Teleproductions, Inc.	152, 218, 247, 262, 274
Cohen Pictures	69
Cohn & Company	218
Collaborative Artists	69, 152
Colomby/Keaton Productions	69, 153
Columbia Pictures/Columbia Tristar Motion Picture Group	69
Columbia TriStar Television	153
Comedy Central	153
Commercials While-U-Wait, Inc.	219
Connection III Entertainment Corp.	69, 153, 274
Constantin Film	69
Conundrum Entertainment	70
Jessica Cooper	287, 290, 292, 302
Coppos Films	219
Cornice Entertainment	70, 153
John Corser	287, 290, 293, 300
The Cort/Madden Company	70, 153
Cosgrove-Meurer Productions	70, 153
Cossette Productions	153
Cindy Cowan Entertainment, Inc.	70, 154
Michael Cowan, Inc.	219
CPC Entertainment	70, 154
CPProds	219, 263
Scott Craig	293
Crane Wexelblatt Entertainment	70, 154
CRAPtv	274
Wes Craven Films	70, 154
Creative Chaos	219
The Creative Department, LLC	219, 247, 263
Creative Impulse Entertainment	70, 154
Cronenweth Films	219
Crossroads Films	219
Crusader Entertainment	71, 154
Crystal Pyramid Productions	154, 247
Ctonic Flikz	71, 274
Bill Curran	287, 290, 293
Madelyn Curtis	287, 293, 300
Cylo	219, 263, 274
D.Film	274
D.L.T. Entertainment Ltd.	154
Dalrymple Productions	154, 219, 248
Danamation Studios	71
Danjaq, Inc.	71
dapTV associates	154, 219, 248, 263
Dark Horse Entertainment	71, 155
Davis Classics	71, 155
Davis Entertainment Co.	71, 155
Beverly Davis	293
Daybreak Productions	71, 155
Rick Days	293
Dayton/Faris, Inc.	263
Dino De Laurentiis Company	71
Heather Dear	287, 290, 293
Deja View Productions, Inc.	71, 155
Dektor Film	220
Diana Demopoulos	293, 302
Denali Productions, Inc.	72, 155, 220, 248
Desert Heart Productions	72, 155
Destination Films	72
Di Novi Pictures	72, 155
DIC Entertainment	72, 155
Steve Dietrich	293
Louis DiGiaimo & Associates	72, 156
Digital Planet	274
Digital Visionaries	248, 275
Digivision Productions	248
Kat Dillon	293
Dimension Films	72
Discovery Networks/Discovery Communications, Inc.	156
The Disney Channel	156
Disney Telefilms	156
The Walt Disney Company	72
Walt Disney Pictures/Touchstone Pictures	72
Walt Disney Television Animation	156
Distant Horizon	73, 156
DNA, Inc.	220, 263
Dockry Productions	73
Carr Donald	293
The Donners' Company	73, 156
Doom, Inc.	220, 248, 263, 275
Bruce Dorn Films	73, 220
Janice Doskey	287, 293, 300
dotcomix	275
Double Whammy Productions	156
Jean Doumanian Productions	73, 157
Helen Dow	293
Bruce Dowad Associates	220
DreamWorks SKG	73, 157
Dreyfuss/James Productions	74, 157
Drive Media	220
Valerie Druckman	293
Duck Soup Studios	74, 220, 263, 275
E! Entertainment Television	157
E.M.E., Inc.	74, 157, 220, 263, 275
Echo Lake Productions	74
Edmonds Entertainment	74, 157
Ralph Edwards/Stu Billett Productions	74, 157
Rona Edwards Productions	74, 157
Egg Pictures	74
El Norte Productions	74, 158
Elephant Walk Entertainment	74, 158
Eleventh Day Entertainment	158, 220, 248
EMK Productions	75, 158
Enchantment Films	75
Peter Engel Productions	158
Ensemble Entertainment	75, 158
Enteraktion, Inc.	75, 158, 275
Entertainment Television Services, Inc.	158
Epiphany Productions, Inc.	75, 158, 248
Erratic Entertainment, Inc.	75, 159
Esparza-Katz Productions	75, 159

Freelance Producer & Production Company Alpha Index

The Robert Evans Company	75
Leslie M. Evers	293, 302
Everyman Pictures	75
Evil Twin Productions	221
Evolution Film	159
Face Broadcast Productions	159, 248
Face Productions	75
Fair Dinkum Productions	76, 159
Fast Carrier Pictures	76, 159
Fat Chance Films	76, 159, 249, 264
Fate Junkie Films, Inc.	76, 221, 264
Franny Faull-La Violette	293
Tom Fauntleroy	288, 293
FDG	221
FDG Internet	275
The Edward S. Feldman Co.	76, 159
Fenady Associates, Inc.	76, 159
Janet Ferrari	288, 293, 303
FGM Entertainment	76
Adam Fields Productions	76, 159
Film Planet	221
Film Roman, Inc.	76, 159
The Film Syndicate	160, 221, 264
FilmColony, Ltd.	76
FilmWorld, Inc.	77
Fine Line Features	77
Wendy Finerman Productions	77
Barry Fink	288, 294, 303
Fireworks Pictures	77
Fireworks Television	160
First Avenue Films	77, 160, 221
Debbie A. Fisher	294
Flip Your Lid, Inc.	77, 160, 275
Flower Films, Inc.	77, 160
Flying Freehold Productions	77
Flying Tiger Films	221
FM Rocks	221, 264
Forest Hills Pictures	78, 160, 249
Fiona Forsyth	294
Fortis Films	78
Forward Pass, Inc.	78, 160
David Foster Productions	78, 160
Foundation Entertainment	78, 160
Fountainbridge Films	78
Fountainhead Pictures	78, 161
Four Sisters Production	222
Four Square Productions, Inc.	78, 161, 222, 249
Fox Broadcasting Company	161
Fox Family Channel	161, 292
Fox Kids Network	161
Fox Searchlight Pictures	78
Fox Television Studios	161
J.P. Fox	294, 303
FR Productions	79
Franchise Pictures, Inc.	79
Tammy A. Franklin	294
Woody Fraser Productions	162, 275
Ruth Frazier	294, 303
Joel Freeman Productions, Inc.	79
Franny Freiberger	294, 303
Fresh Produce Company	79
Fried Films	79, 162
Daniel Fried Productions	79
Nona Sue Friedman	294
Friendly Productions	79
Bruce Fritzberg	288, 290, 294, 300, 305
Mark Frost Productions	79, 162
Fuel	222, 264
Nancy Fulton-Rogers	294
Furman Films, Inc.	162, 249
Further Films	79
Fusion Films	222
FX Networks, LLC	162
Galanty & Company, Inc.	222, 249, 264
Gallo & Gallo, Inc.	162
Debbie Galloway	294
Gartner	222
Kent Gates	294
Gears Communications	162, 249, 264, 275
Genrebend Productions, Inc.	79, 162
Geronimo Film Productions, Inc.	249, 264
Roger Gimbel Productions, Inc.	80, 162
John G. Ginnes	288, 290, 294
Ginty Films	80, 163, 222, 264, 276
Gittes, Inc.	80
Glass Guns	222, 265, 276
Leora Glass	294
GMR Productions	80, 163
Go Film	80, 222, 265
Goepp Circle Productions	80, 163
Jeff Gold Productions, Inc.	80, 163, 223, 249, 265
Golden Eagle Pix	80, 163, 223
Goldenring Productions	81, 163
Bonnie Goldfarb	288, 294
Gold'N Hen Productions	80, 163, 223
The Goldstein Company	81
Samuel Goldwyn Films	81
Good Machine	81
Goodman/Rosen Productions	163
Lawrence Gordon Productions	81
Janice K. Goto	294
Gracie Films	81, 163, 276
Grade A Entertainment	81, 164, 276
Graham/Rosenzweig Films	81
Grammnet Productions (Film)	81
Grammnet Productions (TV)	164
Granada Entertainment USA	164
Graying & Balding, Inc.	223, 265
Grazka Taylor Productions	81, 164
Green Communications	81, 164, 223
Green Dot Films, Inc.	223
Green Grass Blue Sky Company, Inc.	82
Green Moon Productions	82, 164
Katy Greene	233, 294
GreenWater Pictures	223, 249, 265, 276
The Greif Company/A Day With, Inc.	82, 164
The Alan Greisman Company	82
Greystone Communication Group, Inc./Greystone Films	164, 249

Freelance Producer & Production Company Alpha Index

Merv Griffin Entertainment	82, 164
Gross Productions	82, 165, 223
Ken Gross Management	82, 164
Beth Grossbard Productions	82, 165
Grub Street Productions	165
Gullane Pictures	82, 165
H-Gun Labs	83, 165, 223, 265, 276
Carol Haak	294
Hallmark Entertainment	165, 250
Hallmark Hall of Fame Productions, Inc.	165
Hallowes Productions	223
Hallway Pictures	83
Naia Hall-West	295
Halsted Pictures	83, 165
Hammer Films	83
Handprint Entertainment	83, 165
Harbor Lights Productions	83, 166
Dean Hargrove Productions	166
Harpo Films	83, 166
David Haugland Productions	83, 166, 250, 265
Robert Haukoos	288, 290, 295
Havoc Inc.	83
Hawk Entertainment	83, 166, 276
HBO	166
HBO Films	166
HBO Independent Productions/HBO Downtown Productions	166
HBO Original Programming	166
Headquarters	84, 223
Hearst Entertainment Productions	167
Heller Highwater	84, 167
Hennessey Entertainment, Ltd.	84, 167, 276
The Jim Henson Company	84, 167, 224, 250, 265, 277
Paul Hettler	295, 300, 303, 305
Cynthia Hill	295
Debra Hill Productions	84, 167
The History Channel	167
HKM Productions	224
Hodge Film & Video	167, 224, 250, 266
Hofflund-Polone	84, 168
Hogan Moorhouse Pictures	84
Hokus Pokus Productions, Inc.	224
Hollane Corp./Martin Poll Films, Ltd.	85, 168
Lisa Hollingshead	288, 295, 303
Horizon Shine, Inc.	224, 250, 266
Horseshoe Bay Productions	85, 168
Hot Spots Television	224
Craig Houchin	295
Chantal Houle	295
The House Production Company	85, 224, 250
HSI Productions, Inc.	225
Hunt-Tavel Productions	85
Hy-Tone Productions	85, 168, 250, 277
Icebox	277
Icon Productions Inc.	85, 168
Ideal Entertainment, Inc.	85
Image G	85, 168, 225
Image Movers	85
Imaginary Forces	86, 225
Imagine Entertainment	86, 168
IMAX Corporation	86
Impact PSA, Inc.	86, 225, 251
In Play Media Arts	86, 225, 251
Incognito Entertainment	86
IndieGal Productions, LLC	86, 168
Industrial Light + Magic Commercial Productions	225, 266, 277
In-Finn-Ity Productions, Inc.	168, 225, 266
Infomercial Solutions, Inc.	225, 251
InFront Productions	87, 169
Initial Entertainment Group	87
Instinct Pictures	87, 225, 266
Intelliscape Films, LLC	169, 226, 251
Intermedia Films	87
International Television Group (ITG)	87, 169, 226, 251
IPS Productions	226, 251
Irish DreamTime	87
Itasca Pictures, Inc.	87, 169
ITB CineGroup/Television	87, 169
Michael Jacobs Productions	169
The Jacobson Company	87
Jaffilms	87
Jaret Entertainment	88, 169, 277
Jeff Wald Entertainment	88, 205
Jersey Films	88, 169
Jersey Shore Films	88
JGF	226
The Jinks/Cohen Company	88
JKR Productions, Inc.	88, 169, 226, 251
JLT Productions	88
Don Johnson Productions	88, 170
Mark Johnson Productions	88, 170
Bronston Jones	288, 295, 303
The Joneses	226
Quincy Jones Media Group, Inc.	88, 170
Carolyn Judd & Associates, Inc.	226
Jumbo Pictures, Inc.	89, 170
Junction Entertainment	89
Just Singer Entertainment	170
kaboom	226
Leslie A. Kahan	288, 290, 295
Kahn Power Pictures	89, 170
Kandoo Films, Inc.	89, 226
Katie Face Productions	170
Jan Katz	295
Marty Katz Productions	89
Perry Katz Productions	89
The Kaufman Company	89, 170
Doron Kauper	295
Kavich Reynolds Productions, Inc.	236, 251
Dessa Kaye	288, 291, 295
Kedzie Productions	170
David E. Kelley Productions	89, 170
Kelley Productions International	171, 226, 251
The Kennedy/Marshall Company	89, 171
Diana Kerew Productions	171
Killer Films	90, 277
Kandice King Productions, Inc.	90
Kingsgate Films	90, 171
Kingsize Entertainment	90

Freelance Producer & Production Company Alpha Index

Kinowelt USA, Inc.	90
David Kirschner Productions	90, 171
Klasky Csupo, Inc.	90, 171, 226
The Koch Company	90
Konrad Pictures	90
Kontrast Films	91, 171, 227
Kopelson Entertainment	91, 171
Kouf-Bigelow Productions	91, 172
Krainin Productions, Inc.	91, 172
The Jonathan Krane Group	91
Sid & Marty Krofft Pictures	91, 172
Kurtz & Friends	91, 172, 227
Kushner-Locke Company	91, 172
Kuzui Enterprises, Inc.	91, 172
LA Productions	92, 172, 227, 266
The Ladd Company	92, 172
Lakeshore Entertainment Corporation	92
Lakota Productions	92
Patti Lancaster	295
Langley Productions	92, 172, 278
Lawton Entertainment	92, 173
Le Monde Entertainment	92, 173
Leading Pictures, Inc.	92
Stan Lee Media, Inc.	92, 278
Legacy Films	227, 266
Jenny Leimbrook	288, 291, 295, 301
Malcolm Leo Productions	93, 173
Mary Leonard	288, 291, 295, 305
Let There Be Light Productions	93, 173, 227, 251, 266
Level 7 Productions	227
The Levinson/Fontana Company	173
Michael I. Levy Enterprises	93, 173
Simon Lewis Productions, Inc.	93, 173
Licht/Mueller Films	93, 173
The Lieberman Company	227
Life of Riley, Inc.	227
Lifetime Television (East Coast)	173
Lifetime Television (West Coast)	173
Lighthouse Productions	93
Lightmotive, Inc.	93, 174
Lightning Bolt PIX: Barnyard Productions	174, 227, 252, 266
Lightstorm Entertainment	93
Lineup Technologies, Inc.	278
Lion Rock Productions	93, 174
Lions Gate Entertainment	94, 174
Little T Television	227
Si Litvinoff Productions	94, 174
Warren Lockhart Productions, Inc.	94, 174
Logo Entertainment	94, 174
Long Coat Productions	228
Longboard Productions, Inc.	94, 228
Longfellow Pictures	94
Lotus Films	94, 228
Love Spell Entertainment	94
Sonny Lowe	295
LucasFilm Ltd.	95, 175
Martha Lucas	296
Lucid Film	95, 175, 278
Lucid Media	95, 175, 228, 252
Lumiere Films, Inc.	95
Lumination Inc.	175, 228
Luminosity Productions	95, 228
Lux Pictures, Inc.	95, 228
Lyon Studios	228, 252
M.H.S. Productions	95, 175
M-80 Films	228
Don MacBain	288
William J. MacDonald Productions	95, 175
MacGillivray Freeman Films	95
Mad Chance	95
Mad Heart	228
Jeffrey Maier	296
Make It Happen Productions, Inc.	96, 175, 229, 252, 267
Charles Malcolm Video Productions	96, 229, 252
Malpaso Productions	96
Mandalay Pictures	96
Mandalay Television	175
Mandolin Entertainment	96, 175
The Manhattan Project	96, 175
Manifest Film Company	96
Marca-Relli Productions, LLC	96
March Hare Entertainment at Jaffe-Braunstein	175
Jeff Margolis Productions	176
John Marias Productions	229
Mariposa	96, 229, 275, 278
Laurence Mark Productions	96, 176
Mars Media, Inc.	229, 267
Sandy Martin	288, 296, 301, 305
Marvel Characters, Inc.	97, 176
Niki Marvin Productions	97, 176, 252
John Masius Productions, Inc.	176, 321
Matador Pictures	97, 176
Matovich Productions	97
Matrix Communications	97, 229, 252, 267, 278
The Matthau Company, Inc.	97, 176
Maverick Films	97
Ross McCanse & Associates, Inc.	229
Lisa McClelland	296
Colleen McCrary	289, 291, 296, 301, 304, 305
MDP Worldwide	97
Mediatrip	278
Megahertz Pictures	97, 229, 252
Mekanism	229, 278
Carey Melcher Productions, Inc.	229
Barry Mendel Productions	98
Merchant-Ivory Productions	98
Mesita	176, 229
Metafilmics	98, 176, 279
Metro Pictures	230
Metro-Goldwyn-Mayer Studios, Inc.	98
Metro-Goldwyn-Mayer/Worldwide TV	176
Michael/Finney Productions, Inc.	98
The Miller Entertainment Group, Inc.	98, 230, 267
Miller/Boyett Productions	98, 177
Roger Mills	296
Mindfire Entertainment	98, 177, 279
MindStorm Productions, LLC	98, 177
Minervision	99, 177

Freelance Producer & Production Company Alpha Index

Mirage Enterprises 99
Miramax Films 99
Mirella Film Co. 230
Miss Jones 99, 230
MM2K 99, 177, 230, 252, 267
Mo Jo Productions, Inc. 99, 177, 230, 267
Monarex Hollywood Corporation 99, 177, 252
Alison Monico 296
Montage Entertainment 99
The Montecito Picture Company 100
Morgan Creek Productions 100, 177
Sharon Morov 296
Morra, Brezner, Steinberg & Tenenbaum 100, 177
Morton Jankel Zander, Inc. 230
Mostow/Lieberman 100
Moushel Productions 100
Moving Image 230
Moving Pictures 100, 178
Moving Target 100, 178, 231
Moxie Pictures 231, 267
Mozark Productions 100, 178
MPH Films 231
Mr. Mudd Productions 100, 178
MT. Tabor Productions 100
MTV Films 101
MTV Networks (East Coast) 178
MTV Networks (West Coast) 178
Tommy Murov 296
Muse Productions 101, 178
Music Room Pictures 101, 231, 252, 267
Mutant Enemy, Inc. 101, 178
Mutual Film Company 101, 179
MWG Productions 101, 179
National Geographic Feature Films 101, 179
National Lampoon 101, 179, 279
Jack Nayer 296
NBC Entertainment (West Coast) 179
NBC Entertainment, Inc. 179
Neild Street Prod., Inc. 101, 179
Nelvana Entertainment 102, 179
Nemiroff Productions 102, 180, 231, 253, 267, 279
Neo Art & Logic 102
Mace Neufeld Productions 102, 180
Neverland Films, Inc. 102
New & Unique Videos 253
New Concorde 102, 180
New Crime Productions 102
New Line Cinema, Inc. 102
New Millennium Studios 103, 180, 231, 267, 279
New Regency Productions 103, 180
New Screen Concepts, Inc. 180
Merilee Newman 296
Newmark Films, Inc. 103
Nickelodeon Movies 103
Nickelodeon/Nick at Nite 180
Nitestar Productions 103, 231, 253
No Prisoners 104, 231, 268
Noble Productions, Inc. 104, 181
Nonfiction Spots 231
Norah Films 104, 181
North Hall Productions 104, 181
Nova Pictures 104, 181, 231
Nuance Productions 104, 181
NXT Entertainment 104, 181, 232, 253, 279
Nydrle 232
O Entertainment 104
Oak Island Films, Inc. 104
Lynda Obst Productions 105, 181
Ocean Pictures 105
October Productions 181, 232, 253
Lin Oliver Productions 105, 181
Olmos Productions, Inc. 105
Darcy Oltman 296, 301, 304, 305
Omaha Pictures 232
OMNIBUS 105, 182
One Step Productions 105, 182, 253
OneSuch Films 232
Onyx Productions, Inc. 232, 253
Open Road Productions, Ltd. 105
Orange Soda 268
Orbit Entertainment Group 105, 232, 279
Original Film, Inc. 105, 182
Original Voices, Inc. 106
Our Gang Productions 182, 232, 268, 280
Our Productions, Inc. 106, 182, 232, 253, 268
Outerbanks Entertainment 106, 182
Outlaw Productions 106
Ovation Entertainment 233, 253, 268
Overbrook Entertainment 106, 182, 268
P.A.T. Productions 106, 182, 253
Pacific Star Productions 233
Edward Pacio & Associates 233, 254
George Paige Associates, Inc. 106, 183, 233, 254, 268, 280
Paul Papanek 296
Paradox Productions, Inc. 106, 183
Paramount Classics 106
Paramount Domestic Television 183
Paramount International Television 183
Paramount Network Television 183
Paramount Pictures - Motion Picture Group 107
Paramount Television Group 183
Parkway Productions 107
Patchett Kaufman Entertainment 107, 184
Patchwork Productions 107, 184
Pavlic/Raimondi Pictures 107
PaxTV/Paxson Communications 184
PBS 184
Peak Productions 107, 184
Pearson Television 184, 233
Beth Pearson 296
Pendragon Film Ltd. 107, 184
Sandra Penfield 296
James Pentecost Productions 108, 185
Permut Presentations 108, 185
Perseverance Productions 233, 254, 268
Persistent Entertainment, Inc. 108, 185
Lester Persky Productions, Inc. 108, 185
David Persoff 296

Freelance Producer & Production Company Alpha Index

Perspective Films	108, 185, 233, 254, 268, 280
Peters Entertainment	108
Susie Peterson	289, 296
Dorothea G. Petrie Productions, Inc.	185
Pfeffer Film	108
Phase I Productions	108, 185
Philmco	108, 233
Phoenix Pictures	108
Piazzie	297, 304
Pico Creek Productions	109, 185
Picture Mill	109, 254
Picture Park	233
Pie Town Productions	185
The Frederick S. Pierce Company, Inc.	109, 186
Piper Productions	233
Pirates' Cove Entertainment, Inc.	186
Pixar Animation Studios	109
Planet, Inc.	269
PlasterCITY Productions	109, 186
Pleasant Productions	109
Plum Productions	234
PMC Pictures	234
Point of View Productions	186, 234, 254
Polestar Entertainment Group, LLC	109, 186
Polestar Film & Photographic Production	234, 254
Sadie Pollock-Barish	297
Pongo Productions	109, 234
Pop/Art Film Factory	109, 234, 269
Popular Arts Entertainment, Inc.	110, 186
Porter Film Company	234
Post Modern Edit	234, 254
Rick Powers	297
Patricia Priest	289, 291, 301
Producers Group, Ltd.	110, 186, 234, 254
Production Analysis Corporation	110, 186, 234, 254, 269
The Production Asylum	235, 255
Production Partners, Inc.	186
Proletariat Filmworks	110, 186, 235, 255, 269
Propaganda Films	110, 175, 209, 235, 269
Proud Mary Entertainment	110, 187, 235, 269
Jack Provost	297
Punch Productions	110
Joseph Pytka Productions, Inc.	235
Quasar Studios	110, 187, 255, 280
Quinn Productions	110
@radical.media	235
Radar Pictures	111
Radiant Productions	111, 187
Raffaella Productions, Inc.	111, 187
Raimondi Films, Inc.	187, 235
Rainmaker Productions	111, 187
Raintree Productions	111, 235
Ranch Exit Films, Inc.	235
Randwell Productions	111, 187
Martin Ransohoff Productions, Inc.	111
Ron Rapiel	289, 297
Rapport Films, Inc.	235
Ken Raskoff Productions	187
Rastar Productions	111
Raven Productions, Inc.	187, 236
Patrick Raymond Entertainment, Inc.	188, 236, 255, 280
Ken Rayzor Sound Design	236
Realitory Productions	112, 255, 280
Rearguard Productions, Inc.	112, 188
Red Bird Productions	112, 188
Red Hots Entertainment	112, 188, 236, 255, 269
Red Hour Films	112, 188
Red House Entertainment	112, 188
Red Wagon	112
Red-Horse Productions	112, 188, 255
Dan Redler Entertainment	113, 188, 236, 281
Reel Orange	189, 236, 255
Marian Rees Associates	189
Regent Entertainment, Inc.	113, 189
Regent Films, Inc.	236
Tim Reid Productions, Inc.	189
Rick Reinert Pictures	113, 189, 255
Renaissance Pictures	113
Renegade Animation, Inc.	236, 281
Craig Respol	289, 291, 297, 301, 304
Reveal Entertainment	113
Revelations Entertainment	113, 189
Revolution Studios	113
Revolver Films, LLC	113, 189, 236, 256
Lynn Reynolds	289, 297
RGH/Lions Share Pictures	113
Kathryn L. Rhodes	297
Rhythm & Hues Studios	114, 237
Rice & Beans Productions	114, 189, 281
Ridini Entertainment Corporation	114, 189, 256
Christina Ritzmann	297
RJ Lauren	114, 237
RJN Productions, Inc.	114
RKO Pictures, Inc.	114
RoadKill Films	114
Roadside Attractions, LLC	114, 190
Roaring Tiger Films	237
Dolores Robinson Entertainment	114, 190
Phil Alden Robinson	289, 291
Denise Rocchietti	297
Stan Rogow Productions	114, 190
Rogue Entertainment	115, 256
Phil Roman Entertainment	115, 190, 281
Alex Rose Productions	115
Howard Rosenman Productions	115, 190
Freyda Rothstein Productions	190
Roundtable Ink	115, 190
Ruddy Morgan Organization	115, 190
Scott Rudin Productions	115
Rumbalara Films	115
RumRunner Cine Service	190, 237, 256
S.E.R. Filmworks	115, 190
Saban Entertainment	115, 191
Alan Sacks Productions, Inc.	116, 191
Samuelson Productions	116, 191
Amy M. Samuelson	297
Sanford/Pillsbury Productions	116, 191
Santa Monica Pictures	116, 191, 281

Freelance Producer & Production Company Alpha Index

Sarabande Productions. 116, 191
Satellite Films 237, 269
Saturn Films 116
Schapiro Entertainment Group 116
Edgar J. Scherick & Associates, Inc. 116, 191
Paul Schiff Productions 116
George Schlatter Productions 191
Robert Schmidt 291, 297
Sarah Schoessler 297, 301
Scholastic Entertainment 116, 191
Larry Schreiner 297
Joel Schumacher Productions 117
Bernard Schwartz Productions 117, 192
Kristine Schwarz Productions 117, 192, 237, 281
Jan Scott. 289, 297
Scott Free Productions 117, 192
Scotti Productions. 117, 237, 256
Scream, LLC. 237
Screen Gems 117
Section Eight Pictures 117
Dylan Sellers Productions 117, 192
Seven Arts Pictures. 117, 192
Shady Acres Entertainment 118, 192, 269
Shanghai'd Films. 118
Harvey Shapiro. 297
Sharpcut Productions 237, 270
Shearman Entertainment, Inc. 118, 192
Dona Shine 297
Shoelace Productions, Inc. 118
Shonkyte Productions, Inc. 118
Shoreline Entertainment 118, 192
Showtime Networks, Inc. 193
Shukovsky English Entertainment 193
Sí TV 193
Thom Sidoti. 297, 304
Scott Siegal 298
Marc Siegel 298
Sightsound.com. 281
Signature Entertainment 118, 193, 237
Signature Films 118
Karen Silver 298
Silver Lining Productions, Inc. 118, 193, 238, 256, 282
Silver Lion Films 118
Silver Pictures Television 119, 193
Silvereye Productions 119, 193, 238
Silverline Pictures. 119, 193
The Fred Silverman Company 194
Jay Silverman Productions 238
SimEx Digital Studios 119, 238
Simian Films. 119
The Gene Simmons Company 119, 194
Denise Simon 291, 298, 301
Randy Simon Productions 119, 194
The Robert Simonds Company. 119, 194
David A. Simons Productions 194
Single Spark Pictures 119, 194
Sitting Ducks Productions 120, 194
Lindsay Skutch 298
Skylark Entertainment, Inc. 120, 194
Skylark Films, Ltd. 120, 194
Sladek Entertainment Corporation 120, 194
Smillie Films 238
Al Smith. 298
Snapdragon Films, Inc. 120, 195, 256, 282
Sneak Preview Entertainment, Inc. 120, 195, 256, 270
SNL Studios 120, 195
Snow Leopard Productions 120, 195
Sodas & Shoes 238, 270
Sofronski Productions. 195
Sonic Films, Inc. 238
Sonnenfeld/Josephson Worldwide Entertainment 120, 195
Sony Pictures Classics 120
Sony Pictures Entertainment. 121, 195
Sound Concepts Inc. 238
South Fork Productions 121, 195, 238, 256, 270
Southern Skies, Inc. 121, 195
The Spark Factory 121, 238, 282
Spelling Television, Inc.. 196
Spin Pictures Intertainment, LLC 121
SplendidLight Media Productions 196, 239, 257
Spoke Film. 121
Sports' Cinematography Group 239, 270
Spring Creek Productions 196
Spyglass Entertainment. 121, 196
St. Clare Entertainment 121, 196
J. Stack Productions 122, 196, 239, 270
Stagescreen Productions 122, 196
Stampede Entertainment. 122
Star Entertainment Group, Inc. 122
StarBoard Productions 239
Stargazer, Inc.. . . . . 122, 239, 270
StarToons International, LLC. 196
Jane Startz Productions, Inc. 122, 196
Starz Encore Entertainment Group. 197
State Street Pictures 122, 197
Steam 239
Steamroller Productions 122
Stefanino Productions 122, 197, 239, 257, 270
Stereomedia 3D Video Productions. 257, 270, 282
The Howard Stern Production Company 122, 197
Kris Stevens Enterprises Inc. 239
Brad Stevenson 289, 298, 304
Stiefel + Company 239
Stone vs. Stone 123
Stonelock Pictures 123
Storm Entertainment. 123
Steven Strachan 298
Straw Dogs. 123, 239
Streamedia.net 282
Strom Magallon Entertainment 123, 240, 257, 270
Mel Stuart Productions, Inc. 123, 197, 257
Studios USA 197, 312
Mike Sullivan Productions, Inc. 123, 197
Summerland Entertainment 123, 197, 271
Summers Entertainment 123, 197
Sun Spots 240
Sundog Productions 123, 198
Sweet Lorraine Productions, Inc. 198

Freelance Producer & Production Company Alpha Index

Taffner Entertainment	198
Tag Team	240
Martin Tahse Productions	124
Talent Entertainment Group	124, 198
Talisman Pacific	124
Talking Rings Entertainment	124
Tango Films	240, 271
Tapestry Films, Inc.	124
Sal Tassone	289, 291, 298
Taurus Entertainment Company	124, 198
Tavel Entertainment	124, 198, 282
Taylor-Bedell Entertainment	124, 198
TBS Superstation	198
Team Todd	124, 199
Telescene Film Group, Inc.	125, 199
Telling Pictures, Inc.	125, 199, 257
Ten Thirteen Productions	125, 199
Teocalli Entertainment, Inc.	125, 199, 257
Terra Bella Entertainment	125, 199
Threshold Entertainment	125, 199, 283
Tidewater Entertainment	125, 199
Debbie Tietjen	298
Time-Life Video	257
Debby Timmons	298
The Steve Tisch Company	125
TLC Entertainment	125, 199
Joseph P. Tobin	291
Tollin/Robbins Productions	126, 200
Tool of North America	240
Totem Productions	126, 240
Trafficanda Studios, Inc.	240
Lee Trask	298
Tribe Pictures	126, 257
Tribeca Productions	126, 200
The Tribunal	126, 200
Tribune Entertainment Company	200
Triology Entertainment Group	126, 200
Triumph Pictures, Inc.	126, 200
Clarissa Troop	298
Tropix Films	240
True Blue Productions	126, 200
Simon Tse Productions, Inc.	126
Tuesday Films	240
The Turman-Morrissey Company	127, 201
Turner Entertainment Group	201
Turner Network Television (TNT)	201
Jon Turtle Productions	127, 201
Jeffrey S. Tuttle	298, 304
TVA Productions	201, 241, 258
TVP Studios	201, 241, 258, 271
Twentieth Century Fox Pictures	127
Twentieth Century Fox Television	201
Twilight Time Films	127, 202
Two Oceans Entertainment	202
Two Stepp Productions	127, 202
UBU Productions	127, 202
Ufland Productions	127, 202
Unapix Films	127, 202
Undergrace Productions	128, 202
Undergroundfilm.com	283
Unger Productions, Inc.	128, 202
United Artists Films	128
Universal Pictures	128
Universal Studios, Inc.	128, 202
Universal Television	203
UPN (United Paramount Network)	203
Upstart Entertainment	129, 203
USA Films	129
USA Network	203
Val D'Oro Entertainment	203, 283
Renée Valente Productions	129, 203
Valhalla Motion Pictures	129, 203
Vanguard Productions	129, 204, 241, 258, 271
Vault, Inc., The	129
VCA Productions	129, 241
Ventana Films	130, 241, 271
Venture Entertainment Group	130, 204, 241, 258
Venus Entertainment	241
Verdon-Cedric Productions	130
Verhoeven/Marshall Films	130
Verité Productions	204, 258
VH1	204
Viacom Entertainment Group	130, 204
Viacom Productions	204
Video Hollywood Productions	204, 241, 258
Videowerks	204, 241, 258, 283
Videox	205
Vide-U	271
View Askew Productions, Inc.	130, 205
Vihlene & Associates, Inc.	205, 241, 258
Village Roadshow Pictures	130
Villains	242, 271
Vin Di Bona Productions	205
Visionbox	130, 205
Visitor, LLC	242
Susan Vogelfang	289, 291, 299
Raymond Wagner Productions, Inc.	130, 205
Wallach Entertainment	205
Janie Walter	231, 299
Ken Walz Productions	130, 205
Warner Bros.	131
Warner Bros. Animation	131, 206
Warner Bros. International Television	206
Warner Bros. Pictures Production	131
Warner Bros. Telepictures Production	206
Warner Bros. Television	206
Watershed Films	131, 206
WB Television Network	206
Weed Road Pictures	131
Ed Weinberger Productions	206
Francine Weiner	299, 304
Jerry Weintraub Productions	131
Weintraub/Kuhn Productions	131, 206, 258
Roni Weisberg Productions	132, 207, 242
Weller/Grossman Productions	207, 259
John Wells Productions	132, 207
Western Branch Productions, Inc.	207, 242, 259
Jaki West	289, 299

Freelance Producer & Production Company Alpha Index

Bill White Productions	132, 207, 242, 259, 271
Whitewater Films	132, 207
Ree Whitford	299
Wicked Monkey Productions	132, 207
Wild Things Productions	132, 207
WildLife Management	242
WildRice Productions	207
Wildwood Enterprises, Inc./South Fork Pictures	132
Wilshire Court Productions	208
WIN Ventures, LLC.	132, 208
Winchester Films	132
Wind Dancer Production Group	133, 208
Windmill Lane Productions	242, 272
Winkler Films	133
Ralph Winter Productions, Inc.	133, 208
Witt/Thomas/Harris Productions	133
Wolf Films, Inc.	208, 318
The Wolper Organization	208
Wonderland Films	133, 208
The Woofenill Works, Inc.	133, 208
Working Title Films	133
World of Wonder Productions	133, 208
World Wide Pants, Inc.	208
Marvin Worth Productions	133, 209
Linda Wright Productions	209
Norton Wright Productions	134, 209
Wychwood Productions	134, 209
Wyld Spots	242
X-1 Films	242
X-Ray Productions	243, 272
Peter Yacavone	299
Yada/Levine Productions	243, 259
Yak Yak Pictures	134, 209
Mark Yellen Productions	134, 243, 272
Bud Yorkin Productions	134, 209
Yorktown Productions, Inc.	134, 209
Diana Young	299
Gabrielle Yuro-Vickers	231, 299
Z.com	283
Zaloom Film	134, 209
The Zanuck Company	134
Raymond Zarro	299
Zeal Pictures	134, 243, 259, 272
ZeroOneFilms.com	283
Zide/Perry Entertainment	135
Jack Ziga	289, 299
Joel R. Zimmerman	299
Anita Zommers	291, 299
Zooma Zooma Corporation	135, 209, 243, 272, 283
Zucker Productions	135
Zucker/Netter Productions	135, 210
Zuckerman Entertainment	135, 210
Leslie Zurla	289, 299, 301
Zystar Films, Inc.	135, 210, 243, 259, 272

Notes

Advertisers Index

Alliance Post Production, LLC	page 17
Cicada	page 40
Computer Café, Inc.	page 14
Coptervision	page 57
Eastman Kodak	page 12
Fox Studios Production Services	page 33
Giant Studios	page 61
IMAX Corporation	page 56A
Industry Labor Guide	page 34
Kalmenson & Kalmenson Voice Casting	page 212
Keep Me Posted	page 3
Location Connect	page 18
Media Distributors	page 13
Media Services	page 54
Morris Marketing	page 137
Pacific Soundwaves	page 243
Pacific Title Archives	page 210
Panavision	page 22
Play, Inc.	page 30 & IBC
Raleigh Studios	page IFC
Shortenz Digital	page 29
Silicon Graphics, Inc.	page OBC
Tone Dog	page 9
Universal Studios	page 23
Variety/Daily Variety	page 56B

Coming Soon...

A *Variety* Group Publication

How to Get Listed in Producers 411

Listings in Producers 411 and our web service are free – you can't buy one. We grant listings to individuals and businesses on the basis of work in feature film, TV, commercials, video, music videos or interactive multimedia. To apply for a listing, you must mail the application form on the opposite page (including required info). Applications submitted to our editorial staff are thoroughly researched for accuracy and industry experience.

To be considered for the next print edition, make sure you send in all the requested information for your listing by **May 1, 2001.** Applications for listings on our website are accepted at any time. Once approved for an online listing, your company will be included in the subsequent print edition.

Submitting an application does not guarantee a listing.

Ordering Information

Complete this form and send it to:
LA 411, 7083 Hollywood Blvd., Suite 501, Los Angeles, CA 90028-8901

For credit card orders, air and international shipments or questions call: (800) 545-2411 or (323) 460-6304. Credit card orders received by 12 noon PST will be shipped UPS that day. Please allow 5 working days for delivery of all orders.

Quantity	Item		Price	Total
	LA 411 2001*		$69.00	
	NY 411 2001		$49.00	
	411 Digital 2000/2001		$49.00	
	TE 411 2001		$49.00	
	Play 411*		$15.00	
	Producers 411			
	Single Copy circle issue	January July November	$49.00	
	1 year subscription:	3 editions**	$129.00	
	2 year subscription:	6 editions**	$219.00	
	Agents & Managers 411			
	Single Copy circle issue	April October	$49.00	
	1 year subscription:	2 editions**	$79.00	
	2 year subscription:	4 editions**	$139.00	
	Above The Line Subscription 3 editions Producers 411 2 editions Agents & Managers 411		$159.00	

UPS Ground Service
1 Title $6.00
2-3 Titles $5.00 per book
4+ Titles $3.50 per book
Call 800-545-2411 ext.150 for international orders.

Subtotal: _____
Sales Tax (CA orders add 8%, N.Y. 8.25): _____
Shipping (see box at left): _____
Grand Total: _____

* Complimentary Play 411 shipped with each order for LA 411

** Subscriptions begin with the current issue available at the time the order is received.

Make checks payable to LA 411 Publishing Company

Please bill My: ☐ Visa   ☐ MC   ☐ Amex   ☐ Check Enclosed

Name/Title _____

Company/Profession _____

Card# _____ Exp. _____

Address - No P.O. Boxes Please _____ City _____

Name on Card _____

State _____ ZIP Code _____ Telephone _____

Signature _____

APPLICATION FOR PRODUCERS 411™ FREELANCE OR BUSINESS LISTING

Listings in Producers 411 are free - you can't buy one. You may mail in an application at any time; however, to be considered for the next printed book we must have your complete materials by May 1, 2001.

TO BE LISTED, YOU MUST:
1. Be located in North America
2. Be currently involved in the production of feature films, TV shows, commercials, etc. (see complete list on reverse).
3. Include ONE or more of the following: a brief profile on company letterhead, press releases/clippings, demo reel (standard VHS or DVD), or resume/bio.
4. Complete this application form and mail it to:
   7083 Hollywood Blvd., Suite 501, Los Angeles, CA 90028

Submitting an application does not guarantee a listing.

Deadline To Be Included In Summer 2001 Book: May 1, 2001

A. General Information (Required)   ☐ Check here if you are interested in display advertising

PLEASE INDICATE THE CATEGORIES AND SPECIALTIES THAT APPLY TO YOUR COMPANY. SEE REVERSE.

First Name _____ Last Name _____

Company Name _____ Type of Business _____

Street Address _____ Apt./Suite Number _____

City _____ State _____ ZIP Code _____ Print This Address? Yes ☐ or No ☐

( ) Local Phone Number   ( ) Additional Phone/Pager Number   ( ) Fax Number

e-mail Address _____@_____   http://_____ Web Address

Services (if applicable) _____

B. Required Information   ☐ Already Listed in LA411

Include ONE or more of the following: a brief profile on company letterhead, press releases/clippings, demo reel (standard VHS or DVD), or resume/bio.

C. List of Producers/Key Personnel (Name/Title) (For Production Companies only. Attach separate sheet or use additional space on reverse if necessary.)

1. _____   7. _____
2. _____   8. _____
3. _____   9. _____
4. _____   10. _____
5. _____   11. _____
6. _____   12. _____

D. List of Credits (Attach separate sheet or use additional space on reverse if necessary.)

1. _____   3. _____
2. _____   4. _____

E. First Look/Development Deal (Name of studio, network, etc.)

F. Additional Information (Associations/Guilds/Unions, second address, etc.)

☐ Accepts unsolicited material
☐ Does not accept unsolicited material

Form Completed By (Please PRINT your name) _____

Your area code & telephone number _____

Producers 411 is Published by LA 411 Publishing Company
7083 Hollywood Blvd., Suite 501, Los Angeles, CA 90028 (323) 460-6304 (800) 545-2411
www.la411publishing.com

Producers 411 Category List by Tab Section

Please check the main categories and specialties that apply

MAIN ☐ **FEATURE FILM**

SPECIALTIES
- ☐ studio
- ☐ independent
- ☐ direct-to-video
- ☐ shorts
- ☐ documentaries
- ☐ animation
- ☐ large format
- ☐ trailers

MAIN ☐ **TV**

SPECIALTIES
- ☐ network
- ☐ cable
- ☐ animation
- ☐ documentaries
- ☐ made for TV movies
- ☐ miniseries
- ☐ specials

MAIN ☐ **COMMERCIALS**

SPECIALTIES
- ☐ television
- ☐ radio
- ☐ infomercials/direct response
- ☐ promos
- ☐ PSA's

MAIN ☐ **VIDEO**

SPECIALTIES
- ☐ industrial/corporate
- ☐ educational
- ☐ documentaries

MAIN ☐ **MUSIC VIDEO**

SPECIALTIES
- ☐ short form
- ☐ long form

MAIN ☐ **INTERACTIVE MULTIMEDIA**

SPECIALTIES
- ☐ web content
- ☐ movies/film
- ☐ webcasting
- ☐ webisodes
- ☐ animation

OTHER

_____

_____

Use this space for any additional information.